CISSP®

Official (ISC)²®
Practice Tests

CISSP®

Official (ISC)²®

Practice Tests

David Seidl

Mike Chapple

SYBEX®
A Wiley Brand

Executive Editor: Jim Minatel
Development Editor: Kim Wimpsett
Technical Editors: Jeff Parker and Addam Schroll
Production Editor: Christine O'Connor
Copy Editors: Judy Flynn and Elizabeth Welch
Editorial Manager: Mary Beth Wakefield
Production Manager: Kathleen Wisor
Book Designers: Bill Gibson and Judy Fung
Proofreader: Nancy Carrasco
Indexer: Ted Laux
Project Coordinator, Cover: Brent Savage
Cover Designer: Wiley
Cover Image: Getty Images Inc./Jeremy Woodhouse

Published simultaneously in Canada

ISBN: 978-1-119-25228-3
ISBN: 978-1-119-28804-6 (ebk.)
ISBN: 978-1-119-25229-0 (ebk.)

Manufactured in the United States of America

Library of Congress Control Number: 2016941726

10 9 8 7 6 5 4 3 2

For Renee, the most patient and caring person I know. Thank you for being the heart of our family.
—MJC

This book is for Lauren, who supports me through each writing endeavor, and for the wonderful teachers and professors who shared both their knowledge and their lifelong love of learning with me.
—DAS

Acknowledgments

The authors would like to thank the many people who made this book possible. Jim Minatel at Wiley Publishing helped us extend the Sybex CISSP franchise to include this new title and gain important support from the International Information Systems Security Consortium (ISC)². Carole Jelen, our agent, worked on a myriad of logistic details and handled the business side of the book with her usual grace and commitment to excellence. Addam Schroll, our technical editor, pointed out many opportunities to improve our work and deliver a high-quality final product. Jeff Parker's technical proofing ensured a polished product. Kim Wimpsett served as developmental editor and managed the project smoothly. Many other people we'll never meet worked behind the scenes to make this book a success.

About the Authors

Mike Chapple, Ph.D., CISSP is an author of the best-selling *CISSP (ISC)² Certified Information Systems Security Professional Official Study Guide,* Sybex, 2015, now in its seventh edition. He is an information security professional with two decades of experience in higher education, the private sector, and government.

Mike currently serves as Senior Director for IT Service Delivery at the University of Notre Dame. In this role, he oversees the information security, data governance, IT architecture, project management, strategic planning, and product management functions for Notre Dame. Mike also serves as a concurrent assistant professor in the university's Computing and Digital Technologies department, where he teaches undergraduate courses on information security.

Before returning to Notre Dame, Mike served as Executive Vice President and Chief Information Officer of the Brand Institute, a Miami-based marketing consultancy. Mike also spent four years in the information security research group at the National Security Agency and served as an active duty intelligence officer in the U.S. Air Force.

He is a technical editor for *Information Security Magazine* and has written 20 books, including *Cyberwarfare: Information Operations in a Connected World* (Jones & Bartlett, 2015), *the CompTIA Security+ Training Kit* (Microsoft Press, 2013), and the *CISSP Study Guide* (Sybex, 7th edition, 2015).

Mike earned both his BS and Ph.D. degrees from Notre Dame in computer science & engineering. He also holds an MS in computer science from the University of Idaho and an MBA from Auburn University.

David Seidl CISSP is the Senior Director for Campus Technology Services at the University of Notre Dame. As the Senior Director for CTS, David is responsible for central platform and operating system support, database administration and services, identity and access management, application services, and email and digital signage. Prior to his current role, he was Notre Dame's Director of Information Security.

David teaches a popular course on networking and security for Notre Dame's Mendoza College of Business. In addition to his professional and teaching roles, he has co-authored the *CompTIA Security+ Training Kit* (Microsoft Press, 2013) and *Cyberwarfare: Information Operations in a Connected World* (Jones & Bartlett, 2015), and served as the technical editor for the 6th (Sybex, 2012) and 7th (Sybex, 2015) editions of the *CISSP Study Guide.* David holds a bachelor's degree in communication technology and a master's degree in information security from Eastern Michigan University, as well as CISSP, GPEN, and GCIH certifications.

Contents

Introduction

CISSP Official (ISC)^2 Practice Tests is a companion volume to the CISSP (ISC)^2 Certified Information Systems Security Professional Official Study Guide. If you're looking to test your knowledge before you take the CISSP exam, this book will help you by providing a combination of 1,300 questions that cover the CISSP Common Body of Knowledge and easy-to-understand explanations of both right and wrong answers.

If you're just starting to prepare for the CISSP exam, we highly recommend that you use the CISSP (ISC)^2 Certified Information Systems Security Professional Official Study Guide, 7th Edition Stewart/Chapple/Gibson, Sybex, 2015, to help you learn about each of the domains covered by the CISSP exam. Once you're ready to test your knowledge, use this book to help find places where you may need to study more, or to practice for the exam itself.

Since this is a companion to the CISSP Study Guide, this book is designed to be similar to taking the CISSP exam. It contains multipart scenarios as well as standard multiple-choice questions similar to those you may encounter in the certification exam itself. The book itself is broken up into 10 chapters: 8 domain-centric chapters with 100 questions about each domain, and 2 chapters that contain 250-question practice tests to simulate taking the exam itself.

CISSP Certification

The CISSP certification is offered by the International Information System Security Certification Consortium, or (ISC)^2, a global nonprofit. The mission of (ISC)^2 is to support and provide members and constituents with credentials, resources, and leadership to address cyber, information, software, and infrastructure security to deliver value to society. They achieve this mission by delivering the world's leading information security certification program. The CISSP is the flagship credential in this series and is accompanied by several other (ISC)^2 programs:

- Systems Security Certified Practitioner (SSCP)
- Certified Authorization Professional (CAP)
- Certified Secure Software Lifecycle Professional (CSSLP)
- Certified Cyber Forensic Professional (CCFP)
- HealthCare Information Security Privacy Practitioner (HCISPP)
- Certified Cloud Security Professional (CCSP)

There are also three advanced CISSP certifications for those who wish to move on from the base credential to demonstrate advanced expertise in a domain of information security:

- Information Systems Security Architecture Professional (CISSP-ISSAP)
- Information Systems Security Engineering Professional (CISSP-ISSEP)
- Information Systems Security Management Professional (CISSP-ISSMP)

The CISSP certification covers eight domains of information security knowledge. These domains are meant to serve as the broad knowledge foundation required to succeed in the information security profession. They include:

- Security and Risk Management
- Asset Security
- Security Engineering
- Communication and Network Security
- Identity and Access Management
- Security Assessment and Testing
- Security Operations
- Software Development Security

The CISSP domains are periodically updated by (ISC)^2. The last revision in April 2015 changed from 10 domains to the 8 listed here, and included a major realignment of topics and ideas. At the same time, a number of new areas were added or expanded to reflect changes in common information security topics.

Complete details on the CISSP Common Body of Knowledge (CBK) are contained in the Candidate Information Bulletin (CIB). The CIB, which includes a full outline of exam topics, can be found on the ISC^2 website at `www.isc2.org`.

Taking the CISSP Exam

The CISSP exam is a 6-hour exam that consists of 250 questions covering the eight domains. Passing requires achieving a score of at least 700 out of 1,000 points. It's important to understand that this is a scaled score, meaning that not every question is worth the same number of points. Questions of differing difficulty may factor into your score more or less heavily. That said, as you work through these practice exams, you might want to use 70 percent as a yardstick to help you get a sense of whether you're ready to sit for the actual exam. When you're ready, you can schedule an exam via links provided on the (ISC)^2 website—tests are offered in locations throughout the world.

Questions on the CISSP exam are provided in both multiple-choice form and what (ISC)^2 calls "advanced innovative" questions, which are drag and drop and hotspot questions, both of which are offered in computer-based testing environments. Innovative questions are scored the same as traditional multiple-choice questions and have only one right answer.

Computer-Based Testing Environment

Almost all CISSP exams are now administered in a computer-based testing (CBT) format. You'll register for the exam through the Pearson Vue website and may take the exam in the language of your choice. It is offered in English, French, German, Portuguese, Spanish, Japanese, Simplified Chinese, Korean, and a format for the visually impaired.

You'll take the exam in a computer-based testing center located near your home or office. The centers administer many different exams, so you may find yourself sitting in the same room as a student taking a school entrance examination and a healthcare professional earning a medical certification. If you'd like to become more familiar with the testing environment, the Pearson Vue website offers a virtual tour of a testing center:

`https://home.pearsonvue.com/test-taker/Pearson-Professional-Center-Tour.aspx`

When you sit down to take the exam, you'll be seated at a computer that has the exam software already loaded and running. It's a pretty straightforward interface that allows you to navigate through the exam. You can download a practice exam and tutorial from Pearson at:

`http://www.vue.com/athena/athena.asp`

Exam Retake Policy

If you don't pass the CISSP exam, you shouldn't panic. Many individuals don't reach the bar on their first attempt but gain valuable experience that helps them succeed the second time around. When you retake the exam, you'll have the benefit of familiarity with the CBT environment and CISSP exam format. You'll also have time to study up on the areas where you felt less confident.

After your first exam attempt, you must wait 30 days before retaking the computer-based exam. If you're not successful on that attempt, you must then wait 90 days before your third attempt and 180 days before your fourth attempt. You may not take the exam more than three times in a single calendar year.

Work Experience Requirement

Candidates who wish to earn the CISSP credential must not only pass the exam but also demonstrate that they have at least five years of work experience in the information security field. Your work experience must cover activities in at least two of the eight domains of the CISSP program and must be paid, full-time employment. Volunteer experiences or part-time duties are not acceptable to meet the CISSP experience requirement.

You may be eligible to waive one of the five years of the work experience requirement based on your educational achievements. If you hold a bachelor's degree or four-year equivalent, you may be eligible for a degree waiver that covers one of those years. Similarly, if you hold one of the information security certifications on the current (ISC)^2 credential waiver list (`https://www.isc2.org/credential_waiver/default.aspx`), you may also waive a year of the experience requirement. You may not combine these two programs. Holders of both a certification and an undergraduate degree must still demonstrate at least four years of experience.

If you haven't yet completed your work experience requirement, you may still attempt the CISSP exam. Individuals who pass the exam are designated Associates of $(ISC)^2$ and have six years to complete the work experience requirement.

Recertification Requirements

Once you've earned your CISSP credential, you'll need to maintain your certification by paying maintenance fees and participating in continuing professional education (CPE). As long as you maintain your certification in good standing, you will not need to retake the CISSP exam.

Currently, the annual maintenance fees for the CISSP credential are $85 per year. Individuals who hold one of the advanced CISSP concentrations will need to pay an additional $35 annually for each concentration they hold.

The CISSP CPE requirement mandates earning at least 40 CPE credits each year toward the 120-credit three-year requirement. $(ISC)^2$ provides an online portal where certificants may submit CPE completion for review and approval. The portal also tracks annual maintenance fee payments and progress toward recertification.

Using This Book to Practice

This book is composed of 10 chapters. Each of the first eight chapters covers a domain, with a variety of questions that can help you test your knowledge of real-world, scenario, and best practices–based security knowledge. The final two chapters are complete practice exams that can serve as timed practice tests to help determine if you're ready for the CISSP exam.

We recommend taking the first practice exam to help identify where you may need to spend more study time, and then using the domain-specific chapters to test your domain knowledge where it is weak. Once you're ready, take the second practice exam to make sure you've covered all of the material and are ready to attempt the CISSP exam.

Chapter 1

Security and Risk Management (Domain 1)

1. What is the final step of a quantitative risk analysis?
   - A. Determine asset value.
   - B. Assess the annualized rate of occurrence.
   - C. Derive the annualized loss expectancy.
   - D. Conduct a cost/benefit analysis.
2. An evil twin attack that broadcasts a legitimate SSID for an unauthorized network is an example of what category of threat?
   - A. Spoofing
   - B. Information disclosure
   - C. Repudiation
   - D. Tampering
3. Under the Digital Millennium Copyright Act (DMCA), what type of offenses do not require prompt action by an Internet service provider after it receives a notification of infringement claim from a copyright holder?
   - A. Storage of information by a customer on a provider's server
   - B. Caching of information by the provider
   - C. Transmission of information over the provider's network by a customer
   - D. Caching of information in a provider search engine
4. FlyAway Travel has offices in both the European Union and the United States and transfers personal information between those offices regularly. Which of the seven requirements for processing personal information states that organizations must inform individuals about how the information they collect is used?
   - A. Notice
   - B. Choice
   - C. Onward Transfer
   - D. Enforcement
5. Which one of the following is not one of the three common threat modeling techniques?
   - A. Focused on assets
   - B. Focused on attackers
   - C. Focused on software
   - D. Focused on social engineering
6. Which one of the following elements of information is not considered personally identifiable information that would trigger most US state data breach laws?
   - A. Student identification number
   - B. Social Security number

- **C.** Driver's license number
- **D.** Credit card number

7. In 1991, the federal sentencing guidelines formalized a rule that requires senior executives to take personal responsibility for information security matters. What is the name of this rule?

- **A.** Due diligence rule
- **B.** Personal liability rule
- **C.** Prudent man rule
- **D.** Due process rule

8. Which one of the following provides an authentication mechanism that would be appropriate for pairing with a password to achieve multifactor authentication?

- **A.** Username
- **B.** PIN
- **C.** Security question
- **D.** Fingerprint scan

9. What United States government agency is responsible for administering the terms of safe harbor agreements between the European Union and the United States under the EU Data Protection Directive?

- **A.** Department of Defense
- **B.** Department of the Treasury
- **C.** State Department
- **D.** Department of Commerce

10. Yolanda is the chief privacy officer for a financial institution and is researching privacy issues related to customer checking accounts. Which one of the following laws is most likely to apply to this situation?

- **A.** GLBA
- **B.** SOX
- **C.** HIPAA
- **D.** FERPA

11. Tim's organization recently received a contract to conduct sponsored research as a government contractor. What law now likely applies to the information systems involved in this contract?

- **A.** FISMA
- **B.** PCI DSS
- **C.** HIPAA
- **D.** GISRA

12. Chris is advising travelers from his organization who will be visiting many different countries overseas. He is concerned about compliance with export control laws. Which of the following technologies is most likely to trigger these regulations?
    - A. Memory chips
    - B. Office productivity applications
    - C. Hard drives
    - D. Encryption software

13. Bobbi is investigating a security incident and discovers that an attacker began with a normal user account but managed to exploit a system vulnerability to provide that account with administrative rights. What type of attack took place under the STRIDE model?
    - A. Spoofing
    - B. Repudiation
    - C. Tampering
    - D. Elevation of privilege

14. You are completing your business continuity planning effort and have decided that you wish to accept one of the risks. What should you do next?
    - A. Implement new security controls to reduce the risk level.
    - B. Design a disaster recovery plan.
    - C. Repeat the business impact assessment.
    - D. Document your decision-making process.

15. Which one of the following control categories does not accurately describe a fence around a facility?
    - A. Physical
    - B. Detective
    - C. Deterrent
    - D. Preventive

16. Tony is developing a business continuity plan and is having difficulty prioritizing resources because of the difficulty of combining information about tangible and intangible assets. What would be the most effective risk assessment approach for him to use?
    - A. Quantitative risk assessment
    - B. Qualitative risk assessment
    - C. Neither quantitative nor qualitative risk assessment
    - D. Combination of quantitative and qualitative risk assessment

17. What law provides intellectual property protection to the holders of trade secrets?
    - A. Copyright Law
    - B. Lanham Act

C. Glass-Steagall Act

D. Economic Espionage Act

18. Which one of the following principles imposes a standard of care upon an individual that is broad and equivalent to what one would expect from a reasonable person under the circumstances?

A. Due diligence

B. Separation of duties

C. Due care

D. Least privilege

19. Darcy is designing a fault tolerant system and wants to implement RAID-5 for her system. What is the minimum number of physical hard disks she can use to build this system?

A. One

B. Two

C. Three

D. Five

20. Which one of the following is an example of an administrative control?

A. Intrusion detection system

B. Security awareness training

C. Firewalls

D. Security guards

21. Keenan Systems recently developed a new manufacturing process for microprocessors. The company wants to license the technology to other companies for use but wishes to prevent unauthorized use of the technology. What type of intellectual property protection is best suited for this situation?

A. Patent

B. Trade secret

C. Copyright

D. Trademark

22. Which one of the following actions might be taken as part of a business continuity plan?

A. Restoring from backup tapes

B. Implementing RAID

C. Relocating to a cold site

D. Restarting business operations

23. When developing a business impact analysis, the team should first create a list of assets. What should happen next?

- **A.** Identify vulnerabilities in each asset.
- **B.** Determine the risks facing the asset.
- **C.** Develop a value for each asset.
- **D.** Identify threats facing each asset.

24. Mike recently implemented an intrusion prevention system designed to block common network attacks from affecting his organization. What type of risk management strategy is Mike pursuing?

- **A.** Risk acceptance
- **B.** Risk avoidance
- **C.** Risk mitigation
- **D.** Risk transference

25. Which one of the following is an example of physical infrastructure hardening?

- **A.** Antivirus software
- **B.** Hardware-based network firewall
- **C.** Two-factor authentication
- **D.** Fire suppression system

26. Which one of the following is normally used as an authorization tool?

- **A.** ACL
- **B.** Token
- **C.** Username
- **D.** Password

27. The International Information Systems Security Certification Consortium uses the logo below to represent itself online and in a variety of forums. What type of intellectual property protection may it use to protect its rights in this logo?

- **A.** Copyright
- **B.** Patent
- **C.** Trade secret
- **D.** Trademark

28. Mary is helping a computer user who sees the following message appear on his computer screen. What type of attack has occurred?

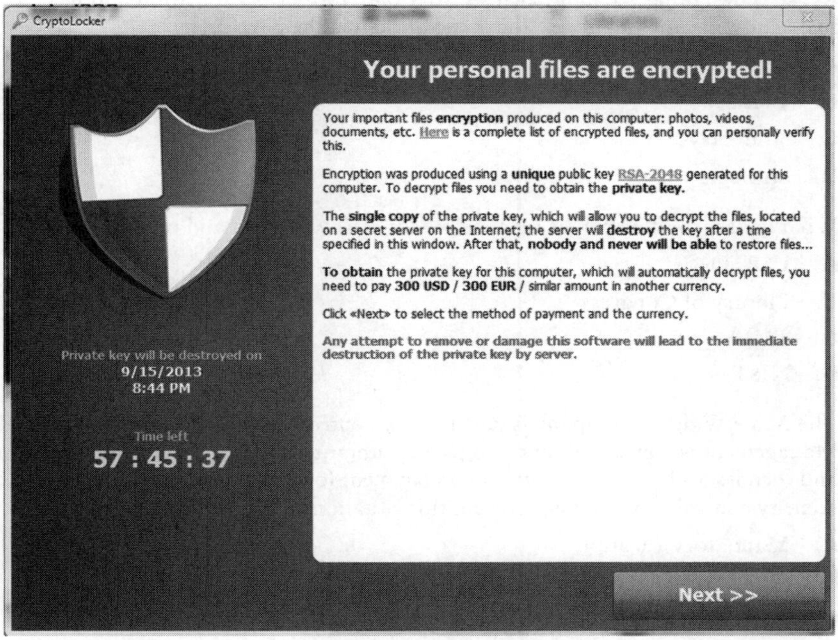

- **A.** Availability
- **B.** Confidentiality
- **C.** Disclosure
- **D.** Distributed

29. Which one of the following organizations would not be automatically subject to the terms of HIPAA if they engage in electronic transactions?

- **A.** Healthcare provider
- **B.** Health and fitness application developer
- **C.** Health information clearinghouse
- **D.** Health insurance plan

30. John's network begins to experience symptoms of slowness. Upon investigation, he realizes that the network is being bombarded with ICMP ECHO REPLY packets and believes that his organization is the victim of a Smurf attack. What principle of information security is being violated?

- **A.** Availability
- **B.** Integrity

C. Confidentiality

D. Denial

31. Renee is designing the long-term security plan for her organization and has a three- to five-year planning horizon. What type of plan is she developing?

A. Operational

B. Tactical

C. Summary

D. Strategic

32. What government agency is responsible for the evaluation and registration of trademarks?

A. USPTO

B. Library of Congress

C. TVA

D. NIST

33. The Acme Widgets Company is putting new controls in place for its accounting department. Management is concerned that a rogue accountant may be able to create a new false vendor and then issue checks to that vendor as payment for services that were never rendered. What security control can best help prevent this situation?

A. Mandatory vacation

B. Separation of duties

C. Defense in depth

D. Job rotation

34. Which one of the following categories of organizations is most likely to be covered by the provisions of FISMA?

A. Banks

B. Defense contractors

C. School districts

D. Hospitals

35. Robert is responsible for securing systems used to process credit card information. What standard should guide his actions?

A. HIPAA

B. PCI DSS

C. SOX

D. GLBA

36. Which one of the following individuals is normally responsible for fulfilling the operational data protection responsibilities delegated by senior management, such as validating data integrity, testing backups, and managing security policies?

A. Data custodian

B. Data owner

C. User

D. Auditor

37. Alan works for an e-commerce company that recently had some content stolen by another website and republished without permission. What type of intellectual property protection would best preserve Alan's company's rights?

A. Trade secret

B. Copyright

C. Trademark

D. Patent

38. Florian receives a flyer from a federal agency announcing that a new administrative law will affect his business operations. Where should he go to find the text of the law?

A. United States Code

B. Supreme Court rulings

C. Code of Federal Regulations

D. Compendium of Laws

39. Tom is installing a next-generation firewall (NGFW) in his data center that is designed to block many types of application attacks. When viewed from a risk management perspective, what metric is Tom attempting to lower?

A. Impact

B. RPO

C. MTO

D. Likelihood

40. Which one of the following individuals would be the most effective organizational owner for an information security program?

A. CISSP-certified analyst

B. Chief information officer

C. Manager of network security

D. President and CEO

41. What important function do senior managers normally fill on a business continuity planning team?

A. Arbitrating disputes about criticality

B. Evaluating the legal environment

C. Training staff

D. Designing failure controls

42. You are the CISO for a major hospital system and are preparing to sign a contract with a Software-as-a-Service (SaaS) email vendor and want to ensure that its business continuity planning measures are reasonable. What type of audit might you request to meet this goal?

A. SOC-1

B. FISMA

C. PCI DSS

D. SOC-2

43. Gary is analyzing a security incident and, during his investigation, encounters a user who denies having performed an action that Gary believes he did perform. What type of threat has taken place under the STRIDE model?

A. Repudiation

B. Information disclosure

C. Tampering

D. Elevation of privilege

44. Beth is the security administrator for a public school district. She is implementing a new student information system and is testing the code to ensure that students are not able to alter their own grades. What principle of information security is Beth enforcing?

A. Integrity

B. Availability

C. Confidentiality

D. Denial

45. Which one of the following issues is not normally addressed in a service-level agreement (SLA)?

A. Confidentiality of customer information

B. Failover time

C. Uptime

D. Maximum consecutive downtime

46. Joan is seeking to protect a piece of computer software that she developed under intellectual property law. Which one of the following avenues of protection would not apply to a piece of software?

A. Trademark

B. Copyright

C. Patent

D. Trade secret

Questions 47–49 refer to the following scenario.

Juniper Content is a web content development company with 40 employees located in two offices: one in New York and a smaller office in the San Francisco Bay Area. Each office has a local area network protected by a perimeter firewall. The LAN contains modern switch equipment connected to both wired and wireless networks.

Each office has its own file server, and the IT team runs software every hour to synchronize files between the two servers, distributing content between the offices. These servers are primarily used to store images and other files related to web content developed by the company. The team also uses a SaaS-based email and document collaboration solution for much of their work.

You are the newly appointed IT manager for Juniper Content and you are working to augment existing security controls to improve the organization's security.

47. Users in the two offices would like to access each other's file servers over the Internet. What control would provide confidentiality for those communications?

- **A.** Digital signatures
- **B.** Virtual private network
- **C.** Virtual LAN
- **D.** Digital content management

48. You are also concerned about the availability of data stored on each office's server. You would like to add technology that would enable continued access to files located on the server even if a hard drive in a server fails. What integrity control allows you to add robustness without adding additional servers?

- **A.** Server clustering
- **B.** Load balancing
- **C.** RAID
- **D.** Scheduled backups

49. Finally, there are historical records stored on the server that are extremely important to the business and should never be modified. You would like to add an integrity control that allows you to verify on a periodic basis that the files were not modified. What control can you add?

- **A.** Hashing
- **B.** ACLs
- **C.** Read-only attributes
- **D.** Firewalls

50. What law serves as the basis for privacy rights in the United States?

- **A.** Privacy Act of 1974
- **B.** Fourth Amendment
- **C.** First Amendment
- **D.** Electronic Communications Privacy Act of 1986

51. Which one of the following is not normally included in business continuity plan documentation?
    - A. Statement of accounts
    - B. Statement of importance
    - C. Statement of priorities
    - D. Statement of organizational responsibility

52. An accounting employee at Doolitte Industries was recently arrested for participation in an embezzlement scheme. The employee transferred money to a personal account and then shifted funds around between other accounts every day to disguise the fraud for months. Which one of the following controls might have best allowed the earlier detection of this fraud?
    - A. Separation of duties
    - B. Least privilege
    - C. Defense in depth
    - D. Mandatory vacation

53. Which one of the following is not normally considered a business continuity task?
    - A. Business impact assessment
    - B. Emergency response guidelines
    - C. Electronic vaulting
    - D. Vital records program

54. Which information security goal is impacted when an organization experiences a DoS or DDoS attack?
    - A. Confidentiality
    - B. Integrity
    - C. Availability
    - D. Denial

55. Yolanda is writing a document that will provide configuration information regarding the minimum level of security that every system in the organization must meet. What type of document is she preparing?
    - A. Policy
    - B. Baseline
    - C. Guideline
    - D. Procedure

56. Who should receive initial business continuity plan training in an organization?
    - A. Senior executives
    - B. Those with specific business continuity roles

C. Everyone in the organization

D. First responders

57. James is conducting a risk assessment for his organization and is attempting to assign an asset value to the servers in his data center. The organization's primary concern is ensuring that it has sufficient funds available to rebuild the data center in the event it is damaged or destroyed. Which one of the following asset valuation methods would be most appropriate in this situation?

A. Purchase cost

B. Depreciated cost

C. Replacement cost

D. Opportunity cost

58. The Computer Security Act of 1987 gave a federal agency responsibility for developing computer security standards and guidelines for federal computer systems. What agency did the act give this responsibility to?

A. National Security Agency

B. Federal Communications Commission

C. Department of Defense

D. National Institute of Standards and Technology

59. Which one of the following is not a requirement for an invention to be patentable?

A. It must be new.

B. It must be invented by an American citizen.

C. It must be nonobvious.

D. It must be useful.

60. Frank discovers a keylogger hidden on the laptop of his company's chief executive officer. What information security principle is the keylogger most likely designed to disrupt?

A. Confidentiality

B. Integrity

C. Availability

D. Denial

61. What is the formula used to determine risk?

A. Risk = Threat * Vulnerability

B. Risk = Threat / Vulnerability

C. Risk = Asset * Threat

D. Risk = Asset / Threat

62. The graphic below shows the NIST risk management framework with step 4 missing. What is the missing step?

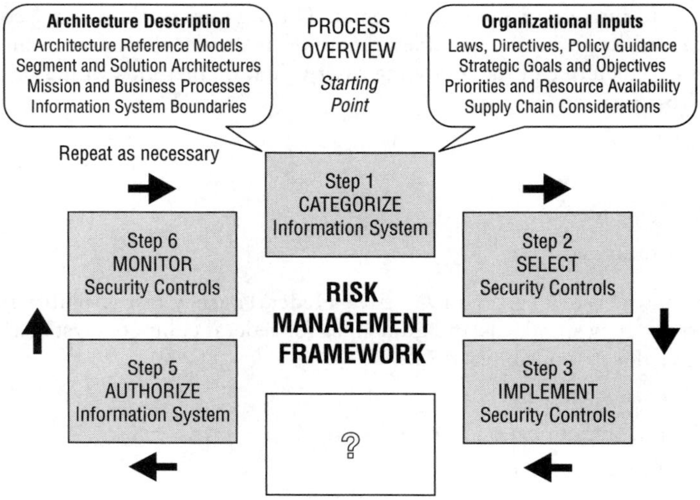

A. Assess security controls

B. Determine control gaps

C. Remediate control gaps

D. Evaluate user activity

63. HAL Systems recently decided to stop offering public NTP services because of a fear that its NTP servers would be used in amplification DDoS attacks. What type of risk management strategy did HAL pursue with respect to its NTP services?

A. Risk mitigation

B. Risk acceptance

C. Risk transference

D. Risk avoidance

64. Susan is working with the management team in her company to classify data in an attempt to apply extra security controls that will limit the likelihood of a data breach. What principle of information security is Susan trying to enforce?

A. Availability

B. Denial

C. Confidentiality

D. Integrity

65. Which one of the following components should be included in an organization's emergency response guidelines?
   A. List of individuals who should be notified of an emergency incident
   B. Long-term business continuity protocols
   C. Activation procedures for the organization's cold sites
   D. Contact information for ordering equipment

66. Who is the ideal person to approve an organization's business continuity plan?
   A. Chief information officer
   B. Chief executive officer
   C. Chief information security officer
   D. Chief operating officer

67. Which one of the following actions is not normally part of the project scope and planning phase of business continuity planning?
   A. Structured analysis of the organization
   B. Review of the legal and regulatory landscape
   C. Creation of a BCP team
   D. Documentation of the plan

68. Gary is implementing a new RAID-based disk system designed to keep a server up and running even in the event of a single disk failure. What principle of information security is Gary seeking to enforce?
   A. Denial
   B. Confidentiality
   C. Integrity
   D. Availability

69. Becka recently signed a contract with an alternate data processing facility that will provide her company with space in the event of a disaster. The facility includes HVAC, power, and communications circuits but no hardware. What type of facility is Becka using?
   A. Cold site
   B. Warm site
   C. Hot site
   D. Mobile site

70. What is the threshold for malicious damage to a federal computer system that triggers the Computer Fraud and Abuse Act?
   A. $500
   B. $2,500
   C. $5,000
   D. $10,000

71. Ben is seeking a control objective framework that is widely accepted around the world and focuses specifically on information security controls. Which one of the following frameworks would best meet his needs?

A. ITIL

B. ISO 27002

C. CMM

D. PMBOK Guide

72. Which one of the following laws requires that communications service providers cooperate with law enforcement requests?

A. ECPA

B. CALEA

C. Privacy Act

D. HITECH Act

73. Every year, Gary receives privacy notices in the mail from financial institutions where he has accounts. What law requires the institutions to send Gary these notices?

A. FERPA

B. GLBA

C. HIPAA

D. HITECH

74. Which one of the following agreements typically requires that a vendor not disclose confidential information learned during the scope of an engagement?

A. NCA

B. SLA

C. NDA

D. RTO

75. Which one of the following is not an example of a technical control?

A. Router ACL

B. Firewall rule

C. Encryption

D. Data classification

76. Which one of the following stakeholders is not typically included on a business continuity planning team?

A. Core business function leaders

B. Information technology staff

C. CEO

D. Support departments

77. Ben is designing a messaging system for a bank and would like to include a feature that allows the recipient of a message to prove to a third party that the message did indeed come from the purported originator. What goal is Ben trying to achieve?

A. Authentication

B. Authorization

C. Integrity

D. Nonrepudiation

78. What principle of information security states that an organization should implement overlapping security controls whenever possible?

A. Least privilege

B. Separation of duties

C. Defense in depth

D. Security through obscurity

79. Which one of the following is not a goal of a formal change management program?

A. Implement change in an orderly fashion.

B. Test changes prior to implementation.

C. Provide rollback plans for changes.

D. Inform stakeholders of changes after they occur.

80. Ben is responsible for the security of payment card information stored in a database. Policy directs that he remove the information from the database, but he cannot do this for operational reasons. He obtained an exception to policy and is seeking an appropriate compensating control to mitigate the risk. What would be his best option?

A. Purchasing insurance

B. Encrypting the database contents

C. Removing the data

D. Objecting to the exception

81. The Domer Industries risk assessment team recently conducted a qualitative risk assessment and developed a matrix similar to the one shown below. Which quadrant contains the risks that require the most immediate attention?

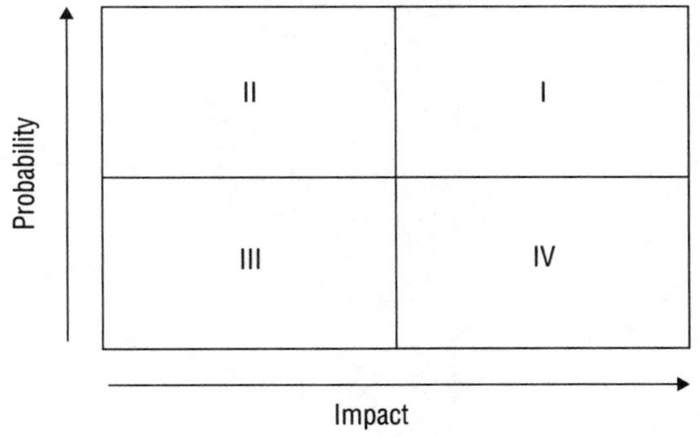

A. I

B. II

C. III

D. IV

82. Tom is planning to terminate an employee this afternoon for fraud and expects that the meeting will be somewhat hostile. He is coordinating the meeting with Human Resources and wants to protect the company against damage. Which one of the following steps is most important to coordinate in time with the termination meeting?

A. Informing other employees of the termination

B. Retrieval of photo ID

C. Calculation of final paycheck

D. Revocation of electronic access rights

83. Rolando is a risk manager with a large-scale enterprise. The firm recently evaluated the risk of California mudslides on its operations in the region and determined that the cost of responding outweighed the benefits of any controls it could implement. The company chose to take no action at this time. What risk management strategy did Rolando's organization pursue?

A. Risk avoidance

B. Risk mitigation

C. Risk transference

D. Risk acceptance

84. Helen is the owner of a website that provides information for middle and high school students preparing for exams. She is concerned that the activities of her site may fall under the jurisdiction of the Children's Online Privacy Protection Act (COPPA). What is the cutoff age below which parents must give consent in advance of the collection of personal information from their children under COPPA?

A. 13

B. 15

C. 17

D. 18

85. Tom is considering locating a business in the downtown area of Miami, Florida. He consults the FEMA flood plain map for the region, shown below, and determines that the area he is considering lies within a 100-year flood plain.

What is the ARO of a flood in this area?

A. 100

B. 1

C. 0.1

D. 0.01

86. You discover that a user on your network has been using the Wireshark tool, as shown in the following screen shot. Further investigation revealed that he was using it for illicit purposes. What pillar of information security has most likely been violated?

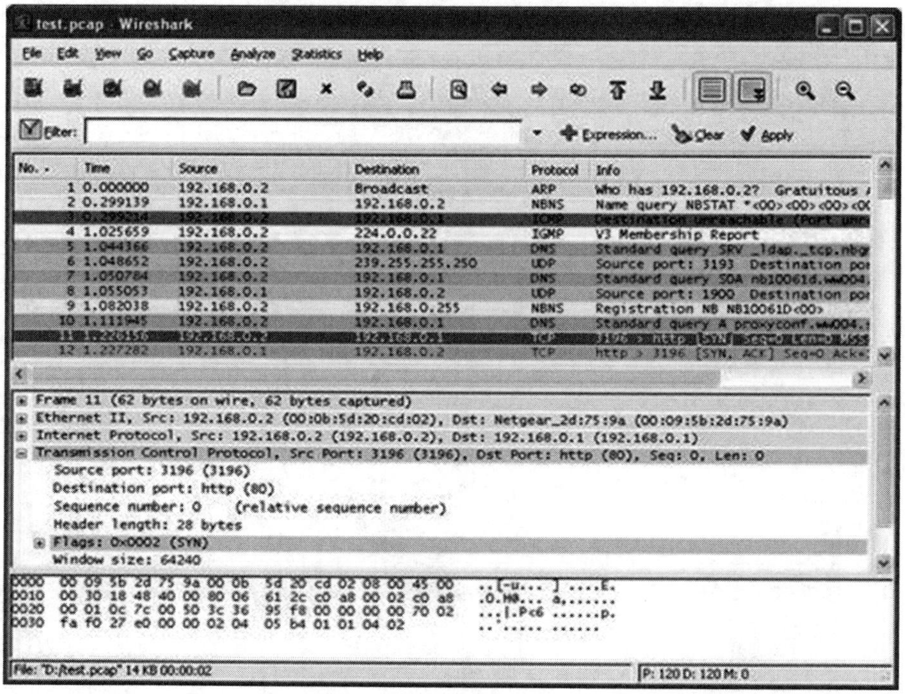

A. Integrity

B. Denial

C. Availability

D. Confidentiality

87. Alan is performing threat modeling and decides that it would be useful to decompose the system into the key elements shown in the following illustration. What tool is he using?

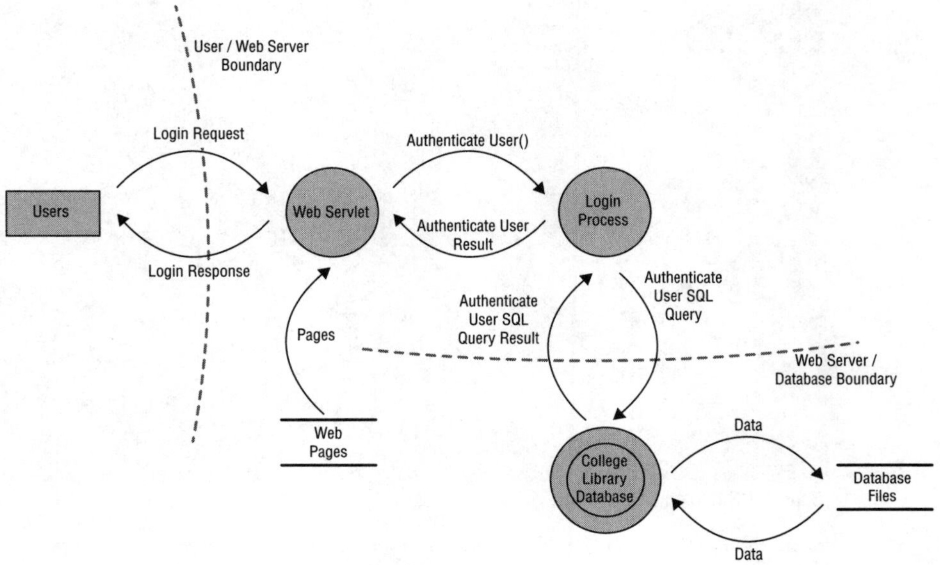

Image reprinted from *CISSP (ISC)² Certified Information Systems Security Professional Official Study Guide, 7th Edition* © John Wiley & Sons 2015, reprinted with permission.

A. Vulnerability assessment

B. Fuzzing

C. Reduction analsis

D. Data modeling

88. What law governs the handling of information related to the financial statements of publicly traded companies?

A. GLBA

B. PCI DSS

C. HIPAA

D. SOX

89. Craig is selecting the site for a new data center and must choose a location somewhere within the United States. He obtained the earthquake risk map below from the United States Geological Survey. Which of the following would be the safest location to build his facility if he were primarily concerned with earthquake risk?

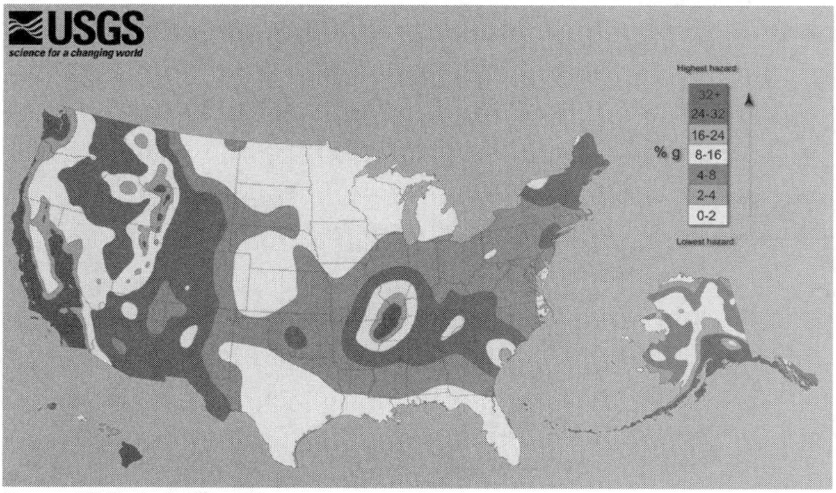

(Source: US Geological Survey)

Image reprinted from *CISSP (ISC)² Certified Information Systems Security Professional Official Study Guide, 7th Edition* © John Wiley & Sons 2015, reprinted with permission.

A. New York

B. North Carolina

C. Indiana

D. Florida

90. Which one of the following tools is most often used for identification purposes and is not suitable for use as an authenticator?

A. Password

B. Retinal scan

C. Username

D. Token

91. Which type of business impact assessment tool is most appropriate when attempting to evaluate the impact of a failure on customer confidence?

A. Quantitative

B. Qualitative

C. Annualized loss expectancy

D. Reduction

92. Which one of the following is the first step in developing an organization's vital records program?

A. Identifying vital records

B. Locating vital records

C. Archiving vital records

D. Preserving vital records

93. Which one of the following security programs is designed to provide employees with the knowledge they need to perform their specific work tasks?

A. Awareness

B. Training

C. Education

D. Indoctrination

94. Which one of the following security programs is designed to establish a minimum standard common denominator of security understanding?

A. Training

B. Education

C. Indoctrination

D. Awareness

95. Ryan is a security risk analyst for an insurance company. He is currently examining a scenario in which a hacker might use a SQL injection attack to deface a web server due to a missing patch in the company's web application. In this scenario, what is the threat?

A. Unpatched web application

B. Web defacement

C. Hacker

D. Operating system

Questions 96–98 refer to the following scenario.

Henry is the risk manager for Atwood Landing, a resort community in the Midwestern United States. The resort's main data center is located in northern Indiana in an area that is prone to tornados. Henry recently undertook a replacement cost analysis and determined that rebuilding and reconfiguring the data center would cost $10 million.

Henry consulted with tornado experts, data center specialists, and structural engineers. Together, they determined that a typical tornado would cause approximately $5 million of damage to the facility. The meteorologists determined that Atwood's facility lies in an area where they are likely to experience a tornado once every 200 years.

96. Based upon the information in this scenario, what is the exposure factor for the effect of a tornado on Atwood Landing's data center?

A. 10%

B. 25%

C. 50%

D. 75%

97. Based upon the information in this scenario, what is the annualized rate of occurrence for a tornado at Atwood Landing's data center?

A. 0.0025

B. 0.005

C. 0.01

D. 0.015

98. Based upon the information in this scenario, what is the annualized loss expectancy for a tornado at Atwood Landing's data center?

A. $25,000

B. $50,000

C. $250,000

D. $500,000

99. John is analyzing an attack against his company in which the attacker found comments embedded in HTML code that provided the clues needed to exploit a software vulnerability. Using the STRIDE model, what type of attack did he uncover?

A. Spoofing

B. Repudiation

C. Information disclosure

D. Elevation of privilege

100. Which one of the following is an administrative control that can protect the confidentiality of information?

A. Encryption

B. Non-disclosure agreement

C. Firewall

D. Fault tolerance

Chapter 2

Asset Security (Domain 2)

1. Angela is an information security architect at a bank and has been assigned to ensure that transactions are secure as they traverse the network. She recommends that all transactions use TLS. What threat is she most likely attempting to stop, and what method is she using to protect against it?
   A. Man-in-the-middle, VPN
   B. Packet injection, encryption
   C. Sniffing, encryption
   D. Sniffing, TEMPEST

2. COBIT, Control Objectives for Information and Related Technology, is a framework for IT management and governance. Which data management role is most likely to select and apply COBIT to balance the need for security controls against business requirements?
   A. Business owners
   B. Data processors
   C. Data owners
   D. Data stewards

3. What term is used to describe a starting point for a minimum security standard?
   A. Outline
   B. Baseline
   C. Policy
   D. Configuration guide

4. When media is labeled based on the classification of the data it contains, what rule is typically applied regarding labels?
   A. The data is labeled based on its integrity requirements.
   B. The media is labeled based on the highest classification level of the data it contains.
   C. The media is labeled with all levels of classification of the data it contains.
   D. The media is labeled with the lowest level of classification of the data it contains.

5. The need to protect sensitive data drives what administrative process?
   A. Information classification
   B. Remanence
   C. Transmitting data
   D. Clearing

6. How can a data retention policy help to reduce liabilities?
   A. By ensuring that unneeded data isn't retained
   B. By ensuring that incriminating data is destroyed
   C. By ensuring that data is securely wiped so it cannot be restored for legal discovery
   D. By reducing the cost of data storage required by law

7. Staff in an IT department who are delegated responsibility for day-to-day tasks hold what data role?

A. Business owner

B. User

C. Data processor

D. Custodian

8. Susan works for an American company that conducts business with customers in the European Union. What is she likely to have to do if she is responsible for handling PII from those customers?

A. Encrypt the data at all times.

B. Label and classify the data according to HIPAA.

C. Conduct yearly assessments to the EU DPD baseline.

D. Comply with the US-EU Safe Harbor requirements.

9. Ben has been tasked with identifying security controls for systems covered by his organization's information classification system. Why might Ben choose to use a security baseline?

A. It applies in all circumstances, allowing consistent security controls.

B. They are approved by industry standards bodies, preventing liability.

C. They provide a good starting point that can be tailored to organizational needs.

D. They ensure that systems are always in a secure state.

10. What term is used to describe overwriting media to allow for its reuse in an environment operating at the same sensitivity level?

A. Clearing

B. Erasing

C. Purging

D. Sanitization

11. Which of the following classification levels is the US government's classification label for data that could cause damage but wouldn't cause serious or grave damage?

A. Top Secret

B. Secret

C. Confidential

D. Classified

12. What issue is common to spare sectors and bad sectors on hard drives as well as overprovisioned space on modern SSDs?

A. They can be used to hide data.

B. They can only be degaussed.

C. They are not addressable, resulting in data remanence.

D. They may not be cleared, resulting in data remanence.

13. What term describes data that remains after attempts have been made to remove the data?

A. Residual bytes

B. Data remanence

C. Slack space

D. Zero fill

For questions 14, 15, and 16, please refer to the following scenario:

Your organization regularly handles three types of data: information that it shares with customers, information that it uses internally to conduct business, and trade secret information that offers the organization significant competitive advantages. Information shared with customers is used and stored on web servers, while both the internal business data and the trade secret information are stored on internal file servers and employee workstations.

14. What civilian data classifications best fit this data?

A. Unclassified, confidential, top secret

B. Public, sensitive, private

C. Public, sensitive, proprietary

D. Public, confidential, private

15. What technique could you use to mark your trade secret information in case it was released or stolen and you need to identify it?

A. Classification

B. Symmetric encryption

C. Watermarks

D. Metadata

16. What type of encryption should you use on the file servers for the proprietary data, and how might you secure the data when it is in motion?

A. TLS at rest and AES in motion

B. AES at rest and TLS in motion

C. VPN at rest and TLS in motion

D. DES at rest and AES in motion

17. What does labeling data allow a DLP system to do?

A. The DLP system can detect labels and apply appropriate protections.

B. The DLP system can adjust labels based on changes in the classification scheme.

C. The DLP system can notify the firewall that traffic should be allowed through.

D. The DLP system can delete unlabeled data.

18. Why is it cost effective to purchase high-quality media to contain sensitive data?

A. Expensive media is less likely to fail.

B. The value of the data often far exceeds the cost of the media.

C. Expensive media is easier to encrypt.

D. More expensive media typically improves data integrity.

19. Chris is responsible for workstations throughout his company and knows that some of the company's workstations are used to handle proprietary information. Which option best describes what should happen at the end of their lifecycle for workstations he is responsible for?

A. Erasing

B. Clearing

C. Sanitization

D. Destruction

20. Which is the proper order from least to most sensitive for US government classifications?

A. Confidential, Secret, Top Secret

B. Confidential, Classified, Secret

C. Top Secret, Secret, Classified, Public, Classified, Top Secret

D. Public, Unclassified, Classified, Top Secret

21. What scenario describes data at rest?

A. Data in an IPsec tunnel

B. Data in an e-commerce transaction

C. Data stored on a hard drive

D. Data stored in RAM

22. If you are selecting a security standard for a Windows 10 system that processes credit cards, what security standard is your best choice?

A. Microsoft's Windows 10 security baseline

B. The CIS Windows 10 baseline

C. PCI DSS

D. The NSA Windows 10 baseline

Use the following scenario for questions 23, 24, and 25.

The Center for Internet Security (CIS) works with subject matter experts from a variety of industries to create lists of security controls for operating systems, mobile devices, server software, and network devices. Your organization has decided to use the CIS benchmarks for your systems. Answer the following questions based on this decision.

23. The CIS benchmarks are an example of what practice?

A. Conducting a risk assessment

B. Implementing data labeling

C. Proper system ownership

D. Using security baselines

24. Adjusting the CIS benchmarks to your organization's mission and your specific IT systems would involve what two processes?

A. Scoping and selection

B. Scoping and tailoring

C. Baselining and tailoring

D. Tailoring and selection

25. How should you determine what controls from the baseline a given system or software package should receive?

A. Consult the custodians of the data.

B. Select based on the data classification of the data it stores or handles.

C. Apply the same controls to all systems.

D. Consult the business owner of the process the system or data supports.

26. What problem with FTP and Telnet makes using SFTP and SSH better alternatives?

A. FTP and Telnet aren't installed on many systems.

B. FTP and Telnet do not encrypt data.

C. FTP and Telnet have known bugs and are no longer maintained.

D. FTP and Telnet are difficult to use, making SFTP and SSH the preferred solution.

27. The government defense contractor that Saria works for has recently shut down a major research project and is planning on reusing the hundreds of thousands of dollars of systems and data storage tapes used for the project for other purposes. When Saria reviews the company's internal processes, she finds that she can't reuse the tapes and that the manual says they should be destroyed. Why isn't Saria allowed to degauss and then reuse the tapes to save her employer money?

A. Data permanence may be an issue.

B. Data remanence is a concern.

C. The tapes may suffer from bitrot.

D. Data from tapes can't be erased by degaussing.

28. Information maintained about an individual that can be used to distinguish or trace their identity is known as what type of information?

A. Personally identifiable information (PII)

B. Personal health information (PHI)

C. Social Security number (SSN)

D. Secure identity information (SII)

29. What is the primary information security risk to data at rest?

A. Improper classification

B. Data breach

C. Decryption

D. Loss of data integrity

30. Full disk encryption like Microsoft's BitLocker is used to protect data in what state?

A. Data in transit

B. Data at rest

C. Unlabeled data

D. Labeled data

31. Sue's employer has asked her to use an IPsec VPN to connect to its network. When Sue connects, what does the IPsec VPN allow her to do?

A. Send decrypted data over a public network and act like she is on her employer's internal network.

B. Create a private encrypted network carried via a public network and act like she is on her employer's internal network.

C. Create a virtual private network using TLS while on her employer's internal network.

D. Create a tunneled network that connects her employer's network to her internal home network.

32. What is the primary purpose of data classification?

A. It quantifies the cost of a data breach.

B. It prioritizes IT expenditures.

C. It allows compliance with breach notification laws.

D. It identifies the value of the data to the organization.

33. Fred's organization allows downgrading of systems for reuse after projects have been finished and the systems have been purged. What concern should Fred raise about the reuse of the systems from his Top Secret classified project for a future project classified as Secret?

A. The Top Secret data may be commingled with the Secret data, resulting in a need to relabel the system.

B. The cost of the sanitization process may exceed the cost of new equipment.

C. The data may be exposed as part of the sanitization process.

D. The organization's DLP system may flag the new system due to the difference in data labels.

34. Which of the following concerns should not be part of the decision when classifying data?

A. The cost to classify the data

B. The sensitivity of the data

C. The amount of harm that exposure of the data could cause

D. The value of the data to the organization

35. Which of the following is the least effective method of removing data from media?

A. Degaussing

B. Purging

C. Erasing

D. Clearing

36. Safe Harbor is part of a US program to meet what European Union law?

A. The EU CyberSafe Act

B. The Network and Information Security (NIS) directives

C. The General Data Protection Regulation (GDPR)

D. The EU Data Protection Directive

Use the following scenario to answer questions 37, 38, and 39.

The healthcare company that Lauren works for handles HIPAA data as well as internal business data, protected health information, and day-to-day business communications. Its internal policy uses the following requirements for securing HIPAA data at rest and in transit.

Classification	Handling Requirements
Confidential (HIPAA)	Encrypt at rest and in transit. Full disk encryption required for all workstations. Files can only be sent in encrypted form, and passwords must be transferred under separate cover. Printed documents must be labeled with "HIPAA handling required."
Private (PHI)	Encrypt at rest and in transit. PHI must be stored on secure servers, and copies should not be kept on local workstations. Printed documents must be labeled with "Private."

Classification	Handling Requirements
Sensitive (business confidential)	Encryption is recommended but not required.
Public	Information can be sent unencrypted.

Using the table, answer the following questions.

37. What type of encryption would be appropriate for HIPAA documents in transit?

A. AES256

B. DES

C. TLS

D. SSL

38. Lauren's employer asks Lauren to classify patient X-ray data that has an internal patient identifier associated with it but does not have any way to directly identify a patient. The company's data owner believes that exposure of the data could cause damage (but not exceptional damage) to the organization. How should Lauren classify the data?

A. Public

B. Sensitive

C. Private

D. Confidential

39. What technology could Lauren's employer implement to help prevent confidential data from being emailed out of the organization?

A. DLP

B. IDS

C. A firewall

D. UDP

40. A US government database contains Secret, Confidential, and Top Secret data. How should it be classified?

A. Top Secret

B. Confidential

C. Secret

D. Mixed classification

41. What tool is used to prevent employees who leave from sharing proprietary information with their new employers?

A. Encryption

B. NDA

C. Classification

D. Purging

42. What encryption algorithm is used by both BitLocker and Microsoft's Encrypting File System?

A. Blowfish

B. Serpent

C. AES

D. 3DES

43. Chris is responsible for his organization's security standards and has guided the selection and implementation of a security baseline for Windows PCs in his organization. How can Chris most effectively make sure that the workstations he is responsible for are being checked for compliance and that settings are being applied as necessary?

A. Assign users to spot-check baseline compliance.

B. Use Microsoft Group Policy.

C. Create startup scripts to apply policy at system start.

D. Periodically review the baselines with the data owner and system owners.

44. What term is used to describe a set of common security configurations, often provided by a third party?

A. Security policy

B. Baseline

C. DSS

D. SP 800

45. What type of policy describes how long data is retained and maintained before destruction?

A. Classification

B. Audit

C. Record retention

D. Availability

46. Which attack helped drive vendors to move away from SSL toward TLS-only by default?

A. POODLE

B. Stuxnet

C. BEAST

D. CRIME

47. What security measure can provide an additional security control in the event that backup tapes are stolen or lost?

A. Keep multiple copies of the tapes.

B. Replace tape media with hard drives.

C. Use appropriate security labels.

D. Use AES256 encryption.

48. Joe works at a major pharmaceutical research and development company and has been tasked with writing his organization's data retention policy. As part of its legal requirements, the organization must comply with the US Food and Drug Administration's Code of Federal Regulations Title 21. To do so, it is required to retain records with electronic signatures. Why would a signature be part of a retention requirement?

A. It ensures that someone has reviewed the data.

B. It provides confidentiality.

C. It ensures that the data has not been changed.

D. It validates who approved the data.

49. What protocol is preferred over Telnet for remote server administration via the command line?

A. SCP

B. SFTP

C. WDS

D. SSH

50. What method uses a strong magnetic field to erase media?

A. Magwipe

B. Degaussing

C. Sanitization

D. Purging

51. What primary issue does personnel retention deal with?

A. Employees quitting

B. Employees not moving on to new positions

C. Knowledge gained after employment

D. Knowledge gained during employment

52. Alex works for a government agency that is required to meet US federal government requirements for data security. To meet these requirements, Alex has been tasked with making sure data is identifiable by its classification level. What should Alex do to the data?

A. Classify the data.

B. Encrypt the data.

C. Label the data.

D. Apply DRM to the data.

53. Ben is following the NIST Special Publication 800-88 guidelines for sanitization and disposition as shown in the following diagram. He is handling information that his organization classified as sensitive, which is a moderate security categorization in the NIST model. If the media is going to be sold as surplus, what process does Ben need to follow?

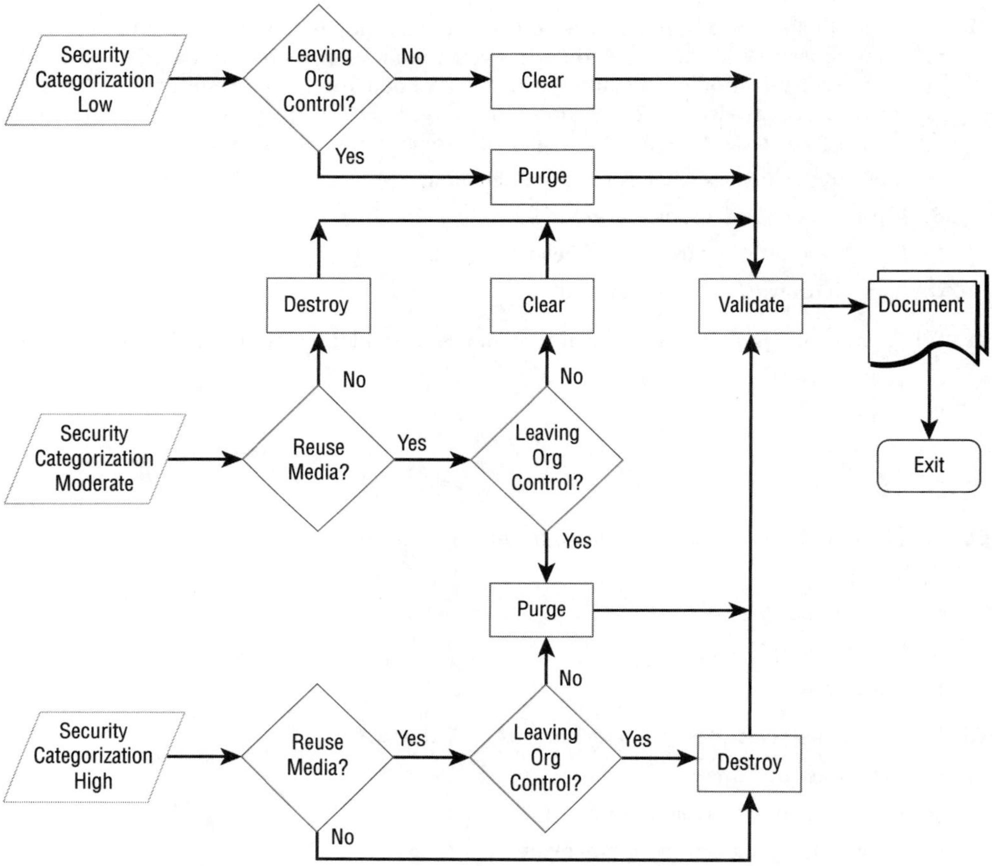

Figure Source: NIST SP 800-88

- **A.** Destroy, validate, document
- **B.** Clear, purge, document
- **C.** Purge, document, validate
- **D.** Purge, validate, document

54. What methods are often used to protect data in transit?

- **A.** Telnet, ISDN, UDP
- **B.** Encrypted storage media
- **C.** AES, Serpent, IDEA
- **D.** TLS, VPN, IPsec

55. Which data role is described as the person who has ultimate organizational responsibility for data?

A. System owners

B. Business owners

C. Data owners

D. Mission owners

56. What US government agency oversees compliance with the Safe Harbor framework for organizations wishing to use the personal data of EU citizens?

A. The FTC

B. The FDA

C. The DoD

D. The Department of Commerce

For questions 57, 58, and 59, use the following scenario.

Chris has recently been hired into a new organization. The organization that Chris belongs to uses the following classification process:

1. Criteria are set for classifying data.
2. Data owners are established for each type of data.
3. Data is classified.
4. Required controls are selected for each classification.
5. Baseline security standards are selected for the organization.
6. Controls are scoped and tailored.
7. Controls are applied and enforced.
8. Access is granted and managed.

Use the classification process to answer the following questions.

57. If Chris is one of the data owners for the organization, what steps in this process is he most likely responsible for?

A. He is responsible for steps 3, 4, and 5.

B. He is responsible for steps 1, 2, and 3.

C. He is responsible for steps 5, 6, and 7.

D. All of the steps are his direct responsibility.

58. Chris manages a team of system administrators. What data role are they fulfilling if they conduct steps 6, 7, and 8 of the classification process?

A. They are system owners and administrators.

B. They are administrators and custodians.

C. They are data owners and administrators.

D. They are custodians and users.

59. If Chris's company operates in the European Union and has been contracted to handle the data for a third party, what role is his company operating in when it uses this process to classify and handle data?

A. Business owners

B. Mission owners

C. Data processors

D. Data administrators

60. Which of the following is not a part of the European Union's Data Protection principles?

A. Notice

B. Reason

C. Security

D. Access

61. Ben's company, which is based in the EU, hires a third-party organization that processes data for it. Who has responsibility to protect the privacy of the data and ensure that it isn't used for anything other than its intended purpose?

A. Ben's company is responsible.

B. The third-party data processor is responsible.

C. The data controller is responsible.

D. Both organizations bear equal responsibility.

62. Major Hunter, a member of the US armed forces, has been entrusted with information that, if exposed, could cause serious damage to national security. Under US government classification standards, how should this data be classified?

A. Unclassified

B. Top Secret

C. Confidential

D. Secret

63. When a computer is removed from service and disposed of, the process that ensures that all storage media has been removed or destroyed is known as what?

A. Sanitization

B. Purging

C. Destruction

D. Declassification

64. Linux systems that use bcrypt are using a tool based on what DES alternative encryption scheme?

A. 3DES

B. AES

C. Diffie-Hellman

D. Blowfish

65. Susan works in an organization that labels all removable media with the classification level of the data it contains, including public data. Why would Susan's employer label all media instead of labeling only the media that contains data that could cause harm if it was exposed?

A. It is cheaper to order all prelabeled media.

B. It prevents sensitive media from not being marked by mistake.

C. It prevents reuse of public media for sensitive data.

D. Labeling all media is required by HIPAA.

66. Data stored in RAM is best characterized as what type of data?

A. Data at rest

B. Data in use

C. Data in transit

D. Data at large

67. What issue is the validation portion of the NIST SP 800-88 sample certificate of sanitization intended to help prevent?

A. Destruction

B. Reuse

C. Data remanence

D. Attribution

68. Why is declassification rarely chosen as an option for media reuse?

A. Purging is sufficient for sensitive data.

B. Sanitization is the preferred method of data removal.

C. It is more expensive than new media and may still fail.

D. Clearing is required first.

69. NIST SP 800-60 provides a process shown in the following diagram to assess information systems. What process does this diagram show?

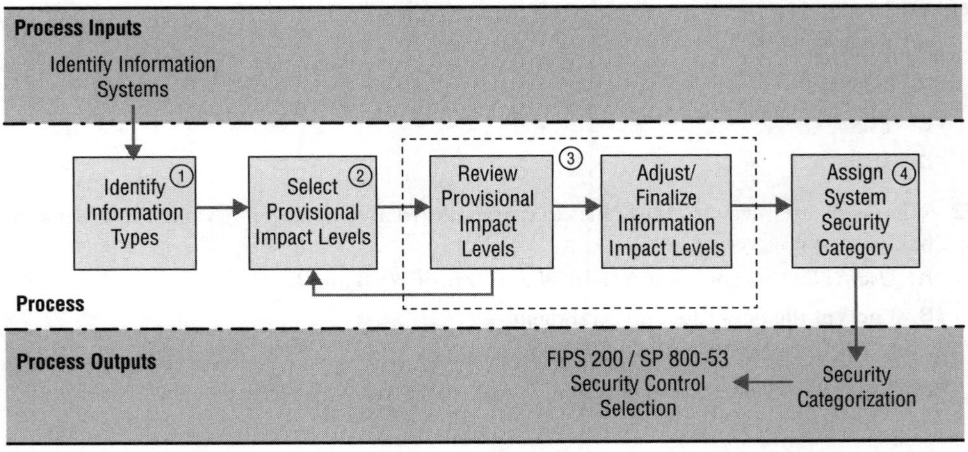

Figure Source: NIST SP 800-60

A. Selecting a standard and implementing it
B. Categorizing and selecting controls
C. Baselining and selecting controls
D. Categorizing and sanitizing

The following image shows a typical workstation and server and their connections to each other and the Internet. Use the image to answer questions 70, 71, and 72.

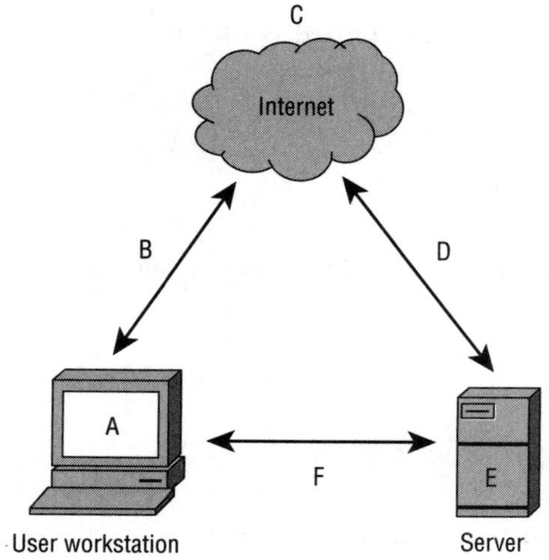

70. Which letters should be associated with data at rest?
A. A, B, and C
B. C and E
C. A and E
D. B, D, and F

71. What would be the best way to secure data at points B, D, and F?
A. AES256
B. SSL
C. TLS
D. 3DES

72. What is the best way to secure files that are sent from workstation A via the Internet service (C) to remote server E?
A. Use AES at rest at point A, and TLS in transit via B and D.
B. Encrypt the data files and send them.
C. Use 3DES and TLS to provide double security.
D. Use full disk encryption at A and E, and use SSL at B and D.

73. Incineration, crushing, shredding, and disintegration all describe what stage in the life cycle of media?
   A. Sanitization
   B. Degaussing
   C. Purging
   D. Destruction

74. The European Union (EU) Data Protection Directive's seven principles do not include which of the following key elements?
   A. The need to inform subjects when their data is being collected
   B. The need to set a limit on how long data is retained
   C. The need to keep the data secure
   D. The need to allow data subjects to be able to access and correct their data

75. Why might an organization use unique screen backgrounds or designs on workstations that deal with data of different classification levels?
   A. To indicate the software version in use
   B. To promote a corporate message
   C. To promote availability
   D. To indicate the classification level of the data or system

76. Charles has been asked to downgrade the media used for storage of private data for his organization. What process should Charles follow?
   A. Degauss the drives, and then relabel them with a lower classification level.
   B. Pulverize the drives, and then reclassify them based on the data they contain.
   C. Follow the organization's purging process, and then downgrade and replace labels.
   D. Relabel the media, and then follow the organization's purging process to ensure that the media matches the label.

77. Which of the following tasks are not performed by a system owner per NIST SP 800-18?
   A. Develops a system security plan
   B. Establishes rules for appropriate use and protection of data
   C. Identifies and implements security controls
   D. Ensures that system users receive appropriate security training

78. Susan needs to provide a set of minimum security requirements for email. What steps should she recommend for her organization to ensure that the email remains secure?
   A. All email should be encrypted.
   B. All email should be encrypted and labeled.
   C. Sensitive email should be encrypted and labeled.
   D. Only highly sensitive email should be encrypted.

79. What term describes the process of reviewing baseline security controls and selecting only the controls that are appropriate for the IT system you are trying to protect?

A. Standard creation

B. CIS benchmarking

C. Baselining

D. Scoping

80. What data role does a system that is used to process data have?

A. Mission owner

B. Data owner

C. Data processor

D. Custodian

81. Which of the following will be superceded in 2018 by the European Union's General Data Protection Regulation (GDPR)

A. The EU Data Protection Directive

B. NIST SP 800-12

C. The EU Personal Data Protection Regulation

D. COBIT

82. What type of health information is the Health Insurance Portability and Accountability Act required to protect?

A. PII

B. PHI

C. SHI

D. HPHI

83. What encryption algorithm would provide strong protection for data stored on a USB thumb drive?

A. TLS

B. SHA1

C. AES

D. DES

84. Lauren's multinational company wants to ensure compliance with the EU Data Protection Directive. If she allows data to be used against the requirements of the notice principle and against what users selected in the choice principle, what principle has her organization violated?

A. Onward transfer

B. Data integrity

C. Enforcement

D. Access

85. What is the best method to sanitize a solid-state drive (SSD)?

A. Clearing

B. Zero fill

C. Disintegration

D. Degaussing

For questions 86, 87, and 88, use the following scenario.

As shown in the following security life cycle diagram (loosely based on the NIST reference architecture), NIST uses a five-step process for risk management. Using your knowledge of data roles and practices, answer the following questions based on the NIST framework process.

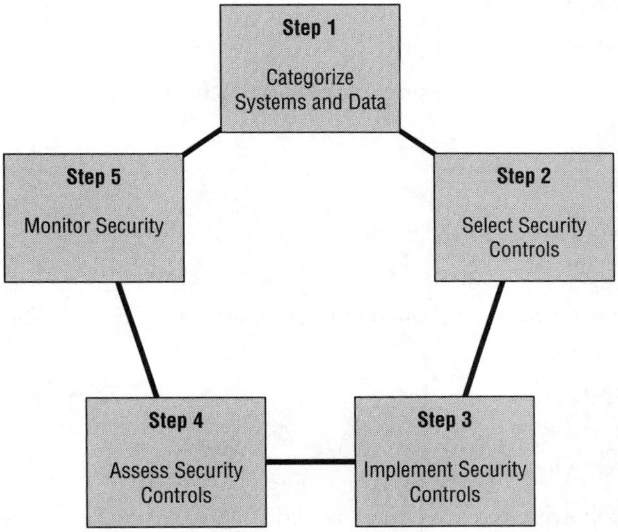

86. What data role will own responsibility for step 1, the categorization of information systems, to whom will they delegate step 2, and what data role will be responsible for step 3?

A. Data owners, system owners, custodians

B. Data processors, custodians, users

C. Business owners, administrators, custodians

D. System owners, business owners, administrators

87. If the systems that are being assessed all handle credit card information (and no other sensitive data), at what step would the PCI DSS first play an important role?

A. Step 1

B. Step 2

C. Step 3

D. Step 4

88. What data security role is primarily responsible for step 5?

A. Data owners

B. Data processors

C. Custodians

D. Users

89. Susan's organization performs a zero fill on hard drives before they are sent to a third-party organization to be shredded. What issue is her organization attempting to avoid?

A. Data remanence while at the third-party site

B. Mishandling of drives by the third party

C. Classification mistakes

D. Data permanence

90. Embedded data used to help identify the owner of a file is an example of what type of label?

A. Copyright notice

B. DLP

C. Digital watermark

D. Steganography

91. Retaining and maintaining information for as long as it is needed is known as what?

A. Data storage policy

B. Data storage

C. Asset maintenance

D. Record retention

92. Which of the following activities is not a consideration during data classification?

A. Who can access the data

B. What the impact would be if the data was lost or breached

C. How much the data cost to create

D. What protection regulations may be required for the data

93. What type of encryption is typically used for data at rest?

A. Asymmetric encryption

B. Symmetric encryption

C. DES

D. OTP

94. Which data role is tasked with granting appropriate access to staff members?

A. Data processors

B. Business owners

C. Custodians

D. Administrators

95. Which California law requires conspicuously posted privacy policies on commercial websites that collect the personal information of California residents?

A. The Personal Information Protection and Electronic Documents Act

B. The California Online Privacy Protection Act

C. California Online Web Privacy Act

D. California Civil Code 1798.82

96. Fred is preparing to send backup tapes off site to a secure third-party storage facility. What steps should Fred take before sending the tapes to that facility?

A. Ensure that the tapes are handled the same way the original media would be handled based on their classification.

B. Increase the classification level of the tapes because they are leaving the possession of the company.

C. Purge the tapes to ensure that classified data is not lost.

D. Encrypt the tapes in case they are lost in transit.

97. Which of the following does not describe data in motion?

A. Data on a backup tape that is being shipped to a storage facility

B. Data in a TCP packet

C. Data in an e-commerce transaction

D. Data in files being copied between locations

98. A new law is passed that would result in significant financial harm to your company if the data that it covers was stolen or inadvertently released. What should your organization do about this?

A. Select a new security baseline.

B. Relabel the data.

C. Encrypt all of the data at rest and in transit.

D. Review its data classifications and classify the data appropriately.

99. Ed has been asked to send data that his organization classifies as confidential and proprietary via email. What encryption technology would be appropriate to ensure that the contents of the files attached to the email remain confidential as they traverse the Internet?

A. SSL

B. TLS

C. PGP

D. VPN

100. Which mapping correctly matches data classifications between nongovernment and government classification schemes?

A. Top Secret - Confidential/Proprietary

Secret – Private

Confidential – Sensitive

B. Secret - Business confidential

Classifed - Proprietary

Confidential - Business Internal

C. Top Secret - Business sensitive

Secret - Business internal

Confidential - Business proprietary

D. Secret - Proprietary

Classified - Private

Unclassified - Public

Chapter 3

Security Engineering (Domain 3)

1. Matthew is the security administrator for a consulting firm and must enforce access controls that restrict users' access based upon their previous activity. For example, once a consultant accesses data belonging to Acme Cola, a consulting client, they may no longer access data belonging to any of Acme's competitors. What security model best fits Matthew's needs?
   - **A.** Clark-Wilson
   - **B.** Biba
   - **C.** Bell-LaPadula
   - **D.** Brewer-Nash

2. Referring to the figure shown below, what is the earliest stage of a fire where it is possible to use detection technology to identify it?

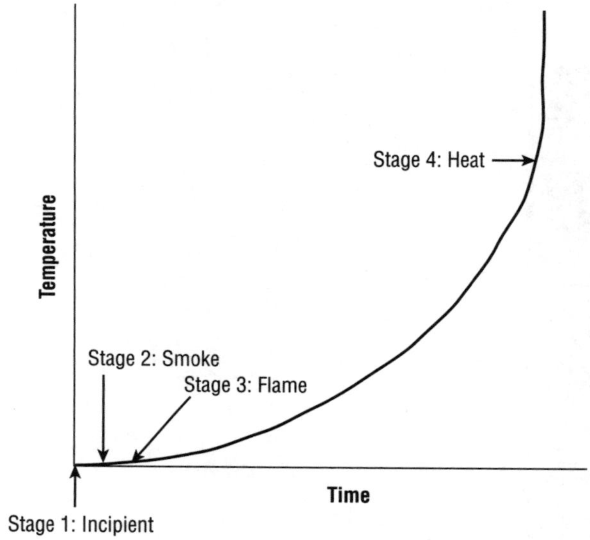

Image reprinted from *CISSP (ISC)² Certified Information Systems Security Professional Official Study Guide, 7th Edition* © John Wiley & Sons 2015, reprinted with permission.

   - **A.** Incipient
   - **B.** Smoke
   - **C.** Flame
   - **D.** Heat

3. Ralph is designing a physical security infrastructure for a new computing facility that will remain largely unstaffed. He plans to implement motion detectors in the facility but would also like to include a secondary verification control for physical presence. Which one of the following would best meet his needs?

A. CCTV
B. IPS
C. Turnstiles
D. Faraday cages

4. Harry would like to retrieve a lost encryption key from a database that uses m of n control with m = 4 and n = 8. What is the minimum number of escrow agents required to retrieve the key?
A. 2
B. 4
C. 8
D. 12

5. Fran's company is considering purchasing a web-based email service from a vendor and eliminating its own email server environment as a cost-saving measure. What type of cloud computing environment is Fran's company considering?
A. SaaS
B. IaaS
C. CaaS
D. PaaS

6. Bob is a security administrator with the federal government and wishes to choose a digital signature approach that is an approved part of the federal Digital Signature Standard under FIPS 186-4. Which one of the following encryption algorithms is not an acceptable choice for use in digital signatures?
A. DSA
B. HAVAL
C. RSA
D. ECDSA

7. Harry would like to access a document owned by Sally and stored on a file server. Applying the subject/object model to this scenario, who or what is the subject of the resource request?
A. Harry
B. Sally
C. Server
D. Document

8. Michael is responsible for forensic investigations and is investigating a medium severity security incident that involved the defacement of a corporate website. The web server in question ran on a virtualization platform, and the marketing team would like to get the website up and running as quickly as possible. What would be the most reasonable next step for Michael to take?

A. Keep the website offline until the investigation is complete.
B. Take the virtualization platform offline as evidence.
C. Take a snapshot of the compromised system and use that for the investigation.
D. Ignore the incident and focus on quickly restoring the website.

9. Helen is a software engineer and is developing code that she would like to restrict to running within an isolated sandbox for security purposes. What software development technique is Helen using?
   A. Bounds
   B. Input validation
   C. Confinement
   D. TCB

10. What concept describes the degree of confidence that an organization has that its controls satisfy security requirements?
    A. Trust
    B. Credentialing
    C. Verification
    D. Assurance

11. What type of security vulnerability are developers most likely to introduce into code when they seek to facilitate their own access, for testing purposes, to software they developed?
    A. Maintenance hook
    B. Cross-site scripting
    C. SQL injection
    D. Buffer overflow

12. In the figure shown below, Sally is blocked from reading the file due to the Biba integrity model. Sally has a Secret security clearance and the file has a Confidential classification. What principle of the Biba model is being enforced?

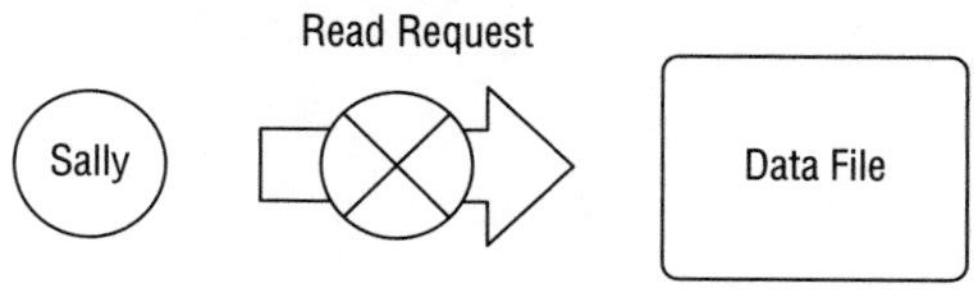

    A. Simple Security Property
    B. Simple Integrity Property
    C. *-Security Property
    D. *-Integrity Property

13. Tom is responsible for maintaining the security of systems used to control industrial processes located within a power plant. What term is used to describe these systems?

A. POWER

B. SCADA

C. HAVAL

D. COBOL

14. Sonia recently removed an encrypted hard drive from a laptop and moved it to a new device because of a hardware failure. She is having difficulty accessing encrypted content on the drive despite the fact that she knows the user's password. What hardware security feature is likely causing this problem?

A. TCB

B. TPM

C. NIACAP

D. RSA

15. Marcy would like to continue using some old DES encryption equipment to avoid throwing it away. She understands that running DES multiple times improves the security of the algorithm. What is the minimum number of times she must run DES on the same data to achieve security that is cryptographically strong by modern standards?

A. 2

B. 3

C. 4

D. 12

Questions 16–19 refer to the following scenario.

Alice and Bob would like to use an asymmetric cryptosystem to communicate with each other. They are located in different parts of the country but have exchanged encryption keys by using digital certificates signed by a mutually trusted certificate authority.

16. If Alice wishes to send Bob an encrypted message, what key does she use to encrypt the message?

A. Alice's public key

B. Alice's private key

C. Bob's public key

D. Bob's private key

17. When Bob receives the encrypted message from Alice, what key does he use to decrypt the message?

A. Alice's public key

B. Alice's private key

C. Bob's public key

D. Bob's private key

18. Which one of the following keys would Bob not possess in this scenario?

A. Alice's public key

B. Alice's private key

C. Bob's public key

D. Bob's private key

19. Alice would also like to digitally sign the message that she sends to Bob. What key should she use to create the digital signature?

A. Alice's public key

B. Alice's private key

C. Bob's public key

D. Bob's private key

20. What name is given to the random value added to a password in an attempt to defeat rainbow table attacks?

A. Hash

B. Salt

C. Extender

D. Rebar

21. Which one of the following is not an attribute of a hashing algorithm?

A. They require a cryptographic key.

B. They are irreversible.

C. It is very difficult to find two messages with the same hash value.

D. They take variable-length input.

22. What type of fire suppression system fills with water when the initial stages of a fire are detected and then requires a sprinkler head heat activation before dispensing water?

A. Wet pipe

B. Dry pipe

C. Deluge

D. Preaction

23. Susan would like to configure IPsec in a manner that provides confidentiality for the content of packets. What component of IPsec provides this capability?

A. AH

B. ESP

C. IKE

D. ISAKMP

24. Which one of the following cryptographic goals protects against the risks posed when a device is lost or stolen?

A. Nonrepudiation

B. Authentication

C. Integrity

D. Confidentiality

25. What logical operation is described by the truth table below?

Input 1	Input 2	Output
0	0	0
0	1	1
1	0	1
1	1	0

A. OR

B. AND

C. XOR

D. NOR

26. How many bits of keying material does the Data Encryption Standard use for encrypting information?

A. 56 bits

B. 64 bits

C. 128 bits

D. 256 bits

27. In the figure shown below, Harry's request to write to the data file is blocked. Harry has a Secret security clearance and the data file has a Confidential classification. What principle of the Bell-LaPadula model blocked this request?

A. Simple Security Property

B. Simple Integrity Property

C. *-Security Property

D. Discretionary Security Property

28. Florian and Tobias would like to begin communicating using a symmetric cryptosystem but they have no prearranged secret and are not able to meet in person to exchange keys. What algorithm can they use to securely exchange the secret key?

A. IDEA

B. Diffie-Hellman

C. RSA

D. MD5

29. Under the Common Criteria, what element describes the security requirements for a product?

A. TCSEC

B. ITSEC

C. PP

D. ST

30. Which one of the following is not one of the basic requirements for a cryptographic hash function?

A. The function must work on fixed-length input.

B. The function must be relatively easy to compute for any input.

C. The function must be one way.

D. The function must be collision free.

31. How many possible keys exist for a cipher that uses a key containing 5 bits?

A. 10

B. 16

C. 32

D. 64

32. What cryptographic principle stands behind the idea that cryptographic algorithms should be open to public inspection?

A. Security through obscurity

B. Kerchoff principle

C. Defense in depth

D. Heisenburg principle

33. Referring to the figure shown below, what is the name of the security control indicated by the arrow?

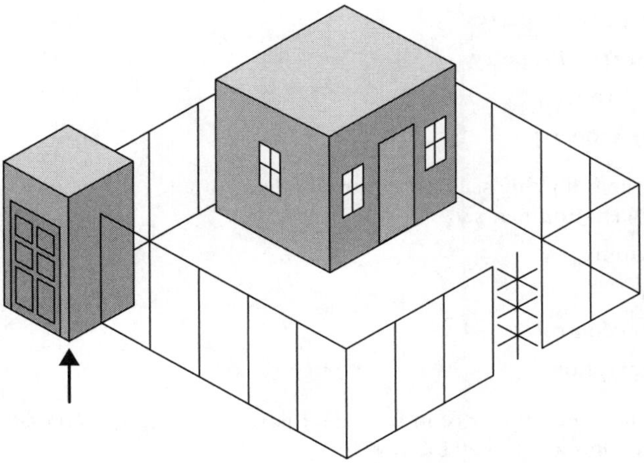

Image reprinted from *CISSP (ISC)² Certified Information Systems Security Professional Official Study Guide, 7th Edition* © John Wiley & Sons 2015, reprinted with permission.

A. Mantrap
B. Turnstile
C. Intrusion prevention system
D. Portal

34. Which one of the following does not describe a standard physical security requirement for wiring closets?
A. Place only in areas monitored by security guards.
B. Do not store flammable items in the closet.
C. Use sensors on doors to log entries.
D. Perform regular inspections of the closet.

35. In the figure shown below, Sally is blocked from writing to the data file by the Biba integrity model. Sally has a Secret security clearance and the file is classified Top Secret. What principle is preventing her from writing to the file?

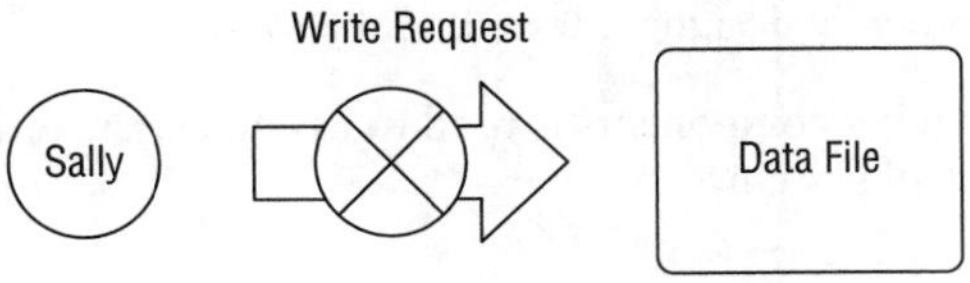

A. Simple Security Property
B. Simple Integrity Property
C. *-Security Property
D. *-Integrity Property

36. Which one of the following security controls is least often required in Bring Your Own Device (BYOD) environments?
A. Remote wiping
B. Passcodes
C. Application control
D. Device encryption

37. What is the minimum number of independent parties necessary to implement the Fair Cryptosystems approach to key escrow?
A. 1
B. 2
C. 3
D. 4

38. In what state does a processor's scheduler place a process when it is prepared to execute but the CPU is not currently available?
A. Ready
B. Running
C. Waiting
D. Stopped

39. Alan is reviewing a system that has been assigned the EAL1 evaluation assurance level under the Common Criteria. What is the degree of assurance that he may have about the system?
A. It has been functionally tested.
B. It has been structurally tested.
C. It has been formally verified, designed, and tested.
D. It has been methodically designed, tested, and reviewed.

40. Which one of the following components is used to assign classifications to objects in a mandatory access control system?
A. Security label
B. Security token
C. Security descriptor
D. Security capability

41. What type of software program exposes the code to anyone who wishes to inspect it?

A. Closed source

B. Open-source

C. Fixed source

D. Unrestricted source

42. Adam recently configured permissions on an NTFS filesystem to describe the access that different users may have to a file by listing each user individually. What did Adam create?

A. An access control list

B. An access control entry

C. Role-based access control

D. Mandatory access control

43. Betty is concerned about the use of buffer overflow attacks against a custom application developed for use in her organization. What security control would provide the strongest defense against these attacks?

A. Firewall

B. Intrusion detection system

C. Parameter checking

D. Vulnerability scanning

44. Which one of the following terms is not used to describe a privileged mode of system operation?

A. User mode

B. Kernel mode

C. Supervisory mode

D. System mode

45. James is working with a Department of Defense system that is authorized to simultaneously handle information classified at the Secret and Top Secret levels. What type of system is he using?

A. Single state

B. Unclassified

C. Compartmented

D. Multistate

46. Kyle is being granted access to a military computer system that uses System High mode. What is not true about Kyle's security clearance requirements?

A. Kyle must have a clearance for the highest level of classification processed by the system, regardless of his access.

B. Kyle must have access approval for all information processed by the system.

C. Kyle must have a valid need to know for all information processed by the system.

D. Kyle must have a valid security clearance.

47. Gary intercepts a communication between two individuals and suspects that they are exchanging secret messages. The content of the communication appears to be the image shown below. What type of technique may the individuals use to hide messages inside this image?

A. Visual cryptography

B. Steganography

C. Cryptographic hashing

D. Transport layer security

48. Which one of the following terms accurately describes the Caesar cipher?

A. Transposition cipher

B. Block cipher

C. Shift cipher

D. Strong cipher

49. In the ring protection model shown below, what ring contains the operating system's kernel?

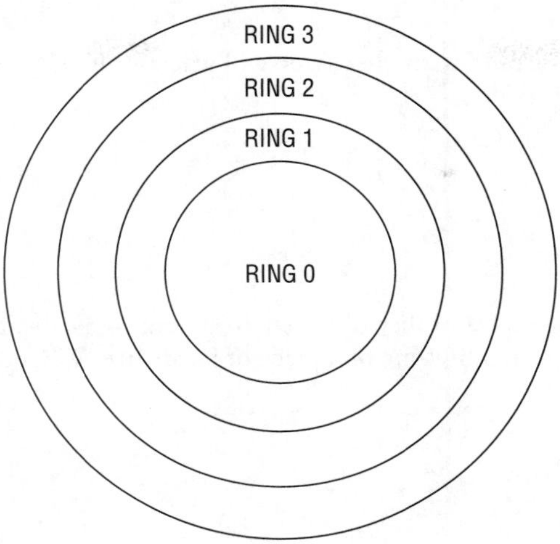

A. Ring 0

B. Ring 1

C. Ring 2

D. Ring 3

50. In an Infrastructure as a Service (IaaS) environment where a vendor supplies a customer with access to storage services, who is normally responsible for removing sensitive data from drives that are taken out of service?

A. Customer's security team

B. Customer's storage team

C. Customer's vendor management team

D. Vendor

51. Which one of the following is an example of a code, not a cipher?

A. Data Encryption Standard

B. "One if by land; two if by sea"

C. Shifting letters by three

D. Word scramble

52. Which one of the following systems assurance processes provides an independent third-party evaluation of a system's controls that may be trusted by many different organizations?

A. Certification

B. Definition

C. Verification

D. Accreditation

53. Process ________ ensures that any behavior will affect only the memory and resources associated with a process.

A. Restriction

B. Isolation

C. Limitation

D. Parameters

54. Harold is assessing the susceptibility of his environment to hardware failures and would like to identify the expected lifetime of a piece of hardware. What measure should he use for this?

A. MTTR

B. MTTF

C. RTO

D. MTO

55. What type of fire extinguisher is useful only against common combustibles?

A. Class A

B. Class B

C. Class C

D. Class D

56. Gary is concerned about applying consistent security settings to the many mobile devices used throughout his organization. What technology would best assist with this challenge?

A. MDM

B. IPS

C. IDS

D. SIEM

57. Alice sent a message to Bob. Bob would like to demonstrate to Charlie that the message he received definitely came from Alice. What goal of cryptography is Bob attempting to achieve?

A. Authentication

B. Confidentiality

C. Nonrepudiation

D. Integrity

58. Rhonda is considering the use of new identification cards for physical access control in her organization. She comes across a military system that uses the card shown below. What type of card is this?

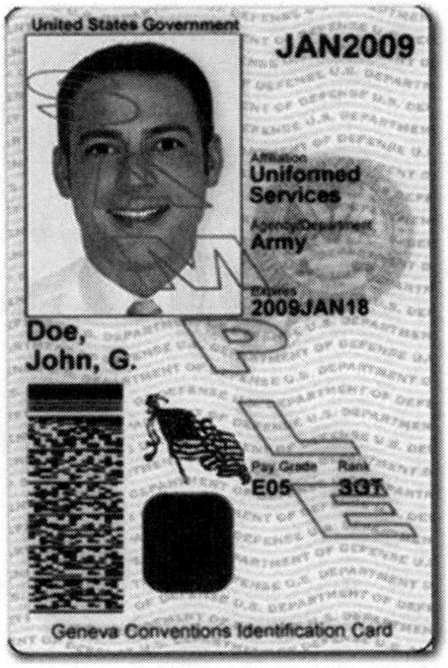

A. Smart card

B. Proximity card

C. Magnetic stripe card

D. Phase three card

59. Gordon is concerned about the possibility that hackers may be able to use the Van Eck radiation phenomenon to remotely read the contents of computer monitors in his facility. What technology would protect against this type of attack?

A. TCSEC

B. SCSI

C. GHOST

D. TEMPEST

60. In the diagram shown below of security boundaries within a computer system, what component's name has been replaced with XXX?

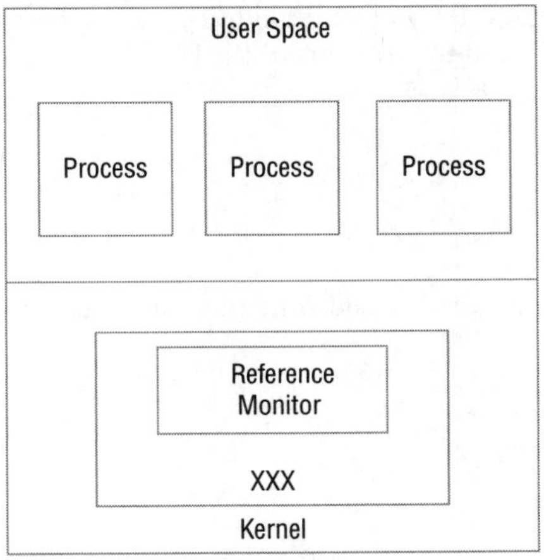

A. Kernel

B. TCB

C. Security perimeter

D. User execution

61. Sherry conducted an inventory of the cryptographic technologies in use within her organization and found the following algorithms and protocols in use. Which one of these technologies should she replace because it is no longer considered secure?

A. MD5

B. 3DES

C. PGP

D. WPA2

62. What action can you take to prevent accidental data disclosure due to wear leveling on an SSD device before reusing the drive?

A. Reformatting

B. Disk encryption

C. Degaussing

D. Physical destruction

63. Tom is a cryptanalyst and is working on breaking a cryptographic algorithm's secret key. He has a copy of an intercepted message that is encrypted and he also has a copy of the decrypted version of that message. He wants to use both the encrypted message and its decrypted plaintext to retrieve the secret key for use in decrypting other messages. What type of attack is Tom engaging in?

A. Chosen ciphertext

B. Chosen plaintext

C. Known plaintext

D. Brute force

64. A hacker recently violated the integrity of data in James's company by modifying a file using a precise timing attack. The attacker waited until James verified the integrity of a file's contents using a hash value and then modified the file between the time that James verified the integrity and read the contents of the file. What type of attack took place?

A. Social engineering

B. TOCTOU

C. Data diddling

D. Parameter checking

65. What standard governs the creation and validation of digital certificates for use in a public key infrastructure?

A. X.509

B. TLS

C. SSL
D. 802.1x

66. What is the minimum fence height that makes a fence difficult to climb easily, deterring most intruders?
A. 3 feet
B. 4 feet
C. 5 feet
D. 6 feet

67. Johnson Widgets strictly limits access to total sales volume information, classifying it as a competitive secret. However, shipping clerks have unrestricted access to order records to facilitate transaction completion. A shipping clerk recently pulled all of the individual sales records for a quarter and totaled them up to determine the total sales volume. What type of attack occurred?
A. Social engineering
B. Inference
C. Aggregation
D. Data diddling

68. What physical security control broadcasts false emanations constantly to mask the presence of true electromagnetic emanations from computing equipment?
A. Faraday cage
B. Copper-infused windows
C. Shielded cabling
D. White noise

69. In a Software as a Service cloud computing environment, who is normally responsible for ensuring that appropriate firewall controls are in place?
A. Customer's security team
B. Vendor
C. Customer's networking team
D. Customer's infrastructure management team

70. Alice has read permissions on an object and she would like Bob to have those same rights. Which one of the rules in the Take-Grant protection model would allow her to complete this operation?
A. Create rule
B. Remove rule
C. Grant rule
D. Take rule

71. In what type of attack does the attacker replace the legitimate BIOS on a computer with a malicious alternative that allows them to take control of the system?

A. Phlashing

B. Phreaking

C. Phishing

D. Phogging

72. Which one of the following computing models allows the execution of multiple concurrent tasks within a single process?

A. Multitasking

B. Multiprocessing

C. Multiprogramming

D. Multithreading

73. Alan intercepts an encrypted message and wants to determine what type of algorithm was used to create the message. He first performs a frequency analysis and notes that the frequency of letters in the message closely matches the distribution of letters in the English language. What type of cipher was most likely used to create this message?

A. Substitution cipher

B. AES

C. Transposition cipher

D. 3DES

74. The Double DES (2DES) encryption algorithm was never used as a viable alternative to the original DES algorithm. What attack is 2DES vulnerable to that does not exist for the DES or 3DES approach?

A. Chosen ciphertext

B. Brute force

C. Man in the middle

D. Meet in the middle

75. Grace would like to implement application control technology in her organization. Users often need to install new applications for research and testing purposes, and she does not want to interfere with that process. At the same time, she would like to block the use of known malicious software. What type of application control would be appropriate in this situation?

A. Blacklisting

B. Greylisting

C. Whitelisting

D. Bluelisting

76. Warren is designing a physical intrusion detection system for his data center and wants to include technology that issues an alert if the communications lines for the alarm system are unexpectedly cut. What technology would meet this requirement?

A. Heartbeat sensor

B. Emanation security

C. Motion detector

D. Faraday cage

77. John and Gary are negotiating a business transaction and John must demonstrate to Gary that he has access to a system. He engages in an electronic version of the "magic door" scenario shown below. What technique is John using?

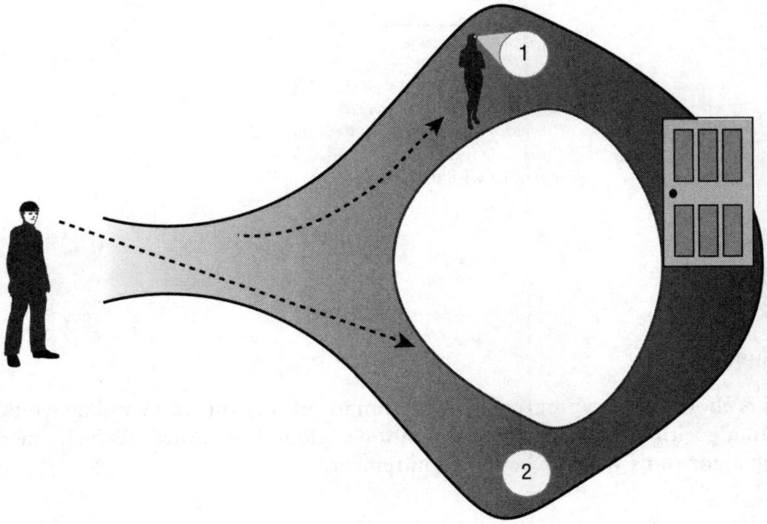

Image reprinted from *CISSP (ISC)² Certified Information Systems Security Professional Official Study Guide, 7th Edition* © John Wiley & Sons 2015, reprinted with permission.

A. Split-knowledge proof

B. Zero-knowledge proof

C. Logical proof

D. Mathematical proof

78. Raj is selecting an encryption algorithm for use in his organization and would like to be able to vary the strength of the encryption with the sensitivity of the information. Which one of the following algorithms allows the use of different key strengths?

A. Blowfish

B. DES

C. Skipjack

D. IDEA

79. Referring to the fire triangle shown below, which one of the following suppression materials attacks a fire by removing the fuel source?

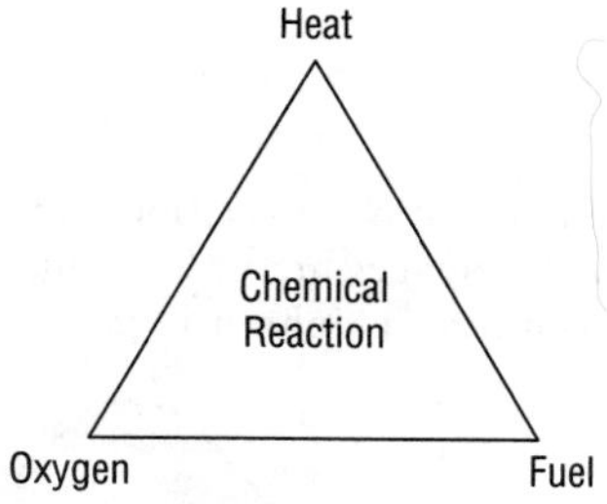

Image reprinted from *CISSP (ISC)² Certified Information Systems Security Professional Official Study Guide, 7th Edition* © John Wiley & Sons 2015, reprinted with permission.

A. Water

B. Soda acid

C. Carbon dioxide

D. Halon

80. Howard is choosing a cryptographic algorithm for his organization and he would like to choose an algorithm that supports the creation of digital signatures. Which one of the following algorithms would meet his requirement?

A. RSA

B. DES

C. AES

D. Blowfish

81. Laura is responsible for securing her company's web-based applications and wishes to conduct an educational program for developers on common web application security vulnerabilities. Where can she turn for a concise listing of the most common web application issues?

A. CVE

B. NSA

C. OWASP

D. CSA

82. The Bell-LaPadula and Biba models implement state machines in a fashion that uses what specific state machine model?

A. Information flow
B. Noninterference
C. Cascading
D. Feedback

83. The ________ of a process consist(s) of the limits set on the memory addresses and resources that the process may access.

A. Perimeter
B. Confinement limits
C. Metes
D. Bounds

84. What type of motion detector senses changes in the electromagnetic fields in monitored areas?

A. Infrared
B. Wave pattern
C. Capacitance
D. Photoelectric

85. Which one of the following fire suppression systems uses a suppressant that is no longer manufactured due to environmental concerns?

A. FM-200
B. Argon
C. Inergen
D. Halon

86. Which one of the following statements is correct about the Biba model of access control?

A. It addresses confidentiality and integrity.
B. It addresses integrity and availability.
C. It prevents covert channel attacks.
D. It focuses on protecting objects from external threats.

87. In Transport Layer Security, what type of key is used to encrypt the actual content of communications between a web server and a client?

A. Ephemeral session key
B. Client's public key
C. Server's public key
D. Server's private key

88. Beth would like to include technology in a secure area of her data center to protect against unwanted electromagnetic emanations. What technology would assist her with this goal?

A. Heartbeat sensor

B. Faraday cage

C. Piggybacking

D. WPA2

89. In a virtualized computing environment, what component is responsible for enforcing separation between guest machines?

A. Guest operating system

B. Hypervisor

C. Kernel

D. Protection manager

90. Rick is an application developer who works primarily in Python. He recently decided to evaluate a new service where he provides his Python code to a vendor who then executes it on their server environment. What type of cloud computing environment is this service?

A. SaaS

B. PaaS

C. IaaS

D. CaaS

91. A software company developed two systems that share information. System A provides information to the input of System B, which then reciprocates by providing information back to System A as input. What type of composition theory best describes this practice?

A. Cascading

B. Feedback

C. Hookup

D. Elementary

92. Tommy is planning to implement a power conditioning UPS for a rack of servers in his data center. Which one of the following conditions will the UPS be unable to protect against if it persists for more than a few minutes?

A. Fault

B. Blackout

C. Sag

D. Noise

93. Which one of the following humidity values is within the acceptable range for a data center operation?

A. 0%

B. 10%

C. 25%

D. 40%

94. Chris is designing a cryptographic system for use within his company. The company has 1,000 employees, and they plan to use an asymmetric encryption system. How many total keys will they need?

A. 500

B. 1,000

C. 2,000

D. 4,950

95. What term is used to describe the formal declaration by a designated approving authority (DAA) that an IT system is approved to operate in a specific environment?

A. Certification

B. Accreditation

C. Evaluation

D. Approval

96. Object-oriented programming languages use a black box approach to development, where users of an object do not necessarily need to know the object's implementation details. What term is used to describe this concept?

A. Layering

B. Abstraction

C. Data hiding

D. Process isolation

97. Todd wants to add a certificate to a certificate revocation list. What element of the certificate goes on the list?

A. Serial number

B. Public key

C. Digital signature

D. Private key

98. Alison is examining a digital certificate presented to her by her bank's website. Which one of the following requirements is not necessary for her to trust the digital certificate?

A. She knows that the server belongs to the bank.

B. She trusts the certificate authority.

C. She verifies that the certificate is not listed on a CRL.

D. She verifies the digital signature on the certificate.

99. Which one of the following is an example of a covert timing channel when used to exfiltrate information from an organization?

A. Sending an electronic mail message

B. Posting a file on a peer-to-peer file sharing service

C. Typing with the rhythm of Morse code

D. Writing data to a shared memory space

100. Which one of the following would be a reasonable application for the use of self-signed digital certificates?

A. E-commerce website

B. Banking application

C. Internal scheduling application

D. Customer portal

Chapter 4

Communication and Network Security (Domain 4)

1. What important factor listed below differentiates Frame Relay from X.25?
   - **A.** Frame Relay supports multiple PVCs over a single WAN carrier connection.
   - **B.** Frame Relay is a cell-switching technology instead of a packet-switching technology like X.25.
   - **C.** Frame Relay does not provide a Committed Information Rate (CIR).
   - **D.** Frame Relay only requires a DTE on the provider side.
2. During a security assessment of a wireless network, Jim discovers that LEAP is in use on a network using WPA. What recommendation should Jim make?
   - **A.** Continue to use LEAP. It provides better security than TKIP for WPA networks.
   - **B.** Use an alternate protocol like PEAP or EAP-TLS and implement WPA2 if supported.
   - **C.** Continue to use LEAP to avoid authentication issues, but move to WPA2.
   - **D.** Use an alternate protocol like PEAP or EAP-TLS, and implement Wired Equivalent Privacy to avoid wireless security issues.
3. Ben has connected his laptop to his tablet PC using an 802.11g connection. What wireless network mode has he used to connect these devices?
   - **A.** Infrastructure mode
   - **B.** Wired extension mode
   - **C.** Ad hoc mode
   - **D.** Stand-alone mode
4. Lauren's and Nick's PCs simultaneously send traffic by transmitting at the same time. What network term describes the range of systems on a network that could be affected by this same issue?
   - **A.** The subnet
   - **B.** The supernet
   - **C.** A collision domain
   - **D.** A broadcast domain
5. Sarah is manually reviewing a packet capture of TCP traffic and finds that a system is setting the RST flag in the TCP packets it sends repeatedly during a short period of time. What does this flag mean in the TCP packet header?
   - **A.** RST flags mean "Rest." The server needs traffic to briefly pause.
   - **B.** RST flags mean "Relay-set." The packets will be forwarded to the address set in the packet.
   - **C.** RST flags mean "Resume Standard." Communications will resume in their normal format.
   - **D.** RST means "Reset." The TCP session will be disconnected.
6. Gary is deploying a wireless network and wants to deploy the fastest possible wireless technology. Of the 802.11 standards listed below, which is the fastest 2.4 GHz option he has?

A. 802.11a

B. 802.11g

C. 802.11n

D. 802.11ac

7. What common applications are associated with each of the following TCP ports: 23, 25, 143, and 515?

A. Telnet, SFTP, NetBIOS, and LPD

B. SSH, SMTP, POP3, and ICMP

C. Telnet, SMTP, IMAP, and LPD

D. Telnet, SMTP, POP3, and X Windows

8. Chris is configuring an IDS to monitor for unencrypted FTP traffic. What ports should Chris use in his configuration?

A. TCP 20 and 21

B. TCP 21 only

C. UDP port 69

D. TCP port 21 and UDP port 21

9. FHSS, DSSS, and OFDM all use what wireless communication method that occurs over multiple frequencies simultaneously?

A. Wi-Fi

B. Spread Spectrum

C. Multiplexing

D. Orthogonal modulation

10. Which authentication protocol commonly used for PPP links encrypts both the username and password and uses a challenge/response dialog that cannot be replayed and periodically reauthenticates remote systems throughout its use in a session?

A. PAP

B. CHAP

C. EAP

D. LEAP

11. Which of the following options is not a common best practice for securing a wireless network?

A. Turn on WPA2.

B. Enable MAC filtering if used for a relatively small group of clients.

C. Enable SSID broadcast.

D. Separate the access point from the wired network using a firewall, thus treating it as external access.

12. What network topology is shown in the image below?

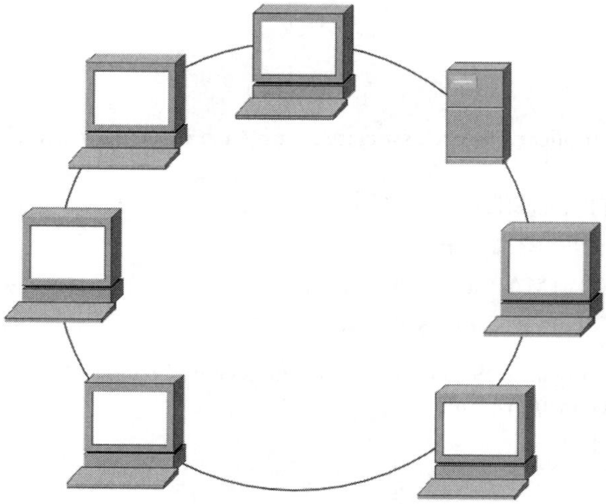

A. A ring
B. A bus
C. A star
D. A mesh

Chris is designing layered network security for his organization. Using the diagram below, answer questions 13 through 15.

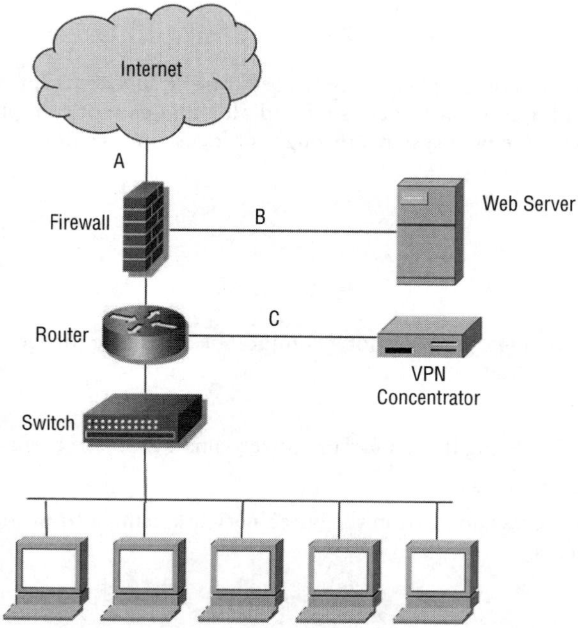

13. What type of firewall design is shown in the diagram?

- **A.** A single-tier firewall
- **B.** A two-tier firewall
- **C.** A three-tier firewall
- **D.** A four-tier firewall

14. If the VPN grants remote users the same access to network and system resources as local workstations have, what security issue should Chris raise?

- **A.** VPN users will not be able to access the web server.
- **B.** There is no additional security issue; the VPN concentrator's logical network location matches the logical network location of the workstations.
- **C.** VPN bypasses the firewall, creating additional risks.
- **D.** VPN users should only connect from managed PCs.

15. If Chris wants to stop cross-site scripting attacks against the web server, what is the best device for this purpose, and where should he put it?

- **A.** A firewall, location A
- **B.** An IDS, location A
- **C.** An IPS, location B
- **D.** A WAF, location C

16. Susan is deploying a routing protocol that maintains a list of destination networks with metrics that include the distance in hops to them and the direction traffic should be sent to them. What type of protocol is she using?

- **A.** A link-state protocol
- **B.** A link-distance protocol
- **C.** A destination metric protocol
- **D.** A distance-vector protocol

17. Ben has configured his network to not broadcast a SSID. Why might Ben disable SSID broadcast, and how could his SSID be discovered?

- **A.** Disabling SSID broadcast prevents attackers from discovering the encryption key. The SSID can be recovered from decrypted packets.
- **B.** Disabling SSID broadcast hides networks from unauthorized personnel. The SSID can be discovered using a wireless sniffer.
- **C.** Disabling SSID broadcast prevents issues with beacon frames. The SSID can be recovered by reconstructing the BSSID.
- **D.** Disabling SSID broadcast helps avoid SSID conflicts. The SSID can be discovered by attempting to connect to the network.

18. What network tool can be used to protect the identity of clients while providing Internet access by accepting client requests, altering the source addresses of the requests, mapping requests to clients, and sending the modified requests out to their destination?

A. A gateway
B. A proxy
C. A router
D. A firewall

19. During troubleshooting, Chris uses the `nslookup` command to check the IP address of a host he is attempting to connect to. The IP he sees in the response is not the IP that should resolve when the lookup is done. What type of attack has likely been conducted?
    A. DNS spoofing
    B. DNS poisoning
    C. ARP spoofing
    D. A Cain attack

20. A remote access tool that copies what is displayed on a desktop PC to a remote computer is an example of what type of technology?
    A. Remote node operation
    B. Screen scraping
    C. Remote control
    D. RDP

21. Which email security solution provides two major usage modes: (1) signed messages that provide integrity, sender authentication, and nonrepudiation; and (2) an enveloped message mode that provides integrity, sender authentication, and confidentiality?
    A. S/MIME
    B. MOSS
    C. PEM
    D. DKIM

22. During a security assessment, Jim discovers that the organization he is working with uses a multilayer protocol to handle SCADA systems and recently connected the SCADA network to the rest of the organization's production network. What concern should he raise about serial data transfers carried via TCP/IP?
    A. SCADA devices that are now connected to the network can now be attacked over the network.
    B. Serial data over TCP/IP cannot be encrypted.
    C. Serial data cannot be carried in TCP packets.
    D. TCP/IP's throughput can allow for easy denial of service attacks against serial devices.

23. What type of key does WEP use to encrypt wireless communications?
    A. An asymmetric key
    B. Unique key sets for each host

C. A predefined shared static key
D. Unique asymmetric keys for each host

24. An attack that causes a service to fail by exhausting all of a system's resources is what type of attack?
   A. A worm
   B. A denial of service attack
   C. A virus
   D. A Smurf attack

25. What speed and frequency range is used by 802.11n?
   A. 54 Mbps, 5 GHz
   B. 200+ Mbps, 5GHz
   C. 200+ Mbps, 2.4 and 5 GHz
   D. 1 Gbps, 5 GHz

26. The Address Resolution Protocol (ARP) and the Reverse Address Resolution Protocol (RARP) operate at what layer of the OSI model?
   A. Layer 1
   B. Layer 2
   C. Layer 3
   D. Layer 4

27. Which of the following is a converged protocol that allows storage mounts over TCP, and which is frequently used as a lower-cost alternative to Fibre Channel?
   A. MPLS
   B. SDN
   C. VoIP
   D. iSCSI

28. Chris is building an Ethernet network and knows that he needs to span a distance of over 150 meters with his 1000Base-T network. What network technology should he use to help with this?
   A. Install a repeater or a concentrator before 100 meters.
   B. Use Category 7 cable, which has better shielding for higher speeds.
   C. Install a gateway to handle the distance.
   D. Use STP cable to handle the longer distance at high speeds.

Lauren's organization has used a popular instant messaging service for a number of years. Recently, concerns have been raised about the use of instant messaging. Using the diagram below, answer questions 29 through 31 about instant messaging.

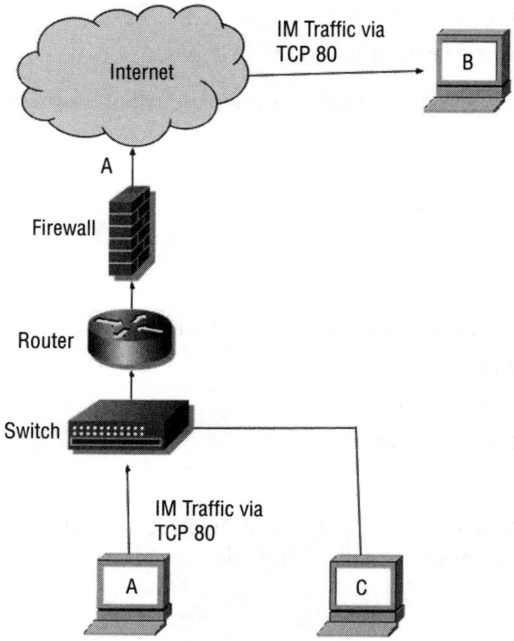

29. What protocol is the instant messaging traffic most likely to use based on the diagram?

A. AOL

B. HTTP

C. SMTP

D. HTTPS

30. What security concern does sending internal communications from A to B cause?

A. The firewall does not protect system B.

B. System C can see the broadcast traffic from system A to B.

C. It is traveling via an unencrypted protocol.

D. IM does not provide nonrepudiation.

31. How could Lauren's company best address a desire for secure instant messaging for users of internal systems A and C?

A. Use a 3rd party instant messaging service.

B. Implement and use a locally hosted IM service.

C. Use HTTPS.

D. Discontinue use of IM and instead use email, which is more secure.

32. Which of the following drawbacks is a concern when multilayer protocols are allowed?

A. A range of protocols may be used at higher layers.

B. Covert channels are allowed.

C. Filters cannot be bypassed.
D. Encryption can't be incorporated at multiple layers.

33. What network topology is shown in the image below?

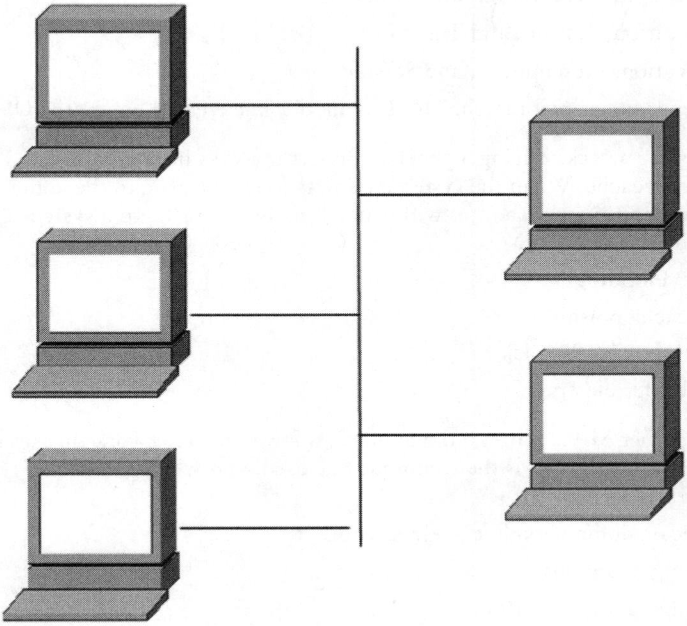

A. A ring
B. A star
C. A bus
D. A mesh

34. Chris uses a cellular hot spot (modem) to provide Internet access when he is traveling. If he leaves the hot spot connected to his PC while his PC is on his organization's corporate network, what security issue might he cause?

A. Traffic may not be routed properly, exposing sensitive data.
B. His system may act as a bridge from the Internet to the local network.
C. His system may be a portal for a reflected DDoS attack.
D. Security administrators may not be able to determine his IP address if a security issue occurs.

35. In her role as an information security professional, Susan has been asked to identify areas where her organization's wireless network may be accessible even though it isn't intended to be. What should Susan do to determine where her organization's wireless network is accessible?

A. A site survey
B. Warwalking

C. Wardriving

D. A design map

36. The DARPA TCP/IP model's Application layer matches up to what three OSI model layers?

A. Application, Presentation, and Transport

B. Presentation, Session, and Transport

C. Application, Presentation, and Session

D. There is not a direct match. The TCP model was created before the OSI model.

37. One of Susan's attacks during a penetration test involves inserting false ARP data into a system's ARP cache. When the system attempts to send traffic to the address it believes belongs to a legitimate system, it will instead send that traffic to a system she controls. What is this attack called?

A. RARP Flooding

B. ARP cache poisoning

C. A denial of ARP attack

D. ARP buffer blasting

38. Sue modifies her MAC address to one that is allowed on a network that uses MAC filtering to provide security. What is the technique Sue used, and what non-security issue could her actions cause?

A. Broadcast domain exploit, address conflict

B. Spoofing, token loss

C. Spoofing, address conflict

D. Sham EUI creation, token loss

39. Jim's audit of a large organization's traditional PBX showed that Direct Inward System Access (DISA) was being abused by third parties. What issue is most likely to lead to this problem?

A. The PBX was not fully patched.

B. The dial-in modem lines use unpublished numbers.

C. DISA is set up to only allow local calls.

D. One or more users' access codes have been compromised.

40. SMTP, HTTP, and SNMP all occur at what layer of the OSI model?

A. Layer 4

B. Layer 5

C. Layer 6

D. Layer 7

41. Lauren uses the ping utility to check whether a remote system is up as part of a penetration testing exercise. If she wants to filter ping out by protocol, what protocol should she filter out from her packet sniffer's logs?

A. UDP

B. TCP

C. IP

D. ICMP

42. Lauren wants to provide port-based authentication on her network to ensure that clients must authenticate before using the network. What technology is an appropriate solution for this requirement?

A. 802.11a

B. 802.3

C. 802.15.1

D. 802.1x

43. Ben has deployed a 1000Base-T 1 gigabit network and needs to run a cable to another building. If Ben is running his link directly from a switch to another switch in that building, what is the maximum distance Ben can cover according to the 1000Base-T specification?

A. 2 kilometers

B. 500 meters

C. 185 meters

D. 100 meters

44. Jim's remote site has only ISDN as an option for connectivity. What type of ISDN should he look for to get the maximum speed possible?

A. BRI

B. BPRI

C. PRI

D. D channel

45. SPIT attacks target what technology?

A. Virtualization platforms

B. Web services

C. VoIP systems

D. Secure Process Internal Transfers

46. What does a bluesnarfing attack target?

A. Data on IBM systems

B. An outbound phone call via Bluetooth

C. 802.11b networks

D. Data from a Bluetooth-enabled device

47. Which of the following options includes standards or protocols that exist in layer 6 of the OSI model?

A. NFS, SQL, and RPC
B. TCP, UDP, and TLS
C. JPEG, ASCII, and MIDI
D. HTTP, FTP, SMTP

48. What network topology is shown below?

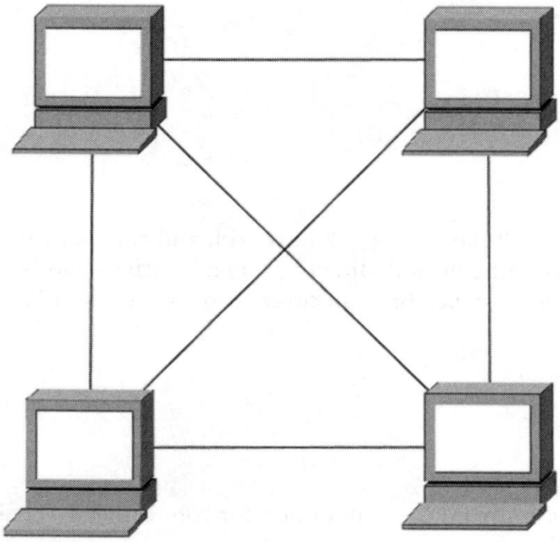

A. A ring
B. A bus
C. A star
D. A mesh

49. There are four common VPN protocols. Which group of four below contains all of the common VPN protocols?

A. PPTP, LTP, L2TP, IPsec
B. PPP, L2TP, IPsec, VNC
C. PPTP, L2F, L2TP, IPsec
D. PPTP, L2TP, IPsec, SPAP

50. What network technology is best described as a token-passing network that uses a pair of rings with traffic flowing in opposite directions?

A. A ring topology
B. Token Ring
C. FDDI
D. SONET

51. Which OSI layer includes electrical specifications, protocols, and interface standards?

A. The Transport layer

B. The Device layer

C. The Physical layer

D. The Data Link layer

52. Ben is designing a Wi-Fi network and has been asked to choose the most secure option for the network. Which wireless security standard should he choose?

A. WPA2

B. WPA

C. WEP

D. AES

53. If your organization needs to allow attachments in email to support critical business processes, what are the two best options for helping to avoid security problems caused by attachments?

A. Train your users and use anti-malware tools.

B. Encrypt your email and use anti-malware tools.

C. Train your users and require S/MIME for all email.

D. Use S/MIME by default and remove all ZIP (`.zip`) file attachments.

54. Segmentation, sequencing, and error checking all occur at what layer of the OSI model that is associated with SSL, TLS, and UDP?

A. The Transport layer

B. The Network layer

C. The Session layer

D. The Presentation layer

55. The Windows `ipconfig` command displays the following information:

BC-5F-F4-7B-4B-7D

What term describes this, and what information can be gathered from it?

A. The IP address, the network location of the system

B. The MAC address, the network interface card's manufacturer

C. The MAC address, the media type in use

D. The IPv6 client ID, the network interface card's manufacturer

56. Chris has been asked to choose between implementing PEAP and LEAP for wireless authentication. What should he choose, and why?

A. LEAP, because it fixes problems with TKIP, resulting in stronger security

B. PEAP, because it implements CCMP for security

C. LEAP, because it implements EAP-TLS for end-to-end session encryption

D. PEAP, because it can provide a TLS tunnel that encapsulates EAP methods, protecting the entire session

57. Ben is troubleshooting a network and discovers that the NAT router he is connected to has the 192.168.x.x subnet as its internal network and that its external IP is 192.168.1.40. What problem is he encountering?

A. 192.168.x.x is a non-routable network and will not be carried to the Internet.

B. 192.168.1.40 is not a valid address because it is reserved by RFC 1918.

C. Double NATing is not possible using the same IP range.

D. The upstream system is unable to de-encapsulate his packets and he needs to use PAT instead.

58. What is the default subnet mask for a Class B network?

A. 255.0.0.0

B. 255.255.0.0

C. 255.254.0.0

D. 255.255.255.0

59. Jim's organization uses a traditional PBX for voice communication. What is the most common security issue that its internal communications are likely to face, and what should he recommend to prevent it?

A. Eavesdropping, encryption

B. Man-in-the-middle attacks, end-to-end encryption

C. Eavesdropping, physical security

D. Wardialing, deploy an IPS

60. What common security issue is often overlooked with cordless phones?

A. Their signal is rarely encrypted and thus can be easily monitored.

B. They use unlicensed frequencies.

C. They can allow attackers access to wireless networks.

D. They are rarely patched and are vulnerable to malware.

61. Lauren's organization has deployed VoIP phones on the same switches that the desktop PCs are on. What security issue could this create, and what solution would help?

A. VLAN hopping, use physically separate switches.

B. VLAN hopping, use encryption.

C. Caller ID spoofing, MAC filtering

D. Denial of service attacks, use a firewall between networks.

62. Which type of firewall can be described as "a device that filters traffic based on its source, destination and the port it is sent from or is going to"?

- **A.** A static packet filtering firewall
- **B.** An Application layer gateway firewall
- **C.** A dynamic packet filtering firewall
- **D.** A stateful inspection firewall

63. A phreaking tool used to manipulate line voltages to steal long-distance service is known as what type of box?

- **A.** A black box
- **B.** A red box
- **C.** A blue box
- **D.** A white box

64. Data streams occur at what three layers of the OSI model?

- **A.** Application, Presentation, and Session
- **B.** Presentation, Session, and Transport
- **C.** Physical, Data Link, and Network
- **D.** Data Link, Network, and Transport

65. Chris needs to design a firewall architecture that can support separately a DMZ, a database, and a private internal network. What type of design should he use, and how many firewalls does he need?

- **A.** A four-tier firewall design with two firewalls
- **B.** A two-tier firewall design with three firewalls
- **C.** A three-tier firewall design with at least one firewall
- **D.** A single-tier firewall design with three firewalls

66. Lauren's networking team has been asked to identify a technology that will allow them to dynamically change the organization's network by treating the network like code. What type of architecture should she recommend?

- **A.** A network that follows the 5-4-3 rule
- **B.** A converged network
- **C.** A software-defined network
- **D.** A hypervisor-based network

67. Jim's organization uses fax machines to receive sensitive data. Since the fax machine is located in a public area, what actions should Jim take to deal with issues related to faxes his organization receives?

- **A.** Encrypt the faxes and purge local memory.
- **B.** Disable automatic printing and purge local memory.
- **C.** Encrypt faxes and disable automatic printing.
- **D.** Use link encryption and enable automatic printing.

68. Cable modems, ISDN, and DSL are all examples of what type of technology?

A. Baseband

B. Broadband

C. Digital

D. Broadcast

69. What type of firewall design is shown in the image below?

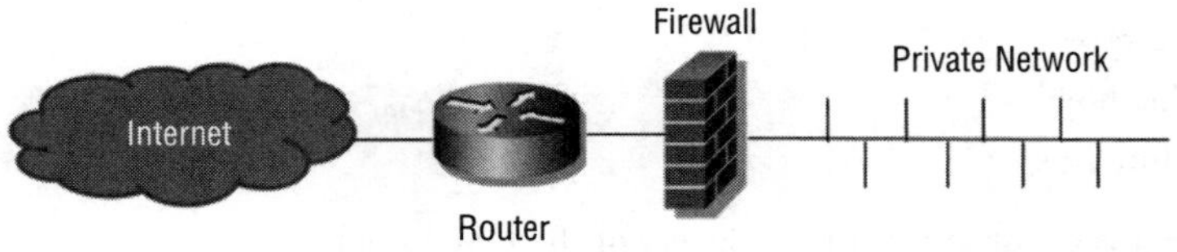

A. Single tier

B. Two tier

C. Three tier

D. Next generation

70. During a review of her organization's network, Angela discovered that it was suffering from broadcast storms and that contractors, guests, and organizational administrative staff were on the same network segment. What design change should Angela recommend?

A. Require encryption for all users.

B. Install a firewall at the network border.

C. Enable spanning tree loop detection.

D. Segment the network based on functional requirements.

71. ICMP, RIP, and network address translation all occur at what layer of the OSI model?

A. Layer 1

B. Layer 2

C. Layer 3

D. Layer 4

Use the following scenario to help guide your answers in the following three questions.

Ben is an information security professional at an organization that is replacing its physical servers with virtual machines. As the organization builds its virtual environment, it is decreasing the number of physical servers it uses while purchasing more powerful servers to act as the virtualization platforms.

72. The IDS Ben is responsible for is used to monitor communications in the data center using a mirrored port on the data center switch. What traffic will Ben see once the majority of servers in the data center have been virtualized?

- **A.** The same traffic he currently sees
- **B.** All inter-VM traffic
- **C.** Only traffic sent outside of the VM environment
- **D.** All inter-hypervisor traffic

73. The VM administrators recommend enabling cut and paste between virtual machines. What security concern should Ben raise about this practice?

- **A.** It can cause a denial of service condition.
- **B.** It can serve as a covert channel.
- **C.** It can allow viruses to spread.
- **D.** It can bypass authentication controls.

74. Ben is concerned about exploits that allow VM escape. What option should Ben suggest to help limit the impact of VM escape exploits?

- **A.** Separate virtual machines onto separate physical hardware based on task or data types.
- **B.** Use VM escape detection tools on the underlying hypervisor.
- **C.** Restore machines to their original snapshots on a regular basis.
- **D.** Use a utility like Tripwire to look for changes in the virtual machines.

75. WPA2's Counter Mode Ciper Block Chaining Message Authentication Mode Protocol (CCMP) is based on which common encryption scheme?

- **A.** DES
- **B.** 3DES
- **C.** AES
- **D.** TLS

76. When a host on an Ethernet network detects a collision and transmits a jam signal, what happens next?

- **A.** The host that transmitted the jam signal is allowed to retransmit while all other hosts pause until that transmission is received successfully.
- **B.** All hosts stop transmitting and each host waits a random period of time before attempting to transmit again.
- **C.** All hosts stop transmitting and each host waits a period of time based on how recently it successfully transmitted.
- **D.** Hosts wait for the token to be passed and then resume transmitting data as they pass the token.

77. IPX, AppleTalk, and NetBEUI are all examples of what?

- **A.** Routing protocols
- **B.** UDP protocols
- **C.** Non-IP protocols
- **D.** TCP protocols

78. What is the speed of a T3 line?

A. 128 kbps

B. 1.544 Mbps

C. 44.736 Mbps

D. 155 Mbps

79. What type of firewall design does the image below show?

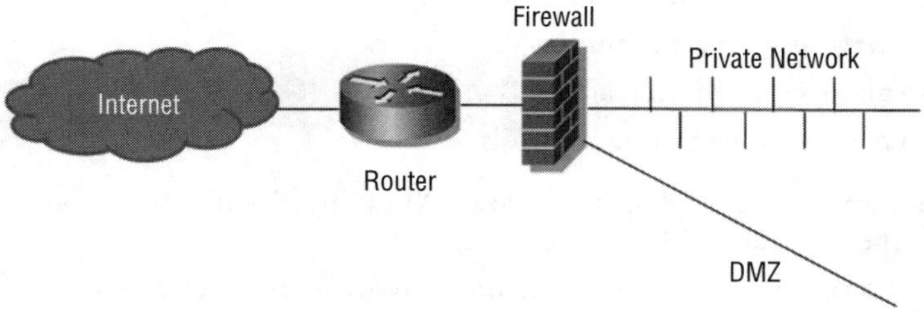

A. A single-tier firewall

B. A two-tier firewall

C. A three-tier firewall

D. A fully protected DMZ firewall

80. What challenge is most common for endpoint security system deployments?

A. Compromises

B. The volume of data

C. Monitoring encrypted traffic on the network

D. Handling non-TCP protocols

81. What type of address is 127.0.0.1?

A. A public IP address

B. An RFC 1918 address

C. An APIPA address

D. A loopback address

82. Susan is writing a best practices statement for her organizational users who need to use Bluetooth. She knows that there are many potential security issues with Bluetooth and wants to provide the best advice she can. Which of the following sets of guidance should Susan include?

A. Use Bluetooth's built-in strong encryption, change the default PIN on your device, turn off discovery mode, and turn off Bluetooth when it's not in active use.

B. Use Bluetooth only for those activities that are not confidential, change the default PIN on your device, turn off discovery mode, and turn off Bluetooth when it's not in active use.

C. Use Bluetooth's built-in strong encryption, use extended (8 digit or longer) Bluetooth PINs, turn off discovery mode, and turn off Bluetooth when it's not in active use.

D. Use Bluetooth only for those activities that are not confidential, use extended (8 digit or longer) Bluetooth PINs, turn off discovery mode, and turn off Bluetooth when it's not in active use.

83. What type of firewall is known as a second-generation firewall?

A. Static packet filtering firewalls

B. Application-level gateway firewalls

C. Stateful inspection firewalls

D. Unified Threat Management

84. Steve has been tasked with implementing a network storage protocol over an IP network. What storage-centric converged protocol is he likely to use in his implementation?

A. MPLS

B. FCoE

C. SDN

D. VoIP

85. What type of network device modulates between an analog carrier signal and digital information for computer communications?

A. A bridge

B. A router

C. A brouter

D. A modem

86. Which list presents the layers of the OSI model in the correct order?

A. Presentation, Application, Session, Transport, Network, Data Link, Physical

B. Application, Presentation, Session, Network, Transport, Data Link, Physical

C. Presentation, Application, Session, Transport, Data Link, Network, Physical

D. Application, Presentation, Session, Transport, Network, Data Link, Physical

87. A denial of service (DoS) attack that sends fragmented TCP packets is known as what kind of attack?

A. Christmas tree

B. Teardrop

C. Stack killer

D. Frag grenade

88. Modern dial-up connections use what dial-up protocol?

A. SLIP

B. SLAP

C. PPTP

D. PPP

89. One of the findings that Jim made when performing a security audit was the use of non-IP protocols in a private network. What issue should Jim point out that may result from the use of these non-IP protocols?

A. They are outdated and cannot be used on modern PCs.

B. They may not be able to be filtered by firewall devices.

C. They may allow Christmas tree attacks.

D. IPX extends on the IP protocol and may not be supported by all TCP stacks.

90. Angela needs to choose between EAP, PEAP, and LEAP for secure authentication. Which authentication protocol should she choose and why?

A. EAP, because it provides strong encryption by default

B. LEAP, because it provides frequent re-authentication and changing of WEP keys

C. PEAP, because it provides encryption and doesn't suffer from the same vulnerabilities that LEAP does

D. None of these options can provide secure authentication, and an alternate solution should be chosen.

91. Lauren has been asked to replace her organization's PPTP implementation with an L2TP implementation for security reasons. What is the primary security reason that L2TP would replace PPTP?

A. L2TP can use IPsec.

B. L2TP creates a point-to-point tunnel, avoiding multipoint issues.

C. PPTP doesn't support EAP.

D. PPTP doesn't properly encapsulate PPP packets.

92. Jim is building a research computing system that benefits from being part of a full mesh topology between systems. In a five-node full mesh topology design, how many connections will an individual node have?

A. Two

B. Three

C. Four

D. Five

93. What topology correctly describes Ethernet?

A. A ring

B. A star

C. A mesh

D. A bus

94. What type of attack is most likely to occur after a successful ARP spoofing attempt?

A. A DoS attack

B. A Trojan

C. A replay attack

D. A man-in-the-middle attack

95. What speed is Category 3 UTP cable rated for?

A. 5 Mbps

B. 10 Mbps

C. 100 Mbps

D. 1000 Mbps

96. What issue occurs when data transmitted over one set of wires is picked up by another set of wires?

A. Magnetic interference

B. Crosstalk

C. Transmission absorption

D. Amplitude modulation

97. What two key issues with the implementation of RC4 make Wired Equivalent Privacy (WEP) even weaker than it might otherwise be?

A. Its use of a static common key and client-set encryption algorithms

B. Its use of a static common key and a limited number of initialization vectors

C. Its use of weak asymmetric keys and a limited number of initialization vectors

D. Its use of a weak asymmetric key and client-set encryption algorithms

98. Chris is setting up a hotel network, and needs to ensure that systems in each room or suite can connect to each other, but systems in other suites or rooms cannot. At the same time, he needs to ensure that all systems in the hotel can reach the Internet. What solution should he recommend as the most effective business solution?

A. Per-room VPNs

B. VLANs

C. Port security

D. Firewalls

99. During a forensic investigation, Charles is able to determine the Media Access Control address of a system that was connected to a compromised network. Charles knows that MAC addresses are tied back to a manufacturer or vendor and are part of the fingerprint of the system. To which OSI layer does a MAC address belong?

A. The Application layer

B. The Session layer

C. The Physical layer

D. The Data Link layer

100. Ben knows that his organization wants to be able to validate the identity of other organizations based on their domain name when receiving and sending email. What tool should Ben recommend?

A. PEM

B. S/MIME

C. DKIM

D. MOSS

Chapter 5

Identity and Access Management (Domain 5)

1. Which of the following is best described as an access control model that focuses on subjects and identifies the objects that each subject can access?
   - **A.** An access control list
   - **B.** An implicit denial list
   - **C.** A capability table
   - **D.** A rights management matrix
2. Jim's organization-wide implementation of IDaaS offers broad support for cloud-based applications. The existing infrastructure for Jim's company does not use centralized identity services but uses Active Directory for AAA services. Which of the following choices is the best option to recommend to handle the company's onsite identity needs?
   - **A.** Integrate onsite systems using OAuth.
   - **B.** Use an on-premise third-party identity service.
   - **C.** Integrate onsite systems using SAML.
   - **D.** Design an in-house solution to handle the organization's unique needs.
3. Which of the following is not a weakness in Kerberos?
   - **A.** The KDC is a single point of failure.
   - **B.** Compromise of the KDC would allow attackers to impersonate any user.
   - **C.** Authentication information is not encrypted.
   - **D.** It is susceptible to password guessing.
4. Voice pattern recognition is what type of authentication factor?
   - **A.** Type 1
   - **B.** Type 2
   - **C.** Type 3
   - **D.** Type 4
5. If Susan's organization requires her to log in with her username, a PIN, a password, and a retina scan, how many distinct types of factor has she used?
   - **A.** One
   - **B.** Two
   - **C.** Three
   - **D.** Four
6. Which of the following items are not commonly associated with restricted interfaces?
   - **A.** Shells
   - **B.** Keyboards
   - **C.** Menus
   - **D.** Database views

7. During a log review, Saria discovers a series of logs that show login failures as shown here:

   Jan 31 11:39:12 ip-10-0-0-2 sshd[29092]: Invalid user admin from remotehost passwd=orange

   Jan 31 11:39:20 ip-10-0-0-2 sshd[29098]: Invalid user admin from remotehost passwd=Orang3

   Jan 31 11:39:23 ip-10-0-0-2 sshd[29100]: Invalid user admin from remotehost passwd=Orange93

   Jan 31 11:39:31 ip-10-0-0-2 sshd[29106]: Invalid user admin from remotehost passwd=Orangutan1

   Jan 31 20:40:53 ip-10-0-0-254 sshd[30520]: Invalid user admin from remotehost passwd=Orangemonkey

   What type of attack has Saria discovered?

   A. A brute force attack
   B. A man-in-the-middle attack
   C. A dictionary attack
   D. A rainbow table attack

8. What type of attack can be prevented by using a trusted path?

   A. Dictionary attacks
   B. Brute force attacks
   C. Man-in-the-middle attacks
   D. Login spoofing

9. What major issue often results from decentralized access control?

   A. Access outages may occur.
   B. Control is not consistent.
   C. Control is too granular.
   D. Training costs are high.

10. Callback to a home phone number is an example of what type of factor?

   A. Type 1
   B. Somewhere you are
   C. Type 3
   D. Geographic

11. Kathleen needs to set up an Active Directory trust to allow authentication with an existing Kerberos K5 domain. What type of trust does she need to create?

   A. A shortcut trust
   B. A forest trust

C. An external trust

D. A realm trust

12. Which of the following AAA protocols is the most commonly used?

A. TACACS

B. TACACS+

C. XTACACS

D. Super TACACS

13. Which of the following is not a single sign-on implementation?

A. Kerberos

B. ADFS

C. CAS

D. RADIUS

14. As seen in the following image, a user on a Windows system is not able to use the "Send Message" functionality. What access control model best describes this type of limitation?

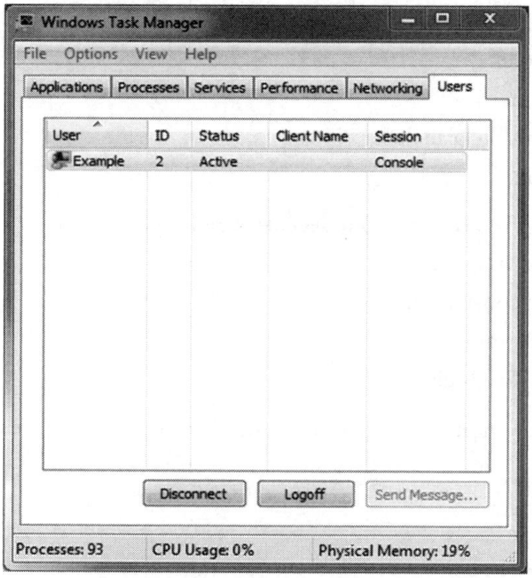

A. Least privilege

B. Need to know

C. Constrained interface

D. Separation of duties

15. What type of access controls allow the owner of a file to grant other users access to it using an access control list?

- **A.** Role based
- **B.** Non-discretionary
- **C.** Rule based
- **D.** Discretionary

16. Alex's job requires him to see personal health information (PHI) to ensure proper treatment of patients. His access to their medical records does not provide access to patient addresses or billing information. What access control concept best describes this control?

- **A.** Separation of duties
- **B.** Constrained interfaces
- **C.** Context-dependent control
- **D.** Need to know

Using your knowledge of the Kerberos logon process and the following diagram, answer questions 17, 18, and 19.

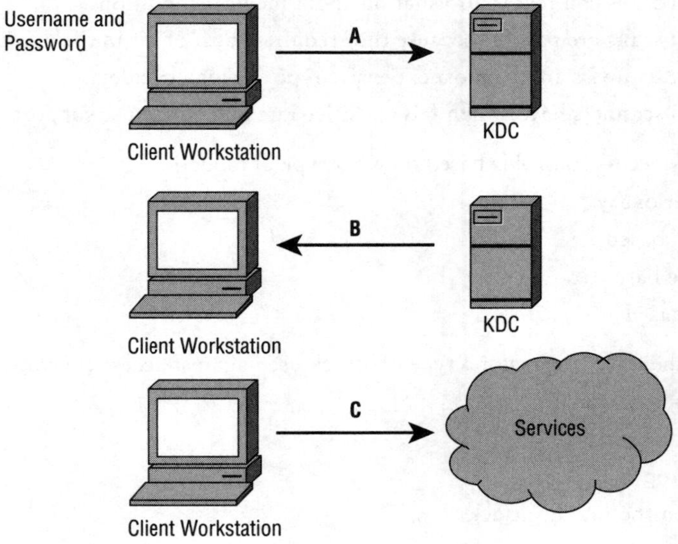

17. At point A in the diagram, the client sends the username and password to the KDC. How is the username and password protected?

- **A.** 3DES encryption
- **B.** TLS encryption
- **C.** SSL encryption
- **D.** AES encryption

18. At point B in the diagram, what two important elements does the KDC send to the client after verifying that the username is valid?
    A. An encrypted TGT and a public key
    B. An access ticket and a public key
    C. An encrypted, time-stamped TGT and a symmetric key encrypted with a hash of the user's password
    D. An encrypted, time-stamped TGT and an access token
19. What tasks must the client perform before it can use the TGT?
    A. It must generate a hash of the TGT and decrypt the symmetric key.
    B. It must install the TGT and decrypt the symmetric key.
    C. It must decrypt the TGT and the symmetric key.
    D. It must send a valid response using the symmetric key to the KDC and must install the TGT.
20. Jacob is planning his organization's biometric authentication system and is considering retina scans. What concern may be raised about retina scans by others in his organization?
    A. Retina scans can reveal information about medical conditions.
    B. Retina scans are painful because they require a puff of air in the user's eye.
    C. Retina scanners are the most expensive type of biometric device.
    D. Retina scanners have a high false positive rate and will cause support issues.
21. Mandatory access control is based on what type of model?
    A. Discretionary
    B. Group based
    C. Lattice based
    D. Rule based
22. Which of the following is not a type of attack used against access controls?
    A. Dictionary attack
    B. Brute force attack
    C. Teardrop
    D. Man-in-the-middle attack
23. What is the best way to provide accountability for the use of identities?
    A. Logging
    B. Authorization
    C. Digital signatures
    D. Type 1 authentication

24. Jim has worked in human relations, payroll, and customer service roles in his company over the past few years. What type of process should his company perform to ensure that he has appropriate rights?

A. Re-provisioning

B. Account review

C. Privilege creep

D. Account revocation

25. Biba is what type of access control model?

A. MAC

B. DAC

C. Role BAC

D. ABAC

26. Which of the following is a client/server protocol designed to allow network access servers to authenticate remote users by sending access request messages to a central server?

A. Kerberos

B. EAP

C. RADIUS

D. OAuth

27. What type of access control is being used in the following permission listing:

Storage Device X

User1: Can read, write, list

User2: Can read, list

User3: Can read, write, list, delete

User4: Can list

A. Resource-based access controls

B. Role-based access controls

C. Mandatory access controls

D. Rule-based access controls

28. Angela uses a sniffer to monitor traffic from a RADIUS server configured with default settings. What protocol should she monitor and what traffic will she be able to read?

A. UDP, none. All RADIUS traffic is encrypted.

B. TCP, all traffic but the passwords, which are encrypted

C. UDP, all traffic but the passwords, which are encrypted

D. TCP, none. All RADIUS traffic is encrypted.

29. Which of the following is not part of a Kerberos authentication system?

A. KDC

B. TGT

C. AS

D. TS

30. When an application or system allows a logged-in user to perform specific actions, it is an example of what?

A. Roles

B. Group management

C. Logins

D. Authorization

31. Alex has been employed by his company for over a decade and has held a number of positions in the company. During an audit, it is discovered that he has access to shared folders and applications due to his former roles. What issue has Alex's company encountered?

A. Excessive provisioning

B. Unauthorized access

C. Privilege creep

D. Account review

32. Which of the following is not a common threat to access control mechanisms?

A. Fake login pages

B. Phishing

C. Dictionary attacks

D. Man-in-the-middle attacks

33. What term properly describes what occurs when two or more processes require access to the same resource and must complete their tasks in the proper order for normal function?

A. Collisions

B. Race conditions

C. Determinism

D. Out-of-order execution

34. What type of access control scheme is shown in the following table?

Highly Sensitive	Red	Blue	Green
Confidential	Purple	Orange	Yellow
Internal Use	Black	Gray	White
Public	Clear	Clear	Clear

A. RBAC

B. DAC

C. MAC

D. TBAC

35. Which of the following is not a valid LDAP DN (distinguished name)?

A. cn=ben+ou=sales

B. ou=example

C. cn=ben,ou=example;

D. ou=example,dc=example,dc=com+dc=org

36. When a subject claims an identity, what process is occurring?

A. Login

B. Identification

C. Authorization

D. Token presentation

37. Dogs, guards, and fences are all common examples of what type of control?

A. Detective

B. Recovery

C. Administrative

D. Physical

38. Susan's organization is updating its password policy and wants to use the strongest possible passwords. What password requirement will have the highest impact in preventing brute force attacks?

A. Change maximum age from 1 year to 180 days.

B. Increase the minimum password length from 8 characters to 16 characters.

C. Increase the password complexity so that at least three character classes (such as uppercase, lowercase, numbers, and symbols) are required.

D. Retain a password history of at least four passwords to prevent reuse.

39. What is the stored sample of a biometric factor called?

A. A reference template

B. A token store

C. A biometric password

D. An enrollment artifact

40. When might an organization using biometrics choose to allow a higher FRR instead of a higher FAR?

A. When security is more important than usability

B. When false rejection is not a concern due to data quality

C. When the CER of the system is not known

D. When the CER of the system is very high

41. Susan is working to improve the strength of her organization's passwords by changing the password policy. The password system that she is using allows upper- and lower-case letters as well as numbers but no other characters. How much additional complexity does adding a single character to the minimum length of passwords for her organization create?

A. 26 times more complex

B. 62 times more complex

C. 36 times more complex

D. 2^62 times more complex

42. Which pair of the following factors are key for user acceptance of biometric identification systems?

A. The FAR

B. The throughput rate and the time required to enroll

C. The CER and the ERR

D. How often users must reenroll and the reference profile requirements

Alex is in charge of SAML integration with a major third-party partner that provides a variety of business productivity services for his organization. Using the following diagram and your knowledge of SAML integrations and security architecture design, answer questions 43, 44, and 45.

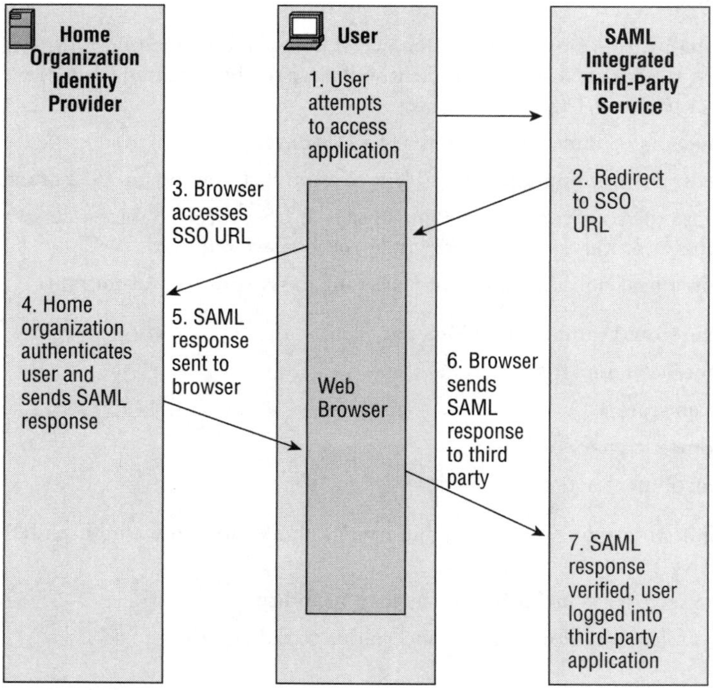

43. Alex is concerned about eavesdropping on the SAML traffic and also wants to ensure that forged assertions will not be successful. What should he do to prevent these potential attacks?

A. Use SAML's secure mode to provide secure authentication.

B. Implement TLS using a strong cipher suite, which will protect against both types of attacks.

C. Implement TLS using a strong cipher suite and use digital signatures.

D. Implement TLS using a strong cipher suite and message hashing.

44. If Alex's organization is one that is primarily made up of offsite, traveling users, what availability risk does integration of critical business applications to onsite authentication create and how could he solve it?

A. Third-party integration may not be trustworthy; use SSL and digital signatures.

B. If the home organization is offline, traveling users won't be able to access third-party applications; implement a hybrid cloud/local authentication system.

C. Local users may not be properly redirected to the third-party services; implement a local gateway.

D. Browsers may not properly redirect; use host files to ensure that issues with redirects are resolved.

45. What solution can best help address concerns about third parties that control SSO directs as shown in step 2 in the diagram?

A. An awareness campaign about trusted third parties

B. TLS

C. Handling redirects at the local site

D. Implementing an IPS to capture SSO redirect attacks

46. Susan has been asked to recommend whether her organization should use a mandatory access control scheme or a discretionary access control scheme. If flexibility and scalability is an important requirement for implementing access controls, which scheme should she recommend and why?

A. MAC, because it provides greater scalability and flexibility because you can simply add more labels as needed

B. DAC, because allowing individual administrators to make choices about the objects they control provides scalability and flexibility

C. MAC, because compartmentalization is well suited to flexibility and adding compartments will allow it to scale well

D. DAC, because a central decision process allows quick responses and will provide scalability by reducing the number of decisions required and flexibility by moving those decisions to a central authority

47. Which of the following tools is not typically used to verify that a provisioning process was followed in a way that ensures that the organization's security policy is being followed?

A. Log review

B. Manual review of permissions

C. Signature-based detection

D. Review the audit trail

48. Lauren needs to send information about services she is provisioning to a third-party organization. What standards-based markup language should she choose to build the interface?

A. SAML

B. SOAP

C. SPML

D. XACML

49. During a penetration test, Chris recovers a file containing hashed passwords for the system he is attempting to access. What type of attack is most likely to succeed against the hashed passwords?

A. A brute force attack

B. A pass-the-hash attack

C. A rainbow table attack

D. A salt recovery attack

50. Google's identity integration with a variety of organizations and applications across domains is an example of which of the following?

A. PKI

B. Federation

C. Single sign-on

D. Provisioning

51. Lauren starts at her new job and finds that she has access to a variety of systems that she does not need access to to accomplish her job. What problem has she encountered?

A. Privilege creep

B. Rights collision

C. Least privilege

D. Excessive privileges

52. When Chris verifies an individual's identity and adds a unique identifier like a user ID to an identity system, what process has occurred?

A. Identity proofing

B. Registration

C. Directory management

D. Session management

53. Jim configures his LDAP client to connect to an LDAP directory server. According to the configuration guide, his client should connect to the server on port 636. What does this indicate to Jim about the configuration of the LDAP server?

A. It requires connections over SSL/TLS.
B. It supports only unencrypted connections.
C. It provides global catalog services.
D. It does not provide global catalog services.

54. The X.500 standards cover what type of important identity systems?
A. Kerberos
B. Provisioning services
C. Biometric authentication systems
D. Directory services

55. Microsoft's Active Directory Domain Services is based on which of the following technologies?
A. RADIUS
B. LDAP
C. SSO
D. PKI

56. Lauren is responsible for building a banking website. She needs proof of the identity of the users who register for the site. How should she validate user identities?
A. Require users to create unique questions that only they will know.
B. Require new users to bring their driver's license or passport in person to the bank.
C. Use information that both the bank and the user have such as questions pulled from their credit report.
D. Call the user on their registered phone number to verify that they are who they claim to be.

57. By default, in what format does OpenLDAP store the value of the userPassword attribute?
A. In the clear
B. Salted and hashed
C. MD5 hashed
D. Encrypted using AES256 encryption

58. A new customer at a bank that uses fingerprint scanners to authenticate its users is surprised when he scans his fingerprint and is logged in to another customer's account. What type of biometric factor error occurred?
A. A registration error
B. A Type 1 error
C. A Type 2 error
D. A time of use, method of use error

59. What type of access control is typically used by firewalls?

A. Discretionary access controls

B. Rule-based access controls

C. Task-based access control

D. Mandatory access controls

60. When you input a user ID and password, you are performing what important identity and access management activity?

A. Authorization

B. Validation

C. Authentication

D. Login

61. Kathleen works for a data center hosting facility that provides physical data center space for individuals and organizations. Until recently, each client was given a magnetic-strip-based keycard to access the section of the facility where their servers are located, and they were also given a key to access the cage or rack where their servers reside. In the past month, a number of servers have been stolen, but the logs for the passcards show only valid IDs. What is Kathleen's best option to make sure that the users of the passcards are who they are supposed to be?

A. Add a reader that requires a PIN for passcard users.

B. Add a camera system to the facility to observe who is accessing servers.

C. Add a biometric factor.

D. Replace the magnetic stripe keycards with smart cards.

62. Which of the following is a ticket-based authentication protocol designed to provide secure communication?

A. RADIUS

B. OAuth

C. SAML

D. Kerberos

63. What type of access control is composed of policies and procedures that support regulations, requirements, and the organization's own policies?

A. Corrective

B. Logical

C. Compensating

D. Administrative

64. In a Kerberos environment, when a user needs to access a network resource, what is sent to the TGS?

A. A TGT

B. An AS

C. The SS

D. A session key

65. Which objects and subjects have a label in a MAC model?

A. Objects and subjects that are classified as Confidential, Secret, or Top Secret have a label.

B. All objects have a label, and all subjects have a compartment.

C. All objects and subjects have a label.

D. All subjects have a label and all objects have a compartment.

Chris is the identity architect for a growing e-commerce website that wants to leverage social identity. To do this, he and his team intend to allow users to use their existing Google accounts as their primary accounts when using the e-commerce site. This means that when a new user initially connects to the e-commerce platform, they are given the choice between using their Google+ account using OAuth 2.0, or creating a new account on the platform using their own email address and a password of their choice.

Using this information and the following diagram of an example authentication flow, answer questions 66, 67, and 68.

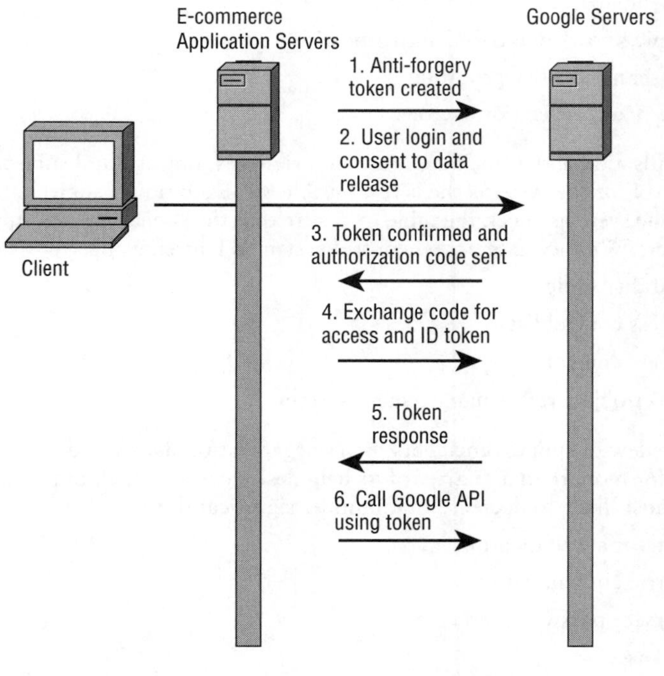

66. When the e-commerce application creates an account for a Google+ user, where should that user's password be stored?

A. The password is stored in the e-commerce application's database.

B. The password is stored in memory on the e-commerce application's server.

C. The password is stored in Google's account management system.

D. The password is never stored; instead, a salted hash is stored in Google's account management system.

67. Which system or systems is/are responsible for user authentication for Google+ users?

A. The e-commerce application

B. Both the e-commerce application and Google servers

C. Google servers

D. The diagram does not provide enough information to determine this.

68. What type of attack is the creation and exchange of state tokens intended to prevent?

A. XSS

B. CSRF

C. SQL injection

D. XACML

69. Questions like "What is your pet's name?" are examples of what type of identity proofing?

A. Knowledge-based authentication

B. Dynamic knowledge-based authentication

C. Out-of-band identity proofing

D. A Type 3 authentication factor

70. Lauren builds a table that includes assigned privileges, objects, and subjects to manage access control for the systems she is responsible for. Each time a subject attempts to access an object, the systems check the table to ensure that the subject has the appropriate rights to the objects. What type of access control system is Lauren using?

A. A capability table

B. An access control list

C. An access control matrix

D. A subject/object rights management system

71. During a review of support incidents, Ben's organization discovered that password changes accounted for more than a quarter of its help desk's cases. Which of the following options would be most likely to decrease that number significantly?

A. Two-factor authentication

B. Biometric authentication

C. Self-service password reset

D. Passphrases

72. Brian's large organization has used RADIUS for AAA services for its network devices for years and has recently become aware of security issues with the unencrypted information transferred during authentication. How should Brian implement encryption for RADIUS?

A. Use the built-in encryption in RADIUS.

B. Implement RADIUS over its native UDP using TLS for protection.

C. Implement RADIUS over TCP using TLS for protection.

D. Use an AES256 pre-shared cipher between devices.

73. Jim wants to allow cloud-based applications to act on his behalf to access information from other sites. Which of the following tools can allow that?

A. Kerberos

B. OAuth

C. OpenID

D. LDAP

74. Ben's organization has had an issue with unauthorized access to applications and workstations during the lunch hour when employees aren't at their desk. What are the best type of session management solutions for Ben to recommend to help prevent this type of access?

A. Use session IDs for all access and verify system IP addresses of all workstations.

B. Set session time-outs for applications and use password protected screensavers with inactivity time-outs on workstations.

C. Use session IDs for all applications, and use password protected screensavers with inactivity time-outs on workstations.

D. Set session time-outs for applications and verify system IP addresses of all workstations.

75. Lauren is an information security analyst tasked with deploying technical access controls for her organization. Which of the following is not a logical or technical access control?

A. Passwords

B. Firewalls

C. RAID arrays

D. Routers

76. The financial services company that Susan works for provides a web portal for its users. When users need to verify their identity, the company uses information from third-party sources to ask questions based on their past credit reports, such as, "Which of the following streets did you live on in 2007?" What process is Susan's organization using?

A. Identity proofing

B. Password verification

C. Authenticating with Type 2 authentication factor

D. Out-of-band identity proofing

77. The US government CAC is an example of what form of Type 2 authentication factor?

A. A token

B. A biometric identifier

C. A smart card

D. A PIV

78. What authentication technology can be paired with OAuth to perform identity verification and obtain user profile information using a RESTful API?

A. SAML

B. Shibboleth

C. OpenID Connect

D. Higgins

79. Jim has Secret clearance and is accessing files that use a mandatory access control scheme to apply the Top Secret, Secret, Confidential, and Unclassified label scheme. If his rights include the ability to access all data of his clearance level or lower, what classification levels of data can he access?

A. Top Secret and Secret

B. Secret, Confidential, and Unclassified

C. Secret data only

D. Secret and Unclassified

80. The security administrators at the company that Susan works for have configured the workstation she uses to allow her to log in only during her work hours. What type of access control best describes this limitation?

A. Constrained interface

B. Context-dependent control

C. Content-dependent control

D. Least privilege

81. When Lauren uses a fingerprint scanner to access her bank account, what type of authentication factor is she using?

A. Type 1

B. Type 2

C. Type 3

D. Type 4

82. Which of the following is not an access control layer?

A. Physical

B. Policy

C. Administrative

D. Technical

83. Ben uses a software based token which changes its code every minute. What type of token is he using?

A. Asynchronous

B. Smart card

C. Synchronous

D. Static

84. What type of token-based authentication system uses a challenge/response process in which the challenge has to be entered on the token?

A. Asynchronous

B. Smart card

C. Synchronous

D. RFID

Ben's organization is adopting biometric authentication for its high-security building's access control system. Using the following chart, answer questions 85, 86, and 87 about the organization's adoption of the technology.

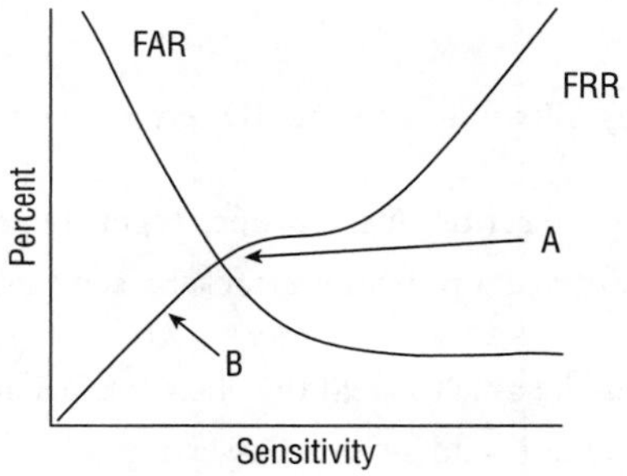

85. Ben's company is considering configuring its systems to work at the level shown by point A on the diagram. To what level is it setting the sensitivity?

A. The FRR crossover

B. The FAR point

C. The CER

D. The CFR

86. At point B, what problem is likely to occur?

A. False acceptance will be very high.

B. False rejection will be very high.

C. False rejection will be very low.

D. False acceptance will be very low.

87. What should Ben do if the FAR and FRR shown in this diagram does not provide an acceptable performance level for his organization's needs?

A. Adjust the sensitivity of the biometric devices.

B. Assess other biometric systems to compare them.

C. Move the CER.

D. Adjust the FRR settings in software.

88. What LDAP authentication mode can provide secure authentication?

- **A.** Anonymous
- **B.** SASL
- **C.** Simple
- **D.** S-LDAP

89. Which of the following Type 3 authenticators is appropriate to use by itself rather than in combination with other biometric factors?

- **A.** Voice pattern recognition
- **B.** Hand geometry
- **C.** Palm scans
- **D.** Heart/pulse patterns

90. What danger is created by allowing the OpenID relying party to control the connection to the OpenID provider?

- **A.** It may cause incorrect selection of the proper OpenID provider.
- **B.** It creates the possibility of a phishing attack by sending data to a fake OpenID provider.
- **C.** The relying party may be able to steal the client's username and password.
- **D.** The relying party may not send a signed assertion.

91. Jim is implementing a cloud identity solution for his organization. What type of technology is he putting in place?

- **A.** Identity as a Service
- **B.** Employee ID as a Service
- **C.** Cloud-based RADIUS
- **D.** OAuth

92. RAID-5 is an example of what type of control?

- **A.** Administrative
- **B.** Recovery
- **C.** Compensation
- **D.** Logical

93. When Alex sets the permissions shown in the following image as one of many users on a Linux server, what type of access control model is he leveraging?

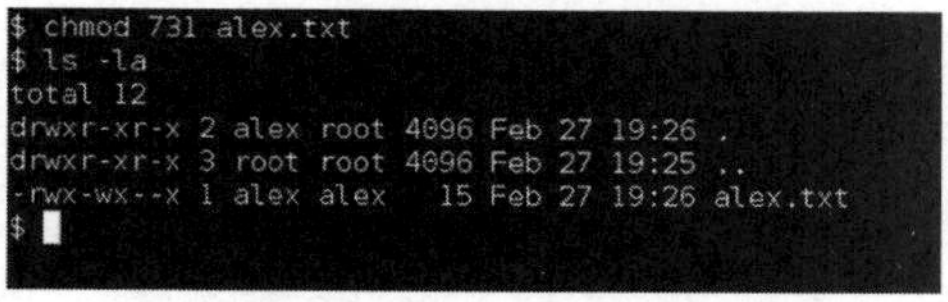

A. Role-based access control
B. Rule-based access control
C. Mandatory access control
D. Discretionary access control

94. What open protocol was designed to replace RADIUS—including support for additional commands and protocols, replacing UDP traffic with TCP, and providing for extensible commands—but does not preserve backward compatibility with RADIUS?

A. TACACS
B. RADIUS-NG
C. Kerberos
D. Diameter

95. LDAP distinguished names (DNs) are made up of comma-separated components called relative distinguished names (RDNs) that have an attribute name and a value. DNs become less specific as they progress from left to right. Which of the following LDAP DN best fits this rule?

A. uid=ben,ou=sales,dc=example,dc=com
B. uid=ben,dc=com,dc=example
C. dc=com,dc=example,ou=sales,uid=ben
D. ou=sales,dc=com,dc=example

96. Susan is troubleshooting Kerberos authentication problems with symptoms including TGTs that are not accepted as valid and an inability to receive new tickets. If the system she is troubleshooting is properly configured for Kerberos authentication, her username and password are correct, and her network connection is functioning, what is the most likely issue?

A. The Kerberos server is offline.
B. There is a protocol mismatch.
C. The client's TGTs have been marked as compromised and de-authorized.
D. The Kerberos server and the local client's time clocks are not synchronized.

97. Kerberos, KryptoKnight, and SESAME are all examples of what type of system?

A. SSO
B. PKI
C. CMS
D. Directory

98. Which of the following types of access controls do not describe a lock?

A. Physical
B. Directive
C. Preventative
D. Deterrent

99. What authentication protocol does Windows use by default for Active Directory systems?

- **A.** RADIUS
- **B.** Kerberos
- **C.** OAuth
- **D.** TACACS+

100. Alex configures his LDAP server to provide services on 636 and 3269. What type of LDAP services has he configured based on LDAP's default ports?

- **A.** Unsecure LDAP and unsecure global directory
- **B.** Unsecure LDAP and secure global directory
- **C.** Secure LDAP and secure global directory
- **D.** Secure LDAP and unsecure global directory

Chapter 6

Security Assessment and Testing (Domain 6)

1. During a port scan, Susan discovers a system running services on TCP and UDP 137-139 and TCP 445, as well as TCP 1433. What type of system is she likely to find if she connects to the machine?
   A. A Linux email server
   B. A Windows SQL server
   C. A Linux file server
   D. A Windows workstation
2. Which of the following is a method used to design new software tests and to ensure the quality of tests?
   A. Code auditing
   B. Static code analysis
   C. Regression testing
   D. Mutation testing
3. During a port scan, Lauren found TCP port 443 open on a system. Which tool is best suited to scanning the service that is most likely running on that port?
   A. zzuf
   B. Nikto
   C. Metasploit
   D. sqlmap
4. What message logging standard is commonly used by network devices, Linux and Unix systems, and many other enterprise devices?
   A. Syslog
   B. Netlog
   C. Eventlog
   D. Remote Log Protocol (RLP)
5. Alex wants to use an automated tool to fill web application forms to test for format string vulnerabilities. What type of tool should he use?
   A. A black box
   B. A brute-force tool
   C. A fuzzer
   D. A static analysis tool
6. Susan needs to scan a system for vulnerabilities, and she wants to use an open source tool to test the system remotely. Which of the following tools will meet her requirements and allow vulnerability scanning?
   A. Nmap
   B. OpenVAS
   C. MBSA
   D. Nessus

7. NIST Special Publication 800-53A describes four major types of assessment objects that can be used to identify items being assessed. If the assessment covers IPS devices, which of the types of assessment objects is being assessed?

A. A specification

B. A mechanism

C. An activity

D. An individual

8. Jim has been contracted to perform a penetration test of a bank's primary branch. In order to make the test as real as possible, he has not been given any information about the bank other than its name and address. What type of penetration test has Jim agreed to perform?

A. A crystal box penetration test

B. A gray box penetration test

C. A black box penetration test

D. A white box penetration test

9. As part of a penetration test, Alex needs to determine if there are web servers that could suffer from the 2014 Heartbleed bug. What type of tool could he use, and what should he check to verify that the tool can identify the problem?

A. A vulnerability scanner, to see whether the scanner has a signature or test for the Heartbleed CVE number

B. A port scanner, to see whether the scanner properly identifies SSL connections

C. A vulnerability scanner, to see whether the vulnerability scanner detects problems with the Apache web server

D. A port scanner, to see whether the port scanner supports TLS connections

10. In a response to a Request for Proposal, Susan receives a SAS-70 Type 1 report. If she wants a report that includes operating effectiveness detail, what should Susan ask for as followup and why?

A. An SAS-70 Type II, because Type I only covers a single point in time

B. An SOC Type 1, because Type II does not cover operating effectiveness

C. An SOC Type 2, because Type I does not cover operating effectiveness

D. An SAC-70 Type 3, because Types 1 and 2 are outdated and no longer accepted

11. During a wireless network penetration test, Susan runs aircrack-ng against the network using a password file. What might cause her to fail in her password-cracking efforts?

A. Use of WPA2 encryption

B. Running WPA2 in Enterprise mode

C. Use of WEP encryption

D. Running WPA2 in PSK mode

12. Which type of SOC report is best suited to provide assurance to users about an organization's security, availability, and the integrity of their service operations?
    - A. An SOC 1 Type 2 report
    - B. An SOC 2 report
    - C. An SOC 3 report
    - D. An SOC 1 Type 1 report

13. What type of testing is used to ensure that separately developed software modules properly exchange data?
    - A. Fuzzing
    - B. Dynamic testing
    - C. Interface testing
    - D. API checksums

14. Which of the following is not a potential problem with active wireless scanning?
    - A. Accidently scanning apparent rogue devices that actually belong to guests
    - B. Causing alarms on the organization's wireless IPS
    - C. Scanning devices that belong to nearby organizations
    - D. Misidentifying rogue devices

15. Ben uses a fuzzing tool that develops data models and creates fuzzed data based on information about how the application uses data to test the application. What type of fuzzing is Ben doing?
    - A. Mutation
    - B. Parametric
    - C. Generational
    - D. Derivative

16. Saria wants to log and review traffic information between parts of her network. What type of network logging should she enable on her routers to allow her to perform this analysis?
    - A. Audit logging
    - B. Flow logging
    - C. Trace logging
    - D. Route logging

17. Jim has been contracted to conduct a gray box penetration test, and his clients have provided him with the following information about their networks so that he can scan them.

    Data center: 10.10.10.0/24

    Sales: 10.10.11.0/24

    Billing: 10.10.12.0/24

    Wireless: 192.168.0.0/16

What problem will Jim encounter if he is contracted to conduct a scan from offsite?

A. The IP ranges are too large to scan efficiently.

B. The IP addresses provided cannot be scanned.

C. The IP ranges overlap and will cause scanning issues.

D. The IP addresses provided are RFC 1918 addresses.

18. Karen's organization has been performing system backups for years but has not used the backups frequently. During a recent system outage, when administrators tried to restore from backups they found that the backups had errors and could not be restored. Which of the following options should Karen avoid when selecting ways to ensure that her organization's backups will work next time?

A. Log review

B. MTD verification

C. Hashing

D. Periodic testing

Questions 19, 20, and 21 refer to the following scenario.

The company that Jennifer works for has implemented a central logging infrastructure, as shown in the following image. Use this diagram and your knowledge of logging systems to answer the following questions.

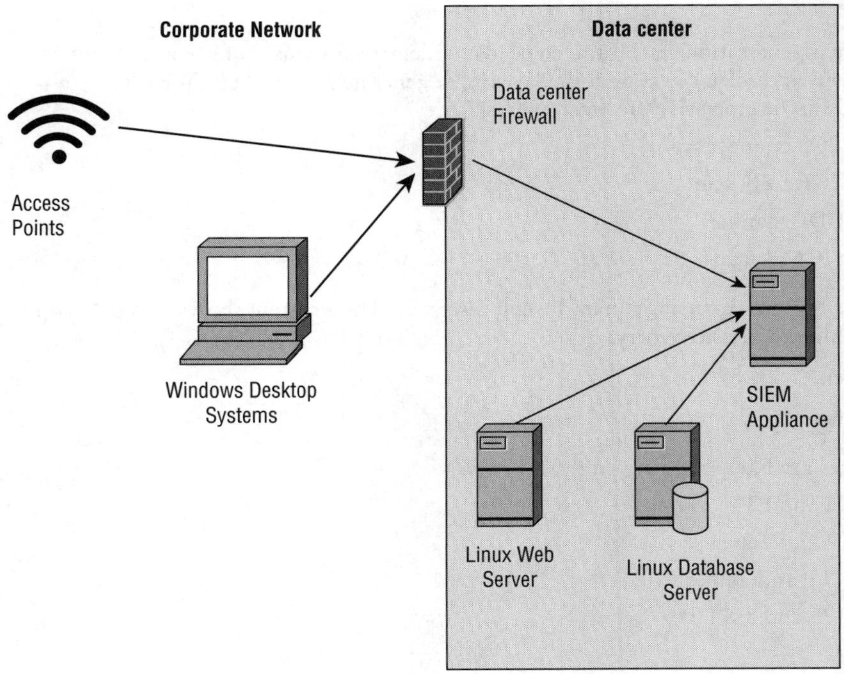

19. Jennifer needs to ensure that all Windows systems provide identical logging information to the SIEM. How can she best ensure that all Windows desktops have the same log settings?

    A. Perform periodic configuration audits.

    B. Use Group Policy.

    C. Use Local Policy.

    D. Deploy a Windows syslog client.

20. During normal operations, Jennifer's team uses the SIEM appliance to monitor for exceptions received via syslog. What system shown does not natively have support for syslog events?

    A. Enterprise wireless access points

    B. Windows desktop systems

    C. Linux web servers

    D. Enterprise firewall devices

21. What technology should an organization use for each of the devices shown in the diagram to ensure that logs can be time sequenced across the entire infrastructure?

    A. Syslog

    B. NTP

    C. Logsync

    D. SNAP

22. During a penetration test, Danielle needs to identify systems, but she hasn't gained sufficient access on the system she is using to generate raw packets. What type of scan should she run to verify the most open services?

    A. A TCP connect scan

    B. A TCP SYN scan

    C. A UDP scan

    D. An ICMP scan

23. During a port scan using nmap, Joseph discovers that a system shows two ports open that cause him immediate worry:

    21/open

    23/open

What services are likely running on those ports?

    A. SSH and FTP

    B. FTP and Telnet

    C. SMTP and Telnet

    D. POP3 and SMTP

24. Saria's team is working to persuade their management that their network has extensive vulnerabilities that attackers could exploit. If she wants to conduct a realistic attack as part of a penetration test, what type of penetration test should she conduct?

A. Crystal box

B. Gray box

C. White box

D. Black box

25. What method is commonly used to assess how well software testing covered the potential uses of a an application?

A. A test coverage analysis

B. A source code review

C. A fuzz analysis

D. A code review report

26. Testing that is focused on functions that a system should not allow are an example of what type of testing?

A. Use case testing

B. Manual testing

C. Misuse case testing

D. Dynamic testing

27. What type of monitoring uses simulated traffic to a website to monitor performance?

A. Log analysis

B. Synthetic monitoring

C. Passive monitoring

D. Simulated transaction analysis

28. Which of the following vulnerabilities is unlikely to be found by a web vulnerability scanner?

A. Path disclosure

B. Local file inclusion

C. Race condition

D. Buffer overflow

29. Jim uses a tool that scans a system for available services, then connects to them to collect banner information to determine what version of the service is running. It then provides a report detailing what it gathers, basing results on service fingerprinting, banner information, and similar details it gathers combined with CVE information. What type of tool is Jim using?

A. A port scanner

B. A service validator

C. A vulnerability scanner

D. A patch management tool

30. Emily builds a script that sends data to a web application that she is testing. Each time the script runs, it sends a series of transactions with data that fits the expected requirements of the web application to verify that it responds to typical customer behavior. What type of transactions is she using, and what type of test is this?

A. Synthetic, passive monitoring

B. Synthetic, use case testing

C. Actual, dynamic monitoring

D. Actual, fuzzing

31. What passive monitoring technique records all user interaction with an application or website to ensure quality and performance?

A. Client/server testing

B. Real user monitoring

C. Synthetic user monitoring

D. Passive user recording

32. Earlier this year, the information security team at Jim's employer identified a vulnerability in the web server that Jim is responsible for maintaining. He immediately applied the patch and is sure that it installed properly, but the vulnerability scanner has continued to flag the system as vulnerable even though Jim is sure the patch is installed. Which of the following options is Jim's best choice to deal with the issue?

A. Uninstall and reinstall the patch.

B. Ask the information security team to flag the system as patched and not vulnerable.

C. Update the version information in the web server's configuration.

D. Review the vulnerability report and use alternate remediation instructions if they are provided.

33. Angela wants to test a web browser's handling of unexpected data using an automated tool. What tool should she choose?

A. Nmap

B. zzuf

C. Nessus

D. Nikto

34. STRIDE, which stands for Spoofing, Tampering, Repudiation, Information Disclosure, Denial of Service, Elevation of Privilege, is useful in what part of application threat modeling?

A. Vulnerability assessment

B. Misuse case testing

C. Threat categorization

D. Penetration test planning

35. Why should passive scanning be conducted in addition to implementing wireless security technologies like wireless intrusion detection systems?

A. It can help identify rogue devices.

B. It can test the security of the wireless network via scripted attacks.

C. Their short dwell time on each wireless channel can allow them to capture more packets.

D. They can help test wireless IDS or IPS systems.

36. During a penetration test, Lauren is asked to test the organization's Bluetooth security. Which of the following is not a concern she should explain to her employers?

A. Bluetooth scanning can be time consuming.

B. Many devices that may be scanned are likely to be personal devices.

C. Bluetooth passive scans may require multiple visits at different times to identify all targets.

D. Bluetooth active scans can't evaluate the security mode of Bluetooth devices.

37. What term describes software testing that is intended to uncover new bugs introduced by patches or configuration changes?

A. Nonregression testing

B. Evolution testing

C. Smoke testing

D. Regression testing

38. Which of the tools cannot identify a target's operating system for a penetration tester?

A. Nmap

B. Nessus

C. Nikto

D. sqlmap

39. Susan needs to predict high-risk areas for her organization and wants to use metrics to assess risk trends as they occur. What should she do to handle this?

A. Perform yearly risk assessments.

B. Hire a penetration testing company to regularly test organizational security.

C. Identify and track key risk indicators.

D. Monitor logs and events using a SIEM device.

40. What major difference separates synthetic and passive monitoring?

A. Synthetic monitoring only works after problems have occurred.

B. Passive monitoring cannot detect functionality issues.

C. Passive monitoring only works after problems have occurred.

D. Synthetic monitoring cannot detect functionality issues.

41. Chris uses the standard penetration testing methodology shown here. Use this methodology and your knowledge of penetration testing to answer the following questions about tool usage during a penetration test.

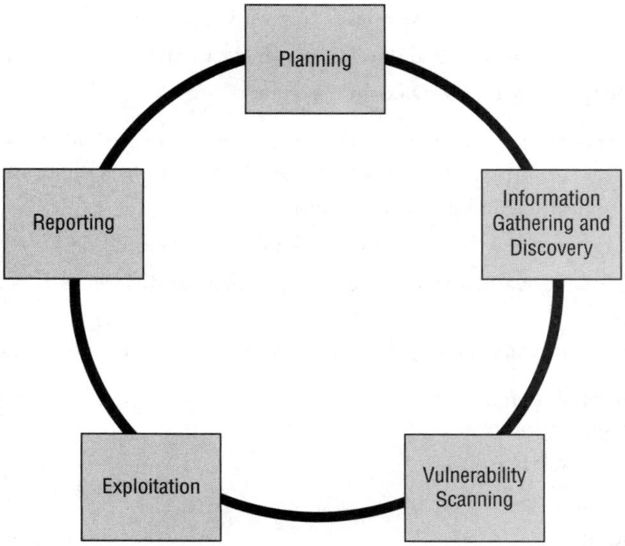

What task is the most important during Phase 1, Planning?

A. Building a test lab

B. Getting authorization

C. Gathering appropriate tools

D. Determining if the test is white, black, or gray box

42. Which of the following tools is most likely to be used during discovery?

A. Nessus

B. john

C. Nmap

D. Nikto

43. Which of these concerns is the most important to address during planning to ensure the reporting phase does not cause problems?

A. Which CVE format to use

B. How the vulnerability data will be stored and sent

C. Which targets are off limits

D. How long the report should be

44. What four types of coverage criteria are commonly used when validating the work of a code testing suite?

A. Input, statement, branch, and condition coverage

B. Function, statement, branch, and condition coverage

C. API, branch, bounds, and condition coverage

D. Bounds, branch, loop, and condition coverage

45. As part of his role as a security manager, Jacob provides the following chart to his organization's management team. What type of measurement is he providing for them?

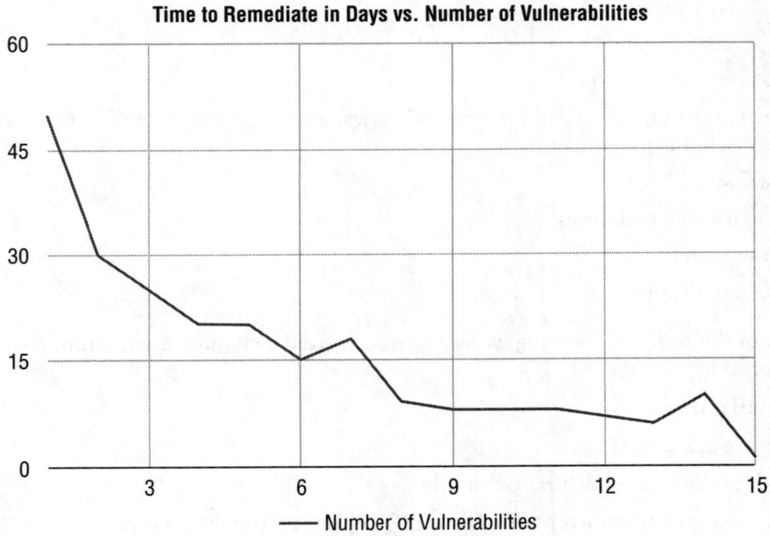

A. A coverage rate measure

B. A key performance indicator

C. A time to live metric

D. A business criticality indicator

46. What does using unique user IDs for all users provide when reviewing logs?

A. Confidentiality

B. Integrity

C. Availability

D. Accountability

47. Which of the following is not an interface that is typically tested during the software testing process?

- **A.** APIs
- **B.** Network interfaces
- **C.** UIs
- **D.** Physical interfaces

48. What protocol is used to handle vulnerability management data?

- **A.** VML
- **B.** SVML
- **C.** SCAP
- **D.** VSCAP

49. Misconfiguration, logical and functional flaws, and poor programming practices are all causes of what type of issue?

- **A.** Fuzzing
- **B.** Security vulnerabilities
- **C.** Buffer overflows
- **D.** Race conditions

50. Which of the following strategies should not be used to handle a vulnerability identified by a vulnerability scanner?

- **A.** Install a patch.
- **B.** Use a workaround fix.
- **C.** Update the banner or version number.
- **D.** Use an application layer firewall or IPS to prevent attacks against the identified vulnerability.

51. During a penetration test Saria calls her target's help desk claiming to be the senior assistance to an officer of the company. She requests that the help desk reset the officer's password because of an issue with his laptop while traveling and persuades them to do so. What type of attack has she successfully completed?

- **A.** Zero knowledge
- **B.** Help desk spoofing
- **C.** Social engineering
- **D.** Black box

52. In this image, what issue may occur due to the log handling settings?

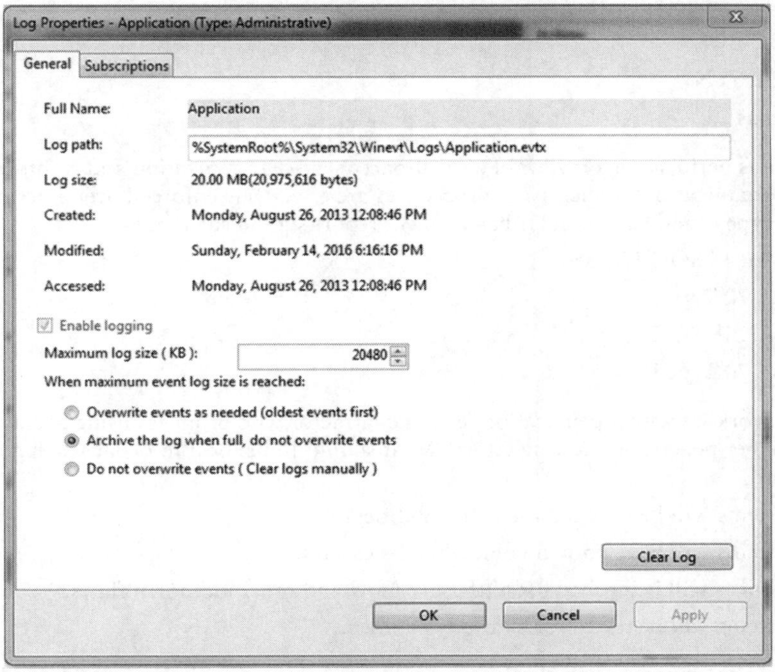

- **A.** Log data may be lost when the log is archived.
- **B.** Log data may be overwritten.
- **C.** Log data may not include needed information.
- **D.** Log data may fill the system disk.

53. Which of the following is not a hazard associated with penetration testing?

- **A.** Application crashes
- **B.** Denial of service
- **C.** Exploitation of vulnerabilities
- **D.** Data corruption

54. Which NIST special publication covers the assessment of security and privacy controls?

- **A.** 800-12
- **B.** 800-53A
- **C.** 800-34
- **D.** 800-86

55. What type of port scanning is known as "half open" scanning?

A. TCP Connect

B. TCP ACK

C. TCP SYN

D. Xmas

56. Lauren is performing a review of a third-party service organization and wants to determine if the organization's policies and procedures are effectively enforced over a period of time. What type of industry standard assessment report should she request?

A. SSAE 16 SOC 1 Type I

B. SAS 70 Type I

C. SSAE 16 SOC 1 Type II

D. SAS 70 Type II

57. Jim is working with a penetration testing contractor who proposes using Metasploit as part of her penetration testing effort. What should Jim expect to occur when Metasploit is used?

A. Systems will be scanned for vulnerabilities.

B. Systems will have known vulnerabilities exploited.

C. Services will be probed for buffer overflow and other unknown flaws.

D. Systems will be tested for zero-day exploits.

58. During a third-party audit, Jim's company receives a finding that states, "The administrator should review backup success and failure logs on a daily basis, and take action in a timely manner to resolve reported exceptions." What is the biggest issue that is likely to result if Jim's IT staff need to restore from a backup?

A. They will not know if the backups succeeded or failed.

B. The backups may not be properly logged.

C. The backups may not be usable.

D. The backup logs may not be properly reviewed.

59. Jim is helping his organization decide on audit standards for use throughout their international organization. Which of the following is not an IT standard that Jim's organization is likely to use as part of its audits?

A. COBIT

B. SSAE-16

C. ITIL

D. ISO27002

60. Which of the following best describes a typical process for building and implementing an Information Security Continuous Monitoring program as described by NIST Special Publication 800-137?

A. Define, establish, implement, analyze and report, respond, review, and update
B. Design, build, operate, analyze, respond, review, revise
C. Prepare, detect and analyze, contain, respond, recover, report
D. Define, design, build, monitor, analyze, react, revise

61. Lauren's team conducts regression testing on each patch that they release. What key performance measure should they maintain to measure the effectiveness of their testing?
A. Time to remediate vulnerabilities
B. A measure of the rate of defect recurrence
C. A weighted risk trend
D. A measure of the specific coverage of their testing

62. Which of the following types of code review is not typically performed by a human?
A. Software inspections
B. Code review
C. Static program analysis
D. Software walkthroughs

Susan is the lead of a Quality Assurance team at her company. They have been tasked with the testing for a major release of their company's core software product. Use your knowledge of code review and testing to answer the following three questions.

63. Susan's team of software testers are required to test every code path, including those that will only be used when an error condition occurs. What type of testing environment does her team need to ensure complete code coverage?
A. White box
B. Gray box
C. Black box
D. Dynamic

64. As part of the continued testing of their new application, Susan's quality assurance team has designed a set of test cases for a series of black box tests. These functional tests are then run, and a report is prepared explaining what has occurred. What type of report is typically generated during this testing to indicate test metrics?
A. A test coverage report
B. A penetration test report
C. A code coverage report
D. A line coverage report

65. As part of their code coverage testing, Susan's team runs the analysis in a nonproduction environment using logging and tracing tools. Which of the following types of code issues is most likely to be missed during testing due to this change in the operating environment?

A. Improper bounds checking
B. Input validation
C. A race condition
D. Pointer manipulation

66. What step should occur after a vulnerability scan finds a critical vulnerability on a system?
A. Patching
B. Reporting
C. Remediation
D. Validation

67. Kathleen is reviewing the code for an application. She first plans the review, conducts an overview session with the reviewers and assigns roles, and then works with the reviewers to review materials and prepare for their roles. Next, she intends to review the code, rework it, and ensure that all defects found have been corrected.

What type of review is Kathleen conducting?
A. A dynamic test
B. Fagan inspection
C. Fuzzing
D. A Roth-Parker review

68. Danielle wants to compare vulnerabilities she has discovered in her data center based on how exploitable they are, if exploit code exists, as well as how hard they are to remediate. What scoring system should she use to compare vulnerability metrics like these?
A. CSV
B. NVD
C. VSS
D. CVSS

69. During a port scan of his network, Alex finds that a number of hosts respond on TCP ports 80, 443, 515, and 9100 in offices throughout his organization. What type of devices is Alex likely discovering?
A. Web servers
B. File servers
C. Wireless access points
D. Printers

70. Nikto, Burp Suite, and Wapiti are all examples of what type of tool?
A. Web application vulnerability scanners
B. Code review tools
C. Vulnerability scanners
D. Port scanners

71. During an nmap scan, what three potential statuses are provided for a port?

A. Open, unknown, closed

B. Open, closed, and filtered

C. Available, denied, unknown

D. Available, unavailable, filtered

72. Which of the following is not a method of synthetic transaction monitoring?

A. Database monitoring

B. Traffic capture and analysis

C. User session monitoring

D. Website performance monitoring

73. Susan needs to ensure that the interactions between the components of her e-commerce application are all handled properly. She intends to verify communications, error handling, and session management capabilities throughout her infrastructure. What type of testing is she planning to conduct?

A. Misuse case testing

B. Fuzzing

C. Regression testing

D. Interface testing

74. Jim is designing his organization's log management systems and knows that he needs to carefully plan to handle the organization's log data. Which of the following is not a factor that Jim should be concerned with?

A. The volume of log data

B. A lack of sufficient log sources

C. Data storage security requirements

D. Network bandwidth

75. Jim has contracted with a software testing organization that uses automated testing tools to validate software. He is concerned that they may not completely test all statements in his software. What measurement should he ask for in their report to provide information about this?

A. A use case count

B. A test coverage report

C. A code coverage report

D. A code review report

76. When a Windows system is rebooted, what type of log is generated?

A. Error

B. Warning

C. Information

D. Failure audit

77. During a review of access logs, Alex notices that Danielle logged into her workstation in New York at 8 a.m. daily, but that she was recorded as logging into her department's main web application shortly after 3 a.m. daily. What common logging issue has Alex likely encountered?

A. Inconsistent log formatting

B. Modified logs

C. Inconsistent timestamps

D. Multiple log sources

78. What type of vulnerability scan accesses configuration information from the systems it is run against as well as information that can be accessed via services available via the network?

A. Authenticated scans

B. Web application scans

C. Unauthenticated scans

D. Port scans

Ben's organization has begun to use STRIDE to assess their software, and has identified threat agents and the business impacts that these threats could have. Now they are working to identify appropriate controls for the issues they have identified. Use the STRIDE model to answer the following three questions.

79. Ben's development team needs to address an authorization issue, resulting in an elevation of privilege threat. Which of the following controls is most appropriate to this type of issue?

A. Auditing and logging is enabled.

B. RBAC is used for specific operations.

C. Data type and format checks are enabled.

D. User input is tested against a whitelist.

80. Ben's team is attempting to categorize a transaction identification issue that is caused by use of a symmetric key shared by multiple servers. What STRIDE category should this fall into?

A. Information disclosure

B. Denial of service

C. Tampering

D. Repudiation

81. Ben wants to prevent or detect tampering with data. Which of the following is not an appropriate solution?

A. Hashes

B. Digital signatures

C. Filtering

D. Authorization controls

82. Which NIST document covers the creation of an Information Security Continuous Monitoring (ISCM)?

A. NIST SP 800-137

B. NIST SP 800-53a

C. NIST SP 800-145

D. NIST SP 800-50

83. Which of the following is not an issue when using fuzzing to find program faults?

A. They often find only simple faults.

B. Fuzz testing bugs are often severe.

C. Fuzzers may not fully cover the code.

D. Fuzzers can't reproduce errors.

84. What term describes an evaluation of the effectiveness of security controls performed by a third party?

A. A security assessment

B. A penetration test

C. A security audit

D. A security test

During a port scan, Ben uses nmap's default settings and sees the following results. Use this information to answer the following three questions.

```
Nmap scan report for 192.168.184.130
Host is up (1.0s latency).
Not shown: 977 closed ports
PORT      STATE SERVICE
21/tcp    open  ftp
22/tcp    open  ssh
23/tcp    open  telnet
25/tcp    open  smtp
53/tcp    open  domain
80/tcp    open  http
111/tcp   open  rpcbind
139/tcp   open  netbios-ssn
445/tcp   open  microsoft-ds
512/tcp   open  exec
513/tcp   open  login
514/tcp   open  shell
1099/tcp open   rmiregistry
1524/tcp open   ingreslock
2049/tcp open   nfs
2121/tcp open   ccproxy-ftp
3306/tcp open   mysql
5432/tcp open   postgresql
5900/tcp open   vnc
6000/tcp open   X11
6667/tcp open   irc
8009/tcp open   ajp13
8180/tcp open   unknown

Nmap done: 1 IP address (1 host up) scanned in 54.69 seconds
```

85. If Ben is conducting a penetration test, what should his next step be after receiving these results?

A. Connect to the web server using a web browser.

B. Connect via Telnet to test for vulnerable accounts.

C. Identify interesting ports for further scanning.

D. Use sqlmap against the open databases.

86. Based on the scan results, what OS was the system that was scanned most likely running?

A. Windows Desktop

B. Linux

C. Network device

D. Windows Server

87. Ben's manager expresses concern about the coverage of his scan. Why might his manager have this concern?

A. Ben did not test UDP services.

B. Ben did not discover ports outside the "well-known ports."

C. Ben did not perform OS fingerprinting.

D. Ben tested only a limited number of ports.

88. What technique relies on reviewing code without running it?

A. Fuzzing

B. Black box analysis

C. Static analysis

D. Gray box analysis

89. Saria needs to write a request for proposal for code review and wants to ensure that the reviewers take the business logic behind her organization's applications into account. What type of code review should she specify in the RFP?

A. Static

B. Fuzzing

C. Manual

D. Dynamic

90. What type of diagram used in application threat modeling includes malicious users as well as descriptions like mitigates and threatens?

A. Threat trees

B. STRIDE charts

C. Misuse case diagrams

D. DREAD diagrams

91. What is the first step that should occur before a penetration test is performed?

A. Data gathering

B. Port scanning

C. Getting permission

D. Planning

92. What international framework was SSAE-16 based on?

A. ISO27001

B. SAS70

C. SOX

D. ISAE 3402

93. During a penetration test of her organization, Kathleen's IPS detects a port scan that has the URG, FIN, and PSH flags set and produces an alarm. What type of scan is the penetration tester attempting?

A. A SYN scan

B. A TCP flag scan

C. An Xmas scan

D. An ACK scan

94. Nmap is an example of what type of tool?

A. Vulnerability scanner

B. Web application fuzzer

C. Network design and layout

D. Port scanner

95. What type of vulnerabilities will not be found by a vulnerability scanner?

A. Local vulnerabilities

B. Service vulnerabilities

C. Zero-day vulnerabilities

D. Vulnerabilities that require authentication

96. MITRE's CVE database provides what type of information?

A. Current versions of software

B. Patching information for applications

C. Vulnerability information

D. A list of costs versus effort required for common processes

97. A zero-day vulnerability is announced for the popular Apache web server in the middle of a workday. In Jacob's role as an information security analyst, he needs to quickly scan his network to determine what servers are vulnerable to the issue. What is Jacob's best route to quickly identify vulnerable systems?

A. Immediately run Nessus against all of the servers to identify which systems are vulnerable.

B. Review the CVE database to find the vulnerability information and patch information.

C. Create a custom IDS or IPS signature.

D. Identify affected versions and check systems for that version number using an automated scanner.

NIST Special Publication 800-115, the Technical Guide to Information Security Testing and Assessment, provides NIST's process for penetration testing. Using this image as well as your knowledge of penetration testing, answer the following questions.

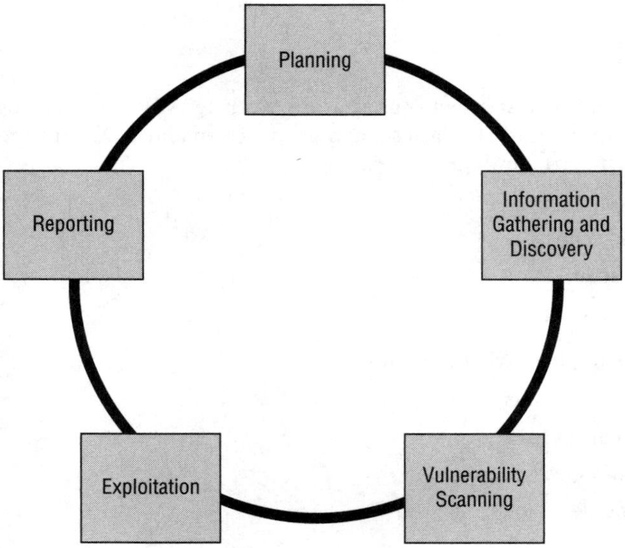

98. Which of the following is not a part of the discovery phase?

A. Hostname and IP address information gathering

B. Service information capture

C. Dumpster diving

D. Privilege escalation

99. NIST specifies four attack phase steps: gaining access, escalating privileges, system browsing, and installing additional tools. Once attackers install additional tools, what phase will a penetration tester typically return to?

A. Discovery

B. Gaining access

C. Escalating privileges

D. System browsing

100. Which of the following is not a typical part of a penetration test report?

A. A list of identified vulnerabilities

B. All sensitive data that was gathered during the test

C. Risk ratings for each issue discovered

D. Mitigation guidance for issues identified

Chapter 7

Security Options (Domain 7)

1. Referring to the figure below, what technology is shown that provides fault tolerance for the database servers?
   - **A.** Failover cluster
   - **B.** UPS
   - **C.** Tape backup
   - **D.** Cold site

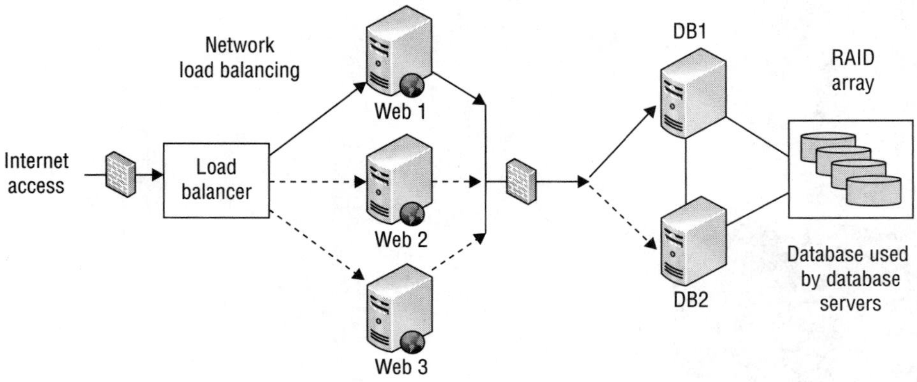

2. Joe is the security administrator for an ERP system. He is preparing to create accounts for several new employees. What default access should he give to all of the new employees as he creates the accounts?
   - **A.** Read only
   - **B.** Editor
   - **C.** Administrator
   - **D.** No access

3. Which one of the following is not a privileged administrative activity that should be automatically sent to a log of superuser actions?
   - **A.** Purging log entries
   - **B.** Restoring a system from backup
   - **C.** Logging into a workstation
   - **D.** Managing user accounts

4. Which one of the following individuals is most likely to lead a regulatory investigation?
   - **A.** CISO
   - **B.** CIO
   - **C.** Government agent
   - **D.** Private detective

5. What type of evidence consists entirely of tangible items that may be brought into a court of law?
   A. Documentary evidence
   B. Parol evidence
   C. Testimonial evidence
   D. Real evidence
6. Which one of the following trusted recovery types does not fail into a secure operating state?
   A. Manual recovery
   B. Automated recovery
   C. Automated recovery without undue loss
   D. Function recovery
7. Which one of the following might a security team use on a honeypot system to consume an attacker's time while alerting administrators?
   A. Honeynet
   B. Pseudoflaw
   C. Warning banner
   D. Darknet
8. Toni responds to the desk of a user who reports slow system activity. Upon checking outbound network connections from that system, Toni notices a large amount of social media traffic originating from the system. The user does not use social media, and when Toni checks the accounts in question, they contain strange messages that appear encrypted. What is the most likely cause of this traffic?
   A. Other users are relaying social media requests through Toni's computer.
   B. Toni's computer is part of a botnet.
   C. Toni is lying about her use of social media.
   D. Someone else is using Toni's computer when she is not present.
9. Under what virtualization model does the virtualization platform separate the network control plane from the data plane and replace complex network devices with simpler devices that simply receive instructions from the controller?
   A. Virtual machines
   B. VSAN
   C. VLAN
   D. SDN
10. Jim would like to identify compromised systems on his network that may be participating in a botnet. He plans to do this by watching for connections made to known command-and-control servers. Which one of the following techniques would be most likely to provide this information if Jim has access to a list of known servers?

A. Netflow records

B. IDS logs

C. Authentication logs

D. RFC logs

Questions 11–14 refer to the following scenario.

Gary was recently hired as the first chief information security officer (CISO) for a local government agency. The agency recently suffered a security breach and is attempting to build a new information security program. Gary would like to apply some best practices for security operations as he is designing this program.

11. As Gary decides what access permissions he should grant to each user, what principle should guide his decisions about default permissions?

A. Separation of duties

B. Least privilege

C. Aggregation

D. Separation of privileges

12. As Gary designs the program, he uses the matrix shown below. What principle of information security does this matrix most directly help enforce?

Roles/Tasks	Application Programmer	Security Administrator	Database Administrator	Database Server Administrator	Budget Analyst	Accounts Receivable	Accounts Payable	Deploy Patches	Verify Patches
Application Programmer		X	X	X					
Security Administrator	X		X	X	X	X	X	X	
Database Administrator	X	X		X					
Database Server Administrator	X	X	X						
Budget Analyst		X				X	X		
Accounts Receivable		X			X		X		
Accounts Payable		X			X	X			
Deploy Patches		X							X
Verify Patches								X	
	Potential Areas of Conflict								

A. Segregation of duties

B. Aggregation

C. Two-person control

D. Defense in depth

13. Gary is preparing to create an account for a new user and assign privileges to the HR database. What two elements of information must Gary verify before granting this access?

    A. Credentials and need to know

    B. Clearance and need to know

    C. Password and clearance

    D. Password and biometric scan

14. Gary is preparing to develop controls around access to root encryption keys and would like to apply a principle of security designed specifically for very sensitive operations. Which principle should he apply?

    A. Least privilege

    B. Defense in depth

    C. Security through obscurity

    D. Two-person control

15. When should an organization conduct a review of the privileged access that a user has to sensitive systems?

    A. On a periodic basis

    B. When a user leaves the organization

    C. When a user changes roles

    D. All of the above

16. Which one of the following terms is often used to describe a collection of unrelated patches released in a large collection?

    A. Hotfix

    B. Update

    C. Security fix

    D. Service pack

17. Which one of the following tasks is performed by a forensic disk controller?

    A. Masking error conditions reported by the storage device

    B. Transmitting write commands to the storage device

    C. Intercepting and modifying or discarding commands sent to the storage device

    D. Preventing data from being returned by a read operation sent to the device

18. Lydia is processing access control requests for her organization. She comes across a request where the user does have the required security clearance, but there is no business justification for the access. Lydia denies this request. What security principle is she following?

    A. Need to know

    B. Least privilege

    C. Separation of duties

    D. Two-person control

19. Which one of the following security tools consists of an unused network address space that may detect unauthorized activity?

A. Honeypot

B. Honeynet

C. Psuedoflaw

D. Darknet

20. Which one of the following mechanisms is not commonly seen as a deterrent to fraud?

A. Job rotation

B. Mandatory vacations

C. Incident response

D. Two-person control

21. Brian recently joined an organization that runs the majority of its services on a virtualization platform located in its own data center but also leverages an IaaS provider for hosting its web services and a SaaS email system. What term best describes the type of cloud environment this organization uses?

A. Public cloud

B. Dedicated cloud

C. Private cloud

D. Hybrid cloud

22. Tom is responding to a recent security incident and is seeking information on the approval process for a recent modification to a system's security settings. Where would he most likely find this information?

A. Change log

B. System log

C. Security log

D. Application log

23. Mark is considering replacing his organization's customer relationship management (CRM) solution with a new product that is available in the cloud. This new solution is completely managed by the vendor and Mark's company will not have to write any code or manage any physical resources. What type of cloud solution is Mark considering?

A. IaaS

B. CaaS

C. PaaS

D. SaaS

24. Which one of the following information sources is useful to security administrators seeking a list of information security vulnerabilities in applications, devices, and operating systems?

A. OWASP

B. Bugtraq

C. Microsoft Security Bulletins

D. CVE

25. Which of the following would normally be considered an example of a disaster when performing disaster recovery planning?

I. Hacking incident

II. Flood

III. Fire

IV. Terrorism

A. II and III only

B. I and IV only

C. II, III, and IV only

D. I, II, III, and IV

26. Glenda would like to conduct a disaster recovery test and is seeking a test that will allow a review of the plan with no disruption to normal information system activities and as minimal a commitment of time as possible. What type of test should she choose?

A. Tabletop exercise

B. Parallel test

C. Full interruption test

D. Checklist review

27. Which one of the following is not an example of a backup tape rotation scheme?

A. Grandfather/Father/Son

B. Meet in the middle

C. Tower of Hanoi

D. Six Cartridge Weekly

28. Helen is implementing a new security mechanism for granting employees administrative privileges in the accounting system. She designs the process so that both the employee's manager and the accounting manager must approve the request before the access is granted. What information security principle is Helen enforcing?

A. Least privilege

B. Two-person control

C. Job rotation

D. Separation of duties

29. Which one of the following is not a requirement for evidence to be admissible in court?

A. The evidence must be relevant.

B. The evidence must be material.

C. The evidence must be tangible.

D. The evidence must be competent.

30. In which cloud computing model does a customer share computing infrastructure with other customers of the cloud vendor where one customer may not know the other's identity?

A. Public cloud

B. Private cloud

C. Community cloud

D. Shared cloud

31. Which of the following organizations would be likely to have a representative on a CSIRT?

I. Information security

II. Legal counsel

III. Senior management

IV. Engineering

A. I, III, and IV

B. I, II, and III

C. I, II, and IV

D. All of the above

32. Sam is responsible for backing up his company's primary file server. He configured a backup schedule that performs full backups every Monday evening at 9 p.m. and differential backups on other days of the week at that same time. Files change according to the information shown in the figure below. How many files will be copied in Wednesday's backup?

A. 2

B. 3

C. 5

D. 6

File Modifications
Monday 8 a.m. - File 1 created
Monday 10 a.m. - File 2 created
Monday 11 a.m. - File 3 created
Monday 4 p.m. - File 1 modified
Monday 5 p.m. - File 4 created
Tuesday 8 a.m. - File 1 modified
Tuesday 9 a.m. - File 2 modified
Tuesday 10 a.m. - File 5 created
Wednesday 8 a.m. - File 3 modified
Wednesday 9 a.m. - File 6 created

33. Which one of the following security tools is not capable of generating an active response to a security event?

A. IPS

B. Firewall

C. IDS

D. Antivirus software

34. In virtualization platforms, what name is given to the module that is responsible for controlling access to physical resources by virtual resources?

A. Guest machine

B. SDN

C. Kernel

D. Hypervisor

35. What term is used to describe the default set of privileges assigned to a user when a new account is created?

A. Aggregation

B. Transitivity

C. Baseline

D. Entitlement

36. Which one of the following types of agreements is the most formal document that contains expectations about availability and other performance parameters between a service provider and a customer?

A. Service-level agreement (SLA)

B. Operations level agreement (OLA)

C. Memorandum of understanding (MOU)

D. Statement of work (SOW)

37. Which one of the following frameworks focuses on IT service management and includes topics such as change management, configuration management, and service-level agreements?

A. ITIL

B. PMBOK

C. PCI DSS

D. TOGAF

38. Richard is experiencing issues with the quality of network service on his organization's network. The primary symptom is that packets are consistently taking too long to travel from their source to their destination. What term describes the issue Richard is facing?

A. Jitter

B. Packet loss

C. Interference

D. Latency

39. Joe is an investigator with a law enforcement agency. He received a tip that a suspect is communicating sensitive information with a third party via a message board. After obtaining a warrant for the message, he obtained the contents and found that the message only contains the image shown in the figure below. If this is the sole content of the communication, what technique could the suspect have used to embed sensitive information in the message?

A. Steganography

B. Watermarking

C. Clipping

D. Sampling

40. Which one of the following is an example of a manmade disaster?

A. Hurricane

B. Flood

C. Mudslide

D. Transformer failure

41. Which of the following is not true about the $(ISC)^2$ code of ethics?

A. Adherence to the code is a condition of certification.

B. Failure to comply with the code may result in revocation of certification.

C. The code applies to all members of the information security profession.

D. Members who observe a breach of the code are required to report the possible violation.

42. Javier is verifying that only IT system administrators have the ability to log on to servers used for administrative purposes. What principle of information security is he enforcing?

- **A.** Need to know
- **B.** Least privilege
- **C.** Two-person control
- **D.** Transitive trust

43. Which one of the following is not a basic preventative measure that you can take to protect your systems and applications against attack?

- **A.** Implement intrusion detection and prevention systems.
- **B.** Maintain current patch levels on all operating systems and applications.
- **C.** Remove unnecessary accounts and services.
- **D.** Conduct forensic imaging of all systems.

44. Tim is a forensic analyst who is attempting to retrieve information from a hard drive. It appears that the user attempted to erase the data, and Tim is trying to reconstruct it. What type of forensic analysis is Tim performing?

- **A.** Software analysis
- **B.** Media analysis
- **C.** Embedded device analysis
- **D.** Network analysis

45. Which one of the following is an example of a computer security incident?

- **A.** Completion of a backup schedule
- **B.** System access recorded in a log
- **C.** Unauthorized vulnerability scan of a file server
- **D.** Update of antivirus signatures

46. Which one of the following technologies would provide the most automation of an inventory control process in a cost-effective manner?

- **A.** IPS
- **B.** Wi-Fi
- **C.** RFID
- **D.** Ethernet

47. Connor's company recently experienced a denial of service attack that Connor believes came from an inside source. If true, what type of event has the company experienced?

- **A.** Espionage
- **B.** Confidentiality breach
- **C.** Sabotage
- **D.** Integrity breach

48. What type of attack is shown in the figure below?

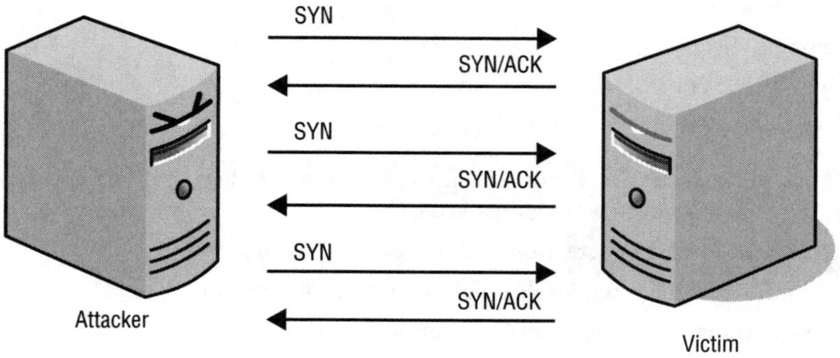

A. SYN flood

B. Ping flood

C. Smurf

D. Fraggle

49. Florian is building a disaster recovery plan for his organization and would like to determine the amount of time that a particular IT service may be down without causing serious damage to business operations. What variable is Florian calculating?

A. RTO

B. MTD

C. RPO

D. SLA

50. Which one of the following statements best describes a zero-day vulnerability?

A. An attacker that is new to the world of hacking

B. A database attack that places the date 00/00/0000 in data tables in an attempt to exploit flaws in business logic

C. An attack previously unknown to the security community

D. An attack that sets the operating system date and time to 00/00/0000 and 00:00:00

51. Which one of the following is not a canon of the (ISC)^2 code of ethics?

A. Protect society, the common good, necessary public trust and confidence, and the infrastructure.

B. Promptly report security vulnerabilities to relevant authorities.

C. Act honorably, honestly, justly, responsibly, and legally.

D. Provide diligent and competent service to principals.

52. During an incident investigation, investigators meet with a system administrator who may have information about the incident but is not a suspect. What type of conversation is taking place during this meeting?

A. Interview

B. Interrogation

C. Both an interview and an interrogation

D. Neither an interview nor an interrogation

53. Beth is selecting a disaster recovery facility for her organization. She would like to choose a facility that has appropriate environmental controls and power for her operations but wants to minimize costs. She is willing to accept a lengthy recovery time. What type of facility should she choose?

A. Hot site

B. Cold site

C. Warm site

D. Service bureau

54. What technique has been used to protect the intellectual property in the image shown below?

A. Steganography

B. Clipping

C. Sampling

D. Watermarking

55. You are working to evaluate the risk of flood to an area and consult the flood maps from the Federal Emergency Management Agency (FEMA). According to those maps, the area lies within a 200-year flood plain. What is the annualized rate of occurrence (ARO) of a flood in that region?

A. 200

B. 0.01

C. 0.02

D. 0.005

56. Which one of the following individuals poses the greatest risk to security in most well-defended organizations?

A. Political activist

B. Malicious insider

C. Script kiddie

D. Thrill attcker

57. Veronica is considering the implementation of a database recovery mechanism recommended by a consultant. In the recommended approach, an automated process will move database backups from the primary facility to an offsite location each night. What type of database recovery technique is the consultant describing?

A. Remote journaling

B. Remote mirroring

C. Electronic vaulting

D. Transaction logging

58. When designing an access control scheme, Hilda set up roles so that the same person does not have the ability to provision a new user account and assign superuser privileges to an account. What information security principle is Hilda following?

A. Least privilege

B. Separation of duties

C. Job rotation

D. Security through obscurity

59. Reggie recently received a letter from his company's internal auditors scheduling the kickoff meeting for an assessment of his group. Which of the following should Reggie not expect to learn during that meeting?

A. Scope of the audit

B. Purpose of the audit

C. Expected timeframe

D. Expected findings

60. Which one of the following events marks the completion of a disaster recovery process?

A. Securing property and life safety

B. Restoring operations in an alternate facility

C. Restoring operations in the primary facility

D. Standing down first responders

61. Melanie suspects that someone is using malicious software to steal computing cycles from her company. Which one of the following security tools would be in the best position to detect this type of incident?

A. NIDS

B. Firewall

C. HIDS

D. DLP

62. Brandon observes that an authorized user of a system on his network recently misused his account to exploit a system vulnerability against a shared server that allowed him to gain root access to that server. What type of attack took place?

A. Denial of service

B. Privilege escalation

C. Reconaissance

D. Brute force

63. Carla has worked for her company for 15 years and has held a variety of different positions. Each time she changed positions, she gained new privileges associated with that position, but no privileges were ever taken away. What concept describes the sets of privileges she has accumulated?

A. Entitlement

B. Aggregation

C. Transitivity

D. Isolation

64. During what phase of the incident response process do administrators take action to limit the effect or scope of an incident?

A. Detection

B. Response

C. Mitigation

D. Recovery

Questions 65–68 refer to the following scenario.

Ann is a security professional for a mid-sized business and typically handles log analysis and security monitoring tasks for her organization. One of her roles is to monitor alerts originating from the organization's intrusion detection system. The system typically generates several dozen alerts each day, and many of those alerts turn out to be false alarms after her investigation.

This morning, the intrusion detection system alerted because the network began to receive an unusually high volume of inbound traffic. Ann received this alert and began looking into the origin of the traffic.

65. At this point in the incident response process, what term best describes what has occurred in Ann's organization?
    A. Security occurrence
    B. Security incident
    C. Security event
    D. Security intrusion

66. Ann continues her investigation and realizes that the traffic generating the alert is abnormally high volumes of inbound UDP traffic on port 53. What service typically uses this port?
    A. DNS
    B. SSH/SCP
    C. SSL/TLS
    D. HTTP

67. As Ann analyzes the traffic further, she realizes that the traffic is coming from many different sources and has overwhelmed the network, preventing legitimate uses. The inbound packets are responses to queries that she does not see in outbound traffic. The responses are abnormally large for their type. What type of attack should Ann suspect?
    A. Reconnaissance
    B. Malicious code
    C. System penetration
    D. Denial of service

68. At this point in the incident response process, what term best describes what has occurred in Ann's organization?
    A. Security occurrence
    B. Security incident
    C. Security event
    D. Security intrusion

69. Frank is seeking to introduce a hacker's laptop in court as evidence against the hacker. The laptop does contain logs that indicate the hacker committed the crime, but the court ruled that the search of the apartment that resulted in police finding the laptop was unconstitutional. What admissibility criteria prevents Frank from introducing the laptop as evidence?
    A. Materiality
    B. Relevance
    C. Hearsay
    D. Competence

70. Gordon suspects that a hacker has penetrated a system belonging to his company. The system does not contain any regulated information and Gordon wishes to conduct an investigation on behalf of his company. He has permission from his supervisor to conduct the investigation. Which of the following statements is true?

A. Gordon is legally required to contact law enforcement before beginning the investigation.

B. Gordon may not conduct his own investigation.

C. Gordon's investigation may include examining the contents of hard disks, network traffic, and any other systems or information belonging to the company.

D. Gordon may ethically perform "hack back" activities after identifying the perpetrator.

71. Which one of the following tools provides an organization with the greatest level of protection against a software vendor going out of business?

A. Service-level agreement

B. Escrow agreeement

C. Mutual assistance agreement

D. PCI DSS compliance agreement

72. Fran is considering new human resources policies for her bank that will deter fraud. She plans to implement a mandatory vacation policy. What is typically considered the shortest effective length of a mandatory vacation?

A. Two days

B. Four days

C. One week

D. One month

73. Which of the following events would constitute a security incident?

1. An attempted network intrusion
2. A successful database intrusion
3. A malware infection
4. A violation of a confidentiality policy
5. An unsuccessful attempt to remove information from a secured area

A. 2, 3, and 4

B. 1, 2, and 3

C. 4 and 5

D. All of the above

74. Which one of the following traffic types should not be blocked by an organization's egress filtering policy?

A. Traffic destined to a private IP address

B. Traffic with a broadcast destination

C. Traffic with a source address from an external network

D. Traffic with a destination address on a external network

75. Allie is responsible for reviewing authentication logs on her organization's network. She does not have the time to review all logs, so she decides to choose only records where there have been four or more invalid authentication attempts. What technique is Allie using to reduce the size of the pool?

A. Sampling

B. Random selection

C. Clipping

D. Statistical analysis

76. You are performing an investigation into a potential bot infection on your network and wish to perform a forensic analysis of the information that passed between different systems on your network and those on the Internet. You believe that the information was likely encrypted. You are beginning your investigation after the activity concluded. What would be the best and easiest way to obtain the source of this information?

A. Packet captures

B. Netflow data

C. Intrusion detection system logs

D. Centralized authentication records

77. Which one of the following tools helps system administrators by providing a standard, secure template of configuration settings for operating systems and applications?

A. Security guidelines

B. Security policy

C. Baseline configuration

D. Running configuration

78. What type of disaster recovery test activates the alternate processing facility and uses it to conduct transactions but leaves the primary site up and running?

A. Full interruption test

B. Parallel test

C. Checklist review

D. Tabletop exercise

79. During which phase of the incident response process would an analyst receive an intrusion detection system alert and verify its accuracy?

A. Response

B. Mitigation

C. Detection

D. Reporting

80. In what virtualization model do full guest operating systems run on top of a virtualization platform?

A. Virtual machines

B. Software-defined networking

C. Virtual SAN

D. Application virtualization

81. What level of RAID is also known as disk mirroring?

A. RAID-0

B. RAID-1

C. RAID-5

D. RAID-10

82. Bruce is seeing quite a bit of suspicious activity on his network. It appears that an outside entity is attempting to connect to all of his systems using a TCP connection on port 22. What type of scanning is the outsider likely engaging in?

A. FTP scanning

B. Telnet scanning

C. SSH scanning

D. HTTP scanning

83. The historic ping of death attack is most similar to which of the following modern attack types?

A. SQL injection

B. Cross-site scripting

C. Buffer overflow

D. Brute force password cracking

84. Roger recently accepted a new position as a security professional at a company that runs its entire IT infrastructure within an IaaS environment. Which one of the following would most likely be the responsibility of Roger's firm?

A. Configuring the network firewall

B. Applying hypervisor updates

C. Patching operating systems

D. Wiping drives prior to disposal

85. What technique can application developers use to test applications in an isolated virtualized environment before allowing them on a production network?

A. Penetration testing

B. Sandboxing

C. White box testing

D. Black box testing

86. Gina is the firewall administrator for a small business and recently installed a new firewall. After seeing signs of unusually heavy network traffic, she checked the intrusion detection system, which reported that a fraggle attack was underway. What firewall configuration change can Gina make to most effectively prevent this attack?

A. Block ICMP echo reply packets from entering the network.

B. Block UDP port 7 and 9 traffic from entering the network.

C. Block the source address of the attack.

D. Block the destination address of the attack.

87. What type of trust relationship extends beyond the two domains participating in the trust to one or more of their subdomains?

A. Transitive trust

B. Inheritable trust

C. Nontransitive trust

D. Noninheritable trust

88. Renee is a software developer who writes code in Node.js for her organization. The company is considering moving from a self-hosted Node.js environment to one where Renee will run her code on application servers managed by a cloud vendor. What type of cloud solution is Renee's company considering?

A. IaaS

B. CaaS

C. PaaS

D. SaaS

89. Timber Industries recently got into a dispute with a customer. During a meeting with his account representative, the customer stood up and declared, "There is no other solution. We will have to take this matter to court." He then left the room. When does Timber Industries have an obligation to begin preserving evidence?

A. Immediately

B. Upon receipt of a notice of litigation from opposing attorneys

C. Upon receipt of a subpoena

D. Upon receipt of a court order

90. What legal protection prevents law enforcement agencies from searching a facility or electronic system without either probable cause or consent?

A. First Amendment

B. Fourth Amendment

C. Fifth Amendment

D. Fifteenth Amendment

91. Darcy is a computer security specialist who is assisting with the prosecution of a hacker. The prosecutor requests that Darcy give testimony in court about whether, in her opinion, the logs and other records in a case are indicative of a hacking attempt. What type of evidence is Darcy being asked to provide?

A. Expert opinion

B. Direct evidence

C. Real evidence

D. Documentary evidence

92. Which one of the following techniques is not commonly used to remove unwanted remnant data from magnetic tapes?

A. Physical destruction

B. Degaussing

C. Overwriting

D. Reformatting

93. What is the minimum number of disks required to implement RAID level 1?

A. One

B. Two

C. Three

D. Five

94. Jerome is conducting a forensic investigation and is reviewing database server logs to investigate query contents for evidence of SQL injection attacks. What type of analysis is he performing?

A. Hardware analysis

B. Software analysis

C. Network analysis

D. Media analysis

95. Quantum Computing regularly ships tapes of backup data across the country to a secondary facility. These tapes contain confidential information. What is the most important security control that Quantum can use to protect these tapes?

A. Locked shipping containers

B. Private couriers

C. Data encryption

D. Media rotation

96. Carolyn is concerned that users on her network may be storing sensitive information, such as Social Security numbers, on their hard drives without proper authorization or security controls. What technology can she use to best detect this activity?

A. IDS

B. IDP

C. DLP

D. TLS

97. Under what type of software license does the recipient of software have an unlimited right to copy, modify, distribute, or resell a software package?

A. GNU Public License

B. Freeware

C. Open source

D. Public domain

98. In what type of attack do attackers manage to insert themselves into a connection between a user and a legitimate website?

A. Man-in-the-middle

B. Fraggle

C. Wardriving

D. Meet-in-the-middle

99. Which one of the following techniques uses statistical methods to select a small number of records from a large pool for further analysis with the goal of choosing a set of records that is representative of the entire pool?

A. Clipping

B. Randomization

C. Sampling

D. Selection

100. Which one of the following controls protects an organization in the event of a sustained period of power loss?

A. Redundant servers

B. Uninterruptible power supply (UPS)

C. Generator

D. RAID

Chapter 8

Software Development Security (Domain 8)

1. When designing an object-oriented model, which of the following situations is ideal?
   - **A.** High cohesion, high coupling
   - **B.** High cohesion, low coupling
   - **C.** Low cohesion, low coupling
   - **D.** Low cohesion, high coupling
2. Which of the following is a common way that attackers leverage botnets?
   - **A.** Sending spam messages
   - **B.** Conducting brute-force attacks
   - **C.** Scanning for vulnerable systems
   - **D.** All of the above
3. Which one of the following statements is not true about code review?
   - **A.** Code review should be a peer-driven process that includes multiple developers.
   - **B.** Code review may be automated.
   - **C.** Code review occurs during the design phase.
   - **D.** Code reviewers may expect to review several hundred lines of code per hour.
4. Harold's company has a strong password policy that requires a minimum length of 12 characters and the use of both alphanumeric characters and symbols. What technique would be the most effective way for an attacker to compromise passwords in Harold's organization?
   - **A.** Brute-force attack
   - **B.** Dictionary attack
   - **C.** Rainbow table attack
   - **D.** Social engineering attack
5. Which process is responsible for ensuring that changes to software include acceptance testing?
   - **A.** Request control
   - **B.** Change control
   - **C.** Release control
   - **D.** Configuration control
6. Which one of the following attack types attempts to exploit the trust relationship that a user's browser has with other websites by forcing the submission of an authenticated request to a third-party site?
   - **A.** XSS
   - **B.** CSRF
   - **C.** SQL injection
   - **D.** Session hijacking

7. When using the SDLC, which one of these steps should you take before the others?
   - **A.** Functional requirements determination
   - **B.** Control specifications development
   - **C.** Code review
   - **D.** Design review

8. Jaime is a technical support analyst and is asked to visit a user whose computer is displaying the error message shown here. What state has this computer entered?

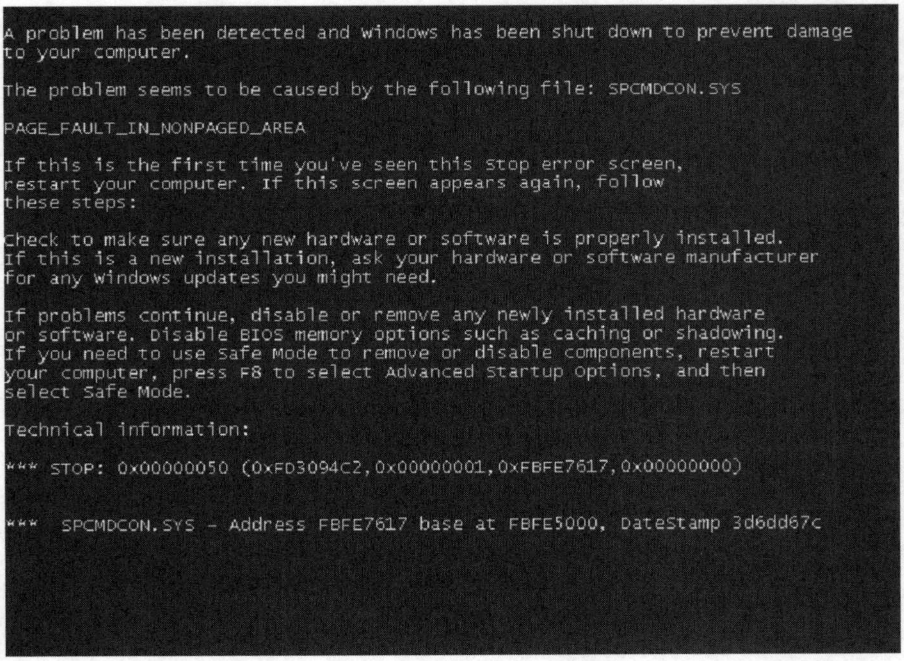

A problem has been detected and windows has been shut down to prevent damage
to your computer.
The problem seems to be caused by the following file: SPCMDCON.SYS
PAGE_FAULT_IN_NONPAGED_AREA
If this is the first time you've seen this Stop error screen,
restart your computer. If this screen appears again, follow
these steps:
Check to make sure any new hardware or software is properly installed.
If this is a new installation, ask your hardware or software manufacturer
for any Windows updates you might need.
If problems continue, disable or remove any newly installed hardware
or software. Disable BIOS memory options such as caching or shadowing.
If you need to use Safe Mode to remove or disable components, restart
your computer, press F8 to select Advanced Startup Options, and then
select Safe Mode.
Technical information:
*** STOP: 0x00000050 (0xFD3094C2,0x00000001,0xFBFE7617,0x00000000)
*** SPCMDCON.SYS - Address FBFE7617 base at FBFE5000, DateStamp 3d6dd67c

   - **A.** Fail open
   - **B.** Irrecoverable error
   - **C.** Memory exhaustion
   - **D.** Fail secure

9. Which one of the following is not a goal of software threat modeling?
   - **A.** To reduce the number of security-related design flaws
   - **B.** To reduce the number of security-related coding flaws
   - **C.** To reduce the severity of non-security-related flaws
   - **D.** To reduce the number of threat vectors

10. In the diagram shown here, which is an example of a method?

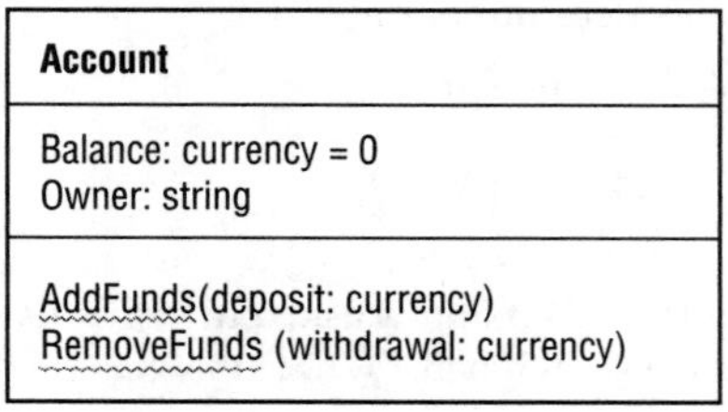

A. `Account`

B. `Owner`

C. `AddFunds`

D. None of the above

11. Which one of the following is considered primary storage?

A. Memory

B. Hard disk

C. Flash drive

D. DVD

12. Which one of the following testing methodologies typically works without access to source code?

A. Dynamic testing

B. Static testing

C. White box testing

D. Code review

13. What concept in object-oriented programming allows a subclass to access methods belonging to a superclass?

A. Polymorphism

B. Inheritance

C. Coupling

D. Cohesion

14. Bobby is investigating how an authorized database user is gaining access to information outside his normal clearance level. Bobby believes that the user is making use of a type of function that summarizes data. What term describes this type of function?

A. Inference

B. Polymorphic

C. Aggregate

D. Modular

15. Which one of the following controls would best protect an application against buffer overflow attacks?

A. Encryption

B. Input validation

C. Firewall

D. Intrusion prevention system

16. Berta is analyzing the logs of the Windows Firewall on one of her servers and comes across the entries shown in this figure. What type of attack do these entries indicate?

```
2016-04-21 05:14:52 DROP TCP 192.168.250.4 192.168.42.14 4004 21  - - - - - - - RECEIVE
2016-04-21 05:14:53 DROP TCP 192.168.250.4 192.168.42.14 4005 22  - - - - - - - RECEIVE
2016-04-21 05:14:54 DROP TCP 192.168.250.4 192.168.42.14 4006 23  - - - - - - - RECEIVE
2016-04-21 05:14:56 DROP TCP 192.168.250.4 192.168.42.14 4007 25  - - - - - - - RECEIVE
2016-04-21 05:14:59 DROP TCP 192.168.250.4 192.168.42.14 4008 53  - - - - - - - RECEIVE
2016-04-21 05:15:02 DROP TCP 192.168.250.4 192.168.42.14 4009 80  - - - - - - - RECEIVE
2016-04-21 05:15:03 DROP TCP 192.168.250.4 192.168.42.14 4010 110  - - - - - - - RECEIVE
2016-04-21 05:15:04 DROP TCP 192.168.250.4 192.168.42.14 4011 111  - - - - - - - RECEIVE
```

A. SQL injection

B. Port scan

C. Teardrop

D. Land

Questions 17–20 refer to the following scenario:

Robert is a consultant who helps organizations create and develop mature software development practices. He prefers to use the Software Capability Maturity Model (SW-CMM) to evaluate the current and future status of organizations using both independent review and self-assessments. He is currently working with two different clients.

Acme Widgets is not very well organized with their software development practices. They have a dedicated team of developers who do "whatever it takes" to get software out the door, but they do not have any formal processes.

Beta Particles is a company with years of experience developing software using formal, documented software development processes. They use a standard model for software development but do not have quantitative management of those processes.

17. What phase of the SW-CMM should Robert report as the current status of Acme Widgets?

A. Defined

B. Repeatable

C. Initial

D. Managed

18. Robert is working with Acme Widgets on a strategy to advance their software development practices. What SW-CMM stage should be their next target milestone?

A. Defined

B. Repeatable

C. Initial

D. Managed

19. What phase of the SW-CMM should Robert report as the current status of Beta Particles?

A. Defined

B. Repeatable

C. Optimizing

D. Managed

20. Robert is also working with Beta Particles on a strategy to advance their software development practices. What SW-CMM stage should be their next target milestone?

A. Defined

B. Repeatable

C. Optimizing

D. Managed

21. Which one of the following database keys is used to enforce referential integrity relationships between tables?

A. Primary key

B. Candidate key

C. Foreign key

D. Master key

22. Which one of the following files is most likely to contain a macro virus?

A. `projections.doc`

B. `command.com`

C. `command.exe`

D. `loopmaster.exe`

23. Victor created a database table that contains information on his organization's employees. The table contains the employee's user ID, three different telephone number fields (home, work, and mobile), the employee's office location, and the employee's job title. There are 16 records in the table. What is the degree of this table?

A. 3

B. 4

C. 6

D. 16

24. Carrie is analyzing the application logs for her web-based application and comes across the following string:

```
../../../../../../../../../etc/passwd
```

What type of attack was likely attempted against Carrie's application?

A. Command injection

B. Session hijacking

C. Directory traversal

D. Brute force

25. When should a design review take place when following an SDLC approach to software development?

A. After the code review

B. After user acceptance testing

C. After the development of functional requirements

D. After the completion of unit testing

26. Tracy is preparing to apply a patch to her organization's enterprise resource planning system. She is concerned that the patch may introduce flaws that did not exist in prior versions, so she plans to conduct a test that will compare previous responses to input with those produced by the newly patched application. What type of testing is Tracy planning?

A. Unit testing

B. Acceptance testing

C. Regression testing

D. Vulnerability testing

27. What term is used to describe the level of confidence that software is free from vulnerabilities, either intentionally designed into the software or accidentally inserted at any time during its life cycle, and that the software functions in the intended manner?

A. Validation

B. Accreditation

C. Confidence interval

D. Assurance

28. Victor recently took a new position at an online dating website and is responsible for leading a team of developers. He realized quickly that the developers are having issues with production code because they are working on different projects that result in conflicting modifications to the production code. What process should Victor invest in improving?

A. Request control

B. Release control

C. Change control

D. Configuration control

29. What type of database security issue exists when a collection of facts has a higher classification than the classification of any of those facts standing alone?

A. Inference

B. SQL injection

C. Multilevel security

D. Aggregation

30. What are the two types of covert channels that are commonly exploited by attackers seeking to surreptitiously exfiltrate information?

A. Timing and storage

B. Timing and firewall

C. Storage and memory

D. Firewall and storage

31. Vivian would like to hire a software tester to come in and evaluate a new web application from a user's perspective. Which of the following tests best simulates that perspective?

A. Black box

B. Gray box

C. Blue box

D. White box

32. Referring to the database transaction shown here, what would happen if no account exists in the Accounts table with account number 1001?

```
BEGIN TRANSACTION
UPDATE accounts
SET balance = balance + 250
WHERE account_number = 1001;

UPDATE accounts
SET balance = balance - 250
WHERE account_number = 2002;

END TRANSACTION
```

A. The database would create a new account with this account number and give it a $250 balance.

B. The database would ignore that command and still reduce the balance of the second account by $250.

C. The database would roll back the transaction, ignoring the results of both commands.

D. The database would generate an error message.

33. What type of malware is characterized by spreading from system to system under its own power by exploiting vulnerabilities that do not require user intervention?

A. Trojan horse

B. Virus

C. Logic bomb

D. Worm

34. Kim is troubleshooting an application firewall that serves as a supplement to the organization's network and host firewalls and intrusion prevention system, providing added protection against web-based attacks. The issue the organization is experiencing is that the firewall technology suffers somewhat frequent restarts that render it unavailable for 10 minutes at a time. What configuration might Kim consider to maintain availability during that period at the lowest cost to the company?

A. High availability cluster

B. Failover device

C. Fail open

D. Redundant disks

35. What type of security issue arises when an attacker can deduce a more sensitive piece of information by analyzing several pieces of information classified at a lower level?

A. SQL injection

B. Multilevel security

C. Aggregation

D. Inference

36. Greg is battling a malware outbreak in his organization. He used specialized malware analysis tools to capture samples of the malware from three different systems and noticed that the code is changing slightly from infection to infection. Greg believes that this is the reason that antivirus software is having a tough time defeating the outbreak. What type of malware should Greg suspect is responsible for this security incident?

A. Stealth virus

B. Polymorphic virus

C. Multipartite virus

D. Encrypted virus

Questions 37–40 refer to the following scenario:

Linda is reviewing posts to a user forum on her company's website and, when she browses a certain post, a message pops up in a dialog box on her screen reading "Alert." She reviews the source code for the post and finds the following code snippet:

```
<script>alert('Alert');</script>
```

37. What vulnerability definitely exists on Linda's message board?

A. Cross-site scripting

B. Cross-site request forgery

C. SQL injection

D. Improper authentication

38. What was the likely motivation of the user who posted the message on the forum containing this code?

A. Reconnaissance

B. Theft of sensitive information

C. Credential stealing

D. Social engineering

39. Linda communicates with the vendor and determines that no patch is available to correct this vulnerability. Which one of the following devices would best help her defend the application against further attack?

A. VPN

B. WAF

C. DLP

D. IDS

40. In further discussions with the vendor, Linda finds that they are willing to correct the issue but do not know how to update their software. What technique would be most effective in mitigating the vulnerability of the application to this type of attack?

A. Bounds checking

B. Peer review

C. Input validation

D. OS patching

41. What property of relational databases ensures that once a database transaction is committed to the database, it is preserved?

A. Atomicity

B. Consistency

C. Durability

D. Isolation

42. Which one of the following programming languages does not make use of a compiler?

A. Java

B. C++

C. C

D. JavaScript

43. Which one of the following is not a technique used by virus authors to hide the existence of their virus from antimalware software?

A. Stealth

B. Multipartitism

C. Polymorphism

D. Encryption

44. Which one of the following types of software testing usually occurs last and is executed against test scenarios?

A. Unit testing

B. Integration testing

C. User acceptance testing

D. System testing

45. What type of requirement specifies what software must do by describing the inputs, behavior, and outputs of software?

A. Derived requirements

B. Structural requirements

C. Behavioral requirements

D. Functional requirements

46. Which of the following organizations is widely considered as the definitive source for information on web-based attack vectors?

A. (ISC)2

B. ISACA

C. OWASP

D. Mozilla Foundation

47. In an object-oriented programming language, what does one object invoke in a second object to interact with the second object?

A. Instance

B. Method

C. Behavior

D. Class

48. Lisa is attempting to prevent her network from being targeted by IP spoofing attacks as well as preventing her network from being the source of those attacks. Which one of the following rules is not a best practice that Lisa can configure at her network border?

A. Block packets with internal source addresses from entering the network.

B. Block packets with external source addresses from leaving the network.

C. Block packets with private IP addresses from exiting the network.

D. Block packets with public IP addresses from entering the network.

49. What type of attack is demonstrated in the C programming language example below?

```
int myarray[10];
myarray[10] = 8;
```

A. Mismatched data types
B. Overflow
C. SQL injection
D. Covert channel

50. Which one of the following database issues occurs when one transaction writes a value to the database that overwrites a value that was needed by transactions with earlier precedence?

A. Dirty read
B. Incorrect summary
C. Lost update
D. SQL injection

51. Which one of the following is the most effective control against session hijacking attacks?

A. TLS
B. Complex session cookies
C. SSL
D. Expiring cookies frequently

52. Faith is looking at the `/etc/passwd` file on a system configured to use shadowed passwords. When she examines a line in the file for a user with interactive login permissions, what should she expect to see in the password field?

A. Plaintext password
B. Hashed password
C. x
D. *

53. What type of vulnerability does a TOC/TOU attack target?

A. Lack of input validation
B. Race condition
C. Injection flaw
D. Lack of encryption

54. While evaluating a potential security incident, Harry comes across a log entry from a web server request showing that a user entered the following input into a form field:

```
CARROT'&1=1;--
```

What type of attack was attempted?

A. Buffer overflow

B. Cross-site scripting

C. SQL injection

D. Cross-site request forgery

55. Which one of the following is not an effective control against SQL injection attacks?

A. Escaping

B. Client-side input validation

C. Parameterization

D. Limiting database permissions

56. What type of project management tool is shown in the figure?

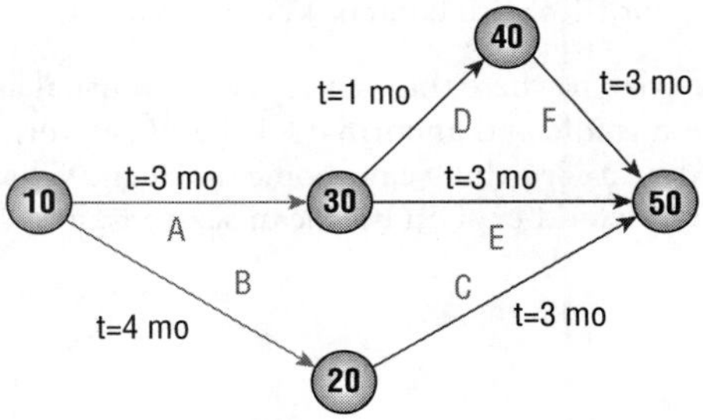

A. WBS chart

B. PERT chart

C. Gantt chart

D. Wireframe diagram

57. In what software testing technique does the evaluator retest a large number of scenarios each time that the software changes to verify that the results are consistent with a standard baseline?

A. Orthogonal array testing

B. Pattern testing

C. Matrix testing

D. Regression testing

58. Which one of the following conditions may make an application most vulnerable to a cross-site scripting (XSS) attack?

A. Input validation

B. Reflected input

C. Unpatched server

D. Promiscuous firewall rules

59. Roger is conducting a software test for a tax preparation application developed by his company. End users will access the application over the web, but Roger is conducting his test on the back end, evaluating the source code on the web server. What type of test is Roger conducting?

A. White box

B. Gray box

C. Blue box

D. Black box

60. Which of the following statements is true about heuristic-based antimalware software?

A. It has a lower false positive rate than signature detection.

B. It requires frequent definition updates to detect new malware.

C. It has a higher likelihood of detecting zero-day exploits than signature detection.

D. It monitors systems for files with content known to be viruses.

61. Martin is inspecting a system where the user reported unusual activity, including disk activity when the system is idle and abnormal CPU and network usage. He suspects that the machine is infected by a virus but scans come up clean. What malware technique might be in use here that would explain the clean scan results?

A. File infector virus

B. MBR virus

C. Service injection virus

D. Stealth virus

62. Tomas discovers a line in his application log that appears to correspond with an attempt to conduct a directory traversal attack. He believes the attack was conducted using URL encoding. The line reads:

```
%252E%252E%252F%252E%252E%252Fetc/passwd
```

What character is represented by the `%252E` value?

A. .

B. ,

C. ;

D. /

63. An attacker posted a message to a public discussion forum that contains an embedded malicious script that is not displayed to the user but executes on the user's system when read. What type of attack is this?

A. Persistent XSRF

B. Nonpersistent XSRF

C. Persistent XSS

D. Nonpersistent XSS

64. Which one of the following is not a principle of the Agile software development process?

A. Welcome changing requirements, even late in the development process.

B. Maximizing the amount of work not done is essential.

C. Clear documentation is the primary measure of progress.

D. Build projects around motivated individuals.

65. Samantha is responsible for the development of three new code modules that will form part of a complex system that her company is developing. She is prepared to publish her code and runs a series of tests against each module to verify that it works as intended. What type of testing is Samantha conducting?

A. Regression testing

B. Integration testing

C. Unit testing

D. System testing

66. What are the two components of an expert system?

A. Decision support system and neural network

B. Inference engine and neural network

C. Neural network and knowledge bank

D. Knowledge bank and inference engine

67. Neal is working with a DynamoDB database. The database is not structured like a relational database but allows Neal to store data using a key-value store. What type of database is DynamoDB?

A. Relational database

B. Graph database

C. Hierarchical database

D. NoSQL database

68. In the transaction shown here, what would happen if the database failed in between the first and second update statement?

```
BEGIN TRANSACTION

UPDATE accounts
SET balance = balance + 250
WHERE account_number = 1001;

UPDATE accounts
SET balance = balance - 250
WHERE account_number = 2002;

COMMIT TRANSACTION
```

A. The database would credit the first account with $250 in funds but then not reduce the balance of the second account.

B. The database would ignore the first command and only reduce the balance of the second account by $250.

C. The database would roll back the transaction, ignoring the results of both commands.

D. The database would successfully execute both commands.

69. In the diagram shown here, which is an example of an attribute?

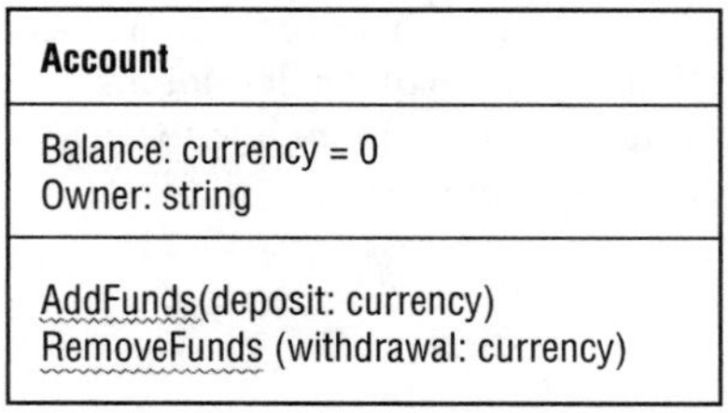

A. `Account`

B. `Owner`

C. `AddFunds`

D. None of the above

70. Which one of the following statements is true about software testing?

A. Static testing works on runtime environments.

B. Static testing performs code analysis.

C. Dynamic testing uses automated tools but static testing does not.

D. Static testing is a more important testing technique than dynamic testing.

71. David is working on developing a project schedule for a software development effort, and he comes across the chart shown here. What type of chart is this?

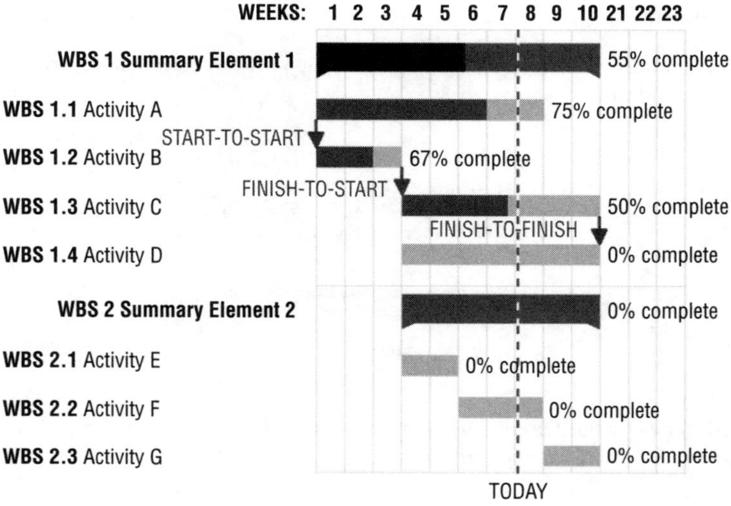

A. Work breakdown structure

B. Functional requirements

C. PERT chart

D. Gantt chart

72. Barry is a software tester who is working with a new gaming application developed by his company. He is playing the game on a smartphone to conduct his testing in an environment that best simulates a normal end user, but he is referencing the source code as he conducts his test. What type of test is Barry conducting?

A. White box

B. Black box

C. Blue box

D. Gray box

73. Miguel recently completed a penetration test of the applications that his organization uses to handle sensitive information. During his testing, he discovered a condition where an attacker can exploit a timing condition to manipulate software into allowing him to perform an unauthorized action. Which one of the following attack types fits this scenario?

A. SQL injection

B. Cross-site scripting

C. Pass the hash

D. TOC/TOU

74. In the diagram shown here, which is an example of a class?

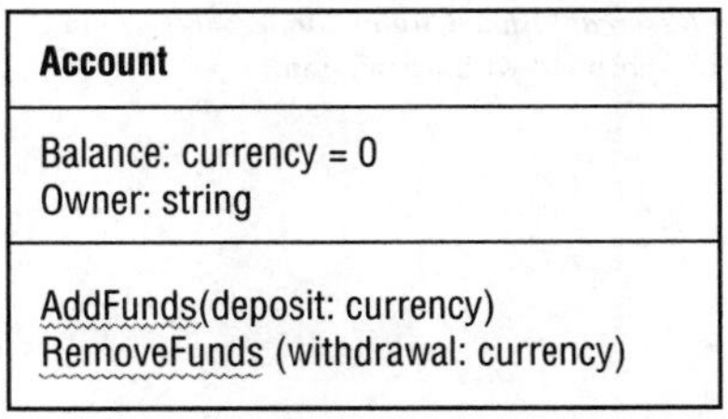

A. `Account`

B. `Owner`

C. `AddFunds`

D. None of the above

75. Gary is designing a database-driven application that relies on the use of aggregate functions. Which one of the following database concurrency issues might occur with aggregate functions and should be one of Gary's top concerns?

A. Lost updates

B. Incorrect summaries

C. SQL injections

D. Dirty reads

76. Which one of the following approaches to failure management is the most conservative from a security perspective?

A. Fail open

B. Fail mitigation

C. Fail clear

D. Fail closed

77. What software development model is shown in the figure?

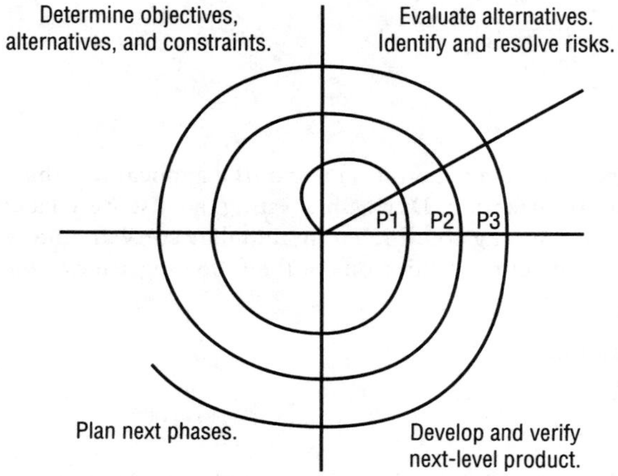
Determine objectives,
alternatives, and constraints.
Evaluate alternatives.
Identify and resolve risks.
P1
P2
P3
Plan next phases.
Develop and verify
next-level product.

Image reprinted from *CISSP (ISC)² Certified Information Systems Security Professional Official Study Guide, 7th Edition* © John Wiley & Sons 2015, reprinted with permission.

A. Waterfall

B. Agile

C. Lean

D. Spiral

78. Which of the following database keys is used by an RDBMS to uniquely identify each row in a database table?

A. Foreign key

B. Primary key

C. Candidate key

D. Referential key

79. Which one of the following change management processes is initiated by users rather than developers?

A. Request control

B. Change control

C. Release control

D. Design review

80. Which one of the following techniques is an effective countermeasure against some inference attacks?

A. Input validation

B. Parameterization

C. Polyinstantiation

D. Server-side validation

81. Ursula is a government web developer who recently created a public application that offers property records. She would like to make it available for other developers to integrate into their applications. What can Ursula create to make it easiest for developers to call her code directly and integrate the output into their applications?

A. Object model

B. Data dictionary

C. API

D. Primary key

82. During what phase of the IDEAL model do organizations develop a specific plan of action for implementing change?

A. Initiating

B. Diagnosing

C. Establishing

D. Acting

83. TJ is inspecting a system where the user reported a strange error message and the inability to access files. He sees the window shown in this figure. What type of malware should TJ suspect?

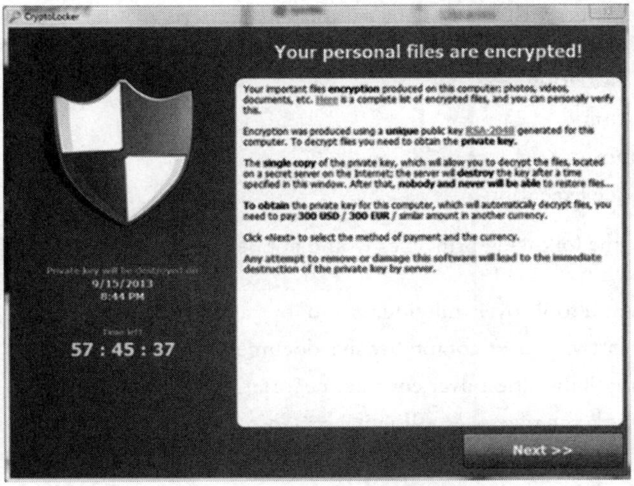

A. Service injection
B. Encrypted virus
C. SQL injection
D. Ransomware

84. What function can be used to convert a string to a safe value for use in passing from a PHP application to a database?
A. `bin2hex()`
B. `hex2bin()`
C. `dechex()`
D. `hexdec()`

85. Which one of the following types of artificial intelligence attempts to use complex computations to replicate the partial function of the human mind?
A. Decision support systems
B. Expert systems
C. Knowledge bank
D. Neural networks

86. At which level of the Software Capability Maturity Model (SW-CMM) does an organization introduce basic life-cycle management processes?
A. Initial
B. Repeatable
C. Defined
D. Managed

87. Lucas runs the accounting systems for his company. The morning after a key employee was fired, systems began mysteriously losing information. Lucas suspects that the fired employee tampered with the systems prior to his departure. What type of attack should Lucas suspect?
A. Privilege escalation
B. SQL injection
C. Logic bomb
D. Remote code execution

88. Which one of the following principles would not be favored in an Agile approach to software development?
A. Processes and tools over individuals and interactions
B. Working software over comprehensive documentation
C. Customer collaboration over contract negotiations
D. Responding to change over following a plan

89. What technique do API developers most commonly use to limit access to an API to authorized individuals and applications?

A. Encryption

B. Input validation

C. API keys

D. IP filters

90. Which one of the following statements about malware is correct?

A. Malware authors do not target Macintosh or Linux systems.

B. The most reliable way to detect known malware is watching for unusual system activity.

C. Signature detection is the most effective technique to combat known malware.

D. APT attackers typically use malware designed to exploit vulnerabilities identified in security bulletins.

91. Which one of the following is the proper order of steps in the waterfall model of software development?

A. Requirements, Design, Testing, Coding, Maintenance

B. Requirements, Design, Coding, Testing, Maintenance

C. Design, Requirements, Coding, Testing, Maintenance

D. Design, Requirements, Testing, Coding, Maintenance

92. Which component of the database ACID model ensures that database transactions are an "all or nothing" affair?

A. Atomicity

B. Consistency

C. Isolation

D. Durability

93. Tom is writing a software program that calculates the sales tax for online orders placed from various jurisdictions. The application includes a user-defined field that allows the entry of the total sale amount. Tom would like to ensure that the data entered in this field is a properly formatted dollar amount. What technique should he use?

A. Limit check

B. Fail open

C. Fail secure

D. Input validation

94. Mal is eavesdropping on the unencrypted communication between the user of a website and the web server. She manages to intercept the cookies from a request header. What type of attack can she perform with these cookies?

A. Session hijacking

B. Cross-site scripting

C. Cross-site request forgery

D. SQL injection

95. Which of the following vulnerabilities might be discovered during a penetration test of a web-based application?

A. Cross-site scripting

B. Cross-site request forgery

C. SQL injection

D. All of the above

96. What approach to technology management integrates the three components of technology management shown in this illustration?

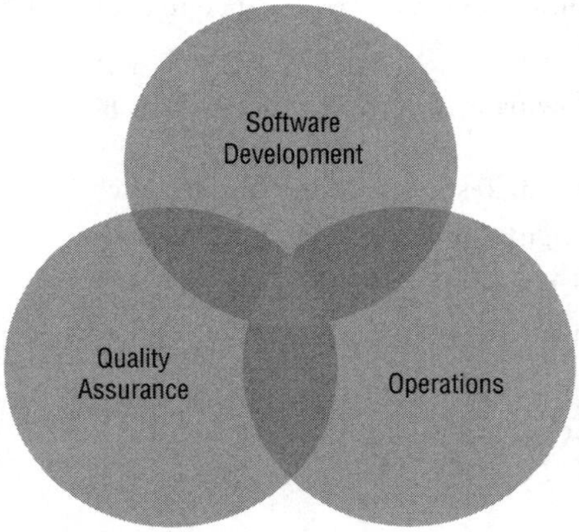

Image reprinted from *CISSP (ISC)² Certified Information Systems Security Professional Official Study Guide, 7th Edition* © John Wiley & Sons 2015, reprinted with permission.

A. Agile

B. Lean

C. DevOps

D. ITIL

97. Which one of the following tools might an attacker use to best identify vulnerabilities in a targeted system?

A. `nmap`

B. `nessus`

C. `ipconfig`

D. `traceroute`

98. Which one of the following database concurrency issues occurs when one transaction reads information that was written to a database by a second transaction that never committed?

A. Lost update

B. SQL injection

C. Incorrect summary

D. Dirty read

99. What type of virus works by altering the system boot process to redirect the BIOS to load malware before the operating system loads?

A. File infector

B. MBR

C. Polymorphic

D. Service injection

100. What type of virus is characterized by the use of two or more different propagation mechanisms to improve its likelihood of spreading between systems?

A. Stealth virus

B. Polymorphic virus

C. Multipartite virus

D. Encrypted virus

Chapter 9

Practice Test 1

1. NIST SP800-53 discusses a set of security controls as what type of security tool?
   - A. A configuration list
   - B. A threat management strategy
   - C. A baseline
   - D. The CIS standard
2. Ed has been tasked with identifying a service that will provide a low-latency, high-performance, and high-availability way to host content for his employer. What type of solution should he seek out to ensure that his employer's customers around the world can access their content quickly, easily, and reliably?
   - A. A hot site
   - B. A CDN
   - C. Redundant servers
   - D. A P2P CDN
3. Which one of the following is not a function of a forensic device controller?
   - A. Preventing the modification of data on a storage device
   - B. Returning data requested from the device
   - C. Reporting errors sent by the device to the forensic host
   - D. Blocking read commands sent to the device
4. Mike is building a fault-tolerant server and wishes to implement RAID 1. How many physical disks are required to build this solution?
   - A. 1
   - B. 2
   - C. 3
   - D. 5
5. Which Kerberos service generates a new ticket and session keys and sends them to the client?
   - A. KDC
   - B. TGT
   - C. AS
   - D. TGS
6. Communication systems that rely on start and stop flags or bits to manage data transmission are known as what type of communication?
   - A. Analog
   - B. Digital
   - C. Synchronous
   - D. Asynchronous

7. What type of motion detector uses high microwave frequency signal transmissions to identify potential intruders?
   - A. Infrared
   - B. Heat-based
   - C. Wave pattern
   - D. Capacitance

8. Susan sets up a firewall that keeps track of the status of the communication between two systems, and allows a remote system to respond to a local system after the local system starts communication. What type of firewall is Susan using?
   - A. A static packet filtering firewall
   - B. An application-level gateway firewall
   - C. A stateful packet inspection firewall
   - D. A circuit-level gateway firewall

Questions 9–11 refer to the following scenario:

Ben owns a coffeehouse and wants to provide wireless Internet service for his customers. Ben's network is simple and uses a single consumer grade wireless router and a cable modem connected via a commercial cable data contract. Using this information about Ben's network, answer the following questions.

9. How can Ben provide access control for his customers without having to provision user IDs before they connect while also gathering useful contact information for his business purposes?
   - A. WPA2 PSK
   - B. A captive portal
   - C. Require customers to use a publicly posted password like "BensCoffee."
   - D. Port security

10. Ben intends to run an open (unencrypted) wireless network. How should he connect his business devices?
    - A. Run WPA2 on the same SSID.
    - B. Set up a separate SSID using WPA2.
    - C. Run the open network in Enterprise mode.
    - D. Set up a separate wireless network using WEP.

11. After implementing the solution from the first question, Ben receives a complaint about users in his cafe hijacking other customers' web traffic, including using their usernames and passwords. How is this possible?
    - A. The password is shared by all users, making traffic vulnerable.
    - B. A malicious user has installed a Trojan on the router.
    - C. A user has ARP spoofed the router, making all traffic broadcast to all users.
    - D. Open networks are unencrypted, making traffic easily sniffable.

12. Which one of the following is not a mode of operation for the Data Encryption Standard?
   A. CBC
   B. CFB
   C. OFB
   D. AES

13. Tom is tuning his security monitoring tools in an attempt to reduce the number of alerts received by administrators without missing important security events. He decides to configure the system to only report failed login attempts if there are five failed attempts to access the same account within a one-hour period of time. What term best describes the technique that Tom is using?
   A. Thresholding
   B. Sampling
   C. Account lockout
   D. Clipping

14. Sally has been tasked with deploying an authentication, authorization, and accounting server for wireless network services in her organization, and needs to avoid using proprietary technology. What technology should she select?
   A. OAuth
   B. RADIUS
   C. TACACS
   D. TACACS+

15. An accounting clerk for Christopher's Cheesecakes does not have access to the salary information for individual employees but wanted to know the salary of a new hire. He pulled total payroll expenses for the pay period before the new person was hired and then pulled the same expenses for the following pay period. He computed the difference between those two amounts to determine the individual's salary. What type of attack occurred?
   A. Aggregation
   B. Data diddling
   C. Inference
   D. Social engineering

16. Alice would like to have read permissions on an object and knows that Bob already has those rights and would like to give them to herself. Which one of the rules in the Take-Grant protection model would allow her to complete this operation if the relationship exists between Alice and Bob?
   A. Take rule
   B. Grant rule
   C. Create rule
   D. Remote rule

17. During a log review, Danielle discovers a series of logs that show login failures:

```
Jan 31 11:39:12 ip-10-0-0-2 sshd[29092]: Invalid user admin from remotehost
passwd=aaaaaaaa
Jan 31 11:39:20 ip-10-0-0-2 sshd[29098]: Invalid user admin from remotehost
passwd=aaaaaaab
Jan 31 11:39:23 ip-10-0-0-2 sshd[29100]: Invalid user admin from remotehost
passwd=aaaaaaac
Jan 31 11:39:31 ip-10-0-0-2 sshd[29106]: Invalid user admin from remotehost
passwd=aaaaaaad
Jan 31 20:40:53 ip-10-0-0-254 sshd[30520]: Invalid user admin from
remotehost passwd=aaaaaaad
```

What type of attack has Danielle discovered?

A. A pass-the-hash attack
B. A brute-force attack
C. A man-in-the-middle attack
D. A dictionary attack

18. What property of a relational database ensures that two executing transactions do not affect each other by storing interim results in the database?

A. Atomicity
B. Isolation
C. Consistency
D. Durability

19. Kim is the system administrator for a small business network that is experiencing security problems. She is in the office in the evening working on the problem and nobody else is there. As she is watching, she can see that systems on the other side of the office that were previously behaving normally are now exhibiting signs of infection. What type of malware is Kim likely dealing with?

A. Virus
B. Worm
C. Trojan horse
D. Logic bomb

20. Which one of the following attack types takes advantage of a vulnerability in the network fragmentation function of some operating systems?

A. Smurf
B. Land
C. Teardrop
D. Fraggle

21. Which of the following sequences properly describes the TCP 3-way handshake?
    A. SYN, ACK, SYN/ACK
    B. PSH, RST, ACK
    C. SYN, SYN/ACK, ACK
    D. SYN, RST, FIN

22. Which one of the following technologies is not normally a capability of Mobile Device Management (MDM) solutions?
    A. Remotely wiping the contents of a mobile device
    B. Assuming control of a nonregistered BYOD mobile device
    C. Enforcing the use of device encyrption
    D. Managing device backups

23. Jim is implementing an IDaaS solution for his organization. What type of technology is he putting in place?
    A. Identity as a Service
    B. Employee ID as a service
    C. Cloud based RADIUS
    D. OAuth

24. Gina recently took the CISSP certification exam and then wrote a blog post that included the text of many of the exam questions that she experienced. What aspect of the $(ISC)^2$ code of ethics is most directly violated in this situation?
    A. Advance and protect the profession.
    B. Act honorably, honestly, justly, responsibly, and legally.
    C. Protect society, the common good, necessary public trust and confidence, and the infrastructure.
    D. Provide diligent and competent service to principals.

25. Gordon is conducting a risk assessment for his organization and determined the amount of damage that flooding is expected to cause to his facilities each year. What metric has Gordon identified?
    A. ALE
    B. ARO
    C. SLE
    D. EF

26. Greg would like to implement application control technology in his organization. He would like to limit users to installing only approved software on their systems. What type of application control would be appropriate in this situation?
    A. Blacklisting
    B. Graylisting

C. Whitelisting

D. Bluelisting

27. Frank is the security administrator for a web server that provides news and information to people located around the world. His server received an unusually high volume of traffic that it could not handle and was forced to reject requests. Frank traced the source of the traffic back to a botnet. What type of attack took place?

A. Denial of service

B. Reconaissance

C. Compromise

D. Malicious insider

28. In the database table shown here, which column would be the best candidate for a primary key?

Company ID	Company Name	Address	City	State	ZIP Code	Telephone	Sales Rep
1	Acme Widgets	234 Main Street	Columbia	MD	21040	(301) 555-1212	14
2	Abrams Consulting	1024 Sample Street	Miami	FL	33131	(305) 555-1995	14
3	Dome Widgets	913 Sorin Street	South Bend	IN	46556	(574) 555-5863	26

A. Company ID

B. Company Name

C. ZIP Code

D. Sales Rep

29. Information about an individual like their name, Social Security number, date and place of birth, or their mother's maiden name is an example of what type of protected information?

A. PHI

B. Proprietary Data

C. PII

D. EDI

30. Bob is configuring egress filtering on his network, examining traffic destined for the Internet. His organization uses the public address range 12.8.195.0/24. Packets with which one of the following destination addresses should Bob permit to leave the network?

A. 12.8.195.15

B. 10.8.15.9

C. 192.168.109.55

D. 129.53.44.124

31. How many possible keys exist in a cryptographic algorithm that uses 6-bit encryption keys?

A. 12

B. 16

C. 32

D. 64

32. What problem drives the recommendation to physically destroy SSD drives to prevent data leaks when they are retired?

A. Degaussing only partially wipes the data on SSDs.

B. SSDs don't have data remanence.

C. SSDs are unable to perform a zero fill.

D. The built-in erase commands are not completely effective on some SSDs.

33. GAD Systems is concerned about the risk of hackers stealing sensitive information stored on a file server. They choose to pursue a risk mitigation strategy. Which one of the following actions would support that strategy?

A. Encrypting the files

B. Deleting the files

C. Purchasing cyberliability insurance

D. Taking no action

34. How should samples be generated when assessing account management practices?

A. They should be generated by administrators.

B. The last 180 days of accounts should be validated.

C. Sampling should be conducted randomly.

D. Sampling is not effective, and all accounts should be audited.

35. The International Safe Harbor Privacy Principles includes seven tenets. Which of the following lists correctly identifies all seven?

A. Awareness, selection, control, security, data integrity, access, enforcement

B. Notice, choice, onward transfer, security, data integrity, access, enforcement

C. Privacy, security, control, notification, data integrity, access, enforcement

D. Submission, editing, updates, confidential, integrity, security, access

36. In what type of software testing does the attacker have complete knowledge of the system implementation prior to beginning the test?

A. Black box

B. Blue box

C. Gray box

D. White box

37. What type of log is shown in the figure?

```
217.69.133.190 - - [11/Apr/2016:09:41:48 -0400] "GET /forum/viewtopic.php?f=4&t=25630 HTTP/1.1" 503 2009 "-
" "Mozilla/5.0 (compatible; Linux x86_64; Mail.RU_Bot/2.0; +http://go.mail.ru/help/robots)"
217.69.133.190 - - [11/Apr/2016:09:41:50 -0400] "GET /forum/viewtopic.php?f=7&t=28513 HTTP/1.1" 503 2009 "-
" "Mozilla/5.0 (compatible; Linux x86_64; Mail.RU_Bot/2.0; +http://go.mail.ru/help/robots)"
188.143.234.155 - - [11/Apr/2016:09:41:50 -0400] "GET /ask-a-pci-dss-question/ HTTP/1.1" 200 6501 "-"
"Mozilla/5.0 (Windows NT 6.1; WOW64; rv:41.0) Gecko/20100101 Firefox/41.0"
217.69.133.242 - - [11/Apr/2016:09:41:51 -0400] "GET /forum/viewtopic.php?f=5&t=27086 HTTP/1.1" 503 2009 "-
" "Mozilla/5.0 (compatible; Linux x86_64; Mail.RU_Bot/2.0; +http://go.mail.ru/help/robots)"
217.69.133.245 - - [11/Apr/2016:09:41:52 -0400] "GET /forum/viewtopic.php?f=6&t=28548 HTTP/1.1" 503 2009 "-
" "Mozilla/5.0 (compatible; Linux x86_64; Mail.RU_Bot/2.0; +http://go.mail.ru/help/robots)"
217.69.133.247 - - [11/Apr/2016:09:41:54 -0400] "GET /forum/viewtopic.php?f=3&t=26497 HTTP/1.1" 503 2009 "-
" "Mozilla/5.0 (compatible; Linux x86_64; Mail.RU_Bot/2.0; +http://go.mail.ru/help/robots)"
217.69.133.247 - - [11/Apr/2016:09:41:55 -0400] "GET /forum/viewtopic.php?f=3&t=27282 HTTP/1.1" 503 2009 "-
" "Mozilla/5.0 (compatible; Linux x86_64; Mail.RU_Bot/2.0; +http://go.mail.ru/help/robots)"
217.69.133.246 - - [11/Apr/2016:09:41:56 -0400] "GET /forum/viewtopic.php?f=6&t=33830 HTTP/1.1" 503 2009 "-
" "Mozilla/5.0 (compatible; Linux x86_64; Mail.RU_Bot/2.0; +http://go.mail.ru/help/robots)"
217.69.133.190 - - [11/Apr/2016:09:41:58 -0400] "GET /forum/viewtopic.php?f=6&t=26425 HTTP/1.1" 503 2009 "-
" "Mozilla/5.0 (compatible; Linux x86_64; Mail.RU_Bot/2.0; +http://go.mail.ru/help/robots)"
217.69.133.245 - - [11/Apr/2016:09:41:59 -0400] "GET /pci-dss/pci-dss-vulnerability-scanning-requirements/
HTTP/1.1" 301 - "-" "Mozilla/5.0 (compatible; Linux x86_64; Mail.RU_Bot/2.0;
+http://go.mail.ru/help/robots)"
217.69.133.247 - - [11/Apr/2016:09:42:01 -0400] "GET /forum/viewtopic.php?f=4&t=26035 HTTP/1.1" 503 2009 "-
" "Mozilla/5.0 (compatible; Linux x86_64; Mail.RU_Bot/2.0; +http://go.mail.ru/help/robots)"
217.69.133.190 - - [11/Apr/2016:09:42:02 -0400] "GET /vulnerability-scanning/pci-dss-vulnerability-
scanning-requirements/ HTTP/1.1" 200 11007 "http://www.pcidssguru.com/pci-dss/pci-dss-vulnerability-
scanning-requirements/" "Mozilla/5.0 (compatible; Linux x86_64; Mail.RU_Bot/2.0;
+http://go.mail.ru/help/robots)"
207.46.13.18 - - [11/Apr/2016:09:42:17 -0400] "GET /category/articles/page/3/ HTTP/1.1" 200 7583 "-"
"Mozilla/5.0 (compatible; bingbot/2.0; +http://www.bing.com/bingbot.htm)"
```

A. Firewall log

B. Change log

C. Application log

D. System log

38. Captain Crunch, famous phone phreak, was known for using a toy whistle to generate the 2600 Hz tones that phone trunk systems used to communicate. What is the common name for a phreaking tool with this capability?

A. A black box

B. A red box

C. A blue box

D. A white box

39. When an attacker calls an organization's help desk and persuades them to reset a password for them due to the help desk employee's trust and willingness to help, what type of attack succeeded?

A. A human Trojan

B. Social engineering

C. Phishing

D. Whaling

40. When a user attempts to log into their online account, Google sends a text message with a code to their cell phone. What type of verification is this?

A. Knowledge-based authentication

B. Dynamic knowledge–based authentication

C. Out-of-band identity proofing

D. Risk-based identity proofing

41. What mathematical operation, when substituted for the blank lines shown here, would make the equations correct?

8____6 = 2
8____4 = 0
10____3 = 1
10____2 = 0

A. MOD

B. XOR

C. NAND

D. DIV

Questions 42–44 refer to the following scenario:

The organization that Ben works for has a traditional onsite Active Directory environment that uses a manual provisioning process for each addition to their 350-employee company. As the company adopts new technologies, they are increasingly using Software as a Service applications to replace their internally developed software stack.

Ben has been tasked with designing an identity management implementation that will allow his company to use cloud services while supporting their existing systems. Using the logical diagram shown here, answer the following questions about the identity recommendations Ben should make.

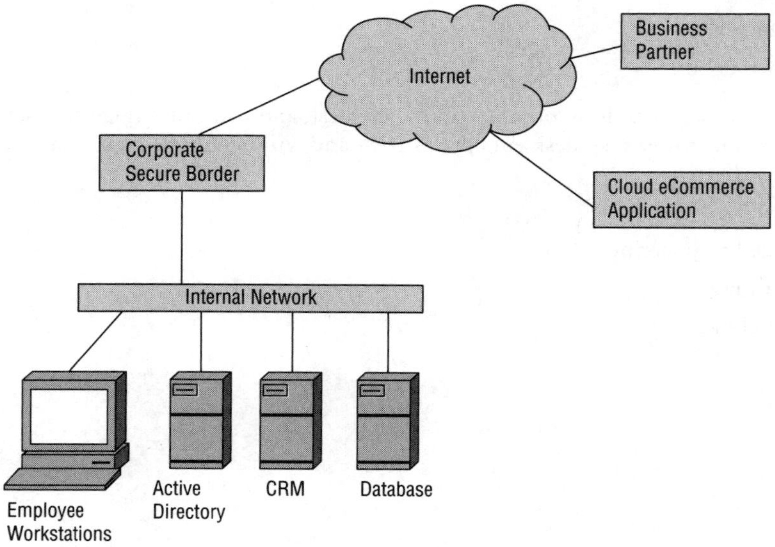

42. If availability of authentication services is the organization's biggest priority, what type of identity platform should Ben recommend?

  A. Onsite
  B. Cloud based
  C. Hybrid
  D. Outsourced

43. If Ben needs to share identity information with the business partner shown, what should he investigate?

  A. Single sign-on
  B. Multifactor authentication
  C. Federation
  D. IDaaS

44. What technology is likely to be involved when Ben's organization needs to provide authentication and authorization assertions to their e-commerce cloud partner?

  A. Active Directory
  B. SAML
  C. RADIUS
  D. SPML

45. Dave is responsible for password security in his organization and would like to strengthen the security of password files. He would like to defend his organization against the use of rainbow tables. Which one of the following techniques is specifically designed to frustrate the use of rainbow tables?

  A. Password expiration policies
  B. Salting
  C. User education
  D. Password complexity policies

46. Which one of the following is a single system designed to attract attackers because it seemingly contains sensitive information or other attractive resources?

  A. Honeynet
  B. Darknet
  C. Honeypot
  D. Pseudoflaw

47. When evaluating biometric devices, what is another term used to describe the equal error rate?

  A. FAR
  B. FRR
  C. CER
  D. ERR

48. A smart card is an example of what type of authentication factor?
   A. Type 1
   B. Type 2
   C. Type 3
   D. Type 4

49. Sean suspects that an individual in his company is smuggling out secret information despite his company's careful use of data loss prevention systems. He discovers that the suspect is posting photos, including the one shown here, to public Internet message boards. What type of technique may the individuals be using to hide messages inside this image?

   A. Watermarking
   B. VPN
   C. Steganography
   D. Covert timing channel

50. Roger is concerned that a third-party firm hired to develop code for an internal application will embed a backdoor in the code. The developer retains rights to the intellectual property and will only deliver the software in its final form. Which one of the following languages would be least susceptible to this type of attack because it would provide Roger with code that is human-readable in its final form?
   A. JavaScript
   B. C
   C. C++
   D. Java

51. Jesse is looking at the `/etc/passwd` file on a system configured to use shadowed passwords. What should she expect to see in the password field of this file?
   A. Plaintext passwords
   B. Encrypted passwords

C. Hashed passwords

D. x

52. Ping of Death, Smurf attacks, and ping floods all abuse features of what important protocol?

A. IGMP

B. UDP

C. IP

D. ICMP

53. What principle states that an individual should make every effort to complete his or her responsibilities in an accurate and timely manner?

A. Least privilege

B. Separation of duties

C. Due care

D. Due diligence

54. Cable modems, ISDN, and DSL are all examples of what type of technology?

A. Baseband

B. Broadband

C. Digital

D. Broadcast

55. What penetration testing technique can best help assess training and awareness issues?

A. Port scanning

B. Discovery

C. Social engineering

D. Vulnerability scanning

56. Bill implemented RAID level 5 on a server that he operates using a total of three disks. How many disks may fail without the loss of data?

A. 0

B. 1

C. 2

D. 3

57. Data is sent as bits at what layer of the OSI model?

A. Transport

B. Network

C. Data Link

D. Physical

58. Bert is considering the use of an infrastructure as a service cloud computing partner to provide virtual servers. Which one of the following would be a vendor responsibility in this scenario?

A. Maintaining the hypervisor

B. Managing operating system security settings

C. Maintaining the host firewall

D. Configuring server access control

59. When Ben records data, then replays it against his test website to verify how it performs based on a real production workload, what type of performance monitoring is he undertaking?

A. Passive

B. Proactive

C. Reactive

D. Replay

60. What technology ensures that an operating system allocates separate memory spaces used by each application on a system?

A. Abstraction

B. Layering

C. Data hiding

D. Process isolation

61. Alan is considering the use of new identification cards in his organization that will be used for physical access control. He comes across a sample card and is unsure of the technology. He breaks it open and sees the following internal construction. What type of card is this?

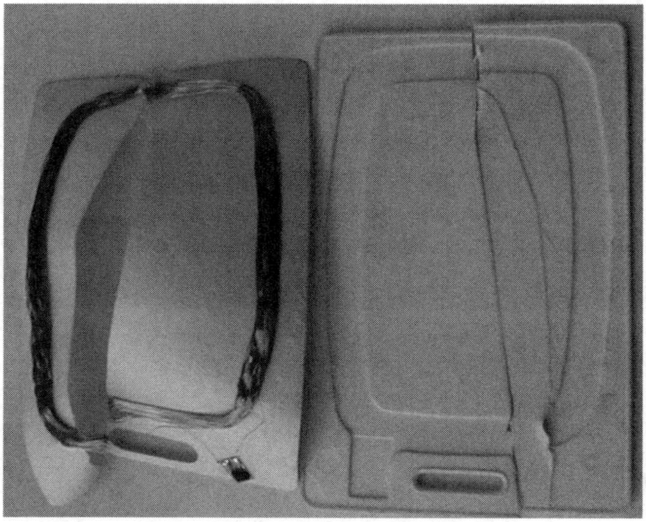

A. Smart card
B. Proximity card
C. Magnetic stripe
D. Phase-two card

62. Mark is planning a disaster recovery test for his organization. He would like to perform a live test of the disaster recovery facility but does not want to disrupt operations at the primary facility. What type of test should Mark choose?
A. Full interruption test
B. Checklist review
C. Parallel test
D. Tabletop exercise

63. Which one of the following is not a principle of the Agile approach to software development?
A. The best architecture, requirements, and designs emerge from self-organizing teams.
B. Deliver working software infrequently, with an emphasis on creating accurate code over longer timelines.
C. Welcome changing requirements, even late in the development process.
D. Simplicity is essential.

64. During a security audit, Susan discovers that the organization is using hand geometry scanners as the access control mechanism for their secure data center. What recommendation should Susan make about the use of hand geometry scanners?
A. They have a high FRR, and should be replaced.
B. A second factor should be added because they are not a good way to reliably distinguish individuals.
C. The hand geometry scanners provide appropriate security for the data center and should be considered for other high-security areas.
D. They may create accessibility concerns and an alternate biometric system should be considered.

65. Colleen is conducting a business impact assessment for her organization. What metric provides important information about the amount of time that the organization may be without a service before causing irreparable harm?
A. MTD
B. ALE
C. RPO
D. RTO

66. An attack that changes a symlink on a Linux system between the time that an account's rights to the file are verified and the file is accessed is an example of what type of attack?
    A. Unlinking
    B. Tick/tock
    C. setuid
    D. TOC/TOU

67. An authentication factor that is "something you have," and that typically includes a microprocessor and one or more certificates, is what type of authenticator?
    A. A smart card
    B. A token
    C. A Type I validator
    D. A Type III authenticator

68. What term best describes an attack that relies on stolen or falsified authentication credentials to bypass an authentication mechanism?
    A. Spoofing
    B. Replay
    C. Masquerading
    D. Modification

69. What speed is a T1 line?
    A. 64 Kbps
    B. 128 Kbps
    C. 1.544 Mbps
    D. 44.736 Mbps

70. Owen recently designed a security access control structure that prevents a single user from simultaneously holding the role required to create a new vendor and the role required to issue a check. What principle is Owen enforcing?
    A. Two-person control
    B. Least privilege
    C. Separation of duties
    D. Job rotation

71. Denise is preparing for a trial relating to a contract dispute between her company and a software vendor. The vendor is claiming that Denise made a verbal agreement that amended their written contract. What rule of evidence should Denise raise in her defense?
    A. Real evidence rule
    B. Best evidence rule

C. Parol evidence rule

D. Testimonial evidence rule

72. While Lauren is monitoring traffic on two ends of a network connection, she sees traffic that is inbound to a public IP address show up inside of the production network bound for an internal host that uses an RFC 1918 reserved address. What technology should she expect is in use at the network border?

A. NAT

B. VLANs

C. S/NAT

D. BGP

73. Which of the following statements about SSAE-16 is not true?

A. It mandates a specific control set.

B. It is an attestation standard.

C. It is used for external audits.

D. It uses a framework, including SOC 1, SOC 2, and SOC 3 reports.

74. What does a constrained user interface do?

A. It prevents unauthorized users from logging in.

B. It limits the data visible in an interface based on the content.

C. It limits the access a user is provided based on what activity they are performing.

D. It limits what users can do or see based on privileges.

75. Greg is building a disaster recovery plan for his organization and would like to determine the amount of time that it should take to restore a particular IT service after an outage. What variable is Greg calculating?

A. MTO

B. RTO

C. RPO

D. SLA

76. In object-oriented programming, what type of variable exists only once and shares the same value across all instances of an object?

A. Instance variable

B. Member variable

C. Class variable

D. Global variable

77. What type of fire extinguisher is useful against liquid-based fires?

A. Class A

B. Class B

C. Class C

D. Class D

78. The company Chris works for has notifications posted at each door reminding employees to be careful to not allow people to enter when they do. Which type of controls best describes this?

A. Detective

B. Physical

C. Preventive

D. Directive

79. Which one of the following principles is not included in the International Safe Harbor Provisions?

A. Access

B. Security

C. Enforcement

D. Nonrepudiation

80. What group is eligible to receive safe harbor protection under the terms of the Digital Millennium Copyright Act (DMCA)?

A. Music producers

B. Book publishers

C. Internet service providers

D. Banks

81. Alex is the system owner for the HR system at a major university. According to NIST SP 800-18, what action should he take when a significant change occurs in the system?

A. He should develop a data confidentiality plan.

B. He should update the system security plan.

C. He should classify the data the system contains.

D. He should select custodians to handle day-to-day operational tasks.

Questions 82–84 refer to the following scenario:

Alex has been with the university he works at for over 10 years. During that time, he has been a system administrator and a database administrator, and he has worked in the university's help desk. He is now a manager for the team that runs the university's web applications. Using the provisioning diagram shown here, answer the following questions.

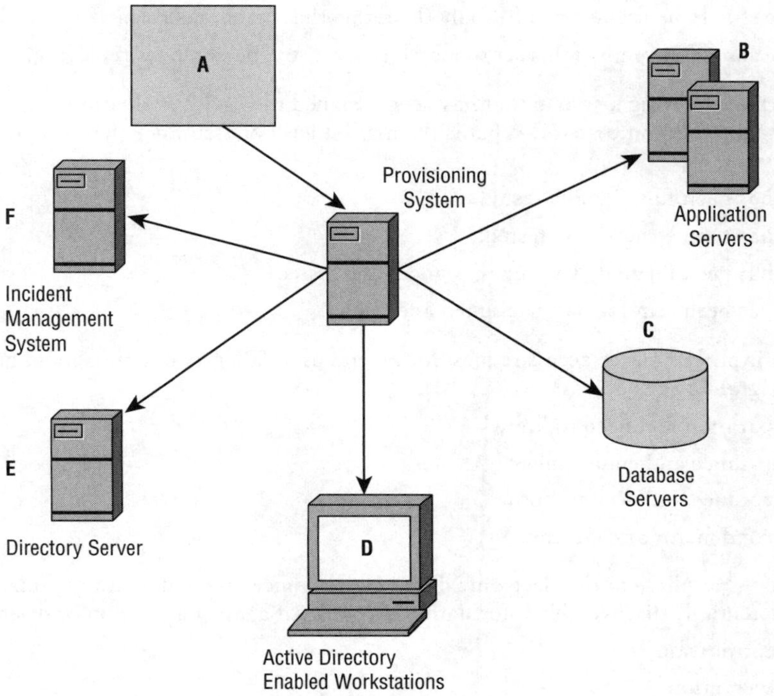

82. If Alex hires a new employee and the employee's account is provisioned after HR manually inputs information into the provisioning system based on data Alex provides via a series of forms, what type of provisioning has occurred?

A. Discretionary account provisioning

B. Workflow-based account provisioning

C. Automated account provisioning

D. Self-service account provisioning

83. Alex has access to B, C, and D. What concern should he raise to the university's identity management team?

A. The provisioning process did not give him the rights he needs.

B. He has excessive privileges.

C. Privilege creep may be taking place.

D. Logging is not properly enabled.

84. When Alex changes roles, what should occur?

A. He should be de-provisioned and a new account should be created.

B. He should have his new rights added to his existing account.

C. He should be provisioned for only the rights that match his role.

D. He should have his rights set to match those of the person he is replacing.

85. Robert is reviewing a system that has been assigned the EAL2 evaluation assurance level under the Common Criteria. What is the highest level of assurance that he may have about the system?

A. It has been functionally tested.

B. It has been structurally tested.

C. It has been formally verified, designed, and tested.

D. It has been semiformally designed and tested.

86. Adam is processing an access request for an end user. What two items should he verify before granting the access?

A. Separation and need to know

B. Clearance and endorsement

C. Clearance and need to know

D. Second factor and clearance

87. During what phase of the electronic discovery reference model does an organization ensure that potentially discoverable information is protected against alteration or deletion?

A. Identification

B. Preservation

C. Collection

D. Production

88. Nessus, OpenVAS, and SAINT are all examples of what type of tool?

A. Port scanners

B. Patch management suites

C. Port mappers

D. Vulnerability scanners

89. Harry would like to access a document owned by Sally stored on a file server. Applying the subject/object model to this scenario, who or what is the object of the resource request?

A. Harry

B. Sally

C. File server

D. Document

90. What is the process that occurs when the session layer removes the header from data sent by the transport layer?

A. Encapsulation

B. Packet unwrapping

C. De-encapsulation

D. Payloading

91. Which of the following tools is best suited to testing known exploits against a system?

A. Nikto

B. Ettercap

C. Metasploit

D. THC Hydra

92. What markup language uses the concepts of a Requesting Authority, a Provisioning Service Point, and a Provisioning Service Target to handle its core functionality?

A. SAML

B. SAMPL

C. SPML

D. XACML

93. What type of risk assessment uses tools such as the one shown here?

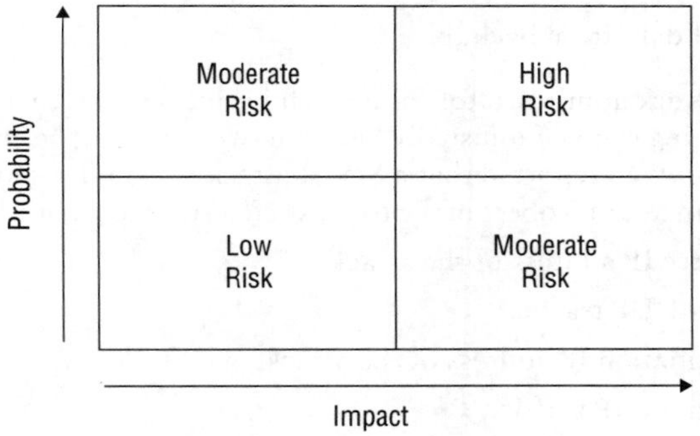

A. Quantitative

B. Loss expectancy

C. Financial

D. Qualitative

94. MAC models use three types of environments. Which of the following is not a mandatory access control design?

A. Hierarchical

B. Bracketed

C. Compartmentalized

D. Hybrid

95. What level of RAID is also called disk striping with parity?

A. RAID 0

B. RAID 1

C. RAID 5

D. RAID 10

96. Sally is wiring a gigabit Ethernet network. What cabling choices should she make to ensure she can use her network at the full 1000 Mbps she wants to provide to her users?

A. Cat 5 and Cat 6

B. Cat 5e and Cat 6

C. Cat 4e and Cat 5e

D. Cat 6 and Cat 7

97. Which one of the following is typically considered a business continuity task?

A. Business impact assessment

B. Alternate facility selection

C. Activation of cold sites

D. Restoration of data from backup

98. Robert is the network administrator for a small business and recently installed a new firewall. After seeing signs of unusually heavy network traffic, he checked his intrusion detection system, which reported that a Smurf attack was under way. What firewall configuration change can Robert make to most effectively prevent this attack.

A. Block the source IP address of the attack.

B. Block inbound UDP traffic.

C. Block the destination IP address of the attack.

D. Block inbound ICMP traffic.

99. Which one of the following types of firewalls does not have the ability to track connection status between different packets?

A. Stateful inspection

B. Application proxy

C. Packet filter

D. Next generation

100. Which of the following is used only to encrypt data in transit over a network and cannot be used to encrypt data at rest?

A. TKIP

B. AES

C. 3DES

D. RSA

101. What type of fuzzing is known as intelligent fuzzing?

A. Zzuf

B. Mutation

C. Generational

D. Code based

102. Matthew is experiencing issues with the quality of network service on his organization's network. The primary symptom is that packets are occasionally taking too long to travel from their source to their destination. What term describes the issue Matthew is facing?

A. Latency

B. Jitter

C. Packet loss

D. Interference

103. Which of the following multifactor authentication technologies provides both low management overhead and flexibility?

A. Biometrics

B. Software tokens

C. Synchronous hardware tokens

D. Asynchronous hardware tokens

104. What type of testing would validate support for all the web browsers that are supported by a web application?

A. Regression testing

B. Interface testing

C. Fuzzing

D. White box testing

105. Kathleen is implementing an access control system for her organization and builds the following array:

Reviewers: update files, delete files

Submitters: upload files

Editors: upload files, update files

Archivists: delete files

What type of access control system has Kathleen implemented?

A. Role-based access control

B. Task-based access control

C. Rule-based access control

D. Discretionary access control

106. Alan is installing a fire suppression system that will kick in after a fire breaks out and protect the equipment in the data center from extensive damage. What metric is Alan attempting to lower?

A. Likelihood

B. RTO

C. RPO

D. Impact

107. Alan's Wrenches recently developed a new manufacturing process for its product. They plan to use this technology internally and not share it with others. They would like it to remain protected for as long as possible. What type of intellectual property protection is best suited for this situation?

A. Patent

B. Copyright

C. Trademark

D. Trade secret

108. Ben wants to interface with the National Vulnerability Database using a standardized protocol. What option should he use to ensure that the tools he builds work with the data contained in the NVD?

A. XACML

B. SCML

C. VSML

D. SCAP

109. Which of the following is not one of the three components of the DevOps model?

A. Software development

B. Change management

C. Quality assurance

D. Operations

110. In the figure shown here, Harry's request to read the data file is blocked. Harry has a Secret security clearance and the data file has a Top Secret classification. What principle of the Bell-LaPadula model blocked this request?

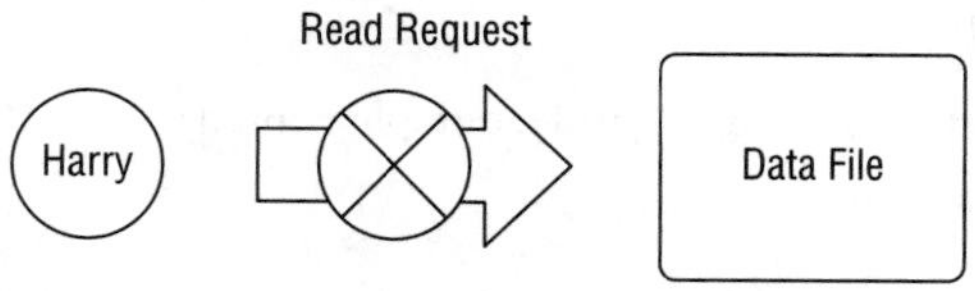

A. Simple Security Property

B. Simple Integrity Property

C. *-Security Property

D. Discretionary Security Property

111. Norm is starting a new software project with a vendor that uses an SDLC approach to development. When he arrives on the job, he receives a document that has the sections shown here. What type of planning document is this?

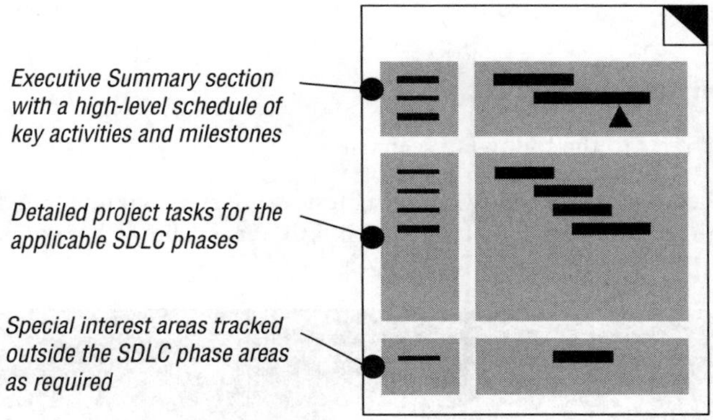

A. Functional requirements

B. Work breakdown structure

C. Test analysis report

D. Project plan

112. Kolin is searching for a network security solution that will allow him to help reduce zero-day attacks while using identities to enforce a security policy on systems before they connect to the network. What type of solution should Kolin implement?

A. A firewall

B. An NAC system

C. An intrusion detection system

D. Port security

113. Gwen comes across an application that is running under a service account on a web server. The service account has full administrative rights to the server. What principle of information security does this violate?

A. Need to know

B. Separation of duties

C. Least privilege

D. Job rotation

114. Which of the following is not a type of structural coverage?

A. Statement

B. Trace

C. Loop

D. Data flow

115. Which of the following tools is best suited to the information gathering phase of a penetration test?

A. Whois

B. zzuf

C. Nessus

D. Metasploit

Questions 116–118 refer to the following scenario:

During a web application vulnerability scanning test, Steve runs Nikto against a web server he believes may be vulnerable to attacks. Using the Nikto output shown here, answer the following questions.

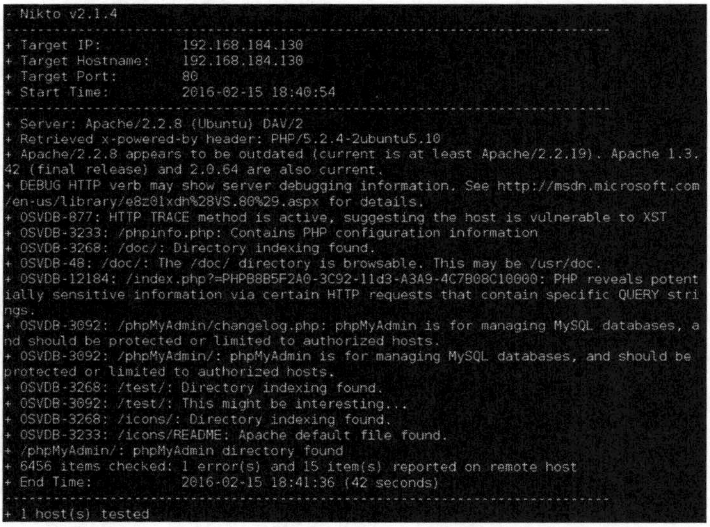

```
- Nikto v2.1.4
---------------------------------------------------------------------------
+ Target IP:          192.168.184.130
+ Target Hostname:    192.168.184.130
+ Target Port:        80
+ Start Time:         2016-02-15 18:40:54
---------------------------------------------------------------------------
+ Server: Apache/2.2.8 (Ubuntu) DAV/2
+ Retrieved x-powered-by header: PHP/5.2.4-2ubuntu5.10
+ Apache/2.2.8 appears to be outdated (current is at least Apache/2.2.19). Apache 1.3.
42 (final release) and 2.0.64 are also current.
+ DEBUG HTTP verb may show server debugging information. See http://msdn.microsoft.com
/en-us/library/e8z01xdh%28VS.80%29.aspx for details.
+ OSVDB-877: HTTP TRACE method is active, suggesting the host is vulnerable to XST
+ OSVDB-3233: /phpinfo.php: Contains PHP configuration information
+ OSVDB-3268: /doc/: Directory indexing found.
+ OSVDB-48: /doc/: The /doc/ directory is browsable. This may be /usr/doc.
+ OSVDB-12184: /index.php?=PHPB8B5F2A0-3C92-11d3-A3A9-4C7B08C10000: PHP reveals potent
ially sensitive information via certain HTTP requests that contain specific QUERY stri
ngs.
+ OSVDB-3092: /phpMyAdmin/changelog.php: phpMyAdmin is for managing MySQL databases, a
nd should be protected or limited to authorized hosts.
+ OSVDB-3092: /phpMyAdmin/: phpMyAdmin is for managing MySQL databases, and should be
protected or limited to authorized hosts.
+ OSVDB-3268: /test/: Directory indexing found.
+ OSVDB-3092: /test/: This might be interesting...
+ OSVDB-3268: /icons/: Directory indexing found.
+ OSVDB-3233: /icons/README: Apache default file found.
+ /phpMyAdmin/: phpMyAdmin directory found
+ 6456 items checked: 1 error(s) and 15 item(s) reported on remote host
+ End Time:           2016-02-15 18:41:36 (42 seconds)
---------------------------------------------------------------------------
+ 1 host(s) tested
```

116. Why does Nikto flag the `/test` directory?

A. The `/test` directory allows administrative access to PHP.

B. It is used to store sensitive data.

C. Test directories often contain scripts that can be misused.

D. It indicates a potential compromise.

117. Why does Nikto identify directory indexing as an issue?

A. It lists files in a directory.

B. It may allow for XDRF.

C. Directory indexing can result in a denial-of-service attack.

D. Directory indexing is off by default, potentially indicating compromise.

118. Nikto lists OSVDB-877, noting that the system may be vulnerable to XST. What would this type of attack allow an attacker to do?

A. Use cross-site targeting.

B. Steal a user's cookies.

C. Counter SQL tracing.

D. Modify a user's TRACE information.

119. Which one of the following memory types is considered volatile memory?

A. Flash

B. EEPROM

C. EPROM

D. RAM

120. Ursula believes that many individuals in her organization are storing sensitive information on their laptops in a manner that is unsafe and potentially violates the organization's security policy. What control can she use to identify the presence of these files?

A. Network DLP

B. Network IPS

C. Endpoint DLP

D. Endpoint IPS

121. In what cloud computing model does the customer build a cloud computing environment in his or her own data center or build an environment in another data center that is for the customer's exclusive use?

A. Public cloud

B. Private cloud

C. Hybrid cloud

D. Shared cloud

122. Which one of the following technologies is designed to prevent a hard drive from becoming a single point of failure in a system?

A. Load balancing

B. Dual-power supplies

C. IPS

D. RAID

123. Alice wants to send Bob a message with the confidence that Bob will know the message was not altered while in transit. What goal of cryptography is Alice trying to achieve?

A. Confidentiality

B. Nonrepudiation

C. Authentication

D. Integrity

124. What network topology is shown here?

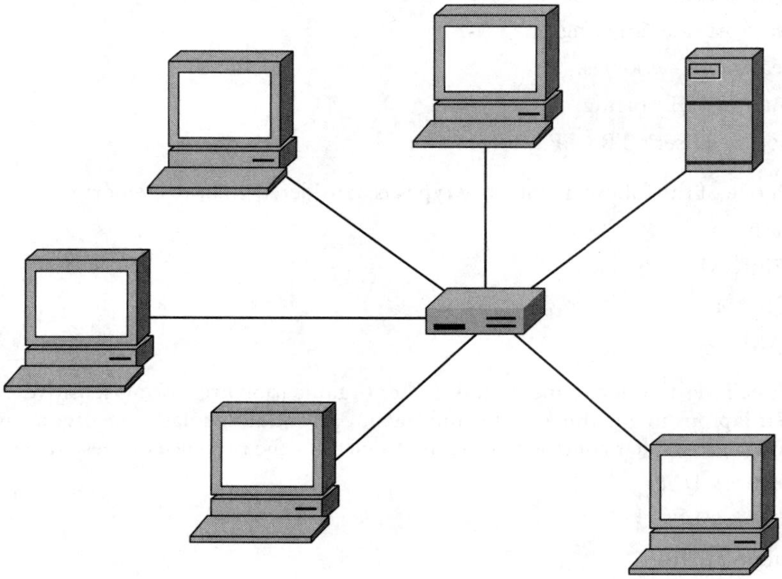

A. A ring

B. A bus

C. A star

D. A mesh

125. Monica is developing a software application that calculates an individual's body mass index for use in medical planning. She would like to include a control on the field where the physician enters an individual's weight to ensure that the weight falls within an expected range. What type of control should Monica use?

A. Fail open

B. Fail secure

C. Limit check

D. Buffer bounds

126. Fred's data role requires him to maintain system security plans and to ensure that system users and support staff get the training they need about security practices and acceptable use. What is the role that Fred is most likely to hold in the organization?

A. Data owner

B. System owner

C. User

D. Custodian

127. Sally is using IPSec's ESP component in transport mode. What important information should she be aware of about transport mode?

A. Transport mode provides full encryption of the entire IP packet.

B. Transport mode adds a new, unencrypted header to ensure that packets reach their destination.

C. Transport mode does not encrypt the header of the packet.

D. Transport mode provides no encryption, only tunnel mode provides encryption.

128. Which one of the following is not a key process area for the Repeatable phase of the Software Capability Maturity Model (SW-CMM)?

A. Software Project Planning

B. Software Quality Management

C. Software Project Tracking

D. Software Subcontract Management

129. Ben wants to provide predictive information about his organization's risk exposure in an automated way as part of an ongoing organizational risk management plan. What should he use to do this?

A. KRIs

B. Quantitative risk assessments

C. KPIs

D. Penetration tests

130. In the image shown here, what does system B send to system A at step 2 of the three-way TCP handshake?

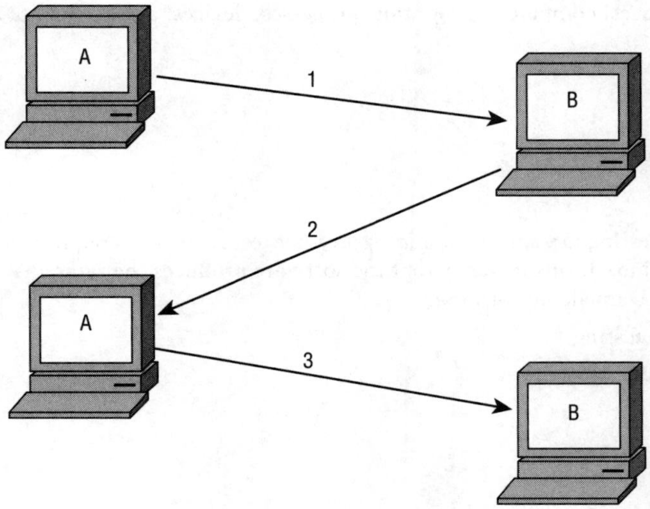

A. SYN

B. ACK

C. FIN/ACK

D. SYN/ACK

131. Chris is conducting reconnaissance on a remote target and discovers that pings are allowed through his target's border firewall. What can he learn by using ping to probe the remote network?

A. Which systems respond to ping, a rough network topology, and potentially the location of additional firewalls

B. A list of all of the systems behind the target's firewall

C. The hostnames and time to live (TTL) for each pingable system, and the ICMP types allowed through the firewall

D. Router advertisements, echo request responses, and potentially which hosts are tarpitted

132. What access management concept defines what rights or privileges a user has?

A. Identification

B. Accountability

C. Authorization

D. Authentication

133. Which one of the following is not a classification level commonly found in commercial data classification schemes?

A. Secret

B. Sensitive

C. Confidential

D. Public

134. Files, databases, computers, programs, processes, devices, and media are all examples of what?

A. Subjects

B. Objects

C. File stores

D. Users

135. Danielle is testing tax software, and part of her testing process requires her to input a variety of actual tax forms to verify that the software produces the right answers. What type of testing is Danielle performing?

A. Use case testing

B. Dynamic testing

C. Fuzzing

D. Misuse testing

136. What is the standard term of protection for a copyrighted work by a known author?

A. 95 years

B. 120 years

C. 70 years from the death of the author

D. 100 years from the death of the author

137. IP addresses like 10.10.10.10 and 172.19.24.21 are both examples of what type of IP address?

A. Public IP addresses

B. Prohibited IP addresses

C. Private IP addresses

D. Class B IP ranges

138. What flaw is a concern with preset questions for cognitive passwords?

A. It prevents the use of tokens.

B. The question's answer may be easy to find on the Internet.

C. Cognitive passwords require users to think to answer the question, and not all users may be able to solve the problems presented.

D. Cognitive passwords don't support long passwords.

139. In the Clark-Wilson integrity model, what type of process is authorized to modify constrained items?

A. CDI

B. UDI

C. IVP

D. TP

140. Kay is selecting an application management approach for her organization. Employees need the flexibility to install software on their systems, but Kay wants to prevent them from installing certain prohibited packages. What type of approach should she use?

A. Antivirus

B. Whitelist

C. Blacklist

D. Heuristic

141. Data relating to the past, present, or future payment for the provision of healthcare to an individual is what type of data per HIPAA?

A. PCI

B. Personal billing data

C. PHI

D. Personally identifiable information (PII)

142. Yagis, panel, cantennas, and parabolic antennas are all examples of what type of antenna?

- **A.** Omnidirectional
- **B.** Rubber duck or base antenna
- **C.** Signal boosting
- **D.** Directional

143. Function, statement, branch, and condition are all types of what?

- **A.** Penetration testing methodologies
- **B.** Fuzzing techniques
- **C.** Code coverage measures
- **D.** Synthetic transaction analysis

144. What is the minimum number of people who should be trained on any specific business continuity plan implementation task?

- **A.** 1
- **B.** 2
- **C.** 3
- **D.** 5

145. Cameron is responsible for backing up his company's primary file server. He configured a backup schedule that performs full backups every Monday evening at 9:00 and incremental backups on other days of the week at that same time. How many files will be copied in Wednesday's backup?

File Modifications
Monday 8AM - File 1 created
Monday 10AM - File 2 created
Monday 11AM - File 3 created
Monday 4PM - File 1 modified
Monday 5PM - File 4 created
Tuesday 8AM - File 1 modified
Tuesday 9AM - File 2 modified
Tuesday 10AM - File 5 created
Wednesday 8AM - File 3 modified
Wednesday 9AM - File 6 created

- **A.** 1
- **B.** 2
- **C.** 5
- **D.** 6

146. Susan uses a span port to monitor traffic to her production website, and uses a monitoring tool to identify performance issues in real time. What type of monitoring is she conducting?

- **A.** Passive monitoring
- **B.** Active monitoring

C. Synthetic monitoring

D. Signature-based monitoring

147. The type of access granted to an object, and the actions that you can take on or with the object, are examples of what?

A. Permissions

B. Rights

C. Priviliges

D. Roles

148. Which one of the following would be considered an example of Infrastructure as a Service cloud computing?

A. Payroll system managed by a vendor and delivered over the web

B. Application platform managed by a vendor that runs customer code

C. Servers provisioned by customers on a vendor-managed virtualization platform

D. Web-based email service provided by a vendor

Questions 149–151 refer to the following scenario.

Darcy is an information security risk analyst for Roscommon Agricultural Products. She is currently trying to decide whether the company should purchase an upgraded fire suppression system for their primary data center. The data center facility has a replacement cost of $2 million.

After consulting with actuaries, data center managers, and fire subject matter experts, Darcy determined that a typical fire would likely require the replacement of all equipment inside the building but not cause significant structural damage. Together, they estimated that recovering from the fire would cost $750,000. They also determined that the company can expect a fire of this magnitude once every 50 years.

149. Based on the information in this scenario, what is the exposure factor for the effect of a fire on the Roscommon Agricultural Products data center?

A. 7.5%

B. 15.0%

C. 27.5%

D. 37.5%

150. Based on the information in this scenario, what is the annualized rate of occurrence for a fire at the Roscommon Agricultural Products data center?

A. 0.002

B. 0.005

C. 0.02

D. 0.05

151. Based on the information in this scenario, what is the annualized loss expectancy for a tornado at the Roscommon Agricultural Products data center?

A. $15,000

B. $25,000

C. $75,000

D. $750,000

152. Two TCP header flags are rarely used. Which two are you unlikely to see in use in a modern network?

A. CWR and ECE

B. URG and FIN

C. ECE and RST

D. CWR and URG

153. Which one of the following is not a tape rotation strategy commonly used in disaster recovery plans?

A. Tower of Hanoi

B. Key Rotation

C. Grandfather, Father, Son

D. First In, First Out

154. Fran is a web developer who works for an online retailer. Her boss asked her to create a way that customers can easily integrate themselves with Fran's company's site. They need to be able to check inventory in real time, place orders, and check order status programatically without having to access the web page. What can Fran create to most directly facilitate this interaction?

A. API

B. Web scraper

C. Data dictionary

D. Call center

155. What type of power issue occurs when a facility experiences a momentary loss of power?

A. Fault

B. Blackout

C. Sag

D. Brownout

156. Lauren's team of system administrators each deal with hundreds of systems with varying levels of security requirements and find it difficult to handle the multitude of usernames and passwords they each have. What type of solution should she recommend to ensure that passwords are properly handled and that features like logging and password rotation occur?

A. A credential management system

B. A strong password policy

C. Separation of duties

D. Single sign-on

157. Ed's Windows system can't connect to the network and `ipconfig` shows the following:

Ethernet adapter Local Area Connection:
Connection-specific DNS Suffix . :
Link-local IPv6 Address . . . . . : fe80::90f1:e9f0:c0f5:b0ba%11
IPv4 Address. . . . . : 169.254.19.21
Subnet Mask . . . . : 255.255.0.0
Default Gateway . . . . :

What has occurred on the system?

A. The system has been assigned in invalid IP address by its DHCP server.

B. The system has a manually assigned IP address.

C. The system has failed to get a DHCP address and has assigned itself an address.

D. The subnet mask is set incorrectly and the system cannot communicate with the gateway.

158. What term is commonly used to describe initial creation of a user account in the provisioning process?

A. Enrollment

B. Clearance verification

C. Background checks

D. Initialization

159. As part of her ongoing duties related to her company's security program, Susan's reports to management include the number of repeated audit findings. This information is an example of what type of useful measure?

A. Key risk indicator

B. Safeguard metrics

C. Key performance indicator

D. Audit tracking indicators

160. There is a significant conflict between the drive for profit and the security requirements that Olivia's organization has standardized. Olivia's role means that decreased usability and loss of profit due to her staff's inability to use the system is her major concern. What is the most likely role that Olivia plays in her organization?

A. Business manager

B. Information security analyst

C. Data processor

D. Mission owner

161. Tom believes that a customer of his Internet service provider has been exploiting a vulnerability in his system to read the email messages of other customers. If true, what law did the customer most likely violate?

A. ECPA

B. CALEA

C. HITECH

D. Privacy Act

162. In the ring protection model shown here, what ring contains user programs and applications?

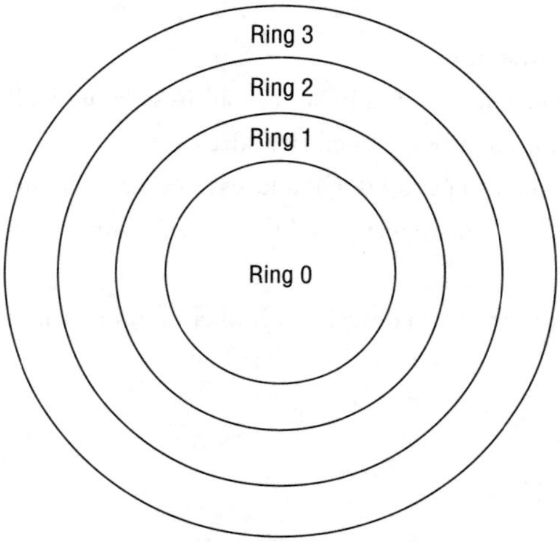

A. Ring 0

B. Ring 1

C. Ring 2

D. Ring 3

163. Metrics like the attack vector, complexity, exploit maturity, and how much user interaction is required are all found in what scoring system?

A. CVE

B. CVSS

C. CNA

D. NVD

164. In which of the following circumstances does an individual not have a reasonable expectation of privacy?

A. Placing a telephone call on your cell phone

B. Sending a letter through the U.S. mail

C. Sending an email at work

D. Retrieving your personal voicemail

165. During which of the following disaster recovery tests does the team sit together and discuss the response to a scenario but not actually activate any disaster recovery controls?

A. Checklist review

B. Full interruption test

C. Parallel test

D. Tabletop exercise

166. Susan wants to integrate her website to allow users to use accounts from sites like Google. What technology should she adopt?

A. Kerberos

B. LDAP

C. OpenID

D. SESAME

167. Tom is conducting a business continuity planning effort for Orange Blossoms, a fruit orchard located in Central Florida. During the assessment process, the committee determined that there is a small risk of snow in the region but that the cost of implementing controls to reduce the impact of that risk is not warranted. They elect to not take any specific action in response to the risk. What risk management strategy is Orange Blossoms pursuing?

A. Risk mitigation

B. Risk transference

C. Risk avoidance

D. Risk acceptance

168. Fred needs to run a network cable for over a kilometer. What wiring option should he choose to ensure that he doesn't encounter issues?

A. 10Base5

B. 10BaseT

C. STP

D. Fiber optic

169. Jack's organization is a multinational nonprofit that has small offices in many developing countries throughout the world. They need to implement an access control system that allows flexibility and which can work despite poor Internet connectivity at their locations. What is the best type of access control design for Jack's organization?

A. Centralized access control

B. Mandatory access control

C. Decentralized access control

D. Rule-based access control

170. What U.S. government classification label is applied to information that, if disclosed, could cause serious damage to national security, and also requires that the damage that would be caused is able to be described or identified by the classification authority?

A. Classified

B. Secret

C. Confidential

D. Top Secret

Questions 171–174 refer to the following scenario.

Mike and Renee would like to use an asymmetric cryptosystem to communicate with each other. They are located in different parts of the country but have exchanged encryption keys by using digital certificates signed by a mutually trusted certificate authority.

171. When the certificate authority (CA) created Renee's digital certificate, what key was contained within the body of the certificate?

A. Renee's public key

B. Renee's private key

C. CA's public key

D. CA's private key

172. When the certificate authority created Renee's digital certificate, what key did it use to digitally sign the completed certificate?

A. Renee's public key

B. Renee's private key

C. CA's public key

D. CA's private key

173. When Mike receives Renee's digital certificate, what key does he use to verify the authenticity of the certificate?

A. Renee's public key

B. Renee's private key

C. CA's public key

D. CA's private key

174. Mike would like to send Renee a private message using the information gained during this exchange. What key should he use to encrypt the message?

A. Renee's public key

B. Renee's private key

C. CA's public key

D. CA's private key

175. Which one of the following tools may be used to directly violate the confidentiality of communications on an unencrypted VoIP network?

A. Nmap

B. Nessus

C. Wireshark

D. Nikto

176. How does single sign-on increase security?

A. It decreases the number of accounts required for a subject.

B. It helps decrease the likelihood users will write down their passwords.

C. It provides logging for each system that it is connected to.

D. It provides better encryption for authentication data.

177. Which one of the following cryptographic algorithms supports the goal of nonrepudiation?

A. Blowfish

B. DES

C. AES

D. RSA

178. Microsoft's STRIDE threat assessment framework uses six categories for threats: Spoofing, Tampering, Repudiation, Information Disclosure, Denial of Service, and Elevation of Privilege. If a penetration tester is able to modify audit logs, what STRIDE categories best describe this issue?

A. Tampering and information disclosure

B. Elevation of privilege and tampering

C. Repudiation and denial of service

D. Repudiation and tampering

179. RIP, OSPF, and BGP are all examples of protocols associated with what type of network device?

A. Switches

B. Bridges

C. Routers

D. Gateways

180. AES-based CCMP and 802.1x replaced what security protocol that was designed as part of WPA to help fix the significant security issues found in WEP?

A. TLS

B. TKIP

C. EAP

D. PEAP

181. The government agency that Ben works at installed a new access control system. The system uses information such as Ben's identity, department, normal working hours, job category, and location to make authorization What type of access control system did Ben's employer adopt?

A. Role-based access control

B. Attribute-based access control

C. Administrative access control

D. System discretionary access control

182. The Low Orbit Ion Cannon (LOIC) attack tool used by Anonymous leverages a multitude of home PCs to attack its chosen targets. This is an example of what type of network attack?

A. DDoS

B. Ionization

C. Zombie horde

D. Teardrop

183. Andrew believes that a digital certificate belonging to his organization was compromised and would like to add it to a Certificate Revocation List. Who must add the certificate to the CRL?

A. Andrew

B. The root authority for the top-level domain

C. The CA that issued the certificate

D. The revocation authority for the top-level domain

184. Amanda is considering the implementation of a database recovery mechanism recommended by a consultant. In the recommended approach, an automated process will move records of transactions from the primary site to a backup site on an hourly basis. What type of database recovery technique is the consultant describing?

A. Electronic vaulting

B. Transaction logging

C. Remote mirroring

D. Remote journaling

185. A process on a system needs access to a file that is currently in use by another process. What state will the process scheduler place this process in until the file becomes available?

A. Running

B. Ready

C. Waiting

D. Stopped

186. Which one of the following investigation types has the loosest standards for the collection and preservation of information?

A. Civil investigation

B. Operational investigation

C. Criminal investigation

D. Regulatory investigation

187. Sue was required to sign an NDA when she took a job at her new company. Why did the company require her to sign it?

A. To protect the confidentiality of their data

B. To ensure that Sue did not delete their data

C. To prevent Sue from directly competing with them in the future

D. To require Sue to ensure the availability for their data as part of her job

188. Susan is concerned about the FAR associated with her biometric technology. What is the best method to deal with the FAR?

A. Adjust the CER.

B. Change the sensitivity of the system to lower the FRR.

C. Add a second factor.

D. Replace the biometric system.

189. What length of time does an SOC 2 report typically cover?

A. Point in time

B. 6 months

C. 12 months

D. 3 months

190. Which of the following is not a code review process?

A. Email pass-around

B. Over the shoulder

C. Pair programming

D. IDE forcing

191. Which one of the following attack types depends on precise timing?

A. TOC/TOU

B. SQL injection

C. Pass the hash

D. Cross-site scripting

192. What process adds a header and a footer to data received at each layer of the OSI model?

A. Attribution

B. Encapsulation

C. TCP wrapping

D. Data hiding

193. Attackers who compromise websites often acquire databases of hashed passwords. What technique can best protect these passwords against automated password cracking attacks that use precomputed values?

A. Using the MD5 hashing algorithm

B. Using the SHA-1 hashing algorithm

C. Salting

D. Double-hashing

194. Jim starts a new job as a system engineer and his boss provides him with a document entitled "Forensic Response Guidelines." Which one of the following statements is not true?

A. Jim must comply with the information in this document.

B. The document contains information about forensic examinations.

C. Jim should read the document thoroughly.

D. The document is likely based on industry best practices.

195. Which one of the following tools is most often used for identification purposes and is not suitable for use as an authenticator?

A. Password

B. Retinal scan

C. Username

D. Token

196. Ben needs to verify that the most recent patch for his organization's critical application did not introduce issues elsewhere. What type of testing does Ben need to conduct to ensure this?

A. Unit testing

B. White box

C. Regression testing

D. Black box

197. Tamara recently decided to purchase cyberliability insurance to cover her company's costs in the event of a data breach. What risk management strategy is she pursuing?

A. Risk acceptance

B. Risk mitigation

C. Risk transference

D. Risk avoidance

198. Which of the following is not one of the four canons of the $(ISC)^2$ code of ethics?

A. Avoid conflicts of interest that may jeopardize impartiality.

B. Protect society, the common good, necessary public trust and confidence, and the infrastructure.

C. Act honorably, honestly, justly, responsibly, and legally.

D. Provide diligent and competent service to principals.

199. Jim wants to allow a partner organization's Active Directory forest (B) to access his domain forest's (A)'s resources but doesn't want to allow users in his domain to access B's resources. He also does not want the trust to flow upward through the domain tree as it is formed. What should he do?

A. Set up a two-way transitive trust.

B. Set up a one-way transitive trust.

C. Set up a one-way nontransitive trust.

D. Set up a two-way nontransitive trust.

200. Susan's team is performing code analysis by manually reviewing the code for flaws. What type of analysis are they performing?

A. Gray box

B. Static

C. Dynamic

D. Fuzzing

201. The IP address 201.19.7.45 is what type of address?

A. A public IP address

B. An RFC 1918 address

C. An APIPA address

D. A loopback address

202. Sam is a security risk analyst for an insurance company. He is currently examining a scenario where a hacker might use a SQL injection attack to deface a web server due to a missing patch in the company's web application. In this scenario, what is the vulnerability?

A. Unpatched web application

B. Web defacement

C. Hacker

D. Operating system

203. Which one of the following categories of secure data removal techniques would include degaussing?

A. Clear

B. Shrink

C. Purge

D. Destroy

204. What type of alternate processing facility includes all of the hardware and data necessary to restore operations in a matter of minutes or seconds?

A. Hot site

B. Warm site

C. Cold site

D. Mobile site

205. What UDP port is typically used by the syslog service?

A. 443

B. 514

C. 515

D. 445

206. Fred finds a packet that his protocol analyzer shows with both PSH and URG set. What type of packet is he looking at, and what do the flags mean?

A. A UDP packet; PSH and URG are used to indicate that the data should be sent at high speed

B. A TCP packet; PSH and URG are used to clear the buffer and indicate that the data is urgent

C. A TCP packet; PSH and URG are used to preset the header and indicate that the speed of the network is unregulated

D. A UDP packet; PSH and URG are used to indicate that the UDP buffer should be cleared and that the data is urgent

207. What code review process is shown here?

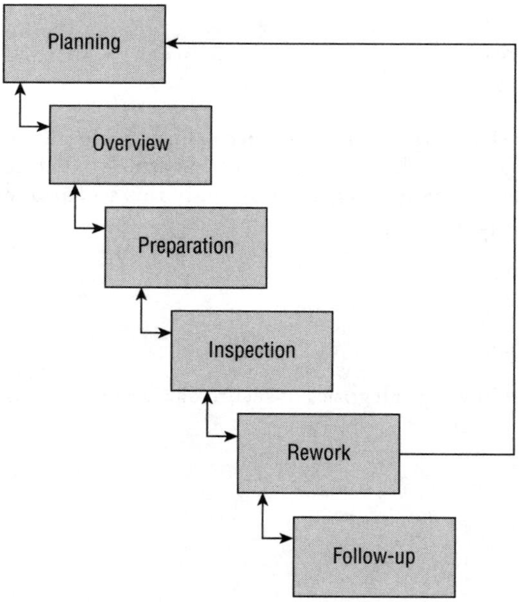

A. Static inspection

B. Fagan inspection

C. Dynamic inspectiom

D. Interface testing

208. During a log review, Karen discovers that the system she needs to gather logs from has the log setting shown here. What problem is Karen likely to encounter?

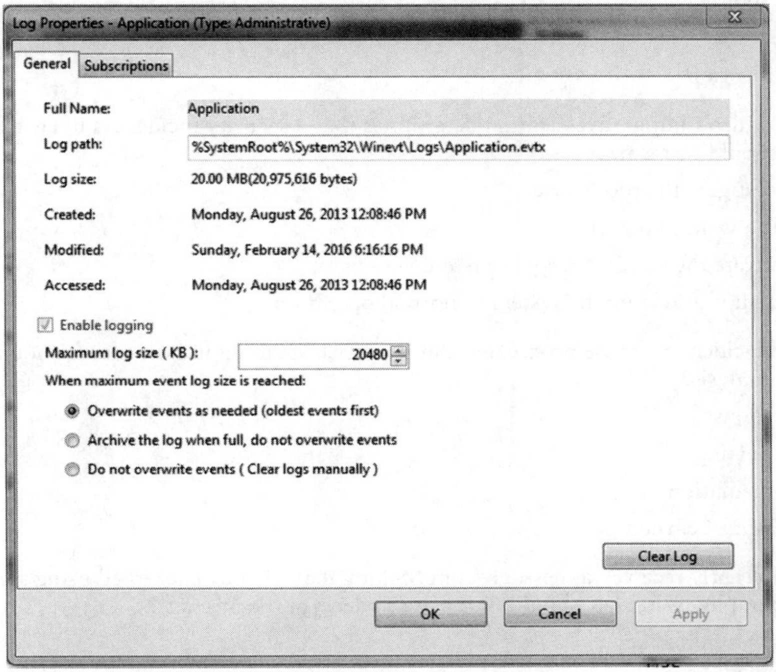

A. Too much log data will be stored on the system.

B. The system is automatically purging archived logs.

C. The logs will not contain the information needed.

D. The logs will only contain the most recent 20 MB of log data.

209. The ESP component of IPSec provides what two functions?

A. Authentication and integrity

B. Confidentiality and authentication

C. Nonrepudiation and authentication

D. Confidentiality and availability

Questions 210–213 refer to the following scenario.

Alejandro is an incident response analyst for a large corporation. He is on the midnight shift when an intrusion detection system alerts him to a potential brute-force password attack against one of the company's critical information systems. He performs an initial triage of the event before taking any additional action.

210. What stage of the incident response process is Alejandro currently conducting?

A. Detection

B. Response

C. Recovery

D. Mitigation

211. If Alejandro's initial investigation determines that a security incident is likely taking place, what should be his next step?

A. Investigate the root cause.

B. File a written report.

C. Activate the incident response team.

D. Attempt to restore the system to normal operations.

212. As the incident response progresses, during which stage should the team conduct a root cause analysis?

A. Response

B. Reporting

C. Remediation

D. Lessons Learned

213. Barry recently received a message from Melody that Melody encrypted using symmetric cryptography. What key should Barry use to decrypt the message?

A. Barry's public key

B. Barry's private key

C. Melody's public key

D. Shared secret key

214. After you do automated functional testing with 100 percent coverage of an application, what type of error is most likely to remain?

A. Business logic errors

B. Input validation errors

C. Runtime errors

D. Error handling errors

215. During what phase of the incident response process would security professionals analyze the process itself to determine whether any improvements are warranted?

A. Lessons Learned

B. Remediation

C. Recovery

D. Reporting

216. What law prevents the removal of protection mechanisms placed on a copyrighted work by the copyright holder?

A. HIPAA

B. DMCA

C. GLBA

D. ECPA

217. Linda is selecting a disaster recovery facility for her organization, and she wishes to retain independence from other organizations as much as possible. She would like to choose a facility that balances cost and recovery time, allowing activation in about one week after a disaster is declared. What type of facility should she choose?

A. Cold site

B. Warm site

C. Mutual assistance agreement

D. Hot site

218. What term is used to describe two-way communications in which only one direction can send at a time?

A. Duplex

B. Half-duplex

C. Simplex

D. Suplex

219. What type of penetration testing provides detail on the scope of a penetration test—including items like what systems would be targeted—but does not provide full visibility into the configuration or other details of the systems or networks the penetration tester must test?

A. Crystal box

B. White box

C. Black box

D. Gray box

220. Test coverage is computed using which of the following formulas?

A. Number of use cases tested/total number of use cases

B. Number of lines of code tested/total number of lines of code

C. Number of functions tested/total number of functions

D. Number of conditional branches tested/Total number of testable branches

221. TCP and UDP both operate at what layer of the OSI model?

A. Layer 2

B. Layer 3

C. Layer 4

D. Layer 5

222. Which one of the following goals of physical security environments occurs first in the functional order of controls?

A. Delay

B. Detection

C. Deterrence

D. Denial

223. In what type of trusted recovery process does the system recover against one or more failure types without administrator intervention with potential data loss?

A. Automated recovery

B. Manual recovery

C. Automated recovery without undue data loss

D. Function recovery

224. Skip needs to transfer files from his PC to a remote server. What protocol should he use instead of FTP?

A. SCP

B. SSH

C. HTTP

D. Telnet

225. Ben's New York–based commercial web service collects personal information from California residents. What does the California Online Privacy Protection Act require Ben to do to be compliant?

A. Ben must encrypt all personal data he receives.

B. Ben must comply with the EU DPD.

C. Ben must have a conspicuously posted privacy policy on his site.

D. Ben must provide notice and choice for users of his website.

226. What process is used to verify that a dial-up user is connecting from the phone number they are preauthorized to use in a way that avoids spoofing?

A. CallerID

B. Callback

C. CHAP

D. PPP

227. In the diagram shown here of security boundaries within a computer system, what component's name has been replaced with XXX?

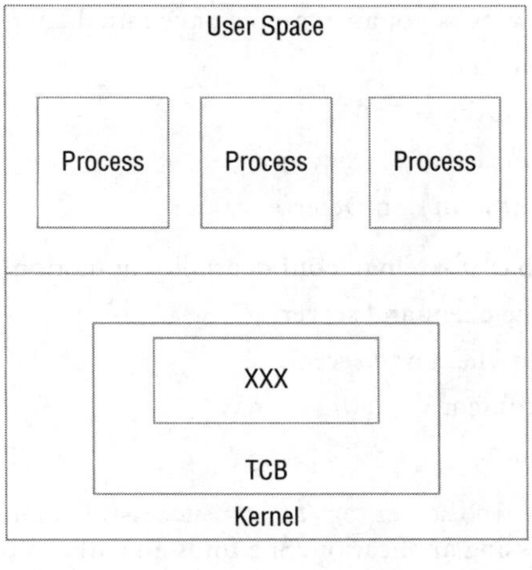

A. Reference monitor

B. Privileged core

C. Security perimeter

D. User kernel

228. Why are iris scans preferable to most other types of biometric factors?

A. Iris scanners are harder to deceive.

B. Irises don't change as much as other factors.

C. Iris scanners are cheaper than other factors.

D. Iris scans cannot be easily replicated.

229. Alex has ensured that all of his staff have signed nondisclosure agreements to help protect his organization's intellectual property and data. What potential issue is Alex working to deal with?

A. Data exfiltration

B. Personnel retention

C. Data breach

D. Nonproprietary data sharing

230. Matthew, Richard, and Christopher would like to exchange messages with each other using symmetric cryptography. They want to ensure that each individual can privately send a message to another individual without the third person being able to read the message. How many keys do they need?

A. 1

B. 2

C. 3

D. 6

231. Which one of the following is not an example of criminal law?

- **A.** Gramm Leach Bliley Act
- **B.** Computer Fraud and Abuse Act
- **C.** Electronic Communications Privacy Act
- **D.** Identity Theft and Assumption Deterrence Act

232. What is the best way to ensure email confidentiality in motion?

- **A.** Use TLS between the client and server.
- **B.** Use SSL between the client and server.
- **C.** Encrypt the email content.
- **D.** Use a digital signature.

233. Brenda is analyzing the web server logs after a successful compromise of her organization's web-based order processing application. She finds an entry in the log file showing that a user entered the following information as his last name when placing an order:

```
Smith';DROP TABLE orders;--
```

What type of attack was attempted?

- **A.** Buffer overflow
- **B.** Cross-site scripting
- **C.** Cross-site request forgery
- **D.** SQL injection

234. What type of policy describes how long data is kept before destruction?

- **A.** Classification
- **B.** Audit
- **C.** Record retention
- **D.** Availability

235. What is the goal of the BCP process?

- **A.** RTO<MTD
- **B.** MTD<RTO
- **C.** RPO<MTD
- **D.** MTD<RPO

236. During which phase of the incident response process would administrators design new security controls intended to prevent a recurrence of the incident?

- **A.** Reporting
- **B.** Recovery
- **C.** Remediation
- **D.** Lessons Learned

237. Bethany received an email from one of her colleagues with an unusual attachment named `smime.p7s`. She does not recognize the attachment and is unsure what to do. What is the most likely scenario?

A. This is an encrypted email message.

B. This is a phishing attack.

C. This is embedded malware.

D. This is a spoofing attack.

Questions 238–241 refer to the following scenario.

Kim is the database security administrator for Aircraft Systems, Inc. (ASI). ASI is a military contractor engaged in the design and analysis of aircraft avionics systems and regularly handles classified information on behalf of the government and other government contractors. Kim is concerned about ensuring the security of information stored in ASI databases.

Kim's database is a multilevel security database, and different ASI employees have different security clearances. The database contains information on the location of military aircraft containing ASI systems to allow ASI staff to monitor those systems.

238. Kim learned that the military is planning a classified mission that involves some ASI aircraft. She is concerned that employees not cleared for the mission may learn of it by noticing the movement of many aircraft to the region. What type of attack is Kim concerned about?

A. Aggregation

B. SQL injection

C. Inference

D. Multilevel security

239. What technique can Kim employ to prevent employees not cleared for the mission from learning the true location of the aircraft?

A. Input validation

B. Polyinstantiation

C. Parameterization

D. Server-side validation

240. Kim's database uniquely identifies aircraft by using their tail number. Which one of the following terms would not necessarily accurately describe the tail number?

A. Database field

B. Foreign key

C. Primary key

D. Candidate key

241. Kim would like to create a key that enforces referential integrity for the database. What type of key does she need to create?

A. Primary key

B. Foreign key

C. Candidate key
D. Master key

242. Doug is choosing a software development life-cycle model for use in a project he is leading to develop a new business application. He has very clearly defined requirements and would like to choose an approach that places an early emphasis on developing comprehensive documentation. He does not have a need for the production of rapid prototypes or iterative improvement. Which model is most appropriate for this scenario?
A. Agile
B. Waterfall
C. Spiral
D. DevOps

243. Which individual bears the ultimate responsibility for data protection tasks?
A. Data owner
B. Data custodian
C. User
D. Auditor

244. What should be true for salts used in password hashes?
A. A single salt should be set so passwords can be de-hashed as needed.
B. A single salt should be used so the original salt can be used to check passwords against their hash.
C. Unique salts should be stored for each user.
D. Unique salts should be created every time a user logs in.

245. What type of assessment methods are associated with mechanisms and activities based on the recommendations of NIST SP800-53A, the Guide for Assessing Security Controls in Federal Information Systems?
A. Examine and interview
B. Test and assess
C. Test and interview
D. Examine and test

246. Which one of the following controls would be most effective in detecting zero-day attack attempts?
A. Signature-based intrusion detection
B. Anomaly-based intrusion detection
C. Strong patch management
D. Full-disk encryption

247. The ability to store and generate passwords, provide logging and auditing capabilities, and allow password check-in and check-out are all features of what type of system?

A. AAA

B. Credential management

C. Two-factor authentication

D. Kerberos

248. Which one of the following components should be included in an organization's emergency response guidelines?

A. Secondary response procedures for first responders

B. Long-term business continuity protocols

C. Activation procedures for the organization's cold sites

D. Contact information for ordering equipment

249. When Jim enters his organization's data center, he has to use a smart card and code to enter, and is allowed through one set of doors. The first set of doors closes, and he must then use his card again to get through a second set, which locks behind him. What type of control is this, and what is it called?

A. A physical control; a one-way trapdoor

B. A logical control; dual-swipe authorization

C. A directive control; one-way access corridor

D. A preventive access control; a mantrap

250. What security control may be used to implement a concept known as two-person control?

A. Mandatory vacation

B. Separation of duties

C. Least privilege

D. Defense in depth

Chapter 10

Practice Test 2

1. James is building a disaster recovery plan for his organization and would like to determine the amount of acceptable data loss after an outage. What variable is James determining?
   A. SLA
   B. RTO
   C. MTD
   D. RPO

2. Fred needs to deploy a network device that can connect his network to other networks while controlling traffic on his network. What type of device is Fred's best choice?
   A. A switch
   B. A bridge
   C. A gateway
   D. A router

3. Alex is preparing to solicit bids for a penetration test of his company's network and systems. He wants to maximize the effectiveness of the testing rather than the realism of the test. What type of penetration test should he require in his bidding process?
   A. Black box
   B. Crystal box
   C. Gray box
   D. Zero box

4. Application banner information is typically recorded during what penetration testing phase?
   A. Planning
   B. Attack
   C. Reporting
   D. Discovery

5. What is the default subnet mask for a Class B network?
   A. 255.0.0.0
   B. 255.255.0.0
   C. 255.254.0.0
   D. 255.255.255.0

6. Jim has been asked to individually identify devices that users are bringing to work as part of a new BYOD policy. The devices will not be joined to a central management system like Active Directory, but he still needs to uniquely identify the systems. Which of the following options will provide Jim with the best means of reliably identifying each unique device?
   A. Record the MAC address of each system.
   B. Require users to fill out a form to register each system.

C. Scan each system using a port scanner.

D. Use device fingerprinting via a web-based registration system.

7. David works in an organization that uses a formal data governance program. He is consulting with an employee working on a project that created an entirely new class of data and wants to work with the appropriate individual to assign a classification level to that information. Who is responsible for the assignment of information to a classification level?

A. Data creator

B. Data owner

C. CISO

D. Data custodian

8. What type of inbound packet is characteristic of a ping flood attack?

A. ICMP echo request

B. ICMP echo reply

C. ICMP destination unreachable

D. ICMP route changed

9. Gabe is concerned about the security of passwords used as a cornerstone of his organization's information security program. Which one of the following controls would provide the greatest improvement in Gabe's ability to authenticate users?

A. More complex passwords

B. User education against social engineering

C. Multifactor authentication

D. Addition of security questions based on personal knowledge

10. The separation of network infrastructure from the control layer, combined with the ability to centrally program a network design in a vendor-neutral, standards-based implementation, is an example of what important concept?

A. MPLS, a way to replace long network addresses with shorter labels and support a wide range of protocols

B. FCoE, a converged protocol that allows common applications over Ethernet

C. SDN, a converged protocol that allows network virtualization

D. CDN, a converged protocol that makes common network designs accessible

11. Susan is preparing to decommission her organization's archival DVD-ROMs that contain Top Secret data. How should she ensure that the data cannot be exposed?

A. Degauss

B. Zero wipe

C. Pulverize

D. Secure erase

12. What is the final stage of the Software Capability Maturity Model (SW-CMM)?
    A. Repeatable
    B. Defined
    C. Managed
    D. Optimizing

13. Angie is configuring egress monitoring on her network to provide added security. Which one of the following packet types should Angie allow to leave the network headed for the Internet?
    A. Packets with a source address from Angie's public IP address block
    B. Packets with a destination address from Angie's public IP address block
    C. Packets with a source address outside of Angie's address block
    D. Packets with a source address from Angie's private address block

14. Matt is conducting a penetration test against a Linux server and successfully gained access to an administrative account. He would now like to obtain the password hashes for use in a brute-force attack. Where is he likely to find the hashes, assuming the system is configured to modern security standards?
    A. `/etc/passwd`
    B. `/etc/hash`
    C. `/etc/secure`
    D. `/etc/shadow`

15. Theresa is implementing a new access control system and wants to ensure that developers do not have the ability to move code from development systems into the production environment. What information security principle is she most directly enforcing?
    A. Separation of duties
    B. Two-person control
    C. Least privilege
    D. Job rotation

16. Which one of the following tools may be used to achieve the goal of nonrepudiation?
    A. Digital signature
    B. Symmetric encryption
    C. Firewall
    D. IDS

17. In the diagram of the TCP three-way handshake here, what should system A send to system B in step 3?

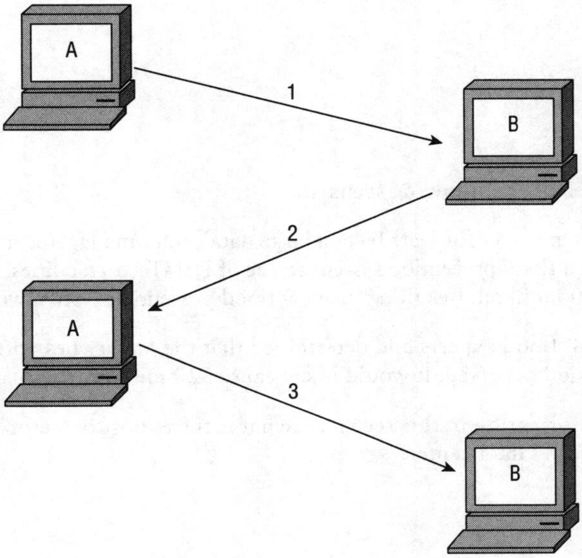

A. ACK

B. SYN

C. FIN

D. RST

18. What RADIUS alternative is commonly used for Cisco network gear and supports two-factor authentication?

A. RADIUS+

B. TACACS+

C. XTACACS

D. Kerberos

19. What two types of attacks are VoIP call managers and VoIP phones most likely to be susceptible to?

A. DoS and malware

B. Worms and Trojans

C. DoS and host OS attacks

D. Host OS attacks and buffer overflows

20. Vivian works for a chain of retail stores and would like to use a software product that restricts the software used on point-of-sale terminals to those packages on a preapproved list. What approach should Vivian use?

A. Antivirus

B. Heuristic

C. Whitelist

D. Blacklist

Questions 21–23 refer to the following scenario.

Hunter is the facilities manager for DataTech, a large data center management firm. He is evaluating the installation of a flood prevention system at one of DataTech's facilities. The facility and contents are valued at $100 million. Installing the new flood prevention system would cost $10 million.

Hunter consulted with flood experts and determined that the facility lies within a 200-year flood plain and that, if a flood occurred, it would likely cause $20 million in damage to the facility.

21. Based on the information in this scenario, what is the exposure factor for the effect of a flood on DataTech's data center?

A. 2%

B. 20%

C. 100%

D. 200%

22. Based on the information in this scenario, what is the annualized rate of occurrence for a flood at DataTech's data center?

A. 0.002

B. 0.005

C. 0.02

D. 0.05

23. Based on the information in this scenario, what is the annualized loss expectancy for a flood at DataTech's data center?

A. $40,000

B. $100,000

C. $400,000

D. $1,000,000

24. Which accounts are typically assessed during an account management assessment?

A. A random sample

B. Highly privileged accounts

C. Recently generated accounts

D. Accounts that have existed for long periods of time

25. In the shared responsibility model, under which tier of cloud computing does the customer take responsibility for securing server operating systems?

A. IaaS

B. PaaS

C. SaaS

D. TaaS

26. What type of error occurs when a valid subject using a biometric authenticator is not authenticated?

A. A Type 1 error

B. A Type 2 error

C. A Type 3 error

D. A Type 4 error

27. Jackie is creating a database that contains the Customers table, shown here. She is designing a new table to contain Orders and plans to use the Company ID in that table to uniquely identify the customer associated with each order. What role does the Company ID field play in the Orders table?

Company ID	Company Name	Address	City	State	ZIP Code	Telephone	Sales Rep
1	Acme Widgets	234 Main Street	Columbia	MD	21040	(301) 555-1212	14
2	Abrams Consulting	1024 Sample Street	Miami	FL	33131	(305) 555-1995	14
3	Dome Widgets	913 Sorin Street	South Bend	IN	46556	(574) 555-5863	26

A. Primary key

B. Foreign key

C. Candidate key

D. Referential key

28. What three types of interfaces are typically tested during software testing?

A. Network, physical, and application interfaces

B. APIs, UIs, and physical interfaces

C. Network interfaces, APIs, and UIs

D. Application, programmatic, and user interfaces

29. George is assisting a prosecutor with a case against a hacker who attempted to break into George's company's computer systems. He provides system logs to the prosecutor for use as evidence but the prosecutor insists that George testify in court about how he gathered the logs. What rule of evidence requires George's testimony?

A. Testimonial evidence rule

B. Parol evidence rule

C. Best evidence rule

D. Hearsay rule

30. Which of the following is not a valid use for key risk indicators?
   A. Provide warnings before issues occur.
   B. Provide real-time incident response information.
   C. Provide historical views of past risks.
   D. Provide insight into risk tolerance for the organization.

31. Which one of the following malware types uses built-in propagation mechanisms that exploit system vulnerabilities to spread?
   A. Trojan horse
   B. Worm
   C. Logic bomb
   D. Virus

32. Don's company is considering the use of an object-based storage system where data is placed in a vendor-managed storage environment through the use of API calls. What type of cloud computing service is in use?
   A. IaaS
   B. PaaS
   C. CaaS
   D. SaaS

33. In what model of cloud computing do two or more organizations collaborate to build a shared cloud computing environment that is for their own use?
   A. Public cloud
   B. Private cloud
   C. Community cloud
   D. Shared cloud

34. Which one of the following is not a principle of the Agile approach to software development?
   A. The most efficient method of conveying information is electronic.
   B. Working software is the primary measure of progress.
   C. Simplicity is essential.
   D. Business people and developers must work together daily.

35. Harry is concerned that accountants within his organization will use data diddling attacks to cover up fraudulent activity in accounts that they normally access. Which one of the following controls would best defend against this type of attack?
   A. Encryption
   B. Access controls
   C. Integrity verification
   D. Firewalls

36. What class of fire extinguisher is capable of fighting electrical fires?

A. Class A

B. Class B

C. Class C

D. Class D

37. What important factor differentiates Frame Relay from X.25?

A. Frame Relay supports multiple PVCs over a single WAN carrier connection.

B. Frame Relay is a cell switching technology instead of a packet switching technology like X.25.

C. Frame Relay does not provide a Committed Information Rate (CIR).

D. Frame Relay only requires a DTE on the provider side.

Using the following table, and your knowledge of the auditing process, answer questions 38–40.

	Report Content	Audience
SOC 1	Internal controls for financial reporting	Users and auditors
SOC 2	Confidentiality, integrity, availability, security, and privacy controls	Auditors, regulators, management, partners, and others under NDA
SOC 3	Confidentiality, integrity, availability, security, and privacy controls	Publicly available, often used for a website seal

38. As they prepare to migrate their data center to an Infrastructure as a Service (IaaS) provider, Susan's company wants to understand the effectiveness of their new provider's security, integrity, and availability controls. What SOC report would provide them with the most detail?

A. SOC 1

B. SOC 2

C. SOC 3

D. None of the SOC reports are suited to this, and they should request another form of report.

39. Susan wants to ensure that the audit report that her organization requested includes input from an external auditor. What type of report should she request?

A. SOC 2, Type 1

B. SOC 3, Type 1

C. SOC 2, Type 2

D. SOC 3, Type 2

40. When Susan requests a SOC2 report, they receive a SAS70 report. What issue should Susan raise?

A. SAS 70 does not include Type 2 reports, so control evaluation is only point in time.

B. SAS 70 has been replaced.

C. SAS 70 is a financial reporting standard and does not cover data centers.

D. SAS 70 only uses a 3-month period for testing.

41. What two logical network topologies can be physically implemented as a star topology?

A. A bus and a mesh

B. A ring and a mesh

C. A bus and a ring

D. It is not possible to implement other topologies as a star.

42. Bell-LaPadula is an example of what type of access control model?

A. DAC

B. RBAC

C. MAC

D. ABAC

43. Martha is the information security officer for a small college and is responsible for safeguarding the privacy of student records. What law most directly applies to her situation?

A. HIPAA

B. HITECH

C. COPPA

D. FERPA

44. What U.S. law mandates the protection of Protected Health Information?

A. FERPA

B. SAFE Act

C. GLBA

D. HIPAA

45. What type of Windows audit record describes events like an OS shutdown or a service being stopped?

A. An application log

B. A security log

C. A system log

D. A setup log

46. Susan is configuring her network devices to use syslog. What should she set to ensure that she is notified about issues but does not receive normal operational issue messages?

   A. The facility code

   B. The log priority

   C. The security level

   D. The severity level

47. What RAID level is also known as disk mirroring?

   A. RAID 0

   B. RAID 1

   C. RAID 3

   D. RAID 5

48. What type of firewall uses multiple proxy servers that filter traffic based on analysis of the protocols used for each service?

   A. A static packet filtering firewall

   B. An application-level gateway firewall

   C. A circuit-level gateway firewall

   D. A stateful inspection firewall

49. Surveys, interviews, and audits are all examples of ways to measure what important part of an organization's security posture?

   A. Code quality

   B. Service vulnerabilities

   C. Awareness

   D. Attack surface

50. Tom is the general counsel for an Internet service provider and he recently received notice of a lawsuit against the firm because of copyrighted content illegally transmitted over the provider's circuits by a customer. What law protects Tom's company in this case?

   A. Computer Fraud and Abuse Act

   B. Digital Millennium Copyright Act

   C. Wiretap Act

   D. Copyright Code

51. A Type 2 authentication factor that generates dynamic passwords based on a time- or algorithm-based system is what type of authenticator?

   A. A PIV

   B. A smart card

   C. A token

   D. A CAC

52. Fred's new employer has hired him for a position with access to their trade secrets and confidential internal data. What legal tool should they use to help protect their data if he chooses to leave to work at a competitor?

A. A stop-loss order

B. An NDA

C. An AUP

D. Encryption

53. Which one of the following computing models allows the execution of multiple processes on a single processor by having the operating system switch between them without requiring modification to the applications?

A. Multitasking

B. Multiprocessing

C. Multiprogramming

D. Multithreading

54. How many possible keys exist when using a cryptographic algorithm that has an 8-bit binary encryption key?

A. 16

B. 128

C. 256

D. 512

55. What activity is being performed when you apply security controls based on the specific needs of the IT system that they will be applied to?

A. Standardizing

B. Baselining

C. Scoping

D. Tailoring

56. During what phase of the electronic discovery process does an organization perform a rough cut of the information gathered to discard irrelevant information?

A. Preservation

B. Identification

C. Collection

D. Processing

57. Ben's job is to ensure that data is labeled with the appropriate sensitivity label. Since Ben works for the US government, he has to apply the labels Unclassified, Confidential, Secret, and Top Secret to systems and media. If Ben is asked to label a system that handles Secret, Confidential, and Unclassified information, how should he label it?

A. Mixed classification

B. Confidential

C. Top Secret

D. Secret

58. Susan has discovered that the smart card-based locks used to keep the facility she works at secure are not effective because staff members are propping the doors open. She places signs on the doors reminding staff that leaving the door open creates a security issue, and adds alarms that will sound if the doors are left open for more than five minutes. What type of controls has she put into place?

A. Physical

B. Administrative

C. Compensation

D. Recovery

59. Ben is concerned about password cracking attacks against his system. He would like to implement controls that prevent an attacker who has obtained those hashes from easily cracking them. What two controls would best meet this objective?

A. Longer passwords and salting

B. Over-the-wire encryption and use of SHA1 instead of MD5

C. Salting and use of MD5

D. Using shadow passwords and salting

60. Which group is best suited to evaluate and report on the effectiveness of administrative controls an organization has put in place to a third party?

A. Internal auditors

B. Penetration testers

C. External auditors

D. Employees who design, implement, and monitor the controls

61. Renee is using encryption to safeguard sensitive business secrets when in transit over the Internet. What risk metric is she attempting to lower?

A. Likelihood

B. RTO

C. MTO

D. Impact

62. As part of hiring a new employee, Kathleen's identity management team creates a new user object and ensures that the user object is available in the directories and systems where it is needed. What is this process called?

A. Registration

B. Provisioning

C. Population

D. Authenticator loading

63. Ricky would like to access a remote file server through a VPN connection. He begins this process by connecting to the VPN and attempting to log in. Applying the subject/object model to this request, what is the subject of Ricky's login attempt?
   A. Ricky
   B. VPN
   C. Remote file server
   D. Files contained on the remote server

64. Alice is designing a cryptosystem for use by six users and would like to use a symmetric encryption algorithm. She wants any two users to be able to communicate with each other without worrying about eavesdropping by a third user. How many symmetric encryption keys will she need to generate?
   A. 6
   B. 12
   C. 15
   D. 30

65. Which one of the following intellectual property protection mechanisms has the shortest duration?
   A. Copyright
   B. Patent
   C. Trademark
   D. Trade secret

66. Gordon is developing a business continuity plan for a manufacturing company's IT operations. The company is located in North Dakota and they are currently evaluating the risk of earthquake. They choose to pursue a risk acceptance strategy. Which one of the following actions is consistent with that strategy?
   A. Purchasing earthquake insurance
   B. Relocating the data center to a safer area
   C. Documenting the decision-making process
   D. Reengineering the facility to withstand the shock of an earthquake

67. Carol would like to implement a control that protects her organization from the momentary loss of power to the data center. Which control is most appropriate for her needs?
   A. Redundant servers
   B. RAID
   C. UPS
   D. Generator

68. Ben has encountered problems with users in his organization reusing passwords, despite a requirement that they change passwords every 30 days. What type of password setting should Ben employ to help prevent this issue?

A. Longer minimum age

B. Increased password complexity

C. Implement password history

D. Implement password length requirements

69. Chris is conducting a risk assessment for his organization and determined the amount of damage that a single flood could be expected to cause to his facilities. What metric has Gordon identified?

A. ALE

B. SLE

C. ARO

D. AV

70. The removal of a hard drive from a PC before it is retired and sold as surplus is an example of what type of action?

A. Purging

B. Sanitization

C. Degaussing

D. Destruction

71. During which phase of the incident response process would an organization determine whether it is required to notify law enforcement officials or other regulators of the incident?

A. Detection

B. Recovery

C. Remediation

D. Reporting

72. What OASIS standard markup language is used to generate provisioning requests both within organizations and with third parties?

A. SAML

B. SPML

C. XACML

D. SOA

73. Which of the following storage mechanisms is not considered secondary storage?

A. Magnetic hard disk

B. Solid state drive

C. DVD
D. RAM

74. Susan's SMTP server does not authenticate senders before accepting and relaying email. What is this security configuration issue known as?
A. An email gateway
B. An SMTP relay
C. An X.400-compliant gateway
D. An open relay

The large business that Jack works for has been using noncentralized logging for years. They have recently started to implement centralized logging, however, and as they reviewed logs they discovered a breach that appeared to have involved a malicious insider. Use this scenario to answer questions 75 through 77 about logging environments.

75. When the breach was discovered and the logs were reviewed, it was discovered that the attacker had purged the logs on the system that they compromised. How can this be prevented in the future?
A. Encrypt local logs
B. Require administrative access to change logs
C. Enable log rotation
D. Send logs to a bastion host

76. How can Jack detect issues like this using his organization's new centralized logging?
A. Deploy and use an IDS
B. Send logs to a central logging server
C. Deploy and use a SIEM
D. Use syslog

77. How can Jack best ensure accountability for actions taken on systems in his environment?
A. Log review and require digital signatures for each log.
B. Require authentication for all actions taken and capture logs centrally.
C. Log the use of administrative credentials and encrypt log data in transit.
D. Require authorization and capture logs centrally.

78. Ed's organization has 5 IP addresses allocated to them by their ISP, but needs to connect over 100 computers and network devices to the Internet. What technology can he use to connect his entire network via the limited set of IP addresses he can use?
A. IPSec
B. PAT
C. SDN
D. IPX

79. What type of attack would the following precautions help prevent?

- Requesting proof of identity
- Requiring callback authorizations on voice-only requests
- Not changing passwords via voice communications

A. DoS attacks
B. Worms
C. Social engineering
D. Shoulder surfing

80. Fred's organization needs to use a non-IP protocol on their VPN. Which of the common VPN protocols should he select to natively handle non-IP protocols?

A. PPTP
B. L2F
C. L2TP
D. IPSec

81. Residual data is another term for what type of data left after attempts have been made to erase it?

A. Leftover data
B. MBR
C. Bitrot
D. Remnant data

82. Which one of the following disaster recovery test types involves the actual activation of the disaster recovery facility?

A. Simulation test
B. Tabletop exercise
C. Parallel test
D. Checklist review

83. What access control system lets owners decide who has access to the objects they own?

A. Role-based access control
B. Task-based access control
C. Discretionary access control
D. Rule-based access control

84. Using a trusted channel and link encryption are both ways to prevent what type of access control attack?

A. Brute force
B. Spoofed login screens

C. Man-in-the-middle attacks

D. Dictionary attacks

85. Which one of the following is not one of the canons of the (ISC)² Code of Ethics?

A. Protect society, the common good, necessary public trust and confidence, and the infrastructure.

B. Act honorably, honestly, justly, responsibly, and legally.

C. Provide diligent and competent service to principals.

D. Maintain competent records of all investigations and assessments.

86. Which one of the following components should be included in an organization's emergency response guidelines?

A. Immediate response procedures

B. Long-term business continuity protocols

C. Activation procedures for the organization's cold sites

D. Contact information for ordering equipment

87. Ben is working on integrating a federated identity management system and needs to exchange authentication and authorization information for browser-based single sign-on. What technology is his best option?

A. HTML

B. XACML

C. SAML

D. SPML

88. What is the minimum interval at which an organization should conduct business continuity plan refresher training for those with specific business continuity roles?

A. Weekly

B. Monthly

C. Semi-annually

D. Annually

89. What is the minimum number of cryptographic keys necessary to achieve strong security when using the 3DES algorithm?

A. 1

B. 2

C. 3

D. 4

90. What type of address is 10.11.45.170?

A. A public IP address

B. An RFC 1918 address

C. An APIPA address

D. A loopback address

91. Lauren wants to monitor her LDAP servers to identify what types of queries are causing problems. What type of monitoring should she use if she wants to be able to use the production servers and actual traffic for her testing?

A. Active

B. Real-time

C. Passive

D. Replay

92. Steve is developing an input validation routine that will protect the database supporting a web application from SQL injection attack. Where should Steve place the input validation code?

A. JavaScript embedded in the web pages

B. Backend code on the web server

C. Stored procedure on the database

D. Code on the user's web browser

93. Ben is selecting an encryption algorithm for use in an organization with 10,000 employees. He must facilitate communication between any two employees within the organization. Which one of the following algorithms would allow him to meet this goal with the least time dedicated to key management?

A. RSA

B. IDEA

C. 3DES

D. Skipjack

94. Grace is considering the use of new identification cards in her organization that will be used for physical access control. She comes across the sample card shown here and is unsure of the technology it uses. What type of card is this?

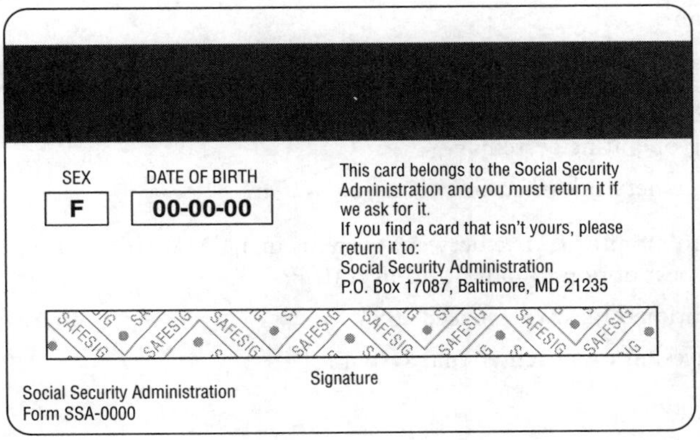

A. Smart card

B. Phase-two card

C. Proximity card

D. Magnetic stripe card

95. What type of log file is shown in this figure?

```
2015-08-09 16:39:01 ALLOW UDP 172.30.0.64 172.30.0.2 62166 53 0 - - - - - - - SEND
2015-08-09 16:39:01 ALLOW UDP 172.30.0.64 172.30.0.2 62167 53 0 - - - - - - - SEND
2015-08-09 16:39:01 ALLOW UDP 172.30.0.64 172.30.0.2 62168 53 0 - - - - - - - SEND
2015-08-09 16:39:01 ALLOW UDP 172.30.0.64 172.30.0.2 62169 53 0 - - - - - - - SEND
2015-08-09 16:39:01 ALLOW UDP 172.30.0.64 172.30.0.2 62170 53 0 - - - - - - - SEND
2015-08-09 16:39:01 ALLOW UDP 172.30.0.64 172.30.0.2 62171 53 0 - - - - - - - SEND
2015-08-09 16:39:01 ALLOW UDP 172.30.0.64 172.30.0.2 62172 53 0 - - - - - - - SEND
2015-08-09 16:39:01 ALLOW UDP 172.30.0.64 172.30.0.2 62173 53 0 - - - - - - - SEND
2015-08-09 16:39:01 ALLOW UDP 172.30.0.64 172.30.0.2 62174 53 0 - - - - - - - SEND
2015-08-09 16:39:01 ALLOW UDP 172.30.0.64 172.30.0.2 62175 53 0 - - - - - - - SEND
2015-08-09 16:39:01 ALLOW UDP 172.30.0.64 172.30.0.2 62176 53 0 - - - - - - - SEND
2015-08-09 16:39:39 ALLOW TCP 54.172.251.189 172.30.0.64 53355 80 0 - 0 0 0 - - - RECEIVE
2015-08-09 16:39:44 ALLOW TCP 54.172.251.189 172.30.0.64 53356 80 0 - 0 0 0 - - - RECEIVE
2015-08-09 16:39:44 ALLOW TCP 127.0.0.1 127.0.0.1 49178 47001 0 - 0 0 0 - - - SEND
2015-08-09 16:39:44 ALLOW TCP 127.0.0.1 127.0.0.1 49178 47001 0 - 0 0 0 - - - RECEIVE
2015-08-09 16:39:47 ALLOW TCP 172.30.0.64 169.254.169.254 49179 80 0 - 0 0 0 - - - SEND
2015-08-09 16:40:37 ALLOW TCP 54.172.251.189 172.30.0.64 53362 80 0 - 0 0 0 - - - RECEIVE
2015-08-09 16:40:47 ALLOW TCP 172.30.0.64 169.254.169.254 49180 80 0 - 0 0 0 - - - SEND
2015-08-09 16:40:55 ALLOW UDP fe80::11ef:7f4f:afb5:7f70 ff02::1:2 546 547 0 - - - - - - - SEND
```

A. Application

B. Web server

C. System

D. Firewall

96. Which one of the following activities transforms a zero-day vulnerability into a less dangerous attack vector?

A. Discovery of the vulnerability

B. Implementation of transport-layer encryption

C. Reconfiguration of a firewall

D. Release of a security patch

97. Which one of the following is an example of a hardening provision that might strengthen an organization's existing physical facilities and avoid implementation of a business continuity plan?

A. Patching a leaky roof

B. Reviewing and updating firewall access control lists

C. Upgrading operating systems

D. Deploying a network intrusion detection system

98. Susan wants to monitor traffic between systems in a VMWare environment. What solution would be her best option to monitor that traffic?

A. Use a traditional hardware-based IPS.

B. Install Wireshark on each virtual system.

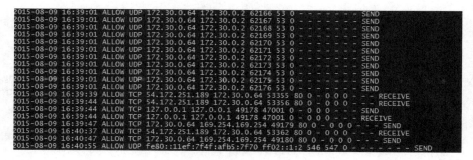

C. Set up a virtual span port and capture data using a VM IDS.

D. Use netcat to capture all traffic sent between VMs.

Questions 99–102 refer to the following scenario.

Matthew and Richard are friends located in different physical locations who would like to begin communicating with each other using cryptography to protect the confidentiality of their communications. They exchange digital certificates to begin this process and plan to use an asymmetric encryption algorithm for the secure exchange of email messages.

99. When Matthew sends Richard a message, what key should he use to encrypt the message?

A. Matthew's public key

B. Matthew's private key

C. Richard's public key

D. Richard's private key

100. When Richard receives the message from Matthew, what key should he use to decrypt the message?

A. Matthew's public key

B. Matthew's private key

C. Richard's public key

D. Richard's private key

101. Matthew would like to enhance the security of his communication by adding a digital signature to the message. What goal of cryptography are digital signatures intended to enforce?

A. Secrecy

B. Availability

C. Confidentiality

D. Nonrepudiation

102. When Matthew goes to add the digital signature to the message, what encryption key does he use to create the digital signature?

A. Matthew's public key

B. Matthew's private key

C. Richard's public key

D. Richard's private key

103. When Jim logs into a system, his password is compared to a hashed value stored in a database. What is this process?

A. Identification

B. Hashing

C. Tokenization

D. Authentication

104. What is the primary advantage of decentralized access control?

A. It provides better redundancy.

B. It provides control of access to people closer to the resources.

C. It is less expensive.

D. It provides more granular control of access.

105. Which of the following types of controls does not describe a mantrap?

A. Deterrent

B. Preventive

C. Compensating

D. Physical

106. Sally's organization needs to be able to prove that certain staff members sent emails, and she wants to adopt a technology that will provide that capability without changing their existing email system. What is the technical term for the capability Sally needs to implement as the owner of the email system, and what tool could she use to do it?

A. Integrity; IMAP

B. Repudiation; encryption

C. Nonrepudiation; digital signatures

D. Authentication; DKIM

107. Which one of the following background checks is not normally performed during normal pre-hire activities?

A. Credit check

B. Reference verification

C. Criminal records check

D. Medical records check

108. Margot is investigating suspicious activity on her network and uses a protocol analyzer to sniff inbound and outbound traffic. She notices an unusual packet that has identical source and destination IP addresses. What type of attack uses this packet type?

A. Fraggle

B. Smurf

C. Land

D. Teardrop

109. Jim wants to perform an audit that will generate an industry recognized report on the design and suitability of his organization's controls as they stand at the time of the report. If this is his only goal, what type of report should he provide?

A. An SSAE-16 Type I

B. An SAS70 Type I

C. An SSAE-16 Type II

D. An SAS-70 Type II

110. In the OSI model, when a packet changes from a datastream to a segment or a datagram, what layer has it traversed?

A. The Transport layer

B. The Application layer

C. The Data Link layer

D. The Physical layer

111. Tommy handles access control requests for his organization. A user approaches him and explains that he needs access to the human resources database in order to complete a headcount analysis requested by the CFO. What has the user demonstrated successfully to Tommy?

A. Clearance

B. Separation of duties

C. Need to know

D. Isolation

112. Kathleen wants to set up a service to provide information about her organization's users and services using a central, open, vendor-neutral, standards-based system that can be easily queried. Which of the following technologies is her best choice?

A. RADIUS

B. LDAP

C. Kerberos

D. Active Directory

113. What type of firewall is capable of inspecting traffic at layer 7 and performing protocol-specific analysis for malicious traffic?

A. Application firewall

B. Stateful inspection firewall

C. Packet filtering firewall

D. Bastion host

114. Alice would like to add another object to a security model and grant herself rights to that object. Which one of the rules in the Take-Grant protection model would allow her to complete this operation?

A. Take rule

B. Grant rule

C. Create rule

D. Remove rule

115. Which of the following concerns should not be on Lauren's list of potential issues when penetration testers suggest using Metasploit during their testing?

A. Metasploit can only test vulnerabilities it has plug-ins for.

B. Penetration testing only covers a point-in-time view of the organization's security.

C. Tools like Metasploit can cause denial-of-service issues.

D. Penetration testing cannot test process and policy.

116. Colin is reviewing a system that has been assigned the EAL7 evaluation assurance level under the Common Criteria. What is the highest level of assurance that he may have about the system?

A. It has been functionally tested.

B. It has been methodically tested and checked.

C. It has been methodically designed, tested, and reviewed.

D. It has been formally verified, designed, and tested.

117. Which ITU-T standard should Alex expect to see in use when he uses his smart card to provide a certificate to an upstream authentication service?

A. X.500

B. SPML

C. X.509

D. SAML

118. What type of websites are regulated under the terms of COPPA?

A. Financial websites not run by financial institutions

B. Healthcare websites that collect personal information

C. Websites that collect information from children

D. Financial websites run by financial institutions

119. Tracy recently accepted an IT compliance position at a federal government agency that works very closely with the Defense Department on classified government matters. Which one of the following laws is least likely to pertain to Tracy's agency?

A. HIPAA

B. FISMA

C. HSA

D. CFAA

120. Referring to the figure shown here, what is the name of the security control indicated by the arrow?

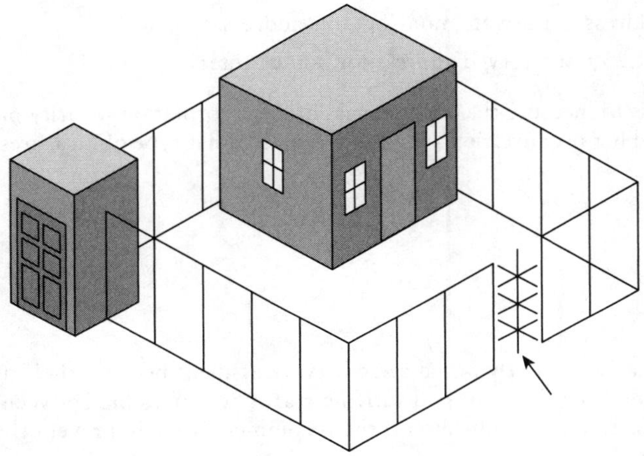

A. Mantrap

B. Intrusion prevention system

C. Turnstile

D. Portal

121. What two important factors does accountability for access control rely on?

A. Identification and authorization

B. Authentication and authorization

C. Identification and authentication

D. Accountability and authentication

122. What key assumption made by EAP can be remedied by using PEAP?

A. EAP assumes that LEAP will replace TKIP, ensuring authentication will occur.

B. EAP originally assumed the use of physically isolated channels and is usually not encrypted.

C. There are no TLS implementations available using EAP.

D. EAP does not allow additional authentication methods, and PEAP adds additional methods.

123. Scott's organization has configured their external IP address to be 192.168.1.25. When traffic is sent to their ISP, it never reaches its destination. What problem is Scott's organization encountering?

A. BGP is not set up properly.

B. They have not registered their IP with their ISP.

C. The IP address is a private, non-routable address.

D. 192.168.1.25 is a reserved address for home routers.

124. Jennifer needs to measure the effectiveness of her information security program as she works toward her organization's long-term goals. What type of measures should she select?

A. Metrics

B. KPIs

C. SLAs

D. OKRs

125. Sue's organization recently failed a security assessment because their network was a single flat broadcast domain, and sniffing traffic was possible between different functional groups. What solution should she recommend to help prevent the issues that were identified?

A. Use VLANs.

B. Change the subnet mask for all systems.

C. Deploy gateways.

D. Turn on port security.

126. Susan is setting up the network for a local coffee house and wants to ensure that users have to authenticate using an email address and agree to the coffee house's acceptable use policy before being allowed on the network. What technology should she use to do this?

A. 802.11

B. NAC

C. A captive portal

D. A wireless gateway

127. What is another term for active monitoring?

A. Synthetic

B. Passive

C. Reactive

D. Span-based

128. The TCP header is made up of elements such as the source port, destination port, sequence number, and others. How many bytes long is the TCP header?

A. 8 bytes

B. 20–60 bytes

C. 64 bytes

D. 64–128 bytes

The company that Fred works for is reviewing the security of their company issued cell phones. They issue 4G capable smartphones running Android and iOS, and use a mobile device management solution to deploy company software to the phones. The mobile device management software also allows the company to remotely wipe the phones if they are lost. Use this information, as well as your knowledge of cellular technology, to answer questions 129–131.

129. What security considerations should Fred's company require for sending sensitive data over the cellular network?

A. They should use the same requirements as data over any public network.

B. Cellular provider networks are private networks and should not require special consideration.

C. Encrypt all traffic to ensure confidentiality.

D. Require the use of WAP for all data sent from the phone.

130. Fred intends to attend a major hacker conference this year. What should he do when connecting to his cellular provider's 4G network while at the conference?

A. Continue normal usage.

B. Discontinue all usage; towers can be spoofed.

C. Only use trusted Wi-Fi networks.

D. Connect to his company's encrypted VPN service.

131. What are the most likely circumstances that would cause a remote wipe of a mobile phone to fail?

A. The phone has a passcode on it.

B. The phone cannot contact a network.

C. The provider has not unlocked the phone.

D. The phone is in use.

132. Elaine is developing a business continuity plan for her organization. What value should she seek to minimize?

A. AV

B. SSL

C. RTO

D. MTO

133. NIST Special Publication 800-53, revision 4, describes two measures of assurance. Which measure of developmental assurance is best described as measuring "the rigor, level of detail, and formality of the artifacts produced during the design and development of the hardware, software, and firmware components of information systems (e.g., functional specifications, high-level design, low-level design, source code)"?

A. Coverage

B. Suitability

C. Affirmation

D. Depth

134. Which one of the following disaster recovery test types does not involve the actual use of any technical disaster recovery controls?

A. Simulation test

B. Parallel test

C. Structured walk-through

D. Full interruption test

135. Chris is experiencing issues with the quality of network service on his organization's network. The primary symptom is that packets are becoming corrupted as they travel from their source to their destination. What term describes the issue Chris is facing?

A. Latency

B. Jitter

C. Interference

D. Packet loss

136. Kathleen has been asked to choose a highly formalized code review process for her software quality assurance team to use. Which of the following software testing processes is the most rigorous and formal?

A. Fagan

B. Fuzzing

C. Over the shoulder

D. Pair programming

137. Frank is attempting to protect his web application against cross-site scripting attacks. Users do not need to provide input containing scripts, so he decided the most effective way to filter would be to write a filter on the server that watches for the `<SCRIPT>` tag and removes it. What is the issue with Frank's approach?

A. Validation should always be performed on the client side.

B. Attackers may use XSS filter evasion techniques against this approach.

C. Server-side validation requires removing all HTML tags, not just the `<SCRIPT>` tag.

D. There is no problem with Frank's approach.

138. Which one of the following is not an object-oriented programming language?

A. C++

B. Java

C. Fortran

D. C#

139. Uptown Records Management recently entered into a contract with a hospital for the secure storage of medical records. The hospital is a HIPAA-covered entity. What type of agreement must the two organizations sign to remain compliant with HIPAA?

A. NDA

B. NCA

C. BAA

D. SLA

140. Norm would like to conduct a disaster recovery test for his organization and wants to choose the most thorough type of test, recognizing that it may be quite disruptive. What type of test should Norm choose?

A. Full interruption test

B. Parallel test

C. Tabletop exercise

D. Checklist review

141. Ed is building a network that supports IPv6 but needs to connect it to an IPv4 network. What type of device should Ed place between the networks?

A. A switch

B. A router

C. A bridge

D. A gateway

142. What encryption standard won the competition for certification as the Advanced Encryption Standard?

A. Blowfish

B. Twofish

C. Rijndael

D. Skipjack

143. Which law can be summarized through these seven key principles: notice, choice, onward transfer, security, data integrity, access, enforcement?

A. COPA

B. NY SAFE Act

C. The EU Data Protection Directive

D. FISMA

144. Which one of the following actions is not required under the EU Data Protection Directive?

A. Organizations must allow individuals to opt out of information sharing.

B. Organizations must provide individuals with lists of employees with access to information.

C. Organizations must use proper mechanisms to protect data against unauthorized disclosure.

D. Organizations must have a dispute resolution process for privacy issues.

145. Tammy is selecting a disaster recovery facility for her organization. She would like to choose a facility that balances the time required to recover operations with the cost involved. What type of facility should she choose?

A. Hot site

B. Warm site

C. Cold site

D. Red site

146. What layer of the OSI model is associated with datagrams?

A. Session

B. Transport

C. Network

D. Data Link

147. Which one of the following is not a valid key length for the Advanced Encryption Standard?

A. 128 bits

B. 192 bits

C. 256 bits

D. 384 bits

148. Which one of the following technologies provides a function interface that allows developers to directly interact with systems without knowing the implementation details of that system?

A. Data dictionary

B. Object model

C. Source code

D. API

149. What email encryption technique is illustrated in this figure?

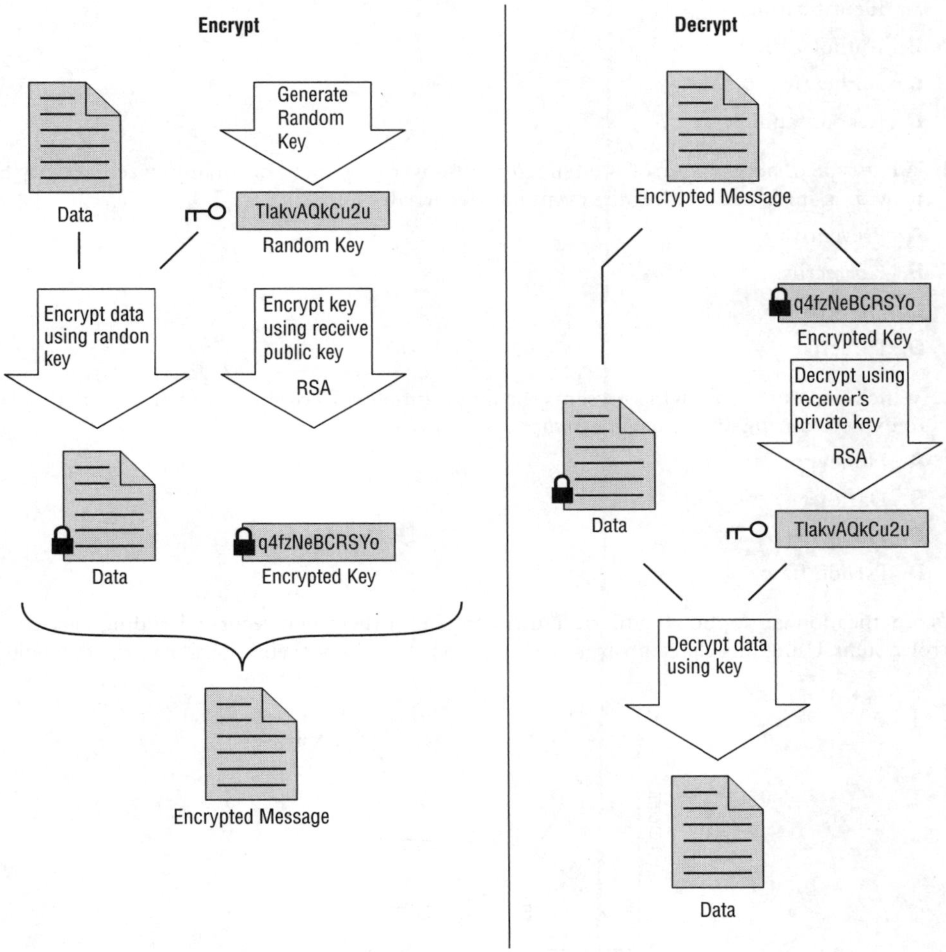

A. MD5

B. Thunderbird

C. S/MIME

D. PGP

150. When Ben lists the files on a Linux system, he sees a set of attributes as shown in the following image.

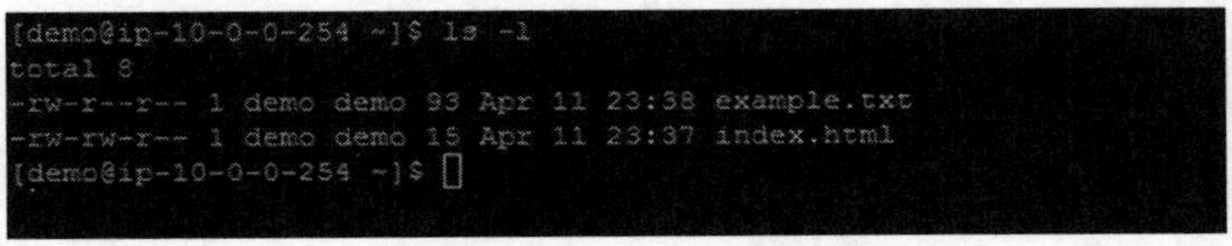

[demo@ip-10-0-0-254 ~]$ ls -l
total 8
-rw-r--r-- 1 demo demo 93 Apr 11 23:38 example.txt
-rw-rw-r-- 1 demo demo 15 Apr 11 23:37 index.html
[demo@ip-10-0-0-254 ~]$

This letters rwx indicate different levels of what?

- **A.** Identification
- **B.** Authorization
- **C.** Authentication
- **D.** Accountability

151. What type of access control is intended to discover unwanted or unauthorized activity by providing information after the event has occurred?

- **A.** Preventive
- **B.** Corrective
- **C.** Detective
- **D.** Directive

152. Which one of the following presents the most complex decoy environment for an attacker to explore during an intrusion attempt?

- **A.** Honeypot
- **B.** Darknet
- **C.** Honeynet
- **D.** Pseudo flaw

Ben's organization is adopting biometric authentication for their high-security building's access control system. Using this chart, answer questions 153–155 about their adoption of the technology.

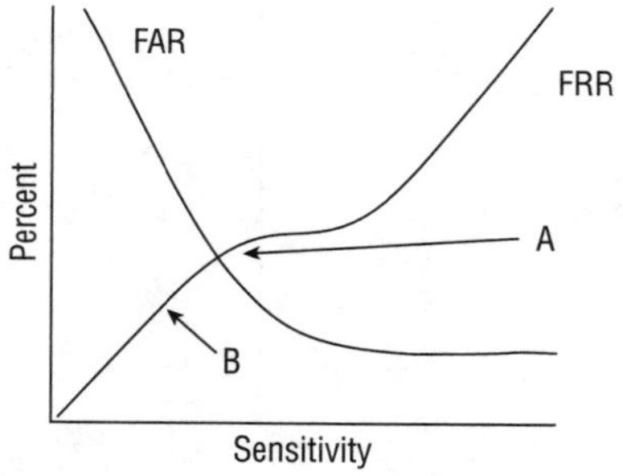

153. Ben's company is considering configuring their systems to work at the level shown by point A on the diagram. What level are they setting the sensitivity to?

- **A.** The FRR crossover
- **B.** The FAR point
- **C.** The CER
- **D.** The CFR

154. At point B, what problem is likely to occur?

- **A.** False acceptance will be very high.
- **B.** False rejection will be very high.

C. False rejection will be very low.

D. False acceptance will be very low.

155. What should Ben do if the FAR and FRR shown in this diagram does not provide an acceptable performance level for his organization's needs?

A. Adjust the sensitivity of the biometric devices.

B. Assess other biometric systems to compare them.

C. Move the CER.

D. Adjust the FRR settings in software.

156. Ed is tasked with protecting information about his organization's customers, including their name, Social Security number, birthdate and place of birth, as well as a variety of other information. What is this information known as?

A. PHI

B. PII

C. Personal Protected Data

D. PID

157. What software development life-cycle model is shown in the following illustration?

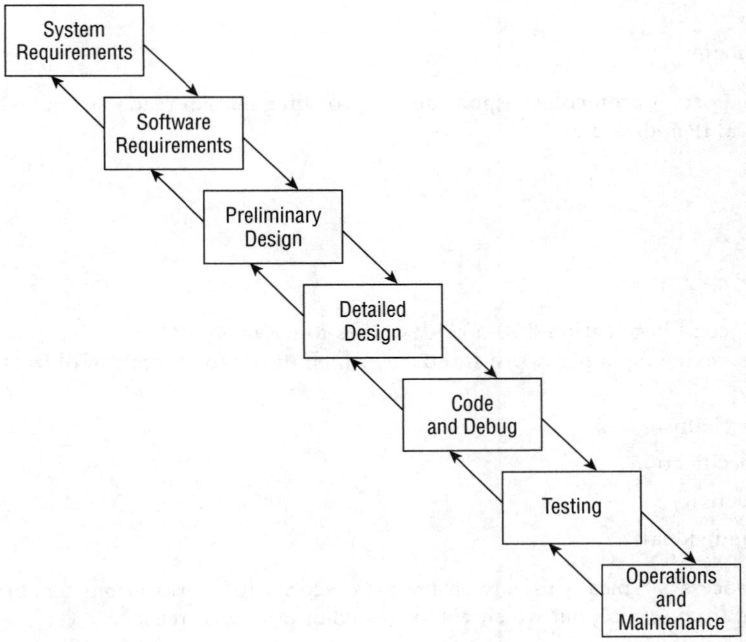

A. Spiral

B. Agile

C. Boehm

D. Waterfall

158. Encapsulation is the core concept that enables what type of protocol?

A. Bridging

B. Multilayer

C. Hashing

D. Storage

159. Which one of the following is not a key principle of the COBIT framework for IT security control objectives?

A. Meeting stakeholder needs

B. Performing exhaustive analysis

C. Covering the enterprise end-to-end

D. Separating governance from management

160. Roscommon Enterprises is an Irish company that handles personal information. They exchange information with many other countries. Which of the following countries would trigger the onward transfer provisions of the International Safe Harbor Privacy Principles?

A. United States

B. United Kingdom

C. Italy

D. Germany

161. What important protocol is responsible for providing human-readable addresses instead of numerical IP addresses?

A. TCP

B. IP

C. DNS

D. ARP

162. NIST Special Publication 800-53A describes four types of objects that can be assessed. If Ben is reviewing a password standard, which of the four types of objects is he assessing?

A. A mechanism

B. A specification

C. An activity

D. An individual

163. What process is typically used to ensure data security for workstations that are being removed from service, but which will be resold or otherwise reused?

A. Destruction

B. Erasing

C. Sanitization

D. Clearing

164. Colleen is conducting a software test that is evaluating code for both security flaws and usability issues. She is working with the application from an end-user perspective and referencing the source code as she works her way through the product. What type of testing is Colleen conducting?

A. White box

B. Blue box

C. Gray box

D. Black box

165. Harold is looking for a software development methodology that will help with a major issue he is seeing in his organization. Currently, developers and operations staff do not work together and are often seen as taking problems and "throwing them over the fence" to the other team. What technology management approach is designed to alleviate this problem?

A. ITIL

B. Lean

C. ITSM

D. DevOps

166. NIST Special Publication 800-92, the Guide to Computer Security Log Management, describes four types of common challenges to log management:

- Many log sources
- Inconsistent log content
- Inconsistent timestamps
- Inconsistent log formats

Which of the following solutions is best suited to solving these issues?

A. Implement SNMP for all logging devices.

B. Implement a SIEM.

C. Standardize on the Windows event log format for all devices and use NTP.

D. Ensure logging is enabled on all endpoints using their native logging formats and set their local time correctly.

167. Mike has a flash memory card that he would like to reuse. The card contains sensitive information. What technique can he use to securely remove data from the card and allow its reuse?

A. Degaussing

B. Physical destruction

C. Overwriting

D. Reformatting

168. Carlos is investigating the compromise of sensitive information in his organization. He believes that attackers managed to retrieve personnel information on all employees from the database and finds the following user-supplied input in a log entry for a web-based personnel management system:

```
Collins'&1=1;--
```

What type of attack took place?

A. SQL injection

B. Buffer overflow

C. Cross-site scripting

D. Cross-site request forgery

169. Which one of the following is a detailed, step-by-step document that describes the exact actions that individuals must complete?

A. Policy

B. Standard

C. Guideline

D. Procedure

170. What principle of relational databases ensures the permanency of transactions that have successfully completed?

A. Atomicity

B. Consistency

C. Isolation

D. Durability

171. Bryan has a set of sensitive documents that he would like to protect from public disclosure. He would like to use a control that, if the documents appear in a public forum, may be used to trace the leak back to the person who was originally given the document copy. What security control would best fulfill this purpose?

A. Digital signature

B. Document staining

C. Hashing

D. Watermarking

172. Carlos is planning a design for a data center that will be constructed within a new four-story corporate headquarters. The building consists of a basement and three above-ground floors. What is the best location for the data center?

A. Basement

B. First floor

C. Second floor

D. Third floor

173. Chris is an information security professional for a major corporation and, as he is walking into the building, he notices that the door to a secure area has been left ajar. Physical security does not fall under his responsibility, but he takes immediate action by closing the door and informing the physical security team of his action. What principle is Chris demonstrating?

A. Due care

B. Due diligence

C. Separation of duties

D. Informed consent

174. Which one of the following investigation types always uses the beyond a reasonable doubt standard of proof?

A. Civil investigation

B. Criminal investigation

C. Operational investigation

D. Regulatory investigation

175. Which one of the following backup types does not alter the status of the archive bit on a file?

A. Full backup

B. Incremental backup

C. Partial backup

D. Differential backup

176. What type of alternate processing facility contains the hardware necessary to restore operations but does not have a current copy of data?

A. Hot site

B. Warm site

C. Cold site

D. Mobile site

177. Which one of the following terms describes a period of momentary high voltage?

A. Sag

B. Brownout

C. Spike

D. Surge

178. A web application accesses information in a database to retrieve user information. What is the web application acting as?

A. A subject

B. An object

C. A user

D. A token

179. The Open Shortest Path First (OSPF) protocol is a routing protocol that keeps a map of all connected remote networks and uses that map to select the shortest path to a remote destination. What type of routing protocol is OSPF?

A. Link state

B. Shortest path first

C. Link mapping

D. Distance vector

180. Which one of the following categories consists of first-generation programming languages?

A. Machine languages

B. Assembly languages

C. Compiled languages

D. Natural language

Questions 181–185 refer to the following scenario.

Concho Controls is a mid-sized business focusing on building automation systems. They host a set of local file servers in their on-premises data center that store customer proposals, building plans, product information, and other data that is critical to their business operations.

Tara works in the Concho Controls IT department and is responsible for designing and implementing the organization's backup strategy, among other tasks. She currently conducts full backups every Sunday evening at 8 p.m. and differential backups on Monday through Friday at noon.

Concho experiences a server failure at 3 p.m. on Wednesday. Tara rebuilds the server and wants to restore data from the backups.

181. What backup should Tara apply to the server first?

A. Sunday's full backup

B. Monday's differential backup

C. Tuesday's differential backup

D. Wednesday's differential backup

182. How many backups in total must Tara apply to the system to make the data it contains as current as possible?

A. 1

B. 2

C. 3

D. 4

183. In this backup approach, some data may be irretrievably lost. How long is the time period where any changes made will have been lost?

A. 3 hours

B. 5 hours

C. 8 hours

D. No data will be lost.

184. If Tara followed the same schedule but switched the differential backups to incremental backups, how many backups in total would she need to apply to the system to make the data it contains as current as possible?

A. 1

B. 2

C. 3

D. 4

185. If Tara made the change from differential to incremental backups and we assume that the same amount of information changes each day, which one of the following files would be the largest?

A. Monday's incremental backup

B. Tuesday's incremental backup

C. Wednesday's incremental backup

D. All three will be the same size.

186. Susan is conducting a STRIDE threat assessment by placing threats into one or more of the following categories: Spoofing, Tampering, Repudiation, Information Disclosure, Denial of Service, and Elevation of Privilege. As part of her assessment, she has discovered an issue that allows transactions to be modified between a web browser and the application server that it accesses. What STRIDE categorization(s) best fit this issue?

A. Tampering and Information Disclosure

B. Spoofing and Tampering

C. Tampering and Repudiation

D. Information Disclosure and Elevation of Privilege

187. Bob has been tasked with writing a policy that describes how long data should be kept and when it should be purged. What concept does this policy deal with?

A. Data remanence

B. Record retention

C. Data redaction

D. Audit logging

188. Which component of IPSec provides authentication, integrity, and nonrepudiation?

A. L2TP

B. Encapsulating Security Payload

C. Encryption Security Header

D. Authentication Header

189. Renee notices that a system on her network recently received connection attempts on all 65,536 TCP ports from a single system during a short period of time. What type of attack did Renee most likely experience?

A. Denial of service

B. Reconnaissance

C. Malicious insider

D. Compromise

190. Which one of the following techniques can an attacker use to exploit a TOC/TOU vulnerability?

A. File locking

B. Exception handling

C. Algorithmic complexity

D. Concurrency control

191. In the ring protection model shown here, what ring does not run in privileged mode?

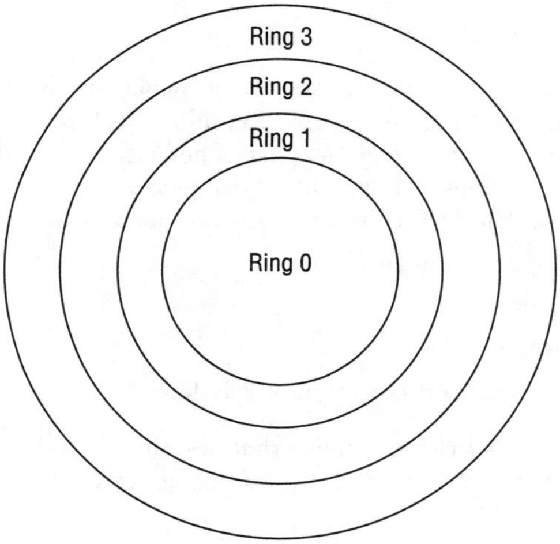

A. Ring 0

B. Ring 1

C. Ring 2

D. Ring 3

192. What level of RAID is also known as disk striping?

A. RAID 0

B. RAID 1

C. RAID 5

D. RAID 10

193. Jacob executes an attack against a system using a valid but low privilege user account by accessing a file pointer that the account has access to. After the access check, but before the file is opened, he quickly switches the file pointer to point to a file that the user account does not have access to. What type of attack is this?

A. TOC/TOU

B. Permissions creep

C. Impersonation

D. Link swap

194. What is the minimum number of disks required to implement RAID level 0?

A. 1

B. 2

C. 3

D. 5

195. Fred's company wants to ensure the integrity of email messages sent via their central email servers. If the confidentiality of the messages is not critical, what solution should Fred suggest?

A. Digitally sign and encrypt all messages to ensure integrity.

B. Digitally sign but don't encrypt all messages.

C. Use TLS to protect messages, ensuring their integrity.

D. Use a hashing algorithm to provide a hash in each message to prove that it hasn't changed.

196. The leadership at Susan's company has asked her to implement an access control system that can support rule declarations like "Only allow access to salespeople from managed devices on the wireless network between 8 a.m. and 6 p.m." What type of access control system would be Susan's best choice?

A. ABAC

B. RBAC

C. DAC

D. MAC

197. What type of communications rely on a timing mechanism using either an independent clock or a time stamp embedded in the communications?

A. Analog

B. Digital

C. Synchronous

D. Asynchronous

198. Chris is deploying a gigabit Ethernet network using Category 6 cable between two buildings. What is the maximum distance he can run the cable according to the Category 6 standard?

A. 50 meters

B. 100 meters

C. 200 meters

D. 300 meters

199. Howard is a security analyst working with an experienced computer forensics investigator. The investigator asks him to retrieve a forensic drive controller, but Howard cannot locate a device in the storage room with this name. What is another name for a forensic drive controller?

A. RAID controller

B. Write blocker

C. SCSI terminator

D. Forensic device analyzer

200. The web application that Saria's development team is working on needs to provide secure session management that can prevent hijacking of sessions using the cookies that the application relies on. Which of the following techniques would be the best for her to recommend to prevent this?

A. Set the Secure attribute for the cookies, thus forcing TLS.

B. Set the Domain cookie attribute to example.com to limit cookie access to servers in the same domain.

C. Set the Expires cookie attribute to less than a week.

D. Set the HTTPOnly attribute to require only unencrypted sessions.

201. Ben's company has recently retired their fleet of multifunction printers. Their information security team has expressed concerns that the printers contain hard drives and that they may still have data from scans and print jobs. What is the technical term for this issue?

A. Data pooling

B. Failed clearing

C. Data permanence

D. Data remanence

202. What access control scheme labels subjects and objects, and allows subjects to access objects when the labels match?

A. DAC

B. MAC

C. Rule BAC

D. Role BAC

203. A cloud-based service that provides account provisioning, management, authentication, authorization, reporting, and monitoring capabilities is known as what type of service?

A. PaaS

B. IDaaS

C. IaaS

D. SaaS

204. Sally wants to secure her organization's VOIP systems. Which of the following attacks is one that she shouldn't have to worry about?

A. Eavesdropping

B. Denial of service

C. Blackboxing

D. Caller ID spoofing

205. Marty discovers that the access restrictions in his organization allow any user to log into the workstation assigned to any other user, even if they are from completely different departments. This type of access most directly violates which information security principle?

A. Separation of duties

B. Two-person control

C. Need to know

D. Least privilege

206. Fred needs to transfer files between two servers on an untrusted network. Since he knows the network isn't trusted, he needs to select an encrypted protocol that can ensure his data remains secure. What protocol should he choose?

A. SSH

B. TCP

C. SFTP

D. IPSec

207. Chris uses a packet sniffer to capture traffic from a TACACS+ server. What protocol should he monitor, and what data should he expect to be readable?

A. UDP; none—TACACS+ encrypts the full session

B. TCP; none—TACACS+ encrypts the full session

C. UDP; all but the username and password, which are encrypted

D. TCP; all but the username and password, which are encrypted

Use your knowledge of Kerberos authentication and authorization as well as the following diagram to answer questions 208–210.

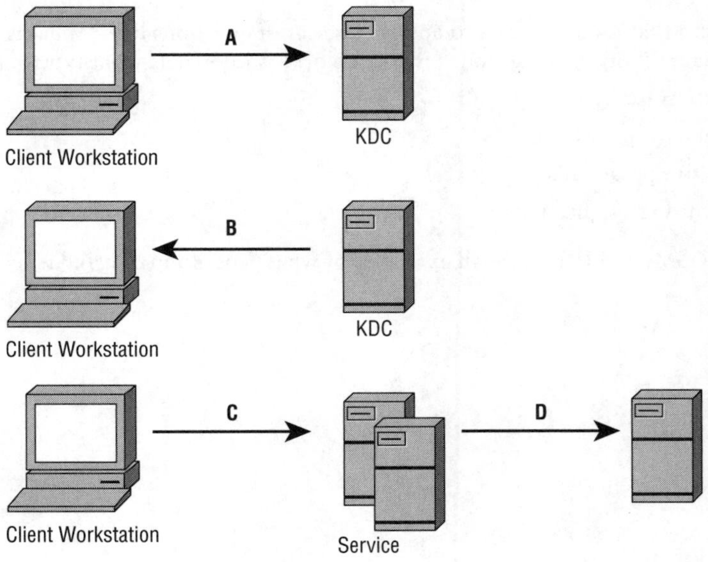

208. If the client has already authenticated to the KDC, what does the client workstation send to the KDC at point A when it wants to access a resource?

A. It re-sends the password.

B. A TGR

C. Its TGT

D. A service ticket

209. What occurs between steps A and B?

A. The KDC verifies the validity of the TGT and whether the user has the right privileges for the requested resource.

B. The KDC updates its access control list based on the data in the TGT.

C. The KDC checks its service listing and prepares an updated TGT based on the service request.

D. The KDC generates a service ticket to issue to the client.

210. What system or systems does the service that is being accessed use to validate the ticket?

A. The KDC

B. The client workstation and the KDC

C. The client workstation supplies it in the form of a client-to-server ticket and an authenticator.

D. The KVS

211. What does a service ticket (ST) provide in Kerberos authentication?

A. It serves as the authentication host.

B. It provides proof that the subject is authorized to access an object.

C. It provides proof that a subject has authenticated through a KDC and can request tickets to access other objects.

D. It provides ticket granting services.

212. A password that requires users to answer a series of questions like "What is your mother's maiden name?" or "What is your favorite color?" is known as what type of password?

A. A passphrase

B. Multifactor passwords

C. Cognitive passwords

D. Password reset questions

213. CDMA, GSM, and IDEN are all examples of what generation of cellular technology?

A. 1G

B. 2G

C. 3G

D. 4G

214. Which one of the following fire suppression systems poses the greatest risk of accidental discharge that damages equipment in a data center?

A. Closed head

B. Dry pipe

C. Deluge

D. Preaction

215. Lauren's healthcare provider maintains such data as details about her health, treatments, and medical billing. What type of data is this?

A. Protected Health Information

B. Personally Identifiable Information

C. Protected Health Insurance

D. Individual Protected Data

216. What type of code review is best suited to identifying business logic flaws?

A. Mutational fuzzing

B. Manual

C. Generational fuzzing

D. Interface testing

217. Something you know is an example of what type of authentication factor?

A. Type 1

B. Type 2

C. Type 3

D. Type 4

218. Saria is the system owner for a healthcare organization. What responsibilities does she have related to the data that resides on or is processed by the systems she owns?

A. She has to classify the data.

B. She has to make sure that appropriate security controls are in place to protect the data.

C. She has to grant appropriate access to personnel.

D. She bears sole responsibility for ensuring that data is protected at rest, in transit, and in use.

219. During software testing, Jack diagrams how a hacker might approach the application he is reviewing and determines what requirements the hacker might have. He then tests how the system would respond to the attacker's likely behavior. What type of testing is Jack conducting?

A. Misuse case testing

B. Use case testing

C. Hacker use case testing

D. Static code analysis

220. When a vendor develops a product that they wish to submit for Common Criteria evaluation, what do they complete to describe the claims of security for their product?

A. PP

B. ITSEC

C. TCSEC

D. ST

221. Chris has been assigned to scan a system on all of its possible TCP and UDP ports. How many ports of each type must he scan to complete his assignment?

A. 65,536 TCP ports and 32,768 UDP ports

B. 1024 common TCP ports and 32,768 ephemeral UDP ports

C. 65,536 TCP and 65,536 UDP ports

D. 16,384 TCP ports, and 16,384 UDP ports

222. CVE and the NVD both provide information about what?

A. Vulnerabilities

B. Markup languages

C. Vulnerability assessment tools

D. Penetration testing methodologies

223. What is the highest level of the military classification scheme?

A. Secret

B. Confidential

C. SBU

D. Top Secret

224. In what type of trusted recovery process does the system recover against one or more failure types without administrator intervention while protecting itself against data loss?

A. Automated recovery

B. Manual recovery

C. Function recovery

D. Automated recovery without undue data loss

225. What three important items should be considered if you are attempting to control the strength of signal for a wireless network as well as where it is accessible?

A. Antenna placement, antenna type, and antenna power levels

B. Antenna design, power levels, use of a captive portal

C. Antenna placement, antenna design, use of a captive portal

D. Power levels, antenna placement, FCC minimum strength requirements

226. What is the best way to ensure that data is unrecoverable from a SSD?

A. Use the built-in erase commands

B. Use a random pattern wipe of 1s and 0s

C. Physically destroy the drive

D. Degauss the drive

227. Alice sends a message to Bob and wants to ensure that Mal, a third party, does not read the contents of the message while in transit. What goal of cryptography is Alice attempting to achieve?

A. Confidentiality

B. Integrity

C. Authentication

D. Nonrepudiation

228. Which one of the following metrics specifies the amount of time that business continuity planners believe it will take to restore a service when it goes down?

A. MTD

B. RTO

C. RPO

D. MTO

229. Gary would like to examine the text of a criminal law on computer fraud to determine whether it applies to a recent act of hacking against his company. Where should he go to read the text of the law?

A. Code of Federal Regulations

B. Supreme Court rulings

C. Compendium of Laws

D. United States Code

230. James has opted to implement an NAC solution that uses a post-admission philosophy for its control of network connectivity. What type of issues can't a strictly post-admission policy handle?

A. Out-of-band monitoring

B. Preventing an unpatched laptop from being exploited immediately after connecting to the network

C. Denying access when user behavior doesn't match an authorization matrix

D. Allowing user access when user behavior is allowed based on an authorization matrix

231. Ben has built an access control list that lists the objects that his users are allowed to access. When users attempt to access an object that they don't have rights to, they are denied access, even though there isn't a specific rule that allows it. What access control principle is key to this behavior?

A. Least privilege

B. Implicit deny

C. Explicit deny

D. Final rule fall-through

232. Mary is a security risk analyst for an insurance company. She is currently examining a scenario where a hacker might use a SQL injection attack to deface a web server due to a missing patch in the company's web application. In this scenario, what is the risk?

A. Unpatched web application

B. Web defacement

C. Hacker

D. Operating system

233. In the diagram shown here of security boundaries within a computer system, what component's name has been replaced with XXX?

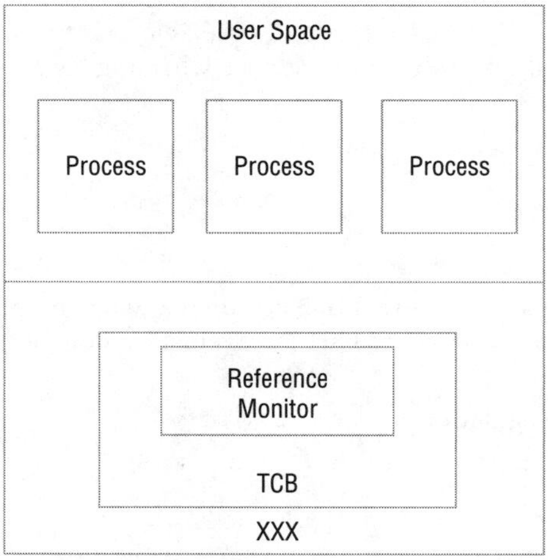

A. Kernel

B. Privileged core

C. User monitor

D. Security perimeter

234. Val is attempting to review security logs but is overwhelmed by the sheer volume of records maintained in her organization's central log repository. What technique can she use to select a representative set of records for further review?

A. Statistical sampling

B. Clipping

C. Choose the first 5% of records from each day.

D. Choose 5% of records from the middle of the day.

235. In Jen's job as the network administrator for an industrial production facility, she is tasked with ensuring that the network is not susceptible to electromagnetic interference due to the large motors and other devices running on the production floor. What type of network cabling should she choose if this concern is more important than cost and difficulty of installation?

A. 10Base2

B. 100BaseT

C. 1000BaseT

D. Fiber-optic

Questions 236–239 refer to the following scenario.

Jasper Diamonds is a jewelry manufacturer that markets and sells custom jewelry through their website. Bethany is the manager of Jasper's software development organization, and she is working to bring the company into line with industry standard practices. She is developing a new change management process for the organization and wishes to follow commonly accepted approaches.

236. Bethany would like to put in place controls that provide an organized framework for company employees to suggest new website features that her team will develop. What change management process facilitates this?

A. Configuration control

B. Change control

C. Release control

D. Request control

237. Bethany would also like to create a process that helps multiple developers work on code at the same time. What change management process facilitates this?

A. Configuration control

B. Change control

C. Release control

D. Request control

238. Bethany is working with her colleagues to conduct user acceptance testing. What change management process includes this task?

A. Configuration control

B. Change control

C. Release control

D. Request control

239. Bethany noticed that some problems arise when system administrators update libraries without informing developers. What change management process can assist with this problem?

A. Configuration control

B. Change control

C. Release control

D. Request control

240. Ben has written the password hashing system for the web application he is building. His hashing code function for passwords results in the following process for a series of passwords:

```
hash (password1 + 07C98BFE4CF67B0BFE2643B5B22E2D7D) =
10B222970537B97919DB36EC757370D2
hash (password2 + 07C98BFE4CF67B0BFE2643B5B22E2D7D) =
F1F16683F3E0208131B46D37A79C8921
```

What flaw has Ben introduced with his hashing implementation?

A. Plaintext salting

B. Salt reuse

C. Use of a short salt

D. Poor salt algorithm selection

241. Which one of the following is an example of risk transference?

A. Building a guard shack

B. Purchasing insurance

C. Erecting fences

D. Relocating facilities

242. What protocol takes the place of certificate revocation lists and adds real-time status verification?

A. RTCP

B. RTVP

C. OCSP

D. CSRTP

243. Jim performs both lexical analysis on a program and produces control flow graphs. What type of software testing is he performing?

A. Dynamic

B. Fuzzing

C. Manual

D. Static

244. What process makes TCP a connection-oriented protocol?

A. It works via network connections.

B. It uses a handshake.

C. It monitors for dropped connections.

D. It uses a complex header.

245. What LDAP operation includes authentication to the LDAP server?

A. Bind

B. Auth

C. StartLDAP

D. AuthDN

246. You are conducting a qualitative risk assessment for your organization. The two important risk elements that should weigh most heavily in your analysis of risk are probability and ______________.

A. Likelihood

B. History

C. Impact

D. Cost

247. Using the OSI model, what format does the Data link Layer use to format messages received from higher up the stack?

A. A datastream

B. A frame

C. A segment

D. A datagram

248. What is the maximum penalty that may be imposed by an $(ISC)^2$ peer review board when considering a potential ethics violation?

A. Revocation of certification

B. Termination of employment

C. Financial penalty

D. Suspension of certification

249. Which one of the following statements about the SDLC is correct?

A. The SDLC requires the use of an iterative approach to software development.

B. The SDLC requires the use of a sequential approach to software development.

C. The SDLC does not include training for end users and support staff.

D. The waterfall methodology is compatible with the SDLC.

250. In the scenario shown here, Harry is prevented from reading a file at a higher classification level than his security clearance. What security model prevents this behavior?

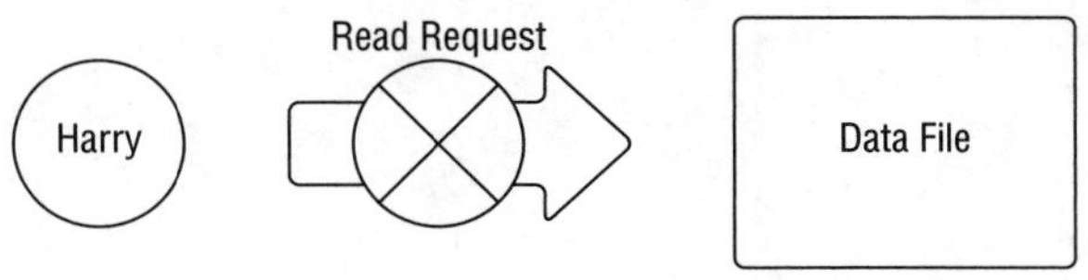

A. Bell-LaPadula

B. Biba

C. Clark-Wilson

D. Brewer-Nash

Appendix

Answers to Review Questions

Chapter 1: Security and Risk Management (Domain 1)

1. D. The final step of a quantitative risk analysis is conducting a cost/benefit analysis to determine whether the organization should implement proposed countermeasure(s).

2. A. Spoofing attacks use falsified identities. Spoofing attacks may use false IP addresses, email addresses, names, or, in the case of an evil twin attack, SSIDs.

3. C. The DMCA states that providers are not responsible for the transitory activities of their users. Transmission of information over a network would qualify for this exemption. The other activities listed are all nontransitory actions that require remediation by the provider.

4. A. The Notice principle says that organizations must inform individuals of the information the organization collects about individuals and how the organization will use it. These principles are based upon the Safe Harbor Privacy Principles issued by the US Department of Commerce in 2000 to help US companies comply with EU and Swiss privacy laws when collecting, storing, processing or transmitting data on EU or Swiss citizens.

5. D. The three common threat modeling techniques are focused on attackers, software, and assets. Social engineering is a subset of attackers.

6. A. Most state data breach notification laws are modeled after California's law, which covers Social Security number, driver's license number, state identification card number, credit/debit card numbers, bank account numbers (in conjunction with a PIN or password), medical records, and health insurance information.

7. C. The prudent man rule requires that senior executives take personal responsibility for ensuring the due care that ordinary, prudent individuals would exercise in the same situation. The rule originally applied to financial matters, but the Federal Sentencing Guidelines applied them to information security matters in 1991.

8. D. A fingerprint scan is an example of a "something you are" factor, which would be appropriate for pairing with a "something you know" password to achieve multifactor authentication. A username is not an authentication factor. PINs and security questions are both "something you know," which would not achieve multifactor authentication when paired with a password because both methods would come from the same category, failing the requirement for multifactor authentication.

9. D. The US Department of Commerce is responsible for implementing the EU-US Safe Harbor agreement. The validity of this agreement was in legal question in the wake of the NSA surveillance disclosures.

10. A. The Gramm-Leach-Bliley Act (GLBA) contains provisions regulating the privacy of customer financial information. It applies specifically to financial institutions.

11. A. The Federal Information Security Management Act (FISMA) specifically applies to government contractors. The Government Information Security Reform Act (GISRA) was the precursor to FISMA and expired in November 2002. HIPAA and PCI DSS apply to healthcare and credit card information, respectively.

12. D. The export of encryption software to certain countries is regulated under US export control laws.

13. D. In an elevation of privilege attack, the attacker transforms a limited user account into an account with greater privileges, powers, and/or access to the system. Spoofing attacks falsify an identity, while repudiation attacks attempt to deny accountability for an action. Tampering attacks attempt to violate the integrity of information or resources.

14. D. Whenever you choose to accept a risk, you should maintain detailed documentation of the risk acceptance process to satisfy auditors in the future. This should happen before implementing security controls, designing a disaster recovery plan, or repeating the business impact analysis (BIA).

15. B. A fence does not have the ability to detect intrusions. It does, however, have the ability to prevent and deter an intrusion. Fences are an example of a physical control.

16. D. Tony would see the best results by combining elements of quantitative and qualitative risk assessment. Quantitative risk assessment excels at analyzing financial risk, while qualitative risk assessment is a good tool for intangible risks. Combining the two techniques provides a well-rounded risk picture.

17. D. The Economic Espionage Act imposes fines and jail sentences on anyone found guilty of stealing trade secrets from a US corporation. It gives true teeth to the intellectual property rights of trade secret owners.

18. C. The due care principle states that an individual should react in a situation using the same level of care that would be expected from any reasonable person. It is a very broad standard. The due diligence principle is a more specific component of due care that states that an individual assigned a responsibility should exercise due care to complete it accurately and in a timely manner.

19. C. RAID level 5, disk striping with parity, requires a minimum of three physical hard disks to operate.

20. B. Awareness training is an example of an administrative control. Firewalls and intrusion detection systems are technical controls. Security guards are physical controls.

21. A. Patents and trade secrets can both protect intellectual property related to a manufacturing process. Trade secrets are appropriate only when the details can be tightly controlled within an organization, so a patent is the appropriate solution in this case.

22. B. RAID technology provides fault tolerance for hard drive failures and is an example of a business continuity action. Restoring from backup tapes, relocating to a cold site, and restarting business operations are all disaster recovery actions.

23. C. After developing a list of assets, the business impact analysis team should assign values to each asset.

24. C. Risk mitigation strategies attempt to lower the probability and/or impact of a risk occurring. Intrusion prevention systems attempt to reduce the probability of a successful attack and are, therefore, examples of risk mitigation.

25. D. Fire suppression systems protect infrastructure from physical damage. Along with uninterruptible power supplies, fire suppression systems are good examples of technology used to harden physical infrastructure. Antivirus software, hardware firewalls, and two-factor authentication are all examples of logical controls.

26. A. Access control lists are used for determining a user's authorization level. Usernames are identification tools. Passwords and tokens are authentication tools.

27. D. Trademark protection extends to words and symbols used to represent an organization, product, or service in the marketplace.

$(ISC)^{2}$®

28. A. The message displayed is an example of ransomware, which encrypts the contents of a user's computer to prevent legitimate use. This is an example of an availability attack.

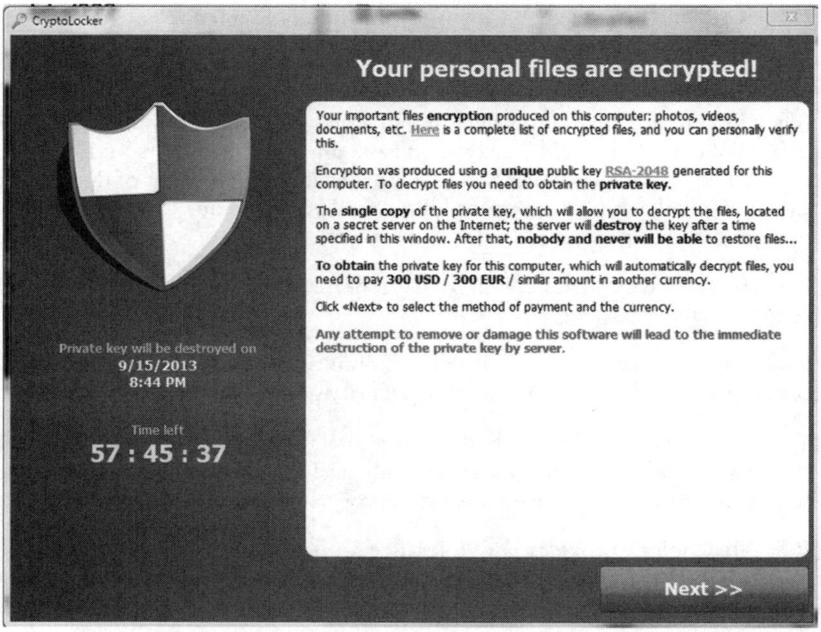

29. B. HIPAA regulates three types of entities—healthcare providers, health information clearinghouses, and health insurance plans—as well as the business associates of any of those covered entities.

30. A. A Smurf attack is an example of a denial of service attack, which jeopardizes the availability of a targeted network.

31. D. Strategic plans have a long-term planning horizon of up to five years in most cases. Operational and tactical plans have shorter horizons of a year or less.

32. A. The United States Patent and Trademark Office (USPTO) bears responsibility for the registration of trademarks.

33. B. When following the separation of duties principle, organizations divide critical tasks into discrete components and ensure that no one individual has the ability to perform both actions. This prevents a single rogue individual from performing that task in an unauthorized manner.

34. B. The Federal Information Security Management Act (FISMA) applies to federal government agencies and contractors. Of the entities listed, a defense contractor is the most likely to have government contracts subject to FISMA.

35. B. The Payment Card Industry Data Security Standard (PCI DSS) governs the storage, processing, and transmission of credit card information.

36. A. The data custodian role is assigned to an individual who is responsible for implementing the security controls defined by policy and senior management. The data owner does bear ultimate responsibility for these tasks, but the data owner is typically a senior leader who delegates operational responsibility to a data custodian.

37. B. Written works, such as website content, are normally protected by copyright law. Trade secret status would not be appropriate here because the content is online and available outside the company. Patents protect inventions and trademarks protect words and symbols used to represent a brand, neither of which is relevant in this scenario.

38. C. The Code of Federal Regulations (CFR) contains the text of all administrative laws promulgated by federal agencies. The United States Code contains criminal and civil law. Supreme Court rulings contain interpretations of law and are not laws themselves. The Compendium of Laws does not exist.

39. D. Installing a device that will block attacks is an attempt to lower risk by reducing the likelihood of a successful application attack.

40. B. The owner of information security programs may be different from the individuals responsible for implementing the controls. This person should be as senior an individual as possible who is able to focus on the management of the security program. The president and CEO would not be an appropriate choice because an executive at this level is unlikely to have the time necessary to focus on security. Of the remaining choices, the CIO is the most senior position who would be the strongest advocate at the executive level.

41. A. Senior managers play several business continuity planning roles. These include setting priorities, obtaining resources, and arbitrating disputes among team members.

42. D. The Service Organizations Control audit program includes business continuity controls in a Type 2, but not Type 1, audit. Although FISMA and PCI DSS may audit business continuity, they would not apply to an email service used by a hospital.

43. A. Repudiation threats allow an attacker to deny having performed an action or activity without the other party being able to prove differently.

44. A. Integrity controls, such as the one Beth is implementing in this example, are designed to prevent the unauthorized modification of information.

45. A. SLAs do not normally address issues of data confidentiality. Those provisions are normally included in a non-disclosure agreement (NDA).

46. A. Trademarks protect words and images that represent a product or service and would not protect computer software.

47. B. Virtual private networks (VPNs) provide secure communications channels over otherwise insecure networks (such as the Internet) using encryption. If you establish a VPN connection between the two offices, users in one office could securely access content located on the other office's server over the Internet. Digital signatures are used to provide nonrepudiation, not confidentiality. Virtual LANs (VLANs) provide network segmentation on local networks but do not cross the Internet. Digital content management solutions are designed to manage web content, not access shared files located on a file server.

48. C. Redundant Array of Inexpensive Disks (RAID) uses additional hard drives to protect the server against the failure of a single device. Load balancing and server clustering do add robustness but require the addition of a server. Scheduled backups protect against data loss but do not provide immediate access to data in the event of a hard drive failure.

49. A. Hashing allows you to computationally verify that a file has not been modified between hash evaluations. ACLs and read-only attributes are useful controls that may help you prevent unauthorized modification, but they cannot verify that files were not modified. Firewalls are network security controls and do not verify file integrity.

50. B. The Fourth Amendment directly prohibits government agents from searching private property without a warrant and probable cause. The courts have expanded the interpretation of the Fourth Amendment to include protections against other invasions of privacy.

51. A. Business continuity plan documentation normally includes the continuity planning goals, a statement of importance, statement of priorities, statement of organizational responsibility, statement of urgency and timing, risk assessment and risk acceptance and mitigation documentation, a vital records program, emergency response guidelines, and documentation for maintaining and testing the plan.

52. D. Mandatory vacation programs require that employees take continuous periods of time off each year and revoke their system privileges during that time. This will hopefully disrupt any attempt to engage in the cover-up actions necessary to hide fraud and result in exposing the threat. Separation of duties, least privilege, and defense in depth controls

all may help prevent the fraud in the first place but are unlikely to speed the detection of fraud that has already occurred.

53. C. Electronic vaulting is a data backup task that is part of disaster recovery, not business continuity, efforts.

54. C. Denial of service (DoS) and distributed denial of service (DDoS) attacks try to disrupt the availability of information systems and networks by flooding a victim with traffic or otherwise disrupting service.

55. B. Baselines provide the minimum level of security that every system throughout the organization must meet.

56. C. Everyone in the organization should receive a basic awareness training for the business continuity program. Those with specific roles, such as first responders and senior executives, should also receive detailed, role-specific training.

57. C. If the organization's primary concern is the cost of rebuilding the data center, James should use the replacement cost method to determine the current market price for equivalent servers.

58. D. The Computer Security Act of 1987 gave the National Institute of Standards and Technology (NIST) responsibility for developing standards and guidelines for federal computer systems. For this purpose, NIST draws upon the technical advice and assistance of the National Security Agency where appropriate.

59. B. There is no requirement that patents be for inventions made by American citizens. Patentable inventions must, on the other hand, be new, nonobvious, and useful.

60. A. Keyloggers monitor the keystrokes of an individual and report them back to an attacker. They are designed to steal sensitive information, a disruption of the goal of confidentiality.

61. A. Risks exist when there is an intersection of a threat and a vulnerability. This is described using the equation Risk = Threat * Vulnerability.

62. A. The fourth step of the NIST risk management framework is assessing security controls.

63. D. HAL Systems decided to stop offering the service because of the risk. This is an example of a risk avoidance strategy. The company altered its operations in a manner that eliminates the risk of NTP misuse.

64. C. Confidentiality controls prevent the disclosure of sensitive information to unauthorized individuals. Limiting the likelihood of a data breach is an attempt to prevent unauthorized disclosure.

65. A. The emergency response guidelines should include the immediate steps an organization should follow in response to an emergency situation. These include immediate response procedures, a list of individuals who should be notified of the emergency and secondary response procedures for first responders. They do not include long-term actions such as activating business continuity protocols, ordering equipment, or activating DR sites.

66. B. Although the CEO will not normally serve on a BCP team, it is best to obtain top-level management approval for your plan to increase the likelihood of successful adoption.

67. D. The project scope and planning phase includes four actions: a structured analysis of the organization, the creation of a BCP team, an assessment of available resources, and an analysis of the legal and regulatory landscape.

68. D. Keeping a server up and running is an example of an availability control because it increases the likelihood that a server will remain available to answer user requests.

69. A. A cold site includes the basic capabilities required for data center operations: space, power, HVAC, and communications, but it does not include any of the hardware required to restore operations.

70. C. The Computer Fraud and Abuse Act (CFAA) makes it a federal crime to maliciously cause damage in excess of $5,000 to a federal computer system during any one-year period.

71. B. ISO 27002 is an international standard focused on information security and titled "Information technology – Security techniques – Code of practice for information security management." The IT Infrastructure Library (ITIL) does contain security management practices, but it is not the sole focus of the document and the ITIL security section is derived from ISO 27002. The Capability Maturity Model (CMM) is focused on software development, and the Project Management Body of Knowledge (PMBOK) Guide focuses on project management.

72. B. The Communications Assistance to Law Enforcement Act (CALEA) requires that all communications carriers make wiretaps possible for law enforcement officials who have an appropriate court order.

73. B. The Gramm-Leach-Bliley Act (GLBA) places strict privacy regulations on financial institutions, including providing written notice of privacy practices to customers.

74. C. Non-disclosure agreements (NDAs) typically require either mutual or one-way confidentiality in a business relationship. Service-level agreements (SLAs) specify service uptime and other performance measures. Non-compete agreements (NCAs) limit the future employment possibilities of employees. Recovery time objectives (RTOs) are used in business continuity planning.

75. D. Router ACLs, encryption, and firewall rules are all examples of technical controls. Data classification is an administrative control.

76. C. While senior management should be represented on the BCP team, it would be highly unusual for the CEO to fill this role personally.

77. D. Nonrepudiation allows a recipient to prove to a third party that a message came from a purported source. Authentication would provide proof to Ben that the sender was authentic, but Ben would not be able to prove this to a third party.

78. C. Defense in depth states that organizations should have overlapping security controls designed to meet the same security objectives whenever possible. This approach provides security in the event of a single control failure.

79. D. Stakeholders should be informed of changes before, not after, they occur. The other items listed are goals of change management programs.

80. B. Ben should encrypt the data to provide an additional layer of protection as a compensating control. The organization has already made a policy exception, so he should not react by objecting to the exception or removing the data without authorization. Purchasing insurance may transfer some of the risk but is not a mitigating control.

81. A. The risk assessment team should pay the most immediate attention to those risks that appear in quadrant I. These are the risks with a high probability of occurring and a high impact on the organization if they do occur.

82. D. Electronic access to company resources must be carefully coordinated. An employee who retains access after being terminated may use that access to take retaliatory action. On the other hand, if access is terminated too early, the employee may figure out that he or she is about to be terminated.

83. D. In a risk acceptance strategy, the organization decides that taking no action is the most beneficial route to managing a risk.

84. A. COPPA requires that websites obtain advance parental consent for the collection of personal information from children under the age of 13.

85. D. The annualized rate of occurrence (ARO) is the frequency at which you should expect a risk to materialize each year. In a 100-year flood plain, risk analysts expect a flood to occur once every 100 years, or 0.01 times per year.

86. D. Wireshark is a protocol analyzer and may be used to eavesdrop on network connections. Eavesdropping is an attack against confidentiality.

87. C. In reduction analysis, the security professional breaks the system down into five key elements: trust boundaries, data flow paths, input points, privileged operations, and details about security controls.

88. D. The Sarbanes-Oxley Act (SOX) governs the financial reporting of publicly traded companies and includes requirements for security controls that ensure the integrity of that information.

89. D. Of the states listed, Florida is the only one that is not shaded to indicate a serious risk of a major earthquake.

90. C. Usernames are an identification tool. They are not secret, so they are not suitable for use as a password.

91. B. Qualitative tools are often used in business impact assessment to capture the impact on intangible factors such as customer confidence, employee morale, and reputation.

92. A. An organization pursuing a vital records management program should begin by identifying all of the documentation that qualifies as a vital business record. This should include all of the records necessary to restart the business in a new location should the organization invoke its business continuity plan.

93. B. Security training is designed to provide employees with the specific knowledge they need to fulfill their job functions. It is usually designed for individuals with similar job functions.

94. D. Awareness establishes a minimum standard of information security understanding. It is designed to accommodate all personnel in an organization, regardless of their assigned tasks.

95. C. Risks are the combination of a threat and a vulnerability. Threats are the external forces seeking to undermine security, such as the hacker in this case. Vulnerabilities are the internal weaknesses that might allow a threat to succeed. In this case, the missing patch is the vulnerability. In this scenario, if the hacker (threat) attempts a SQL injection attack against the unpatched server (vulnerability), the result is website defacement.

96. C. The exposure factor is the percentage of the facility that risk managers expect will be damaged if a risk materializes. It is calculated by dividing the amount of damage by the asset value. In this case, that is $5 million in damage divided by the $10 million facility value, or 50%.

97. B. The annualized rate of occurrence is the number of times that risk analysts expect a risk to happen in any given year. In this case, the analysts expect tornados once every 200 years, or 0.005 times per year.

98. A. The annualized loss expectancy is calculated by multiplying the single loss expectancy (SLE) by the annualized rate of occurrence (ARO). In this case, the SLE is $5,000,000 and the ARO is 0.005. Multiplying these numbers together gives you the ALE of $25,000.

99. C. Information disclosure attacks rely upon the revelation of private, confidential, or controlled information. Programming comments embedded in HTML code are an example of this type of attack.

100. B. Non-disclosure agreements (NDAs) protect the confidentiality of sensitive information by requiring that employees and affiliates not share confidential information with third parties. NDAs normally remain in force after an employee leaves the company.

Chapter 2: Asset Security (Domain 2)

1. C. Encryption is often used to protect traffic like bank transactions from sniffing. While packet injection and man-in-the-middle attacks are possible, they are far less likely to occur, and if a VPN were used, it would be used to provide encryption. TEMPEST is a specification for techniques used to prevent spying using electromagnetic emissions and wouldn't be used to stop attacks at any normal bank.

2. A. Business owners have to balance the need to provide value with regulatory, security, and other requirements. This makes the adoption of a common framework like COBIT attractive. Data owners are more likely to ask that those responsible for control selection identify a standard to use. Data processors are required to perform specific actions under

regulations like the EU DPD. Finally, in many organizations, data stewards are internal roles that oversee how data is used.

3. B. A baseline is used to ensure a minimum security standard. A policy is the foundation that a standard may point to for authority, and a configuration guide may be built from a baseline to help staff who need to implement it to accomplish their task. An outline is helpful, but *outline* isn't the term you're looking for here.

4. B. Media is typically labeled with the highest classification level of data it contains. This prevents the data from being handled or accessible at a lower classification level. Data integrity requirements may be part of a classification process but don't independently drive labeling in a classification scheme.

5. A. The need to protect sensitive data drives information classification. This allows organizations to focus on data that needs to be protected rather than spending effort on less important data. Remanence describes data left on media after an attempt is made to remove the data. Transmitting data isn't a driver for an administrative process to protect sensitive data, and clearing is a technical process for removing data from media.

6. A. A data retention policy can help to ensure that outdated data is purged, removing potential additional costs for discovery. Many organizations have aggressive retention policies to both reduce the cost of storage and limit the amount of data that is kept on hand and discoverable.

Data retention policies are not designed to destroy incriminating data, and legal requirements for data retention must still be met.

7. D. Custodians are delegated the role of handling day-to-day tasks by managing and overseeing how data is handled, stored, and protected. Data processors are systems used to process data. Business owners are typically project or system owners who are tasked with making sure systems provide value to their users or customers.

8. D. Safe Harbor compliance helps US companies meet the EU Data Protection Directive. Yearly assessments may be useful, but they aren't required. HIPAA is a US law that applies specifically to healthcare and related organizations, and encrypting all data all the time is impossible (at least if you want to use the data!).

9. C. Security baselines provide a starting point to scope and tailor security controls to your organization's needs. They aren't always appropriate to specific organizational needs, they cannot ensure that systems are always in a secure state, nor do they prevent liability.

10. A. *Clearing* describes preparing media for reuse. When media is cleared, unclassified data is written over all addressable locations on the media. Once that's completed, the media can be reused. Erasing is the deletion of files or media. Purging is a more intensive form of clearing for reuse in lower security areas, and sanitization is a series of processes that removes data from a system or media while ensuring that the data is unrecoverable by any means.

11. C. The US government uses the label Confidential for data that could cause damage if it was disclosed without authorization. Exposure of Top Secret data is considered to potentially cause grave damage, while Secret data could cause serious damage. Classified is not a level in the US government classification scheme.

12. D. Spare sectors, bad sectors, and space provided for wear leveling on SSDs (overprovisioned space) may all contain data that was written to the space that will not be cleared when the drive is wiped. Most wiping utilities only deal with currently addressable space on the drive. SSDs cannot be degaussed, and wear leveling space cannot be reliably used to hide data. These spaces are still addressable by the drive, although they may not be seen by the operating system.

13. B. *Data remanence* is a term used to describe data left after attempts to erase or remove data. Slack space describes unused space in a disk cluster, zero fill is a wiping methodology that replaces all data bits with zeroes, and *residual bytes* is a made-up term.

14. C. Information shared with customers is public, internal business could be sensitive or private, and trade secrets are proprietary. Thus public, sensitive, proprietary matches this most closely. Confidential is a military classification, which removes two of the remaining options, and trade secrets are more damaging to lose than a private classification would allow.

15. C. A watermark is used to digitally label data and can be used to indicate ownership. Encryption would have prevented the data from being accessed if it was lost, while classification is part of the set of security practices that can help make sure the right controls are in place. Finally, metadata is used to label data and might help a data loss prevention system flag it before it leaves your organization.

16. B. AES is a strong modern symmetric encryption algorithm that is appropriate for encrypting data at rest. TLS is frequently used to secure data when it is in transit. A virtual private network is not necessarily an encrypted connection and would be used for data in motion, while DES is an outdated algorithm and should not be used for data that needs strong security.

17. A. Data loss prevention (DLP) systems can use labels on data to determine the appropriate controls to apply to the data. DLP systems won't modify labels in real time and typically don't work directly with firewalls to stop traffic. Deleting unlabeled data would cause big problems for organizations that haven't labeled every piece of data!

18. B. The value of the data contained on media often exceeds the cost of the media, making more expensive media that may have a longer life span or additional capabilities like encryption support a good choice. While expensive media may be less likely to fail, the reason it makes sense is the value of the data, not just that it is less likely to fail. In general, the cost of the media doesn't have anything to do with the ease of encryption, and data integrity isn't ensured by better media.

19. C. Sanitization is a combination of processes that ensure that data from a system cannot be recovered by any means.

    Erasing and clearing are both prone to mistakes and technical problems that can result in remnant data and don't make sense for systems that handled proprietary information. Destruction is the most complete method of ensuring that data cannot be exposed, and some organizations opt to destroy the entire workstation, but that is not a typical solution due to the cost involved.

20. A. The US government's classification levels from least to most sensitive are Confidential, Secret, and Top Secret.

21. C. Data at rest is inactive data that is physically stored. Data in an IPsec tunnel or part of an e-commerce transaction is data in motion. Data in RAM is ephemeral and is not inactive

22. C. PCI DSS, the Payment Card Industry Data Security Standard, provides the set of requirements for credit card processing systems. The Microsoft, NSA, and CIS baseline are all useful for building a Windows 10 security standard, but they aren't as good of an answer as the PCI DSS standard itself.

23. D. The CIS benchmarks are an example of a security baseline. A risk assessment would help identify which controls were needed, and proper system ownership is an important part of making sure baselines are implemented and maintained. Data labeling can help ensure that controls are applied to the right systems and data.

24. B. Scoping involves selecting only the controls that are appropriate for your IT systems, while tailoring matches your organization's mission and the controls from a selected baseline. Baselining is the process of configuring a system or software to match a baseline, or building a baseline itself. *Selection* isn't a technical term used for any of these processes.

25. B. The controls implemented from a security baseline should match the data classification of the data used or stored on the system. Custodians are trusted to ensure the day-to-day security of the data and should do so by ensuring that the baseline is met and maintained. Business owners often have a conflict of interest between functionality and data security, and of course, applying the same controls everywhere is expensive and may not meet business needs or be a responsible use of resources.

26. B. FTP and Telnet do not provide encryption for the data they transmit and should not be used if they can be avoided. SFTP and SSH provide encryption to protect both the data they send and the credentials that are used to log in via both utilities.

27. B. Many organizations require the destruction of media that contains data at higher levels of classification. Often the cost of the media is lower than the potential costs of data exposure, and it is difficult to guarantee that reused media doesn't contain remnant data. Tapes can be erased by degaussing, but degaussing is not always fully effective. Bitrot describes the slow loss of data on aging media, while *data permanence* is a term sometimes used to describe the life span of data and media.

28. A. NIST Special Publication 800-122 defines PII as any information that can be used to distinguish or trace an individual's identity, such as name, Social Security number, date and place of birth, mother's maiden name, biometric records, and other information that is linked or linkable to an individual such as medical, educational, financial, and employment information. PHI is health-related information about a specific person, Social Security numbers are issued to individuals in the United States, and *SII* is a made-up term.

29. B. The biggest threat to data at rest is typically a data breach. Data at rest with a high level of sensitivity is often encrypted to help prevent this. Decryption is not as significant of a threat if strong encryption is used and encryption keys are well secured. Data integrity issues could occur, but proper backups can help prevent this, and of course data could be improperly classified, but this is not the primary threat to the data.

30. B. Full disk encryption only protects data at rest. Since it encrypts the full disk, it does not distinguish between labeled and unlabeled data.

31. B. One way to use an IPsec VPN is to create a private, encrypted network (or tunnel) via a public network, allowing users to be a virtual part of their employer's internal network. IPsec is distinct from TLS, provides encryption for confidentiality and integrity, and of course, in this scenario Sue is connecting to her employer's network rather than the employer connecting to hers.

32. D. Classification identifies the value of data to an organization. This can often help drive IT expenditure prioritization and could help with rough cost estimates if a breach occurred, but that's not the primary purpose. Finally, most breach laws call out specific data types for notification rather than requiring organizations to classify data themselves.

33. B. Downgrading systems and media is rare due to the difficulty of ensuring that sanitization is complete. The need to completely wipe (or destroy) the media that systems use means that the cost of reuse is often significant and may exceed the cost of purchasing a new system or media. The goal of purging is to ensure that no data remains, so commingling data should not be a concern, nor should the exposure of the data; only staff with the proper clearance should handle the systems! Finally, a DLP system should flag data based on labels, not on the system it comes from.

34. A. Classification should be conducted based on the value of the data to the organization, its sensitivity, and the amount of harm that could result from exposure of the data. Cost should be considered when implementing controls and is weighed against the damage that exposure would create.

35. C. Erasing, which describes a typical deletion process in many operating systems, typically removes only the link to the file, and leaves the data that makes up the file itself. The data will remain in place but not indexed until the space is needed and it is overwritten. Degaussing works only on magnetic media, but it can be quite effective on it. Purging and clearing both describe more elaborate removal processes.

36. D. Safe Harbor is a framework intended to bridge the different privacy protection laws between the United States and the European Union and is run by the US Department of Commerce. At the time of this writing, Safe Harbor had been declared "invalid" by the European Court of Justice, although the US Department of Commerce has stated that it will continue the Safe Harbor program.

    Both the GDPR and NIS are pending EU regulations, and there is no EU CyberSafe Act.

37. C. TLS is a modern encryption method used to encrypt and protect data in transit. AES256 is a symmetric cipher often used to protect data at rest. DES and SSL are both outdated encryption methods and should not be used for data that requires high levels of security.

38. C. Private data is typically considered data that could cause damage. Loss of confidential data is normally classified as able to cause exceptionally grave damage, while exposure of private data could cause serious damage. As you'd expect, public data exposure won't cause damage.

39. A. A data loss prevention (DLP) system or software is designed to identify labeled data or data that fits specific patterns and descriptions to help prevent it from leaving the organization. An IDS is designed to identify intrusions. Although some IDS systems can detect specific types of sensitive data using pattern matching, they have no ability to stop traffic. A firewall uses rules to control traffic routing, while UDP is a network protocol.

40. A. When data is stored in a mixed classification environment, it is typically classified based on the highest classification of data included. In this case, the US government's highest classification is Top Secret. Mixed classification is not a valid classification in this scheme.

41. B. A non-disclosure agreement, or NDA, is a legal agreement that prevents employees from sharing proprietary data with their new employers. Purging is used on media, while classification is used on data. Encryption can help secure data, but it doesn't stop employees who can decrypt or copy the data from sharing it.

42. C. By default, BitLocker and Microsoft's Encrypting File System (EFS) both use AES (Advanced Encryption Standard), which is the NIST-approved replacement for DES (Data Encryption Standard). Serpent was a competitor of AES, and 3DES was created as a possible replacement for DES.

43. B. Group Policy provides the ability to monitor and apply settings in a security baseline. Manual checks by users or using startup scripts provide fewer reviews and may be prone to failure, while periodic review of the baseline won't result in compliance being checked.

44. B. A baseline is a set of security configurations that can be adopted and modified to fit an organization's security needs. A security policy is written to describe an organization's approach to security, while DSS is the second half of the Payment Card Industry Data Security Standard. The NIST SP-800 series of documents address computer security in a variety of areas.

45. C. Record retention policies describe how long an organization should retain data and may also specify how and when destruction should occur. Classification policies describe how and why classification should occur and who is responsible, while availability and audit policies may be created for specific purposes.

46. A. The POODLE (or Padding Oracle On Downgraded Legacy Encryption) attack helped force the move from SSL 3.0 to TLS because it allowed attackers to easily access SSL encrypted messages. Stuxnet was a worm aimed at the Iranian nuclear program, while CRIME and BEAST were earlier attacks against SSL.

47. D. Using strong encryption, like AES256, can help ensure that loss of removable media like tapes doesn't result in a data breach. Security labels may help with handling processes, but they won't help once the media is stolen or lost. Having multiple copies will ensure that you can still access the data but won't increase the security of the media. Finally, using hard drives instead of tape only changes the media type and not the risk from theft or loss.

48. D. Electronic signatures, as used in this rule, prove that the signature was provided by the intended signer. Electronic signatures as part of the FDA code are intended to ensure that

electronic records are "trustworthy, reliable, and generally equivalent to paper records and handwritten signatures executed on paper." Signatures cannot provide confidentiality, or integrity, and don't ensure that someone has reviewed the data.

49. D. Secure Shell (SSH) is an encrypted protocol for remote login and command-line access. SCP and SFTP are both secure file transfer protocols, while WDS is the acronym for Windows Deployment Services, which provides remote installation capabilities for Windows operating systems.

50. B. Degaussing uses strong magnetic fields to erase magnetic media. *Magwipe* is a made-up term. Sanitization is a combination of processes used to remove data from a system or media to ensure that it cannot be recovered. Purging is a form of clearing used on media that will be reused in a lower classification or lower security environment.

51. D. Personnel retention deals with the knowledge that employees gain while employed. Issues related to the knowledge they may leave with and share are often handled with nondisclosure agreements. Knowledge gained after employment, as well as how soon (or how late) employees leave the organization, is not central to this issue.

52. C. One of the most important parts of labeling the data is ensuring that it receives a mark or label that provides the classification of the data. Digital rights management (DRM) tools provide ways to control how data is used, while encrypting it can help maintain the confidentiality and integrity of the data. Classifying the data is necessary to label it, but it doesn't automatically place a label on the data.

53. D. The NIST SP 800-88 process for sanitization and disposition shows that media that will be reused and was classified at a moderate level should be purged and then that purge should be validated. Finally, it should be documented.

54. D. Data in transit is data that is traversing a network or is otherwise in motion. TLS, VPNs, and IPsec tunnels are all techniques used to protect data in transit. AES, Serpent, and IDEA are all symmetric algorithms, while Telnet, ISDN, and UDP are all protocols. Encrypting your storage media before it is transported is a good practice, but transporting media isn't the type of transit that is meant by the phrase.

55. C. The data owner has ultimate responsibility for data belonging to an organization and is typically the CEO, president, or another senior employee. Business and mission owners typically own processes or programs. System owners own a system that processes sensitive data.

56. A. The Federal Trade Commission, or FTC, is the US government agency that deals with Safe Harbor. The Food and Drug Administration, Department of Defense, and Department of Commerce do not oversee Safe Harbor.

57. A. Chris is most likely to be responsible for classifying the data that he owns as well as assisting with or advising the system owners on security requirements and control selection. In an organization with multiple data owners, Chris is unlikely to set criteria for classifying data on his own. As a data owner, Chris will also not typically have direct responsibility for scoping, tailoring, applying, or enforcing those controls.

58. B. The system administrators are acting in the roles of data administrators who grant access and will also act as custodians who are tasked with the day-to-day application of security controls. They are not acting as data owners who own the data itself. Typically, system administrators are delegated authority by system owners, such as a department head, and of course they are tasked with providing access to users.

59. C. According to the European Union's Data Protection Directive, third-party organizations that process personal data on behalf of a data controller are known as data processors. The organization that they are contracting with would act in the role of the business or mission owners, and others within Chris's organization would have the role of data administrators, granting access as needed to the data based on their operational procedures and data classification.

60. B. The European Data Protection Directive has seven primary tenets:

- Notice
- Choice
- Onward transfer
- Security
- Data integrity
- Access
- Enforcement

Reason is not included in this list.

61. B. Under the EU's DPD, data processors like the third-party company in this question bear responsibility for ensuring that the data is not used for anything other than the purpose for which it is intended. Ben's company is the data controller, while the third party is the data processor, leaving the third party with that role.

62. D. The US government specifies Secret as the classification level for information that, if disclosed, could cause serious harm to national security. Top Secret is reserved for information that could cause exceptionally grave harm, while confidential data could be expected to cause less harm. Unclassified is not an actual classification but only indicates that the data may be released to unclassified individuals. Organizations may still restrict access to unclassified information.

63. A. Sanitization is the combination of processes used to remove data from a system or media. When a PC is disposed of, sanitization includes the removal or destruction of drives, media, and any other storage devices it may have. Purging, destruction, and declassification are all other handling methods.

64. D. Bcrypt is based on Blowfish (the *b* is a key hint here). AES and 3DES are both replacements for DES, while Diffie-Hellman is a protocol for key exchange.

65. C. Requiring all media to have a label means that when unlabeled media is found, it should immediately be considered suspicious. This helps to prevent mistakes that might leave sensitive data un-labeled. Prelabeled media is not necessarily cheaper (nor may it make sense to buy!), while reusing public media simply means that it must be classified based on the data it now contains. HIPAA does not have specific media labeling requirements.

66. B. Data in use is data that is in a temporary storage location while an application or process is using it. Thus, data in memory is best described as data in use or ephemeral data. Data at rest is in storage, while data in transit is traveling over a network or other channel. *Data at large* is a made-up term.

67. C. Validation processes are conducted to ensure that the sanitization process was completed, avoiding data remanence. A form like this one helps to ensure that each device has been checked and that it was properly wiped, purged, or sanitized. This can allow reuse, does not prevent destruction, and does not help with attribution, which is a concept used with encryption to prove who created or sent a file.

68. C. Ensuring that data cannot be recovered is difficult, and the time and effort required to securely and completely wipe media as part of declassification can exceed the cost of new media. Sanitization, purging, and clearing may be part of declassification, but they are not reasons that it is not frequently chosen as an option for organizations with data security concerns.

69. B. In the NIST SP 800-60 diagram, the process determines appropriate categorization levels resulting in security categorization and then uses that as an input to determine controls. Standard selection would occur at an organizational level, while baselining occurs when systems are configured to meet a baseline. Sanitization would require the intentional removal of data from machines or media.

70. C. A and E can both be expected to have data at rest. C, the Internet, is an unknown, and the data can't be guaranteed to be at rest. B, D, and F are all data in transit across network links.

71. C. B, D, and F all show network links. Of the answers provided, Transport Layer Security (TLS) provides the best security for data in motion. AES256 and 3DES are both symmetric ciphers and are more likely to be used for data at rest. SSL has been replaced with TLS and should not be a preferred solution.

72. B. Sending a file that is encrypted before it leaves means that exposure of the file in transit will not result in a confidentiality breach and the file will remain secure until decrypted at location E. Since answers A, C, and D do not provide any information about what happens at point C, they should be considered insecure, as the file may be at rest at point C in an unencrypted form.

73. D. Destruction is the final stage in the life cycle of media and can be done via disintegration, incineration, or a variety of other methods that result in the media and data being nonrecoverable. Sanitization is a combination of processes used when data is being removed from a system or media. Purging is an intense form of clearing, and degaussing uses strong magnetic fields to wipe data from magnetic media.

74. B. The Data Protection Directive's principles do not address data retention time periods. The seven principles are notice, purpose, consent, security, disclosure, access, and accountability.

75. D. Visual indicators like a distinctive screen background can help employees remember what level of classification they are dealing with and thus the handling requirements that they are expected to follow.

76. C. If an organization allows media to be downgraded, the purging process should be followed, and then the media should be relabeled. Degaussing may be used for magnetic media but won't handle all types of media. Pulverizing would destroy the media, preventing reuse, while relabeling first could lead to mistakes that result in media that hasn't been purged entering use.

77. B. The data owner sets the rules for use and protection of data. The remaining options all describe tasks for the system owner, including implementation of security controls.

78. C. Encrypting and labeling sensitive email will ensure that it remains confidential and can be identified. Performing these actions only on sensitive email will reduce the cost and effort of encrypting all email, allowing only sensitive email to be the focus of the organization's efforts. Only encrypting highly sensitive email not only skips labeling but might expose other classifications of email that shouldn't be exposed.

79. D. Scoping is performed when you match baseline controls to the IT system you're working to secure. Creation of standards is part of the configuration process and may involve the use of baselines. Baselining can mean the process of creating a security baseline or configuring systems to meet the baseline. CIS, the Center for Internet Security, provides a variety of security baselines.

80. C. Systems used to process data are data processors. Data owners are typically CEOs or other very senior staff, custodians are granted rights to perform day-to-day tasks when handling data, and mission owners are typically program or information system owners.

81. A. The EU GDPR is slated to replace the EU DPD, with adoption starting in 2015 and 2016 and full enforcement occurring in 2017 and 2018. NIST standards and special publications apply to the United States, while COBIT is an IT management framework. There is no EU Personal Data Protection Regulation.

82. B. Protected health information, or PHI, includes a variety of data in multiple formats, including oral and recorded data, such as that created or received by healthcare providers, employers, and life insurance providers. PHI must be protected by HIPAA. PII is personally identifiable information. SHI and HPHI are both made-up acronyms.

83. C. AES is a strong symmetric cipher that is appropriate for use with data at rest. SHA1 is a cryptographic hash, while TLS is appropriate for data in motion. DES is an outdated and insecure symmetric encryption method.

84. B. The principle of data integrity states that data should be reliable and that information should not be used for purposes other than those that users are made aware of by notice and that they have accepted through choice.

Enforcement is aimed at ensuring that compliance with principles is assured. Access allows individuals to correct, change, or delete their information, while onward transfer limits transfers to other organizations that comply with the principles of notice and choice.

85. C. Due to problems with remnant data, the US National Security Agency requires physical destruction of SSDs. This process, known as disintegration, results in very small fragments via a shredding process. Zero fill wipes a drive by replacing data with zeros, degaussing uses magnets to wipe magnetic media, and clearing is the process of preparing media for reuse.

86. A. The data owner bears responsibility for categorizing information systems and delegates selection of controls to system owners, while custodians implement the controls. Users don't perform any of these actions, while business owners are tasked with ensuring that systems are fulfilling their business purpose.

87. B. PCI DSS provides a set of required security controls and standards. Step 2 would be guided by the requirements of PCI DSS. PCI DSS will not greatly influence step 1 because all of the systems handle credit card information, making PCI DSS apply to all systems covered. Steps 3 and 4 will be conducted after PCI DSS has guided the decisions in step 2.

88. C. Custodians are tasked with the day-to-day monitoring of the integrity and security of data. Step 5 requires monitoring, which is a custodial task. A data owner may grant rights to custodians but will not be responsible for conducting monitoring. Data processors process data on behalf of the data controller, and a user simply uses the data via a computing system.

89. B. Susan's organization is limiting its risk by sending drives that have been sanitized before they are destroyed. This limits the possibility of a data breach if drives are mishandled by the third party, allowing them to be stolen, resold, or simply copied. The destruction of the drives will handle any issues with data remanence, while classification mistakes are not important if the drives have been destroyed. Data permanence and the life span of the data are not important on a destroyed drive.

90. C. A digital watermark is used to identify the owner of a file or to otherwise label it. A copyright notice provides information about the copyright asserted on the file, while data loss prevention (DLP) is a solution designed to prevent data loss. Steganography is the science of hiding information, often in images or files.

91. D. Record retention is the process of retaining and maintaining information for as long as it is needed. A data storage policy describes how and why data is stored, while data storage is the process of actually keeping the data. Asset maintenance is a non-information-security-related process for maintaining physical assets.

92. C. The cost of the data is not directly included in the classification process. Instead, the impact to the organization if the data were exposed or breached is considered. Who can access the data and what regulatory or compliance requirements cover the data are also important considerations.

93. B. Symmetric encryption like AES is typically used for data at rest. Asymmetric encryption is often used during transactions or communications when the ability to have public and private keys is necessary. DES is an outdated encryption standard, and OTP is the acronym for *one-time password*.

94. D. Administrators have the rights to assign permissions to access and handle data. Custodians are trusted to handle day-to-day data handling tasks. Business owners are typically system or project owners, and data processors are systems used to process data.

95. B. The California Online Privacy Protection Act (COPPA) requires that operators of commercial websites and services post a prominently displayed privacy policy if they collect personal information on California residents.

The Personal Information Protection and Electronic Documents Act is a Canadian privacy law, while California Civil Code 1798.82 is part of the set of California codes that requires breach notification. The California Online Web Privacy Act does not exist.

96. A. Tapes are frequently exposed due to theft or loss in transit. That means that tapes that are leaving their normal storage facility should be handled according to the organization's classification schemes and handling requirements. Purging the tapes would cause the loss of data, while increasing the classification level of the tapes or encrypting them may create extra work that isn't required by the classification level of the tapes.

97. A. The correct answer is the tape that is being shipped to a storage facility. You might think that the tape in shipment is "in motion," but the key concept is that the data is not being accessed and is instead in storage. Data in a TCP packet, in an e-commerce transaction, or in local RAM is in motion and is actively being used.

98. D. When the value of data changes due to legal, compliance, or business reasons, reviewing classifications and reclassifying the data is an appropriate response. Once the review is complete, data can be reclassified and handled according to its classification level. Simply relabeling the data avoids the classification process and may not result in the data being handled appropriately. Similarly, selecting a new baseline or simply encrypting the data may not handle all of the needs that the changes affecting the data create.

99. C. PGP, or Pretty Good Privacy (or its open-source alternative, GPG) provide strong encryption of files, which can then be sent via email. Email traverses multiple servers and will be unencrypted at rest at multiple points along its path as it is stored and forwarded to its destination.

100. A. While many non-government organizations create their own classification schemes, a common model with levels that align with the U.S. government's classification labels is shown below. In the given options, B and D do not match the US government's Top Secret, Secret, Confidential scheme, and C incorrectly matches business proprietary data with confidential data as well as Top Secret data with business sensitive data. Business internal is often another term for business sensitive, meaning that it is used to match two classifications!

US Government Classification	DAMAGE DESCRIPTION	CIVILIAN CLASSIFICATION
Top Secret	Exceptionally grave damage	Confidential/Proprietary
Secret	Serious damage	Private
Confidential	Damage	Sensitive

Chapter 3: Security Engineering (Domain 3)

1. D. The Brewer-Nash model allows access controls to change dynamically based upon a user's actions. It is often used in environments like Matthew's to implement a "Chinese wall" between data belonging to different clients.

2. A. Fires may be detected as early as the incipient stage. During this stage, air ionization takes place and specialized incipient fire detection systems can identify these changes to provide early warning of a fire.

3. A. Closed circuit television (CCTV) systems act as a secondary verification mechanism for physical presence because they allow security officials to view the interior of the facility when a motion alarm sounds to determine the current occupants and their activities.

4. B. In an m of n control system, at least m of n possible escrow agents must collaborate to retrieve an encryption key from the escrow database.

5. A. This is an example of a vendor offering a fully functional application as a web-based service. Therefore, it fits under the definition of Software as a Service (SaaS). In Infrastructure as a Service (IaaS), Compute as a Service (CaaS), and Platform as a Service (PaaS) approaches, the customer provides their own software. In this example, the vendor is providing the email software, so none of those choices are appropriate.

6. B. The Digital Signature Standard approves three encryption algorithms for use in digital signatures: the Digital Signature Algorithm (DSA); the Rivest, Shamir, Adleman (RSA) algorithm; and the Elliptic Curve DSA (ECDSA) algorithm. HAVAL is a hash function, not an encryption algorithm. While hash functions are used as part of the digital signature process, they do not provide encryption.

7. A. In the subject/object model of access control, the user or process making the request for a resource is the subject of that request. In this example, Harry is requesting resource access and is, therefore, the subject.

8. C. Michael should conduct his investigation, but there is a pressing business need to bring the website back online. The most reasonable course of action would be to take a snapshot of the compromised system and use the snapshot for the investigation, restoring the website to operation as quickly as possible while using the results of the investigation to improve the security of the site.

9. C. The use of a sandbox is an example of confinement, where the system restricts the access of a particular process to limit its ability to affect other processes running on the same system.

10. D. Assurance is the degree of confidence that an organization has that its security controls are correctly implemented. It must be continually monitored and re-verified.

11. A. Maintenance hooks, otherwise known as backdoors, provide developers with easy access to a system, bypassing normal security controls. If not removed prior to finalizing code, they pose a significant security vulnerability if an attacker discovers the maintenance hook.

12. B. The Simple Integrity Property states that an individual may not read a file classified at a lower security level than the individual's security clearance.

13. B. Supervisory control and data acquisition (SCADA) systems are used to control and gather data from industrial processes. They are commonly found in power plants and other industrial environments.

14. B. The Trusted Platform Module (TPM) is a hardware security technique that stores an encryption key on a chip on the motherboard and prevents someone from accessing an encrypted drive by installing it in another computer.

15. B. Running DES three times produces a strong encryption standard known as Triple DES, or 3DES. In order for this to provide additional security, DES must also be run using at least two different keys. NIST recommends use of three independent keys for the strongest version.

16. C. In an asymmetric cryptosystem, the sender of a message always encrypts the message using the recipient's public key.

17. D. When Bob receives the message, he uses his own private key to decrypt it. Since he is the only one with his private key, he is theB.

18. B. Each user retains their private key as secret information. In this scenario, Bob would only have access to his own private key and would not have access to the private key of Alice or any other user.

19. B. Alice creates the digital signature using her own private key. Then Bob, or any other user, can verify the digital signature using Alice's public key.

20. B. The salt is a random value added to a password before it is hashed by the operating system. The salt is then stored in a password file with the hashed password. This increases the complexity of cryptanalytic attacks by negating the usefulness of attacks that use precomputed hash values, such as rainbow tables.

21. A. Hash functions do not include any element of secrecy and, therefore, do not require a cryptographic key.

22. D. A preaction fire suppression system activates in two steps. The pipes fill with water once the early signs of a fire are detected. The system does not dispense water until heat sensors on the sprinkler heads trigger the second phase.

23. B. The Encapsulating Security Payload (ESP) protocol provides confidentiality and integrity for packet contents. It encrypts packet payloads and provides limited authentication and protection against replay attacks.

24. D. The greatest risk when a device is lost or stolen is that sensitive data contained on the device will fall into the wrong hands. Confidentiality protects against this risk.

25. C. The exclusive or (XOR) operation is true when one and only one of the input values is true.

26. A. DES uses a 64-bit encryption key but only 56 of those bits are actually used as keying material in the encryption operation. The remaining 8 bits are used to detect tampering or corruption of the key.

27. C. The *-Security Property states that an individual may not write to a file at a lower classification level than that of the individual. This is also known as the confinement property.

28. B. The Diffie-Hellman algorithm allows for the secure exchange of symmetric encryption keys over a public network.

29. C. Protection Profiles (PPs) specify the security requirements and protections that must be in place for a product to be accepted under the Common Criteria.

30. A. Hash functions must be able to work on any variable-length input and produce a fixed-length output from that input, regardless of the length of the input.

31. C. Binary keyspaces contain a number of keys equal to two raised to the power of the number of bits. Two to the fifth power is 32, so a 5-bit keyspace contains 32 possible keys.

32. B. Kerchoff's principle says that a cryptographic system should be secure even if everything about the system, except the key, is public knowledge.

33. A. Mantraps use a double set of doors to prevent piggybacking by allowing only a single individual to enter a facility at a time.

34. A. While it would be ideal to have wiring closets in a location where they are monitored by security staff, this is not feasible in most environments. Wiring closets must be distributed geographically in multiple locations across each building used by an organization.

35. D. The *-Integrity Property states that a subject cannot modify an object at a higher security level than that possessed by the subject.

36. C. Companies with BYOD environments often require nonintrusive security controls, such as remote wiping capability, device passcodes, and full device encryption. They do not normally use application control to restrict applications because users object to the use of this technology to personally owned devices.

37. B. In the Fair Cryptosystem approach to key escrow, the secret keys used in communications are divided into two or more pieces, each of which is given to an independent third party.

38. A. The Ready state is used when a process is prepared to execute but the CPU is not available. The Running state is used when a process is executing on the CPU. The Waiting state is used when a process is blocked waiting for an external event. The Stopped state is used when a process terminates.

39. A. EAL1 assurance applies when the system in question has been functionally tested. It is the lowest level of assurance under the Common Criteria.

40. A. Administrators and processes may attach security labels to objects that provide information on an object's attributes. Labels are commonly used to apply classifications in a mandatory access control system.

41. B. Open-source software exposes the source code to public inspection and modification. The open-source community includes major software packages, including the Linux operating system.

42. A. Adam created a list of individual users that may access the file. This is an access control list, which consists of multiple access control entries. It includes the names of users, so it is not role-based, and Adam was able to modify the list, so it is not mandatory access control.

43. C. Parameter checking, or input validation, is used to ensure that input provided by users to an application matches the expected parameters for the application. Developers may use parameter checking to ensure that input does not exceed the expected length, preventing a buffer overflow attack.

44. A. *Kernel mode*, *supervisory mode*, and *system mode* are all terms used to describe privileged modes of system operation. User mode is an unprivileged mode.

45. D. Multistate systems are certified to handle data from different security classifications simultaneously by implementing protection mechanisms that segregate data appropriately.

46. C. For systems running in System High mode, the user must have a valid security clearance for all information processed by the system, access approval for all information processed by the system, and a valid need to know for some, but not necessarily all, information processed by the system.

47. B. Steganography is the art of using cryptographic techniques to embed secret messages within other content. Some steganographic algorithms work by making alterations to the least significant bits of the many bits that make up image files.

48. C. The Caesar cipher is a shift cipher that works on a stream of text and is also a substitution cipher. It is not a block cipher or a transposition cipher. It is extremely weak as a cryptographic algorithm.

49. A. The kernel lies within the central ring, Ring 0. Conceptually, Ring 1 contains other operating system components. Ring 2 is used for drivers and protocols. User-level programs and applications run at Ring 3. Rings 0 through 2 run in privileged mode while Ring 3 runs in user mode. It is important to note that many modern operating systems do not fully implement this model.

50. D. In an Infrastructure as a Service environment, security duties follow a shared responsibility model. Since the vendor is responsible for managing the storage hardware, the vendor would retain responsibility for destroying or wiping drives as they are taken out of service. However, it is still the customer's responsibility to validate that the vendor's sanitization procedures meet their requirements prior to utilizing the vendor's storage services.

51. B. The major difference between a code and a cipher is that ciphers alter messages at the character or bit level, not at the word level. DES, shift ciphers, and word scrambles all work at the character or bit level and are ciphers. "One if by land; two if by sea" is a message with hidden meaning in the words and is an example of a code.

52. C. The verification process is similar to the certification process in that it validates security controls. Verification may go a step further by involving a third-party testing service and compiling results that may be trusted by many different organizations. Accreditation is the act of management formally accepting an evaluating system, not evaluating the system itself.

53. B. When a process is confined within certain access bounds, that process runs in isolation. Isolation protects the operating environment, the operating system kernel, and other processes running on the system.

54. B. The mean time to failure (MTTF) provides the average amount of time before a device of that particular specification fails.

55. A. Class A fire extinguishers are useful only against common combustible materials. They use water or soda acid as their suppressant. Class B extinguishers are for liquid fires. Class C extinguishers are for flammable gasses, and Class D fire extinguishers are for combustible metals.

56. A. Mobile Device Management (MDM) products provide a consistent, centralized interface for applying security configuration settings to mobile devices.

57. C. Nonrepudiation occurs when the recipient of a message is able to demonstrate to a third party that the message came from the purported sender.

58. A. The card shown in the image has a smart chip underneath the American flag. Therefore, it is an example of a smart card. This is the most secure type of identification card technology.

59. D. The TEMPEST program creates technology that is not susceptible to Van Eck phreaking attacks because it reduces or suppresses natural electromagnetic emanations.

60. B. The Trusted Computing Base (TCB) is a small subset of the system contained within the kernel that carries out critical system activities.

61. A. The MD5 hash algorithm has known collisions and, as of 2005, is no longer considered secure for use in modern environments.

62. B. Encrypting data on SSD drives does protect against wear leveling. Disk formatting does not effectively remove data from any device. Degaussing is only effective for magnetic media. Physically destroying the drive would not permit reuse.

63. C. In a known plaintext attack, the attacker has a copy of the encrypted message along with the plaintext message used to generate that ciphertext.

64. B. In a Time of Check/Time of Use (TOCTOU) attack, the attacker exploits the difference in time between when a security control is verified and the data protected by the control is actually used.

65. A. The X.509 standard, developed by the International Telecommunications Union, contains the specification for digital certificates.

66. D. Fences designed to deter more than the casual intruder should be at least 6 feet high. If a physical security system is designed to deter even determined intruders, it should be at least 8 feet high and topped with three strands of barbed wire.

67. C. In an aggregation attack, individual(s) use their access to specific pieces of information to piece together a larger picture that they are not authorized to access.

68. D. While all of the controls mentioned protect against unwanted electromagnetic emanations, only white noise is an active control. White noise generates false emanations that effectively "jam" the true emanations from electronic equipment.

69. B. In a Software as a service environment, the customer has no access to any underlying infrastructure, so firewall management is a vendor responsibility under the cloud computing shared responsibility model.

70. C. The grant rule allows a subject to grant rights that it possesses on an object to another subject.

71. A. In a phlashing attack, the attacker introduces a custom, malicious BIOS that grants the attacker some level of control over the attacked system.

72. D. Multithreading permits multiple tasks to execute concurrently within a single process. These tasks are known as threads and may be alternated between without switching processes.

73. C. This message was most likely encrypted with a transposition cipher. The use of a substitution cipher, a category that includes AES and 3DES, would change the frequency distribution so that it did not mirror that of the English language.

74. D. The meet-in-the-middle attack uses a known plaintext message and uses both encryption of the plaintext and decryption of the ciphertext simultaneously in a brute force manner to identify the encryption key in approximately double the time of a brute force attack against the basic DES algorithm.

75. A. The blacklisting approach to application control allows users to install any software they wish except for packages specifically identified by the administrator as prohibited. This would be an appropriate approach in a scenario where users should be able to install any nonmalicious software they wish to use.

76. A. Heartbeat sensors send periodic status messages from the alarm system to the monitoring center. The monitoring center triggers an alarm if it does not receive a status message for a prolonged period of time, indicating that communications were disrupted.

77. B. In a zero-knowledge proof, one individual demonstrates to another that they can achieve a result that requires sensitive information without actually disclosing the sensitive information.

78. A. Blowfish allows the user to select any key length between 32 and 448 bits.

79. B. Soda acid and other dry powder extinguishers work to remove the fuel supply. Water suppresses temperature, while halon and carbon dioxide remove the oxygen supply from a fire.

80. A. Digital signatures are possible only when using an asymmetric encryption algorithm. Of the algorithms listed, only RSA is asymmetric and supports digital signature capabilities.

81. C. The Open Web Application Security Project (OWASP) produces an annual list of the top ten web application security issues that developers and security professionals around the world rely upon for education and training purposes. The OWASP vulnerabilities form the basis for many web application security testing products.

82. A. The information flow model applies state machines to the flow of information. The Bell-LaPadula model applies the information flow model to confidentiality while the Biba model applies it to integrity.

83. D. Each process that runs on a system is assigned certain physical or logical bounds for resource access, such as memory.

84. C. Capacitance motion detectors monitor the electromagnetic field in a monitored area, sensing disturbances that correspond to motion.

85. D. Halon fire suppression systems use a chlorofluorocarbon (CFC) suppressant material that was banned in the Montreal Protocol because it depletes the ozone layer.

86. D. The Biba model focuses only on protecting integrity and does not provide protection against confidentiality or availability threats. It also does not provide protection against covert channel attacks. The Biba model focuses on external threats and assumes that internal threats are addressed programatically.

87. A. In TLS, both the server and the client first communicate using an ephemeral symmetric session key. They exchange this key using asymmetric cryptography, but all encrypted content is protected using symmetric cryptography.

88. B. A Faraday cage is a metal skin that prevents electromagnetic emanations from exiting. It is a rarely used technology because it is unwieldy and expensive, but it is quite effective at blocking unwanted radiation.

89. B. The hypervisor is responsible for coordinating access to physical hardware and enforcing isolation between different virtual machines running on the same physical platform.

90. B. Cloud computing systems where the customer only provides application code for execution on a vendor-supplied computing platform are examples of Platform as a Service (PaaS) computing.

91. B. The feedback model of composition theory occurs when one system provides input for a second system and then the second system provides input for the first system. This is a specialized case of the cascading model, so the feedback model is the most appropriate answer.

92. B. UPSes are designed to protect against short-term power losses, such as power faults. When they conduct power conditioning, they are also able to protect against sags and noise. UPSes have limited-life batteries and are not able to maintain continuous operating during a sustained blackout.

93. D. Data center humidity should be maintained between 40% and 60%. Values below this range increase the risk of static electricity, while values above this range may generate moisture that damages equipment.

94. C. Asymmetric cryptosystems use a pair of keys for each user. In this case, with 1,000 users, the system will require 2,000 keys.

95. B. Accreditation is the formal approval by a DAA that an IT system may operate in a described risk environment.

96. B. Abstraction uses a black box approach to hide the implementation details of an object from the users of that object.

97. A. The certificate revocation list contains the serial numbers of digital certificates issued by a certificate authority that have later been revoked.

98. A. The point of the digital certificate is to prove to Alison that the server belongs to the bank, so she does not need to have this trust in advance. To trust the certificate, she must verify the CA's digital signature on the certificate, trust the CA, verify that the certificate is not listed on a CRL, and verify that the certificate contains the name of the bank.

99. C. Covert channels use surreptitious communications' paths. Covert timing channels alter the use of a resource in a measurable fashion to exfiltrate information. If a user types using a specific rhythm of Morse code, this is an example of a covert timing channel. Someone watching or listening to the keystrokes could receive a secret message with no trace of the message left in logs.

100. C. Self-signed digital certificates should only be used for internal-facing applications, where the user base trusts the internally generated digital certificate.

Chapter 4: Communication and Network Security (Domain 4)

1. A. Frame Relay supports multiple private virtual circuits (PVCs), unlike X.25. It is a packet-switching technology that provides a Committed Information Rate (CIR), which is a minimum bandwidth guarantee provided by the service provider to customers. Finally, Frame Relay requires a DTE/DCE at each connection point, with the DTE providing access to the Frame Relay network, and a provider-supplied DCE, which transmits the data over the network.

2. B. LEAP, the Lightweight Extensible Authentication Protocol. is a Cisco proprietary protocol designed to handle problems with TKIP. Unfortunately, LEAP has significant security issues as well and should not be used. Any modern hardware should support WPA2 and technologies like PEAP or EAP-TLS. Using WEP, the predecessor to WPA and WPA2, would be a major step back in security for any network.

3. C. Ben is using ad hoc mode, which directly connects two clients. It can be easy to confuse this with stand-alone mode, which connects clients using a wireless access point, but not to wired resources like a central network. Infrastructure mode connects endpoints to a central network, not directly to each other. Finally, wired extension mode uses a wireless access point to link wireless clients to a wired network.

4. C. A collision domain is the set of systems that could cause a collision if they transmitted at the same time. Systems outside of a collision domain cannot cause a collision if they send at the same time. This is important, as the number of systems in a collision domain increases the likelihood of network congestion due to an increase in collisions. A broadcast domain is the set of systems that can receive a broadcast from each other. A subnet is a logical division of a network, while a supernet is made up of two or more networks.

5. D. The RST flag is used to reset or disconnect a session. It can be resumed by restarting the connection via a new three-way handshake.

6. C. He should choose 802.11n, which supports 200+ Mbps in the 2.4 GHz or the 5 GHz frequency range. 802.11a and 802.11ac are both 5 GHz only, while 802.11g is only capable of 54 Mbps.

7. C. These common ports are important to know, although some of the protocols are becoming less common. TCP 23 is used for Telnet; TCP 25 is used for SMTP (the Simple Mail Transfer Protocol); 143 is used for IMAP, the Internet Message Access Protocol; and 515 is associated with LPD, the Line Printer Daemon protocol used to send print jobs to printers.

   POP3 operates on TCP 110, SSH operates on TCP 22 (and SFTP operates over SSH), and X Windows operates on a range of ports between 6000 and 6063.

8. A. The File Transfer Protocol (FTP) operates on TCP ports 20 and 21. UDP port 69 is used for the Trivial File Transfer Protocol, or TFTP, while UDP port 21 is not used for any common file transfer protocol.

9. B. Frequency Hopping Spread Spectrum (FHSS), Direct Sequence Spread Spectrum (DSSS), and Orthogonal Frequency-Division Multiplexing (OFDM) all use spread spectrum techniques to transmit on more than one frequency at the same time. Neither FHSS nor DHSS uses orthogonal modulation, while multiplexing describes combining multiple signals over a shared medium of any sort. Wi-Fi may receive interference from FHSS systems but doesn't use it.

10. B. The Challenge-Handshake Authentication Protocol, or CHAP, is used by PPP servers to authenticate remote clients. It encrypts both the username and password and performs periodic reauthentication while connected using techniques to prevent replay attacks. LEAP provides reauthentication but was designed for WEP, while PAP sends passwords unencrypted. EAP is extensible and was used for PPP connections, but it doesn't directly address the listed items.

11. C. SSID broadcast is typically disabled for secure networks. While this won't stop a determined attacker, it will stop casual attempts to connect. Separating the network from other wired networks, turning on the highest level of encryption supported (like WPA2), and using MAC filtering for small groups of clients that can reasonably be managed by hand are all common best practices for wireless networks.

12. A. A ring connects all systems like points on a circle. A ring topology was used with Token Ring networks, and a token was passed between systems around the ring to allow each system to communicate. More modern networks may be described as a ring but are only physically a ring and not logically using a ring topology.

13. B. The firewall in the diagram has two protected zones behind it, making it a two-tier firewall design.

14. D. Remote PCs that connect to a protected network need to comply with security settings and standards that match those required for the internal network. The VPN concentrator logically places remote users in the protected zone behind the firewall, but that means that user workstations (and users) must be trusted in the same way that local workstations are.

15. C. An intrusion protection system can scan traffic and stop both known and unknown attacks. A web application firewall, or WAF, is also a suitable technology, but placing it at location C would only protect from attacks via the organization's VPN, which should only be used by trusted users. A firewall typically won't have the ability to identify and stop cross-site scripting attacks, and IDS systems only monitor and don't stop attacks.

16. D. Distance-vector protocols use metrics including the direction and distance in hops to remote networks to make decisions. A link-state routing protocol considers the shortest distance to a remote network. Destination metric and link-distance protocols don't exist.

17. B. Disabling SSID broadcast can help prevent unauthorized personnel from attempting to connect to the network. Since the SSID is still active, it can be discovered by using a wireless sniffer. Encryption keys are not related to SSID broadcast, beacon frames are used to broadcast the SSID, and it is possible to have multiple networks with the same SSID.

18. B. A proxy is a form of gateway that provide clients with a filtering, caching, or other service that protects their information from remote systems. A router connects networks, while a firewall uses rules to limit traffic permitted through it. A gateway translates between protocols.

19. B. DNS poisoning occurs when an attacker changes the domain name to IP address mappings of a system to redirect traffic to alternate systems. DNS spoofing occurs when an attacker sends false replies to a requesting system, beating valid replies from the actual DNS server. ARP spoofing provides a false hardware address in response to queries about an IP, and Cain & Abel is a powerful Windows hacking tool, but a Cain attack is not a specific type of attack.

20. B. Screen scrapers copy the actual screen displayed and display it at a remote location. RDP provides terminal sessions without doing screen scraping, remote node operation is the same as dial-up access, and remote control is a means of controlling a remote system (screen scraping is a specialized subset of remote control).

21. A. S/MIME supports both signed messages and a secure envelope method. While the functionality of S/MIME can be replicated with other tools, the secure envelope is an S/MIME-specific concept. MOSS, or MIME Object Security Services, and PEM can also both provide authentication, confidentiality, integrity, and nonrepudiation, while DKIM, or Domain Keys Identified Mail, is a domain validation tool.

22. A. Multilayer protocols like DNP3 allow SCADA and other systems to use TCP/IP-based networks to communicate. Many SCADA devices were never designed to be exposed to a network, and adding them to a potentially insecure network can create significant risks. TLS or other encryption can be used on TCP packets, meaning that even serial data can be protected. Serial data can be carried via TCP packets because TCP packets don't care about their content; it is simply another payload. Finally, TCP/IP does not have a specific throughput as designed, so issues with throughput are device-level issues.

23. C. WEP has a very weak security model that relies on a single, predefined, shared static key. This means that modern attacks can break WEP encryption in less than a minute.

24. B. A denial of service attack is an attack that causes a service to fail or to be unavailable. Exhausting a system's resources to cause a service to fail is a common form of denial of service attack. A worm is a self-replicating form of malware that propagates via a network, a virus is a type of malware that can copy itself to spread, and a Smurf attack is a distributed denial of service attack (DDoS) that spoofs a victim's IP address to systems using an IP broadcast, resulting in traffic from all of those systems to the target.

25. C. 802.11n can operate at speeds over 200 Mbps, and it can operate on both the 2.4 and 5 GHz frequency range. 802.11g operates at 54 Mbps using the 2.4 GHz frequency range, and 802.11ac is capable of 1 Gbps using the 5 GHz range. 802.11a and b are both outdated and are unlikely to be encountered in modern network installations.

26. B. ARP and RARP operate at the Data Link layer, the second layer of the OSI model. Both protocols deal with physical hardware addresses, which are used above the Physical layer (layer 1) and below the Network layer (layer 3), thus falling at the Data Link layer.

27. D. iSCSI is a converged protocol that allows location-independent file services over traditional network technologies. It costs less than traditional Fibre Channel. VoIP is Voice over IP, SDN is Software-defined networking, and MPLS is Multiprotocol Label Switching, a technology that uses path labels instead of network addresses.

28. A. A repeater or concentrator will amplify the signal, ensuring that the 100-meter distance limitation of 1000Base-T is not an issue. A gateway would be useful if network protocols were changing, while Cat7 cable is appropriate for a 10Gbps network at much shorter distances. STP cable is limited to 155 Mbps and 100 meters, which would leave Chris with network problems.

29. B. TCP 80 is typically HTTP.

30. C. HTTP traffic is typically sent via TCP 80. Unencrypted HTTP traffic can be easily captured at any point between A and B, meaning that the instant messaging solution chosen does not provide confidentiality for the organization's corporate communications.

31. B. If a business need requires instant messaging, using a local instant messaging server is the best option. This prevents traffic from traveling to a third-party server and can offer additional benefits such as logging, archiving, and control of security options like the use of encryption.

32. B. Multilayer protocols create three primary concerns for security practitioners: They can conceal covert channels (and thus covert channels are allowed), filters can be bypassed by traffic concealed in layered protocols, and the logical boundaries put in place by network segments can be bypassed under some circumstances. Multilayer protocols allow encryption at various layers and support a range of protocols at higher layers.

33. C. A bus can be linear or tree-shaped and connects each system to trunk or backbone cable. Ethernet networks operate on a bus topology.

34. B. When a workstation or other device is connected simultaneously to both a secure and a nonsecure network like the Internet, it may act as a bridge, bypassing the security protections located at the edge of a corporate network. It is unlikely that traffic will be routed improperly leading to the exposure of sensitive data, as traffic headed to internal systems and networks is unlikely to be routed to the external network. Reflected DDoS attacks are used to hide identities rather than to connect through to an internal network, and security administrators of managed systems should be able to determine both the local and wireless IP addresses his system uses.

35. A. Wardriving and warwalking are both processes used to locate wireless networks, but are not typically as detailed and thorough as a site survey, and design map is a made-up term.

36. C. The DARPA TCP/IP model was used to create the OSI model, and the designers of the OSI model made sure to map the OSI model layers to it. The Application layer of the TCP model maps to the Application, Presentation, and Session layers, while the TCP and OSI models both have a distinct Transport layer.

37. B. ARP cache poisoning occurs when false ARP data is inserted into a system's ARP cache, allowing the attacker to modify its behavior. *RARP flooding*, *denial of ARP attacks*, and *ARP buffer blasting* are all made-up terms.

38. C. The process of using a fake MAC (Media Access Control) address is called spoofing, and spoofing a MAC address already in use on the network can lead to an address collision, preventing traffic from reaching one or both systems. Tokens are used in token ring networks, which are outdated, and EUI refers to an *Extended Unique Identifier*, another term for *MAC address*, but token loss is still not the key issue. *Broadcast domains* refers to the set of machines a host can send traffic to via a broadcast message.

39. D. Direct Inward System Access uses access codes assigned to users to add a control layer for external access and control of the PBX. If the codes are compromised, attackers can make calls through the PBX or even control it. Not updating a PBX can lead to a range of issues, but this question is looking for a DISA issue. Allowing only local calls and using unpublished numbers are both security controls and might help keep the PBX more secure.

40. D. Application-specific protocols are handled at layer 7, the Application layer of the OSI model.

41. D. Ping uses ICMP, the Internet Control Message Protocol, to determine whether a system responds and how many hops there are between the originating system and the remote system. Lauren simply needs to filter out ICMP to not see her pings.

42. D. 802.1x provides port-based authentication and can be used with technologies like EAP, the Extensible Authentication Protocol. 802.11a is a wireless standard, 802.3 is the standard for Ethernet, and 802.15.1 was the original Bluetooth IEEE standard.

43. D. 1000Base-T is capable of a 100 meter run according to its specifications. For longer distances, a fiber-optic cable is typically used in modern networks.

44. C. PRI, or Primary Rate Interface, can use between 2 and 23 64 Kbps channels, with a maximum potential bandwidth of 1.544 Mbps. Actual speeds will be lower due to the D channel, which can't be used for actual data transmission, but PRI beats BRI's two B channels paired with a D channel for 144 Kbps of bandwidth.

45. C. SPIT stands for Spam over Internet Telephony and targets VoIP systems.

46. D. Bluesnarfing targets the data or information on Bluetooth-enabled devices. Bluejacking occurs when attackers send unsolicited messages via Bluetooth.

47. C. Layer 6, the Presentation layer, transforms data from the Application layer into formats that other systems can understand by formatting and standardizing the data. That means that standards like JPEG, ASCII, and MIDI are used at the Presentation layer for data. TCP, UDP, and TLS are used at the Transport layer; NFS, SQL, and RPC operate at the Session layer; and HTTP, FTP, and SMTP are Application layer protocols.

48. D. Fully connected mesh networks provide each system with a direct physical link to every other system in the mesh. This is very expensive but can provide performance advantages for specific types of computational work.

49. C. PPTp, L2F, L2TP, and IPsec are the most common VPN protocols. TLS is also used for an increasingly large percentage of VPN connections and may appear at some point in the CISSP exam. PPP is a dial-up protocol, LTP is not a protocol, and SPAP is the Shiva Password Authentication Protocol sometimes used with PPTP.

50. C. FDDI, or Fiber Distributed Data Interface, is a token-passing network that uses a pair of rings with traffic flowing in opposite directions. It can bypass broken segments by dropping the broken point and using the second, unbroken ring to continue to function. Token Ring also uses tokens, but it does not use a dual loop. SONET is a protocol for sending multiple optical streams over fiber, and a ring topology is a design, not a technology.

51. C. The Physical Layer includes electrical specifications, protocols, and standards that allow control of throughput, handling line noise, and a variety of other electrical interface and signaling requirements. The OSI layer doesn't have a Device layer. The Transport layer connects the Network and Session layers, and the Data Link layer packages packets from the network layer for transmission and receipt by devices operating on the Physical layer.

52. A. WPA2, the replacement for WPA, does not suffer from the security issues that WEP, the original wireless security protocol, and WPA, its successor, both suffer from. AES is used in WPA2 but is not specifically a wireless security standard.

53. A. User awareness is one of the most important tools when dealing with attachments. Attachments are often used as a vector for malware, and aware users can help prevent successful attacks by not opening the attachments. Anti-malware tools, including antivirus software, can help detect known threats before users even see the attachments. Encryption, including tools like S/MIME, won't help prevent attachment-based security problems, and removing ZIP file attachments will only stop malware that is sent via those ZIP files.

54. A. The Transport layer provides logical connections between devices, including end-to-end transport services to ensure that data is delivered. Transport layer protocols include TCP, UDP, SSL, and TLS.

55. B. Machine Access Control (MAC) addresses are the hardware address the machine uses for layer 2 communications. The MAC addresses include an organizationally unique identifier (OUI), which identifies the manufacturer. MAC addresses can be changed, so this is not a guarantee of accuracy, but under normal circumstances you can tell what manufacturer made the device by using the MAC address.

56. D. PEAP provides encryption for EAP methods and can provide authentication. It does not implement CCMP, which was included in the WPA2 standard. LEAP is dangerously insecure and should not be used due to attack tools that have been available since the early 2000s.

57. C. Double NATing isn't possible with the same IP range; the same IP addresses cannot appear inside and outside of a NAT router. RFC 1918 addresses are reserved, but only so they are not used and routable on the Internet, and changing to PAT would not fix the issue.

58. B. A Class B network holds 2^16 systems, and its default network mask is 255.255.0.0.

59. C. Traditional private branch exchange (PBX) systems are vulnerable to eavesdropping because voice communications are carried directly over copper wires. Since standard telephones don't provide encryption (and you're unlikely to add encrypted phones unless you're the NSA), physically securing access to the lines and central connection points is the best strategy available.

60. A. Most cordless phones don't use encryption, and even modern phones that use DECT (which does provide encryption) have already been cracked. This means that a determined attacker can almost always eavesdrop on cordless phones, and makes them a security risk if they're used for confidential communication.

61. A. VLAN hopping between the voice and computer VLANs can be accomplished when devices share the same switch infrastructure. Using physically separate switches can prevent this attack. Encryption won't help with VLAN hopping because it relies on header data that the switch needs to read (and this is unencrypted), while Caller ID spoofing is an inherent problem with VoIP systems. A denial of service is always a possibility, but it isn't specifically a VoIP issue and a firewall may not stop the problem if it's on a port that must be allowed through.

62. A. A static packet filtering firewall is only aware of the information contained in the message header of packets: the source, destination, and port it is sent from and headed to. This means that they're not particularly smart, unlike Application layer firewalls that proxy traffic based on the service they support or stateful inspection firewalls (also known as dynamic packet inspection firewalls) that understand the relationship between systems and their communications.

63. A. Black boxes are designed to steal long-distance service by manipulating line voltages. Red boxes simulate tones of coins being deposited into payphones; blue boxes were tone generators used to simulate the tones used for telephone networks; and white boxes included a dual tone, multifrequency generator to control phone systems.

64. A. Data streams are associated with the Application, Presentation, and Session layers. Once they reach the Transport layer, they become segments (TCP) or datagrams (UDP). From there, they are converted to packets at the Network layer, frames at the Data Link layer, and bits at the Physical layer.

65. C. A three-tier design separates three distinct protected zones and can be accomplished with a single firewall that has multiple interfaces. Single- and two-tier designs don't support the number of protected networks needed in this scenario, while a four-tier design would provide a tier that isn't needed.

66. C. Software-defined networking provides a network architecture than can be defined and configured as code or software. This will allow Lauren's team to quickly change the network based on organizational requirements. The 5-4-3 rule is an old design rule for networks that relied on repeaters or hubs. A converged network carries multiple types of traffic like voice, video, and data. A hypervisor-based network may be software defined, but it could also use traditional network devices running as virtual machines.

67. B. Sensitive information contained in faxes should not be left in a public area. Disabling automatic printing will help prevent unintended viewing of the faxes. Purging local memory after the faxes are printed will ensure that unauthorized individuals can't make additional copies of faxes. Encryption would help keep the fax secure during transmission but won't help with the public location and accessibility of the fax machine itself, and of course, enabling automatic printing will only make casual access easier.

68. B. ISDN, cable modems, DSL, and T1 and T3 lines are all examples of broadband technology that can support multiple simultaneous signals. They are analog, not digital, and are not broadcast technologies.

69. A. A single-tier firewall deployment is very simple and does not offer useful design options like a DMZ or separate transaction subnets.

70. D. Network segmentation can reduce issues with performance as well as diminish the chance of broadcast storms by limiting the number of systems in a segment. This decreases broadcast traffic visible to each system and can reduce congestion. Segmentation can also help provide security by separating functional groups who don't need to be able to access each other's systems. Installing a firewall at the border would only help with inbound and outbound traffic, not cross-network traffic. Spanning tree loop

prevention helps prevent loops in Ethernet networks (for example, when you plug a switch into a switch via two ports on each), but it won't solve broadcast storms that aren't caused by a loop or security issues. Encryption might help prevent some problems between functional groups, but it won't stop them from scanning other systems, and it definitely won't stop a broadcast storm!

71. C. ICMP, RIP, and network address translation all occur at layer 3, the Network layer.

72. C. One of the visibility risks of virtualization is that communication between servers and systems using virtual interfaces can occur "inside" of the virtual environment. This means that visibility into traffic in the virtualization environment has to be purpose built as part of its design. Option D is correct but incomplete because inter-hypervisor traffic isn't the only traffic the IDS will see.

73. B. Cut and paste between virtual machines can bypass normal network-based data loss prevention tools and monitoring tools like an IDS or IPS. Thus, it can act as a covert channel, allowing the transport of data between security zones. So far, cut and paste has not been used as a method for malware spread in virtual environments and has not been associated with denial of service attacks. Cut and paste requires users to be logged in and does not bypass authentication requirements.

74. A. While virtual machine escape has only been demonstrated in laboratory environments, the threat is best dealt with by limiting what access to the underlying hypervisor can prove to a successful tracker. Segmenting by data types or access levels can limit the potential impact of a hypervisor compromise. If attackers can access the underlying system, restricting the breach to only similar data types or systems will limit the impact. Escape detection tools are not available on the market, restoring machines to their original snapshots will not prevent the exploit from occuring again, and Tripwire detects file changes and is unlikely to catch exploits that escape the virtual machines themselves.

75. C. WPA2's CCMP encryption scheme is based on AES. As of the writing of this book, there have not been any practical real-world attacks against WPA2.

DES has been successfully broken, and neither 3DES nor TLS is used for WPA2.

76. B. Ethernet networks use Carrier-Sense Multiple Access with Collision Detection (CSMA/CD) technology. When a collision is detected and a jam signal is sent, hosts wait a random period of time before attempting retransmission.

77. C. IPX, AppleTalk, and NetBEUI are all examples of non-IP protocols. TCP and UDP are both IP protocols, while routing protocols are used to send information about how traffic should be routed through networks.

78. C. A T3 (DS-3) line is capable of 44.736 Mbps. This is often referred to as 45 Mbps. A T1 is 1.544 Mbps, ATM is 155 Mbps, and ISDN is often 64 or 128 Mbps.

79. B. A two-tier firewall uses a firewall with multiple interfaces or multiple firewalls in series. This image shows a firewall with two protected interfaces, with one used for a DMZ and one used for a protected network. This allows traffic to be filtered between each of the zones (Internet, DMZ, and private network).

80. B. Endpoint security solutions face challenges due to the sheer volume of data that they can create. When each workstation is generating data about events, this can be a massive amount of data. Endpoint security solutions should reduce the number of compromises when properly implemented, and they can also help by monitoring traffic after it is decrypted on the local host. Finally, non-TCP protocols are relatively uncommon on modern networks, making this a relatively rare concern for endpoint security system implementations.

81. D. The IP address 127.0.0.1 is a loopback address and will resolve to the local machine. Public addresses are non-RFC 1918, non-reserved addresses. RFC 1918 addresses are reserved and include ranges like 10.x.x.x. An APIPA address is a self-assigned address used when a DHCP server cannot be found.

82. B. Since Bluetooth doesn't provide strong encryption, it should only be used for activities that are not confidential. Bluetooth PINs are four-digit codes that often default to 0000. Turning it off and ensuring that your devices are not in discovery mode can help prevent Bluetooth attacks.

83. B. Application-level gateway firewalls are known as second-generation firewalls. Static packet filtering firewalls are known as first-generation firewalls, and stateful packet inspection firewalls are known as third-generation firewalls. UTM, or Unified Threat Management is a concept used in next generation firewalls.

84. B. Fiber Channel over Ethernet allows Fiber Channel communications over Ethernet networks, allowing existing high-speed networks to be used to carry storage traffic. This avoids the cost of a custom cable plant for a Fiber Channel implementation. MPLS, or Multiprotocol label Switching, is used for high performance networking; VoIP is Voice over IP; and SDN is Software-Defined Networking.

85. D. A modem (MOdulator/DEModulator) modulates between an analog carrier like a phone line and digital communications like those used between computers. While modems aren't in heavy use in most areas, they are still in place for system control and remote system contact and in areas where phone lines are available but other forms of communication are too expensive or not available.

86. D. The OSI layers in order are Application, Presentation, Session, Transport, Network, Data Link, and Physical.

87. B. A teardrop attack uses fragmented packets to target a flaw in how the TCP stack on a system handles fragment reassembly. If the attack is successful, the TCP stack fails, resulting in a denial of service. Christmas tree attacks set all of the possible TCP flags on a packet, thus "lighting it up like a Christmas tree." Stack killer and frag grenade attacks are made-up answers.

88. D. The Point-to-Point Protocol (PPP) is used for dial-up connections for modems, IDSN, Frame Relay, and other technologies. It replaced SLIP in almost all cases. PPTP is the Point-to-Point Tunneling Protocol used for VPNs, and SLAP is not protocol at all!

89. B. While non-IP protocols like IPX/SPX, NetBEUI, and AppleTalk are rare in modern networks, they can present a challenge because many firewalls are not capable of filtering them. This can create risks when they are necessary for an application or system's function because they may have to be passed without any inspection. Christmas tree attacks set all of the possible flags on a TCP packet (and are thus related to an IP protocol), IPX is not an IP-based protocol, and while these protocols are outdated, there are ways to make even modern PCs understand them.

90. C. Of the three answers, PEAP is the best solution. It encapsulates EAP in a TLS tunnel, providing strong encryption. LEAP is a Cisco proprietary protocol that was originally designed to help deal with problems in WEP. LEAP's protections have been defeated, making it a poor choice.

91. A. L2TP can use IPsec to provide encryption of traffic, ensuring confidentiality of the traffic carried via an L2TP VPN. PPTP sends the initial packets of a session in plaintext, potentially including usernames and hashed passwords. PPTP does support EAP and was designed to encapsulate PPP packets. All VPNs are point to point, and multipoint issues are not a VPN problem.

92. C. A full mesh topology directly connects each machine to every other machine on the network. For five systems, this means four connections per system.

93. D. Ethernet uses a bus topology. While devices may be physically connected to a switch in a physical topology that looks like a star, systems using Ethernet can all transmit on the bus simultaneously, possibly leading to collisions.

94. D. ARP spoofing is often done to replace a target's cache entry for a destination IP, allowing the attacker to conduct a man-in-the-middle attack. A denial of service attack would be aimed at disrupting services rather than spoofing an ARP response, a replay attack will involve existing sessions, and a Trojan is malware that is disguised in a way that makes it look harmless.

95. B. Category 3 UTP cable is primarily used for phone cables and was also used for early Ethernet networks where it provided 10 Mbps of throughput. Cat 5 cable provides 100 Mbps (and 1000 Mbps if it is Cat 5e). Cat 6 cable can also provide 1000 Mbps.

96. B. Crosstalk occurs when data transmitted on one set of wires is picked up on another set of wires. Interference like this is electromagnetic rather than simply magnetic, *transmission absorption* is a made-up term, and amplitude modulation is how AM radio works.

97. B. WEP's implementation of RC4 is weakened by its use of a static common key and a limited number of initialization vectors. It does not use asymmetric encryption, and clients do not select encryption algorithms.

98. B. VLANs can be used to logically separate groups of network ports while still providing access to an uplink. Per-room VPNs would create significant overhead for support as well as create additional expenses. Port security is used to limit what systems can connect to ports, but it doesn't provide network security between systems. Finally, while firewalls might work, they would add additional expense and complexity without adding any benefits over a VLAN solution.

99. D. MAC addresses and their organizationally unique identifiers are used at the Data Link layer to identify systems on a network. The Application and Session layers don't care about physical addresses, while the Physical layer involves electrical connectivity and handling physical interfaces rather than addressing.

100. C. Domain Keys Identified Mail, or DKIM, is designed to allow assertions of domain identity to validate email. S/MIME, PEM, and MOSS are all solutions that can provide authentication, integrity, nonrepudiation, and confidentiality, depending on how they are used.

Chapter 5: Identity and Access Management (Domain 5)

1. C. Capability tables list the privileges assigned to subjects and identify the objects that subjects can access. Access control lists are object-focused rather than subject-focused. Implicit deny is a principle that states that anything that is not explicitly allowed is denied, and a rights management matrix is not an access control model.

2. B. Since Jim's organization is using a cloud-based Identity as a Service solution, a third party, on-premise identity service can provide the ability to integrate with the IDaaS solution, and the company's use of Active Directory is widely supported by third-party vendors. OAuth is used to log into third-party websites using existing credentials and would not meet the needs described. SAML is a markup language and would not meet the full set of AAA needs. Since the organization is using Active Directory, a custom in-house solution is unlikely to be as effective as a preexisting third-party solution and may take far more time and expense to implement.

3. C. Kerberos encrypts messages using secret keys, providing protection for authentication traffic. The KDC is both a single point of failure and can cause problems if compromised because keys are stored on the KDC that would allow attackers to impersonate any user. Like many authentication methods, Kerberos can be susceptible to password guessing.

4. C. Voice pattern recognition is "something you are," a Type 3 authentication factor. Type 1 factors are "something you know," and Type 2 factors are "something you have." Type 4 is made up and is not a valid type of authentication factor.

5. B. Susan has used two distinct types of factors: the PIN and password are both Type 1 factors, and the retina scan is a Type 3 factor. Her username is not a factor.

6. B. Menus, shells, and database views are all commonly used for constrained interfaces. A keyboard is not typically a constrained interface, although physically constrained interfaces like those found on ATMs, card readers, and other devices are common.

7. C. Dictionary attacks use a dictionary or list of common passwords as well as variations of those words to attempt to log in as an authorized user. This attack shows a variety of passwords based on a similar base word, which is often a good indicator of a dictionary attack. A brute force attack will typically show simple iteration of passwords, while a

man-in-the-middle attack would not be visible in the authentication log. A rainbow table attack is used when attackers already have password hashes in their possession and would also not show up in logs.

8. D. The Common Criteria defines trusted paths as a way to protect data between users and a security component. This includes attacks like replacing login windows for systems and is the reason Windows uses Ctrl+Alt_Del as a login sequence. Man-in-the-middle attacks can be prevented by using a trusted channel, which is often implemented with encryption and certificates. Brute force and dictionary attacks are often discouraged by using a back-off algorithm to slow down or prevent attacks.

9. B. Decentralized access control can result in less consistency because the individuals tasked with control may interpret policies and requirements differently and may perform their roles in different ways. Access outages, overly granular control, and training costs may occur, depending on specific implementations, but they are not commonly identified issues with decentralized access control.

10. B. A callback to a home phone number is an example of a "somewhere you are" factor. This could potentially be spoofed by call forwarding or using a VoIP system. Type 1 factors are "something you know," Type 3 factors are biometric, and geographic factors are typically based on IP addresses or access to a GPS.

11. D. Kerberos uses realms, and the proper type of trust to set up for an Active Directory environment that needs to connect to a K5 domain is a realm trust. A shortcut trust is a transitive trust between parts of a domain tree or forest that shortens the trust path, a forest trust is a transitive trust between two forest root domains, and an external trust is a non-transitive trust between AD domains in separate forests.

12. B. TACACS+ is the only modern protocol on the list. It provides advantages of both TACACS and XTACACS as well as some benefits over RADIUS, including encryption of all authentication information. Super TACACS is not an actual protocol.

13. D. Kerberos, Active Directory Federation Services (ADFS), and Central Authentication Services (CAS) are all SSO implementations. RADIUS is not a single-sign on implementation, although some vendors use it behind the scenes to provide authentication for proprietary SSO.

14. C. Interface restrictions based on user privileges is an example of a constrained interface. Least privilege describes the idea of providing users with only the rights they need to accomplish their job, while need to know limits access based on whether a subject needs to know the information to accomplish an assigned task. Separation of duties focuses on preventing fraud or mistakes by splitting tasks between multiple subjects.

15. D. When the owner of a file makes the decisions about who has rights or access privileges to it, they are using discretionary access control. Role-based access controls would grant accessed based on a subject's role, while rule-based controls would base the decision on a set of rules or requirements. Non-discretionary access controls apply a fixed set of rules to an environment to manage access. Non-discretionary access controls include rule-, role-, and lattice-based access controls.

16. D. Need to know is applied when subjects like Alex have access to only the data they need to accomplish their job. Separation of duties is used to limit fraud and abuse by having multiple employees perform parts of a task. Constrained interfaces restrict what a user can see or do and would be a reasonable answer if need to know did not describe his access more completely in this scenario. Context-dependent control relies on the activity being performed to apply controls, and this question does not specify a workflow or process.

17. D. The client in Kerberos logins uses AES to encrypt the username and password prior to sending it to the KDC.

18. C. The KDC uses the user's password to generate a hash and then uses that hash to encrypt a symmetric key. It transmits both the encrypted symmetric key and an encrypted time-stamped TGT to the client.

19. B. The client needs to install the TGT for use until it expires, and must also decrypt the symmetric key using a hash of the user's password.

20. A. Retina scans can reveal additional information, including high blood pressure and pregnancy, causing privacy concerns. Newer retina scans don't require a puff of air, and retina scanners are not the most expensive biometric factor. Their false positive rate can typically be adjusted in software, allowing administrators to adjust their acceptance rate as needed to balance usability and security.

21. C. Mandatory access control systems are based on a lattice-based model. Lattice-based models use a matrix of classification labels to compartmentalize data. Discretionary access models allow object owners to determine access to the objects they control, role-based access controls are often group based, and rule-based access controls like firewall ACLs apply rules to all subjects they apply to.

22. C. Dictionary, brute force, and man-in-the-middle attacks are all types of attacks that are frequently aimed at access controls. Teardrop attacks are a type of denial of service attack.

23. A. Logging systems can provide accountability for identity systems by tracking the actions, changes, and other activities a user or account performs.

24. B. As an employee's role changes, they often experience privilege creep, which is the accumulation of old rights and roles. Account review is the process of reviewing accounts and ensuring that their rights match their owners' role and job requirements. Account revocation removes accounts, while re-provisioning might occur if an employee was terminated and returned or took a leave of absence and returned.

25. A. Biba uses a lattice to control access and is a form of the mandatory access control (MAC) model. It does not use rules, roles, or attributes, nor does it allow user discretion. Users can create content at their level or lower but cannot decide who gets access, levels are not roles, and attributes are not used to make decisions on access control.

26. C. RADIUS is an AAA protocol used to provide authentication and authorization; it's often used for modems, wireless networks, and network devices. It uses network access

servers to send access requests to central RADIUS servers. Kerberos is a ticket-based authentication protocol; OAuth is an open standard for authentication allowing the use of credentials from one site on third-party sites; and EAP is the Extensible Authentication Protocol, an authentication framework often used for wireless networks.

27. A. Resource-based access controls match permissions to resources like a storage volume. Resource-based access controls are becoming increasingly common in cloud-based Infrastructure as a Service environments. The lack of roles, rules, or a classification system indicate that role-based, rule-based, and mandatory access controls are not in use here.

28. C. By default, RADIUS uses UDP and only encrypts passwords. RADIUS supports TCP and TLS, but this is not a default setting.

29. D. A key distribution center (KDC) provides authentication services, and ticket-granting tickets (TGTs) provide proof that a subject has authenticated and can request tickets to access objects. Authentication services (ASs) are part of the KDC. There is no TS in a Kerberos infrastructure.

30. D. Authorization provides a user with capabilities or rights. Roles and group management are both methods that could be used to match users with rights. Logins are used to validate a user.

31. C. Privilege creep occurs when users retain from roles they held previously rights they do not need to accomplish their current job. Unauthorized access occurs when an unauthorized user accesses files. *Excessive provisioning* is not a term used to describe permissions issues, and account review would help find issues like this.

32. B. Phishing is not an attack against an access control mechanism. While phishing can result in stolen credentials, the attack itself is not against the control system and is instead against the person being phished. Dictionary attacks and man-in-the-middle attacks both target access control systems.

33. B. Race conditions occur when two or more processes need to access the same resource in the right order. If an attacker can disrupt this order, they may be able to affect the normal operations of the system and gain unauthorized access or improper rights. Collisions occur when two different files produce the same result from a hashing operation, out-of-order execution is a CPU architecture feature that allows the use of otherwise unused cycles, and *determinism* is a philosophical term rather than something you should see on the CISSP exam!

34. C. Mandatory access controls use a lattice to describe how classification labels relate to each other. In this image, classification levels are set for each of the labels shown. A discretionary access control (DAC) system would show how the owner of the objects allows access. RBAC could be either rule- or role-based access control and would either use system-wide rules or roles. Task-based access control (TBAC) would list tasks for users.

35. C. LDAP distinguished names are made up of zero or more comma-separate components known as relative distinguished names. cn=ben,ou=example; ends with a semicolon and is not a valid DN. It is possible to have additional values in the same RDN by using a plus sign between then.

36. B. The process of a subject claiming or professing an identity is known as identification. Authorization verifies the identity of a subject by checking a factor like a password. Logins typically include both identification and authorization, and token presentation is a type of authentication.

37. D. Dogs, guards, and fences are all examples of physical controls. While dogs and guards might detect a problem, fences cannot, so they are not all examples of detective controls. None of these controls would help repair or restore functionality after an issue, and thus none are recovery controls, nor are they administrative controls that involve policy or procedures, although the guards might refer to them when performing their duties.

38. B. Password complexity is driven by length, and a longer password will be more effective against brute force attacks than a shorter password. Each character of additional length increases the difficulty by the size of the potential character set (for example, a single lowercase character makes the passwords 26 times more difficult to crack). While each of the other settings is useful for a strong password policy, they won't have the same impact on brute force attacks.

39. A. The stored sample of a biometric factor is called a reference profile or a reference template. None of the other answers are common terms used for biometric systems.

40. A. Organizations that have very strict security requirements that don't have a tolerance for false acceptance want to lower the false acceptance rate, or FAR, to be as near to zero as possible. That often means that the false rejection rate, or FRR, increases. Different biometric technologies or a better registration method can help improve biometric performance, but false rejections due to data quality are not typically a concern with modern biometric systems. In this case, knowing the crossover error rate, or CER, or having a very high CER doesn't help the decision.

41. B. The complexity of brute forcing a password increases based on both the number of potential characters and the number of letters added. In this case, there are 26 lowercase letters, 26 uppercase letters, and 10 possible digits. That creates 62 possibilities. Since we added only a single letter of length, we get 62^1, or 62 possibilities, and thus, the new passwords would be 62 times harder to brute force on average.

42. B. Biometric systems can face major usability challenges if the time to enroll is long (over a couple of minutes) and if the speed at which the biometric system is able to scan and accept or reject the user is too slow. FAR and FRR may be important in the design decisions made by administrators or designers, but they aren't typically visible to users. CER and ERR are the same and are the point where FAR and FRR meet. Reference profile requirements are a system requirement, not a user requirement.

43. C. TLS provides message confidentiality and integrity, which can prevent eavesdropping. When paired with digital signatures, which provide integrity and authentication, forged assertions can also be defeated. SAML does not have a security mode and relies on TLS and digital signatures to ensure security if needed. Message hashing without a signature would help prevent modification of the message but won't necessarily provide authentication.

44. B. Integration with cloud-based third parties that rely on local authentication can fail if the local organization's Internet connectivity or servers are offline. Adopting a hybrid cloud and

local authentication system can ensure that Internet or server outages are handled, allowing authentication to work regardless of where the user is or if their home organization is online. Using encrypted and signed communication does not address availability, redirects are a configuration issue with the third party, and a local gateway won't handle remote users. Also, host files don't help with availability issues with services other than DNS.

45. A. While many solutions are technical, if a trusted third party redirects to an unexpected authentication site, awareness is often the best defense. Using TLS would keep the transaction confidential but would not prevent the redirect. Handling redirects locally only works for locally hosted sites, and using a third-party service requires offsite redirects. An IPS might detect an attacker's redirect, but tracking the multitude of load-balanced servers most large providers use can be challenging, if not impossible. In addition, an IPS relies on visibility into the traffic, and SAML integrations should be encrypted for security, which would require a man-in-the-middle type of IPS to be configured.

46. B. Discretionary access control (DAC) can provide greater scalability by leveraging many administrators, and those administrators can add flexibility by making decisions about access to their objects without fitting into an inflexible mandatory access control system (MAC). MAC is more secure due to the strong set of controls it provides, but it does not scale as well as DAC and is relatively inflexible in comparison.

47. C. While signature-based detection is used to detect attacks, review of provisioning processes typically involves checking logs, reviewing the audit trail, or performing a manual review of permissions granted during the provisioning process.

48. C. Service Provisioning Markup Language, or SPML is an XML-based language designed to allow platforms to generate and respond to provisioning requests. SAML is used to make authorization and authentication data, while XACML is used to describe access controls. SOAP, or Simple Object Access Protocol, is a messaging protocol and could be used for any XML messaging, but is not a markup language itself.

49. C. Rainbow tables are databases of prehashed passwords paired with high-speed lookup functions. Since they can quickly compare known hashes against those in a file, using rainbow tables is the fastest way to quickly determine passwords from hashes. A brute force attack may eventually succeed but will be very slow against most hashes. Pass-the-hash attacks rely on sniffed or otherwise acquired NTLM or LanMan hashes being sent to a system to avoid the need to know a user's password. Salts are data added to a hash to avoid the use of tools like rainbow tables. A salt added to a password means the hash won't match a rainbow table generated without the same salt.

50. B. Google's federation with other applications and organizations allows single-sign on as well as management of their electronic identity and its related attributes. While this is an example of SSO, it goes beyond simple single-sign on. Provisioning provides accounts and rights, and a public key infrastructure is used for certificate management.

51. D. When users have more rights than they need to accomplish their job, they have excessive privileges. This is a violation of the concept of least privilege. Unlike creeping privileges, this is a provisioning or rights management issue rather than a problem of retention of rights the user needed but no longer requires. *Rights collision* is a made-up term, and thus is not an issue here.

52. B. Registration is the process of adding a user to an identity management system. This includes creating their unique identifier and adding any attribute information that is associated with their identity. Proofing occurs when the user provides information to prove who they are. Directories are managed to maintain lists of users, services, and other items. Session management tracks application and user sessions.

53. A. Port 636 is the default port for LDAP-S, which provides LDAP over SSL or TLS, thus indicating that the server supports encrypted connections. Since neither port 3268 nor 3269 is mentioned, we do not know if the server provides support for a global catalog.

54. D. The X.500 series of standards covers directory services. Kerberos is described in RFCs; biometric systems are covered by a variety of standards, including ISO standards; and provisioning standards include SCIM, SPML, and others.

55. B. Active Directory Domain Services is based on LDAP, the Lightweight Directory Access Protocol. Active Directory also uses Kerberos for authentication.

56. C. Identity proofing can be done by comparing user information that the organization already has, like account numbers or personal information. Requiring users to create unique questions can help with future support by providing a way for them to do password resets. Using a phone call only verifies that the individual who created the account has the phone that they registered and won't prove their identity. In-person verification would not fit the business needs of most websites.

57. A. By default, OpenLDAP stored the userPassword attribute in the clear. This means that ensuring that the password is provided to OpenLDAP in a secure format is the responsibility of the administrator or programmer who builds its provisioning system.

58. C. Type 2 errors occur in biometric systems when an invalid subject is incorrectly authenticated as a valid user. In this case, nobody except the actual customer should be validated when fingerprints are scanned. Type 1 errors occur when a valid subject is not authenticated; if the existing customer was rejected, it would be a Type 1 error. Registration is the process of adding users, but registration errors and time of use, method of use errors are not specific biometric authentication terms.

59. B. Firewalls use rule-based access control, or Rule-BAC, in their access control lists and apply rules created by administrators to all traffic that pass through them. DAC, or discretionary access control, allows owners to determine who can access objects they control, while task-based access control lists tasks for users. MAC, or mandatory access control, uses classifications to determine access.

60. C. When you input a username and password, you are authenticating yourself by providing a unique identifier and a verification that you are the person who should have that identifier (the password). Authorization is the process of determining what a user is allowed to do. Validation and login both describe elements of what is happening in the process; however, they aren't the most important identity and access management activity.

61. C. Kathleen should implement a biometric factor. The cards and keys are an example of a Type 2 factor, or "something you have." Using a smart card replaces this with another

Type 2 factor, but the cards could still be loaned out or stolen. Adding a PIN suffers from the same problem: A PIN can be stolen. Adding cameras doesn't prevent access to the facility and thus doesn't solve the immediate problem (but it is a good idea!).

62. D. Kerberos is an authentication protocol that uses tickets, and provides secure communications between the client, key distribution center (KDC), ticket-granting service (TGS), authentication server (AS), and endpoint services. RADIUS does not provide the same level of security by default, SAML is a markup language, and OAuth is designed to allow third-party websites to rely on credentials from other sites like Google or Microsoft.

63. D. Administrative access controls are procedures and the policies from which they derive. They are based on regulations, requirements, and the organization's own policies. Corrective access controls return an environment to its original status after an issue, while logical controls are technical access controls that rely on hardware or software to protect systems and data. Compensating controls are used in addition to or as an alternative to other controls.

64. A. When clients perform a client service authorization, they send a TGT and the ID of the requested service to the TGS, and the TGS responds with a client-to-server ticket and session key back to the client if the request is validated. An AS is an authentication server and the SS is a service server, neither of which can be sent.

65. C. In a mandatory access control system, all subjects and objects have a label. Compartments may or may not be used, but there is not a specific requirement for either subjects or objects to be compartmentalized. The specific labels of Confidential, Secret, and Top Secret are not required by MAC.

66. D. Passwords are never stored for web applications in a well-designed environment. Instead, salted hashes are stored and compared to passwords after they are salted and hashed. If the hashes match, the user is authenticated.

67. C. When a third-party site integrates via OAuth 2.0, authentication is handled by the service provider's servers. In this case, Google is acting as the service provider for user authentication. Authentication for local users who create their own accounts would occur in the e-commerce application (or a related server), but that is not the question that is asked here.

68. B. The anti-forgery state token exchanged during OAuth sessions is intended to prevent cross-site request forgery. This makes sure that the unique session token with the authentication response from Google's OAuth service is available to verify that the user, not an attacker, is making a request. XSS attacks focus on scripting and would have script tags involved, SQL injection would have SQL code included, and XACML is the eXtensible Access Control Markup Language, not a type of attack.

69. A. Knowledge-based authentication relies on preset questions "What is your pet's name?" and the answers. It can be susceptible to attacks due to the availability of the answers on social media or other sites. Dynamic knowledge based authentication relies on facts or data that the user already knows which can be used to create questions they can answer on an as needed basis (for example, a previous address, or a school they attended).

Out-of-band identity proofing relies on an alternate channel like a phone call or text message. Finally, Type 3 authentication factors are biometric, or "something you are," rather than knowledge based.

70. C. An access control matrix is a table that lists objects, subjects, and their privileges. Access control lists focus on objects and which subjects can access them. Capability tables list subjects and what objects they can access. Subject/object rights management systems are not based on an access control model.

71. C. Self-service password reset tools typically have a significant impact on the number of password reset contacts that a help desk has. Two-factor and biometric authentication both add additional complexity and may actually increase the number of contacts. Passphrases can be easier to remember than traditional complex passwords and may decrease calls, but they don't have the same impact that a self-service system does.

72. C. RADIUS supports TLS over TCP. RADIUS does not have a supported TLS mode over UDP. AES pre-shared symmetric ciphers are not a supported solution and would be very difficult to both implement and maintain in a large environment, and the built-in encryption in RADIUS only protects passwords.

73. B. OAuth provides the ability to access resources from another service and would meet Jim's needs. OpenID would allow him to use an account from another service with his application, and Kerberos and LDAP are used more frequently for in-house services.

74. B. Since physical access to the workstations is part of the problem, setting application time-outs and password-protected screensavers with relatively short inactivity time-outs can help prevent unauthorized access. Using session IDs for all applications and verifying system IP addresses would be helpful for online attacks against applications.

75. C. Firewalls, routers, and passwords are all examples of technical access controls and are software or hardware systems used to manage and protect access. RAID-5 is an example of a recovery control. If you're questioning why routers are a technical access control, remember that router access control lists (ACLs) are quite often used to control network access or traffic flows.

76. A. Verifying information that an individual should know about themselves using third-party factual information (a Type 1 authentication factor) is sometimes known as dynamic knowledge-based authentication and is a type of identity proofing. Out-of-band identity proofing would use another means of contacting the user, like a text message or phone call, and password verification requires a password.

77. C. The US government's Common Access Card is a smart card. The US government also issues PIV cards, or personal identity verification cards.

78. C. OpenID Connect is a RESTful, JSON-based authentication protocol that, when paired with OAuth, can provide identity verification and basic profile information. SAML is the Security Assertion Markup Language, Shibboleth is a federated identity solution designed to allow web-based SSO, and Higgins is an open-source project designed to provide users with control over the release of their identity information.

79. C. In a mandatory access control system, classifications do not have to include rights to lower levels. This means that the only label we can be sure Jim has rights to is Secret. Despite the fact that it is unclassified, Unclassified data remains a different label, and Jim may not be authorized to access it.

80. B. Time-based controls are an example of context-dependent controls. A constrained interface would limit what Susan was able to do in an application or system interface, while content-dependent control would limit her access to content based on her role or rights. Least privilege is used to ensure that subjects only receive the rights they need to perform their role.

81. C. A Type 3 authentication factor is: something you are: like a biometric identifier. A Type 1 authentication factor is "something you know." A Type 2 factor is "something you have," like a smart card or hardware token. There is not a Type 4 authentication factor.

82. B. Policy is a subset of the administrative layer of access controls. Administrative, technical, and physical access controls all play an important role in security.

83. C. Google Authenticator's constantly changing codes are part of a synchronous token that uses a time-based algorithm to generate codes. Asynchronous tokens typically require a challenge to be entered on the token to allow it to calculate a response, which the server compares to the response it expects. Smart cards typically present a certificate but may have other token capabilities built in. Static tokens are physical devices that can contain credentials and include smart cards and memory cards.

84. A. Asynchronous tokens use a challenge/response process in which the system sends a challenge and the user responds with a PIN and a calculated response to the challenge. The server performs the same calculations, and if both match, it authenticates the user. Synchronous tokens use a time-based calculation to generate codes. Smart cards are paired with readers and don't need to have challenges entered, and RFID devices are not used for challenge/response tokens.

85. C. The crossover error rate is the point where false acceptance rate and false rejection rate cross over and is a standard assessment used to compare the accuracy of biometric devices.

86. A. At point B, the false acceptance rate, or FAR, is quite high, while the false rejection rate, or FRR, is relatively low. This may be acceptable in some circumstances, but in organizations where a false acceptance can cause a major problem, it is likely that they should instead choose a point to the right of pointA.

87. B. CER is a standard used to assess biometric devices. If the CER for this device does not fit the needs of the organization, Ben should assess other biometric systems to find one with a lower CER. Sensitivity is already accounted for in CER charts, and moving the CER isn't something Ben can do. FRR is not a setting in software, so Ben can't use that as an option either.

88. B. The Simple Authentication and Security Layer (SASL) for LDAP provides support for a range of authentication types, including secure methods. Anonymous authentication does not require or provide security, and simple authentication can be tunneled over SSL or TLS but does not provide security by itself. S-LDAP is not an LDAP protocol.

89. C. Palm scans compare the vein patterns in the palm to a database to authenticate a user. Vein patterns are unique, and this method is a better single-factor authentication method than voice pattern recognition, hand geometry, and pulse patterns, each of which can be more difficult to uniquely identify between individuals or can be fooled more easily.

90. B. Allowing the relying party to provide the redirect to the OpenID provider could allow a phishing attack by directing clients to a fake OpenID provider that can capture valid credentials. Since the OpenID provider URL is provided by the client, the relying party cannot select the wrong provider. The relying party never receives the user's password, which means that they can't steal it. Finally, the relying party receives the signed assertion but does not send one.

91. A. IDaaS, or Identity as a Service, provides an identity platform as a third-party service. This can provide benefits including integration with cloud services and removing overhead for maintenance of traditional on-premise identity systems, but it can also create risk due to third-party control of identity services and reliance on an offsite identity infrastructure.

92. B. Drives in a RAID-5 array are intended to handle failure of a drive. This is an example of a recovery control, which is used to return operations to normal function after a failure. Administrative controls are policies and procedures. Compensation controls help cover for issues with primary controls or improve them. Logical controls are software and hardware mechanisms used to protect resources and systems.

93. D. The Linux filesystem allows the owners of objects to determine the access rights that subjects have to them. This means that it is a discretionary access control. If the system enforced a role-based access control, Alex wouldn't set the controls; they would be set based on the roles assigned to each subject. A rule-based access control system would apply rules throughout the system, and a mandatory access control system uses classification labels.

94. D. Diameter was designed to provide enhanced, modern features to replace RADIUS. Diameter provides better reliability and a broad range of improved functionality. RADIUS-NG does not exist, Kerberos is not a direct competitor for RADIUS, and TACACS is not an open protocol.

95. A. In this example, uid=ben,ou=sales,dc=example,dc=com, the items proceed from most specific to least specific (broadest) from left to right, as required by a DN.

96. D. Kerberos relies on properly synchronized time on each end of a connection to function. If the local system time is more than 5 minutes out of sync, otherwise valid TGTs will be invalid and the system won't receive any new tickets.

97. A. Kerberos, KryptoKnight, and SESAME are all single sign-on, or SSO, systems. PKI systems are public key infrastructure systems, CMS systems are content management systems, and LDAP and other directory servers provide information about services, resources, and individuals.

98. B. Locks can be preventative access controls by stopping unwanted access, can deter potential intruders by making access difficult, and are physical access controls. They are not directive controls because they don't control the actions of subjects.

99. B. Windows uses Kerberos for authentication. RADIUS is typically used for wireless networks, modems, and network devices, while OAuth is primarily used for web applications. TACACS+ is used for network devices.

100. C. The default ports for SSL/TLS LDAP directory information and global catalog services are 636 and 3269, respectively. Unsecure LDAP uses 389, and unsecure global directory services use 3268.

Chapter 6: Security Assessment and Testing (Domain 6)

1. B. TCP and UDP ports 137-139 are used for NetBIOS services, whereas 445 is used for Active Directory. TCP 1433 is the default port for Microsoft SQL, indicating that this is probably a Windows server providing SQL services.

2. D. Mutation testing modifies a program in small ways, and then tests that mutant to determine if it behaves as it should or if it fails. This technique is used to design and test software tests through mutation. Static code analysis and regression testing are both means of testing code, whereas code auditing is an analysis of source code rather than a means of designing and testing software tests.

3. B. TCP port 443 normally indicates an HTTPS server. Nikto is useful for vulnerability scanning web servers and applications and is the best choice listed for a web server. Metasploit includes some scanning functionality but is not a purpose-built tool for vulnerability scanning. zzuf is a fuzzing tool and isn't relevant for vulnerability scans, whereas sqlmap is a SQL injection testing tool.

4. A. Syslog is a widely used protocol for event and message logging. Eventlog, netlog, and Remote Log Protocol are all made-up terms.

5. C. Fuzzers are tools that are designed to provide invalid or unexpected input to applications, testing for vulnerabilities like format string vulnerabilities, buffer overflow issues, and other problems. A static analysis relies on examining code without running the application or code, and thus would not fill forms as part of a web application. Brute-force tools attempt to bypass security by trying every possible combination for passwords or other values. A black box is a type of penetration test where the testers do not know anything about the environment.

6. B. OpenVAS is an open source vulnerability scanning tool that will provide Susan with a report of the vulnerabilities that it can identify from a remote, network-based scan. Nmap is an open source port scanner. Both the Microsoft Baseline Security Analyzer (MBSA) and Nessus are closed source tools, although Nessus was originally open source.

7. B. An IPS is an example of a mechanism like a hardware-, software-, or firmware-based control or system. Specifications are document-based artifacts like policies or designs,

activities are actions that support an information system that involves people, and an individual is one or more people applying specifications, mechanisms, or activities.

8. C. Jim has agreed to a black box penetration test, which provides no information about the organization, its systems, or its defenses. A crystal or white box penetration test provides all of the information an attacker needs, whereas a gray box penetration test provides some, but not all, information.

9. A. A vulnerability scanner that has a test (sometimes called a signature or plugin) that provides a detection method for CVE-2014-0160, also known as the Heartbleed bug, a vulnerability in OpenSSL will detect and report on the issue on any system it can connect to. Port scanners do not determine whether services are vulnerable, and Heartbleed was not a vulnerability in the Apache web server—but even without knowing this, the CVE number is a better indicator of whether the issue will be found than a generic detect for a service.

10. C. Service Organization Control (SOC) reports replaced SAS-70 reports in 2010. A Type 1 report only covers a point in time, so Susan needs an SOC Type 2 report to have the information she requires to make a design and operating effectiveness decision based on the report.

11. B. WPA2 enterprise uses RADIUS authentication for users rather than a preshared key. This means a password attack is more likely to fail as password attempts for a given user may result in account lock-out. WPA2 encryption will not stop a password attack, and WPA2's preshared key mode is specifically targeted by password attacks that attempt to find the key. Not only is WEP encryption outdated, but it can also frequently be cracked quickly by tools like aircrack-ng.

12. C. SOC 3 reports are intended to be shared with a broad community, often with a website seal, and support the organization's claims about their ability to provide integrity, availability, and confidentiality. SOC 1 reports report on controls over financial reporting, whereas SOC 2 reports cover security, availability, integrity, and privacy for business partners, regulators, and other similar organizations in detail that would not typically be provided to a broad audience.

13. C. Interface testing is used to ensure that software modules properly meet interface specifications and thus will properly exchange data. Dynamic testing tests software in a running environment, whereas fuzzing is a type of dynamic testing that feeds invalid input to running software to test error and input handling. API checksums are not a testing technique.

14. B. Not only should active scanning be expected to cause wireless IPS alarms, but they may actually be desired if the test is done to test responses. Accidently scanning guests, neighbors, or misidentifying devices belonging to third parties are all potential problems with active scanning and require the security assessor to carefully verify the systems that she is scanning.

15. C. Generational fuzzing relies on models for application input and conducts fuzzing attacks based on that information. Mutation based fuzzers are sometimes called "dumb" fuzzers because they simply mutate or modify existing data samples to create new test samples. Neither parametric nor derivative is a term used to describe types of fuzzers.

16. B. Flows, also often called network flows, are captured to provide insight into network traffic for security, troubleshooting, and performance management. Audit logging provides information about events on the routers, route logging is not a common network logging function, and trace logs are used in troubleshooting specific software packages as they perform their functions.

17. D. The IP addresses that his clients have provided are RFC 1918 non-routable IP addresses, and Jim will not be able to scan them from offsite. To succeed in his penetration test, he will either have to first penetrate their network border or place a machine inside their network to scan from the inside. IP addresses overlapping is not a real concern for scanning, and the ranges can easily be handled by current scanning systems.

18. B. Karen can't use MTD verification because MTD is the Maximum Tolerable Downtime. Verifying it will only tell her how long systems can be offline without significant business impact. Reviewing logs, using hashing to verify that the logs are intact, and performing periodic tests are all valid ways to verify that the backups are working properly.

19. B. Group Policy enforced by Active Directory can ensure consistent logging settings and can provide regular enforcement of policy on systems. Periodic configuration audits won't catch changes made between audits, and local policies can drift due to local changes or differences in deployments. A Windows syslog client will enable the Windows systems to send syslog to the SIEM appliance but won't ensure consistent logging of events.

20. B. Windows systems generate logs in the Windows native logging format. To send syslog events, Windows systems require a helper application or tool. Enterprise wireless access points, firewalls, and Linux systems all typically support syslog.

21. B. Network Time Protocol (NTP) can ensure that systems are using the same time, allowing time sequencing for logs throughout a centralized logging infrastructure. Syslog is a way for systems to send logs to a logging server and won't address time sequencing. Neither logsync nor SNAP is an industry term.

22. A. When a tester does not have raw packet creation privileges, such as when they have not escalated privileges on a compromised host, a TCP connect scan can be used. TCP SYN scans require elevated privileges on most Linux systems due to the need to write raw packets. A UDP scan will miss most services that are provided via TCP, and an ICMP is merely a ping sweep of systems that respond to pings and won't identify services at all.

23. B. Joseph may be surprised to discover FTP (TCP port 21) and Telnet (TCP port 23) open on his network since both services are unencrypted and have been largely replaced by SSH, and SCP or SFTP. SSH uses port 22, SMTP uses port 25, and POP3 uses port 110.

24. D. Black box testing is the most realistic type of penetration test because it does not provide the penetration tester with inside information about the configuration or design of systems, software, or networks. A gray box test provides some information, whereas a white or crystal box test provides significant or full detail.

25. A. A test coverage analysis is often used to provide insight into how well testing covered the set of use cases that an application is being tested for. Source code reviews look at the

code of a program for bugs, not necessarily at a use case analysis, whereas fuzzing tests invalid inputs. A code review report might be generated as part of a source code review.

26. C. Testing how a system could be misused, or misuse testing, focuses on behaviors that are not what the organization desires or that are counter to the proper function of a system or application. Use case testing is used to verify whether a desired functionality works. Dynamic testing is used to determine how code handles variables that change over time, whereas manual testing is just what it implies: testing code by hand.

27. B. Synthetic monitoring uses emulated or recorded transactions to monitor for performance changes in response time, functionality, or other performance monitors. Passive monitoring uses a span port or other method to copy traffic and monitor it in real time. Log analysis is typically performed against actual log data but can be performed on simulated traffic to identify issues. Simulated transaction analysis is not an industry term.

28. C. Path disclosures, local file inclusions, and buffer overflows are all vulnerabilities that may be found by a web vulnerability scanner, but race conditions that take advantage of timing issues tend to be found either by code analysis or using automated tools that specifically test for race conditions as part of software testing.

29. C. Vulnerability scanners that do not have administrative rights to access a machine or that are not using an agent scan remote machines to gather information, including fingerprints from responses to queries and connections, banner information from services, and related data. CVE information is Common Vulnerability and Exposure information, or vulnerability information. A port scanner gathers information about what service ports are open, although some port scanners blur the line between port and vulnerability scanners. Patch management tools typically run as an agent on a system to allow them to both monitor patch levels and update the system as needed. Service validation typically involves testing the functionality of a service, not its banner and response patterns.

30. B. Emily is using synthetic transactions, which can use recorded or generated transactions, and is conducting use case testing to verify that the application responds properly to actual use cases. Neither actual data nor dynamic monitoring is an industry term. Fuzzing involves sending unexpected inputs to a program to see how it responds. Passive monitoring uses a network tap or other capture technology to allow monitoring of actual traffic to a system or application.

31. B. Real user monitoring (RUM) is a passive monitoring technique that records user interaction with an application or system to ensure performance and proper application behavior. RUM is often used as part of a predeployment process using the actual user interface. The other answers are all made up—synthetic monitoring uses simulated behavior, but synthetic user monitoring is not a testing method. Similarly, passive monitoring monitors actual traffic, but passive user recording is not an industry term or technique. Client/server testing merely describes one possible architecture.

32. B. Jim should ask the information security team to flag the issue as resolved if he is sure the patch was installed. Many vulnerability scanners rely on version information or banner information, and may flag patched versions if the software provider does not update the information they see. Uninstalling and reinstalling the patch will not change this. Changing the version information may not change all of the details that are being flagged

by the scanner, and may cause issues at a later date. Reviewing the vulnerability information for a workaround may be a good idea but should not be necessary if the proper patch is installed; it can create maintenance issues later.

33. B. zzuf is the only fuzzer on the list, and zzuf is specifically designed to work with tools like web browsers, image viewers, and similar software by modifying network and file input to application. Nmap is a port scanner, Nessus is a vulnerability scanner, and Nikto is a web server scanner.

34. C. An important part of application threat modeling is threat categorization. It helps to assess attacker goals that influence the controls that should be put in place. The other answers all involve topics that are not directly part of application threat modeling.

35. A. Passive scanning can help identify rogue devices by capturing MAC address vendor IDs that do not match deployed devices, by verifying that systems match inventories of organizationally owned hardware by hardware address, and by monitoring for rogue SSIDs or connections.

Scripted attacks are part of active scanning rather than passive scanning, and active scanning is useful for testing IDS or IPS systems, whereas passive scanning will not be detected by detection systems. Finally, a shorter dwell time can actually miss troublesome traffic, so balancing dwell time versus coverage is necessary for passive wireless scanning efforts.

36. D. Bluetooth active scans can determine both the strength of the PIN and what security mode the device is operating in. Unfortunately, Bluetooth scans can be challenging due to the limited range of Bluetooth and the prevalence of personally owned Bluetooth enabled devices. Passive Bluetooth scanning only detects active connections and typically requires multiple visits to have a chance of identifying all devices.

37. D. Regression testing, which is a type of functional or unit testing, tests to ensure that changes have not introduced new issues. Nonregression testing checks to see if a change has had the effect it was supposed to, smoke testing focuses on simple problems with impact on critical functionality, and evolution testing is not a software testing technique.

38. D. Nmap, Nessus, and Nikto all have OS fingerprinting or other operating system identification capabilities. sqlmap is designed to perform automated detection and testing of SQL injection flaws, and does not provide OS detection.

39. C. Key risk indicators are used to tell those in charge of risk management how risky an activity is and how much impact changes are having on that risk profile. Identifying key risk indicators and monitoring them can help to identify high-risk areas earlier in their life cycle. Yearly risk assessments may be a good idea, but only provide a point in time view, whereas penetration tests may miss out on risks that are not directly security related. Monitoring logs and events using a SIEM device can help detect issues as they occur but won't necessarily show trends in risk.

40. C. Passive monitoring only works after issues have occurred because it requires actual traffic. Synthetic monitoring uses simulated or recorded traffic, and thus can be used to proactively identify problems. Both synthetic and passive monitoring can be used to detect functionality issues.

41. B. Getting authorization is the most critical element in the planning phase. Permission, and the "get out of jail free card" that demonstrates that organizational leadership is aware of the issues that a penetration test could cause, is the first step in any penetration test. Gathering tools and building a lab, as well as determining what type of test will be conducted, are all important, but nothing should happen without permission.

42. C. Discovery can include both active and passive discovery. Port scanning is commonly done during discovery to assess what services the target provides, and nmap is one of the most popular tools used for this purpose. Nessus and Nikto might be used during the vulnerability scanning phase, and john, a password cracker, can be used to recover passwords during the exploitation phase.

43. B. Penetration test reports often include information that could result in additional exposure if they were accidently released or stolen. Therefore, determining how vulnerability data should be stored and sent is critical. Problems with off-limits targets are more likely to result in issues during the vulnerability assessment and exploitation phase, and reports should not be limited in length but should be as long as they need to be to accomplish the goals of the test.

44. B. Code coverage testing most frequently requires that every function has been called, that each statement has been executed, that all branches have been fully explored, and that each condition has been evaluated for all possibilities. API, input, and loop testing are not common types of code coverage testing measures.

45. B. Time to remediate a vulnerability is a commonly used key performance indicator for security teams. Time to live measures how long a packet can exist in hops, business criticality is a measure used to determine how important a service or system is to an organization, and coverage rates are used to measure how effective code testing is.

46. D. Unique user IDs provide accountability when paired with auditable logs to provide that a specific user took any given action. Confidentiality, availability, and integrity can be provided through other means like encryption, systems design, and digital signatures.

47. B. Application programming interfaces (APIs), user interfaces (UIs), and physical interfaces are all important to test when performing software testing. Network interfaces are not a part of the typical list of interfaces tested in software testing.

48. C. The Security Content Automation Protocol (SCAP) is a community sourced specification for security flaw and security configuration information and is defined in NIST SP 800-126. SVML, VSCAP, and VML are not information security–related terms.

49. B. Security vulnerabilities can be created by misconfiguration, logical or functional design or implementation issues, or poor programming practices. Fuzzing is a method of software testing and is not a type of issue. Buffer overflows and race conditions are both caused by logical or programming flaws, but they are not typically caused by misconfiguration or functional issues.

50. C. Simply updating the version that an application provides may stop the vulnerability scanner from flagging it, but it won't fix the underlying issue. Patching, using workarounds, or installing an application layer firewall or IPS can all help to remediate or limit the impact of the vulnerability.

51. C. Saria's social-engineering attack succeeded in persuading a staff member at the help desk to change a password for someone who they not only couldn't see, but who they couldn't verify actually needed their password reset. Black box and zero knowledge are both terms describing penetration tests without information about the organization or system, and help desk spoofing is not an industry term.

52. D. The menu shown will archive logs when they reach the maximum size allowed (20 MB). These archives will be retained, which could fill the disk. Log data will not be overwritten, and log data should not be lost when the data is archived. The question does not include enough information to determine if needed information may not be logged.

53. C. Penetration tests are intended to help identify vulnerabilities, and exploiting them is part of the process rather than a hazard. Application crashes; denial of service due to system, network, or application failures; and even data corruption can all be hazards of penetration tests.

54. B. NIST SP 800-53A is titled "Assessing Security and Privacy Controls in Federal Information Systems and Organizations: Building Effective Assessment Plans," and covers methods for assessing and measuring controls.

    NIST 800-12 is an introduction to computer security, 800-34 covers contingency planning, and 800-86 is the "Guide to Integrating Forensic Techniques into Incident Response."

55. C. TCP SYN scans only open a connection halfway; they do not complete the TCP connection with an ACK, thus leaving the connection open. TCP Connect scans complete the connection, whereas TCP ACK scans attempt to appear like an open connection. Xmas, or Christmas tree, scans set the FIN, PSH, and URG flags, thereby "lighting up" the TCP packet.

56. C. SOC 1 reports are prepared according to the Statement on Standards for Attestation Engagements, or SSAE number 16 (typically shortened to SSAE-16). An SOC 1 Type I report validates policies and procedures at a point in time, whereas SOC 1 Type II reports cover a period of time of at least six months. SOC 1 reports replaced SAS 70 reports in 2011, meaning that a current report should be an SSAE-16 SOC 1 report.

57. B. Metasploit is an exploitation package that is designed to assist penetration testers. A tester using Metasploit can exploit known vulnerabilities for which an exploit has been created or can create their own exploits using the tool. While Metasploit provides built-in access to some vulnerability scanning functionality, a tester using Metasploit should primarily be expected to perform actual tests of exploitable vulnerabilities. Similarly, Metasploit supports creating buffer overflow attacks, but it is not a purpose-built buffer overflow testing tool, and of course testing systems for zero-day exploits doesn't work unless they have been released.

58. C. The audit finding indicates that the backup administrator may not be monitoring backup logs and taking appropriate action based on what they report, thus resulting in potentially unusable backups. Issues with review, logging, or being aware of the success or failure of backups are less important than not having usable backups.

59. C. ITIL, which originally stood for IT Infrastructure Library, is a set of practices for IT service management, and is not typically used for auditing. COBIT, or the Control Objectives for Information and Related Technology, ISO 27002, and SSAE-16, or the Statement on Standards for Attestation Engagements number 16, are all used for auditing.

60. A. NIST SP 800-137 outlines the process for organizations that are establishing, implementing, and maintaining an ICSM as define, establish, implement, analyze and report, respond, review, and update. Prepare, detect and analyze, contain, respond, recover, report is an incident response plan, and the others do not match the NIST process.

61. B. Lauren's team is using regression testing, which is intended to prevent the recurrence of issues. This means that measuring the rate of defect recurrence is an appropriate measure for their work. Time to remediate vulnerabilities is associated with activities like patching, rather than preparing the patch, whereas a weighted risk trend is used to measure risk over time to an organization. Finally, specific coverage may be useful to determine if they are fully testing their effort, but regression testing is more specifically covered by defect recurrence rates.

62. C. Static program reviews are typically performed by an automated tool. Program understanding, program comprehension, code review, software inspections and software walkthroughs are all human-centric methods for reviewing code.

63. A. In order to fully test code, a white box test is required. Without full visibility of the code, error conditions or other code could be missed, making a gray box or black box test an inappropriate solution. Using dynamic testing that runs against live code could also result in some conditions being missed due to sections of code not being exposed to typical usage.

64. A. A test coverage report measures how many of the test cases have been completed and is used as a way to provide test metrics when using test cases. A penetration test report is provided when a penetration test is conducted—this is not a penetration test. A code coverage report covers how much of the code has been tested, and a line coverage report is a type of code coverage report.

65. C. The changes from a testing environment with instrumentation inserted into the code and the production environment for the code can mask timing-related issues like race conditions. Bounds checking, input validation, and pointer manipulation are all related to coding issues rather than environmental issues and are more likely to be discoverable in a test environment.

66. D. Once a vulnerability scanner identifies a potential problem, validation is necessary to verify that the issue exists. Reporting, patching, or other remediation actions can be conducted once the vulnerability has been confirmed.

67. B. Fagan testing is a detailed code review that steps through planning, overview, preparation, inspection, rework, and follow-up phases. Dynamic tests test the code in a real runtime environment, whereas fuzzing is a type of dynamic testing that feeds invalid inputs to software to test its exception-handling capabilities. Roth-Parker reviews were made up for this question.

68. D. The Common Vulnerability Scoring System (CVSS) includes metrics and calculation tools for exploitability, impact, how mature exploit code is, and how vulnerabilities can be remediated, as well as a means to score vulnerabilities against users' unique requirements. NVD is the National Vulnerability Database, CSV is short for Comma-Separated Values, and VSS is a made-up term.

69. D. Network-enabled printers often provided services via TCP 515 and 9100, and have both nonsecure and secure web-enabled management interfaces on TCP 80 and 443. Web servers, access points, and file servers would not typically provide service on the LPR and LPD ports (515 and 9100).

70. A. Nikto, Burp Suite, and Wapiti are all web application vulnerability scanners, tools designed specifically to scan web servers and applications. While they share some functionality with broader vulnerability scanners and port scanning tools, they have a narrower focus and typically have deeper capabilities than vulnerability scanners.

71. B. Nmap reports one of three statuses: Open, which means that the port is open and that an application responds; Closed, which means that the port is accessible but there is no application response; and Filtered, which means that a firewall is not allowing nmap to determine if the port is open or closed.

72. C. User session monitoring is not a means of conducting synthetic performance monitoring. Synthetic performance monitoring uses scripted or recorded data, not actual user sessions. Traffic capture, database performance monitoring, and website performance monitoring can all be used during synthetic performance monitoring efforts.

73. D. Susan is conducting interface testing. Interface testing involves testing system or application components to ensure that they work properly together. Misuse case testing focuses on how an attacker might misuse the application and would not test normal cases. Fuzzing attempts to send unexpected input and might be involved in interface testing, but it won't cover the full set of concerns. Regression testing is conducted when testing changes and is used to ensure that the application or system functions as it did before the update or change.

74. B. Not having enough log sources is not a key consideration in log management system design, although it may be a worry for security managers who can't capture the data they need. Log management system designs must take into account the volume of log data and the network bandwidth it consumes, the security of the data, and the amount of effort required to analyze the data.

75. C. Jim should ask for a code coverage report, which provides information on the functions, statements, branches, and conditions or other elements that were covered in the testing. Use cases are used as part of a test coverage calculation that divides the tested use cases by the total use cases, but use cases may not cover all possible functions or branches. A code review report would be generated if the organization was manually reviewing the application's source code.

76. C. Rebooting a Windows machine results in an information log entry. Windows defines five types of events: errors, which indicate a significant problem; warnings, which may indicate future problems; information, which describes successful operation; success audits, which record successful security accesses; and failure audits, which record failed security access attempts.

77. C. Inconsistent timestamps are a common problem, often caused by improperly set time zones or due to differences in how system clocks are set. In this case, a consistent time difference often indicates that one system uses local time, and the other is using Greenwich Mean Time (GMT). Logs from multiple sources tend to cause problems with centralization and collection, whereas different log formats can create challenges in parsing log data. Finally, modified logs are often a sign of intrusion or malicious intent.

78. A. Authenticated scans use a read-only account to access configuration files, allowing more accurate testing of vulnerabilities. Web application, unauthenticated scans, and port scans don't have access to configuration files unless they are inadvertently exposed.

Microsoft's STRIDE threat assessment model places threats into one of six categories:

- Spoofing—threats that involve user credentials and authentication, or falsifying legitimate communications
- Tampering—threats that involve the malicious modification of data
- Repudiation—threats that cause actions to occur that cannot be denied by a user
- Information disclosure—threats that involve exposure of data to unauthorized individuals
- Denial of service—threats that deny service to legitimate users
- Elevation of privilege—threats that provide higher privileges to unauthorized users

79. B. Using role-based access controls (RBACs) for specific operations will help to ensure that users cannot perform actions that they should not be able to. Auditing and logging can help detect abuse but won't prevent it, and data type, format checks, and whitelisting are all useful for preventing attacks like SQL injection and buffer overflow attacks but are not as directly aimed at authorization issues.

80. D. Since a shared symmetric key could be used by any of the servers, transaction identification problems caused by a shared key are likely to involve a repudiation issue. If encrypted transactions cannot be uniquely identified by server, they cannot be proved to have come from a specific server.

81. C. Filtering is useful for preventing denial of service attacks but won't prevent tampering with data. Hashes and digital signatures can both be used to verify the integrity of data, and authorization controls can help ensure that only those with the proper rights can modify the data.

82. A. NIST SP 800-137 is titled "Information Security Continuous Monitoring (ISCM) for Federal Systems and Organizations" and describes the process of building and maintaining an ISCM. NIST SP 800-145 defines cloud computing, whereas NIST SP 800-53A covers assessing security and privacy controls for federal systems and organizations. NIST SP 800-50 focuses on information security awareness programs.

83. B. Finding severe bugs is not a fault—in fact, fuzzing often finds important issues that would otherwise have been exploitable. Fuzzers can reproduce errors, but typically don't fully cover the code—code coverage tools are usually paired with fuzzers to validate how much coverage was possible. Fuzzers are often limited to simple errors because they won't handle business logic or attacks that require knowledge from the application user.

84. C. Security audits are security assessments performed by third parties and are intended to evaluate the effectiveness of security controls. Security assessments are conducted by internal staff, and security tests are used to verify that a control is functioning effectively. Penetration tests can be conducted by internal or external staff and test systems by using actual exploitation techniques.

85. C. After scanning for open ports using a port scanning tool like nmap, penetration testers will identify interesting ports and then conduct vulnerability scans to determine what services may be vulnerable. This will perform many of the same activities that connecting via a web server will, and will typically be more useful than trying to manually test for vulnerable accounts via Telnet. sqlmap would typically be used after a vulnerability scanner identifies additional information about services, and the vulnerability scanner will normally provide a wider range of useful information.

86. B. The system is likely a Linux system. The system shows X11, as well as login, shell, and nfs ports, all of which are more commonly found on Linux systems than Windows systems or network devices. This system is also very poorly secured; many of the services running on it should not be exposed in a modern secure network.

87. D. Nmap only scans 1000 TCP and UDP ports by default, including ports outside of the 0–1024 range of "well-known" ports. By using the defaults for nmap, Ben missed 64,535 ports. OS fingerprinting won't cover more ports but would have provided a best guess of the OS running on the scanned system.

88. C. Static analysis is the process of reviewing code without running it. It relies on techniques like data flow analysis to review what the code does if it was run with a given set of inputs. Black and gray box analyses are not types of code review, although black box and gray box both describe types of penetration testing. Fuzzing provides unexpected or invalid data inputs to test how software responds.

89. C. A manual code review, which is performed by humans who review code line by line, is the best option when it is important to understand the context and business logic in the code. Fuzzing, dynamic, and static code review can all find bugs that manual code review might not, but won't take the intent of the programmers into account.

90. C. Misuse case diagrams use language beyond typical use case diagrams, including threatens and mitigates. Threat trees are used to map threats but don't use specialized languages like threatens and mitigates. STRIDE is a mnemonic and model used in threat modeling, and DREAD is a risk assessment model.

91. C. The most important first step for a penetration test is getting permission. Once permission has been received, planning, data gathering, and then elements of the actual test like port scanning can commence.

92. D. SSAE-16 is based on ISAE 3402, the International Standard on Assurance Engagements. It differs in a number of ways, including how it handles purposeful acts by service organizational personnel as well as anomalies, but the two share many elements. SAS-70 has been replaced by SSAE-16, whereas ISO27001 is a formal specification for an information security management system (ISMS). SOX is the Sarbanes–Oxley Act, a U.S. law that impacts accounting and investor protection.

93. C. A TCP scan that sets all or most of the possible TCP flags is called a Christmas tree, or Xmas, scan since it is said to "light up like a Christmas tree" with the flags. A SYN scan would attempt to open TCP connections, whereas an ACK scan sends packets with the ACK flag set. There is no such type of scan known as a TCP flag scan.

94. D. Nmap is a very popular open source port scanner. Nmap is not a vulnerability scanner, nor is it a web application fuzzer. While port scanners can be used to partially map a network, and its name stands for Network Mapper, it is not a network design tool.

95. C. Vulnerability scanners cannot detect vulnerabilities for which they do not have a test, plug-in, or signature. Signatures often include version numbers, service fingerprints, or configuration data. They can detect local vulnerabilities as well as those that require authentication if they are provided with credentials, and of course, they can detect service vulnerabilities.

96. C. The Common Vulnerabilities and Exposures (CVE) dictionary provides a central repository of security vulnerabilities and issues. Patching information for applications and software versions are sometimes managed using central patch management tools, but a single central database is not available for free or public use. Costs versus effort is also not what CVE stands for.

97. D. In many cases when an exploit is initially reported, there are no prebuilt signatures or detections for vulnerability scanners, and the CVE database may not have information about the attack immediately. Jacob's best option is to quickly gather information and review potentially vulnerable servers based on their current configuration. As more information becomes available, signatures and CVE information are likely to be published. Unfortunately for Jacob, IDS and IPS signatures will only detect attacks, and won't detect whether systems are vulnerable unless he sees the systems being exploited.

98. D. Privilege escalation occurs during the attack phase of a penetration test. Host and service information gathering, as well as activities like dumpster diving that can provide information about the organization, its systems, and security, are all part of the discovery phase.

99. B. Once additional tools have been installed, penetration testers will typically use them to gain additional access. From there they can further escalate privileges, search for new targets or data, and once again, install more tools to allow them to pivot further into infrastructure or systems.

100. B. Penetration testing reports often do not include the specific data captured during the assessment, as the readers of the report may not be authorized to access all of the data, and exposure of the report could result in additional problems for the organization. A listing of the issues discovered, risk ratings, and remediation guidance are all common parts of a penetration test report.

Chapter 7: Security Operations (Domain 7)

1. A. The illustration shows an example of a failover cluster, where DB1 and DB2 are both configured as database servers. At any given time, only one will function as the active database server, while the other remains ready to assume responsibility if the first one fails. While the environment may use UPS, tape backup, and cold sites as disaster recovery and business continuity controls, they are not shown in the diagram.

2. D. The principle of least privilege should guide Joe in this case. He should apply no access permissions by default and then give each user the necessary permissions to perform their job responsibilities. Read only, editor, and administrator permissions may be necessary for one or more of these users, but those permissions should be assigned based upon business need and not by default.

3. C. While most organizations would want to log attempts to log in to a workstation, this is not considered a privileged administrative activity and would go through normal logging processes.

4. C. Regulatory investigations attempt to uncover whether an individual or organization has violated administrative law. These investigations are almost always conducted by government agents.

5. D. Real evidence consists of things that may actually be brought into a courtroom as evidence. For example, real evidence includes hard disks, weapons, and items containing fingerprints. Documentary evidence consists of written items that may or may not be in tangible form. Testimonial evidence is verbal testimony given by witnesses with relevant information. The parol evidence rule says that when an agreement is put into written form, the written document is assumed to contain all the terms of the agreement.

6. A. In a manual recovery approach, the system does not fail into a secure state but requires an administrator to manually restore operations. In an automated recovery, the system can recover itself against one or more failure types. In an automated recovery without undue loss, the system can recover itself against one or more failure types and also preserve data against loss. In function recovery, the system can restore functional processes automatically.

7. B. A pseudoflaw is a false vulnerability in a system that may attract an attacker. A honeynet is a network of multiple honeypots that creates a more sophisticated environment for intruders to explore. A darknet is a segment of unused network address space that should have no network activity and, therefore, may be easily used to monitor for illicit activity. A warning banner is a legal tool used to notify intruders that they are not authorized to access a system.

8. B. Social media is commonly used as a command-and-control system for botnet activity. The most likely scenario here is that Toni's computer was infected with malware and joined to a botnet. This accounts for both the unusual social media traffic and the slow system activity.

9. D. Software-defined networking separates the control plane from the data plane. Network devices then do not contain complex logic themselves but receive instructions from the SDN.

10. A. Netflow records contain an entry for every network communication session that took place on a network and can be compared to a list of known malicious hosts. IDS logs may contain a relevant record but it is less likely because they would only create log entries if the traffic triggers the IDS, as opposed to netflow records which encompass all communications. Authentication logs and RFC logs would not have records of any network traffic.

11. B. Gary should follow the least privilege principle and assign users only the permissions they need to perform their job responsibilities. *Aggregation* is a term used to describe the unintentional accumulation of privileges over time, also known as privilege creep. Separation of duties and separation of privileges are principles used to secure sensitive processes.

12. A. The matrix shown in the figure is known as a segregation of duties matrix. It is used to ensure that one person does not obtain two privileges that would create a potential conflict. *Aggregation* is a term used to describe the unintentional accumulation of privileges over time, also known as privilege creep. Two-person control is used when two people must work together to perform a sensitive action. Defense in depth is a general security principle used to describe a philosophy of overlapping security controls.

13. B. Before granting access, Gary should verify that the user has a valid security clearance and a business need to know the information. Gary is performing an authorization task, so he does not need to verify the user's credentials, such as a password or biometric scan.

14. D. Gary should follow the principle of two-person control by requiring simultaneous action by two separate authorized individuals to gain access to the encryption keys. He should also apply the principles of least privilege and defense in depth, but these principles apply to all operations and are not specific to sensitive operations. Gary should avoid the security through obscurity principle, the reliance upon the secrecy of security mechanisms to provide security for a system or process.

15. D. Privileged access reviews are one of the most critical components of an organization's security program because they ensure that only authorized users have access to perform the most sensitive operations. They should take place whenever a user with privileged access leaves the organization or changes roles as well as on a regular, recurring basis.

16. D. Hotfixes, updates, and security fixes are all synonyms for single patches designed to correct a single problem. Service packs are collections of many different updates that serve as a major update to an operating system or application.

17. C. A forensic disk controller performs four functions. One of those, write blocking, intercepts write commands sent to the device and prevents them from modifying data on the device. The other three functions include returning data requested by a read operation, returning access-significant information from the device, and reporting errors from the device back to the forensic host.

18. A. Lydia is following the need to know principle. While the user may have the appropriate security clearance to access this information, there is no business justification provided, so she does not know that the user has an appropriate need to know the information.

19. D. A darknet is a segment of unused network address space that should have no network activity and, therefore, may be easily used to monitor for illicit activity. A honeypot is a decoy computer system used to bait intruders into attacking. A honeynet is a network of multiple honeypots that creates a more sophisticated environment for intruders to explore. A pseudoflaw is a false vulnerability in a system that may attract an attacker.

20. C. Job rotation and mandatory vacations deter fraud by increasing the likelihood that it will be detected. Two-person control deters fraud by requiring collusion between two employees. Incident response does not normally serve as a deterrent mechanism.

21. D. The scenario describes a mix of public cloud and private cloud services. This is an example of a hybrid cloud environment.

22. A. The change log contains information about approved changes and the change management process. While other logs may contain details about the change's effect, the audit trail for change management would be found in the change log.

23. D. In a Software as a Service solution, the vendor manages both the physical infrastructure and the complete application stack, providing the customer with access to a fully managed application.

24. D. The Common Vulnerability and Exposures (CVE) dictionary contains standardized information on many different security issues. The Open Web Application Security Project (OWASP) contains general guidance on web application security issues but does not track specific vulnerabilities or go beyond web applications. The Bugtraq mailing list and Microsoft Security Bulletins are good sources of vulnerability information but are not comprehensive databases of known issues.

25. D. A disaster is any event that can disrupt normal IT operations and can be either natural or manmade. Hacking and terrorism are examples of manmade disasters, while flooding and fire are examples of natural disasters.

26. D. The checklist review is the least disruptive type of disaster recovery test. During a checklist review, team members each review the contents of their disaster recovery checklists on their own and suggest any necessary changes. During a tabletop exercise, team members come together and walk through a scenario without making any changes to information systems. During a parallel test, the team actually activates the disaster recovery site for testing, but the primary site remains operational. During a full interruption test, the team takes down the primary site and confirms that the disaster recovery site is capable of handling regular operations. The full interruption test is the most thorough test but also the most disruptive.

27. B. The Grandfather/Father/Son, Tower of Hanoi, and Six Cartridge Weekly schemes are all different approaches to rotating backup media that balance reuse of media with data retention concerns. Meet-in-the-middle is a cryptographic attack against 2DES encryption.

28. B. In this scenario, Helen designed a process that requires the concurrence of two people to perform a sensitive action. This is an example of two-person control.

29. C. Evidence provided in court must be relevant to determining a fact in question, material to the case at hand, and competently obtained. Evidence does not need to be tangible. Witness testimony is an example of intangible evidence that may be offered in court.

30. A. In the public cloud computing model, the vendor builds a single platform that is shared among many different customers. This is also known as the shared tenancy model.

31. D. CSIRT representation normally includes at least representatives of senior management, information security professionals, legal representatives, public affairs staff, and engineering/technical staff.

32. C. In this scenario, all of the files on the server will be backed up on Monday evening during the full backup. The differential backup on Wednesday will then copy all files modified since the last full backup. These include files 1, 2, 3, 5, and 6: a total of five files.

File Modifications
Monday 8 a.m. - File 1 created
Monday 10 a.m. - File 2 created
Monday 11 a.m. - File 3 created
Monday 4 p.m. - File 1 modified
Monday 5 p.m. - File 4 created
Tuesday 8 a.m. - File 1 modified
Tuesday 9 a.m. - File 2 modified
Tuesday 10 a.m. - File 5 created
Wednesday 8 a.m. - File 3 modified
Wednesday 9 a.m. - File 6 created

33. C. Intrusion detection systems (IDSs) provide only passive responses, such as alerting administrators to a suspected attack. Intrusion prevention systems and firewalls, on the other hand, may take action to block an attack attempt. Antivirus software also may engage in active response by quarantining suspect files.

34. D. The hypervisor runs within the virtualization platform and serves as the moderator between virtual resources and physical resources.

35. D. *Entitlement* refers to the privileges granted to users when an account is first provisioned.

36. A. The service-level agreement (SLA) is between a service provider and a customer and documents in a formal manner expectations around availability, performance, and other parameters. An MOU may cover the same items but is not as formal a document. An OLA is between internal service organizations and does not involve customers. An SOW is an addendum to a contract describing work to be performed.

37. A. The IT Infrastructure Library (ITIL) framework focuses on IT service management. The Project Management Body of Knowledge (PMBOK) provides a common core of project management expertise. The Payment Card Industry Data Security Standard (PCI DSS) contains regulations for credit card security. The Open Group Architecture Framework (TOGAF) focuses on IT architecture issues.

38. D. Latency is a delay in the delivery of packets from their source to their destination. Jitter is a variation in the latency for different packets. Packet loss is the disappearance of packets in transit that requires retransmission. Interference is electrical noise or other disruptions that corrupt the contents of packets.

39. A. Steganography is a technique used to hide information in an otherwise innocuous-seeming file. The suspect may have used this technique to embed hidden information in the image file. Watermarking also manipulates images but does so in an attempt to protect intellectual property. Clipping and sampling are techniques used to reduce a large set of data to a small quantity that may be used for analysis.

40. D. A transformer failure is a failure of a manmade electrical component. Flooding, mudslides, and hurricanes are all examples of natural disasters.

41. C. The $(ISC)^2$ code of ethics applies only to information security professionals who are members of $(ISC)^2$. Adherence to the code is a condition of certification, and individuals found in violation of the code may have their certifications revoked. (ISC)² members who observe a breach of the code are required to report the possible violation by following the ethics complaint procedures.

42. B. The principle of least privilege says that an individual should only have the privileges necessary to complete their job functions. Removing administrative privileges from non-administrative users is an example of least privilege.

43. D. There is no need to conduct forensic imaging as a preventative measure. Rather, forensic imaging should be used during the incident response process. Maintaining patch levels, implementing intrusion detection/prevention, and removing unnecessary services and accounts are all basic preventative measures.

44. B. The scrutiny of hard drives for forensic purposes is an example of media analysis. Embedded device analysis looks at the computers included in other large systems, such as automobiles or security systems. Software analysis analyzes applications and their logs. Network analysis looks at network traffic and logs.

45. C. Security incidents negatively affect the confidentiality, integrity, or availability of information or assets and/or violate a security policy. The unauthorized vulnerability scan of a server does violate security policy and may negatively affect the security of that system, so it qualifies as a security incident. The completion of a backup schedule, logging of system access, and update of antivirus signatures are all routine actions that do not violate policy or jeopardize security, so they are all events rather than incidents.

46. C. Radio Frequency IDentification (RFID) technology is a cost-effective way to track items around a facility. While Wi-Fi could be used for the same purpose, it would be much more expensive to implement.

47. C. An attack committed against an organization by an insider, such as an employee, is known as sabotage. Espionage and confidentiality breaches involve the theft of sensitive information, which is not alleged to have occurred in this case. Integrity breaches involve the unauthorized modification of information, which is not described in this scenario.

48. A. In a SYN flood attack, the attacker sends a large number of SYN packets to a system but does not respond to the SYN/ACK packets, attempting to overwhelm the attacked system's connection state table with half-open connections.

49. B. The maximum tolerable downtime (MTD) is the longest amount of time that an IT service or component may be unavailable without causing serious damage to the organization. The recovery time objective (RTO) is the amount of time expected to return an IT service or component to operation after a failure. The recovery point objective (RPO) identifies the maximum amount of data, measured in time, that may be lost during a recovery effort. Service-level agreements (SLAs) are written contracts that document service expectations.

50. C. Zero-day attacks are those that are previously unknown to the security community and, therefore, have no available patch. These are especially dangerous attacks because they may be highly effective until a solution becomes available.

51. B. The four canons of the (ISC)^2 code of ethics are to protect society, the common good, necessary public trust and confidence and the infrastructure; act honorably, honestly, justly, responsibly and legally; provide diligent and competent service to principals; and advance and protect the profession.

52. A. Interviews occur when investigators meet with an individual who may have information relevant to their investigation but is not a suspect. If the individual is a suspect, then the meeting is an interrogation.

53. B. Beth should choose a cold site. This type of facility meets her requirements for environmental controls and power but, does not have the equipment or data found in a warm site, hot site, or service bureau. However, it does have the lowest cost of the four options.

54. D. The image clearly contains the watermark of the US Geological Survey (USGS), which ensures that anyone seeing the image knows its origin. It is not possible to tell from looking at the image whether steganography was used. Sampling and clipping are data analysis techniques and are not used to protect images.

55. D. The annualized rate of occurrence (ARO) is the expected number of times an incident will occur each year. In the case of a 200-year flood plain, planners should expect a flood once every 200 years. This is equivalent to a 1/200 chance of a flood in any given year, or 0.005 floods per year.

56. B. While all hackers with malicious intent pose a risk to the organization, the malicious insider poses the greatest risk to security because they likely have legitimate access to sensitive systems that may be used as a launching point for an attack. Other attackers do not begin with this advantage.

57. C. In an electronic vaulting approach, automated technology moves database backups from the primary database server to a remote site on a scheduled basis, typically daily. Transaction logging is not a recovery technique alone; it is a process for generating the logs used in remote journaling. Remote journaling transfers transaction logs to a remote site on a more frequent basis than electronic vaulting, typically hourly. Remote mirroring maintains a live database server at the backup site and mirrors all transactions at the primary site on the server at the backup site.

58. B. Hilda's design follows the principle of separation of duties. Giving one user the ability to both create new accounts and grant administrative privileges combines two actions that would result in a significant security change that should be divided among two users.

59. D. An audit kickoff meeting should clearly describe the scope and purpose of the audit as well as the expected timeframe. Auditors should never approach an audit with any expectations about what they will discover because the findings should only be developed based upon the results of audit examinations.

60. C. The end goal of the disaster recovery process is restoring normal business operations in the primary facility. All of the other actions listed may take place during the disaster recovery process but the process is not complete until the organization is once again functioning normally in its primary facilities.

61. C. A host-based intrusion detection system (HIDS) may be able to detect unauthorized processes running on a system. The other controls mentioned, network intrusion detection systems (NIDSs), firewalls, and DLP systems, are network-based and may not notice rogue processes.

62. B. The scenario describes a privilege escalation attack where a malicious insider with authorized access to a system misused that access to gain privileged credentials.

63. B. Carla's account has experienced aggregation, where privileges accumulated over time. This condition is also known as privilege creep and likely constitutes a violation of the least privilege principle.

64. C. The Mitigation phase of incident response focuses on actions that can contain the damage incurred during an incident. This includes limiting the scope and or effectiveness of the incident.

65. C. At this point in the process, Ann has no reason to believe that any actual security compromise or policy violation took place, so this situation does not meet the criteria for a security incident or intrusion. Rather, the alert generated by the intrusion detection system is simply a security event requiring further investigation. *Security occurrence* is not a term commonly used in incident handling.

66. A. DNS traffic commonly uses port 53 for both TCP and UDP communications. SSH and SCP use TCP port 22. SSL and TLS do not have ports assigned to them but are commonly used for HTTPS traffic on port 443. Unencrypted web traffic over HTTP often uses port 80.

67. D. The attack described in this scenario has all of the hallmarks of a denial of service attack. More specifically, Ann's organization is likely experiencing a DNS amplification attack where an attacker sends false requests to third-party DNS servers with a forged source IP address belonging to the targeted system. Because the attack uses UDP requests, there is no three-way handshake. The attack packets are carefully crafted to elicit a lengthy response from a short query. The purpose of these queries is to generate responses headed to the target system that are sufficiently large and numerous enough to overwhelm the targeted network or system.

68. B. Now that Ann suspects an attack against her organization, she has sufficient evidence to declare a security incident. The attack underway seems to have undermined the availability of her network, meeting one of the criteria for a security incident. This is an escalation beyond a security event but does not reach the level of an intrusion because there is no evidence that the attacker has even attempted to gain access to systems on Ann's network. *Security occurrence* is not a term commonly used in incident handling.

69. D. To be admissible, evidence must be relevant, material, and competent. The laptop in this case is clearly material because it contains logs related to the crime in question. It is also relevant because it provides evidence that ties the hacker to the crime. It is not competent because the evidence was not legally obtained.

70. C. Gordon may conduct his investigation as he wishes and use any information that is legally available to him, including information and systems belonging to his employer.

There is no obligation to contact law enforcement. However, Gordon may not perform "hack back" activities because those may constitute violations of the law and/or (ISC)^2 Code of Ethics.

71. B. Software escrow agreements place a copy of the source code for a software package in the hands of an independent third party who will turn the code over to the customer if the vendor ceases business operations. Service-level agreements, mutual assistance agreements, and compliance agreements all lose some or all of their effectiveness if the vendor goes out of business.

72. C. Most security professionals recommend at least one, and preferably two, weeks of vacation to deter fraud. The idea is that fraudulent schemes will be uncovered during the time that the employee is away and does not have the access required to perpetuate a cover-up.

73. D. Any attempt to undermine the security of an organization or violation of a security policy is a security incident. Each of the events described meets this definition and should be treated as an incident.

74. D. Egress filtering scans outbound traffic for potential security policy violations. This includes traffic with a private IP address as the destination, traffic with a broadcast address as the destination, and traffic that has a falsified source address not belonging to the organization.

75. C. The two main methods of choosing records from a large pool for further analysis are sampling and clipping. Sampling uses statistical techniques to choose a sample that is representative of the entire pool, while clipping uses threshold values to select those records that exceed a predefined threshold because they may be of most interest to analysts.

76. B. Netflow data contains information on the source, destination, and size of all network communications and is routinely saved as a matter of normal activity. Packet capture data would provide relevant information, but it must be captured during the suspicious activity and cannot be re-created after the fact unless the organization is already conducting 100 percent packet capture, which is very rare. Additionally, the use of encryption limits the effectiveness of packet capture. Intrusion detection system logs would not likely contain relevant information because the encrypted traffic would probably not match intrusion signatures. Centralized authentication records would not contain information about network traffic.

77. C. Baseline configurations serve as the starting point for configuring secure systems and applications. They contain the security settings necessary to comply with an organization's security policy and may then be customized to meet the specific needs of an implementation. While security policies and guidelines may contain information needed to secure a system, they do not contain a set of configuration settings that may be applied to a system. The running configuration of a system is the set of currently applied settings, which may or may not be secure.

78. B. During a parallel test, the team actually activates the disaster recovery site for testing but the primary site remains operational. During a full interruption test, the team takes down the primary site and confirms that the disaster recovery site is capable of handling regular operations. The full interruption test is the most thorough test but also the most disruptive. The checklist review is the least disruptive type of disaster recovery test. During a checklist review, team members each review the contents of their disaster recovery checklists on their own and suggest any necessary changes. During a tabletop exercise, team members come together and walk through a scenario without making any changes to information systems.

79. C. Both the receipt of alerts and the verification of their accuracy occurs during the Detection phase of the incident response process.

80. A. Virtual machines run full guest operating systems on top of a host platform known as the hypervisor.

81. B. RAID level 1 is also known as disk mirroring. RAID-0 is called disk striping. RAID-5 is called disk striping with parity. RAID-10 is known as a stripe of mirrors.

82. C. SSH uses TCP port 22, so this attack is likely an attempt to scan for open or weakly secured SSH servers. FTP uses ports 20 and 21. Telnet uses port 23, and HTTP uses port 80.

83. C. The ping of death attack placed more data than allowed by the specification in the payload of an ICMP echo request packet. This is similar to the modern-day buffer overflow attack where attackers attempt to place more data in a targeted system's memory that consumes more space than is allocated for that data.

84. C. In an Infrastructure as a Service environment, the vendor is responsible for hardware- and network-related responsibilities. These include configuring network firewalls, maintaining the hypervisor, and managing physical equipment. The customer retains responsibility for patching operating systems on its virtual machine instances.

85. B. Sandboxing is a technique where application developers (or the recipients of an untrusted application) may test the code in a virtualized environment that is isolated from production systems. White box testing, black box testing, and penetration testing are all common software testing techniques but do not require the use of an isolated system.

86. B. Fraggle attacks use a distributed attack approach to send UDP traffic at a targeted system from many different source addresses on ports 7 and 9. The most effective way to block this attack would be to block inbound UDP traffic on those ports. Blocking the source addresses is not feasible because the attacker would likely simply change the source addresses. Blocking destination addresses would likely disrupt normal activity. The fraggle attack does not use ICMP, so blocking that traffic would have no effect.

87. A. Transitive trusts go beyond the two domains directly involved in the trust relationship and extend to their subdomains.

88. C. In a Platform as a Service solution, the customer supplies application code that the vendor then executes on its own infrastructure.

89. A. Companies have an obligation to preserve evidence whenever they believe that the threat of litigation is imminent. The statement made by this customer that "we will have

to take this matter to court" is a clear threat of litigation and should trigger the preservation of any related documents and records.

90. B. The Fourth Amendment states, in part, that "the right of the people to be secure in their persons, houses, papers and effects, against unreasonable searches and seizures, shall not be violated, and no Warrants shall issue, but upon probable cause, supported by Oath or affirmation, and particularly describing the place to be searched, and the persons or things to be seized." The First Amendment contains protections related to freedom of speech. The Fifth Amendment ensures that no person will be required to serve as a witness against themselves. The Fifteenth Amendment protects the voting rights of citizens.

91. A. Expert opinion evidence allows individuals to offer their opinion based upon the facts in evidence and their personal knowledge. Expert opinion evidence may be offered only if the court accepts the witness as an expert in a particular field. Direct evidence is when witnesses testify about their direct observations. Real evidence consists of tangible items brought into court as evidence. Documentary evidence consists of written records used as evidence in court.

92. D. The standard methods for clearing magnetic tapes, according to the NIST Guidelines for Media Sanitization, are overwriting the tape with nonsensitive data, degaussing, and physical destruction via shredding or incineration. Reformatting a tape does not remove remnant data.

93. B. RAID level 1, also known as disk mirroring, uses two disks that contain identical information. If one disk fails, the other contains the data needed for the system to continue operation.

94. B. The analysis of application logs is one of the core tasks of software analysis because SQL injection attacks are application attacks.

95. C. Quantum may choose to use any or all of these security controls, but data encryption is, by far, the most important control. It protects the confidentiality of data stored on the tapes, which are most vulnerable to theft while in transit between two secure locations.

96. C. Data loss prevention (DLP) systems may identify sensitive information stored on endpoint systems or in transit over a network. This is their primary purpose. Intrusion detection and prevention systems (IDS/IDP) may be used to identify some sensitive information using signatures built for that purpose, but this is not the primary role of those tools and they would not be as effective as DLP systems at this task. TLS is a network encryption protocol that may be used to protect sensitive information, but it does not have any ability to identify sensitive information.

97. D. If software is released into the public domain, anyone may use it for any purpose, without restriction. All other license types contain at least some level of restriction.

98. A. In a man-in-the-middle attack, attackers manage to insert themselves into a connection between a user and a legitimate website, relaying traffic between the two parties while eavesdropping on the connection. Although similarly named, the meet-in-the-middle attack is a cryptographic attack that does not necessarily involve connection tampering. Fraggle is a network-based denial of service attack using UDP packets. Wardriving is a reconnaissance technique for discovering open or weakly secured wireless networks.

99. C. The two main methods of choosing records from a large pool for further analysis are sampling and clipping. Sampling uses statistical techniques to choose a sample that is representative of the entire pool, while clipping uses threshold values to select those records that exceed a predefined threshold because they may be of most interest to analysts.

100. C. Generators are capable of providing backup power for a sustained period of time in the event of a power loss, but they take time to activate. Uninterruptible power supplies (UPS) provide immediate, battery-driven power for a short period of time to cover momentary losses of power, which would not cover a sustained period of power loss. RAID and redundant servers are high availability controls but do not cover power loss scenarios.

Chapter 8: Software Development Security (Domain 8)

1. B. Coupling is a description of the level of interaction between objects. Cohesion is the strength of the relationship between the purposes of methods within the same class. When you are developing an object-oriented model, it is desirable to have high cohesion and low coupling.

2. D. Botnets are used for a wide variety of malicious purposes, including scanning the network for vulnerable systems, conducting brute-force attacks against other systems, and sending out spam messages.

3. C. Code review takes place after code has been developed, which occurs after the design phase of the system's development life cycle (SDLC). Code review may use a combination of manual and automated techniques, or rely solely on one or the other. It should be a peer-driven process that includes developers who did not write the code. Developers should expect to complete the review of around 300 lines per hour, on average.

4. D. A social engineering attack may trick a user into revealing their password to the attacker. Other attacks that depend on guessing passwords, such as brute-force attacks, rainbow table attacks, and dictionary attacks, are unlikely to be successful in light of the organization's strong password policy.

5. C. One of the responsibilities of the release control process is ensuring that the process includes acceptance testing that confirms that any alterations to end-user work tasks are understood and functional prior to code release. The request control, change control, and configuration control processes do not include acceptance testing.

6. B. Cross-site request forgery (XSRF or CSRF) attacks exploit the trust that sites have in a user's browser by attempting to force the submission of authenticated requests to third-party sites. Session hijacking attacks attempt to steal previously authenticated sessions but do not force the browser to submit requests. SQL injection directly attacks a database through a web application. Cross-site scripting uses reflected input to trick a user's browser into executing untrusted code from a trusted site.

7. A. The SDLC consists of seven phases, in the following order: conceptual definition, functional requirements determination, control specifications development, design review, code review, system test review, and maintenance and change management.

8. D. The error message shown in the figure is the infamous "Blue Screen of Death" that occurs when a Windows system experiences a dangerous failure and enters a fail secure state. If the system had "failed open," it would have continued operation. The error described is a memory fault that is likely recoverable by rebooting the system. There is no indication that the system has run out of usable memory.

9. D. Software threat modeling is designed to reduce the number of security-related design and coding flaws as well as the severity of other flaws. The developer or evaluator of software has no control over the threat environment, because it is external to the organization.

10. C. In the diagram, `Account` is the name of the class. `Owner` and `Balance` are attributes of that class. `AddFunds` and `RemoveFunds` are methods of the class.

11. A. Primary storage is a technical term used to refer to the memory that is directly available to the CPU. Nonvolatile storage mechanisms, such as flash drives, DVDs, and hard drives, are classified as secondary storage.

12. A. Dynamic testing of software typically occurs in a black box environment where the tester does not have access to the source code. Static testing, white box testing, and code review approaches all require access to the source code of the application.

13. B. Inheritance occurs when a subclass (or child class) is able to use methods belonging to a superclass (or parent class). Polymorphism occurs when different subclasses may have different methods using the same interfaces that respond differently. Coupling is a description of the level of interaction between objects. Cohesion is the strength of the relationship between the purposes of methods within the same class.

14. C. Aggregate functions summarize large amounts of data and provide only summary information as a result. When carefully crafted, aggregate functions may unintentionally reveal sensitive information.

15. B. The best protection against buffer overflow attacks is server-side input validation. This technique limits user input to approved ranges of values that fit within allocated buffers. While firewalls and intrusion prevention systems may contain controls that limit buffer overflows, it would be more effective to perform filtering on the application server. Encryption cannot protect against buffer overflow attacks.

16. B. The log entries show the characteristic pattern of a port scan. The attacking system sends connection attempts to the target system against a series of commonly used ports.

17. C. Acme Widgets is clearly in the initial stage of the SW-CMM. This stage is characterized by the absence of formal process. The company may still produce working code, but they do so in a disorganized fashion.

18. B. The Repeatable stage is the second stage in the SW-CMM, following the Initial stage. It should be the next milestone goal for Acme Widgets. The Repeatable stage is characterized by basic life-cycle management processes.

19. A. The Defined stage of the SW-CMM is marked by the presence of basic life-cycle management processes and reuse of code. It includes the use of requirements management, software project planning, quality assurance, and configuration management practices.

20. D. The Managed stage is the fourth stage in the SW-CMM, following the Defined stage. It should be the next milestone goal for Beta Particles. The Repeatable stage is characterized by the use of quantitative software development measures.

21. C. Referential integrity ensures that records exist in a secondary table when they are referenced with a foreign key from another table. Foreign keys are the mechanism used to enforce referential integrity.

22. A. Macro viruses are most commonly found in office productivity documents, such as Microsoft Word documents that end in the `.doc` or `.docx` extension. They are not commonly found in executable files with the `.com` or `.exe` extensions.

23. C. The degree of a database table is the number of attributes in the table. Victor's table has six attributes: the employee's user ID, home telephone, office telephone, mobile telephone, office location, and job title.

24. C. The string shown in the logs is characteristic of a directory traversal attack where the attacker attempts to force the web application to navigate up the file hierarchy and retrieve a file that should not normally be provided to a web user, such as the password file. The series of "double dots" is indicative of a directory traversal attack because it is the character string used to reference the directory one level up in a hierarchy.

25. C. Design reviews should take place after the development of functional and control specifications but before the creation of code. The code review, unit testing, and functional testing all take place after the creation of code and, therefore, after the design review.

26. C. Regression testing is software testing that runs a set of known inputs against an application and then compares the results to those produced by an earlier version of the software. It is designed to capture unanticipated consequences of deploying new code versions prior to introducing them into a production environment.

27. D. Assurance, when it comes to software, is the level of confidence that software is free from vulnerabilities, either intentionally designed into the software or accidentally inserted at any time during its life cycle, and that the software functions in the intended manner. It is a term typically used in military and defense environments.

28. C. The change control process is responsible for providing an organized framework within which multiple developers can create and test a solution prior to rolling it out in a production environment. Request control provides a framework for user requests. Release control manages the deployment of code into production. Configuration control ensures that changes to software versions are made in accordance with the change and configuration management policies.

29. D. Aggregation is a security issue that arises when a collection of facts has a higher classification than the classification of any of those facts standing alone. An inference problem

occurs when an attacker can pull together pieces of less sensitive information and use them to derive information of greater sensitivity. SQL injection is a web application exploit. Multilevel security is a system control that allows the simultaneous processing of information at different classification levels.

30. A. The two major classifications of covert channels are timing and storage. A covert timing channel conveys information by altering the performance of a system component or modifying a resource's timing in a predictable manner. A covert storage channel conveys information by writing data to a common storage area where another process can read it. There is no such thing as a covert firewall channel. Memory is a type of storage, so a memory-based covert channel would fit into the covert storage channel category.

31. A. Black box testing begins with no prior knowledge of the system implementation, simulating a user perspective. White box and gray box testing provide full and partial knowledge of the system, respectively, in advance of the test. Blue boxes are a phone hacking tool and are not used in software testing.

32. B. In this example, the two SQL commands are indeed bundled in a transaction, but it is not an error to issue an update command that does not match any rows. Therefore, the first command would "succeed" in updating zero rows and not generate an error or cause the transaction to rollback. The second command would then execute, reducing the balance of the second account by $250.

```
BEGIN TRANSACTION
UPDATE accounts
SET balance = balance + 250
WHERE account_number = 1001;

UPDATE accounts
SET balance = balance - 250
WHERE account_number = 2002;

END TRANSACTION
```

33. D. Worms have built-in propagation mechanisms that do not require user interaction, such as scanning for systems containing known vulnerabilities and then exploiting those vulnerabilities to gain access. Viruses and Trojan horses typically require user interaction to spread. Logic bombs do not spread from system to system but lie in wait until certain conditions are met, triggering the delivery of their payload.

34. C. A fail open configuration may be appropriate in this case. In this configuration, the firewall would continue to pass traffic without inspection while it is restarting. This would minimize downtime, and the traffic would still be protected by the other security controls described in the scenario. Failover devices and high availability clusters would indeed increase availability, but at potentially significant expense. Redundant disks would not help in this scenario because no disk failure is described.

35. D. An inference problem occurs when an attacker can pull together pieces of less sensitive information and use them to derive information of greater sensitivity. Aggregation is a security issue that arises when a collection of facts has a higher classification than the classification of any of those facts standing alone. SQL injection is a web application exploit. Multilevel security is a system control that allows the simultaneous processing of information at different classification levels.

36. B. Polymorphic viruses mutate each time they infect a system by making adjustments to their code that assists them in evading signature detection mechanisms. Encrypted viruses also mutate from infection to infection but do so by encrypting themselves with different keys on each device.

37. A. The message forum is clearly susceptible to a cross-site scripting (XSS) attack. The code that Linda discovered in the message is a definitive example of an attempt to conduct cross-site scripting, and the alert box that she received demonstrates that the vulnerability exists. The website may also be vulnerable to cross-site request forgery, SQL injection, improper authentication, and other attacks, but there is no evidence of this provided in the scenario.

38. A. The script that Linda discovered merely pops up a message on a user's screen and does not perform any more malicious action. This type of script, using an `alert()` call, is commonly used to probe websites for cross-site scripting vulnerabilities.

39. B. Web application firewalls (WAFs) sit in front of web applications and watch for potentially malicious web attacks, including cross-site scripting. They then block that traffic from reaching the web application. An intrusion detection system (IDS) may detect the attack but is unable to take action to prevent it. DLP and VPN solutions are unable to detect web application attacks.

40. C. Input validation verifies that user-supplied input does not violate security conditions and is the most effective defense against cross-site scripting attacks. Bounds checking is a form of input validation, but it is used to ensure that numeric input falls within an acceptable range and is not applicable against cross-site scripting attacks. Peer review and OS patching are both good security practices but are unlikely to be effective against a cross-site scripting attack.

41. C. Durability requires that once a transaction is committed to the database it must be preserved. Atomicity ensures that if any part of a database transaction fails, the entire transaction must be rolled back as if it never occurred. Consistency ensures that all transactions are consistent with the logical rules of the database, such as having a primary key. Isolation requires that transactions operate separately from each other.

42. D. JavaScript is an interpreted language that does not make use of a compiler to transform code into an executable state. Java, C, and C++ are all compiled languages.

43. B. Multipartite viruses use multiple propagation mechanisms to defeat system security controls but do not necessarily include techniques designed to hide the malware from antivirus software. Stealth viruses tamper with the operating system to hide their existence. Polymorphic viruses alter their code on each system they infect to defeat signature detection. Encrypted viruses use a similar technique, employing encryption to alter their appearance and avoid signature detection mechanisms.

44. C. User acceptance testing (UAT) is typically the last phase of the testing process. It verifies that the solution developed meets user requirements and validates it against use cases. Unit testing, integration testing, and system testing are all conducted earlier in the process leading up to UAT.

45. D. Functional requirements specify the inputs, behavior, and outputs of software. Derived requirements are requirements developed from other requirement definitions. Structural and behavioral requirements focus on the overall structure of a system and the behaviors it displays.

46. C. The Open Web Application Security Project (OWASP) is widely considered as the most authoritative source on web application security issues. They publish the OWASP Top Ten list that publicizes the most critical web application security issues.

47. B. When one object wishes to interact with another object, it does so by invoking one of the second object's methods, including required and, perhaps, optional arguments to that method.

48. D. It is perfectly normal for packets with public IP addresses to enter the network from external locations. However, packets with internal addresses should never originate from the outside and should be blocked as spoofed traffic. Similarly, traffic leaving the network should have an internal source address. In no case should packets with private IP addresses cross the network border.

49. B. This is an example of a specific type of buffer overflow known as an off-by-one error. The first line of the code defines an array of 10 elements, which would be numbered 0 through 9. The second line of code tries to place a value in the 11th element of the array (remember, array counting begins at 0!), which would cause an overflow.

50. C. Lost updates occur when one transaction writes a value to the database that overwrites a value needed by transactions that have earlier precedence, causing those transactions to read an incorrect value. Dirty reads occur when one transaction reads a value from a database that was written by another transaction that did not commit. Incorrect summaries occur when one transaction is using an aggregate function to summarize data stored in a database while a second transaction is making modifications to the database, causing the summary to include incorrect information. SQL injection is a web application security flaw, not a database concurrency problem.

51. A. Transport Layer Security (TLS) provides the most effective defense against session hijacking because it encrypts all traffic between the client and server, preventing the attacker from stealing session credentials. Secure Sockets Layer (SSL) also encrypts traffic, but it is vulnerable to attacks against its encryption technology. Complex and expiring cookies are a good idea, but they are not sufficient protection against session hijacking.

52. C. When a system uses shadowed passwords, the hashed password value is stored in `/etc/shadow` instead of `/etc/passwd`. The `/etc/passwd` file would not contain the password in plaintext or hashed form. Instead, it would contain an x to indicate that the password hash is in the shadow file. The * character is normally used to disable interactive logins to an account.

53. B. Time of check to time of use (TOC/TOU) attacks target situations where there is a race condition, meaning that a dependence on the timing of actions allows impermissible actions to take place.

54. C. The single quotation mark in the input field is a telltale sign that this is a SQL injection attack. The quotation mark is used to escape outside of the SQL code's input field, and the text following is used to directly manipulate the SQL command sent from the web application to the database.

55. B. Client-side input validation is not an effective control against any type of attack because the attacker can easily bypass the validation by altering the code on the client. Escaping restricted characters prevents them from being passed to the database, as does parameterization. Limiting database permissions prevents dangerous code from executing.

56. B. PERT charts use nodes to represent milestones or deliverables and then show the estimated time to move between milestones. Gantt charts use a different format with a row for each task and lines showing the expected duration of the task. Work breakdown structures are an earlier deliverable that divides project work into achievable tasks. Wireframe diagrams are used in web design.

57. D. Regression testing is performed after developers make changes to an application. It reruns a number of test cases and compares the results to baseline results. Orthogonal array testing is a method for generating test cases based on statistical analysis. Pattern testing uses records of past software bugs to inform the analysis. Matrix testing develops a matrix of all possible inputs and outputs to inform the test plan.

58. B. Cross-site scripting (XSS) attacks may take advantage of the use of reflected input in a web application where input provided by one user is displayed to another user. Input validation is a control used to prevent XSS attacks. XSS does not require an unpatched server or any firewall rules beyond those permitting access to the web application.

59. A. In a white box test, the attacker has access to full implementation details of the system, including source code, prior to beginning the test. In gray box testing, the attacker has partial knowledge. In black box testing, the attacker has no knowledge of the system and tests it from a user perspective. Blue boxes are a phone hacking tool and are not used in software testing.

60. C. Heuristic-based anti-malware software has a higher likelihood of detecting a zero-day exploit than signature-based methods. Heuristic-based software does not require frequent signature updates because it does not rely upon monitoring systems for the presence of known malware. The trade-off with this approach is that it has a higher false positive rate than signature detection methods.

61. D. One possibility for the clean scan results is that the virus is using stealth techniques, such as intercepting read requests from the antivirus software and returning a correct-looking version of the infected file. The system may also be the victim of a zero-day attack, using a virus that is not yet included in the signature definition files provided by the antivirus vendor.

62. A. In URL encoding, the . character is replaced by `%252E` and the / character is replaced by `%252F`. You can see this in the log entry, where the expected pattern of ../../ is replaced by `%252E%252E%252F%252E%252E%252F`.

63. C. Attacks where the malicious user tricks the victim's web browser into executing a script through the use of a third-party site are known as cross-site scripting (XSS) attacks. This particular attack is a persistent XSS attack because it remains on the discussion forum until an administrator discovers and deletes it, giving it the ability to affect many users.

64. C. The Agile Manifesto includes 12 principles for software development. Three of those are listed as answer choices: maximizing the amount of work not done is essential, build projects around motivated individuals, and welcome changing requirements throughout the development process. Agile does not, however, consider clear documentation the primary measure of progress. Instead, working software is the primary measure of progress.

65. C. Unit testing works on individual system components, such as code modules. Regression testing is used to validate updates to code by comparing the output of the new version with previous versions. Samantha is developing new modules, so regression testing is not relevant. Integration and system testing require a broader scope than individual modules.

66. D. Expert systems have two components: a knowledge bank that contains the collected wisdom of human experts and an inference engine that allows the expert systems to draw conclusions about new situations based on the information contained within the knowledge bank.

67. D. A key-value store is an example of a NoSQL database that does not follow a relational or hierarchical model like traditional databases. A graph database is another example of a NoSQL database, but it uses nodes and edges to store data rather than keys and values.

68. C. A database failure in the middle of a transaction causes the rollback of the entire transaction. In this scenario, the database would not execute either command.

69. B. In the diagram, `Account` is the name of the class. `Owner` and `Balance` are attributes of that class. `AddFunds` and `RemoveFunds` are methods of the class.

70. B. Static testing performs code analysis in an offline fashion, without actually executing the code. Dynamic testing evaluates code in a runtime environment. Both static and dynamic testing may use automated tools, and both are important security testing techniques.

71. D. The chart shown in the figure is a Gantt chart, showing the proposed start and end dates for different activities. It is developed based on the work breakdown structure (WBS), which is developed based on functional requirements. Program Evaluation Review Technique (PERT) charts show the project schedule as a series of numbered nodes.

72. D. In a gray box test, the tester evaluates the software from a user perspective but has access to the source code as the test is conducted. White box tests also have access to the source code but perform testing from a developer's perspective. Black box tests work from a user's perspective but do not have access to source code. Blue boxes are a telephone hacking tool and not a software testing technique.

73. D. The Time of Check to Time of Use (TOC/TOU) attack exploits timing differences between when a system verifies authorization and software uses that authorization to perform an action. It is an example of a race condition attack. The other three attacks mentioned do not depend on precise timing.

74. A. In the diagram, `Account` is the name of the class. `Owner` and `Balance` are attributes of that class. `AddFunds` and `RemoveFunds` are methods of the class.

75. B. Incorrect summaries occur when one transaction is using an aggregate function to summarize data stored in a database while a second transaction is making modifications to the database, causing the summary to include incorrect information. Dirty reads occur when one transaction reads a value from a database that was written by another transaction that did not commit. Lost updates occur when one transaction writes a value to the database that overwrites a value needed by transactions that have earlier precedence, causing those transactions to read an incorrect value. SQL injection is a web application security flaw, not a database concurrency problem.

76. D. The fail closed approach prevents any activity from taking place during a system security failure and is the most conservative approach to failure management. Fail open takes the opposite philosophy, allowing all activity in the event of a security control failure. Fail clear and fail mitigation are not failure management approaches.

77. D. The illustration shows the spiral model of software development. In this approach, developers use multiple iterations of a waterfall-style software development process. This becomes a "loop" of iterations through similar processes. The waterfall approach does not iterate through the entire process repeatedly but rather only allows movement backward and forward one stage. The agile approach to software development focuses on iterative improvement and does not follow a rigorous SDLC model. Lean is a process improvement methodology and not a software development model.

78. B. Relational databases use the primary key to uniquely identify each of the rows in a table. The primary key is selected by the database designer from the set of candidate keys that are able to uniquely identify each row, but the RDBMS only uses the primary key for this purpose. Foreign keys are used to establish relationships between tables. Referential keys are not a type of database key.

79. A. The request process begins with a user-initiated request for a feature. Change and release control are initiated by developers seeking to implement changes. Design review is a phase of the change approval process initiated by developers when they have a completed design.

80. C. Polyinstantiation allows the storage of multiple different pieces of information in a database at different classification levels to prevent attackers from inferring anything about the absence of information. Input validation, server-side validation, and parameterization are all techniques used to prevent web application attacks and are not effective against inference attacks.

81. C. While Ursula may certainly use an object model, data dictionary, and primary key in her development effort, external developers cannot directly use them to access her code. An application programming interface (API) allows other developers to call Ursula's code from within their own without knowing the details of Ursula's implementation.

82. C. In the Establishing phase of the IDEAL model, the organization takes the general recommendations from the Diagnosing phase and develops a specific plan of action that achieves those changes.

83. D. Messages similar to the one shown in the figure are indicative of a ransomware attack. The attacker encrypts files on a user's hard drive and then demands a ransom, normally paid in Bitcoin, for the decryption key required to restore access to the original content. Encrypted viruses, on the other hand, use encryption to hide themselves from antivirus mechanisms and do not alter other contents on the system.

84. A. The `bin2hex()` function converts a string to a hexadecimal value that may then be passed to a database safely. The `dechex()` function performs a similar function but will not work for a string as it only functions on numeric values. The `hex2bin()` and `hexdec()` functions work in the reverse manner.

85. D. Neural networks attempt to use complex computational techniques to model the behavior of the human mind. Knowledge banks are a component of expert systems, which are designed to capture and reapply human knowledge. Decision support systems are designed to provide advice to those carrying out standard procedures and are often driven by expert systems.

86. B. In level 2, the Repeatable level of the SW-CMM, an organization introduces basic life-cycle management processes. Reuse of code in an organized fashion begins, and repeatable results are expected from similar projects. The key process areas for this level include Requirements Management, Software Project Planning, Software Project Tracking and Oversight, Software Subcontract Management, Software Quality Assurance, and Software Configuration Management.

87. C. The key to this question is that Lucas suspects the tampering took place before the employee departed. This is the signature of a logic bomb: malicious code that lies dormant until certain conditions are met. The other attack types listed here: privilege escalation, SQL injection, and remote code execution would more likely take place in real time.

88. A. The Agile approach to software development embraces four principles. It values individuals and interactions over processes and tools, working software over comprehensive documentation, customer collaboration over contract negotiation, and responding to change over following a plan.

89. C. API developers commonly use API keys to limit access to authorized users and applications. Encryption provides for confidentiality of information exchanged using an API but does not provide authentication. Input validation is an application security technique used to protect against malicious input. IP filters may be used to limit access to an API, but they are not commonly used because it is difficult to deploy an API with IP filters since the filters require constant modification and maintenance as endpoints change.

90. C. Signature detection is extremely effective against known strains of malware because it uses a very reliable pattern matching technique to identify known malware. Signature detection is, therefore, the most reliable way to detect known malware. This technique is not, however, effective against the zero-day malware typically used by advanced persistent threats (APTs) that does not exploit vulnerabilities identified in security bulletins. While malware authors once almost exclusively targeted Windows systems, malware now exists for all major platforms.

91. B. In the waterfall model, the software development process follows five sequential steps which are, in order: Requirements, Design, Coding, Testing, and Maintenance.

92. A. Atomicity ensures that database transactions either execute completely or not at all. Consistency ensures that all transactions must begin operating in an environment that is consistent with all of the database's rules. The isolation principle requires that transactions operate separately from each other. Durability ensures that database transactions, once committed, are permanent.

93. D. Input validation ensures that the data provided to a program as input matches the expected parameters. Limit checks are a special form of input validation that ensure the value remains within an expected range, but there was no range specified in this scenario. Fail open and fail secure are options when planning for possible system failures.

94. A. Cookies are used to maintain authenticated sessions, even when IP addresses change. Therefore, Mal can use the stolen cookies to conduct a session hijacking attack, taking over an authorized user's session with the website, potentially without the knowledge of the legitimate user.

95. D. Penetration tests of web-based systems may detect any possible web application security flaw, including cross-site request forgery (XSRF), cross-site scripting (XSS), and SQL injection vulnerabilities.

96. C. The DevOps approach to technology management seeks to integrate software development, operations, and quality assurance in a seamless approach that builds collaboration between the three disciplines.

97. B. `nessus` is a vulnerability testing tool designed for use by security professionals but also available to attackers. `nmap` may also assist attackers, but it only shows open ports and has limited capability to identify vulnerabilities. `ipconfig` displays network configuration information about a system, whereas `traceroute` identifies the network path between two systems.

98. D. Dirty reads occur when one transaction reads a value from a database that was written by another transaction that did not commit. Lost updates occur when one transaction writes a value to the database that overwrites a value needed by transactions that have earlier precedence, causing those transactions to read an incorrect value. Incorrect summaries occur when one transaction is using an aggregate function to summarize data stored in a database while a second transaction is making modifications to the database, causing the summary to include incorrect information. SQL injection is a web application security flaw, not a database concurrency problem.

99. B. A master boot record (MBR) virus redirects the boot process to load malware during the operating system loading process. File infector viruses infect one or more normal files stored on the system. Polymorphic viruses alter themselves to avoid detection. Service injection viruses compromise trusted components of the operating system.

100. C. Multipartite viruses use multiple propagation mechanisms to spread between systems. This improves their likelihood of successfully infecting a system because it provides alternative infection mechanisms that may be successful against systems that are not vulnerable to the primary infection mechanism.

Chapter 9: Practice Test 1

1. C. NIST SP 800-53 discusses security control baselines as a list of security controls. CIS releases security baselines, and a baseline is a useful part of a threat management strategy and may contain a list of acceptable configuration items.

2. B. A Content Distribution Network (CDN) is designed to provide reliable, low-latency, geographically distributed content distribution. In this scenario, a CDN is an ideal solution. A P2P CDN like BitTorrent isn't a typical choice for a commercial entity, whereas redundant servers or a hot site can provide high availability but won't provide the remaining requirements.

3. D. A forensic disk controller performs four functions. One of those, write blocking, intercepts write commands sent to the device and prevents them from modifying data on the device. The other three functions include returning data requested by a read operation, returning access-significant information from the device, and reporting errors from the device back to the forensic host. The controller should not prevent read commands from being sent to the device because those commands may return crucial information.

4. B. RAID 1, disk mirroring, requires two physical disks that will contain copies of the same data.

5. D. The TGS, or Ticket-Granting Service (which is usually on the same server as the KDC) receives a TGT from the client. It validates the TGT and the user's rights to access the service they are requesting to use. The TGS then issues a ticket and session keys to the client. The AS serves as the authentication server, which forwards the username to the KDC.

6. D. Asynchronous communications rely on a a built-in stop and start flag or bit. This makes asynchronous communications less efficient than synchronous communications, but better suited to some types of communication.

7. C. Wave pattern motion detectors transmit ultrasonic or microwave signals into the monitor area, watching for changes in the returned signals bouncing off objects.

8. C. Stateful packet inspection firewalls, also known as dynamic packet filtering firewalls, track the state of a conversation, and can allow a response from a remote system based on an internal system being allowed to start the communication. Static packet filtering and circuit level gateways only filter based on source, destination, and ports, whereas application-level gateway firewalls proxy traffic for specific applications.

9. B. A captive portal can require those who want to connect to and use Wi-Fi to provide an email address to connect. This allows Ben to provide easy-to-use wireless while meeting his business purposes. WPA2 PSK is the preshared key mode of WPA and won't provide information about users who are given a key. Sharing a password doesn't allow for data gathering either. Port security is designed to protect wired network ports based on MAC addresses.

10. B. Many modern wireless routers can provide multiple SSIDs. Ben can create a private, secure network for his business operations, but he will need to make sure that the customer and business networks are firewalled or otherwise logically separated from each other. Running WPA2 on the same SSID isn't possible without creating another wireless network and would cause confusion for customers (SSIDs aren't required to be unique). Running a network in Enterprise mode isn't used for open networks, and WEP is outdated and incredibly vulnerable.

11. D. Unencrypted open networks broadcast traffic in the clear. This means that unencrypted sessions to websites can be easily captured with a packet sniffer. Some tools like FireSheep have been specifically designed to capture sessions from popular websites. Fortunately, many now use TLS by default, but other sites still send user session information in the clear. Shared passwords are not the cause of the vulnerability, ARP spoofing isn't an issue with wireless networks, and a Trojan is designed to look like safe software, not to compromise a router.

12. D. The DES modes of operation are Electronic Codebook (ECB), Cipher Block Chaining (CBC), Cipher Feedback (CFB), Output Feedback (OFB), and Counter (CTR). The Advanced Encryption Standard (AES) is a separate encryption algorithm.

13. D. Clipping is an analysis technique that only reports alerts after they exceed a set threshold. It is a specific form of sampling, which is a more general term that describes any attempt to excerpt records for review. Thresholding is not a commonly used term. Administrators may choose to configure automatic or manual account lockout after failed login attempts but that is not described in the scenario.

14. B. RADIUS is a common AAA technology used to provide services for dial-up, wireless networks, network devices, and a range of other systems. OAuth is an authentication protocol used to allow applications to act on a user's behalf without sharing the password, and is used for many web applications. While both TACACS and TACACS+ provide the functionality Sally is looking for, both are Cisco proprietary protocols.

15. C. In an inference attack, the attacker uses several pieces of generic nonsensitive information to determine a specific sensitive value.

16. A. The take rule allows a subject to take the rights belonging to another object. If Alice has take rights on Bob, she can give herself the same permissions that Bob already possesses.

17. B. Brute-force attacks try every possible password. In this attack, the password is changing by one letter at each attempt, which indicates that it is a brute-force attack. A dictionary attack would use dictionary words for the attack, whereas a man-in-the-middle or pass-the-hash attack would most likely not be visible in an authentication log except as a successful login.

18. B. Isolation requires that transactions operate separately from each other. Atomicity ensures that if any part of a database transaction fails, the entire transaction must be rolled back as if it never occurred. Consistency ensures that all transactions are consistent with the logical rules of the database, such as having a primary key. Durability requires that once a transaction is committed to the database it must be preserved.

19. B. Worms have built-in propagation mechanisms that do not require user interaction, such as scanning for systems containing known vulnerabilities and then exploiting those vulnerabilities to gain access. Viruses and Trojan horses typically require user interaction to spread. Logic bombs do not spread from system to system but lie in wait until certain conditions are met, triggering the delivery of their payload.

20. C. In a teardrop attack, the attacker fragments traffic in such a way that the system is unable to reassemble them. Modern systems are not vulnerable to this attack if they run current operating systems, but the concept of this attack illustrates the danger of relying upon users following protocol specifications instead of performing proper exception handling.

21. C. The TCP three-way handshake consists of initial contact via a SYN, or synchronize flagged packet, which receives a response with a SYN/ACK, or synchronize and acknowledge flagged packet, which is acknowledged by the original sender with an ACK, or acknowledge packet. RST is used in TCP to reset a connection, PSH is used to send data immediately, and FIN is used to end a connection.

22. B. MDM products do not have the capability of assuming control of a device not currently managed by the organization. This would be equivalent to hacking into a device owned by someone else and might constitute a crime.

23. A. Identity as a Service (IDaaS) provides an identity platform as a third-party service. This can provide benefits, including integration with cloud services and removing overhead for maintenance of traditional on-premise identity systems, but can also create risk due to third-party control of identity services and reliance on an offsite identity infrastructure.

24. A. Gina's actions harm the CISSP certification and information security community by undermining the integrity of the examination process. While Gina also is acting dishonestly, the harm to the profession is more of a direct violation of the code of ethics.

25. A. The annualized loss expectancy is the amount of damage that the organization expects to occur each year as the result of a given risk.

26. C. The whitelisting approach to application control allows users to install only those software packages specifically approved by administrators.. This would be an appropriate approach in a scenario where application installation needs to be tightly controlled.

27. A. This is a clear example of a denial-of-service attack—denying legitimate users authorized access to the system through the use of overwhelming traffic. It goes beyond a reconnaissance attack because the attacker is affecting the system, but it is not a compromise because the attacker did not attempt to gain access to the system. There is no reason to believe that a malicious insider was involved.

28. A. The Company ID is likely unique for each row in the table, making it the best choice for a primary key. There may be multiple companies that share the same name or ZIP code. Similarly, a single sales representative likely serves more than one company, making those fields unsuitable for use as a unique identifier.

29. C. Personally Identifiable Information (PII) includes data that can be used to distinguish or trace that person's identity, and also includes information like their medical, educational, financial, and employment information. PHI is personal health information, EDI is electronic data interchange, and proprietary data is used to maintain an organization's competitive advantage.

30. D. 129.53.44.124 is a valid public IP address and a legitimate destination for traffic leaving Bob's network. 12.8.195.15 is a public address on Bob's network and should not be a destination address on a packet leaving the network. 10.8.15.9 and 192.168.109.55 are both private IP addresses that should not be routed to the Internet.

31. D. Binary keyspaces contain a number of keys equal to 2 raised to the power of the number of bits. Two to the sixth power is 64, so a 6-bit keyspace contains 64 possible keys. The number of viable keys is usually smaller in most algorithms due to the presence of parity bits and other algorithmic overhead or security issues that restrict the use of some key values.

32. D. Research has shown that traditional methods of sanitizing files on SSDs were not reliable. SSDs remap data sectors as part of wear leveling, and erase commands are not consistently effective across multiple SSD brands. Zero fills can be performed on SSDs but may not be effective, much like erase commands. Degaussing doesn't work on SSDs because they are flash media, rather than magnetic media. SSDs don't have data remanence issues, but that doesn't create the need to destroy them.

33. A. Encrypting the files reduces the probability that the data will be successfully stolen, so it is an example of risk mitigation. Deleting the files would be risk avoidance. Purchasing insurance would be risk transference. Taking no action would be risk acceptance.

34. C. Sampling should be done randomly to avoid human bias. Choosing a timeframe may miss historic issues or only account for the current administrator's processes. Sampling is an effective process if it is done on a truly random sample of sufficient size to provide effective coverage of the userbase.

35. B. The European Data Protection Directive's seven primary tenets are:

Notice

Choice

Onward transfer

Security

Data integrity

Access

Enforcement

36. D. In a white box test, the attacker has access to full implementation details of the system, including source code, prior to beginning the test. In gray box testing, the attacker has partial knowledge. In black box testing, the attacker has no knowledge of the system and tests it from a user perspective. Blue boxes are a phone hacking tool and are not used in software testing.

37. C. The file clearly shows HTTP requests, as evidenced by the many GET commands. Therefore, this is an example of an application log from an HTTP server.

38. C. A blue box was used to generate the 2600 Hz tones that trunking systems required. White boxes included a dual-tone, multifrequency generator to control phone systems. Black boxes were designed to steal long-distance service by manipulating line voltages, and red boxes simulated the tones of coins being deposited into payphones.

39. B. Social engineering exploits humans to allow attacks to succeed. Since help desk employees are specifically tasked with being helpful, they may be targeted by attackers posing as legitimate employees. Trojans are a type of malware, whereas phishing is a targeted attack via electronic communication methods intended to capture passwords or other sensitive data. Whaling is a type of phishing aimed at high-profile or important targets.

40. C. Identity proofing that relies on a type of verification outside of the initial environment that required the verification is out-of-band identity proofing. This type of verification relies on the owner of the phone or phone number having control of it but removes the ability for attackers to use only Internet-based resources to compromise an account. Knowledge-based authentication relies on answers to preselected information, whereas dynamic knowledge–based authentication builds questions using facts or data about the user. Risk-based identity proofing uses risk-based metrics to determine whether identities should be permitted or denied access. It is used to limit fraud in financial transactions, such as credit card purchases. This is a valid form of proofing but does not necessairly use an out-of-band channel, such as SMS.

41. A. The modulo function is the remainder value left over after an integer division operation takes place.

42. C. A hybrid authentication service can provide authentication services in both the cloud and on-premise, ensuring that service outages due to interrupted links are minimized. An onsite service would continue to work during an Internet outage but would not allow the e-commerce website to authenticate. A cloud service would leave the corporate location offline. Outsourcing authentication does not indicate whether the solution is on or off-premise, and thus isn't a useful answer.

43. C. Federation links identity information between multiple organizations. Federating with a business partner can allow identification and authorization to occur between them, making integration much easier. Single sign-on would reduce the number of times a user has to log in but will not facilitate the sharing of identity information. Multifactor can help secure authentication, but again, doesn't help integrate with a third party. Finally, an Identity as a Service provider might provide federation but doesn't guarantee it.

44. B. Security Assertion Markup Language (SAML) is frequently used to integrate cloud services and provides the ability to make authentication and authorization assertions.

Active Directory integrations are possible but are less common for cloud service providers, and RADIUS is not typically used for integrations like this. Service Provisioning Markup Language (SPML) is used to provision users, resources, and services, not for authentication and authorization.

45. B. Rainbow tables use precomputed password hashes to conduct cracking attacks against password files. They may be frustrated by the use of salting, which adds a specified value to the password prior to hashing, making it much more difficult to perform precomputation. Password expiration policies, password complexity policies, and user education may all contribute to password security, but they are not direct defenses against the use of rainbow tables.

46. C. A honeypot is a decoy computer system used to bait intruders into attacking. A honeynet is a network of multiple honeypots that creates a more sophisticated environment for intruders to explore. A pseudoflaw is a false vulnerability in a system that may attract an attacker. A darknet is a segment of unused network address space that should have no network activity and, therefore, may be easily used to monitor for illicit activity.

47. C. The crossover error rate (CER) is the point where both the false acceptance rate and the false rejection rate cross. CER and ERR, or equal error rate, mean the same thing and are used interchangeably.

48. B. A Type 2 is something you have, like a smart card or hardware token. A Type 1 authentication factor is something you know. A Type 3 authentication factor is something you are, like a biometric identifier. There is no such thing as a Type 4 authentication factor.

49. C. Steganography is the art of using cryptographic techniques to embed secret messages within other content. Steganographic algorithms work by making invisible alterations to files, such as modifying the least significant bits of the many bits that make up image files. VPNs may be used to obscure secret communications, but they provide protection in transit and can't be used to embed information in an image. Watermarking does embed information in an image but with the intent of protecting intellectual property. A still image would not be used for a covert timing channel because it is a fixed file.

50. A. JavaScript is an interpreted language so the code is not compiled prior to execution, allowing Roger to inspect the contents of the code. C, C++, and Java are all compiled languages—a compiler produces an executable file that is not human-readable.

51. D. When a system is configured to use shadowed passwords, the `/etc/passwd` file contains only the character x in the place of a password. It would not contain any passwords, in either plaintext, encrypted, or hashed form.

52. D. Internet Control Message Protocol (ICMP) is used for normal pings, as well as Pings of Death. Ping of Death describes attacks that were used to overflow poorly implemented ICMP handlers; Smurf attacks, which spoof broadcast pings to create huge amounts of traffic on a network; and ping floods, which are a type of denial-of-service attack.

53. D. The due care principle states that an individual should react in a situation using the same level of care that would be expected from any reasonable person. It is a very broad standard. The due diligence principle is a more specific component of due care that states an individual assigned a responsibility should exercise due care to complete it accurately and in a timely manner.

54. B. ISDN, cable modems, DSL, and T1 and T3 lines are all examples of broadband technology that can support multiple simultaneous signals. They are analog, not digital, and are not broadcast technologies.

55. C. Social engineering is the best answer, as it can be useful to penetration testers who are asked to assess whether staff members are applying security training and have absorbed the awareness messages the organization uses. Port and vulnerability scanning find technical issues that may be related to awareness or training issues but that are less likely to be directly related. Discovery can involve port scanning or other data-gathering efforts, but is also less likely to be directly related to training and awareness.

56. B. RAID level 5 is also known as disk striping with parity. It uses three or more disks, with one disk containing parity information used to restore data to another disk in the event of failure. When used with three disks, RAID 5 is able to withstand the loss of a single disk.

57. D. The Physical layer deals with the electrical impulses or optical pulses that are sent as bits to convey data.

58. A. In an IaaS server environment, the customer retains responsibility for most server security operations under the shared responsibility model. This includes managing OS security settings, maintaining host firewalls, and configuring server access control. The vendor would be responsible for all security mechanisms at the hypervisor layer and below.

59. B. Proactive monitoring, aka synthetic monitoring, uses recorded or generated traffic to test systems and software. Passive monitoring uses a network span, tap, or other device to capture traffic to be analyzed. Reactive and replay are not industry terms for types of monitoring.

60. D. Process isolation ensures that the operating system allocates a separate area of memory for each process, preventing processes from seeing each other's data. This is a requirement for multilevel security systems.

61. B. The use of an eletcromagnetic coil inside the card indicates that this is a proximity card.

62. C. During a parallel test, the team actually activates the disaster recovery site for testing, but the primary site remains operational. During a full interruption test, the team takes down the primary site and confirms that the disaster recovery site is capable of handling regular operations. The full interruption test is the most thorough test but also the most disruptive. The checklist review is the least disruptive type of disaster recovery test. During a checklist review, team members each review the contents of their disaster recovery checklists on their own and suggest any necessary changes. During a tabletop exercise, team members come together and walk through a scenario without making any changes to information systems.

63. B. The Agile approach to software development embraces 12 core principles, found in the Agile Manifesto. One of these principles is that the best architecture, requirements, and designs emerge from self-organizing teams. Another is that teams should welcome changing requirements at any step in the process. A third is that simplicity is essential. The Agile approach emphasizes delivering software frequently, not infrequently.

64. B. Hand geometry scanners assess the physical dimensions of an individual's hand, but do not verify other unique factors about the individual, or even verify if they are alive. This means that hand geometry scanners should not be implemented as the sole authentication factor for secure environments. Hand geometry scanners do not have an abnormally high FRR, and do not stand out as a particular issue from an accessibility standpoint compared to other biometric systems.

65. A. The maximum tolerable downtime (MTD) is the amount of time that a business may be without a service before irreparable harm occurs. This measure is sometimes also called maximum tolerable outage (MTO).

66. D. Attacks that change a symlink between the time that rights are checked and the file is accessed, in order to access a file that the account does not have rights to, are time of check/time of use (TOC/TOU) attacks, a form of race condition. Unlinking removes names from a Linux filesystem, setuid allows a user to run an executable with the permissions of its owner, and tick/tock is not a type of attack or Linux command.

67. A. Smart cards are a Type II authentication factor, and include both a microprocessor and at least one certificate. Since they are something you have, they're not a Type I or III authentication factor. Tokens do not necessarily contain certificates.

68. C. Masquerading (or impersonation) attacks use stolen or falsified credentials to bypass authentication mechanisms. Spoofing attacks rely on falsifying an identity like an IP address or hostname without credentials. Replay attacks are a more specific type of masquerading attack that relies on captured network traffic to reestablish authorized connections. Modification attacks occur when captured packets are modified and replayed to a system to attempt to perform an action.

69. C. A T1 (DS1) line is rated at 1.544 Mbps. ISDN is often 64 or 128 Kbps, and T3 lines are 44.736 Mbps.

70. C. This scenario describes separation of duties—not allowing the same person to hold two roles that, when combined, are sensitive. While two-person control is a similar concept, it does not apply in this case because the scenario does not say that either action requires the concurrence of two users.

71. C. The parol evidence rule states that when an agreement between two parties is put into written form, it is assumed to be the entire agreement unless amended in writing. The best evidence rule says that a copy of a document is not admissible if the original document is available. Real evidence and testimonial evidence are evidence types, not rules of evidence.

72. A. Network Address Translation (NAT) translates an internal address to an external address. VLANs are used to logically divide networks, BGP is a routing protocol, and S/NAT is a made-up term.

73. A. SSAE-16 does not assert specific controls. Instead it reviews the use and application of controls in an audited organization. It is an attestation standard, used for external audits, and forms part of the underlying framework for SOC 1, 2, and 3 reports.

74. D. A constrained user interface restricts what users can see or do based on their privileges. This can result in grayed-out or missing menu items, or other interface changes. Activity-based controls are called context-dependent controls, whereas controls based on the content of an object are content-dependent controls. Preventing unauthorized users from logging in is a basic authentication function.

75. B. The recovery time objective (RTO) is the amount of time expected to return an IT service or component to operation after a failure. The maximum tolerable downtime (MTD) is the longest amount of time that an IT service or component may be unavailable without causing serious damage to the organization. The recovery point objective (RPO) identifies the maximum amount of data, measured in time, that may be lost during a recovery effort. Service-level agreements (SLAs) are written contracts that document service expectations.

76. C. Class variables exist only once and share their value across all instances of that object class. Instance variables have different values for each instance. Member variables are the combination of class and instance variables associated with a particular class. Global variables do not exist in an object-oriented programming language.

77. B. Class B fire extinguishers use carbon dioxide, halon, or soda acid as their suppression material and are useful against liquid-based fires. Water may not be used against liquid-based fires because it may cause the burning liquid to splash, and many burning liquids, such as oil, will float on water.

78. D. Notifications and procedures like the signs posted at the company Chris works for are examples of directive access controls. Detective controls are designed to operate after the fact. The doors and the locks on them are examples of physical controls. Preventive controls are designed to stop an event, and could also include the locks that are present on the doors.

79. D. The seven principles that the International Safe Harbor Provisions spell out for handling personal information are notice, choice, onward transfer, access, security, data integrity, and enforcement.

80. C. The DMCA provides safe harbor protection for the operators of Internet service providers who only handle information as a common carrier for transitory purposes.

81. B. According to NIST SP 800-18, a system owner should update the system security plan when the system they are responsible for undergoes a significant change. Classification, selection of custodians, and designing ways to protect data confidentiality might occur if new data was added, but should have already been done otherwise.

82. B. Provisioning that occurs through an established workflow, such as through an HR process, is workflow-based account provisioning. If Alex had set up accounts for his new hire on the systems he manages, he would have been using discretionary account provisioning. If the provisioning system allowed the new hire to sign up for an account on their own, they would have used self-service account provisioning, and if there was a central, software-driven process, rather than HR forms, it would have been automated account provisioning.

83. C. As Alex has changed roles, he retained access to systems that he no longer administers. The provisioning system has provided rights to workstations and the application servers he manages, but he should not have access to the databases he no longer administers. Privilege levels are not specified, so we can't determine if he has excessive rights. Logging may or may not be enabled, but it isn't possible to tell from the diagram or problem.

84. C. When a user's role changes, they should be provisioned based on their role and other access entitlements. De-provisioning and re-provisioning is time consuming and can lead to problems with changed IDs and how existing credentials work. Simply adding new rights leads to privilege creep, and matching another user's rights can lead to excessive privileges due to privilege creep for that other user.

85. B. EAL2 assurance applies when the system has been structurally tested. It is the second-to-lowest level of assurance under the Common Criteria.

86. C. Before granting any user access to information, Adam should verify that the user has an appropriate security clearance as well as a business need to know the information in question.

87. B. During the preservation phase, the organization ensures that information related to the matter at hand is protected against intentional or unintentional alteration or deletion. The identification phase locates relevant information but does not preserve it. The collection phase occurs after preservation and gathers responsive information. The processing phase performs a rough cut of the collected information for relevance.

88. D. Nessus, OpenVAS, the Open Vulnerability Assessment scanner and manager, and SAINT are all vulnerability scanning tools. All provide port scanning capabilities as well but are more than simple port scanning tools.

89. D. In the subject/object model, the object is the resource being requested by a subject. In this example, Harry would like access to the document, making the document the object of the request.

90. C. The process of removing a header (and possibly a footer) from the data received from a previous layer in the OSI model is known as de-encapsulation. Encapsulation occurs when the header and/or footer are added. Payloads are part of a virus or malware package that are delivered to a target, and packet unwrapping is a made-up term.

91. C. Metasploit is a tool used to exploit known vulnerabilities. Nikto is a web application and server vulnerability scanning tool, Ettercap is a man-in-the-middle attack tool, and THC Hydra is a password brute-force tool.

92. C. Service Provisioning Markup Language (SPML) uses Requesting Authorities to issue SPML requests to a Provisioning Service Point. Provisioning Service Targets are often user accounts, and are required to be allowed unique identification of the data in its implementation. SAML is used for security assertions, SAMPL is an algebraic modeling language, and XACML is an access control markup language used to describe and process access control policies in an XML format.

93. D. The use of a probability/impact matrix is the hallmark of a qualitative risk assessment It uses subjective measures of probability and impact, such as "high" and "low," in place of quantitative measures.

94. B. Mandatory access control systems can be hierarchical, where each domain is ordered and related to other domains above and below it; compartmentalized, where there is no relationship between each domain; or hybrid, where both hierarchy and compartments are used. There is no concept of bracketing in mandatory access control design.

95. C. RAID level 5 is also known as disk striping with parity. RAID 0 is called disk striping. RAID 1 is called disk mirroring. RAID 10 is known as a stripe of mirrors.

96. B. Category 5e and Category 6 UTP cable are both rated to 1000 Mbps. Cat 5 (not Cat 5e) is only rated to 100 Mbps, whereas Cat 7 is rated to 10 Gbps. There is no Cat 4e.

97. A. Developing a business impact assessment is an integral part of the business continuity planning effort. The selection of alternate facilities, activation of those facilities, and restoration of data from backup are all disaster recovery tasks.

98. D. Smurf attacks use a distributed attack approach to send ICMP echo replies at a targeted system from many different source addresses. The most effective way to block this attack would be to block inbound ICMP traffic. Blocking the source addresses is not feasible because the attacker would likely simply change the source addresses. Blocking destination addresses would likely disrupt normal activity. The Smurf attack does not use UDP, so blocking that traffic would have no effect.

99. C. Static packet filtering firewalls are known as first-generation firewalls and do not track connection state. Stateful inspection, application proxying, and next-generation firewalls all add connection state tracking capability.

100. A. TKIP is only used as a means to encrypt transmissions and is not used for data at rest. RSA, AES, and 3DES are all used on data at rest as well as data in transit.

101. C. Generational fuzzing is also known as intelligent fuzzing because it relies on the development of data models using an understanding of how the data is used by the program. Zzuf is a fuzzing program. Mutation simply modifies the inputs each time, and code based is not a description used for a type of fuzzing.

102. B. Latency is a delay in the delivery of packets from their source to their destination. Jitter is a variation in the latency for different packets. Packet loss is the disappearance of packets in transit that requires retransmission. Interference is electrical noise or other disruptions that corrupt the contents of packets.

103. B. Software tokens are flexible, with delivery options including mobile applications, SMS, and phone delivery. They have a relatively low administrative overhead, as users can typically self-manage. Biometrics require significant effort to register users and to deploy and maintain infrastructure, and require hardware at each authentication location. Both types of hardware tokens can require additional overhead for distribution and maintenance, and token failure can cause support challenges.

104. B. Web applications communicate with web browsers via an interface, making interface testing the best answer here. Regression testing might be used as part of the interface test, but is too specific to be the best answer. Similarly, the test might be a white box, or full knowledge test, but interface testing better describes this specific example. Fuzzing is less likely as part of a browser compatibility test, as it tests unexpected inputs, rather than functionality.

105. A. Role-based access control gives each user an array of permissions based on their position in the organization, such as the scheme shown here. Task-based access control is not a standard approach. Rule-based access controls use rules that apply to all subjects, which isn't something we see in the list. Discretionary access control gives object owners rights to choose how the objects they own are accessed, which is not what this list shows.

106. D. Fire suppression systems do not stop a fire from occurring but do reduce the damage that fires cause. This is an example of reducing risk by lowering the impact of an event.

107. D. Patents and trade secrets can both protect intellectual property in the form of a process. Patents require public disclosure and have expiration dates while trade secrets remain in force for as long as they remain secret. Therefore, trade secret protection most closely aligns with the company's goals.

108. D. The Security Content Automation Protocol (SCAP) is a suite of specifications used to handle vulnerability and security configuration information. The National Vulnerability Database provided by NIST uses SCAP. XACML is the eXtensible Access Control Markup Language, an OASIS standard used for access control decisions, and neither VSML nor SCML are industry terms.

109. B. The three components of the DevOps model are software development, operations, and quality assurance.

110. A. The Simple Security Property prevents an individual from reading information at a higher security level than his or her clearance allows. This is also known as the "no read up" rule. The Simple Integrity Property says that a user can't write data to a higher integrity level than their own. The *-Security Property says that users can't write data to a lower security level than their own. The Discretionary Security Property allows the use of a matrix to determine access permissions.

111. B. The work breakdown structure (WBS) is an important project management tool that divides the work done for a large project into smaller components. It is not a project plan because it does not describe timing or resources. Test analyses are used during later phases of the development effort to report test results. Functional requirements may be included in a work breakdown structure, but they are not the full WBS.

112. B. Network Access Control (NAC) systems can be used to authenticate users, and then validate their system's compliance with a security standard before they are allowed to connect to the network. Enforcing security profiles can help reduce zero-day attacks, making

NAC a useful solution. A firewall can't enforce system security policies, whereas an IDS can only monitor for attacks and alarm when they happen. Thus neither a firewall nor an IDS meets Kolin's needs. Finally, port security is a MAC address–based security feature that can only restrict which systems or devices can connect to a given port.

113. C. This scenario violates the least privilege principle because an application should never require full administrative rights to run. Gwen should update the service account to have only the privileges necessary to support the application.

114. B. Trace coverage is not a type of structural coverage. Common types of structural coverage include statement, branch or decision coverage, loop coverage, path coverage, and data flow coverage.

115. A. During the information gathering and discovery phase of a penetration test, testers will gather information about the target. Whois can provide information about an organization, including IP ranges, physical addresses, and staff contacts. Nessus would be useful during a vulnerability detection phase, and Metasploit would be useful during exploitation. zzuf is a fuzzing tool and is less likely to be used during a penetration test.

116. C. Test directories often include scripts that may have poor protections or may have other data that can be misused. There is not a default test directory that allows administrative access to PHP. Test directories are not commonly used to store sensitive data, nor is the existence of a test directory a common indicator of compromise.

117. A. Directory indexing may not initially seem like an issue during a penetration test, but simply knowing the name and location of files can provide an attacker with quite a bit of information about an organization, as well as a list of potentially accessible files. XDRF is not a type of attack, and indexing is not a denial-of-service attack vector. Directory indexing being turned on is typically either due to misconfiguration or design, or because the server was not properly configured at setup, rather than being a sign of attack.

118. B. Cross-site tracing (XST) leverages the HTTP TRACE or TRACK methods, and could be used to steal a user's cookies via cross-site scripting (XSS). The other options are not industry terms for web application or web server attacks or vulnerabilities.

119. D. The contents of RAM are volatile, meaning that they are only available while power is applied to the memory chips. EPROM, EEPROM, and flash memory are all nonvolatile, meaning that they retain their contents even when powered off.

120. C. Data loss prevention (DLP) systems specialize in the identification of sensitive information. In this case, Ursula would like to identify the presence of this information on endpoint devices, so she should choose an endpoint DLP control. Network-based DLP would not detect stored information unless the user transmits it over the network. Intrusion prevention systems (IPSs) are designed to detect and block attacks in progress, not necessarily the presence of sensitive information.

121. B. In the private cloud computing model, the cloud computing environment is dedicated to a single organization and does not follow the shared tenancy model. The environment may be built by the company in its own data center or built by a vendor at a co-location site.

122. D. Redundant Arrays of Inexpensive Disks (RAID) is designed to allow a system to continue operating without data loss in the event of a hard drive failure. Load balancing is designed to spread work across multiple servers. Intrusion prevention systems (IPSs) monitor systems and/or networks for potential attacks. Dual-power supplies protect against power supplies becoming a single point of failure.

123. D. Integrity ensures that unauthorized changes are not made to data while stored or in transit.

124. C. A star topology uses a central connection device. Ethernet networks may look like a star, but they are actually a logical bus topology that is sometimes deployed in a physical star.

125. C. Input validation ensures that the data provided to a program as input matches the expected parameters. Limit checks are a special form of input validation that ensure the value remains within an expected range, as is the case described in this scenario. Fail open and fail secure are options when planning for possible system failures. Buffer bounds are not a type of software control.

126. B. NIST SP 800-18 describes system owner responsibilities that include helping to develop system security plans, maintaining the plan, ensuring training, and identifying, implementing, and assessing security controls. A data owner is more likely to delegate these tasks to the system owner. Custodians may be asked to enforce those controls, whereas a user will be directly affected by them.

127. C. ESP's Transport mode encrypts IP packet data but leaves the packet header unencrypted. Tunnel mode encrypts the entire packet and adds a new header to support transmission through the tunnel.

128. B. In level 2, the Repeatable level of the SW-CMM, an organization introduces basic life-cycle management processes. Reuse of code in an organized fashion begins and repeatable results are expected from similar projects. The key process areas for this level include Requirements Management, Software Project Planning, Software Project Tracking and Oversight, Software Subcontract Management, Software Quality Assurance and Software Configuration Management. Software Quality Management is a process that occurs during level 4, the Managed stage of the SW-CMM.

129. A. Key risk indicators (KRIs) are often used to monitor risk for organizations that establish an ongoing risk management program. Using automated data gathering and tools that allow data to be digested and summarized can provide predictive information about how organizational risks are changing. KPIs are key performance indicators, which are used to assess how an organization is performing. Quantitative risk assessments are good for point-in-time views with detailed valuation and measurement-based risk assessments, whereas a penetration test would provide details of how well an organization's security controls are working.

130. D. The three-way handshake is SYN, SYN/ACK, ACK. System B should respond with "Synchronize and Acknowledge" to System A after it receives a SYN.

131. A. Systems that respond to ping will show the time to live for packets that reach them. Since TTL is decremented at each hop, this can help build a rough network topology map.

In addition, some firewalls respond differently to ping than a normal system, which means pinging a network can sometimes reveal the presence of firewalls that would otherwise be invisible. Hostnames are revealed by a DNS lookup, and ICMP types allowed through a firewall are not revealed by only performing a ping. ICMP can be used for router advertisements, but pinging won't show them!

132. C. Authorization defines what a subject can or can't do. Identification occurs when a subject claims an identity, accountability is provided by the logs and audit trail that track what occurs on a system, and authorization occurs when that identity is validated.

133. A. The commercial classification scheme discussed by $(ISC)^2$ includes four primary classification levels: confidential, private, sensitive, and public. Secret is a part of the military classification scheme.

134. B. All of these are objects. Although some of these items can be subjects, files, databases, and storage media can't be. Processes and programs aren't file stores, and of course none of these are users.

135. A. Testing for desired functionality is use case testing. Dynamic testing is used to determine how code handles variables that change over time. Misuse testing focuses on how code handles examples of misuse, and fuzzing feeds unexpected data as an input to see how the code responds.

136. C. When the author of a work is known, copyright protects that work for 70 years after the death of the author. Works created by a corporate author are protected for 95 years from publication or 120 years from creation, whichever expires first.

137. C. These are examples of private IP addresses. RFC1918 defines a set of private IP addresses for use in internal networks. These private addresses including 10.0.0.0-10.255.255.255, 172.16.0.0-172.31.255.255, and 192.168.0.0-196.168.255.255 should never be routable on the public Internet.

138. B. A cognitive password authenticates users based on a series of facts or answers to questions that they know. Preset questions for cognitive passwords typically rely on common information about a user like their mother's maiden name, or the name of their pet, and that information can frequently be found on the Internet. The best cognitive password systems let users make up their own questions.

139. D. A transformation procedure (TP) is the only process authorized to modify constrained data items (CDIs) within the Clark-Wilson model.

140. C. The blacklist approach to application control blocks certain prohibited packages but allows the installation of other software on systems. The whitelist approach uses the reverse philosophy and only allows approved software. Antivirus software would only detect the installation of malicious software after the fact. Heuristic detection is a variant of antivirus software.

141. C. Personal Health Information (PHI) is specifically defined by HIPAA to include information about an individual's medical bills. PCI could refer to the payment card industry's security standard but would only apply in relation to credit cards. PII is a broadly defined term for personally identifiable information, and personal billing data isn't a broadly used industry term.

142. D. Yagis, panel antennas, cantennas, and parabolic antennas are all types of directional antenna. Omnidirectional antennas radiate in all directions, whereas these types of antennas are not necessarily signal boosting. Finally, rubber duck antennas are a type of omnidirectional pole antenna.

143. C. Function, statement, branch, and condition are all types of code coverage metrics. Penetration testing methodologies use phases like planning, discovery, scanning, exploit, and reporting. Fuzzing techniques focus on ways to provide unexpected inputs, whereas synthetic transactions are generated test data provided to validate applications and performance.

144. B. Organizations should train at least two individuals on every business continuity plan task. This provides a backup in the event the primary responder is not available.

145. B. In this scenario, all of the files on the server will be backed up on Monday evening during the full backup. Tuesday's incremental backup will include all files changed since Monday's full backup: files 1, 2, and 5. Wednesday's incremental backup will then include all files modified since Tuesday's incremental backup: files 3 and 6.

File Modifications
Monday 8AM - File 1 created
Monday 10AM - File 2 created
Monday 11AM - File 3 created
Monday 4PM - File 1 modified
Monday 5PM - File 4 created
Tuesday 8AM - File 1 modified
Tuesday 9AM - File 2 modified
Tuesday 10AM - File 5 created
Wednesday 8AM - File 3 modified
Wednesday 9AM - File 6 created

146. A. Susan is performing passive monitoring, which uses a network tap or span port to capture traffic to analyze it without impacting the network or devices that it is used to monitor. Synthetic, or active, monitoring uses recorded or generated traffic to test for performance and other issues. Signature based technologies include IDS, IPS, and anti-malware systems.

147. A. While the differences between rights, permissions, and roles can be confusing, typically permissions include both the access and actions that you can take on an object. Rights usually refer to the ability to take action on an object, and don't include the access to it. Privileges combine rights and permissions, and roles describe sets of privileges based on job tasks or other organizational artifacts.

148. C. One of the core capabilities of Infrastructure as a Service is providing servers on a vendor-managed virtualization platform. Web-based payroll and email systems are examples of Software as a Service. An application platform managed by a vendor that runs customer code is an example of Platform as a Service.

149. D. The exposure factor is the percentage of the facility that risk managers expect will be damaged if a risk materializes. It is calculated by dividing the amount of damage by the asset value. In this case, that is $750,000 in damage divided by the $2 million facility value, or 37.5%.

150. C. The annualized rate of occurrence is the number of times each year that risk analysts expect a risk to happen. In this case, the analysts expect fires will occur once every 50 years, or 0.02 times per year.

151. A. The annualized loss expectancy is calculated by multiplying the single loss expectancy (SLE) by the annualized rate of occurrence (ARO). In this case, the SLE is $750,000 and the ARO is 0.02. Multiplying these numbers together gives you the ALE of $15,000.

152. A. Congestion Window Reduced (CWR) and ECN-Echo (ECE) are used to manage transmission over congested links, and are rarely seen in modern TCP networks.

153. B. The Tower of Hanoi; Grandfather, Father, Son; and First In, First Out backup rotation strategies are all used to rotate backup tapes and other media. Key rotation is a cryptographic concept not related to disaster recovery media.

154. A. An application programming interface (API) allows external users to directly call routines within Fran's code. They can embed API calls within scripts and other programs to automate interactions with Fran's company. A web scraper or call center might facilitate the same tasks, but they do not do so in a direct integration. Data dictionaries might provide useful information but they also do not allow direct integration.

155. A. A fault is a momentary loss of power. Blackouts are sustained complete losses of power. Sags and brownouts are not complete power disruptions but rather periods of low voltage conditions.

156. A. Lauren's team would benefit from a credential management system. Credential management systems offer features like password management, multifactor authentication to retrieve passwords, logging, audit, and password rotation capabilities. A strong password policy would only make maintenance of passwords for many systems a more difficult task if done manually. Single sign-on would help if all of the systems had the same sensitivity levels, but different credentials are normally required for higher sensitivity systems.

157. C. Windows systems will assign themselves an APIPA address between 169.254.0.1 and 169.254.255.254 if they cannot contact a DHCP server.

158. A. Enrollment, or registration, is the initial creation of a user account in the provisioning process. Clearance verification and background checks are sometimes part of the process that ensures that the identity of the person being enrolled matches who they claim to be. Initialization is not used to describe the provisioning process.

159. C. Repeated audit findings indicate a performance issue, making this a key performance indicator for Susan's organization. Audit findings may demonstrate risk, but are not guaranteed to do so. Safeguard metrics and audit tracking metrics are not common industry terms.

160. D. The business or mission owner's role is responsible for making sure systems provide value. When controls decrease the value that an organization gets, the business owner bears responsibility for championing the issue to those involved. There is not a business manager or information security analyst role in the list of NIST-defined data security roles. A data processor is defined but acts as a third-party data handler, and would not have to represent this issue in Olivia's organization.

161. A. The Electronic Communications Privacy Act (ECPA) makes it a crime to invade the electronic privacy of an individual. It prohibits the unauthorized monitoring of email and voicemail communications.

162. D. The kernel lies within the central ring, Ring 0. Ring 1 contains other operating system components. Ring 2 is used for drivers and protocols. User-level programs and applications run at Ring 3. Rings 0–2 run in privileged mode whereas Ring 3 runs in user mode.

163. B. The Common Vulnerability Scoring System (CVSS) uses measures such as attack vector, complexity, exploit maturity, and how much user interaction is required as well as measures suited to local concerns. CVE is the Common Vulnerabilities and Exposures dictionary, CNA is the CVE Numbering Authority, and NVD is the National Vulnerability Database.

164. C. An individual does not have a reasonable expectation of privacy when any communication takes place using employer-owned communications equipment or accounts.

165. D. During a tabletop exercise, team members come together and walk through a scenario without making any changes to information systems. The checklist review is the least disruptive type of disaster recovery test. During a checklist review, team members each review the contents of their disaster recovery checklists on their own and suggest any necessary changes. During a parallel test, the team actually activates the disaster recovery site for testing but the primary site remains operational. During a full interruption test, the team takes down the primary site and confirms that the disaster recovery site is capable of handling regular operations. The full interruption test is the most thorough test but also the most disruptive.

166. C. OpenID is a widely supported standard that allows a user to use a single account to log into multiple sites, and Google accounts are frequently used with OpenID.

167. D. Risk acceptance occurs when an organization determines that the costs involved in pursuing other risk management strategies are not justified and they choose not to pursue any action.

168. D. Fred should choose a fiber-optic cable. Copper cable types like 10Base2, 5, and 10BaseT, as well as 100Base-T and 1000BaseT, fall far short of the distance required, whereas fiber-optic cable can run for miles.

169. C. Decentralized access control makes sense because it allows local control over access. When network connectivity to a central control point is a problem, or if rules and regulations may vary significantly from location to location, centralized control can be less desirable than decentralized control despite its challenges with consistency. Since the problem does not describe specific control needs, mandatory access control and rule-based access controls could fit the need but aren't the best answer.

170. B. The U.S. government classifies data that could reasonably be expected to cause damage to national security if disclosed, and for which the damage can be identified or described, as Secret. The U.S. government does not use Classified in its formal four levels of classification. Top Secret data could cause exceptionally grave damage, whereas Confidential data could be expected to cause damage.

171. A. The purpose of a digital certificate is to provide the general public with an authenticated copy of the certificate subject's public key.

172. D. The last step of the certificate creation process is the digital signature. During this step, the certificate authority signs the certificate using its own private key.

173. C. When an individual receives a copy of a digital certificate, he or she verifies the authenticity of that certificate by using the CA's public key to validate the digital signature contained on the certificate.

174. A. Mike uses the public key that he extracted from Renee's digital certificate to encrypt the message that he would like to send to Renee.

175. C. Wireshark is a network monitoring tool that can capture and replay communications sent over a data network, including Voice over IP (VoIP) communications. Nmap, Nessus, and Nikto are all security tools that may identify security flaws in the network, but they do not directly undermine confidentiality because they do not have the ability to capture communications.

176. B. Studies consistently show that users are more likely to write down passwords if they have more accounts. Central control of a single account is also easier to shut off if something does go wrong. Simply decreasing the number of accounts required for a subject doesn't increase security by itself, and SSO does not guarantee individual system logging, although it should provide central logging of SSO activity. Since a SSO system was not specified, there is no way of determining whether a given SSO system provides better or worse encryption for authentication data.

177. D. Nonrepudiation is only possible with an asymmetric encryption algorithm. RSA is an asymmetric algorithm. AES, DES, and Blowfish are all symmetric encryption algorithms that do not provide nonrepudiation.

178. D. Modification of audit logs will prevent repudiation because the data cannot be trusted, and thus actions cannot be provably denied. The modification of the logs is also a direct example of tampering. It might initially be tempting to answer elevation of privileges and tampering, as the attacker made changes to files that should be protected, but this is an unknown without more information. Similarly, the attacker may have accessed the files, resulting in information disclosure in addition to tampering, but again, this is not specified in the question. Finally, this did not cause a denial of service, and thus that answer can be ignored.

179. C. Routing Information Protocol (RIP), Open Shortest Path First (OSPF), and Border Gateway Protocol (BGP) are all routing protocols and are associated with routers.

180. B. The Temporal Key Integrity Protocol (TKIP) was used with WPA on existing hardware to replace WEP. TKIP has been replaced by CCMP and 802.1x since 2012. PEAP and

EAP are both authentication protocols. Transport Layer Security (TLS) is used to secure web transactions and other network communications.

181. B. Each of the attributes linked to Ben's access provides information for an attribute-based information control system. Attribute-based information controls like those described in NIST SP 800-162 can take many details about the user, actions, and objects into consideration before allowing access to occur. A role-based access control would simply consider Ben's role, whereas both administrative and system discretionary access controls are not commonly used terms to describe access controls.

182. A. LOIC is an example of a distributed denial-of-service attack. It uses many systems to attack targets, combining their bandwidth and making it difficult to shut down the attack because of the number and variety of attackers. Ionization and Zombie horde attacks are both made-up answers. Teardrop attacks are an older type of attack that sends fragmented packets as a denial-of-service attack.

183. C. Certificates may only be added to a Certificate Revocation List by the certificate authority that created the digital certificate.

184. D. Remote journaling transfers transaction logs to a remote site on a more frequent basis than electronic vaulting, typically hourly. Transaction logging is not a recovery technique alone; it is a process for generating the logs used in remote journaling. In an electronic vaulting approach, automated technology moves database backups from the primary database server to a remote site on a scheduled basis, typically daily. Remote mirroring maintains a live database server at the backup site and mirrors all transactions at the primary site on the server at the backup site.

185. C. The Waiting state is used when a process is blocked waiting for an external event. The Running state is used when a process is executing on the CPU. The Ready state is used when a process is prepared to execute, but the CPU is not available. The Stopped state is used when a process terminates.

186. B. Operational investigations are performed by internal teams to troubleshoot performance or other technical issues. They are not intended to produce evidence for use in court and, therefore, do not have the rigid collection standards of criminal, civil, or regulatory investigations.

187. A. Non-disclosure agreements (NDAs) are designed to protect the confidentiality of an organization's data, including trade secrets during and after the person's employment. NDAs do not protect against deletion or availability issues, and non-compete agreements would be required to stop competition.

188. C. Adding a second factor can ensure that users who might be incorrectly accepted are not given access due to a higher than desired false acceptance rate (FAR) from accessing a system. The CER is the crossover between the false acceptance and false rejection rate (FRR), and is used as a way to measure the accuracy of biometric systems. Changing the sensitivity to lower the FRR may actually increase the FAR, and replacing a biometric system can be time consuming and expensive in terms of time and cost.

189. B. SOC 2 reports typically cover 6 months of operations. SOC 1 reports cover a point in time.

190. D. Over-the-shoulder reviews require the original developer to explain her code to a peer while walking through it. Email pass-around code reviews are done by sending code for review to peers. Pair programming requires two developers, only one of whom writes code while both collaborate. IDE forcing is not a type of code review; an IDE is an integrated development environment.

191. A. The Time of Check to Time of Use (TOC/TOU) attack exploits timing differences between when a system verifies authorization and software uses that authorization to perform an action. It is an example of a race condition attack. The other three attacks mentioned do not depend on precise timing.

192. B. Encapsulation is a process that adds a header and possibly a footer to data received at each layer before handoff to the next layer. TCP wrappers are a host-based network access control system, attribution is determining who or what performed an action or sent data, and data hiding is a term from object-oriented programming that is not relevant here.

193. C. Salting adds random text to the password before hashing in an attempt to defeat automated password cracking attacks that use precomputed values. MD5 and SHA-1 are both common hashing algorithms, so using them does not add any security. Double-hashing would only be a minor inconvenience for an attacker and would not be as effective as the use of salting.

194. A. Guidelines provide advice based on best practices developed throughout industry and organizations, but they are not compulsory. Compliance with guidelines is optional.

195. C. Usernames are an identification tool. They are not secret, so they are not suitable for use as a password.

196. C. Regression testing ensures proper functionality of an application or system after it has been changed. Unit testing focuses on testing each module of a program instead of against its previous functional state. White and black box testing both describe the amount of knowledge about a system or application, rather than a specific type or intent for testing.

197. C. Risk transference involves shifting the impact of a potential risk from the organization incurring the risk to another organization. Insurance is a common example of risk transference.

198. A. The four canons of the $(ISC)^2$ code of ethics are to protect society, the common good, necessary public trust and confidence, and the infrastructure; act honorably, honestly, justly, responsibly, and legally; provide diligent and competent service to principals; and advance and protect the profession.

199. C. A trust that allows one forest to access another's resources without the reverse being possible is an example of a one-way trust. Since Jim doesn't want the trust path to flow as the domain tree is formed, this trust has to be nontransitive.

200. B. Susan's team is performing static analysis, which analyzes nonrunning code. Dynamic analysis uses running code, whereas gray box assessments are a type of assessment done without full knowledge. Fuzzing feeds unexpected inputs to a program as part of dynamic analysis.

201. A. 201.19.7.45 is a public IP address. RFC 1918 addresses are in the ranges 10.0.0.0–0.255.255.255, 172.16.0.0–172.31.255.255, and 192.168.0.0–192.168.255.255. APIPA addresses are assigned between 169.254.0.0 to 169.254.255.254, and 127.0.0.1 is a loopback address (although technically the entire 127.x.x.x network is reserved for loopback).

202. A. Risks are the combination of a threat and a vulnerability. Threats are the external forces seeking to undermine security, such as the hacker in this case. Vulnerabilities are the internal weaknesses that might allow a threat to succeed. In this case the missing patch is the vulnerability. In this scenario, if the hacker attempts a SQL injection attack (threat) against the unpatched server (vulnerability), the result is website defacement.

203. C. The three categories of data destruction are clear (overwriting with nonsensitive data), purge (removing all data), and destroy (physical destruction of the media). Degaussing is an example of a purging technique.

204. A. Hot sites contain all of the hardware and data necessary to restore operations and may be activated very quickly.

205. B. Syslog uses UDP port 514. TCP-based implementations of syslog typically use port 6514. The other ports may look familiar because they are commonly used TCP ports: 443 is HTTPS, 515 is the LPD print service, and 445 is used for Windows SMB.

206. B. PSH is a TCP flag used to clear the buffer, resulting in immediately sending data, and URG is the TCP urgent flag. These flags are not present in UDP headers.

207. B. Fagan inspection is a highly formalized review and testing process that uses planning, overview, preparation, inspection, rework, and follow-up steps. Static inspection looks at code without running it, dynamic inspection uses live programs, and interface testing tests where code modules interact.

208. D. The system is set to overwrite the logs and will replace the oldest log entries with new log entries when the file reaches 20 MB. The system is not purging archived logs because it is not archiving logs. Since there can only be 20 MB of logs, this system will not have stored too much log data, and the question does not provide enough information to know if there will be an issue with not having the information needed.

209. B. Encapsulating Security Payload (ESP) provides the ability to encrypt and thus provides confidentiality, as well as limited authentication capabilities. It does not provide availability, nonrepudiation, or integrity validation.

210. A. Alejandro is in the first stage of the incident response process, detection. During this stage, the intrusion detection system provides the initial alert, and Alejandro performs preliminary triaging to determine if an intrusion is actually taking place and whether the scenario fits the criteria for activating further steps of the incident response process (which include response, mitigation, reporting, recovery, remediation, and lessons learned).

211. C. After detection of a security incident, the next step in the process is response, which should follow the organization's formal incident response procedure. The first step of this procedure is activating the appropriate teams, including the organization's computer security incident response team (CSIRT).

212. C. The root cause analysis examines the incident to determine what allowed it to happen and provides critical information for repairing systems so that the incident does not recur. This is a component of the remediation step of the incident response process because the root cause analysis output is necessary to fully remediate affected systems and processes.

213. D. When using symmetric cryptography, the sender encrypts a message using a shared secret key and the recipient then decrypts the message with that same key. Only asymmetric cryptography uses the concept of public and private key pairs.

214. A. Business logic errors are most likely to be missed by automated functional testing. If a complete coverage code test was conducted, runtime, input validation, and error handling issues are likely to have been discovered by automated testing. Any automated system is more likely to miss business logic errors, because humans are typically necessary to understand business logic issues.

215. A. During the Lessons Learned phase, analysts close out an incident by conducting a review of the entire incident response process. This may include making recommendations for improvements to the process that will streamline the efficiency and effectiveness of future incident response efforts.

216. B. The Digital Millennium Copyright Act (DMCA) prohibits attempts to circumvent copyright protection mechanisms placed on a protected work by the copyright holder.

217. B. Linda should choose a warm site. This approach balances cost and recovery time. Cold sites take a very long time to activate, measured in weeks or months. Hot sites activate immediately but are quite expensive. Mutual assistance agreements depend on the support of another organization.

218. B. Half-duplex communications allow only one side to send at a time. Full-duplex communications allow both parties to send simultaneously, whereas simplex communications describe one-way communications. A suplex would be a bad idea for most communications—it is a wrestling move!

219. D. Gray box testing is a blend of crystal (or white) box testing that provides full information about a target, and black box testing, which provides little or no knowledge about the target.

220. A. Test coverage is computed using the formula test coverage = number of use cases tested/total number of use cases. Code coverage is assessed by the other formulas, including function, conditional, and total code coverage.

221. C. TCP, UDP, and other transport layer protocols like SSL and TLS operate at the Transport layer.

222. C. Deterrence is the first functional goal of physical security mechanisms. If a physical security control presents a formidable challenge to a potential attacker, they may not attempt the attack in the first place.

223. A. In an automated recovery, the system can recover itself against one or more failure types. In a manual recovery approach, the system does not fail into a secure state but requires an administrator to manually restore operations. In an automated recovery without undue loss, the system can recover itself against one or more failure types and also preserve data against loss. In function recovery, the system can restore functional processes automatically.

224. A. Skip should use SCP—Secure Copy is a secure file transfer method. SSH is a secure command-line and login protocol, whereas HTTP is used for unencrypted web traffic. Telnet is an unencrypted command-line and login protocol.

225. C. The California Online Privacy Protection Act requires that commercial websites that collect personal information from users in California conspicuously post a privacy policy. The Act does not require compliance with the EU DPD, nor does it use the DPD concepts of notice or choice, and it does not require encryption of all personal data.

226. B. Callback disconnects a remote user after their initial connection, and then calls them back at a preauthorized number. CallerID can help with this but can be spoofed, making callback a better solution. CHAP is an authentication protocol, and PPP is a dial-up protocol. Neither will verify a phone number.

227. A. The reference monitor is a component of the Trusted Computing Base (TCB) that validates access to resources.

228. B. Iris scans have a longer useful life than many other types of biometric factors because they don't change throughout a person's lifespan (unless the eye itself is damaged). Iris scanners can be fooled in some cases by high-resolution images of an eye, and iris scanners are not significantly cheaper than other scanners.

229. B. Personnel retention deals with what happens when employees leave and share proprietary data. A data breach occurs when data is stolen or lost, and data exfiltration occurs when attackers or insiders extract data from an organization. Finally, nonproprietary data sharing should result in very little harm.

230. C. They need a key for every possible pair of users in the cryptosystem. The first key would allow communication between Matthew and Richard. The second key would allow communication between Richard and Christopher. The third key would allow communication between Christopher and Matthew.

231. A. The Gramm Leach Bliley Act is an example of civil law. The Computer Fraud and Abuse Act, Electronic Communications Privacy Act, and Identity Theft and Assumption Deterrence Act are all examples of criminal law.

232. C. The SMTP protocol does not guarantee confidentiality between servers, making TLS or SSL between the client and server only a partial measure. Encrypting the email content can provide confidentiality; digital signatures can provide nonrepudiation.

233. D. The single quotation mark in the input field is a telltale sign that this is a SQL injection attack. The quotation mark is used to escape outside of the SQL code's input field, and the text following is used to directly manipulate the SQL command sent from the web application to the database.

234. C. Record retention policies describe how long the organization should retain data and may also specify how and when destruction should occur. Classification policies describe how and why classification should occur and who is responsible, whereas availability and audit policies may be created for specific purposes.

235. A. The goal of the business continuity planning process is to ensure that your recovery time objectives are all less than your maximum tolerable downtimes.

236. C. The Remediation phase of incident handling focuses on conducting a root cause analysis to identify the factors contributing to an incident and implementing new security controls, as needed.

237. A. The S/MIME secure email format uses the P7S format for encrypted email messages. If the recipient does not have a mail reader that supports S/MIME, the message will appear with an attachment named `smime.p7s`.

238. A. Aggregation is a security issue that arises when a collection of facts has a higher classification than the classification of any of those facts standing alone. An inference problem occurs when an attacker can pull together pieces of less sensitive information from multiple sources and use them to derive information of greater sensitivity. In this case, only a single source was used. SQL injection is a web application exploit. Multilevel security is a system control that allows the simultaneous processing of information at different classification levels.

239. B. Polyinstantiation allows the storage of multiple different pieces of information in a database at different classification levels to prevent attackers from conducting aggregation or inference attacks. Kim could store incorrect location information in the database at lower classification levels to prevent the aggregation attack in this scenario. Input validation, server-side validation, and parameterization are all techniques used to prevent web application attacks and are not effective against inference attacks.

240. B. The tail number is a database field because it is stored in the database. It is also a primary key because the question states that the database uniquely identifies aircraft using this field. Any primary key is, by definition, also a candidate key. There is no information provided that the tail number is a foreign key used to reference a different database table.

241. B. Foreign keys are used to create relationships between tables in a database. The database enforces referential integrity by ensuring that the foreign key used in a table has a corresponding record with that value as the primary key in the referenced table.

242. B. The waterfall model uses an approach that develops software sequentially, spending quite a bit of time up front on the development and documentation of requirements and design. The spiral and agile models focus on iterative development and are appropriate when requirements are not well understood or iterative development is preferred. DevOps is an approach to integrating development and operations activities and is not an SDLC model.

243. A. The data owner is a senior manager who bears ultimate responsibility for data protection tasks. The data owner typically delegates this responsibility to one or more data custodians.

244. C. A unique salt should be created for each user using a secure generation method and stored in that user's record. Since attacks against hashes rely on building tables to compare the hashes against, unique salts for each user make building tables for an entire database essentially impossible—the work to recover a single user account may be feasible, but large scale recovery requires complete regeneration of the table each time. A single salt allows rainbow tables to be generated if the salt is stolen or can be guessed based on frequently used passwords. Creating a unique salt each time a user logs in does not allow a match against a known salted hashed password.

245. D. NIST SP800-53 describes three processes:

- Examination, which is reviewing or analyzing assessment objects like specifications, mechanisms, or activities
- Interviews, which are conducted with individuals or groups of individuals
- Testing, which involves evaluating activities or mechanisms for expected behavior when used or exercised

Knowing the details of a given NIST document in depth can be challenging. To address a question like this, first eliminate responses that do not make sense; here, a mechanism cannot be interviewed, and test and assess both mean the same thing. This leaves only one correct answer.

246. B. Anomaly-based intrusion detection systems may identify a zero-day vulnerability because it deviates from normal patterns of activity. Signature-based detection methods would not be effective because there are no signatures for zero-day vulnerabilities. Strong patch management would not be helpful because, by definition, zero-day vulnerabilities do not have patches available. Full-disk encryption would not detect an attack because it is not a detective control.

247. B. Credential management systems provide features designed to make using and storing credentials in a secure and controllable way. AAA systems are authorization, authentication, and accounting systems. Two-factor authentication and Kerberos are examples of protocols.

248. A. The emergency response guidelines should include the immediate steps an organization should follow in response to an emergency situation. These include immediate response procedures, a list of individuals who should be notified of the emergency, and secondary response procedures for first responders. They do not include long-term actions such as activating business continuity protocols, ordering equipment, or activating disaster recovery sites.

249. D. A mantrap uses two sets of doors, only one of which can open at a time. A mantrap is a type of preventive access control, although its implementation is a physical control.

250. B. When following the separation-of-duties principle, organizations divide critical tasks into discrete components and ensure that no one individual has the ability to perform both actions. This prevents a single rogue individual from performing that task in an unauthorized manner and is also known as two-person control.

Chapter 10: Practice Test 2

1. D. The recovery point objective (RPO) identifies the maximum amount of data, measured in time, that may be lost during a recovery effort. The recovery time objective (RTO) is the amount of time expected to return an IT service or component to operation after a failure. The maximum tolerable downtime (MTD) is the longest amount of time that an IT service or component may be unavailable without causing serious damage to the organization. Service-level agreements (SLAs) are written contracts that document service expectations.

2. D. Fred should choose a router. Routers are designed to control traffic on a network while connecting to other similar networks. If the networks were very different, a bridge can help connect them. Gateways are used to connect to networks that use other protocols by transforming traffic to the appropriate protocol or format as it passes through them. Switches are often used to create broadcast domains and to connect endpoint systems or other devices.

3. B. Crystal box penetration testing, which is also sometimes called white box penetration testing, provides the tester with information about networks, systems, and configurations, allowing highly effective testing. It doesn't simulate an actual attack like black and gray box testing can, and thus does not have the same realism, and it can lead to attacks succeeding that would fail in a zero- or limited-knowledge attack.

4. D. The discovery phase includes activities like gathering IP addresses, network ranges, and hostnames, as well as gathering information about employees, locations, systems, and of course, the services those systems provide. Banner information is typically gathered as part of discovery to provide information about what version and type of service is being provided.

5. B. A class B network holds 2^16 systems, and its default network mask is 255.255.0.0.

6. D. Device fingerprinting via a web portal can require user authentication and can gather data like operating systems, versions, software information, and many other factors that can uniquely identify systems. Using an automated fingerprinting system is preferable to handling manual registration, and pairing user authentication with data gathering provides more detail than a port scan. MAC addresses can be spoofed, and systems may have more than one depending on how many network interfaces they have, which can make unique identification challenging.

7. B. The data owner is normally responsible for classifying information at an appropriate level. This role is typically filled by a senior manager or director, who then delegates operational responsibility to a data custodian.

8. A. The ping flood attack sends echo requests at a targeted system. These pings use inbound ICMP echo request packets, causing the system to respond with an outbound ICMP echo reply.

9. C. While all of the listed controls would improve authentication security, most simply strengthen the use of knowledge-based authentication. The best way to improve the authentication process would be to add a factor not based on knowledge through the use of multifactor authentication. This may include the use of biometric controls or token-based authentication.

10. C. Software-defined networking (SDN) is a converged protocol that allows virtualization concepts and practices to be applied to networks. MPLS handles a wide range of protocols like ATM, DSL, and others, but isn't intended to provide the centralization capabilities that SDN does. Content Distribution Network (CDN) is not a converged protocol, and FCoE is Fiber Channel over Ethernet, a converged protocol for storage.

11. C. The best way to ensure that data on DVDs is fully gone is to destroy them, and pulverizing DVDs is an appropriate means of destruction. DVDs are write-only media, meaning that secure erase and zero wipes won't work. Degaussing only works on magnetic media and cannot guarantee that there will be zero data remnance.

12. D. The five stages of the SW-CMM are, in order, Initial, Repeatable, Defined, Managed, and Optimizing. In the Optimizing stage, a process of continuous improvement occurs.

13. A. All packets leaving Angie's network should have a source address from her public IP address block. Packets with a destination address from Angie's network should not be leaving the network. Packets with source addresses from other networks are likely spoofed and should be blocked by egress filters. Packets with private IP addresses as sources or destinations should never be routed onto the Internet.

14. D. Security best practices dictate the use of shadowed password files that move the password hashes from the widely accessible `/etc/passwd` file to the more restricted `/etc/shadow` file.

15. A. While developers may feel like they have a business need to be able to move code into production, the principle of separation of duties dictates that they should not have the ability to both write code and place it on a production server. The deployment of code is often performed by change management staff.

16. A. Applying a digital signature to a message allows the sender to achieve the goal of nonrepudiation. This allows the recipient of a message to prove to a third party that the message came from the purported sender. Symmetric encryption does not support nonrepudiation. Firewalls and IDS are network security tools that are not used to provide nonrepudiation.

17. A. System A should send an ACK to end the three-way handshake. The TCP three-way handshake is SYN, SYN/ACK, ACK.

18. B. TACACS+ is the most modern version of TACACS, the Terminal Access Controller Access-Control System. It is a Cisco proprietary protocol with added features beyond what RADIUS provides, meaning it is commonly used on Cisco networks. XTACACS is an earlier version, Kerberos is a network authentication protocol rather than a remote user authentication protocol, and RADIUS+ is a made-up term.

19. C. Call managers and VoIP phones can be thought of as servers or appliances and embedded or network devices. That means that the most likely threats that they will face are denial-of-service (DoS) attacks and attacks against the host operating system. Malware and Trojans are less likely to be effective against a server or embedded system that doesn't browse the Internet or exchange data files; buffer overflows are usually aimed at specific applications or services.

20. C. The blacklist approach to application control blocks certain prohibited packages but allows the installation of other software on systems. The whitelist approach uses the reverse philosophy and only allows approved software. Antivirus software would only detect the installation of malicious software after the fact. Heuristic detection is a variant of antivirus software.

21. B. The exposure factor is the percentage of the facility that risk managers expect will be damaged if a risk materializes. It is calculated by dividing the amount of damage by the asset value. In this case, that is $20 million in damage divided by the $100 million facility value, or 20%.

22. B. The annualized rate of occurrence is the number of times each year that risk analysts expect a risk to happen in any given year. In this case, the analysts expect floods once every 200 years, or 0.005 times per year.

23. B. The annualized loss expectancy is calculated by multiplying the single loss expectancy (SLE) by the annualized rate of occurrence (ARO). In this case, the SLE is $20 million and the ARO is 0.005. Multiplying these numbers together gives you the ALE of $100,000.

24. B. The most frequent target of account management reviews are highly privileged accounts, as they create the greatest risk. Random samples are the second most likely choice. Accounts that have existed for a longer period of time are more likely to have a problem due to privilege creep than recently created accounts, but neither of these choices is likely unless there is a specific organizational reason to choose them.

25. A. In an Infrastructure as a Service (IaaS) cloud computing model, the customer retains responsibility for managing operating system security while the vendor manages security at the hypervisor level and below.

26. A. Type 1 errors occur when a valid subject is not authenticated. Type 2 errors occur when an invalid subject is incorrectly authenticated. Type 3 and Type 4 errors are not associated with biometric authentication.

27. B. The Company ID is a field used to identify the corresponding record in another table. This makes it a foreign key. Each customer may place more than one order, making Company ID unsuitable for use as a primary or candidate key in this table. Referential keys are not a type of database key.

28. B. Application programming interfaces (APIs), user interfaces (UIs), and physical interfaces are all tested during the software testing process. Network interfaces are not typically tested, and programmatic interfaces is another term for APIs.

29. D. The hearsay rule says that a witness cannot testify about what someone else told them, except under very specific exceptions. The courts have applied the hearsay rule to include

the concept that attorneys may not introduce logs into evidence unless they are authenticated by the system administrator. The best evidence rule states that copies of documents may not be submitted into evidence if the originals are available. The parol evidence rule states that if two parties enter into a written agreement, that written document is assumed to contain all of the terms of the agreement. Testimonial evidence is a type of evidence, not a rule of evidence.

30. B. While key risk indicators can provide useful information for organizational planning and a deeper understanding of how organizations view risk, KRIs are not a great way to handle a real-time security response. Monitoring and detection systems like IPS, SIEM, and other tools are better suited to handling actual attacks.

31. B. Worms have built-in propagation mechanisms that do not require user interaction, such as scanning for systems containing known vulnerabilities and then exploiting those vulnerabilities to gain access. Viruses and Trojan horses typically require user interaction to spread. Logic bombs do not spread from system to system but lie in wait until certain conditions are met, triggering the delivery of their payload.

32. A. In this scenario, the vendor is providing object-based storage, a core infrastructure service. Therefore, this is an example of Infrastructure as a Service (IaaS).

33. C. In the community cloud computing model, two or more organizations pool their resources to create a cloud environment that they then share.

34. A. The Agile approach to software development states that working software is the primary measure of progress, that simplicity is essential, and that business people and developers must work together daily. It also states that the most efficient method of conveying information is face-to-face, not electronic.

35. C. Encryption, access controls, and firewalls would not be effective in this example because the accountants have legitimate access to the data. Integrity verification software would protect against this attack by identifying unexpected changes in protected data.

36. C. Class C fire extinguishers use carbon dioxide or halon suppressants and are useful against electrical fires. Water-based extinguishers should never be used against electrical fires due to the risk of electrocution.

37. A. Frame Relay supports multiple private virtual circuits (PVCs), unlike X.25. It is a packet switching technology that provides a Committed Information Rate, which is a minimum bandwidth guarantee provided by the service provider to customers. Finally, Frame Relay requires a DTE/DCE at each connection point, with the DTE providing access to the Frame Relay network, and a provider supplied DCE which transmits the data over the network.

38. B. SOC 2 reports are released under NDA to select partners or customers, and can provide detail on the controls and any issues they may have. A SOC 1 report would only provide financial control information, and a SOC 3 report provides less information since it is publicly available.

39. C. A SOC 2, Type 2 report includes information about a data center's security, availability, processing integrity, confidentiality, and privacy, and includes an auditor's opinion on the operational effectiveness of the controls. SOC 3 does not have types, and an SOC 2 Type 1 only requires the organization's own attestation.

40. B. SAS 70 was superseded in 2010 by the SSAE 16 standard with three SOC levels for reporting. SAS 70 included Type 2 reports, covered data centers, and used 6-month testing periods for Type 2 reports.

41. C. Both a logical bus and a logical ring can be implemented as a physical star. Ethernet is commonly deployed as a physical star but placing a switch as the center of a star, but Ethernet still operates as a bus. Similarly, Token Ring deployments using multistation access unit (MAU) were deployed as physical stars, but operated as rings.

42. C. Bell-LaPadula uses security labels on objects and clearances for subjects, and is therefore a MAC model. It does not use discretionary, rule-based, role-based, or attribute-based access control.

43. D. The Family Educational Rights and Privacy Act (FERPA) protects the privacy of students in any educational institution that accepts any form of federal funding.

44. D. The Health Insurance Portability and Accountability Act (HIPAA) mandates the protection of Protected Health Information (PHI). The SAFE Act deals with mortgages, the Graham Leach Bliley Act (GLBA) covers financial institutions, and FERPA deals with student data.

45. C. Windows system logs include reboots, shutdowns, and service state changes. Application logs record events generated by programs, security logs track events like logins and uses of rights, and setup logs track application setup.

46. D. Implementations of syslog vary, but most provide a setting for severity level, allowing configuration of a value that determines what messages are sent. Typical severity levels include debug, informational, notice, warning, error, critical, alert, and emergency. The facility code is also supported by syslog, but is associated with which services are being logged. Security level and log priority are not typical syslog settings.

47. B. In RAID 1, also known as disk mirroring, systems contain two physical disks. Each disk contains copies of the same data, and either one may be used in the event the other disk fails.

48. B. An application-level gateway firewall uses proxies for each service it filters. Each proxy is designed to analyze traffic for its specific traffic type, allowing it to better understand valid traffic and to prevent attacks. Static packet filters and circuit-level gateways simply look at the source, destination, and ports in use, whereas a stateful packet inspection firewall can track the status of communication and allow or deny traffic based on that understanding.

49. C. Interviews, surveys, and audits are all useful for assessing awareness. Code quality is best judged by code review, service vulnerabilities are tested using vulnerability scanners and related tools, and the attack surface of an organization requires both technical and administrative review.

50. B. The Digital Millennium Copyright Act extends common carrier protection to Internet service providers who are not liable for the "transitory activities" of their customers.

51. C. Tokens are hardware devices (something you have) that generate a one-time password based on time or an algorithm. They are typically combined with another factor like a password to authenticate users. CAC and PIV cards are US government–issued smart cards.

52. B. A non-disclosure agreement (NDA) is a legal agreement between two parties that specifies what data they will not disclose. NDAs are common in industries that have sensitive or trade secret information they do not want employees to take to new jobs. Encryption would only help in transit or at rest, and Fred will likely have access to the data in unencrypted form as part of his job. An AUP is an acceptable use policy, and a stop-loss order is used on the stock market.

53. A. Multitasking handles multiple processes on a single processor by switching between them using the operating system. Multiprocessing uses multiple processors to perform multiple processes simultaneously. Multiprogramming requires modifications to the underlying applications. Multithreading runs multiple threads within a single process.

54. C. Binary keyspaces contain a number of keys equal to 2 raised to the power of the number of bits. Two to the eighth power is 256, so an 8-bit keyspace contains 256 possible keys.

55. C. Scoping is the process of reviewing and selecting security controls based on the system that they will be applied to. Tailoring is the process of matching a list of security controls to the mission of an organization. Baselines are used as a base set of security controls, often from a third-party organization that creates them. Standardization isn't a relevant term here.

56. D. During the preservation phase, the organization ensures that information related to the matter at hand is protected against intentional or unintentional alteration or deletion. The identification phase locates relevant information but does not preserve it. The collection phase occurs after preservation and gathers responsive information. The processing phase performs a rough cut of the collected information for relevance.

57. D. Systems and media should be labeled with the highest level of sensitivity that they store or handle. In this case, based on the US government classification scheme, the highest classification level in use on the system is Secret. Mixed classification provides no useful information about the level, whereas Top Secret and Confidential are too high and too low, respectively.

58. C. She has placed compensation controls in place. Compensation controls are used when controls like the locks in this example are not sufficient. While the alarm is a physical control, the signs she posted are not. Similarly, the alarms are not administrative controls. None of these controls help to recover from an issue and are thus not recovery controls.

59. A. Rainbow tables rely on being able to use databases of precomputed hashes to quickly search for matches to known hashes acquired by an attacker. Making passwords longer can greatly increase the size of the rainbow table required to find the matching hash, and adding a salt to the password will make it nearly impossible for the attacker to generate a table that will match unless they can acquire the salt value. MD5 and SHA1 are both poor choices for password hashing compared to modern password hashes, which are designed

to make hashing easy and recovery difficult. Rainbow tables are often used against lists of hashes acquired by attacks rather than over-the-wire attacks, so over-the-wire encryption is not particularly useful here. Shadow passwords simply make the traditionally world-readable list of password hashes on Unix and Linux systems available in a location readable only by root. This doesn't prevent a rainbow table attack once the hashes are obtained.

60. C. External auditors can provide an unbiased and impartial view of an organization's controls to third parties. Internal auditors are useful when reporting to senior management of the organization but are typically not asked to report to third parties. Penetration tests test technical controls but are not as well suited to testing many administrative controls. The employees who build and maintain controls are more likely to bring a bias to the testing of those controls and should not be asked to report on them to third parties.

61. A. Using encryption reduces risk by lowering the likelihood that an eavesdropper will be able to gain access to sensitive information.

62. B. Provisioning includes the creation, maintenance, and removal of user objects from applications, systems, and directories. Registration occurs when users are enrolled in a biometric system; population and authenticator loading are not common industry terms.

63. A. In the subject/object model of access control, the user or process making the request for a resource is the subject of that request. In this example, Ricky is requesting access to the VPN (the object of the request) and is, therefore, the subject.

64. C. The formula for determining the number of encryption keys required by a symmetric algorithm is ((n*(n-1))/2). With six users, you will need ((6*5)/2), or 15 keys.

65. B. Patents have the shortest duration of the techniques listed: 20 years. Copyrights last for 70 years beyond the death of the author. Trademarks are renewable indefinitely and trade secrets are protected as long as they remain secret.

66. C. In a risk acceptance strategy, the organization chooses to take no action other than documenting the risk. Purchasing insurance would be an example of risk transference. Relocating the data center would be risk avoidance. Reengineering the facility is an example of a risk mitigation strategy.

67. C. Uninterruptible power supplies (UPSs) provide immediate, battery-driven power for a short period of time to cover momentary losses of power. Generators are capable of providing backup power for a sustained period of time in the event of a power loss, but they take time to activate. RAID and redundant servers are high-availability controls but do not cover power loss scenarios.

68. C. Password histories retain a list of previous passwords (or, preferably, a list of salted hashed for previous passwords) to ensure that users don't reuse their previous passwords. Longer minimum age can help prevent users from changing their passwords, then changing them back, but won't prevent a determined user from eventually getting their old password back. Length requirements and complexity requirements tend to drive users to reuse passwords if they're not paired with tools like single-sign on, password storage systems, or other tools that decrease the difficulty of password management.

69. B. The Single Loss Expectancy (SLE) is the amount of damage that a risk is expected to cause each time that it occurs.

70. B. Sanitization includes steps like removing the hard drive and other local storage from PCs before they are sold as surplus. Degaussing uses magnetic fields to wipe media; purging is an intense form of clearing used to ensure that data is removed and unrecoverable from media; and removing does not necessarily imply destruction of the drive.

71. D. During the Reporting phase, incident responders assess their obligations under laws and regulations to report the incident to government agencies and other regulators.

72. B. Service Provisioning Markup Language (SPML) is an OASIS developed markup language designed to provide service, user, and resource provisioning between organizations. Security Assertion Markup Language (SAML) is used to exchange user authentication and authorization data. Extensible Access Control Markup Language (XACML) is used to describe access controls. Service-oriented architecture (SOA) is not a markup language.

73. D. RAM is a type of primary storage. Secondary storage includes hard drives, solid state disks, and optical drives.

74. D. SMTP servers that don't authenticate users before relaying their messages are known as open relays. Open relays that are Internet exposed are typically quickly exploited to send email for spammers.

75. D. Sending logs to a secure log server, sometimes called a bastion host, is the most effective way to ensure that logs survive a breach. Encrypting local logs won't stop an attacker from deleting them, and requiring administrative access won't stop attackers who have breached a machine and acquired escalated privileges. Log rotation archives logs based on time or file size, and can also purge logs after a threshold is hit. Rotation won't prevent an attacker from purging logs.

76. C. A Security Information and Event Management tool (SIEM) is designed to provide automated analysis and monitoring of logs and security events. A SIEM that receives access to logs can help detect and alert on events like logs being purged or other breach indicators. An IDS can help detect intrusions, but IDSs are not typically designed to handle central logs. A central logging server can receive and store logs, but won't help with analysis without taking additional actions. Syslog is simply a log format.

77. B. Requiring authentication can help provide accountability by ensuring that any action taken can be tracked back to a specific user. Storing logs centrally ensures that users can't erase the evidence of actions that they have taken. Log review can be useful when identifying issues, but digital signatures are not a typical part of a logging environment. Logging the use of administrative credentials helps for those users but won't cover all users, and encrypting the logs doesn't help with accountability. Authorization helps, but being able to specifically identify users through authentication is more important.

78. B. Port Address Translation (PAT) is used to allow a network to use any IP address set inside without causing a conflict with the public Internet. PAT is often confused with

Network Address Translation (NAT), which maps one internal address to one external address. IPSec is a security protocol suite, Software Defined Networking (SDN) is a method of defining networks programmatically, and IPX is a non-IP network protocol.

79. C. Each of the precautions listed helps to prevent social engineering by helping prevent exploitation of trust. Avoiding voice-only communications is particularly important, since establishing identity over the phone is difficult. The other listed attacks would not be prevented by these techniques.

80. C. L2TP is the only one of the four common VPN protocols that can natively support non-IP protocols. PPTP, L2F, and IPSec are all IP-only protocols.

81. D. Remnant data is data that is left after attempts have been made to remove or erase it. Bitrot is a term used to describe aging media that decays over time. MBR is the master boot record, a boot sector found on hard drives and other media. Leftover data is not an industry term.

82. C. During a parallel test, the team activates the disaster recovery site for testing but the primary site remains operational. A simulation test involves a roleplay of a prepared scenario overseen by a moderator. Responses are assessed to help improve the organization's response process. The checklist review is the least disruptive type of disaster recovery test. During a checklist review, team members each review the contents of their disaster recovery checklists on their own and suggest any necessary changes. During a tabletop exercise, team members come together and walk through a scenario without making any changes to information systems.

83. C. Discretionary access control gives owners the right to decide who has access to the objects they own. Role-based access control uses administrators to make that decision for roles or groups of people with a role, task-based access control uses lists of tasks for each user, and rule-based access control applies a set of rules to all subjects.

84. C. Trusted paths that secure network traffic from capture and link encryption are both ways to help prevent man-in-the-middle attacks. Brute-force and dictionary attacks can both be prevented using back-off algorithms that slow down repeated attacks. Log analysis tools can also create dynamic firewall rules, or an IPS can block attacks like these in real time. Spoofed login screens can be difficult to prevent, although user awareness training can help.

85. D. The four canons of the (ISC)^2 code of ethics are to protect society, the common good, necessary public trust and confidence, and the infrastructure; act honorably, honestly, justly, responsibly, and legally; provide diligent and competent service to principals; and advance and protect the profession.

86. A. The emergency response guidelines should include the immediate steps an organization should follow in response to an emergency situation. These include immediate response procedures, a list of individuals who should be notified of the emergency, and secondary response procedures for first responders. They do not include long-term actions such as activating business continuity protocols, ordering equipment, or activating DR sites.

87. C. Security Assertion Markup Language (SAML) is the best choice for providing authentication and authorization information, particularly for browser-based SSO. HTML is primarily used for web pages, SPML is used to exchange user information for SSO, and XACML is used for access control policy markup.

88. D. Individuals with specific business continuity roles should receive training on at least an annual basis.

89. B. Triple DES functions by using either two or three encryption keys. When used with only one key, 3DES produces weakly encrypted ciphertext that is the insecure equivalent of DES.

90. B. RFC 1918 addresses are in the range 10.0.0.0–10.255.255.255, 172.16.0.0–172.31.255.255, and 192.168.0.0–192.168.255.255. APIPA addresses are assigned between 169.254.0.01 and 169.254.255.254, and 127.0.0.1 is a loopback address (although technically the entire 127.x.x.x network is reserved for loopback). Public IP addresses are the rest of the addresses in the space.

91. C. Since Lauren wants to monitor her production server she should use passive monitoring by employing a network tap, span port, or other means of copying actual traffic to a monitoring system that can identify performance and other problems. This will avoid introducing potentially problematic traffic on purpose while capturing actual traffic problems. Active monitoring relies on synthetic or previously recorded traffic, and both replay and real time are not common industry terms used to describe types of monitoring.

92. B. For web applications, input validation should always be performed on the web application server. By the time the input reaches the database, it is already part of a SQL command that is properly formatted and input validation would be far more difficult, if it is even possible. Input validation controls should never reside in the client's browser, as is the case with JavaScript, because the user may remove or tamper with the validation code.

93. A. RSA is an asymmetric encryption algorithm that requires only two keys for each user. IDEA, 3DES, and Skipjack are all symmetric encryption algorithms and would require a key for every unique pair of users in the system.

94. D. The image clearly shows a black magnetic stripe running across the card, making this an example of a magnetic stripe card.

95. D. The log entries contained in this example show the allow/deny status for inbound and outbound TCP and UDP sessions. This is, therefore, an example of a firewall log.

96. D. Zero-day vulnerabilities remain in the dangerous zero-day category until the release of a patch that corrects the vulnerability. At that time, it becomes the responsibility of IT professionals to protect their systems by applying the patch. Implementation of other security controls, such as encryption or firewalls, does not change the nature of the zero-day vulnerability.

97. A. All of the techniques listed are hardening methods, but only patching the leaky roof is an example of physical infrastructure hardening.

98. C. Using a virtual machine to monitor a virtual span port allows the same type of visibility that it would in a physical network if implemented properly. Installing Wireshark would allow monitoring on each system but doesn't scale well. A physical appliance would require all traffic to be sent out of the VM environment, losing many of the benefits of the design. Finally, netcat is a network tool used to send or receive data, but it isn't a tool that allows packet capture of traffic between systems.

99. C. The sender of a message encrypts the message using the public key of the message recipient.

100. D. The recipient of a message uses his or her own private key to decrypt messages that were encrypted with the recipient's public key. This ensures that nobody other than the intended recipient can decrypt the message.

101. D. Digital signatures enforce nonrepudiation. They prevent an individual from denying that he or she was the actual originator of the message.

102. B. An individual creates a digital signature by encrypting the message digest with his or her own private key.

103. D. The comparison of a factor to validate an identity is known as authorization. Identification would occur when Jim presented his user ID. Tokenization is a process that converts a sensitive data element to a nonsensitive representation of that element. Hashing transforms a string of characters into a fixed-length value or key that represents the original string.

104. B. Decentralized access control empowers people closer to the resources to control access but does not provide consistent control. It does not provide redundancy, since it merely moves control points, the cost of access control depends on its implementation and methods, and granularity can be achieved in both centralized and decentralized models.

105. C. A mantrap, which is composed of a pair of doors with an access mechanism that allows only one door to open at a time, is an example of a preventive access control because it can stop unwanted access by keeping intruders from accessing a facility due to an opened door or following legitimate staff in. It can serve as a deterrent by discouraging intruders who would be trapped in it without proper access, and of course, doors with locks are an example of a physical control. A compensating control attempts to make up for problems with an existing control or to add additional controls to improve a primary control.

106. C. Sally needs to provide nonrepudiation, the ability to provably associate a given email with a sender. Digital signatures can provide nonrepudiation and are her best option. IMAP is a mail protocol, encryption can provide confidentiality, and DKIM is a tool for identifying domains that send email.

107. D. In most situations, employers may not access medical information due to healthcare privacy laws. Reference checks, criminal records checks, and credit history reports are all typically found during pre-employment background checks.

108. C. In a land attack, the attacker sends a packet that has identical source and destination IP addresses in an attempt to crash systems that are not able to handle this out-of-specification traffic.

109. A. An SSAE-16 Type I report covers controls and design of controls at the time of the report. A Type II report adds a historical element, covering controls over time. SAS-70 is outdated and should not be used.

110. A. When a data stream is converted into a segment (TCP) or a datagram (UDP) it transitions from the Session layer to the Transport layer. This change from a message sent to an encoded segment allows it to then traverse the network layer.

111. C. The user has successfully explained a valid need to know the data—completing the report requested by the CFO requires this access. However, the user has not yet demonstrated that he or she has appropriate clearance to access the information. A note from the CFO would meet this requirement.

112. B. Kathleen's needs point to a directory service, and the Lightweight Directory Access Protocol (LDAP) would meet her needs. LDAP is an open, industry standard and vendor-neutral protocol for directory services. Kerberos and RADIUS are both authentication protocols, and Active Directory is a Microsoft product and is not vendor neutral, although it does support a number of open standards.

113. A. Application firewalls add Layer 7 functionality to other firewall solutions. This includes the ability to inspect application-layer details such as analyzing HTTP, DNS, FTP, and other application protocols.

114. C. The create rule allows a subject to create new objects and also creates an edge from the subject to that object, granting rights on the new object.

115. A. Metasploit provides an extensible framework, allowing penetration testers to create their own exploits in addition to those that are built into the tool. Unfortunately, penetration testing can only cover the point in time when it is conducted. When conducting a penetration test, the potential to cause a denial of service due to a fragile service always exists, but it can test process and policy through social engineering and operational testing that validates how those processes and policies work.

116. D. EAL7 is the highest level of assurance under the Common Criteria. It applies when a system has been formally verified, designed, and tested.

117. C. X.509 defines standards for public key certificates like those used with many smart cards. X.500 is a series of standards defining directory services. The Service Provisioning Markup Language (SPML) and the Security Assertion Markup Language (SAML) aren't standards that Alex should expect to see when using a smart card to authenticate.

118. C. The Children's Online Privacy Protection Act (COPPA) regulates websites that cater to children or knowingly collect information from children under the age of 13.

119. A. The Health Insurance Portability and Accountability Act (HIPAA) applies to healthcare information and is unlikely to apply in this situation. The Federal Information Security Management Act (FISMA) and Government Information Security Reform Act regulate the activities of all government agencies. The Homeland Security Act (HSA) created the US Department of Homeland Security, and more importantly for this question included the Cyber Security Enhancement Act of 2002 and the Critical Infrastructure

Information Act of 2002. The Computer Fraud and Abuse Act (CFAA) provides specific protections for systems operated by government agencies.

120. C. Turnstiles are unidirectional gates that prevent more than a single person from entering a facility at a time.

121. C. Access control systems rely on identification and authentication to provide accountability. Effective authorization systems are desirable, but not required, since logs can provide information about who accessed what resources, even if access to those resources are not managed well. Of course, poor authorization management can create many other problems.

122. B. EAP was originally intended to be used on physically isolated network channels and did not include encryption. Fortunately, it was designed to be extensible, and PEAP can provide TLS encryption. EAP isn't limited to PEAP as an option as EAP-TLS also exists, providing an EAP TLS implementation, and the same extensibility allows a multitude of other authentication methods.

123. C. The 192.168.0.0-192.168.255.255 address range is one of the ranges defined by RFC 1918 as private, non-routable IP ranges. Scott's ISP (and any other organization with a properly configured router) will not route traffic from these addresses over the public Internet.

124. B. She should use a KPI (Key Performance Indicator). KPIs are used to measure success, typically in relation to an organization's long-term goals. Metrics are measures, and although a KPI can be a metric, metrics are not all KPIs. SLAs are service-level agreements, and metrics can help determine whether they are being met. Objectives and key results (OKRs) are used to connect employee performance to results using subjective measures for objectives and quantitative measures for key results.

125. A. A well-designed set of VLANs based on functional groupings will logically separate segments of the network, making it difficult to have data exposure issues between VLANs. Changing the subnet mask will only modify the broadcast domain and will not fix issues with packet sniffing. Gateways would be appropriate if network protocols were different on different segments. Port security is designed to limit which systems can connect to a given port.

126. C. Captive portals are designed to show a page that can require actions like accepting an agreement or recording an email address before connecting clients to the Internet. NAC is designed to verify whether clients meet a security profile, which doesn't match the needs of most coffee shops. A wireless gateway is a tool to access a cellular or other network, rather than a way to interact with users before they connect, and 802.11 is the family of IEEE wireless standards.

127. A. Active monitoring is also known as synthetic monitoring and relies on prerecorded or generated traffic to test systems for performance and other issues. Passive monitoring uses span ports, network taps, or similar technologies to capture actual traffic for analysis. Reactive monitoring is not a commonly used industry term.

128. B. TCP headers can be 20 to 60 bytes long depending on options that are set.

129. A. Cellular networks have the same issues that any public network does. Encryption requirements should match those that the organization selects for other public networks like hotels, conference Wi-Fi, and similar scenarios. Encrypting all data is difficult, and adds overhead, so it should not be the default answer unless the company specifically requires it. WAP is a dated wireless application protocol and is not in broad use; requiring it would be difficult. WAP does provide TLS, which would help when in use.

130. D. Fred's best option is to use an encrypted, trusted VPN service to tunnel all of his data usage. Trusted Wi-Fi networks are unlikely to exist at a hacker conference, normal usage is dangerous due to the proliferation of technology that allows fake towers to be set up, and discontinuing all usage won't support Fred's business needs.

131. B. Remote wipe tools are a useful solution, but they only work if the phone can access either a cellular or Wi-Fi network. Remote wipe solutions are designed to wipe data from the phone regardless of whether it is in use or has a passcode. Providers unlock phones for use on other cellular networks rather than for wiping or other feature support.

132. C. The goal of business continuity planning exercises is to reduce the amount of time required to restore operations. This is done by minimizing the recovery time objective (RTO).

133. D. NIST Special Publication 800-53 describes depth and coverage. These terms describe depth, specifying the level of detail. Coverage measures breadth by using multiple assessment types and ensuring that each line of code is covered. If you encounter a question like this and are not familiar with the details of a standard like NIST 800-53, or may not remember them, focus on the meanings of each word and the details of the question. We can easily rule out affirmation, which isn't a measure. Suitability is a possibility, but depth fits better than suitability or coverage.

134. C. A structured walk-through uses only role-playing to test a disaster recovery plan. It does not involve the use of any technical controls. Simulation tests, parallel tests, and full interruption tests actually use some or all of the disaster recovery controls.

135. C. Interference is electrical noise or other disruptions that corrupt the contents of packets. Latency is a delay in the delivery of packets from their source to their destination. Jitter is a variation in the latency for different packets. Packet loss is the disappearance of packets in transit that requires retransmission.

136. A. Fagan inspections follow a rigorous, highly structured process to perform code review, using a planning, overview, preparation, inspection, rework, and follow-up cycle. Fuzzing feeds unexpected input to programs, while over-the-shoulder code review is simply a review by having another developer meet with them to review code using a walk-through. Pair programming uses a pair of developers, one of whom writes code while both talk through the coding and development process.

137. B. While removing the `<SCRIPT>` tag from user input, it is not sufficient, as a user may easily evade this filter by encoding the tag with an XSS filter evasion technique. Frank was correct to perform validation on the server rather than at the client, but he should use validation that limits user input to allowed values, rather than filtering out one potentially malicious tag.

138. C. Fortran is a functional programming language. Java, C++, and C# are all object-oriented languages, meaning that they use the object model and approach programming as describing the interactions between objects.

139. C. HIPAA requires that anyone working with personal health information on behalf of a HIPAA-covered entity be subject to the terms of a business associates agreement (BAA).

140. A. During a full interruption test, the team takes down the primary site and confirms that the disaster recovery site is capable of handling regular operations. The full interruption test is the most thorough test but also the most disruptive. During a parallel test, the team actually activates the disaster recovery site for testing but the primary site remains operational. The checklist review is the least disruptive type of disaster recovery test. During a checklist review, team members each review the contents of their disaster recovery checklists on their own and suggest any necessary changes. During a tabletop exercise, team members come together and walk through a scenario without making any changes to information systems.

141. D. Ed's best option is to install an IPv6 to IPv4 gateway that can translate traffic between the networks. A bridge would be appropriate for different types of networks, whereas a router would make sense if the networks were similar. A modern switch might be able to carry both types of traffic but wouldn't be much help translating between the two protocols.

142. C. The Rijndael block cipher was selected as the winner and is the cryptographic algorithm underlying the Advanced Encryption Standard (AES).

143. C. The International Safe Harbor Privacy Principles listed here are part of the Safe Harbor provisions intended to address the European Union's Data Privacy Directive. The DPD provides seven slightly different key principles to ensure data security and privacy. The Children's Online Privacy Act (COPA), the NY SAFE Act is not an information security or privacy law, and the Federal Information Security Modernization Act (FISMA) is a key part of the US federal government's security posture.

144. B. The EU Data Protection Directive does not require that organizations provide individuals with employee lists.

145. B. Tammy should choose a warm site. This type of facility meets her requirements for a good balance between cost and recovery time. It is less expensive than a hot site but facilitates faster recovery than a cold site. A red site is not a type of disaster recovery facility.

146. B. When data reaches the Transport layer, it is sent as segments (TCP) or datagrams (UDP). Above the Transport layer, data becomes a data stream, while below the Transport layer they are converted to packets at the Network layer, frames at the Data Link layer, and bits at the Physical layer.

147. D. The Advanced Encryption Standard supports encryption with 128-bit keys, 192-bit keys, and 256-bit keys.

148. D. An application programming interface (API) allows developers to create a direct method for other users to interact with their systems through an abstraction that does not require knowledge of the implementation details. Access to object models, source code, and data dictionaries also indirectly facilitate interaction but do so in a manner that provides other developers with implementation details.

149. D. The PGP email system, invented by Phil Zimmerman, uses the "web of trust" approach to secure email. The commercial version uses RSA for key exchange, IDEA for encryption/decryption, and MD5 for message digest production. The freeware version uses Diffie-Hellman key exchange, the Carlisle Adams/Stafford Tavares (CAST) encryption/decryption, and SHA hashing.

150. B. The permissions granted on files in Linux designate what authorized users can do with those files—read, write, or execute. In the image shown, all users can read, write, and execute `index.html`, whereas the owner can read, write, and execute `example.txt`, the group cannot, and everyone can write and execute it.

151. C. Detective access controls operate after the fact and are intended to detect or discover unwanted access or activity. Preventive access controls are designed to prevent the activity from occurring, whereas corrective controls return an environment to its original status after an issue occurs. Directive access controls limit or direct the actions of subjects to ensure compliance with policies.

152. C. A honeypot is a decoy computer system used to bait intruders into attacking. A honeynet is a network of multiple honeypots that creates a more sophisticated environment for intruders to explore. A pseudo flaw is a false vulnerability in a system that may attract an attacker. A darknet is a segment of unused network address space that should have no network activity and, therefore, may be easily used to monitor for illicit activity.

153. C. The CER is the point where FAR and FRR cross over, and it is a standard assessment used to compare the accuracy of biometric devices.

154. A. At point B, the false acceptance rate (FAR) is quite high, whereas the false rejection rate (FRR) is relatively low. This may be acceptable in some circumstances, but in organizations where a false acceptance can cause a major problem, it is likely that they should instead choose a point to the right of point A.

155. B. CER is a standard used to assess biometric devices. If the CER for this device does not fit the needs of the organization, Ben should assess other biometric systems to find one with a lower CER. Sensitivity is already accounted for in CER charts, and moving the CER isn't something Ben can do. FRR is not a setting in software, so Ben can't use that as an option either.

156. B. Personally Identifiable Information (PII) can be used to distinguish a person's identity. Personal Health Information (PHI) includes data like medical history, lab results, insurance information, and other details about a patient. Personal Protected Data is a made-up term, and PID is an acronym for process ID, the number associated with a running program or process.

157. D. The figure shows the waterfall model, developed by Winston Royce. The key characteristic of this model is a series of sequential steps that include a feedback loop that allows the process to return one step prior to the current step when necessary.

158. B. Encapsulation creates both the benefits and potential issues with multilayer protocols. Bridging can use various protocols but does not rely on encapsulation. Hashing and storage protocols typically do not rely on encapsulation as a core part of their functionality.

159. B. The five COBIT principles are meeting stakeholder needs, covering the enterprise end-to-end, applying a single integrated framework, enabling a holistic approach, and separating governance from management.

160. A. The onward transfer principle requires that organizations only exchange personal information with other organizations bound by the EU Data Protection Directive's privacy principles. The United Kingdom, Italy, and Germany, as EU member states, are all bound by those principles. The United States does not have a comprehensive privacy law codifying those principles, so the onward transfer requirement applies.

161. C. The Domain Name System (DNS) provides human-friendly domain names that resolve to IP addresses, making it possible to easily remember websites and hostnames. ARP is used to resolve IP addresses into MAC addresses, whereas TCP is used to control the network traffic that travels between systems.

162. B. Ben is assessing a specification. Specifications are document-based artifacts like policies or designs. Activities are actions that support an information system that involves people. Mechanisms are the hardware-, software-, or firmware-based controls or systems in an information system, and an individual is one or more people applying specifications, mechanisms, or activities.

163. C. When done properly, a sanitization process fully ensures that data is not remnant on the system before it is reused. Clearing and erasing can both be failure prone, and of course destruction wouldn't leave a machine or device to reuse.

164. C. In a gray box test, the tester evaluates the software from a user perspective but has access to the source code as the test is conducted. White box tests also have access to the source code but perform testing from a developer's perspective. Black box tests work from a user's perspective but do not have access to source code. Blue boxes are a telephone hacking tool and not a software testing technique.

165. D. The DevOps approach to technology management seeks to integrate software development, operations, and quality assurance in a cohesive effort. It specifically attempts to eliminate the issue of "throwing problems over the fence" by building collaborative relationships between members of the IT team.

166. B. A Security Information and Event Management (SIEM) tool is designed to centralize logs from many locations in many formats, and to ensure that logs are read and analyzed despite differences between different systems and devices. The Simple Network Management Protocol (SNMP) is used for some log messaging but is not a solution that solves all of these problems. Most non-Windows devices, including network devices among others, are not designed to use the Windows event log format, although using NTP for time synchronization is a good idea. Finally, local logging is useful, but setting clocks individually will result in drift over time and won't solve the issue with many log sources.

167. C. Mike should use overwriting to protect this device. While degaussing is a valid secure data removal technique, it would not be effective in this case, since degaussing only works on magnetic media. Physical destruction would prevent the reuse of the device. Reformatting is not a valid secure data removal technique.

168. A. The single quotation mark in the input field is a telltale sign that this is a SQL injection attack. The quotation mark is used to escape outside the SQL code's input field and the text that follows is used to directly manipulate the SQL command sent from the web application to the database.

169. D. Procedures are formal, mandatory documents that provide detailed, step-by-step actions required from individuals performing a task.

170. D. Durability requires that once a transaction is committed to the database it must be preserved. Atomicity ensures that if any part of a database transaction fails, the entire transaction must be rolled back as if it never occurred. Consistency ensures that all transactions are consistent with the logical rules of the database, such as having a primary key. Isolation requires that transactions operate separately from each other.

171. D. Watermarking alters a digital object to embed information about the source, either in a visible or hidden form. Digital signatures may identify the source of a document but they are easily removed. Hashing would not provide any indication of the document source, since anyone could compute a hash value. Document staining is not a security control.

172. C. Data centers should be located in the core of a building. Locating it on lower floors makes it susceptible to flooding and physical break-ins. Locating it on the top floor makes it vulnerable to wind and roof damage.

173. A. The due care principle states that an individual should react in a situation using the same level of care that would be expected from any reasonable person. It is a very broad standard. The due diligence principle is a more specific component of due care that states an individual assigned a responsibility should exercise due care to complete it accurately and in a timely manner.

174. B. Criminal investigations have high stakes with severe punishment for the offender that may include incarceration. Therefore, they use the strictest standard of evidence of all investigations: beyond a reasonable doubt. Civil investigations use a preponderance of the evidence standard. Regulatory investigations may use whatever standard is appropriate for the venue where the evidence will be heard. This may include the beyond-a-reasonable-doubt standard, but it is not always used in regulatory investigations. Operational investigations do not use a standard of evidence.

175. D. Differential backups do not alter the archive bit on a file, whereas incremental and full backups reset the archive bit to 0 after the backup completes. Partial backups are not a backup type.

176. B. Warm sites contain the hardware necessary to restore operations but do not have a current copy of data.

177. C. A power spike is a momentary period of high voltage. A surge is a prolonged period of high voltage. Sags and brownouts are periods of low voltage.

178. A. Subjects are active entities that can access a passive object to retrieve information from or about an object. Subjects can also make changes to objects when they are properly authorized. Users are often subjects, but not all subjects are users.

179. A. OSPF is a link state protocol. Link state protocols maintain a topographical map of all connected networks and preferentially select the shortest path to remote networks for traffic. A distance vector protocol would map the direction and distance in hops to a remote network, whereas shortest path first and link mapping are not types of routing protocols.

180. A. Machine languages are examples of first-generation programming languages. Second-generation languages include assembly languages. Third-generation languages include compiled languages. Fourth- and fifth-generation languages go beyond standard compiled languages to include natural languages and declarative approaches to programming.

181. A. Tara first must achieve a system baseline. She does this by applying the most recent full backup to the new system. This is Sunday's full backup. Once Tara establishes this baseline, she may then proceed to apply differential backups to bring the system back to a more recent state.

182. B. To restore the system to as current a state as possible, Tara must first apply Sunday's full backup. She may then apply the most recent differential backup, from Tuesday evening. Differential backups include all files that have changed since the most recent full backup, so the contents of Tuesday's backup contain all of the data that would be contained in Monday's backup, making the Monday backup irrelevant for this scenario.

183. A. In this scenario, the differential backup was made at noon and the server failed at 3 p.m. Therefore, any data modified or created between noon and 3 p.m. will not be contained on any backup and will be irretrievably lost.

184. D. By switching from differential to incremental backups, Tara's weekday backups will only contain the information changed since the previous day. Therefore, she must apply all of the available incremental backups. She would begin by restoring the Sunday full backup and then apply the Monday, Tuesday, and Wednesday incremental backups.

185. D. Each incremental backup contains only the information changed since the most recent full or incremental backup. If we assume that the same amount of information changes every day, each of the incremental backups would be roughly the same size.

186. A. Information that is modifiable between a client and a server also means that it is accessible, pointing to both tampering and information disclosure. Spoofing in STRIDE is aimed at credentials and authentication, and there is no mention of this in the question. Repudiation would require that proving who performed an action was important, and elevation of privilege would come into play if privilege levels were involved.

187. B. Record retention ensures that data is kept and maintained as long as it is needed, and that it is purged when it is no longer necessary. Data remanence occurs when data is left behind after an attempt is made to remove it, whereas data redaction is not a technical term used to describe this effort. Finally, audit logging may be part of the records retained but doesn't describe the life cycle of data.

188. D. The Authentication Header provides authentication, integrity, and nonrepudiation for IPSec connections. The Encapsulating Security Payload provides encryption and thus provides confidentiality. It can also provide limited authentication. L2TP is an independent VPN protocol, and Encryption Security Header is a made-up term.

189. B. The attack described in the scenario is a classic example of TCP scanning, a network reconnaissance technique that may precede other attacks. There is no evidence that the attack disrupted system availability, which would characterize a denial-of-service attack, that it was waged by a malicious insider, or that the attack resulted in the compromise of a system.

190. C. Attackers may use algorithmic complexity as a tool to exploit a TOC/TOU race condition. By varying the workload on the CPU, attackers may exploit the amount of time required to process requests and use that variance to effectively schedule the exploit's execution. File locking, exception handling, and concurrency controls are all methods used to defend against TOC/TOU attacks.

191. D. The kernel lies within the central ring, Ring 0. Ring 1 contains other operating system components. Ring 2 is used for drivers and protocols. User-level programs and applications run at Ring 3. Rings 0-2 run in privileged mode, whereas Ring 3 runs in user mode.

192. A. RAID level 0 is also known as disk striping. RAID 1 is called disk mirroring. RAID 5 is called disk striping with parity. RAID 10 is known as a stripe of mirrors.

193. A. This is an example of a time of check/time of use, or TOC/TOU attack. It exploits the difference between the times when a system checks for permission to perform an action and when the action is actually performed. Permissions creep would occur if the account had gained additional rights over time as the other's role or job changed. Impersonation occurs when an attacker pretends to be a valid user, and link swap is not a type of attack.

194. B. RAID 0, or disk striping, requires at least two disks to implement. It improves performance of the storage system but does not provide fault tolerance.

195. B. Fred's company needs to protect integrity, which can be accomplished by digitally signing messages. Any change will cause the signature to be invalid. Encrypting isn't necessary because the company does not want to protect confidentiality. TLS can provide in-transit protection but won't protect integrity of the messages, and of course a hash used without a way to verify that the hash wasn't changed won't ensure integrity either.

196. A. An attribute-based access control (ABAC) system will allow Susan to specify details about subjects, objects, and access, allowing granular control. Although a rule-based access control system (RBAC) might allow this, the attribute-based access control system can be more specific and thus is more flexible. Discretionary access control (DAC) would allow object owners to make decisions, and mandatory access controls (MACs) would use classifications; neither of these capabilities was described in the requirements.

197. C. Synchronous communications use a timing or clock mechanism to control the data stream. This can permit very fast communication.

198. B. The maximum allowed length of a Cat 6 cable is 100 meters, or 328 feet. Long distances are typically handled by a fiber run or by using network devices like switches or repeaters.

199. B. One of the main functions of a forensic drive controller is preventing any command sent to a device from modifying data stored on the device. For this reason, forensic drive controllers are also often referred to as write blockers.

200. A. Setting the Secure cookie will only allow cookies to be sent via HTTPS TLS or SSL sessions, preventing man-in-the-middle attacks that target cookies. The rest of the settings are problematic: Cookies are vulnerable to DNS spoofing. Domain cookies should usually have the narrowest possible scope, which is actually accomplished by not setting the Domain cookie. This allows only the originating server to access the cookie. Cookies without the Expires or Max-age attributes are ephemeral and will only be kept for the session, making them less vulnerable than stored cookies. Normally, the HTTPOnly attribute is a good idea, but it prevents scripting rather than requiring unencrypted HTTP sessions.

201. D. Data remanence describes data that is still on media after an attempt has been made to remove it. Failed clearing and data pooling are not technical terms, and data permanence describes how long data lasts.

202. B. Mandatory access control (MAC) applies labels to subjects and objects and allows subjects to access objects when their labels match. Discretionary access control (DAC) is controlled by the owner of objects, rule-based access control applies rules throughout a system, and role-based access control bases rights on roles, which are often handled as groups of users.

203. B. Identity as a Service (IDaaS) provides capabilities such as account provisioning, management, authentication, authorization, reporting, and monitoring. PaaS is Platform as a Service, IaaS is Infrastructure as a Service, and SaaS is Software as a Service.

204. C. Eavesdropping, denial-of-service attacks, and caller ID spoofing are all common VoIP attacks. Blackboxing is a made-up answer, although various types of colored boxes were associated with phone phreaking.

205. D. This broad access may indirectly violate all of the listed security principles, but it is most directly a violation of least privilege because it grants users privileges that they do not need for their job functions.

206. C. The Secure File Transfer Protocol (SFTP) is specifically designed for encrypted file transfer. SSH is used for secure command-line access, whereas TCP is one of the bundles of Internet protocols commonly used to transmit data across a network. IPSec could be used to create a tunnel to transfer the data but is not specifically designed for file transfer.

207. B. TACACS+ uses TCP, and encrypts the entire session, unlike RADIUS, which only encrypts the password and operates via UDP.

208. C. The client sends its existing valid TGT to the KDC and requests access to the resource.

209. A. The KDC must verify that the TGT is valid and whether the user has the right privileges to access the service it is requesting access to. If it does, it generates a service ticket and sends it to the client (step B).

210. C. The server or service that is being accessed receives all of the data it needs in the service ticket. To do so, the client uses a client-to-server ticket received from the Ticket Granting Service.

211. B. The service ticket in Kerberos authentication provides proof that a subject is authorized to access an object. Ticket granting services are provided by the TGS. Proof that a subject has authenticated and can request tickets to other objects, uses ticket granting tickets, and authentication host is a made-up term.

212. C. A series of questions that the user has previously provided the answer to or which the user knows the answers to like the questions listed is known as a cognitive password. A passphrase consists of a phrase or series of words, whereas multifactor authentication consists of two or more authenticators, like a password and a biometric factor or a one-time token-based code.

213. B. CDMA, GSM, and IDEN are all 2G technologies. EDGE, DECT, and UTMS are all examples of 3G technologies, whereas 4G technologies include WiMax, LTE, and IEE 802.20 mobile broadband.

214. A. Dry pipe, deluge, and preaction systems all use pipes that remain empty until the system detects signs of a fire. Closed-head systems use pipes filled with water that may damage equipment if there is damage to a pipe.

215. A. Protected Health Information (PHI) is defined by HIPAA to include health information used by healthcare providers, like medical treatment, history, and billing. Personally Identifiable Information is information that can be used to identify an individual, which may be included in the PHI but isn't specifically this type of data. Protected Health Insurance and Individual Protected Data are both made-up terms.

216. B. Manual testing uses human understanding of business logic to assess program flow and responses. Mutation or generational fuzzing will help determine how the program responds to expected inputs but does not test the business logic. Interface testing ensures that data exchange between modules works properly but does not focus on the logic of the program or application.

217. A. A Type 1 authentication factor is something you know. A Type 2 is something you have, like a smart card or hardware token. A Type 3 authentication factor is something you are, like a biometric identifier. There is no such thing as a Type 4 authentication factor.

218. B. System owners have to ensure that the systems they are responsible for are properly labeled based on the highest level of data that their system processes, and they have to ensure that appropriate security controls are in place on those systems. System owners also share responsibility for data protection with data owners. Administrators grant appropriate access, whereas data owners own the classification process.

219. A. Jack is performing misuse case analysis, a process that tests code based on how it would perform if it was misused instead of used properly. Use case testing tests valid use cases, whereas static code analysis involves reviewing the code itself for flaws rather than testing the live software. Hacker use case testing isn't an industry term for a type of testing.

220. D. Vendors complete security targets (STs) to describe the controls that exist within their product. During the review process, reviewers compare those STs to the entity's Protection Profile (PP) to determine whether the product meets the required security controls.

221. C. Both TCP and UDP port numbers are a 16-digit binary number, which means there can be 2^{16} ports, or 65,536 ports, numbered from 0 to 65,535.

222. A. MITRE's Common Vulnerabilities and Exploits (CVE) dictionary and NIST's National Vulnerability Database (NVD) both provide information about vulnerabilities.

223. D. The military classification scheme contains three major levels. They are, in descending order of sensitivity: Top Secret, Secret, and Confidential. Unclassified is a default, and not a classification, whereas Sensitive But Unclassified (SBU) has been replaced with Controlled Unclassified Information (CUI).

224. D. In an automated recovery, the system can recover itself against one or more failure types. In an automated recovery without undue loss, the system can recover itself against one or more failure types and also preserve data against loss. In function recovery, the system can restore functional processes automatically. In a manual recovery approach, the system does not fail into a secure state but requires an administrator to manually restore operations.

225. A. Antenna placement, antenna design, and power level control are the three important factors in determining where a signal can be accessed and how usable it is. A captive portal can be used to control user logins, and antenna design is part of antenna types. The FCC does provide maximum broadcast power guidelines but does not require a minimum power level.

226. C. Physically destroying the drive is the best way to ensure that there is no remnant data on the drive. SSDs are flash media, which means that you can't degauss them, whereas both random pattern writes and the built-in erase commands have been shown to be problematic due to the wear leveling built into SSDs as well as differences in how they handle erase commands.

227. A. Confidentiality ensures that data cannot be read by unauthorized individuals while stored or in transit.

228. B. The recovery time objective (RTO) is the amount of time that a business believes it will take to restore a function in the event of a disruption.

229. D. The United States Code (USC) contains the text of all federal criminal and civil laws passed by the legislative branch and signed by the President (or where the President's veto was overruled by Congress).

230. B. A post-admission philosophy allows or denies access based on user activity after connection. Since this doesn't check the status of a machine before it connects, it can't prevent the exploit of the system immediately after connection. This doesn't preclude out-of-band or in-band monitoring, but it does mean that a strictly post-admission policy won't handle system checks before the systems are admitted to the network.

231. B. The principle of implicit denial states that any action that is not explicitly allowed is denied. This is an important concept for firewall rules and other access control systems. Implementing least privilege ensures that subjects have only the rights they need to accomplish their job. While explicit deny and final rule fall-through may sound like important access control concepts, neither is.

232. B. Risks are the combination of a threat and a vulnerability. Threats are the external forces seeking to undermine security, such as the hacker in this case. Vulnerabilities are the internal weaknesses that might allow a threat to succeed. In this case, web defacement is the risk. In this scenario, if the hacker attempts a SQL injection attack (threat) against the unpatched server (vulnerability), the result is website defacement (risk).

233. A. The kernel of an operating system is the collection of components that work together to implement a secure, reliable operating system. The kernel contains both the Trusted Computing Base (TCB) and the reference monitor.

234. A. Val can use statistical sampling techniques to choose a set of records for review that are representative of the entire day's data. Clipping chooses only records that exceed a set threshold so it is not a representative sample. Choosing records based on the time they are recorded may not produce a representative sample because it may capture events that occur at the same time each day and miss many events that simply don't occur during the chosen time period.

235. D. Fiber-optic cable is more expensive and can be much harder to install than stranded copper cable or coaxial cable, but it isn't susceptible to electromagnetic interference (EMI). That makes it a great solution for Jen's problem, especially if she is deploying EMI-hardened systems to go with her EMI-resistant network cables.

236. D. The request control process provides an organized framework within which users can request modifications, managers can conduct cost/benefit analyses, and developers can prioritize tasks.

237. B. Change control provides an organized framework within which multiple developers can create and test solutions prior to rolling them out into a production environment.

238. C. Release control ensures that any code inserted as a programming aid during the change process is removed before releasing the new software to production. It also includes acceptance testing to ensure that any alterations to end-user work tasks are understood and functional.

239. A. Configuration control ensures that changes to software versions are made in accordance with the change control and configuration management process. Updates can be made only from authorized distributions in accordance with those policies.

240. B. Ben is reusing his salt. When the same salt is used for each hash, all users with the same password will have the same hash, and the attack can either attempt to steal the salt or may attempt to guess the salt by targeting the most frequent hash occurrences based on commonly used passwords. Short salts are an issue, but the salts used here are 32 bytes (256 bits) long. There is no salting algorithm used or mentioned here; salt is an added value for a hash, and plaintext salting is a made-up term.

241. B. Risk transference involves actions that shift risk from one party to another. Purchasing insurance is an example of risk transference because it moves risk from the insured to the insurance company.

242. C. The Online Certificate Status Protocol (OCSP) eliminates the latency inherent in the use of certificate revocation lists by providing a means for real-time certificate verification.

243. D. Static code analysis uses techniques like control flow graphs, lexical analysis, and data flow analysis to assess code without running it. Dynamic code analysis runs code on a real or virtual processor and uses actual inputs for testing. Fuzzing provides unexpected or invalid input to test how programs handle input outside of the norm. Manual analysis is performed by reading code line by line to identify bugs or other issues.

244. B. TCP's use of a handshake process to establish communications makes it a connection-oriented protocol. TCP does not monitor for dropped connections. nor does the fact that it works via network connections make it connection-oriented.

245. A. The LDAP bind operation authenticates and specifies the LDAP protocol version. Auth, StartLDAP, and AuthDN operations do not exist in the LDAP protocol.

246. C. The two most important elements of a qualitative risk assessment are determining the probability and impact of each risk upon the organization. Likelihood is another word for probability. Cost should be taken into account but is only one element of impact, which also includes reputational damage, operational disruption, and other ill effects.

247. B. When a message reaches the Data Link layer, it is called a frame. Data streams exist at the application, presentation, and session layers, whereas segments and datagrams exist at the transport layer (for TCP and UDP, respectively).

248. A. If the $(ISC)^2$ peer review board finds that a certified individual has violated the $(ISC)^2$ code of ethics, the board may revoke their certification. The board is not able to terminate an individual's employment or assess financial penalties.

249. D. SDLC approaches include steps to provide operational training for support staff as well as end-user training. The SDLC may use one of many development models, including the waterfall and spiral models. The SDLC does not mandate the use of an iterative or sequential approach; it allows for either approach.

250. A. The Bell-LaPadula model includes the Simple Security Property, which prevents an individual from reading information that is classified at a level higher than the individual's security clearance.

Index

A

B

C

D

E

F

G

H

I

J

K

N

O

P

Q

R

S

T

U

V

W

X

Z

Comprehensive Online Learning Environment

Register on Sybex.com to gain access to the online interactive test bank to help you study for your CISSP certification—included with your purchase of this book! All of the practice tests in this book are included in the online test bank so you can practice in a timed and graded setting.

Go to `www.wiley.com/go/sybextestprep` to register and gain access to this study tool.

Do you need more? If you have not already read Sybex's CISSP (ISC)² Certified Information Systems Security Professional Official Study Guide, 7th Edition by James M. Stewart, Mike Chapple, and Darril Gibson (ISBN: 978-1-119-04271-6) and are not seeing passing grades on these practice tests, this book is an excellent resource to master any CISSP topics causing problems. This book maps every official exam objective to the corresponding chapter in the book to help track exam prep objective by objective, challenging review questions in each chapter to prepare for exam day, and online test prep materials with flashcards and additional practice tests.

CISSP®

Study Guide

Seventh Edition

CISSP®

Certified Information Systems Security Professional Study Guide

Seventh Edition

James Michael Stewart

Mike Chapple

Darril Gibson

SYBEX

A Wiley Brand

Development Editor: Alexa Murphy
Technical Editors: David Seidl, Brian O'Hara, Paul Calatayud
Production Editor: Rebecca Anderson
Copy Editors: Elizabeth Welch, Linda Recktenwald
Editorial Manager: Mary Beth Wakefield
Production Manager: Kathleen Wisor
Associate Publisher: Jim Minatel
Media Supervising Producer: Richard Graves
Book Designers: Judy Fung and Bill Gibson
Proofreaders: Josh Chase, Sarah Kaikini and Louise Watson, Word One New York
Indexer: J & J Indexing
Project Coordinator, Cover: Brent Savage
Cover Designer: Wiley
Cover Image: ©Getty Images Inc./Jeremy Woodhouse

Published simultaneously in Canada

ISBN: 978-1-119-04271-6

ISBN: 978-1-119-04272-3 (ebk.)

ISBN: 978-1-119-04275-4 (ebk.)

Library of Congress Control Number: 2015948797

10 9 8 7 6 5

Whenever we look toward the future, we have to first look back and think about where we came from. Back in 1989, (ISC)^2 was established by a handful of passionate volunteers who wanted to create a set of standards for a new concept, not yet a full-fledged career field, called information security. In the minds of those volunteers, having the initial 500 applicants sign up to take the Certified Information Systems Security Professional (CISSP®) exam was considered quite a success. Little did they imagine that 26 years later, not only would those 500 applicants grow to a cadre of 100,000 CISSP credential holders across more than 160 countries, the CISSP would also become recognized as the standard certification for the information security industry.

Advancements in technology bring about the need for updates, and we work tirelessly to ensure that our content is always relevant to the industry. As the information security industry continues to transition, and cybersecurity becomes a global focus, the CISSP Common Body of Knowledge (CBK) is even more relevant to today's challenges.

The new (ISC)^2 *CISSP Study Guide* is part of a concerted effort to enhance and increase our education and training offerings. The *CISSP Study Guide* reflects the most relevant topics in our ever-changing field and is a learning tool for (ISC)^2 certification exam candidates. It provides a comprehensive study guide to the eight CISSP domains and the most current topics in the industry.

If you are on the path to getting certified, you have no doubt heard of the *(ISC)^2 Official Guides to the CBK*. While our *Official Guides to the CBK* are the authoritative references to the Common Body of Knowledge, the new study guides are learning tools focused on educating the reader in preparation for exams. As an ANSI accredited certification body under the ISO/IEC 17024 standard, (ISC)^2 does not teach the CISSP exam. Rather, we strive to generate or endorse content that teaches the CISSP's CBK. Candidates who have a strong understanding of the CBK are best prepared for success with the exam and within the profession.

(ISC)^2 is also breaking new ground by partnering with Wiley, a recognized industry leading brand. Developing a partnership with renowned content provider Wiley allows (ISC)^2 to grow its offerings on the scale required to keep our content fresh and aligned with the constantly changing environment. The power of combining the expertise of our two organizations benefits certification candidates and the industry alike.

I look forward to your feedback on the (ISC)^2 *CISSP Study Guide*. Congratulations on taking the first step toward earning the certification that *SC Magazine* named "Best Professional Certification Program." Good luck with your studies!

Best Regards,

David P. Shearer, CISSP, PMP
CEO
(ISC)^2

To Cathy, your perspective on the world and life often surprises me, challenges me, and makes me love you even more.
—James Michael Stewart

To Dewitt Latimer, my mentor, friend, and colleague. I miss you dearly.
—Mike Chapple

To Nimfa: Thanks for sharing your life with me for the past 23 years and letting me share mine with you.
—Darril Gibson

Acknowledgments

I'd like to express my thanks to Sybex for continuing to support this project. Thanks to Mike Chapple and Darril Gibson for continuing to contribute to this project. Thanks also to all my CISSP course students who have provided their insight and input to improve my training courseware and ultimately this tome. Extra thanks to the seventh edition developmental editor, Alexa Murphy, and technical editor, David Seidl, who performed amazing feats in guiding us to improve this book. Thanks as well to my agent, Carole Jelen, for continuing to assist in nailing down these projects.

To my adoring wife, Cathy: Building a life and a family together has been more wonderful than I could have ever imagined. To Slayde and Remi: You are growing up so fast and learning at an outstanding pace, and you continue to delight and impress me daily. You are both growing into amazing individuals. To my mom, Johnnie: It is wonderful to have you close by. To Mark: No matter how much time has passed or how little we see each other, I have been and always will be your friend. And finally, as always, to Elvis: You were way ahead of the current bacon obsession, with your peanut butter-banana-bacon sandwich; I think that's proof you traveled through time!

—James Michael Stewart

Special thanks go to the information security team at the University of Notre Dame, who provided hours of interesting conversation and debate on security issues that inspired and informed much of the material in this book.

I would like to thank the team at Wiley who provided invaluable assistance throughout the book development process. I also owe a debt of gratitude to my literary agent, Carole Jelen of Waterside Productions. My coauthors, James Michael Stewart and Darril Gibson, were great collaborators. David Seidl, our diligent and knowledgeable technical editor, provided valuable insight as we brought this edition to press.

I'd also like to thank the many people who participated in the production of this book but whom I never had the chance to meet: the graphics team, the production staff, and all of those involved in bringing this book to press.

—Mike Chapple

Thanks to Carol Long and Carole Jelen for helping get this update in place before (ISC)^2 released the objectives. This helped us get a head start on this new edition and we appreciate your efforts. It's been a pleasure working with talented people like James Michael Stewart and Mike Chapple. Thanks to both of you for all your work and collaborative efforts on this project. The technical editor, Dave Seidl, provided us with some outstanding feedback and this book is better because of his efforts. Thanks again, David. Last, thanks to the team at Sybex (including project managers, editors, and graphics artists) for all the work you did helping us get this book to print.

—Darril Gibson

About the Authors

James Michael Stewart, CISSP, has been writing and training for more than 20 years, with a current focus on security. He has been teaching CISSP training courses since 2002, not to mention other courses on Internet security and ethical hacking/penetration testing. He is the author of and contributor to more than 75 books and numerous courseware sets on security certification, Microsoft topics, and network administration. More information about Michael can be found at his website: `www.impactonline.com`.

Mike Chapple, CISSP, Ph.D., is Senior Director for IT Service Delivery at the University of Notre Dame. In the past, he was chief information officer of Brand Institute and an information security researcher with the National Security Agency and the U.S. Air Force. His primary areas of expertise include network intrusion detection and access controls. Mike is a frequent contributor to TechTarget's SearchSecurity site and the author of more than 25 books including *CompTIA Security+ Training Kit* and *Information Security Illuminated*. Mike can be found on Twitter @mchapple.

Darril Gibson, CISSP, is the CEO of YCDA, LLC (short for You Can Do Anything) and he has authored or coauthored more than 35 books. Darril regularly writes, consults, and teaches on a wide variety of technical and security topics and holds several certifications. He regularly posts blog articles at `http://blogs.getcertifiedgetahead.com/` about certification topics and uses that site to help people stay abreast of changes in certification exams. He loves hearing from readers, especially when they pass an exam after using one of his books, and you can contact him through the blogging site.

Contents at a Glance

Contents

Introduction

The *CISSP: Certified Information Systems Security Professional Study Guide, Seventh Edition,* offers you a solid foundation for the Certified Information Systems Security Professional (CISSP) exam. By purchasing this book, you've shown a willingness to learn and a desire to develop the skills you need to achieve this certification. This introduction provides you with a basic overview of this book and the CISSP exam.

This book is designed for readers and students who want to study for the CISSP certification exam. If your goal is to become a certified security professional, then the CISSP certification and this study guide are for you. The purpose of this book is to adequately prepare you to take the CISSP exam.

Before you dive into this book, you need to have accomplished a few tasks on your own. You need to have a general understanding of IT and of security. You should have the necessary five years of full-time paid work experience (or four years if you have a college degree) in two or more of the eight domains covered by the CISSP exam. If you are qualified to take the CISSP exam according to $(ISC)^2$, then you are sufficiently prepared to use this book to study for it. For more information on $(ISC)^2$, see the next section.

$(ISC)^2$

The CISSP exam is governed by the International Information Systems Security Certification Consortium $(ISC)^2$. $(ISC)^2$ is a global not-for-profit organization. It has four primary mission goals:

- Maintain the Common Body of Knowledge (CBK) for the field of information systems security.
- Provide certification for information systems security professionals and practitioners.
- Conduct certification training and administer the certification exams.
- Oversee the ongoing accreditation of qualified certification candidates through continued education.

The $(ISC)^2$ is operated by a board of directors elected from the ranks of its certified practitioners.

$(ISC)^2$ supports and provides a wide variety of certifications, including CISSP, SSCP, CAP, CSSLP, CCFP, HCISPP, and CCSP. These certifications are designed to verify the knowledge and skills of IT security professionals across all industries. You can obtain more information about $(ISC)^2$ and its other certifications from its website at `www.isc2.org`.

The Certified Information Systems Security Professional (CISSP) credential is for security professionals responsible for designing and maintaining security infrastructure within an organization.

Topical Domains

The CISSP certification covers material from the eight topical domains. These eight domains are as follows:

- Security and Risk Management
- Asset Security
- Security Engineering
- Communication and Network Security
- Identity and Access Management
- Security Assessment and Testing
- Security Operations
- Software Development Security

These eight domains provide a vendor-independent overview of a common security framework. This framework is the basis for a discussion on security practices that can be supported in all type of organizations worldwide.

The topical domains underwent a major revision as of April 2015. The domains were reduced from ten to eight, and many topics and concepts were re-organized. For a complete view of the breadth of topics covered on the CISSP exam from these eight new domain groupings, visit the $(ISC)^2$ website at `www.isc2.org` to request a copy of the Candidate Information Bulletin. This document includes a complete exam outline as well as other relevant facts about the certification.

Prequalifications

$(ISC)^2$ has defined the qualification requirements you must meet to become a CISSP. First, you must be a practicing security professional with at least five years' full-time paid work experience or with four years' experience and a recent IT or IS degree. Professional experience is defined as security work performed for salary or commission within two or more of the eight CBK domains.

Second, you must agree to adhere to a formal code of ethics. The CISSP Code of Ethics is a set of guidelines the $(ISC)^2$ wants all CISSP candidates to follow to maintain professionalism in the field of information systems security. You can find it in the Information section on the $(ISC)^2$ website at `www.isc2.org`.

$(ISC)^2$ also offers an entry program known as an Associate of $(ISC)^2$. This program allows someone without any or enough experience to qualify as a CISSP to take the CISSP exam anyway and then obtain experience afterward. Associates are granted six years to obtain five years' of security experience. Only after providing proof of such experience, usually by means of endorsement and a resume, can the individual be awarded CISSP certification.

Overview of the CISSP Exam

The CISSP exam focuses on security from a 30,000-foot view; it deals more with theory and concept than implementation and procedure. It is very broad but not very deep. To successfully complete this exam, you'll need to be familiar with every domain but not necessarily be a master of each domain.

The CISSP exam consists of 250 questions, and you have six hours to complete it. The exam can be taken in PBT (paper-based test) form or in CBT (computer-based test) form. You'll need to register for the exam through the (ISC)^2 website at `www.isc2.org` for the PBT form or at `www.pearsonvue.com/isc2` for the CBT form. The CBT form of the exam is administered at a Pearson Vue testing facility (`www.pearsonvue.com/isc2`).

The PBT form of the exam is administered using a paper booklet and answer sheet. This means you'll be using a pencil to fill in answer bubbles. If you take a PBT exam, be sure to arrive at the testing center around 8 a.m., and keep in mind that absolutely no one will be admitted into the exam after 8:30 a.m. Once all test takers are signed in and seated, the exam proctors will pass out the testing materials and read a few pages of instructions. This may take 30 minutes or more. Once that process is finished, the six-hour window for taking the test will begin.

CISSP Exam Question Types

Most of the questions on the CISSP exam are four-option, multiple-choice questions with a single correct answer. Some are straightforward, such as asking you to select a definition. Some are a bit more involved, asking you to select the appropriate concept or best practice. And some questions present you with a scenario or situation and ask you to select the best response. Here's an example:

1. What is the most important goal and top priority of a security solution?
   - **A.** Preventing disclosure
   - **B.** Maintaining integrity
   - **C.** Maintaining human safety
   - **D.** Sustaining availability

You must select the one correct or best answer and mark it on your answer sheet. In some cases, the correct answer will be very obvious to you. In other cases, several answers may seem correct. In these instances, you must choose the best answer for the question asked. Watch for general, specific, universal, superset, and subset answer selections. In other cases, none of the answers will seem correct. In these instances, you'll need to select the least incorrect answer.

NOTE: By the way, the correct answer for this sample question is C. Maintaining human safety is always your first priority.

In addition to the standard multiple-choice question format, ISC^2 has added in a few new question formats. These include drag-and-drop and hotspot questions. The drag-and-drop questions require the test taker to move labels or icons to mark items on an image. The hotspot questions require the test taker to pinpoint a location on an image with a cross-hair marker. Both of these question concepts are easy to work with and understand, but be careful about your accuracy of dropping or marking.

NOTE To see live examples of these new question types, access the Exam Outline: Candidate Information Bulletin. In a later section titled "Sample Exam Questions," a URL is provided that leads to a tutorial of these question formats.

Advice on Taking the Exam

The CISSP exam consists of two key elements. First, you need to know the material from the eight domains. Second, you must have good test-taking skills. With six hours to complete a 250-question exam, you have just less than 90 seconds for each question. Thus, it is important to work quickly, without rushing but also without wasting time.

One key factor to remember is that guessing is better than not answering a question. If you don't answer a question, you will not get any credit. But if you guess, you have at least a chance of improving your score. Wrong answers are not counted against you. So, near the end of the sixth hour, be sure you've selected an answer for every question.

In the PBT form of the exam, you can write on the test booklet, but nothing written on it will count for or against your score. Use the booklet to make notes and keep track of your progress. We recommend circling your selected answer in the question booklet before you mark it on your answer sheet.

In the CBT form of the exam, you will be provided a dry-erase board and a marker to jot down thoughts and make notes. But nothing written on that board will be used to alter your score. And that board must be returned to the test administrator prior to departing the test facility.

To maximize your test-taking activities, here are some general guidelines:

- Answer easy questions first.
- Skip harder questions, and return to them later. Either use the CBT bookmarking feature or jot down a list of question numbers in a PBT.
- Eliminate wrong answers before selecting the correct one.
- Watch for double negatives.
- Be sure you understand what the question is asking.

Manage your time. You should try to complete about 50 questions per hour. This will leave you with about an hour to focus on skipped questions and double-check your work.

Be sure to bring food and drink to the test site. You will not be allowed to leave to obtain sustenance. Your food and drink will be stored for you away from the testing area. You can eat and drink at any time, but that break time will count against your total time limit. Be sure to bring any medications or other essential items, but leave all things electronic at home or in your car. Wear a watch, but make sure it is not a programmable one. If you are taking a PBT, bring pencils, a manual pencil sharpener, and an eraser. We also recommend bringing foam ear plugs, wearing comfortable clothes, and taking a light jacket with you (some testing locations are a bit chilly).

If English is not your first language, you can register for one of several other language versions of the exam. Or, if you choose to use the English version of the exam, a translation dictionary is allowed. You must be able to prove that you need such a dictionary; this is usually accomplished with your birth certificate or your passport.

NOTE

Occasionally, small changes are made to the exam or exam objectives. When that happens, Sybex will post updates to its website. Visit `www.sybex.com/go/cissp7e` before you sit for the exam to make sure you have the latest information.

Study and Exam Preparation Tips

We recommend planning for a month or so of nightly intensive study for the CISSP exam. Here are some suggestions to maximize your learning time; you can modify them as necessary based on your own learning habits:

- Take one or two evenings to read each chapter in this book and work through its review material.
- Answer all the review questions and take the practice exams provided in the book and in the test engine. Complete the written labs from each chapter, and use the review questions for each chapter to help guide you to topics for which more study or time spent working through key concepts and strategies might be beneficial.
- Review the (ISC)²'s Exam Outline: Candidate Information Bulletin from `www.isc2.org`.
- Use the flashcards included with the study tools to reinforce your understanding of concepts.

TIP

We recommend spending about half of your study time reading and reviewing concepts and the other half taking practice exams. Students have reported that the more time they spent taking practice exams, the better they retained test topics. You might also consider visiting online resources such as `www.cccure.org` and other CISSP-focused websites.

Completing the Certification Process

Once you have been informed that you successfully passed the CISSP certification, there is one final step before you are actually awarded the CISSP certification. That final step is known as *endorsement*. Basically, this involves getting someone who is a CISSP, or other (ISC)^2 certification holder, in good standing and familiar with your work history to submit an endorsement form on your behalf. The endorsement form is accessible through the email notifying you of your achievement in passing the exam. The endorser must review your resume, ensure that you have sufficient experience in the eight CISSP domains, and then submit the signed form to (ISC)^2 digitally or via fax or post mail. You must have submitted the endorsement files to (ISC)^2 within 90 days after receiving the confirmation-of-passing email. Once (ISC)^2 receives your endorsement form, the certification process will be completed and you will be sent a welcome packet via USPS.

If you happen to fail the exam, you may take the exam a second time, but you must wait 30 days. If a third attempt is needed, you must wait 90 days. If a fourth attempt is needed, you must wait 180 days. You can attempt the exam only three times in any calendar year. You will need to pay full price for each additional exam attempt.

Post-CISSP Concentrations

(ISC)^2 has three concentrations offered only to CISSP certificate holders. The (ISC)^2 has taken the concepts introduced on the CISSP exam and focused on specific areas, namely, architecture, management, and engineering. These three concentrations are as follows:

Information Systems Security Architecture Professional (ISSAP) Aimed at those who specialize in information security architecture. Key domains covered here include access control systems and methodology; cryptography; physical security integration; requirements analysis and security standards, guidelines, and criteria; technology-related aspects of business continuity planning and disaster recovery planning; and telecommunications and network security. This is a credential for those who design security systems or infrastructure or for those who audit and analyze such structures.

Information Systems Security Management Professional (ISSMP) Aimed at those who focus on management of information security policies, practices, principles, and procedures. Key domains covered here include enterprise security management practices; enterprise-wide system development security; law, investigations, forensics, and ethics; oversight for operations security compliance; and understanding business continuity planning, disaster recovery planning, and continuity of operations planning. This is a credential for professionals who are responsible for security infrastructures, particularly where mandated compliance comes into the picture.

Information Systems Security Engineering Professional (ISSEP) Aimed at those who focus on the design and engineering of secure hardware and software information systems, components, or applications. Key domains covered include certification and accreditation, systems security engineering, technical management, and U.S. government information assurance rules and regulations. Most ISSEPs work for the U.S. government or for a government contractor that manages government security clearances.

For more details about these concentration exams and certifications, please see the (ISC)[2] website at `www.isc2.org`.

Notes on This Book's Organization

This book is designed to cover each of the eight CISSP Common Body of Knowledge domains in sufficient depth to provide you with a clear understanding of the material. The main body of this book comprises 21 chapters. The domain/chapter breakdown is as follows:

Chapters 1, 2, 3, and 4: Security and Risk Management

Chapter 5: Asset Security

Chapters 6, 7, 8, 9, and 10: Security Engineering

Chapters 11 and 12: Communication and Network Security

Chapters 13 and 14: Identity and Access Management

Chapters 15: Security Assessment and Testing

Chapters 16, 17, 18, and 19: Security Operations

Chapters 20 and 21: Software Development Security

Each chapter includes elements to help you focus your studies and test your knowledge, detailed in the following sections. Note: please see the table of contents and chapter introductions for a detailed list of domain topics covered in each chapter.

The Elements of This Study Guide

You'll see many recurring elements as you read through this study guide. Here are descriptions of some of those elements:

Summaries The summary is a brief review of the chapter to sum up what was covered.

Exam Essentials The Exam Essentials highlight topics that could appear on the exam in some form. While we obviously do not know exactly what will be included in a particular exam, this section reinforces significant concepts that are key to understanding the Common Body of Knowledge (CBK) area and the test specs for the CISSP exam.

Chapter Review Questions Each chapter includes practice questions that have been designed to measure your knowledge of key ideas that were discussed in the chapter. After you finish each chapter, answer the questions; if some of your answers are incorrect, it's an indication that you need to spend some more time studying the corresponding topics. The answers to the practice questions can be found at the end of each chapter.

Written Labs Each chapter includes written labs that synthesize various concepts and topics that appear in the chapter. These raise questions that are designed to help you put together various pieces you've encountered individually in the chapter and assemble them to propose or describe potential security strategies or solutions.

Real-World Scenarios As you work through each chapter, you'll find descriptions of typical and plausible workplace situations where an understanding of the security strategies and approaches relevant to the chapter content could play a role in fixing problems or in fending off potential difficulties. This gives readers a chance to see how specific security policies, guidelines, or practices should or may be applied to the workplace.

What's Included with the Additional Study Tools

Readers of this book can get access to a number of additional study tools. We worked really hard to provide some essential tools to help you with your certification process. All of the following gear should be loaded on your workstation when studying for the test.

> NOTE: Readers can get access to the following tools by visiting `sybextestbanks.wiley.com`.

The Sybex Test Preparation Software

The test preparation software, made by experts at Sybex, prepares you for the CISSP exam. In this test engine, you will find all the review and assessment questions from the book plus additional bonus practice exams that are included with the study tools. You can take the assessment test, test yourself by chapter, take the practice exams, or take a randomly generated exam comprising all the questions.

Electronic Flashcards

Sybex's electronic flashcards include hundreds of questions designed to challenge you further for the CISSP exam. Between the review questions, practice exams, and flashcards, you'll have more than enough practice for the exam!

Glossary of Terms in PDF

Sybex offers a robust glossary of terms in PDF format. This comprehensive glossary includes all of the key terms you should understand for the CISSP, in a searchable format.

Bonus Practice Exams

Sybex includes bonus practice exams, each comprising questions meant to survey your understanding of key elements in the CISSP CBK. This book has four bonus exams, each comprising 250 full-length questions. These exams are available digitally at `http://sybextestbanks.wiley.com`.

How to Use This Book's Study Tools

This book has a number of features designed to guide your study efforts for the CISSP certification exam. It assists you by listing at the beginning of each chapter the CISSP Common Body of Knowledge domain topics covered in the chapter and by ensuring that each topic is fully discussed within the chapter. The review questions at the end of each chapter and the practice exams are designed to test your retention of the material you've read to make sure you are aware of areas in which you should spend additional study time. Here are some suggestions for using this book and study tools (found at `sybextestbanks.wiley.com`):

- Take the assessment test before you start reading the material. This will give you an idea of the areas in which you need to spend additional study time as well as those areas in which you may just need a brief refresher.
- Answer the review questions after you've read each chapter; if you answer any incorrectly, go back to the chapter and review the topic, or utilize one of the additional resources if you need more information.
- Download the flashcards to your mobile device, and review them when you have a few minutes during the day.
- Take every opportunity to test yourself. In addition to the assessment test and review questions, there are bonus practice exams included with the additional study tools. Take these exams without referring to the chapters and see how well you've done—go back and review any topics you've missed until you fully understand and can apply the concepts.

Finally, find a study partner if possible. Studying for, and taking, the exam with someone else will make the process more enjoyable, and you'll have someone to help you understand topics that are difficult for you. You'll also be able to reinforce your own knowledge by helping your study partner in areas where they are weak.

Assessment Test

1. Which of the following types of access control seeks to discover evidence of unwanted, unauthorized, or illicit behavior or activity?
   - **A.** Preventive
   - **B.** Deterrent
   - **C.** Detective
   - **D.** Corrective
2. Define and detail the aspects of password selection that distinguish good password choices from ultimately poor password choices.
   - **A.** Difficult to guess or unpredictable
   - **B.** Meet minimum length requirements
   - **C.** Meet specific complexity requirements
   - **D.** All of the above
3. Which of the following is most likely to detect DoS attacks?
   - **A.** Host-based IDS
   - **B.** Network-based IDS
   - **C.** Vulnerability scanner
   - **D.** Penetration testing
4. Which of the following is considered a denial of service attack?
   - **A.** Pretending to be a technical manager over the phone and asking a receptionist to change their password
   - **B.** While surfing the Web, sending to a web server a malformed URL that causes the system to consume 100 percent of the CPU
   - **C.** Intercepting network traffic by copying the packets as they pass through a specific subnet
   - **D.** Sending message packets to a recipient who did not request them simply to be annoying
5. At which layer of the OSI model does a router operate?
   - **A.** Network layer
   - **B.** Layer 1
   - **C.** Transport layer
   - **D.** Layer 5
6. Which type of firewall automatically adjusts its filtering rules based on the content of the traffic of existing sessions?
   - **A.** Static packet filtering
   - **B.** Application-level gateway

C. Stateful inspection
D. Dynamic packet filtering

7. A VPN can be established over which of the following?
A. Wireless LAN connection
B. Remote access dial-up connection
C. WAN link
D. All of the above

8. What type of malware uses social engineering to trick a victim into installing it?
A. Viruses
B. Worms
C. Trojan horse
D. Logic bomb

9. The CIA Triad comprises what elements?
A. Contiguousness, interoperable, arranged
B. Authentication, authorization, accountability
C. Capable, available, integral
D. Availability, confidentiality, integrity

10. Which of the following is not a required component in the support of accountability?
A. Auditing
B. Privacy
C. Authentication
D. Authorization

11. Which of the following is not a defense against collusion?
A. Separation of duties
B. Restricted job responsibilities
C. Group user accounts
D. Job rotation

12. A data custodian is responsible for securing resources after ________________ has assigned the resource a security label.
A. Senior management
B. Data owner
C. Auditor
D. Security staff

13. In what phase of the Capability Maturity Model for Software (SW-CMM) are quantitative measures utilized to gain a detailed understanding of the software development process?
    - **A.** Repeatable
    - **B.** Defined
    - **C.** Managed
    - **D.** Optimizing
14. Which one of the following is a layer of the ring protection scheme that is not normally implemented in practice?
    - **A.** Layer 0
    - **B.** Layer 1
    - **C.** Layer 3
    - **D.** Layer 4
15. What is the last phase of the TCP/IP three-way handshake sequence?
    - **A.** SYN packet
    - **B.** ACK packet
    - **C.** NAK packet
    - **D.** SYN/ACK packet
16. Which one of the following vulnerabilities would best be countered by adequate parameter checking?
    - **A.** Time of check to time of use
    - **B.** Buffer overflow
    - **C.** SYN flood
    - **D.** Distributed denial of service
17. What is the value of the logical operation shown here?

```
X:          0 1 1 0 1 0
Y:          0 0 1 1 0 1

-----------------
X ∨ Y:      ?
```

    - **A.** 0 1 1 1 1 1
    - **B.** 0 1 1 0 1 0
    - **C.** 0 0 1 0 0 0
    - **D.** 0 0 1 1 0 1
18. In what type of cipher are the letters of the plain-text message rearranged to form the cipher text?
    - **A.** Substitution cipher
    - **B.** Block cipher

C. Transposition cipher
D. One-time pad

19. What is the length of a message digest produced by the MD5 algorithm?
    A. 64 bits
    B. 128 bits
    C. 256 bits
    D. 384 bits

20. If Renee receives a digitally signed message from Mike, what key does she use to verify that the message truly came from Mike?
    A. Renee's public key
    B. Renee's private key
    C. Mike's public key
    D. Mike's private key

21. Which of the following is not a composition theory related to security models?
    A. Cascading
    B. Feedback
    C. Iterative
    D. Hookup

22. The collection of components in the TCB that work together to implement reference monitor functions is called the __________________.
    A. Security perimeter
    B. Security kernel
    C. Access matrix
    D. Constrained interface

23. Which of the following statements is true?
    A. The less complex a system, the more vulnerabilities it has.
    B. The more complex a system, the less assurance it provides.
    C. The less complex a system, the less trust it provides.
    D. The more complex a system, the less attack surface it generates.

24. Ring 0, from the design architecture security mechanism known as protection rings, can also be referred to as all but which of the following?
    A. Privileged mode
    B. Supervisory mode
    C. System mode
    D. User mode

25. Audit trails, logs, CCTV, intrusion detection systems, antivirus software, penetration testing, password crackers, performance monitoring, and cyclic redundancy checks (CRCs) are examples of what?
    - A. Directive controls
    - B. Preventive controls
    - C. Detective controls
    - D. Corrective controls
26. System architecture, system integrity, covert channel analysis, trusted facility management, and trusted recovery are elements of what security criteria?
    - A. Quality assurance
    - B. Operational assurance
    - C. Life cycle assurance
    - D. Quantity assurance
27. Which of the following is a procedure designed to test and perhaps bypass a system's security controls?
    - A. Logging usage data
    - B. War dialing
    - C. Penetration testing
    - D. Deploying secured desktop workstations
28. Auditing is a required factor to sustain and enforce what?
    - A. Accountability
    - B. Confidentiality
    - C. Accessibility
    - D. Redundancy
29. What is the formula used to compute the ALE?
    - A. ALE = AV * EF * ARO
    - B. ALE = ARO * EF
    - C. ALE = AV * ARO
    - D. ALE = EF * ARO
30. What is the first step of the business impact assessment process?
    - A. Identification of priorities
    - B. Likelihood assessment
    - C. Risk identification
    - D. Resource prioritization

31. Which of the following represent natural events that can pose a threat or risk to an organization?

A. Earthquake

B. Flood

C. Tornado

D. All of the above

32. What kind of recovery facility enables an organization to resume operations as quickly as possible, if not immediately, upon failure of the primary facility?

A. Hot site

B. Warm site

C. Cold site

D. All of the above

33. What form of intellectual property is used to protect words, slogans, and logos?

A. Patent

B. Copyright

C. Trademark

D. Trade secret

34. What type of evidence refers to written documents that are brought into court to prove a fact?

A. Best evidence

B. Payroll evidence

C. Documentary evidence

D. Testimonial evidence

35. Why are military and intelligence attacks among the most serious computer crimes?

A. The use of information obtained can have far-reaching detrimental strategic effects on national interests in an enemy's hands.

B. Military information is stored on secure machines, so a successful attack can be embarrassing.

C. The long-term political use of classified information can impact a country's leadership.

D. The military and intelligence agencies have ensured that the laws protecting their information are the most severe.

36. What type of detected incident allows the most time for an investigation?

A. Compromise

B. Denial of service

C. Malicious code

D. Scanning

37. If you want to restrict access into or out of a facility, which would you choose?

A. Gate

B. Turnstile

C. Fence

D. Mantrap

38. What is the point of a secondary verification system?

A. To verify the identity of a user

B. To verify the activities of a user

C. To verify the completeness of a system

D. To verify the correctness of a system

39. Spamming attacks occur when numerous unsolicited messages are sent to a victim. Because enough data is sent to the victim to prevent legitimate activity, it is also known as what?

A. Sniffing

B. Denial of service

C. Brute-force attack

D. Buffer overflow attack

40. Which type of intrusion detection system (IDS) can be considered an expert system?

A. Host-based

B. Network-based

C. Knowledge-based

D. Behavior-based

Answers to Assessment Test

1. C. Detective access controls are used to discover (and document) unwanted or unauthorized activity.

2. D. Strong password choices are difficult to guess, unpredictable, and of specified minimum lengths to ensure that password entries cannot be computationally determined. They may be randomly generated and utilize all the alphabetic, numeric, and punctuation characters; they should never be written down or shared; they should not be stored in publicly accessible or generally readable locations; and they shouldn't be transmitted in the clear.

3. B. Network-based IDSs are usually able to detect the initiation of an attack or the ongoing attempts to perpetrate an attack (including denial of service, or DoS). They are, however, unable to provide information about whether an attack was successful or which specific systems, user accounts, files, or applications were affected. Host-based IDSs have some difficulty with detecting and tracking down DoS attacks. Vulnerability scanners don't detect DoS attacks; they test for possible vulnerabilities. Penetration testing may cause a DoS or test for DoS vulnerabilities, but it is not a detection tool.

4. B. Not all instances of DoS are the result of a malicious attack. Errors in coding OSs, services, and applications have resulted in DoS conditions. Some examples of this include a process failing to release control of the CPU or a service consuming system resources out of proportion to the service requests it is handling. Social engineering and sniffing are typically not considered DoS attacks.

5. A. Network hardware devices, including routers, function at layer 3, the Network layer.

6. D. Dynamic packet-filtering firewalls enable the real-time modification of the filtering rules based on traffic content.

7. D. A VPN link can be established over any other network communication connection. This could be a typical LAN cable connection, a wireless LAN connection, a remote access dial-up connection, a WAN link, or even an Internet connection used by a client for access to the office LAN.

8. C. A Trojan horse is a form of malware that uses social engineering tactics to trick a victim into installing it—the trick is to make the victim believe that the only thing they have downloaded or obtained is the host file, when in fact it has a malicious hidden payload.

9. D. The components of the CIA Triad are confidentiality, availability, and integrity.

10. B. Privacy is not necessary to provide accountability.

11. C. Group user accounts allow for multiple people to log in under a single user account. This allows collusion because it prevents individual accountability.

12. B. The data owner must first assign a security label to a resource before the data custodian can secure the resource appropriately.

13. C. The Managed phase of the SW-CMM involves the use of quantitative development metrics. The Software Engineering Institute (SEI) defines the key process areas for this level as Quantitative Process Management and Software Quality Management.

14. B. Layers 1 and 2 contain device drivers but are not normally implemented in practice. Layer 0 always contains the security kernel. Layer 3 contains user applications. Layer 4 does not exist.

15. B. The SYN packet is first sent from the initiating host to the destination host. The destination host then responds with a SYN/ACK packet. The initiating host sends an ACK packet, and the connection is then established.

16. B. Parameter checking is used to prevent the possibility of buffer overflow attacks.

17. A. The ~OR symbol represents the OR function, which is true when one or both of the input bits are true.

18. C. Transposition ciphers use an encryption algorithm to rearrange the letters of the plaintext message to form a cipher text message.

19. B. The MD5 algorithm produces a 128-bit message digest for any input.

20. C. Any recipient can use Mike's public key to verify the authenticity of the digital signature.

21. C. Iterative is not one of the composition theories related to security models. Cascading, feedback, and hookup are the three composition theories.

22. B. The collection of components in the TCB that work together to implement reference monitor functions is called the security kernel.

23. B. The more complex a system, the less assurance it provides. More complexity means more areas for vulnerabilities to exist and more areas that must be secured against threats. More vulnerabilities and more threats mean that the subsequent security provided by the system is less trustworthy.

24. D. Ring 0 has direct access to the most resources; thus user mode is not an appropriate label because user mode requires restrictions to limit access to resources.

25. C. Examples of detective controls are audit trails, logs, CCTV, intrusion detection systems, antivirus software, penetration testing, password crackers, performance monitoring, and CRCs.

26. B. Assurance is the degree of confidence you can place in the satisfaction of security needs of a computer, network, solution, and so on. Operational assurance focuses on the basic features and architecture of a system that lend themselves to supporting security.

27. C. Penetration testing is the attempt to bypass security controls to test overall system security.

28. A. Auditing is a required factor to sustain and enforce accountability.

29. A. The annualized loss expectancy (ALE) is computed as the product of the asset value (AV) times the exposure factor (EF) times the annualized rate of occurrence (ARO). This is the longer form of the formula ALE = SLE * ARO. The other formulas displayed here do not accurately reflect this calculation.

30. A. Identification of priorities is the first step of the business impact assessment process.

31. D. Natural events that can threaten organizations include earthquakes, floods, hurricanes, tornados, wildfires, and other acts of nature as well. Thus options A, B, and C are correct because they are natural and not man made.

32. A. Hot sites provide backup facilities maintained in constant working order and fully capable of taking over business operations. Warm sites consist of preconfigured hardware and software to run the business, neither of which possesses the vital business information. Cold sites are simply facilities designed with power and environmental support systems but no configured hardware, software, or services. Disaster recovery services can facilitate and implement any of these sites on behalf of a company.

33. C. Trademarks are used to protect the words, slogans, and logos that represent a company and its products or services.

34. C. Written documents brought into court to prove the facts of a case are referred to as documentary evidence.

35. A. The purpose of a military and intelligence attack is to acquire classified information. The detrimental effect of using such information could be nearly unlimited in the hands of an enemy. Attacks of this type are launched by very sophisticated attackers. It is often very difficult to ascertain what documents were successfully obtained. So when a breach of this type occurs, you sometimes cannot know the full extent of the damage.

36. D. Scanning incidents are generally reconnaissance attacks. The real damage to a system comes in the subsequent attacks, so you may have some time to react if you detect the scanning attack early.

37. B. A turnstile is a form of gate that prevents more than one person from gaining entry at a time and often restricts movement to one direction. It is used to gain entry but not exit, or vice versa.

38. D. Secondary verification mechanisms are set in place to establish a means of verifying the correctness of detection systems and sensors. This often means combining several types of sensors or systems (CCTV, heat and motion sensors, and so on) to provide a more complete picture of detected events.

39. B. A spamming attack (sending massive amounts of unsolicited email) can be used as a type of denial-of-service attack. It doesn't use eavesdropping methods so it isn't sniffing. Brute force methods attempt to crack passwords. Buffer overflow attacks send strings of data to a system in an attempt to cause it to fail.

40. D. A behavior-based IDS can be labeled an expert system or a pseudo-artificial intelligence system because it can learn and make assumptions about events. In other words, the IDS can act like a human expert by evaluating current events against known events. A knowledge-based IDS uses a database of known attack methods to detect attacks. Both host-based and network-based systems can be either knowledge-based, behavior-based, or a combination of both.

Chapter 1

Security Governance Through Principles and Policies

THE CISSP EXAM TOPICS COVERED IN THIS CHAPTER INCLUDE:

✓ **Security and Risk Management (e.g., Security, Risk, Compliance, Law, Regulations, Business Continuity)**

- A. Understand and apply concepts of confidentiality, integrity and availability
- B. Apply security governance principles through:
  - B.1 Alignment of security function to strategy, goals, mission, and objectives (e.g., business case, budget and resources)
  - B.2 Organizational processes (e.g., acquisitions, divestitures, governance committees)
  - B.3 Security roles and responsibilities
  - B.4 Control frameworks
  - B.5 Due care
  - B.6 Due diligence
- F. Develop and implement documented security policy, standards, procedures, and guidelines
- J. Understand and apply threat modeling
  - J.1 Identifying threats (e.g., adversaries, contractors, employees, trusted partners)
  - J.2 Determining and diagramming potential attacks (e.g., social engineering, spoofing)
  - J.3 Performing reduction analysis
  - J.4 Technologies and processes to remediate threats (e.g., software architecture and operations)

- K. Integrate security risk considerations into acquisition strategy and practice
  - K.1 Hardware, software, and services
  - K.2 Third-party assessment and monitoring (e.g., on-site assessment, document exchange and review, process/policy review)
  - K.3 Minimum security requirements
  - K.4 Service-level requirements

The Security and Risk Management domain of the Common Body of Knowledge (CBK) for the CISSP certification exam deals with many of the foundational elements of security solutions. These include elements essential to the design, implementation, and administration of security mechanisms. Additional elements of this domain are discussed in various chapters: Chapter 2, "Personal Security and Risk Management Concepts"; Chapter 3, "Business Continuity Planning"; and Chapter 4, "Laws, Regulations, and Compliance." Please be sure to review all of these chapters to have a complete perspective on the topics of this domain.

Understand and Apply Concepts of Confidentiality, Integrity, and Availability

Security management concepts and principles are inherent elements in a security policy and solution deployment. They define the basic parameters needed for a secure environment. They also define the goals and objectives that both policy designers and system implementers must achieve to create a secure solution. It is important for real-world security professionals, as well as CISSP exam students, to understand these items thoroughly.

The primary goals and objectives of security are contained within the CIA Triad (see Figure 1.1), which is the name given to the three primary security principles:

FIGURE 1.1 The CIA Triad

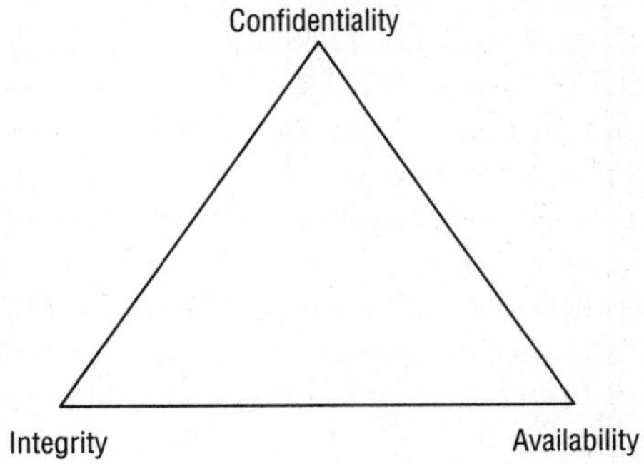

- Confidentiality
- Integrity
- Availability

Security controls are typically evaluated on how well they address these core information security tenets. Overall, a complete security solution should adequately address each of these tenets. Vulnerabilities and risks are also evaluated based on the threat they pose against one or more of the CIA Triad principles. Thus, it is a good idea to be familiar with these principles and use them as guidelines for judging all things related to security.

These three principles are considered the most important within the realm of security. However important each specific principle is to a specific organization depends on the organization's security goals and requirements and on the extent to which the organization's security might be threatened.

Confidentiality

The first principle of the CIA Triad is confidentiality. If a security mechanism offers confidentiality, it offers a high level of assurance that data, objects, or resources are restricted from unauthorized subjects. If a threat exists against confidentiality, unauthorized disclosure could take place.

In general, for confidentiality to be maintained on a network, data must be protected from unauthorized access, use, or disclosure while in storage, in process, and in transit. Unique and specific security controls are required for each of these states of data, resources, and objects to maintain confidentiality.

Numerous attacks focus on the violation of confidentiality. These include capturing network traffic and stealing password files as well as social engineering, port scanning, shoulder surfing, eavesdropping, sniffing, and so on.

Violations of confidentiality are not limited to directed intentional attacks. Many instances of unauthorized disclosure of sensitive or confidential information are the result of human error, oversight, or ineptitude. Events that lead to confidentiality breaches include failing to properly encrypt a transmission, failing to fully authenticate a remote system before transferring data, leaving open otherwise secured access points, accessing malicious code that opens a back door, misrouted faxes, documents left on printers, or even walking away from an access terminal while data is displayed on the monitor. Confidentiality violations can result from the actions of an end user or a system administrator. They can also occur because of an oversight in a security policy or a misconfigured security control.

Numerous countermeasures can help ensure confidentiality against possible threats. These include encryption, network traffic padding, strict access control, rigorous authentication procedures, data classification, and extensive personnel training.

Confidentiality and integrity depend on each other. Without object integrity, confidentiality cannot be maintained. Other concepts, conditions, and aspects of confidentiality include the following:

Sensitivity Sensitivity refers to the quality of information, which could cause harm or damage if disclosed. Maintaining confidentiality of sensitive information helps to prevent harm or damage.

Discretion Discretion is an act of decision where an operator can influence or control disclosure in order to minimize harm or damage.

Criticality The level to which information is mission critical is its measure of criticality. The higher the level of criticality, the more likely the need to maintain the confidentiality of the information. High levels of criticality are essential to the operation or function of an organization.

Concealment Concealment is the act of hiding or preventing disclosure. Often concealment is viewed as a means of cover, obfuscation, or distraction.

Secrecy Secrecy is the act of keeping something a secret or preventing the disclosure of information.

Privacy Privacy refers to keeping information confidential that is personally identifiable or that might cause harm, embarrassment, or disgrace to someone if revealed.

Seclusion Seclusion involves storing something in an out-of-the-way location. This location can also provide strict access controls. Seclusion can help enforcement confidentiality protections.

Isolation Isolation is the act of keeping something separated from others. Isolation can be used to prevent commingling of information or disclosure of information.

Each organization needs to evaluate the nuances of confidentiality they wish to enforce. Tools and technology that implements one form of confidentiality might not support or allow other forms.

Integrity

The second principle of the CIA Triad is integrity. For integrity to be maintained, objects must retain their veracity and be intentionally modified by only authorized subjects. If a security mechanism offers integrity, it offers a high level of assurance that the data, objects, and resources are unaltered from their original protected state. Alterations should not occur while the object is in storage, in transit, or in process. Thus, maintaining integrity means the object itself is not altered and the operating system and programming entities that manage and manipulate the object are not compromised.

Integrity can be examined from three perspectives:

- Preventing unauthorized subjects from making modifications
- Preventing authorized subjects from making unauthorized modifications, such as mistakes
- Maintaining the internal and external consistency of objects so that their data is a correct and true reflection of the real world and any relationship with any child, peer, or parent object is valid, consistent, and verifiable

For integrity to be maintained on a system, controls must be in place to restrict access to data, objects, and resources. Additionally, activity logging should be employed to ensure that only authorized users are able to access their respective resources. Maintaining and validating object integrity across storage, transport, and processing requires numerous variations of controls and oversight.

Numerous attacks focus on the violation of integrity. These include viruses, logic bombs, unauthorized access, errors in coding and applications, malicious modification, intentional replacement, and system back doors.

As with confidentiality, integrity violations are not limited to intentional attacks. Human error, oversight, or ineptitude accounts for many instances of unauthorized alteration of sensitive information. Events that lead to integrity breaches include accidentally deleting files; entering invalid data; altering configurations, including errors in commands, codes, and scripts; introducing a virus; and executing malicious code such as a Trojan horse. Integrity violations can occur because of the actions of any user, including administrators. They can also occur because of an oversight in a security policy or a misconfigured security control.

Numerous countermeasures can ensure integrity against possible threats. These include strict access control, rigorous authentication procedures, intrusion detection systems, object/data encryption, hash total verifications (see Chapter 6, "Cryptography and Symmetric Key Algorithms"), interface restrictions, input/function checks, and extensive personnel training.

Integrity is dependent on confidentiality. Without confidentiality, integrity cannot be maintained. Other concepts, conditions, and aspects of integrity include accuracy, truthfulness, authenticity, validity, nonrepudiation, accountability, responsibility, completeness, and comprehensiveness.

Availability

The third principle of the CIA Triad is availability, which means authorized subjects are granted timely and uninterrupted access to objects. If a security mechanism offers availability, it offers a high level of assurance that the data, objects, and resources are accessible to authorized subjects. Availability includes efficient uninterrupted access to objects and prevention of denial-of-service (DoS) attacks. Availability also implies that the supporting infrastructure—including network services, communications, and access control mechanisms—is functional and allows authorized users to gain authorized access.

For availability to be maintained on a system, controls must be in place to ensure authorized access and an acceptable level of performance, to quickly handle interruptions, to provide for redundancy, to maintain reliable backups, and to prevent data loss or destruction.

There are numerous threats to availability. These include device failure, software errors, and environmental issues (heat, static, flooding, power loss, and so on). There are also some forms of attacks that focus on the violation of availability, including DoS attacks, object destruction, and communication interruptions.

As with confidentiality and integrity, violations of availability are not limited to intentional attacks. Many instances of unauthorized alteration of sensitive information are caused by human error, oversight, or ineptitude. Some events that lead to availability breaches include accidentally deleting files, overutilizing a hardware or software component, underallocating resources, and mislabeling or incorrectly classifying objects. Availability violations can occur because of the actions of any user, including administrators. They can also occur because of an oversight in a security policy or a misconfigured security control.

Numerous countermeasures can ensure availability against possible threats. These include designing intermediary delivery systems properly, using access controls effectively, monitoring performance and network traffic, using firewalls and routers to prevent DoS attacks, implementing redundancy for critical systems, and maintaining and testing backup systems. Most security policies, as well as business continuity planning (BCP), focus on the use of fault tolerance features at the various levels of access/storage/security (that is, disk, server, or site) with the goal of eliminating single points of failure to maintain availability of critical systems.

Availability depends on both integrity and confidentiality. Without integrity and confidentiality, availability cannot be maintained. Other concepts, conditions, and aspects of availability include usability, accessibility, and timeliness.

Real World Scenario

CIA Priority

Every organization has unique security requirements. On the CISSP exam, most security concepts are discussed in general terms, but in the real world, general concepts and best practices don't get the job done. The management team and security team must work together to prioritize an organization's security needs. This includes establishing a budget and spending plan, allocating expertise and hours, and focusing the IT and security staff efforts. One key aspect of this effort is to prioritize the security requirements of the organization. Knowing which tenet or asset is more important than another guides the creation of a security stance and ultimately the deployment of a security solution. Often, getting started in establishing priorities is a challenge. A possible solution to this challenge is to start with prioritizing the three primary security tenets of confidentiality, integrity, and availability. Defining which of these elements is most important to the organization is essential in crafting a sufficient security solution. This establishes a pattern that can be replicated from concept through design, architecture, deployment, and finally, maintenance.

Do you know the priority your organization places on each of the components of the CIA Triad? If not, find out.

An interesting generalization of this concept of CIA prioritization is that in many cases military and government organizations tend to prioritize confidentiality above integrity and availability, whereas private companies tend to prioritize availability above confidentiality and integrity. Although such prioritization focuses efforts on one aspect of security over another, it does not imply that the second or third prioritized items are ignored or improperly addressed.

Other Security Concepts

In addition to the CIA Triad, you need to consider a plethora of other security-related concepts and principles when designing a security policy and deploying a security solution. The following sections discuss identification, authentication, authorization, auditing, accountability (see Figure 1.2), and nonrepudiation.

FIGURE 1.2 The five elements of AAA services

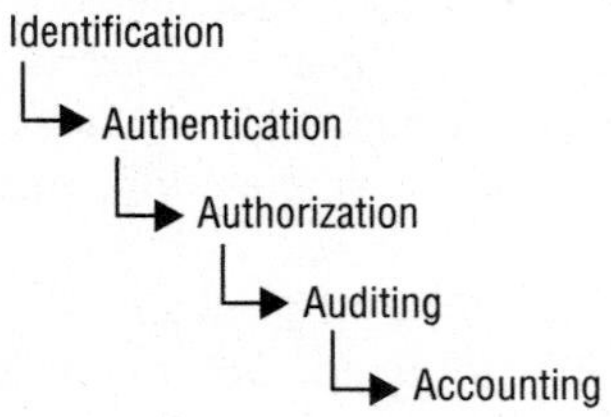

Identification

Identification is the process by which a subject professes an identity and accountability is initiated. A subject must provide an identity to a system to start the process of authentication, authorization, and accountability (AAA). Providing an identity can involve typing in a username; swiping a smart card; waving a proximity device; speaking a phrase; or positioning your face, hand, or finger for a camera or scanning device. Providing a process ID number also represents the identification process. Without an identity, a system has no way to correlate an authentication factor with the subject.

Once a subject has been identified (that is, once the subject's identity has been recognized and verified), the identity is accountable for any further actions by that subject. IT systems track activity by identities, not by the subjects themselves. A computer doesn't know one human from another, but it does know that your user account is different from all other user accounts. A subject's identity is typically labeled as, or considered to be, public information. However, simply claiming an identity does not imply access or authority. The identity must be proven or verified before access to controlled resources is allowed. That process is authentication.

Authentication

The process of verifying or testing that the claimed identity is valid is authentication. Authentication requires from the subject additional information that must exactly correspond to the identity indicated. The most common form of authentication is using a password (this includes the password variations of PINs and passphrases). Authentication verifies the identity of the subject by comparing one or more factors against the database of valid identities (that is, user accounts). The authentication factor used to verify identity is typically labeled as, or considered to be, private information. The capability of the subject and system to maintain the secrecy of the authentication factors for identities directly reflects the level of security of that system. If the process of illegitimately obtaining and using the authentication factor of a target user is relatively easy, then the authentication system is insecure. If that process is relatively difficult, then the authentication system is reasonably secure.

Identification and authentication are always used together as a single two-step process. Providing an identity is the first step, and providing the authentication factor(s) is the second step. Without both, a subject cannot gain access to a system—neither element alone is useful in terms of security.

A subject can provide several types of authentication (for example, something you know, something you have, and so on). Each authentication technique or factor has its unique benefits and drawbacks. Thus, it is important to evaluate each mechanism in light of the environment in which it will be deployed to determine viability. (We discuss authentication at length in Chapter 13, "Managing Identity and Authentication.")

Authorization

Once a subject is authenticated, access must be authorized. The process of authorization ensures that the requested activity or access to an object is possible given the rights and privileges assigned to the authenticated identity. In most cases, the system evaluates an access control matrix that compares the subject, the object, and the intended activity. If the specific action is allowed, the subject is authorized. If the specific action is not allowed, the subject is not authorized.

Keep in mind that just because a subject has been identified and authenticated does not mean they have been authorized to perform any function or access all resources within the controlled environment. It is possible for a subject to be logged onto a network (that is, identified and authenticated) but to be blocked from accessing a file or printing to a printer (that is, by not being authorized to perform that activity). Most network users are authorized to perform only a limited number of activities on a specific collection of resources. Identification and authentication are all-or-nothing aspects of access control. Authorization has a wide range of variations between all or nothing for each object within the environment. A user may be able to read a file but not delete it, print a document but not alter the print queue, or log on to a system but not access any resources. Authorization is usually defined using one of the concepts of access control, such as discretionary access control (DAC), mandatory access control (MAC), or role-based access control (RBAC); see Chapter 14, "Controlling and Monitoring Access."

AAA Services

You may have heard of the concept of AAA services. The three As in this acronym refer to authentication, authorization, and accounting (or sometimes auditing). However, what is not as clear is that although there are three letters in the acronym, it actually refers to five elements: identification, authentication, authorization, auditing, and accounting. Thus, the first and the third/last A actually represent two concepts instead of just one. These five elements represent the following processes of security:

Identification claiming an identity when attempting to access a secured area or system

Authentication proving that you are that identity

Authorization defining the allows and denials of resource and object access for a specific identity

Auditing recording a log of the events and activities related to the system and subjects

Accounting (aka accountability) reviewing log files to check for compliance and violations in order to hold subjects accountable for their actions

Although AAA is often referenced in relation to authentication systems, it is in fact a foundational concept of all forms of security. As without any one of these five elements, a security mechanism would be incomplete.

Auditing

Auditing, or monitoring, is the programmatic means by which a subject's actions are tracked and recorded for the purpose of holding the subject accountable for their actions while authenticated on a system. It is also the process by which unauthorized or abnormal activities are detected on a system. Auditing is recording activities of a subject and its objects as well as recording the activities of core system functions that maintain the operating environment and the security mechanisms. The audit trails created by recording system events to logs can be used to evaluate the health and performance of a system. System crashes may indicate faulty programs, corrupt drivers, or intrusion attempts. The event logs leading up to a crash can often be used to discover the reason a system failed. Log files provide an audit trail for re-creating the history of an event, intrusion, or system failure. Auditing is needed to detect malicious actions by subjects, attempted intrusions, and system failures and to reconstruct events, provide evidence for prosecution, and produce problem reports and analysis. Auditing is usually a native feature of operating systems and most applications and services. Thus, configuring the system to record information about specific types of events is fairly straightforward.

Accountability

An organization's security policy can be properly enforced only if accountability is maintained. In other words, you can maintain security only if subjects are held accountable for their actions. Effective accountability relies on the capability to prove a subject's identity and track their activities. Accountability is established by linking a human to the activities of an online identity through the security services and mechanisms of auditing, authorization, authentication, and identification. Thus, human accountability is ultimately dependent on the strength of the authentication process. Without a strong authentication process, there is doubt that the human associated with a specific user account was the actual entity controlling that user account when the undesired action took place.

To have viable accountability, you must be able to support your security in a court of law. If you are unable to legally support your security efforts, then you will be unlikely to be able to hold a human accountable for actions linked to a user account. With only a password as authentication, there is significant room for doubt. Passwords are the least secure form of authentication, with dozens of different methods available to compromise them. However, with the use of multifactor authentication, such as a password, smartcard, and fingerprint scan in combination, there is very little possibility that any other human could have compromised the authentication process in order to impersonate the human responsible for the user account.

Legally Defensible Security

The point of security is to keep bad things from happening while supporting the occurrence of good things. When bad things do happen, organizations often desire assistance from law enforcement and the legal system for compensation. To obtain legal restitution, you must demonstrate that a crime was committed, that the suspect committed that crime, and that you took reasonable efforts to prevent the crime. This means your organization's security needs to be legally defensible. If you are unable to convince a court that your log files are accurate and that no other person other than the subject could have committed the crime, you will not obtain restitution. Ultimately, this requires a complete security solution that has strong multifactor authentication techniques, solid authorization mechanisms, and impeccable auditing systems. Additionally, you must show that the organization complied with all applicable laws and regulations, that proper warnings and notifications were posted, that both logical and physical security were not otherwise compromised, and that there are no other possible reasonable interpretations of the electronic evidence. This is a fairly challenging standard to meet. If you are not going to make the effort to design and implement legally defensible security, what is the point in attempting subpar security?

Nonrepudiation

Nonrepudiation ensures that the subject of an activity or event cannot deny that the event occurred. Nonrepudiation prevents a subject from claiming not to have sent a message, not to have performed an action, or not to have been the cause of an event. It is made possible through identification, authentication, authorization, accountability, and auditing. Nonrepudiation can be established using digital certificates, session identifiers, transaction logs, and numerous other transactional and access control mechanisms. If nonrepudiation is not built into a system and properly enforced, you will not be able to verify that a specific entity performed a certain action. Nonrepudiation is an essential part of accountability. A suspect cannot be held accountable if they can repudiate the claim against them.

Protection Mechanisms

Another aspect of understanding and apply concepts of confidentiality, integrity, and availability is the concept of protection mechanisms. Protection mechanisms are common characteristics of security controls. Not all security controls must have them, but many controls offer their protection for confidentiality, integrity, and availability through the use of these mechanisms. These mechanisms include using multiple layers or levels of access, employing abstraction, hiding data, and using encryption.

Layering

Layering, also known as defense in depth, is simply the use of multiple controls in a series. No one control can protect against all possible threats. Using a multilayered solution allows for numerous, different controls to guard against whatever threats come to pass. When security solutions are designed in layers, most threats are eliminated, mitigated, or thwarted.

Using layers in a series rather than in parallel is important. Performing security restrictions in a series means to perform one after the other in a linear fashion. Only through a series configuration will each attack be scanned, evaluated, or mitigated by every security control. In a series configuration, failure of a single security control does not render the entire solution ineffective. If security controls were implemented in parallel, a threat could pass through a single checkpoint that did not address its particular malicious activity.

Serial configurations are very narrow but very deep, whereas parallel configurations are very wide but very shallow. Parallel systems are useful in distributed computing applications, but parallelism is not often a useful concept in the realm of security.

Think of physical entrances to buildings. A parallel configuration is used for shopping malls. There are many doors in many locations around the entire perimeter of the mall. A series configuration would most likely be used in a bank or an airport. A single entrance is provided, and that entrance is actually several gateways or checkpoints that must be passed in sequential order to gain entry into active areas of the building.

Layering also includes the concept that networks comprise numerous separate entities, each with its own unique security controls and vulnerabilities. In an effective security solution, there is a synergy between all networked systems that creates a single security front. Using separate security systems creates a layered security solution.

Abstraction

Abstraction is used for efficiency. Similar elements are put into groups, classes, or roles that are assigned security controls, restrictions, or permissions as a collective. Thus, the concept of abstraction is used when classifying objects or assigning roles to subjects. The concept of abstraction also includes the definition of object and subject types or of objects themselves (that is, a data structure used to define a template for a class of entities). Abstraction is used to define what types of data an object can contain, what types of functions can be performed on or by that object, and what capabilities that object has. Abstraction simplifies security by enabling you to assign security controls to a group of objects collected by type or function.

Data Hiding

Data hiding is exactly what it sounds like: preventing data from being discovered or accessed by a subject by positioning the data in a logical storage compartment that is not accessible or seen by the subject. Forms of data hiding include keeping a database from being accessed by unauthorized visitors and restricting a subject at a lower classification level from accessing data at a higher classification level. Preventing an application from accessing hardware directly is also a form of data hiding. Data hiding is often a key element in security controls as well as in programming.

Encryption

Encryption is the art and science of hiding the meaning or intent of a communication from unintended recipients. Encryption can take many forms and be applied to every type of electronic communication, including text, audio, and video files as well as applications themselves. Encryption is an important element in security controls, especially in regard to the transmission of data between systems. There are various strengths of encryption, each of which is designed and/or appropriate for a specific use or purpose. Encryption is discussed at length in Chapter 6, "Cryptography and Symmetric Key Algorithms," and Chapter 7, "PKI and Cryptographic Applications."

Apply Security Governance Principles

Security governance is the collection of practices related to supporting, defining, and directing the security efforts of an organization. Security governance is closely related to and often intertwined with corporate and IT governance. The goals of these three governance agendas are often the same or interrelated. For example, a common goal of organizational governance is to ensure that the organization will continue to exist and will grow or expand over time. Thus, the common goal of governance is to maintain business processes while striving toward growth and resiliency.

Some aspects of governance are imposed on organizations due to legislative and regulatory compliance needs, whereas others are imposed by industry guidelines or license requirements. All forms of governance, including security governance, must be assessed and verified from time to time. Various requirements for auditing and validation may be present due to government regulations or industry best practices. Governance compliance issues often vary from industry to industry and from country to country. As many organizations expand and adapt to deal with a global market, governance issues become more complex. This is especially problematic when laws in different countries differ or in fact conflict. The organization as a whole should be given the direction, guidance, and tools to provide sufficient oversight and management to address threats and risks with a focus on eliminating downtime and keeping potential loss or damage to a minimum.

As you can tell, the definitions of security governance are often rather stilted and high level. Ultimately, security governance is the implementation of a security solution and a management method that are tightly interconnected. Security governance directly oversees and gets involved in all levels of security. Security is not and should not be treated as an IT issue only. Instead, security affects every aspect of an organization. It is no longer just something the IT staff can handle on their own. Security is a business operations issue. Security is an organizational process, not just something the IT geeks do behind the scenes. Using the term *security governance* is an attempt to emphasize this point by indicating that security needs to be managed and governed throughout the organization, not just in the IT department.

Alignment of Security Function to Strategy, Goals, Mission, and Objectives

Security management planning ensures proper creation, implementation, and enforcement of a security policy. Security management planning aligns the security functions to the strategy, goals, mission, and objectives of the organization. This includes designing and implementing security based on a business case, budget restrictions, or scarcity of resources. A business case is usually a documented argument or stated position in order to define a need to make a decision or take some form of action. To make a business case is to demonstrate a business-specific need to alter an existing process or choose an approach to a business task. A business case is often made to justify the start of a new project, especially a project related to security. It is also important to consider the budget that can be allocated to a business need–based security project. Security can be expensive, but it is often an essential element of reliable and long-term business operation. In most organizations, money and resources, such as people, technology, and space, are limited. Due to resource limitations like these, the maximum benefit needs to be obtained from any endeavor.

One of the most effective ways to tackle security management planning is to use a top-down approach. Upper, or senior, management is responsible for initiating and defining policies for the organization. Security policies provide direction for all levels of the organization's hierarchy. It is the responsibility of middle management to flesh out the security policy into standards, baselines, guidelines, and procedures. The operational managers or security professionals must then implement the configurations prescribed in the security management documentation. Finally, the end users must comply with all the security policies of the organization.

NOTE

The opposite of the top-down approach is the bottom-up approach. In a bottom-up approach environment, the IT staff makes security decisions directly without input from senior management. The bottom-up approach is rarely used in organizations and is considered problematic in the IT industry.

Security management is a responsibility of upper management, not of the IT staff, and is considered a business operations issue rather than an IT administration issue. The team or department responsible for security within an organization should be autonomous. The information security (InfoSec) team should be led by a designated chief security officer (CSO) who must report directly to senior management. Placing the autonomy of the CSO and the CSO's team outside the typical hierarchical structure in an organization can improve security management across the entire organization. It also helps to avoid cross-department and internal political issues.

Elements of security management planning include defining security roles; prescribing how security will be managed, who will be responsible for security, and how security will be tested for effectiveness; developing security policies; performing risk analysis; and requiring security education for employees. These efforts are guided through the development of management plans.

The best security plan is useless without one key factor: approval by senior management. Without senior management's approval of and commitment to the security policy, the policy will not succeed. It is the responsibility of the policy development team to educate senior management sufficiently so it understands the risks, liabilities, and exposures that remain even after security measures prescribed in the policy are deployed. Developing and implementing a security policy is evidence of due care and due diligence on the part of senior management. If a company does not practice due care and due diligence, managers can be held liable for negligence and held accountable for both asset and financial losses.

A security management planning team should develop three types of plans, as shown in Figure 1.3.

FIGURE 1.3 Strategic, tactical, and operational plan timeline comparison

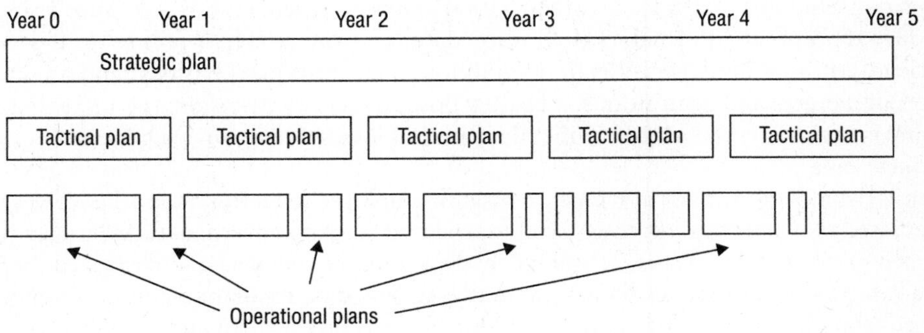

Strategic Plan A strategic plan is a long-term plan that is fairly stable. It defines the organization's security purpose. It also helps to understand security function and align it to goals, mission, and objectives of the organization. It's useful for about five years if it is maintained and updated annually. The strategic plan also serves as the planning horizon. Long-term goals and visions for the future are discussed in a strategic plan. A strategic plan should include a risk assessment.

Tactical plan The tactical plan is a midterm plan developed to provide more details on accomplishing the goals set forth in the strategic plan or can be crafted ad-hoc based upon unpredicted events. A tactical plan is typically useful for about a year and often prescribes and schedules the tasks necessary to accomplish organizational goals. Some examples of tactical plans are project plans, acquisition plans, hiring plans, budget plans, maintenance plans, support plans, and system development plans.

Operational Plan An operational plan is a short-term, highly detailed plan based on the strategic and tactical plans. It is valid or useful only for a short time. Operational plans must be updated often (such as monthly or quarterly) to retain compliance with tactical plans. Operational plans spell out how to accomplish the various goals of the organization. They include resource allotments, budgetary requirements, staffing assignments, scheduling, and step-by-step or implementation procedures. Operational plans include details on how the implementation processes are in compliance with the organization's security policy. Examples of operational plans are training plans, system deployment plans, and product design plans.

Security is a continuous process. Thus, the activity of security management planning may have a definitive initiation point, but its tasks and work are never fully accomplished or complete. Effective security plans focus attention on specific and achievable objectives, anticipate change and potential problems, and serve as a basis for decision making for the entire organization. Security documentation should be concrete, well defined, and clearly stated. For a security plan to be effective, it must be developed, maintained, and actually used.

Organizational Processes

Security governance needs to address every aspect of an organization. This includes the organizational processes of acquisitions, divestitures, and governance committees. Acquisitions and mergers place an organization at an increased level of risk. Such risks include inappropriate information disclosure, data loss, downtime, or failure to achieve sufficient return on investment (ROI). In addition to all the typical business and financial aspects of mergers and acquisitions, a healthy dose of security oversight and increased scrutiny is often essential to reduce the likelihood of losses during such a period of transformation.

Similarly, a divestiture or any form of asset or employee reduction is another time period of increased risk and thus increased need for focused security governance. Assets need to be sanitized to prevent data leakage. Storage media should be removed and destroyed, because media sanitization techniques do not guarantee against data remnant recovery. Employees released from duty need to be debriefed. This process is often called an exit interview.

This process usually involves reviewing any nondisclosure agreements as well as any other binding contracts or agreements that will continue after employment has ceased.

Often, security governance is managed by a governance committee or at least a board of directors. This is the group of influential knowledge experts whose primary task is to oversee and guide the actions of security and operations for an organization. Security is a complex task. Organizations are often large and difficult to understand from a single viewpoint. Having a group of experts work together toward the goal of reliable security governance is a solid strategy.

Two additional examples of organizational processes that are essential to strong security governance are change control/change management and data classification.

Change Control/Management

Another important aspect of security management is the control or management of change. Change in a secure environment can introduce loopholes, overlaps, missing objects, and oversights that can lead to new vulnerabilities. The only way to maintain security in the face of change is to systematically manage change. This usually involves extensive planning, testing, logging, auditing, and monitoring of activities related to security controls and mechanisms. The records of changes to an environment are then used to identify agents of change, whether those agents are objects, subjects, programs, communication pathways, or even the network itself.

The goal of change management is to ensure that any change does not lead to reduced or compromised security. Change management is also responsible for making it possible to roll back any change to a previous secured state. Change management can be implemented on any system despite the level of security. It is a requirement for systems complying with the Information Technology Security Evaluation and Criteria (ITSEC) classifications of B2, B3, and A1. Ultimately, change management improves the security of an environment by protecting implemented security from unintentional, tangential, or affected diminishments. Although an important goal of change management is to prevent unwanted reductions in security, its primary purpose is to make all changes subject to detailed documentation and auditing and thus able to be reviewed and scrutinized by management.

Change management should be used to oversee alterations to every aspect of a system, including hardware configuration and OS and application software. Change management should be included in design, development, testing, evaluation, implementation, distribution, evolution, growth, ongoing operation, and modification. It requires a detailed inventory of every component and configuration. It also requires the collection and maintenance of complete documentation for every system component, from hardware to software and from configuration settings to security features.

The change control process of configuration or change management has several goals or requirements:

- Implement changes in a monitored and orderly manner. Changes are always controlled.
- A formalized testing process is included to verify that a change produces expected results.
- All changes can be reversed (also known as backout or rollback plans/procedures).

- Users are informed of changes before they occur to prevent loss of productivity.
- The effects of changes are systematically analyzed.
- The negative impact of changes on capabilities, functionality, and performance is minimized.
- Changes are reviewed and approved by a CAB (change approval board).

One example of a change management process is a parallel run, which is a type of new system deployment testing where the new system and the old system are run in parallel. Each major or significant user process is performed on each system simultaneously to ensure that the new system supports all required business functionality that the old system supported or provided.

Data Classification

Data classification, or categorization, is the primary means by which data is protected based on its need for secrecy, sensitivity, or confidentiality. It is inefficient to treat all data the same way when designing and implementing a security system because some data items need more security than others. Securing everything at a low security level means sensitive data is easily accessible. Securing everything at a high security level is too expensive and restricts access to unclassified, noncritical data. Data classification is used to determine how much effort, money, and resources are allocated to protect the data and control access to it. Data classification, or categorization, is the process of organizing items, objects, subjects, and so on into groups, categories, or collections with similarities. These similarities could include value, cost, sensitivity, risk, vulnerability, power, privilege, possible levels of loss or damage, or need to know.

The primary objective of data classification schemes is to formalize and stratify the process of securing data based on assigned labels of importance and sensitivity. Data classification is used to provide security mechanisms for storing, processing, and transferring data. It also addresses how data is removed from a system and destroyed.

The following are benefits of using a data classification scheme:

- It demonstrates an organization's commitment to protecting valuable resources and assets.
- It assists in identifying those assets that are most critical or valuable to the organization.
- It lends credence to the selection of protection mechanisms.
- It is often required for regulatory compliance or legal restrictions.
- It helps to define access levels, types of authorized uses, and parameters for declassification and/or destruction of resources that are no longer valuable.
- It helps with data life-cycle management which in part is the storage length (retention), usage, and destruction of the data.

The criteria by which data is classified vary based on the organization performing the classification. However, you can glean numerous generalities from common or standardized classification systems:

- Usefulness of the data
- Timeliness of the data

- Value or cost of the data
- Maturity or age of the data
- Lifetime of the data (or when it expires)
- Association with personnel
- Data disclosure damage assessment (that is, how the disclosure of the data would affect the organization)
- Data modification damage assessment (that is, how the modification of the data would affect the organization)
- National security implications of the data
- Authorized access to the data (that is, who has access to the data)
- Restriction from the data (that is, who is restricted from the data)
- Maintenance and monitoring of the data (that is, who should maintain and monitor the data)
- Storage of the data

Using whatever criteria is appropriate for the organization, data is evaluated, and an appropriate data classification label is assigned to it. In some cases, the label is added to the data object. In other cases, labeling occurs automatically when the data is placed into a storage mechanism or behind a security protection mechanism.

To implement a classification scheme, you must perform seven major steps, or phases:

1. Identify the custodian, and define their responsibilities.
2. Specify the evaluation criteria of how the information will be classified and labeled.
3. Classify and label each resource. (The owner conducts this step, but a supervisor should review it.)
4. Document any exceptions to the classification policy that are discovered, and integrate them into the evaluation criteria.
5. Select the security controls that will be applied to each classification level to provide the necessary level of protection.
6. Specify the procedures for declassifying resources and the procedures for transferring custody of a resource to an external entity.
7. Create an enterprise-wide awareness program to instruct all personnel about the classification system.

Declassification is often overlooked when designing a classification system and documenting the usage procedures. Declassification is required once an asset no longer warrants or needs the protection of its currently assigned classification or sensitivity level. In other words, if the asset were new, it would be assigned a lower sensitivity label than it currently is assigned. When assets fail to be declassified as needed, security resources are wasted, and the value and protection of the higher sensitivity levels is degraded.

The two common classification schemes are government/military classification (Figure 1.4) and commercial business/private sector classification. There are five levels of government/military classification (listed here from highest to lowest):

FIGURE 1.4 Levels of government/military classification

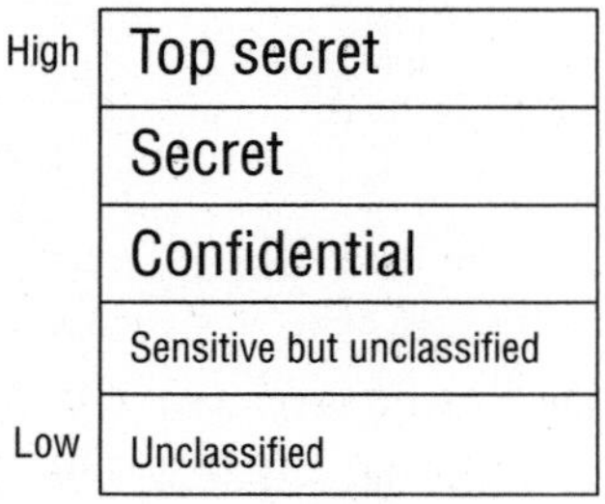

Top Secret The highest level of classification. The unauthorized disclosure of top-secret data will have drastic effects and cause grave damage to national security.

Secret Used for data of a restricted nature. The unauthorized disclosure of data classified as secret will have significant effects and cause critical damage to national security.

Confidential Used for data of a private, sensitive, proprietary, or highly valuable nature. The unauthorized disclosure of data classified as confidential will have noticeable effects and cause serious damage to national security. This classification is used for all data between secret and sensitive but unclassified classifications.

Unclassified The lowest level of classification. This is used for data that is neither sensitive nor classified. The disclosure of unclassified data does not compromise confidentiality or cause any noticeable damage.

TIP

An easy way to remember the names of the five levels of the government or military classification scheme in least secure to most secure order is with a memorization acronym: U.S. Can Stop Terrorism. Notice that the five uppercase letters represent the five named classification levels, from least secure on the left to most secure on the right (or from bottom to top in the preceding list of items).

Items labeled as confidential, secret, and top secret are collectively known as classified. Often, revealing the actual classification of data to unauthorized individuals is a violation of that data. Thus, the term *classified* is generally used to refer to any data that is ranked above the unclassified level. All classified data is exempt from the Freedom of Information Act as well as many other laws and regulations. The US military classification scheme is most concerned with the sensitivity of data and focuses on the protection of confidentiality (that is, the prevention of disclosure). You can roughly define each level or label of classification by the level of damage that would be caused in the event of a confidentiality violation. Data from the top-secret level would cause grave damage to national security, whereas data from the unclassified level would not cause any serious damage to national or localized security.

Commercial business/private sector classification systems can vary widely because they typically do not have to adhere to a standard or regulation. The CISSP exam focuses on four common or possible business classification levels (listed highest to lowest and shown in Figure 1.5):

FIGURE 1.5 Commercial business/private sector classification levels

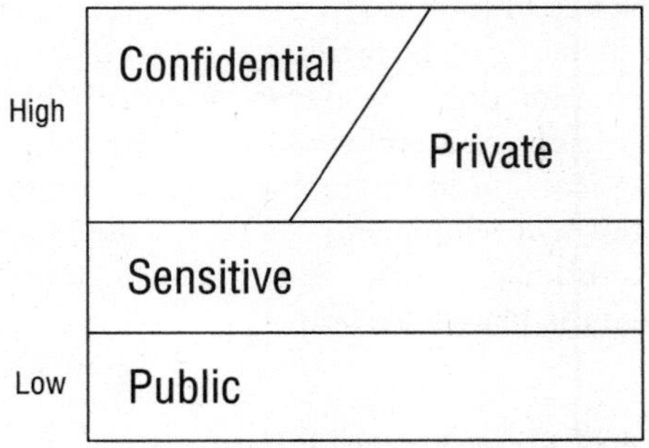

Confidential The highest level of classification. This is used for data that is extremely sensitive and for internal use only. A significant negative impact could occur for a company if confidential data is disclosed. Sometimes the label *proprietary* is substituted for *confidential*. Sometimes proprietary data is considered a specific form of confidential information. If proprietary data is disclosed, it can have drastic effects on the competitive edge of an organization.

Private Used for data that is of a private or personal nature and intended for internal use only. A significant negative impact could occur for the company or individuals if private data is disclosed.

NOTE

Confidential and private data in a commercial business/private sector classification scheme both require roughly the same level of security protection. The real difference between the two labels is that confidential data is company data whereas private data is data related to individuals, such as medical data.

Sensitive Used for data that is more classified than public data. A negative impact could occur for the company if sensitive data is disclosed.

Public The lowest level of classification. This is used for all data that does not fit in one of the higher classifications. Its disclosure does not have a serious negative impact on the organization.

Another consideration related to data classification or categorization is ownership. Ownership is the formal assignment of responsibility to an individual or group. Ownership can be made clear and distinct within an operating system where files or other types of objects can be assigned an owner. Often, an owner has full capabilities and privileges over the object they own. The ability to take ownership is often granted to the most powerful accounts in an operating system, such as the administrator in Windows or root in Unix or Linux. In most cases, the subject that creates a new object is by default the owner of that object. In some environments, the security policy mandates that when new objects are created, a formal change of ownership from end users to an administrator or management user is necessary. In this situation, the admin account can simply take ownership of the new objects.

Ownership of objects outside of formal IT structures is often not as obvious. A company document can define owners for the facility, business tasks, processes, assets, and so on. However, such documentation does not always "enforce" this ownership in the real world. The ownership of a file object is enforced by the operating system and file system, whereas ownership of a physical object, intangible asset, or organizational concept (such as the research department or a development project) is defined only on paper and can be more easily undermined. Additional security governance must be implemented to provide enforcement of ownership in the physical world.

Security Roles and Responsibilities

A security role is the part an individual plays in the overall scheme of security implementation and administration within an organization. Security roles are not necessarily prescribed in job descriptions because they are not always distinct or static. Familiarity with security roles will help in establishing a communications and support structure within an organization. This structure will enable the deployment and enforcement of the security policy. The following six roles are presented in the logical order in which they appear in a secured environment:

Senior Manager The organizational owner (senior manager) role is assigned to the person who is ultimately responsible for the security maintained by an organization and who should be most concerned about the protection of its assets. The senior manager must sign off on all policy issues. In fact, all activities must be approved by and signed off on by the senior manager before they can be carried out. There is no effective security policy if the senior manager does not authorize and support it. The senior manager's endorsement of the security policy indicates the accepted ownership of the implemented security within the organization. The senior manager is the person who will be held liable for the overall success or failure of a security solution and is responsible for exercising due care and due diligence in establishing security for an organization.

Even though senior managers are ultimately responsible for security, they rarely implement security solutions. In most cases, that responsibility is delegated to security professionals within the organization.

Security Professional The security professional, information security (InfoSec) officer, or computer incident response team (CIRT) role is assigned to a trained and experienced network, systems, and security engineer who is responsible for following the directives mandated by senior management. The security professional has the functional responsibility for security, including writing the security policy and implementing it. The role of security professional can be labeled as an IS/IT function role. The security professional role is often filled by a team that is responsible for designing and implementing security solutions based on the approved security policy. Security professionals are not decision makers; they are implementers. All decisions must be left to the senior manager.

Data Owner The data owner role is assigned to the person who is responsible for classifying information for placement and protection within the security solution. The data owner is typically a high-level manager who is ultimately responsible for data protection. However, the data owner usually delegates the responsibility of the actual data management tasks to a data custodian.

Data Custodian The data custodian role is assigned to the user who is responsible for the tasks of implementing the prescribed protection defined by the security policy and senior management. The data custodian performs all activities necessary to provide adequate protection for the CIA Triad (confidentiality, integrity, and availability) of data and to fulfill the requirements and responsibilities delegated from upper management. These activities can include performing and testing backups, validating data integrity, deploying security solutions, and managing data storage based on classification.

User The user (end user or operator) role is assigned to any person who has access to the secured system. A user's access is tied to their work tasks and is limited so they have only enough access to perform the tasks necessary for their job position (the principle of least privilege). Users are responsible for understanding and upholding the security policy of an organization by following prescribed operational procedures and operating within defined security parameters.

Auditor An auditor is responsible for reviewing and verifying that the security policy is properly implemented and the derived security solutions are adequate. The auditor role may be assigned to a security professional or a trained user. The auditor produces compliance and effectiveness reports that are reviewed by the senior manager. Issues discovered through these reports are transformed into new directives assigned by the senior manager to security professionals or data custodians. However, the auditor is listed as the last or final role because the auditor needs a source of activity (that is, users or operators working in an environment) to audit or monitor.

All of these roles serve an important function within a secured environment. They are useful for identifying liability and responsibility as well as for identifying the hierarchical management and delegation scheme.

Control Frameworks

Crafting a security stance for an organization often involves a lot more than just writing down a few lofty ideals. In most cases, a significant amount of planning goes into developing a solid security policy. Many Dilbert fans may recognize the seemingly absurd concept of holding a meeting to plan a meeting for a future meeting. But it turns out that planning for security must start with planning to plan, then move into planning for standards and compliance, and finally move into the actual plan development and design. Skipping any of these "planning to plan" steps can derail an organization's security solution before it even gets started.

One of the first and most important security planning steps is to consider the overall control framework or structure of the security solution desired by the organization. You can choose from several options in regard to security concept infrastructure; however, the one covered on the CISSP exam is Control Objectives for Information and Related Technology (COBIT). COBIT is a documented set of best IT security practices crafted by the Information Systems Audit and Control Association (ISACA). It prescribes goals and requirements for security controls and encourages the mapping of IT security ideals to business objectives. COBIT 5 is based on five key principles for governance and management of enterprise IT: Principle 1: Meeting Stakeholder Needs, Principle 2: Covering the Enterprise End-to-End, Principle 3: Applying a Single, Integrated Framework, Principle 4: Enabling a Holistic Approach, and Principle 5: Separating Governance From Management. COBIT is used not only to plan the IT security of an organization but also as a guideline for auditors.

Fortunately, COBIT is only modestly referenced on the exam, so further details are not necessary. However, if you have interest in this concept, please visit the ISACA website (`www.isaca.org`), or if you want a general overview, read the COBIT entry on Wikipedia.

There are many other standards and guidelines for IT security. A few of these are Open Source Security Testing Methodology Manual (OSSTMM), ISO/IEC 27002 (which replaced ISO 17799), and the Information Technology Infrastructure Library (ITIL) (see `www.itlibrary.org` for more information).

Due Care and Due Diligence

Why is planning to plan security so important? One reason is the requirement for due care and due diligence. Due care is using reasonable care to protect the interests of an organization. Due diligence is practicing the activities that maintain the due care effort. For example, due care is developing a formalized security structure containing a security policy, standards, baselines, guidelines, and procedures. Due diligence is the continued application of this security structure onto the IT infrastructure of an organization. Operational security is the ongoing maintenance of continued due care and due diligence by all responsible parties within an organization.

In today's business environment, prudence is mandatory. Showing due care and due diligence is the only way to disprove negligence in an occurrence of loss. Senior management must show due care and due diligence to reduce their culpability and liability when a loss occurs.

Develop and Implement Documented Security Policy, Standards, Procedures, and Guidelines

For most organizations, maintaining security is an essential part of ongoing business. If their security were seriously compromised, many organizations would fail. To reduce the likelihood of a security failure, the process of implementing security has been somewhat formalized with a hierarchical organization of documentation. Each level focuses on a specific type or category of information and issues. Developing and implementing documented security policy, standards, procedures, and guidelines produces a solid and reliable security infrastructure. This formalization has greatly reduced the chaos and complexity of designing and implementing security solutions for IT infrastructures.

Security Policies

The top tier of the formalization is known as a security policy. A security policy is a document that defines the scope of security needed by the organization and discusses the assets that require protection and the extent to which security solutions should go to provide the necessary protection. The security policy is an overview or generalization of an organization's security needs. It defines the main security objectives and outlines the security framework of an organization. It also identifies the major functional areas of data processing and clarifies and defines all relevant terminology. It should clearly define why security is important and what assets are valuable. It is a strategic plan for implementing security. It should broadly outline the security goals and practices that should be employed to protect the organization's vital interests. The document discusses the importance of security to every aspect of daily business operation and the importance of the support of the senior staff for the implementation of security. The security policy is used to assign responsibilities, define roles, specify audit requirements, outline enforcement processes, indicate compliance requirements, and define acceptable risk levels. This document is often used as the proof that senior management has exercised due care in protecting itself against intrusion, attack, and disaster. Security policies are compulsory.

Many organizations employ several types of security policies to define or outline their overall security strategy. An organizational security policy focuses on issues relevant to every aspect of an organization. An issue-specific security policy focuses on a specific network service, department, function, or other aspect that is distinct from the organization as a whole. A system-specific security policy focuses on individual systems or types of systems and prescribes approved hardware and software, outlines methods for locking down a system, and even mandates firewall or other specific security controls.

In addition to these focused types of security policies, there are three overall categories of security policies: regulatory, advisory, and informative. A regulatory policy is required whenever industry or legal standards are applicable to your organization. This policy discusses the regulations that must be followed and outlines the procedures that should be used to elicit compliance. An advisory policy discusses behaviors and activities that are acceptable and defines consequences of violations. It explains senior management's desires for security and compliance within an organization. Most policies are advisory. An informative policy is designed to provide information or knowledge about a specific subject, such as company goals, mission statements, or how the organization interacts with partners and customers. An informative policy provides support, research, or background information relevant to the specific elements of the overall policy.

From the security policies flow many other documents or subelements necessary for a complete security solution. Policies are broad overviews, whereas standards, baselines, guidelines, and procedures include more specific, detailed information on the actual security solution. Standards are the next level below security policies.

Security Policies and Individuals

As a rule of thumb, security policies (as well as standards, guidelines, and procedures) should not address specific individuals. Instead of assigning tasks and responsibilities to a person, the policy should define tasks and responsibilities to fit a role. That role is a function of administrative control or personnel management. Thus, a security policy does not define who is to do what but rather defines what must be done by the various roles within the security infrastructure. Then these defined security roles are assigned to individuals as a job description or an assigned work task.

Acceptable Use Policy

An *acceptable use policy* is a commonly produced document that exists as part of the overall security documentation infrastructure. The acceptable use policy is specifically designed to assign security roles within the organization as well as ensure the responsibilities tied to those roles. This policy defines a level of acceptable performance and expectation of behavior and activity. Failure to comply with the policy may result in job action warnings, penalties, or termination.

Security Standards, Baselines, and Guidelines

Once the main security policies are set, then the remaining security documentation can be crafted under the guidance of those policies. Standards define compulsory requirements for the homogenous use of hardware, software, technology, and security controls. They provide a course of action by which technology and procedures are uniformly implemented throughout an organization. Standards are tactical documents that define steps or methods to accomplish the goals and overall direction defined by security policies.

At the next level are baselines. A baseline defines a minimum level of security that every system throughout the organization must meet. All systems not complying with the baseline should be taken out of production until they can be brought up to the baseline. The baseline establishes a common foundational secure state on which all additional and more stringent security measures can be built. Baselines are usually system specific and often refer to an industry or government standard, like the Trusted Computer System Evaluation Criteria (TCSEC) or Information Technology Security Evaluation and Criteria (ITSEC) or NIST (National Institute of Standards and Technology) standards.

Guidelines are the next element of the formalized security policy structure. A guideline offers recommendations on how standards and baselines are implemented and serves as an operational guide for both security professionals and users. Guidelines are flexible so they can be customized for each unique system or condition and can be used in the creation of new procedures. They state which security mechanisms should be deployed instead of prescribing a specific product or control and detailing configuration settings. They outline methodologies, include suggested actions, and are not compulsory.

Security Procedures

Procedures are the final element of the formalized security policy structure. A procedure is a detailed, step-by-step how-to document that describes the exact actions necessary to implement a specific security mechanism, control, or solution. A procedure could discuss the entire system deployment operation or focus on a single product or aspect, such as deploying a firewall or updating virus definitions. In most cases, procedures are system and software specific. They must be updated as the hardware and software of a system evolve. The purpose of a procedure is to ensure the integrity of business processes. If everything is accomplished by following a detailed procedure, then all activities should be in compliance with policies, standards, and guidelines. Procedures help ensure standardization of security across all systems.

All too often, policies, standards, baselines, guidelines, and procedures are developed only as an afterthought at the urging of a consultant or auditor. If these documents are not used and updated, the administration of a secured environment will be unable to use them as guides. And without the planning, design, structure, and oversight provided by these documents, no environment will remain secure or represent proper diligent due care.

It is also common practice to develop a single document containing aspects of all these elements. This should be avoided. Each of these structures must exist as a separate entity because each performs a different specialized function. At the top of the formalization security policy documentation structure there are fewer documents because they contain general broad discussions of overview and goals. There are more documents further down the formalization structure (in other words, guidelines and procedures) because they contain details specific to a limited number of systems, networks, divisions, and areas.

Keeping these documents as separate entities provides several benefits:

- Not all users need to know the security standards, baselines, guidelines, and procedures for all security classification levels.
- When changes occur, it is easier to update and redistribute only the affected material rather than updating a monolithic policy and redistributing it throughout the organization.

Crafting the totality of security policy and all supporting documentation can be a daunting task. Many organizations struggle just to define the foundational parameters of their security, much less detail every single aspect of their day-to-day activities. However, in theory, a detailed and complete security policy supports real-world security in a directed, efficient, and specific manner. Once the security policy documentation is reasonably complete, it can be used to guide decisions, train new users, respond to problems, and predict trends for future expansion. A security policy should not be an afterthought but a key part of establishing an organization.

There are a few additional perspectives to understand about the documentation that comprises a complete security policy. Figure 1.6 shows the dependencies of these components: policies, standards, guidelines, and procedures. The security policies are the foundation of the overall structure of organized security documentation. Then, standards are based on those policies as well as mandated by regulations and contracts. From these the guidelines are derived. Finally, procedures are based on the three underlying layers of the structure. The inverted pyramid is used to convey the volume or size of each of these documents. There are typically significantly more procedures than any other element in a complete security policy. Comparatively, there are fewer guidelines than policies, fewer still standards, and usually even fewer still of overarching or organization-wide security policies.

FIGURE 1.6 The comparative relationships of security policy components

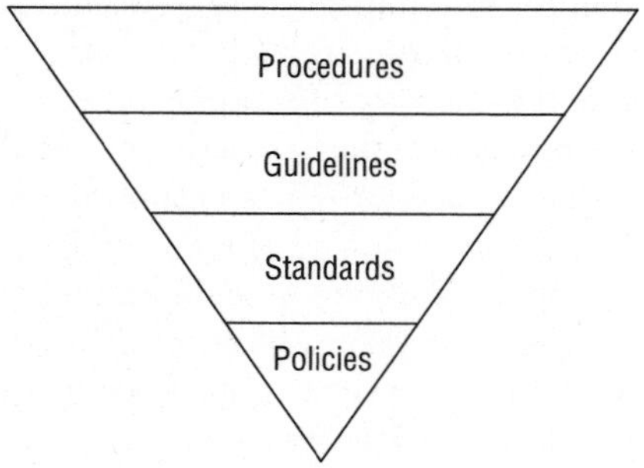

Understand and Apply Threat Modeling

Threat modeling is the security process where potential threats are identified, categorized, and analyzed. Threat modeling can be performed as a proactive measure during design and development or as a reactive measure once a product has been deployed. In either case, the process identifies the potential harm, the probability of occurrence, the priority of concern, and the means to eradicate or reduce the threat.

Threat modeling isn't meant to be a single event. Instead it's common for an organization to begin threat modeling early in the design process of a system and continue throughout its life cycle. For example, Microsoft uses a Security Development Lifecycle (SDL) process to consider and implement security at each stage of a product's development. This supports the motto of "Secure by Design, Secure by Default, Secure in Deployment and Communication" (also known as SD3+C). It has two goals in mind with this process:

- To reduce the number of security-related design and coding defects
- To reduce the severity of any remaining defects

In other words, it attempts to reduce vulnerabilities and reduce the impact of any vulnerabilities that remain. The overall result is reduced risk.

A proactive approach to threat modeling takes place during early stages of systems development, specifically during initial design and specifications establishment. This type of threat modeling is also known as a defensive approach. This method is based on predicting threats and designing in specific defenses during the coding and crafting process, rather than relying on postdeployment updates and patches. In most cases, integrated security solutions are more cost effective and more successful than those shoehorned in later. Unfortunately, not all threats can be predicted during the design phase, so reactive approach threat modeling is still needed to address unforeseen issues.

A reactive approach to threat modeling takes place after a product has been created and deployed. This deployment could be in a test or laboratory environment or to the general marketplace. This type of threat modeling is also known as the adversarial approach. This technique of threat modeling is the core concept behind ethical hacking, penetration testing, source code review, and fuzz testing. Although these processes are often useful in finding flaws and threats that need to be addressed, they unfortunately result in additional effort in coding to add in new countermeasures. Returning back to the design phase might produce better products in the long run, but starting over from scratch is massively expensive and causes significant time delays to product release. Thus, the shortcut is to craft updates or patches to be added to the product after deployment. This results in less effective security improvements (over-proactive threat modeling) at the cost of potentially reducing functionality and user-friendliness.

NOTE

Fuzz testing is a specialized dynamic testing technique that provides many different types of input to software to stress its limits and find previously undetected flaws. Fuzz testing software supplies invalid input to the software, either randomly generated or specially crafted to trigger known software vulnerabilities. The fuzz tester then monitors the performance of the application, watching for software crashes, buffer overflows, or other undesirable and/or unpredictable outcomes. See Chapter 15, "Security Assessment and Testing," for more on fuzz testing.

Identifying Threats

There's an almost infinite possibility of threats, so it's important to use a structured approach to accurately identify relevant threats. For example, some organizations use one or more of the following three approaches:

Focused on Assets This method uses asset valuation results and attempts to identify threats to the valuable assets. For example, a specific asset can be evaluated to determine if it is susceptible to an attack. If the asset hosts data, access controls can be evaluated to identify threats that can bypass authentication or authorization mechanisms.

Focused on Attackers Some organizations are able to identify potential attackers and can identify the threats they represent based on the attacker's goals. For example, a government is often able to identify potential attackers and recognize what the attackers want to achieve. They can then use this knowledge to identify and protect their relevant assets. A challenge with this approach is that new attackers can appear that weren't previously considered a threat.

Focused on Software If an organization develops software, it can consider potential threats against the software. Although organizations didn't commonly develop their own software years ago, it's common to do so today. Specifically, most organizations have a web presence, and many create their own web pages. Fancy web pages drive more traffic, but they also require more sophisticated programming and present additional threats.

If the threat is identified as an attacker (as opposed to a natural threat), threat modeling attempts to identify what the attacker may be trying to accomplish. Some attackers may want to disable a system, whereas other attackers may want to steal data. Once such threats are identified, they are categorized based on their goals or motivations. Additionally, it's common to pair threats with vulnerabilities to identify threats that can exploit vulnerabilities and represent significant risks to the organization. An ultimate goal of threat modeling is to prioritize the potential threats against an organization's valuable assets.

When attempting to inventory and categorize threats, it is often helpful to use a guide or reference. Microsoft developed a threat categorization scheme known as STRIDE. STRIDE is often used in relation to assessing threats against applications or operating systems. However, it can also be used in other contexts as well. STRIDE is an acronym standing for the following:

- Spoofing—An attack with the goal of gaining access to a target system through the use of a falsified identity. Spoofing can be used against IP addresses, MAC address, usernames, system names, wireless network SSIDs, email addresses, and many other types of logical identification. When an attacker spoofs their identity as a valid or authorized entity, they are often able to bypass filters and blockades against unauthorized access. Once a spoofing attack has successfully granted an attacker access to a target system, subsequent attacks of abuse, data theft, or privilege escalation can be initiated.
- Tampering—Any action resulting in the unauthorized changes or manipulation of data, whether in transit or in storage. Tampering is used to falsify communications or alter static information. Such attacks are a violation of integrity as well as availability.

- Repudiation—The ability for a user or attacker to deny having performed an action or activity. Often attackers engage in repudiation attacks in order to maintain plausible deniability so as not to be held accountable for their actions. Repudiation attacks can also result in innocent third parties being blamed for security violations.
- Information disclosure —The revelation or distribution of private, confidential, or controlled information to external or unauthorized entities. This could include customer identity information, financial information, or proprietary business operation details. Information disclosure can take advantage of system design and implementation mistakes, such as failing to remove debugging code, leaving sample applications and accounts, not sanitizing programming notes from client visible content (such as comments in HTML documents), using hidden form fields, or allowing overly detailed error messages to be shown to users.
- Denial of service (DoS)—An attack that attempts to prevent authorized use of a resource. This can be done through flaw exploitation, connection overloading, or traffic flooding. A DoS attack does not necessarily result in full interruption to a resource; it could instead reduce throughput or introduce latency in order to hamper productive use of a resource. Although most DoS attacks are temporary and last only as long as the attacker maintains the onslaught, there are some permanent DoS attacks. A permanent DoS attack might involve the destruction of a dataset, the replacement of software with malicious alternatives, or forcing a firmware flash operation that could be interrupted or that installs faulty firmware. Any of these DoS attacks would render a permanently damaged system that is not able to be restored to normal operation with a simple reboot or by waiting out the attackers. A full system repair and backup restoration would be required to recover from a permanent DoS attack.
- Elevation of privilege—An attack where a limited user account is transformed into an account with greater privileges, powers, and access. This might be accomplished through theft or exploitation of the credentials of a higher-level account, such as that of an administrator or root. It also might be accomplished through a system or application exploit that temporarily or permanently grants additional powers to an otherwise limited account.

Although STRIDE is typically used to focus on application threats, it is applicable to other situations, such as network threats and host threats. Other attacks may be more specific to network and host concerns, such as sniffing and hijacking for networks and malware and arbitrary code execution for hosts, but the six threat concepts of STRIDE are fairly broadly applicable.

Generally, the purpose of STRIDE and other tools in threat modeling is to consider the range of compromise concerns and to focus on the goal or end results of an attack. Attempting to identify each and every specific attack method and technique is an impossible task—new attacks are being developed constantly. Although the goals or purposes of attacks can be loosely categorized and grouped, they remain relatively constant over time.

Be Alert for Individual Threats

Competition is often a key part of business growth, but overly adversarial competition can increase the threat level from individuals. In addition to criminal hackers and disgruntled employees, adversaries, contractors, employees, and even trusted partners can be a threat to an organization if relationships go sour.

- Never assume that a consultant or contractor has the same loyalty to your organization as a long-term employee. Contractors and consultants are effectively mercenaries who will work for the highest bidder. Don't take employee loyalty for granted either. Employees who are frustrated with their working environment or feel they've been treated unfairly may attempt to retaliate. An employee experiencing financial hardship may consider unethical and illegal activities that pose a threat to your business for their own gain.
- A trusted partner is only a trusted partner as long as it is in your mutual self-interest to be friendly and cooperative toward each other. Eventually a partnership might sour or become adversarial; then, your former partner might take actions that pose a threat to your business.

Potential threats to your business are broad and varied. A company faces threats from nature, technology, and people. Most businesses focus on natural disasters and IT attacks in preparing for threats, but it's also important to consider threat potential from individuals. Always consider the best and worst possible outcomes of your organization's activities, decisions, interactions. Identifying threats is the first step toward designing defenses to help reduce or eliminate downtime, compromise, and loss.

Determining and Diagramming Potential Attacks

Once an understanding has been gained in regard to the threats facing your development project or deployed infrastructure, the next step in threat modeling is to determine the potential attack concepts that could be realized. This is often accomplished through the creation of a diagram of the elements involved in a transaction along with indications of data flow and privilege boundaries (Figure 1.7).

Such data flow diagrams are useful in gaining a better understanding of the relationships of resources and movement of data through a visual representation. This process of diagramming is also known as crafting an architecture diagram. The creation of the diagram helps to detail the functions and purpose of each element of a business task, development process, or work activity. It is important to include users, processors, applications, datastores, and all other essential elements needed to perform the specific task or operation. This is a high-level overview and not a detailed evaluation of the coding logic. However, for more complex systems, multiple diagrams may need to be created at various focus points and at varying levels of detail magnification.

FIGURE 1.7 An example of diagramming to reveal threat concerns

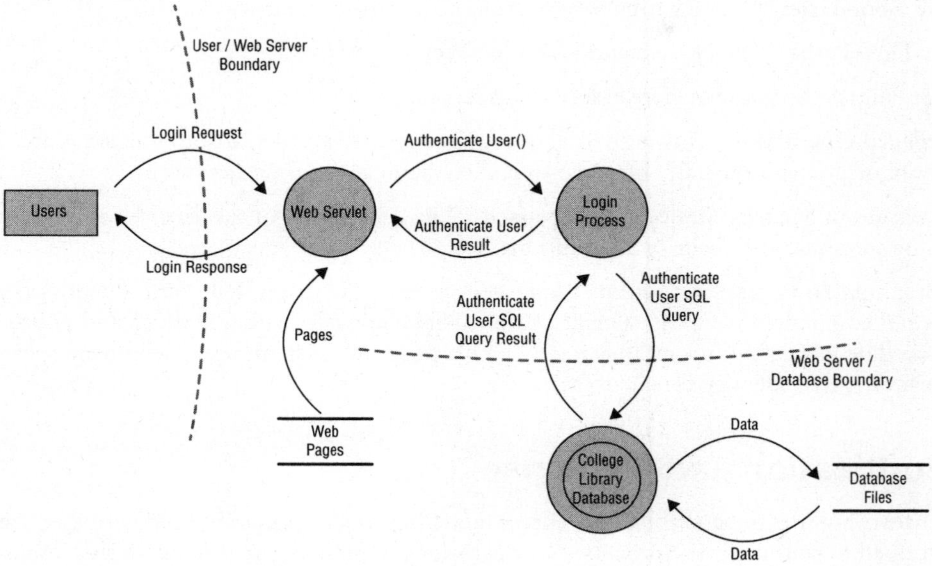

Once a diagram has been crafted, identify all of the technologies involved. This would include operating systems, applications (network service and client based), and protocols. Be specific as to the version numbers and update/patch level in use.

Next, identify attacks that could be targeted at each element of the diagram. Keep in mind that all forms of attacks should be considered, including logical/technical, physical, and social. For example, be sure to include spoofing, tampering, and social engineering. This process will quickly lead you into the next phase of threat modeling: reduction analysis.

Performing Reduction Analysis

The next step in threat modeling is to perform reduction analysis. Reduction analysis is also known as decomposing the application, system, or environment. The purpose of this task is to gain a greater understanding of the logic of the product as well as its interactions with external elements. Whether an application, a system, or an entire environment, it needs to be divided into smaller containers or compartments. Those might be subroutines, modules, or objects if you're focusing on software, computers, or operating systems; they might be protocols if you're focusing on systems or networks; or they might be departments, tasks, and networks if you're focusing on an entire business infrastructure. Each identified subelement should be evaluated in order to understand inputs, processing, security, data management, storage, and outputs.

In the decomposition process, you must identify five key concepts:

Trust Boundaries Any location where the level of trust or security changes

Data Flow Paths The movement of data between locations

Input Points Locations where external input is received

Privileged Operations Any activity that requires greater privileges than of a standard user account or process, typically required to make system changes or alter security

Details about Security Stance and Approach The declaration of the security policy, security foundations, and security assumptions

Breaking down a system into its constituent parts makes it much easier to identity the essential components of each element as well as take notice of vulnerabilities and points of attack. The more you understand exactly how a program, system, or environment operates, the easier it is to identity threats to it.

Prioritization and Response

As threats are identified through the threat modeling procedure, additional activities are prescribed to round out the process. Next is to fully document the threats. In this documentation, you should define the means, target, and consequences of a threat. Consider including the techniques required to implement an exploitation as well as list potential countermeasures and safeguards.

After documentation, rank or rate the threats. This can be accomplished using a wide range of techniques, such as Probability × Damage Potential ranking, high/medium/low rating, or the DREAD system.

The ranking technique of Probability × Damage Potential produces a risk severity number on a scale of 1 to 100, with 100 the most severe risk possible. Each of the two initial values can be assigned numbers between 1 and 10, with 1 being lowest and 10 being highest. These rankings can be somewhat arbitrary and subjective, but since the same person or team will be assigning the numbers for their own organization, it should still result in assessment values that are accurate on a relative basis.

The high/medium/low rating process is even simpler. Each threat is assigned one of these three priority labels. Those given the high-priority label need to be addressed immediately. Those given the medium-priority label should be addressed eventually, but they don't require immediate action. Those given the low-priority level might be addressed, but they could be deemed optional if they require too much effort or expense in comparison to the project as a whole.

The DREAD rating system is designed to provide a flexible rating solution that is based on the answers to five main questions about each threat:

- Damage potential—How severe is the damage likely to be if the threat is realized?
- Reproducibility—How complicated is it for attackers to reproduce the exploit?
- Exploitability—How hard is it to perform the attack?

- Affected users—How many users are likely to be affected by the attack (as a percentage)?
- Discoverability—How hard is it for an attacker to discover the weakness?

By asking these and potentially additional customized questions, along with assigning H/M/L or 3/2/1 values to the answers, you can establish a detailed threat prioritization.

Once threat priorities are set, responses to those threats need to be determined. Technologies and processes to remediate threats should be considered and weighted according to their cost and effectiveness. Response options should include making adjustments to software architecture, altering operations and processes, as well as implementing defensive and detective components.

Integrate Security Risk Considerations into Acquisition Strategy and Practice

Integrating cyber security risk management with acquisition strategies and practices is a means to ensure a more robust and successful security strategy in organizations of all sizes. When purchases are made without security considerations, the risks inherent in those products remain throughout their deployment lifespan. Minimizing inherent threats in acquired elements will reduce security management costs and likely reduce security violations.

Selecting hardware, software, and services that have resilient integrated security are often more expensive products and solutions than those that fail to have a security foundation. However, this additional initial expense is often a much more cost-effective expenditure than addressing security needs over the life of a poorly designed product. Thus, when considering the cost of acquisition, it is important to consider the total cost of ownership over the life of the product's deployment rather than just initial purchase and implementation.

Acquisition does not relate exclusively to hardware and software. Outsourcing, contracting with suppliers, and engaging consultants are also elements of acquisition. Integrating security assessments when working with external entities is just as important as ensuring a product was designed with security in mind.

In many cases, ongoing security monitoring, management, and assessment may be required. This could be an industry best practice or a regulation. Such assessment and monitoring might be performed by the organization internally or may require the use of external auditors. When engaging third-party assessment and monitoring services, keep in mind that the external entity needs to show security-mindedness in their business operations. If an external organization is unable to manage their own internal operations on a secure basis, how can they provide reliable security management functions for yours?

When evaluating a third party for your security integration, consider the following processes:

On-Site Assessment Visit the site of the organization to interview personnel and observe their operating habits.

Document Exchange and Review Investigate the means by which datasets and documentation are exchanged as well as the formal processes by which they perform assessments and reviews.

Process/Policy Review Request copies of their security policies, processes/procedures, and documentation of incidents and responses for review.

For all acquisitions, establish minimum security requirements. These should be modeled from your existing security policy. The security requirements for new hardware, software, or services should always meet or exceed the security of your existing infrastructure. When working with an external service, be sure to review any SLA (service-level agreements) to ensure security is a prescribed component of the contracted services. This could include customization of service-level requirements for your specific needs.

Here are some excellent resources related to security integrated with acquisition:

- Improving Cybersecurity and Resilience through Acquisition. Final Report of the Department of Defense and General Services Administration, published November 2013 (`www.gsa.gov/portal/getMediaData?mediaId=185371`)
- NIST Special Publication 800-64 Revision 2: Security Considerations in the System Development Life Cycle (`http://csrc.nist.gov/publications/nistpubs/800-64-Rev2/SP800-64-Revision2.pdf`)

Summary

Security governance, management concepts, and principles are inherent elements in a security policy and in solution deployment. They define the basic parameters needed for a secure environment. They also define the goals and objectives that both policy designers and system implementers must achieve in order to create a secure solution.

The primary goals and objectives of security are contained within the CIA Triad: confidentiality, integrity, and availability. These three principles are considered the most important within the realm of security. Their importance to an organization depends on the organization's security goals and requirements and on how much of a threat to security exists in its environment.

The first principle from the CIA Triad is confidentiality, the principle that objects are not disclosed to unauthorized subjects. Security mechanisms that offer confidentiality offer a high level of assurance that data, objects, or resources are not exposed to unauthorized subjects. If a threat exists against confidentiality, there is the possibility that unauthorized disclosure could take place.

The second principle from the CIA Triad is integrity, the principle that objects retain their veracity and are intentionally modified by only authorized subjects. Security mechanisms that offer integrity offer a high level of assurance that the data, objects, and resources are unaltered from their original protected state. This includes alterations occurring while the object is in storage, in transit, or in process. Maintaining integrity means the object itself is not altered and the operating system and programming entities that manage and manipulate the object are not compromised.

The third principle from the CIA Triad is availability, the principle that authorized subjects are granted timely and uninterrupted access to objects. Security mechanisms that offer availability offer a high level of assurance that the data, objects, and resources are accessible to authorized subjects. Availability includes efficient uninterrupted access to objects and prevention of denial-of-service attacks. It also implies that the supporting infrastructure is functional and allows authorized users to gain authorized access.

Other security-related concepts and principles that should be considered and addressed when designing a security policy and deploying a security solution are privacy, identification, authentication, authorization, accountability, nonrepudiation, and auditing.

Other aspects of security solution concepts and principles are the elements of protection mechanisms: layering, abstraction, data hiding, and encryption. These are common characteristics of security controls, and although not all security controls must have them, many controls use these mechanisms to protect confidentiality, integrity, and availability.

Security roles determine who is responsible for the security of an organization's assets. Those assigned the senior management role are ultimately responsible and liable for any asset loss, and they are the ones who define security policy. Security professionals are responsible for implementing security policy, and users are responsible for complying with the security policy. The person assigned the data owner role is responsible for classifying information, and a data custodian is responsible for maintaining the secure environment and backing up data. An auditor is responsible for making sure a secure environment is properly protecting assets.

A formalized security policy structure consists of policies, standards, baselines, guidelines, and procedures. These individual documents are essential elements to the design and implementation of security in any environment.

The control or management of change is an important aspect of security management practices. When a secure environment is changed, loopholes, overlaps, missing objects, and oversights can lead to new vulnerabilities. You can, however, maintain security by systematically managing change. This typically involves extensive logging, auditing, and monitoring of activities related to security controls and security mechanisms. The resulting data is then used to identify agents of change, whether objects, subjects, programs, communication pathways, or even the network itself.

Data classification is the primary means by which data is protected based on its secrecy, sensitivity, or confidentiality. Because some data items need more security than others, it is inefficient to treat all data the same when designing and implementing a security system. If everything is secured at a low security level, sensitive data is easily accessible, but securing everything at a high security level is too expensive and restricts access to unclassified, noncritical data. Data classification is used to determine how much effort, money, and resources are allocated to protect the data and control access to it.

An important aspect of security management planning is the proper implementation of a security policy. To be effective, the approach to security management must be a top-down approach. The responsibility of initiating and defining a security policy lies with upper or senior management. Security policies provide direction for the lower levels of the organization's hierarchy. Middle management is responsible for fleshing out the security policy into standards, baselines, guidelines, and procedures. It is the responsibility of the operational managers or security professionals to implement the configurations prescribed in the security management documentation. Finally, the end users' responsibility is to comply with all security policies of the organization.

Security management planning includes defining security roles, developing security policies, performing risk analysis, and requiring security education for employees. These responsibilities are guided by the developments of management plans. The security management team should develop strategic, tactical, and operational plans.

Threat modeling is the security process where potential threats are identified, categorized, and analyzed. Threat modeling can be performed as a proactive measure during design and development or as a reactive measure once a product has been deployed. In either case, the process identifies the potential harm, the probability of occurrence, the priority of concern, and the means to eradicate or reduce the threat.

Integrating cyber security risk management with acquisition strategies and practices is a means to ensure a more robust and successful security strategy in organizations of all sizes. When purchases are made without security considerations, the risks inherent in those products remain throughout their deployment lifespan.

Exam Essentials

Understand the CIA Triad elements of confidentiality, integrity, and availability. Confidentiality is the principle that objects are not disclosed to unauthorized subjects. Integrity is the principle that objects retain their veracity and are intentionally modified by only authorized subjects. Availability is the principle that authorized subjects are granted timely and uninterrupted access to objects. Know why these are important, the mechanisms that support them, the attacks that focus on each, and the effective countermeasures.

Be able to explain how identification works. Identification is the process by which a subject professes an identity and accountability is initiated. A subject must provide an identity to a system to start the process of authentication, authorization, and accountability.

Understand the process of authentication. Authentication is the process of verifying or testing that a claimed identity is valid. Authentication requires information from the subject that must exactly correspond to the identity indicated.

Know how authorization fits into a security plan. Once a subject is authenticated, its access must be authorized. The process of authorization ensures that the requested activity or object access is possible given the rights and privileges assigned to the authenticated identity.

Understand security governance. Security governance is the collection of practices related to supporting, defining, and directing the security efforts of an organization.

Be able to explain the auditing process. Auditing, or monitoring, is the programmatic means by which subjects are held accountable for their actions while authenticated on a system. Auditing is also the process by which unauthorized or abnormal activities are detected on a system. Auditing is needed to detect malicious actions by subjects, attempted intrusions, and system failures and to reconstruct events, provide evidence for prosecution, and produce problem reports and analysis.

Understand the importance of accountability. An organization's security policy can be properly enforced only if accountability is maintained. In other words, security can be maintained only if subjects are held accountable for their actions. Effective accountability relies on the capability to prove a subject's identity and track their activities.

Be able to explain nonrepudiation. Nonrepudiation ensures that the subject of an activity or event cannot deny that the event occurred. It prevents a subject from claiming not to have sent a message, not to have performed an action, or not to have been the cause of an event.

Understand security management planning. Security management is based on three types of plans: strategic, tactical, and operational. A strategic plan is a long-term plan that is fairly stable. It defines the organization's goals, mission, and objectives. The tactical plan is a midterm plan developed to provide more details on accomplishing the goals set forth in the strategic plan. Operational plans are short-term and highly detailed plans based on the strategic and tactical plans.

Know the elements of a formalized security policy structure. To create a comprehensive security plan, you need the following items in place: security policy, standards, baselines, guidelines, and procedures. Such documentation clearly states security requirements and creates due diligence on the part of the responsible parties.

Understand key security roles. The primary security roles are senior manager, organizational owner, upper management, security professional, user, data owner, data custodian, and auditor. By creating a security role hierarchy, you limit risk overall.

Know how to implement security awareness training. Before actual training can take place, awareness of security as a recognized entity must be created for users. Once this is accomplished, training, or teaching employees to perform their work tasks and to comply with the security policy, can begin. All new employees require some level of training so they will be able to comply with all standards, guidelines, and procedures mandated by the security policy. Education is a more detailed endeavor in which students/users learn much more than they actually need to know to perform their work tasks. Education is most often associated with users pursuing certification or seeking job promotion.

Know how layering simplifies security. Layering is the use of multiple controls in series. Using a multilayered solution allows for numerous controls to guard against threats.

Be able to explain the concept of abstraction. Abstraction is used to collect similar elements into groups, classes, or roles that are assigned security controls, restrictions, or permissions as a collective. It adds efficiency to carrying out a security plan.

Understand data hiding. Data hiding is exactly what it sounds like: preventing data from being discovered or accessed by a subject. It is often a key element in security controls as well as in programming.

Understand the need for encryption. Encryption is the art and science of hiding the meaning or intent of a communication from unintended recipients. It can take many forms and be applied to every type of electronic communication, including text, audio, and video files, as well as programs themselves. Encryption is an important element in security controls, especially in regard to the transmission of data between systems.

Be able to explain the concepts of change control and change management. Change in a secure environment can introduce loopholes, overlaps, missing objects, and oversights that can lead to new vulnerabilities. The only way to maintain security in the face of change is to systematically manage change.

Know why and how data is classified. Data is classified to simplify the process of assigning security controls to groups of objects rather than to individual objects. The two common classification schemes are government/military and commercial business/private sector. Know the five levels of government/military classification and the four levels of commercial business/private sector classification.

Understand the importance of declassification. Declassification is required once an asset no longer warrants the protection of its currently assigned classification or sensitivity level.

Know the basics of COBIT. Control Objectives for Information and Related Technology (COBIT) is a security concept infrastructure used to organize the complex security solutions of companies.

Know the basics of threat modeling. Threat modeling is the security process where potential threats are identified, categorized, and analyzed. Threat modeling can be performed as a proactive measure during design and development or as a reactive measure once a product has been deployed. Key concepts include assets/attackers/software, STRIDE, diagramming, reduction/decomposing, and DREAD.

Understand the need for security-minded acquisitions. Integrating cyber security risk management with acquisition strategies and practices is a means to ensure a more robust and successful security strategy in organizations of all sizes. When purchases are made without security considerations, the risks inherent in those products remain throughout their deployment lifespan.

Written Lab

1. Discuss and describe the CIA Triad.
2. What are the requirements to hold a person accountable for the actions of their user account?
3. Describe the benefits of change control management.
4. What are the seven major steps or phases in the implementation of a classification scheme?
5. Name the six primary security roles as defined by $(ISC)^2$ for CISSP.
6. What are the four components of a complete organizational security policy and their basic purpose?

Review Questions

1. Which of the following contains the primary goals and objectives of security?
   - **A.** A network's border perimeter
   - **B.** The CIA Triad
   - **C.** A stand-alone system
   - **D.** The Internet

2. Vulnerabilities and risks are evaluated based on their threats against which of the following?
   - **A.** One or more of the CIA Triad principles
   - **B.** Data usefulness
   - **C.** Due care
   - **D.** Extent of liability

3. Which of the following is a principle of the CIA Triad that means authorized subjects are granted timely and uninterrupted access to objects?
   - **A.** Identification
   - **B.** Availability
   - **C.** Encryption
   - **D.** Layering

4. Which of the following is *not* considered a violation of confidentiality?
   - **A.** Stealing passwords
   - **B.** Eavesdropping
   - **C.** Hardware destruction
   - **D.** Social engineering

5. Which of the following is not true?
   - **A.** Violations of confidentiality include human error.
   - **B.** Violations of confidentiality include management oversight.
   - **C.** Violations of confidentiality are limited to direct intentional attacks.
   - **D.** Violations of confidentiality can occur when a transmission is not properly encrypted.

6. STRIDE is often used in relation to assessing threats against applications or operating systems. Which of the following is not an element of STRIDE?
   - **A.** Spoofing
   - **B.** Elevation of privilege

C. Repudiation
D. Disclosure

7. If a security mechanism offers availability, then it offers a high level of assurance that authorized subjects can ______________________ the data, objects, and resources.
   A. Control
   B. Audit
   C. Access
   D. Repudiate

8. ___________ refers to keeping information confidential that is personally identifiable or which might cause harm, embarrassment, or disgrace to someone if revealed.
   A. Seclusion
   B. Concealment
   C. Privacy
   D. Criticality

9. All but which of the following items requires awareness for all individuals affected?
   A. Restricting personal email
   B. Recording phone conversations
   C. Gathering information about surfing habits
   D. The backup mechanism used to retain email messages

10. What element of data categorization management can override all other forms of access control?
    A. Classification
    B. Physical access
    C. Custodian responsibilities
    D. Taking ownership

11. What ensures that the subject of an activity or event cannot deny that the event occurred?
    A. CIA Triad
    B. Abstraction
    C. Nonrepudiation
    D. Hash totals

12. Which of the following is the most important and distinctive concept in relation to layered security?
    A. Multiple
    B. Series

C. Parallel

D. Filter

13. Which of the following is *not* considered an example of data hiding?

A. Preventing an authorized reader of an object from deleting that object

B. Keeping a database from being accessed by unauthorized visitors

C. Restricting a subject at a lower classification level from accessing data at a higher classification level

D. Preventing an application from accessing hardware directly

14. What is the primary goal of change management?

A. Maintaining documentation

B. Keeping users informed of changes

C. Allowing rollback of failed changes

D. Preventing security compromises

15. What is the primary objective of data classification schemes?

A. To control access to objects for authorized subjects

B. To formalize and stratify the process of securing data based on assigned labels of importance and sensitivity

C. To establish a transaction trail for auditing accountability

D. To manipulate access controls to provide for the most efficient means to grant or restrict functionality

16. Which of the following is typically *not* a characteristic considered when classifying data?

A. Value

B. Size of object

C. Useful lifetime

D. National security implications

17. What are the two common data classification schemes?

A. Military and private sector

B. Personal and government

C. Private sector and unrestricted sector

D. Classified and unclassified

18. Which of the following is the lowest military data classification for classified data?

A. Sensitive

B. Secret

C. Proprietary

D. Private

19. Which commercial business/private sector data classification is used to control information about individuals within an organization?
    A. Confidential
    B. Private
    C. Sensitive
    D. Proprietary

20. Data classifications are used to focus security controls over all but which of the following?
    A. Storage
    B. Processing
    C. Layering
    D. Transfer

Chapter

2

Personnel Security and Risk Management Concepts

THE CISSP EXAM TOPICS COVERED IN THIS CHAPTER INCLUDE:

✓ **Security and Risk Management (e.g., Security, Risk, Compliance, Law, Regulations, Business Continuity)**

- H. Contribute to personnel security policies
  - H.1 Employment candidate screening (e.g., reference checks, education verification)
  - H.2 Employment agreements and policies
  - H.3 Employment termination processes
  - H.4 Vendor, consultant, and contractor controls
  - H.5 Compliance
  - H.6 Privacy
- I. Understand and apply risk management concepts
  - I.1 Identify threats and vulnerabilities
  - I.2 Risk assessment/analysis (qualitative, quantitative, hybrid)
  - I.3 Risk assignment/acceptance (e.g., system authorization)
  - I.4 Countermeasure selection
  - I.5 Implementation
  - I.6 Types of controls (preventive, detective, corrective, etc.)
  - I.7 Control assessment
  - I.8 Monitoring and measurement
  - I.9 Asset valuation

        - I.10 Reporting
        - I.11 Continuous improvement
        - I.12 Risk frameworks
    - L. Establish and manage information security education, training, and awareness
        - L.1 Appropriate levels of awareness, training, and education required within organization
        - L.2 Periodic reviews for content relevancy

✓ **Security Assessment and Testing (Designing, Performing, and Analyzing Security Testing)**

- C.5 Training and awareness

The Security and Risk Management domain of the Common Body of Knowledge (CBK) for the CISSP certification exam deals with many of the foundational elements of security solutions. These include elements essential to the design, implementation, and administration of security mechanisms.

Additional elements of this domain are discussed in various chapters: Chapter 1, "Security Governance Through Principles and Policies"; Chapter 3, "Business Continuity Planning"; and Chapter 4, "Laws, Regulations, and Compliance". Please be sure to review all of these chapters to have a complete perspective on the topics of this domain.

Because of the complexity and importance of hardware and software controls, security management for employees is often overlooked in overall security planning. This chapter explores the human side of security, from establishing secure hiring practices and job descriptions to developing an employee infrastructure. Additionally, we look at how employee training, management, and termination practices are considered an integral part of creating a secure environment. Finally, we examine how to assess and manage security risks.

Contribute to Personnel Security Policies

Humans are the weakest element in any security solution. No matter what physical or logical controls are deployed, humans can discover ways to avoid them, circumvent or subvert them, or disable them. Thus, it is important to take into account the humanity of your users when designing and deploying security solutions for your environment. To understand and apply security governance, you must address the weakest link in your security chain—namely, people.

Issues, problems, and compromises related to humans occur at all stages of a security solution development. This is because humans are involved throughout the development, deployment, and ongoing administration of any solution. Therefore, you must evaluate the effect users, designers, programmers, developers, managers, and implementers have on the process.

Hiring new staff typically involves several distinct steps: creating a job description, setting a classification for the job, screening employment candidates, and hiring and training the one best suited for the job. Without a job description, there is no consensus on what type of individual should be hired. Thus, crafting job descriptions is the first step in defining security needs related to personnel and being able to seek out new hires. Personnel should be added to an organization because there is a need for their specific skills and experience. Any job description for any position within an organization should address relevant security issues. You must consider items such as whether the position requires the handling of sensitive material or access to classified information. In effect, the job description defines the roles to which an employee needs to be assigned to perform their work tasks. The job description should define the type and extent of access the position requires on the secured network. Once these issues have been resolved, assigning a security classification to the job description is fairly standard.

TIP

The Importance of Job Descriptions

Job descriptions are important to the design and support of a security solution. However, many organizations either have overlooked this or have allowed job descriptions to become stale and out-of-sync with reality. Try to track down your job description. Do you even have one? If so, when was it last updated? Does it accurately reflect your job? Does it describe the type of security access you need to perform the prescribed job responsibilities? Some organizations must craft job descriptions to be in compliance with SOC-2, while others following ISO 27001 require annual reviews of job descriptions.

Important elements in constructing job descriptions that are in line with organizational processes include separation of duties, job responsibilities, and job rotation.

Separation of Duties Separation of duties is the security concept in which critical, significant, and sensitive work tasks are divided among several individual administrators or high-level operators (Figure 2.1). This prevents any one person from having the ability to undermine or subvert vital security mechanisms. Think of separation of duties as the application of the principle of least privilege to administrators. Separation of duties is also a protection against *collusion*, which is the occurrence of negative activity undertaken by two or more people, often for the purposes of fraud, theft, or espionage.

FIGURE 2.1 An example of separation of duties related to five admin tasks and seven administrators

Admin Tasks	Database Management	Firewall Management	User Account Management	File Management	Network Management
Assigned to Admins	Admin 1	Admin 2	Admin 3 & 4	Admin 5	Admin 6 & 7

Job Responsibilities Job responsibilities are the specific work tasks an employee is required to perform on a regular basis. Depending on their responsibilities, employees require access to various objects, resources, and services. On a secured network, users must be granted access privileges for those elements related to their work tasks. To maintain the greatest security, access should be assigned according to the principle of least privilege. The principle of least privilege states that in a secured environment, users should be granted the minimum amount of access necessary for them to complete their required work tasks or job responsibilities. True application of this principle requires low-level granular access control over all resources and functions.

Job Rotation Job rotation, or rotating employees among multiple job positions, is simply a means by which an organization improves its overall security (Figure 2.2). Job rotation serves two functions. First, it provides a type of knowledge redundancy. When multiple employees are all capable of performing the work tasks required by several job positions, the organization is less likely to experience serious downtime or loss in productivity if an illness or other incident keeps one or more employees out of work for an extended period of time.

FIGURE 2.2 An example of job rotation among management positions

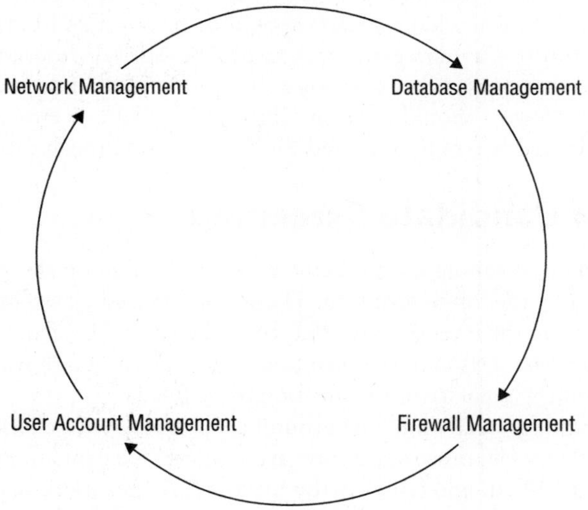

Second, moving personnel around reduces the risk of fraud, data modification, theft, sabotage, and misuse of information. The longer a person works in a specific position, the more likely they are to be assigned additional work tasks and thus expand their privileges and access. As a person becomes increasingly familiar with their work tasks, they may abuse their privileges for personal gain or malice. If misuse or abuse is committed by one employee, it will be easier to detect by another employee who knows the job position and work responsibilities. Therefore, job rotation also provides a form of peer auditing and protects against collusion.

Cross-training

Cross-training is often discussed as an alternative to job rotation. In both cases, workers learn the responsibilities and tasks of multiple job positions. However, in cross-training the workers are just prepared to perform the other job positions; they are not rotated through them on a regular basis. Cross-training enables existing personnel to fill the work gap when the proper employee is unavailable as a type of emergency response procedure.

When several people work together to perpetrate a crime, it's called *collusion*. Employing the principles of separation of duties, restricted job responsibilities, and job rotation reduces the likelihood that a co-worker will be willing to collaborate on an illegal or abusive scheme because of the higher risk of detection. Collusion and other privilege abuses can be reduced through strict monitoring of special privileges, such as those of an administrator, backup operator, user manager, and others.

Job descriptions are not used exclusively for the hiring process; they should be maintained throughout the life of the organization. Only through detailed job descriptions can a comparison be made between what a person should be responsible for and what they actually are responsible for. It is a managerial task to ensure that job descriptions overlap as little as possible and that one worker's responsibilities do not drift or encroach on those of another. Likewise, managers should audit privilege assignments to ensure that workers do not obtain access that is not strictly required for them to accomplish their work tasks.

Employment Candidate Screening

Employment candidate screening for a specific position is based on the sensitivity and classification defined by the job description. The sensitivity and classification of a specific position is dependent on the level of harm that could be caused by accidental or intentional violations of security by a person in the position. Thus, the thoroughness of the screening process should reflect the security of the position to be filled.

Employment candidate screening, background checks, reference checks, education verification, and security clearance validation are essential elements in proving that a candidate is adequate, qualified, and trustworthy for a secured position. Background checks include obtaining a candidate's work and educational history; reference checks; education verification; interviewing colleagues, neighbors, and friends; checking police and government records for arrests or illegal activities; verifying identity through fingerprints, driver's license, and birth certificate; and holding a personal interview. This process could also include a polygraph test, drug testing, and personality testing/evaluation.

Performing online background checks and reviewing the social networking accounts of applicants has become standard practice for many organizations. If a potential employee has posted inappropriate materials to their photo sharing site, social networking biographies, or public instant messaging services, then they are not as attractive a candidate as those who did not. Our actions in the public eye become permanent when they are recorded in text, photo, or video and then posted online. A general picture of a person's attitude, intelligence, loyalty, common sense, diligence, honesty, respect, consistency, and adherence to social norms and/or corporate culture can be gleaned quickly by viewing a person's online identity.

Employment Agreements and Policies

When a new employee is hired, they should sign an employment agreement. Such a document outlines the rules and restrictions of the organization, the security policy, the acceptable use and activities policies, details of the job description, violations and consequences, and the length of time the position is to be filled by the employee. These items might be separate documents. In such a case, the employment agreement is used to verify that the employment candidate has read and understood the associated documentation for their prospective job position.

In addition to employment agreements, there may be other security-related documentation that must be addressed. One common document is a *nondisclosure agreement (NDA)*. An NDA is used to protect the confidential information within an organization from being disclosed by a former employee. When a person signs an NDA, they agree not to disclose any information that is defined as confidential to anyone outside the organization. Violations of an NDA are often met with strict penalties.

Real World Scenario

NCA: The NDA's Evil Twin

The NDA has a common companion contract known as the *noncompete agreement (NCA)*. The noncompete agreement attempts to prevent an employee with special knowledge of secrets from one organization from working in a competing organization in order to prevent that second organization from benefiting from the worker's special knowledge of secrets. NCAs are also used to prevent workers from jumping from one company to another competing company just because of salary increases or other incentives. Often NCAs have a time limit, such as six months, one year, or even three years. The goal is to allow the original company to maintain its competitive edge by keeping its human resources working for its benefit rather than against it.

Many companies require new hires to sign NCAs. However, fully enforcing an NCA in court is often a difficult battle. The court recognizes the need for a worker to be able to work using the skills and knowledge they have in order to provide for themselves and their families. If the NCA would prevent a person from earning a reasonable income, the courts often invalidate the NCA or prevent its consequences from being realized.

Even if an NCA is not always enforceable in court, however, that does not mean it doesn't have benefits to the original company, such as the following:

- The threat of a lawsuit because of NCA violations is often sufficient incentive to prevent a worker from violating the terms of secrecy when they seek employment with a new company.
- If a worker does violate the terms of the NCA, then even without specifically defined consequences being levied by court restrictions, the time and effort, not to mention the cost, of battling the issue in court is a deterrent.

Did you sign an NCA when you were hired? If so, do you know the terms and the potential consequences if you break that NCA?

Throughout the employment lifetime of personnel, managers should regularly audit the job descriptions, work tasks, privileges, and responsibilities for every staff member. It is common for work tasks and privileges to drift over time. This can cause some tasks to be overlooked and others to be performed multiple times. Drifting can also result in security violations. Regularly reviewing the boundaries of each job description in relation to what is actually occurring aids in keeping security violations to a minimum.

A key part of this review process is enforcing mandatory vacations. In many secured environments, mandatory vacations of one to two weeks are used to audit and verify the work tasks and privileges of employees. The vacation removes the employee from the work environment and places a different worker in their position, which makes it easier to detect abuse, fraud, or negligence on the part of the original employee.

Employment Termination Processes

When an employee must be terminated, numerous issues must be addressed. A strong relationship between the security department and HR is essential to maintain control and minimize risks during termination. An employee termination process or procedure policy is essential to maintaining a secure environment when a disgruntled employee must be removed from the organization. The reactions of terminated employees can range from calm, understanding acceptance to violent, destructive rage. A sensible procedure for handling terminations must be designed and implemented to reduce incidents.

The termination of an employee should be handled in a private and respectful manner. However, this does not mean that precautions should not be taken. Terminations should take place with at least one witness, preferably a higher-level manager and/or a security guard. Once the employee has been informed of their release, they should be escorted off the premises and not allowed to return to their work area without an escort for any reason. Before the employee is released, all organization-specific identification, access, or security badges as well as cards, keys, and access tokens should be collected (Figure 2.3). Generally, the best time to terminate an employee is at the end of their shift midweek. A early to mid-week termination provides the ex-employee with time to file for unemployment and/or start looking for new employment before the weekend. Also, end-of-shift terminations allow the worker to leave with other employees in a more natural departure, thus reducing stress.

FIGURE 2.3 Ex-employees must return all company property.

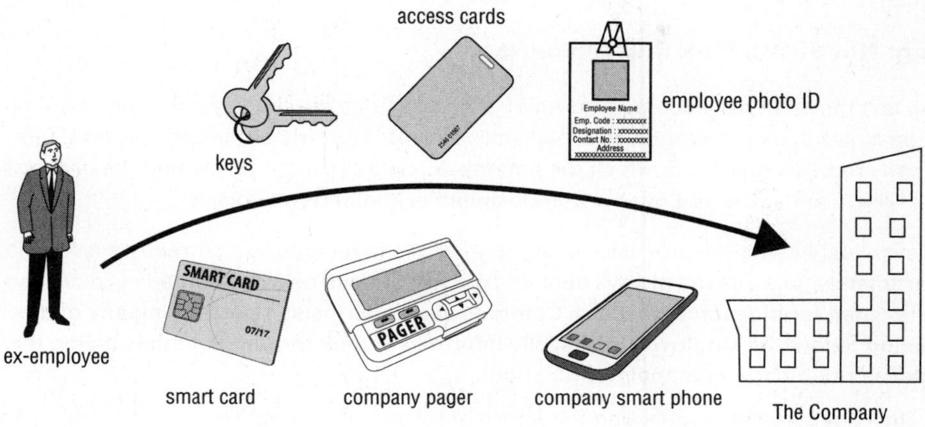

When possible, an exit interview should be performed. However, this typically depends on the mental state of the employee upon release and numerous other factors. If an exit interview is unfeasible immediately upon termination, it should be conducted as soon as possible. The primary purpose of the exit interview is to review the liabilities and restrictions placed on the former employee based on the employment agreement, nondisclosure agreement, and any other security-related documentation.

The following list includes some other issues that should be handled as soon as possible:

- Make sure the employee returns any organizational equipment or supplies from their vehicle or home.
- Remove or disable the employee's network user account.
- Notify human resources to issue a final paycheck, pay any unused vacation time, and terminate benefit coverage.
- Arrange for a member of the security department to accompany the released employee while they gather their personal belongings from the work area.
- Inform all security personnel and anyone else who watches or monitors any entrance point to ensure that the ex-employee does not attempt to reenter the building without an escort.

In most cases, you should disable or remove an employee's system access at the same time or just before they are notified of being terminated. This is especially true if that employee is capable of accessing confidential data or has the expertise or access to alter or damage data or services. Failing to restrict released employees' activities can leave your organization open to a wide range of vulnerabilities, including theft and destruction of both physical property and logical data.

Real World Scenario

Firing: Not Just a Pink Slip Anymore

Firing an employee has become a complex process. Gone are the days of firing merely by placing a pink slip in an employee's mail slot. In most IT-centric organizations, termination can create a situation in which the employee could cause harm, putting the organization at risk. That's why you need a well-designed exit interview process.

However, just having the process isn't enough. It has to be followed correctly every time. Unfortunately, this doesn't always happen. You might have heard of some fiasco caused by a botched termination procedure. Common examples include performing any of the following before the employee is officially informed of their termination (thus giving the employee prior warning of their termination):

- The IT department requesting the return of a notebook computer
- Disabling a network account
- Blocking a person's PIN or smartcard for building entrance
- Revoking a parking pass
- Distributing a company reorganization chart
- Positioning a new employee in the cubicle
- Allowing layoff information to be leaked to the media

It should go without saying that in order for the exit interview and safe termination processes to function properly, they must be implemented in the correct order and at the correct time (that is, at the start of the exit interview), as in the following example:

- Inform the person that they are relieved of their job.
- Request the return of all access badges, keys, and company equipment.
- Disable the person's electronic access to all aspects of the organization.
- Remind the person about the NDA obligations.
- Escort the person off the premises.

Vendor, Consultant, and Contractor Controls

Vendor, consultant, and contractor controls are used to define the levels of performance, expectation, compensation, and consequences for entities, persons, or organizations that are external to the primary organization. Often these controls are defined in a document or policy known as a service-level agreement (SLA).

Using SLAs is an increasingly popular way to ensure that organizations providing services to internal and/or external customers maintain an appropriate level of service agreed on by both the service provider and the vendor. It's a wise move to put SLAs in place for any data circuits, applications, information processing systems, databases, or other critical components that are vital to your organization's continued viability. SLAs are important when using any type of third-party service provider, which would include cloud services. The following issues are commonly addressed in SLAs:

- System uptime (as a percentage of overall operating time)
- Maximum consecutive downtime (in seconds/minutes/and so on)
- Peak load
- Average load
- Responsibility for diagnostics
- Failover time (if redundancy is in place)

SLAs also commonly include financial and other contractual remedies that kick in if the agreement is not maintained. For example, if a critical circuit is down for more than 15 minutes, the service provider might agree to waive all charges on that circuit for one week.

SLAs and vendor, consultant, and contractor controls are an important part of risk reduction and risk avoidance. By clearly defining the expectations and penalties for external parties, everyone involved knows what is expected of them and what the consequences are in the event of a failure to meet those expectations. Although it may be very cost effective to use outside providers for a variety of business functions or services, it does increase potential risk by expanding the potential attack surface and range of vulnerabilities. SLAs should include a focus on protecting and improving security in addition to ensuring quality and timely services at a reasonable price.

Compliance

Compliance is the act of conforming to or adhering to rules, policies, regulations, standards, or requirements. Compliance is an important concern to security governance. On a personnel level, compliance is related to whether individual employees follow company policy and perform their job tasks in accordance to defined procedures. Many organizations rely on employee compliance in order to maintain high levels of quality, consistency, efficiency, and cost savings. If employees do not maintain compliance, it could cost the organization in terms of profit, market share, recognition, and reputation. Employees need to be trained in regard to what they need to do; only then can they be held accountable for violations or lacking compliance.

Privacy

Privacy can be a difficult concept to define. The term is used frequently in numerous contexts without much quantification or qualification. Here are some partial definitions of privacy:

- Active prevention of unauthorized access to information that is personally identifiable (that is, data points that can be linked directly to a person or organization)

- Freedom from unauthorized access to information deemed personal or confidential
- Freedom from being observed, monitored, or examined without consent or knowledge

NOTE A concept that comes up frequently in discussions of privacy is *personally identifiable information (PII).* PII is any data item that can be easily and/or obviously traced back to the person of origin or concern. A phone number, email address, mailing address, social security number, and name are all PII. A MAC address, IP address, OS type, favorite vacation spot, name of high school mascot, and so forth are not typically PII.

When addressing privacy in the realm of IT, there is usually a balancing act between individual rights and the rights or activities of an organization. Some claim that individuals have the right to control whether information can be collected about them and what can be done with it. Others claim that any activity performed in public view—such as most activities performed over the Internet or activities performed on company equipment—can be monitored without knowledge of or permission from the individuals being watched and that the information gathered from such monitoring can be used for whatever purposes an organization deems appropriate or desirable.

Protecting individuals from unwanted observation, direct marketing, and disclosure of private, personal, or confidential details is usually considered a worthy effort. However, some organizations profess that demographic studies, information gleaning, and focused marketing improve business models, reduce advertising waste, and save money for all parties.

There are many legislative and regulatory compliance issues in regard to privacy. Many US regulations—such as the Health Insurance Portability and Accountability Act (HIPAA), the Sarbanes-Oxley Act of 2002 (SOX), and the Gramm-Leach-Bliley Act—as well as the EU's Directive 95/46/EC (aka the Data Protection Directive) and the contractual requirement Payment Card Industry Data Security Standard (PCI DSS)—include privacy requirements. It is important to understand all government regulations that your organization is required to adhere to and ensure compliance, especially in the areas of privacy protection.

Whatever your personal or organizational stance is on the issue of online privacy, it must be addressed in an organizational security policy. Privacy is an issue not just for external visitors to your online offerings but also for your customers, employees, suppliers, and contractors. If you gather any type of information about any person or company, you must address privacy.

In most cases, especially when privacy is being violated or restricted, the individuals and companies must be informed; otherwise, you may face legal ramifications. Privacy issues must also be addressed when allowing or restricting personal use of email, retaining email, recording phone conversations, gathering information about surfing or spending habits, and so on.

Security Governance

Security governance is the collection of practices related to supporting, defining, and directing the security efforts of an organization. Security governance is closely related to and often intertwined with corporate and IT governance. The goals of these three governance agendas often interrelate or are the same. For example, a common goal of organizational governance is to ensure that the organization will continue to exist and will grow or expand over time. Thus, the goal of all three forms of governance is to maintain business processes while striving toward growth and resiliency.

Third-party governance is the system of oversight that may be mandated by law, regulation, industry standards, contractual obligation, or licensing requirements. The actual method of governance may vary, but it generally involves an outside investigator or auditor. These auditors might be designated by a governing body or might be consultants hired by the target organization.

Another aspect of third-party governance is the application of security oversight on third parties that your organization relies on. Many organizations choose to outsource various aspects of their business operations. Outsourced operations can include security guards, maintenance, technical support, and accounting services. These parties need to stay in compliance with the primary organization's security stance. Otherwise, they present additional risks and vulnerabilities to the primary organization.

Third-party governance focuses on verifying compliance with stated security objectives, requirements, regulations, and contractual obligations. On-site assessments can provide firsthand exposure to the security mechanisms employed at a location. Those performing on-site assessment or audits need to follow auditing protocols (such as COBIT) and have a specific checklist of requirements to investigate.

In the auditing and assessment process, both the target and the governing body should participate in full and open document exchange and review. An organization needs to know the full details of all requirements it must comply with. The organization should submit security policy and self-assessment reports back to the governing body. This open document exchange ensures that all parties involved are in agreement about all the issues of concern. It reduces the chances of unknown requirements or unrealistic expectations. Document exchange does not end with the transmission of paperwork or electronic files. Instead, it leads into the process of documentation review.

Documentation review is the process of reading the exchanged materials and verifying them against standards and expectations. The documentation review is typically performed before any on-site inspection takes place. If the exchanged documentation is sufficient and meets expectations (or at least requirements), then an on-site review will be able to focus on compliance with the stated documentation. However, if the documentation is incomplete, inaccurate, or otherwise insufficient, the on-site review is postponed until the documentation can be updated and corrected. This step is important because if the documentation is not in compliance, chances are the location will not be in compliance either.

In many situations, especially related to government or military agencies or contractors, failing to provide sufficient documentation to meet requirements of third-party governance can result in a loss of or a voiding of authorization to operate (ATO). Complete and sufficient documentation can often maintain existing ATO or provide a temporary ATO (TATO). However, once an ATO is lost or revoked, a complete documentation review and on-site review showing full compliance is usually necessary to reestablish the ATO.

A portion of the documentation review is the logical and practical investigation of the business processes and organizational policies. This review ensures that the stated and implemented business tasks, systems, and methodologies are practical, efficient, and cost effective and most of all (at least in relation to security governance) that they support the goal of security through the reduction of vulnerabilities and the avoidance, reduction, or mitigation of risk. Risk management, risk assessment, and addressing risk are all methods and techniques involved in performing process/policy review.

Understand and Apply Risk Management Concepts

Security is aimed at preventing loss or disclosure of data while sustaining authorized access. The possibility that something could happen to damage, destroy, or disclose data or other resources is known as *risk*. Understanding risk management concepts is not only important for the CISSP exam, it's also essential to the establishment of a sufficient security stance, proper security governance, and legal proof of due care and due diligence.

Managing risk is therefore an element of sustaining a secure environment. Risk management is a detailed process of identifying factors that could damage or disclose data, evaluating those factors in light of data value and countermeasure cost, and implementing cost-effective solutions for mitigating or reducing risk. The overall process of risk management is used to develop and implement information security strategies. The goal of these strategies is to reduce risk and to support the mission of the organization.

The primary goal of risk management is to reduce risk to an acceptable level. What that level actually is depends on the organization, the value of its assets, the size of its budget, and many other factors. What is deemed acceptable risk to one organization may be an unreasonably high level of risk to another. It is impossible to design and deploy a totally risk-free environment; however, significant risk reduction is possible, often with little effort.

Risks to an IT infrastructure are not all computer based. In fact, many risks come from noncomputer sources. It is important to consider all possible risks when performing risk evaluation for an organization. Failing to properly evaluate and respond to all forms of risk will leave a company vulnerable. Keep in mind that IT security, commonly referred to as logical or technical security, can provide protection only against logical or technical attacks. To protect IT against physical attacks, physical protections must be erected.

The process by which the goals of risk management are achieved is known as *risk analysis*. It includes examining an environment for risks, evaluating each threat event as to its likelihood of occurring and the cost of the damage it would cause if it did occur, assessing the cost of various countermeasures for each risk, and creating a cost/benefit report for safeguards to present to upper management. In addition to these risk-focused activities, risk management requires evaluation, assessment, and the assignment of value for all assets within the organization. Without proper asset valuations, it is not possible to prioritize and compare risks with possible losses.

Risk Terminology

Risk management employs a vast terminology that must be clearly understood, especially for the CISSP exam. This section defines and discusses all the important risk-related terminology:

Asset An asset is anything within an environment that should be protected. It is anything used in a business process or task. It can be a computer file, a network service, a system resource, a process, a program, a product, an IT infrastructure, a database, a hardware device, furniture, product recipes/formulas, personnel, software, facilities, and so on. If an organization places any value on an item under its control and deems that item important enough to protect, it is labeled an asset for the purposes of risk management and analysis. The loss or disclosure of an asset could result in an overall security compromise, loss of productivity, reduction in profits, additional expenditures, discontinuation of the organization, and numerous intangible consequences.

Asset Valuation Asset valuation is a dollar value assigned to an asset based on actual cost and nonmonetary expenses. These can include costs to develop, maintain, administer, advertise, support, repair, and replace an asset; they can also include more elusive values, such as public confidence, industry support, productivity enhancement, knowledge equity, and ownership benefits. Asset valuation is discussed in detail later in this chapter.

Threats Any potential occurrence that may cause an undesirable or unwanted outcome for an organization or for a specific asset is a threat. Threats are any action or inaction that could cause damage, destruction, alteration, loss, or disclosure of assets or that could block access to or prevent maintenance of assets. Threats can be large or small and result in large or small consequences. They can be intentional or accidental. They can originate from people, organizations, hardware, networks, structures, or nature. Threat agents intentionally exploit vulnerabilities. Threat agents are usually people, but they could also be programs, hardware, or systems. Threat events are accidental and intentional exploitations of vulnerabilities. They can also be natural or manmade. Threat events include fire, earthquake, flood, system failure, human error (due to a lack of training or ignorance), and power outage.

Vulnerability The weakness in an asset or the absence or the weakness of a safeguard or countermeasure is a vulnerability.

In other words, a vulnerability is a flaw, loophole, oversight, error, limitation, frailty, or susceptibility in the IT infrastructure or any other aspect of an organization. If a vulnerability is exploited, loss or damage to assets can occur.

Exposure Exposure is being susceptible to asset loss because of a threat; there is the possibility that a vulnerability can or will be exploited by a threat agent or event. Exposure doesn't mean that a realized threat (an event that results in loss) is actually occurring (the exposure to a realized threat is called *experienced exposure*). It just means that if there is a vulnerability and a threat that can exploit it, there is the possibility that a threat event, or potential exposure, can occur.

Risk Risk is the possibility or likelihood that a threat will exploit a vulnerability to cause harm to an asset. It is an assessment of probability, possibility, or chance. The more likely it is that a threat event will occur, the greater the risk. Every instance of exposure is a risk. When written as a formula, risk can be defined as follows:

```
risk = threat * vulnerability
```

Thus, reducing either the threat agent or the vulnerability directly results in a reduction in risk.

When a risk is realized, a threat agent or a threat event has taken advantage of a vulnerability and caused harm to or disclosure of one or more assets. The whole purpose of security is to prevent risks from becoming realized by removing vulnerabilities and blocking threat agents and threat events from jeopardizing assets. As a risk management tool, security is the implementation of safeguards.

Safeguards A *safeguard*, or *countermeasure*, is anything that removes or reduces a vulnerability or protects against one or more specific threats. A safeguard can be installing a software patch, making a configuration change, hiring security guards, altering the infrastructure, modifying processes, improving the security policy, training personnel more effectively, electrifying a perimeter fence, installing lights, and so on. It is any action or product that reduces risk through the elimination or lessening of a threat or a vulnerability anywhere within an organization. Safeguards are the only means by which risk is mitigated or removed. It is important to remember that a safeguard, security control, or countermeasure need not involve the purchase of a new product; reconfiguring existing elements and even removing elements from the infrastructure are also valid safeguards.

Attack An attack is the exploitation of a vulnerability by a threat agent. In other words, an attack is any intentional attempt to exploit a vulnerability of an organization's security infrastructure to cause damage, loss, or disclosure of assets. An attack can also be viewed as any violation or failure to adhere to an organization's security policy.

Breach A breach is the occurrence of a security mechanism being bypassed or thwarted by a threat agent. When a breach is combined with an attack, a penetration, or intrusion, can result. A penetration is the condition in which a threat agent has gained access to an organization's infrastructure through the circumvention of security controls and is able to directly imperil assets.

The elements asset, threat, vulnerability, exposure, risk, and safeguard are related, as shown in Figure 2.4. Threats exploit vulnerabilities, which results in exposure. Exposure is risk, and risk is mitigated by safeguards. Safeguards protect assets that are endangered by threats.

FIGURE 2.4 The elements of risk

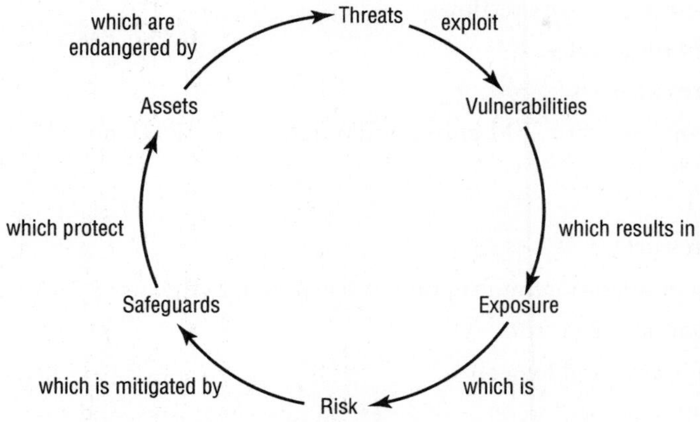

Identify Threats and Vulnerabilities

An essential part of risk management is identifying and examining threats. This involves creating an exhaustive list of all possible threats for the organization's identified assets. The list should include threat agents as well as threat events. It is important to keep in mind that threats can come from anywhere. Threats to IT are not limited to IT sources. When compiling a list of threats, be sure to consider the following:

- Viruses
- Cascade errors (a series of escalating errors) and dependency faults (caused by relying on events or items that don't exist)
- Criminal activities by authorized users
- Movement (vibrations, jarring, etc.)
- Intentional attacks
- Reorganization
- Authorized user illness or epidemics
- Malicious hackers
- Disgruntled employees
- User errors
- Natural disasters (earthquakes, floods, fire, volcanoes, hurricanes, tornadoes, tsunamis, and so on)
- Physical damage (crushing, projectiles, cable severing, and so on)
- Misuse of data, resources, or services
- Changes or compromises to data classification or security policies

- Government, political, or military intrusions or restrictions
- Processing errors, buffer overflows
- Personnel privilege abuse
- Temperature extremes
- Energy anomalies (static, EM pulses, radio frequencies [RFs], power loss, power surges, and so on)
- Loss of data
- Information warfare
- Bankruptcy or alteration/interruption of business activity
- Coding/programming errors
- Intruders (physical and logical)
- Environmental factors (presence of gases, liquids, organisms, and so on)
- Equipment failure
- Physical theft
- Social engineering

In most cases, a team rather than a single individual should perform risk assessment and analysis. Also, the team members should be from various departments within the organization. It is not usually a requirement that all team members be security professionals or even network/system administrators. The diversity of the team based on the demographics of the organization will help to exhaustively identify and address all possible threats and risks.

The Consultant Cavalry

Risk assessment is a highly involved, detailed, complex, and lengthy process. Often risk analysis cannot be properly handled by existing employees because of the size, scope, or liability of the risk; thus, many organizations bring in risk management consultants to perform this work. This provides a high level of expertise, does not bog down employees, and can be a more reliable measurement of real-world risk. But even risk management consultants do not perform risk assessment and analysis on paper only; they typically employ complex and expensive risk assessment software. This software streamlines the overall task, provides more reliable results, and produces standardized reports that are acceptable to insurance companies, boards of directors, and so on.

Risk Assessment/Analysis

Risk management/analysis is primarily an exercise for upper management. It is their responsibility to initiate and support risk analysis and assessment by defining the scope and purpose of the endeavor. The actual processes of performing risk analysis are often delegated to security professionals or an evaluation team. However, all risk assessments, results, decisions, and outcomes must be understood and approved by upper management as an element in providing prudent due care.

All IT systems have risk. There is no way to eliminate 100 percent of all risks. Instead, upper management must decide which risks are acceptable and which are not. Determining which risks are acceptable requires detailed and complex asset and risk assessments.

Once you develop a list of threats, you must individually evaluate each threat and its related risk. There are two risk assessment methodologies: quantitative and qualitative. *Quantitative risk analysis* assigns real dollar figures to the loss of an asset. *Qualitative risk analysis* assigns subjective and intangible values to the loss of an asset. Both methods are necessary for a complete risk analysis. Most environments employ a hybrid of both risk assessment methodologies in order to gain a balanced view of their security concerns.

Quantitative Risk Analysis

The quantitative method results in concrete probability percentages. That means the end result is a report that has dollar figures for levels of risk, potential loss, cost of countermeasures, and value of safeguards. This report is usually fairly easy to understand, especially for anyone with knowledge of spreadsheets and budget reports. Think of quantitative analysis as the act of assigning a quantity to risk—in other words, placing a dollar figure on each asset and threat. However, a purely quantitative analysis is not sufficient; not all elements and aspects of the analysis can be quantified because some are qualitative, subjective, or intangible.

The process of quantitative risk analysis starts with asset valuation and threat identification. Next, you estimate the potential and frequency of each risk. This information is then used to calculate various cost functions that are used to evaluate safeguards.

The six major steps or phases in quantitative risk analysis are as follows (Figure 2.5):

FIGURE 2.5 The six major elements of quantitative risk analysis

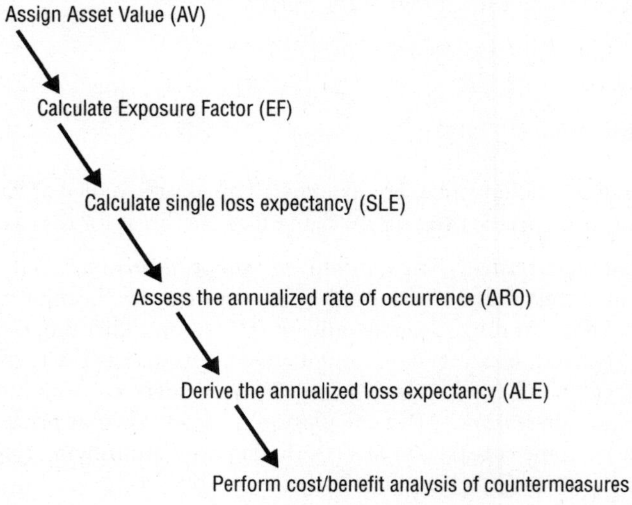
Assign Asset Value (AV)
Calculate Exposure Factor (EF)
Calculate single loss expectancy (SLE)
Assess the annualized rate of occurrence (ARO)
Derive the annualized loss expectancy (ALE)
Perform cost/benefit analysis of countermeasures

1. Inventory assets, and assign a value (asset value, or AV). (Asset value is detailed further in a later section of this chapter named "Asset Valuation.")
2. Research each asset, and produce a list of all possible threats of each individual asset. For each listed threat, calculate the exposure factor (EF) and single loss expectancy (SLE).
3. Perform a threat analysis to calculate the likelihood of each threat being realized within a single year—that is, the annualized rate of occurrence (ARO).
4. Derive the overall loss potential per threat by calculating the annualized loss expectancy (ALE).
5. Research countermeasures for each threat, and then calculate the changes to ARO and ALE based on an applied countermeasure.
6. Perform a cost/benefit analysis of each countermeasure for each threat for each asset. Select the most appropriate response to each threat.

The cost functions associated with quantitative risk analysis include the exposure factor, single loss expectancy, annualized rate of occurrence, and annualized loss expectancy:

Exposure Factor The *exposure factor (EF)* represents the percentage of loss that an organization would experience if a specific asset were violated by a realized risk. The EF can also be called the *loss potential*. In most cases, a realized risk does not result in the total loss of an asset. The EF simply indicates the expected overall asset value loss because of a single realized risk. The EF is usually small for assets that are easily replaceable, such as hardware. It can be very large for assets that are irreplaceable or proprietary, such as product designs or a database of customers. The EF is expressed as a percentage.

Single Loss Expectancy The EF is needed to calculate the SLE. The *single loss expectancy (SLE)* is the cost associated with a single realized risk against a specific asset. It indicates the exact amount of loss an organization would experience if an asset were harmed by a specific threat occurring.

The SLE is calculated using the following formula:

SLE = asset value (AV) * exposure factor (EF)

or more simply:

SLE = AV * EF

The SLE is expressed in a dollar value. For example, if an asset is valued at $200,000 and it has an EF of 45 percent for a specific threat, then the SLE of the threat for that asset is $90,000.

Annualized Rate of Occurrence The *annualized rate of occurrence (ARO)* is the expected frequency with which a specific threat or risk will occur (that is, become realized) within a single year. The ARO can range from a value of 0.0 (zero), indicating that the threat or risk will never be realized, to a very large number, indicating that the threat or risk occurs often. Calculating the ARO can be complicated. It can be derived from historical records, statistical analysis, or guesswork. ARO calculation is also known as *probability determination*. The ARO for some threats or risks is calculated by multiplying the likelihood of a single occurrence by the number of users who could initiate the threat. For example, the ARO of an earthquake in Tulsa may be .00001, whereas the ARO of an email virus in an office in Tulsa may be 10,000,000.

Annualized Loss Expectancy The *annualized loss expectancy (ALE)* is the possible yearly cost of all instances of a specific realized threat against a specific asset.

The ALE is calculated using the following formula:

ALE = single loss expectancy (SLE) * annualized rate of occurrence (ARO)

Or more simply:

ALE = SLE * ARO

For example, if the SLE of an asset is $90,000 and the ARO for a specific threat (such as total power loss) is .5, then the ALE is $45,000. On the other hand, if the ARO for a specific threat (such as compromised user account) were 15, then the ALE would be $1,350,000.

The task of calculating EF, SLE, ARO, and ALE for every asset and every threat/risk is a daunting one. Fortunately, quantitative risk assessment software tools can simplify and automate much of this process. These tools produce an asset inventory with valuations and then, using predefined AROs along with some customizing options (that is, industry, geography, IT components, and so on), produce risk analysis reports. The following calculations are often involved:

Calculating Annualized Loss Expectancy with a Safeguard In addition to determining the annual cost of the safeguard, you must calculate the ALE for the asset if the safeguard is implemented. This requires a new EF and ARO specific to the safeguard. In most cases, the EF to an asset remains the same even with an applied safeguard. (Recall that the EF is the amount of loss incurred if the risk becomes realized.) In other words, if the safeguard fails, how much damage does the asset receive? Think about it this way: If you have on body armor but the body armor fails to prevent a bullet from piercing your heart, you are still experiencing the same damage that would have occurred without the body armor. Thus, if the safeguard fails, the loss on the asset is usually the same as when there is no safeguard. However, some safeguards *do* reduce the resultant damage even when they fail to fully stop an attack. For example, though a fire might still occur and the facility may be damaged by the fire and the water from the sprinklers, the total damage is likely to be less than having the entire building burn down.

Even if the EF remains the same, a safeguard changes the ARO. In fact, the whole point of a safeguard is to reduce the ARO. In other words, a safeguard should reduce the number of times an attack is successful in causing damage to an asset. The best of all possible safeguards would reduce the ARO to zero. Although there are some perfect safeguards, most are not. Thus, many safeguards have an applied ARO that is smaller (you hope much smaller) than the nonsafeguarded ARO, but it is not often zero. With the new ARO (and possible new EF), a new ALE with the application of a safeguard is computed.

With the pre-safeguard ALE and the post-safeguard ALE calculated, there is yet one more value needed to perform a cost/benefit analysis. This additional value is the annual cost of the safeguard.

Calculating Safeguard Costs For each specific risk, you must evaluate one or more safeguards, or countermeasures, on a cost/benefit basis. To perform this evaluation, you must first compile a list of safeguards for each threat. Then you assign each safeguard a deployment value. In fact, you must measure the deployment value or the cost of the safeguard against the value of the protected asset. The value of the protected asset therefore determines the maximum expenditures for protection mechanisms. Security should be cost effective, and thus it is not prudent to spend more (in terms of cash or resources) protecting an asset than its value to the organization. If the cost of the countermeasure is greater than the value of the asset (that is, the cost of the risk), then you should accept the risk.

Numerous factors are involved in calculating the value of a countermeasure:

- Cost of purchase, development, and licensing
- Cost of implementation and customization
- Cost of annual operation, maintenance, administration, and so on
- Cost of annual repairs and upgrades
- Productivity improvement or loss
- Changes to environment
- Cost of testing and evaluation

Once you know the potential cost of a safeguard, it is then possible to evaluate the benefit of that safeguard if applied to an infrastructure. As mentioned earlier, the annual costs of safeguards should not exceed the expected annual cost of asset loss.

Calculating Safeguard Cost/Benefit One of the final computations in this process is the cost/benefit calculation to determine whether a safeguard actually improves security without costing too much. To make the determination of whether the safeguard is financially equitable, use the following formula:

> ALE before safeguard – ALE after implementing the safeguard – annual cost of safeguard (ACS) = value of the safeguard to the company

If the result is negative, the safeguard is not a financially responsible choice. If the result is positive, then that value is the annual savings your organization may reap by deploying the safeguard because the rate of occurrence is not a guarantee of occurrence.

The annual savings or loss from a safeguard should not be the only consideration when evaluating safeguards. You should also consider the issues of legal responsibility and prudent due care. In some cases, it makes more sense to lose money in the deployment of a safeguard than to risk legal liability in the event of an asset disclosure or loss.

In review, to perform the cost/benefit analysis of a safeguard, you must calculate the following three elements:

- The pre-countermeasure ALE for an asset-and-threat pairing
- The post-countermeasure ALE for an asset-and-threat pairing
- The ACS

With those elements, you can finally obtain a value for the cost/benefit formula for this specific safeguard against a specific risk against a specific asset:

(pre-countermeasure ALE – post-countermeasure ALE) – ACS

Or, even more simply:

(ALE1 – ALE2) – ACS

The countermeasure with the greatest resulting value from this cost/benefit formula makes the most economic sense to deploy against the specific asset-and-threat pairing.

Table 2.1 illustrates the various formulas associated with quantitative risk analysis.

TABLE 2.1 Quantitative risk analysis formulas

Concept	Formula
Exposure factor (EF)	%
Single loss expectancy (SLE)	SLE = AV * EF
Annualized rate of occurrence (ARO)	# / year
Annualized loss expectancy (ALE)	ALE = SLE * ARO or ALE = AV * EF * ARO
Annual cost of the safeguard (ACS)	$ / year
Value or benefit of a safeguard	(ALE1 – ALE2) – ACS

Yikes, So Much Math!

Yes, quantitative risk analysis involves a lot of math. Math questions on the exam are likely to involve basic multiplication. Most likely, you will be asked definition, application, and concept synthesis questions on the CISSP exam. This means you need to know the definition of the equations/formulas and values, what they mean, why they are important, and how they are used to benefit an organization. The concepts you must know are AV, EF, SLE, ARO, ALE, and the cost/benefit formula.

It is important to realize that with all the calculations used in the quantitative risk assessment process, the end values are used for prioritization and selection. The values themselves do not truly reflect real-world loss or costs due to security breaches. This should be obvious because of the level of guesswork, statistical analysis, and probability predictions required in the process.

Once you have calculated a cost/benefit for each safeguard for each risk that affects each asset, you must then sort these values. In most cases, the cost/benefit with the highest value is the best safeguard to implement for that specific risk against a specific asset. But as with all things in the real world, this is only one part of the decision-making process. Although very important and often the primary guiding factor, it is not the sole element of data.

Other items include actual cost, security budget, compatibility with existing systems, skill/knowledge base of IT staff, and availability of product as well as political issues, partnerships, market trends, fads, marketing, contracts, and favoritism. As part of senior management or even the IT staff, it is your responsibility to either obtain or use all available data and information to make the best security decision for your organization.

Most organizations have a limited and all-too-finite budget to work with. Thus, obtaining the best security for the cost is an essential part of security management. To effectively manage the security function, you must assess the budget, the benefit and performance metrics, and the necessary resources of each security control. Only after a thorough evaluation can you determine which controls are essential and beneficial not only to security, but also to your bottom line.

Qualitative Risk Analysis

Qualitative risk analysis is more scenario based than it is calculator based. Rather than assigning exact dollar figures to possible losses, you rank threats on a scale to evaluate their risks, costs, and effects. Since a purely quantitative risk assessment is not possible, balancing the results of a quantitative analysis is essential. The method of combining quantitative and qualitative analysis into a final assessment of organizational risk is known as hybrid assessment or hybrid analysis. The process of performing qualitative risk analysis involves judgment, intuition, and experience. You can use many techniques to perform qualitative risk analysis:

- Brainstorming
- Delphi technique
- Storyboarding
- Focus groups
- Surveys
- Questionnaires
- Checklists
- One-on-one meetings
- Interviews

Determining which mechanism to employ is based on the culture of the organization and the types of risks and assets involved. It is common for several methods to be employed simultaneously and their results compared and contrasted in the final risk analysis report to upper management.

Scenarios

The basic process for all these mechanisms involves the creation of scenarios. A *scenario* is a written description of a single major threat. The description focuses on how a threat would be instigated and what effects its occurrence could have on the organization, the IT infrastructure, and specific assets. Generally, the scenarios are limited to one page of text to keep them manageable. For each scenario, one or more safeguards are described that would completely or partially protect against the major threat discussed in the scenario. The analysis participants then assign to the scenario a threat level, a loss potential, and the advantages of each safeguard. These assignments can be grossly simple—such as High, Medium, and Low or a basic number scale of 1 to 10—or they can be detailed essay responses. The responses from all participants are then compiled into a single report that is presented to upper management. For examples of reference ratings and levels, please see Table 3-6 and Table 3-7 in NIST SP 800-30:

`http://csrc.nist.gov/publications/nistpubs/800-30/sp800-30.pdf`

The usefulness and validity of a qualitative risk analysis improves as the number and diversity of the participants in the evaluation increases. Whenever possible, include one or more people from each level of the organizational hierarchy, from upper management to end user. It is also important to include a cross section from each major department, division, office, or branch.

Delphi Technique

The *Delphi technique* is probably the only mechanism on the previous list that is not immediately recognizable and understood. The Delphi technique is simply an anonymous feedback-and-response process used to enable a group to reach an anonymous consensus. Its primary purpose is to elicit honest and uninfluenced responses from all participants. The participants are usually gathered into a single meeting room. To each request for feedback, each participant writes down their response on paper anonymously. The results are compiled and presented to the group for evaluation. The process is repeated until a consensus is reached.

Both the quantitative and qualitative risk analysis mechanisms offer useful results. However, each technique involves a unique method of evaluating the same set of assets and risks. Prudent due care requires that both methods be employed. Table 2.2 describes the benefits and disadvantages of these two systems.

TABLE 2.2 Comparison of quantitative and qualitative risk analysis

Characteristic	Qualitative	Quantitative
Employs complex functions	No	Yes
Uses cost/benefit analysis	No	Yes
Results in specific values	No	Yes
Requires guesswork	Yes	No
Supports automation	No	Yes
Involves a high volume of information	No	Yes
Is objective	No	Yes
Uses opinions	Yes	No
Requires significant time and effort	No	Yes
Offers useful and meaningful results	Yes	Yes

Risk Assignment/Acceptance

The results of risk analysis are many:

- Complete and detailed valuation of all assets
- An exhaustive list of all threats and risks, rate of occurrence, and extent of loss if realized
- A list of threat-specific safeguards and countermeasures that identifies their effectiveness and ALE
- A cost/benefit analysis of each safeguard

This information is essential for management to make educated, intelligent decisions about safeguard implementation and security policy alterations.

Once the risk analysis is complete, management must address each specific risk. There are four possible responses to risk:

- Reduce or mitigate
- Assign or transfer
- Accept
- Reject or ignore

You need to know the following information about the four responses:

Risk Mitigation Reducing risk, or risk mitigation, is the implementation of safeguards and countermeasures to eliminate vulnerabilities or block threats. Picking the most cost-effective or beneficial countermeasure is part of risk management, but it is not an element of risk assessment. In fact, countermeasure selection is a post-risk-assessment or post-risk-analysis activity. Another potential variation of risk mitigation is risk avoidance. The risk is avoided by eliminating the risk cause. A simple example is removing the FTP protocol from a server to avoid FTP attacks, and a larger example is to move to an inland location to avoid the risks from hurricanes.

Risk Assignment Assigning risk or transferring risk is the placement of the cost of loss a risk represents onto another entity or organization. Purchasing insurance and outsourcing are common forms of assigning or transferring risk.

Risk Acceptance Accepting risk, or acceptance of risk, is the valuation by management of the cost/benefit analysis of possible safeguards and the determination that the cost of the countermeasure greatly outweighs the possible cost of loss due to a risk. It also means that management has agreed to accept the consequences and the loss if the risk is realized. In most cases, accepting risk requires a clearly written statement that indicates why a safeguard was not implemented, who is responsible for the decision, and who will be responsible for the loss if the risk is realized, usually in the form of a sign-off letter. An organization's decision to accept risk is based on its risk tolerance. Risk tolerance is the ability of an organization to absorb the losses associated with realized risks. This is also known as risk tolerance or risk appetite.

Risk Rejection A final but unacceptable possible response to risk is to reject or ignore risk. Denying that a risk exists and hoping that it will never be realized are not valid or prudent due-care responses to risk.

Once countermeasures are implemented, the risk that remains is known as *residual risk*. Residual risk comprises threats to specific assets against which upper management chooses not to implement a safeguard. In other words, residual risk is the risk that management has chosen to accept rather than mitigate. In most cases, the presence of residual risk indicates that the cost/benefit analysis showed that the available safeguards were not cost-effective deterrents.

Total risk is the amount of risk an organization would face if no safeguards were implemented. A formula for total risk is as follows:

threats * vulnerabilities * asset value = total risk

(Note that the * here does not imply multiplication, but a combination function; this is not a true mathematical formula.) The difference between total risk and residual risk is known as the *controls gap*. The controls gap is the amount of risk that is reduced by implementing safeguards. A formula for residual risk is as follows:

total risk – controls gap = residual risk

As with risk management in general, handling risk is not a one-time process. Instead, security must be continually maintained and reaffirmed. In fact, repeating the risk assessment and analysis process is a mechanism to assess the completeness and effectiveness of the security program over time. Additionally, it helps locate deficiencies and areas where change has occurred. Because security changes over time, reassessing on a periodic basis is essential to maintaining reasonable security.

Countermeasure Selection and Assessment

Selecting a countermeasure within the realm of risk management relies heavily on the cost/benefit analysis results. However, you should consider several other factors when assessing the value or pertinence of a security control:

- The cost of the countermeasure should be less than the value of the asset.
- The cost of the countermeasure should be less than the benefit of the countermeasure.
- The result of the applied countermeasure should make the cost of an attack greater for the perpetrator than the derived benefit from an attack.
- The countermeasure should provide a solution to a real and identified problem. (Don't install countermeasures just because they are available, are advertised, or sound cool.)
- The benefit of the countermeasure should not be dependent on its secrecy. This means that "security through obscurity" is not a viable countermeasure and that any viable countermeasure can withstand public disclosure and scrutiny.
- The benefit of the countermeasure should be testable and verifiable.
- The countermeasure should provide consistent and uniform protection across all users, systems, protocols, and so on.
- The countermeasure should have few or no dependencies to reduce cascade failures.
- The countermeasure should require minimal human intervention after initial deployment and configuration.

- The countermeasure should be tamperproof.
- The countermeasure should have overrides accessible to privileged operators only.
- The countermeasure should provide fail-safe and/or fail-secure options.

Keep in mind that security should be designed to support and enable business tasks and functions. Thus countermeasures and safeguards need to be evaluated in the context of a business task.

Implementation

Security controls, countermeasures, and safeguards can be implemented administratively, logically/technically, or physically. These three categories of security mechanisms should be implemented in a defense-in-depth manner in order to provide maximum benefit (Figure 2.6).

FIGURE 2.6 The categories of security controls in a defense-in-depth implementation

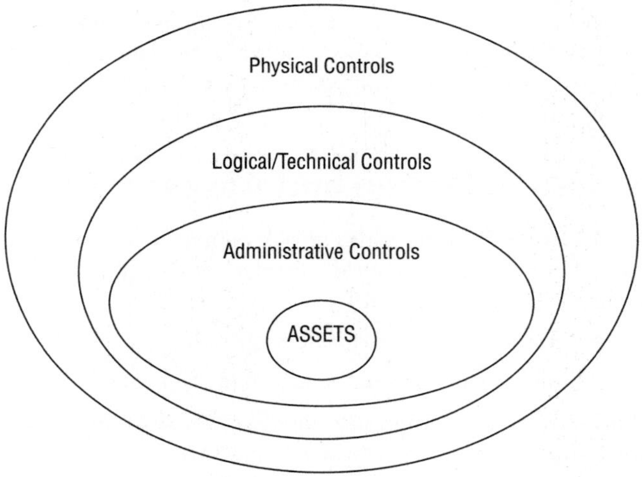

Technical

Technical or logical access involves the hardware or software mechanisms used to manage access and to provide protection for resources and systems. As the name implies, it uses technology. Examples of logical or technical access controls include authentication methods (such as usernames, passwords, smartcards, and biometrics), encryption, constrained interfaces, access control lists, protocols, firewalls, routers, intrusion detection systems (IDSs), and clipping levels.

Administrative

Administrative access controls are the policies and procedures defined by an organization's security policy and other regulations or requirements. They are sometimes referred to as management controls. These controls focus on personnel and business practices. Examples of administrative access controls include policies, procedures, hiring practices, background checks, data classifications and labeling, security awareness and training efforts, vacation history, reports and reviews, work supervision, personnel controls, and testing.

Physical

Physical access controls are items you can physically touch. They include physical mechanisms deployed to prevent, monitor, or detect direct contact with systems or areas within a facility. Examples of physical access controls include guards, fences, motion detectors, locked doors, sealed windows, lights, cable protection, laptop locks, badges, swipe cards, guard dogs, video cameras, mantraps, and alarms.

Types of Controls

The term *access control* refers to a broad range of controls that perform such tasks as ensuring that only authorized users can log on and preventing unauthorized users from gaining access to resources. Controls mitigate a wide variety of information security risks.

Whenever possible, you want to prevent any type of security problem or incident. Of course, this isn't always possible, and unwanted events occur. When they do, you want to detect the events as soon as possible. And once you detect an event, you want to correct it.

As you read the control descriptions, notice that some are listed as examples of more than one access-control type. For example, a fence (or perimeter-defining device) placed around a building can be a preventive control (physically barring someone from gaining access to a building compound) and/or a deterrent control (discouraging someone from trying to gain access).

Deterrent

A deterrent access control is deployed to discourage violation of security policies. Deterrent and preventive controls are similar, but deterrent controls often depend on individuals deciding not to take an unwanted action. In contrast, a preventive control actually blocks the action. Some examples include policies, security-awareness training, locks, fences, security badges, guards, mantraps, and security cameras.

Preventive

A preventive access control is deployed to thwart or stop unwanted or unauthorized activity from occurring. Examples of preventive access controls include fences, locks, biometrics, mantraps, lighting, alarm systems, separation of duties, job rotation, data classification, penetration testing, access-control methods, encryption, auditing, presence of security cameras or CCTV, smartcards, callback procedures, security policies, security-awareness training, antivirus software, firewalls, and intrusion prevention systems (IPSs).

Detective

A detective access control is deployed to discover or detect unwanted or unauthorized activity. Detective controls operate after the fact and can discover the activity only after it has occurred. Examples of detective access controls include security guards, motion detectors, recording and reviewing of events captured by security cameras or CCTV, job rotation, mandatory vacations, audit trails, honeypots or honeynets, IDSs, violation reports, supervision and reviews of users, and incident investigations.

Compensating

A compensation access control is deployed to provide various options to other existing controls to aid in enforcement and support of security policies. They can be any controls used in addition to, or in place of, another control. For example, an organizational policy may dictate that all PII must be encrypted. A review discovers that a preventive control is encrypting all PII data in databases, but PII transferred over the network is sent in cleartext. A compensation control can be added to protect the data in transit.

Corrective

A corrective access control modifies the environment to return systems to normal after an unwanted or unauthorized activity has occurred. It attempts to correct any problems that occurred as a result of a security incident. Corrective controls can be simple, such as terminating malicious activity or rebooting a system. They also include antivirus solutions that can remove or quarantine a virus, backup and restore plans to ensure that lost data can be restored, and active IDs that can modify the environment to stop an attack in progress. The access control is deployed to repair or restore resources, functions, and capabilities after a violation of security policies.

Recovery

Recovery controls are an extension of corrective controls but have more advanced or complex abilities. Examples of recovery access controls include backups and restores, fault-tolerant drive systems, system imaging, server clustering, antivirus software, and database or virtual machine shadowing.

Directive

A directive access control is deployed to direct, confine, or control the actions of subjects to force or encourage compliance with security policies. Examples of directive access controls include security policy requirements or criteria, posted notifications, escape route exit signs, monitoring, supervision, and procedures.

Monitoring and Measurement

Security controls should provide benefits that can be monitored and measured. If a security control's benefits cannot be quantified, evaluated, or compared, then it does not actually provide any security. A security control may provide native or internal monitoring, or external monitoring might be required. You should take this into consideration when making initial countermeasure selections.

Measuring the effectiveness of a countermeasure is not always an absolute value. Many countermeasures offer degrees of improvement rather than specific hard numbers as to the number of breaches prevented or attack attempts thwarted. Often to obtain countermeasure success or failure measurements, monitoring and recording of events both prior to and after safeguard installation is necessary. Benefits can only be accurately measured if the starting point (that is, the normal point or initial risk level) is known. Part of the cost/benefit equation takes countermeasure monitoring and measurement into account. Just because a security control provides some level of increased security does not necessarily mean that the benefit gained is cost effective. A significant improvement in security should be identified to clearly justify the expense of new countermeasure deployment.

Asset Valuation

An important step in risk analysis is to appraise the value of an organization's assets. If an asset has no value, then there is no need to provide protection for it. A primary goal of risk analysis is to ensure that only cost-effective safeguards are deployed. It makes no sense to spend $100,000 protecting an asset that is worth only $1,000. The value of an asset directly affects and guides the level of safeguards and security deployed to protect it. As a rule, the annual costs of safeguards should not exceed the expected annual cost of asset loss.

When the cost of an asset is evaluated, there are many aspects to consider. The goal of *asset valuation* is to assign to an asset a specific dollar value that encompasses tangible costs as well as intangible ones. Determining an exact value is often difficult if not impossible, but nevertheless, a specific value must be established. (Note that the discussion of qualitative versus quantitative risk analysis in the next section may clarify this issue.) Improperly assigning value to assets can result in failing to properly protect an asset or implementing financially infeasible safeguards. The following list includes some of the tangible and intangible issues that contribute to the valuation of assets:

- Purchase cost
- Development cost
- Administrative or management cost
- Maintenance or upkeep cost
- Cost in acquiring asset
- Cost to protect or sustain asset
- Value to owners and users
- Value to competitors
- Intellectual property or equity value
- Market valuation (sustainable price)
- Replacement cost
- Productivity enhancement or degradation
- Operational costs of asset presence and loss

- Liability of asset loss
- Usefulness

Assigning or determining the value of assets to an organization can fulfill numerous requirements. It serves as the foundation for performing a cost/benefit analysis of asset protection through safeguard deployment. It serves as a means for selecting or evaluating safeguards and countermeasures. It provides values for insurance purposes and establishes an overall net worth or net value for the organization. It helps senior management understand exactly what is at risk within the organization. Understanding the value of assets also helps to prevent negligence of due care and encourages compliance with legal requirements, industry regulations, and internal security policies. Risk reporting is a key task to perform at the conclusion of a risk analysis. Risk reporting involves the production of a risk report and a presentation of that report to the interested/relevant parties. For many organizations, risk reporting is an internal concern only, whereas other organizations may have regulations that mandate third-party or public reporting of their risk findings.

A risk report should be accurate, timely, comprehensive of the entire organization, clear and precise to support decision making, and updated on a regular basis.

Continuous Improvement

Risk analysis is performed to provide upper management with the details necessary to decide which risks should be mitigated, which should be transferred, and which should be accepted. The result is a cost/benefit comparison between the expected cost of asset loss and the cost of deploying safeguards against threats and vulnerabilities. Risk analysis identifies risks, quantifies the impact of threats, and aids in budgeting for security. It helps integrate the needs and objectives of the security policy with the organization's business goals and intentions. The risk analysis/risk assessment is a "point in time" metric. Threats and vulnerabilities constantly change, and the risk assessment needs to be redone periodically in order to support continuous improvement.

Security is always changing. Thus any implemented security solution requires updates and changes over time. If a continuous improvement path is not provided by a selected countermeasure, then it should be replaced with one that offers scalable improvements to security.

Risk Frameworks

A risk framework is a guideline or recipe for how risk is to be assessed, resolved, and monitored. The primary example of a risk framework referenced by the CISSP exam is that defined by NIST in Special Publication 800-37 (`http://nvlpubs.nist.gov/nistpubs/SpecialPublications/NIST.SP.800-37r1.pdf`). We encourage you to review this publication in its entirety, but here are a few excerpts of relevance to CISSP:

> Abstract
>
> This publication provides guidelines for applying the Risk Management Framework (RMF) to federal information systems. The six-step RMF includes security categorization, security control selection, security

control implementation, security control assessment, information system authorization, and security control monitoring. The RMF promotes the concept of near real-time risk management and ongoing information system authorization through the implementation of robust continuous monitoring processes, provides senior leaders the necessary information to make cost-effective, risk-based decisions with regard to the organizational information systems supporting their core missions and business functions, and integrates information security into the enterprise architecture and system development life cycle. Applying the RMF within enterprises links risk management processes at the information system level to risk management processes at the organization level through a risk executive (function) and establishes lines of responsibility and accountability for security controls deployed within organizational information systems and inherited by those systems (i.e., common controls). The RMF has the following characteristics:

- Promotes the concept of near real-time risk management and ongoing information system authorization through the implementation of robust continuous monitoring processes;
- Encourages the use of automation to provide senior leaders the necessary information to make cost-effective, risk-based decisions with regard to the organizational information systems supporting their core missions and business functions;
- Integrates information security into the enterprise architecture and system development life cycle;
- Provides emphasis on the selection, implementation, assessment, and monitoring of security controls, and the authorization of information systems;
- Links risk management processes at the information system level to risk management processes at the organization level through a risk executive (function); and

Establishes responsibility and accountability for security controls deployed within organizational information systems and inherited by those systems (i.e., common controls)"The RMF steps include [(see Figure 2.7)]:

- **Categorize** the information system and the information processed, stored, and transmitted by that system based on an impact analysis.
- **Select** an initial set of baseline security controls for the information system based on the security categorization; tailoring and supplementing the security control baseline as needed based on an organizational assessment of risk and local conditions.
- **Implement** the security controls and describe how the controls are employed within the information system and its environment of operation.
- **Assess** the security controls using appropriate assessment procedures to determine the extent to which the controls are implemented correctly, operating as intended, and producing the desired outcome with respect to meeting the security requirements for the system.

- **Authorize** information system operation based on a determination of the risk to organizational operations and assets, individuals, other organizations, and the Nation resulting from the operation of the information system and the decision that this risk is acceptable.
- **Monitor** the security controls in the information system on an ongoing basis including assessing control effectiveness, documenting changes to the system or its environment of operation, conducting security impact analyses of the associated changes, and reporting the security state of the system to designated organizational officials."

  [From NIST SP 800-37]

FIGURE 2.7 The six steps of the risk management framework

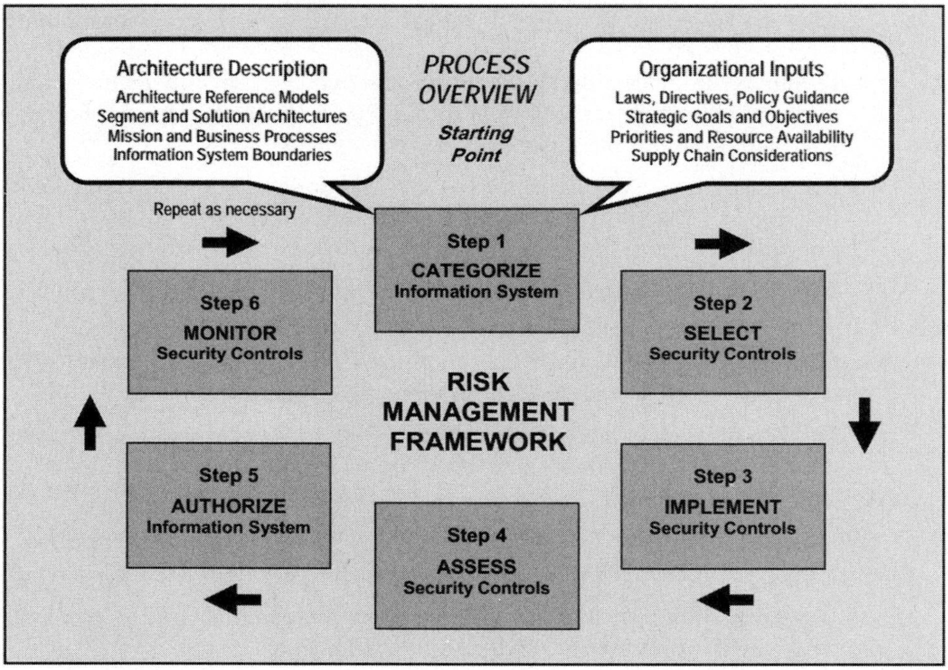

There is significantly more detail about RMF in the NIST publication; please review that document for a complete perspective on risk frameworks.

The NIST RMF is the primary focus of the CISSP exam, but you might want to review other risk management frameworks for use in the real world. Please consider operationally critical threat, asset, and vulnerability evaluation (OCTAVE), factor analysis of information risk (FAIR), and threat agent risk assessment (TARA). For further research, you'll find a useful article here: `www.csoonline.com/article/2125140/metrics-budgets/`

`it-risk-assessment-frameworks--real-world-experience.html`. Understanding that there are a number of well-recognized frameworks and that selecting one that fits your organization's requirements and style is important.

Establish and Manage Information Security Education, Training, and Awareness

The successful implementation of a security solution requires changes in user behavior. These changes primarily consist of alterations in normal work activities to comply with the standards, guidelines, and procedures mandated by the security policy. Behavior modification involves some level of learning on the part of the user. To develop and manage security education, training, and awareness, all relevant items of knowledge transference must be clearly identified and programs of presentation, exposure, synergy, and implementation crafted.

A prerequisite to security training is *awareness*. The goal of creating awareness is to bring security to the forefront and make it a recognized entity for users. Awareness establishes a common baseline or foundation of security understanding across the entire organization and focuses on key or basic topics and issues related to security that all employees must understand and comprehend. Awareness is not exclusively created through a classroom type of exercise but also through the work environment. Many tools can be used to create awareness, such as posters, notices, newsletter articles, screen savers, T-shirts, rally speeches by managers, announcements, presentations, mouse pads, office supplies, and memos as well as the traditional instructor-led training courses.

Awareness establishes a minimum standard common denominator or foundation of security understanding. All personnel should be fully aware of their security responsibilities and liabilities. They should be trained to know what to do and what not to do.

The issues that users need to be aware of include avoiding waste, fraud, and unauthorized activities. All members of an organization, from senior management to temporary interns, need the same level of awareness. The awareness program in an organization should be tied in with its security policy, incident-handling plan, and disaster recovery procedures. For an awareness-building program to be effective, it must be fresh, creative, and updated often. The awareness program should also be tied to an understanding of how the corporate culture will affect and impact security for individuals as well as the organization as a whole. If employees do not see enforcement of security policies and standards, especially at the awareness level, then they may not feel obligated to abide by them.

Training is teaching employees to perform their work tasks and to comply with the security policy. Training is typically hosted by an organization and is targeted to groups of employees with similar job functions. All new employees require some level of training so they will be able to comply with all standards, guidelines, and procedures mandated by the security policy. New users need to know how to use the IT infrastructure, where data is stored, and how and why resources are classified. Many organizations choose to train new employees before they are granted access to the network, whereas others will grant new users limited access until their training in their specific job position is complete. Training is an ongoing activity that must be sustained throughout the lifetime of the organization for every employee. It is considered an administrative security control.

Awareness and training are often provided in-house. That means these teaching tools are created and deployed by and within the organization itself. However, the next level of knowledge distribution is usually obtained from an external third-party source.

Education is a more detailed endeavor in which students/users learn much more than they actually need to know to perform their work tasks. Education is most often associated with users pursuing certification or seeking job promotion. It is typically a requirement for personnel seeking security professional positions. A security professional requires extensive knowledge of security and the local environment for the entire organization and not just their specific work tasks.

An assessment of the appropriate levels of awareness, training, and education required within organization should be revised on a regular basis. Training efforts need to be updated and tuned as the organization evolves over time. Additionally, new bold and subtle means of awareness should be implemented as well to keep the content fresh and relevant. Without periodic reviews for content relevancy, materials will become stale and workers will likely being to make up their own guidelines and procedures. It is the responsibility of the security governance team to establish security rules as well as provide training and education to further the implementation of those rules.

Manage the Security Function

To manage the security function, an organization must implement proper and sufficient security governance. The act of performing a risk assessment to drive the security policy is the clearest and most direct example of management of the security function.

Security must be cost effective. Organizations do not have infinite budgets and thus must allocate their funds appropriately. Additionally, an organizational budget includes a percentage of monies dedicated to security just as most other business tasks and processes require capital, not to mention payments to employees, insurance, retirement, and so on. Security should be sufficient to withstand typical or standard threats to the organization but not when such security is more expensive than the assets being protected. As discussed in "Understand and Apply Risk Management Concepts" earlier in this chapter, a countermeasure that is more costly than the value of the asset itself is not usually an effective solution.

Security must be measurable. Measurable security means that the various aspects of the security mechanisms function, provide a clear benefit, and have one or more metrics that can be recorded and analyzed. Similar to performance metrics, security metrics are measurements of performance, function, operation, action, and so on as related to the operation of a security feature. When a countermeasure or safeguard is implemented, security metrics should show a reduction in unwanted occurrences or an increase in the detection of attempts. Otherwise, the security mechanism is not providing the expected benefit. The act of measuring and evaluating security metrics is the practice of assessing the completeness and effectiveness of the security program. This should also include measuring it against common security guidelines and tracking the success of its controls. Tracking and assessing security metrics are part of effective security governance. However, it is worth noting that choosing incorrect security metrics can cause significant problems, such as choosing to monitor or measure something the security staff has little control over or that is based on external drivers.

Resources will be consumed both by the security mechanisms themselves and by the security governance processes. Obviously, security mechanisms should consume as few resources as possible and impact the productivity or throughput of a system at as low a level as feasible. However, every hardware and software countermeasure as well as every policy and procedure users must follow will consume resources. Being aware of and evaluating resource consumption before and after countermeasure selection, deployment, and tuning is an important part of security governance and managing the security function.

Managing the security function includes the development and implementation of information security strategies. Most of the content of the CISSP exam, and hence this book, addresses the various aspects of development and implementation of information security strategies.

Summary

When planning a security solution, it's important to consider the fact that humans are often the weakest element in organizational security. Regardless of the physical or logical controls deployed, humans can discover ways to avoid them, circumvent or subvert them, or disable them. Thus, it is important to take users into account when designing and deploying security solutions for your environment. The aspects of secure hiring practices, roles, policies, standards, guidelines, procedures, risk management, awareness training, and management planning all contribute to protecting assets. The use of these security structures provides some protection from the threat humans present against your security solutions.

Secure hiring practices require detailed job descriptions. Job descriptions are used as a guide for selecting candidates and properly evaluating them for a position. Maintaining security through job descriptions includes the use of separation of duties, job responsibilities, and job rotation.

A termination policy is needed to protect an organization and its existing employees. The termination procedure should include witnesses, return of company property, disabling network access, an exit interview, and an escort from the property.

Third-party governance is a system of oversight that is sometimes mandated by law, regulation, industry standards, or licensing requirements. The method of governance can vary, but it generally involves an outside investigator or auditor. Auditors might be designated by a governing body, or they might be consultants hired by the target organization.

The process of identifying, evaluating, and preventing or reducing risks is known as risk management. The primary goal of risk management is to reduce risk to an acceptable level. Determining this level depends on the organization, the value of its assets, and the size of its budget. Although it is impossible to design and deploy a completely risk-free environment, it is possible to significantly reduce risk with little effort. Risk analysis is the process by which risk management is achieved and includes analyzing an environment for risks, evaluating each risk as to its likelihood of occurring and the cost of the resulting damage, assessing the cost of various countermeasures for each risk, and creating a cost/benefit report for safeguards to present to upper management.

For a security solution to be successfully implemented, user behavior must change. Such changes primarily consist of alterations in normal work activities to comply with the standards, guidelines, and procedures mandated by the security policy. Behavior modification involves some level of learning on the part of the user. There are three commonly recognized learning levels: awareness, training, and education.

Exam Essentials

Know how privacy fits into the realm of IT security. Know the multiple meanings/definitions of privacy, why it is important to protect, and the issues surrounding it, especially in a work environment.

Be able to discuss third-party governance of security. Third-party governance is the system of oversight that may be mandated by law, regulation, industry standards, or licensing requirements.

Be able to define overall risk management. The process of identifying factors that could damage or disclose data, evaluating those factors in light of data value and countermeasure cost, and implementing cost-effective solutions for mitigating or reducing risk is known as risk management. By performing risk management, you lay the foundation for reducing risk overall.

Understand risk analysis and the key elements involved. Risk analysis is the process by which upper management is provided with details to make decisions about which risks are to be mitigated, which should be transferred, and which should be accepted. To fully evaluate risks and subsequently take the proper precautions, you must analyze the following: assets, asset valuation, threats, vulnerability, exposure, risk, realized risk, safeguards, countermeasures, attacks, and breaches.

Know how to evaluate threats. Threats can originate from numerous sources, including IT, humans, and nature. Threat assessment should be performed as a team effort to provide the widest range of perspectives. By fully evaluating risks from all angles, you reduce your system's vulnerability.

Understand quantitative risk analysis. Quantitative risk analysis focuses on hard values and percentages. A complete quantitative analysis is not possible because of intangible aspects of risk. The process involves asset valuation and threat identification and then determining a threat's potential frequency and the resulting damage; the result is a cost/benefit analysis of safeguards.

Be able to explain the concept of an exposure factor (EF). An exposure factor is an element of quantitative risk analysis that represents the percentage of loss that an organization would experience if a specific asset were violated by a realized risk. By calculating exposure factors, you are able to implement a sound risk management policy.

Know what single loss expectancy (SLE) is and how to calculate it. SLE is an element of quantitative risk analysis that represents the cost associated with a single realized risk against a specific asset. The formula is SLE = asset value (AV) * exposure factor (EF).

Understand annualized rate of occurrence (ARO). ARO is an element of quantitative risk analysis that represents the expected frequency with which a specific threat or risk will occur (in other words, become realized) within a single year. Understanding AROs further enables you to calculate the risk and take proper precautions.

Know what annualized loss expectancy (ALE) is and how to calculate it. ALE is an element of quantitative risk analysis that represents the possible yearly cost of all instances of a specific realized threat against a specific asset. The formula is ALE = single loss expectancy (SLE) * annualized rate of occurrence (ARO).

Know the formula for safeguard evaluation. In addition to determining the annual cost of a safeguard, you must calculate the ALE for the asset if the safeguard is implemented. Use the formula: ALE before safeguard - ALE after implementing the safeguard - annual cost of safeguard = value of the safeguard to the company, or (ALE1 - ALE2) - ACS.

Understand qualitative risk analysis. Qualitative risk analysis is based more on scenarios than calculations. Exact dollar figures are not assigned to possible losses; instead, threats are ranked on a scale to evaluate their risks, costs, and effects. Such an analysis assists those responsible in creating proper risk management policies.

Understand the Delphi technique. The Delphi technique is simply an anonymous feedback-and-response process used to arrive at a consensus. Such a consensus gives the responsible parties the opportunity to properly evaluate risks and implement solutions.

Know the options for handling risk. Reducing risk, or risk mitigation, is the implementation of safeguards and countermeasures. Assigning risk or transferring a risk places the cost of loss a risk represents onto another entity or organization. Purchasing insurance is one form of assigning or transferring risk. Accepting risk means the management has evaluated the cost/benefit analysis of possible safeguards and has determined that the cost of the countermeasure greatly outweighs the possible cost of loss due to a risk. It also means that management has agreed to accept the consequences and the loss if the risk is realized.

Be able to explain total risk, residual risk, and controls gap. Total risk is the amount of risk an organization would face if no safeguards were implemented. To calculate total risk, use this formula: threats * vulnerabilities * asset value = total risk. Residual risk is the risk that management has chosen to accept rather than mitigate. The difference between total risk and residual risk is the controls gap, which is the amount of risk that is reduced by implementing safeguards. To calculate residual risk, use the following formula: total risk - controls gap = residual risk.

Understand control types. The term access control refers to a broad range of controls that perform such tasks as ensuring that only authorized users can log on and preventing unauthorized users from gaining access to resources. Control types include preventive, detective, corrective, deterrent, recovery, directive, and compensation. Controls can also be categorized by how they are implemented: administrative, logical, or physical.

Understand the security implications of hiring new employees. To properly plan for security, you must have standards in place for job descriptions, job classification, work tasks, job responsibilities, preventing collusion, candidate screening, background checks, security clearances, employment agreements, and nondisclosure agreements. By deploying such mechanisms, you ensure that new hires are aware of the required security standards, thus protecting your organization's assets.

Be able to explain separation of duties. Separation of duties is the security concept of dividing critical, significant, sensitive work tasks among several individuals. By separating duties in this manner, you ensure that no one person can compromise system security.

Understand the principle of least privilege. The principle of least privilege states that in a secured environment, users should be granted the minimum amount of access necessary for them to complete their required work tasks or job responsibilities. By limiting user access only to those items that they need to complete their work tasks, you limit the vulnerability of sensitive information.

Know why job rotation and mandatory vacations are necessary. Job rotation serves two functions. It provides a type of knowledge redundancy, and moving personnel around reduces the risk of fraud, data modification, theft, sabotage, and misuse of information. Mandatory vacations of one to two weeks are used to audit and verify the work tasks and privileges of employees. This often results in easy detection of abuse, fraud, or negligence.

Understand vendor, consultant, and contractor controls. Vendor, consultant, and contractor controls are used to define the levels of performance, expectation, compensation, and consequences for entities, persons, or organizations that are external to the primary organization. Often these controls are defined in a document or policy known as a service-level agreement (SLA).

Be able to explain proper termination policies. A termination policy defines the procedure for terminating employees. It should include items such as always having a witness, disabling the employee's network access, and performing an exit interview. A termination policy should also include escorting the terminated employee off the premises and requiring the return of security tokens and badges and company property.

Know how to implement security awareness training and education. Before actual training can take place, awareness of security as a recognized entity must be created for users. Once this is accomplished, training, or teaching employees to perform their work tasks and to comply with the security policy can begin. All new employees require some level of training so they will be able to comply with all standards, guidelines, and procedures mandated by the security policy. Education is a more detailed endeavor in which students/users learn much more than they actually need to know to perform their work tasks. Education is most often associated with users pursuing certification or seeking job promotion.

Understand how to manage the security function. To manage the security function, an organization must implement proper and sufficient security governance. The act of performing a risk assessment to drive the security policy is the clearest and most direct example of management of the security function. This also relates to budget, metrics, resources, information security strategies, and assessing the completeness and effectiveness of the security program.

Know the six steps of the risk management framework. The six steps of the risk management framework are: Categorize, Select, Implement, Assess, Authorize, and Monitor.

Written Lab

1. Name six different administrative controls used to secure personnel.
2. What are the basic formulas used in quantitative risk assessment?
3. Describe the process or technique used to reach an anonymous consensus during a qualitative risk assessment?
4. Discuss the need to perform a balanced risk assessment. What are the techniques that can be used and why is this necessary?

Review Questions

1. Which of the following is the weakest element in any security solution?
   - **A.** Software products
   - **B.** Internet connections
   - **C.** Security policies
   - **D.** Humans
2. When seeking to hire new employees, what is the first step?
   - **A.** Create a job description.
   - **B.** Set position classification.
   - **C.** Screen candidates.
   - **D.** Request resumes.
3. Which of the following is a primary purpose of an exit interview?
   - **A.** To return the exiting employee's personal belongings
   - **B.** To review the nondisclosure agreement
   - **C.** To evaluate the exiting employee's performance
   - **D.** To cancel the exiting employee's network access accounts
4. When an employee is to be terminated, which of the following should be done?
   - **A.** Inform the employee a few hours before they are officially terminated.
   - **B.** Disable the employee's network access just as they are informed of the termination.
   - **C.** Send out a broadcast email informing everyone that a specific employee is to be terminated.
   - **D.** Wait until you and the employee are the only people remaining in the building before announcing the termination.
5. If an organization contracts with outside entities to provide key business functions or services, such as account or technical support, what is the process called that is used to ensure that these entities support sufficient security?
   - **A.** Asset identification
   - **B.** Third-party governance
   - **C.** Exit interview
   - **D.** Qualitative analysis
6. A portion of the ____________ is the logical and practical investigation of business processes and organizational policies. This process/policy review ensures that the stated and implemented business tasks, systems, and methodologies are practical, efficient, cost-effective, but most of all (at least in relation to security governance) that they support security through the reduction of vulnerabilities and the avoidance, reduction, or mitigation of risk.
   - **A.** Hybrid assessment
   - **B.** Risk aversion process

C. Countermeasure selection

D. Documentation review

7. Which of the following statements is *not* true?

A. IT security can provide protection only against logical or technical attacks.

B. The process by which the goals of risk management are achieved is known as risk analysis.

C. Risks to an IT infrastructure are all computer based.

D. An asset is anything used in a business process or task.

8. Which of the following is *not* an element of the risk analysis process?

A. Analyzing an environment for risks

B. Creating a cost/benefit report for safeguards to present to upper management

C. Selecting appropriate safeguards and implementing them

D. Evaluating each threat event as to its likelihood of occurring and cost of the resulting damage

9. Which of the following would generally *not* be considered an asset in a risk analysis?

A. A development process

B. An IT infrastructure

C. A proprietary system resource

D. Users' personal files

10. Which of the following represents accidental or intentional exploitations of vulnerabilities?

A. Threat events

B. Risks

C. Threat agents

D. Breaches

11. When a safeguard or a countermeasure is not present or is not sufficient, what remains?

A. Vulnerability

B. Exposure

C. Risk

D. Penetration

12. Which of the following is *not* a valid definition for risk?

A. An assessment of probability, possibility, or chance

B. Anything that removes a vulnerability or protects against one or more specific threats

C. Risk = threat * vulnerability

D. Every instance of exposure

13. When evaluating safeguards, what is the rule that should be followed in most cases?
    A. The expected annual cost of asset loss should not exceed the annual costs of safeguards.
    B. The annual costs of safeguards should equal the value of the asset.
    C. The annual costs of safeguards should not exceed the expected annual cost of asset loss.
    D. The annual costs of safeguards should not exceed 10 percent of the security budget.

14. How is single loss expectancy (SLE) calculated?
    A. Threat + vulnerability
    B. Asset value ($) * exposure factor
    C. Annualized rate of occurrence * vulnerability
    D. Annualized rate of occurrence * asset value * exposure factor

15. How is the value of a safeguard to a company calculated?
    A. ALE before safeguard - ALE after implementing the safeguard - annual cost of safeguard
    B. ALE before safeguard * ARO of safeguard
    C. ALE after implementing safeguard + annual cost of safeguard - controls gap
    D. Total risk - controls gap

16. What security control is directly focused on preventing collusion?
    A. Principle of least privilege
    B. Job descriptions
    C. Separation of duties
    D. Qualitative risk analysis

17. What process or event is typically hosted by an organization and is targeted to groups of employees with similar job functions?
    A. Education
    B. Awareness
    C. Training
    D. Termination

18. Which of the following is *not* specifically or directly related to managing the security function of an organization?
    A. Worker job satisfaction
    B. Metrics
    C. Information security strategies
    D. Budget

19. While performing a risk analysis, you identify a threat of fire and a vulnerability because there are no fire extinguishers. Based on this information, which of the following is a possible risk?

    A. Virus infection

    B. Damage to equipment

    C. System malfunction

    D. Unauthorized access to confidential information

20. You've performed a basic quantitative risk analysis on a specific threat/vulnerability/risk relation. You select a possible countermeasure. When performing the calculations again, which of the following factors will change?

    a. Exposure factor

    b. Single loss expectancy

    c. Asset value

    d. Annualized rate of occurrence

Chapter 3

Business Continuity Planning

THE CISSP EXAM TOPICS COVERED IN THIS CHAPTER INCLUDE:

✓ **Security and Risk Management (e.g. Security, Risk, Compliance, Law, Regulations, Business Continuity)**

- G. Understand business continuity requirements
  - G.1 Develop and document project scope and plan
  - G.2 Conduct business impact analysis

✓ **Security Operations (e.g. Foundational Concepts, Investigations, Incident Management, Disaster Recovery)**

- N. Participate in business continuity planning and exercises

Despite our best wishes, disasters of one form or another eventually strike every organization. Whether it's a natural disaster such as a hurricane or earthquake or a man-made calamity such as a building fire or burst water pipes, every organization will encounter events that threaten their operations or even their very existence.

Resilient organizations have plans and procedures in place to help mitigate the effects a disaster has on their continuing operations and to speed the return to normal operations. Recognizing the importance of planning for business continuity and disaster recovery, the International Information Systems Security Certification Consortium (ISC)² included these two processes in the Common Body of Knowledge for the CISSP program. Knowledge of these fundamental topics will help you prepare for the exam and help you prepare your organization for the unexpected.

In this chapter, we'll explore the concepts behind business continuity planning. Chapter 18, "Disaster Recovery Planning," will continue our discussion and delve into the specifics of what happens if business continuity controls fail and the organization needs to get its operations back up and running again after a disaster strikes.

Planning for Business Continuity

Business continuity planning (BCP) involves assessing the risks to organizational processes and creating policies, plans, and procedures to minimize the impact those risks might have on the organization if they were to occur. BCP is used to maintain the continuous operation of a business in the event of an emergency situation. The goal of BCP planners is to implement a combination of policies, procedures, and processes such that a potentially disruptive event has as little impact on the business as possible.

BCP focuses on maintaining business operations with reduced or restricted infrastructure capabilities or resources. As long as the continuity of the organization's ability to perform its mission-critical work tasks is maintained, BCP can be used to manage and restore the environment. If the continuity is broken, then business processes have stopped and the organization is in disaster mode; thus, disaster recovery planning (DRP) takes over.

TIP

The top priority of BCP and DRP is always *people*. The primary concern is to get people out of harm's way; then you can address IT recovery and restoration issues.

Business Continuity Planning vs. Disaster Recovery Planning

You should understand the distinction between business continuity planning and disaster recovery planning. One easy way to remember the difference is that BCP comes first, and if the BCP efforts fail, DRP steps in to fill the gap. For example, consider the case of a datacenter located downstream from a dam. BCP efforts might involve verifying that municipal authorities perform appropriate preventive maintenance on the dam and reinforcing the datacenter to protect it from floodwaters.

Despite your best efforts, it's possible that your business continuity efforts will fail. Pressure on the dam might increase to the point that the dam fails and the area beneath it floods. The level of those floodwaters might be too much for the datacenter reinforcements to handle, causing flooding of the datacenter and a disruption in business operations. At this point, your business continuity efforts have failed, and it's time to invoke your disaster recovery plan.

We'll discuss disaster recovery planning in Chapter 18. The eventual goal of those efforts is to restore business operations in the primary datacenter as quickly as possible.

The overall goal of BCP is to provide a quick, calm, and efficient response in the event of an emergency and to enhance a company's ability to recover from a disruptive event promptly. The BCP process, as defined by $(ISC)^2$, has four main steps:

- Project scope and planning
- Business impact assessment
- Continuity planning
- Approval and implementation

The next four sections of this chapter cover each of these phases in detail. The last portion of this chapter will introduce some of the critical elements you should consider when compiling documentation of your organization's business continuity plan.

Project Scope and Planning

As with any formalized business process, the development of a strong business continuity plan requires the use of a proven methodology. This requires the following:

- Structured analysis of the business's organization from a crisis planning point of view
- The creation of a BCP team with the approval of senior management
- An assessment of the resources available to participate in business continuity activities
- An analysis of the legal and regulatory landscape that governs an organization's response to a catastrophic event

The exact process you use will depend on the size and nature of your organization and its business. There isn't a "one-size-fits-all" guide to business continuity project planning. You should consult with project planning professionals within your organization and determine the approach that will work best within your organizational culture.

Business Organization Analysis

One of the first responsibilities of the individuals responsible for business continuity planning is to perform an analysis of the business organization to identify all departments and individuals who have a stake in the BCP process. Here are some areas to consider:

- Operational departments that are responsible for the core services the business provides to its clients
- Critical support services, such as the information technology (IT) department, plant maintenance department, and other groups responsible for the upkeep of systems that support the operational departments
- Senior executives and other key individuals essential for the ongoing viability of the organization

This identification process is critical for two reasons. First, it provides the groundwork necessary to help identify potential members of the BCP team (see the next section). Second, it provides the foundation for the remainder of the BCP process.

Normally, the business organization analysis is performed by the individuals spearheading the BCP effort. This is acceptable, given that they normally use the output of the analysis to assist with the selection of the remaining BCP team members. However, a thorough review of this analysis should be one of the first tasks assigned to the full BCP team when it is convened. This step is critical because the individuals performing the original analysis may have overlooked critical business functions known to BCP team members that represent other parts of the organization. If the team were to continue without revising the organizational analysis, the entire BCP process may be negatively affected, resulting in the development of a plan that does not fully address the emergency-response needs of the organization as a whole.

TIP

When developing a business continuity plan, be sure to account for both your headquarters location as well as any branch offices. The plan should account for a disaster that occurs at any location where your organization conducts its business.

BCP Team Selection

In many organizations, the IT and/or security departments are given sole responsibility for BCP and no arrangements are made for input from other operational and support departments. In fact, those departments may not even know of the plan's existence until disaster strikes or is imminent. This is a critical flaw! The isolated development of a business continuity plan can spell disaster in two ways. First, the plan itself may not take into account knowledge possessed only by the individuals responsible for the day-to-day operation of the business. Second, it keeps operational elements "in the dark" about plan specifics until implementation becomes necessary. This reduces the possibility that operational elements will agree with the provisions of the plan and work effectively to implement it. It also denies organizations the benefits achieved by a structured training and testing program for the plan.

To prevent these situations from adversely impacting the BCP process, the individuals responsible for the effort should take special care when selecting the BCP team. The team should include, at a minimum, the following individuals:

- Representatives from each of the organization's departments responsible for the core services performed by the business
- Representatives from the key support departments identified by the organizational analysis
- IT representatives with technical expertise in areas covered by the BCP
- Security representatives with knowledge of the BCP process
- Legal representatives familiar with corporate legal, regulatory, and contractual responsibilities
- Representatives from senior management

Tips for Selecting an Effective BCP Team

Select your team carefully! You need to strike a balance between representing different points of view and creating a team with explosive personality differences. Your goal should be to create a group that is as diverse as possible and still operates in harmony.

Take some time to think about the BCP team membership and who would be appropriate for your organization's technical, financial, and political environment. Who would you include?

Each one of the individuals mentioned in the preceding list brings a unique perspective to the BCP process and will have individual biases. For example, the representatives from each of the operational departments will often consider their department the most critical to the organization's continued viability. Although these biases may at first seem divisive, the leader of the BCP effort should embrace them and harness them in a productive manner. If used effectively, the biases will help achieve a healthy balance in the final plan as each representative advocates the needs of their department. On the other hand, if proper leadership isn't provided, these biases may devolve into destructive turf battles that derail the BCP effort and harm the organization as a whole.

Senior Management and BCP

The role of senior management in the BCP process varies widely from organization to organization and depends on the internal culture of the business, interest in the plan from above, and the legal and regulatory environment in which the business operates. Important roles played by senior management usually include setting priorities, providing staff and financial resources, and arbitrating disputes about the criticality (i.e., relative importance) of services.

One of the authors recently completed a BCP consulting engagement with a large nonprofit institution. At the beginning of the engagement, he had a chance to sit down with one of the organization's senior executives to discuss his goals and objectives for their work together. During that meeting, the senior executive asked him, "Is there anything you need from me to complete this engagement?"

He must have expected a perfunctory response because his eyes widened when the response began with, "Well, as a matter of fact..." He was then told that his active participation in the process was critical to its success.

When you work on a business continuity plan, you, as the BCP team leader, must seek and obtain as active a role as possible from a senior executive. This conveys the importance of the BCP process to the entire organization and fosters the active participation of individuals who might otherwise write BCP off as a waste of time better spent on operational activities. Furthermore, laws and regulations might require the active participation of those senior leaders in the planning process. If you work for a publicly traded company, you may want to remind executives that the officers and directors of the firm might be found personally liable if a disaster cripples the business and they are found not to have exercised due diligence in their contingency planning.

You may also have to convince management that BCP and DRP spending should not be viewed as a discretionary expense. Management's fiduciary responsibilities to the organization's shareholders require them to at least ensure that adequate BCP measures are in place.

In the case of this BCP engagement, the executive acknowledged the importance of his support and agreed to participate. He sent an email to all employees introducing the effort and stating that it had his full backing. He also attended several of the high-level planning sessions and mentioned the effort in an organization-wide "town hall" meeting.

Resource Requirements

After the team validates the business organization analysis, it should turn to an assessment of the resources required by the BCP effort. This involves the resources required by three distinct BCP phases:

BCP Development The BCP team will require some resources to perform the four elements of the BCP process (project scope and planning, business impact assessment, continuity planning, and approval and implementation). It's more than likely that the major resource consumed by this BCP phase will be effort expended by members of the BCP team and the support staff they call on to assist in the development of the plan.

BCP Testing, Training, and Maintenance The testing, training, and maintenance phases of BCP will require some hardware and software commitments, but once again, the major commitment in this phase will be effort on the part of the employees involved in those activities.

BCP Implementation When a disaster strikes and the BCP team deems it necessary to conduct a full-scale implementation of the business continuity plan, this implementation will require significant resources. This includes a large amount of effort (BCP will likely become the focus of a large part, if not all, of the organization) and the utilization of hard resources. For this reason, it's important that the team uses its BCP implementation powers judiciously yet decisively.

An effective business continuity plan requires the expenditure of a large amount of resources, ranging all the way from the purchase and deployment of redundant computing facilities to the pencils and paper used by team members scratching out the first drafts of the plan. However, as you saw earlier, personnel are one of the most significant resources consumed by the BCP process. Many security professionals overlook the importance of accounting for labor, but you can rest assured that senior management will not. Business leaders are keenly aware of the effect that time-consuming side activities have on the operational productivity of their organizations and the real cost of personnel in terms of salary, benefits, and lost opportunities. These concerns become especially paramount when you are requesting the time of senior executives.

You should expect that leaders responsible for resource utilization management will put your BCP proposal under a microscope, and you should be prepared to defend the necessity of your plan with coherent, logical arguments that address the business case for BCP.

Real World Scenario

Explaining the Benefits of BCP

At a recent conference, one of the authors discussed business continuity planning with the chief information security officer (CISO) of a health system from a medium-sized U.S. city. The CISO's attitude was shocking. His organization had not conducted a formal BCP process, and he was confident that a "seat-of-the-pants" approach would work fine in the unlikely event of a disaster.

This "seat-of-the-pants" attitude is one of the most common arguments against committing resources to BCP. In many organizations, the attitude that the business has always survived and the key leaders will figure something out in the event of a disaster pervades corporate thinking. If you encounter this objection, you might want to point out to management the costs that will be incurred by the business (both direct costs and the indirect cost of lost opportunities) for each day that the business is down. Then ask them to consider how long a "seat-of-the-pants" recovery might take when compared to an orderly, planned continuity of operations.

Legal and Regulatory Requirements

Many industries may find themselves bound by federal, state, and local laws or regulations that require them to implement various degrees of BCP. We've already discussed one example in this chapter—the officers and directors of publicly traded firms have a fiduciary responsibility to exercise due diligence in the execution of their business continuity duties. In other circumstances, the requirements (and consequences of failure) might be more severe. Emergency services, such as police, fire, and emergency medical operations, have a responsibility to the community to continue operations in the event of a disaster. Indeed, their services become even more critical in an emergency when public safety is threatened. Failure on their part to implement a solid BCP could result in the loss of life and/or property and the decreased confidence of the population in their government.

In many countries, financial institutions, such as banks, brokerages, and the firms that process their data, are subject to strict government and international banking and securities regulations designed to facilitate their continued operation to ensure the viability of the national economy. When pharmaceutical manufacturers must produce products in less-than-optimal circumstances following a disaster, they are required to certify the purity of their products to government regulators. There are countless other examples of industries that are required to continue operating in the event of an emergency by various laws and regulations.

Even if you're not bound by any of these considerations, you might have contractual obligations to your clients that require you to implement sound BCP practices. If your contracts include some type of *service-level agreement (SLA)*, you might find yourself in breach of those contracts if a disaster interrupts your ability to service your clients. Many clients may feel sorry for you and want to continue using your products/services, but their own business requirements might force them to sever the relationship and find new suppliers.

On the flip side of the coin, developing a strong, documented business continuity plan can help your organization win new clients and additional business from existing clients. If you can show your customers the sound procedures you have in place to continue serving them in the event of a disaster, they'll place greater confidence in your firm and might be more likely to choose you as their preferred vendor. Not a bad position to be in!

All of these concerns point to one conclusion—it's essential to include your organization's legal counsel in the BCP process. They are intimately familiar with the legal, regulatory, and contractual obligations that apply to your organization and can help your team implement a plan that meets those requirements while ensuring the continued viability of the organization to the benefit of all—employees, shareholders, suppliers, and customers alike.

WARNING

Laws regarding computing systems, business practices, and disaster management change frequently and vary from jurisdiction to jurisdiction. Be sure to keep your attorneys involved throughout the lifetime of your BCP, including the testing and maintenance phases. If you restrict their involvement to a pre-implementation review of the plan, you may not become aware of the impact that changing laws and regulations have on your corporate responsibilities.

Business Impact Assessment

Once your BCP team completes the four stages of preparing to create a business continuity plan, it's time to dive into the heart of the work—the *business impact assessment (BIA)*. The BIA identifies the resources that are critical to an organization's ongoing viability and the threats posed to those resources. It also assesses the likelihood that each threat will actually occur and the impact those occurrences will have on the business. The results of the BIA provide you with quantitative measures that can help you prioritize the commitment of business continuity resources to the various local, regional, and global risk exposures facing your organization.

It's important to realize that there are two different types of analyses that business planners use when facing a decision:

Quantitative Decision Making Quantitative decision making involves the use of numbers and formulas to reach a decision. This type of data often expresses options in terms of the dollar value to the business.

Qualitative Decision Making Qualitative decision making takes non-numerical factors, such as emotions, investor/customer confidence, workforce stability, and other concerns, into account. This type of data often results in categories of prioritization (such as high, medium, and low).

NOTE

Quantitative analysis and qualitative analysis both play an important role in the BCP process. However, most people tend to favor one type of analysis over the other. When selecting the individual members of the BCP team, try to achieve a balance between people who prefer each strategy. This will result in the development of a well-rounded BCP and benefit the organization in the long run.

The BIA process described in this chapter approaches the problem from both quantitative and qualitative points of view. However, it's tempting for a BCP team to "go with the numbers" and perform a quantitative assessment while neglecting the somewhat more difficult qualitative assessment. It's important that the BCP team performs a qualitative analysis of the factors affecting your BCP process. For example, if your business is highly dependent on a few very important clients, your management team is probably willing to suffer significant short-term financial loss in order to retain those clients in the long term. The BCP team must sit down and discuss (preferably with the involvement of senior management) qualitative concerns to develop a comprehensive approach that satisfies all stakeholders.

Identify Priorities

The first BIA task facing the BCP team is identifying business priorities. Depending on your line of business, there will be certain activities that are most essential to your day-to-day operations when disaster strikes. The priority identification task, or criticality prioritization, involves creating a comprehensive list of business processes and ranking them in order of importance. Although this task may seem somewhat daunting, it's not as hard as it seems.

A great way to divide the workload of this process among the team members is to assign each participant responsibility for drawing up a prioritized list that covers the business functions for which their department is responsible. When the entire BCP team convenes, team members can use those prioritized lists to create a master prioritized list for the entire organization.

This process helps identify business priorities from a qualitative point of view. Recall that we're describing an attempt to simultaneously develop both qualitative and quantitative BIAs. To begin the quantitative assessment, the BCP team should sit down and draw up a list of organization assets and then assign an *asset value (AV)* in monetary terms to each asset. These numbers will be used in the remaining BIA steps to develop a financially based BIA.

The second quantitative measure that the team must develop is the *maximum tolerable downtime (MTD)*, sometimes also known as maximum tolerable outage (MTO). The MTD is the maximum length of time a business function can be inoperable without causing irreparable harm to the business. The MTD provides valuable information when you're performing both BCP and DRP planning.

This leads to another metric, the *recovery time objective (RTO)*, for each business function. This is the amount of time in which you think you can feasibly recover the function in the event of a disruption. Once you have defined your recovery objectives, you can design and plan the procedures necessary to accomplish the recovery tasks.

The goal of the BCP process is to ensure that your RTOs are less than your MTDs, resulting in a situation in which a function should never be unavailable beyond the maximum tolerable downtime.

Risk Identification

The next phase of the BIA is the identification of risks posed to your organization. Some elements of this organization-specific list may come to mind immediately. The identification of other, more obscure risks might take a little creativity on the part of the BCP team.

Risks come in two forms: natural risks and man-made risks. The following list includes some events that pose natural threats:

- Violent storms/hurricanes/tornadoes/blizzards
- Earthquakes
- Mudslides/avalanches
- Volcanic eruptions

Man-made threats include the following events:

- Terrorist acts/wars/civil unrest
- Theft/vandalism
- Fires/explosions

- Prolonged power outages
- Building collapses
- Transportation failures

Remember, these are by no means all-inclusive lists. They merely identify some common risks that many organizations face. You may want to use them as a starting point, but a full listing of risks facing your organization will require input from all members of the BCP team.

The risk identification portion of the process is purely qualitative in nature. At this point in the process, the BCP team should not be concerned about the likelihood that each type of risk will actually materialize or the amount of damage such an occurrence would inflict upon the continued operation of the business. The results of this analysis will drive both the qualitative and quantitative portions of the remaining BIA tasks.

Business Impact Assessment and the Cloud

As you conduct your business impact assessment, don't forget to take any cloud vendors on which your organization relies into account. Depending on the nature of the cloud service, the vendor's own business continuity arrangements may have a critical impact on your organization's business operations as well.

Consider, for example, a firm that outsourced email and calendaring to a third-party Software-as-a-Service (SaaS) provider. Does the contract with that provider include details about the provider's SLA and commitments for restoring operations in the event of a disaster?

Also remember that a contract is not normally sufficient due diligence when choosing a cloud provider. You should also verify that they have the controls in place to deliver on their contractual commitments. Although it may not be possible for you to physically visit the vendor's facilities to verify their control implementation, you can always do the next best thing—send someone else!

Now, before you go off identifying an emissary and booking flights, realize that many of your vendor's customers are probably asking the same question. For this reason, the vendor may have already hired an independent auditing firm to conduct an assessment of their controls. They can make the results of this assessment available to you in the form of a service organization control (SOC) report.

Keep in mind that there are three different versions of the SOC report. The simplest of these, a SOC-1 report, covers only internal controls over financial reporting. If you want to verify the security, privacy, and availability controls, you'll want to review either an SOC-2 or SOC-3 report. The American Institute of Certified Public Accountants (AICPA) sets and maintains the standards surrounding these reports to maintain consistency between auditors from different accounting firms.

Likelihood Assessment

The preceding step consisted of the BCP team's drawing up a comprehensive list of the events that can be a threat to an organization. You probably recognized that some events are much more likely to happen than others. For example, a business in Southern California is much more likely to face the risk of an earthquake than to face the risk posed by a volcanic eruption. A business based in Hawaii might have the exact opposite likelihood that each risk would occur.

To account for these differences, the next phase of the business impact assessment identifies the likelihood that each risk will occur. To keep calculations consistent, this assessment is usually expressed in terms of an *annualized rate of occurrence (ARO)* that reflects the number of times a business expects to experience a given disaster each year.

The BCP team should sit down and determine an ARO for each risk identified in the previous section. These numbers should be based on corporate history, professional experience of team members, and advice from experts, such as meteorologists, seismologists, fire prevention professionals, and other consultants, as needed.

TIP

In addition to the government resources identified in this chapter, insurance companies develop large repositories of risk information as part of their actuarial processes. You may be able to obtain this information from them to assist in your BCP efforts. After all, you have a mutual interest in preventing damage to your business!

In many cases, you may be able to find likelihood assessments for some risks prepared by experts at no cost to you. For example, the U.S. Geological Survey (USGS) developed the earthquake hazard map shown in Figure 3.1. This map illustrates the ARO for earthquakes in various regions of the United States. Similarly, the Federal Emergency Management Agency (FEMA) coordinates the development of detailed flood maps of local communities throughout the United States. These resources are available online and offer a wealth of information to organizations performing a business impact assessment.

Impact Assessment

As you may have surmised based on its name, the impact assessment is one of the most critical portions of the business impact assessment. In this phase, you analyze the data gathered during risk identification and likelihood assessment and attempt to determine what impact each one of the identified risks would have on the business if it were to occur.

From a quantitative point of view, we will cover three specific metrics: the exposure factor, the single loss expectancy, and the annualized loss expectancy. Each one of these values is computed for each specific risk/asset combination evaluated during the previous phases.

The *exposure factor (EF)* is the amount of damage that the risk poses to the asset, expressed as a percentage of the asset's value. For example, if the BCP team consults with fire experts and determines that a building fire would cause 70 percent of the building to be destroyed, the exposure factor of the building to fire is 70 percent.

FIGURE 3.1 Earthquake hazard map of the United States

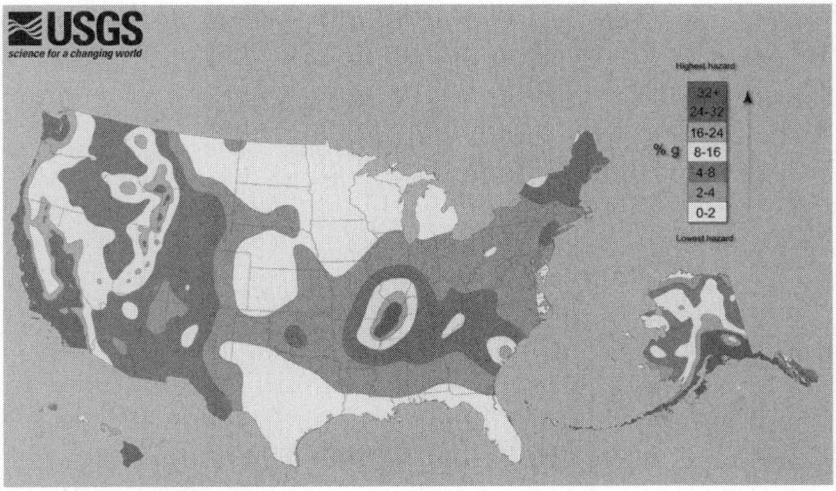

(Source: U.S. Geological Survey)

The *single loss expectancy (SLE)* is the monetary loss that is expected each time the risk materializes. You can compute the SLE using the following formula:

SLE = AV × EF

Continuing with the preceding example, if the building is worth $500,000, the single loss expectancy would be 70 percent of $500,000, or $350,000. You can interpret this figure to mean that a single fire in the building would be expected to cause $350,000 worth of damage.

The *annualized loss expectancy (ALE)* is the monetary loss that the business expects to occur as a result of the risk harming the asset over the course of a year. You already have all the data necessary to perform this calculation. The SLE is the amount of damage you expect each time a disaster strikes, and the ARO (from the likelihood analysis) is the number of times you expect a disaster to occur each year. You compute the ALE by simply multiplying those two numbers:

ALE = SLE × ARO

Returning once again to our building example, if fire experts predict that a fire will occur in the building once every 30 years, the ARO is ~1/30, or 0.03. The ALE is then 3 percent of the $350,000 SLE, or $11,667. You can interpret this figure to mean that the business should expect to lose $11,667 each year due to a fire in the building.

Obviously, a fire will not occur each year—this figure represents the average cost over the 30 years between fires. It's not especially useful for budgeting considerations but proves invaluable when attempting to prioritize the assignment of BCP resources to a given risk. These concepts were also covered in Chapter 2, "Personnel Security and Risk Management Concepts."

> TIP: Be certain you're familiar with the quantitative formulas contained in this chapter and the concepts of asset value, exposure factor, annualized rate of occurrence, single loss expectancy, and annualized loss expectancy. Know the formulas and be able to work through a scenario.

From a qualitative point of view, you must consider the nonmonetary impact that interruptions might have on your business. For example, you might want to consider the following:

- Loss of goodwill among your client base
- Loss of employees to other jobs after prolonged downtime
- Social/ethical responsibilities to the community
- Negative publicity

It's difficult to put dollar values on items like these in order to include them in the quantitative portion of the impact assessment, but they are equally important. After all, if you decimate your client base, you won't have a business to return to when you're ready to resume operations!

Resource Prioritization

The final step of the BIA is to prioritize the allocation of business continuity resources to the various risks that you identified and assessed in the preceding tasks of the BIA.

From a quantitative point of view, this process is relatively straightforward. You simply create a list of all the risks you analyzed during the BIA process and sort them in descending order according to the ALE computed during the impact assessment phase. This provides you with a prioritized list of the risks that you should address. Select as many items as you're willing and able to address simultaneously from the top of the list and work your way down. Eventually, you'll reach a point at which you've exhausted either the list of risks (unlikely!) or all your available resources (much more likely!).

Recall from the previous section that we also stressed the importance of addressing qualitatively important concerns. In previous sections about the BIA, we treated quantitative and qualitative analysis as mainly separate functions with some overlap in the analysis. Now it's time to merge the two prioritized lists, which is more of an art than a science. You must sit down with the BCP team and representatives from the senior management team and combine the two lists into a single prioritized list.

Qualitative concerns may justify elevating or lowering the priority of risks that already exist on the ALE-sorted quantitative list. For example, if you run a fire suppression company, your number-one priority might be the prevention of a fire in your principal place of business despite the fact that an earthquake might cause more physical damage. The potential loss of reputation within the business community resulting from the destruction of a fire suppression company by fire might be too difficult to overcome and result in the eventual collapse of the business, justifying the increased priority.

Continuity Planning

The first two phases of the BCP process (project scope and planning and the business impact assessment) focus on determining how the BCP process will work and prioritizing the business assets that must be protected against interruption. The next phase of BCP development, continuity planning, focuses on developing and implementing a continuity strategy to minimize the impact realized risks might have on protected assets.

In this section, you'll learn about the subtasks involved in continuity planning:

- Strategy development
- Provisions and processes
- Plan approval
- Plan implementation
- Training and education

Strategy Development

The strategy development phase bridges the gap between the business impact assessment and the continuity planning phases of BCP development. The BCP team must now take the prioritized list of concerns raised by the quantitative and qualitative resource prioritization exercises and determine which risks will be addressed by the business continuity plan. Fully addressing all the contingencies would require the implementation of provisions and processes that maintain a zero-downtime posture in the face of every possible risk. For obvious reasons, implementing a policy this comprehensive is simply impossible.

The BCP team should look back to the MTD estimates created during the early stages of the BIA and determine which risks are deemed acceptable and which must be mitigated by BCP continuity provisions. Some of these decisions are obvious—the risk of a blizzard striking an operations facility in Egypt is negligible and would be deemed an acceptable risk. The risk of a monsoon in New Delhi is serious enough that it must be mitigated by BCP provisions.

TIP

Keep in mind that there are four possible responses to a risk: reduce, assign, accept, and reject. Each may be an acceptable response based upon the circumstances.

Once the BCP team determines which risks require mitigation and the level of resources that will be committed to each mitigation task, they are ready to move on to the provisions and processes phase of continuity planning.

Provisions and Processes

The provisions and processes phase of continuity planning is the meat of the entire business continuity plan. In this task, the BCP team designs the specific procedures and mechanisms that will mitigate the risks deemed unacceptable during the strategy development stage. Three categories of assets must be protected through BCP provisions and processes: people, buildings/facilities, and infrastructure. In the next three sections, we'll explore some of the techniques you can use to safeguard these categories.

People

First and foremost, you must ensure that the people within your organization are safe before, during, and after an emergency. Once you've achieved that goal, you must make provisions to allow your employees to conduct both their BCP and operational tasks in as normal a manner as possible given the circumstances.

WARNING

Don't lose sight of the fact that people are your most valuable asset. The safety of people must always come before the organization's business goals. Make sure that your business continuity plan makes adequate provisions for the security of your employees, customers, suppliers, and any other individuals who may be affected!

People should be provided with all the resources they need to complete their assigned tasks. At the same time, if circumstances dictate that people be present in the workplace for extended periods of time, arrangements must be made for shelter and food. Any continuity plan that requires these provisions should include detailed instructions for the BCP team in the event of a disaster. The organization should maintain stockpiles of provisions sufficient to feed the operational and support teams for an extended period of time in an accessible location. Plans should specify the periodic rotation of those stockpiles to prevent spoilage.

Buildings and Facilities

Many businesses require specialized facilities in order to carry out their critical operations. These might include standard office facilities, manufacturing plants, operations centers, warehouses, distribution/logistics centers, and repair/maintenance depots, among others. When you perform your BIA, you will identify those facilities that play a critical role in your organization's continued viability. Your continuity plan should address two areas for each critical facility:

Hardening Provisions Your BCP should outline mechanisms and procedures that can be put in place to protect your existing facilities against the risks defined in the strategy development phase. This might include steps as simple as patching a leaky roof or as complex as installing reinforced hurricane shutters and fireproof walls.

Alternate Sites In the event that it's not feasible to harden a facility against a risk, your BCP should identify alternate sites where business activities can resume immediately (or at least in a period of time that's shorter than the maximum tolerable downtime for all affected critical business functions). Chapter 18, "Disaster Recovery Planning," describes a few of the facility types that might be useful in this stage.

Infrastructure

Every business depends on some sort of infrastructure for its critical processes. For many businesses, a critical part of this infrastructure is an IT backbone of communications and computer systems that process orders, manage the supply chain, handle customer interaction, and perform other business functions. This backbone consists of a number of servers, workstations, and critical communications links between sites. The BCP must address how these systems will be protected against risks identified during the strategy development phase. As with buildings and facilities, there are two main methods of providing this protection:

Physically Hardening Systems You can protect systems against the risks by introducing protective measures such as computer-safe fire suppression systems and uninterruptible power supplies.

Alternative Systems You can also protect business functions by introducing redundancy (either redundant components or completely redundant systems/communications links that rely on different facilities).

These same principles apply to whatever infrastructure components serve your critical business processes—transportation systems, electrical power grids, banking and financial systems, water supplies, and so on.

Plan Approval and Implementation

Once the BCP team completes the design phase of the BCP document, it's time to gain top-level management endorsement of the plan. If you were fortunate enough to have senior management involvement throughout the development phases of the plan, this should be a relatively straightforward process. On the other hand, if this is your first time approaching management with the BCP document, you should be prepared to provide a lengthy explanation of the plan's purpose and specific provisions.

TIP

Senior management approval and buy-in is essential to the success of the overall BCP effort.

Plan Approval

If possible, you should attempt to have the plan endorsed by the top executive in your business—the chief executive officer, chairman, president, or similar business leader. This move demonstrates the importance of the plan to the entire organization and showcases the business leader's commitment to business continuity. The signature of such an individual on the plan also gives it much greater weight and credibility in the eyes of other senior managers, who might otherwise brush it off as a necessary but trivial IT initiative.

Plan Implementation

Once you've received approval from senior management, it's time to dive in and start implementing your plan. The BCP team should get together and develop an implementation schedule that utilizes the resources dedicated to the program to achieve the stated process and provision goals in as prompt a manner as possible given the scope of the modifications and the organizational climate.

After all the resources are fully deployed, the BCP team should supervise the conduct of an appropriate BCP maintenance program to ensure that the plan remains responsive to evolving business needs.

Training and Education

Training and education are essential elements of the BCP implementation. All personnel who will be involved in the plan (either directly or indirectly) should receive some sort of training on the overall plan and their individual responsibilities.

Everyone in the organization should receive at least a plan overview briefing to provide them with the confidence that business leaders have considered the possible risks posed to continued operation of the business and have put a plan in place to mitigate the impact on the organization should business be disrupted.

People with direct BCP responsibilities should be trained and evaluated on their specific BCP tasks to ensure that they are able to complete them efficiently when disaster strikes. Furthermore, at least one backup person should be trained for every BCP task to ensure redundancy in the event personnel are injured or cannot reach the workplace during an emergency.

BCP Documentation

Documentation is a critical step in the business continuity planning process. Committing your BCP methodology to paper provides several important benefits:

- It ensures that BCP personnel have a written continuity document to reference in the event of an emergency, even if senior BCP team members are not present to guide the effort.
- It provides a historical record of the BCP process that will be useful to future personnel seeking to both understand the reasoning behind various procedures and implement necessary changes in the plan.
- It forces the team members to commit their thoughts to paper—a process that often facilitates the identification of flaws in the plan. Having the plan on paper also allows draft documents to be distributed to individuals not on the BCP team for a "sanity check."

In the following sections, we'll explore some of the important components of the written business continuity plan.

Continuity Planning Goals

First, the plan should describe the goals of continuity planning as set forth by the BCP team and senior management. These goals should be decided on at or before the first BCP team meeting and will most likely remain unchanged throughout the life of the BCP.

The most common goal of the BCP is quite simple: to ensure the continuous operation of the business in the face of an emergency situation. Other goals may also be inserted in this section of the document to meet organizational needs. For example, you might have goals that your customer call center experience no more than 15 consecutive minutes of downtime or that your backup servers be able to handle 75 percent of your processing load within 1 hour of activation.

Statement of Importance

The statement of importance reflects the criticality of the BCP to the organization's continued viability. This document commonly takes the form of a letter to the organization's employees stating the reason that the organization devoted significant resources to the BCP development process and requesting the cooperation of all personnel in the BCP implementation phase.

Here's where the importance of senior executive buy-in comes into play. If you can put out this letter under the signature of the CEO or an officer at a similar level, the plan will carry tremendous weight as you attempt to implement changes throughout the organization. If you have the signature of a lower-level manager, you may encounter resistance as you attempt to work with portions of the organization outside of that individual's direct control.

Statement of Priorities

The statement of priorities flows directly from the identify priorities phase of the business impact assessment. It simply involves listing the functions considered critical to continued business operations in a prioritized order. When listing these priorities, you should also include a statement that they were developed as part of the BCP process and reflect the importance of the functions to continued business operations in the event of an emergency and nothing more. Otherwise, the list of priorities could be used for unintended purposes and result in a political turf battle between competing organizations to the detriment of the business continuity plan.

Statement of Organizational Responsibility

The statement of organizational responsibility also comes from a senior-level executive and can be incorporated into the same letter as the statement of importance. It basically echoes the sentiment that "business continuity is everyone's responsibility!" The statement of organizational responsibility restates the organization's commitment to business continuity planning and informs employees, vendors, and affiliates that they are individually expected to do everything they can to assist with the BCP process.

Statement of Urgency and Timing

The statement of urgency and timing expresses the criticality of implementing the BCP and outlines the implementation timetable decided on by the BCP team and agreed to by upper management. The wording of this statement will depend on the actual urgency assigned to the BCP process by the organization's leadership. If the statement itself is included in the same letter as the statement of priorities and statement of organizational responsibility, the timetable should be included as a separate document. Otherwise, the timetable and this statement can be put into the same document.

Risk Assessment

The risk assessment portion of the BCP documentation essentially recaps the decision-making process undertaken during the business impact assessment. It should include a discussion of all the risks considered during the BIA as well as the quantitative and qualitative analyses performed to assess these risks. For the quantitative analysis, the actual AV, EF, ARO, SLE, and ALE figures should be included. For the qualitative analysis, the thought process behind the risk analysis should be provided to the reader. It's important to note that the risk assessment must be updated on a regular basis because it reflects a point-in-time assessment.

Risk Acceptance/Mitigation

The risk acceptance/mitigation section of the BCP documentation contains the outcome of the strategy development portion of the BCP process. It should cover each risk identified in the risk analysis portion of the document and outline one of two thought processes:

- For risks that were deemed acceptable, it should outline the reasons the risk was considered acceptable as well as potential future events that might warrant reconsideration of this determination.
- For risks that were deemed unacceptable, it should outline the risk management provisions and processes put into place to reduce the risk to the organization's continued viability.

WARNING

It's far too easy to look at a difficult risk mitigation challenge and say "we accept this risk" before moving on to easier things. Business continuity planners should resist these statements and ask business leaders to formally document their risk acceptance decisions. If auditors later scrutinize your business continuity plan, they will most certainly look for formal artifacts of any risk acceptance decisions made in the BCP process.

Vital Records Program

The BCP documentation should also outline a vital records program for the organization. This document states where critical business records will be stored and the procedures for making and storing backup copies of those records.

One of the biggest challenges in implementing a vital records program is often identifying the vital records in the first place! As many organizations transitioned from paper-based to digital workflows, they often lost the rigor that existed around creating and maintaining formal file structures. Vital records may now be distributed among a wide variety of IT systems and cloud services. Some may be stored on central servers accessible to groups whereas others may be located in digital repositories assigned to an individual employee.

If that messy state of affairs sounds like your current reality, you may wish to begin your vital records program by identifying the records that are truly critical to your business. Sit down with functional leaders and ask, "If we needed to rebuild the organization today in a completely new location without access to any of our computers or files, what records would you need?" Asking the question in this way forces the team to visualize the actual process of re-creating operations and, as they walk through the steps in their minds, will produce an inventory of the organization's vital records. This inventory may evolve over time as people remember other important information sources, so you should consider using multiple conversations to finalize it.

Once you've identified the records that your organization considers vital, the next task is a formidable one: find them! You should be able to identify the storage locations for each record identified in your vital records inventory. Once you've completed this task, you can then use this vital records inventory to inform the rest of your business continuity planning efforts.

Emergency-Response Guidelines

The emergency-response guidelines outline the organizational and individual responsibilities for immediate response to an emergency situation. This document provides the first employees to detect an emergency with the steps they should take to activate provisions of the BCP that do not automatically activate. These guidelines should include the following:

- Immediate response procedures (security and safety procedures, fire suppression procedures, notification of appropriate emergency-response agencies, etc.)
- A list of the individuals who should be notified of the incident (executives, BCP team members, etc.)
- Secondary response procedures that first responders should take while waiting for the BCP team to assemble

Your guidelines should be easily accessible to everyone in the organization who may be among the first responders to a crisis incident. Any time a disruption strikes, time is of the essence. Slowdowns in activating your business continuity procedures may result in undesirable downtime for your business operations.

Maintenance

The BCP documentation and the plan itself must be living documents. Every organization encounters nearly constant change, and this dynamic nature ensures that the business's continuity requirements will also evolve. The BCP team should not be disbanded after the plan is developed but should still meet periodically to discuss the plan and review the results of plan tests to ensure that it continues to meet organizational needs.

Obviously, minor changes to the plan do not require conducting the full BCP development process from scratch; they can simply be made at an informal meeting of the BCP team by unanimous consent. However, keep in mind that drastic changes in an organization's mission or resources may require going back to the BCP drawing board and beginning again.

Any time you make a change to the BCP, you must practice good version control. All older versions of the BCP should be physically destroyed and replaced by the most current version so that no confusion exists as to the correct implementation of the BCP.

It is also a good practice to include BCP components in job descriptions to ensure that the BCP remains fresh and is performed correctly. Including BCP responsibilities in an employee's job description also makes them fair game for the performance review process.

Testing and Exercises

The BCP documentation should also outline a formalized exercise program to ensure that the plan remains current and that all personnel are adequately trained to perform their duties in the event of a disaster. The testing process is quite similar to that used for the disaster recovery plan, so we'll reserve the discussion of the specific test types for Chapter 18.

Summary

Every organization dependent on technological resources for its survival should have a comprehensive business continuity plan in place to ensure the sustained viability of the organization when unforeseen emergencies take place. There are a number of important concepts that underlie solid business continuity planning (BCP) practices, including project scope and planning, business impact assessment, continuity planning, and approval and implementation.

Every organization must have plans and procedures in place to help mitigate the effects a disaster has on continuing operations and to speed the return to normal operations. To determine the risks that your business faces and that require mitigation, you must conduct a business impact assessment from both quantitative and qualitative points of view. You must take the appropriate steps in developing a continuity strategy for your organization and know what to do to weather future disasters.

Finally, you must create the documentation required to ensure that your plan is effectively communicated to present and future BCP team participants. Such documentation should include continuity planning guidelines. The business continuity plan must also contain statements of importance, priorities, organizational responsibility, and urgency and timing. In addition, the documentation should include plans for risk assessment, acceptance, and mitigation; a vital records program; emergency-response guidelines; and plans for maintenance and testing.

Chapter 18 will take this planning to the next step—developing and implementing a disaster recovery plan. The disaster recovery plan kicks in where the business continuity plan leaves off. When an emergency occurs that interrupts your business in spite of the BCP measures, the disaster recovery plan guides the recovery efforts necessary to restore your business to normal operations as quickly as possible.

Exam Essentials

Understand the four steps of the business continuity planning process. Business continuity planning (BCP) involves four distinct phases: project scope and planning, business impact assessment, continuity planning, and approval and implementation. Each task contributes to the overall goal of ensuring that business operations continue uninterrupted in the face of an emergency situation.

Describe how to perform the business organization analysis. In the business organization analysis, the individuals responsible for leading the BCP process determine which departments and individuals have a stake in the business continuity plan. This analysis is used as the foundation for BCP team selection and, after validation by the BCP team, is used to guide the next stages of BCP development.

List the necessary members of the business continuity planning team. The BCP team should contain, at a minimum, representatives from each of the operational and support departments; technical experts from the IT department; security personnel with BCP skills; legal representatives familiar with corporate legal, regulatory, and contractual responsibilities; and representatives from senior management. Additional team members depend on the structure and nature of the organization.

Know the legal and regulatory requirements that face business continuity planners. Business leaders must exercise due diligence to ensure that shareholders' interests are protected in the event disaster strikes. Some industries are also subject to federal, state, and local regulations that mandate specific BCP procedures. Many businesses also have contractual obligations to their clients that must be met, before and after a disaster.

Explain the steps of the business impact assessment process. The five steps of the business impact assessment process are identification of priorities, risk identification, likelihood assessment, impact assessment, and resource prioritization.

Describe the process used to develop a continuity strategy. During the strategy development phase, the BCP team determines which risks will be mitigated. In the provisions and processes phase, mechanisms and procedures that will mitigate the risks are designed. The plan must then be approved by senior management and implemented. Personnel must also receive training on their roles in the BCP process.

Explain the importance of fully documenting an organization's business continuity plan. Committing the plan to writing provides the organization with a written record of the procedures to follow when disaster strikes. It prevents the "it's in my head" syndrome and ensures the orderly progress of events in an emergency.

Written Lab

1. Why is it important to include legal representatives on your business continuity planning team?
2. What is wrong with the "seat-of-the-pants" approach to business continuity planning?
3. What is the difference between quantitative and qualitative risk assessment?
4. What critical components should be included in your business continuity training plan?
5. What are the four main steps of the business continuity planning process?

Review Questions

1. What is the first step that individuals responsible for the development of a business continuity plan should perform?
   A. BCP team selection
   B. Business organization analysis
   C. Resource requirements analysis
   D. Legal and regulatory assessment
2. Once the BCP team is selected, what should be the first item placed on the team's agenda?
   A. Business impact assessment
   B. Business organization analysis
   C. Resource requirements analysis
   D. Legal and regulatory assessment
3. What is the term used to describe the responsibility of a firm's officers and directors to ensure that adequate measures are in place to minimize the effect of a disaster on the organization's continued viability?
   A. Corporate responsibility
   B. Disaster requirement
   C. Due diligence
   D. Going concern responsibility
4. What will be the major resource consumed by the BCP process during the BCP phase?
   A. Hardware
   B. Software
   C. Processing time
   D. Personnel
5. What unit of measurement should be used to assign quantitative values to assets in the priority identification phase of the business impact assessment?
   A. Monetary
   B. Utility
   C. Importance
   D. Time
6. Which one of the following BIA terms identifies the amount of money a business expects to lose to a given risk each year?
   A. ARO
   B. SLE

C. ALE
D. EF

7. What BIA metric can be used to express the longest time a business function can be unavailable without causing irreparable harm to the organization?
A. SLE
B. EF
C. MTD
D. ARO

8. You are concerned about the risk that an avalanche poses to your $3 million shipping facility. Based on expert opinion, you determine that there is a 5 percent chance that an avalanche will occur each year. Experts advise you that an avalanche would completely destroy your building and require you to rebuild on the same land. Ninety percent of the $3 million value of the facility is attributed to the building and 10 percent is attributed to the land itself. What is the single loss expectancy of your shipping facility to avalanches?
A. $3,000,000
B. $2,700,000
C. $270,000
D. $135,000

9. Referring to the scenario in question 8, what is the annualized loss expectancy?
A. $3,000,000
B. $2,700,000
C. $270,000
D. $135,000

10. You are concerned about the risk that a hurricane poses to your corporate headquarters in South Florida. The building itself is valued at $15 million. After consulting with the National Weather Service, you determine that there is a 10 percent likelihood that a hurricane will strike over the course of a year. You hired a team of architects and engineers who determined that the average hurricane would destroy approximately 50 percent of the building. What is the annualized loss expectancy (ALE)?
A. $750,000
B. $1.5 million
C. $7.5 million
D. $15 million

11. Which task of BCP bridges the gap between the business impact assessment and the continuity planning phases?
A. Resource prioritization
B. Likelihood assessment
C. Strategy development
D. Provisions and processes

12. Which resource should you protect first when designing continuity plan provisions and processes?
    A. Physical plant
    B. Infrastructure
    C. Financial
    D. People

13. Which one of the following concerns is not suitable for quantitative measurement during the business impact assessment?
    A. Loss of a plant
    B. Damage to a vehicle
    C. Negative publicity
    D. Power outage

14. Lighter Than Air Industries expects that it would lose $10 million if a tornado struck its aircraft operations facility. It expects that a tornado might strike the facility once every 100 years. What is the single loss expectancy for this scenario?
    A. 0.01
    B. $10,000,000
    C. $100,000
    D. 0.10

15. Referring to the scenario in question 14, what is the annualized loss expectancy?
    A. 0.01
    B. $10,000,000
    C. $100,000
    D. 0.10

16. In which business continuity planning task would you actually design procedures and mechanisms to mitigate risks deemed unacceptable by the BCP team?
    A. Strategy development
    B. Business impact assessment
    C. Provisions and processes
    D. Resource prioritization

17. What type of mitigation provision is utilized when redundant communications links are installed?
    A. Hardening systems
    B. Defining systems
    C. Reducing systems
    D. Alternative systems

18. What type of plan outlines the procedures to follow when a disaster interrupts the normal operations of a business?
   - A. Business continuity plan
   - B. Business impact assessment
   - C. Disaster recovery plan
   - D. Vulnerability assessment

19. What is the formula used to compute the single loss expectancy for a risk scenario?
   - A. $SLE = AV \times EF$
   - B. $SLE = RO \times EF$
   - C. $SLE = AV \times ARO$
   - D. $SLE = EF \times ARO$

20. Of the individuals listed, who would provide the best endorsement for a business continuity plan's statement of importance?
   - A. Vice president of business operations
   - B. Chief information officer
   - C. Chief executive officer
   - D. Business continuity manager

Chapter 4

Laws, Regulations, and Compliance

THE CISSP EXAM TOPICS COVERED IN THIS CHAPTER INCLUDE:

✓ **Security and Risk Management (e.g., Security, Risk, Compliance, Law, Regulations, Business Continuity)**

- C. Compliance
  - C.1 Legislative and regulatory compliance
  - C.2 Privacy requirements compliance
- D. Understand legal and regulatory issues that pertain to information security in a global context
  - D.1 Computer crimes
  - D.2 Licensing and intellectual property (e.g. copyright, trademark, digital-rights management)
  - D.3 Import/export controls
  - D.4 Trans-border data flow
  - D.5 Privacy
  - D.6 Data breaches

In the early days of computer security, information security professionals were pretty much left on their own to defend their systems against attacks. They didn't have much help from the criminal and civil justice systems. When they did seek assistance from law enforcement, they were met with reluctance by overworked agents who didn't have a basic understanding of how something that involved a computer could actually be a crime. The legislative branch of government hadn't addressed the issue of computer crime, and the executive branch thought they simply didn't have statutory authority or obligation to pursue those matters.

Fortunately, both our legal system and the men and women of law enforcement have come a long way over the past three decades. The legislative branches of governments around the world have at least attempted to address issues of computer crime. Many law enforcement agencies have full-time, well-trained computer crime investigators with advanced security training. Those who don't usually know where to turn when they require this sort of experience.

In this chapter, we'll cover the various types of laws that deal with computer security issues. We'll examine the legal issues surrounding computer crime, privacy, intellectual property, and a number of other related topics. We'll also cover basic investigative techniques, including the pros and cons of calling in assistance from law enforcement.

Categories of Laws

Three main categories of laws play a role in our legal system. Each is used to cover a variety of circumstances, and the penalties for violating laws in the different categories vary widely. In the following sections, you'll learn how criminal law, civil law, and administrative law interact to form the complex web of our justice system.

Criminal Law

Criminal law forms the bedrock of the body of laws that preserve the peace and keep our society safe. Many high-profile court cases involve matters of criminal law; these are the laws that the police and other law enforcement agencies concern themselves with. Criminal law contains prohibitions against acts such as murder, assault, robbery, and arson. Penalties for violating criminal statutes fall in a range that includes mandatory hours of community service, monetary penalties in the form of fines (small and large), and deprivation of civil liberties in the form of prison sentences.

Real World Scenario

Cops Are Smart!

A good friend of one of the authors is a technology crime investigator for the local police department. He often receives cases of computer abuse involving threatening emails and website postings.

Recently, he shared a story about a bomb threat that had been emailed to a local high school. The perpetrator sent a threatening note to the school principal declaring that the bomb would explode at 1 p.m. and warning him to evacuate the school. The author's friend received the alert at 11 a.m., leaving him with only two hours to investigate the crime and advise the principal on the best course of action.

He quickly began issuing emergency subpoenas to Internet service providers and traced the email to a computer in the school library. At 12:15 p.m., he confronted the suspect with surveillance tapes showing him at the computer in the library as well as audit logs conclusively proving that he had sent the email. The student quickly admitted that the threat was nothing more than a ploy to get out of school a couple of hours early. His explanation? "I didn't think there was anyone around here who could trace stuff like that."

He was wrong.

A number of criminal laws serve to protect society against computer crime. In later sections of this chapter, you'll learn how some laws, such as the Computer Fraud and Abuse Act, the Electronic Communications Privacy Act, and the Identity Theft and Assumption Deterrence Act (among others), provide criminal penalties for serious cases of computer crime. Technically savvy prosecutors teamed with concerned law enforcement agencies have dealt serious blows to the "hacking underground" by using the court system to slap lengthy prison terms on offenders guilty of what used to be considered harmless pranks.

In the United States, legislative bodies at all levels of government establish criminal laws through elected representatives. At the federal level, both the House of Representatives and the Senate must pass criminal law bills by a majority vote (in most cases) in order for the bill to become law. Once passed, these laws then become federal law and apply in all cases where the federal government has jurisdiction (mainly cases that involve interstate commerce, cases that cross state boundaries, or cases that are offenses against the federal government itself). If federal jurisdiction does not apply, state authorities handle the case using laws passed in a similar manner by state legislators.

All federal and state laws must comply with the ultimate authority that dictates how the U.S. system of government works—the U.S. Constitution. All laws are subject to judicial review by regional courts with the right of appeal all the way to the Supreme Court of the United States. If a court finds that a law is unconstitutional, it has the power to strike it down and render it invalid.

Keep in mind that criminal law is a serious matter. If you find yourself involved—as a witness, defendant, or victim—in a matter where criminal authorities become involved, you'd be well advised to seek advice from an attorney familiar with the criminal justice system and specifically with matters of computer crime. It's not wise to "go it alone" in such a complex system.

Civil Law

Civil laws form the bulk of our body of laws. They are designed to provide for an orderly society and govern matters that are not crimes but that require an impartial arbiter to settle between individuals and organizations. Examples of the types of matters that may be judged under civil law include contract disputes, real estate transactions, employment matters, and estate/probate procedures. Civil laws also are used to create the framework of government that the executive branch uses to carry out its responsibilities. These laws provide budgets for governmental activities and lay out the authority granted to the executive branch to create administrative laws (see the next section).

Civil laws are enacted in the same manner as criminal laws. They must pass through the legislative process before enactment and are subject to the same constitutional parameters and judicial review procedures. At the federal level, both criminal and civil laws are embodied in the United States Code (USC).

The major difference between civil laws and criminal laws is the way in which they are enforced. Usually, law enforcement authorities do not become involved in matters of civil law beyond taking action necessary to restore order. In a criminal prosecution, the government, through law enforcement investigators and prosecutors, brings action against a person accused of a crime. In civil matters, it is incumbent upon the person who thinks they have been wronged to obtain legal counsel and file a civil lawsuit against the person they think is responsible for their grievance. The government (unless it is the plaintiff or defendant) does not take sides in the dispute or argue one position or the other. The only role of the government in civil matters is to provide the judges, juries, and court facilities used to hear civil cases and to play an administrative role in managing the judicial system in accordance with the law.

As with criminal law, it is best to obtain legal assistance if you think you need to file a civil lawsuit or if someone files a civil lawsuit against you. Although civil law does not impose the threat of imprisonment, the losing party may face severe financial penalties. You don't need to look any further than the nightly news for examples—multimillion-dollar cases against tobacco companies, major corporations, and wealthy individuals are filed every day.

Administrative Law

The executive branch of our government charges numerous agencies with wide-ranging responsibilities to ensure that government functions effectively. It is the duty of these agencies to abide by and enforce the criminal and civil laws enacted by the legislative branch. However, as can be easily imagined, criminal and civil law can't possibly lay out rules and procedures that should be followed in any possible situation. Therefore, executive branch agencies have some leeway to enact administrative law, in the form of policies, procedures, and regulations that govern the daily operations of the agency. Administrative law covers topics as mundane as the procedures to be used within a federal agency to obtain a desk telephone to more substantial issues such as the immigration policies that will be used to enforce the laws passed by Congress. Administrative law is published in the Code of Federal Regulations, often referred to as the CFR.

Although administrative law does not require an act of the legislative branch to gain the force of law, it must comply with all existing civil and criminal laws. Government agencies may not implement regulations that directly contradict existing laws passed by the legislature. Furthermore, administrative laws (and the actions of government agencies) must also comply with the U.S. Constitution and are subject to judicial review.

In order to understand compliance requirements and procedures, it is necessary to be fully versed in the complexities of the law. From administrative law to civil law to criminal law (and, in some countries, even religious law), navigating the regulatory environment is a daunting task. The CISSP exam focuses on the generalities of law, regulations, investigations, and compliance as they affect organizational security efforts. However, it is your responsibility to seek out professional help (i.e., an attorney) to guide and support you in your efforts to maintain legal and legally supportable security.

Laws

Throughout these sections, we'll examine a number of laws that relate to information technology. By necessity, this discussion is U.S.-centric, as is the material covered by the CISSP exam. We'll look briefly at several high-profile foreign laws, such as the European Union's data privacy act. However, if you operate in an environment that involves foreign jurisdictions, you should retain local legal counsel to guide you through the system.

WARNING Every information security professional should have a basic understanding of the law as it relates to information technology. However, the most important lesson to be learned is knowing when it's necessary to call in an attorney. If you think you're in a legal "gray area," it's best to seek professional advice.

Computer Crime

The first computer security issues addressed by legislators were those involving computer crime. Early computer crime prosecutions were attempted under traditional criminal law, and many were dismissed because judges thought that applying traditional law to this modern type of crime was too far of a stretch. Legislators responded by passing specific statutes that defined computer crime and laid out specific penalties for various crimes. In the following sections, we'll cover several of those statutes.

> **TIP** The U.S. laws discussed in this chapter are federal laws. But keep in mind that almost every state in the union has also enacted some form of legislation regarding computer security issues. Because of the global reach of the Internet, most computer crimes cross state lines and, therefore, fall under federal jurisdiction and are prosecuted in the federal court system. However, in some circumstances, state laws can be more restrictive than federal laws and impose harsher penalties.

Computer Fraud and Abuse Act

Congress first enacted computer crime law as part of the Comprehensive Crime Control Act (CCCA) of 1984, and it remains in force today, with several amendments. This law was carefully written to exclusively cover computer crimes that crossed state boundaries to avoid infringing on states' rights and treading on thin constitutional ice. The major provisions of the act are that it is a crime to perform the following:

- Access classified information or financial information in a federal system without authorization or in excess of authorized privileges
- Access a computer used exclusively by the federal government without authorization
- Use a federal computer to perpetrate a fraud (unless the only object of the fraud was to gain use of the computer itself)
- Cause malicious damage to a federal computer system in excess of $1,000
- Modify medical records in a computer when doing so impairs or may impair the examination, diagnosis, treatment, or medical care of an individual
- Traffic in computer passwords if the trafficking affects interstate commerce or involves a federal computer system

Computer crime law enacted as part of the CCCA was amended by the more well-known Computer Fraud and Abuse Act (CFAA) in 1986 to change the scope of the regulation. Instead of merely covering federal computers that processed sensitive information, the act was changed to cover all "federal interest" computers. This widened the coverage of the act to include the following:

- Any computer used exclusively by the U.S. government
- Any computer used exclusively by a financial institution
- Any computer used by the government or a financial institution when the offense impedes the ability of the government or institution to use that system
- Any combination of computers used to commit an offense when they are not all located in the same state

> **TIP** When preparing for the CISSP exam, be sure you're able to briefly describe the purpose of each law discussed in this chapter.

1994 CFAA Amendments

In 1994, Congress recognized that the face of computer security had drastically changed since the CFAA was last amended in 1986 and made a number of sweeping changes to the act. Collectively, these changes are referred to as the Computer Abuse Amendments Act of 1994 and included the following provisions:

- Outlawed the creation of any type of malicious code that might cause damage to a computer system
- Modified the CFAA to cover any computer used in interstate commerce rather than just "federal interest" computer systems
- Allowed for the imprisonment of offenders, regardless of whether they actually intended to cause damage
- Provided legal authority for the victims of computer crime to pursue civil action to gain injunctive relief and compensation for damages

In 2015, President Barack Obama proposed significant changes to the Computer Fraud and Abuse Act that would bring computer crimes into the scope of the Racketeer Influenced and Corrupt Organizations Act (RICO) statutes used to combat organized crime. That proposal was still pending as this book went to press.

Computer Security Act of 1987

After amending the CFAA in 1986 to cover a wider variety of computer systems, Congress turned its view inward and examined the current state of computer security in federal government systems. Members of Congress were not satisfied with what they saw and they enacted the Computer Security Act (CSA) of 1987 to mandate baseline security requirements for all federal agencies. In the introduction to the CSA, Congress specified four main purposes of the act:

- To give the National Institute of Standards and Technology (NIST) responsibility for developing standards and guidelines for federal computer systems. For this purpose, NIST draws on the technical advice and assistance (including work products) of the National Security Agency where appropriate.
- To provide for the enactment of such standards and guidelines.
- To require the establishment of security plans by all operators of federal computer systems that contain sensitive information.
- To require mandatory periodic training for all people involved in management, use, or operation of federal computer systems that contain sensitive information.

This act clearly set out a number of requirements that formed the basis of federal computer security policy for many years. It also divided responsibility for computer security among two federal agencies. The National Security Agency (NSA), which formerly had authority over all computer security issues, retained authority over classified systems, but NIST gained responsibility for securing all other federal government systems. NIST produces the 800 series of Special Publications related to computer security in the federal government. These are useful for all security practitioners and are available for free online here:

`http://csrc.nist.gov/publications/PubsSPs.html`

Federal Sentencing Guidelines

The Federal Sentencing Guidelines released in 1991 provided punishment guidelines to help federal judges interpret computer crime laws. Three major provisions of these guidelines have had a lasting impact on the information security community:

- The guidelines formalized the *prudent man rule*, which requires senior executives to take personal responsibility for ensuring the due care that ordinary, prudent individuals would exercise in the same situation. This rule, developed in the realm of fiscal responsibility, now applies to information security as well.
- The guidelines allowed organizations and executives to minimize punishment for infractions by demonstrating that they used due diligence in the conduct of their information security duties.
- The guidelines outlined three burdens of proof for negligence. First, the person accused of negligence must have a legally recognized obligation. Second, the person must have failed to comply with recognized standards. Finally, there must be a causal relationship between the act of negligence and subsequent damages.

National Information Infrastructure Protection Act of 1996

In 1996, Congress passed yet another set of amendments to the Computer Fraud and Abuse Act designed to further extend the protection it provides. The National Information Infrastructure Protection Act included the following main new areas of coverage:

- Broadens CFAA to cover computer systems used in international commerce in addition to systems used in interstate commerce
- Extends similar protections to portions of the national infrastructure other than computing systems, such as railroads, gas pipelines, electric power grids, and telecommunications circuits
- Treats any intentional or reckless act that causes damage to critical portions of the national infrastructure as a felony

Paperwork Reduction Act of 1995

The Paperwork Reduction Act of 1995 requires that agencies obtain Office of Management and Budget (OMB) approval before requesting most types of information from the public. Information collections include forms, interviews, record-keeping requirements, and a wide variety of other things. The Government Information Security Reform Act (GISRA) of 2000 amended this act, as described in the next section.

Government Information Security Reform Act of 2000

The Government Information Security Reform Act (GISRA) of 2000 amended the Paperwork Reduction Act to implement additional information security policies and procedures. In the text of the act, Congress laid out five basic purposes for establishing the GISRA:

- To provide a comprehensive framework for establishing and ensuring the effectiveness of controls over information resources that support federal operations and assets
- To recognize the highly networked nature of the federal computing environment, including the need for federal government interoperability, and in the implementation of improved security management measures, to assure that opportunities for interoperability are not adversely affected
- To provide effective government-wide management and oversight of the related information security risks, including coordination of information security efforts throughout the civilian, national security, and law enforcement communities
- To provide for development and maintenance of minimum controls required to protect federal information and information systems
- To provide a mechanism for improved oversight of federal agency information security programs

The provisions of the GISRA continue to charge the National Institute of Standards and Technology and the National Security Agency with security oversight responsibilities for unclassified and classified information processing systems, respectively. However, GISRA places the burden of maintaining the security and integrity of government information and information systems squarely on the shoulders of individual agency leaders.

GISRA also creates a new category of computer system. A mission-critical system meets one of the following criteria:

- It is defined as a national security system by other provisions of law.
- It is protected by procedures established for classified information.
- The loss, misuse, disclosure, or unauthorized access to or modification of any information it processes would have a debilitating impact on the mission of an agency.

GISRA provides specific evaluation and auditing authority for mission-critical systems to the secretary of defense and the director of central intelligence. This is an attempt to ensure that all government agencies, even those that do not routinely deal with classified national security information, implement adequate security controls on systems that are absolutely critical to the continued functioning of the agency.

NOTE

For the past 10 years, Congress failed to pass any new significant regulation of computer crime, but there has been a recent push to enact new laws. Notable failures include the Cybersecurity Act of 2012 and the Cyber Intelligence Sharing and Protection Act of 2013.

Although these bills failed to become law, it is likely that the push to enact new cybercrime law will continue, and new regulations loom on the horizon.

Federal Information Security Management Act

The Federal Information Security Management Act (FISMA), passed in 2002, requires that federal agencies implement an information security program that covers the agency's operations. FISMA also requires that government agencies include the activities of contractors in their security management programs. The National Institute of Standards and Technology (NIST), responsible for developing the FISMA implementation guidelines, outlines the following elements of an effective information security program:

- Periodic assessments of risk, including the magnitude of harm that could result from the unauthorized access, use, disclosure, disruption, modification, or destruction of information and information systems that support the operations and assets of the organization
- Policies and procedures that are based on risk assessments, cost-effectively reduce information security risks to an acceptable level, and ensure that information security is addressed throughout the life cycle of each organizational information system
- Subordinate plans for providing adequate information security for networks, facilities, information systems, or groups of information systems, as appropriate
- Security awareness training to inform personnel (including contractors and other users of information systems that support the operations and assets of the organization) of the information security risks associated with their activities and their responsibilities in complying with organizational policies and procedures designed to reduce these risks
- Periodic testing and evaluation of the effectiveness of information security policies, procedures, practices, and security controls to be performed with a frequency depending on risk, but no less than annually
- A process for planning, implementing, evaluating, and documenting remedial actions to address any deficiencies in the information security policies, procedures, and practices of the organization
- Procedures for detecting, reporting, and responding to security incidents
- Plans and procedures to ensure continuity of operations for information systems that support the operations and assets of the organization.

FISMA places a significant burden on federal agencies and government contractors, who must develop and maintain substantial documentation of their FISMA compliance activities.

Intellectual Property

America's role in the global economy is shifting away from a manufacturer of goods and toward a provider of services. This trend also shows itself in many of the world's large industrialized nations. With this shift toward providing services, intellectual property takes on an increasingly important role in many firms. Indeed, it is arguable that the most valuable assets of many large multinational companies are simply the brand names that we've all come to recognize. Company names such as Dell, Procter & Gamble, and Merck bring instant credibility to any product. Publishing companies, movie producers, and artists depend on their creative output to earn their livelihood. Many products depend on secret recipes or production techniques—take the legendary secret formula for Coca-Cola or KFC's secret blend of herbs and spices, for example.

These intangible assets are collectively referred to as *intellectual property*, and a whole host of laws exist to protect the rights of their owners. After all, it simply wouldn't be fair if a music store bought only one copy of each artist's CD and burned copies for all of its customers—that would deprive the artist of the benefits of their labor. In the following sections, we'll explore the laws surrounding the four major types of intellectual property—copyrights, trademarks, patents, and trade secrets. We'll also discuss how these concepts specifically concern information security professionals. Many countries protect (or fail to protect) these rights in different ways, but the basic concepts ring true throughout the world.

WARNING Some countries are notorious for violating intellectual property rights. The most notable example is China. China is world renowned for its blatant disregard of copyright and patent law. If you're planning to do business in this region of the world, you should definitely consult with an attorney who specializes in this area.

Copyrights and the Digital Millennium Copyright Act

Copyright law guarantees the creators of "original works of authorship" protection against the unauthorized duplication of their work. Eight broad categories of works qualify for copyright protection:

- Literary works
- Musical works
- Dramatic works
- Pantomimes and choreographic works
- Pictorial, graphical, and sculptural works
- Motion pictures and other audiovisual works
- Sound recordings
- Architectural works

There is precedent for copyrighting computer software—it's done under the scope of literary works. However, it's important to note that copyright law protects only the expression inherent in computer software—that is, the actual source code. It does not protect the ideas or process behind the software. There has also been some question over whether copyrights can be extended to cover the "look and feel" of a software package's graphical user interface. Court decisions have gone in both directions on this matter; if you will be involved in this type of issue, you should consult a qualified intellectual property attorney to determine the current state of legislation and case law.

There is a formal procedure to obtain a copyright that involves sending copies of the protected work along with an appropriate registration fee to the U.S. Copyright Office. For more information on this process, visit the office's website at `www.copyright.gov`. However, it is important to note that officially registering a copyright is not a prerequisite for copyright enforcement. Indeed, the law states that the creator of a work has an automatic copyright from the instant the work is created. If you can prove in court that you were the creator of a work (perhaps by publishing it), you will be protected under copyright law. Official registration merely provides the government's acknowledgment that they received your work on a specific date.

Copyright ownership always defaults to the creator of a work. The exceptions to this policy are works for hire. A work is considered "for hire" when it is made for an employer during the normal course of an employee's workday. For example, when an employee in a company's public relations department writes a press release, the press release is considered a work for hire. A work may also be considered a work for hire when it is made as part of a written contract declaring it as such.

Current copyright law provides for a very lengthy period of protection. Works by one or more authors are protected until 70 years after the death of the last surviving author. Works for hire and anonymous works are provided protection for 95 years from the date of first publication or 120 years from the date of creation, whichever is shorter.

In 1998, Congress recognized the rapidly changing digital landscape that was stretching the reach of existing copyright law. To help meet this challenge, it enacted the hotly debated Digital Millennium Copyright Act (DMCA). The DMCA also serves to bring U.S. copyright law into compliance with terms of two World Intellectual Property Organization (WIPO) treaties.

The first major provision of the DMCA is the prohibition of attempts to circumvent copyright protection mechanisms placed on a protected work by the copyright holder. This clause was designed to protect copy-prevention mechanisms placed on digital media such as CDs and DVDs. The DMCA provides for penalties of up to $1,000,000 and 10 years in prison for repeat offenders. Nonprofit institutions such as libraries and schools are exempted from this provision.

The DMCA also limits the liability of Internet service providers when their circuits are used by criminals violating the copyright law. The DMCA recognizes that ISPs have a legal status similar to the "common carrier" status of telephone companies and does not hold them liable for the "transitory activities" of their users. To qualify for this exemption, the service provider's activities must meet the following requirements (quoted directly from the Digital Millennium Copyright Act of 1998, U.S. Copyright Office Summary, December 1998):

- The transmission must be initiated by a person other than the provider.
- The transmission, routing, provision of connections, or copying must be carried out by an automated technical process without selection of material by the service provider.
- The service provider must not determine the recipients of the material.

- Any intermediate copies must not ordinarily be accessible to anyone other than anticipated recipients, and must not be retained for longer than reasonably necessary.
- The material must be transmitted with no modification to its content.

The DMCA also exempts activities of service providers related to system caching, search engines, and the storage of information on a network by individual users. However, in those cases, the service provider must take prompt action to remove copyrighted materials upon notification of the infringement.

Congress also included provisions in the DMCA that allow the creation of backup copies of computer software and any maintenance, testing, or routine usage activities that require software duplication. These provisions apply only if the software is licensed for use on a particular computer, the usage is in compliance with the license agreement, and any such copies are immediately deleted when no longer required for a permitted activity.

Finally, the DMCA spells out the application of copyright law principles to the emerging field of *webcasting*, or broadcasting audio and/or video content to recipients over the Internet. This technology is often referred to as *streaming audio* or *streaming video*. The DMCA states that these uses are to be treated as "eligible nonsubscription transmissions." The law in this area is still under development, so if you plan to engage in this type of activity, you should contact an attorney to ensure that you are in compliance with current law.

TIP

Keep an eye on the development of the Anti-Counterfeiting Trade Agreement (ACTA), which proposes a framework for international enforcement of intellectual property protections. As of February 2015, the treaty awaited ratification by the European Union member states, the United States, and five other nations.

Trademarks

Copyright laws are used to protect creative works; there is also protection for *trademarks*, which are words, slogans, and logos used to identify a company and its products or services. For example, a business might obtain a copyright on its sales brochure to ensure that competitors can't duplicate its sales materials. That same business might also seek to obtain trademark protection for its company name and the names of specific products and services that it offers to its clients.

The main objective of trademark protection is to avoid confusion in the marketplace while protecting the intellectual property rights of people and organizations. As with copyright protection, trademarks do not need to be officially registered to gain protection under the law. If you use a trademark in the course of your public activities, you are automatically protected under any relevant trademark law and can use the ™ symbol to show that you intend to protect words or slogans as trademarks. If you want official recognition of your trademark, you can register it with the United States Patent and Trademark Office (USPTO). This process generally requires an attorney to perform a due diligence comprehensive search for existing trademarks that might preclude your registration. The entire registration process can take more than a year from start to finish. Once you've received your registration certificate from the USPTO, you can denote your mark as a registered trademark with the ® symbol.

One major advantage of trademark registration is that you may register a trademark that you intend to use but are not necessarily already using. This type of application is called an *intent to use* application and conveys trademark protection as of the date of filing provided that you actually use the trademark in commerce within a certain time period. If you opt not to register your trademark with the PTO, your protection begins only when you first use the trademark.

The acceptance of a trademark application in the United States depends on two main requirements:

- The trademark must not be confusingly similar to another trademark—you should determine this during your attorney's due diligence search. There will be an open opposition period during which other companies may dispute your trademark application.
- The trademark should not be descriptive of the goods and services that you will offer. For example, "Mike's Software Company" would not be a good trademark candidate because it describes the product produced by the company. The USPTO may reject an application if it considers the trademark descriptive.

In the United States, trademarks are granted for an initial period of 10 years and can be renewed for unlimited successive 10-year periods.

Patents

Patents protect the intellectual property rights of inventors. They provide a period of 20 years during which the inventor is granted exclusive rights to use the invention (whether directly or via licensing agreements). At the end of the patent exclusivity period, the invention is in the public domain available for anyone to use.

Patents have three main requirements:

- The invention must be new. Inventions are patentable only if they are original ideas.
- The invention must be useful. It must actually work and accomplish some sort of task.
- The invention must not be obvious. You could not, for example, obtain a patent for your idea to use a drinking cup to collect rainwater. This is an obvious solution. You might, however, be able to patent a specially designed cup that optimizes the amount of rainwater collected while minimizing evaporation.

In the technology field, patents have long been used to protect hardware devices and manufacturing processes. There is plenty of precedent on the side of inventors in those areas. Recent patents have also been issued covering software programs and similar mechanisms, but the jury is still out on whether these patents will hold up to the scrutiny of the courts.

Trade Secrets

Many companies have intellectual property that is absolutely critical to their business and significant damage would result if it were disclosed to competitors and/or the public—in other words, *trade secrets*. We previously mentioned two examples of this type of information from popular culture—the secret formula for Coca-Cola and KFC's "secret blend of herbs and spices." Other examples are plentiful—a manufacturing company may want to keep secret a certain manufacturing process that only a few key employees fully understand, or a statistical analysis company might want to safeguard an advanced model developed for in-house use.

Two of the previously discussed intellectual property tools—copyrights and patents—could be used to protect this type of information, but with two major disadvantages:

- Filing a copyright or patent application requires that you publicly disclose the details of your work or invention. This automatically removes the "secret" nature of your property and may harm your firm by removing the mystique surrounding a product or by allowing unscrupulous competitors to copy your property in violation of international intellectual property laws.
- Copyrights and patents both provide protection for a limited period of time. Once your legal protection expires, other firms are free to use your work at will (and they have all the details from the public disclosure you made during the application process!).

There actually is an official process regarding trade secrets—by their nature you don't register them with anyone; you keep them to yourself. To preserve trade secret status, you must implement adequate controls within your organization to ensure that only authorized personnel with a need to know the secrets have access to them. You must also ensure that anyone who does have this type of access is bound by a nondisclosure agreement (NDA) that prohibits them from sharing the information with others and provides penalties for violating the agreement. Consult an attorney to ensure that the agreement lasts for the maximum period permitted by law. In addition, you must take steps to demonstrate that you value and protect your intellectual property. Failure to do so may result in the loss of trade secret protection.

Trade secret protection is one of the best ways to protect computer software. As discussed in the previous section, patent law does not provide adequate protection for computer software products. Copyright law protects only the actual text of the source code and doesn't prohibit others from rewriting your code in a different form and accomplishing the same objective. If you treat your source code as a trade secret, it keeps it out of the hands of your competitors in the first place. This is the technique used by large software development companies such as Microsoft to protect its core base of intellectual property.

Economic Espionage Act of 1996

Trade secrets are very often the crown jewels of major corporations, and the U.S. government recognized the importance of protecting this type of intellectual property when Congress enacted the Economic Espionage Act of 1996. This law has two major provisions:

- Anyone found guilty of stealing trade secrets from a U.S. corporation with the intention of benefiting a foreign government or agent may be fined up to $500,000 and imprisoned for up to 15 years.
- Anyone found guilty of stealing trade secrets under other circumstances may be fined up to $250,000 and imprisoned for up to 10 years.

The terms of the Economic Espionage Act give true teeth to the intellectual property rights of trade secret owners. Enforcing this law requires that companies take adequate steps to ensure that their trade secrets are well protected and not accidentally placed into the public domain.

Licensing

Security professionals should also be familiar with the legal issues surrounding software licensing agreements. Four common types of license agreements are in use today:

- Contractual license agreements use a written contract between the software vendor and the customer, outlining the responsibilities of each. These agreements are commonly found for high-priced and/or highly specialized software packages.
- Shrink-wrap license agreements are written on the outside of the software packaging. They commonly include a clause stating that you acknowledge agreement to the terms of the contract simply by breaking the shrink-wrap seal on the package.
- Click-through license agreements are becoming more commonplace than shrink-wrap agreements. In this type of agreement, the contract terms are either written on the software box or included in the software documentation. During the installation process, you are required to click a button indicating that you have read the terms of the agreement and agree to abide by them. This adds an active consent to the process, ensuring that the individual is aware of the agreement's existence prior to installation.
- Cloud services license agreements take click-through agreements to the extreme. Most cloud services do not require any form of written agreement and simply flash legal terms on the screen for review. In some cases, they may simply provide a link to legal terms and a check box for users to confirm that they read and agree to the terms. Most users, in their excitement to access a new service, simply click their way through the agreement without reading it and may unwittingly bind their entire organization to onerous terms and conditions.

Uniform Computer Information Transactions Act

The Uniform Computer Information Transactions Act (UCITA) is a federal law designed for adoption by each of the 50 states to provide a common framework for the conduct of computer-related business transactions. UCITA contains provisions that address software licensing. The terms of UCITA give legal backing to the previously questionable practices of shrink-wrap licensing and click-wrap licensing by giving them status as legally binding contracts. UCITA also requires that manufacturers provide software users with the option to reject the terms of the license agreement before completing the installation process and receive a full refund of the software's purchase price.

NOTE

Industry groups provide guidance and enforcement activities regarding software licensing. You can get more information from their websites. One major group is the Software Alliance at `www.bsa.org`.

Import/Export

The federal government recognizes that the very same computers and encryption technologies that drive the Internet and e-commerce can be extremely powerful tools in the hands of a military force. For this reason, during the Cold War, the government developed a complex set of regulations governing the export of sensitive hardware and software products to other nations. The regulations include the management of trans-border data flow of new technologies, intellectual property, and personally identifying information.

Until recently, it was very difficult to export high-powered computers outside the United States, except to a select handful of allied nations. The controls on exporting encryption software were even more severe, rendering it virtually impossible to export any encryption technology outside the country. Recent changes in federal policy have relaxed these restrictions and provided for more open commerce.

Computer Export Controls

Currently, U.S. firms can export high-performance computing systems to virtually any country without receiving prior approval from the government. There are exceptions to this rule for countries designated by the Department of Commerce's Bureau of Industry and Security as countries of concern based on the fact that they pose a threat of nuclear proliferation, are classified as state sponsors of terrorism, or other concerns. These countries include India, Pakistan, Afghanistan, Cuba, North Korea, the Sudan, and Syria.

NOTE

You can find a list of countries and their corresponding computer export tiers on the Department of Commerce's website at `www.bis.doc.gov`.

Encryption Export Controls

The Department of Commerce's Bureau of Industry and Security sets forth regulations on the export of encryption products outside the United States. Under previous regulations, it was virtually impossible to export even relatively low-grade encryption technology outside the United States. This placed U.S. software manufacturers at a great competitive disadvantage to foreign firms that faced no similar regulations. After a lengthy lobbying campaign by the software industry, the president directed the Commerce Department to revise its regulations to foster the growth of the American security software industry.

Current regulations now designate the categories of retail and mass market security software. The rules now permit firms to submit these products for review by the Commerce Department, but the review will take no longer than 30 days. After successful completion of this review, companies may freely export these products.

Privacy

The right to privacy has for years been a hotly contested issue in the United States. The main source of this contention is that the Constitution's Bill of Rights does not explicitly provide for a right to privacy. However, this right has been upheld by numerous courts and is vigorously pursued by organizations such as the American Civil Liberties Union (ACLU).

Europeans have also long been concerned with their privacy. Indeed, countries such as Switzerland are world renowned for their ability to keep financial secrets. Later in this chapter, we'll examine how the European Union data privacy laws impact companies and Internet users.

U.S. Privacy Law

Although there is no constitutional guarantee of privacy, a myriad of federal laws (many enacted in recent years) are designed to protect the private information the government maintains about citizens as well as key portions of the private sector such as financial, educational, and health-care institutions. In the following sections, we'll examine a number of these federal laws.

Fourth Amendment The basis for privacy rights is in the Fourth Amendment to the U.S. Constitution. It reads as follows:

> The right of the people to be secure in their persons, houses, papers, and effects, against unreasonable searches and seizures, shall not be violated, and no warrants shall issue, but upon probable cause, supported by oath or affirmation, and particularly describing the place to be searched, and the persons or things to be seized.

The direct interpretation of this amendment prohibits government agents from searching private property without a warrant and probable cause. The courts have expanded their interpretation of the Fourth Amendment to include protections against wiretapping and other invasions of privacy.

Privacy Act of 1974 The Privacy Act of 1974 is perhaps the most significant piece of privacy legislation restricting the way the federal government may deal with private information about individual citizens. It severely limits the ability of federal government agencies to disclose private information to other persons or agencies without the prior written consent of the affected individual(s). It does provide for exceptions involving the census, law enforcement, the National Archives, health and safety, and court orders.

The Privacy Act mandates that agencies maintain only the records that are necessary for conducting their business and that they destroy those records when they are no longer needed for a legitimate function of government. It provides a formal procedure for individuals to gain access to records the government maintains about them and to request that incorrect records be amended.

Electronic Communications Privacy Act of 1986 The Electronic Communications Privacy Act (ECPA) makes it a crime to invade the electronic privacy of an individual. This act broadened the Federal Wiretap Act, which previously covered communications traveling via a physical wire, to apply to any illegal interception of electronic communications or to the intentional, unauthorized access of electronically stored data. It prohibits the interception or disclosure of electronic communication and defines those situations in which disclosure is legal. It protects against the monitoring of email and voicemail communications and prevents providers of those services from making unauthorized disclosures of their content.

One of the most notable provisions of the ECPA is that it makes it illegal to monitor mobile telephone conversations. In fact, such monitoring is punishable by a fine of up to $500 and a prison term of up to five years.

Communications Assistance for Law Enforcement Act (CALEA) of 1994 The Communications Assistance for Law Enforcement Act (CALEA) of 1994 amended the Electronic Communications Privacy Act of 1986. CALEA requires all communications carriers to make wiretaps possible for law enforcement with an appropriate court order, regardless of the technology in use.

Economic and Protection of Proprietary Information Act of 1996 The Economic and Protection of Proprietary Information Act of 1996 extends the definition of property to include proprietary economic information so that the theft of this information can be considered industrial or corporate espionage. This changed the legal definition of theft so that it was no longer restricted by physical constraints.

Health Insurance Portability and Accountability Act of 1996 In 1996, Congress passed the Health Insurance Portability and Accountability Act (HIPAA), which made numerous changes to the laws governing health insurance and health maintenance organizations (HMOs). Among the provisions of HIPAA are privacy and security regulations requiring strict security measures for hospitals, physicians, insurance companies, and other organizations that process or store private medical information about individuals.

HIPAA also clearly defines the rights of individuals who are the subject of medical records and requires organizations that maintain such records to disclose these rights in writing.

TIP

The HIPAA privacy and security regulations are quite complex. You should be familiar with the broad intentions of the act, as described here. If you work in the health-care industry, consider devoting time to an in-depth study of this law's provisions.

Health Information Technology for Economic and Clinical Health Act of 2009 In 2009, Congress amended HIPAA by passing the Health Information Technology for Economic and Clinical Health (HITECH) Act. This law updated many of HIPAA's privacy and security requirements and was implemented through the HIPAA Omnibus Rule in 2013.

One of the changes mandated by the new regulations is a change in the way the law treats business associates (BAs), organizations who handle protected health information (PHI) on behalf of a HIPAA covered entity. Any relationship between a covered entity and a BA must be governed by a written contract known as a business associate agreement (BAA). Under the new regulation, BAs are directly subject to HIPAA and HIPAA enforcement actions in the same manner as a covered entity.

HITECH also introduced new data breach notification requirements. Under the HITECH Breach Notification Rule, HIPAA-covered entities who experience a data breach must notify affected individuals of the breach and must also notify both the Secretary of Health and Human Services and the media when the breach affects more than 500 individuals.

Data Breach Notification Laws

HITECH's data breach notification rule is unique in that it is a federal law mandating the notification of affected individuals. Outside of this requirement for health-care records, data breach notification requirements vary widely from state to state.

In 2002, California passed SB 1386 and became the first state to immediately disclose to individuals the known or suspected breach of personally identifiable information. This includes unencrypted copies of a person's name in conjunction with any of the following information:

- Social Security number
- Driver's license number
- State identification card number
- Credit or debit card number
- Bank account number in conjunction with the security code, access code, or password that would permit access to the account
- Medical records
- Health insurance information

In the years following SB 1386, many (but not all) other states passed similar laws modeled on the California data breach notification law. As of 2015, only Alabama, New Mexico, and South Dakota did not have state breach notification laws.

NOTE For a complete listing of state data breach notification laws, see `www.ncsl.org/research/telecommunications-and-information-technology/security-breach-notification-laws.aspx`.

Children's Online Privacy Protection Act of 1998 In April 2000, provisions of the Children's Online Privacy Protection Act (COPPA) became the law of the land in the United States. COPPA makes a series of demands on websites that cater to children or knowingly collect information from children:

- Websites must have a privacy notice that clearly states the types of information they collect and what it's used for, including whether any information is disclosed to third parties. The privacy notice must also include contact information for the operators of the site.
- Parents must be provided with the opportunity to review any information collected from their children and permanently delete it from the site's records.

- Parents must give verifiable consent to the collection of information about children younger than the age of 13 prior to any such collection. Exceptions in the law allow websites to collect minimal information solely for the purpose of obtaining such parental consent.

Gramm-Leach-Bliley Act of 1999 Until the Gramm-Leach-Bliley Act (GLBA) became law in 1999, there were strict governmental barriers between financial institutions. Banks, insurance companies, and credit providers were severely limited in the services they could provide and the information they could share with each other. GLBA somewhat relaxed the regulations concerning the services each organization could provide. When Congress passed this law, it realized that this increased latitude could have far-reaching privacy implications. Because of this concern, it included a number of limitations on the types of information that could be exchanged even among subsidiaries of the same corporation and required financial institutions to provide written privacy policies to all their customers by July 1, 2001.

USA PATRIOT Act of 2001 Congress passed the Uniting and Strengthening America by Providing Appropriate Tools Required to Intercept and Obstruct Terrorism (USA PATRIOT) Act of 2001 in direct response to the September 11, 2001, terrorist attacks in New York City and Washington, DC. The PATRIOT Act greatly broadened the powers of law enforcement organizations and intelligence agencies across a number of areas, including when monitoring electronic communications.

One of the major changes prompted by the PATRIOT Act revolves around the way government agencies obtain wiretapping authorizations. Previously, police could obtain warrants for only one circuit at a time, after proving that the circuit was used by someone subject to monitoring. Provisions of the PATRIOT Act allow authorities to obtain a blanket authorization for a person and then monitor all communications to or from that person under the single warrant.

Another major change is in the way the government deals with Internet service providers (ISPs). Under the terms of the PATRIOT Act, ISPs may voluntarily provide the government with a large range of information. The PATRIOT Act also allows the government to obtain detailed information on user activity through the use of a subpoena (as opposed to a wiretap).

Finally, the USA PATRIOT Act amends the Computer Fraud and Abuse Act (yes, another set of amendments!) to provide more severe penalties for criminal acts. The PATRIOT Act provides for jail terms of up to 20 years and once again expands the coverage of the CFAA.

Family Educational Rights and Privacy Act The Family Educational Rights and Privacy Act (FERPA) is another specialized privacy bill that affects any educational institution that accepts any form of funding from the federal government (the vast majority of schools). It grants certain privacy rights to students older than 18 and the parents of minor students. Specific FERPA protections include the following:

- Parents/students have the right to inspect any educational records maintained by the institution on the student.
- Parents/students have the right to request correction of records they think are erroneous and the right to include a statement in the records contesting anything that is not corrected.
- Schools may not release personal information from student records without written consent, except under certain circumstances.

Identity Theft and Assumption Deterrence Act In 1998, the president signed the Identity Theft and Assumption Deterrence Act into law. In the past, the only legal victims of identity theft were the creditors who were defrauded. This act makes identity theft a crime against the person whose identity was stolen and provides severe criminal penalties (up to a 15-year prison term and/or a $250,000 fine) for anyone found guilty of violating this law.

Real World Scenario

Privacy in the Workplace

One of the authors of this book had an interesting conversation with a relative who works in an office environment. At a family Christmas party, the author's relative casually mentioned a story he had read online about a local company that had fired several employees for abusing their Internet privileges. He was shocked and couldn't believe that a company would violate their employees' right to privacy.

As you've read in this chapter, the U.S. court system has long upheld the traditional right to privacy as an extension of basic constitutional rights. However, the courts have maintained that a key element of this right is that privacy should be guaranteed only when there is a "reasonable expectation of privacy." For example, if you mail a letter to someone in a sealed envelope, you may reasonably expect that it will be delivered without being read along the way—you have a reasonable expectation of privacy. On the other hand, if you send your message on a postcard, you do so with the awareness that one or more people might read your note before it arrives at the other end—you do not have a reasonable expectation of privacy.

Recent court rulings have found that employees do not have a reasonable expectation of privacy while using employer-owned communications equipment in the workplace. If you send a message using an employer's computer, Internet connection, telephone, or other communications device, your employer can monitor it as a routine business procedure.

That said, if you're planning to monitor the communications of your employees, you should take reasonable precautions to ensure that there is no implied expectation of privacy. Here are some common measures to consider:

- Clauses in employment contracts that state the employee has no expectation of privacy while using corporate equipment
- Similar written statements in corporate acceptable use and privacy policies
- Logon banners warning that all communications are subject to monitoring
- Warning labels on computers and telephones warning of monitoring

As with many of the issues discussed in this chapter, it's a good idea to consult with your legal counsel before undertaking any communications-monitoring efforts.

European Union Privacy Law

On October 24, 1995, the European Union (EU) Parliament passed a sweeping directive outlining privacy measures that must be in place for protecting personal data processed by information systems. The directive went into effect three years later in October 1998. The directive requires that all processing of personal data meet one of the following criteria:

- Consent
- Contract
- Legal obligation
- Vital interest of the data subject
- Balance between the interests of the data holder and the interests of the data subject

The directive also outlines key rights of individuals about whom data is held and/or processed:

- Right to access the data
- Right to know the data's source
- Right to correct inaccurate data
- Right to withhold consent to process data in some situations
- Right of legal action should these rights be violated

Even organizations based outside of Europe must consider the applicability of these rules due to trans-border data flow requirements. In cases where personal information about European Union citizens leaves the EU, those sending the data must ensure that it remains protected. American companies doing business in Europe can obtain protection under a treaty between the EU and the United States that allows the Department of Commerce to certify businesses that comply with regulations and offer them "safe harbor" from prosecution.

To qualify for the safe harbor provision, U.S. companies conducting business in Europe must meet seven requirements for the processing of personal information:

Notice They must inform individuals of what information they collect about them and how the information will be used.

Choice They must allow individuals to opt out if the information will be used for any other purpose or shared with a third party. For information considered sensitive, an opt-in policy must be used.

Onward Transfer Organizations can share data only with other organizations that comply with the safe harbor principles.

Access Individuals must be granted access to any records kept containing their personal information.

Security Proper mechanisms must be in place to protect data against loss, misuse, and unauthorized disclosure.

Data Integrity Organizations must take steps to ensure the reliability of the information they maintain.

Enforcement Organizations must make a dispute resolution process available to individuals and provide certifications to regulatory agencies that they comply with the safe harbor provisions.

> **TIP** For more information on the safe harbor protections available to American companies, visit the Department of Commerce's Safe Harbor website at `http://export.gov/safeharbor`.

Compliance

Over the past decade, the regulatory environment governing information security has grown increasingly complex. Organizations may find themselves subject to a wide variety of laws (many of which were outlined earlier in this chapter) and regulations imposed by regulatory agencies or contractual obligations.

Real World Scenario

Payment Card Industry Data Security Standard

The Payment Card Industry Data Security Standard (PCI DSS) is an excellent example of a compliance requirement that is not dictated by law but by contractual obligation. PCI DSS governs the security of credit card information and is enforced through the terms of a merchant agreement between a business that accepts credit cards and the bank that processes the business's transactions.

PCI DSS has 12 main requirements:

1. Install and maintain a firewall configuration to protect cardholder data.
2. Do not use vendor-supplied defaults for system passwords and other security parameters.
3. Protect stored cardholder data.
4. Encrypt transmission of cardholder data across open, public networks.
5. Protect all systems against malware and regularly update antivirus software or programs
6. Develop and maintain secure systems and applications.
7. Restrict access to cardholder data by business need-to-know.
8. Identify and authenticate access to system components.
9. Restrict physical access to cardholder data.
10. Track and monitor all access to network resources and cardholder data.
11. Regularly test security systems and processes.
12. Maintain a policy that addresses information security for all personnel.

Each of these requirements is spelled out in detail in the full PCI DSS standard, which may be found at `www.pcisecuritystandards.org/`.

Dealing with the many overlapping, and sometimes contradictory, compliance requirements facing an organization requires careful planning. Many organizations employ full-time IT compliance staff responsible for tracking the regulatory environment, monitoring controls to ensure ongoing compliance, facilitating compliance audits, and meeting the organization's compliance reporting obligations.

WARNING

Organizations who are not merchants but store, process, or transmit credit card information on behalf of merchants must also comply with PCI DSS. For example, the requirements apply to shared hosting providers who must protect the cardholder data environment.

Organizations may be subject to compliance audits, either by their standard internal and external auditors or by regulators or their agents. For example, an organization's financial auditors may conduct an IT controls audit designed to ensure that the information security controls for an organization's financial systems are sufficient to ensure compliance with the Sarbanes-Oxley Act. Some regulations, such as PCI DSS, may require the organization to retain approved independent auditors to verify controls and provide a report directly to regulators.

In addition to formal audits, organizations often must report regulatory compliance to a number of internal and external stakeholders. For example, an organization's Board of Directors (or, more commonly, that board's Audit Committee) may require periodic reporting on compliance obligations and status. Similarly, PCI DSS requires organizations that are not compelled to conduct a formal third-party audit to complete and submit a self-assessment report outlining their compliance status.

Contracting and Procurement

The increased use of cloud services and other external vendors to store, process, and transmit sensitive information leads organizations to a new focus on implementing security reviews and controls in their contracting and procurement processes. Security professionals should conduct reviews of the security controls put in place by vendors, both during the initial vendor selection and evaluation process, and as part of ongoing vendor governance reviews.

Some questions to cover during these vendor governance reviews include:

- What types of sensitive information are stored, processed, or transmitted by the vendor?
- What controls are in place to protect the organization's information?
- How is our organization's information segregated from that of other clients?
- If encryption is relied on as a security control, what encryption algorithms and key lengths are used? How is key management handled?

- What types of security audits does the vendor perform and what access does the client have to those audits?
- Does the vendor rely on any other third parties to store, process, or transmit data? How do the provisions of the contract related to security extend to those third parties?
- Where will data storage, processing, and transmission take place? If outside the home country of the client and/or vendor, what implications does that have?
- What is the vendor's incident response process and when will clients be notified of a potential security breach?
- What provisions are in place to ensure the ongoing integrity and availability of client data?

This is just a brief listing of some of the concerns that you may have. Tailor the scope of your security review to the specific concerns of your organization, the type of service provided by the vendor, and the information that will be shared with them.

Summary

Computer security necessarily entails a high degree of involvement from the legal community. In this chapter, you learned about the laws that govern security issues such as computer crime, intellectual property, data privacy, and software licensing.

There are three major categories of law that impact information security professionals. Criminal law outlines the rules and sanctions for major violations of the public trust. Civil law provides us with a framework for conducting business. Government agencies use administrative law to promulgate the day-to-day regulations that interpret existing law.

The laws governing information security activities are diverse and cover all three categories. Some, such as the Electronic Communications Privacy Act and the Digital Millennium Copyright Act, are criminal laws where violations may result in criminal fines and/or prison time. Others, such as trademark and patent law, are civil laws that govern business transactions. Finally, many government agencies promulgate administrative law, such as the HIPAA Security Rule, that affects specific industries and data types.

Information security professionals should be aware of the compliance requirements specific to their industry and business activities. Tracking these requirements is a complex task and should be assigned to one or more compliance specialists who monitor changes in the law, changes in the business environment, and the intersection of those two realms.

It's also not sufficient to simply worry about your own security and compliance. With increased adoption of cloud computing, many organizations now share sensitive and personal data with vendors who act as service providers. Security professionals must take steps to ensure that vendors treat data with as much care as the organization itself would and also meet any applicable compliance requirements.

Exam Essentials

Understand the differences between criminal law, civil law, and administrative law. Criminal law protects society against acts that violate the basic principles we believe in. Violations of criminal law are prosecuted by federal and state governments. Civil law provides the framework for the transaction of business between people and organizations. Violations of civil law are brought to the court and argued by the two affected parties. Administrative law is used by government agencies to effectively carry out their day-to-day business.

Be able to explain the basic provisions of the major laws designed to protect society against computer crime. The Computer Fraud and Abuse Act (as amended) protects computers used by the government or in interstate commerce from a variety of abuses. The Computer Security Act outlines steps the government must take to protect its own systems from attack. The Government Information Security Reform Act further develops the federal government information security program.

Know the differences among copyrights, trademarks, patents, and trade secrets. Copyrights protect original works of authorship, such as books, articles, poems, and songs. Trademarks are names, slogans, and logos that identify a company, product, or service. Patents provide protection to the creators of new inventions. Trade secret law protects the operating secrets of a firm.

Be able to explain the basic provisions of the Digital Millennium Copyright Act of 1998. The Digital Millennium Copyright Act prohibits the circumvention of copy protection mechanisms placed in digital media and limits the liability of Internet service providers for the activities of their users.

Know the basic provisions of the Economic Espionage Act of 1996. The Economic Espionage Act provides penalties for individuals found guilty of the theft of trade secrets. Harsher penalties apply when the individual knows that the information will benefit a foreign government.

Understand the various types of software license agreements. Contractual license agreements are written agreements between a software vendor and user. Shrink-wrap agreements are written on software packaging and take effect when a user opens the package. Click-wrap agreements are included in a package but require the user to accept the terms during the software installation process.

Explain the impact of the Uniform Computer Information Transactions Act on software licensing. The Uniform Computer Information Transactions Act provides a framework for the enforcement of shrink-wrap and click-wrap agreements by federal and state governments.

Understand the notification requirements placed on organizations that experience a data breach. California's SB 1386 implemented the first statewide requirement to notify individuals of a breach of their personal information. All but three states eventually followed suit with similar laws. Currently, federal law only requires the notification of individuals when a HIPAA-covered entity breaches their protected health information.

Understand the major laws that govern privacy of personal information in both the United States and the European Union. The United States has a number of privacy laws that affect the government's use of information as well as the use of information by specific industries, such as financial services companies and health-care organizations that handle sensitive information. The EU has a more comprehensive directive on data privacy that regulates the use and exchange of personal information.

Explain the importance of a well-rounded compliance program. Most organizations are subject to a wide variety of legal and regulatory requirements related to information security. Building a compliance program ensures that you become and remain compliant with these often overlapping requirements.

Know how to incorporate security into the procurement and vendor governance process. The expanded use of cloud services by many organizations requires added attention to conducting reviews of information security controls during the vendor selection process and as part of ongoing vendor governance.

Written Lab

1. What are the key rights guaranteed to individuals under the European Union's directive on data privacy?
2. What are some common questions that organizations should ask when considering outsourcing information storage, processing, or transmission?
3. What are some common steps that employers take to notify employees of system monitoring?

Review Questions

1. Which criminal law was the first to implement penalties for the creators of viruses, worms, and other types of malicious code that cause harm to computer system(s)?
   - **A.** Computer Security Act
   - **B.** National Infrastructure Protection Act
   - **C.** Computer Fraud and Abuse Act
   - **D.** Electronic Communications Privacy Act
2. Which law first required operators of federal interest computer systems to undergo periodic training in computer security issues?
   - **A.** Computer Security Act
   - **B.** National Infrastructure Protection Act
   - **C.** Computer Fraud and Abuse Act
   - **D.** Electronic Communications Privacy Act
3. What type of law does not require an act of Congress to implement at the federal level but rather is enacted by the executive branch in the form of regulations, policies, and procedures?
   - **A.** Criminal law
   - **B.** Common law
   - **C.** Civil law
   - **D.** Administrative law
4. Which federal government agency has responsibility for ensuring the security of government computer systems that are not used to process sensitive and/or classified information?
   - **A.** National Security Agency
   - **B.** Federal Bureau of Investigation
   - **C.** National Institute of Standards and Technology
   - **D.** Secret Service
5. What is the broadest category of computer systems protected by the Computer Fraud and Abuse Act, as amended?
   - **A.** Government-owned systems
   - **B.** Federal interest systems
   - **C.** Systems used in interstate commerce
   - **D.** Systems located in the United States
6. What law protects the right of citizens to privacy by placing restrictions on the authority granted to government agencies to search private residences and facilities?
   - **A.** Privacy Act
   - **B.** Fourth Amendment

C. Second Amendment

D. Gramm-Leach-Bliley Act

7. Matthew recently authored an innovative algorithm for solving a mathematical problem, and he wants to share it with the world. However, prior to publishing the software code in a technical journal, he wants to obtain some sort of intellectual property protection. Which type of protection is best suited to his needs?

A. Copyright

B. Trademark

C. Patent

D. Trade secret

8. Mary is the cofounder of Acme Widgets, a manufacturing firm. Together with her partner, Joe, she has developed a special oil that will dramatically improve the widget manufacturing process. To keep the formula secret, Mary and Joe plan to make large quantities of the oil by themselves in the plant after the other workers have left. They want to protect this formula for as long as possible. What type of intellectual property protection best suits their needs?

A. Copyright

B. Trademark

C. Patent

D. Trade secret

9. Richard recently developed a great name for a new product that he plans to begin using immediately. He spoke with his attorney and filed the appropriate application to protect his product name but has not yet received a response from the government regarding his application. He wants to begin using the name immediately. What symbol should he use next to the name to indicate its protected status?

A. ©

B. ®

C. ™

D. †

10. What law prevents government agencies from disclosing personal information that an individual supplies to the government under protected circumstances?

A. Privacy Act

B. Electronic Communications Privacy Act

C. Health Insurance Portability and Accountability Act

D. Gramm-Leach-Bliley Act

11. What law formalizes many licensing arrangements used by the software industry and attempts to standardize their use from state to state?

A. Computer Security Act

B. Uniform Computer Information Transactions Act

C. Digital Millennium Copyright Act
D. Gramm-Leach-Bliley Act

12. The Children's Online Privacy Protection Act was designed to protect the privacy of children using the Internet. What is the minimum age a child must be before companies can collect personal identifying information from them without parental consent?
    A. 13
    B. 14
    C. 15
    D. 16
13. Which one of the following is not a requirement that Internet service providers must satisfy in order to gain protection under the "transitory activities" clause of the Digital Millennium Copyright Act?
    A. The service provider and the originator of the message must be located in different states.
    B. The transmission, routing, provision of connections, or copying must be carried out by an automated technical process without selection of material by the service provider.
    C. Any intermediate copies must not ordinarily be accessible to anyone other than anticipated recipients and must not be retained for longer than reasonably necessary.
    D. The transmission must be originated by a person other than the provider.
14. Which one of the following laws is not designed to protect the privacy rights of consumers and Internet users?
    A. Health Insurance Portability and Accountability Act
    B. Identity Theft Assumption and Deterrence Act
    C. USA PATRIOT Act
    D. Gramm-Leach-Bliley Act
15. Which one of the following types of licensing agreements does not require that the user acknowledge that they have read the agreement prior to executing it?
    A. Standard license agreement
    B. Shrink-wrap agreement
    C. Click-wrap agreement
    D. Verbal agreement
16. What industry is most directly impacted by the provisions of the Gramm-Leach-Bliley Act?
    A. Health care
    B. Banking
    C. Law enforcement
    D. Defense contractors

17. What is the standard duration of patent protection in the United States?

A. 14 years from the application date

B. 14 years from the date the patent is granted

C. 20 years from the application date

D. 20 years from the date the patent is granted

18. Which one of the following is not a valid legal reason for processing information about an individual under the European Union's data privacy directive?

A. Contract

B. Legal obligation

C. Marketing needs

D. Consent

19. What compliance obligation relates to the processing of credit card information?

A. SOX

B. HIPAA

C. PCI DSS

D. FERPA

20. What act updated the privacy and security requirements of the Health Insurance Portability and Accountability Act (HIPAA)?

A. HITECH

B. CALEA

C. CFAA

D. CCCA

Chapter 5

Protecting Security of Assets

THE CISSP EXAM TOPICS COVERED IN THIS CHAPTER INCLUDE:

ASSET SECURITY

✓ **A. Classify information and supporting assets (e.g., sensitivity, criticality)**

✓ **B. Determine and maintain ownership (e.g., data owners, system owners, business/mission owners)**

✓ **C. Protect privacy**

- C.1 Data owners
- C.2 Data processers
- C.3 Data remanence
- C.4 Collection limitation

✓ **D. Ensure appropriate retention (e.g., media, hardware, personnel)**

✓ **E. Determine data security controls (e.g., data at rest, data in transit)**

- E.1 Baselines
- E.2 Scoping and tailoring
- E.3 Standards selection
- E.4 Cryptography

✓ **F. Establish handling requirements (markings, labels, storage, destruction of sensitive information)**

The Asset Security domain focuses on collecting, handling, and protecting information throughout its life cycle. A primary step in this domain is classifying information based on its value to the organization.

All follow-on actions vary depending on the classification. For example, highly classified data requires stringent security controls. In contrast, unclassified data uses fewer security controls.

Classifying and Labeling Assets

One of the first steps in asset security is classifying and labeling assets. Organizations often include classification definitions within a security policy. Personnel then label assets appropriately based on the security policy requirements. In this context, assets include sensitive data, the hardware used to process it, and the media used to hold it.

Defining Sensitive Data

Sensitive data is any information that isn't public or unclassified. It can include confidential, proprietary, protected, or any other type of data that an organization needs to protect due to its value to the organization, or to comply with existing laws and regulations.

Personally Identifiable Information

Personally identifiable information (PII) is any information that can identify an individual. National Institute of Standards and Technology (NIST) Special Publication (SP) 800-122 provides a more formal definition:

> Any information about an individual maintained by an agency, including
>
> (1) any information that can be used to distinguish or trace an individual's identity, such as name, social security number, date and place of birth, mother's maiden name, or biometric records; and
>
> (2) any other information that is linked or linkable to an individual, such as medical, educational, financial, and employment information.

The key is that organizations have a responsibility to protect PII. This includes PII related to employees and customers. Many laws require organizations to notify individuals if a data breach results in a compromise of PII.

> **TIP** Protection for personally identifiable information (PII) drives privacy and confidentiality requirements for rules, regulations, and legislation all over the world (especially in North America and the European Union). NIST SP 800-122, *Guide to Protecting the Confidentiality of Personally Identifiable Information (PII)*, provides more information on how to protect PII. It is available from the NIST Special Publications (800 Series) download page:
>
> `http://csrc.nist.gov/publications/PubsSPs.html`

Protected Health Information

Protected health information (PHI) is any health-related information that can be related to a specific person. In the United States, the Health Insurance Portability and Accountability Act (HIPAA) mandates the protection of PHI. HIPAA provides a more formal definition of PHI:

> Health information means any information, whether oral or recorded in any form or medium, that—
>
> (A) is created or received by a health care provider, health plan, public health authority, employer, life insurer, school or university, or health care clearinghouse; and
>
> (B) relates to the past, present, or future physical or mental health or condition of any individual, the provision of health care to an individual, or the past, present, or future payment for the provision of health care to an individual.

Some people think that only medical care providers such as doctors and hospitals need to protect PHI. However, HIPAA defines PHI much more broadly. Any employer that provides, or supplements, health-care policies collects and handles PHI. It's very common for organizations to provide or supplement health-care policies, so HIPAA applies to a large percentage of organizations in the US.

Proprietary Data

Proprietary data refers to any data that helps an organization maintain a competitive edge. It could be software code it developed, technical plans for products, internal processes, intellectual property, or trade secrets. If competitors are able to access the proprietary data, it can seriously affect the primary mission of an organization.

Although copyrights, patents, and trade secret laws provide a level of protection for proprietary data, this isn't always enough. Many criminals don't pay attention to copyrights, patents, and laws. Similarly, foreign entities have stolen a significant amount of proprietary data.

As an example, information security company Mandiant released a report in 2013 documenting a group operating out of China that they named APT1. Mandiant attributes a significant number of data thefts to this advanced persistent threat (APT). They observed APT1 compromise 141 companies spanning 20 major industries. In one instance, they observed APT1 stealing 6.5 TB of compressed intellectual property data over a ten-month period.

NOTE In 2014, FireEye, a US network security company, purchased Mandiant for about $1 billion. However, you can still access Mandiant's APT1 report online by searching on "Mandiant APT1."

Defining Classifications

Organizations typically include data classifications in their security policy, or in a separate data policy. A data classification identifies the value of the data to the organization and is critical to protect data confidentiality and integrity. The policy identifies classification labels used within the organization. It also identifies how data owners can determine the proper classification, and personnel should protect data based on its classification.

As an example, government data classifications include top secret, secret, confidential, and unclassified. Anything above unclassified is sensitive data, but clearly, these have different values. The US government provides clear definitions for these classifications. As you read them, note that the wording of each definition is close except for a few key words. Top secret uses the phrase "exceptionally grave damage," secret uses the phrase "serious damage," and confidential uses the term "damage."

Top Secret The *top secret* label is "applied to information, the unauthorized disclosure of which reasonably could be expected to cause exceptionally grave damage to the national security that the original classification authority is able to identify or describe."

Secret The *secret* label is "applied to information, the unauthorized disclosure of which reasonably could be expected to cause serious damage to the national security that the original classification authority is able to identify or describe."

Confidential The *confidential* label is "applied to information, the unauthorized disclosure of which reasonably could be expected to cause damage to the national security that the original classification authority is able to identify or describe."

Unclassified *Unclassified* refers to any data that doesn't meet one of the descriptions for top secret, secret, or confidential data. Within the US, unclassified data is available to anyone, though it often requires individuals to request the information using procedures identified in the Freedom of Information Act (FOIA).

A classification authority is the entity that applies the original classification to the sensitive data and strict rules identify who can do so. For example, the US president, vice president, and agency heads can classify data in the US. Additionally, individuals in any of these positions can delegate permission for others to classify data.

TIP Although the focus of classifications is often on data, these classifications also apply to hardware. This includes any computing system or media that processes or holds this data.

Nongovernment organizations rarely need to classify their data based on potential damage to the national security. However, management is concerned about potential damage to the organization. For example, if attackers accessed the organization's data, what is the potential adverse impact? In other words, an organization doesn't just consider the sensitivity of the data but also the criticality of the data. They could use the same phrases of "exceptionally grave damage," "serious damage," and "damage" that the US government uses when describing top secret, secret, and confidential data.

Some nongovernment organizations use labels such as Class 3, Class 2, Class 1, and Class 0. Other organizations use more meaningful labels such as confidential (or proprietary), private, sensitive, and public. Figure 5.1 shows the relationship between these different classifications with the government classifications on the left and the non-government (or civilian) classifications on the right. Just as the government can define the data based on the potential adverse impact from a data breach, organizations can use similar descriptions.

FIGURE 5.1 Data classifications

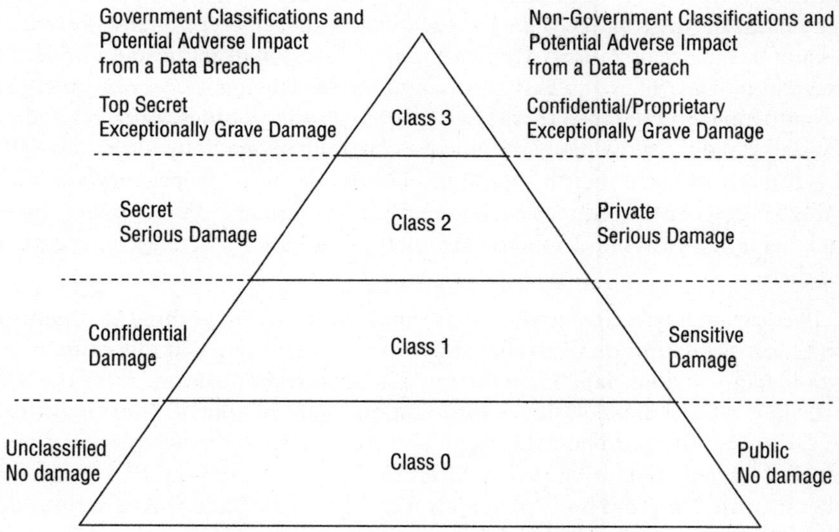

Both government and civilian classifications identify the relative value of the data to the organization, with top secret representing the highest classification for governments and confidential representing the highest classification for organizations in Figure 5.1. However, it's important to remember that organizations can use any labels they desire. When the labels in Figure 5.1 are used, sensitive information is any information that isn't unclassified (when using the government labels) or isn't public (when using the civilian classifications). The following sections identify the meaning of the nongovernment classifications.

Sony Attacks

You may remember the attacks on Sony during November and December of 2014. Kevin Mandia (founder of Mandiant) stated "the scope of this attack differs from any we have responded to in the past, as its purpose was to both destroy property and release confidential information to the public. The bottom line is that this was an unparalleled and well planned crime, carried out by an organized group."

Attackers obtained over 100 TB of data, including full-length versions of unreleased movies, salary information, and internal emails. Some of this data was more valuable to the organization than other data. As you're reading the definitions of nongovernment data classifications, think about the seriousness of the damage that it caused Sony and the appropriate classification for this data. Note that anyone might label data with a different classification than the data owners at Sony. There's no right or wrong here. However, the attack does provide us with some realistic examples.

Confidential or Proprietary The confidential or propriety label refers to the highest level of classified data. In this context, a data breach would cause exceptionally grave damage to the mission of the organization. After the Sony attack, attackers posted unreleased versions of several movies. These quickly showed up on file-sharing sites and security experts estimate that people downloaded these movies up to a million times. With pirated versions of the movies available, many people skipped seeing them when Sony ultimately released them. This directly affected their bottom line. The movies were proprietary and the organization might have considered it as exceptionally grave damage. In retrospect, they may choose to label movies as confidential or proprietary and use the strongest access controls to protect them.

Private The private label refers to data that should stay private within the organization but doesn't meet the definition of confidential or proprietary data. In this context, a data breach would cause serious damage to the mission of the organization. After the Sony attack, attackers posted detailed salary information on more than 30,000 employees, including the multimillion-dollar salaries of 17 top executives. As these details came out and employees started comparing their salaries to their peers (and the 17 top executives), you can bet it caused internal problems. Sony may have considered this as serious damage and, in retrospect, may choose to label this type of data as private.

Sensitive Sensitive data is similar to confidential data. In this context, a data breach would cause damage to the mission of the organization. After the Sony attack, attackers posted a spreadsheet with a list of all employees who were laid off or terminated. It included the reason for termination and the cost to terminate each employee. They also posted several email threads that included embarrassing comments. For example, one producer referred to a movie star as a "minimally talented spoiled brat" and some emails included what many people viewed as racially insensitive comments. These were embarrassing and potentially caused damage to the organization. In retrospect, they may choose to label this type of data as sensitive and protect it appropriately.

Public Public data is similar to unclassified data. It includes information posted in websites, brochures, or any other public source. Although an organization doesn't protect the confidentiality of public data, it does take steps to protect its integrity. For example, anyone can view public data posted on a website. However, an organization doesn't want attackers to modify this data so it takes steps to protect it.

> TIP Although the CISSP Candidate Information Bulletin (CIB) refers to sensitive information as any data that isn't public or unclassified, some organizations use sensitive as a label. In other words, the term "sensitive information" might mean something different in one organization when compared to what it means for the CISSP exam. For the exam, remember that "sensitive information" refers to any information that isn't public or unclassified.

Civilian organizations aren't required to use any specific classification labels. However, it is important to classify data in some manner and ensure personnel understand the classifications. No matter what labels an organization uses, it still has an obligation to protect sensitive information.

After classifying the data, an organization takes additional steps to manage it based on its classification. Unauthorized access to sensitive information can result in significant losses to an organization. However, basic security practices, such as properly marking, handling, storing, and destroying data based on its classification, help to prevent losses.

Defining Data Security Requirements

After defining data classifications, it's important to define the security requirements. For example, what steps should an organization take to protect email?

At a minimum, an organization should label and encrypt sensitive email. Encryption converts cleartext data into scrambled ciphertext and makes it more difficult to read. Using strong encryption methods such as Advanced Encryption Standard with 256-bit cryptography keys (AES 256) makes it almost impossible for unauthorized personnel to read the text. Table 5.1 shows possible security requirements for email that an organization could implement.

TABLE 5.1 Securing email data

Classification	Security requirements for email
Confidential/Proprietary	Email and attachments must be encrypted with AES 256.
	Email and attachments remain encrypted except when viewed.
	Email can only be sent to recipients within the organization.
	Email can only be opened and viewed by recipients (forwarded emails cannot be opened).
	Attachments can be opened and viewed, but not saved.
	Email content cannot be copied and pasted into other documents.
	Email cannot be printed.

TABLE 5.1 Securing email data *(continued)*

Classification	Security requirements for email
Private	Email and attachments must be encrypted with AES 256. Email and attachments remain encrypted except when viewed. Can only be sent to recipients within the organization.
Sensitive	Email and attachments must be encrypted with AES 256.
Public	Email and attachments can be sent in cleartext.

NOTE The requirements listed in Table 5.1 are provided as an example only. Any organization could use these requirements or define other requirements that work for them.

Although it's possible to meet all of the requirements in Table 5.1, they require implementing other solutions. For example, Boldon James sells several products that organizations can use to automate these tasks. Users apply relevant labels (such as confidential, private, sensitive, and public) to emails before sending them. These emails pass through a data loss prevention (DLP) server that detects the labels, and applies the required protection.

Table 5.1 shows possible requirements that an organization might want to apply to email. However, an organization wouldn't stop there. Any type of data that an organization wants to protect needs similar security definitions. For example, organizations would define requirements for data stored on servers, data backups stored onsite and offsite, and proprietary data such as full-length unreleased films.

Understanding Data States

It's important to protect data while it is at rest, in motion, and in use. Data at rest is any data stored on media such as system hard drives, external USB drives, storage area networks (SANs), and backup tapes. Data in transit (sometimes called data in motion) is any data transmitted over a network. This includes data transmitted over an internal network using wired or wireless methods and data transmitted over public networks such as the Internet. Data in use refers to data in temporary storage buffers while an application is using it.

The best way to protect the confidentiality of data is to use strong encryption protocols, discussed later in this chapter. Additionally, strong authentication and authorization controls help prevent unauthorized access.

As an example, consider a web application that retrieves credit card data for an e-commerce transaction. The credit card data is stored on a separate database server and is protected while at rest, while in motion, and while in use.

Database administrators take steps to encrypt sensitive data stored on the database server (data at rest). For example, they would encrypt columns holding sensitive data such as credit card data. Additionally, they would implement strong authentication and authorization controls to prevent unauthorized entities from accessing the database.

When the web application sends a request for data from the web server, the database server verifies the web application is authorized to retrieve the data and, if so, the database server sends it. However, this entails several steps. For example, the database management system first retrieves and decrypts the data and formats it in a way that the web application can read it. The database server then uses a transport encryption algorithm to encrypt the data before transmitting it. This ensures that the data in transit is secure.

The web application server receives the data in an encrypted format. It decrypts the data and sends it to the web application. The web application stores the data in temporary buffers while it uses it to authorize the transaction. When the web application no longer needs the data, it takes steps to purge memory buffers, ensuring all residual sensitive data is completely removed from memory.

Managing Sensitive Data

A key goal of managing sensitive data is to prevent data breaches. A data breach is any event in which an unauthorized entity is able to view or access sensitive data. If you pay attention to the news, you probably hear about data breaches quite often. Big breaches such as the Sony breach of 2014 hit the mainstream news. However, even though you might never hear about smaller data breaches, they are happening regularly, with an average of 15 reported data breaches a week. The following sections identify basic steps people within an organization follow to limit the possibility of data breaches.

NOTE

The Identity Theft Resource Center (ITRC) routinely tracks data breaches. They post reports through their website (`www.idtheftcenter.org/`) that are free to anyone. In 2014, they tracked 783 data breaches, exposing over 85 million records. This equated to approximately 15 data breaches a week and follows a trend of more data breaches every year.)

Marking Sensitive Data

Marking (often called labeling) sensitive information ensures that users can easily identify the classification level of any data. The most important information that a mark or a label provides is the classification of the data. For example, a label of top secret makes it clear to anyone who sees the label that the information is classified top secret. When users know the value of the data, they are more likely to take appropriate steps to control and protect it based on the classification. Marking includes both physical and electronic marking and labels.

Physical labels indicate the security classification for the data stored on media or processed on a system. For example, if a backup tape includes secret data, a physical label attached to the tape makes it clear to users that it holds secret data. Similarly, if a computer processes sensitive information, the computer would have a label indicating the highest classification of information that it processes. A computer used to process confidential, secret, and top secret data should be marked with a label indicating that it processes top secret data. Physical labels remain on the system or media throughout its lifetime.

TIP Many organizations use color-coded hardware to help mark it. For example, some organizations purchase red-colored USB flash drives in bulk, with the intent that personnel can only copy classified data onto these flash drives. Technical security controls identify these flash drives using a universally unique identifier (UUID) and can enforce security policies. DLP systems can block users from copying data to other USB devices and ensure that data is encrypted when a user copies it to one of these devices.

Marking also includes using digital marks or labels. A simple method is to include the classification as a header and/or footer in a document, or embed it as a watermark. A benefit of these methods is that they also appear on printouts. Even when users include headers and footers on printouts, most organizations require users to place printed sensitive documents within a folder that includes a label or cover page clearly indicating the classification. Headers aren't limited to files. Backup tapes often include header information, and the classification can be included in this header.

Another benefit of headers, footers, and watermarks is that DLP systems can identify documents that include sensitive information, and apply the appropriate security controls. Some DLP systems will also add metadata tags to the document when they detect that the document is classified. These tags provide insight into the document's contents and help the DLP system handle it appropriately.

Similarly, some organizations mandate specific desktop backgrounds on their computers. For example, a system used to process proprietary data might have a black desktop background with the word Proprietary in white and a wide orange border. The background could also include statements such as "This computer processes proprietary data" and statements reminding users of their responsibilities to protect the data.

In many secure environments, personnel also use labels for unclassified media and equipment. This prevents an error of omission where sensitive information isn't marked. For example, if a backup tape holding sensitive data isn't marked, a user might assume it only holds unclassified data. However, if the organization marks unclassified data too, the user would view it with suspicion.

Organizations often identify procedures to downgrade media. For example, if a backup tape includes confidential information, an administrator might want to downgrade the tape to unclassified. The organization would identify trusted procedures that will purge the tape of all usable data. After administrators purge the tape, they can then downgrade it and replace the labels.

However, many organizations prohibit downgrading media at all. For example, a data policy might prohibit downgrading a backup tape that contains top secret data. Instead, the policy might mandate destroying this tape when it reaches the end of its life cycle. Similarly, it is rare to downgrade a system. In other words, if a system has been processing top secret data, it would be rare to downgrade it and relabel it as an unclassified system.

> **NOTE** If media or a system needs to be downgraded to a less sensitive classification, it must be sanitized using appropriate procedures as described in the section "Destroying Sensitive Data" later in this chapter. However, it's often safer and easier just to purchase new media or equipment rather than follow through with the sanitization steps for reuse. Many organizations adopt a policy that prohibits downgrading any media or systems.

Handling Sensitive Data

Handling refers to the secure transportation of media through its lifetime. Personnel handle data differently based on its value and classification, and as you'd expect, highly classified information needs much greater protection. Even though this is common sense, people still make mistakes. Many times people get accustomed to handling sensitive information and become lackadaisical with protecting it.

For example, it was reported in April 2011 that the United Kingdom's Ministry of Defense mistakenly published classified information on nuclear submarines, in addition to other sensitive information, in response to Freedom of Information requests. They redacted the classified data by using image-editing software to black it out. However, anyone who tried to copy the data was able to copy all the text, including the blacked-out data.

A common occurrence is the loss of control of backup tapes. Backup tapes should be protected with the same level of protection as the data that is backed up. In other words, if confidential information is on a backup tape, the backup tape should be protected as confidential information. However, there are many examples where this just isn't followed. In 2011, Science Applications International Corporation (SAIC), a government contractor, lost control of backup tapes that included PII and PHI for 4.9 million patients. Because it is PHI, it falls under HIPAA and required specific actions to protect it that SAIC personnel apparently didn't implement.

Policies and procedures need to be in place to ensure that people understand how to handle sensitive data. This starts by ensuring systems and media are labeled appropriately. Additionally, as President Reagan famously said when discussing relations with the Soviet Union, "Trust, but verify." Chapter 17, "Preventing and Responding to Incidents," discusses the importance of logging, monitoring, and auditing. These controls verify that sensitive information is handled appropriately before a significant loss occurs. If a loss does occur, investigators use audit trails to help discover what went wrong. Any incidents that occur because personnel didn't handle data appropriately should be quickly investigated and actions taken to prevent a reoccurrence.

Storing Sensitive Data

Sensitive data should be stored in such a way that it is protected against any type of loss. The obvious protection is encryption. As of this writing, AES 256 provides strong encryption and there are many applications available to encrypt data with AES 256. Additionally, many operating systems include built-in capabilities to encrypt data at both the file level and the disk level.

If sensitive data is stored on physical media such as portable disk drives or backup tapes, personnel should follow basic physical security practices to prevent losses due to theft. This includes storing these devices in locked safes or vaults and/or within a secure room, that includes several additional physical controls. For example, a server room includes physical security measures to prevent unauthorized access so storing portable media within a locked cabinet in a server would provide strong protection.

Additionally, environmental controls should be used to protect the media. This includes temperature and humidity controls such as heating, ventilation, and air conditioning (HVAC) systems.

Here's a point that end users often forget: the value of any sensitive data is much greater than the value of the media holding the sensitive data. In other words, it's cost effective to purchase high-quality media, especially if the data will be stored for a long time, such as on backup tapes. Similarly, the purchase of high-quality USB flash drives with built-in encryption is worth the cost. Some of these USB flash drives include biometric authentication mechanisms using fingerprints, which provide added protection.

NOTE Encryption of sensitive data provides an additional layer of protection and should be considered for any data at rest. If data is encrypted, it becomes much more difficult for an attacker to access it, even if it is stolen.

Destroying Sensitive Data

When an organization no longer needs sensitive data, personnel should destroy it. Proper destruction ensures that it cannot fall into the wrong hands and result in unauthorized disclosure. Highly classified data requires different steps to destroy it than data classified at a lower level. An organization's security policy or data policy should define the acceptable methods of destroying data based on the data's classification. For example, an organization may require the complete destruction of media holding highly classified data, but allow personnel to use software tools to overwrite data files classified at a lower level.

Data remanence is the data that remains on a hard drive as residual magnetic flux. Using system tools to delete data generally leaves much of the data remaining on the media, and widely available tools can easily undelete it. Even when you use sophisticated tools to overwrite the media, traces of the original data may remain as less perceptible magnetic fields. This is similar to a ghost image that can remain on some TV and computer monitors if the same data is displayed for long periods of time. Forensics experts and attackers have tools they can use to retrieve this data even after it has been supposedly overwritten.

One way to remove data remanence is with a degausser. A degausser generates a heavy magnetic field, which realigns the magnetic fields in magnetic media such as traditional hard drives, magnetic tape, and floppy disk drives. Degaussers using power will reliably rewrite these magnetic fields and remove data remanence. However, they are only effective on magnetic media.

In contrast, solid state drives (SSDs) use integrated circuitry instead of magnetic flux on spinning platters. Because of this, SSDs do not have data remanence and degaussing them won't remove data. However, even when using other methods to remove data from SSDs, data remnants often remain. In a research paper titled "Reliably Erasing Data from Flash-Based Solid State Drives," (available at `www.usenix.org/legacy/event/fast11/tech/full_papers/wei.pdf`) the authors found that none of the traditional methods of sanitizing individual files was effective. Some SSDs include built-in erase commands to sanitize the entire disk, but unfortunately, these weren't effective on some SSDs from different manufacturers. Due to these risks, the best method of sanitizing SSDs is destruction. The US National Security Agency (NSA) requires the destruction of SSDs using an approved disintegrator. Approved disintegrators shred the SSDs to a size of 2 millimeters (mm) or smaller. Security Engineered Machinery (SEM) sells multiple information destruction and sanitization solutions, including many approved by the NSA.

WARNING Be careful when performing any type of clearing, purging, or sanitization process. The human operator or the tool involved in the activity may not properly perform the task of completely removing data from the media. Software can be flawed, magnets can be faulty, and either can be used improperly. Always verify that the desired result is achieved after performing any sanitization process.

The following list includes some of the common terms associated with destroying data:

Erasing *Erasing* media is simply performing a delete operation against a file, a selection of files, or the entire media. In most cases, the deletion or removal process removes only the directory or catalog link to the data. The actual data remains on the drive. As new files are written to the media, the system eventually overwrites the erased data, but depending on the size of the drive, how much free space it has, and several other factors, the data may not be overwritten for months. Anyone can typically retrieve the data using widely available undelete tools.

Clearing *Clearing*, or *overwriting*, is a process of preparing media for reuse and assuring that the cleared data cannot be recovered using traditional recovery tools. When media is cleared, unclassified data is written over all addressable locations on the media. One method writes a single character, or a specific bit pattern, over the entire media. A more thorough method writes a single character over the entire media, writes the character's complement over the entire media, and finishes by writing random bits over the entire media. It repeats this in three separate passes, as shown in Figure 5.2. Although this sounds like the original data is lost forever, it is sometimes possible to retrieve some of the original data using sophisticated laboratory or forensics techniques. Additionally, some types of data storage don't respond well to clearing techniques. For example, spare sectors on hard drives, sectors labeled as "bad," and areas on many modern SSDs are not necessarily cleared and may still retain data.

FIGURE 5.2 Clearing a hard drive

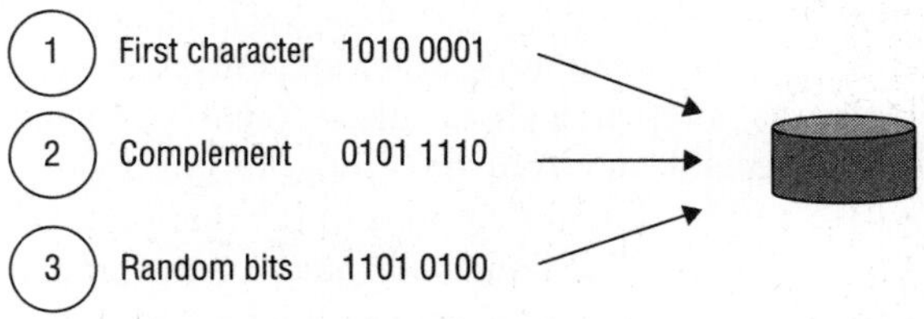

Purging *Purging* is a more intense form of clearing that prepares media for reuse in less secure environments. It provides a level of assurance that the original data is not recoverable using any known methods. A purging process will repeat the clearing process multiple times and may combine it with another method such as degaussing to completely remove the data. Even though purging is intended to remove all data remnants, it isn't always trusted. For example, the US government doesn't consider any purging method acceptable to purge top secret data. Media labeled top secret will always remain top secret until it is destroyed.

Declassification *Declassification* involves any process that purges media or a system in preparation for reuse in an unclassified environment. Purging can be used to prepare media for declassification, but often the efforts required to securely declassify media are significantly greater than the cost of new media for a less secure environment. Additionally, even though purged data is not recoverable using any known methods, there is a remote possibility that an unknown method is available. Instead of taking the risk, many organizations choose not to declassify any media.

Sanitization *Sanitization* is a combination of processes that removes data from a system or from media. It ensures that data cannot be recovered by any means. When a computer is disposed of, sanitization includes ensuring that all nonvolatile memory has been removed or destroyed, the system doesn't have CD/DVDs in any drive, and internal drives (hard drives and SSDs) have been purged, removed, and/or destroyed. Sanitization can refer to the destruction of media or using a trusted method to purge classified data from the media without destroying it.

Degaussing A degausser creates a strong magnetic field that erases data on some media in a process called *degaussing*. Technicians commonly use degaussing methods to remove data from magnetic tapes with the goal of returning the tape to its original state. It is possible to degauss hard disks, but we don't recommend it. Degaussing a hard disk will normally destroy the electronics used to access the data. However, you won't have any assurance that all of the data on the disk has actually been destroyed. Someone could open the drive in a clean room and install the platters on a different drive to read the data. Degaussing does not affect optical CDs, DVDs, or SSDs.

Destruction Destruction is the final stage in the life cycle of media and is the most secure method of sanitizing media. When destroying media it's important to ensure that the media cannot be reused or repaired and that data cannot be extracted from the destroyed media. Methods of destruction include incineration, crushing, shredding, disintegration, and dissolving using caustic or acidic chemicals. Some organizations remove the platters in highly classified disk drives and destroy them separately.

NOTE When organizations donate or sell used computer equipment, they often remove and destroy storage devices that hold sensitive data rather than attempting to purge them. This eliminates the risk that the purging process wasn't complete, thus resulting in a loss of confidentiality.

Retaining Assets

Retention requirements apply to data or records, media holding sensitive data, systems that process sensitive data, and personnel who have access to sensitive data. Record retention and media retention is the most important element of asset retention.

Record retention involves retaining and maintaining important information as long as it is needed and destroying it when it is no longer needed. An organization's security policy or data policy typically identifies retention timeframes. Some laws and regulations dictate the length of time that an organization should retain data, such as three years, seven years, or even indefinitely. However, even in the absence of external requirements, an organization should still identify how long to retain data.

As an example, many organizations require the retention of all audit logs for three years or longer. This allows the organization to reconstruct the details of past security incidents. When an organization doesn't have a retention policy, administrators may delete valuable data earlier than management expects them to or attempt to keep data indefinitely. The longer data is retained, the more it costs in terms of media, locations to store it, and personnel to protect it.

Most hardware is on a refresh cycle, where it is replaced every three to five years. Hardware retention primarily refers to retaining it until it has been properly sanitized.

Personnel retention in this context refers to the knowledge that personnel gain while employed by an organization. It's common for organizations to include nondisclosure agreements (NDAs) when hiring new personnel. These NDAs prevent employees from leaving the job and sharing proprietary data with others.

Real World Scenario

Retention Policies Can Reduce Liabilities

Saving data longer than necessary also presents unnecessary legal issues. As an example, aircraft manufacturer Boeing was once the target of a class action lawsuit. Attorneys for the claimants learned that Boeing had a warehouse filled with 14,000 email backup tapes and demanded the relevant tapes. Not all of the tapes were relevant to the lawsuit, but Boeing had to first restore the 14,000 tapes and examine the content before they could turn them over. It ended up settling the lawsuit for $92.5 million, and analysts speculated that there would have been a different outcome if those 14,000 tapes hadn't existed.

The Boeing example is an extreme example, but it's not the only one. These events have prompted many companies to implement aggressive email retention policies. It is not uncommon for an email policy to require the deletion of all emails older than six months. These policies are often implemented using automated tools that search for old emails and delete them without any user or administrator intervention.

A company cannot legally delete potential evidence after a lawsuit is filed. However, if a retention policy dictates deleting data after a specific amount of time, it is legal to delete this data before any lawsuits have been filed. Not only does this practice prevent wasting resources to store unneeded data, it also provides an added layer of legal protection against wasting resources by looking through old information.

Protecting Confidentiality with Cryptography

One of the primary methods of protecting the confidentiality of data is encryption. Chapter 6, "Cryptography and Symmetric Key Algorithms," and Chapter 7, "PKI and Cryptographic Applications," cover cryptographic algorithms in more depth. However, it's worth pointing out the differences between algorithms used for data at rest and data in transit.

As an introduction, encryption converts cleartext data into scrambled ciphertext. Anyone can read the data when it is in cleartext format. However, when strong encryption algorithms are used, it is almost impossible to read the scrambled ciphertext.

Protecting Data with Symmetric Encryption

Symmetric encryption uses the same key to encrypt and decrypt data. In other words, if an algorithm encrypted data with a key of 123, it would decrypt it with the same key of 123. Symmetric algorithms don't use the same key for different data. For example, if it encrypted one set of data using a key of 123, it might encrypt the next set of data with a key of 456. The important point here is that a file encrypted using a key of 123 can only be decrypted using the same key of 123. In practice, the key size is much larger. For example, AES uses key sizes of 128 bits or 192 bits and AES 256 uses a key size of 256 bits.

The following list identifies some of the commonly used symmetric encryption algorithms. Although many of these algorithms are used in applications to encrypt data at rest, some of them are also used in transport encryption algorithms discussed in the next section. Additionally, this is by no means a complete list of encryption algorithms, but Chapter 6 covers more of them.

Advanced Encryption Standard The Advanced Encryption Standard (AES) is one of the most popular symmetric encryption algorithms. NIST selected it as a standard replacement for the older Data Encryption Standard (DES) in 2001. Since then, developers have steadily been implementing AES into many other algorithms and protocols. For example, BitLocker (a full disk encryption application used with a Trusted Platform Module) uses AES. The Microsoft Encrypting File System (EFS) uses AES for file and folder encryption. AES supports key sizes of 128 bits, 192 bits, and 256 bits, and the US government has approved its use to protect classified data up to top secret. Larger key sizes add additional security, making it more difficult for unauthorized personnel to decrypt the data.

Triple DES Developers created Triple DES (or 3DES) as a possible replacement for DES. The first implementation used 56-bit keys but newer implementations use 112-bit or 168-bit keys. Larger keys provide a higher level of security. Microsoft OneNote and System Center Configuration Manager use 3DES to protect some content and passwords.

Blowfish Security expert Bruce Schneier developed Blowfish as a possible alternative to DES. It can use key sizes of 32 bits to 448 bits and is a strong encryption protocol. Linux systems use bcrypt to encrypt passwords, and bcrypt is based on Blowfish. Bcrypt adds 128 additional bits as a salt to protect against rainbow table attacks.

Protecting Data with Transport Encryption

Transport encryption methods encrypt data before it is transmitted, providing protection of data in transit. The primary risk of sending unencrypted data over a network is a sniffing attack. Attackers can use a sniffer or protocol analyzer to capture traffic sent over a network. The sniffer allows attackers to read all the data sent in cleartext. However, attackers are unable to read data encrypted with a strong encryption protocol.

As an example, web browsers use Hypertext Transfer Protocol Secure (HTTPS) to encrypt e-commerce transactions. This prevents attackers from capturing the data and using credit card information to rack up charges. In contrast, Hypertext Transfer Protocol (HTTP) transmits data in cleartext.

Almost all HTTPS transmissions use Transport Layer Security (TLS) as the underlying encryption protocol. Secure Sockets Layer (SSL) was the precursor to TLS. Netscape created and released SSL in 1995. Later, the Internet Engineering Task Force (IETF) released TLS as a replacement. In 2014, Google discovered that SSL is susceptible to the POODLE attack (Padding Oracle On Downgraded Legacy Encryption). As a result, many organizations have disabled SSL in their applications.

Organizations often enable remote access solutions such as virtual private networks (VPNs). VPNs allow employees to access the organization's internal network from their home or while traveling. VPN traffic goes over a public network, such as the Internet, so encryption is important. VPNs use encryption protocols such as TLS and Internet Protocol security (IPsec).

IPsec is often combined with Layer 2 Tunneling Protocol (L2TP) for VPNs. L2TP transmits data in cleartext, but L2TP/IPsec encrypts data and sends it over the Internet using Tunnel mode to protect it while in transit. IPsec includes an Authentication Header (AH), which provides authentication and integrity, and Encapsulating Security Payload (ESP) to provide confidentiality.

It's also appropriate to encrypt sensitive data before transmitting it on internal networks, and IPsec and Secure Shell (SSH) are commonly used to protect data in transit on internal networks. SSH is a strong encryption protocol included with other protocols such as Secure Copy (SCP) and Secure File Transfer Protocol (SFTP). Both SCP and SFTP are secure protocols used to transfer encrypted files over a network. Protocols such as File Transfer Protocol (FTP) transmit data in cleartext and so are not appropriate for transmitting sensitive data over a network.

Many administrators use SSH instead of Telnet when administering remote servers. Telnet should not be used because it sends traffic over the network in cleartext. When connecting to remote servers, administrators need to log on to the server, so Telnet also sends their credentials over the network in cleartext. However, SSH encrypts all of the traffic, including the administrator's credentials.

NOTE

When Telnet must be used to connect to a remote server, administrators typically use a VPN to encrypt the Telnet traffic within a tunnel.

Identifying Data Roles

Many people within an organization manage, handle, and use data, and they have different requirements based on their roles. Different documentation refers to these roles a little differently. Some of the terms used in the CISSP Candidate Information Bulletin (CIB) match the terminology in some NIST documents, and some of the terminology matches the *Safe Harbor* program related to the European Union (EU) Data Protection law. When appropriate, we've listed the source so that you can dig into of these terms a little deeper if desired.

Data Owners

The *data owner* is the person who has ultimate organizational responsibility for data. The owner is typically the CEO, president, or a department head (DH). Data owners identify the classification of data and ensure that it is labeled properly. They also ensure it has adequate security controls based on the classification and the organization's security policy requirements. Owners may be liable for negligence if they fail to perform due diligence in establishing and enforcing security policies to protect and sustain sensitive data.

NIST SP 800-18 outlines the following responsibilities for the information owner, which can be interpreted the same as the data owner.

- Establishes the rules for appropriate use and protection of the subject data/information (rules of behavior)
- Provides input to information system owners regarding the security requirements and security controls for the information system(s) where the information resides
- Decides who has access to the information system and with what types of privileges or access rights
- Assists in the identification and assessment of the common security controls where the information resides.

NOTE

NIST SP 800-18 frequently uses the phrase "rules of behavior," which is effectively the same as an acceptable usage policy (AUP). Both outline the responsibilities and expected behavior of individuals and state the consequences of not complying with the rules or AUP. Additionally, individuals are required to periodically acknowledge that they have read, understand, and agree to abide by the rules or AUP. Many organizations post these on a website and allow users to acknowledge they understand and agree to abide by them using an online electronic digital signature.

System Owners

The system owner is the person who owns the system that processes sensitive data. NIST SP 800-18 outlines the following responsibilities for the system owner:

- Develops a system security plan in coordination with information owners, the system administrator, and functional end users
- Maintains the system security plan and ensures that the system is deployed and operated according to the agreed-upon security requirements
- Ensures that system users and support personnel receive appropriate security training, such as instruction on rules of behavior (or an AUP)
- Updates the system security plan whenever a significant change occurs
- Assists in the identification, implementation, and assessment of the common security controls

The system owner is typically the same person as the data owner, but it can sometimes be someone different, such as a different department head (DH). As an example, consider a web server used for e-commerce that interacts with a back-end database server. A software development department might perform database development and database administration for the database and the database server, but the IT department maintains the web server. In this case, the software development DH is the system owner for the database server, and the IT DH is the system owner for the web server. However, it's more common for one person (such as a single department head) to control both servers, and this one person would be the system owner for both systems.

The system owner is responsible for ensuring that data processed on the system remains secure. This includes identifying the highest level of data that the system processes. The system owner then ensures that the system is labeled accurately and that appropriate security controls are in place to protect the data. System owners interact with data owners to ensure the data is protected while at rest on the system, in transit between systems, and in use by applications operating on the system.

Business/Mission Owners

The business/mission owner is role is viewed differently in different organizations. NIST SP 800-18 refers to the business/mission owner as a program manager or an information system owner. As such, the responsibilities of the business/mission owner can overlap with the responsibilities of the system owner or be the same role.

Business owners might own processes that use systems managed by other entities. As an example, the sales department could be the business owner but the IT department and the software development department could be the system owners for systems used in sales processes. Imagine that the sales department focuses on online sales using an e-commerce website and the website accesses a back-end database server. As in the previous example, the IT department manages the web server as its system owner, and the software development department manages the database server as its system owner. Even though the sales department doesn't own these systems, it does own the business processes that generate sales using these systems.

In businesses, business owners are responsible for ensuring systems provide value to the organization. This sounds obvious. However, IT departments sometimes become overzealous and implement security controls without considering the impact on the business or its mission.

A potential area of conflict in many businesses is the comparison between cost centers and profit centers. The IT department doesn't generate revenue. Instead, it is a cost center generating costs. In contrast, the business side generates revenue as a profit center. Costs generated by the IT department eat up profits generated by the business side. Additionally, many of the security controls implemented by the IT department reduce usability of systems in the interest of security. If you put these together, you can see that the business side sometimes views the IT department as spending money, reducing profits, and making it more difficult for the business to generate profits.

Organizations often implement IT governance methods such as Control Objectives for Information and Related Technology (COBIT). These methods help business owners and mission owners balance security control requirements with business or mission needs.

Data Processors

Generically, a data processor is any system used to process data. However, in the context of the EU Data Protection law, *data processor* has a more specific meaning. The EU Data Protection law defines a *data processor* as "a natural or legal person which processes personal data solely on behalf of the data controller." In this context, the *data controller* is the person or entity that controls processing of the data.

As an example, a company that collects personal information on employees for payroll is a data controller. If they pass this information to a third-party company to process payroll, the payroll company is the data processor. In this example, the payroll company (the data processor) must not use the data for anything other than processing payroll at the direction of the data controller.

The EU Data Protection Directive (Directive 95/46/EC) restricts data transfers to countries outside of the EU. These countries must meet specific requirements that indicate they meet an adequate level of data protection. The US Department of Commerce runs the Safe Harbor program, which is a regulatory mechanism that includes a set of Safe Harbor Principles. The goal is to prevent unauthorized disclosure of information, handled by data processors, and transmitted between data processors and the data controller. US companies can voluntarily opt into the program if they agree to abide by seven principles and the requirements outlined in 15 frequently asked questions satisfactorily. The principles have a lot of legalese embedded within them but are paraphrased in the following bullets:

- Notice: An organization must inform individuals about the purposes for which it collects and uses information about them.
- Choice: An organization must offer individuals the opportunity to opt out.
- Onward transfer: Organizations can only transfer data to other than organizations that comply with the Notice and Choice principles.
- Security: Organizations must take reasonable precautions to protect data.
- Data integrity: Organizations may not use information for purposes other than what they stated in the Notice principle and users selected in the Choice principle. Additionally, organizations should take steps to ensure the data is reliable.
- Access: Individuals must have access to personal information an organization holds about them. Individuals also have the ability to correct, amend, or delete information, when it is inaccurate.
- Enforcement: Organizations must implement mechanisms to assure compliance with the principles.

NOTE

The US Department of Commerce maintains a site with many resources on Safe Harbor starting here: `www.export.gov/safeharbor/`. You can view the full text of the principles and the list of frequently asked questions by searching their site with Safe Harbor Principles and Safe Harbor Frequently Asked Questions, respectively.

Administrators

A data administrator is responsible for granting appropriate access to personnel. They don't necessarily have full administrator rights and privileges, but they do have the ability to assign permissions. Administrators assign permissions based on the principles of least privilege and the need to know, granting users access to only what they need for their job.

Administrators typically assign permissions using a role-based access control model. In other words, they add user accounts to groups and then grant permissions to the groups. When users no longer need access to the data, administrators remove their account from the group. Chapter 13, "Managing Identity and Authentication," covers the role-based access control model in more depth.

Custodians

Data owners often delegate day-to-day tasks to a *custodian*. A custodian helps protect the integrity and security of data by ensuring it is properly stored and protected. For example, custodians would ensure the data is backed up in accordance with a backup policy. If administrators have configured auditing on the data, custodians would also maintain these logs.

In practice, personnel within an IT department or system security administrators would typically be the custodians. They might be the same administrators responsible for assigning permissions to data.

Users

A *user* is any person who accesses data via a computing system to accomplish work tasks. Users have access to only the data they need to perform their work tasks. You can also think of users as employees or end users.

Protecting Privacy

Organizations have an obligation to protect data that they collect and maintain. This is especially true for both PII and PHI data (described earlier in this chapter). Many laws and regulations mandate the protection of privacy data, and organizations have an obligation to learn which laws and regulations apply to them. Additionally, organizations need to ensure their practices comply with these laws and regulations.

Many laws require organizations to disclose what data they collect, why they collect it, and how they plan to use the information. Additionally, these laws prohibit organizations from using the information in ways that are outside the scope of what they intend to use it for. For example, if an organization states it is collecting email addresses to communicate with a customer about purchases, the organization should not sell the email addresses to third parties.

It's common for organizations to use an online privacy policy on their websites. Some of the entities that require strict adherence to privacy laws include the US (with HIPAA privacy rules), the state of California (with the California Online Privacy Protection Act of 2003), Canada (with the Personal Information Protection and Electronic Documents Act), and the EU with the Data Protection Directive.

NOTE The EU has drafted the General Data Protection Regulation (GDPR) as a replacement for the EU Data Protection Directive. The planned timeline is for organizations to begin adopting the requirements in 2015 and 2016, and begin enforcing the requirements in 2017 and 2018.

Many of these laws require organizations to follow these requirements if they operate in the jurisdiction of the law. For example, the California Online Privacy Protection Act (COPA) requires a conspicuously posted privacy policy for any commercial websites or online services that collect personal information on California residents. In effect, this potentially applies to any website in the world that collects personal information because if the website is accessible on the Internet, any California residents can access it. Many people consider COPA to be one of the most stringent laws in the United States, and US-based organizations that follow the requirements of the California law typically meet the requirements in other locales. However, an organization has an obligation to determine what laws apply to it and follow them.

When protecting privacy, an organization will typically use several different security controls. Selecting the proper security controls can be a daunting task, especially for new organizations. However, using security baselines and identifying relevant standards makes the task a little easier.

Using Security Baselines

Baselines provide a starting point and ensure a minimum security standard. One common baseline that organizations use is imaging. Chapter 16, "Managing Security Operations," covers imaging in the context of configuration management in more depth. As an introduction, administrators configure a single system with desired settings, capture it as an image, and then deploy the image to other systems. This ensures all of the systems are deployed in a similar secure state.

After deploying systems in a secure state, auditing processes periodically check the systems to ensure they remain in a secure state. As an example, Microsoft Group Policy can periodically check systems and reapply settings to match the baseline.

NIST SP 800-53 discusses *security control baselines* as a list of security controls. It stresses that a single set of security controls does not apply to all situations, but any organization can select a set of baseline security controls and tailor it to its needs. Appendix D of SP 800-53 includes four prioritized sets of security controls that organizations can implement to provide basic security. These give organizations insight into what they should implement first, second, and last.

As an example, consider Table 5.2, which is a partial list of some security controls in the access control family. NIST has assigned the control number and the control name for these controls and has provided a recommended priority. P-1 indicates the highest priority, P-2 is next, and P-3 is last. NIST SP 800-53 explains all of these controls in more depth in Appendix F.

TABLE 5.2 Security control baselines

Control no.	Control name	Priority
AC-1	Access Control Policy and Procedures	P-1
AC-2	Account Management	P-1
AT-2	Security Awareness Training	P-1
AC-5	Separation of Duties	P-1
AC-6	Least Privilege	P-1
AC-7	Unsuccessful Logon Attempts	P-2
AC-10	Concurrent Session Control	P-3

It's worth noting that many of the items labeled as P-1 are basic security practices. Access control policies and procedures ensure that users have unique identifications (such as usernames) and can prove their identity with authentication procedures. Administrators grant users access to resources based on their proven identity (using authorization processes). Similarly, implementing basic security principles such as separation of duties and the principle of least privilege shouldn't be a surprise to anyone studying for the CISSP exam. Of course, just because these are basic security practices, it doesn't mean organizations implement them. Unfortunately, many organizations have yet to discover, or enforce, the basics.

Scoping and Tailoring

Scoping refers to reviewing baseline security controls and selecting only those controls that apply to the IT system you're trying to protect. For example, if a system doesn't allow any two people to log on to it at the same time, there's no need to apply a concurrent session control.

Tailoring refers to modifying the list of security controls within a baseline so that they align with the mission of the organization. For example, an organization might decide that a set of baseline controls applies perfectly to computers in their main location, but some controls aren't appropriate or feasible in a remote office location. In this situation, the organization can select compensating security controls to tailor the baseline to the remote location.

Selecting Standards

When selecting security controls within a baseline, or otherwise, organizations need to ensure that the controls comply with certain external security standards. External elements typically define compulsory requirements for an organization. As an example, the Payment Card Industry Data Security Standard (PCI DSS) defines requirements that businesses must follow to process major credit cards. Similarly, organizations that want to transfer data to and from EU countries must abide by the principles in the Safe Harbor standard.

Obviously, not all organizations have to comply with these standards. Organizations that don't process credit card transactions do not need to comply with PCI DSS. Similarly, organizations that do not transfer data to and from EU countries do not need to comply with the Safe Harbor standard. With this in mind, organizations need to identify the standards that apply, and ensure the security controls they select comply with these standards.

Summary

Asset security focuses on collecting, handling, and protecting information throughout its life cycle. This includes sensitive information stored, processed, or transmitted on computing systems. Sensitive information is any information that an organization keeps private and can include multiple levels of classifications.

A key step in this process is defining classification labels in a security policy or data policy. Governments use labels such as top secret, secret, confidential, and unclassified. Nongovernment organizations can use any labels they choose. The key is that they define the labels in a security policy or a data policy. Data owners (typically senior management personnel) provide the data definitions.

Organizations take specific steps to mark, handle, store, and destroy sensitive information, and these steps help prevent the loss of confidentiality due to unauthorized disclosure. Additionally, organizations commonly define specific rules for record retention to ensure that data is available when it is needed. Data retention policies also reduce liabilities resulting from keeping data for too long.

A key method of protecting the confidentiality of data is with encryption. Symmetric encryption protocols (such as AES) can encrypt data at rest (stored on media). Transport encryption protocols protect data in transit by encrypting it before transmitting it (data in transit).

Personnel can fulfill many different roles when handling data. Data owners are ultimately responsible for classifying, labeling, and protecting data. System owners are responsible for the systems that process the data. Business and mission owners own the processes and ensure the systems provide value to the organization. Data processors are typically third-party entities that process data for an organization. Administrators grant access to data based on guidelines provided by the data owners. A custodian is delegated day-to-day responsibilities for properly storing and protecting data. A user (often called an end user) accesses data on a system.

The EU Data Protection law mandates protection of privacy data. A data controller can hire a third party to process data, and in this context, the third party is the data processor. Data processors have a responsibility to protect the privacy of the data and not use it for any other purpose than directed by the data controller. The Safe Harbor program includes seven principles that organizations agree to abide by so that they follow the requirements within the EU Data Protection law.

Security baselines provide a set of security controls that an organization can implement as a secure starting point. Some publications (such as NIST SP 800-53) identify security control baselines. However, these baselines don't apply equally to all organizations. Instead, organizations use scoping and tailoring techniques to identify the security controls to implement in their baselines. Additionally, organizations ensure that they implement security controls mandated by external standards that apply to their organization.

Exam Essentials

Understand the importance of data classifications. Data owners are responsible for defining data classifications and ensuring systems and data are properly marked. Additionally, data owners define requirements to protect data at different classifications, such as encrypting sensitive data at rest and in transit. Data classifications are typically defined within security policies or data policies.

Know about PII and PHI. Personally identifiable information (PII) is any information that can identify an individual. Protected health information (PHI) is any health-related information that can be related to a specific person. Many laws and regulations mandate the protection of PII and PHI.

Know how to manage sensitive information. Sensitive information is any type of classified information, and proper management helps prevent unauthorized disclosure resulting in a loss of confidentiality. Proper management includes marking, handling, storing, and destroying sensitive information. The two areas where organizations often miss the mark are adequately protecting backup media holding sensitive information and sanitizing media or equipment when it is at the end of its life cycle.

Understand record retention. Record retention policies ensure that data is kept in a usable state while it is needed and destroyed when it is no longer needed. Many laws and regulations mandate keeping data for a specific amount of time, but in the absence of formal regulations, organizations specify the retention period within a policy. Audit trail data needs to be kept long enough to reconstruct past incidents, but the organization must identify how far back they want to investigate. A current trend with many organizations is to reduce legal liabilities by implementing short retention policies with email.

Know the difference between different roles. The data owner is the person responsible for classifying, labeling, and protecting data. System owners are responsible for the systems that process the data. Business and mission owners own the processes and ensure the systems provide value to the organization. Data processors are typically third-party entities that process data for an organization. Administrators grant access to data based on guidelines provided by the data owners. A user accesses data in the course of performing work tasks. A custodian has day-to-day responsibilities for protecting and storing data.

Understand the seven Safe Harbor principles. The EU Data Protection law mandates protection of privacy data. Third parties agree to abide by the seven Safe Harbor principles as a method of ensuring that they are complying with the EU Data Protection law. The seven principles are notice, choice, onward transfer, security, data integrity, access, and enforcement.

Know about security control baselines. Security control baselines provide a listing of controls that an organization can apply as a baseline. Not all baselines apply to all organizations. However, an organization can apply scoping and tailoring techniques to adopt a baseline to its needs.

Written Lab

1. Describe PII and PHI.
2. Describe the best method to sanitize SSDs.
3. Name four classification levels that an organization can implement for data.
4. List the seven principles outlined by the Safe Harbor program.

Review Questions

1. Which one of the following identifies the primary a purpose of information classification processes?
   A. Define the requirements for protecting sensitive data.
   B. Define the requirements for backing up data.
   C. Define the requirements for storing data.
   D. Define the requirements for transmitting data.
2. When determining the classification of data, which one of the following is the most important consideration?
   A. Processing system
   B. Value
   C. Storage media
   D. Accessibility
3. Which of the following answers would not be included as sensitive data?
   A. Personally identifiable information (PII)
   B. Protected health information (PHI)
   C. Proprietary data
   D. Data posted on a website
4. What is the most important aspect of marking media?
   A. Date labeling
   B. Content description
   C. Electronic labeling
   D. Classification
5. Which would an administrator do to classified media before reusing it in a less secure environment?
   A. Erasing
   B. Clearing
   C. Purging
   D. Overwriting
6. Which of the following statements correctly identifies a problem with sanitization methods?
   A. Methods are not available to remove data ensuring that unauthorized personnel cannot retrieve data.
   B. Even fully incinerated media can offer extractable data.
   C. Personnel can perform sanitization steps improperly.
   D. Stored data is physically etched into the media.

7. Which of the following choices is the most reliable method of destroying data on a solid state drive?
   A. Erasing
   B. Degaussing
   C. Deleting
   D. Purging
8. Which of the following is the most secure method of deleting data on a DVD?
   A. Formatting
   B. Deleting
   C. Destruction
   D. Degaussing
9. Which of the following does not erase data?
   A. Clearing
   B. Purging
   C. Overwriting
   D. Remanence
10. Which one of the following is based on Blowfish and helps protect against rainbow table attacks?
    A. 3DES
    B. AES
    C. Bcrypt
    D. SCP
11. Which one of the following would administrators use to connect to a remote server securely for administration?
    A. Telnet
    B. Secure File Transfer Protocol (SFTP)
    C. Secure Copy (SCP)
    D. Secure Shell (SSH)
12. Which one of the following tasks would a custodian most likely perform?
    A. Access the data
    B. Classify the data
    C. Assign permissions to the data
    D. Back up data
13. Which one of the following data roles is most likely to assign permissions to grant users access to data?
    A. Administrator
    B. Custodian

C. Owner

D. User

14. Which of the following best defines "rules of behavior" established by a data owner?

A. Ensuring users are granted access to only what they need

B. Determining who has access to a system

C. Identifying appropriate use and protection of data

D. Applying security controls to a system

15. Within the context of the European Union (EU) Data Protection law, what is a data processor?

A. The entity that processes personal data on behalf of the data controller

B. The entity that controls processing of data

C. The computing system that processes data

D. The network that processes data

16. What do the principles of notice, choice, onward transfer, and access closely apply to?

A. Privacy

B. Identification

C. Retention

D. Classification

17. An organization is implementing a preselected baseline of security controls, but finds not all of the controls apply. What should they do?

A. Implement all of the controls anyway.

B. Identify another baseline.

C. Re-create a baseline.

D. Tailor the baseline to their needs.

Refer the following scenario when answering questions 18 through 20.

An organization has a datacenter manned 24 hours a day that processes highly sensitive information. The datacenter includes email servers, and administrators purge email older than six months to comply with the organization's security policy. Access to the datacenter is controlled, and all systems that process sensitive information are marked. Administrators routinely back up data processed in the datacenter. They keep a copy of the backups on site and send an unmarked copy to one of the company warehouses. Warehouse workers organize the media by date, and they have backups from the last 20 years. Employees work at the warehouse during the day and lock it when they leave at night and over the weekends. Recently a theft at the warehouse resulted in the loss of all of the offsite backup tapes. Later, copies of their data, including sensitive emails from years ago, began appearing on Internet sites, exposing the organization's internal sensitive data.

18. Of the following choices, what would have prevented this loss without sacrificing security?

A. Mark the media kept offsite.

B. Don't store data offsite.

C. Destroy the backups offsite.

D. Use a secure offsite storage facility.

19. Which of the following administrator actions might have prevented this incident?

A. Mark the tapes before sending them to the warehouse.

B. Purge the tapes before backing up data to them.

C. Degauss the tapes before backing up data to them.

D. Add the tapes to an asset management database.

20. Of the following choices, what policy was not followed regarding the backup media?

A. Media destruction

B. Record retention

C. Configuration management

D. Versioning

Chapter 6

Cryptography and Symmetric Key Algorithms

THE CISSP EXAM TOPICS COVERED IN THIS CHAPTER INCLUDE:

✓ **Security Engineering**

- I. Apply cryptography
  - I.1 Cryptographic life cycle (e.g., cryptographic limitations, algorithm/protocol governance)
  - I.2 Cryptographic types (e.g. symmetric, asymmetric, elliptic curves)
  - I.7 Non-repudiation
  - I.8 Integrity (hashing and salting)

Cryptography provides added levels of security to data during processing, storage, and communications. Over the years, mathematicians and computer scientists have developed a series of increasingly complex algorithms designed to ensure confidentiality, integrity, authentication, and nonrepudiation. While cryptographers spent time developing strong encryption algorithms, hackers and governments alike devoted significant resources to undermining them. This led to an "arms race" in cryptography and resulted in the development of the extremely sophisticated algorithms in use today. This chapter looks at the history of cryptography, the basics of cryptographic communications, and the fundamental principles of private key cryptosystems. The next chapter continues the discussion of cryptography by examining public key cryptosystems and the various techniques attackers use to defeat cryptography.

Historical Milestones in Cryptography

Since the beginning of mankind, human beings have devised various systems of written communication, ranging from ancient hieroglyphics written on cave walls to flash storage devices stuffed with encyclopedias full of information in modern English. As long as mankind has been communicating, we've used secretive means to hide the true meaning of those communications from the uninitiated. Ancient societies used a complex system of secret symbols to represent safe places to stay during times of war. Modern civilizations use a variety of codes and ciphers to facilitate private communication between individuals and groups. In the following sections, you'll look at the evolution of modern cryptography and several famous attempts to covertly intercept and decipher encrypted communications.

Caesar Cipher

One of the earliest known cipher systems was used by Julius Caesar to communicate with Cicero in Rome while he was conquering Europe. Caesar knew that there were several risks when sending messages—one of the messengers might be an enemy spy or might be ambushed while en route to the deployed forces. For that reason, Caesar developed a cryptographic system now known as the *Caesar cipher*. The system is extremely simple. To encrypt a message, you simply shift each letter of the alphabet three places to the right. For example, *A* would become *D*, and *B* would become *E*. If you reach the end of the alphabet during this process, you simply wrap around to the beginning so that *X* becomes *A*, *Y* becomes *B*, and Z becomes C. For this reason, the Caesar cipher also became known as the ROT3 (or Rotate 3) cipher. The Caesar cipher is a substitution cipher that is monoalphabetic; it's also known as a C3 cipher.

NOTE Although the Caesar cipher uses a shift of 3, the more general shift cipher uses the same algorithm to shift any number of characters desired by the user. For example, the ROT12 cipher would turn an *A* into an *M*, a *B* into an *N*, and so on.

Here's an example of the Caesar cipher in action. The first line contains the original sentence, and the second line shows what the sentence looks like when it is encrypted using the Caesar cipher:

```
THE DIE HAS BEEN CAST
WKH GLH KDV EHHQ FDVW
```

To decrypt the message, you simply shift each letter three places to the left.

WARNING Although the Caesar cipher is easy to use, it's also easy to crack. It's vulnerable to a type of attack known as frequency analysis. As you may know, the most common letters in the English language are *E, T, A, O, N, R, I, S,* and *H*. An attacker seeking to break a Caesar-style cipher merely needs to find the most common letters in the encrypted text and experiment with substitutions of these common letters to help determine the pattern.

American Civil War

Between the time of Caesar and the early years of the United States, scientists and mathematicians made significant advances beyond the early ciphers used by ancient civilizations. During the American Civil War, Union and Confederate troops both used relatively advanced cryptographic systems to secretly communicate along the front lines because each side was tapping into the telegraph lines to spy on the other side. These systems used complex combinations of word substitutions and transposition (see the section "Ciphers," later in this chapter, for more details) to attempt to defeat enemy decryption efforts. Another system used widely during the Civil War was a series of flag signals developed by army doctor Albert J. Myer.

NOTE Photos of many of the items discussed in this chapter are available online at www.nsa.gov/about/cryptologic_heritage/museum.

Ultra vs. Enigma

Americans weren't the only ones who expended significant resources in the pursuit of superior code-making machines. Prior to World War II, the German military-industrial complex adapted a commercial code machine nicknamed Enigma for government use. This machine used a series of three to six rotors to implement an extremely complicated substitution cipher. The only possible way to decrypt the message with contemporary technology was to use a similar machine with the same rotor settings used by the transmitting device. The Germans recognized the importance of safeguarding these devices and made it extremely difficult for the Allies to acquire one.

The Allied forces began a top-secret effort known by the code name Ultra to attack the Enigma codes. Eventually, their efforts paid off when the Polish military successfully reconstructed an Enigma prototype and shared their findings with British and American cryptology experts. The Allies successfully broke the Enigma code in 1940, and historians credit this triumph as playing a significant role in the eventual defeat of the Axis powers.

The Japanese used a similar machine, known as the Japanese Purple Machine, during World War II. A significant American attack on this cryptosystem resulted in breaking the Japanese code prior to the end of the war. The Americans were aided by the fact that Japanese communicators used very formal message formats that resulted in a large amount of similar text in multiple messages, easing the cryptanalytic effort.

Cryptographic Basics

The study of any science must begin with a discussion of some of the fundamental principles upon which it is built. The following sections lay this foundation with a review of the goals of cryptography, an overview of the basic concepts of cryptographic technology, and a look at the major mathematical principles used by cryptographic systems.

Goals of Cryptography

Security practitioners use cryptographic systems to meet four fundamental goals: confidentiality, integrity, authentication, and nonrepudiation. Achieving each of these goals requires the satisfaction of a number of design requirements, and not all cryptosystems are intended to achieve all four goals. In the following sections, we'll examine each goal in detail and give a brief description of the technical requirements necessary to achieve it.

Confidentiality

Confidentiality ensures that data remains private while at rest, such as when stored on a disk, or in transit, such as during transmission between two or more parties. This is perhaps the most widely cited goal of cryptosystems—the preservation of secrecy for stored information or for communications between individuals and groups. Two main types of cryptosystems enforce confidentiality. Symmetric key cryptosystems use a shared secret key available to all users of the cryptosystem. Asymmetric cryptosystems use individual combinations of public and private keys for each user of the system. Both of these concepts are explored in the section "Modern Cryptography" later in this chapter.

TIP The concept of protecting data at rest and data in transit is often covered on the CISSP exam. You should also know that data in transit is also commonly called data "on the wire," referring to the network cables that carry data communications.

When developing a cryptographic system for the purpose of providing confidentiality, you must think about two different types of data:

Data at rest, or stored data, is that which resides in a permanent location awaiting access. Examples of data at rest include data stored on hard drives, backup tapes, cloud storage services, USB devices, and other storage media.

Data in motion, or data "on the wire," is data being transmitted across a network between two systems. Data in motion might be traveling on a corporate network, a wireless network, or the public Internet.

Both data in motion and data at rest pose different types of confidentiality risks that cryptography can protect against. For example, data in motion may be susceptible to eavesdropping attacks, whereas data at rest is more susceptible to the theft of physical devices.

Integrity

Integrity ensures that data is not altered without authorization. If integrity mechanisms are in place, the recipient of a message can be certain that the message received is identical to the message that was sent. Similarly, integrity checks can ensure that stored data was not altered between the time it was created and the time it was accessed. Integrity controls protect against all forms of alteration: intentional alteration by a third party attempting to insert false information and unintentional alteration by faults in the transmission process.

Message integrity is enforced through the use of encrypted message digests, known as digital signatures created upon transmission of a message. The recipient of the message simply verifies that the message's digital signature is valid, ensuring that the message was not altered in transit. Integrity can be enforced by both public and secret key cryptosystems. This concept is discussed in detail in the section "Digital Signatures" in Chapter 7, "PKI and Cryptographic Applications." The use of cryptographic hash functions to protect file integrity is discussed in Chapter 21, "Malicious Code and Application Attacks."

Authentication

Authentication verifies the claimed identity of system users and is a major function of cryptosystems. For example, suppose that Bob wants to establish a communications session with Alice and they are both participants in a shared secret communications system. Alice might use a challenge-response authentication technique to ensure that Bob is who he claims to be.

Figure 6.1 shows how this challenge-response protocol would work in action. In this example, the shared-secret code used by Alice and Bob is quite simple—the letters of each word are simply reversed. Bob first contacts Alice and identifies himself. Alice then sends a challenge message to Bob, asking him to encrypt a short message using the secret code known only to Alice and Bob. Bob replies with the encrypted message. After Alice verifies that the encrypted message is correct, she trusts that Bob himself is truly on the other end of the connection.

FIGURE 6.1 Challenge-response authentication protocol

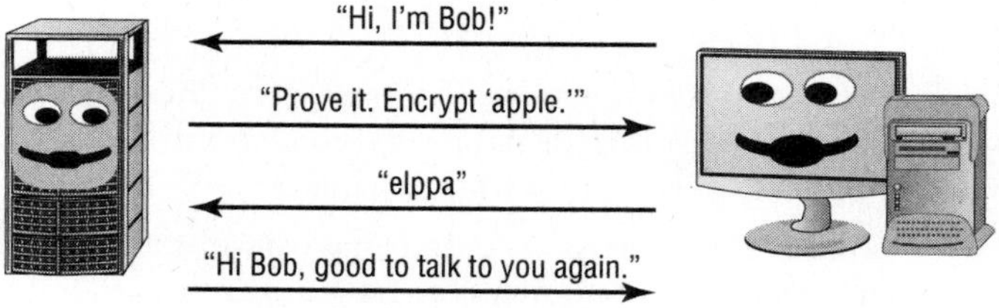
"Hi, I'm Bob!"
"Prove it. Encrypt 'apple.'"
"elppa"
"Hi Bob, good to talk to you again."

Nonrepudiation

Nonrepudiation provides assurance to the recipient that the message was originated by the sender and not someone masquerading as the sender. It also prevents the sender from claiming that they never sent the message in the first place (also known as *repudiating* the message). Secret key, or symmetric key, cryptosystems (such as simple substitution ciphers) do not provide this guarantee of nonrepudiation. If Jim and Bob participate in a secret key communication system, they can both produce the same encrypted message using their shared secret key. Nonrepudiation is offered only by public key, or asymmetric, cryptosystems, a topic discussed in greater detail in Chapter 7.

Cryptography Concepts

As with any science, you must be familiar with certain terminology before studying cryptography. Let's take a look at a few of the key terms used to describe codes and ciphers. Before a message is put into a coded form, it is known as a *plaintext* message and is represented by the letter P when encryption functions are described. The sender of a message uses a cryptographic algorithm to *encrypt* the plaintext message and produce a *ciphertext* message, represented by the letter C. This message is transmitted by some physical or electronic means to the recipient. The recipient then uses a predetermined algorithm to decrypt the ciphertext message and retrieve the plaintext version. (For an illustration of this process, see Figure 6.3 later in this chapter.)

All cryptographic algorithms rely on *keys* to maintain their security. For the most part, a key is nothing more than a number. It's usually a very large binary number, but a number nonetheless. Every algorithm has a specific *key space*. The key space is the range of values that are valid for use as a key for a specific algorithm. A key space is defined by its *bit size*.

Bit size is nothing more than the number of binary bits (0s and 1s) in the key. The key space is the range between the key that has all 0s and the key that has all 1s. Or to state it another way, the key space is the range of numbers from 0 to $2n$, where n is the bit size of the key. So, a 128-bit key can have a value from 0 to 2^{128} (which is roughly 3.40282367 * 10^{38}, a very big number!). It is absolutely critical to protect the security of secret keys. In fact, all of the security you gain from cryptography rests on your ability to keep the keys used private.

The Kerchoff Principle

All cryptography relies on algorithms. An *algorithm* is a set of rules, usually mathematical, that dictates how enciphering and deciphering processes are to take place. Most cryptographers follow the Kerchoff principle, a concept that makes algorithms known and public, allowing anyone to examine and test them. Specifically, the *Kerchoff principle* (also known as Kerchoff's assumption) is that a cryptographic system should be secure even if everything about the system, except the key, is public knowledge. The principle can be summed up as "The enemy knows the system."

A large number of cryptographers adhere to this principle, but not all agree. In fact, some believe that better overall security can be maintained by keeping both the algorithm and the key private. Kerchoff's adherents retort that the opposite approach includes the dubious practice of "security through obscurity" and believe that public exposure produces more activity and exposes more weaknesses more readily, leading to the abandonment of insufficiently strong algorithms and quicker adoption of suitable ones.

As you'll learn in this chapter and the next, different types of algorithms require different types of keys. In private key (or secret key) cryptosystems, all participants use a single shared key. In public key cryptosystems, each participant has their own pair of keys. Cryptographic keys are sometimes referred to as *cryptovariables*.

The art of creating and implementing secret codes and ciphers is known as *cryptography*. This practice is paralleled by the art of *cryptanalysis*—the study of methods to defeat codes and ciphers. Together, cryptography and cryptanalysis are commonly referred to as *cryptology*. Specific implementations of a code or cipher in hardware and software are known as *cryptosystems*. Federal Information Processing Standard (FIPS) 140–2, "Security Requirements for Cryptographic Modules," defines the hardware and software requirements for cryptographic modules that the federal government uses.

TIP

Be sure to understand the meanings of the terms in this section before continuing your study of this chapter and the following chapter. They are essential to understanding the technical details of the cryptographic algorithms presented in the following sections.

Cryptographic Mathematics

Cryptography is no different from most computer science disciplines in that it finds its foundations in the science of mathematics. To fully understand cryptography, you must first understand the basics of binary mathematics and the logical operations used to manipulate binary values. The following sections present a brief look at some of the most fundamental concepts with which you should be familiar.

Boolean Mathematics

Boolean mathematics defines the rules used for the bits and bytes that form the nervous system of any computer. You're most likely familiar with the decimal system. It is a base 10 system in which an integer from 0 to 9 is used in each place and each place value is a multiple of 10. It's likely that our reliance on the decimal system has biological origins—human beings have 10 fingers that can be used to count.

> **TIP** Boolean math can be very confusing at first, but it's worth the investment of time to learn how logical functions work. You need to understand these concepts to truly understand the inner workings of cryptographic algorithms.

Similarly, the computer's reliance upon the Boolean system has electrical origins. In an electrical circuit, there are only two possible states—on (representing the presence of electrical current) and off (representing the absence of electrical current). All computation performed by an electrical device must be expressed in these terms, giving rise to the use of Boolean computation in modern electronics. In general, computer scientists refer to the on condition as a *true* value and the off condition as a *false* value.

Logical Operations

The Boolean mathematics of cryptography uses a variety of logical functions to manipulate data. We'll take a brief look at several of these operations.

AND

The AND operation (represented by the $\wedge$ symbol) checks to see whether two values are both true. The truth table that follows illustrates all four possible outputs for the AND function. Remember, the AND function takes only two variables as input. In Boolean math, there are only two possible values for each of these variables, leading to four possible inputs to the AND function. It's this finite number of possibilities that makes it extremely easy for computers to implement logical functions in hardware. Notice in the following truth table that only one combination of inputs (where both inputs are true) produces an output value of true:

X	Y	X ∧ Y
0	0	0
0	1	0
1	0	0
1	1	1

Logical operations are often performed on entire Boolean words rather than single values. Take a look at the following example:

```
    X:   0 1 1 0 1 1 0 0
    Y:   1 0 1 0 0 1 1 1
---------------------------
X ∧ Y:   0 0 1 0 0 1 0 0
```

Notice that the AND function is computed by comparing the values of `X` and `Y` in each column. The output value is true only in columns where both `X` and `Y` are true.

OR

The OR operation (represented by the ∨ symbol) checks to see whether at least one of the input values is true. Refer to the following truth table for all possible values of the OR function. Notice that the only time the OR function returns a false value is when both of the input values are false:

X	Y	X ∨ Y
0	0	0
0	1	1
1	0	1
1	1	1

We'll use the same example we used in the previous section to show you what the output would be if `X` and `Y` were fed into the OR function rather than the AND function:

```
    X:   0 1 1 0 1 1 0 0
    Y:   1 0 1 0 0 1 1 1
---------------------------
X ∨ Y:   1 1 1 0 1 1 1 1
```

NOT

The NOT operation (represented by the ~ or ! symbol) simply reverses the value of an input variable. This function operates on only one variable at a time. Here's the truth table for the NOT function:

X	~X
0	1
1	0

In this example, you take the value of X from the previous examples and run the NOT function against it:

```
 X:     0 1 1 0 1 1 0 0
--------------------------
~X:     1 0 0 1 0 0 1 1
```

Exclusive OR

The final logical function you'll examine in this chapter is perhaps the most important and most commonly used in cryptographic applications—the exclusive OR (XOR) function. It's referred to in mathematical literature as the XOR function and is commonly represented by the ⊕ symbol. The XOR function returns a true value when only one of the input values is true. If both values are false or both values are true, the output of the XOR function is false. Here is the truth table for the XOR operation:

X	Y	X ⊕ Y
0	0	0
0	1	1
1	0	1
1	1	0

The following operation shows the X and Y values when they are used as input to the XOR function:

```
    X:   0 1 1 0 1 1 0 0
    Y:   1 0 1 0 0 1 1 1
--------------------------
X ⊕ Y:   1 1 0 0 1 0 1 1
```

Modulo Function

The *modulo* function is extremely important in the field of cryptography. Think back to the early days when you first learned division. At that time, you weren't familiar with decimal numbers and compensated by showing a remainder value each time you performed a division operation. Computers don't naturally understand the decimal system either, and these remainder values play a critical role when computers perform many mathematical functions. The modulo function is, quite simply, the remainder value left over after a division operation is performed.

TIP: The modulo function is just as important to cryptography as the logical operations are. Be sure you're familiar with its functionality and can perform simple modular math.

The modulo function is usually represented in equations by the abbreviation *mod*, although it's also sometimes represented by the % operator. Here are several inputs and outputs for the modulo function:

```
 8 mod 6 = 2
 6 mod 8 = 6
10 mod 3 = 1
10 mod 2 = 0
32 mod 8 = 0
```

We'll revisit this function in Chapter 7 when we explore the RSA public key encryption algorithm (named after Rivest, Shamir, and Adleman, its inventors).

One-Way Functions

A *one-way function* is a mathematical operation that easily produces output values for each possible combination of inputs but makes it impossible to retrieve the input values. Public key cryptosystems are all based on some sort of one-way function. In practice, however, it's never been proven that any specific known function is truly one way. Cryptographers rely on functions that they suspect may be one way, but it's theoretically possible that they might be broken by future cryptanalysts.

Here's an example. Imagine you have a function that multiplies three numbers together. If you restrict the input values to single-digit numbers, it's a relatively straightforward matter to reverse-engineer this function and determine the possible input values by looking at the numerical output. For example, the output value 15 was created by using the input values 1, 3, and 5. However, suppose you restrict the input values to five-digit prime numbers. It's still quite simple to obtain an output value by using a computer or a good calculator, but reverse-engineering is not quite so simple. Can you figure out what three prime numbers were used to obtain the output value 10,718,488,075,259? Not so simple, eh? (As it turns out, the number is the product of the prime numbers 17,093; 22,441; and 27,943.) There are actually 8,363 five-digit prime numbers, so this problem might be attacked using a computer and a brute-force algorithm, but there's no easy way to figure it out in your head, that's for sure!

Nonce

Cryptography often gains strength by adding randomness to the encryption process. One method by which this is accomplished is through the use of a nonce. A *nonce* is a random number that acts as a placeholder variable in mathematical functions. When the function is executed, the nonce is replaced with a random number generated at the moment of processing for one-time use. The nonce must be a unique number each time it is used. One of the more recognizable examples of a nonce is an initialization vector (IV), a random bit string that is the same length as the block size and is XORed with the message. IVs are used to create unique ciphertext every time the same message is encrypted using the same key.

Zero-Knowledge Proof

One of the benefits of cryptography is found in the mechanism to prove your knowledge of a fact to a third party without revealing the fact itself to that third party. This is often done with passwords and other secret authenticators.

The classic example of a *zero-knowledge proof* involves two individuals: Peggy and Victor. Peggy knows the password to a secret door located inside a circular cave, as shown in Figure 6.2. Victor would like to buy the password from Peggy, but he wants Peggy to prove that she knows the password before paying her for it. Peggy doesn't want to tell Victor the password for fear that he won't pay later. The zero-knowledge proof can solve their dilemma.

FIGURE 6.2 The magic door

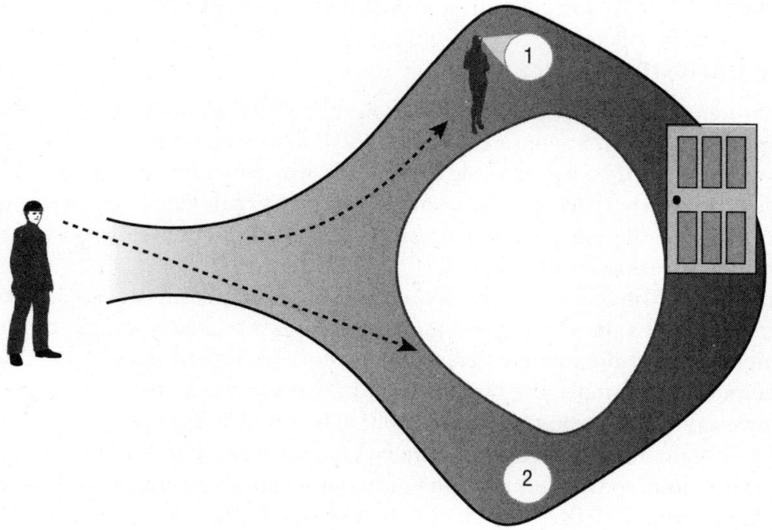

Victor can stand at the entrance to the cave and watch Peggy depart down the path. Peggy then reaches the door and opens it using the password. She then passes through the door and returns via path 2. Victor saw her leave down path 1 and return via path 2, proving that she must know the correct password to open the door.

Split Knowledge

When the information or privilege required to perform an operation is divided among multiple users, no single person has sufficient privileges to compromise the security of an environment. This separation of duties and two-person control contained in a single solution is called *split knowledge*. The best example of split knowledge is seen in the concept of *key escrow*. Using key escrow, cryptographic keys, digital signatures, and even digital certificates can be stored or backed up in a special database called the *key escrow database*. In the event a user loses or damages their key, that key can be extracted from the backup. However, if only a single key escrow recovery agent exists, there is opportunity for fraud and abuse of this privilege. *M of N Control* requires that a minimum number of agents (`M`) out of the total number of agents (`N`) work together to perform high-security tasks. So, implementing three of eight controls would require three people out of the eight with the assigned work task of key escrow recovery agent to work together to pull a single key out of the key escrow database (thereby also illustrating that `M` is always less than or equal to `N`).

Work Function

You can measure the strength of a cryptography system by measuring the effort in terms of cost and/or time using a *work function* or work factor. Usually the time and effort required to perform a complete brute-force attack against an encryption system is what the work function represents. The security and protection offered by a cryptosystem is directly proportional to the value of the work function/factor. The size of the work function should be matched against the relative value of the protected asset. The work function need be only slightly greater than the time value of that asset. In other words, all security, including cryptography, should be cost effective and cost efficient. Spend no more effort to protect an asset than it warrants, but be sure to provide sufficient protection. Thus, if information loses its value over time, the work function needs to be only large enough to ensure protection until the value of the data is gone.

Ciphers

Cipher systems have long been used by individuals and governments interested in preserving the confidentiality of their communications. In the following sections, we'll cover the definition of a cipher and explore several common cipher types that form the basis of modern ciphers. It's important to remember that these concepts seem somewhat basic, but when used in combination, they can be formidable opponents and cause cryptanalysts many hours of frustration.

Codes vs. Ciphers

People often use the words *code* and *cipher* interchangeably, but technically, they aren't interchangeable. There are important distinctions between the two concepts. *Codes*, which are cryptographic systems of symbols that represent words or phrases, are sometimes secret, but they are not necessarily meant to provide confidentiality. A common example of a code is the "10 system" of communications used by law enforcement agencies. Under this system, the sentence "I received your communication and understand the contents" is represented by the code phrase "10-4." This code is commonly known by the public, but it does provide for ease of communication. Some codes are secret. They may convey confidential information using a secret codebook where the meaning of the code is known only to the sender and recipient. For example, a spy might transmit the sentence "The eagle has landed" to report the arrival of an enemy aircraft.

Ciphers, on the other hand, are always meant to hide the true meaning of a message. They use a variety of techniques to alter and/or rearrange the characters or bits of a message to achieve confidentiality. Ciphers convert messages from plain text to ciphertext on a bit basis (that is, a single digit of a binary code), character basis (that is, a single character of an ASCII message), or block basis (this is, a fixed-length segment of a message, usually expressed in number of bits). The following sections cover several common ciphers in use today.

TIP An easy way to keep the difference between codes and ciphers straight is to remember that codes work on words and phrases whereas ciphers work on individual characters and bits.

Transposition Ciphers

Transposition ciphers use an encryption algorithm to rearrange the letters of a plaintext message, forming the ciphertext message. The decryption algorithm simply reverses the encryption transformation to retrieve the original message.

In the challenge-response protocol example in Figure 6.1 earlier in this chapter, a simple transposition cipher was used to reverse the letters of the message so that *apple* became *elppa*. Transposition ciphers can be much more complicated than this. For example, you can use a keyword to perform a *columnar transposition*. In the following example, we're attempting to encrypt the message "The fighters will strike the enemy bases at noon" using the secret key *attacker*. Our first step is to take the letters of the keyword and number them in alphabetical order. The first appearance of the letter *A* receives the value 1; the second appearance is numbered 2. The next letter in sequence, *C*, is numbered 3, and so on. This results in the following sequence:

```
A T T A C K E R
1 7 8 2 3 5 4 6
```

Next, the letters of the message are written in order underneath the letters of the keyword:

```
A T T A C K E R
1 7 8 2 3 5 4 6
T H E F I G H T
E R S W I L L S
T R I K E T H E
E N E M Y B A S
E S A T N O O N
```

Finally, the sender enciphers the message by reading down each column; the order in which the columns are read corresponds to the numbers assigned in the first step. This produces the following ciphertext:

```
T E T E E F W K M T I I E Y N H L H A O G L T B O T S E S N H R R N S E S I E A
```

On the other end, the recipient reconstructs the eight-column matrix using the ciphertext and the same keyword and then simply reads the plaintext message across the rows.

Substitution Ciphers

Substitution ciphers use the encryption algorithm to replace each character or bit of the plaintext message with a different character. The Caesar cipher discussed in the beginning of this chapter is a good example of a substitution cipher. Now that you've learned a little bit about cryptographic math, we'll take another look at the Caesar cipher. Recall that we simply shifted each letter three places to the right in the message to generate the ciphertext. However, we ran into a problem when we got to the end of the alphabet and ran out of letters. We solved this by wrapping around to the beginning of the alphabet so that the plaintext character *Z* became the ciphertext character *C*.

You can express the ROT3 cipher in mathematical terms by converting each letter to its decimal equivalent (where *A* is 0 and *Z* is 25). You can then add three to each plaintext letter to determine the ciphertext. You account for the wrap-around by using the modulo function discussed in the section "Cryptographic Mathematics." The final encryption function for the Caesar cipher is then this:

```
C = (P + 3) mod 26
```

The corresponding decryption function is as follows:

```
P = (C - 3) mod 26
```

As with transposition ciphers, there are many substitution ciphers that are more sophisticated than the examples provided in this chapter. Polyalphabetic substitution ciphers use multiple alphabets in the same message to hinder decryption efforts. One of the most notable examples of a polyalphabetic substitution cipher system is the Vigenère cipher. The Vigenère cipher uses a single encryption/decryption chart as shown here:

A	B	C	D	E	F	G	H	I	J	K	L	M	N	O	P	Q	R	S	T	U	V	W	X	Y	Z
A	B	C	D	E	F	G	H	I	J	K	L	M	N	O	P	Q	R	S	T	U	V	W	X	Y	Z

B	C	D	E	F	G	H	I	J	K	L	M	N	O	P	Q	R	S	T	U	V	W	X	Y	Z	A
C	D	E	F	G	H	I	J	K	L	M	N	O	P	Q	R	S	T	U	V	W	X	Y	Z	A	B
D	E	F	G	H	I	J	K	L	M	N	O	P	Q	R	S	T	U	V	W	X	Y	Z	A	B	C
E	F	G	H	I	J	K	L	M	N	O	P	Q	R	S	T	U	V	W	X	Y	Z	A	B	C	D
F	G	H	I	J	K	L	M	N	O	P	Q	R	S	T	U	V	W	X	Y	Z	A	B	C	D	E
G	H	I	J	K	L	M	N	O	P	Q	R	S	T	U	V	W	X	Y	Z	A	B	C	D	E	F
H	I	J	K	L	M	N	O	P	Q	R	S	T	U	V	W	X	Y	Z	A	B	C	D	E	F	G
I	J	K	L	M	N	O	P	Q	R	S	T	U	V	W	X	Y	Z	A	B	C	D	E	F	G	H
J	K	L	M	N	O	P	Q	R	S	T	U	V	W	X	Y	Z	A	B	C	D	E	F	G	H	I
K	L	M	N	O	P	Q	R	S	T	U	V	W	X	Y	Z	A	B	C	D	E	F	G	H	I	J
L	M	N	O	P	Q	R	S	T	U	V	W	X	Y	Z	A	B	C	D	E	F	G	H	I	J	K
M	N	O	P	Q	R	S	T	U	V	W	X	Y	Z	A	B	C	D	E	F	G	H	I	J	K	L
N	O	P	Q	R	S	T	U	V	W	X	Y	Z	A	B	C	D	E	F	G	H	I	J	K	L	M
O	P	Q	R	S	T	U	V	W	X	Y	Z	A	B	C	D	E	F	G	H	I	J	K	L	M	N
P	Q	R	S	T	U	V	W	X	Y	Z	A	B	C	D	E	F	G	H	I	J	K	L	M	N	O
Q	R	S	T	U	V	W	X	Y	Z	A	B	C	D	E	F	G	H	I	J	K	L	M	N	O	P
R	S	T	U	V	W	X	Y	Z	A	B	C	D	E	F	G	H	I	J	K	L	M	N	O	P	Q
S	T	U	V	W	X	Y	Z	A	B	C	D	E	F	G	H	I	J	K	L	M	N	O	P	Q	R
T	U	V	W	X	Y	Z	A	B	C	D	E	F	G	H	I	J	K	L	M	N	O	P	Q	R	S
U	V	W	X	Y	Z	A	B	C	D	E	F	G	H	I	J	K	L	M	N	O	P	Q	R	S	T
V	W	X	Y	Z	A	B	C	D	E	F	G	H	I	J	K	L	M	N	O	P	Q	R	S	T	U
W	X	Y	Z	A	B	C	D	E	F	G	H	I	J	K	L	M	N	O	P	Q	R	S	T	U	V
X	Y	Z	A	B	C	D	E	F	G	H	I	J	K	L	M	N	O	P	Q	R	S	T	U	V	W
Y	Z	A	B	C	D	E	F	G	H	I	J	K	L	M	N	O	P	Q	R	S	T	U	V	W	X
Z	A	B	C	D	E	F	G	H	I	J	K	L	M	N	O	P	Q	R	S	T	U	V	W	X	Y

Notice that the chart is simply the alphabet written repeatedly (26 times) under the master heading, shifting by one letter each time. You need a key to use the Vigenère system. For example, the key could be *secret*. Then, you would perform the following encryption process:

1. Write out the plain text.
2. Underneath, write out the encryption key, repeating the key as many times as needed to establish a line of text that is the same length as the plain text.
3. Convert each letter position from plain text to ciphertext.
    a. Locate the column headed by the first plaintext character (*a*).
    b. Next, locate the row headed by the first character of the key (*s*).
    c. Finally, locate where these two items intersect, and write down the letter that appears there (*s*). This is the ciphertext for that letter position.
4. Repeat steps 1 through 3 for each letter in the plaintext version.

Plain text:	a t t a c k a t d a w n
Key:	s e c r e t s e c r e t
Ciphertext:	s x v r g d s x f r a g

Although polyalphabetic substitution protects against direct frequency analysis, it is vulnerable to a second-order form of frequency analysis called *period analysis*, which is an examination of frequency based on the repeated use of the key.

One-Time Pads

A *one-time pad* is an extremely powerful type of substitution cipher. One-time pads use a different substitution alphabet for each letter of the plaintext message. They can be represented by the following encryption function, where *K* is the encryption key used to encrypt the plaintext letter *P* into the ciphertext letter *C*:

```
C = (P + K) mod 26
```

Usually, one-time pads are written as a very long series of numbers to be plugged into the function.

NOTE: One-time pads are also known as *Vernam ciphers*, after the name of their inventor, Gilbert Sandford Vernam of AT&T Bell Labs.

The great advantage of one-time pads is that, when used properly, they are an unbreakable encryption scheme. There is no repeating pattern of alphabetic substitution, rendering cryptanalytic efforts useless. However, several requirements must be met to ensure the integrity of the algorithm:

- The one-time pad must be randomly generated. Using a phrase or a passage from a book would introduce the possibility that cryptanalysts could break the code.
- The one-time pad must be physically protected against disclosure. If the enemy has a copy of the pad, they can easily decrypt the enciphered messages.

NOTE: You may be thinking at this point that the Caesar cipher, Vigenère cipher, and one-time pad sound very similar. They are! The only difference is the key length. The Caesar shift cipher uses a key of length one, the Vigenère cipher uses a longer key (usually a word or sentence), and the one-time pad uses a key that is as long as the message itself.

- Each one-time pad must be used only once. If pads are reused, cryptanalysts can compare similarities in multiple messages encrypted with the same pad and possibly determine the key values used.
- The key must be at least as long as the message to be encrypted. This is because each character of the key is used to encode only one character of the message.

> **TIP** These one-time pad security requirements are essential knowledge for any network security professional. All too often, people attempt to implement a one-time pad cryptosystem but fail to meet one or more of these fundamental requirements. Read on for an example of how an entire Soviet code system was broken because of carelessness in this area.

If any one of these requirements is not met, the impenetrable nature of the one-time pad instantly breaks down. In fact, one of the major intelligence successes of the United States resulted when cryptanalysts broke a top-secret Soviet cryptosystem that relied on the use of one-time pads. In this project, code-named VENONA, a pattern in the way the Soviets generated the key values used in their pads was discovered. The existence of this pattern violated the first requirement of a one-time pad cryptosystem: the keys must be randomly generated without the use of any recurring pattern. The entire VENONA project was recently declassified and is publicly available on the National Security Agency website at

`www.nsa.gov/about/_files/cryptologic_heritage/publications/coldwar/venona_story.pdf`

One-time pads have been used throughout history to protect extremely sensitive communications. The major obstacle to their widespread use is the difficulty of generating, distributing, and safeguarding the lengthy keys required. One-time pads can realistically be used only for short messages, because of key lengths.

Running Key Ciphers

Many cryptographic vulnerabilities surround the limited length of the cryptographic key. As you learned in the previous section, one-time pads avoid these vulnerabilities by using a key that is at least as long as the message. However, one-time pads are awkward to implement because they require the physical exchange of pads.

One common solution to this dilemma is the use of a *running key cipher* (also known as a *book cipher*). In this cipher, the encryption key is as long as the message itself and is often chosen from a common book. For example, the sender and recipient might agree in advance to use the text of a chapter from *Moby Dick*, beginning with the third paragraph, as the key. They would both simply use as many consecutive characters as necessary to perform the encryption and decryption operations.

Let's look at an example. Suppose you wanted to encrypt the message "Richard will deliver the secret package to Matthew at the bus station tomorrow" using the key just described. This message is 66 characters in length, so you'd use the first 66 characters of the running key: "With much interest I sat watching him. Savage though he was, and hideously marred." Any algorithm could then be used to encrypt the plaintext message using this key. Let's look at the example of modulo 26 addition, which converts each letter to a decimal equivalent, adds the plain text to the key, and then performs a modulo 26 operation to yield the ciphertext. If you assign the letter *A* the value 0 and the letter *Z* the value 25, you have the following encryption operation for the first two words of the ciphertext:

Plain text	R	I	C	H	A	R	D	W	I	L	L
Key	W	I	T	H	M	U	C	H	I	N	T
Numeric plain text	17	8	2	7	0	17	3	22	8	11	11
Numeric key	22	8	19	7	12	20	2	7	8	13	19
Numeric ciphertext	13	16	21	14	12	11	5	3	16	24	4
Ciphertext	N	Q	V	O	M	L	F	D	Q	Y	E

When the recipient receives the ciphertext, they use the same key and then subtract the key from the ciphertext, perform a modulo 26 operation, and then convert the resulting plain text back to alphabetic characters.

Block Ciphers

Block ciphers operate on "chunks," or blocks, of a message and apply the encryption algorithm to an entire message block at the same time. The transposition ciphers are examples of block ciphers. The simple algorithm used in the challenge-response algorithm takes an entire word and reverses its letters. The more complicated columnar transposition cipher works on an entire message (or a piece of a message) and encrypts it using the transposition algorithm and a secret keyword. Most modern encryption algorithms implement some type of block cipher.

Stream Ciphers

Stream ciphers operate on one character or bit of a message (or data stream) at a time. The Caesar cipher is an example of a stream cipher. The one-time pad is also a stream cipher because the algorithm operates on each letter of the plaintext message independently. Stream ciphers can also function as a type of block cipher. In such operations there is a buffer that fills up to real-time data that is then encrypted as a block and transmitted to the recipient.

Confusion and Diffusion

Cryptographic algorithms rely on two basic operations to obscure plaintext messages—confusion and diffusion. *Confusion* occurs when the relationship between the plain text and the key is so complicated that an attacker can't merely continue altering the plain text and analyzing the resulting ciphertext to determine the key. *Diffusion* occurs when a change in the plain text results in multiple changes spread throughout the ciphertext. Consider, for example, a cryptographic algorithm that first performs a complex substitution and then uses transposition to rearrange the characters of the substituted ciphertext. In this example, the substitution introduces confusion and the transposition introduces diffusion.

Modern Cryptography

Modern cryptosystems use computationally complex algorithms and long cryptographic keys to meet the cryptographic goals of confidentiality, integrity, authentication, and nonrepudiation. The following sections cover the roles cryptographic keys play in the world of data security and examine three types of algorithms commonly used today: symmetric encryption algorithms, asymmetric encryption algorithms, and hashing algorithms.

Cryptographic Keys

In the early days of cryptography, one of the predominant principles was "security through obscurity." Some cryptographers thought the best way to keep an encryption algorithm secure was to hide the details of the algorithm from outsiders. Old cryptosystems required communicating parties to keep the algorithm used to encrypt and decrypt messages secret from third parties. Any disclosure of the algorithm could lead to compromise of the entire system by an adversary.

Modern cryptosystems do not rely on the secrecy of their algorithms. In fact, the algorithms for most cryptographic systems are widely available for public review in the accompanying literature and on the Internet. Opening algorithms to public scrutiny actually improves their security. Widespread analysis of algorithms by the computer security community allows practitioners to discover and correct potential security vulnerabilities and ensure that the algorithms they use to protect their communications are as secure as possible.

Instead of relying on secret algorithms, modern cryptosystems rely on the secrecy of one or more cryptographic keys used to personalize the algorithm for specific users or groups of users. Recall from the discussion of transposition ciphers that a keyword is used with the columnar transposition to guide the encryption and decryption efforts. The algorithm used to perform columnar transposition is well known—you just read the details of it in this book! However, columnar transposition can be used to securely communicate between parties as long as a keyword is chosen that would not be guessed by an outsider. As long as the security of this keyword is maintained, it doesn't matter that third parties know the details of the algorithm.

NOTE Although the public nature of the algorithm does not compromise the security of columnar transposition, the method does possess several inherent weaknesses that make it vulnerable to cryptanalysis. It is therefore an inadequate technology for use in modern secure communication.

In the discussion of one-time pads earlier in this chapter, you learned that the main strength of the one-time pad algorithm is derived from the fact that it uses an extremely long key. In fact, for that algorithm, the key is at least as long as the message itself. Most modern cryptosystems do not use keys quite that long, but the length of the key is still an extremely important factor in determining the strength of the cryptosystem and the likelihood that the encryption will not be compromised through cryptanalytic techniques.

The rapid increase in computing power allows you to use increasingly long keys in your cryptographic efforts. However, this same computing power is also in the hands of cryptanalysts attempting to defeat the algorithms you use. Therefore, it's essential that you outpace adversaries by using sufficiently long keys that will defeat contemporary cryptanalysis efforts. Additionally, if you want to improve the chance that your data will remain safe from cryptanalysis some time into the future, you must strive to use keys that will outpace the projected increase in cryptanalytic capability during the entire time period the data must be kept safe.

Several decades ago, when the Data Encryption Standard was created, a 56-bit key was considered sufficient to maintain the security of any data. However, there is now widespread agreement that the 56-bit DES algorithm is no longer secure because of advances in cryptanalysis techniques and supercomputing power. Modern cryptographic systems use at least a 128-bit key to protect data against prying eyes. Remember, the length of the key directly relates to the work function of the cryptosystem: the longer the key, the harder it is to break the cryptosystem.

Symmetric Key Algorithms

Symmetric key algorithms rely on a "shared secret" encryption key that is distributed to all members who participate in the communications. This key is used by all parties to both encrypt and decrypt messages, so the sender and the receiver both possess a copy of the shared key. The sender encrypts with the shared secret key and the receiver decrypts with it. When large-sized keys are used, symmetric encryption is very difficult to break. It is primarily employed to perform bulk encryption and provides only for the security service of confidentiality. Symmetric key cryptography can also be called *secret key cryptography* and *private key cryptography*. Figure 6.3 illustrates the symmetric key encryption and decryption processes.

FIGURE 6.3 Symmetric key cryptography

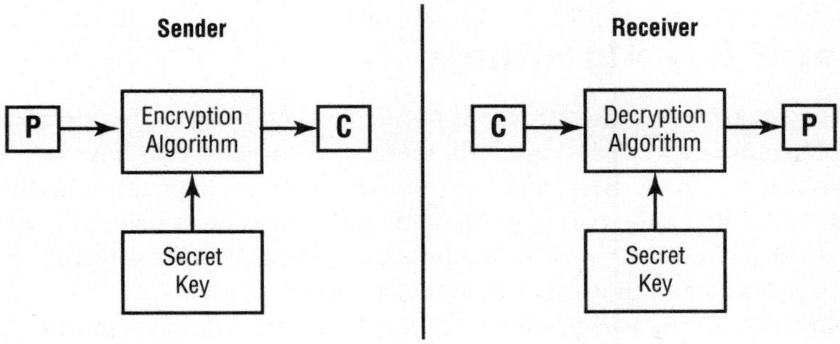

NOTE The use of the term *private key* can be tricky because it is part of three different terms that have two different meanings. The term *private key* by itself always means the private key from the key pair of public key cryptography (aka asymmetric). However, both *private key cryptography* and *shared private key* refer to symmetric cryptography. The meaning of the word *private* is stretched to refer to two people sharing a secret that they keep confidential. (The true meaning of *private* is that only a single person has a secret that's kept confidential.) Be sure to keep these confusing terms straight in your studies.

Symmetric key cryptography has several weaknesses:

Key distribution is a major problem. Parties must have a secure method of exchanging the secret key before establishing communications with a symmetric key protocol. If a secure electronic channel is not available, an offline key distribution method must often be used (that is, out-of-band exchange).

Symmetric key cryptography does not implement nonrepudiation. Because any communicating party can encrypt and decrypt messages with the shared secret key, there is no way to prove where a given message originated.

The algorithm is not scalable. It is extremely difficult for large groups to communicate using symmetric key cryptography. Secure private communication between individuals in the group could be achieved only if each possible combination of users shared a private key.

Keys must be regenerated often. Each time a participant leaves the group, all keys known by that participant must be discarded.

The major strength of symmetric key cryptography is the great speed at which it can operate. Symmetric key encryption is very fast, often 1,000 to 10,000 times faster than asymmetric algorithms. By nature of the mathematics involved, symmetric key cryptography also naturally lends itself to hardware implementations, creating the opportunity for even higher-speed operations.

The section "Symmetric Cryptography" later in this chapter provides a detailed look at the major secret key algorithms in use today.

Asymmetric Key Algorithms

Asymmetric key algorithms, also known as *public key algorithms*, provide a solution to the weaknesses of symmetric key encryption. In these systems, each user has two keys: a public key, which is shared with all users, and a private key, which is kept secret and known only to the user. But here's a twist: opposite and related keys must be used in tandem to encrypt and decrypt. In other words, if the public key encrypts a message, then only the corresponding private key can decrypt it, and vice versa.

Figure 6.4 shows the algorithm used to encrypt and decrypt messages in a public key cryptosystem. Consider this example. If Alice wants to send a message to Bob using public key cryptography, she creates the message and then encrypts it using Bob's public key. The only possible way to decrypt this ciphertext is to use Bob's private key, and the only user with access to that key is Bob. Therefore, Alice can't even decrypt the message herself after she encrypts it. If Bob wants to send a reply to Alice, he simply encrypts the message using Alice's public key, and then Alice reads the message by decrypting it with her private key.

FIGURE 6.4 Asymmetric key cryptography

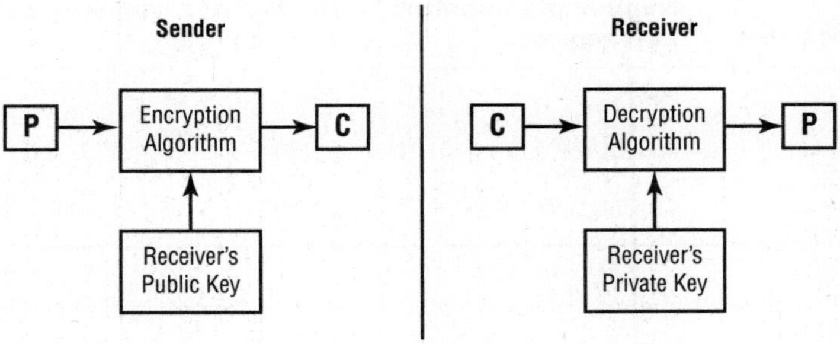

Real World Scenario

Key Requirements

In a class one of the authors of this book taught recently, a student wanted to see an illustration of the scalability issue associated with symmetric encryption algorithms. The fact that symmetric cryptosystems require each pair of potential communicators to have a shared private key makes the algorithm nonscalable. The total number of keys required to completely connect n parties using symmetric cryptography is given by the following formula:

$$\text{Number of Keys} = \frac{n^{*}(n-1)}{2}$$

Now, this might not sound so bad (and it's not for small systems), but consider the following figures. Obviously, the larger the population, the less likely a symmetric cryptosystem will be suitable to meet its needs.

Number of participants	Number of symmetric keys required	Number of asymmetric keys required
2	1	4
3	3	6
4	6	8
5	10	10
10	45	20

Number of participants	Number of symmetric keys required	Number of asymmetric keys required
100	4,950	200
1,000	499,500	2,000
10,000	49,995,000	20,000

Asymmetric key algorithms also provide support for digital signature technology. Basically, if Bob wants to assure other users that a message with his name on it was actually sent by him, he first creates a message digest by using a hashing algorithm (you'll find more on hashing algorithms in the next section). Bob then encrypts that digest using his private key. Any user who wants to verify the signature simply decrypts the message digest using Bob's public key and then verifies that the decrypted message digest is accurate. Chapter 7 explains this process in greater detail.

The following is a list of the major strengths of asymmetric key cryptography:

The addition of new users requires the generation of only one public-private key pair. This same key pair is used to communicate with all users of the asymmetric cryptosystem. This makes the algorithm extremely scalable.

Users can be removed far more easily from asymmetric systems. Asymmetric cryptosystems provide a key revocation mechanism that allows a key to be canceled, effectively removing a user from the system.

Key regeneration is required only when a user's private key is compromised. If a user leaves the community, the system administrator simply needs to invalidate that user's keys. No other keys are compromised and therefore key regeneration is not required for any other user.

Asymmetric key encryption can provide integrity, authentication, and nonrepudiation. If a user does not share their private key with other individuals, a message signed by that user can be shown to be accurate and from a specific source and cannot be later repudiated.

Key distribution is a simple process. Users who want to participate in the system simply make their public key available to anyone with whom they want to communicate. There is no method by which the private key can be derived from the public key.

No preexisting communication link needs to exist. Two individuals can begin communicating securely from the moment they start communicating. Asymmetric cryptography does not require a preexisting relationship to provide a secure mechanism for data exchange.

The major weakness of public key cryptography is its slow speed of operation. For this reason, many applications that require the secure transmission of large amounts of data use public key cryptography to establish a connection and then exchange a symmetric secret key. The remainder of the session then uses symmetric cryptography. Table 6.1 compares the symmetric and asymmetric cryptography systems. Close examination of this table reveals that a weakness in one system is matched by a strength in the other.

TABLE 6.1 Comparison of symmetric and asymmetric cryptography systems

Symmetric	Asymmetric
Single shared key	Key pair sets
Out-of-band exchange	In-band exchange
Not scalable	Scalable
Fast	Slow
Bulk encryption	Small blocks of data, digital signatures, digital envelopes, digital certificates
Confidentiality	Confidentiality, integrity, authenticity, nonrepudiation

NOTE: Chapter 7 provides technical details on modern public key encryption algorithms and some of their applications.

Hashing Algorithms

In the previous section, you learned that public key cryptosystems can provide digital signature capability when used in conjunction with a message digest. Message digests are summaries of a message's content (not unlike a file checksum) produced by a hashing algorithm. It's extremely difficult, if not impossible, to derive a message from an ideal hash function, and it's very unlikely that two messages will produce the same hash value.

The following are some of the more common hashing algorithms in use today:

- Message Digest 2 (MD2)
- Message Digest 5 (MD5)
- Secure Hash Algorithm (SHA-0, SHA-1, and SHA-2)
- Hashed Message Authentication Code (HMAC)

Chapter 7, "PKI and Cryptographic Applications," provides details on these contemporary hashing algorithms and explains how they are used to provide digital signature capability, which helps meet the cryptographic goals of integrity and nonrepudiation.

Symmetric Cryptography

You've learned the basic concepts underlying symmetric key cryptography, asymmetric key cryptography, and hashing functions. In the following sections, we'll take an in-depth look at several common symmetric cryptosystems: the Data Encryption Standard (DES), Triple DES (3DES), International Data Encryption Algorithm (IDEA), Blowfish, Skipjack, and the Advanced Encryption Standard (AES).

Data Encryption Standard

The US government published the Data Encryption Standard in 1977 as a proposed standard cryptosystem for all government communications. Due to flaws in the algorithm, cryptographers and the federal government no longer consider DES secure. It is widely believed that intelligence agencies routinely decrypt DES-encrypted information. DES was superseded by the Advanced Encryption Standard in December 2001. It is still important to understand DES because it is the building block of Triple DES (3DES), a strong encryption algorithm discussed in the next section.

DES is a 64-bit block cipher that has five modes of operation: Electronic Codebook (ECB) mode, Cipher Block Chaining (CBC) mode, Cipher Feedback (CFB) mode, Output Feedback (OFB) mode, and Counter (CTR) mode. These modes are explained in the following sections. All of the DES modes operate on 64 bits of plain text at a time to generate 64-bit blocks of ciphertext. The key used by DES is 56 bits long.

DES uses a long series of exclusive OR (XOR) operations to generate the ciphertext. This process is repeated 16 times for each encryption/decryption operation. Each repetition is commonly referred to as a *round* of encryption, explaining the statement that DES performs 16 rounds of encryption.

NOTE

As mentioned, DES uses a 56-bit key to drive the encryption and decryption process. However, you may read in some literature that DES uses a 64-bit key. This is not an inconsistency—there's a perfectly logical explanation. The DES specification calls for a 64-bit key. However, of those 64 bits, only 56 actually contain keying information. The remaining 8 bits are supposed to contain parity information to ensure that the other 56 bits are accurate. In practice, however, those parity bits are rarely used. You should commit the 56-bit figure to memory.

Electronic Codebook Mode

Electronic Codebook (ECB) mode is the simplest mode to understand and the least secure. Each time the algorithm processes a 64-bit block, it simply encrypts the block using the chosen secret key. This means that if the algorithm encounters the same block multiple times, it will produce the same encrypted block. If an enemy were eavesdropping on the communications, they could simply build a "code book" of all the possible encrypted values. After a sufficient number of blocks were gathered, cryptanalytic techniques could be used to decipher some of the blocks and break the encryption scheme.

This vulnerability makes it impractical to use ECB mode on all but the shortest transmissions. In everyday use, ECB is used only for exchanging small amounts of data, such as keys and parameters used to initiate other DES modes as well as the cells in a database.

Cipher Block Chaining Mode

In Cipher Block Chaining (CBC) mode, each block of unencrypted text is XORed with the block of ciphertext immediately preceding it before it is encrypted using the DES algorithm. The decryption process simply decrypts the ciphertext and reverses the XOR operation. CBC implements an IV and XORs it with the first block of the message, producing a unique output every time the operation is performed. The IV must be sent to the recipient, perhaps by tacking the IV onto the front of the completed ciphertext in plain form or by protecting it with ECB mode encryption using the same key used for the message. One important consideration when using CBC mode is that errors propagate—if one block is corrupted during transmission, it becomes impossible to decrypt that block and the next block as well.

Cipher Feedback Mode

Cipher Feedback (CFB) mode is the streaming cipher version of CBC. In other words, CFB operates against data produced in real time. However, instead of breaking a message into blocks, it uses memory buffers of the same block size. As the buffer becomes full, it is encrypted and then sent to the recipient(s). Then the system waits for the next buffer to be filled as the new data is generated before it is in turn encrypted and then transmitted. Other than the change from preexisting data to real-time data, CFB operates in the same fashion as CBC. It uses an IV and it uses chaining.

Output Feedback Mode

In Output Feedback (OFB) mode, DES operates in almost the same fashion as it does in CFB mode. However, instead of XORing an encrypted version of the previous block of ciphertext, DES XORs the plain text with a seed value. For the first encrypted block, an initialization vector is used to create the seed value. Future seed values are derived by running the DES algorithm on the previous seed value. The major advantages of OFB mode are that there is no chaining function and transmission errors do not propagate to affect the decryption of future blocks.

Counter Mode

DES that is run in Counter (CTR) mode uses a stream cipher similar to that used in CFB and OFB modes. However, instead of creating the seed value for each encryption/decryption operation from the results of the previous seed values, it uses a simple counter that increments for each operation. As with OFB mode, errors do not propagate in CTR mode.

TIP

CTR mode allows you to break an encryption or decryption operation into multiple independent steps. This makes CTR mode well suited for use in parallel computing.

Triple DES

As mentioned in previous sections, the Data Encryption Standard's 56-bit key is no longer considered adequate in the face of modern cryptanalytic techniques and supercomputing power. However, an adapted version of DES, Triple DES (3DES), uses the same algorithm to produce a more secure encryption.

There are four versions of 3DES. The first simply encrypts the plain text three times, using three different keys: K_1, K_2, and K_3. It is known as DES-EEE3 mode (the *E*s indicate that there are three encryption operations, whereas the numeral 3 indicates that three different keys are used). DES-EEE3 can be expressed using the following notation, where `E(K,P)` represents the encryption of plaintext *P* with key *K*:

$$E(K_1,E(K_2,E(K_3,P)))$$

DES-EEE3 has an effective key length of 168 bits.

The second variant (DES-EDE3) also uses three keys but replaces the second encryption operation with a decryption operation:

$$E(K_1,D(K_2,E(K_3,P)))$$

The third version of 3DES (DES-EEE2) uses only two keys, K_1 and K_2, as follows:

$$E(K_1,E(K_2,E(K_1,P)))$$

The fourth variant of 3DES (DES-EDE2) also uses two keys but uses a decryption operation in the middle:

$$E(K_1,D(K_2,E(K_1,P)))$$

Both the third and fourth variants have an effective key length of 112 bits.

NOTE

Technically, there is a fifth variant of 3DES, DES-EDE1, which uses only one cryptographic key. However, it results in the same algorithm as standard DES, which is unacceptably weak for most applications. It is provided only for backward-compatibility purposes.

These four variants of 3DES were developed over the years because several cryptologists put forth theories that one variant was more secure than the others. However, the current belief is that all modes are equally secure.

TIP

Take some time to understand the variants of 3DES. Sit down with a pencil and paper and be sure you understand the way each variant uses two or three keys to achieve stronger encryption.

NOTE: This discussion raises an obvious question—what happened to Double DES (2DES)? You'll read in Chapter 7 that Double DES was tried but quickly abandoned when it was proven that an attack existed that rendered it no more secure than standard DES.

International Data Encryption Algorithm

The International Data Encryption Algorithm (IDEA) block cipher was developed in response to complaints about the insufficient key length of the DES algorithm. Like DES, IDEA operates on 64-bit blocks of plain text/ciphertext. However, it begins its operation with a 128-bit key. This key is broken up in a series of operations into 52 16-bit subkeys. The subkeys then act on the input text using a combination of XOR and modulus operations to produce the encrypted/decrypted version of the input message. IDEA is capable of operating in the same five modes used by DES: ECB, CBC, CFB, OFB, and CTR.

WARNING: All of this material on key length block size and the number of rounds of encryption may seem dreadfully boring; however, it's important material, so be sure to brush up on it while preparing for the exam.

The IDEA algorithm is patented by its Swiss developers. However, they have granted an unlimited license to anyone who wants to use IDEA for noncommercial purposes. One popular implementation of IDEA is found in Phil Zimmerman's popular Pretty Good Privacy (PGP) secure email package. Chapter 7 covers PGP in further detail.

Blowfish

Bruce Schneier's Blowfish block cipher is another alternative to DES and IDEA. Like its predecessors, Blowfish operates on 64-bit blocks of text. However, it extends IDEA's key strength even further by allowing the use of variable-length keys ranging from a relatively insecure 32 bits to an extremely strong 448 bits. Obviously, the longer keys will result in a corresponding increase in encryption/decryption time. However, time trials have established Blowfish as a much faster algorithm than both IDEA and DES. Also, Mr. Schneier released Blowfish for public use with no license required. Blowfish encryption is built into a number of commercial software products and operating systems. A number of Blowfish libraries are also available for software developers.

Skipjack

The Skipjack algorithm was approved for use by the US government in Federal Information Processing Standard (FIPS) 185, the Escrowed Encryption Standard (EES). Like many block ciphers, Skipjack operates on 64-bit blocks of text. It uses an 80-bit key and supports the same four modes of operation supported by DES. Skipjack was quickly embraced by the US government and provides the cryptographic routines supporting the Clipper and Capstone encryption chips.

However, Skipjack has an added twist—it supports the escrow of encryption keys. Two government agencies, the National Institute of Standards and Technology (NIST) and the Department of the Treasury, hold a portion of the information required to reconstruct a Skipjack key. When law enforcement authorities obtain legal authorization, they contact the two agencies, obtain the pieces of the key, and are able to decrypt communications between the affected parties.

Skipjack and the Clipper chip were not embraced by the cryptographic community at large because of its mistrust of the escrow procedures in place within the US government.

Rivest Cipher 5 (RC5)

Rivest Cipher 5, or RC5, is a symmetric algorithm patented by Rivest, Shamir, and Adleman (RSA) Data Security, the people who developed the RSA asymmetric algorithm. RC5 is a block cipher of variable block sizes (32, 64, or 128 bits) that uses key sizes between 0 (zero) length and 2,040 bits.

Advanced Encryption Standard

In October 2000, the National Institute of Standards and Technology (NIST) announced that the Rijndael (pronounced "rhine-doll") block cipher had been chosen as the replacement for DES. In November 2001, NIST released FIPS 197, which mandated the use of AES/Rijndael for the encryption of all sensitive but unclassified data by the US government.

The AES cipher allows the use of three key strengths: 128 bits, 192 bits, and 256 bits. AES only allows the processing of 128-bit blocks, but Rijndael exceeded this specification, allowing cryptographers to use a block size equal to the key length. The number of encryption rounds depends on the key length chosen:

- 128-bit keys require 10 rounds of encryption.
- 192-bit keys require 12 rounds of encryption.
- 256-bit keys require 14 rounds of encryption.

Twofish

The Twofish algorithm developed by Bruce Schneier (also the creator of Blowfish) was another one of the AES finalists. Like Rijndael, Twofish is a block cipher. It operates on 128-bit blocks of data and is capable of using cryptographic keys up to 256 bits in length.

Twofish uses two techniques not found in other algorithms:

Prewhitening involves XORing the plain text with a separate subkey before the first round of encryption.

Postwhitening uses a similar operation after the 16th round of encryption.

AES is just one of the many symmetric encryption algorithms you need to be familiar with. Table 6.2 lists several common and well-known symmetric encryption algorithms along with their block size and key size.

TABLE 6.2 Symmetric memorization chart

Name	Block size	Key size
Advanced Encryption Standard (AES)	128	128, 192, 256
Rijndael	Variable	128, 192, 256
Blowfish (often used in SSH)	64	32–448
Data Encryption Standard (DES)	64	56
IDEA (used in PGP)	64	128
Rivest Cipher 2 (RC2)	64	128
Rivest Cipher 4 (RC4)	Streaming	128
Rivest Cipher 5 (RC5)	32, 64, 128	0–2,040
Skipjack	64	80
Triple DES (3DES)	64	112 or 168
Twofish	128	1–256

Symmetric Key Management

Because cryptographic keys contain information essential to the security of the cryptosystem, it is incumbent upon cryptosystem users and administrators to take extraordinary measures to protect the security of the keying material. These security measures are collectively known as key management practices. They include safeguards surrounding the creation, distribution, storage, destruction, recovery, and escrow of secret keys.

Creation and Distribution of Symmetric Keys

As previously mentioned, one of the major problems underlying symmetric encryption algorithms is the secure distribution of the secret keys required to operate the algorithms. The three main methods used to exchange secret keys securely are offline distribution, public key encryption, and the Diffie-Hellman key exchange algorithm.

Offline Distribution The most technically simple method involves the physical exchange of key material. One party provides the other party with a sheet of paper or piece of storage media containing the secret key. In many hardware encryption devices, this key material comes in the form of an electronic device that resembles an actual key that is inserted into the encryption device. However, every offline key distribution method has its own inherent flaws. If keying material is sent through the mail, it might be intercepted. Telephones can be wiretapped. Papers containing keys might be inadvertently thrown in the trash or lost.

Public Key Encryption Many communicators want to obtain the speed benefits of secret key encryption without the hassles of key distribution. For this reason, many people use public key encryption to set up an initial communications link. Once the link is successfully established and the parties are satisfied as to each other's identity, they exchange a secret key over the secure public key link. They then switch communications from the public key algorithm to the secret key algorithm and enjoy the increased processing speed. In general, secret key encryption is thousands of times faster than public key encryption.

Diffie-Hellman In some cases, neither public key encryption nor offline distribution is sufficient. Two parties might need to communicate with each other, but they have no physical means to exchange key material, and there is no public key infrastructure in place to facilitate the exchange of secret keys. In situations like this, key exchange algorithms like the Diffie-Hellman algorithm prove to be extremely useful mechanisms.

TIP

Secure RPC (S-RPC) employs Diffie-Hellman for key exchange.

About the Diffie-Hellman Algorithm

The Diffie-Hellman algorithm represented a major advance in the state of cryptographic science when it was released in 1976. It's still in use today. The algorithm works as follows:

1. The communicating parties (we'll call them Richard and Sue) agree on two large numbers: *p* (which is a prime number) and *g* (which is an integer) such that $1 < g < p$.
2. Richard chooses a random large integer *r* and performs the following calculation:

   $R = g^r \bmod p$

3. Sue chooses a random large integer *s* and performs the following calculation:

   $S = g^s \bmod p$

4. Richard sends *R* to Sue and Sue sends *S* to Richard.
5. Richard then performs the following calculation:

$K = S^r \bmod p$

6. Sue then performs the following calculation:

$K = R^s \bmod p$

At this point, Richard and Sue both have the same value, *K*, and can use this for secret key communication between the two parties.

Storage and Destruction of Symmetric Keys

Another major challenge with the use of symmetric key cryptography is that all of the keys used in the cryptosystem must be kept secure. This includes following best practices surrounding the storage of encryption keys:

- Never store an encryption key on the same system where encrypted data resides. This just makes it easier for the attacker!
- For sensitive keys, consider providing two different individuals with half of the key. They then must collaborate to re-create the entire key. This is known as the principle of *split knowledge* (discussed earlier in this chapter).

When a user with knowledge of a secret key leaves the organization or is no longer permitted access to material protected with that key, the keys must be changed and all encrypted materials must be reencrypted with the new keys. The difficulty of destroying a key to remove a user from a symmetric cryptosystem is one of the main reasons organizations turn to asymmetric algorithms, as discussed in Chapter 7.

Key Escrow and Recovery

Cryptography is a powerful tool. Like most tools, it can be used for a number of beneficent purposes, but it can also be used with malicious intent. To gain a handle on the explosive growth of cryptographic technologies, governments around the world have floated ideas to implement key escrow systems. These systems allow the government, under limited circumstances such as a court order, to obtain the cryptographic key used for a particular communication from a central storage facility.

There are two major approaches to key escrow that have been proposed over the past decade:

Fair Cryptosystems In this escrow approach, the secret keys used in a communication are divided into two or more pieces, each of which is given to an independent third party. Each of these pieces is useless on its own but may be recombined to obtain the secret key. When the government obtains legal authority to access a particular key, it provides evidence of the court order to each of the third parties and then reassembles the secret key.

Escrowed Encryption Standard This escrow approach provides the government with a technological means to decrypt ciphertext. This standard is the basis behind the Skipjack algorithm discussed earlier in this chapter.

It's highly unlikely that government regulators will ever overcome the legal and privacy hurdles necessary to implement key escrow on a widespread basis. The technology is certainly available, but the general public will likely never accept the potential government intrusiveness it facilitates.

Cryptographic Life Cycle

With the exception of the one-time pad, all cryptographic systems have a limited life span. Moore's law, a commonly cited trend in the advancement of computing power, states that the processing capabilities of a state-of-the-art microprocessor will double approximately every two years. This means that, eventually, processors will reach the amount of strength required to simply guess the encryption keys used for a communication.

Security professionals must keep this cryptographic life cycle in mind when selecting an encryption algorithm and have appropriate governance controls in place to ensure that the algorithms, protocols, and key lengths selected are sufficient to preserve the integrity of a cryptosystem for however long it is necessary to keep the information it is protecting secret. Security professionals can use the following algorithm and protocol governance controls:

- Specifying the cryptographic algorithms (such as AES, 3DES, and RSA) acceptable for use in an organization
- Identifying the acceptable key lengths for use with each algorithm based on the sensitivity of information transmitted
- Enumerating the secure transaction protocols (such as SSL and TLS) that may be used

For example, if you're designing a cryptographic system to protect the security of business plans that you expect to execute next week, you don't need to worry about the theoretical risk that a processor capable of decrypting them might be developed a decade from now. On the other hand, if you're protecting the confidentiality of information that could be used to construct a nuclear bomb, it's virtually certain that you'll still want that information to remain secret 10 years in the future!

Summary

Cryptographers and cryptanalysts are in a never-ending race to develop more secure cryptosystems and advanced cryptanalytic techniques designed to circumvent those systems.

Cryptography dates back as early as Caesar and has been an ongoing topic for study for many years. In this chapter, you learned some of the fundamental concepts underlying the field of cryptography, gained a basic understanding of the terminology used by cryptographers, and looked at some historical codes and ciphers used in the early days of cryptography.

This chapter also examined the similarities and differences between symmetric key cryptography (where communicating parties use the same key) and asymmetric key cryptography (where each communicator has a pair of public and private keys).

We then analyzed some of the symmetric algorithms currently available and their strengths and weaknesses. We wrapped up the chapter by taking a look at the cryptographic life cycle and the role of algorithm/protocol governance in enterprise security.

The next chapter expands this discussion to cover contemporary public key cryptographic algorithms. Additionally, some of the common cryptanalytic techniques used to defeat both types of cryptosystems will be explored.

Exam Essentials

Understand the role that confidentiality, integrity, and nonrepudiation play in cryptosystems. Confidentiality is one of the major goals of cryptography. It protects the secrecy of data while it is both at rest and in transit. Integrity provides the recipient of a message with the assurance that data was not altered (intentionally or unintentionally) between the time it was created and the time it was accessed. Nonrepudiation provides undeniable proof that the sender of a message actually authored it. It prevents the sender from subsequently denying that they sent the original message.

Know how cryptosystems can be used to achieve authentication goals. Authentication provides assurances as to the identity of a user. One possible scheme that uses authentication is the challenge-response protocol, in which the remote user is asked to encrypt a message using a key known only to the communicating parties. Authentication can be achieved with both symmetric and asymmetric cryptosystems.

Be familiar with the basic terminology of cryptography. When a sender wants to transmit a private message to a recipient, the sender takes the plaintext (unencrypted) message and encrypts it using an algorithm and a key. This produces a ciphertext message that is transmitted to the recipient. The recipient then uses a similar algorithm and key to decrypt the ciphertext and re-create the original plaintext message for viewing.

Understand the difference between a code and a cipher and explain the basic types of ciphers. Codes are cryptographic systems of symbols that operate on words or phrases and are sometimes secret but don't always provide confidentiality. Ciphers, however, are always meant to hide the true meaning of a message. Know how the following types of ciphers work: transposition ciphers, substitution ciphers (including one-time pads), stream ciphers, and block ciphers.

Know the requirements for successful use of a one-time pad. For a one-time pad to be successful, the key must be generated randomly without any known pattern. The key must be at least as long as the message to be encrypted. The pads must be protected against physical disclosure, and each pad must be used only one time and then discarded.

Understand the concept of zero-knowledge proof. Zero-knowledge proof is a communication concept. A specific type of information is exchanged but no real data is transferred, as with digital signatures and digital certificates.

Understand split knowledge. Split knowledge means that the information or privilege required to perform an operation is divided among multiple users. This ensures that no single person has sufficient privileges to compromise the security of the environment. M of N Control is an example of split knowledge.

Understand work function (work factor). Work function, or work factor, is a way to measure the strength of a cryptography system by measuring the effort in terms of cost and/or time to decrypt messages. Usually the time and effort required to perform a complete brute-force attack against an encryption system is what a work function rating represents. The security and protection offered by a cryptosystem is directly proportional to the value of its work function/factor.

Understand the importance of key security. Cryptographic keys provide the necessary element of secrecy to a cryptosystem. Modern cryptosystems utilize keys that are at least 128 bits long to provide adequate security. It's generally agreed that the 56-bit key of the Data Encryption Standard (DES) is no longer sufficiently long to provide security.

Know the differences between symmetric and asymmetric cryptosystems. Symmetric key cryptosystems (or secret key cryptosystems) rely on the use of a shared secret key. They are much faster than asymmetric algorithms, but they lack support for scalability, easy key distribution, and nonrepudiation. Asymmetric cryptosystems use public-private key pairs for communication between parties but operate much more slowly than symmetric algorithms.

Be able to explain the basic operational modes of the Data Encryption Standard (DES) and Triple DES (3DES). The Data Encryption Standard operates in four modes: Electronic Codebook (ECB) mode, Cipher Block Chaining (CBC) mode, Cipher Feedback (CFB) mode, and Output Feedback (OFB) mode. ECB mode is considered the least secure and is used only for short messages. 3DES uses three iterations of DES with two or three different keys to increase the effective key strength to 112 or 168 bits, respectively.

Know the Advanced Encryption Standard (AES). The Advanced Encryption Standard (AES) uses the Rijndael algorithm and is the US government standard for the secure exchange of sensitive but unclassified data. AES uses key lengths of 128, 192, and 256 bits and a fixed block size of 128 bits to achieve a much higher level of security than that provided by the older DES algorithm.

Written Lab

1. What is the major hurdle preventing the widespread adoption of one-time pad cryptosystems to ensure data confidentiality?
2. Encrypt the message "I will pass the CISSP exam and become certified next month" using columnar transposition with the keyword SECURE.
3. Decrypt the message "F R Q J U D W X O D W L R Q V B R X J R W L W" using the Caesar ROT3 substitution cipher.

Review Questions

1. How many possible keys exist in a 4-bit key space?
   A. 4
   B. 8
   C. 16
   D. 128
2. John recently received an email message from Bill. What cryptographic goal would need to be met to convince John that Bill was actually the sender of the message?
   A. Nonrepudiation
   B. Confidentiality
   C. Availability
   D. Integrity
3. What is the length of the cryptographic key used in the Data Encryption Standard (DES) cryptosystem?
   A. 56 bits
   B. 128 bits
   C. 192 bits
   D. 256 bits
4. What type of cipher relies on changing the location of characters within a message to achieve confidentiality?
   A. Stream cipher
   B. Transposition cipher
   C. Block cipher
   D. Substitution cipher
5. Which one of the following is not a possible key length for the Advanced Encryption Standard Rijndael cipher?
   A. 56 bits
   B. 128 bits
   C. 192 bits
   D. 256 bits
6. Which one of the following cannot be achieved by a secret key cryptosystem?
   A. Nonrepudiation
   B. Confidentiality
   C. Availability
   D. Key distribution

7. When correctly implemented, what is the only cryptosystem known to be unbreakable?
   A. Transposition cipher
   B. Substitution cipher
   C. Advanced Encryption Standard
   D. One-time pad

8. What is the output value of the mathematical function `16 mod 3`?
   A. 0
   B. 1
   C. 3
   D. 5

9. In the 1940s, a team of cryptanalysts from the United States successfully broke a Soviet code based on a one-time pad in a project known as VENONA. What rule did the Soviets break that caused this failure?
   A. Key values must be random.
   B. Key values must be the same length as the message.
   C. Key values must be used only once.
   D. Key values must be protected from physical disclosure.

10. Which one of the following cipher types operates on large pieces of a message rather than individual characters or bits of a message?
    A. Stream cipher
    B. Caesar cipher
    C. Block cipher
    D. ROT3 cipher

11. What is the minimum number of cryptographic keys required for secure two-way communications in symmetric key cryptography?
    A. One
    B. Two
    C. Three
    D. Four

12. Dave is developing a key escrow system that requires multiple people to retrieve a key but does not depend on every participant being present. What type of technique is he using?
    A. Split knowledge
    B. M of N Control
    C. Work function
    D. Zero-knowledge proof

13. Which one of the following Data Encryption Standard (DES) operating modes can be used for large messages with the assurance that an error early in the encryption/decryption process won't spoil results throughout the communication?

A. Cipher Block Chaining (CBC)

B. Electronic Codebook (ECB)

C. Cipher Feedback (CFB)

D. Output Feedback (OFB)

14. Many cryptographic algorithms rely on the difficulty of factoring the product of large prime numbers. What characteristic of this problem are they relying on?

A. It contains diffusion.

B. It contains confusion.

C. It is a one-way function.

D. It complies with Kerchoff's principle.

15. How many keys are required to fully implement a symmetric algorithm with 10 participants?

A. 10

B. 20

C. 45

D. 100

16. What block size is used by the Advanced Encryption Standard?

A. 32 bits

B. 64 bits

C. 128 bits

D. Variable

17. What kind of attack makes the Caesar cipher virtually unusable?

A. Meet-in-the-middle attack

B. Escrow attack

C. Frequency analysis attack

D. Transposition attack

18. What type of cryptosystem commonly makes use of a passage from a well-known book for the encryption key?

A. Vernam cipher

B. Running key cipher

C. Skipjack cipher

D. Twofish cipher

19. Which AES finalist makes use of prewhitening and postwhitening techniques?

A. Rijndael

B. Twofish

C. Blowfish

D. Skipjack

20. How many encryption keys are required to fully implement an asymmetric algorithm with 10 participants?

A. 10

B. 20

C. 45

D. 100

Chapter 7

PKI and Cryptographic Applications

THE CISSP EXAM TOPICS COVERED IN THIS CHAPTER INCLUDE:

✓ **Security Engineering**

- I. Applying Cryptographics
- I.2 Cryptographic types (e.g. symmetric, asymmetric, elliptic curves)
- I.3 Public Key Infrastructure (PKI)
- I.4 Key management practices
- I.5 Digital signatures
- I.6 Digital rights management
- I.7 Non-repudiation
- I.8 Integrity (hashing and salting)
- I.9 Methods of cryptanalytic attacks (e.g. brute force, cipher-text only, known plaintext)

In Chapter 6, "Cryptography and Symmetric Key Algorithms," we introduced basic cryptography concepts and explored a variety of private key cryptosystems. These symmetric cryptosystems offer fast, secure communication but introduce the substantial challenge of key exchange between previously unrelated parties.

This chapter explores the world of asymmetric (or public key) cryptography and the public key infrastructure (PKI) that supports worldwide secure communication between parties that don't necessarily know each other prior to the communication. Asymmetric algorithms provide convenient key exchange mechanisms and are scalable to very large numbers of users, both challenges for users of symmetric cryptosystems.

This chapter also explores several practical applications of asymmetric cryptography: securing email, web communications, electronic commerce, digital rights management, and networking. The chapter concludes with an examination of a variety of attacks malicious individuals might use to compromise weak cryptosystems.

Asymmetric Cryptography

The section "Modern Cryptography" in Chapter 6 introduced the basic principles behind both private (symmetric) and public (asymmetric) key cryptography. You learned that symmetric key cryptosystems require both communicating parties to have the same shared secret key, creating the problem of secure key distribution. You also learned that asymmetric cryptosystems avoid this hurdle by using pairs of public and private keys to facilitate secure communication without the overhead of complex key distribution systems. The security of these systems relies on the difficulty of reversing a one-way function.

In the following sections, we'll explore the concepts of public key cryptography in greater detail and look at three of the more common public key cryptosystems in use today: RSA, El Gamal, and the elliptic curve cryptosystem (ECC).

Public and Private Keys

Recall from Chapter 6 that *public key cryptosystems* rely on pairs of keys assigned to each user of the cryptosystem. Every user maintains both a public key and a private key. As the names imply, public key cryptosystem users make their public keys freely available to anyone with whom they want to communicate. The mere possession of the public key by third parties does not introduce any weaknesses into the cryptosystem. The private key, on the other hand, is reserved for the sole use of the individual who owns the keys. It is never shared with any other cryptosystem user.

Normal communication between public key cryptosystem users is quite straightforward. Figure 7.1 shows the general process.

FIGURE 7.1 Asymmetric key cryptography

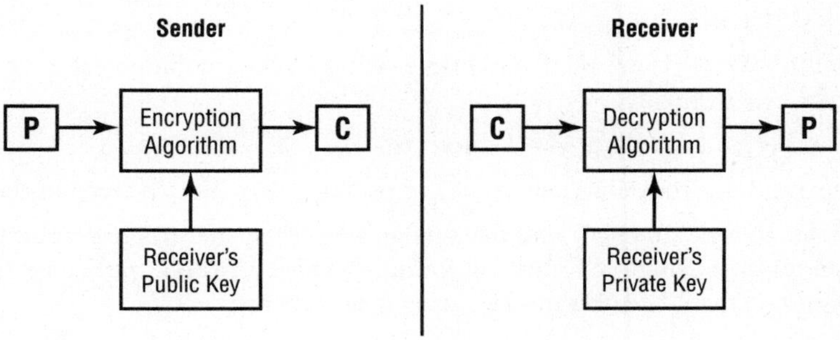

Notice that the process does not require the sharing of private keys. The sender encrypts the plaintext message (*P*) with the recipient's public key to create the ciphertext message (*C*). When the recipient opens the ciphertext message, they decrypt it using their private key to re-create the original plaintext message.

Once the sender encrypts the message with the recipient's public key, no user (including the sender) can decrypt that message without knowing the recipient's private key (the second half of the public-private key pair used to generate the message). This is the beauty of public key cryptography—public keys can be freely shared using unsecured communications and then used to create secure communications channels between users previously unknown to each other.

You also learned in the previous chapter that public key cryptography entails a higher degree of computational complexity. Keys used within public key systems must be longer than those used in private key systems to produce cryptosystems of equivalent strengths.

RSA

The most famous public key cryptosystem is named after its creators. In 1977, Ronald Rivest, Adi Shamir, and Leonard Adleman proposed the *RSA public key algorithm* that remains a worldwide standard today. They patented their algorithm and formed a commercial venture known as RSA Security to develop mainstream implementations of their security technology. Today, the RSA algorithm forms the security backbone of a large number of well-known security infrastructures produced by companies like Microsoft, Nokia, and Cisco.

The RSA algorithm depends on the computational difficulty inherent in factoring large prime numbers. Each user of the cryptosystem generates a pair of public and private keys using the algorithm described in the following steps:

1. Choose two large prime numbers (approximately 200 digits each), labeled p and q.
2. Compute the product of those two numbers: $n = p * q$.
3. Select a number, e, that satisfies the following two requirements:
   a. e is less than n.
   b. e and $(n – 1)(q – 1)$ are relatively prime—that is, the two numbers have no common factors other than 1.
4. Find a number, d, such that $(ed – 1) \bmod (p – 1)(q – 1) = 0$.
5. Distribute e and n as the public key to all cryptosystem users. Keep d secret as the private key.

If Alice wants to send an encrypted message to Bob, she generates the ciphertext (C) from the plain text (P) using the following formula (where e is Bob's public key and n is the product of p and q created during the key generation process):

$$C = P^e \bmod n$$

When Bob receives the message, he performs the following calculation to retrieve the plaintext message:

$$P = C^d \bmod n$$

Merkle-Hellman Knapsack

Another early asymmetric algorithm, the Merkle-Hellman Knapsack algorithm, was developed the year after RSA was publicized. Like RSA, it's based on the difficulty of performing factoring operations, but it relies on a component of set theory known as *super-increasing sets* rather than on large prime numbers. Merkle-Hellman was proven ineffective when it was broken in 1984.

Importance of Key Length

The length of the cryptographic key is perhaps the most important security parameter that can be set at the discretion of the security administrator. It's important to understand the capabilities of your encryption algorithm and choose a key length that provides an appropriate level of protection. This judgment can be made by weighing the difficulty of defeating a given key length (measured in the amount of processing time required to defeat the cryptosystem) against the importance of the data.

Generally speaking, the more critical your data, the stronger the key you use to protect it should be. Timeliness of the data is also an important consideration. You must take into account the rapid growth of computing power—Moore's law suggests that computing power doubles approximately every 18 months. If it takes current computers one year of processing time to break your code, it will take only three months if the attempt is made with contemporary technology three years down the road. If you expect that your data will still be sensitive at that time, you should choose a much longer cryptographic key that will remain secure well into the future.

The strengths of various key lengths also vary greatly according to the cryptosystem you're using. The key lengths shown in the following table for three asymmetric cryptosystems all provide equal protection:

Cryptosystem	Key length
RSA	1,024 bits
DSA	1,024 bits
Elliptic curve	160 bits

El Gamal

In Chapter 6, you learned how the Diffie-Hellman algorithm uses large integers and modular arithmetic to facilitate the secure exchange of secret keys over insecure communications channels. In 1985, Dr. T. El Gamal published an article describing how the mathematical principles behind the Diffie-Hellman key exchange algorithm could be extended to support an entire public key cryptosystem used for encrypting and decrypting messages.

At the time of its release, one of the major advantages of El Gamal over the RSA algorithm was that it was released into the public domain. Dr. El Gamal did not obtain a patent on his extension of Diffie-Hellman, and it is freely available for use, unlike the then-patented RSA technology. (RSA released its algorithm into the public domain in 2000.)

However, El Gamal also has a major disadvantage—the algorithm doubles the length of any message it encrypts. This presents a major hardship when encrypting long messages or data that will be transmitted over a narrow bandwidth communications circuit.

Elliptic Curve

Also in 1985, two mathematicians, Neal Koblitz from the University of Washington and Victor Miller from IBM, independently proposed the application of *elliptic curve cryptography* (ECC) theory to develop secure cryptographic systems.

NOTE: The mathematical concepts behind elliptic curve cryptography are quite complex and well beyond the scope of this book. However, you should be generally familiar with the elliptic curve algorithm and its potential applications when preparing for the CISSP exam. If you are interested in learning the detailed mathematics behind elliptic curve cryptosystems, an excellent tutorial exists at `www.certicom.com/index.php/ecc-tutorial`.

Any elliptic curve can be defined by the following equation:

$$y^2 = x^3 + ax + b$$

In this equation, *x*, *y*, *a*, and *b* are all real numbers. Each elliptic curve has a corresponding *elliptic curve group* made up of the points on the elliptic curve along with the point *O*, located at infinity. Two points within the same elliptic curve group (*P* and *Q*) can be added together with an elliptic curve addition algorithm. This operation is expressed, quite simply, as follows:

$$P + Q$$

This problem can be extended to involve multiplication by assuming that *Q* is a multiple of *P*, meaning the following:

$$Q = xP$$

Computer scientists and mathematicians believe that it is extremely hard to find *x*, even if *P* and *Q* are already known. This difficult problem, known as the elliptic curve discrete logarithm problem, forms the basis of elliptic curve cryptography. It is widely believed that this problem is harder to solve than both the prime factorization problem that the RSA cryptosystem is based on and the standard discrete logarithm problem utilized by Diffie-Hellman and El Gamal. This is illustrated by the data shown in the table in the sidebar "Importance of Key Length," which noted that a 1,088-bit RSA key is cryptographically equivalent to a 160-bit elliptic curve cryptosystem key.

Hash Functions

Later in this chapter, you'll learn how cryptosystems implement digital signatures to provide proof that a message originated from a particular user of the cryptosystem and to ensure that the message was not modified while in transit between the two parties. Before you can completely understand that concept, we must first explain the concept of *hash functions*. We will explore the basics of hash functions and look at several common hash functions used in modern digital signature algorithms.

Hash functions have a very simple purpose—they take a potentially long message and generate a unique output value derived from the content of the message. This value is commonly referred to as the *message digest*. Message digests can be generated by the sender of a message and transmitted to the recipient along with the full message for two reasons.

First, the recipient can use the same hash function to recompute the message digest from the full message. They can then compare the computed message digest to the transmitted one to ensure that the message sent by the originator is the same one received by the recipient. If the message digests do not match, that means the message was somehow modified while in transit.

Second, the message digest can be used to implement a digital signature algorithm. This concept is covered in "Digital Signatures" later in this chapter.

NOTE The term *message digest* is used interchangeably with a wide variety of synonyms, including *hash, hash value, hash total, CRC, fingerprint, checksum*, and *digital ID*.

In most cases, a message digest is 128 bits or larger. However, a single-digit value can be used to perform the function of parity, a low-level or single-digit checksum value used to provide a single individual point of verification. In most cases, the longer the message digest, the more reliable its verification of integrity.

According to RSA Security, there are five basic requirements for a cryptographic hash function:

- The input can be of any length.
- The output has a fixed length.
- The hash function is relatively easy to compute for any input.
- The hash function is one-way (meaning that it is extremely hard to determine the input when provided with the output). One-way functions and their usefulness in cryptography are described in Chapter 6.
- The hash function is collision free (meaning that it is extremely hard to find two messages that produce the same hash value).

In the following sections, we'll look at four common hashing algorithms: SHA, MD2, MD4, and MD5. HMAC is also discussed later in this chapter.

TIP There are numerous hashing algorithms not addressed in this exam. But in addition to SHA, MD2, MD4, MD5, and HMAC, you should recognize HAVAL. Hash of Variable Length (HAVAL) is a modification of MD5. HAVAL uses 1,024-bit blocks and produces hash values of 128, 160, 192, 224, and 256 bits.

SHA

The Secure Hash Algorithm (SHA) and its successors, SHA-1 and SHA-2, are government standard hash functions developed by the National Institute of Standards and Technology (NIST) and are specified in an official government publication—the Secure Hash Standard (SHS), also known as Federal Information Processing Standard (FIPS) 180.

SHA-1 takes an input of virtually any length (in reality, there is an upper bound of approximately 2,097,152 terabytes on the algorithm) and produces a 160-bit message digest. The SHA-1 algorithm processes a message in 512-bit blocks. Therefore, if the message length is not a multiple of 512, the SHA algorithm pads the message with additional data until the length reaches the next highest multiple of 512.

Recent cryptanalytic attacks demonstrated that there are weaknesses in the SHA-1 algorithm. This led to the creation of SHA-2, which has four variants:

- SHA-256 produces a 256-bit message digest using a 512-bit block size.
- SHA-224 uses a truncated version of the SHA-256 hash to produce a 224-bit message digest using a 512-bit block size.
- SHA-512 produces a 512-bit message digest using a 1,024-bit block size.
- SHA-384 uses a truncated version of the SHA-512 hash to produce a 384-bit digest using a 1,024-bit block size.

TIP

Although it might seem trivial, you should take the time to memorize the size of the message digests produced by each one of the hash algorithms described in this chapter.

The cryptographic community generally considers the SHA-2 algorithms secure, but they theoretically suffer from the same weakness as the SHA-1 algorithm. In 2012, the federal government announced the selection of the Keccak algorithm as the SHA-3 standard. However, the SHA-3 standard remains in draft form and some technical details still require finalization. Observers expect that, once NIST finalizes SHA-3, SHA-2 will remain an accepted part of NIST's Secure Hash Standard (SHS) until someone demonstrates an effective practical attack against SHA-2.

MD2

The Message Digest 2 (MD2) hash algorithm was developed by Ronald Rivest (the same Rivest of Rivest, Shamir, and Adleman fame) in 1989 to provide a secure hash function for 8-bit processors. MD2 pads the message so that its length is a multiple of 16 bytes. It then computes a 16-byte checksum and appends it to the end of the message. A 128-bit message digest is then generated by using the entire original message along with the appended checksum.

Cryptanalytic attacks exist against the MD2 algorithm. Specifically, Nathalie Rogier and Pascal Chauvaud discovered that if the checksum is not appended to the message before digest computation, collisions may occur. Frederic Mueller later proved that MD2 is not a one-way function. Therefore, it should no longer be used.

MD4

In 1990, Rivest enhanced his message digest algorithm to support 32-bit processors and increase the level of security. This enhanced algorithm is known as MD4. It first pads the message to ensure that the message length is 64 bits smaller than a multiple of 512 bits. For example, a 16-bit message would be padded with 432 additional bits of data to make it 448 bits, which is 64 bits smaller than a 512-bit message.

The MD4 algorithm then processes 512-bit blocks of the message in three rounds of computation. The final output is a 128-bit message digest.

TIP

The MD2, MD4, and MD5 algorithms are no longer accepted as suitable hashing functions. However, the details of the algorithms may still appear on the CISSP exam.

Several mathematicians have published papers documenting flaws in the full version of MD4 as well as improperly implemented versions of MD4. In particular, Hans Dobbertin published a paper in 1996 outlining how a modern PC could be used to find collisions for MD4 message digests in less than one minute. For this reason, MD4 is no longer considered to be a secure hashing algorithm, and its use should be avoided if at all possible.

MD5

In 1991, Rivest released the next version of his message digest algorithm, which he called MD5. It also processes 512-bit blocks of the message, but it uses four distinct rounds of computation to produce a digest of the same length as the MD2 and MD4 algorithms (128 bits). MD5 has the same padding requirements as MD4—the message length must be 64 bits less than a multiple of 512 bits.

MD5 implements additional security features that reduce the speed of message digest production significantly. Unfortunately, recent cryptanalytic attacks demonstrated that the MD5 protocol is subject to collisions, preventing its use for ensuring message integrity. Specifically, Arjen Lenstra and others demonstrated in 2005 that it is possible to create two digital certificates from different public keys that have the same MD5 hash.

Table 7.1 lists well-known hashing algorithms and their resultant hash value lengths in bits. Earmark this page for memorization.

TABLE 7.1 Hash algorithm memorization chart

Name	Hash value length
Hash of Variable Length (HAVAL)—an MD5 variant	128, 160, 192, 224, and 256 bits
Hash Message Authenticating Code (HMAC)	Variable
Message Digest 2 (MD2)	128
Message Digest 4 (MD4)	128

TABLE 7.1 Hash algorithm memorization chart *(continued)*

Name	Hash value length
Message Digest 5 (MD5)	128
Secure Hash Algorithm (SHA-1)	160
SHA-224	224
SHA-256	256
SHA-384	384
SHA-512	512

Digital Signatures

Once you have chosen a cryptographically sound hashing algorithm, you can use it to implement a *digital signature* system. Digital signature infrastructures have two distinct goals:

- Digitally signed messages assure the recipient that the message truly came from the claimed sender. They enforce nonrepudiation (that is, they preclude the sender from later claiming that the message is a forgery).
- Digitally signed messages assure the recipient that the message was not altered while in transit between the sender and recipient. This protects against both malicious modification (a third party altering the meaning of the message) and unintentional modification (because of faults in the communications process, such as electrical interference).

Digital signature algorithms rely on a combination of the two major concepts already covered in this chapter—public key cryptography and hashing functions.

If Alice wants to digitally sign a message she's sending to Bob, she performs the following actions:

1. Alice generates a message digest of the original plaintext message using one of the cryptographically sound hashing algorithms, such as SHA-512.
2. Alice then encrypts only the message digest using her private key. This encrypted message digest is the digital signature.
3. Alice appends the signed message digest to the plaintext message.
4. Alice transmits the appended message to Bob.

When Bob receives the digitally signed message, he reverses the procedure, as follows:

1. Bob decrypts the digital signature using Alice's public key.
2. Bob uses the same hashing function to create a message digest of the full plaintext message received from Alice.
3. Bob then compares the decrypted message digest he received from Alice with the message digest he computed himself. If the two digests match, he can be assured that the message he received was sent by Alice. If they do not match, either the message was not sent by Alice or the message was modified while in transit.

NOTE Digital signatures are used for more than just messages. Software vendors often use digital signature technology to authenticate code distributions that you download from the Internet, such as applets and software patches.

Note that the digital signature process does not provide any privacy in and of itself. It only ensures that the cryptographic goals of integrity, authentication, and nonrepudiation are met. However, if Alice wanted to ensure the privacy of her message to Bob, she could add a step to the message creation process. After appending the signed message digest to the plaintext message, Alice could encrypt the entire message with Bob's public key. When Bob received the message, he would decrypt it with his own private key before following the steps just outlined.

HMAC

The Hashed Message Authentication Code (HMAC) algorithm implements a partial digital signature—it guarantees the integrity of a message during transmission, but it does not provide for nonrepudiation.

Real World Scenario

Which Key Should I Use?

If you're new to public key cryptography, selecting the correct key for various applications can be quite confusing. Encryption, decryption, message signing, and signature verification all use the same algorithm with different key inputs. Here are a few simple rules to help keep these concepts straight in your mind when preparing for the CISSP exam:

- If you want to encrypt a message, use the recipient's public key.
- If you want to decrypt a message sent to you, use your private key.
- If you want to digitally sign a message you are sending to someone else, use your private key.
- If you want to verify the signature on a message sent by someone else, use the sender's public key.

These four rules are the core principles of public key cryptography and digital signatures. If you understand each of them, you're off to a great start!

HMAC can be combined with any standard message digest generation algorithm, such as SHA-2, by using a shared secret key. Therefore, only communicating parties who know the key can generate or verify the digital signature. If the recipient decrypts the message digest but cannot successfully compare it to a message digest generated from the plaintext message, that means the message was altered in transit.

Because HMAC relies on a shared secret key, it does not provide any nonrepudiation functionality (as previously mentioned). However, it operates in a more efficient manner than the digital signature standard described in the following section and may be suitable for applications in which symmetric key cryptography is appropriate. In short, it represents a halfway point between unencrypted use of a message digest algorithm and computationally expensive digital signature algorithms based on public key cryptography.

Digital Signature Standard

The National Institute of Standards and Technology specifies the digital signature algorithms acceptable for federal government use in Federal Information Processing Standard (FIPS) 186-4, also known as the Digital Signature Standard (DSS). This document specifies that all federally approved digital signature algorithms must use the SHA-2 hashing functions.

DSS also specifies the encryption algorithms that can be used to support a digital signature infrastructure. There are three currently approved standard encryption algorithms:

- The Digital Signature Algorithm (DSA) as specified in FIPS 186-4
- The Rivest, Shamir, Adleman (RSA) algorithm as specified in ANSI X9.31
- The Elliptic Curve DSA (ECDSA) as specified in ANSI X9.62

TIP

Two other digital signature algorithms you should recognize, at least by name, are Schnorr's signature algorithm and Nyberg-Rueppel's signature algorithm.

Public Key Infrastructure

The major strength of public key encryption is its ability to facilitate communication between parties previously unknown to each other. This is made possible by the *public key infrastructure (PKI)* hierarchy of trust relationships. These trusts permit combining asymmetric cryptography with symmetric cryptography along with hashing and digital certificates, giving us hybrid cryptography.

In the following sections, you'll learn the basic components of the public key infrastructure and the cryptographic concepts that make global secure communications possible. You'll learn the composition of a digital certificate, the role of certificate authorities, and the process used to generate and destroy certificates.

Certificates

Digital *certificates* provide communicating parties with the assurance that the people they are communicating with truly are who they claim to be. Digital certificates are essentially endorsed copies of an individual's public key. When users verify that a certificate was signed by a trusted certificate authority (CA), they know that the public key is legitimate.

Digital certificates contain specific identifying information, and their construction is governed by an international standard—X.509. Certificates that conform to X.509 contain the following data:

- Version of X.509 to which the certificate conforms
- Serial number (from the certificate creator)
- Signature algorithm identifier (specifies the technique used by the certificate authority to digitally sign the contents of the certificate)
- Issuer name (identification of the certificate authority that issued the certificate)
- Validity period (specifies the dates and times—a starting date and time and an ending date and time—during which the certificate is valid)
- Subject's name (contains the distinguished name, or DN, of the entity that owns the public key contained in the certificate)
- Subject's public key (the meat of the certificate—the actual public key the certificate owner used to set up secure communications)

The current version of X.509 (version 3) supports certificate extensions—customized variables containing data inserted into the certificate by the certificate authority to support tracking of certificates or various applications.

NOTE

If you're interested in building your own X.509 certificates or just want to explore the inner workings of the public key infrastructure, you can purchase the complete official X.509 standard from the International Telecommunications Union (ITU). It's part of the Open Systems Interconnection (OSI) series of communication standards and can be purchased electronically on the ITU website at `www.itu.int`.

X.509 has not been officially accepted as a standard, and implementations can vary from vendor to vendor. However, both Microsoft and Mozilla have adopted X.509 as their de facto standard for Secure Sockets Layer (SSL) communication between their web clients and servers. SSL is covered in greater detail in the section "Applied Cryptography" later in this chapter.

Certificate Authorities

Certificate authorities (CAs) are the glue that binds the public key infrastructure together. These neutral organizations offer notarization services for digital certificates. To obtain a digital certificate from a reputable CA, you must prove your identify to the satisfaction of the CA. The following list includes the major CAs:

- Symantec
- Thawte
- GeoTrust
- GlobalSign
- Comodo Limited
- Starfield Technologies
- GoDaddy
- DigiCert
- Network Solutions, LLC
- Entrust

Nothing is preventing any organization from simply setting up shop as a CA. However, the certificates issued by a CA are only as good as the trust placed in the CA that issued them. This is an important item to consider when receiving a digital certificate from a third party. If you don't recognize and trust the name of the CA that issued the certificate, you shouldn't place any trust in the certificate at all. PKI relies on a hierarchy of trust relationships. If you configure your browser to trust a CA, it will automatically trust all of the digital certificates issued by that CA. Browser developers preconfigure browsers to trust the major CAs to avoid placing this burden on users.

Registration authorities (RAs) assist CAs with the burden of verifying users' identities prior to issuing digital certificates. They do not directly issue certificates themselves, but they play an important role in the certification process, allowing CAs to remotely validate user identities.

Real World Scenario

Certificate Path Validation

You may have heard of *certificate path validation* (CPV) in your studies of certificate authorities. CPV means that each certificate in a certificate path from the original start or root of trust down to the server or client in question is valid and legitimate. CPV can be important if you need to verify that every link between "trusted" endpoints remains current, valid, and trustworthy.

This issue arises from time to time when intermediary systems' certificates expire or are replaced; this can break the chain of trust or the verification path. By forcing a reverification of all stages of trust, you can reestablish all trust links and prove that the assumed trust remains assured.

Certificate Generation and Destruction

The technical concepts behind the public key infrastructure are relatively simple. In the following sections, we'll cover the processes used by certificate authorities to create, validate, and revoke client certificates.

Enrollment

When you want to obtain a digital certificate, you must first prove your identity to the CA in some manner; this process is called *enrollment*. As mentioned in the previous section, this sometimes involves physically appearing before an agent of the certification authority with the appropriate identification documents. Some certificate authorities provide other means of verification, including the use of credit report data and identity verification by trusted community leaders.

Once you've satisfied the certificate authority regarding your identity, you provide them with your public key. The CA next creates an X.509 digital certificate containing your identifying information and a copy of your public key. The CA then digitally signs the certificate using the CA's private key and provides you with a copy of your signed digital certificate. You may then safely distribute this certificate to anyone with whom you want to communicate securely.

Verification

When you receive a digital certificate from someone with whom you want to communicate, you *verify* the certificate by checking the CA's digital signature using the CA's public key. Next, you must check and ensure that the certificate was not published on a *certificate revocation list* (CRL). At this point, you may assume that the public key listed in the certificate is authentic, provided that it satisfies the following requirements:

- The digital signature of the CA is authentic.
- You trust the CA.
- The certificate is not listed on a CRL.
- The certificate actually contains the data you are trusting.

The last point is a subtle but extremely important item. Before you trust an identifying piece of information about someone, be sure that it is actually contained within the certificate. If a certificate contains the email address (`billjones@foo.com`) but not the individual's name, you can be certain only that the public key contained therein is associated with that email address. The CA is not making any assertions about the actual identity of the `billjones@foo.com` email account. However, if the certificate contains the name Bill Jones along with an address and telephone number, the CA is vouching for that information as well.

Digital certificate verification algorithms are built in to a number of popular web browsing and email clients, so you won't often need to get involved in the particulars of the process. However, it's important to have a solid understanding of the technical details taking place behind the scenes to make appropriate security judgments for your organization. It's also the reason that, when purchasing a certificate, you choose a CA that is widely trusted. If a CA is not included in, or is later pulled from, the list of CAs trusted by a major browser, it will greatly limit the usefulness of your certificate.

Revocation

Occasionally, a certificate authority needs to *revoke* a certificate. This might occur for one of the following reasons:

- The certificate was compromised (for example, the certificate owner accidentally gave away the private key).
- The certificate was erroneously issued (for example, the CA mistakenly issued a certificate without proper verification).
- The details of the certificate changed (for example, the subject's name changed).
- The security association changed (for example, the subject is no longer employed by the organization sponsoring the certificate).

TIP

The revocation request grace period is the maximum response time within which a CA will perform any requested revocation. This is defined in the *certificate practice statement* (CPS). The CPS states the practices a CA employs when issuing or managing certificates.

You can use two techniques to verify the authenticity of certificates and identify revoked certificates:

Certificate Revocation Lists Certificate revocation lists (CRLs) are maintained by the various certificate authorities and contain the serial numbers of certificates that have been issued by a CA and have been revoked along with the date and time the revocation went into effect. The major disadvantage to certificate revocation lists is that they must be downloaded and cross-referenced periodically, introducing a period of latency between the time a certificate is revoked and the time end users are notified of the revocation. However, CRLs remain the most common method of checking certificate status in use today.

Online Certificate Status Protocol (OCSP) This protocol eliminates the latency inherent in the use of certificate revocation lists by providing a means for real-time certificate verification. When a client receives a certificate, it sends an OCSP request to the CA's OCSP server. The server then responds with a status of valid, invalid, or unknown.

Asymmetric Key Management

When working within the public key infrastructure, it's important that you comply with several best practice requirements to maintain the security of your communications.

First, choose your encryption system wisely. As you learned earlier, "security through obscurity" is not an appropriate approach. Choose an encryption system with an algorithm in the public domain that has been thoroughly vetted by industry experts. Be wary of systems that use a "black-box" approach and maintain that the secrecy of their algorithm is critical to the integrity of the cryptosystem.

You must also select your keys in an appropriate manner. Use a key length that balances your security requirements with performance considerations. Also, ensure that your key is truly random. Any patterns within the key increase the likelihood that an attacker will be able to break your encryption and degrade the security of your cryptosystem.

When using public key encryption, keep your private key secret! Do not, under any circumstances, allow anyone else to gain access to your private key. Remember, allowing someone access even once permanently compromises all communications that take place (past, present, or future) using that key and allows the third party to successfully impersonate you.

Retire keys when they've served a useful life. Many organizations have mandatory key rotation requirements to protect against undetected key compromise. If you don't have a formal policy that you must follow, select an appropriate interval based on the frequency with which you use your key. You might want to change your key pair every few months, if practical.

Back up your key! If you lose the file containing your private key because of data corruption, disaster, or other circumstances, you'll certainly want to have a backup available. You may want to either create your own backup or use a key escrow service that maintains the backup for you. In either case, ensure that the backup is handled in a secure manner. After all, it's just as important as your primary key file!

Applied Cryptography

Up to this point, you've learned a great deal about the foundations of cryptography, the inner workings of various cryptographic algorithms, and the use of the public key infrastructure to distribute identity credentials using digital certificates. You should now feel comfortable with the basics of cryptography and prepared to move on to higher-level applications of this technology to solve everyday communications problems.

In the following sections, we'll examine the use of cryptography to secure data at rest, such as that stored on portable devices, as well as data in transit, using techniques that include secure email, encrypted web communications, and networking.

Portable Devices

The now ubiquitous nature of notebook computers, netbooks, smartphones, and tablets brings new risks to the world of computing. Those devices often contain highly sensitive information that, if lost or stolen, could cause serious harm to an organization and its customers, employees, and affiliates. For this reason, many organizations turn to encryption to protect the data on these devices in the event they are misplaced.

Current versions of popular operating systems now include disk encryption capabilities that make it easy to apply and manage encryption on portable devices. For example, Microsoft Windows includes the BitLocker and Encrypting File System (EFS) technologies, Mac OS X includes FileVault encryption, and the TrueCrypt open source package allows the encryption of disks on Linux, Windows, and Mac systems.

A wide variety of commercial tools are available that provide added features and management capability. The major differentiators between these tools are how they protect keys stored in memory, whether they provide full disk or volume-only encryption, and whether they integrate with hardware-based Trusted Platform Modules (TPMs) to provide added security. Any effort to select encryption software should include an analysis of how well the alternatives compete on these characteristics.

TIP

Don't forget about smartphones when developing your portable device encryption policy. Most major smartphone and tablet platforms include enterprise-level functionality that supports encryption of data stored on the phone.

Email

We have mentioned several times that security should be cost effective. When it comes to email, simplicity is the most cost-effective option, but sometimes cryptography functions provide specific security services that you can't avoid using. Since ensuring security is also cost effective, here are some simple rules about encrypting email:

- If you need confidentiality when sending an email message, encrypt the message.
- If your message must maintain integrity, you must hash the message.
- If your message needs authentication, integrity and/or nonrepudiation, you should digitally sign the message.
- If your message requires confidentiality, integrity, authentication, and nonrepudiation, you should encrypt and digitally sign the message.

It is always the responsibility of the sender to put proper mechanisms in place to ensure that the security (that is, confidentiality, integrity, authenticity, and nonrepudiation) of a message or transmission is maintained.

One of the most in-demand applications of cryptography is encrypting and signing email messages. Until recently, encrypted email required the use of complex, awkward software that in turn required manual intervention and complicated key exchange procedures. An increased emphasis on security in recent years resulted in the implementation of strong encryption technology in mainstream email packages. Next, we'll look at some of the secure email standards in widespread use today.

Pretty Good Privacy

Phil Zimmerman's Pretty Good Privacy (PGP) secure email system appeared on the computer security scene in 1991. It combines the CA hierarchy described earlier in this chapter with the "web of trust" concept—that is, you must become trusted by one or more PGP users to begin using the system. You then accept their judgment regarding the validity of additional users and, by extension, trust a multilevel "web" of users descending from your initial trust judgments.

PGP initially encountered a number of hurdles to widespread use. The most difficult obstruction was the US government export regulations, which treated encryption technology as munitions and prohibited the distribution of strong encryption technology outside the United States. Fortunately, this restriction has since been repealed, and PGP may be freely distributed to most countries.

PGP is available in two versions. The commercial version uses RSA for key exchange, IDEA for encryption/decryption, and MD5 for message digest production. The freeware version (based on the extremely similar OpenPGP standard) uses Diffie-Hellman key exchange, the Carlisle Adams/Stafford Tavares (CAST) 128-bit encryption/decryption algorithm, and the SHA-1 hashing function.

Many commercial providers also offer PGP-based email services as web-based cloud email offerings, mobile device applications, or webmail plug-ins. These services appeal to administrators and end users because they remove the complexity of configuring and maintaining encryption certificates and provide users with a managed secure email service. Some products in this category include StartMail, Mailvelope, SafeGmail, and Hushmail.

S/MIME

The Secure Multipurpose Internet Mail Extensions (S/MIME) protocol has emerged as a de facto standard for encrypted email. S/MIME uses the RSA encryption algorithm and has received the backing of major industry players, including RSA Security. S/MIME has already been incorporated in a large number of commercial products, including these:

- Microsoft Outlook and Outlook Web Access
- Mozilla Thunderbird
- Mac OS X Mail

S/MIME relies on the use of X.509 certificates for exchanging cryptographic keys. The public keys contained in these certificates are used for digital signatures and for the exchange of symmetric keys used for longer communications sessions. RSA is the only public key cryptographic protocol supported by S/MIME. The protocol supports the AES and 3DES symmetric encryption algorithms.

Despite strong industry support for the S/MIME standard, technical limitations have prevented its widespread adoption. Although major desktop mail applications support S/MIME email, mainstream web-based email systems do not support it out of the box (the use of browser extensions is required).

Web Applications

Encryption is widely used to protect web transactions. This is mainly because of the strong movement toward e-commerce and the desire of both e-commerce vendors and consumers to securely exchange financial information (such as credit card information) over the Web. We'll look at the two technologies that are responsible for the small lock icon within web browsers—Secure Sockets Layer (SSL) and Transport Layer Security (TLS).

SSL was developed by Netscape to provide client/server encryption for web traffic. Hypertext Transfer Protocol over Secure Sockets Layer (HTTPS) uses port 443 to negotiate encrypted communications sessions between web servers and browser clients. Although SSL originated as a standard for Netscape browsers, Microsoft also adopted it as a security standard for its popular Internet Explorer browser. The incorporation of SSL into both of these products made it the de facto Internet standard.

SSL relies on the exchange of server digital certificates to negotiate encryption/decryption parameters between the browser and the web server. SSL's goal is to create secure communications channels that remain open for an entire web browsing session. It depends on a combination of symmetric and asymmetric cryptography. The following steps are involved:

1. When a user accesses a website, the browser retrieves the web server's certificate and extracts the server's public key from it.
2. The browser then creates a random symmetric key, uses the server's public key to encrypt it, and then sends the encrypted symmetric key to the server.
3. The server then decrypts the symmetric key using its own private key, and the two systems exchange all future messages using the symmetric encryption key.

This approach allows SSL to leverage the advanced functionality of asymmetric cryptography while encrypting and decrypting the vast majority of the data exchanged using the faster symmetric algorithm.

In 1999, security engineers proposed TLS as a replacement for the SSL standard, which was at the time in its third version. As with SSL, TLS uses TCP port 443. Based on SSL technology, TLS incorporated many security enhancements and was eventually adopted as a replacement for SSL in most applications. Early versions of TLS supported downgrading communications to SSL v3.0 when both parties did not support TLS. However, in 2011, TLS v1.2 dropped this backward compatibility.

In 2014, an attack known as the Padding Oracle On Downgraded Legacy Encryption (POODLE) demonstrated a significant flaw in the SSL 3.0 fallback mechanism of TLS. In an effort to remediate this vulnerability, many organizations completely dropped SSL support and now rely solely on TLS security.

TIP

Even though TLS has been in existence for more than a decade, many people still mistakenly call it SSL. For this reason, TLS has gained the nickname SSL 3.1.

Steganography and Watermarking

Steganography is the art of using cryptographic techniques to embed secret messages within another message. Steganographic algorithms work by making alterations to the least significant bits of the many bits that make up image files. The changes are so minor that there is no appreciable effect on the viewed image. This technique allows communicating parties to hide messages in plain sight—for example, they might embed a secret message within an illustration on an otherwise innocent web page.

Steganographers often embed their secret messages within images or WAV files because these files are often so large that the secret message would easily be missed by even the most observant inspector. Steganography techniques are often used for illegal or questionable activities, such as espionage and child pornography.

Steganography can also be used for legitimate purposes, however. Adding digital watermarks to documents to protect intellectual property is accomplished by means of steganography. The hidden information is known only to the file's creator. If someone later creates an unauthorized copy of the content, the watermark can be used to detect the copy and (if uniquely watermarked files are provided to each original recipient) trace the offending copy back to the source.

Steganography is an extremely simple technology to use, with free tools openly available on the Internet. Figure 7.2 shows the entire interface of one such tool, iSteg. It simply requires that you specify a text file containing your secret message and an image file that you wish to use to hide the message. Figure 7.3 shows an example of a picture with an embedded secret message; the message is impossible to detect with the human eye.

FIGURE 7.2 Steganography tool

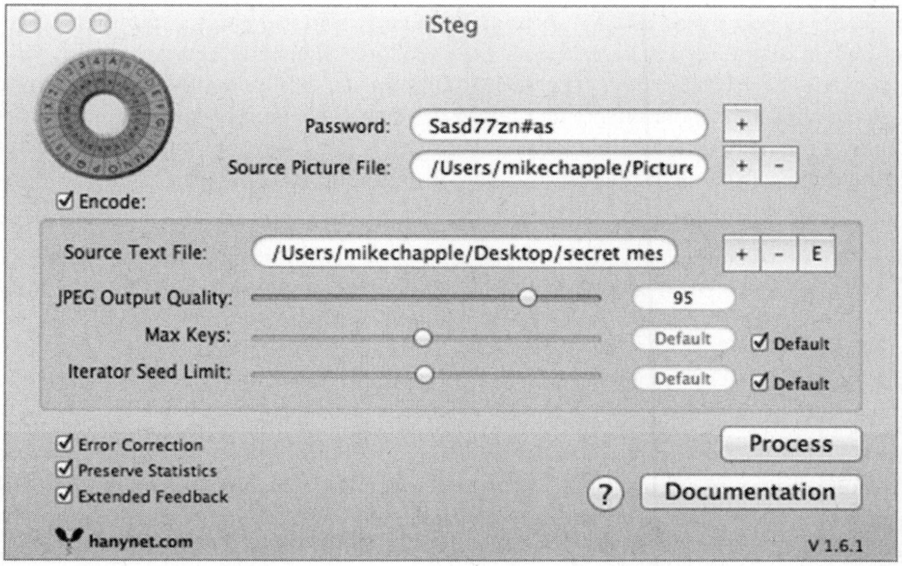

FIGURE 7.3 Image with embedded message

Digital Rights Management

Digital rights management (DRM) software uses encryption to enforce copyright restrictions on digital media. Over the past decade, publishers attempted to deploy DRM schemes across a variety of media types, including music, movies and books. In many cases, particularly with music, opponents met DRM deployment attempts with fierce opposition, arguing that the use of DRM violated their rights to freely enjoy and make backup copies of legitimately licensed media files.

NOTE As you will read in this section, many commercial attempts to deploy DRM on a widespread basis failed when users rejected the technology as intrusive and/or obstructive.

Music DRM

The music industry has battled pirates for years, dating back to the days of homemade cassette tape duplication and carrying through compact disc and digital formats. Music distribution companies attempted to use a variety of DRM schemes, but most backed away from the technology under pressure from consumers.

The use of DRM for purchased music slowed dramatically when, facing this opposition, Apple rolled back their use of FairPlay DRM for music sold through the iTunes Store. Apple co-founder Steve Jobs foreshadowed this move when, in 2007, he issued an open letter to the music industry calling on them to allow Apple to sell DRM-free music. That letter read, in part:

> The third alternative is to abolish DRMs entirely. Imagine a world where every online store sells DRM-free music encoded in open licensable formats. In such a world, any player can play music purchased from any store, and any store can sell music which is playable on all players. This is clearly the best alternative for consumers, and Apple would embrace it in a heartbeat. If the big four music companies would license Apple their music without the requirement that it be protected with a DRM, we would switch to selling only DRM-free music on our iTunes store. Every iPod ever made will play this DRM-free music.

The full essay is no longer available on Apple's website, but an archived copy may be found at `http://bit.ly/1TyBm5e`.

Currently, the major use of DRM technology in music is for subscription-based services such as Napster and Kazaa, which use DRM to revoke a user's access to downloaded music when their subscription period ends.

NOTE Do the descriptions of DRM technology in this section seem a little vague? There's a reason for that: manufacturers typically do not disclose the details of their DRM functionality due to fears that pirates will use that information to defeat the DRM scheme.

Movie DRM

The movie industry has used a variety of DRM schemes over the years to stem the worldwide problem of movie piracy. Two of the major technologies used to protect mass-distributed media are as follows:

Content Scrambling System (CSS) Enforces playback and region restrictions on DVDs. This encryption scheme was broken with the release of a tool known as DeCSS that enabled the playback of CSS-protected content on Linux systems.

Advanced Access Content System (AACS) Protects the content stored on Blu-Ray and HD DVD media. Hackers have demonstrated attacks that retrieved AACS encryption keys and posted them on the Internet.

Industry publishers and hackers continue the cat-and-mouse game today; media companies try to protect their content and hackers seek to gain continued access to unencrypted copies.

E-book DRM

Perhaps the most successful deployment of DRM technology is in the area of book and document publishing. Most e-books made available today use some form of DRM, and these technologies also protect sensitive documents produced by corporations with DRM capabilities.

> **TIP** All DRM schemes in use today share a fatal flaw: the device used to access the content must have access to the decryption key. If the decryption key is stored on a device possessed by the end user, there is always a chance that the user will manipulate the device to gain access to the key.

Adobe Systems offers the Adobe Digital Experience Protection Technology (ADEPT) to provide DRM technology for e-books sold in a variety of formats. ADEPT uses a combination of AES technology to encrypt the media content and RSA encryption to protect the AES key. Many e-book readers, with the notable exception of the Amazon Kindle, use this technology to protect their content. Amazon's Kindle e-readers use a variety of formats for book distribution, and each contains its own encryption technology.

Video Game DRM

Many video games implement DRM technology that depends on consoles using an active Internet connection to verify the game license with a cloud-based service. These technologies, such as Ubisoft's Uplay, once typically required a constant Internet connection to facilitate gameplay. If a player lost connection, the game would cease functioning.

In March 2010, the Uplay system came under a denial-of-service attack and players of Uplay-enabled games around the world were unable to play games that previously functioned properly because their consoles were unable to access the Uplay servers. This led to public outcry, and Ubisoft later removed the always-on requirement, shifting to a DRM approach that only requires an initial activation of the game on the console and then allows unrestricted use.

Document DRM

Although the most common uses of DRM technology protect entertainment content, organizations may also use DRM to protect the security of sensitive information stored in PDF files, office productivity documents, and other formats. Commercial DRM products, such as Vitrium and FileOpen, use encryption to protect source content and then enable organizations to carefully control document rights.

Here are some of the common permissions restricted by document DRM solutions:

- Reading a file
- Modifying the contents of a file
- Removing watermarks from a file
- Downloading/saving a file
- Printing a file
- Taking screenshots of file content

DRM solutions allow organizations to control these rights by granting them when needed, revoking them when no longer necessary, and even automatically expiring rights after a specified period of time.

Networking

The final application of cryptography we'll explore in this chapter is the use of cryptographic algorithms to provide secure networking services. In the following sections, we'll take a brief look at two methods used to secure communications circuits. We'll also look at IPsec and Internet Security Association and Key Management Protocol (ISAKMP) as well as some of the security issues surrounding wireless networking.

Circuit Encryption

Security administrators use two types of encryption techniques to protect data traveling over networks:

- *Link encryption* protects entire communications circuits by creating a secure tunnel between two points using either a hardware solution or a software solution that encrypts all traffic entering one end of the tunnel and decrypts all traffic entering the other end of the tunnel. For example, a company with two offices connected via a data circuit might use link encryption to protect against attackers monitoring at a point in between the two offices.
- *End-to-end encryption* protects communications between two parties (for example, a client and a server) and is performed independently of link encryption. An example of end-to-end encryption would be the use of TLS to protect communications between a user and a web server. This protects against an intruder who might be monitoring traffic on the secure side of an encrypted link or traffic sent over an unencrypted link.

The critical difference between link and end-to-end encryption is that in link encryption, all the data, including the header, trailer, address, and routing data, is also encrypted. Therefore, each packet has to be decrypted at each hop so it can be properly routed to the next hop and then re-encrypted before it can be sent along its way, which slows the routing. End-to-end encryption does not encrypt the header, trailer, address, and routing data, so it moves faster from point to point but is more susceptible to sniffers and eavesdroppers.

When encryption happens at the higher OSI layers, it is usually end-to-end encryption, and if encryption is done at the lower layers of the OSI model, it is usually link encryption.

Secure Shell (SSH) is a good example of an end-to-end encryption technique. This suite of programs provides encrypted alternatives to common Internet applications such as FTP, Telnet, and rlogin. There are actually two versions of SSH. SSH1 (which is now considered insecure) supports the DES, 3DES, IDEA, and Blowfish algorithms. SSH2 drops support for DES and IDEA but adds support for several other algorithms.

IPsec

Various security architectures are in use today, each one designed to address security issues in different environments. One such architecture that supports secure communications is the Internet Protocol Security (IPsec) standard. IPsec is a standard architecture set forth by the Internet Engineering Task Force (IETF) for setting up a secure channel to exchange information between two entities.

The entities communicating via IPsec could be two systems, two routers, two gateways, or any combination of entities. Although generally used to connect two networks, IPsec can be used to connect individual computers, such as a server and a workstation or a pair of workstations (sender and receiver, perhaps). IPsec does not dictate all implementation details but is an open, modular framework that allows many manufacturers and software developers to develop IPsec solutions that work well with products from other vendors.

IPsec uses public key cryptography to provide encryption, access control, nonrepudiation, and message authentication, all using IP-based protocols. The primary use of IPsec is for virtual private networks (VPNs), so IPsec can operate in either transport or tunnel mode. IPsec is commonly paired with the Layer 2 Tunneling Protocol (L2TP) as L2TP/IPsec.

The IP Security (IPsec) protocol provides a complete infrastructure for secured network communications. IPsec has gained widespread acceptance and is now offered in a number of commercial operating systems out of the box. IPsec relies on security associations, and there are two main components:

- The Authentication Header (AH) provides assurances of message integrity and nonrepudiation. AH also provides authentication and access control and prevents replay attacks.
- The Encapsulating Security Payload (ESP) provides confidentiality and integrity of packet contents. It provides encryption and limited authentication and prevents replay attacks.

NOTE

ESP also provides some limited authentication, but not to the degree of the AH. Though ESP is sometimes used without AH, it's rare to see AH used without ESP.

IPsec provides for two discrete modes of operation. When IPsec is used in *transport mode*, only the packet payload is encrypted. This mode is designed for peer-to-peer communication. When it's used in *tunnel mode*, the entire packet, including the header, is encrypted. This mode is designed for gateway-to-gateway communication.

TIP

IPsec is an extremely important concept in modern computer security. Be certain that you're familiar with the component protocols and modes of IPsec operation.

At runtime, you set up an IPsec session by creating a *security association* (SA). The SA represents the communication session and records any configuration and status information about the connection. The SA represents a simplex connection. If you want a two-way channel, you need two SAs, one for each direction. Also, if you want to support a bidirectional channel using both AH and ESP, you will need to set up four SAs.

Some of IPsec's greatest strengths come from being able to filter or manage communications on a per-SA basis so that clients or gateways between which security associations exist can be rigorously managed in terms of what kinds of protocols or services can use an IPsec connection. Also, without a valid security association defined, pairs of users or gateways cannot establish IPsec links.

Further details of the IPsec algorithm are provided in Chapter 11, "Secure Network Architecture and Securing Network Components."

ISAKMP

The Internet Security Association and Key Management Protocol (ISAKMP) provides background security support services for IPsec by negotiating, establishing, modifying, and deleting security associations. As you learned in the previous section, IPsec relies on a system of security associations (SAs). These SAs are managed through the use of ISAKMP. There are four basic requirements for ISAKMP, as set forth in Internet RFC 2408:

- Authenticate communicating peers
- Create and manage security associations
- Provide key generation mechanisms
- Protect against threats (for example, replay and denial-of-service attacks)

Wireless Networking

The widespread rapid adoption of wireless networks poses a tremendous security risk. Many traditional networks do not implement encryption for routine communications between hosts on the local network and rely on the assumption that it would be too difficult for an attacker to gain physical access to the network wire inside a secure location to eavesdrop on the network. However, wireless networks transmit data through the air, leaving them extremely vulnerable to interception. There are two main types of wireless security:

Wired Equivalent Privacy Wired Equivalent Privacy (WEP) provides 64- and 128-bit encryption options to protect communications within the wireless LAN. WEP is described in IEEE 802.11 as an optional component of the wireless networking standard.

WARNING

Cryptanalysis has conclusively demonstrated that significant flaws exist in the WEP algorithm, making it possible to completely undermine the security of a WEP-protected network within seconds. You should never use WEP encryption to protect a wireless network. In fact, the use of WEP encryption on a store network was the root cause behind the TJX security breach that was widely publicized in 2007. Again, you should *never* use WEP encryption on a wireless network.

WiFi Protected Access WiFi Protected Access (WPA) improves on WEP encryption by implementing the Temporal Key Integrity Protocol (TKIP), eliminating the cryptographic weaknesses that undermined WEP. A further improvement to the technique, dubbed WPA2, adds AES cryptography. WPA2 provides secure algorithms appropriate for use on modern wireless networks.

WARNING Remember that WPA does not provide an end-to-end security solution. It encrypts traffic only between a mobile computer and the nearest wireless access point. Once the traffic hits the wired network, it's in the clear again.

Another commonly used security standard, IEEE 802.1x, provides a flexible framework for authentication and key management in wired and wireless networks. To use 802.1x, the client runs a piece of software known as the *supplicant*. The supplicant communicates with the authentication server. After successful authentication, the network switch or wireless access point allows the client to access the network. WPA was designed to interact with 802.1x authentication servers.

Cryptographic Attacks

As with any security mechanism, malicious individuals have found a number of attacks to defeat cryptosystems. It's important that you understand the threats posed by various cryptographic attacks to minimize the risks posed to your systems:

Analytic Attack This is an algebraic manipulation that attempts to reduce the complexity of the algorithm. Analytic attacks focus on the logic of the algorithm itself.

Implementation Attack This is a type of attack that exploits weaknesses in the implementation of a cryptography system. It focuses on exploiting the software code, not just errors and flaws but the methodology employed to program the encryption system.

Statistical Attack A statistical attack exploits statistical weaknesses in a cryptosystem, such as floating-point errors and inability to produce truly random numbers. Statistical attacks attempt to find a vulnerability in the hardware or operating system hosting the cryptography application.

Brute Force Brute-force attacks are quite straightforward. Such an attack attempts every possible valid combination for a key or password. They involve using massive amounts of processing power to methodically guess the key used to secure cryptographic communications.

For a nonflawed protocol, the average amount of time required to discover the key through a brute-force attack is directly proportional to the length of the key. A brute-force attack will always be successful given enough time. Every additional bit of key length doubles the time to perform a brute-force attack because the number of potential keys doubles.

There are two modifications that attackers can make to enhance the effectiveness of a brute-force attack:

- Rainbow tables provide precomputed values for cryptographic hashes. These are commonly used for cracking passwords stored on a system in hashed form.
- Specialized, scalable computing hardware designed specifically for the conduct of brute-force attacks may greatly increase the efficiency of this approach.

Salting Saves Passwords

Salt might be hazardous to your health, but it can save your password! To help combat the use of brute-force attacks, including those aided by dictionaries and rainbow tables, cryptographers make use of a technology known as *cryptographic salt*.

The cryptographic salt is a random value that is added to the end of the password before the operating system hashes the password. The salt is then stored in the password file along with the hash. When the operating system wishes to compare a user's proffered password to the password file, it first retrieves the salt and appends it to the password. It feeds the concatenated value to the hash function and compares the resulting hash with the one stored in the password file.

Going to this extra trouble dramatically increases the difficulty of brute-force attacks. Anyone attempting to build a rainbow table must build a separate table for each possible value of the cryptographic salt.

Frequency Analysis and the Ciphertext Only Attack In many cases, the only information you have at your disposal is the encrypted ciphertext message, a scenario known as the *ciphertext only attack*. In this case, one technique that proves helpful against simple ciphers is frequency analysis—counting the number of times each letter appears in the ciphertext. Using your knowledge that the letters *E*, *T*, *O*, *A*, *I*, and *N* are the most common in the English language, you can then test several hypotheses:

- If these letters are also the most common in the ciphertext, the cipher was likely a transposition cipher, which rearranged the characters of the plain text without altering them.
- If other letters are the most common in the ciphertext, the cipher is probably some form of substitution cipher that replaced the plaintext characters.

This is a simple overview of frequency analysis, and many sophisticated variations on this technique can be used against polyalphabetic ciphers and other sophisticated cryptosystems.

Known Plaintext In the known plaintext attack, the attacker has a copy of the encrypted message along with the plaintext message used to generate the ciphertext (the copy). This knowledge greatly assists the attacker in breaking weaker codes. For example, imagine the ease with which you could break the Caesar cipher described in Chapter 6 if you had both a plaintext copy and a ciphertext copy of the same message.

Chosen Ciphertext In a chosen ciphertext attack, the attacker has the ability to decrypt chosen portions of the ciphertext message and use the decrypted portion of the message to discover the key.

Chosen Plaintext In a chosen plaintext attack, the attacker has the ability to encrypt plaintext messages of their choosing and can then analyze the ciphertext output of the encryption algorithm.

Meet in the Middle Attackers might use a meet-in-the-middle attack to defeat encryption algorithms that use two rounds of encryption. This attack is the reason that Double DES (2DES) was quickly discarded as a viable enhancement to the DES encryption (it was replaced by Triple DES, or 3DES).

In the meet-in-the-middle attack, the attacker uses a known plaintext message. The plain text is then encrypted using every possible key (k1), and the equivalent ciphertext is decrypted using all possible keys (k2). When a match is found, the corresponding pair (k1, k2) represents both portions of the double encryption. This type of attack generally takes only double the time necessary to break a single round of encryption (or 2^n rather than the anticipated $2^n * 2^n$), offering minimal added protection.

Man in the Middle In the man-in-the-middle attack, a malicious individual sits between two communicating parties and intercepts all communications (including the setup of the cryptographic session). The attacker responds to the originator's initialization requests and sets up a secure session with the originator. The attacker then establishes a second secure session with the intended recipient using a different key and posing as the originator. The attacker can then "sit in the middle" of the communication and read all traffic as it passes between the two parties.

TIP

Be careful not to confuse the meet-in-the-middle attack with the man-in-the-middle attack. They may have similar names, but they are quite different!

Birthday The birthday attack, also known as a *collision attack* or *reverse hash matching* (see the discussion of brute-force and dictionary attacks in Chapter 14, "Controlling and Monitoring Access"), seeks to find flaws in the one-to-one nature of hashing functions. In this attack, the malicious individual seeks to substitute in a digitally signed communication a different message that produces the same message digest, thereby maintaining the validity of the original digital signature.

NOTE

Don't forget that social engineering techniques can also be used in cryptanalysis. If you're able to obtain a decryption key by simply asking the sender for it, that's much easier than attempting to crack the cryptosystem!

Replay The replay attack is used against cryptographic algorithms that don't incorporate temporal protections. In this attack, the malicious individual intercepts an encrypted message between two parties (often a request for authentication) and then later "replays" the captured message to open a new session. This attack can be defeated by incorporating a time stamp and expiration period into each message.

Summary

Asymmetric key cryptography, or public key encryption, provides an extremely flexible infrastructure, facilitating simple, secure communication between parties that do not necessarily know each other prior to initiating the communication. It also provides the framework for the digital signing of messages to ensure nonrepudiation and message integrity.

This chapter explored public key encryption, which provides a scalable cryptographic architecture for use by large numbers of users. We also described some popular cryptographic algorithms, such as link encryption and end-to-end encryption. Finally, we introduced you to the public key infrastructure, which uses certificate authorities (CAs) to generate digital certificates containing the public keys of system users and digital signatures, which rely on a combination of public key cryptography and hashing functions.

We also looked at some of the common applications of cryptographic technology in solving everyday problems. You learned how cryptography can be used to secure email (using PGP and S/MIME), web communications (using SSL and TLS), and both peer-to-peer and gateway-to-gateway networking (using IPsec and ISAKMP) as well as wireless communications (using WPA and WPA2).

Finally, we covered some of the more common attacks used by malicious individuals attempting to interfere with or intercept encrypted communications between two parties. Such attacks include birthday, cryptanalytic, replay, brute-force, known plaintext, chosen plaintext, chosen ciphertext, meet-in-the-middle, man-in-the-middle, and birthday attacks. It's important for you to understand these attacks in order to provide adequate security against them.

Exam Essentials

Understand the key types used in asymmetric cryptography. Public keys are freely shared among communicating parties, whereas private keys are kept secret. To encrypt a message, use the recipient's public key. To decrypt a message, use your own private key. To sign a message, use your own private key. To validate a signature, use the sender's public key.

Be familiar with the three major public key cryptosystems. RSA is the most famous public key cryptosystem; it was developed by Rivest, Shamir, and Adleman in 1977. It depends on the difficulty of factoring the product of prime numbers. El Gamal is an extension of the Diffie-Hellman key exchange algorithm that depends on modular arithmetic. The elliptic curve algorithm depends on the elliptic curve discrete logarithm problem and provides more security than other algorithms when both are used with keys of the same length.

Know the fundamental requirements of a hash function. Good hash functions have five requirements. They must allow input of any length, provide fixed-length output, make it relatively easy to compute the hash function for any input, provide one-way functionality, and be collision free.

Be familiar with the major hashing algorithms. The successors to the Secure Hash Algorithm (SHA), SHA-1 and SHA-2, make up the government standard message digest function. SHA-1 produces a 160-bit message digest whereas SHA-2 supports variable lengths, ranging up to 512 bits. SHA-3 remains in development and NIST may release it in final form soon.

Know how cryptographic salts improve the security of password hashing. When straightforward hashing is used to store passwords in a password file, attackers may use rainbow tables of precomputed values to identify commonly used passwords. Adding salts to the passwords before hashing them reduces the effectiveness of rainbow table attacks.

Understand how digital signatures are generated and verified. To digitally sign a message, first use a hashing function to generate a message digest. Then encrypt the digest with your private key. To verify the digital signature on a message, decrypt the signature with the sender's public key and then compare the message digest to one you generate yourself. If they match, the message is authentic.

Know the components of the Digital Signature Standard (DSS). The Digital Signature Standard uses the SHA-1 and SHA-2 message digest functions along with one of three encryption algorithms: the Digital Signature Algorithm (DSA); the Rivest, Shamir, Adleman (RSA) algorithm; or the Elliptic Curve DSA (ECDSA) algorithm.

Understand the public key infrastructure (PKI). In the public key infrastructure, certificate authorities (CAs) generate digital certificates containing the public keys of system users. Users then distribute these certificates to people with whom they want to communicate. Certificate recipients verify a certificate using the CA's public key.

Know the common applications of cryptography to secure email. The emerging standard for encrypted messages is the S/MIME protocol. Another popular email security tool is Phil Zimmerman's Pretty Good Privacy (PGP). Most users of email encryption rely on having this technology built into their email client or their web-based email service.

Know the common applications of cryptography to secure web activity. The de facto standard for secure web traffic is the use of HTTP over Transport Layer Security (TLS) or the older Secure Sockets Layer (SSL). Most web browsers support both standards, but many websites are dropping support for SSL due to security concerns.

Know the common applications of cryptography to secure networking. The IPsec protocol standard provides a common framework for encrypting network traffic and is built into a number of common operating systems. In IPsec transport mode, packet contents are encrypted for peer-to-peer communication. In tunnel mode, the entire packet, including header information, is encrypted for gateway-to-gateway communications.

Be able to describe IPsec. IPsec is a security architecture framework that supports secure communication over IP. IPsec establishes a secure channel in either transport mode or tunnel mode. It can be used to establish direct communication between computers or to set up a VPN between networks. IPsec uses two protocols: Authentication Header (AH) and Encapsulating Security Payload (ESP).

Be able to explain common cryptographic attacks. Brute-force attacks are attempts to randomly find the correct cryptographic key. Known plaintext, chosen ciphertext, and chosen plaintext attacks require the attacker to have some extra information in addition to the ciphertext. The meet-in-the-middle attack exploits protocols that use two rounds of encryption. The man-in-the-middle attack fools both parties into communicating with the attacker instead of directly with each other. The birthday attack is an attempt to find collisions in hash functions. The replay attack is an attempt to reuse authentication requests.

Understand uses of digital rights management (DRM). Digital rights management (DRM) solutions allow content owners to enforce restrictions on the use of their content by others. DRM solutions commonly protect entertainment content, such as music, movies, and e-books but are occasionally found in the enterprise, protecting sensitive information stored in documents.

Written Lab

1. Explain the process Bob should use if he wants to send a confidential message to Alice using asymmetric cryptography.
2. Explain the process Alice would use to decrypt the message Bob sent in question 1.
3. Explain the process Bob should use to digitally sign a message to Alice.
4. Explain the process Alice should use to verify the digital signature on the message from Bob in question 3.

Review Questions

1. In the RSA public key cryptosystem, which one of the following numbers will always be largest?
   A. *e*
   B. *n*
   C. *p*
   D. *q*
2. Which cryptographic algorithm forms the basis of the El Gamal cryptosystem?
   A. RSA
   B. Diffie-Hellman
   C. 3DES
   D. IDEA
3. If Richard wants to send an encrypted message to Sue using a public key cryptosystem, which key does he use to encrypt the message?
   A. Richard's public key
   B. Richard's private key
   C. Sue's public key
   D. Sue's private key
4. If a 2,048-bit plaintext message were encrypted with the El Gamal public key cryptosystem, how long would the resulting ciphertext message be?
   A. 1,024 bits
   B. 2,048 bits
   C. 4,096 bits
   D. 8,192 bits
5. Acme Widgets currently uses a 1,024-bit RSA encryption standard companywide. The company plans to convert from RSA to an elliptic curve cryptosystem. If it wants to maintain the same cryptographic strength, what ECC key length should it use?
   A. 160 bits
   B. 512 bits
   C. 1,024 bits
   D. 2,048 bits
6. John wants to produce a message digest of a 2,048-byte message he plans to send to Mary. If he uses the SHA-1 hashing algorithm, what size will the message digest for this particular message be?
   A. 160 bits
   B. 512 bits

C. 1,024 bits

D. 2,048 bits

7. Which one of the following technologies is considered flawed and should no longer be used?

A. SHA-2

B. PGP

C. WEP

D. TLS

8. What encryption technique does WPA use to protect wireless communications?

A. TKIP

B. DES

C. 3DES

D. AES

9. Richard received an encrypted message sent to him from Sue. Which key should he use to decrypt the message?

A. Richard's public key

B. Richard's private key

C. Sue's public key

D. Sue's private key

10. Richard wants to digitally sign a message he's sending to Sue so that Sue can be sure the message came from him without modification while in transit. Which key should he use to encrypt the message digest?

A. Richard's public key

B. Richard's private key

C. Sue's public key

D. Sue's private key

11. Which one of the following algorithms is not supported by the Digital Signature Standard?

A. Digital Signature Algorithm

B. RSA

C. El Gamal DSA

D. Elliptic Curve DSA

12. Which International Telecommunications Union (ITU) standard governs the creation and endorsement of digital certificates for secure electronic communication?

A. X.500

B. X.509

C. X.900

D. X.905

13. What cryptosystem provides the encryption/decryption technology for the commercial version of Phil Zimmerman's Pretty Good Privacy secure email system?
    A. ROT13
    B. IDEA
    C. ECC
    D. El Gamal
14. What TCP/IP communications port is used by Transport Layer Security traffic?
    A. 80
    B. 220
    C. 443
    D. 559
15. What type of cryptographic attack rendered Double DES (2DES) no more effective than standard DES encryption?
    A. Birthday attack
    B. Chosen ciphertext attack
    C. Meet-in-the-middle attack
    D. Man-in-the-middle attack
16. Which of the following tools can be used to improve the effectiveness of a brute-force password cracking attack?
    A. Rainbow tables
    B. Hierarchical screening
    C. TKIP
    D. Random enhancement
17. Which of the following links would be protected by WPA encryption?
    A. Firewall to firewall
    B. Router to firewall
    C. Client to wireless access point
    D. Wireless access point to router
18. What is the major disadvantage of using certificate revocation lists?
    A. Key management
    B. Latency
    C. Record keeping
    D. Vulnerability to brute-force attacks
19. Which one of the following encryption algorithms is now considered insecure?
    A. El Gamal
    B. RSA

C. Skipjack

D. Merkle-Hellman Knapsack

20. What does IPsec define?

A. All possible security classifications for a specific configuration

B. A framework for setting up a secure communication channel

C. The valid transition states in the Biba model

D. TCSEC security categories

Chapter 8

Principles of Security Models, Design, and Capabilities

THE CISSP EXAM TOPICS COVERED IN THIS CHAPTER INCLUDE:

✓ **3) Security Engineering (Engineering and Management of Security)**

- A. Implement and manage engineering processes using secure design principles
- B. Understand the fundamental concepts of security models (e.g., Confidentiality, Integrity, and Multi-level Models)
- C. Select controls and countermeasures based upon systems security evaluation models
- D. Understand security capabilities of information systems (e.g., memory protection, virtualization, trusted platform module, interfaces, fault tolerance)

Understanding the philosophy behind security solutions helps to limit your search for the best controls for specific security needs. In this chapter, we discuss security models, including state machine, Bell-LaPadula, Biba, Clark-Wilson, Take-Grant, and Brewer and Nash. This chapter also describes Common Criteria and other methods governments and corporations use to evaluate information systems from a security perspective, with particular emphasis on US Department of Defense and international security evaluation criteria. Finally, we discuss commonly encountered design flaws and other issues that can make information systems susceptible to attack.

The process of determining how secure a system is can be difficult and time-consuming. In this chapter, we describe the process of evaluating a computer system's level of security. We begin by introducing and explaining basic concepts and terminology used to describe information system security concepts and talk about secure computing, secure perimeters, security and access monitors, and kernel code. We turn to security models to explain how access and security controls can be implemented. We also briefly explain how system security may be categorized as either open or closed; describe a set of standard security techniques used to ensure confidentiality, integrity, and availability of data; discuss security controls; and introduce a standard suite of secure networking protocols.

Additional elements of this domain are discussed in various chapters: Chapter 6, "Cryptography and Symmetric Key Algorithms," Chapter 7, "PKI and Cryptographic Applications," Chapter 9, "Security Vulnerabilities, Threats, and Countermeasures," and Chapter 10, "Physical Security Requirements." Please be sure to review all of these chapters to have a complete perspective on the topics of this domain.

Implement and Manage Engineering Processes Using Secure Design Principles

Security should be a consideration at every stage of a system's development. Programmers should strive to build security into every application they develop, with greater levels of security provided to critical applications and those that process sensitive information. It's extremely important to consider the security implications of a development project from the early stages because it's much easier to build security into a system than it is to add security onto an existing system. The following sections discuss several essential security design principles that should be implemented and managed early in the engineering process of a hardware or software project.

Objects and Subjects

Controlling access to any resource in a secure system involves two entities. The *subject* is the user or process that makes a request to access a resource. Access can mean reading from or writing to a resource. The *object* is the resource a user or process wants to access. Keep in mind that the subject and object refer to some specific access request, so the same resource can serve as a subject and an object in different access requests.

For example, process A may ask for data from process B. To satisfy process A's request, process B must ask for data from process C. In this example, process B is the object of the first request and the subject of the second request:

First request	process A (subject)	process B (object)
Second request	process B (subject)	process C (object)

This also serves as an example of transitive trust. Transitive trust is the concept that if A trusts B and B trusts C, then A inherits trust of C through the transitive property—which works like it would in a mathematical equation: if a = b, and b = c, then a = c. In the previous example, when A requests data from B and then B requests data from C, the data that A receives is essentially from C. Transitive trust is a serious security concern because it may enable bypassing of restrictions or limitations between A and C, especially if A and C both support interaction with B. An example of this would be when an organization blocks access to Facebook or YouTube to increase worker productivity. Thus, workers (A) do not have access to certain Internet sites (C). However, if workers are able to access to a web proxy, VPN, or anonymization service, then this can serve as a means to bypass the local network restriction. In other words, workers (A) accessing VPN service (B), then the VPN service (B), can access the blocked Internet service (C); thus A is able to access C through B via a transitive trust exploitation.

Closed and Open Systems

Systems are designed and built according to one of two differing philosophies: A *closed system* is designed to work well with a narrow range of other systems, generally all from the same manufacturer. The standards for closed systems are often proprietary and not normally disclosed. *Open systems*, on the other hand, are designed using agreed-upon industry standards. Open systems are much easier to integrate with systems from different manufacturers that support the same standards.

Closed systems are harder to integrate with unlike systems, but they can be more secure. A closed system often comprises proprietary hardware and software that does not incorporate industry standards. This lack of integration ease means that attacks on many generic system components either will not work or must be customized to be successful. In many cases, attacking a closed system is harder than launching an attack on an open system.

Many software and hardware components with known vulnerabilities may not exist on a closed system. In addition to the lack of known vulnerable components on a closed system, it is often necessary to possess more in-depth knowledge of the specific target system to launch a successful attack.

Open systems are generally far easier to integrate with other open systems. It is easy, for example, to create a LAN with a Microsoft Windows Server machine, a Linux machine, and a Macintosh machine. Although all three computers use different operating systems and could represent up to three different hardware architectures, each supports industry standards and makes it easy for networked (or other) communications to occur. This ease comes at a price, however. Because standard communications components are incorporated into each of these three open systems, there are far more predictable entry points and methods for launching attacks. In general, their openness makes them more vulnerable to attack, and their widespread availability makes it possible for attackers to find (and even to practice on) plenty of potential targets. Also, open systems are more popular than closed systems and attract more attention. An attacker who develops basic attacking skills will find more targets on open systems than on closed ones. This larger "market" of potential targets usually means that there is more emphasis on targeting open systems. Inarguably, there's a greater body of shared experience and knowledge on how to attack open systems than there is for closed systems.

Open Source vs. Close Source

It's also helpful to keep in mind the distinction between open source and closed source systems. An open source solution is one where the source code and other internal logic is exposed to the public. A closed source solution is one where the source code and other internal logic is hidden from the public. Open source solutions often depend on public inspection and review to improve the product over time. Closed source solutions are more dependent on the vendor/programmer to revise the product over time. Both open source and closed source solutions can be available for sale or at no charge, but the term *commercial* typically implies closed source. However, closed source code is often revealed through either vendor compromise or through decompiling. The former is always a breach of ethics and often the law, whereas the latter is a standard element in ethical reverse engineering or systems analysis.

It is also the case that a closed source program can be either an open system or a closed system, and an open source program can be either an open system or a closed system.

Techniques for Ensuring Confidentiality, Integrity, and Availability

To guarantee the confidentiality, integrity, and availability of data, you must ensure that all components that have access to data are secure and well behaved. Software designers use different techniques to ensure that programs do only what is required and nothing more. Suppose a program writes to and reads from an area of memory that is being used by another program. The first program could potentially violate all three security tenets: confidentiality, integrity, and availability. If an affected program is processing sensitive or secret data, that data's confidentiality is no longer guaranteed. If that data is overwritten or altered in an unpredictable way (a common problem when multiple readers and writers inadvertently access the same shared data), there is no guarantee of integrity. And, if data modification results in corruption or outright loss, it could become unavailable for future use. Although the concepts we discuss in the following sections all relate to software programs, they are also commonly used in all areas of security. For example, physical confinement guarantees that all physical access to hardware is controlled.

Confinement

Software designers use process confinement to restrict the actions of a program. Simply put, process *confinement* allows a process to read from and write to only certain memory locations and resources. This is also known as *sandboxing*. The operating system, or some other security component, disallows illegal read/write requests. If a process attempts to initiate an action beyond its granted authority, that action will be denied. In addition, further actions, such as logging the violation attempt, may be taken. Systems that must comply with higher security ratings usually record all violations and respond in some tangible way. Generally, the offending process is terminated. Confinement can be implemented in the operating system itself (such as through process isolation and memory protection), through the use of a confinement application or service (for example, Sandboxie at `www.sandboxie.com`), or through a virtualization or hypervisor solution (such as VMware or Oracle's VirtualBox).

Bounds

Each process that runs on a system is assigned an authority level. The authority level tells the operating system what the process can do. In simple systems, there may be only two authority levels: user and kernel. The authority level tells the operating system how to set the bounds for a process. The *bounds* of a process consist of limits set on the memory addresses and resources it can access. The bounds state the area within which a process is confined or contained. In most systems, these bounds segment logical areas of memory for each process to use. It is the responsibility of the operating system to enforce these logical bounds and to disallow access to other processes. More secure systems may require physically bounded processes. Physical bounds require each bounded process to run in an area of memory that is physically separated from other bounded processes, not just logically bounded in the same memory space. Physically bounded memory can be very expensive, but it's also more secure than logical bounds.

Isolation

When a process is confined through enforcing access bounds, that process runs in *isolation*. Process isolation ensures that any behavior will affect only the memory and resources associated with the isolated process. Isolation is used to protect the operating environment, the kernel of the OS, and other independent applications. Isolation is an essential component of a stable operating system. Isolation is what prevents an application from accessing the memory or resources of another application, whether for good or ill. The operating system may provide intermediary services, such as cut-and-paste and resource sharing (such as the keyboard, network interface, and storage device access).

These three concepts (confinement, bounds, and isolation) make designing secure programs and operating systems more difficult, but they also make it possible to implement more secure systems.

Controls

To ensure the security of a system, you need to allow subjects to access only authorized objects. A *control* uses access rules to limit the access of a subject to an object. Access rules state which objects are valid for each subject. Further, an object might be valid for one type of access and be invalid for another type of access. One common control is for file access. A file can be protected from modification by making it read-only for most users but read-write for a small set of users who have the authority to modify it.

There are both mandatory and discretionary access controls, often called MAC and DAC, respectively. With mandatory controls, static attributes of the subject and the object are considered to determine the permissibility of an access. Each subject possesses attributes that define its clearance, or authority, to access resources. Each object possesses attributes that define its classification. Different types of security methods classify resources in different ways. For example, subject A is granted access to object B if the security system can find a rule that allows a subject with subject A's clearance to access an object with object B's classification. This is called *rule-based access control* (RBAC). The predefined rules state which subjects can access which objects.

Discretionary controls differ from mandatory controls in that the subject has some ability to define the objects to access. Within limits, discretionary access controls allow the subject to define a list of objects to access as needed. This access control list serves as a dynamic access rule set that the subject can modify. The constraints imposed on the modifications often relate to the subject's identity. Based on the identity, the subject may be allowed to add or modify the rules that define access to objects.

Both mandatory and discretionary access controls limit the access to objects by subjects. The primary goal of controls is to ensure the confidentiality and integrity of data by disallowing unauthorized access by authorized or unauthorized subjects.

Trust and Assurance

Proper security concepts, controls, and mechanisms must be integrated before and during the design and architectural period in order to produce a reliably secure product. Security issues should not be added on as an afterthought; this causes oversights, increased costs, and less reliability. Once security is integrated into the design, it must be engineered, implemented, tested, audited, evaluated, certified, and finally accredited.

A *trusted system* is one in which all protection mechanisms work together to process sensitive data for many types of users while maintaining a stable and secure computing environment. *Assurance* is simply defined as the degree of confidence in satisfaction of security needs. Assurance must be continually maintained, updated, and reverified. This is true if the trusted system experiences a known change or if a significant amount of time has passed. In either case, change has occurred at some level. Change is often the antithesis of security; it often diminishes security. So, whenever change occurs, the system needs to be reevaluated to verify that the level of security it provided previously is still intact. Assurance varies from one system to another and must be established on individual systems. However, there are grades or levels of assurance that can be placed across numerous systems of the same type, systems that support the same services, or systems that are deployed in the same geographic location. Thus, trust can be built into a system by implementing specific security features, whereas assurance is an assessment of the reliability and usability of those security features in a real-world situation.

Understand the Fundamental Concepts of Security Models

In information security, models provide a way to formalize security policies. Such models can be abstract or intuitive (some are decidedly mathematical), but all are intended to provide an explicit set of rules that a computer can follow to implement the fundamental security concepts, processes, and procedures that make up a security policy. These models offer a way to deepen your understanding of how a computer operating system should be designed and developed to support a specific security policy.

A security model provides a way for designers to map abstract statements into a security policy that prescribes the algorithms and data structures necessary to build hardware and software. Thus, a security model gives software designers something against which to measure their design and implementation. That model, of course, must support each part of the security policy. In this way, developers can be sure their security implementation supports the security policy.

Tokens, Capabilities, and Labels

Several different methods are used to describe the necessary security attributes for an object. A security *token* is a separate object that is associated with a resource and describes its security attributes. This token can communicate security information about an object prior to requesting access to the actual object. In other implementations, various lists are used to store security information about multiple objects. A *capabilities list* maintains a row of security attributes for each controlled object. Although not as flexible as the token approach, capabilities lists generally offer quicker lookups when a subject requests access to an object. A third common type of attribute storage is called a *security label*, which is generally a permanent part of the object to which it's attached. Once a security label is set, it usually cannot be altered. This permanence provides another safeguard against tampering that neither tokens nor capabilities lists provide.

You'll explore several security models in the following sections; all of them can shed light on how security enters into computer architectures and operating system design:

- Trusted computing base
- State machine model
- Information flow model
- Noninterference model
- Take-Grant model
- Access control matrix
- Bell-LaPadula model
- Biba model
- Clark-Wilson model
- Brewer and Nash model (also known as Chinese Wall)
- Goguen-Meseguer model
- Sutherland model
- Graham-Denning model

Although no system can be totally secure, it is possible to design and build reasonably secure systems. In fact, if a secured system complies with a specific set of security criteria, it can be said to exhibit a level of trust. Therefore, trust can be built into a system and then evaluated, certified, and accredited. But before we can discuss each security model, we have to establish a foundation on which most security models are built. This foundation is the trusted computing base.

Trusted Computing Base

An old US Department of Defense standard known colloquially as the Orange Book (DoD Standard 5200.28, covered in more detail later in this chapter in the section "Rainbow Series") describes a *trusted computing base* (TCB) as a combination of hardware, software, and controls that work together to form a trusted base to enforce your security policy. The TCB is a subset of a complete information system. It should be as small as possible so that a detailed analysis can reasonably ensure that the system meets design specifications and requirements. The TCB is the only portion of that system that can be trusted to adhere to and enforce the security policy. It is not necessary that every component of a system be trusted. But any time you consider a system from a security standpoint, your evaluation should include all trusted components that define that system's TCB.

In general, TCB components in a system are responsible for controlling access to the system. The TCB must provide methods to access resources both inside and outside the TCB itself. TCB components commonly restrict the activities of components outside the TCB. It is the responsibility of TCB components to ensure that a system behaves properly in all cases and that it adheres to the security policy under all circumstances.

Security Perimeter

The *security perimeter* of your system is an imaginary boundary that separates the TCB from the rest of the system (Figure 8.1). This boundary ensures that no insecure communications or interactions occur between the TCB and the remaining elements of the computer system. For the TCB to communicate with the rest of the system, it must create secure channels, also called *trusted paths*. A trusted path is a channel established with strict standards to allow necessary communication to occur without exposing the TCB to security vulnerabilities. A trusted path also protects system users (sometimes known as *subjects*) from compromise as a result of a TCB interchange. As you learn more about formal security guidelines and evaluation criteria later in this chapter, you'll also learn that trusted paths are required in systems that seek to deliver high levels of security to their users. According to the TCSEC guidelines, trusted paths are required for high trust level systems such as those at level B2 or higher of TCSEC.

FIGURE 8.1 The TCB, security perimeter, and reference monitor

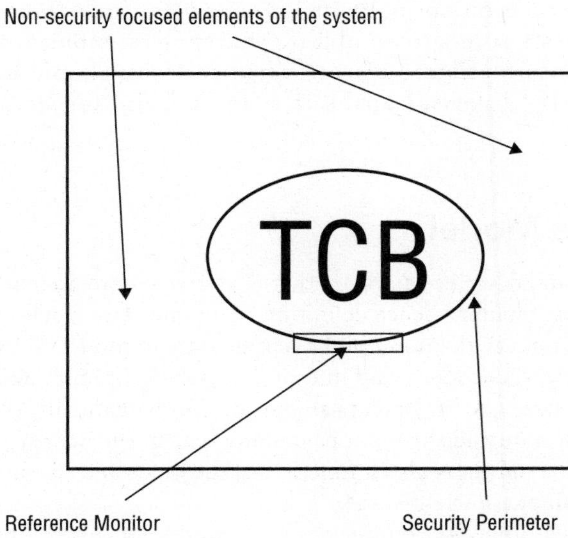

Reference Monitors and Kernels

When the time comes to implement a secure system, it's essential to develop some part of the TCB to enforce access controls on system assets and resources (sometimes known as *objects*). The part of the TCB that validates access to every resource prior to granting access requests is called the *reference monitor* (Figure 8.1). The reference monitor stands between every subject and object, verifying that a requesting subject's credentials meet the object's access requirements before any requests are allowed to proceed. If such access requirements aren't met, access requests are turned down. Effectively, the reference monitor is the access control enforcer for the TCB. Thus, authorized and secured actions and activities are allowed to occur, whereas unauthorized and insecure activities and actions are denied and blocked from occurring. The reference monitor enforces access control or authorization based the desired security model, whether discretionary, mandatory, role-based, or some other form of access control. The reference monitor may be a conceptual part of the TCB; it doesn't need to be an actual, stand-alone, or independent working system component.

The collection of components in the TCB that work together to implement reference monitor functions is called the *security kernel*. The reference monitor is a concept or theory that is put into practice via the implementation of a security kernel in software and hardware. The purpose of the security kernel is to launch appropriate components to enforce reference monitor functionality and resist all known attacks. The security kernel uses a trusted path to communicate with subjects. It also mediates all resource access requests, granting only those requests that match the appropriate access rules in use for a system.

The reference monitor requires descriptive information about each resource that it protects. Such information normally includes its classification and designation. When a subject requests access to an object, the reference monitor consults the object's descriptive information to discern whether access should be granted or denied (see the sidebar "Tokens, Capabilities, and Labels" for more information on how this works).

State Machine Model

The *state machine model* describes a system that is always secure no matter what state it is in. It's based on the computer science definition of a finite state machine (FSM). An FSM combines an external input with an internal machine state to model all kinds of complex systems, including parsers, decoders, and interpreters. Given an input and a state, an FSM transitions to another state and may create an output. Mathematically, the next state is a function of the current state and the input next state; that is, the next state = F(input, current state). Likewise, the output is also a function of the input and the current state output; that is, the output = F(input, current state).

Many security models are based on the secure state concept. According to the state machine model, a *state* is a snapshot of a system at a specific moment in time. If all aspects of a state meet the requirements of the security policy, that state is considered secure. A transition occurs when accepting input or producing output. A transition always results in a new state (also called a *state transition*). All state transitions must be evaluated. If each possible state transition results in another secure state, the system can be called a *secure state machine*. A secure state machine model system always boots into a secure state, maintains a secure state across all transitions, and allows subjects to access resources only in a secure manner compliant with the security policy. The secure state machine model is the basis for many other security models.

Information Flow Model

The *information flow model* focuses on the flow of information. Information flow models are based on a state machine model. The Bell-LaPadula and Biba models, which we will discuss in detail later in this chapter, are both information flow models. Bell-LaPadula is concerned with preventing information flow from a high security level to a low security level. Biba is concerned with preventing information flow from a low security level to a high security level. Information flow models don't necessarily deal with only the direction of information flow; they can also address the type of flow.

Information flow models are designed to prevent unauthorized, insecure, or restricted information flow, often between different levels of security (these are often referred to as multilevel models). Information flow can be between subjects and objects at the same classification level as well as between subjects and objects at different classification levels. An information flow model allows all authorized information flows, whether within the same classification level or between classification levels. It prevents all unauthorized information flows, whether within the same classification level or between classification levels.

Another interesting perspective on the information flow model is that it is used to establish a relationship between two versions or states of the same object when those two versions or states exist at different points in time. Thus, information flow dictates the transformation of an object from one state at one point in time to another state at another point in time. The information flow model also addresses covert channels by specifically excluding all nondefined flow pathways.

Noninterference Model

The *noninterference model* is loosely based on the information flow model. However, instead of being concerned about the flow of information, the noninterference model is concerned with how the actions of a subject at a higher security level affect the system state or the actions of a subject at a lower security level. Basically, the actions of subject A (high) should not affect the actions of subject B (low) or even be noticed by subject B. The real concern is to prevent the actions of subject A at a high level of security classification from affecting the system state at a lower level. If this occurs, subject B may be placed into an insecure state or be able to deduce or infer information about a higher level of classification. This is a type of information leakage and implicitly creates a covert channel. Thus, the noninterference model can be imposed to provide a form of protection against damage caused by malicious programs such as Trojan horses.

Real World Scenario

Composition Theories

Some other models that fall into the information flow category build on the notion of how inputs and outputs between multiple systems relate to one another—which follows how information flows between systems rather than within an individual system. These are called *composition theories* because they explain how outputs from one system relate to inputs to another system. There are three recognized types of composition theories:

- *Cascading*: Input for one system comes from the output of another system.
- *Feedback*: One system provides input to another system, which reciprocates by reversing those roles (so that system A first provides input for system B and then system B provides input to system A).
- *Hookup*: One system sends input to another system but also sends input to external entities.

Take-Grant Model

The *Take-Grant model* employs a directed graph (Figure 8.2) to dictate how rights can be passed from one subject to another or from a subject to an object. Simply put, a subject with the grant right can grant another subject or another object any other right they possess. Likewise, a subject with the take right can take a right from another subject. In addition to these two primary rules, the Take-Grant model may adopt a create rule and a remove rule to generate or delete rights. The key to this model is that using these rules allows you to figure out when rights in the system can change and where leakage (that is, unintentional distribution of permissions) can occur.

Take rule	Allows a subject to take rights over an object
Grant rule	Allows a subject to grant rights to an object
Create rule	Allows a subject to create new rights
Remove rule	Allows a subject to remove rights it has

Access Control Matrix

An *access control matrix* is a table of subjects and objects that indicates the actions or functions that each subject can perform on each object. Each column of the matrix is an access control list (ACL). Each row of the matrix is a *capabilities list*. An ACL is tied to the object; it lists valid actions each subject can perform. A capability list is tied to the subject; it lists valid actions that can be taken on each object. From an administration perspective, using only capability lists for access control is a management nightmare. A capability list method of access control can be accomplished by storing on each subject a list of rights the subject has for every object. This effectively gives each user a key ring of accesses and rights to objects within the security domain. To remove access to a particular object, every user (subject) that has access to it must be individually manipulated. Thus, managing access on each user account is much more difficult than managing access on each object (in other words, via ACLs).

FIGURE 8.2 The Take Grant model's directed graph

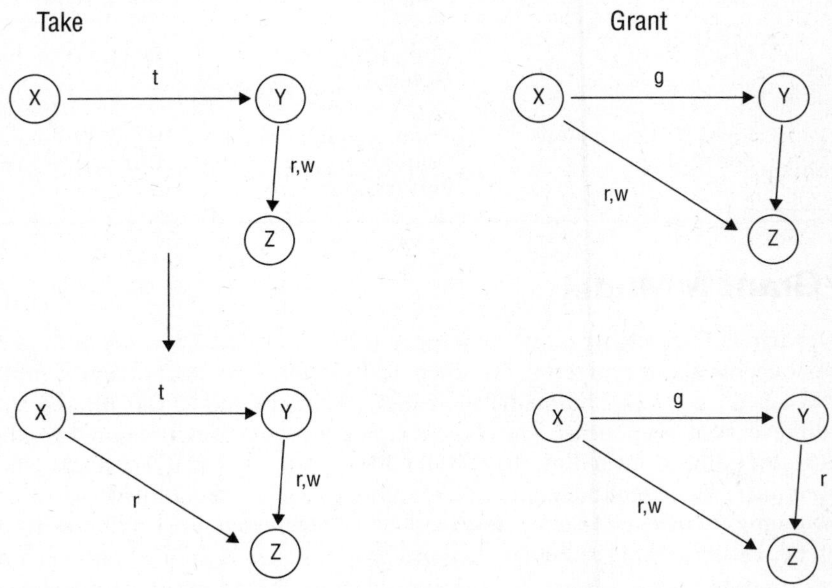

- Implementing an access control matrix model usually involves the following: Constructing an environment that can create and manage lists of subjects and objects
- Crafting a function that can return the type associated with whatever object is supplied to that function as input (this is important because an object's type determines what kind of operations may be applied to it)

The access control matrix shown in Table 8.1 is for a discretionary access control system. A mandatory or rule-based matrix can be constructed simply by replacing the subject names with classifications or roles. Access control matrixes are used by systems to quickly determine whether the requested action by a subject for an object is authorized.

TABLE 8.1 An access control matrix

Subjects	Document File	Printer	Network Folder Share
Bob	Read	No Access	No Access
Mary	No Access	No Access	Read
Amanda	Read, Write	Print	No Access

TABLE 8.1 An access control matrix *(continued)*

Subjects	Document File	Printer	Network Folder Share
Mark	Read, Write	Print	Read, Write
Kathryn	Read, Write	Print, Manage Print Queue	Read, Write, Execute
Colin	Read, Write, Change Permissions	Print, Manage Print Queue, Change Permissions	Read, Write, Execute, Change Permissions

Bell-LaPadula Model

The US Department of Defense (DoD) developed the *Bell-LaPadula model* in the 1970s to address concerns about protecting classified information. The DoD manages multiple levels of classified resources, and the Bell-LaPadula multilevel model was derived from the DoD's multilevel security policies. The classifications the DoD uses are numerous; however, discussions of classifications within the CISSP CBK are usually limited to unclassified, sensitive but unclassified, confidential, secret, and top secret. The multilevel security policy states that a subject with any level of clearance can access resources at or below its clearance level. However, within the higher clearance levels, access is granted only on a need-to-know basis. In other words, access to a specific object is granted to the classified levels only if a specific work task requires such access. For example, any person with a secret security clearance can access secret, confidential, sensitive but unclassified, and unclassified documents but not top-secret documents. Also, to access a document within the secret level, the person seeking access must also have a need to know for that document.

By design, the Bell-LaPadula model prevents the leaking or transfer of classified information to less secure clearance levels. This is accomplished by blocking lower-classified subjects from accessing higher-classified objects. With these restrictions, the Bell-LaPadula model is focused on maintaining the confidentiality of objects. Thus, the complexities involved in ensuring the confidentiality of documents are addressed in the Bell-LaPadula model. However, Bell-LaPadula does not address the aspects of integrity or availability for objects. Bell-LaPadula is also the first mathematical model of a multilevel security policy.

Real World Scenario

Lattice-Based Access Control

This general category for nondiscretionary access controls is covered in Chapter 13, "Managing Identity and Authentication." Here's a quick preview on that more detailed coverage of this subject (which drives the underpinnings for most access control security models): Subjects under lattice-based access controls are assigned positions in a lattice. These positions fall between defined security labels or classifications. Subjects can access only those objects that fall into the range between the least upper bound (the nearest security label or classification higher than their lattice position) and the highest lower bound (the nearest security label or classification lower than their lattice position) of the labels or classifications for their lattice position. Thus, a subject that falls between the private and sensitive labels in a commercial scheme that reads bottom up as public, sensitive, private, proprietary, and confidential can access only public and sensitive data but not private, proprietary, or confidential data. Lattice-based access controls also fit into the general category of information flow models and deal primarily with confidentiality (that's the reason for the connection to Bell-LaPadula).

This model is built on a state machine concept and the information flow model. It also employs mandatory access controls and the lattice concept. The lattice tiers are the *classification levels* used by the security policy of the organization. The state machine supports multiple states with explicit transitions between any two states; this concept is used because the correctness of the machine, and guarantees of document confidentiality, can be proven mathematically. There are three basic properties of this state machine:

- The *Simple Security Property* states that a subject may not read information at a higher sensitivity level (no read up).
- The ** (star) Security Property* states that a subject may not write information to an object at a lower sensitivity level (no write down). This is also known as the *Confinement Property*.
- The *Discretionary Security Property* states that the system uses an access matrix to enforce discretionary access control.

These first two properties define the states into which the system can transition. No other transitions are allowed. All states accessible through these two rules are secure states. Thus, Bell-LaPadula–modeled systems offer state machine model security (see Figure 8.3).

FIGURE 8.3 The Bell-LaPadula model

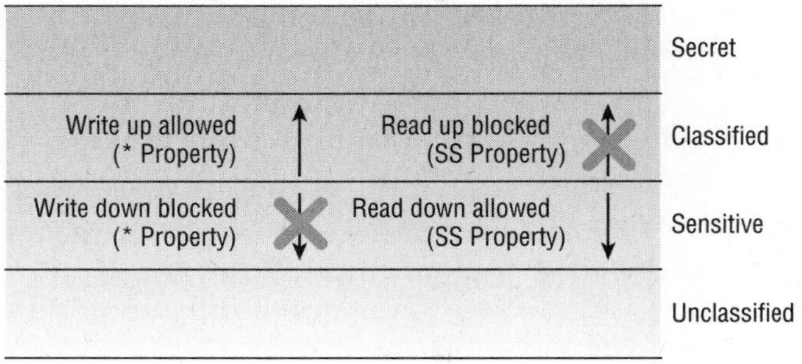

NOTE An exception in the Bell-LaPadula model states that a "trusted subject" is not constrained by the * Security Property. A trusted subject is defined as "a subject that is guaranteed not to consummate a security-breaching information transfer even if it is possible." This means that a trusted subject is allowed to violate the * Security Property and perform a write-down, which is necessary when performing valid object declassification or reclassification.

The Bell-LaPadula properties are in place to protect data confidentiality. A subject cannot read an object that is classified at a higher level than the subject is cleared for. Because objects at one level have data that is more sensitive or secret than data in objects at a lower level, a subject (who is not a trusted subject) cannot write data from one level to an object at a lower level. That action would be similar to pasting a top-secret memo into an unclassified document file. The third property enforces a subject's need to know in order to access an object.

The Bell-LaPadula model addresses only the confidentiality of data. It does not address its integrity or availability. Because it was designed in the 1970s, it does not support many operations that are common today, such as file sharing and networking. It also assumes secure transitions between security layers and does not address covert channels (covered in Chapter 9, "Security Vulnerabilities, Threats, and Countermeasures"). Bell-LaPadula does handle confidentiality well, so it is often used in combination with other models that provide mechanisms to handle integrity and availability.

Biba Model

For many nonmilitary organizations, integrity is more important than confidentiality. Out of this need, several integrity-focused security models were developed, such as those developed by Biba and by Clark-Wilson. The *Biba model* was designed after the Bell-LaPadula model. Where the Bell-LaPadula model addresses confidentiality, the Biba model addresses integrity. The Biba model is also built on a state machine concept, is based on information flow, and is a multilevel model. In fact, Biba appears to be pretty similar to the Bell-LaPadula model, except inverted. Both use states and transitions. Both have basic properties. The biggest difference is their primary focus: Biba primarily protects data integrity. Here are the basic properties or axioms of the Biba model state machine:

- The *Simple Integrity Property* states that a subject cannot read an object at a lower integrity level (no read-down).
- The ** (star) Integrity Property* states that a subject cannot modify an object at a higher integrity level (no write-up).

NOTE In both the Biba and Bell-LaPadula models, there are two properties that are inverses of each other: simple and * (star). However, they may also be labeled as axioms, principles, or rules. What you should focus on is the *simple* and *star* designations. Take note that *simple* is always about reading, and *star* is always about writing. Also, in both cases, simple and star are rules that define what cannot or should not be done. In most cases, what is not prevented or disallowed is supported or allowed.

Figure 8.4 illustrates these Biba model axioms.

FIGURE 8.4 The Biba model

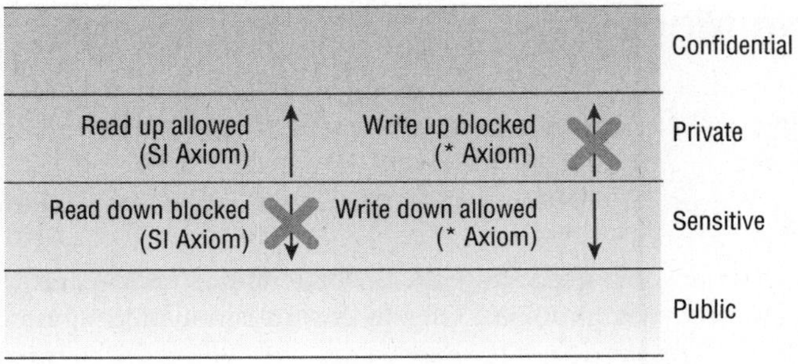

When you compare Biba to Bell-LaPadula, you will notice that they look like they are opposites. That's because they focus on different areas of security. Where the Bell-LaPadula model ensures data confidentiality, Biba ensures data integrity.

Biba was designed to address three integrity issues:

- Prevent modification of objects by unauthorized subjects.
- Prevent unauthorized modification of objects by authorized subjects.
- Protect internal and external object consistency.

As with Bell-LaPadula, Biba requires that all subjects and objects have a classification label. Thus, data integrity protection is dependent on data classification.

Consider the Biba properties. The second property of the Biba model is pretty straightforward. A subject cannot write to an object at a higher integrity level. That makes sense. What about the first property? Why can't a subject read an object at a lower integrity level? The answer takes a little thought. Think of integrity levels as being like the purity level of air. You would not want to pump air from the smoking section into the clean room environment. The same applies to data. When integrity is important, you do not want unvalidated data read into validated documents. The potential for data contamination is too great to permit such access.

Critiques of the Biba model reveal a few drawbacks:

- It addresses only integrity, not confidentiality or availability.
- It focuses on protecting objects from external threats; it assumes that internal threats are handled programmatically.
- It does not address access control management, and it doesn't provide a way to assign or change an object's or subject's classification level.
- It does not prevent covert channels.

Because the Biba model focuses on data integrity, it is a more common choice for commercial security models than the Bell-LaPadula model. Most commercial organizations are more concerned with the integrity of their data than its confidentiality.

Clark-Wilson Model

Although the Biba model works in commercial applications, another model was designed in 1987 specifically for the commercial environment. The *Clark-Wilson model* uses a multifaceted approach to enforcing data integrity. Instead of defining a formal state machine, the Clark-Wilson model defines each data item and allows modifications through only a small set of programs.

The Clark-Wilson model does not require the use of a lattice structure; rather, it uses a three-part relationship of subject/program/object (or subject/transaction/object) known as a *triple* or an *access control triple*. Subjects do not have direct access to objects. Objects can be accessed only through programs. Through the use of two principles—well-formed transactions and separation of duties—the Clark-Wilson model provides an effective means to protect integrity.

Well-formed transactions take the form of programs. A subject is able to access objects only by using a program, interface, or access portal (Figure 8.5). Each program has specific limitations on what it can and cannot do to an object (such as a database or other resource). This effectively limits the subject's capabilities. This is known as a constrained interface. If the programs are properly designed, then the triple relationship provides a means to protect the integrity of the object.

FIGURE 8.5 The Clark-Wilson model

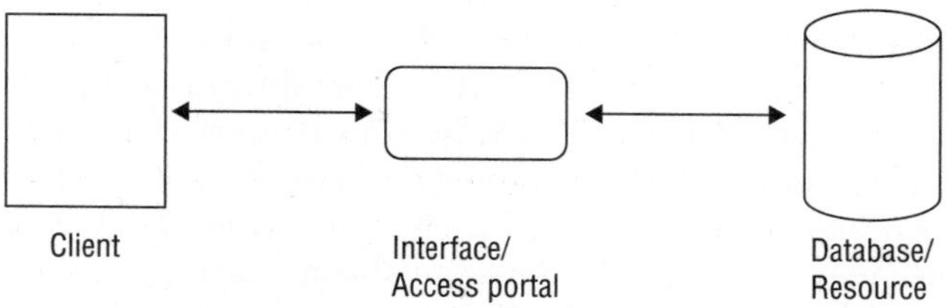

Clark-Wilson defines the following items and procedures:

- A constrained data item (CDI) is any data item whose integrity is protected by the security model.

- An unconstrained data item (UDI) is any data item that is not controlled by the security model. Any data that is to be input and hasn't been validated, or any output, would be considered an unconstrained data item.
- An integrity verification procedure (IVP) is a procedure that scans data items and confirms their integrity.
- Transformation procedures (TPs) are the only procedures that are allowed to modify a CDI. The limited access to CDIs through TPs forms the backbone of the Clark-Wilson integrity model. (We wonder whether this is where TPS reports come from...see the movie *Office Space*.)

The Clark-Wilson model uses security labels to grant access to objects, but only through transformation procedures and a *restricted interface model*. A restricted interface model uses classification-based restrictions to offer only subject-specific authorized information and functions. One subject at one classification level will see one set of data and have access to one set of functions, whereas another subject at a different classification level will see a different set of data and have access to a different set of functions. The different functions made available to different levels or classes of users may be implemented by either showing all functions to all users but disabling those that are not authorized for a specific user or by showing only those functions granted to a specific user. Through these mechanisms, the Clark-Wilson model ensures that data is protected from unauthorized changes from any user. In effect, the Clark-Wilson model enforces separation of duties. The Clark-Wilson design makes it a good model for commercial applications.

Brewer and Nash Model (aka Chinese Wall)

This model was created to permit access controls to change dynamically based on a user's previous activity (making it a kind of state machine model as well). This model applies to a single integrated database; it seeks to create security domains that are sensitive to the notion of conflict of interest (for example, someone who works at Company C who has access to proprietary data for Company A should not also be allowed access to similar data for Company B if those two companies compete with each other). This model is known as the *Chinese Wall* because it creates a class of data that defines which security domains are potentially in conflict and prevents any subject with access to one domain that belongs to a specific conflict class from accessing any other domain that belongs to the same conflict class. Metaphorically, this puts a wall around all other information in any conflict class. Thus, this model also uses the principle of data isolation within each conflict class to keep users out of potential conflict-of-interest situations (for example, management of company datasets). Because company relationships change all the time, dynamic updates to members of and definitions for conflict classes are important.

Another way of looking at or thinking of the Brewer and Nash model is of an administrator having full control access to a wide range of data in a system based on their assigned job responsibilities and work tasks. However, at the moment an action is taken against any data item, the administrator's access to any conflicting data items is temporarily blocked. Only data items that relate to the initial data item can be accessed during the operation. Once the task is completed, the administrator's access returns to full control.

Goguen-Meseguer Model

The Goguen-Meseguer model is an integrity model, although not as well known as Biba and the others. In fact, this model is said to be the foundation of noninterference conceptual theories. Often when someone refers to a noninterference model, they are actually referring to the Goguen-Meseguer model.

The Goguen-Meseguer model is based on predetermining the set or domain—a list of objects that a subject can access. This model is based on automation theory and domain separation. This means subjects are allowed only to perform predetermined actions against predetermined objects. When similar users are grouped into their own domain (that is, collective), the members of one subject domain cannot interfere with the members of another subject domain. Thus, subjects are unable to interfere with each other's activities.

Sutherland Model

The Sutherland model is an integrity model. It focuses on preventing interference in support of integrity. It is formally based on the state machine model and the information flow model. However, it does not directly indicate specific mechanisms for protection of integrity. Instead, the model is based on the idea of defining a set of system states, initial states, and state transitions. Through the use of only these predetermined secure states, integrity is maintained and interference is prohibited.

A common example of the Sutherland model is its use to prevent a covert channel from being used to influence the outcome of a process or activity. (For a discussion of covert channels, see Chapter 9.)

Graham-Denning Model

The Graham-Denning model is focused on the secure creation and deletion of both subjects and objects. Graham-Denning is a collection of eight primary protection rules or actions that define the boundaries of certain secure actions:

- Securely create an object.
- Securely create a subject.
- Securely delete an object.
- Securely delete a subject.
- Securely provide the read access right.
- Securely provide the grant access right.
- Securely provide the delete access right.
- Securely provide the transfer access right.

Usually the specific abilities or permissions of a subject over a set of objects is defined in an access matrix (aka access control matrix).

Select Controls and Countermeasures Based on Systems Security Evaluation Models

Those who purchase information systems for certain kinds of applications—think, for example, about national security agencies where sensitive information may be extremely valuable (or dangerous in the wrong hands) or central banks or securities traders where certain data may be worth billions of dollars—often want to understand their security strengths and weaknesses. Such buyers are often willing to consider only systems that have been subjected to formal evaluation processes in advance and have received some kind of security rating. Buyers want to know what they're buying and, usually, what steps they must take to keep such systems as secure as possible.

When formal evaluations are undertaken, systems are usually subjected to a two-step process:

1. The system is tested and a technical evaluation is performed to make sure that the system's security capabilities meet criteria laid out for its intended use.
2. The system is subjected to a formal comparison of its design and security criteria and its actual capabilities and performance, and individuals responsible for the security and veracity of such systems must decide whether to adopt them, reject them, or make some changes to their criteria and try again.

Often trusted third parties are hired to perform such evaluations; the most important result from such testing is their "seal of approval" that the system meets all essential criteria.

Regardless of whether the evaluations are conducted inside an organization or out of house, the adopting organization must decide to accept or reject the proposed systems. An organization's management must take formal responsibility if and when a system is adopted and be willing to accept any risks associated with its deployment and use.

The three main product evaluation models or classification criteria models addressed here are TCSEC, ITSEC, and Common Criteria.

NOTE You should be aware that TCSEC was repealed and replaced by the Common Criteria (as well as many other DoD directives). It is still included here as a historical reference and as an example of static-based assessment criteria to offset the benefits of dynamic (although subjective) assessment criteria. Keep in mind that the CISSP exam focuses on the "why" of security more than the "how"—in other words, it focuses on the concepts and theories more than the technologies and implementations. Thus, some of this historical information could be present in questions on the exam.

Rainbow Series

Since the 1980s, governments, agencies, institutions, and business organizations of all kinds have faced the risks involved in adopting and using information systems. This led to a historical series of information security standards that attempted to specify minimum acceptable security criteria for various categories of use. Such categories were important as purchasers attempted to obtain and deploy systems that would protect and preserve their contents or that would meet various mandated security requirements (such as those that contractors must routinely meet to conduct business with the government). The first such set of standards resulted in the creation of the Trusted Computer System Evaluation Criteria (TCSEC) in the 1980s, as the US Department of Defense (DoD) worked to develop and impose security standards for the systems it purchased and used. In turn, this led to a whole series of such publications through the mid-1990s. Since these publications were routinely identified by the color of their covers, they are known collectively as the *rainbow series*.

Following in the DoD's footsteps, other governments or standards bodies created computer security standards that built and improved on the rainbow series elements. Significant standards in this group include a European model called the Information Technology Security Evaluation Criteria (ITSEC), which was developed in 1990 and used through 1998. Eventually TCSEC and ITSEC were replaced with the so-called Common Criteria, adopted by the United States, Canada, France, Germany, and the United Kingdom in 1998 but more formally known as the "Arrangement on the Recognition of Common Criteria Certificates in the Field of IT Security." Both ITSEC and the Common Criteria will be discussed in later sections.

When governments or other security-conscious agencies evaluate information systems, they make use of various standard evaluation criteria. In 1985, the National Computer Security Center (NCSC) developed the TCSEC, usually called the Orange Book because of the color of this publication's covers. The TCSEC established guidelines to be used when evaluating a stand-alone computer from the security perspective. These guidelines address basic security functionality and allow evaluators to measure and rate a system's functionality and trustworthiness. In the TSCEC, in fact, functionality and security assurance are combined and not separated as they are in security criteria developed later. TCSEC guidelines were designed to be used when evaluating vendor products or by vendors to ensure that they build all necessary functionality and security assurance into new products.

Next, we'll take a look at some of the details in the Orange Book itself and then talk about some of the other important elements in the rainbow series.

TCSEC Classes and Required Functionality

TCSEC combines the functionality and assurance rating of the confidentiality protection offered by a system into four major categories. These categories are then subdivided into additional subcategories identified with numbers, such as C1 and C2. Furthermore, TCSEC's categories are assigned through the evaluation of a target system. Applicable systems are stand-alone systems that are not networked. TCSEC defines the following major categories:

Category A Verified protection. The highest level of security.

Category B Mandatory protection.

Category C Discretionary protection.

Category D Minimal protection. Reserved for systems that have been evaluated but do not meet requirements to belong to any other category.

The list that follows includes brief discussions of categories A through C, along with numeric suffixes that represent any applicable subcategories (Figure 8.6).

FIGURE 8.6 The levels of TCSEC

Level Label	Requirements
D	Minimal Protection
C1	Discretionary Protection
C2	Controlled Access Protection
B1	Labeled Security
B2	Structured Protection
B3	Security Domains
A1	Verified Protection

Discretionary Protection (Categories C1, C2) Discretionary protection systems provide basic access control. Systems in this category do provide some security controls but are lacking in more sophisticated and stringent controls that address specific needs for secure systems. C1 and C2 systems provide basic controls and complete documentation for system installation and configuration.

Discretionary Security Protection (C1) A discretionary security protection system controls access by user IDs and/or groups. Although there are some controls in place that limit object access, systems in this category provide only weak protection.

Controlled Access Protection (C2) Controlled access protection systems are stronger than C1 systems. Users must be identified individually to gain access to objects. C2 systems must also enforce media cleansing. With media cleansing, any media that are reused by another user must first be thoroughly cleansed so that no remnant of the previous data remains available for inspection or use. Additionally, strict logon procedures must be enforced that restrict access for invalid or unauthorized users.

Mandatory Protection (Categories B1, B2, B3) Mandatory protection systems provide more security controls than category C or D systems. More granularity of control is mandated, so security administrators can apply specific controls that allow only very limited sets of subject/object access. This category of systems is based on the Bell-LaPadula model. Mandatory access is based on security labels.

Labeled Security (B1) In a labeled security system, each subject and each object has a security label. A B1 system grants access by matching up the subject and object labels and comparing their permission compatibility. B1 systems support sufficient security to house classified data.

Structured Protection (B2) In addition to the requirement for security labels (as in B1 systems), B2 systems must ensure that no covert channels exist. Operator and administrator functions are separated, and process isolation is maintained. B2 systems are sufficient for classified data that requires more security functionality than a B1 system can deliver.

Security Domains (B3) Security domain systems provide more secure functionality by further increasing the separation and isolation of unrelated processes. Administration functions are clearly defined and separate from functions available to other users. The focus of B3 systems shifts to simplicity to reduce any exposure to vulnerabilities in unused or extra code. The secure state of B3 systems must also be addressed during the initial boot process. B3 systems are difficult to attack successfully and provide sufficient secure controls for very sensitive or secret data.

Verified Protection (Category A1) Verified protection systems are similar to B3 systems in the structure and controls they employ. The difference is in the development cycle. Each phase of the development cycle is controlled using formal methods. Each phase of the design is documented, evaluated, and verified before the next step is taken. This forces extreme security consciousness during all steps of development and deployment and is the only way to formally guarantee strong system security.

A verified design system starts with a design document that states how the resulting system will satisfy the security policy. From there, each development step is evaluated in the context of the security policy. Functionality is crucial, but assurance becomes more important than in lower security categories. A1 systems represent the top level of security and are designed to handle top-secret data. Every step is documented and verified, from the design all the way through to delivery and installation.

Other Colors in the Rainbow Series

Altogether, there are nearly 30 titles in the collection of DoD documents that either add to or further elaborate on the Orange Book. Although the colors don't necessarily mean anything, they're used to identify publications in this series.

NOTE

It is important to understand that most of the books in the rainbow series are now outdated and have been replaced by updated standards, guidelines, and directives. However, they are still included here for reference to address any exam items.

Other important elements in this collection of documents include the following:

Red Book Because the Orange Book applies only to stand-alone computers not attached to a network, and so many systems were used on networks (even in the 1980s), the Red Book was developed to interpret the TCSEC in a networking context. In fact, the official title of the Red Book is ***Trusted Network Interpretation of the TCSEC*** so it could be considered an interpretation of the Orange Book with a bent on networking. Quickly the Red Book became more relevant and important to system buyers and builders than the Orange Book. The following list includes a few other functions of the Red Book:

- Rates confidentiality and integrity
- Addresses communications integrity
- Addresses denial of service protection
- Addresses compromise (in other words, intrusion) protection and prevention
- Is restricted to a limited class of networks that are labeled as "centralized networks with a single accreditation authority"
- Uses only four rating levels: None, C1 (Minimum), C2 (Fair), and B2 (Good)

Green Book The Green Book, or the *Department of Defense Password Management Guidelines*, provides password creation and management guidelines; it's important for those who configure and manage trusted systems.

Table 8.2 has a more complete list of books in the rainbow series. For more information and to download the books, see the Rainbow Series web page here:

`http://csrc.nist.gov/publications/secpubs/index.html`

TABLE 8.2 Important rainbow series elements

Publication Number	Title	Book name
5200.28-STD	*DoD Trusted Computer System Evaluation Criteria*	Orange Book
CSC-STD-002-85	*DoD Password Management Guidelines*	Green Book
CSC-STD-003-85	*Guidance for Applying TCSEC in Specific Environments*	Yellow Book
NCSC-TG-001	*A Guide to Understanding Audit in Trusted Systems*	Tan Book
NCSC-TG-002	*Trusted Product Evaluation: A Guide for Vendors*	Bright Blue Book
NCSC-TG-002-85	*PC Security Considerations*	Light Blue Book

TABLE 8.2 Important rainbow series elements *(continued)*

Publication Number	Title	Book name
NCSC-TG-003	*A Guide to Understanding Discretionary Access Controls in Trusted Systems*	Neon Orange Book
NCSC-TG-004	*Glossary of Computer Security Terms*	Aqua Book
NCSC-TG-005	*Trusted Network Interpretation*	Red Book
NCSC-TG-006	*A Guide to Understanding Configuration Management in Trusted Systems*	Amber Book
NCSC-TG-007	*A Guide to Understanding Design Documentation in Trusted Systems*	Burgundy Book
NCSC-TG-008	*A Guide to Understanding Trusted Distribution in Trusted Systems*	Lavender Book
NCSC-TG-009	*Computer Security Subsystem Interpretation of the TCSEC*	Venice Blue Book

Given all the time and effort that went into formulating the TCSEC, it's not unreasonable to wonder why evaluation criteria have evolved to newer, more advanced standards. The relentless march of time and technology aside, these are the major critiques of TCSEC; they help to explain why newer standards are now in use worldwide:

- Although the TCSEC puts considerable emphasis on controlling user access to information, it doesn't exercise control over what users do with information once access is granted. This can be a problem in military and commercial applications alike.
- Given the origins of evaluation standards at the US Department of Defense, it's understandable that the TCSEC focuses its concerns entirely on confidentiality, which assumes that controlling how users access data is of primary importance and that concerns about data accuracy or integrity are irrelevant. This doesn't work in commercial environments where concerns about data accuracy and integrity can be more important than concerns about confidentiality.
- Outside the evaluation standards' own emphasis on access controls, the TCSEC does not carefully address the kinds of personnel, physical, and procedural policy matters or safeguards that must be exercised to fully implement security policy. They don't deal much with how such matters can impact system security either.
- The Orange Book, per se, doesn't deal with networking issues (though the Red Book, developed later in 1987, does).

To some extent, these criticisms reflect the unique security concerns of the military, which developed the TCSEC. Then, too, the prevailing computing tools and technologies widely available at the time (networking was just getting started in 1985) had an impact as well. Certainly, an increasingly sophisticated and holistic view of security within organizations helps to explain why and where the TCSEC also fell short, procedurally and policy-wise. But because ITSEC has been largely superseded by the Common Criteria, coverage in the next section explains ITSEC as a step along the way toward the Common Criteria (covered in the section after that).

ITSEC Classes and Required Assurance and Functionality

The ITSEC represents an initial attempt to create security evaluation criteria in Europe. It was developed as an alternative to the TCSEC guidelines. The ITSEC guidelines evaluate the functionality and assurance of a system using separate ratings for each category. In this context, a system's functionality is a measurement of the system's utility value for users. The functionality rating of a system states how well the system performs all necessary functions based on its design and intended purpose. The assurance rating represents the degree of confidence that the system will work properly in a consistent manner.

ITSEC refers to any system being evaluated as a target of evaluation (TOE). All ratings are expressed as TOE ratings in two categories. ITSEC uses two scales to rate functionality and assurance.

The functionality of a system is rated from F-D through F-B3 (there is no F-A1). The assurance of a system is rated from E0 through E6. Most ITSEC ratings generally correspond with TCSEC ratings (for example, a TCSEC C1 system corresponds to an ITSEC F-C1, E1 system). See Table 8.4 (at the end of the section "Structure of the Common Criteria") for a comparison of TCSEC, ITSEC, and Common Criteria ratings.

NOTE There are some instances where the F ratings of ITSEC are defined using F1 through F5 rather than reusing the labels from TCSEC. These alternate labels are F1 = F-C1, F2 = F-C2, F3 = F-B1, F4 = F-B2, and F5 = F-B3. There is no numbered F rating for F-D, but there are a few cases where F0 is used. This is a fairly ridiculous label because if there are no functions to rate, there is no need for a rating label.

Differences between TCSEC and ITSEC are many and varied. The following are some of the most important differences between the two standards:

- Although the TCSEC concentrates almost exclusively on confidentiality, ITSEC addresses concerns about the loss of integrity and availability in addition to confidentiality, thereby covering all three elements so important to maintaining complete information security.
- ITSEC does not rely on the notion of a TCB, and it doesn't require that a system's security components be isolated within a TCB.
- Unlike TCSEC, which required any changed systems to be reevaluated anew—be it for operating system upgrades, patches, or fixes; application upgrades or changes; and so forth—ITSEC includes coverage for maintaining targets of evaluation after such changes occur without requiring a new formal evaluation.

For more information on ITSEC (now largely supplanted by the Common Criteria, covered in the next section), please view the overview document at `https://www.bsi.bund.de/cae/servlet/contentblob/471346/publicationFile/30220/itsec-en_pdf.pdf`

Or you can view the original ITSEC specification here:

`http://www.ssi.gouv.fr/uploads/2015/01/ITSEC-uk.pdf`

Common Criteria

The Common Criteria represents a more or less global effort that involves everybody who worked on TCSEC and ITSEC as well as other global players. Ultimately, it results in the ability to purchase CC-evaluated products (where CC, of course, stands for Common Criteria). The Common Criteria defines various levels of testing and confirmation of systems' security capabilities, and the number of the level indicates what kind of testing and confirmation has been performed. Nevertheless, it's wise to observe that even the highest CC ratings do not equate to a guarantee that such systems are completely secure or that they are entirely devoid of vulnerabilities or susceptibilities to exploit. The Common Criteria was designed as a product evaluation model.

Recognition of Common Criteria

Caveats and disclaimers aside, a document titled "Arrangement on the Recognition of Common Criteria Certificates in the Field of IT Security" was signed by representatives from government organizations in Canada, France, Germany, the United Kingdom, and the United States in 1998, making it an international standard. This document was converted by ISO into an official standard: ISO 15408, Evaluation Criteria for Information Technology Security. The objectives of the CC guidelines are as follows:

- To add to buyers' confidence in the security of evaluated, rated IT products
- To eliminate duplicate evaluations (among other things, this means that if one country, agency, or validation organizations follows the CC in rating specific systems and configurations, others elsewhere need not repeat this work)
- To keep making security evaluations and the certification process more cost effective and efficient
- To make sure evaluations of IT products adhere to high and consistent standards
- To promote evaluation and increase availability of evaluated, rated IT products
- To evaluate the functionality (in other words, what the system does) and assurance (in other words, how much can you trust the system) of the TOE

Common Criteria documentation is available at `www.niap-ccevs.org/cc-scheme/`. Visit this site to get information on the current version of the CC guidelines and guidance on using the CC along with lots of other useful, relevant information.

The Common Criteria process is based on two key elements: protection profiles and security targets. *Protection profiles* (PPs) specify for a product that is to be evaluated (the TOE) the security requirements and protections, which are considered the security desires or the "I want" from a customer. *Security targets* (STs) specify the claims of security from the vendor that are built into a TOE. STs are considered the implemented security measures or the "I will provide" from the vendor. In addition to offering security targets, vendors may offer packages of additional security features. A *package* is an intermediate grouping of security requirement components that can be added or removed from a TOE (like the option packages when purchasing a new vehicle).

The PP is compared to various STs from the selected vendor's TOEs. The closest or best match is what the client purchases. The client initially selects a vendor based on published or marketed evaluation assurance levels (EALs) (see the next section for more details on EALs), for currently available systems. Using Common Criteria to choose a vendor allows clients to request exactly what they need for security rather than having to use static fixed security levels. It also allows vendors more flexibility on what they design and create. A well-defined set of Common Criteria supports subjectivity and versatility, and it automatically adapts to changing technology and threat conditions. Furthermore, the EALs provide a method for comparing vendor systems that is more standardized (like the old TCSEC).

Structure of the Common Criteria

The CC guidelines are divided into three areas, as follows:

Part 1 Introduction and General Model describes the general concepts and underlying model used to evaluate IT security and what's involved in specifying targets of evaluation. It contains useful introductory and explanatory material for those unfamiliar with the workings of the security evaluation process or who need help reading and interpreting evaluation results.

Part 2 Security Functional Requirements describes various functional requirements in terms of security audits, communications security, cryptographic support for security, user data protection, identification and authentication, security management, TOE security functions (TSFs), resource utilization, system access, and trusted paths. Covers the complete range of security functions as envisioned in the CC evaluation process, with additional appendices (called *annexes*) to explain each functional area.

Part 3 Security Assurance covers assurance requirements for TOEs in the areas of configuration management, delivery and operation, development, guidance documents, and life-cycle support plus assurance tests and vulnerability assessments. Covers the complete range of security assurance checks and protects profiles as envisioned in the CC evaluation process, with information on evaluation assurance levels that describe how systems are designed, checked, and tested.

Most important of all, the information that appears in these various CC documents (worth at least a cursory read-through) are the evaluation assurance levels commonly known as EALs. Table 8.3 summarizes EALs 1 through 7. For a complete description of EALs, consult the CC documents hosted at `https://www.niap-ccevs.org/` and view Part 3 of the latest revision.

TABLE 8.3 CC evaluation assurance levels

Level	Assurance level	Description
EAL1	Functionally tested	Applies when some confidence in correct operation is required but where threats to security are not serious. This is of value when independent assurance that due care has been exercised in protecting personal information is necessary.
EAL2	Structurally tested	Applies when delivery of design information and test results are in keeping with good commercial practices. This is of value when developers or users require low to moderate levels of independently assured security. IT is especially relevant when evaluating legacy systems.
EAL3	Methodically tested and checked	Applies when security engineering begins at the design stage and is carried through without substantial subsequent alteration. This is of value when developers or users require a moderate level of independently assured security, including thorough investigation of TOE and its development.
EAL4	Methodically designed, tested, and reviewed	Applies when rigorous, positive security engineering and good commercial development practices are used. This does not require substantial specialist knowledge, skills, or resources. It involves independent testing of all TOE security functions.
EAL5	Semi-formally designed and tested	Uses rigorous security engineering and commercial development practices, including specialist security engineering techniques, for semi-formal testing. This applies when developers or users require a high level of independently assured security in a planned development approach, followed by rigorous development.
EAL6	Semi-formally verified, designed, and tested	Uses direct, rigorous security engineering techniques at all phases of design, development, and testing to produce a premium TOE. This applies when TOEs for high-risk situations are needed, where the value of protected assets justifies additional cost. Extensive testing reduces risks of penetration, probability of cover channels, and vulnerability to attack.
EAL7	Formally verified, designed, and tested	Used only for highest-risk situations or where high-value assets are involved. This is limited to TOEs where tightly focused security functionality is subject to extensive formal analysis and testing.

Though the CC guidelines are flexible and accommodating enough to capture most security needs and requirements, they are by no means perfect. As with other evaluation criteria, the CC guidelines do nothing to make sure that how users act on data is also secure. The CC guidelines also do not address administrative issues outside the specific purview of security. As with other evaluation criteria, the CC guidelines do not include evaluation of security *in situ*—that is, they do not address controls related to personnel, organizational practices and procedures, or physical security. Likewise, controls over electromagnetic emissions are not addressed, nor are the criteria for rating the strength of cryptographic algorithms explicitly laid out. Nevertheless, the CC guidelines represent some of the best techniques whereby systems may be rated for security. To conclude this discussion of security evaluation standards, Table 8.4 summarizes how various ratings from the TCSEC, ITSEC, and the CC can be compared. Table 8.4 shows that ratings from each standard have similar, but not identical evaluation criteria.

TABLE 8.4 Comparing security evaluation standards

TCSEC	ITSEC	CC description	
D	F-D+E0	EAL0, EAL1	Minimal/no protection
C1	F-C1+E1	EAL2	Discretionary security mechanisms
C2	F-C2+E2	EAL3	Controlled access protection
B1	F-B1+E3	EAL4	Labeled security protection
B2	F-B2+E4	EAL5	Structured security protection
B3	F-B3+E5	EAL6	Security domains
A1	F-B3+E6	EAL7	Verified security design

Industry and International Security Implementation Guidelines

In addition to overall security access models, such as Common Criteria, there are many other more specific or focused security standards for various aspects of storage, communication, transactions, and the like. Two of these standards you should be familiar with are Payment Card Industry–Data Security Standard (PCI-DSS) and International Organization for Standardization (ISO).

PCI-DSS is a collection of requirements for improving the security of electronic payment transactions. These standards were defined by the PCI Security Standards Council members, who are primarily credit card banks and financial institutions. The PCI-DSS defines requirements for security management, policies, procedures, network architecture, software design, and other critical protective measures. For more information on PCI-DSS, please visit the website at `www.pcisecuritystandards.org`.

ISO is a worldwide standards-setting group of representatives from various national standards organizations. ISO defines standards for industrial and commercial equipment, software, protocols, and management, among others. It issues six main products: International Standards, Technical Reports, Technical Specifications, Publicly Available Specifications, Technical Corrigenda, and Guides. ISO standards are widely accepted across many industries and have even been adopted as requirements or laws by various governments. For more information in ISO, please visit the website at `www.iso.org`.

Certification and Accreditation

Organizations that require secure systems need one or more methods to evaluate how well a system meets their security requirements. The formal evaluation process is divided into two phases, called *certification* and *accreditation*. The actual steps required in each phase depend on the evaluation criteria an organization chooses. A CISSP candidate must understand the need for each phase and the criteria commonly used to evaluate systems. The two evaluation phases are discussed in the next two sections, and then we present various evaluation criteria and considerations you must address when assessing the security of a system. Certification and accreditation processes are used to assess the effectiveness of application security as well as operating system and hardware security.

The process of evaluation provides a way to assess how well a system measures up to a desired level of security. Because each system's security level depends on many factors, all of them must be taken into account during the evaluation. Even though a system is initially described as secure, the installation process, physical environment, and general configuration details all contribute to its true general security. Two identical systems could be assessed at different levels of security because of configuration or installation differences.

TIP

The terms *certification*, *accreditation*, and *maintenance* as used in the following sections are official terms used by the defense establishment, and you should be familiar with them.

Certification and accreditation are additional steps in the software and IT systems development process normally required from defense contractors and others working in a military environment. The official definitions of these terms as used by the US government are from Department of Defense Instruction 5200.40, Enclosure 2.

Certification

The first phase in a total evaluation process is *certification*. Certification is the comprehensive evaluation of the technical and nontechnical security features of an IT system and other safeguards made in support of the accreditation process to establish the extent to which a particular design and implementation meets a set of specified security requirements.

System certification is the technical evaluation of each part of a computer system to assess its concordance with security standards. First, you must choose evaluation criteria (we will present criteria alternatives in later sections). Once you select criteria to use, you analyze each system component to determine whether it satisfies the desired security goals. The certification analysis includes testing the system's hardware, software, and configuration. All controls are evaluated during this phase, including administrative, technical, and physical controls.

After you assess the entire system, you can evaluate the results to determine the security level the system supports in its current environment. The environment of a system is a critical part of the certification analysis, so a system can be more or less secure depending on its surroundings. The manner in which you connect a secure system to a network can change its security standing. Likewise, the physical security surrounding a system can affect the overall security rating. You must consider all factors when certifying a system.

You complete the certification phase when you have evaluated all factors and determined the level of security for the system. Remember that the certification is valid only for a system in a specific environment and configuration. Any changes could invalidate the certification. Once you have certified a security rating for a specific configuration, you are ready to seek acceptance of the system. Management accepts the certified security configuration of a system through the accreditation process.

Accreditation

In the certification phase, you test and document the security capabilities of a system in a specific configuration. With this information in hand, the management of an organization compares the capabilities of a system to the needs of the organization. It is imperative that the security policy clearly states the requirements of a security system. Management reviews the certification information and decides whether the system satisfies the security needs of the organization. If management decides the certification of the system satisfies their needs, the system is *accredited*. Accreditation is the formal declaration by the designated approving authority (DAA) that an IT system is approved to operate in a particular security mode using a prescribed set of safeguards at an acceptable level of risk. Once accreditation is performed, management can formally accept the adequacy of the overall security performance of an evaluated system.

NOTE

Certification and accreditation do seem similar, and thus it is often a challenge to understand them. One perspective you might consider is that certification is often an internal verification of security and the results of that verification are trusted only by your organization. Accreditation is often performed by a third-party testing service, and the results are trusted by everyone in the world who trusts the specific testing group involved.

The process of certification and accreditation is often iterative. In the accreditation phase, it is not uncommon to request changes to the configuration or additional controls to address security concerns. Remember that whenever you change the configuration, you must recertify the new configuration. Likewise, you need to recertify the system when a specific time period elapses or when you make any configuration changes. Your security policy should specify what conditions require recertification. A sound policy would list the amount of time a certification is valid along with any changes that would require you to restart the certification and accreditation process.

Certification and Accreditation Systems

Two government standards are currently in place for the certification and accreditation of computing systems. The current DoD standard is Risk Management Framework (RMF) (`www.dtic.mil/whs/directives/corres/pdf/851001_2014.pdf`) which recently replaced DoD Information Assurance Certification and Accreditation Process (DIACAP), which itself replaced the Defense Information Technology Security Certification and Accreditation Process (DITSCAP). The standard for all other US government executive branch departments, agencies, and their contractors and consultants is the Committee on National Security Systems (CNSS) Policy (CNSSP) (`www.ncix.gov/publications/policy/docs/CNSSP_22.pdf`) which replaced National Information Assurance Certification and Accreditation Process (NIACAP). However, the CISSP may refer to either the current standards or the previous ones. Both of these processes are divided into four phases:

Phase 1: Definition Involves the assignment of appropriate project personnel; documentation of the mission need; and registration, negotiation, and creation of a System Security Authorization Agreement (SSAA) that guides the entire certification and accreditation process

Phase 2: Verification Includes refinement of the SSAA, systems development activities, and a certification analysis

Phase 3: Validation Includes further refinement of the SSAA, certification evaluation of the integrated system, development of a recommendation to the DAA, and the DAA's accreditation decision

Phase 4: Post Accreditation Includes maintenance of the SSAA, system operation, change management, and compliance validation

The NIACAP process, administered by the Information Systems Security Organization of the National Security Agency, outlines three types of accreditation that may be granted. The definitions of these types of accreditation (from National Security Telecommunications and Information Systems Security Instruction 1000) are as follows:

- For a system accreditation, a major application or general support system is evaluated.
- For a site accreditation, the applications and systems at a specific, self-contained location are evaluated.
- For a type accreditation, an application or system that is distributed to a number of different locations is evaluated.

Understand Security Capabilities of Information Systems

The security capabilities of information systems include memory protection, virtualization, Trusted Platform Module, interfaces, and fault tolerance. It is important to carefully assess each aspect of the infrastructure to ensure that it sufficiently supports security. Without an understanding of the security capabilities of information systems, it is impossible to evaluate them, nor is it possible to implement them properly.

Memory Protection

Memory protection is a core security component that must be designed and implemented into an operating system. It must be enforced regardless of the programs executing in the system. Otherwise instability, violation of integrity, denial of service, and disclosure are likely results. Memory protection is used to prevent an active process from interacting with an area of memory that was not specifically assigned or allocated to it.

Memory protection is discussed throughout Chapter 9 in relation to the topics of isolation, virtual memory, segmentation, memory management, and protection rings.

Virtualization

Virtualization technology is used to host one or more operating systems within the memory of a single host computer. This mechanism allows virtually any OS to operate on any hardware. It also allows multiple OSs to work simultaneously on the same hardware. Common examples include VMware, Microsoft's Virtual PC, Microsoft Virtual Server, Hyper-V with Windows Server, Oracle's VirtualBox, XenServer, and Parallels Desktop for Mac.

Virtualization has several benefits, such as being able to launch individual instances of servers or services as needed, real-time scalability, and being able to run the exact OS version needed for a specific application. Virtualized servers and services are indistinguishable from traditional servers and services from a user's perspective. Additionally, recovery from damaged, crashed, or corrupted virtual systems is often quick, simply consisting of replacing the virtual system's main hard drive file with a clean backup version and then relaunching it. (Additional coverage of virtualization and some of its associated risks are covered in Chapter 9 along with cloud computing.)

Trusted Platform Module

The Trusted Platform Module (TPM) is both a specification for a cryptoprocessor chip on a mainboard and the general name for implementation of the specification. A TPM chip is used to store and process cryptographic keys for the purposes of a hardware supported/implemented hard drive encryption system. Generally, a hardware implementation, rather than a software-only implementation of hard drive encryption, is considered to be more secure.

When TPM-based whole-disk encryption is in use, the user/operator must supply a password or physical USB token device to the computer to authenticate and allow the TPM chip to release the hard drive encryption keys into memory. While this seems similar to a software implementation, the key difference is that if the hard drive is removed from its original system, it cannot be decrypted. Only with the original TPM chip can an encryption be decrypted and accessed. With software-only hard drive encryption, the hard drive can be moved to a different computer without any access or use limitations.

A hardware security module (HSM) is a cryptoprocessor used to manage/store digital encryption keys, accelerate crypto operations, support faster digital signatures, and improve authentication. An HSM is often an add-on adapter or peripheral or can be a TCP/IP network device. HSMs include tamper protection to prevent their misuse even if physical access is gained by an attacker. A TPM is just one example of an HSM.

HSMs provide an accelerated solution for large (2,048+ bit) asymmetric encryption calculations and a secure vault for key storage. Many certificate authority systems use HSMs to store certificates; ATM and POS bank terminals often employ proprietary HSMs; hardware SSL accelerators can include HSM support; and DNSSEC-compliant DNS servers use HSM for key and zone file storage.

Interfaces

A constrained or restricted interface is implemented within an application to restrict what users can do or see based on their privileges. Users with full privileges have access to all the capabilities of the application. Users with restricted privileges have limited access.

Applications constrain the interface using different methods. A common method is to hide the capability if the user doesn't have permissions to use it. Commands might be available to administrators via a menu or by right-clicking an item, but if a regular user doesn't have permissions, the command does not appear. Other times, the command is shown but is dimmed or disabled. The regular user can see it but will not be able to use it.

The purpose of a constrained interface is to limit or restrict the actions of both authorized and unauthorized users. The use of such an interface is a practical implementation of the Clark-Wilson model of security.

Fault Tolerance

Fault tolerance is the ability of a system to suffer a fault but continue to operate. Fault tolerance is achieved by adding redundant components such as additional disks within a redundant array of inexpensive disks (RAID) array, or additional servers within a failover clustered configuration. Fault tolerance is an essential element of security design. It is also considered part of avoiding single points of failure and the implementation of redundancy. For more details on fault tolerance, redundant servers, RAID, and failover solutions, see Chapter 18, "Disaster Recovery Planning."

Summary

Secure systems are not just assembled; they are designed to support security. Systems that must be secure are judged for their ability to support and enforce the security policy. This process of evaluating the effectiveness of a computer system is certification. The certification process is the technical evaluation of a system's ability to meet its design goals. Once a system has satisfactorily passed the technical evaluation, the management of an organization begins the formal acceptance of the system. The formal acceptance process is accreditation.

The entire certification and accreditation process depends on standard evaluation criteria. Several criteria exist for evaluating computer security systems. The earliest, TCSEC, was developed by the US Department of Defense. TCSEC, also called the Orange Book, provides criteria to evaluate the functionality and assurance of a system's security components. ITSEC is an alternative to the TCSEC guidelines and is used more often in European countries. Regardless of which criteria you use, the evaluation process includes reviewing each security control for compliance with the security policy. The better a system enforces the good behavior of subjects' access to objects, the higher the security rating.

When security systems are designed, it is often helpful to create a security model to represent the methods the system will use to implement the security policy. We discussed several security models in this chapter. The Bell-LaPadula model supports data confidentiality only. It was designed for the military and satisfies military concerns. The Biba model and the Clark-Wilson model address the integrity of data and do so in different ways. These two security models are appropriate for commercial applications.

All of this understanding must culminate into an effective system security implementation in terms of preventive, detective, and corrective controls. That's why you must also know the access control models and their functions. This includes the state machine model, Bell-LaPadula, Biba, Clark-Wilson, the information flow model, the noninterference model, the Take-Grant model, the access control matrix model, and the Brewer and Nash model.

Exam Essentials

Know details about each of the access control models. Know the access control models and their functions. The state machine model ensures that all instances of subjects accessing objects are secure. The information flow model is designed to prevent unauthorized, insecure, or restricted information flow. The noninterference model prevents the actions of one subject from affecting the system state or actions of another subject. The Take-Grant model dictates how rights can be passed from one subject to another or from a subject to an object. An access control matrix is a table of subjects and objects that indicates the actions or functions that each subject can perform on each object. Bell-LaPadula subjects have a clearance level that allows them to access only those objects with the corresponding classification levels. This enforces confidentiality. Biba prevents subjects with lower security levels from writing to objects at higher security levels. Clark-Wilson is an integrity model that relies on auditing to ensure that unauthorized subjects cannot access objects and that authorized users access objects properly. Biba and Clark-Wilson enforce integrity. Goguen-Meseguer and Sutherland focus on integrity. Graham-Denning focuses on the secure creation and deletion of both subjects and objects.

Know the definitions of certification and accreditation. Certification is the technical evaluation of each part of a computer system to assess its concordance with security standards. Accreditation is the process of formal acceptance of a certified configuration from a designated authority.

Be able to describe open and closed systems. Open systems are designed using industry standards and are usually easy to integrate with other open systems. Closed systems are generally proprietary hardware and/or software. Their specifications are not normally published, and they are usually harder to integrate with other systems.

Know what confinement, bounds, and isolation are. Confinement restricts a process to reading from and writing to certain memory locations. Bounds are the limits of memory a process cannot exceed when reading or writing. Isolation is the mode a process runs in when it is confined through the use of memory bounds.

Be able to define *object* and *subject* in terms of access. The subject is the user or process that makes a request to access a resource. The object is the resource a user or process wants to access.

Know how security controls work and what they do. Security controls use access rules to limit the access by a subject to an object.

Be able to list the classes of TCSEC, ITSEC, and the Common Criteria. The classes of TCSEC include verified protection, mandatory protection, discretionary protection, and minimal protection. Table 8.4 covers and compares equivalent and applicable rankings for TCSEC, ITSEC, and the CC (remember that functionality ratings from F7 to F10 in ITSEC have no corresponding ratings in TCSEC).

Define a trusted computing base (TCB). A TCB is the combination of hardware, software, and controls that form a trusted base that enforces the security policy.

Be able to explain what a security perimeter is. A security perimeter is the imaginary boundary that separates the TCB from the rest of the system. TCB components communicate with non-TCB components using trusted paths.

Know what the reference monitor and the security kernel are. The reference monitor is the logical part of the TCB that confirms whether a subject has the right to use a resource prior to granting access. The security kernel is the collection of the TCB components that implement the functionality of the reference monitor.

Understand the security capabilities of information systems. Common security capabilities include memory protection, virtualization, and Trusted Platform Module (TPM).

Written Lab

1. Name at least seven security models.
2. Describe the primary components of TCB.
3. What are the two primary rules or principles of the Bell-LaPadula security model? Also, what are the two rules of Biba?
4. What is the difference between open and closed systems and open and closed source?

Review Questions

1. What is system certification?
   - **A.** Formal acceptance of a stated system configuration
   - **B.** A technical evaluation of each part of a computer system to assess its compliance with security standards
   - **C.** A functional evaluation of the manufacturer's goals for each hardware and software component to meet integration standards
   - **D.** A manufacturer's certificate stating that all components were installed and configured correctly
2. What is system accreditation?
   - **A.** Formal acceptance of a stated system configuration
   - **B.** A functional evaluation of the manufacturer's goals for each hardware and software component to meet integration standards
   - **C.** Acceptance of test results that prove the computer system enforces the security policy
   - **D.** The process to specify secure communication between machines
3. What is a closed system?
   - **A.** A system designed around final, or closed, standards
   - **B.** A system that includes industry standards
   - **C.** A proprietary system that uses unpublished protocols
   - **D.** Any machine that does not run Windows
4. Which best describes a confined or constrained process?
   - **A.** A process that can run only for a limited time
   - **B.** A process that can run only during certain times of the day
   - **C.** A process that can access only certain memory locations
   - **D.** A process that controls access to an object
5. What is an access object?
   - **A.** A resource a user or process wants to access
   - **B.** A user or process that wants to access a resource
   - **C.** A list of valid access rules
   - **D.** The sequence of valid access types
6. What is a security control?
   - **A.** A security component that stores attributes that describe an object
   - **B.** A document that lists all data classification types

C. A list of valid access rules

D. A mechanism that limits access to an object

7. For what type of information system security accreditation are the applications and systems at a specific, self-contained location evaluated?

A. System accreditation

B. Site accreditation

C. Application accreditation

D. Type accreditation

8. How many major categories do the TCSEC criteria define?

A. Two

B. Three

C. Four

D. Five

9. What is a trusted computing base (TCB)?

A. Hosts on your network that support secure transmissions

B. The operating system kernel and device drivers

C. The combination of hardware, software, and controls that work together to enforce a security policy

D. The software and controls that certify a security policy

10. What is a security perimeter? (Choose all that apply.)

A. The boundary of the physically secure area surrounding your system

B. The imaginary boundary that separates the TCB from the rest of the system

C. The network where your firewall resides

D. Any connections to your computer system

11. What part of the TCB concept validates access to every resource prior to granting the requested access?

A. TCB partition

B. Trusted library

C. Reference monitor

D. Security kernel

12. What is the best definition of a security model?

A. A security model states policies an organization must follow.

B. A security model provides a framework to implement a security policy.

C. A security model is a technical evaluation of each part of a computer system to assess its concordance with security standards.

D. A security model is the process of formal acceptance of a certified configuration.

13. Which security models are built on a state machine model?

A. Bell-LaPadula and Take-Grant

B. Biba and Clark-Wilson

C. Clark-Wilson and Bell-LaPadula

D. Bell-LaPadula and Biba

14. Which security model addresses data confidentiality?

A. Bell-LaPadula

B. Biba

C. Clark-Wilson

D. Brewer and Nash

15. Which Bell-LaPadula property keeps lower-level subjects from accessing objects with a higher security level?

A. (star) Security Property

B. No write up property

C. No read up property

D. No read down property

16. What is the implied meaning of the simple property of Biba?

A. Write down

B. Read up

C. No write up

D. No read down

17. When a trusted subject violates the star property of Bell-LaPadula in order to write an object into a lower level, what valid operation could be taking place?

A. Perturbation

B. Polyinstantiation

C. Aggregation

D. Declassification

18. What security method, mechanism, or model reveals a capabilities list of a subject across multiple objects?

A. Separation of duties

B. Access control matrix

C. Biba

D. Clark-Wilson

19. What security model has a feature that in theory has one name or label, but when implemented into a solution, takes on the name or label of the security kernel?

A. Graham-Denning model

B. Deployment modes

C. Trusted computing base

D. Chinese Wall

20. Which of the following is not part of the access control relationship of the Clark-Wilson model?

A. Object

B. Interface

C. Programming language

D. Subject

Chapter 9

Security Vulnerabilities, Threats, and Countermeasures

THE CISSP EXAM TOPICS COVERED IN THIS CHAPTER INCLUDE:

✓ **3) Security Engineering (Engineering and Management of Security)**

- E. Assess and mitigate the vulnerabilities of security architectures, designs, and solution elements
  - E.1 Client-based (e.g., applets, local caches)
  - E.2 Server-based (e.g., data flow control)
  - E.3 Database security (e.g., inference, aggregation, data mining, data analytics, warehousing)
  - E.4 Large-scale parallel data systems
  - E.5 Distributed systems (e.g., cloud computing, grid computing, peer to peer)
  - E.6 Cryptographic systems
  - E.7 Industrial control systems (e.g., SCADA)
- F. Assess and mitigate vulnerabilities in web-based systems (e.g., XML, OWASP)
- G. Assess and mitigate vulnerabilities in mobile systems
- H. Assess and mitigate vulnerabilities in embedded devices and cyber-physical systems (e.g., network-enabled devices, Internet of things (IoT))

In previous chapters of this book, we've covered basic security principles and the protective mechanisms put in place to prevent violation of them. We've also examined some of the specific types of attacks used by malicious individuals seeking to circumvent those protective mechanisms. Until this point, when discussing preventive measures, we have focused on policy measures and the software that runs on a system. However, security professionals must also pay careful attention to the system itself and ensure that their higher-level protective controls are not built on a shaky foundation. After all, the most secure firewall configuration in the world won't do a bit of good if the computer it runs on has a fundamental security flaw that allows malicious individuals to simply bypass the firewall completely.

In this chapter, we'll cover those underlying security concerns by conducting a brief survey of a field known as *computer architecture*: the physical design of computers from various components. We'll examine each of the major physical components of a computing system—hardware and firmware—from a security perspective. Obviously, the detailed analysis of a system's hardware components is not always a luxury available to you because of resource and time constraints. However, all security professionals should have at least a basic understanding of these concepts in case they encounter a security incident that reaches down to the system design level.

The Security Engineering domain addresses a wide range of concerns and issues, including secure design elements, security architecture, vulnerabilities, threats, and associated countermeasures. Additional elements of this domain are discussed in various chapters: Chapter 6, "Cryptography and Symmetric Key Algorithms," Chapter 7, "PKI and Cryptographic Applications," Chapter 8, "Principles of Security Models, Design, and Capabilities," and Chapter 10, "Physical Security Requirements." Please be sure to review all of these chapters to have a complete perspective on the topics of this domain.

Assess and Mitigate Security Vulnerabilities

Computer architecture is an engineering discipline concerned with the design and construction of computing systems at a logical level. Many college-level computer engineering and computer science programs find it difficult to cover all the basic principles of computer architecture in a single semester, so this material is often divided into two one-semester courses for undergraduates. Computer architecture courses delve into the design of central processing unit (CPU) components, memory devices, device communications, and similar topics at the bit level, defining processing paths for individual logic devices that make simple "0 or 1" decisions. Most security professionals do not need that level of knowledge, which is well beyond the scope of this book and the CISSP exam. However, if you will be involved in the security aspects of the design of computing systems at this level, you would be well advised to conduct a more thorough study of this field.

This initial discussion of computer architecture may seem at first to be irrelevant to CISSP, but most of the security architectures and design elements are based on a solid understanding and implementation of computer hardware.

TIP The more complex a system, the less assurance it provides. More complexity means more areas for vulnerabilities exist and more areas must be secured against threats. More vulnerabilities and more threats mean that the subsequent security provided by the system is less trustworthy.

Hardware

Any computing professional is familiar with the concept of hardware. As in the construction industry, hardware is the physical "stuff" that makes up a computer. The term *hardware* encompasses any tangible part of a computer that you can actually reach out and touch, from the keyboard and monitor to its CPU(s), storage media, and memory chips. Take careful note that although the physical portion of a storage device (such as a hard disk or flash memory) may be considered hardware, the contents of those devices—the collections of 0s and 1s that make up the software and data stored within them—may not. After all, you can't reach inside the computer and pull out a handful of bits and bytes!

Processor

The central processing unit (CPU), generally called the *processor*, is the computer's nerve center—it is the chip (or chips in a multiprocessor system) that governs all major operations and either directly performs or coordinates the complex symphony of calculations that allows a computer to perform its intended tasks. Surprisingly, the CPU is capable of performing only a limited set of computational and logical operations, despite the complexity of the tasks it allows the computer to perform. It is the responsibility of the operating system and compilers to translate high-level programming languages used to design software into simple assembly language instructions that a CPU understands. This limited range of functionality is intentional—it allows a CPU to perform computational and logical operations at blazing speeds.

NOTE For an idea of the magnitude of the progress in computing technology over the years, view the Moore's Law article at `http://en.wikipedia.org/wiki/Moore's_law`.

Execution Types

As computer processing power increased, users demanded more advanced features to enable these systems to process information at greater rates and to manage multiple functions simultaneously. Computer engineers devised several methods to meet these demands:

> **TIP** At first blush, the terms *multitasking, multiprocessing, multiprogramming,* and *multithreading* may seem nearly identical. However, they describe very different ways of approaching the "doing two things at once" problem. We strongly advise that you take the time to review the distinctions between these terms until you feel comfortable with them.

Multitasking In computing, *multitasking* means handling two or more tasks simultaneously. In reality, most systems do not truly multitask; they rely on the operating system to simulate multitasking by carefully structuring the sequence of commands sent to the CPU for execution. After all, when your processor is humming along at multiple gigahertz, it's hard to tell that it's switching between tasks rather than working on two tasks at once. However, you can assume that a multitasking system is able to juggle more than one task or process at any given time.

Multiprocessing In a *multiprocessing* environment, a multiprocessor computing system (that is, one with more than one CPU) harnesses the power of more than one processor to complete the execution of a single application. For example, a database server might run on a system that contains four, six, or more processors. If the database application receives a number of separate queries simultaneously, it might send each query to a separate processor for execution.

Two types of multiprocessing are most common in modern systems with multiple CPUs. The scenario just described, where a single computer contains multiple processors that are treated equally and controlled by a single operating system, is called *symmetric multiprocessing (SMP)*. In SMP, processors share not only a common operating system but also a common data bus and memory resources. In this type of arrangement, systems may use a large number of processors. Fortunately, this type of computing power is more than sufficient to drive most systems.

Some computationally intensive operations, such as those that support the research of scientists and mathematicians, require more processing power than a single operating system can deliver. Such operations may be best served by a technology known as *massively parallel processing (MPP)*. MPP systems house hundreds or even thousands of processors, each of which has its own operating system and memory/bus resources. When the software that coordinates the entire system's activities and schedules them for processing encounters a computationally intensive task, it assigns responsibility for the task to a single processor. This processor in turn breaks the task up into manageable parts and distributes them to other processors for execution. Those processors return their results to the coordinating processor where they are assembled and returned to the requesting application. MPP systems are extremely powerful (not to mention extremely expensive!) and are used in a great deal of computing or computational-based research.

Both types of multiprocessing provide unique advantages and are suitable for different types of situations. SMP systems are adept at processing simple operations at extremely high rates, whereas MPP systems are uniquely suited for processing very large, complex, computationally intensive tasks that lend themselves to decomposition and distribution into a number of subordinate parts.

Next-Generation Multiprocessing

Until the release of dual-core and quad-core processors, the only way to create a multiprocessing system was to place two or more CPUs onto the motherboard. However, today we have several options of multicore CPUs so that with a single CPU chip on the motherboard, there are two or four (or more!) execution paths. This truly allows single CPU multiprocessing because it enables two (or more) calculations to occur simultaneously.

Multiprogramming *Multiprogramming* is similar to multitasking. It involves the pseudosimultaneous execution of two tasks on a single processor coordinated by the operating system as a way to increase operational efficiency. For the most part, multiprogramming is a way to batch or serialize multiple processes so that when one process stops to wait on a peripheral, its state is saved and the next process in line begins to process. The first program does not return to processing until all other processes in the batch have had their chance to execute and they in turn stop for a peripheral. For any single program, this methodology causes significant delays in completing a task. However, across all processes in the batch, the total time to complete all tasks is reduced.

Multiprogramming is considered a relatively obsolete technology and is rarely found in use today except in legacy systems. There are two main differences between multiprogramming and multitasking:

- Multiprogramming usually takes place on large-scale systems, such as mainframes, whereas multitasking takes place on PC operating systems, such as Windows and Linux.
- Multitasking is normally coordinated by the operating system, whereas multiprogramming requires specially written software that coordinates its own activities and execution through the operating system.

Multithreading *Multithreading* permits multiple concurrent tasks to be performed within a single process. Unlike multitasking, where multiple tasks occupy multiple processes, multithreading permits multiple tasks to operate within a single process. A thread is a self-contained sequence of instructions that can execute in parallel with other threads that are part of the same parent process. Multithreading is often used in applications where frequent context switching between multiple active processes consumes excessive overhead and reduces efficiency. In multithreading, switching between threads incurs far less overhead and is therefore more efficient. In modern Windows implementations, for example, the overhead involved in switching from one thread to another within a single process is on the order of 40 to 50 instructions, with no substantial memory transfers needed. By contrast, switching from one process to another involves 1,000 instructions or more and requires substantial memory transfers as well.

A good example of multithreading occurs when multiple documents are opened at the same time in a word processing program. In that situation, you do not actually run multiple instances of the word processor—this would place far too great a demand on the system. Instead, each document is treated as a single thread within a single word processor process, and the software chooses which thread it works on at any given moment.

Symmetric multiprocessing systems use threading at the operating system level. As in the word processing example just described, the operating system also contains a number of threads that control the tasks assigned to it. In a single-processor system, the OS sends one thread at a time to the processor for execution. SMP systems send one thread to each available processor for simultaneous execution.

Processing Types

Many high-security systems control the processing of information assigned to various security levels, such as the classification levels of unclassified, sensitive, confidential, secret, and top secret that the US government assigns to information related to national defense. Computers must be designed so that they do not—ideally, so that they cannot—inadvertently disclose information to unauthorized recipients.

Computer architects and security policy administrators have addressed this problem at the processor level in two different ways. One is through a policy mechanism, whereas the other is through a hardware solution. The following list explores each of those options:

Single State *Single-state systems* require the use of policy mechanisms to manage information at different levels. In this type of arrangement, security administrators approve a processor and system to handle only one security level at a time. For example, a system might be labeled to handle only secret information. All users of that system must then be approved to handle information at the secret level. This shifts the burden of protecting the information being processed on a system away from the hardware and operating system and onto the administrators who control access to the system.

Multistate *Multistate systems* are capable of implementing a much higher level of security. These systems are certified to handle multiple security levels simultaneously by using specialized security mechanisms such as those described in the next section, "Protection Mechanisms." These mechanisms are designed to prevent information from crossing between security levels. One user might be using a multistate system to process secret information, while another user is processing top-secret information at the same time. Technical mechanisms prevent information from crossing between the two users and thereby crossing between security levels.

In actual practice, multistate systems are relatively uncommon owing to the expense of implementing the necessary technical mechanisms. This expense is sometimes justified; however, when you're dealing with a very expensive resource, such as a massively parallel system, the cost of obtaining multiple systems far exceeds the cost of implementing the additional security controls necessary to enable multistate operation on a single such system.

Protection Mechanisms

If a computer isn't running, it's an inert lump of plastic, silicon, and metal doing nothing. When a computer is running, it operates a runtime environment that represents the combination of the operating system and whatever applications may be active. When running, the computer also has the capability to access files and other data as the user's security permissions allow. Within that runtime environment, it's necessary to integrate security information and controls to protect the integrity of the operating system itself, to manage which users are allowed to access specific data items, to authorize or deny operations requested against such data, and so forth. The ways in which running computers implement and handle security at runtime may be broadly described as a collection of protection mechanisms. What follows are descriptions of various protection mechanisms such as protection rings, operational states, and security modes.

TIP

Because the ways in which computers implement and use protection mechanisms are so important to maintaining and controlling security, you should understand how all three mechanisms covered here—rings, operational states, and security modes—are defined and how they behave. Don't be surprised to see exam questions about specifics in all three areas because this is such important stuff!

Protection Rings The ring protection scheme is an oldie but a goodie. It dates all the way back to work on the Multics operating system. This experimental operating system was designed and built between 1963 and 1969 through the collaboration of Bell Labs, MIT, and General Electric. It saw commercial use in implementations from Honeywell. Multics has left two enduring legacies in the computing world. First, it inspired the creation of a simpler, less intricate operating system called Unix (a play on the word *multics*), and second, it introduced the idea of protection rings to OS design.

From a security standpoint, *protection rings* organize code and components in an operating system (as well as applications, utilities, or other code that runs under the operating system's control) into concentric rings, as shown in Figure 9.1. The deeper inside the circle you go, the higher the privilege level associated with the code that occupies a specific ring. Though the original Multics implementation allowed up to seven rings (numbered 0 through 6), most modern operating systems use a four-ring model (numbered 0 through 3).

As the innermost ring, 0 has the highest level of privilege and can basically access any resource, file, or memory location. The part of an operating system that always remains resident in memory (so that it can run on demand at any time) is called the *kernel*. It occupies ring 0 and can preempt code running at any other ring. The remaining parts of the operating system—those that come and go as various tasks are requested, operations performed, processes switched, and so forth—occupy ring 1. Ring 2 is also somewhat privileged in that it's where I/O drivers and system utilities reside; these are able to access peripheral devices, special files, and so forth that applications and other programs cannot themselves access directly. Those applications and programs occupy the outermost ring, ring 3.

FIGURE 9.1 In the commonly used four-ring model, protection rings segregate the operating system into kernel, components, and drivers in rings 0 through 2 and applications and programs run at ring 3.

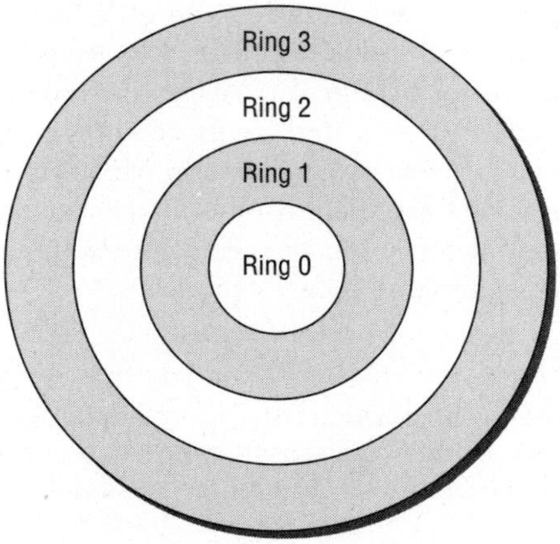

Ring 0: OS Kernel/Memory (Resident Components)
Ring 1: Other OS Components
Ring 2: Drivers, Protocols, etc.
Ring 3: User-Level Programs and Applications

Rings 0–2 run in supervisory or privileged mode.
Ring 3 runs in user mode.

The essence of the ring model lies in priority, privilege, and memory segmentation. Any process that wants to execute must get in line (a pending process queue). The process associated with the lowest ring number always runs before processes associated with higher-numbered rings. Processes in lower-numbered rings can access more resources and interact with the operating system more directly than those in higher-numbered rings. Those processes that run in higher-numbered rings must generally ask a handler or a driver in a lower-numbered ring for services they need; this is sometimes called a *mediated-access model*. In its strictest implementation, each ring has its own associated memory segment. Thus, any request from a process in a higher-numbered ring for an address in a lower-numbered ring must call on a helper process in the ring associated with that address. In practice, many modern operating systems break memory into only two segments: one for system-level access (rings 0 through 2), often called *kernel mode* or *privileged mode*, and one for user-level programs and applications (ring 3), often called *user mode*.

From a security standpoint, the ring model enables an operating system to protect and insulate itself from users and applications. It also permits the enforcement of strict boundaries between highly privileged operating system components (such as the kernel) and less privileged parts of the operating system (such as other parts of the operating system, plus drivers and utilities). Within this model, direct access to specific resources is possible only within certain rings; likewise, certain operations (such as process switching, termination, and scheduling) are allowed only within certain rings.

The ring that a process occupies determines its access level to system resources (and determines what kinds of resources it must request from processes in lower-numbered, more privileged rings). Processes may access objects directly only if they reside within their own ring or within some ring outside its current boundaries (in numerical terms, for example, this means a process at ring 1 can access its own resources directly, plus any associated with rings 2 and 3, but it can't access any resources associated only with ring 0). The mechanism whereby mediated access occurs—that is, the driver or handler request mentioned previously—is usually known as a *system call* and usually involves invocation of a specific system or programming interface designed to pass the request to an inner ring for service. Before any such request can be honored, however, the called ring must check to make sure that the calling process has the right credentials and authorization to access the data and to perform the operation(s) involved in satisfying the request.

Process States Also known as *operating states*, *process states* are various forms of execution in which a process may run. Where the operating system is concerned, it can be in one of two modes at any given moment: operating in a privileged, all-access mode known as *supervisor state* or operating in what's called the *problem state* associated with user mode, where privileges are low and all access requests must be checked against credentials for authorization before they are granted or denied. The latter is called the problem state not because problems are guaranteed to occur but because the unprivileged nature of user access means that problems can occur and the system must take appropriate measures to protect security, integrity, and confidentiality.

Processes line up for execution in an operating system in a processing queue, where they will be scheduled to run as a processor becomes available. Because many operating systems allow processes to consume processor time only in fixed increments or chunks, when a new process is created, it enters the processing queue for the first time; should a process consume its entire chunk of processing time (called a *time slice*) without completing, it returns to the processing queue for another time slice the next time its turn comes around. Also, the process scheduler usually selects the highest-priority process for execution, so reaching the front of the line doesn't always guarantee access to the CPU (because a process may be preempted at the last instant by another process with higher priority).

According to whether a process is running, it can operate in one of several states:

Ready In the ready state, a process is ready to resume or begin processing as soon as it is scheduled for execution. If the CPU is available when the process reaches this state, it will transition directly into the running state; otherwise, it sits in the ready state until its turn comes up. This means the process has all the memory and other resources it needs to begin executing immediately.

Waiting Waiting can also be understood as "waiting for a resource"—that is, the process is ready for continued execution but is waiting for a device or access request (an interrupt of some kind) to be serviced before it can continue processing (for example, a database application that asks to read records from a file must wait for that file to be located and opened and for the right set of records to be found). Some references label this state as a blocked state because the process could be said to be blocked from further execution until an external event occurs.

Running The running process executes on the CPU and keeps going until it finishes, its time slice expires, or it is blocked for some reason (usually because it has generated an interrupt for access to a device or the network and is waiting for that interrupt to be serviced). If the time slice ends and the process isn't completed, it returns to the ready state (and queue); if the process blocks while waiting for a resource to become available, it goes into the waiting state (and queue).

TIP

The running state is also often called the *problem state*. However, don't associate the word *problem* with an error. Instead, think of the problem state as you would think of a math problem being solved to obtain the answer. But keep in mind that it is called the problem state because it is possible for problems or errors to occur, just as you could do a math problem incorrectly. The problem state is separated from the supervisory state so that any errors that might occur do not easily affect the stability of the overall system; they affect only the process that experienced the error.

Supervisory The supervisory state is used when the process must perform an action that requires privileges that are greater than the problem state's set of privileges, including modifying system configuration, installing device drivers, or modifying security settings. Basically, any function not occurring in the user mode (ring 3) or problem state takes place in the supervisory mode.

Stopped When a process finishes or must be terminated (because an error occurs, a required resource is not available, or a resource request can't be met), it goes into a stopped state. At this point, the operating system can recover all memory and other resources allocated to the process and reuse them for other processes as needed.

Figure 9.2 shows a diagram of how these various states relate to one another. New processes always transition into the ready state. From there, ready processes always transition into the running state. While running, a process can transition into the stopped state if it completes or is terminated, return to the ready state for another time slice, or transition to the waiting state until its pending resource request is met. When the operating system decides which process to run next, it checks the waiting queue and the ready queue and takes the highest-priority job that's ready to run (so that only waiting jobs whose pending requests have been serviced, or are ready to service, are eligible in this consideration). A special part of the kernel, called the *program executive* or the *process scheduler*, is always around (waiting in memory) so that when a process state transition must occur, it can step in and handle the mechanics involved.

In Figure 9.2, the process scheduler manages the processes awaiting execution in the ready and waiting states and decides what happens to running processes when they transition into another state (ready, waiting, or stopped).

FIGURE 9.2 The process scheduler

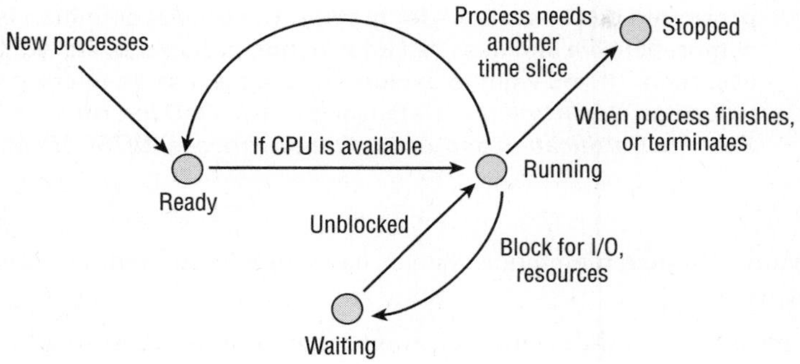

Security Modes The US government has designated four approved security modes for systems that process classified information. These are described next. In Chapter 1, "Security Governance Through Principles and Policies," we reviewed the classification system used by the federal government and the concepts of security clearances and access approval. The only new term in this context is *need to know*, which refers to an access authorization scheme in which a subject's right to access an object takes into consideration not just a privilege level but also the relevance of the data involved in the role the subject plays (or the job they perform). This indicates that the subject requires access to the object to perform their job properly or to fill some specific role. Those with no need to know may not access the object, no matter what level of privilege they hold. If you need a refresher on those concepts, please review them in Chapter 1 before proceeding. Three specific elements must exist before the security modes themselves can be deployed:

- A hierarchical MAC environment
- Total physical control over which subjects can access the computer console
- Total physical control over which subjects can enter into the same room as the computer console

TIP You will rarely, if ever, encounter the following modes outside of the world of government agencies and contractors. However, you may discover this terminology in other contexts, so you'd be well advised to commit the terms to memory.

Dedicated Mode Dedicated mode systems are essentially equivalent to the single-state system described in the section "Processing Types" earlier in this chapter. Three requirements exist for users of dedicated systems:

- Each user must have a security clearance that permits access to all information processed by the system.
- Each user must have access approval for all information processed by the system.
- Each user must have a valid need to know for all information processed by the system.

NOTE In the definitions of each of these modes, we use "all information processed by the system" for brevity. The official definition is more comprehensive and uses "all information processed, stored, transferred, or accessed." If you want to explore the source, use an Internet search engine to locate: *Department of Defense 8510.1-M DoD Information Technology Security Certification and Accreditation Process (DITSCAP) Manual.*

System High Mode System high mode systems have slightly different requirements that must be met by users:

- Each user must have a valid security clearance that permits access to all information processed by the system.
- Each user must have access approval for all information processed by the system.
- Each user must have a valid need to know for some information processed by the system but not necessarily all information processed by the system.

Note that the major difference between the dedicated mode and the system high mode is that all users do not necessarily have a need to know for all information processed on a system high mode computing device. Thus, although the same user could access both a dedicated mode system and a system high mode system, that user could access all data on the former but be restricted from some of the data on the latter.

Compartmented mode Compartmented mode systems weaken these requirements one step further:

- Each user must have a valid security clearance that permits access to all information processed by the system.
- Each user must have access approval for any information they will have access to on the system.
- Each user must have a valid need to know for all information they will have access to on the system.

Notice that the major difference between compartmented mode systems and system high mode systems is that users of a compartmented mode system do not necessarily have access approval for all the information on the system. However, as with system high and dedicated systems, all users of the system must still have appropriate security clearances. In a special implementation of this mode called *compartmented mode workstations* (CMWs), users with the necessary clearances can process multiple compartments of data at the same time.

CMWs require that two forms of security labels be placed on objects: sensitivity levels and information labels. Sensitivity levels describe the levels at which objects must be protected. These are common among all four of the modes. Information labels prevent data overclassification and associate additional information with the objects, which assists in proper and accurate data labeling not related to access control.

Multilevel Mode The government's definition of multilevel mode systems pretty much parallels the technical definition given in the previous section. However, for consistency, we'll express it in terms of clearance, access approval, and need to know:

- Some users do not have a valid security clearance for all information processed by the system. Thus, access is controlled by whether the subject's clearance level dominates the object's sensitivity label.
- Each user must have access approval for all information they will have access to on the system.
- Each user must have a valid need to know for all information they will have access to on the system.

As you look through the requirements for the various modes of operation approved by the federal government, you'll notice that the administrative requirements for controlling the types of users that access a system decrease as you move from dedicated systems down to multilevel systems. However, this does not decrease the importance of limiting individual access so that users can obtain only the information they are legitimately entitled to access. As discussed in the previous section, it's simply a matter of shifting the burden of enforcing these requirements from administrative personnel—who physically limit access to a computer—to the hardware and software—which control what information can be accessed by each user of a multiuser system.

NOTE: Multilevel security mode can also be called the *controlled security mode.*

Table 9.1 summarizes and compares these four security modes according to security clearances required, need to know, and the ability to process data from multiple clearance levels (abbreviated PDMCL). When comparing all four security modes, it is generally understood that the multilevel mode is exposed to the highest level of risk.

TABLE 9.1 Comparing security modes

Mode	Clearance	Need to know	PDMCL
Dedicated	Same	None	None
System high	Same	Yes	None
Compartmented	Same	Yes	Yes
Multilevel	Different	Yes	Yes

Clearance is **Same** if all users must have the same security clearances, **Different** if otherwise.

Need to Know is **None** if it does not apply and is not used or if it is used but all users have the need to know all data present on the system, **Yes** if access is limited by need-to-know restrictions.

PDMCL applies if and when CMW implementations are used (**Yes**); otherwise, PDMCL is **None**.

Operating Modes

Modern processors and operating systems are designed to support multiuser environments in which individual computer users might not be granted access to all components of a system or all the information stored on it. For that reason, the processor itself supports two modes of operation: user mode and privileged mode.

User Mode User mode is the basic mode used by the CPU when executing user applications. In this mode, the CPU allows the execution of only a portion of its full instruction set. This is designed to protect users from accidentally damaging the system through the execution of poorly designed code or the unintentional misuse of that code. It also protects the system and its data from a malicious user who might try to execute instructions designed to circumvent the security measures put in place by the operating system or who might mistakenly perform actions that could result in unauthorized access or damage to the system or valuable information assets.

Often processes within user mode are executed within a controlled environment called a *virtual machine* (VM) or a *virtual subsystem machine*. A virtual machine is a simulated environment created by the OS to provide a safe and efficient place for programs to execute. Each VM is isolated from all other VMs, and each VM has its own assigned memory address space that can be used by the hosted application. It is the responsibility of the elements in privileged mode (aka kernel mode) to create and support the VMs and prevent the processes in one VM from interfering with the processes in other VMs.

Privileged Mode CPUs also support privileged mode, which is designed to give the operating system access to the full range of instructions supported by the CPU. This mode goes by a number of names, and the exact terminology varies according to the CPU manufacturer. Some of the more common monikers are included in the following list:

- Privileged mode
- Supervisory mode
- System mode
- Kernel mode

No matter which term you use, the basic concept remains the same—this mode grants a wide range of permissions to the process executing on the CPU. For this reason, well-designed operating systems do not let any user applications execute in privileged mode. Only those processes that are components of the operating system itself are allowed to execute in this mode, for both security and system integrity purposes.

TIP

Don't confuse processor modes with any type of user access permissions. The fact that the high-level processor mode is sometimes called *privileged* or *supervisory* mode has no relationship to the role of a user. All user applications, including those of system administrators, run in user mode. When system administrators use system tools to make configuration changes to the system, those tools also run in user mode. When a user application needs to perform a privileged action, it passes that request to the operating system using a system call, which evaluates it and either rejects the request or approves it and executes it using a privileged mode process outside the user's control.

Memory

The second major hardware component of a system is *memory*, the storage bank for information that the computer needs to keep readily available. There are many different kinds of memory, each suitable for different purposes, and we'll take a look at each in the sections that follow.

Read-Only Memory

Read-only memory (ROM) works like the name implies—it's memory the PC can read but can't change (no writing allowed). The contents of a standard ROM chip are burned in at the factory, and the end user simply cannot alter it. ROM chips often contain "bootstrap" information that computers use to start up prior to loading an operating system from disk. This includes the familiar power-on self-test (POST) series of diagnostics that run each time you boot a PC.

ROM's primary advantage is that it can't be modified. There is no chance that user or administrator error will accidentally wipe out or modify the contents of such a chip. This attribute makes ROM extremely desirable for orchestrating a computer's innermost workings.

There is a type of ROM that may be altered by administrators to some extent. It is known as programmable read-only memory (PROM), and its several subtypes are described next:

Programmable Read-Only Memory (PROM) A basic programmable read-only memory (PROM) chip is similar to a ROM chip in functionality, but with one exception. During the manufacturing process, a PROM chip's contents aren't "burned in" at the factory as with standard ROM chips. Instead, a PROM incorporates special functionality that allows an end user to burn in the chip's contents later. However, the burning process has a similar outcome—once data is written to a PROM chip, no further changes are possible. After it's burned in, a PROM chip essentially functions like a ROM chip.

PROM chips provide software developers with an opportunity to store information permanently on a high-speed, customized memory chip. PROMs are commonly used for hardware applications where some custom functionality is necessary but seldom changes once programmed.

Erasable Programmable Read-Only Memory (EPROM) Combine the relatively high cost of PROM chips and software developers' inevitable desires to tinker with their code once it's written and you have the rationale that led to the development of erasable PROM (EPROM). These chips have a small window that, when illuminated with a special ultraviolet light, causes the contents of the chip to be erased. After this process is complete, end users can burn new information into the EPROM as if it had never been programmed before.

Electronically Erasable Programmable Read-Only Memory (EEPROM) Although it's better than no erase function at all, EPROM erasure is pretty cumbersome. It requires the physical removal of the chip from the computer and exposure to a special kind of ultraviolet light. A more flexible, friendly alternative is electronically erasable PROM (EEPROM), which uses electric voltages delivered to the pins of the chip to force erasure. EEPROM chips can be erased without removing them from the computer, which makes them much more attractive than standard PROM or EPROM chips.

Flash Memory Flash memory is a derivative concept from EEPROM. It is a nonvolatile form of storage media that can be electronically erased and rewritten. The primary difference between EEPROM and flash memory is that EEPROM must be fully erased to be rewritten whereas flash memory can be erased and written in blocks or pages. The most common type of flash memory is NAND flash. It is widely used in memory cards, thumb drives, mobile devices, and SSD (solid-state drives).

Random Access Memory

Random access memory (RAM) is readable and writable memory that contains information a computer uses during processing. RAM retains its contents only when power is continuously supplied to it. Unlike with ROM, when a computer is powered off, all data stored in RAM disappears. For this reason, RAM is useful only for temporary storage. Critical data should never be stored solely in RAM; a backup copy should always be kept on another storage device to prevent its disappearance in the event of a sudden loss of electrical power. The following are types of RAM:

Real Memory Real memory (also known as *main memory*or *primary memory*) is typically the largest RAM storage resource available to a computer. It is normally composed of a number of dynamic RAM chips and, therefore, must be refreshed by the CPU on a periodic basis (see the sidebar "Dynamic vs. Static RAM" for more information on this subject).

Cache RAM Computer systems contain a number of caches that improve performance by taking data from slower devices and temporarily storing it in faster devices when repeated use is likely; this is cache RAM. The processor normally contains an onboard cache of extremely fast memory used to hold data on which it will operate. This on-chip, or level 1, cache is often backed up by a static RAM cache on a separate chip, called a *level 2 cache*, which holds data from the computer's main bank of real memory. Likewise, real memory often contains a cache of information stored on magnetic media or SSD. This chain continues down through the memory/storage hierarchy to enable computers to improve performance by keeping data that's likely to be used next closer at hand (be it for CPU instructions, data fetches, file access, or what have you).

Many peripherals also include onboard caches to reduce the storage burden they place on the CPU and operating system. For example, many higher-end printers include large RAM caches so that the operating system can quickly spool an entire job to the printer. After that, the processor can forget about the print job; it won't be forced to wait for the printer to actually produce the requested output, spoon-feeding it chunks of data one at a time. The printer can preprocess information from its onboard cache, thereby freeing the CPU and operating system to work on other tasks.

Real World Scenario

Dynamic vs. Static RAM

There are two main types of RAM: dynamic RAM and static RAM. Most computers contain a combination of both types and use them for different purposes.

To store data, dynamic RAM uses a series of capacitors, tiny electrical devices that hold a charge. These capacitors either hold a charge (representing a 1 bit in memory) or do not hold a charge (representing a 0 bit). However, because capacitors naturally lose their charges over time, the CPU must spend time refreshing the contents of dynamic RAM to ensure that 1 bits don't unintentionally change to 0 bits, thereby altering memory contents.

Static RAM uses more sophisticated technology—a logical device known as a *flip-flop*, which to all intents and purposes is simply an on/off switch that must be moved from one position to another to change a 0 to 1 or vice versa. More important, static memory maintains its contents unaltered as long as power is supplied and imposes no CPU overhead for periodic refresh operations.

Dynamic RAM is cheaper than static RAM because capacitors are cheaper than flip-flops. However, static RAM runs much faster than dynamic RAM. This creates a trade-off for system designers, who combine static and dynamic RAM modules to strike the right balance of cost versus performance.

Registers

The CPU also includes a limited amount of onboard memory, known as *registers*, that provide it with directly accessible memory locations that the brain of the CPU, the arithmetic-logical unit (ALU), uses when performing calculations or processing instructions. In fact, any data that the ALU is to manipulate must be loaded into a register unless it is directly supplied as part of the instruction. The main advantage of this type of memory is that it is part of the ALU itself and, therefore, operates in lockstep with the CPU at typical CPU speeds.

Memory Addressing

When using memory resources, the processor must have some means of referring to various locations in memory. The solution to this problem is known as *addressing*, and there are several different addressing schemes used in various circumstances. The following are five of the more common addressing schemes:

Register Addressing As you learned in the previous section, registers are small memory locations directly in the CPU. When the CPU needs information from one of its registers to complete an operation, it uses a register address (for example, "register 1") to access its contents.

Immediate Addressing Immediate addressing is not a memory addressing scheme per se but rather a way of referring to data that is supplied to the CPU as part of an instruction. For example, the CPU might process the command "Add 2 to the value in register 1." This command uses two addressing schemes. The first is immediate addressing—the CPU is being told to add the value 2 and does not need to retrieve that value from a memory location—it's supplied as part of the command. The second is register addressing; it's instructed to retrieve the value from register 1.

Direct Addressing In direct addressing, the CPU is provided with an actual address of the memory location to access. The address must be located on the same memory page as the instruction being executed. Direct addressing is more flexible than immediate addressing since the contents of the memory location can be changed more readily than reprogramming the immediate addressing's hard-coded data.

Indirect Addressing Indirect addressing uses a scheme similar to direct addressing. However, the memory address supplied to the CPU as part of the instruction doesn't contain the actual value that the CPU is to use as an operand. Instead, the memory address contains another memory address (perhaps located on a different page). The CPU reads the indirect address to learn the address where the desired data resides and then retrieves the actual operand from that address.

Base+Offset Addressing Base+offset addressing uses a value stored in one of the CPU's registers as the base location from which to begin counting. The CPU then adds the offset supplied with the instruction to that base address and retrieves the operand from that computed memory location.

Secondary Memory

Secondary memory is a term commonly used to refer to magnetic, optical, or flash-based media or other storage devices that contain data not immediately available to the CPU. For the CPU to access data in secondary memory, the data must first be read by the operating system and stored in real memory. However, secondary memory is much more inexpensive than primary memory and can be used to store massive amounts of information. In this context, hard disks, floppy drives, and optical media such as CDs and DVDs can all function as secondary memory.

Virtual memory is a special type of secondary memory that the operating system manages to make look and act just like real memory. The most common type of virtual memory is the pagefile that most operating systems manage as part of their memory management functions. This specially formatted file contains data previously stored in memory but not recently used. When the operating system needs to access addresses stored in the pagefile, it checks to see whether the page is memory-resident (in which case it can access it immediately) or whether it has been swapped to disk, in which case it reads the data from disk back into real memory (this process is called *paging*).

Using virtual memory is an inexpensive way to make a computer operate as if it had more real memory than is physically installed. Its major drawback is that the paging operations that occur when data is exchanged between primary and secondary memory are relatively slow (memory functions in nanoseconds, disk systems in microseconds; usually, this means three orders of magnitude difference!) and consume significant computer overhead, slowing down the entire system.

Memory Security Issues

Memory stores and processes your data—some of which may be extremely sensitive. It's essential that you understand the various types of memory and know how they store and retain data. Any memory devices that may retain sensitive data should be purged before they are allowed to leave your organization for any reason. This is especially true for secondary memory and ROM/PROM/EPROM/EEPROM devices designed to retain data even after the power is turned off.

However, memory data retention issues are not limited to those types of memory designed to retain data. Remember that static and dynamic RAM chips store data through the use of capacitors and flip-flops (see the sidebar "Dynamic vs. Static RAM"). It is technically possible that those electrical components could retain some of their charge for a limited period of time after power is turned off. A technically sophisticated individual could theoretically take electrical measurements of those components and retrieve portions of the data stored on such devices. However, this requires a good deal of technical expertise and is not a likely threat unless you have adversaries with mind-bogglingly deep pockets.

There is also an attack that freezes memory chips to delay the decay of resident data when the system is turned off or the RAM is pulled out of the motherboard. See `http://en.wikipedia.org/wiki/Cold_boot_attack`.

WARNING The greatest security threat posed by RAM chips is a simple one. They are highly pilferable and are quite often stolen. After all, who checks to see how much memory is in their computer at the start of each day? Someone could easily remove a single memory module from each of a large number of systems and walk out the door with a small bag containing valuable chips. Today, this threat is diminishing as the price of memory chips continues to fall.

One of the most important security issues surrounding memory is controlling who may access data stored in memory while a computer is in use. This is primarily the responsibility of the operating system and is the main memory security issue underlying the various processing modes described in previous sections in this chapter. In the section "Essential Security Protection Mechanisms" later in this chapter, you'll learn how the principle of process isolation can be used to ensure that processes don't have access to read or write to memory spaces not allocated to them. If you're operating in a multilevel security environment, it's especially important to ensure that adequate protections are in place to prevent the unwanted leakage of memory contents between security levels, through either direct memory access or covert channels (a full discussion of covert channels appears later in this chapter).

Storage

Data storage devices make up the third class of computer system components we'll discuss. These devices are used to store information that may be used by a computer any time after it's written. We'll first examine a few common terms that relate to storage devices and then cover some of the security issues related to data storage.

Primary vs. Secondary

The concepts of primary and secondary storage can be somewhat confusing, especially when compared to primary and secondary memory. There's an easy way to keep it straight—they're the same thing! *Primary memory*, also known as *primary storage*, is the RAM that a computer uses to keep necessary information readily available to the CPU while the computer is running. *Secondary memory* (or *secondary storage*) includes all the familiar long-term storage devices that you use every day. Secondary storage consists of magnetic and optical media such as hard drives, solid-state drives (SSDs), floppy disks, magnetic tapes, compact discs (CDs), digital video disks (DVDs), flash memory cards, and the like.

Volatile vs. Nonvolatile

You're already familiar with the concept of volatility from our discussion of memory, although you may not have heard it described using that term before. The volatility of a storage device is simply a measure of how likely it is to lose its data when power is turned off. Devices designed to retain their data (such as magnetic media) are classified as *nonvolatile*, whereas devices such as static or dynamic RAM modules, which are designed to lose their data, are classified as *volatile*. Recall from the discussion in the previous section that sophisticated technology may sometimes be able to extract data from volatile memory after power is removed, so the lines between the two may sometimes be blurry.

Random vs. Sequential

Storage devices may be accessed in one of two fashions. *Random access storage* devices allow an operating system to read (and sometimes write) immediately from any point within the device by using some type of addressing system. Almost all primary storage devices are random access devices. You can use a memory address to access information stored at any point within a RAM chip without reading the data that is physically stored before it. Most secondary storage devices are also random access. For example, hard drives use a movable head system that allows you to move directly to any point on the disk without spinning past all the data stored on previous tracks; likewise, CD and DVD devices use an optical scanner that can position itself anywhere on the platter surface.

Sequential storage devices, on the other hand, do not provide this flexibility. They require that you read (or speed past) all the data physically stored prior to the desired location. A common example of a sequential storage device is a magnetic tape drive. To provide access to data stored in the middle of a tape, the tape drive must physically scan through the entire tape (even if it's not necessarily processing the data that it passes in fast-forward mode) until it reaches the desired point.

Obviously, sequential storage devices operate much slower than random access storage devices. However, here again you're faced with a cost/benefit decision. Many sequential storage devices can hold massive amounts of data on relatively inexpensive media. This property makes tape drives uniquely suited for backup tasks associated with a disaster recovery/business continuity plan (see Chapter 3, "Business Continuity Planning," and Chapter 18, "Disaster Recovery Planning"). In a backup situation, you often have extremely large amounts of data that need to be stored, and you infrequently need to access that stored information. The situation just begs for a sequential storage device!

Storage Media Security

We discussed the security problems that surround primary storage devices in the previous section. There are three main concerns when it comes to the security of secondary storage devices; all of them mirror concerns raised for primary storage devices:

- Data may remain on secondary storage devices even after it has been erased. This condition is known as *data remanence.* Most technically savvy computer users know that utilities are available that can retrieve files from a disk even after they have been deleted. It's also technically possible to retrieve data from a disk that has been reformatted. If you truly want to remove data from a secondary storage device, you must use a specialized utility designed to destroy all traces of data on the device or damage or destroy it beyond possible repair (commonly called *sanitizing*).
- SSDs present a unique problem in relation to sanitization. SSD wear leveling means that there are often blocks of data that are not marked as "live" but that hold a copy of the data when it was copied off to lower wear leveled blocks. This means that a traditional zero wipe is ineffective as a data security measure for SSDs.
- Secondary storage devices are also prone to theft. Economic loss is not the major factor (after all, how much does a CD-R disc or even a hard drive cost?), but the loss of confidential information poses great risks. If someone copies your trade secrets onto a removable media disc and walks out the door with it, it's worth a lot more than the cost of the disc itself. For this reason, it is important to use full disk encryption to reduce the risk of an unauthorized entity gaining access to your data. It is good security practice to encrypt SSDs prior to storing any data on them due to their wear leveling technology. This will minimize the chance of any plaintext data residing in dormant blocks. Fortunately, many HDD and SSD devices offer on-device native encryption.
- Access to data stored on secondary storage devices is one of the most critical issues facing computer security professionals. For hard disks, data can often be protected through a combination of operating system access controls. Removable media pose a greater challenge, so securing them often requires encryption technologies.

Input and Output Devices

Input and output devices are often seen as basic, primitive peripherals and usually don't receive much attention until they stop working properly. However, even these basic devices can present security risks to a system. Security professionals should be aware of these risks and ensure that appropriate controls are in place to mitigate them. The next four sections examine some of the risks posed by specific input and output devices.

Monitors

Monitors seem fairly innocuous. After all, they simply display the data presented by the operating system. When you turn them off, the data disappears from the screen and can't be recovered. However, technology from a program known as TEMPEST can compromise the security of data displayed on a monitor.

TEMPEST is a technology that allows the electronic emanations that every monitor produces (known as *Van Eck radiation*) to be read from a distance (this process is known as *Van Eck phreaking*) and even from another location. The technology is also used to protect against such activity. Various demonstrations have shown that you can easily read the screens of monitors inside an office building using gear housed in a van parked outside on the street. Unfortunately, the protective controls required to prevent Van Eck radiation (lots and lots of copper!) are expensive to implement and cumbersome to use. Generally, CRT monitors are more prone to radiate significantly, whereas LCD monitors leak much less (some claim not enough to reveal critical data). It is arguable that the biggest risk with any monitor is still shoulder surfing or telephoto lenses on cameras.

Printers

Printers also may represent a security risk, albeit a simpler one. Depending on the physical security controls used at your organization, it may be much easier to walk out with sensitive information in printed form than to walk out with a floppy disk or other magnetic media. If printers are shared, users may forget to retrieve their sensitive printouts, leaving them vulnerable to prying eyes. Many modern printers also store data locally, often on a hard drive, and some retain copies of printouts indefinitely. Printers are usually exposed on the network for convenient access and are often not designed to be secure systems. These are all issues that are best addressed by an organization's security policy.

Keyboards/Mice

Keyboards, mice, and similar input devices are not immune to security vulnerabilities either. All of these devices are vulnerable to TEMPEST monitoring. Also, keyboards are vulnerable to less sophisticated bugging. A simple device can be placed inside a keyboard or along its connection cable to intercept all the keystrokes that take place and transmit them to a remote receiver using a radio signal. This has the same effect as TEMPEST monitoring but can be done with much less expensive gear. Additionally, if your keyboard and mouse are wireless, including Bluetooth, their radio signals can be intercepted.

Modems

With the advent of ubiquitous broadband and wireless connectivity, modems are becoming a scarce legacy computer component. If your organization is still using older equipment, there is a chance that a modem is part of the hardware configuration. The presence of a modem on a user system is often one of the greatest woes of a security administrator. Modems allow users to create uncontrolled access points into your network. In the worst case, if improperly configured, they can create extremely serious security vulnerabilities that allow an outsider to bypass all your perimeter protection mechanisms and directly access your network resources. At best, they create an alternate egress channel that insiders can use to funnel data outside your organization. But keep in mind, these vulnerabilities can only be exploited if the modem is connected to an operational telephone land line.

You should seriously consider an outright ban on modems in your organization's security policy unless you truly need them for business reasons. In those cases, security officials should know the physical and logical locations of all modems on the network, ensure that they are correctly configured, and make certain that appropriate protective measures are in place to prevent their illegitimate use.

Input/Output Structures

Certain computer activities related to general input/output (I/O) operations, rather than individual devices, also have security implications. Some familiarity with manual input/output device configuration is required to integrate legacy peripheral devices (those that do not autoconfigure or support Plug and Play, or PnP, setup) in modern PCs as well. Three types of operations that require manual configuration on legacy devices are involved here:

Memory-Mapped I/O For many kinds of devices, memory-mapped I/O is a technique used to manage input/output. That is, a part of the address space that the CPU manages functions to provide access to some kind of device through a series of mapped memory addresses or locations. Thus, by reading mapped memory locations, you're actually reading the input from the corresponding device (which is automatically copied to those memory locations at the system level when the device signals that input is available). Likewise, by writing to those mapped memory locations, you're actually sending output to that device (automatically handled by copying from those memory locations to the device at the system level when the CPU signals that the output is available).

From a configuration standpoint, it's important to make sure that only one device maps into a specific memory address range and that the address range is used for no other purpose than to handle device I/O. From a security standpoint, access to mapped memory locations should be mediated by the operating system and subject to proper authorization and access controls.

Interrupt (IRQ) Interrupt (IRQ) is an abbreviation for *interrupt request*, a technique for assigning specific signal lines to specific devices through a special interrupt controller. When a device wants to supply input to the CPU, it sends a signal on its assigned IRQ (which usually falls in a range of 0 to 16 on older PCs for two cascaded 8-line interrupt controllers and 0 to 23 on newer ones with three cascaded 8-line interrupt controllers). Where newer PnP-compatible devices may actually share a single interrupt (IRQ number), older legacy devices must generally have exclusive use of a unique IRQ number (a well-known pathology called *interrupt conflict* occurs when two or more devices are assigned the same IRQ number and is best recognized by an inability to access all affected devices). From a configuration standpoint, finding unused IRQ numbers that will work with legacy devices can be a sometimes trying exercise. From a security standpoint, only the operating system should be able to mediate access to IRQs at a sufficiently high level of privilege to prevent tampering or accidental misconfiguration.

Direct Memory Access (DMA) Direct Memory Access (DMA) works as a channel with two signal lines, where one line is a DMA request (DMQ) line and the other is a DMA acknowledgment (DACK) line. Devices that can exchange data directly with real memory (RAM) without requiring assistance from the CPU use DMA to manage such access. Using its DRQ line, a device signals the CPU that it wants to make direct access (which may be read or write or some combination of the two) to another device, usually real memory. The CPU authorizes access and then allows the access to proceed independently while blocking other access to the memory locations involved. When the access is complete, the device uses the DACK line to signal that the CPU may once again permit access to previously blocked memory locations. This is faster than requiring the CPU to mediate such access and permits the CPU to move on to other tasks while the memory access is underway. DMA is used most commonly to permit disk drives, optical drives, display cards, and multimedia cards to manage large-scale data transfers to and from real memory. From a configuration standpoint, it's important to manage DMA addresses to keep device addresses unique and to make sure such addresses are used only for DMA signaling. From a security standpoint, only the operating system should be able to mediate DMA assignment and the use of DMA to access I/O devices.

If you understand common IRQ assignments, how memory-mapped I/O and DMA work, and related security concerns, you know enough to tackle the CISSP exam. If not, some additional reading may be warranted. In that case, PC Guide's excellent overview of system memory (`www.pcguide.com/ref/ram/`) should tell you everything you need to know.

Firmware

Firmware (also known as *microcode* in some circles) is a term used to describe software that is stored in a ROM chip. This type of software is changed infrequently (actually, never, if it's stored on a true ROM chip as opposed to an EPROM/EEPROM) and often drives the basic operation of a computing device. There are two types of firmware: BIOS on a motherboard and general internal and external device firmware.

BIOS

The Basic Input/Output System (BIOS) contains the operating system–independent primitive instructions that a computer needs to start up and load the operating system from disk. The BIOS is contained in a firmware device that is accessed immediately by the computer at boot time. In most computers, the BIOS is stored on an EEPROM chip to facilitate version updates. The process of updating the BIOS is known as "flashing the BIOS."

There have been a few examples of malicious code embedding itself into BIOS/firmware. There is also an attack known as *phlashing*, in which a malicious variation of official BIOS or firmware is installed that introduces remote control or other malicious features into a device.

Since 2011, most system manufacturers have replaced the traditional BIOS system on their motherboards with UEFI (unified extensible firmware interface). UEFI is a more advanced interface between hardware and the operating system, which maintains support for legacy BIOS services.

Device Firmware

Many hardware devices, such as printers and modems, also need some limited processing power to complete their tasks while minimizing the burden placed on the operating system itself. In many cases, these "mini" operating systems are entirely contained in firmware chips onboard the devices they serve. As with a computer's BIOS, device firmware is frequently stored on an EEPROM device so it can be updated as necessary.

Client-Based

Client-based vulnerabilities place the user, their data, and their system at risk of compromise and destruction. A client-side attack is any attack that is able to harm a client. Generally, when attacks are discussed, it's assumed that the primary target is a server or a server-side component. A client-side or client-focused attack is one where the client itself, or a process on the client, is the target. A common example of a client-side attack is a malicious website that transfers malicious mobile code (such as an applet) to a vulnerable browser running on the client. Client-side attacks can occur over any communications protocol, not just HTTP. Another potential vulnerability that is client based is the risk of poisoning of local caches.

Applets

Recall that agents are code objects sent from a user's system to query and process data stored on remote systems. *Applets* perform the opposite function; these code objects are sent from a server to a client to perform some action. In fact, applets are actually self-contained miniature programs that execute independently of the server that sent them.

Imagine a web server that offers a variety of financial tools to web users. One of these tools might be a mortgage calculator that processes a user's financial information and provides a monthly mortgage payment based on the loan's principal and term and the borrower's credit information. Instead of processing this data and returning the results to the client system, the remote web server might send to the local system an applet that enables it to perform those calculations itself. This provides a number of benefits to both the remote server and the end user:

- The processing burden is shifted to the client, freeing up resources on the web server to process requests from more users.
- The client is able to produce data using local resources rather than waiting for a response from the remote server. In many cases, this results in a quicker response to changes in the input data.
- In a properly programmed applet, the web server does not receive any data provided to the applet as input, therefore maintaining the security and privacy of the user's financial data.

However, just as with agents, applets introduce a number of security concerns. They allow a remote system to send code to the local system for execution. Security administrators must take steps to ensure that code sent to systems on their network is safe and properly screened for malicious activity. Also, unless the code is analyzed line by line, the end user can never be certain that the applet doesn't contain a Trojan horse component. For example, the mortgage calculator might indeed transmit sensitive financial information to the web server without the end user's knowledge or consent.

Two common applet types are Java applets and ActiveX controls:

Java Applets Java is a platform-independent programming language developed by Sun Microsystems. Most programming languages use compilers that produce applications custom-tailored to run under a specific operating system. This requires the use of multiple compilers to produce different versions of a single application for each platform it must support. Java overcomes this limitation by inserting the Java Virtual Machine (JVM) into the picture. Each system that runs Java code downloads the version of the JVM supported by its operating system. The JVM then takes the Java code and translates it into a format executable by that specific system. The great benefit of this arrangement is that code can be shared between operating systems without modification. Java applets are simply short Java programs transmitted over the Internet to perform operations on a remote system.

Security was of paramount concern during the design of the Java platform, and Sun's development team created the "sandbox" concept to place privilege restrictions on Java code. The sandbox isolates Java code objects from the rest of the operating system and enforces strict rules about the resources those objects can access. For example, the sandbox would prohibit a Java applet from retrieving information from areas of memory not specifically allocated to it, preventing the applet from stealing that information. Unfortunately, while sandboxing reduces the forms of malicious events that can be launched via Java, there are still plenty of other vulnerabilities that have been widely exploited.

ActiveX Controls ActiveX controls are Microsoft's answer to Sun's Java applets. They operate in a similar fashion, but they are implemented using a variety of languages, including Visual Basic, C, C++, and Java. There are two key distinctions between Java applets and ActiveX controls. First, ActiveX controls use proprietary Microsoft technology and, therefore, can execute only on systems running Microsoft browsers. Second, ActiveX controls are not subject to the sandbox restrictions placed on Java applets. They have full access to the Windows operating environment and can perform a number of privileged actions. Therefore, you must take special precautions when deciding which ActiveX controls to download and execute. Some security administrators have taken the somewhat harsh position of prohibiting the download of any ActiveX content from all but a select handful of trusted sites.

Microsoft has announced and released previews of its new browser code named Project Spartan. This new browser will not include ActiveX support. While plans to ship Internet Explorer 10 will still include ActiceX, this signals that even Microsoft may be phasing out ActiveX.

Local Caches

A local cache is anything that is temporarily stored on the client for future reuse. There are many local caches on a typical client, including ARP cache, DNS cache, and Internet files cache. ARP cache poisoning is caused by an attack responding to ARP broadcast queries in order to send back falsified replies. If the false reply is received by the client before the valid reply, then the false reply is used to populate the ARP cache and the valid reply is discarded as being outside of an open query. The dynamic content of ARP cache, whether poisoned or legitimate, will remain in cache until a timeout occurs (which is usually under 10 minutes). ARP is used to resolve an IP address into the appropriate MAC address in order to craft the Ethernet header for data transmission. Once an IP-to-MAC mapping falls out of cache, then the attacker gains another opportunity to poison the ARP cache when the client re-performs the ARP broadcast query.

A second form of ARP cache poisoning is to create static ARP entries. This is done via the ARP command and must be done locally. But this is easily accomplished through a script that gets executed on the client either through a Trojan horse, buffer overflow, or social engineering attack. Static ARP entries are permanent, even across system reboots. Once ARP poisoning has occurred, whether against a permanent entry or a dynamic one, the traffic transmitted from the client will be sent to a different system than intended. This is due to have the wrong or a different hardware address (that is, the MAC address) associated with an IP address. ARP cache poisoning or just ARP poisoning is one means of setting up a man-in-the-middle attack.

Another popular means of performing a man-in-the-middle attack is through DNS cache poisoning. Similar to ARP cache, once a client receives a response from DNS, that response will be cached for future use. If false information can be fed into the cache, then misdirecting communications is trivially easy. There are many means of performing DNS cache poisoning, including HOSTS poisoning, authorized DNS server attacks, caching DNS server attacks, DNS lookup address changing, and DNS query spoofing.

The HOSTS file is the static file found on TCP/IP supporting system that contains hard-coded references for domain names and their associated IP addresses. The HOSTS file was used prior to the dynamic query–based DNS system of today, but it serves as a fallback measure or a means to force resolution. Administrators or hackers can add content to the HOSTS file that sets up a relationship between a FQDN (fully qualified domain name) and the IP address of choice. If an attacker is able to plant false information into the HOSTS file, then when the system boots the contents of the HOSTS file will be read into memory where they will take precedence. Unlike dynamic queries, which eventually time out and expire from cache, entries from the HOSTS file are permanent.

Authorized DNS server attacks aim at altering the primary record of a FQDN on its original host system. The authoritative DNS server hosts the zone file or domain database. If this original dataset is altered, then eventually those changes will propagate across the entire Internet. However, an attack on an authoritative DNS server typically gets noticed very quickly, so this rarely results in widespread exploitation. So, most attackers focus on caching DNS servers instead. A caching DNS server is any DNS system deployed to cache DNS information from other DNS servers. Most companies and ISPs provide a caching

DNS server for their users. The content hosted on a caching DNS server is not being watched by the worldwide security community, just the local operators. Thus, an attack against a caching DNS server can potentially occur without notice for a significant period of time. For detailed information on how caching DNS server attacks can occur, see "An Illustrated Guide to the Kaminsky DNS Vulnerability" at `http://unixwiz.net/techtips/iguide-kaminsky-dns-vuln.html`. Although both of these attacks focus on DNS servers, they ultimately affect clients. Once a client has performed a dynamic DNS resolution, the information received from an authoritative DNS server or a caching DNS server will be temporarily stored in the client's local DNS cache. If that information is false, then the client's DNS cache has been poisoned.

A fourth example of DNS poisoning focuses on sending an alternate IP address to the client to be used as the DNS server the client uses for resolving queries. The DNS server address is typically distributed to clients through DHCP but it can also be assigned statically. Even if all of the other elements of IP configuration have been assigned by DHCP, a local alteration can easily staticly assign a DNS server address. Attacks to alter a client's DNS server lookup address can be performed through a script (similar to the ARP attack mentioned earlier) or by compromising DHCP. Once the client has the wrong DNS server, they will be sending their queries to a hacker-controlled DNS server, which will respond with poisoned results.

A fifth example of DNS poisoning is that of DNS query spoofing. This attack occurs when the hacker is able to eavesdrop on a client's query to a DNS server. The attacker then sends back a reply with false information. If the client accepts the false reply, they will put that information in their local DNS cache. When the real reply arrives, it will be discarded since the original query will have already been answered. No matter which of these five means of DNS attack is performed, false entries will be present in the local DNS cache of the client. Thus, all of the IP communications will be sent to the wrong endpoint. This allows the hacker to set up a man-in-the-middle attack by operating that false endpoint and then forwarding traffic on to the correct destination.

A third area of concern in regard to local cache is that of the temporary Internet files or the Internet files cache. This is the temporary storage of files downloaded from Internet sites that are being held by the client's utility for current and possibly future use. Mostly this cache contains website content, but other Internet services can use a file cache as well. A variety of exploitations, such as the split-response attack, can cause the client to download content and store it in the cache that was not an intended element of a requested web page. Mobile code scripting attacks could also be used to plant false content in the cache. Once files have been poisoned in the cache, then even when a legitimate web document calls on a cached item, the malicious item will be activated.

Mitigating or resolving these attacks is not simple or straightforward. There is not an easy patch or update that will prevent these exploits from being waged against a client. This is due to the fact that these attacks take advantage of the normal and proper mechanisms built into various protocols, services, and applications. Thus, instead of a patch to fix a flaw, the defense is more of a detective and preventive concern. Generally as a start, keep operating systems and applications current with patches from their respective vendors. Next, install both host-IDS and network-IDS tools to watch for abuses of these types. Regularly review the logs of your DNS and DHCP systems, as well as local client system logs and potentially firewall, switch, and router logs for entries indicating abnormal or questionable occurrences.

Server-Based

An important area of server-based concern, which may include clients as well, is the issue of data flow control. Data flow is the movement of data between processes, between devices, across a network, or over communication channels. Management of data flow ensures not only efficient transmission with minimal delays or latency, but also reliable throughput using hashing and protection confidentiality with encryption. Data flow control also ensures that receiving systems are not overloaded with traffic, especially to the point of dropping connections or being subject to a malicious or even self-inflicted denial of service. When data overflow occurs, data may be lost or corrupted or may trigger a need for retransmission. These results are undesirable, and data flow control is often implemented to prevent these issues from occurring. Data flow control may be provided by networking devices, including routers and switches, as well as network applications and services.

Database Security

Database security is an important part of any organization that uses large sets of data as an essential asset. Without database security efforts, business tasks can be interrupted and confidential information disclosed. For the CISSP exam, it is important that you are aware of several topics in relation to database security. These include aggregation, inference, data mining, data warehousing, and data analytics.

Aggregation

SQL provides a number of functions that combine records from one or more tables to produce potentially useful information. This process is called *aggregation*. Aggregation is not without its security vulnerabilities. Aggregation attacks are used to collect numerous low-level security items or low-value items and combine them to create something of a higher security level or value.

These functions, although extremely useful, also pose a risk to the security of information in a database. For example, suppose a low-level military records clerk is responsible for updating records of personnel and equipment as they are transferred from base to base. As part of his duties, this clerk may be granted the database permissions necessary to query and update personnel tables.

The military might not consider an individual transfer request (in other words, Sergeant Jones is being moved from Base X to Base Y) to be classified information. The records clerk has access to that information because he needs it to process Sergeant Jones's transfer.

However, with access to aggregate functions, the records clerk might be able to count the number of troops assigned to each military base around the world. These force levels are often closely guarded military secrets, but the low-ranking records clerk could deduce them by using aggregate functions across a large number of unclassified records.

For this reason, it's especially important for database security administrators to strictly control access to aggregate functions and adequately assess the potential information they may reveal to unauthorized individuals.

Inference

The database security issues posed by inference attacks are similar to those posed by the threat of data aggregation. Inference attacks involve combining several pieces of nonsensitive information to gain access to information that should be classified at a higher level. However, inference makes use of the human mind's deductive capacity rather than the raw mathematical ability of modern database platforms.

A commonly cited example of an inference attack is that of the accounting clerk at a large corporation who is allowed to retrieve the total amount the company spends on salaries for use in a top-level report but is not allowed to access the salaries of individual employees. The accounting clerk often has to prepare those reports with effective dates in the past and so is allowed to access the total salary amounts for any day in the past year. Say, for example, that this clerk must also know the hiring and termination dates of various employees and has access to this information. This opens the door for an inference attack. If an employee was the only person hired on a specific date, the accounting clerk can now retrieve the total salary amount on that date and the day before and deduce the salary of that particular employee—sensitive information that the user would not be permitted to access directly.

As with aggregation, the best defense against inference attacks is to maintain constant vigilance over the permissions granted to individual users. Furthermore, intentional blurring of data may be used to prevent the inference of sensitive information. For example, if the accounting clerk were able to retrieve only salary information rounded to the nearest million, they would probably not be able to gain any useful information about individual employees. Finally, you can use database partitioning (discussed earlier in this chapter) to help subvert these attacks.

Data Mining and Data Warehousing

Many organizations use large databases, known as *data warehouses*, to store large amounts of information from a variety of databases for use with specialized analysis techniques. These data warehouses often contain detailed historical information not normally stored in production databases because of storage limitations or data security concerns.

A *data dictionary* is commonly used for storing critical information about data, including usage, type, sources, relationships, and formats. DBMS software reads the data dictionary to determine access rights for users attempting to access data.

Data mining techniques allow analysts to comb through data warehouses and look for potential correlated information. For example, an analyst might discover that the demand for lightbulbs always increases in the winter months and then use this information when planning pricing and promotion strategies. Data mining techniques result in the development of data models that can be used to predict future activity.

The activity of data mining produces metadata. Metadata is data about data or information about data. Metadata is not exclusively the result of data mining operations; other functions or services can produce metadata as well. Think of metadata from a data mining operation as a concentration of data. It can also be a superset, a subset, or a representation of a larger dataset. Metadata can be the important, significant, relevant, abnormal, or aberrant elements from a dataset.

One common security example of metadata is that of a security incident report. An incident report is the metadata extracted from a data warehouse of audit logs through the use of a security auditing data mining tool. In most cases, metadata is of a greater value or sensitivity (due to disclosure) than the bulk of data in the warehouse. Thus, metadata is stored in a more secure container known as the *data mart*.

Data warehouses and data mining are significant to security professionals for two reasons. First, as previously mentioned, data warehouses contain large amounts of potentially sensitive information vulnerable to aggregation and inference attacks, and security practitioners must ensure that adequate access controls and other security measures are in place to safeguard this data. Second, data mining can actually be used as a security tool when it's used to develop baselines for statistical anomaly–based intrusion detection systems.

Data Analytics

Data analytics is the science of raw data examination with the focus of extracting useful information out of the bulk information set. The results of data analytics could focus on important outliers or exceptions to normal or standard items, a summary of all data items, or some focused extraction and organization of interesting information. Data analytics is a growing field as more organizations are gathering an astounding volume of data from their customers and products. The sheer volume of information to be processed has demanded a whole new category of database structures and analysis tools. It has even picked up the nickname of "big data."

Big data refers to collections of data that have become so large that traditional means of analysis or processing are ineffective, inefficient, and insufficient. Big data involves numerous difficult challenges, including collection, storage, analysis, mining, transfer, distribution, and results presentation. Such large volumes of data have the potential to reveal nuances and idiosyncrasies that more mundane sets of data fail to address. The potential to learn from big data is tremendous, but the burdens of dealing with big data are equally great. As the volume of data increases, the complexity of data analysis increases as well. Big data analysis requires high-performance analytics running on massively parallel or distributed processing systems. With regard to security, organizations are endeavoring to collect an ever more detailed and exhaustive range of event data and access data. This data is collected with the goal of assessing compliance, improving efficiencies, improving productivity, and detecting violations.

Large-Scale Parallel Data Systems

Parallel data systems or parallel computing is a computation system designed to perform numerous calculations simultaneously. But parallel data systems often go far beyond basic multiprocessing capabilities. They often include the concept of dividing up a large task into smaller elements, and then distributing each subelement to a different processing subsystem for parallel computation. This implementation is based on the idea that some problems can be solved efficiently if broken into smaller tasks that can be worked on concurrently. Parallel data processing can be accomplished by using distinct CPUs or multicode CPUs, using virtual systems, or any combination of these. Large-scale parallel data systems must also be concerned with performance, power consumption, and reliability/stability issues. The complexity of involving 1,000 or more processing units often results in an unexpected increase in problems and risks along with the enormous levels of computational capabilities.

The arena of large-scale parallel data systems is still evolving. It is likely that many management issues are yet to be discovered and solutions to known issues are still being sought. Large-scale parallel data management is likely a key tool in managing big data and will often involve cloud computing, grid computing, or peer-to-peer computing solutions. These three concepts are covered in the following sections.

Distributed Systems

As computing has evolved from a host/terminal model (where users could be physically distributed but all functions, activity, data, and resources reside on a single centralized system) to a client-server model (where users operate independent, fully functional desktop computers but also access services and resources on networked servers), security controls and concepts have had to evolve to follow suit. This means that clients have computing and storage capabilities and, typically, that multiple servers do likewise. Thus, security must be addressed everywhere instead of at a single centralized host. From a security standpoint, this means that because processing and storage are distributed on multiple clients and servers, all those computers must be properly secured and protected. It also means that the network links between clients and servers (and in some cases, these links may not be purely local) must also be secured and protected. When evaluating security architecture, be sure to include an assessment of the needs and risks related to distributed architectures.

Distributed architectures are prone to vulnerabilities unthinkable in monolithic host/terminal systems. Desktop systems can contain sensitive information that may be at some risk of being exposed and must therefore be protected. Individual users may lack general security savvy or awareness, and therefore the underlying architecture has to compensate for those deficiencies. Desktop PCs, workstations, and laptops can provide avenues of access into critical information systems elsewhere in a distributed environment because users require access to networked servers and services to do their jobs. By permitting user machines to access a network and its distributed resources, organizations must also recognize that those user machines can become threats if they are misused or compromised. Such software and system vulnerabilities and threats must be assessed and addressed properly.

Communications equipment can also provide unwanted points of entry into a distributed environment. For example, modems attached to a desktop machine that's also attached to an organization's network can make that network vulnerable to dial-in attacks. There is also a risk that wireless adapters on client systems can be used to create open networks. Likewise, users who download data from the Internet increase the risk of infecting their own and other systems with malicious code, Trojan horses, and so forth. Desktops, laptops, and workstations—and associated disks or other storage devices—may not be secure from physical intrusion or theft. Finally, when data resides only on client machines, it may not be secured with a proper backup (it's often the case that although servers are backed up routinely, the same is not true for client computers).

You should see that the foregoing litany of potential vulnerabilities in distributed architectures means that such environments require numerous safeguards to implement appropriate security and to ensure that such vulnerabilities are eliminated, mitigated, or remedied. Clients must be subjected to policies that impose safeguards on their contents and their users' activities. These include the following:

- Email must be screened so that it cannot become a vector for infection by malicious software; email should also be subject to policies that govern appropriate use and limit potential liability.
- Download/upload policies must be created so that incoming and outgoing data is screened and suspect materials blocked.
- Systems must be subject to robust access controls, which may include multifactor authentication and/or biometrics to restrict access to desktops and to prevent unauthorized access to servers and services.
- Graphical user interface mechanisms and database management systems should be installed, and their use required, to restrict and manage access to critical information.
- File encryption may be appropriate for files and data stored on client machines (indeed, drive-level encryption is a good idea for laptops and other mobile computing gear that is subject to loss or theft outside an organization's premises).
- It's essential to separate and isolate processes that run in user and supervisory modes so that unauthorized and unwanted access to high-privilege processes and capabilities is prevented.
- Protection domains should be created so that compromise of a client won't automatically compromise an entire network.
- Disks and other sensitive materials should be clearly labeled as to their security classification or organizational sensitivity; procedural processes and system controls should combine to help protect sensitive materials from unwanted or unauthorized access.
- Files on desktop machines should be backed up, as well as files on servers—ideally, using some form of centralized backup utility that works with client agent software to identify and capture files from clients stored in a secure backup storage archive.

- Desktop users need regular security awareness training to maintain proper security awareness; they also need to be notified about potential threats and instructed on how to deal with them appropriately.
- Desktop computers and their storage media require protection against environmental hazards (temperature, humidity, power loss/fluctuation, and so forth).
- Desktop computers should be included in disaster recovery and business continuity planning because they're potentially as important (if not more important) to getting their users back to work as other systems and services within an organization.
- Developers of custom software built in and for distributed environments also need to take security into account, including using formal methods for development and deployment, such as code libraries, change control mechanisms, configuration management, and patch and update deployment.

In general, safeguarding distributed environments means understanding the vulnerabilities to which they're subject and applying appropriate safeguards. These can (and do) range from technology solutions and controls to policies and procedures that manage risk and seek to limit or avoid losses, damage, unwanted disclosure, and so on.

A reasonable understanding of countermeasure principles is always important when responding to vulnerabilities and threats. Some specific countermeasure principles are discussed in Chapter 2, "Personnel Security and Risk Management Concepts," in the section "Risk Management." But a common general principle is that of defense in depth. *Defense in depth* is a common security strategy used to provide a protective multilayer barrier against various forms of attack. It's reasonable to assume that there is greater difficulty in passing bad traffic or data through a network heavily fortified by a firewall, an IDS, and a diligent administration staff than one with a firewall alone. Why shouldn't you double up your defenses? Defense in depth is the use of multiple types of access controls in literal or theoretical concentric circles. This form of layered security helps an organization avoid a monolithic security stance. A monolithic or fortress mentality is the belief that a single security mechanism is all that is required to provide sufficient security. Unfortunately, every individual security mechanism has a flaw or a workaround just waiting to be discovered and abused by a hacker. Only through the intelligent combination of countermeasures is a defense constructed that will resist significant and persistent attempts of compromise.

Cloud Computing

Cloud computing is the popular term referring to a concept of computing where processing and storage are performed elsewhere over a network connection rather than locally. Cloud computing is often thought of as Internet-based computing. Ultimately, processing and storage still occurs on computers somewhere, but the distinction is that the local operator no longer needs to have that capacity or capability locally. This also allows a larger group of users to leverage cloud resources on demand. From the end-user perspective, all the work of computing is now performed "in the cloud" and thus the complexity is isolated from them.

Cloud computing is a natural extension and evolution of virtualization, the Internet, distributed architecture, and the need for ubiquitous access to data and resources. However, it does have some issues, including privacy concerns, regulation compliance difficulties, use of open/closed-source solutions, adoption of open standards, and whether or not cloud-based data is actually secured (or even securable).

Some of the concepts in cloud computing are listed here:

Platform-as-a-Service Platform-as-a-Service (PaaS) is the concept of providing a computing platform and software solution stack as a virtual or cloud-based service. Essentially, this type of cloud solution provides all the aspects of a platform (that is, the operating system and complete solution package). The primary attraction of PaaS is the avoidance of having to purchase and maintain high-end hardware and software locally.

Software-as-a-Service Software-as-a-Service (SaaS) is a derivative of PaaS. SaaS provides on-demand online access to specific software applications or suites without the need for local installation. In many cases, there are few local hardware and OS limitations. SaaS can be implemented as a subscription service (for example, Microsoft Office 365), a pay-as-you-go service, or a free service (for example, Google Docs).

Infrastructure-as-a-Service Infrastructure-as-a-Service (IaaS) takes the PaaS model yet another step forward and provides not just on-demand operating solutions but complete outsourcing options. This can include utility or metered computing services, administrative task automation, dynamic scaling, virtualization services, policy implementation and management services, and managed/filtered Internet connectivity. Ultimately, IaaS allows an enterprise to scale up new software or data-based services/solutions through cloud systems quickly and without having to install massive hardware locally.

Grid Computing

Grid computing is a form of parallel distributed processing that loosely groups a significant number of processing nodes to work toward a specific processing goal. Members of the grid can enter and leave the grid at random intervals. Often, grid members join the grid only when their processing capacities are not being taxed for local workloads. When a system is otherwise in an idle state, it could join a grid group, download a small portion of work, and begin calculations. When a system leaves the grid, it saves its work and may upload completed or partial work elements back to the grid. Many interesting uses of grid computing have developed, ranging from projects seeking out intelligent aliens, performing protein folding, predicting weather, modeling earthquakes, planning financial decisions, and solving for primes.

The biggest security concern with grid computing is that the content of each work packet is potentially exposed to the world. Many grid computing projects are open to the world, so there is no restriction on who can run the local processing application and participate in the grid's project. This also means that grid members could keep copies of each work packet and examine the contents. Thus, grid projects will not likely be able to maintain secrecy and are not appropriate for private, confidential, or proprietary data.

Grid computing can also vary greatly in the computational capacity from moment to moment. Work packets are sometimes not returned, returned late, or returned corrupted. This requires significant reworking and causes instability in the speed, progress, responsiveness, and latency of the project as a whole and with individual grid members. Time-sensitive projects might not be given sufficient computational time to finish by a specific chronological deadline.

Grid computing often uses a central primary core of servers to manage the project, track work packets, and integrate returned work segments. If the central servers are overloaded or go offline, complete failure or crashing of the grid can occur. However, usually when central grid systems are inaccessible, grid members complete their current local tasks and then regularly poll to discover when the central servers come back online. There is also a potential risk that a compromise of the central grid servers could be leveraged to attack grid members or trick grid members into performing malicious actions instead of the intended purpose of the grid community.

Peer to Peer

Peer-to-peer (P2P) technologies are networking and distributed application solutions that share tasks and workloads among peers. This is similar to grid computing; the primary differences are that there is no central management system and the services provided are usually real time rather than as a collection of computational power. Common examples of P2P include many VoIP services, such as Skype, BitTorrent (for data/file distribution), and Spotify (for streaming audio/music distribution).

Security concerns with P2P solutions include a perceived inducement to pirate copyrighted materials, the ability to eavesdrop on distributed content, a lack of central control/oversight/management/filtering, and the potential for services to consume all available bandwidth.

NOTE

Cryptographic systems are covered in detail in Chapter 6, "Cryptography and Symmetric Key Algorithms," and Chapter 7, "PKI and Cryptographic Applications."

Industrial Control Systems

An industrial control system (ICS) is a form of computer-management device that controls industrial processes and machines. ICSs are used across a wide range of industries, including manufacturing, fabrication, electricity generation and distribution, water distribution, sewage processing, and oil refining. There are several forms of ICS, including distributed control systems (DCSs), programmable logic controllers (PLCs), and supervisory control and data acquisition (SCADA).

DCS units are typically found in industrial process plans where the need to gather data and implement control over a large-scale environment from a single location is essential. An important aspect of DCS is that the controlling elements are distributed across the monitored environment, such as a manufacturing floor or a production line, and the centralized monitoring location sends commands out of those localized controllers while gathering status and performance data. A DCS might be analog or digital in nature, depending on the task being performed or the device being controlled. For example, a liquid flow value DCS would be an analog system whereas an electric voltage regulator DCS would likely be a digital system.

PLC units are effectively single-purpose or focused-purpose digital computers. They are typically deployed for the management and automation of various industrial electromechanical operations, such as controlling systems on an assembly line or a large-scale digital light display (such as a giant display system in a stadium or on a Las Vegas Strip marquee).

A SCADA system can operate as a stand-alone device, be networked together with other SCADA systems, or be networked with traditional IT systems. Most SCADA systems are designed with minimal human interfaces. Often, they use mechanical buttons and knobs or simple LCD screen interfaces (similar to what you might have on a business printer or a GPS navigation device). However, networked SCADA devices may have more complex remote-control software interfaces.

In theory, the static design of SCADA, PLC, and DCS units and their minimal human interfaces should make the system fairly resistant to compromise or modification. Thus, little security was built into these industrial control devices, especially in the past. But there have been several well-known compromises of industrial control systems in recent years; for example, Stuxnet delivered the first-ever rootkit to a SCADA system located in a nuclear facility. Many SCADA vendors have started implementing security improvements into their solutions in order to prevent or at least reduce future compromises.

Assess and Mitigate Vulnerabilities in Web-Based Systems

There is a wide variety of application and system vulnerabilities and threats in web-based systems, and the range is constantly expanding. Vulnerabilities include concerns related to XML and SAML plus many other concerns discussed by the open community-focused web project known as the Open Web Application Security Project (OWASP).

XML exploitation is a form of programming attack that is used to either falsify information being sent to a visitor or cause their system to give up information without authorization. One area of growing concern in regard to XML attacks is Security Association Markup Language (SAML). SAML abuses are often focused on web-based authentication. SAML is an XML-based convention for the organization and exchange of communication authentication and authorization details between security domains, often over web protocols. SAML is often used to provide a web-based SSO (single sign-on) solution. If an attacker can falsify SAML communications or steal a visitor's access token, they may be able to bypass authentication and gain unauthorized access to a site.

OWASP is a nonprofit security project focusing on improving security for online or web-based applications. OWASP is not just an organization—it is also a large community that works together to freely share information, methodology, tools, and techniques related to better coding practices and more secure deployment architectures. For more information on OWASP and to participate in the community, visit the website at `www.owasp.org`.

Assess and Mitigate Vulnerabilities in Mobile Systems

Smartphones and other mobile devices present an ever-increasing security risk as they become more and more capable of interacting with the Internet as well as corporate networks. When personally owned devices are allowed to enter and leave a secured facility without limitation, oversight, or control, the potential for harm is significant.

Malicious insiders can bring in malicious code from outside on various storage devices, including mobile phones, audio players, digital cameras, memory cards, optical discs, and USB drives. These same storage devices can be used to leak or steal internal confidential and private data in order to disclose it to the outside world. (Where do you think most of the content on WikiLeaks comes from?) Malicious insiders can execute malicious code, visit dangerous websites, or intentionally perform harmful activities.

Mobile devices often contain sensitive data such as contacts, text messages, email, and possibly notes and documents. Any mobile device with a camera feature can take photographs of sensitive information or locations. The loss or theft of a mobile device could mean the compromise of personal and/or corporate secrets.

NOTE

A device owned by an individual can be referenced using any of these terms: portable device, mobile device, personal mobile device (PMD), personal electronic device or portable electronic device (PED), and personally owned device (POD).

Mobile devices are common targets of hackers and malicious code. It's important to keep nonessential information off portable devices, run a firewall and antivirus product (if available), and keep the system locked and/or encrypted (if possible).

Many mobile devices also support USB connections to perform synchronization of communications and contacts with desktop and/or notebook computers as well as the transfer of files, documents, music, video, and so on.

Additionally, mobile devices aren't immune to eavesdropping. With the right type of sophisticated equipment, most mobile phone conversations can be tapped into—not to mention the fact that anyone within 15 feet can hear you talking. Be careful what you discuss over a mobile phone, especially when you're in a public place.

A wide range of security features are available on mobile devices. However, support for a feature isn't the same thing as having a feature properly configured and enabled.

A security benefit is gained only when the security function is in force. Be sure to check that all desired security features are operating as expected on your device.

Android

Android is a mobile device OS based on Linux, which was acquired by Google in 2005. In 2008, the first devices hosting Android were made available to the public. The Android source code is made open source through the Apache license, but most devices also include proprietary software. Although it's mostly intended for use on phones and tablets, Android is being used on a wide range of devices, including televisions, game consoles, digital cameras, microwaves, watches, e-readers, cordless phones, and ski goggles.

The use of Android in phones and tablets allows for a wide range of user customization: you can install both Google Play Store apps as well as apps from unknown external sources (such as Amazon's App Store), and many devices support the replacement of the default version of Android with a customized or alternate version. However, when Android is used on other devices, it can be implemented as something closer to a static system.

Whether static or not, Android has numerous security vulnerabilities. These include exposure to malicious apps, running scripts from malicious websites, and allowing insecure data transmissions. Android devices can often be rooted (breaking their security and access limitations) in order to grant the user full root-level access to the device's low-level configuration settings. Rooting increases a device's security risk, because all running code inherits root privileges.

Improvements are made to Android security as new updates are released. Users can adjust numerous configuration settings to reduce vulnerabilities and risks. Also, users may be able to install apps that add additional security features to the platform.

iOS

iOS is the mobile device OS from Apple that is available on the iPhone, iPad, iPod, and Apple TV. iOS isn't licensed for use on any non-Apple hardware. Thus, Apple is in full control of the features and capabilities of iOS. However, iOS is not an example of a static environment, because users can install any of over one million apps from the Apple App Store. Also, it's often possible to jailbreak iOS (breaking Apple's security and access restrictions), allowing users to install apps from third parties and gain greater control over low-level settings. Jailbreaking an iOS device reduces its security and exposes the device to potential compromise. Users can adjust device settings to increase an iOS device's security and install many apps that can add security features.

Device Security

Device security is the range of potential security options or features that may be available for a mobile device. Not all portable electronic devices (PEDs) have good security features. But even if devices have security features, they're of no value unless they're enabled and properly configured. Be sure to consider the security options of a new device before you make a purchase decision.

Full Device Encryption

Some mobile devices, including portable computers, tablets, as well as mobile phones, may offer device encryption. If most or all the storage media of a device can be encrypted, this is usually a worthwhile feature to enable. However, encryption isn't a guarantee of protection for data, especially if the device is stolen while unlocked or if the system itself has a known backdoor attack vulnerability.

Voice encryption may be possible on mobile devices when voice-over IP (VOIP) services are used. VOIP service between computer-like devices is more likely to offer an encryption option than VOIP connections to a traditional land-line phone or typical mobile phone. When a voice conversation is encrypted, eavesdropping becomes worthless because the contents of the conversation are undecipherable.

Remote Wiping

It's becoming common for a remote wipe or remote sanitation to be performed if a device is lost or stolen. A remote wipe lets you delete all data and possibly even configuration settings from a device remotely. The wipe process can be triggered over mobile phone service or sometimes over any Internet connection. However, a remote wipe isn't a guarantee of data security. Thieves may be smart enough to prevent connections that would trigger the wipe function while they dump out the data. Additionally, a remote wipe is mostly a deletion operation. The use of an undelete or data recovery utility can often recover data on a wiped device. To ensure that a remote wipe destroys data beyond recovery, the device should be encrypted. Thus the undeletion operation would only be recovering encrypted data, which the attacker would be unable to decipher.

Lockout

Lockout on a mobile device is similar to account lockout on a company workstation. When a user fails to provide their credentials after repeated attempts, the account or device is disabled (locked out) for a period of time or until an administrator clears the lockout flag.

Mobile devices may offer a lockout feature, but it's in use only if a screen lock has been configured. Otherwise, a simple screen swipe to access the device doesn't provide sufficient security, because an authentication process doesn't occur. Some devices trigger ever longer delays between access attempts as a greater number of authentication failures occur. Some devices allow for a set number of attempts (such as three) before triggering a lockout that lasts minutes. Other devices trigger a persistent lockout and require the use of a different account or master password/code to regain access to the device.

Screen Locks

A screen lock is designed to prevent someone from casually picking up and being able to use your phone or mobile device. However, most screen locks can be unlocked by swiping a pattern or typing a number on a keypad display. Neither of these is truly a secure operation. Screen locks may have workarounds, such as accessing the phone application through the emergency calling feature. And a screen lock doesn't necessarily protect the device if a hacker connects to it over Bluetooth, wireless, or a USB cable.

Screen locks are often triggered after a timeout period of nonuse. Most PCs autotrigger a password-protected screen saver if the system is left idle for a few minutes. Similarly, many tablets and mobile phones trigger a screen lock and dim or turn off the display after 30–60 seconds. The lockout feature ensures that if you leave your device unattended or it's lost or stolen, it will be difficult for anyone else to be able to access your data or applications. To unlock the device, you must enter a password, code, or PIN; draw a pattern; offer your eyeball or face for recognition; scan your fingerprint; or use a proximity device such as a near-field communication (NFC) or radio-frequency identification (RFID) ring or tile.

NOTE

Near field communication (NFC) is a standard to establish radio communications between devices in close proximity. It lets you perform a type of automatic synchronization and association between devices by touching them together or bringing them within inches of each other. NFC is commonly found on smartphones and many mobile device accessories. It's often used to perform device-to-device data exchanges, set up direct communications, or access more complex services such as WPA-2 encrypted wireless networks by linking with the wireless access point via NFC. Because NFC is a radio-based technology, it isn't without its vulnerabilities. NFC attacks can include man-in-the-middle, eavesdropping, data manipulation, and replay attacks.

GPS

Many mobile devices include a GPS chip to support and benefit from localized services, such as navigation, so it's possible to track those devices. The GPS chip itself is usually just a receiver of signals from orbiting GPS satellites. However, applications on the mobile device can record the GPS location of the device and then report it to an online service. You can use GPS tracking to monitor your own movements, track the movements of others (such as minors or delivery personnel), or track down a stolen device. But for GPS tracking to work, the mobile device must have Internet or wireless phone service over which to communicate its location information.

Application Control

Application control is a device-management solution that limits which applications can be installed onto a device. It can also be used to force specific applications to be installed or to enforce the settings of certain applications, in order to support a security baseline or maintain other forms of compliance. Using application control can often reduce exposure to malicious applications by limiting the user's ability to install apps that come from unknown sources or that offer non-work-related features.

Storage Segmentation

Storage segmentation is used to artificially compartmentalize various types or values of data on a storage medium. On a mobile device, the device manufacturer and/or the service provider may use storage segmentation to isolate the device's OS and preinstalled apps from user-installed apps and user data. Some mobile device-management systems further impose storage segmentation in order to separate company data and apps from user data and apps.

Asset Tracking

Asset tracking is the management process used to maintain oversight over an inventory, such as deployed mobile devices. An asset-tracking system can be passive or active. Passive systems rely on the asset itself to check in with the management service on a regular basis, or the device is detected as being present in the office each time the employee arrives at work. An active system uses a polling or pushing technology to send out queries to devices in order to elicit a response.

You can use asset tracking to verify that a device is still in the possession of the assigned authorized user. Some asset-tracking solutions can locate missing or stolen devices.

Some asset-tracking solutions expand beyond hardware inventory management and can oversee the installed apps, app usage, stored data, and data access on a device. You can use this type of monitoring to verify compliance with security guidelines or check for exposure of confidential information to unauthorized entities.

Inventory Control

The term *inventory control* may describe hardware asset tracking (as discussed in the previous topic). However, it can also refer to the concept of using a mobile device as a means of tracking inventory in a warehouse or storage cabinet. Most mobile devices have a camera. Using a mobile device camera, apps that can take photos or scan bar codes can be used to track physical goods. Those mobile devices with RFID or NFC capabilities may be able to interact with objects or their containers that have been electronically tagged.

Mobile Device Management

Mobile device management (MDM) is a software solution to the challenging task of managing the myriad mobile devices that employees use to access company resources. The goals of MDM are to improve security, provide monitoring, enable remote management, and support troubleshooting. Many MDM solutions support a wide range of devices and can operate across many service providers. You can use MDM to push or remove apps, manage data, and enforce configuration settings both over the air (across a carrier network) and over Wi-Fi connections. MDM can be used to manage company-owned devices as well as personally owned devices (such as in a bring-your-own-device [BYOD] environment).

Device Access Control

A strong password would be a great idea on a phone or other mobile device if locking the phone provided true security. But most mobile devices aren't secure, so even with a strong password, the device is still accessible over Bluetooth, wireless, or a USB cable. If a specific mobile device blocked access to the device when the system lock was enabled, this would be a worthwhile feature to set to trigger automatically after a period of inactivity or manual initialization. This benefit is usually obtained when you enable both a device password and storage encryption.

You should consider any means that reduces unauthorized access to a mobile device. Many MDM solutions can force screen-lock configuration and prevent a user from disabling the feature.

Removable Storage

Many mobile devices support removable storage. Some devices support microSD cards, which can be used to expand available storage on a mobile device. However, most mobile phones require the removal of a back plate and sometimes removal of the battery in order to add or remove a storage card. Larger mobile phones, tablets, and notebook computers may support an easily accessible card slot on the side of the device.

Many mobile devices also support external USB storage devices, such as flash drives and external hard drives. These may require a special on-the-go (OTG) cable.

In addition, there are mobile storage devices that can provide Bluetooth- or Wi-Fi-based access to stored data through an on-board wireless interface.

Disabling Unused Features

Although enabling security features is essential for them to have any beneficial effect, it's just as important to remove apps and disable features that aren't essential to business tasks or common personal use. The wider the range of enabled features and installed apps, the greater the chance that an exploitation or software flaw will cause harm to the device and/or the data it contains. Following common security practices, such as hardening, reduces the attack surface of mobile devices.

Application Security

In addition to managing the security of mobile devices, you also need to focus on the applications and functions used on those devices. Most of the software security concerns on desktop or notebook systems apply to mobile devices just as much as common-sense security practices do.

Key Management

Key management is always a concern when cryptography is involved. Most of the failures of a cryptosystem are based on the key management rather than on the algorithms. Good key selection is based on the quality and availability of random numbers. Most mobile devices must rely locally on poor random-number-producing mechanisms or access more robust random number generators (RNGs) over a wireless link. Once keys are created, they need to be stored in such a way as to minimize exposure to loss or compromise. The best option for key storage is usually removable hardware or the use of a Trusted Platform Module (TPM), but these are rarely available on mobile phones and tablets.

Credential Management

The storage of credentials in a central location is referred to as credential management. Given the wide range of Internet sites and services, each with its own particular logon requirements, it can be a burden to use unique names and passwords. Credential management solutions offer a means to securely store a plethora of credential sets. Often these tools employ a master credential set (multifactor being preferred) to unlock the dataset when needed. Some credential-management options can even provide auto-login options for apps and websites.

Authentication

Authentication on or to a mobile device is often fairly simple, especially for mobile phones and tablets. However, a swipe or pattern access shouldn't be considered true authentication. Whenever possible, use a password, provide a PIN, offer your eyeball or face for recognition, scan your fingerprint, or use a proximity device such as an NFC or RFID ring or tile. These means of device authentication are much more difficult for a thief to bypass if properly implemented. As mentioned previously, it's also prudent to combine device authentication with device encryption to block access to stored information via a connection cable.

Geotagging

Mobile devices with GPS support enable the embedding of geographical location in the form of latitude and longitude as well as date/time information on photos taken with these devices. This allows a would-be attacker (or angry ex) to view photos from social networking or similar sites and determine exactly when and where a photo was taken. This geotagging can be used for nefarious purposes, such as determining when a person normally performs routine activities.

Once a geotagged photo has been uploaded to the Internet, a potential cyber-stalker may have access to more information than the uploader intended. This is prime material for security-awareness briefs for end users.

Encryption

Encryption is often a useful protection mechanism against unauthorized access to data, whether in storage or in transit. Most mobile devices provide some form of storage encryption. When this is available, it should be enabled. Some mobile devices offer native support for communications encryption, but most can run add-on software (apps) that can add encryption to data sessions, voice calls, and/or video conferences.

Application Whitelisting

Application whitelisting is a security option that prohibits unauthorized software from being able to execute. Whitelisting is also known as *deny by default* or *implicit deny*. In application security, whitelisting prevents any and all software, including malware, from executing unless it's on the preapproved exception list: the whitelist. This is a significant departure from the typical device-security stance, which is to allow by default and deny by exception (also known as blacklisting).

Due to the growth of malware, an application whitelisting approach is one of the few options remaining that shows real promise in protecting devices and data. However, no security solution is perfect, including whitelisting. All known whitelisting solutions can be circumvented with kernel-level vulnerabilities and application configuration issues.

BYOD Concerns

BYOD is a policy that allows employees to bring their own personal mobile devices into work and use those devices to connect to (or through) the company network to business resources and/or the Internet. Although BYOD may improve employee morale and job satisfaction, it increases security risk to the organization. If the BYOD policy is open-ended, any device is allowed to connect to the company network. Not all mobile devices have security features, and thus such a policy allows noncompliant devices onto the production network. A BYOD policy that mandates specific devices may reduce this risk, but it may in turn require the company to purchase devices for employees who are unable to purchase their own compliant device. Many other BYOD concerns are discussed in the following sections.

Users need to understand the benefits, restrictions, and consequences of using their own devices at work. Reading and signing off on the BYOD policy along with attending an overview or training program may be sufficient to accomplish reasonable awareness.

Data Ownership

When a personal device is used for business tasks, comingling of personal data and business data is likely to occur. Some devices can support storage segmentation, but not all devices can provide data-type isolation. Establishing data ownership can be complicated. For example, if a device is lost or stolen, the company may wish to trigger a remote wipe, clearing the device of all valuable information. However, the employee will often be resistant to this, especially if there is any hope that the device will be found or returned. A wipe may remove all business and personal data, which may be a significant loss to the individual — especially if the device is recovered, because then the wipe would seem to have been an overreaction. Clear policies about data ownership should be established. Some MDM solutions can provide data isolation/segmentation and support business data sanitization without affecting personal data.

The BYOD policy regarding data ownership should address backups for mobile devices. Business data and personal data should be protected by a backup solution—either a single solution for all data on the device or separate solutions for each type or class of data. This reduces the risk of data loss in the event of a remote-wipe event as well as device failure or damage.

Support Ownership

When an employee's mobile device experiences a failure, a fault, or damage, who is responsible for the device's repair, replacement, or technical support? The BYOD policy should define what support will be provided by the company and what support is left to the individual and, if relevant, their service provider.

Patch Management

The BYOD policy should define the means and mechanisms of patch management for a personally owned mobile device. Is the user responsible for installing updates? Should the user install all available updates? Should the organization test updates prior to on-device installation? Are updates to be handled over the air (via service provider) or over Wi-Fi? Are there versions of the mobile OS that cannot be used? What patch or update level is required?

Antivirus Management

The BYOD policy should dictate whether antivirus, anti-malware, and anti-spyware scanners are to be installed on mobile devices. The policy should indicate which products/apps are recommended for use, as well as the settings for those solutions.

Forensics

The BYOD policy should address forensics and investigations as related to mobile devices. Users need to be aware that in the event of a security violation or a criminal activity, their devices might be involved. This would mandate gathering evidence from those devices. Some processes of evidence gathering can be destructive, and some legal investigations require the confiscation of devices.

Privacy

The BYOD policy should address privacy and monitoring. When a personal device is used for business tasks, the user often loses some or all of the privacy they enjoyed prior to using their mobile device at work. Workers may need to agree to be tracked and monitored on their mobile device, even when not on company property and outside of work hours. A personal device in use under BYOD should be considered by the individual to be quasi-company property.

On-boarding/Off-boarding

The BYOD policy should address personal mobile device on-boarding and off-boarding procedures. BYOD on-boarding includes installing security, management, and productivity apps along with implementing secure and productive configuration settings. BYOD off-boarding includes a formal wipe of the business data along with the removal of any business-specific applications. In some cases, a full device wipe and factory reset may be prescribed.

Adherence to Corporate Policies

A BYOD policy should clearly indicate that using a personal mobile device for business activities doesn't exclude a worker from adhering to corporate policies. A worker should treat BYOD equipment as company property and thus stay in compliance with all restrictions, even when off premises and off hours.

User Acceptance

A BYOD policy needs to be clear and specific about all the elements of using a personal device at work. For many users, the restrictions, security settings, and MDM tracking implemented under BYOD will be much more onerous than they expect. Thus, organizations should make the effort to fully explain the details of a BYOD policy prior to allowing a personal device into the production environment. Only after an employee has expressed consent and acceptance, typically through a signature, should their device be on-boarded.

Architecture/Infrastructure Considerations

When implementing BYOD, organizations should evaluate their network and security design, architecture, and infrastructure. If every worker brings in a personal device, the number of devices on the network may double. This requires planning to handle IP assignments, communications isolation, data-priority management, increased intrusion detection system (IDS)/intrusion prevention system (IPS) monitoring load, as well as increased bandwidth consumption, both internally and across any Internet link. Most mobile devices are wireless enabled, so this will likely require a more robust wireless network and dealing with Wi-Fi congestion and interference. BYOD needs to be considered in light of the additional infrastructure costs it will trigger.

Legal Concerns

Company attorneys should evaluate the legal concerns of BYOD. Using personal devices in the execution of business tasks probably means an increased burden of liability and risk of data leakage. BYOD may make employees happy, but it might not be a worthwhile or cost-effective endeavor for the organization.

Acceptable Use Policy

The BYOD policy should either reference the company acceptable use policy or include a mobile device-specific version focusing on unique issues. With the use of personal mobile devices at work, there is an increased risk of information disclosure, distraction, and access of inappropriate content. Workers should remain mindful that the primary goal when at work is to accomplish productivity tasks.

On-board Camera/Video

The BYOD policy needs to address mobile devices with on-board cameras. Some environments disallow cameras of any type. This would require that BYOD equipment be without a camera. If cameras are allowed, a description of when they may and may not be used should be clearly documented and explained to workers. A mobile device can act as a storage device, provide an alternate wireless connection pathway to an outside provider or service, and also be used to collect images and video that disclose confidential information or equipment.

Assess and Mitigate Vulnerabilities in Embedded Devices and Cyber-Physical Systems

An embedded system is a computer implemented as part of a larger system. The embedded system is typically designed around a limited set of specific functions in relation to the larger product of which it's a component. It may consist of the same components found in a typical computer system, or it may be a microcontroller (an integrated chip with on-board memory and peripheral ports). Examples of embedded systems include network-attached printers, smart TVs, HVAC controls, smart appliances, smart thermostats, Ford SYNC (a Microsoft embedded system in vehicles), and medical devices.

Another similar concept to that of embedded systems are static systems (aka static environments). A static environment is a set of conditions, events, and surroundings that don't change. In theory, once understood, a static environment doesn't offer new or surprising elements. A static IT environment is any system that is intended to remain unchanged by users and administrators. The goal is to prevent, or at least reduce, the possibility of a user implementing change that could result in reduced security or functional operation.

In technology, static environments are applications, OSs, hardware sets, or networks that are configured for a specific need, capability, or function, and then set to remain unaltered. However, although the term *static* is used, there are no truly static systems. There is always the chance that a hardware failure, a hardware configuration change, a software bug, a software-setting change, or an exploit may alter the environment, resulting in undesired operating parameters or actual security intrusions.

Examples of Embedded and Static Systems

Network-enabled devices are any type of portable or nonportable device that has native network capabilities. This generally assumes the network in question is a wireless type of network, primarily that provided by a mobile telecommunications company. However, it can also refer to devices that connect to Wi-Fi (especially when they can connect automatically), devices that share data connectivity from a wireless telco service (such as a mobile hot spot), and devices with RJ-45 jacks to receive a standard Ethernet cable for a wired connection. Network-enabled devices include smartphones, mobile phones, tablets, smart TVs, set-top boxes, or an HDMI stick streaming media players (such as a Roku Player, Amazon Fire TV, or Google Android TV/Chromecast), network-attached printers, game systems, and much more.

NOTE In some cases, network-enabled devices might include equipment supporting Bluetooth, NFC, and other radio-based connection technologies. Additionally, some vendors offer devices to add network capabilities to devices that are not network enabled on their own. These add-on devices might be viewed as network-enabled devices themselves (or more specifically, network-enabling devices) and their resultant enhanced device might be deemed a network-enabled device.

Cyber-physical systems refer to devices that offer a computational means to control something in the physical world. In the past these might have been referred to as embedded systems, but the category of cyber-physical seems to focus more on the physical world results rather than the computational aspects. Cyber-physical devices and systems are essentially key elements in robotics and sensor networks. Basically, any computational device that can cause a movement to occur in the real world is considered a robotic element, whereas any such device that can detect physical conditions (such as temperature, light, movement, and humidity) are sensors. Examples of cyber-physical systems include prosthetics to provide human augmentation or assistance, collision avoidance in vehicles, air traffic control coordination, precision in robot surgery, remote operation in hazardous conditions, and energy conservation in vehicles, equipment, mobile devices, and buildings.

A new extension of cyber-physical systems, embedded systems, and network-enabled devices is that of the Internet of Things (IoT). The IoT is the collection of devices that can communicate over the Internet with one another or with a control console in order to affect and monitor the real world. IoT devices might be labeled as smart devices or smart-home equipment. Many of the ideas of industrial environmental control found in office buildings are finding their way into more consumer-available solutions for small offices or personal homes. IoT is not limited to static location equipment but can also be used in association with land, air, or water vehicles or on mobile devices.

Mainframes are high-end computer systems used to perform highly complex calculations and provide bulk data processing. Older mainframes may be considered static environments because they were often designed around a single task or supported a single mission-critical application. These configurations didn't offer significant flexibility, but they did provide for high stability and long-term operation. Many mainframes were able to operate for decades.

Modern mainframes are much more flexible and are often used to provide high-speed computation power in support of numerous virtual machines. Each virtual machine can be used to host a unique OS and in turn support a wide range of applications. If a modern mainframe is implemented to provide fixed or static support of one OS or application, it may be considered a static environment.

Game consoles, whether home systems or portable systems, are potentially examples of static systems. The OS of a game console is generally fixed and is changed only when the vendor releases a system upgrade. Such upgrades are often a mixture of OS, application, and firmware improvements. Although game console capabilities are generally focused on playing games and media, modern consoles may offer support for a range of cultivated and third-party applications. The more flexible and open-ended the app support, the less of a static system it becomes.

In-vehicle computing systems can include the components used to monitor engine performance and optimize braking, steering, and suspension, but can also include in-dash elements related to driving, environment controls, and entertainment. Early in-vehicle systems were static environments with little or no ability to be adjusted or changed, especially by the owner/driver. Modern in-vehicle systems may offer a wider range of capabilities, including linking a mobile device or running custom apps.

Methods of Securing

Security concerns regarding embedded and static systems include the fact that most are designed with a focus on minimizing costs and extraneous features. This often leads to a lack of security and difficulty with upgrades or patches. Because an embedded system is in control of a mechanism in the physical world, a security breach could cause harm to people and property.

Static environments, embedded systems, and other limited or single-purpose computing environments need security management. Although they may not have as broad an attack surface and aren't exposed to as many risks as a general-purpose computer, they still require proper security government.

Network Segmentation

Network segmentation involves controlling traffic among networked devices. Complete or physical network segmentation occurs when a network is isolated from all outside communications, so transactions can only occur between devices within the segmented network. You can impose logical network segmentation with switches using VLANs, or through other traffic-control means, including MAC addresses, IP addresses, physical ports, TCP or UDP ports, protocols, or application filtering, routing, and access control management. Network segmentation can be used to isolate static environments in order to prevent changes and/or exploits from reaching them.

Security Layers

Security layers exist where devices with different levels of classification or sensitivity are grouped together and isolated from other groups with different levels. This isolation can be absolute or one-directional. For example, a lower level may not be able to initiate communication with a higher level, but a higher level may initiate with a lower level. Isolation can also be logical or physical. Logical isolation requires the use of classification labels on data and packets, which must be respected and enforced by network management, OSs, and applications. Physical isolation requires implementing network segmentation or air gaps between networks of different security levels.

Application Firewalls

An application firewall is a device, server add-on, virtual service, or system filter that defines a strict set of communication rules for a service and all users. It's intended to be an application-specific server-side firewall to prevent application-specific protocol and payload attacks.

A network firewall is a hardware device, typically called an appliance, designed for general network filtering. A network firewall is designed to provide broad protection for an entire network.

Both of these types of firewalls are important and may be relevant in many situations. Every network needs a network firewall. Many application servers need an application firewall. However, the use of an application firewall generally doesn't negate the need for a network firewall. You should use both firewalls in a series to complement each other, rather than seeing them as competitive solutions.

Manual Updates

Manual updates should be used in static environments to ensure that only tested and authorized changes are implemented. Using an automated update system would allow for untested updates to introduce unknown security reductions.

Firmware Version Control

Similar to manual software updates, strict control over firmware in a static environment is important. Firmware updates should be implemented on a manual basis, only after testing and review. Oversight of firmware version control should focus on maintaining a stable operating platform while minimizing exposure to downtime or compromise.

Wrappers

A wrapper is something used to enclose or contain something else. Wrappers are well known in the security community in relation to Trojan horse malware. A wrapper of this sort is used to combine a benign host with a malicious payload.

Wrappers are also used as encapsulation solutions. Some static environments may be configured to reject updates, changes, or software installations unless they're introduced through a controlled channel. That controlled channel can be a specific wrapper. The wrapper may include integrity and authentication features to ensure that only intended and authorized updates are applied to the system.

Control Redundancy and Diversity

As with any security solution, relying on a single security mechanism is unwise. Defense in depth uses multiple types of access controls in literal or theoretical concentric circles or layers. This form of layered security helps an organization avoid a monolithic security stance. A monolithic mentality is the belief that a single security mechanism is all that is required to provide sufficient security. By having security control redundancy and diversity, a static environment can avoid the pitfalls of a single security feature failing; the environment has several opportunities to deflect, deny, detect, and deter any threat. Unfortunately, no security mechanism is perfect. Each individual security mechanism has a flaw or a workaround just waiting to be discovered and abused by a hacker.

Essential Security Protection Mechanisms

The need for security mechanisms within an operating system comes down to one simple fact: software should not be trusted. Third-party software is inherently untrustworthy, no matter who or where it comes from. This is not to say that all software is evil. Instead, this is a protection stance—because all third-party software is written by someone other than the OS creator, that software might cause problems. Thus, treating all non-OS software as potentially damaging allows the OS to prevent many disastrous occurrences through the use of software management protection mechanisms. The OS must employ protection mechanisms to keep the computing environment stable and to keep processes isolated from each other. Without these efforts, the security of data could never be reliable or even possible.

Computer system designers should adhere to a number of common protection mechanisms when designing secure systems. These principles are specific instances of the more general security rules that govern safe computing practices. Designing security into a system during the earliest stages of development will help ensure that the overall security architecture has the best chance for success and reliability. In the following sections, we'll divide the discussion into two areas: technical mechanisms and policy mechanisms.

Technical Mechanisms

Technical mechanisms are the controls that system designers can build right into their systems. We'll look at five: layering, abstraction, data hiding, process isolation, and hardware segmentation.

Layering

By *layering* processes, you implement a structure similar to the ring model used for operating modes (and discussed earlier in this chapter) and apply it to each operating system process. It puts the most sensitive functions of a process at the core, surrounded by a series of increasingly larger concentric circles with correspondingly lower sensitivity levels (using a slightly different approach, this is also sometimes explained in terms of upper and lower layers, where security and privilege decrease when climbing up from lower to upper layers). In discussions of OS architectures, the protected ring concept is common, and it is not exclusive. There are other ways of representing the same basic ideas with levels rather than rings. In such a system, the highest level is the most privileged, while the lowest level is the least privileged.

Levels Compared to Rings

Many of the features and restrictions of the protecting ring concept apply also to a multilayer or multilevel system. Think about a high-rise apartment building. The low-rent apartments are often found in the lower floors. As you reach the middle floors, the apartments are often larger and offer better views. Finally, the top floor (or floors) is the most lavish and expensive (often deemed the penthouse). Usually, if you are living in a low-rent apartment in the building, you are unable to ride the elevators any higher than the highest floor of the low-rent apartments. If you are a middle-floor apartment resident, you can ride the elevators everywhere except to the penthouse floor(s). And if you are a penthouse resident, you can ride the elevators anywhere you want to go. You may also find this floor restriction system in office buildings and hotels.

The top of a layered or multilevel system is the same as the center ring of a protection ring scheme. Likewise, the bottom of a layered or multilevel system is the same as the outer ring of a protection ring scheme. In terms of protection and access concepts, *levels*, *layers*, and *rings* are similar. The term *domain* (that is, a collection of objects with a singular characteristic) might also be used.

Communication between layers takes place only through the use of well-defined, specific interfaces to provide necessary security. All inbound requests from outer (less-sensitive) layers are subject to stringent authentication and authorization checks before they're allowed to proceed (or denied, if they fail such checks). Using layering for security is similar to using security domains and lattice-based security models in that security and access controls over certain subjects and objects are associated with specific layers and privileges and that access increases as you move from outer to inner layers.

In fact, separate layers can communicate only with one another through specific interfaces designed to maintain a system's security and integrity. Even though less secure outer layers depend on services and data from more secure inner layers, they know only how to interface with those layers and are not privy to those inner layers' internal structure, characteristics, or other details. So that layer integrity is maintained, inner layers neither know about nor depend on outer layers. No matter what kind of security relationship may exist between any pair of layers, neither can tamper with the other (so that each layer is protected from tampering by any other layer). Finally, outer layers cannot violate or override any security policy enforced by an inner layer.

Abstraction

Abstraction is one of the fundamental principles behind the field known as *object-oriented programming*. It is the "black-box" doctrine that says that users of an object (or operating system component) don't necessarily need to know the details of how the object works; they need to know just the proper syntax for using the object and the type of data that will be returned as a result (that is, how to send input and receive output). This is very much what's involved in mediated access to data or services, such as when user mode applications use system calls to request administrator mode services or data (and where such requests may be granted or denied depending on the requester's credentials and permissions) rather than obtaining direct, unmediated access.

Another way in which abstraction applies to security is in the introduction of object groups, sometimes called *classes*, where access controls and operation rights are assigned to groups of objects rather than on a per-object basis. This approach allows security administrators to define and name groups easily (the names are often related to job roles or responsibilities) and helps make the administration of rights and privileges easier (when you add an object to a class, you confer rights and privileges rather than having to manage rights and privileges for each object separately).

Data Hiding

Data hiding is an important characteristic in multilevel secure systems. It ensures that data existing at one level of security is not visible to processes running at different security levels. The key concept behind data hiding is a desire to make sure those who have no need to know the details involved in accessing and processing data at one level have no way to learn or observe those details covertly or illicitly. From a security perspective, data hiding relies on placing objects in security containers that are different from those that subjects occupy to hide object details from those with no need to know about them.

Process Isolation

Process isolation requires that the operating system provide separate memory spaces for each process's instructions and data. It also requires that the operating system enforce those boundaries, preventing one process from reading or writing data that belongs to another process. There are two major advantages to using this technique:

- It prevents unauthorized data access. Process isolation is one of the fundamental requirements in a multilevel security mode system.
- It protects the integrity of processes. Without such controls, a poorly designed process could go haywire and write data to memory spaces allocated to other processes, causing the entire system to become unstable rather than affecting only the execution of the errant process. In a more malicious vein, processes could attempt (and perhaps even succeed at) reading or writing to memory spaces outside their scope, intruding on or attacking other processes.

Many modern operating systems address the need for process isolation by implementing virtual machines on a per-user or per-process basis. A virtual machine presents a user or process with a processing environment—including memory, address space, and other key system resources and services—that allows that user or process to behave as though they have sole, exclusive access to the entire computer. This allows each user or process to operate independently without requiring it to take cognizance of other users or processes that might be active simultaneously on the same machine. As part of the mediated access to the system that the operating system provides, it maps virtual resources and access in user mode so that they use supervisory mode calls to access corresponding real resources. This not only makes things easier for programmers, it also protects individual users and processes from one another.

Hardware Segmentation

Hardware segmentation is similar to process isolation in purpose—it prevents the access of information that belongs to a different process/security level. The main difference is that hardware segmentation enforces these requirements through the use of physical hardware controls rather than the logical process isolation controls imposed by an operating system. Such implementations are rare, and they are generally restricted to national security implementations where the extra cost and complexity is offset by the sensitivity of the information involved and the risks inherent in unauthorized access or disclosure.

Security Policy and Computer Architecture

Just as security policy guides the day-to-day security operations, processes, and procedures in organizations, it has an important role to play when designing and implementing systems. This is equally true whether a system is entirely hardware based, entirely software based, or a combination of both. In this case, the role of a security policy is to inform and guide the design, development, implementation, testing, and maintenance of a particular system. Thus, this kind of security policy tightly targets a single implementation effort. (Although it may be adapted from other, similar efforts, it should reflect the target as accurately and completely as possible.)

For system developers, a security policy is best encountered in the form of a document that defines a set of rules, practices, and procedures that describe how the system should manage, protect, and distribute sensitive information. Security policies that prevent information flow from higher security levels to lower security levels are called multilevel security policies. As a system is developed, the security policy should be designed, built, implemented, and tested as it relates to all applicable system components or elements, including any or all of the following: physical hardware components, firmware, software, and how the organization interacts with and uses the system. The overall point is that security needs be considered for the entire life of the project. When security is applied only at the end, it typically fails.

Policy Mechanisms

As with any security program, policy mechanisms should also be put into place. These mechanisms are extensions of basic computer security doctrine, but the applications described in this section are specific to the field of computer architecture and design.

Principle of Least Privilege

Chapter 13, "Managing Identity and Authentication," discusses the general security *principle of least privilege* and how it applies to users of computing systems. This principle is also important to the design of computers and operating systems, especially when applied to system modes. When designing operating system processes, you should always ensure that they run in user mode whenever possible. The greater the number of processes that execute in privileged mode, the higher the number of potential vulnerabilities that a malicious individual could exploit to gain supervisory access to the system. In general, it's better to use APIs to ask for supervisory mode services or to pass control to trusted, well-protected supervisory mode processes as they're needed from within user mode applications than it is to elevate such programs or processes to supervisory mode altogether.

Separation of Privilege

The principle of *separation of privilege* builds on the principle of least privilege. It requires the use of granular access permissions; that is, different permissions for each type of privileged operation. This allows designers to assign some processes rights to perform certain supervisory functions without granting them unrestricted access to the system. It also allows individual requests for services or access to resources to be inspected, checked against access controls, and granted or denied based on the identity of the user making the requests or on the basis of groups to which the user belongs or security roles that the user occupies.

Think of separation of duties as the application of the principle of least privilege to administrators. In most moderate to large organizations, there are many administrators, each with different assigned tasks. Thus, there are usually few or no individual administrators with complete and total need for access across the entire environment or infrastructure. For example, a user administrator has no need for privileges that enable reconfiguring network routing, formatting storage devices, or performing backup functions.

Separation of duties is also a tool used to prevent conflicts of interest in the assignment of access privileges and work tasks. For example, those persons responsible for programming code should not be tasked to test and implement that code. Likewise, those who work in accounts payable should not also have accounts receivable responsibilities. There are many such job or task conflicts that can be securely managed through the proper implementation of separation of duties.

Accountability

Accountability is an essential component in any security design. Many high-security systems contain physical devices (such as paper-and-pen visitor logs and nonmodifiable audit trails) that enforce individual accountability for privileged functionality. In general, however, such capabilities rely on a system's ability to monitor activity on and interactions with a system's resources and configuration data and to protect resulting logs from unwanted access or alteration so that they provide an accurate and reliable record of activity and interaction that documents every user's (including administrators or other trusted individuals with high levels of privilege) history on that system. In addition to the need for reliable auditing and monitoring systems to support accountability, there must be a resilient authorization system and an impeccable authentication system.

Common Architecture Flaws and Security Issues

No security architecture is complete and totally secure. Every computer system has weaknesses and vulnerabilities. The goal of security models and architectures is to address as many known weaknesses as possible. Due to this fact, corrective actions must be taken to resolve security issues. The following sections present some of the more common security issues that affect computer systems in relation to vulnerabilities of security architectures. You should understand each of the issues and how they can degrade the overall security of your system. Some issues and flaws overlap one another and are used in creative ways to attack systems. Although the following discussion covers the most common flaws, the list is not exhaustive. Attackers are very clever.

Covert Channels

A *covert channel* is a method that is used to pass information over a path that is not normally used for communication. Because the path is not normally used for communication, it may not be protected by the system's normal security controls. Using a covert channel provides a means to violate, bypass, or circumvent a security policy undetected. Covert channels are one of the important examples of vulnerabilities of security architectures.

As you might imagine, a covert channel is the opposite of an *overt channel*. An overt channel is a known, expected, authorized, designed, monitored, and controlled method of communication.

There are two basic types of covert channels:

Covert Timing Channel A covert timing channel conveys information by altering the performance of a system component or modifying a resource's timing in a predictable manner. Using a covert timing channel is generally a method to secretly transfer data and is very difficult to detect.

Covert Storage Channel A covert storage channel conveys information by writing data to a common storage area where another process can read it. When assessing the security of software, be diligent for any process that writes to any area of memory that another process can read.

Both types of covert channels rely on the use of communication techniques to exchange information with otherwise unauthorized subjects. Because the covert channel is outside the normal data transfer environment, detecting it can be difficult. The best defense is to implement auditing and analyze log files for any covert channel activity.

Attacks Based on Design or Coding Flaws and Security Issues

Certain attacks may result from poor design techniques, questionable implementation practices and procedures, or poor or inadequate testing. Some attacks may result from deliberate design decisions when special points of entry built into code to circumvent access controls, login, or other security checks often added to code while under development are not removed when that code is put into production. For what we hope are obvious reasons, such points of egress are properly called *back doors* because they avoid security measures by design (they're covered later in this chapter in "Maintenance Hooks and Privileged Programs"). Extensive testing and code review are required to uncover such covert means of access, which are easy to remove during final phases of development but can be incredibly difficult to detect during the testing and maintenance phases.

Although functionality testing is commonplace for commercial code and applications, separate testing for security issues has been gaining attention and credibility only in the past few years, courtesy of widely publicized virus and worm attacks, SQL injection attacks, cross-site scripting attacks, and occasional defacements of or disruptions to widely used public sites online. In the sections that follow, we cover common sources of attack or vulnerabilities of security architectures that can be attributed to failures in design, implementation, prerelease code cleanup, or out-and-out coding mistakes. Although they're avoidable, finding and fixing such flaws requires rigorous security-conscious design from the beginning of a development project and extra time and effort spent in testing and analysis. This helps to explain the often lamentable state of software security, but it does not excuse it!

Initialization and Failure States

When an unprepared system crashes and subsequently recovers, two opportunities to compromise its security controls may arise. Many systems unload security controls as part of their shutdown procedures. *Trusted recovery* ensures that all controls remain intact in the event of a crash. During a trusted recovery, the system ensures that there are no opportunities for access to occur when security controls are disabled. Even the recovery phase runs with all controls intact.

For example, suppose a system crashes while a database transaction is being written to disk for a database classified as top secret. An unprotected system might allow an unauthorized user to access that temporary data before it gets written to disk. A system that supports trusted recovery ensures that no data confidentiality violations occur, even during the crash. This process requires careful planning and detailed procedures for handling system failures. Although automated recovery procedures may make up a portion of the entire recovery, manual intervention may still be required. Obviously, if such manual action is needed, appropriate identification and authentication for personnel performing recovery is likewise essential.

Input and Parameter Checking

One of the most notorious security violations is a buffer overflow. This violation occurs when programmers fail to validate input data sufficiently, particularly when they do not impose a limit on the amount of data their software will accept as input. Because such data is usually stored in an input buffer, when the normal maximum size of the buffer is exceeded, the extra data is called *overflow*. Thus, the type of attack that results when someone attempts to supply malicious instructions or code as part of program input is called a *buffer overflow*. Unfortunately, in many systems such overflow data is often executed directly by the system under attack at a high level of privilege or at whatever level of privilege attaches to the process accepting such input. For nearly all types of operating systems, including Windows, Unix, Linux, and others, buffer overflows expose some of the most glaring and profound opportunities for compromise and attack of any kind of known security vulnerability.

The party responsible for a buffer overflow vulnerability is always the programmer whose code allowed nonsanitized input. Due diligence from programmers can eradicate buffer overflows completely, but only if programmers check all input and parameters before storing them in any data structure (and limit how much data can be proffered as input). Proper data validation is the only way to do away with buffer overflows. Otherwise, discovery of buffer overflows leads to a familiar pattern of critical security updates that must be applied to affected systems to close the point of attack.

Real World Scenario

Checking Code for Buffer Overflows

In early 2002, Bill Gates acted in his traditional role as the archetypal Microsoft spokesperson when he announced something he called the "Trustworthy Computing Initiative," a series of design philosophy changes intended to beef up the often questionable standing of Microsoft's operating systems and applications when viewed from a security perspective. As discussion on this subject continued through 2002 and 2003, the topic of buffer overflows occurred repeatedly. As is the case for many other development organizations and also for the builders of software development environments (the software tools that developers use to create other software), increased awareness of buffer overflow exploits has caused changes at many stages during the development process:

- Designers must specify bounds for input data or state acceptable input values and set hard limits on how much data will be accepted, parsed, and handled when input is solicited.
- Developers must follow such limitations when building code that solicits, accepts, and handles input.
- Testers must check to make sure that buffer overflows can't occur and attempt to circumvent or bypass security settings when testing input handling code.

In his book *Secrets & Lies: Digital Security in a Networked World* (Wiley, 2004), noted information security expert Bruce Schneier makes a great case that security testing is in fact quite different from standard testing activities like unit testing, module testing, acceptance testing, and quality assurance checks that software companies have routinely performed as part of the development process for years and years. What's not yet clear at Microsoft (and at other development companies as well, to be as fair to the colossus of Redmond as possible) is whether this change in design and test philosophy equates to the right kind of rigor necessary to foil all buffer overflows. (Some of the most serious security holes that Microsoft Windows continues to be plagued by are still buffer overflows or "buffer overruns," or the cause is identified as an "unchecked buffer.")

Maintenance Hooks and Privileged Programs

Maintenance hooks are entry points into a system that are known only by the developer of the system. Such entry points are also called *back doors*. Although the existence of maintenance hooks is a clear violation of security policy, they still pop up in many systems. The original purpose of back doors was to provide guaranteed access to the system for maintenance reasons or if regular access was inadvertently disabled. The problem is that this type of access bypasses all security controls and provides free access to anyone who knows that the back doors exist. It is imperative that you explicitly prohibit such entry points and monitor your audit logs to uncover any activity that may indicate unauthorized administrator access.

Another common system vulnerability is the practice of executing a program whose security level is elevated during execution. Such programs must be carefully written and tested so they do not allow any exit and/or entry points that would leave a subject with a higher security rating. Ensure that all programs that operate at a high security level are accessible only to appropriate users and that they are hardened against misuse.

Incremental Attacks

Some forms of attack occur in slow, gradual increments rather than through obvious or recognizable attempts to compromise system security or integrity. Two such forms of attack are data diddling and the salami attack.

Data diddling occurs when an attacker gains access to a system and makes small, random, or incremental changes to data during storage, processing, input, output, or transaction rather than obviously altering file contents or damaging or deleting entire files. Such changes can be difficult to detect unless files and data are protected by encryption or unless some kind of integrity check (such as a checksum or message digest) is routinely performed and applied each time a file is read or written. Encrypted file systems, file-level encryption techniques, or some form of file monitoring (which includes integrity checks like those performed by applications such as Tripwire) usually offer adequate guarantees that no data diddling is underway. Data diddling is often considered an attack performed more often by insiders rather than outsiders (in other words, external intruders). It should be obvious that since data diddling is an attack that alters data, it is considered an active attack.

The *salami attack* is more mythical by all published reports. The name of the attack refers to a systematic whittling at assets in accounts or other records with financial value, where very small amounts are deducted from balances regularly and routinely. Metaphorically, the attack may be explained as stealing a very thin slice from a salami each time it's put on the slicing machine when it's being accessed by a paying customer. In reality, though no documented examples of such an attack are available, most security experts concede that salami attacks are possible, especially when organizational insiders could be involved. Only by proper separation of duties and proper control over code can organizations completely prevent or eliminate such an attack. Setting financial transaction monitors to track very small transfers of funds or other items of value should help to detect such activity; regular employee notification of the practice should help to discourage attempts at such attacks.

NOTE If you want an entertaining method of learning about the salami attack or the salami technique, view the movies *Office Space*, *Sneakers*, and *Superman III*.

Programming

We have already mentioned the biggest flaw in programming: the buffer overflow, which can occur if the programmer fails to check or sanitize the format and/or the size of input data. There are other potential flaws with programs. Any program that does not handle any exception gracefully is in danger of exiting in an unstable state. It is possible to cleverly crash a program after it has increased its security level to carry out a normal task. If an attacker is successful in crashing the program at the right time, they can attain the higher security level and cause damage to the confidentiality, integrity, and availability of your system.

All programs that are executed directly or indirectly must be fully tested to comply with your security model. Make sure you have the latest version of any software installed, and be aware of any known security vulnerabilities. Because each security model, and each security policy, is different, you must ensure that the software you execute does not exceed the authority you allow. Writing secure code is difficult, but it's certainly possible. Make sure all programs you use are designed to address security concerns.

Timing, State Changes, and Communication Disconnects

Computer systems perform tasks with rigid precision. Computers excel at repeatable tasks. Attackers can develop attacks based on the predictability of task execution. The common sequence of events for an algorithm is to check that a resource is available and then access it if you are permitted. The *time of check* (TOC) is the time at which the subject checks on the status of the object. There may be several decisions to make before returning to the object to access it. When the decision is made to access the object, the procedure accesses it at the *time of use* (TOU). The difference between the TOC and the TOU is sometimes large enough for an attacker to replace the original object with another object that suits their own needs. *Time-of-check-to-time-of-use* (TOCTTOU) attacks are often called *race conditions* because the attacker is racing with the legitimate process to replace the object before it is used.

A classic example of a TOCTTOU attack is replacing a data file after its identity has been verified but before data is read. By replacing one authentic data file with another file of the attacker's choosing and design, an attacker can potentially direct the actions of a program in many ways. Of course, the attacker would have to have in-depth knowledge of the program and system under attack.

Likewise, attackers can attempt to take action between two known states when the state of a resource or the entire system changes. Communication disconnects also provide small windows that an attacker might seek to exploit. Anytime a status check of a resource precedes action on the resource, a window of opportunity exists for a potential attack in the brief interval between check and action. These attacks must be addressed in your security policy and in your security model. TOCTTOU attacks, race condition exploits, and communication disconnects are known as *state attacks* because they attack timing, data flow control, and transition between one system state to another.

Technology and Process Integration

It is important to evaluate and understand the vulnerabilities in system architectures, especially in regard to technology and process integration. As multiple technologies and complex processes are intertwined in the act of crafting new and unique business functions, new issues and security problems often surface. As systems are integrated, attention should be paid to potential single points of failure as well as to emergent weaknesses in service-oriented architecture (SOA). An SOA constructs new applications or functions out of existing but separate and distinct software services. The resulting application is often new; thus, its security issues are unknown, untested, and unprotected. All new deployments, especially new applications or functions, need to be thoroughly vetted before they are allowed to go live into a production network or the public Internet.

Electromagnetic Radiation

Simply because of the kinds of electronic components from which they're built, many computer hardware devices emit electromagnetic (EM) radiation during normal operation. The process of communicating with other machines or peripheral equipment creates emanations that can be intercepted. It's even possible to re-create keyboard input or monitor output by intercepting and processing electromagnetic radiation from the keyboard and computer monitor. You can also detect and read network packets passively (that is, without actually tapping into the cable) as they pass along a network segment. These emanation leaks can cause serious security issues but are generally easy to address.

The easiest way to eliminate electromagnetic radiation interception is to reduce emanation through cable shielding or conduit and block unauthorized personnel and devices from getting too close to equipment or cabling by applying physical security controls. By reducing the signal strength and increasing the physical buffer around sensitive equipment, you can dramatically reduce the risk of signal interception.

As discussed previously, several TEMPEST technologies could provide protection against EM radiation eavesdropping. These include Faraday cages, jamming or noise generators, and control zones. A *Faraday cage* is a special enclosure that acts as an EM capacitor. When a Faraday cage is in use, no EM signals can enter or leave the enclosed area. *Jamming* or *noise generators* use the idea that it is difficult or impossible to retrieve a signal when there is too much interference. Thus, by broadcasting your own interference, you can prevent unwanted EM interception. The only issue with this concept is that you have to ensure that the interference won't affect the normal operations of your devices. One way to ensure that is to use *control zones*, which are Faraday cages used to block purposely broadcast interference. For example, if you wanted to use wireless networking within a few rooms of your office but not allow it anywhere else, you could enclose those rooms in a single Faraday cage and then plant several noise generators outside the control zone. This would allow normal wireless networking within the designated rooms but completely prevent normal use and eavesdropping anywhere outside those designated areas.

Summary

Designing secure computing systems is a complex task, and many security engineers have dedicated their entire careers to understanding the innermost workings of information systems and ensuring that they support the core security functions required to safely operate in the current environment. Many security professionals don't necessarily require an in-depth knowledge of these principles, but they should have at least a broad understanding of the basic fundamentals that drive the process to enhance security within their own organizations.

Such understanding begins with an investigation of hardware, software, and firmware and how those pieces fit into the security puzzle. It's important to understand the principles of common computer and network organizations, architectures, and designs, including addressing (both physical and symbolic), the difference between address space and memory space, and machine types (real, virtual, multistate, multitasking, multiprogramming, multiprocessing, multiprocessor, and multiuser).

Additionally, a security professional must have a solid understanding of operating states (single state, multistate), operating modes (user, supervisor, privileged), storage types (primary, secondary, real, virtual, volatile, nonvolatile, random, sequential), and protection mechanisms (layering, abstraction, data hiding, process isolation, hardware segmentation, principle of least privilege, separation of privilege, accountability).

No matter how sophisticated a security model is, flaws exist that attackers can exploit. Some flaws, such as buffer overflows and maintenance hooks, are introduced by programmers, whereas others, such as covert channels, are architectural design issues. It is important to understand the impact of such issues and modify the security architecture when appropriate to compensate.

Exam Essentials

Be able to explain the differences between multitasking, multithreading, multiprocessing, and multiprogramming. Multitasking is the simultaneous execution of more than one application on a computer and is managed by the operating system. Multithreading permits multiple concurrent tasks to be performed within a single process. Multiprocessing is the use of more than one processor to increase computing power. Multiprogramming is similar to multitasking but takes place on mainframe systems and requires specific programming.

Understand the differences between single state processors and multistate processors. Single state processors are capable of operating at only one security level at a time, whereas multistate processors can simultaneously operate at multiple security levels.

Describe the four security modes approved by the federal government for processing classified information. Dedicated systems require that all users have appropriate clearance, access permissions, and need to know for all information stored on the system. System high mode removes the need-to-know requirement. Compartmented mode removes the need-to-know requirement and the access permission requirement. Multilevel mode removes all three requirements.

Explain the two layered operating modes used by most modern processors. User applications operate in a limited instruction set environment known as user mode. The operating system performs controlled operations in privileged mode, also known as system mode, kernel mode, and supervisory mode.

Describe the different types of memory used by a computer. ROM is nonvolatile and can't be written to by the end user. The end user can write data to PROM chips only once. EPROM chips may be erased through the use of ultraviolet light and then can have new data written to them. EEPROM chips may be erased with electrical current and then have new data written to them. RAM chips are volatile and lose their contents when the computer is powered off.

Know the security issues surrounding memory components. Three main security issues surround memory components: the fact that data may remain on the chip after power is removed, the fact that memory chips are highly pilferable, and the control of access to memory in a multiuser system.

Describe the different characteristics of storage devices used by computers. Primary storage is the same as memory. Secondary storage consists of magnetic and optical media that must be first read into primary memory before the CPU can use the data. Random access storage devices can be read at any point, whereas sequential access devices require scanning through all the data physically stored before the desired location.

Know the security issues surrounding secondary storage devices. There are three main security issues surrounding secondary storage devices: removable media can be used to steal data, access controls and encryption must be applied to protect data, and data can remain on the media even after file deletion or media formatting.

Understand security risks that input and output devices can pose. Input/output devices can be subject to eavesdropping and tapping, used to smuggle data out of an organization, or used to create unauthorized, insecure points of entry into an organization's systems and networks. Be prepared to recognize and mitigate such vulnerabilities.

Understand I/O addresses, configuration, and setup. Working with legacy PC devices requires some understanding of IRQs, DMA, and memory-mapped I/O. Be prepared to recognize and work around potential address conflicts and misconfigurations and to integrate legacy devices with Plug and Play (PnP) counterparts.

Know the purpose of firmware. Firmware is software stored on a ROM chip. At the computer level, it contains the basic instructions needed to start a computer. Firmware is also used to provide operating instructions in peripheral devices such as printers.

Be able to describe process isolation, layering, abstraction, data hiding, and hardware segmentation. Process isolation ensures that individual processes can access only their own data. Layering creates different realms of security within a process and limits communication between them. Abstraction creates "black-box" interfaces for programmers to use without requiring knowledge of an algorithm's or device's inner workings. Data hiding prevents information from being read from a different security level. Hardware segmentation enforces process isolation with physical controls.

Understand how a security policy drives system design, implementation, testing, and deployment. The role of a security policy is to inform and guide the design, development, implementation, testing, and maintenance of some particular system.

Understand cloud computing. Cloud computing is the popular term referring to a concept of computing where processing and storage are performed elsewhere over a network connection rather than locally. Cloud computing is often thought of as Internet-based computing.

Understand mobile device security. Device security involves the range of potential security options or features that may be available for a mobile device. Not all portable electronic devices (PEDs) have good security features. PED security features include full device encryption, remote wiping, lockout, screen locks, GPS, application control, storage segmentation, asset tracking, inventory control, mobile device management, device access control, removable storage, and the disabling of unused features.

Understand mobile device application security. The applications and functions used on a mobile device need to be secured. Related concepts include key management, credential management, authentication, geotagging, encryption, application whitelisting, and transitive trust/authentication.

Understand BYOD. Bring your own device (BYOD) is a policy that allows employees to bring their own personal mobile devices to work and then use those devices to connect to (or through) the company network to business resources and/or the Internet. Although BYOD may improve employee morale and job satisfaction, it increases security risks to the organization. Related issues include data ownership, support ownership, patch management, antivirus management, forensics, privacy, on-boarding/off-boarding, adherence to corporate policies, user acceptance, architecture/infrastructure considerations, legal concerns, acceptable use policies, and on-board cameras/video.

Understand embedded systems and static environments. An embedded system is typically designed around a limited set of specific functions in relation to the larger product of which it's a component. Static environments are applications, OSs, hardware sets, or networks that are configured for a specific need, capability, or function, and then set to remain unaltered.

Understand embedded systems and static environment security concerns. Static environments, embedded systems, and other limited or single-purpose computing environments need security management. These techniques may include network segmentation, security layers, application firewalls, manual updates, firmware version control, wrappers, and control redundancy and diversity.

Understand how the principle of least privilege, separation of privilege, and accountability apply to computer architecture. The principle of least privilege ensures that only a minimum number of processes are authorized to run in supervisory mode. Separation of privilege increases the granularity of secure operations. Accountability ensures that an audit trail exists to trace operations back to their source.

Be able to explain what covert channels are. A covert channel is any method that is used to pass information but that is not normally used for information.

Understand what buffer overflows and input checking are. A buffer overflow occurs when the programmer fails to check the size of input data prior to writing the data into a specific memory location. In fact, any failure to validate input data could result in a security violation.

Describe common flaws to security architectures. In addition to buffer overflows, programmers can leave back doors and privileged programs on a system after it is deployed. Even well-written systems can be susceptible to time-of-check-to-time-of-use (TOCTTOU) attacks. Any state change could be a potential window of opportunity for an attacker to compromise a system.

Written Lab

1. What are the terms used to describe the various computer mechanisms that allow multiple simultaneous activities?
2. What are the four security modes for systems processing classified information?
3. Name the three pairs of aspects or features used to describe storage.
4. Name some vulnerabilities found in distributed architectures.

Review Questions

1. Many PC operating systems provide functionality that enables them to support the simultaneous execution of multiple applications on single-processor systems. What term is used to describe this capability?
   - **A.** Multiprogramming
   - **B.** Multithreading
   - **C.** Multitasking
   - **D.** Multiprocessing
2. What technology provides an organization with the best control over BYOD equipment?
   - **A.** Application whitelisting
   - **B.** Mobile device management
   - **C.** Encrypted removable storage
   - **D.** Geotagging
3. You have three applications running on a single-core single-processor system that supports multitasking. One of those applications is a word processing program that is managing two threads simultaneously. The other two applications are using only one thread of execution. How many application threads are running on the processor at any given time?
   - **A.** One
   - **B.** Two
   - **C.** Three
   - **D.** Four
4. What type of federal government computing system requires that all individuals accessing the system have a need to know all of the information processed by that system?
   - **A.** Dedicated
   - **B.** System high
   - **C.** Compartmented
   - **D.** Multilevel
5. What is a security risk of an embedded system that is not commonly found in a standard PC?
   - **A.** Software flaws
   - **B.** Access to the Internet
   - **C.** Control of a mechanism in the physical world
   - **D.** Power loss
6. What type of memory chip allows the end user to write information to the memory only one time and then preserves that information indefinitely without the possibility of erasure?
   - **A.** ROM
   - **B.** PROM

C. EPROM

D. EEPROM

7. Which type of memory chip can be erased only when it is removed from the computer and exposed to a special type of ultraviolet light?

A. ROM

B. PROM

C. EPROM

D. EEPROM

8. Which one of the following types of memory might retain information after being removed from a computer and, therefore, represent a security risk?

A. Static RAM

B. Dynamic RAM

C. Secondary memory

D. Real memory

9. What is the most effective means of reducing the risk of losing the data on a mobile device, such as a notebook computer?

A. Defining a strong logon password

B. Minimizing sensitive data stored on the mobile device

C. Using a cable lock

D. Encrypting the hard drive

10. What type of electrical component serves as the primary building block for dynamic RAM chips?

A. Capacitor

B. Resistor

C. Flip-flop

D. Transistor

11. Which one of the following storage devices is most likely to require encryption technology in order to maintain data security in a networked environment?

A. Hard disk

B. Backup tape

C. Removable drives

D. RAM

12. In which of the following security modes can you be assured that all users have access permissions for all information processed by the system but will not necessarily need to know of all that information?

A. Dedicated

B. System high

C. Compartmented
D. Multilevel

13. The most commonly overlooked aspect of mobile phone eavesdropping is related to which of the following?
A. Storage device encryption
B. Screen locks
C. Overhearing conversations
D. Wireless networking

14. What type of memory device is usually used to contain a computer's motherboard BIOS?
A. PROM
B. EEPROM
C. ROM
D. EPROM

15. What type of memory is directly available to the CPU and is often part of the CPU?
A. RAM
B. ROM
C. Register memory
D. Virtual memory

16. In what type of addressing scheme is the data actually supplied to the CPU as an argument to the instruction?
A. Direct addressing
B. Immediate addressing
C. Base+offset addressing
D. Indirect addressing

17. What type of addressing scheme supplies the CPU with a location that contains the memory address of the actual operand?
A. Direct addressing
B. Immediate addressing
C. Base+offset addressing
D. Indirect addressing

18. What security principle helps prevent users from accessing memory spaces assigned to applications being run by other users?
A. Separation of privilege
B. Layering
C. Process isolation
D. Least privilege

19. Which security principle mandates that only a minimum number of operating system processes should run in supervisory mode?

   A. Abstraction

   B. Layering

   C. Data hiding

   D. Least privilege

20. Which security principle takes the concept of process isolation and implements it using physical controls?

   A. Hardware segmentation

   B. Data hiding

   C. Layering

   D. Abstraction

Chapter 10

Physical Security Requirements

THE CISSP EXAM TOPICS COVERED IN THIS CHAPTER INCLUDE:

✓ **3) Security Engineering (Engineering and Management of Security)**

- J. Apply secure principles to site and facility design
- K. Design and implement physical security
  - K.1 Wiring closets
  - K.2 Server rooms
  - K.3 Media storage facilities
  - K.4 Evidence storage
  - K.5 Restricted and work area security (e.g., operations centers)
  - K.6 Data center security
  - K.7 Utilities and HVAC considerations
  - K.8 Water issues (e.g., leakage, flooding)
  - K.9 Fire prevention, detection and suppression

✓ **7) Security Operations (e.g., Foundational Concepts, Investigations, Incident Management, Disaster Recovery)**

- O. Implement and manage physical security
  - O.1 Perimeter (e.g., access control and monitoring)
  - O.2 Internal security (e.g., escort requirements/visitor control, keys and locks)

The topic of physical and environmental security is referenced in several domains. The two primary occurrences are in domain 3) Security Engineering (Engineering and Management of Security) and domain 7) Security Operations (e.g., Foundational Concepts, Investigations, Incident Management, Disaster Recovery). Several sub-sections of these two domains of the Common Body of Knowledge (CBK) for the CISSP certification exam deal with topics and issues related to facility security, including foundational principles, design and implementation, fire protection, perimeter security, internal security, and many more.

The purpose of physical security is to protect against physical threats. The following physical threats are among the most common: fire and smoke, water (rising/falling), earth movement (earthquakes, landslides, volcanoes), storms (wind, lightning, rain, snow, sleet, ice), sabotage/vandalism, explosion/destruction, building collapse, toxic materials, utility loss (power, heating, cooling, air, water), equipment failure, theft, and personnel loss (strikes, illness, access, transport).

This chapter explores these issues and discusses safeguards and countermeasures to protect against them. In many cases, you'll need a disaster recovery plan or a business continuity plan should a serious physical threat (such as an explosion, sabotage, or natural disaster) occur. Chapter 3, "Business Continuity Planning," and Chapter 18, "Disaster Recovery Planning," cover those topics in detail.

Apply Secure Principles to Site and Facility Design

It should be blatantly obvious at this point that without control over the physical environment, no collection of administrative, technical, or logical access controls can provide adequate security. If a malicious person can gain physical access to your facility or equipment, they can do just about anything they want, from destruction to disclosure or alteration. Physical controls are your first line of defense, and people are your last.

There are many aspects of implementing and maintaining physical security. A core element is selecting or designing the facility to house your IT infrastructure and your organization's operations. The process of selecting or designing facilities security always starts with a plan.

Secure Facility Plan

A secure facility plan outlines the security needs of your organization and emphasizes methods or mechanisms to employ to provide security. Such a plan is developed through a process known as *critical path analysis*. Critical path analysis is a systematic effort to identify relationships between mission-critical applications, processes, and operations and all the necessary supporting elements. For example, an e-commerce server used to sell products over the Web relies on Internet access, computer hardware, electricity, temperature control, storage facility, and so on.

When critical path analysis is performed properly, a complete picture of the interdependencies and interactions necessary to sustain the organization is produced. Once that analysis is complete, its results serve as a list of items to secure. The first step in designing a secure IT infrastructure is providing security for the basic requirements of the organization and its computers. These basic requirements include electricity, environmental controls (in other words, a building, air conditioning, heating, humidity control, and so on), and water/sewage.

While examining for critical paths, it is also important to evaluate completed or potential technology convergence. *Technology convergence* is the tendency for various technologies, solutions, utilities, and systems to evolve and merge over time. Often this results in multiple systems performing similar or redundant tasks or one system taking over the feature and abilities of another. While in some instances this can result in improved efficiency and cost savings, it can also represent a single point of failure and become a more valuable target for hackers and intruders. For example, if voice, video, fax, and data traffic all share a single connection path rather than individual paths, a single act of sabotage to the main connection is all that is required for intruders or thieves to sever external communications.

Security staff should participate in site and facility design considerations. Otherwise, many important aspects of physical security essential for the existence of logical security may be overlooked. With security staff involved in the physical facility design, you can be assured that your long-term security goals as an organization will be supported not just by your policies, personnel, and electronic equipment, but by the building itself.

Site Selection

Site selection should be based on the security needs of the organization. Cost, location, and size are important, but addressing the requirements of security should always take precedence. When choosing a site on which to build a facility or selecting a preexisting structure, be sure to examine every aspect of its location carefully.

Securing assets depends largely on site security, which involves numerous considerations and situational elements. Site location and construction play a crucial role in the overall site selection process. Susceptibility to riots, looting, break-ins, and vandalism or location within a high-crime area are obviously all poor choices but cannot always be dictated or controlled. Environmental threats such as fault lines, tornado/hurricane regions, and close proximity to other natural disasters present significant issues for the site selection process as well because you can't always avoid such threats.

Proximity to other buildings and businesses is another crucial consideration. What sorts of attention do they draw, and how does that affect your operation or facility? If a nearby business attracts too many visitors, generates lots of noise, causes vibrations, or handles dangerous materials, they could harm your employees or buildings. Proximity to emergency-response personnel is another consideration, along with other elements. Some companies can afford to buy or build their own campuses to keep neighboring elements out of play and to enable tighter access control and monitoring. However, not every company can exercise this option and must make do with what's available and affordable instead.

At a minimum, ensure that the building is designed to withstand fairly extreme weather conditions and that it can deter or fend off overt break-in attempts. Vulnerable entry points such as windows and doors tend to dominate such analysis, but you should also evaluate objects (trees, shrubs, or man-made items) that can obscure break-in attempts.

Visibility

Visibility is important. What is the surrounding terrain? Would it be easy to approach the facility by vehicle or on foot without being seen? The makeup of the surrounding area is also important. Is it in or near a residential, business, or industrial area? What is the local crime rate? Where are the closest emergency services located (fire, medical, police)? What unique hazards may be found in the vicinity (chemical plants, homeless shelters, universities, construction sites, and so on)?

Natural Disasters

Another concern is the potential impact that natural disasters could make in the area. Is it prone to earthquakes, mudslides, sinkholes, fires, floods, hurricanes, tornadoes, falling rocks, snow, rainfall, ice, humidity, heat, extreme cold, and so on? You must prepare for natural disasters and equip your IT environment to either survive an event or be replaced easily. As mentioned earlier, the topics of business continuity and disaster planning are covered in Chapters 3 and 18, respectively.

Facility Design

When designing the construction of a facility, you must understand the level of security that your organization needs. A proper level of security must be planned and designed before construction begins.

Important issues to consider include combustibility, fire rating, construction materials, load rating, placement, and control of items such as walls, doors, ceilings, flooring, HVAC, power, water, sewage, gas, and so on. Forced intrusion, emergency access, resistance to entry, direction of entries and exits, use of alarms, and conductivity are other important aspects to evaluate. Every element within a facility should be evaluated in terms of how it could be used for and against the protection of the IT infrastructure and personnel (for example, positive flows for air and water from inside a facility to outside its boundaries).

There's also a well-established school of thought on "secure architecture" that's often called crime prevention through environmental design (CPTED). The guiding idea is to structure the physical environment and surroundings to influence individual decisions that potential offenders make before committing any criminal acts. The International CPTED Association is an excellent source for information on this subject (`www.cpted.net`), as is Oscar Newman's book *Creating Defensible Space,* published by HUD's Office of Policy Development and Research (you can obtain a free PDF download at `www.defensiblespace.com/book.htm`).

Design and Implement Physical Security

The security controls implemented to manage physical security can be divided into three groups: administrative, technical, and physical. Because these are the same categories used to describe access controls, it is vital to focus on the physical security aspects of these controls. *Administrative physical security controls* include facility construction and selection, site management, personnel controls, awareness training, and emergency response and procedures. *Technical physical security controls* include access controls; intrusion detection; alarms; closed-circuit television (CCTV); monitoring; heating, ventilating, and air conditioning (HVAC); power supplies; and fire detection and suppression. *Physical controls for physical security* include fencing, lighting, locks, construction materials, mantraps, dogs, and guards.

Real World Scenario

Corporate vs. Personal Property

Many business environments have both visible and invisible physical security controls. You see them at the post office, at the corner store, and in certain areas of your own computing environment. They are so pervasive that some people choose where they live based on their presence, as in gated access communities or secure apartment complexes.

Alison is a security analyst for a major technology corporation that specializes in data management. This company includes an in-house security staff (guards, administrators, and so on) that is capable of handling physical security breaches.

Brad experienced an intrusion—into his personal vehicle in the company parking lot. He asks Alison whether she observed or recorded anyone breaking into and entering his vehicle, but this is a personal item and not a company possession, and she has no control or regulation over damage to employee assets.

> This is understandably unnerving for Brad, but he understands that she's protecting the business and not his belongings. When or where would you think it would be necessary to implement security measures for both? The usual answer is anywhere business assets are or might be involved. Had Brad been using a company vehicle parked in the company parking lot, then perhaps Alison could make allowances for an incidental break-in involving Brad's things, but even then she isn't responsible for their safekeeping. On the other hand, where key people are also important assets (executive staff at most enterprises, security analysts who work in sensitive positions, heads of state, and so forth), protection and safeguards usually extend to embrace them and their belongings as part of asset protection and risk mitigation. Of course, if danger to employees or what they carry with them becomes a problem, securing the parking garage with key cards and installing CCTV monitors on every floor begins to make sense. Simply put, if the costs of allowing break-ins to occur exceeds that of installing preventive measures, it's prudent to put them in place.

When designing physical security for an environment, focus on the functional order in which controls should be used. The order is as follows:

1. Deterrence
2. Denial
3. Detection
4. Delay

Security controls should be deployed so that initial attempts to access physical assets are *deterred* (boundary restrictions accomplish this). If deterrence fails, then direct access to physical assets should be *denied* (for example, locked vault doors). If denial fails, your system needs to *detect* intrusion (for example, using motion sensors), and the intruder should be *delayed* sufficiently in their access attempts to enable authorities to respond (for example, a cable lock on the asset). It's important to remember this order when deploying physical security controls: first deterrence, then denial, then detection, then delay.

Equipment Failure

No matter the quality of the equipment your organization chooses to purchase and install, eventually it will fail. Understanding and preparing for this eventuality helps ensure the ongoing availability of your IT infrastructure and should help you to protect the integrity and availability of your resources.

Preparing for equipment failure can take many forms. In some non-mission-critical situations, simply knowing where you can purchase replacement parts for a 48-hour replacement timeline is sufficient. In other situations, maintaining onsite replacement parts is mandatory. Keep in mind that the response time in returning a system to a fully functioning state is directly proportional to the cost involved in maintaining such a solution. Costs include storage, transportation, pre-purchasing, and maintaining onsite installation and restoration expertise. In some cases, maintaining onsite replacements is not feasible. For those cases, establishing a service-level agreement (SLA) with the hardware vendor is essential. An SLA clearly defines the response time a vendor will provide in the event of an equipment failure emergency.

Aging hardware should be scheduled for replacement and/or repair. The schedule for such operations should be based on the mean time to failure (MTTF) and mean time to repair (MTTR) estimates established for each device or on prevailing best organizational practices for managing the hardware life cycle. MTTF is the expected typical functional lifetime of the device given a specific operating environment. MTTR is the average length of time required to perform a repair on the device. A device can often undergo numerous repairs before a catastrophic failure is expected. Be sure to schedule all devices to be replaced before their MTTF expires. An additional measurement is that of the mean time between failures (MTBF). This is an estimation of the time between the first and any subsequent failures. If the MTTF and MTBF values are the same or fairly similar, manufacturers often only list the MTTF to represent both values.

When a device is sent out for repairs, you need to have an alternate solution or a backup device to fill in for the duration of the repair time. Often, waiting until a minor failure occurs before a repair is performed is satisfactory, but waiting until a complete failure occurs before replacement is an unacceptable security practice.

Wiring Closets

Wiring closets used to be a small closet where the telecommunications cables were organized for the building using punch-down blocks. Today, a wiring closet is still used for organizational purposes, but it serves as an important infrastructure purpose as well. A modern wiring closet is where the networking cables for a whole building or just a floor are connected to other essential equipment, such as patch panels, switches, routers, LAN extenders, and backbone channels. A more technical name for wiring closet is *premises wire distribution room*. It is fairly common to have one or more racks of interconnection devices stationed in a wiring closet (see Figure 10.1).

Larger buildings may require multiple wiring closets in order to stay within the maximum cable run limitations. For the common copper-based twisted-pair cabling, the maximum run length is 100 meters. However, in electrically noisy environments, this run length can be significantly reduced. Wiring closets also serve as a convenient location to link multiple floors together. In such a multistory configuration, the wiring closets are often located directly above or below each other on their respective floor.

Wiring closets are also commonly used to house and manage the wiring for many other important elements of a building, including alarm systems, circuit breaker panels, telephone punch-down blocks, wireless access points, and video systems, including security cameras.

FIGURE 10.1 A typical wiring closet
Source: https://www.flickr.com/photos/clonedmilkmen/4390901323/

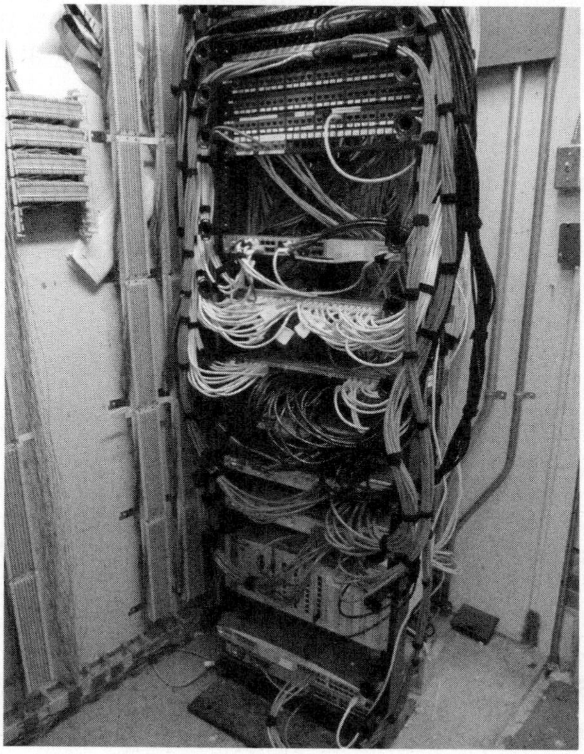

Wiring closet security is extremely important. Most of the security for a wiring closet focuses on preventing physical unauthorized access. If an unauthorized intruder gains access to the area, they may be able to steal equipment, pull or cut cables, or even plant a listening device. Thus, the security policy for the wiring closet should include a few ground rules, such as the following:

- Never use the wiring closet as a general storage area.
- Have adequate locks.
- Keep the area tidy.
- Do not store flammable items in the area.
- Set up video surveillance to monitor activity inside the wiring closet.
- Use a door open sensor to log entries.
- Do not give keys to anyone except the authorized administrator.
- Perform regular physical inspections of the wiring closet's security and contents.

- Include the wiring closet in the organization's environmental management and monitoring, in order to ensure appropriate environmental control and monitoring, as well as detect damaging conditions such as flooding or fire.

It is also important to notify your building management of your wiring closet security policy and access restrictions. This will further reduce unauthorized access attempts.

Server Rooms

Server rooms, datacenters, communications rooms, wiring closets, server vaults, and IT closets are enclosed, restricted, and protected rooms where your mission-critical servers and network devices are housed. Centralized server rooms need not be human compatible. In fact, the more human incompatible a server room is, the more protection it will offer against casual and determined attacks. Human incompatibility can be accomplished by including Halotron, PyroGen, or other halon-substitute oxygen-displacement fire detection and extinguishing systems, low temperatures, little or no lighting, and equipment stacked with little room to maneuver. Server rooms should be designed to support optimal operation of the IT infrastructure and to block unauthorized human access or intervention.

Server rooms should be located at the core of the building. Try to avoid locating these rooms on the ground floor, the top floor, and the basement whenever possible. Additionally, the server room should be located away from water, gas, and sewage lines. These pose too large a risk of leakage or flooding, which can cause serious damage and downtime.

TIP: The walls of your server room should also have a one-hour minimum fire rating.

Real World Scenario

Making Servers Inaccessible

The running joke in the IT security realm is that the most secure computer is one that is disconnected from the network and sealed in a room with no doors or windows. No, seriously, that's the joke. But there's a massive grain of truth and irony in it as well.

Carlos operates security processes and platforms for a financial banking firm, and he knows all about one-way systems and unreachable devices. Sensitive business transactions occur in fractions of a second, and one wrong move could pose serious risks to data and involved parties.

In his experience, Carlos knows that the least accessible and least human-friendly places are his most valuable assets, so he stores many of his machines inside a separate bank vault. You'd have to be a talented burglar, a skilled safecracker, and a determined computer attacker to breach his security defenses.

Not all business applications and processes warrant this extreme sort of prevention. What security recommendations might you suggest to make a server more inconvenient or inaccessible, short of dedicating a vault? A basement with limited access or an interior room with no windows and only one entry/exit point makes an excellent substitute when an empty vault isn't available. The key is to select a space with limited access and then to establish serious hurdles to entry (especially unauthorized entry). CCTV monitoring on the door and motion detectors inside the space can also help maintain proper attention to who is coming and going.

Media Storage Facilities

Media storage facilities should be designed to securely store blank media, reusable media, and installation media. Whether hard drives, flash memory devices, optical disks, or tapes, media should be controlled against theft and corruption. New blank media should be secured to prevent someone from stealing it or planting malware on it.

Media that is reused, such as thumb drives, flash memory cards, or portable hard drives, should be protected against theft and data remnant recovery. *Data remnants* are the remaining data elements left on a storage device after a standard deletion or formatting process. Such a process clears out the directory structure and marks clusters as available for use but leaves the original data in the clusters. A simple un-deletion utility or data recovery scanner can often recover access to these files. Restricting access to media and using secure wiping solutions can reduce this risk.

Installation media needs to be protected against theft and malware planting. This will ensure that when a new installation needs to be performed, the media is available and safe for use.

Here are some means of implementing secure media storage facilities:

- Store media in a locked cabinet or safe.
- Have a librarian or custodian who manages access to the locked media cabinet.
- Use a check-in/check-out process to track who retrieves, uses, and returns media from storage
- For reusable media, when the device is returned, run a secure drive sanitization or *zeroization* (a procedure that erases data by replacing it with meaningless data such as zeroes) process to remove all data remnants.

For more security-intensive organizations, it may be necessary to place a security notification label on media to indicate its use classification or employ RFID/NFC asset tracking tags on media. It also might be important to use a storage cabinet that is more like a safe than an office supply shelf. Higher levels of protection could also include fire, flood, electromagnetic field, and temperature monitoring and protection.

Evidence Storage

Evidence storage is quickly becoming a necessity for all businesses, not just law enforcement–related organizations. As cybercrime events continue to increase, it is important to retain logs, audit trails, and other records of digital events. It also may be necessary to retain image copies of drives or snapshots of virtual machines for future comparison. This may be related to internal corporate investigations or to law enforcement–based forensic analysis. In either case, preserving datasets that might be used as evidence is essential to the favorable conclusion to a corporate internal investigation or a law enforcement investigation of cybercrime.

Secure evidence storage is likely to involve the following:

- A dedicated storage system distinct from the production network
- Potentially keeping the storage system offline when not actively having new datasets transferred to it
- Blocking Internet connectivity to and from the storage system
- Tracking all activities on the evidence storage system
- Calculating hashes for all datasets stored on the system
- Limiting access to the security administrator and legal counsel
- Encrypting all datasets stored on the system

There may be additional security requirements for an evidence storage solution based on your local regulations, industry, or contractual obligations.

Restricted and Work Area Security (e.g., Operations Centers)

The design and configuration of internal security, including work areas and visitor areas, should be considered carefully. There should not be equal access to all locations within a facility. Areas that contain assets of higher value or importance should have more restricted access. For example, anyone who enters the facility should be able to access the restrooms and the public telephone without going into sensitive areas, but only network administrators and security staff should have access to the server room. Valuable and confidential assets should be located in the heart or center of protection provided by a facility. In effect, you should focus on deploying concentric circles of physical protection. This type of configuration requires increased levels of authorization to gain access into more sensitive areas inside the facility.

Walls or partitions can be used to separate similar but distinct work areas. Such divisions deter casual shoulder surfing or eavesdropping (*shoulder surfing* is the act of gathering information from a system by observing the monitor or the use of the keyboard by the operator). Floor-to-ceiling walls should be used to separate areas with differing levels of sensitivity and confidentiality (where false or suspended ceilings are present, walls should cut these off as well to provide an unbroken physical barrier between more and less secure areas).

Each work area should be evaluated and assigned a classification just as IT assets are classified. Only people with clearance or classifications corresponding to the classification of the work area should be allowed access. Areas with different purposes or uses should be assigned different levels of access or restrictions. The more access to assets the equipment within an area offers, the more important become the restrictions that are used to control who enters those areas and what activities they are allowed to perform.

Your facility security design process should support the implementation and operation of internal security. In addition to the management of workers in proper work spaces, you should address visitors and visitor control. Should there be an escort requirement for visitors, and what other forms of visitor control should be implemented? In addition to basic physical security tools such as keys and locks, mechanisms such as mantraps, video cameras, written logs, security guards, and RFID ID tags should be implemented.

Datacenter Security

For many organizations their datacenter and their server room are one and the same. The previous section, "Server Rooms," includes discussion of topics that apply to datacenters as well as server rooms, whether or not you consider these label synonymous.

For some organizations, a datacenter is an external location used to house the bulk of their backend computer servers, data storage equipment, and network management equipment. This could be a separate building nearby the primary offices or it could be a remote location. A datacenter might be owned and managed exclusively by your organization, or it could be a leased service from a datacenter provider. A datacenter could be a single-tenant configuration or a multitenant configuration. No matter what the variation, in addition to the concerns of a server room, many other concepts are likely relevant.

In many datacenters and server rooms, a variety of technical controls are employed as access control mechanisms to manage physical access. These include smart/dumb cards, proximity readers, and intrusion detection systems (IDSs).

Smartcards

Smartcards are credit-card-sized IDs, badges, or security passes with an embedded magnetic strip, bar code, or integrated circuit chip. They contain information about the authorized bearer that can be used for identification and/or authentication purposes. Some smartcards can even process information or store reasonable amounts of data in a memory chip. A smartcard may be known by several phrases or terms:

- An identity token containing integrated circuits (ICs)
- A processor IC card
- An IC card with an ISO 7816 interface

Smartcards are often viewed as a complete security solution, but they should not be considered complete by themselves. As with any single security mechanism, smartcards are subject to weaknesses and vulnerabilities. Smartcards can fall prey to physical attacks, logical attacks, Trojan horse attacks, or social-engineering attacks. In most cases, a smartcard is used in a multifactor configuration. Thus, theft or loss of a smartcard does not result in easy impersonation. The most common form of multifactor used in relation to a smartcard is the requirement of a PIN. You'll find additional information about smartcards in Chapter 13, "Managing Identity and Authentication."

Memory cards are machine-readable ID cards with a magnetic strip. Like a credit card, debit card, or ATM card, memory cards can retain a small amount of data but are unable to process data like a smartcard. Memory cards often function as a type of two-factor control: the card is "something you have" and its PIN is "something you know." However, memory cards are easy to copy or duplicate and are insufficient for authentication purposes in a secure environment.

Proximity Readers

In addition to smart/dumb cards, proximity readers can be used to control physical access. A *proximity reader* can be a passive device, a field-powered device, or a transponder. The proximity device is worn or held by the authorized bearer. When it passes a proximity reader, the reader is able to determine who the bearer is and whether they have authorized access. A passive device reflects or otherwise alters the electromagnetic field generated by the reader. This alteration is detected by the reader.

The passive device has no active electronics; it is just a small magnet with specific properties (like antitheft devices commonly found on DVDs). A field-powered device has electronics that activate when the device enters the electromagnetic field that the reader generates. Such devices actually generate electricity from an EM field to power themselves (such as card readers that require only that the access card be waved within inches of the reader to unlock doors). A transponder device is self-powered and transmits a signal received by the reader. This can occur consistently or only at the press of a button (like a garage door opener or car alarm key fob).

In addition to smart/dumb cards and proximity readers, physical access can be managed with radio frequency identification (RFID) or biometric access control devices. See Chapter 13 for a description of biometric devices. These and other devices, such as cable locks, can support the protection and securing of equipment.

Intrusion Detection Systems

Intrusion detection systems are systems—automated or manual—designed to detect an attempted intrusion, breach, or attack; the use of an unauthorized entry point; or the occurrence of some specific event at an unauthorized or abnormal time. Intrusion detection systems used to monitor physical activity may include security guards, automated access controls, and motion detectors as well as other specialty monitoring techniques. (These are discussed in more detail in the previous section, "Motion Detectors," and later in the section "Intrusion Alarms.")

Physical intrusion detection systems, also called *burglar alarms*, detect unauthorized activities and notify the authorities (internal security or external law enforcement). The most common type of system uses a simple circuit (aka dry contact switches) consisting of foil tape in entrance points to detect when a door or window has been opened.

An intrusion detection mechanism is useful only if it is connected to an intrusion alarm. (See "Intrusion Alarms," later in this chapter.) An intrusion alarm notifies authorities about a breach of physical security.

There are two aspects of any intrusion detection and alarm system that can cause it to fail: how it gets its power and how it communicates. If the system loses power, the alarm will not function. Thus, a reliable detection and alarm system has a battery backup with enough stored power for 24 hours of operation.

If communication lines are cut, an alarm may not function and security personnel and emergency services will not be notified. Thus, a reliable detection and alarm system incorporates a *heartbeat sensor* for line supervision. A heartbeat sensor is a mechanism by which the communication pathway is either constantly or periodically checked with a test signal. If the receiving station detects a failed heartbeat signal, the alarm triggers automatically. Both measures are designed to prevent intruders from circumventing the detection and alarm system.

Access Abuses

No matter what form of physical access control is used, a security guard or other monitoring system must be deployed to prevent abuse, masquerading, and piggybacking. Examples of abuses of physical access controls are propping open secured doors and bypassing locks or access controls. *Masquerading* is using someone else's security ID to gain entry into a facility. *Piggybacking* is following someone through a secured gate or doorway without being identified or authorized personally. Detecting abuses like these can be done by creating audit trails and retaining access logs.

Audit trails and access logs are useful tools even for physical access control. They may need to be created manually by security guards. Or they can be generated automatically if sufficient automated access control mechanisms (such as smartcards and certain proximity readers) are in use. The time at which a subject requests entry, the result of the authentication process, and the length of time the secured gate remains open are important elements to include in audit trails and access logs. In addition to using the electronic or paper trail, consider monitoring entry points with CCTV. CCTV enables you to compare the audit trails and access logs with a visual recording of the events. Such information is critical to reconstruct the events for an intrusion, breach, or attack.

Emanation Security

Many electrical devices emanate electrical signals or radiation that can be intercepted by unauthorized individuals. These signals may contain confidential, sensitive, or private data. Obvious examples of emanation devices are wireless networking equipment and mobile phones, but many other devices are vulnerable to interception. Other examples include monitors, modems, and internal or external media drives (hard drives, USB thumb drives, CDs, and so on). With the right equipment, unauthorized users can intercept electromagnetic or radio frequency signals (collectively known as *emanations*) from these devices and interpret them to extract confidential data.

Clearly, if a device emits a signal that someone outside your organization can intercept, some security protection is needed. The types of countermeasures and safeguards used to protect against emanation attacks are known as TEMPEST countermeasures. TEMPEST was originally a government research study aimed at protecting electronic equipment from the electromagnetic pulse (EMP) emitted during nuclear explosions. It has since expanded to a general study of monitoring emanations and preventing their interception. Thus, TEMPEST is now a formal name for a broad category of activities.

TEMPEST countermeasures include Faraday cages, white noise, and control zones.

Faraday Cage A *Faraday cage* is a box, mobile room, or entire building designed with an external metal skin, often a wire mesh that fully surrounds an area on all sides (in other words, front, back, left, right, top, and bottom). This metal skin acts as an EMI absorbing capacitor (which is why it's named after Michael Faraday, a pioneer in the field of electromagnetism) that prevents electromagnetic signals (emanations) from exiting or entering the area that the cage encloses. Faraday cages are quite effective at blocking EM signals. In fact, inside an active Faraday cage, mobile phones do not work, and you can't pick up broadcast radio or television stations.

White Noise White noise simply means broadcasting false traffic at all times to mask and hide the presence of real emanations. White noise can consist of a real signal from another source that is not confidential, a constant signal at a specific frequency, a randomly variable signal (such as the white noise heard between radio stations or television stations), or even a jam signal that causes interception equipment to fail. White noise is most effective when created around the perimeter of an area so that it is broadcast outward to protect the internal area where emanations may be needed for normal operations.

NOTE

White noise describes any random sound, signal, or process that can drown out meaningful information. This can vary from audible frequencies to inaudible electronic transmissions, and it may even involve the deliberate act of creating line or traffic noise to disguise origins or disrupt listening devices.

Control Zone A third type of TEMPEST countermeasure, a *control zone*, is simply the implementation of either a Faraday cage or white noise generation or both to protect a specific area in an environment; the rest of the environment is not affected. A control zone can be a room, a floor, or an entire building. Control zones are those areas where emanation signals are supported and used by necessary equipment, such as wireless networking, mobile phones, radios, and televisions. Outside the control zones, emanation interception is blocked or prevented through the use of various TEMPEST countermeasures.

Utilities and HVAC Considerations

Power supplied by electric companies is not always consistent and clean. Most electronic equipment demands clean power to function properly. Equipment damage from power fluctuations is a common occurrence. Many organizations opt to manage their own power through various means. An *uninterruptible power supply* (UPS) is a type of self-charging battery that can be used to supply consistent clean power to sensitive equipment. A UPS functions by taking power in from the wall outlet, storing it in a battery, pulling power out of the battery, and then feeding that power to whatever devices are connected to it. By directing current through its battery, it is able to maintain a consistent clean power supply. A UPS has a second function, one that is often used as a selling point: it provides continuous power even after the primary power source fails. A UPS can continue to supply power for minutes or hours, depending on its capacity and how much power the equipment attached to it needs. In some cases, a backup battery is used to provide emergency power. However, such a basic device should not be considered a UPS.

Another means to ensure that equipment is not harmed by power fluctuations requires use of power strips with surge protectors. A surge protector includes a fuse that will blow before power levels change enough to cause damage to equipment. However, once a surge protector's fuse or circuit is tripped, current flow is completely interrupted. Surge protectors should be used only when instant termination of electricity will not cause damage or loss to the equipment. Otherwise, a UPS should be employed instead.

If maintaining operations for considerable time in spite of a brownout or blackout is a necessity, onsite electric generators are required. Such generators turn on automatically when a power failure is detected. Most generators operate using a fuel tank of liquid or gaseous propellant that must be maintained to ensure reliability. Electric generators are considered alternate or backup power sources.

The problems with power are numerous. Here is a list of terms associated with power issues you should know:

Fault A momentary loss of power

Blackout A complete loss of power

Sag Momentary low voltage

Brownout Prolonged low voltage

Spike Momentary high voltage

Surge Prolonged high voltage

Inrush An initial surge of power usually associated with connecting to a power source, whether primary or alternate/secondary

Noise A steady interfering power disturbance or fluctuation

Transient A short duration of line noise disturbance

Clean Nonfluctuating pure power

Ground The wire in an electrical circuit that is grounded

A brownout is an interesting power issue because its definition references ANSI standards for power. Those standards allow for an 8 percent drop in power between the power source and the facility meter and a drop of 3.5 percent between the facility meter and the wall outlet before any prolonged instance of low voltage is labeled as a brownout. The ANSI standard further distinguishes that low voltage outside your meter is to be repaired by the power company, whereas an internal brownout is your responsibility.

Noise

Noise can cause more than just problems with how equipment functions; it can also interfere with the quality of communications, transmissions, and playback. Noise generated by electric current can affect any means of data transmission that relies on electromagnetic transport mechanisms, such as telephone, cellular, television, audio, radio, and network mechanisms.

There are two types of *electromagnetic interference* (EMI): common mode and traverse mode. *Common mode noise* is generated by a difference in power between the hot and ground wires of a power source or operating electrical equipment. *Traverse mode noise* is generated by a difference in power between the hot and neutral wires of a power source or operating electrical equipment.

Radio frequency interference (RFI) is another source of noise and interference that can affect many of the same systems as EMI. A wide range of common electrical appliances generate RFI, including fluorescent lights, electrical cables, electric space heaters, computers, elevators, motors, and electric magnets, so it's important to locate all such equipment when deploying IT systems and infrastructure elements.

Protecting your power supply and your equipment from noise is an important part of maintaining a productive and functioning environment for your IT infrastructure. Steps to take for this kind of protection include providing for sufficient power conditioning, establishing proper grounding, shielding all cables, and limiting exposure to EMI and RFI sources.

Temperature, Humidity, and Static

In addition to power considerations, maintaining the environment involves control over the HVAC mechanisms. Rooms intended primarily to house computers should generally be kept at 60 to 75 degrees Fahrenheit (15 to 23 degrees Celsius). However, there are some extreme environments that run their equipment as low as 50 degrees Fahrenheit and others that run above 90 degrees Fahrenheit. Humidity in a computer room should be maintained between 40 and 60 percent. Too much humidity can cause corrosion. Too little humidity causes static electricity. Even on antistatic carpeting, if the environment has low humidity it is still possible to generate 20,000-volt static discharges. As you can see in Table 10.1, even minimal levels of static discharge can destroy electronic equipment.

TABLE 10.1 Static voltage and damage

Static voltage	Possible damage
40	Destruction of sensitive circuits and other electronic components
1,000	Scrambling of monitor displays
1,500	Destruction of data stored on hard drives
2,000	Abrupt system shutdown
4,000	Printer jam or component damage
17,000	Permanent circuit damage

Water Issues (e.g., Leakage, Flooding)

Water issues, such as leakage and flooding, should be addressed in your environmental safety policy and procedures. Plumbing leaks are not an everyday occurrence, but when they do happen, they can cause significant damage.

Water and electricity don't mix. If your computer systems come in contact with water, especially while they are operating, damage is sure to occur. Plus, water and electricity create a serious risk of electrocution for nearby personnel. Whenever possible, locate server rooms, datacenters, and critical computer equipment away from any water source or transport pipes. You may also want to install water detection circuits on the floor around mission-critical systems. Water-detection circuits will sound an alarm and alert you if water is encroaching upon the equipment.

To minimize emergencies, be familiar with shutoff valves and drainage locations. In addition to monitoring for plumbing leaks, you should evaluate your facility's ability to handle severe rain or flooding in its vicinity. Is the facility located on a hill or in a valley? Is there sufficient drainage? Is there a history of flooding or accumulation of standing water? Is a server room in the basement or on the first floor?

Fire Prevention, Detection, and Suppression

Fire prevention, detection, and suppression must not be overlooked. Protecting personnel from harm should always be the most important goal of any security or protection system. In addition to protecting people, fire detection and suppression is designed to keep damage caused by fire, smoke, heat, and suppression materials to a minimum, especially as regards the IT infrastructure.

Basic fire education involves knowledge of the fire triangle (see Figure 10.2). The three corners of the triangle represent fire, heat, and oxygen. The center of the triangle represents the chemical reaction among these three elements. The point of the fire triangle is to illustrate that if you can remove any one of the four items from the fire triangle, the fire can be extinguished. Different suppression mediums address different aspects of the fire:

- Water suppresses the temperature.
- Soda acid and other dry powders suppress the fuel supply.
- CO2 suppresses the oxygen supply.
- Halon substitutes and other nonflammable gases interfere with the chemistry of combustion and/or suppress the oxygen supply.

When selecting a suppression medium, consider what aspect of the fire triangle it addresses, what this really represents, how effective the suppression medium usually is, and what impact the suppression medium will exert on your environment.

In addition to understanding the fire triangle, you should understand the stages of fire. Fires go through numerous stages, and Figure 10.3 addresses the four most vital stages.

FIGURE 10.2 The fire triangle

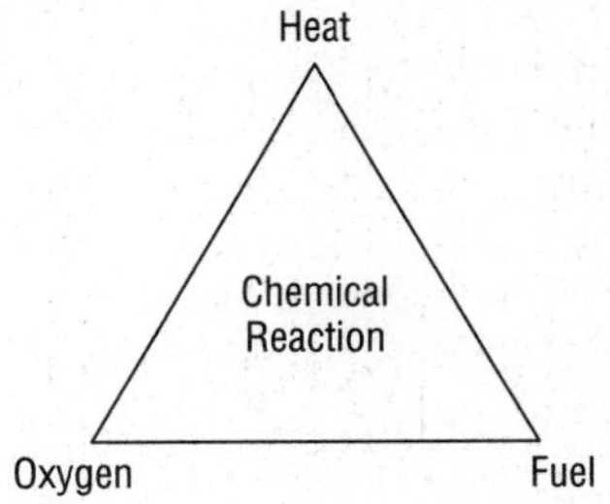

FIGURE 10.3 The four primary stages of fire

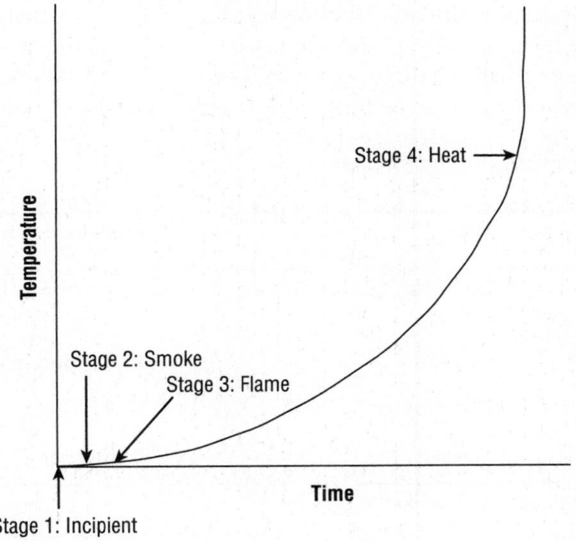

Stage 1: The Incipient Stage At this stage, there is only air ionization but no smoke.

Stage 2: The Smoke Stage In Stage 2, smoke is visible from the point of ignition.

Stage 3: The Flame Stage This is when a flame can be seen with the naked eye.

Stage 4: The Heat Stage At Stage 4, the fire is considerably further down the timescale to the point where there is an intense heat buildup and everything in the area burns.

The earlier a fire is detected, the easier it is to extinguish and the less damage it and its suppression medium(s) can cause.

One of the basics of fire management is proper personnel awareness training. Everyone should be thoroughly familiar with the fire suppression mechanisms in their facility. Everyone should also be familiar with at least two evacuation routes from their primary work area and know how to locate evacuation routes elsewhere in the facility. Personnel should be trained in the location and use of fire extinguishers. Other items to include in fire or general emergency-response training include cardiopulmonary resuscitation (CPR), emergency shutdown procedures, and a pre-established rendezvous location or safety verification mechanism (such as voicemail).

TIP Most fires in a datacenter are caused by overloaded electrical distribution outlets.

Fire Extinguishers

There are several types of fire extinguishers. Understanding what type to use on various forms of fire is essential to effective fire suppression. If a fire extinguisher is used improperly or the wrong form of fire extinguisher is used, the fire could spread and intensify instead of being quenched. Fire extinguishers are to be used only when a fire is still in the incipient stage. Table 10.2 lists the three common types of fire extinguishers.

TABLE 10.2 Fire extinguisher classes

Class	Type	Suppression material
A	Common combustibles	Water, soda acid (a dry powder or liquid chemical)
B	Liquids	CO2, halon*, soda acid
C	Electrical	CO2, halon*
D	Metal	Dry powder

* Halon or an EPA-approved halon substitute

TIP Water cannot be used on Class B fires because it splashes the burning liquids and such liquids usually float on water. Water cannot be used on Class C fires because of the potential for electrocution. Oxygen suppression cannot be used on metal fires because burning metal produces its own oxygen.

Fire Detection Systems

To properly protect a facility from fire requires installing an automated detection and suppression system. There are many types of fire detection systems. Fixed-temperature detection systems trigger suppression when a specific temperature is reached. The trigger is usually a metal or plastic component that is in the sprinkler head and melts at a specific temperature. Rate-of-rise detection systems trigger suppression when the speed at which the temperature changes reaches a specific level. Flame-actuated systems trigger suppression based on the infrared energy of flames. Smoke-actuated systems use photoelectric or radioactive ionization sensors as triggers.

Most fire-detection systems can be linked to fire response service notification mechanisms. When suppression is triggered, such linked systems will contact the local fire response team and request aid using an automated message or alarm.

To be effective, fire detectors need to be placed strategically. Don't forget to place them inside dropped ceilings and raised floors, in server rooms, in private offices and public areas, in HVAC vents, in elevator shafts, in the basement, and so on.

As for suppression mechanisms used, they can be based on water or on a fire suppression gas system. Water is common in human-friendly environments, whereas gaseous systems are more appropriate for computer rooms where personnel typically do not reside.

Water Suppression Systems

There are four main types of water suppression systems:

- A *wet pipe system* (also known as a *closed head system*) is always full of water. Water discharges immediately when suppression is triggered.
- A *dry pipe system* contains compressed air. Once suppression is triggered, the air escapes, opening a water valve that in turn causes the pipes to fill and discharge water into the environment.
- A *deluge system* is another form of dry pipe system that uses larger pipes and therefore delivers a significantly larger volume of water. Deluge systems are inappropriate for environments that contain electronics and computers.
- A *preaction system* is a combination dry pipe/wet pipe system. The system exists as a dry pipe until the initial stages of a fire (smoke, heat, and so on) are detected, and then the pipes are filled with water. The water is released only after the sprinkler head activation triggers are melted by sufficient heat. If the fire is quenched before sprinklers are triggered, pipes can be manually emptied and reset. This also allows manual intervention to stop the release of water before sprinkler triggering occurs.

Preaction systems are the most appropriate water-based system for environments that house both computers and humans together.

TIP

The most common cause of failure for a water-based system is human error, such as turning off a water source when a fire occurs or triggering water release when there is no fire.

Gas Discharge Systems

Gas discharge systems are usually more effective than water discharge systems. However, gas discharge systems should not be used in environments in which people are located. Gas discharge systems usually remove the oxygen from the air, thus making them hazardous to personnel. They employ a pressurized gaseous suppression medium, such as CO2, halon, or FM-200 (a halon replacement).

Halon is an effective fire suppression compound (it starves a fire of oxygen by disrupting the chemical reaction between oxygen and combustible materials), but it degrades into toxic gases at 900 degrees Fahrenheit. Also, it is not environmentally friendly (it is an ozone-depleting substance). In 1994, the EPA banned the manufacture of halon in the United States. It is also illegal to import halon manufactured after 1994. (Production of halon 1301, halon 1211, and halon 2403 ceased in developed countries on December 31, 2003.) However, according to the Montreal Protocol, you can obtain halon by contacting a halon recycling facility. The EPA seeks to exhaust existing stocks of halon to take this substance out of circulation.

Owing to issues with halon, it is often replaced by a more ecologically friendly and less toxic medium. The following list itemizes various EPA-approved substitutes for halon (see `http://www.epa.gov/ozone/snap/fire/halonreps.html` for more information):

- FM-200 (HFC-227ea)
- CEA-410 or CEA-308
- NAF-S-III (HCFC Blend A)
- FE-13 (HCFC-23)
- Argon (IG55) or Argonite (IG01)
- Inergen (IG541)

You can also replace halon substitutes with low-pressure water mists, but such systems are usually not employed in computer rooms or electrical equipment storage facilities. A low-pressure water mist is a vapor cloud used to quickly reduce the temperature in an area.

Damage

Addressing fire detection and suppression includes dealing with possible contamination and damage caused by a fire. The destructive elements of a fire include smoke and heat, but they also include the suppression media, such as water or soda acid. Smoke is damaging to most storage devices. Heat can damage any electronic or computer component. For example, temperatures of 100 degrees Fahrenheit can damage storage tapes, 175 degrees can damage computer hardware (that is, CPU and RAM), and 350 degrees can damage paper products (through warping and discoloration).

Suppression media can cause short circuits, initiate corrosion, or otherwise render equipment useless. All these issues must be addressed when designing a fire response system.

WARNING

Don't forget that in the event of a fire, in addition to damage caused by the flames and your chosen suppression medium, members of the fire department may inflict damage using their hoses to spray water and their axes while searching for hot spots.

Implement and Manage Physical Security

Many types of physical access control mechanisms can be deployed in an environment to control, monitor, and manage access to a facility. These range from deterrents to detection mechanisms. The various sections, divisions, or areas within a site or facility should be clearly designated as public, private, or restricted. Each of these areas requires unique and focused physical access controls, monitoring, and prevention mechanisms. The following sections discuss many such mechanisms that may be used to separate, isolate, and control access to various areas of a site, including perimeter and internal security.

Perimeter (e.g., Access Control and Monitoring)

The accessibility to the building or campus location is also important. Single entrances are great for providing security, but multiple entrances are better for evacuation during emergencies. What types of roads are nearby? What means of transportation are easily accessible (trains, highway, airport, shipping)? What about traffic levels throughout the day?

Keep in mind that accessibility is also constrained by the need for perimeter security. The needs of access and use should meld and support the implementation and operation of perimeter security. The use of physical access controls and monitoring personnel and equipment entering and leaving as well as auditing/logging all physical events are key elements in maintaining overall organizational security.

Fences, Gates, Turnstiles, and Mantraps

A *fence* is a perimeter-defining device. Fences are used to clearly differentiate between areas that are under a specific level of security protection and those that aren't. Fencing can include a wide range of components, materials, and construction methods. It can consist of stripes painted on the ground, chain link fences, barbed wire, concrete walls, and even invisible perimeters using laser, motion, or heat detectors. Various types of fences are effective against different types of intruders:

- Fences 3 to 4 feet high deter casual trespassers.
- Fences 6 to 7 feet high are too hard to climb easily and deter most intruders, except determined ones.
- Fences 8 or more feet high with three strands of barbed wire deter even determined intruders.

A *gate* is a controlled exit and entry point in a fence. The deterrent level of a gate must be equivalent to the deterrent level of the fence to sustain the effectiveness of the fence as a whole. Hinges and locking/closing mechanisms should be hardened against tampering, destruction, or removal. When a gate is closed, it should not offer any additional access vulnerabilities. Keep the number of gates to a minimum. They can be manned by guards. When they're not protected by guards, use of dogs or CCTV is recommended.

A *turnstile* (see Figure 10.4) is a form of gate that prevents more than one person at a time from gaining entry and often restricts movement in one direction. It is used to gain entry but not to exit, or vice versa. A turnstile is basically the fencing equivalent of a secured revolving door.

FIGURE 10.4 A secure physical boundary with a mantrap and a turnstile

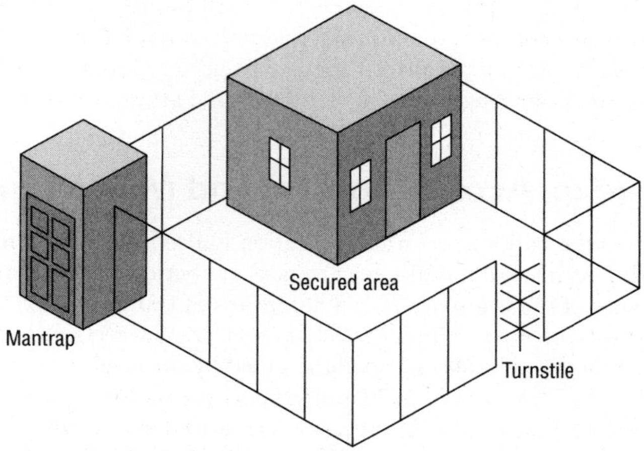

A *mantrap* is a double set of doors that is often protected by a guard (also shown in Figure 10.4) or some other physical layout that prevents piggybacking and can trap individuals at the discretion of security personnel. The purpose of a mantrap is to immobilize a subject until their identity and authentication is verified. If a subject is authorized for entry, the inner door opens, allowing entry into the facility or onto the premises. If a subject is not authorized, both doors remain closed and locked until an escort (typically a guard or a police officer) arrives to escort the subject off the property or arrest the subject for trespassing (this is called a *delay feature*). Often a mantrap includes a scale to prevent piggybacking or tailgating.

Lighting

Lighting is a commonly used form of perimeter security control. The primary purpose of lighting is to discourage casual intruders, trespassers, prowlers, or would-be thieves who would rather perform their misdeeds in the dark. However, lighting is not a strong deterrent. It should not be used as the primary or sole protection mechanism except in areas with a low threat level.

Lighting should not illuminate the positions of guards, dogs, patrol posts, or other similar security elements. It should be combined with guards, dogs, CCTV, or some other form of intrusion detection or surveillance mechanism. Lighting must not cause a nuisance or problem for nearby residents, roads, railways, airports, and so on. It should also never cause glare or reflective distraction to guards, dogs, and monitoring equipment, which could otherwise aid attackers during break-in attempts.

It is generally accepted as a de facto standard that lighting used for perimeter protection should illuminate critical areas with 2 candle feet of power. Another common issue for the use of lighting is the placement of the lights. Standards seem to indicate that light poles should be placed the same distance apart as the diameter of the illuminated area created by illumination elements. Thus, if a lighted area is 40 feet in diameter, poles should be 40 feet apart.

Security Guards and Dogs

All physical security controls, whether static deterrents or active detection and surveillance mechanisms, ultimately rely on personnel to intervene and stop actual intrusions and attacks. Security guards exist to fulfill this need. Guards can be posted around a perimeter or inside to monitor access points or watch detection and surveillance monitors. The real benefit of guards is that they are able to adapt and react to various conditions or situations. Guards can learn and recognize attack and intrusion activities and patterns, can adjust to a changing environment, and can make decisions and judgment calls. Security guards are often an appropriate security control when immediate situation handling and decision making onsite is necessary.

Unfortunately, using security guards is not a perfect solution. There are numerous disadvantages to deploying, maintaining, and relying on security guards. Not all environments and facilities support security guards. This may be because of actual human incompatibility or the layout, design, location, and construction of the facility. Not all security guards are themselves reliable. Prescreening, bonding, and training do not guarantee that you won't end up with an ineffective or unreliable security guard.

Even if a guard is initially reliable, guards are subject to physical injury and illness, take vacations, can become distracted, are vulnerable to social engineering, and may become unemployable because of substance abuse. In addition, security guards usually offer protection only up to the point at which their life is endangered. Additionally, security guards are usually unaware of the scope of the operations within a facility and are therefore not thoroughly equipped to know how to respond to every situation. Finally, security guards are expensive.

Guard dogs can be an alternative to security guards. They can often be deployed as a perimeter security control. As a detection and deterrent, dogs are extremely effective. However, dogs are costly, require a high level of maintenance, and impose serious insurance and liability requirements.

Internal Security (e.g., Escort Requirements/Visitor Control, Keys, and Locks)

If a facility employs restricted areas to control physical security, a mechanism to handle visitors is required. Often an escort is assigned to visitors, and their access and activities are monitored closely. Failing to track the actions of outsiders when they are allowed into a protected area can result in malicious activity against the most protected assets. Visitor control can also benefit from the use of keys, combination locks, badges, motion detectors, intrusion alarms, and more.

Keys and Combination Locks

Locks keep closed doors closed. They are designed and deployed to prevent access to everyone without proper authorization. A *lock* is a crude form of an identification and authorization mechanism. If you possess the correct key or combination, you are considered authorized and permitted entry. Key-based locks are the most common and inexpensive forms of physical access control devices. These are often known as *preset locks*. These types of locks are subject to picking, which is often categorized under a class of lock mechanism attacks called *shimming*.

Real World Scenario

Using Locks

Keys or combination locks—which do you choose and for what purposes?

Ultimately, there will always be forgetful users. Elise constantly forgets her combination, and Francis can never remember to bring his security key card to work. Gino maintains a pessimistic outlook in his administrative style, so he's keen on putting combinations and key card accesses in all the right places.

Under what circumstances or conditions might you employ a combination lock, and where might you instead opt for a key or key card? What options put you at greater risk of loss if someone discovers the combination or finds the key? Can you be certain that these single points of failure do not significantly pose a risk to the protected assets?

Many organizations typically utilize separate forms of key or combination accesses throughout several areas of the facility. Key and key card access is granted at select shared entry points (exterior access into the building, access into interior rooms), and combination locks control access to individual entry points (storage lockers, file cabinets, and so on).

Programmable or combination locks offer a broader range of control than preset locks. Some programmable locks can be configured with multiple valid access combinations or may include digital or electronic controls employing keypads, smartcards, or cipher devices. For instance, an *electronic access control (EAC) lock* incorporates three elements: an electromagnet to keep the door closed, a credential reader to authenticate subjects and to disable the electromagnet, and a sensor to reengage the electromagnet when the door is closed.

Locks serve as an alternative to security guards as a perimeter entrance access control device. A gate or door can be opened and closed to allow access by a security guard who verifies your identity before granting access, or the lock itself can serve as the verification device that also grants or restricts entry.

Badges

Badges, *identification cards*, and *security IDs* are forms of physical identification and/or electronic access control devices. A badge can be as simple as a name tag indicating whether you are a valid employee or a visitor. Or it can be as complex as a smartcard or token device that employs multifactor authentication to verify and prove your identity and provide authentication and authorization to access a facility, specific rooms, or secured workstations. Badges often include pictures, magnetic strips with encoded data, and personal details to help a security guard verify identity.

Badges can be used in environments in which physical access is primarily controlled by security guards. In such conditions, the badge serves as a visual identification tool for the guards. They can verify your identity by comparing your picture to your person and consult a printed or electronic roster of authorized personnel to determine whether you have valid access.

Badges can also serve in environments guarded by scanning devices rather than security guards. In such conditions, a badge can be used either for identification or for authentication. When a badge is used for identification, it is swiped in a device, and then the badge owner must provide one or more authentication factors, such as a password, passphrase, or biological trait (if a biometric device is used). When a badge is used for authentication, the badge owner provides an ID, username, and so on and then swipes the badge to authenticate.

Motion Detectors

A *motion detector*, or *motion sensor*, is a device that senses movement or sound in a specific area. Many types of motion detectors exist, including infrared, heat, wave pattern, capacitance, photoelectric, and passive audio.

- An *infrared motion detector* monitors for significant or meaningful changes in the infrared lighting pattern of a monitored area.
- A *heat-based motion detector* monitors for significant or meaningful changes in the heat levels and patterns in a monitored area.
- A *wave pattern motion detector* transmits a consistent low ultrasonic or high microwave frequency signal into a monitored area and monitors for significant or meaningful changes or disturbances in the reflected pattern.
- A *capacitance motion detector* senses changes in the electrical or magnetic field surrounding a monitored object.
- A *photoelectric motion detector* senses changes in visible light levels for the monitored area. Photoelectric motion detectors are usually deployed in internal rooms that have no windows and are kept dark.
- A *passive audio motion detector* listens for abnormal sounds in the monitored area.

Intrusion Alarms

Whenever a motion detector registers a significant or meaningful change in the environment, it triggers an alarm. An *alarm* is a separate mechanism that triggers a deterrent, a repellent, and/or a notification.

Deterrent Alarms Alarms that trigger deterrents may engage additional locks, shut doors, and so on. The goal of such an alarm is to make further intrusion or attack more difficult.

Repellant Alarms Alarms that trigger repellants usually sound an audio siren or bell and turn on lights. These kinds of alarms are used to discourage intruders or attackers from continuing their malicious or trespassing activities and force them off the premises.

Notification Alarms Alarms that trigger notification are often silent from the intruder/attacker perspective but record data about the incident and notify administrators, security guards, and law enforcement. A recording of an incident can take the form of log files and/or CCTV tapes. The purpose of a silent alarm is to bring authorized security personnel to the location of the intrusion or attack in hopes of catching the person(s) committing the unwanted or unauthorized acts.

Alarms are also categorized by where they are located: local, centralized or proprietary, or auxiliary.

Local Alarm System *Local alarm systems* must broadcast an audible (up to 120 decibel [db]) alarm signal that can be easily heard up to 400 feet away. Additionally, they must be protected from tampering and disablement, usually by security guards. For a local alarm system to be effective, there must be a security team or guards positioned nearby who can respond when the alarm is triggered.

Central Station System The alarm is usually silent locally, but offsite monitoring agents are notified so they can respond to the security breach. Most residential security systems are of this type. Most central station systems are well-known or national security companies, such as Brinks and ADT. A *proprietary system* is similar to a central station system, but the host organization has its own onsite security staff waiting to respond to security breaches.

Auxiliary Station *Auxiliary alarm systems* can be added to either local or centralized alarm systems. When the security perimeter is breached, emergency services are notified to respond to the incident and arrive at the location. This could include fire, police, and medical services.

Two or more of these types of intrusion and alarm systems can be incorporated in a single solution.

Secondary Verification Mechanisms

When motion detectors, sensors, and alarms are used, secondary verification mechanisms should be in place. As the sensitivity of these devices increases, false triggers occur more often. Innocuous events such as the presence of animals, birds, bugs, or authorized personnel can trigger false alarms. Deploying two or more detection and sensor systems and requiring two or more triggers in quick succession to occur before an alarm is issued may significantly reduce false alarms and increase the likelihood that alarms indicate actual intrusions or attacks.

CCTV is a security mechanism related to motion detectors, sensors, and alarms. However, CCTV is not an automated detection-and-response system. CCTV requires personnel to watch the captured video to detect suspicious and malicious activities and to trigger alarms. Security cameras can expand the effective visible range of a security guard, therefore increasing the scope of the oversight. In many cases, CCTV is not used as a primary detection tool because of the high cost of paying a person to sit and watch the video screens. Instead, it is used as a secondary or follow-up mechanism that is reviewed after a trigger from an automated system occurs. In fact, the same logic used for auditing and audit trails is used for CCTV and recorded events. A CCTV is a preventive measure, whereas reviewing recorded events is a detective measure.

Real World Scenario

Secondary Verification

As illustrated in the previous real-world scenario, Gino was at constant risk of security breaches because Elise is constantly forgetting (and therefore writes down) every password, whereas Francis is habitually forgetful about the location of his key card. What happens when someone else comes into possession of either of these items and has knowledge of how or where to use them?

Gino's biggest advantage will be any secondary verification mechanisms he has established in the workplace. This may include a CCTV system that identifies the face of the person who uses a key card for access or inputs a combination in some area designated under surveillance. Even videotape logs of ingress and egress through checkpoints can be helpful when it comes to chasing down accidental or deliberate access abuses.

With known "problem users" or "problem identities," many security systems can issue notifications or alerts when those identities are used. Depending on the systems that are available, and the risks that unauthorized access could pose, human follow-up may or may not be warranted. But any time Elise (or somebody who uses that identity) logs onto a system or anytime Francis's key card is used, a floating or roving security guard could be dispatched to ensure that everything is on the up and up. Of course, it's probably also a good idea to have Elise's and Francis's managers counsel them on the appropriate use (and storage) of passwords and key cards, just to make sure they understand the potential risks involved too.

Real World Scenario

Deploying Physical Access Controls

In the real world, you will deploy multiple layers of physical access controls to manage the traffic of authorized and unauthorized individuals within your facility. The outermost layer will be lighting. The entire outer perimeter of your site should be clearly lit. This enables easy identification of personnel and makes it easier to notice intrusions and intimidate potential intruders. Just inside the lighted area, place a fence or wall designed to prevent intrusion. Specific controlled points along that fence or wall should be points for entry or exit. These should have gates, turnstiles, or mantraps all monitored by CCTV and security guards. Identification and authentication should be required at all entry points before entrance is granted.

Within the facility, areas of different sensitivity or confidentiality levels should be distinctly separated and compartmentalized. This is especially true for public areas and areas accessible to visitors. An additional identification/authentication process to validate the need to enter should be required when anyone moves from one area to another. The most sensitive resources and systems should be isolated from all but the most privileged personnel and located at the center or core of the facility.

Environment and Life Safety

An important aspect of physical access control and maintaining the security of a facility is protecting the basic elements of the environment and protecting human life. In all circumstances and under all conditions, the most important aspect of security is protecting people. Thus, preventing harm to people is the most important goal for all security solutions.

Part of maintaining safety for personnel is maintaining the basic environment of a facility. For short periods of time, people can survive without water, food, air conditioning, and power. But in some cases, the loss of these elements can have disastrous results, or they can be symptoms of more immediate and dangerous problems. Flooding, fires, release of toxic materials, and natural disasters all threaten human life as well as the stability of a facility. Physical security procedures should focus on protecting human life and then on restoring the safety of the environment and restoring the utilities necessary for the IT infrastructure to function.

People should always be your top priority. Only after personnel are safe can you consider addressing business continuity. Many organizations adopt occupant emergency plans (OEPs) to guide and assist with sustaining personnel safety in the wake of a disaster. The OEP provides guidance on how to minimize threats to life, prevent injury, manage duress, handle travel, provide for safety monitoring, and protect property from damage in the event of a destructive physical event. The OEP does not address IT issues or business continuity, just personnel and general property. The BCP and DRP address IT and business continuity and recovery issues.

Privacy Responsibilities and Legal Requirements

The safety of personal information also needs to be addressed in any organization's security policy. In addition, the security policy must conform to the regulatory requirements of the industry and jurisdictions in which it is active.

Privacy means protecting personal information from disclosure to any unauthorized individual or entity. In today's online world, the line between public and private information is often blurry. For example, is information about your web-surfing habits private or public? Can that information be gathered legally without your consent? And can the gathering organization sell that information for a profit that you don't share in? In addition, your personal information includes more than information about your online habits; it also includes who you are (name, address, phone, race, religion, age, and so on), your health and medical records, your financial records, and even your criminal or legal records. In general such information falls under the heading of personally identifiable information (PII), as described in the NIST publication *Guide to Protecting the Confidentiality of Personally Identifiable Information (PII)* available online at `http://csrc.nist.gov/publications/nistpubs/800-122/sp800-122.pdf`.

Dealing with privacy is a requirement for any organization that has employees. Thus, privacy is a central issue for all organizations. Protection of privacy should be a core mission or goal set forth in the security policy for any organization. Personnel privacy issues are discussed at greater length in Chapter 4, "Laws, Regulations, and Compliance."

Regulatory Requirements

Every organization operates within a certain industry and jurisdiction. Both of these entities (and possibly additional ones) impose legal requirements, restrictions, and regulations on the practices of organizations that fall within their realm. These *legal requirements* can apply to licensed use of software, hiring restrictions, handling of sensitive materials, and compliance with safety regulations.

Complying with all applicable legal requirements is a key part of sustaining security. The legal requirements for an industry and a country (and often also a state and city) must be considered a baseline or foundation on which the remainder of the security infrastructure is built.

Summary

If you don't have control over the physical environment, no amount of administrative or technical/logical access controls can provide adequate security. If a malicious person gains physical access to your facility or equipment, they own it.

Several elements are involved in implementing and maintaining physical security. One core element is selecting or designing the facility to house your IT infrastructure and the operations of your organization. You must start with a plan that outlines the security needs for your organization and emphasizes methods or mechanisms to employ to provide such security. Such a plan is developed through a process known as *critical path analysis*.

The security controls implemented to manage physical security can be divided into three groups: administrative, technical, and physical. Administrative physical security controls include facility construction and selection, site management, personnel controls, awareness training, and emergency response and procedures. Technical physical security controls include access controls, intrusion detection, alarms, CCTV, monitoring, HVAC, power supplies, and fire detection and suppression. Examples of physical controls for physical security include fencing, lighting, locks, construction materials, mantraps, dogs, and guards.

There are many types of physical access control mechanisms that can be deployed in an environment to control, monitor, and manage access to a facility. These range from deterrents to detection mechanisms. They can be fences, gates, turnstiles, mantraps, lighting, security guards, security dogs, key locks, combination locks, badges, motion detectors, sensors, and alarms.

The technical controls most often employed as access control mechanisms to manage physical access include smart/dumb cards and biometrics. In addition to access control, physical security mechanisms can take the form of audit trails, access logs, and intrusion detection systems.

Wiring closets and server rooms are important infrastructure elements that require protection. They often house core networking devices and other sensitive equipment. Protections include adequate locks, surveillance, access control, and regular physical inspections.

Media storage security should include a library checkout system, storage in a locked cabinet or safe, and sanitization of reusable media.

An important aspect of physical access control and maintaining the security of a facility is protecting the basic elements of the environment and protecting human life. In all circumstances and under all conditions, the most important goal of security is protecting people. Preventing harm is the utmost goal of all security solutions. Providing clean power sources and managing the environment are also important.

Fire detection and suppression must not be overlooked. In addition to protecting people, fire detection and suppression is designed to keep damage caused by fire, smoke, heat, and suppression materials to a minimum, especially in regard to the IT infrastructure.

People should always be your top priority. Only after personnel are safe can you consider addressing business continuity.

Exam Essentials

Understand why there is no security without physical security. Without control over the physical environment, no amount of administrative or technical/logical access controls can provide adequate security. If a malicious person can gain physical access to your facility or equipment, they can do just about anything they want, from destruction to disclosure and alteration.

Be able to list administrative physical security controls. Examples of administrative physical security controls are facility construction and selection, site management, personnel controls, awareness training, and emergency response and procedures.

Be able to list the technical physical security controls. Technical physical security controls can be access controls, intrusion detection, alarms, CCTV, monitoring, HVAC, power supplies, and fire detection and suppression.

Be able to name the physical controls for physical security. Physical controls for physical security are fencing, lighting, locks, construction materials, mantraps, dogs, and guards.

Know the functional order of controls. These are deterrence, then denial, then detection, and then delay.

Know the key elements in making a site selection and designing a facility for construction. The key elements in making a site selection are visibility, composition of the surrounding area, area accessibility, and the effects of natural disasters. A key element in designing a facility for construction is understanding the level of security needed by your organization and planning for it before construction begins.

Know how to design and configure secure work areas. There should not be equal access to all locations within a facility. Areas that contain assets of higher value or importance should have restricted access. Valuable and confidential assets should be located in the heart or center of protection provided by a facility. Also, centralized server or computer rooms need not be human compatible.

Understand the security concerns of a wiring closet. A wiring closet is where the networking cables for a whole building or just a floor are connected to other essential equipment, such as patch panels, switches, routers, LAN extenders, and backbone channels. Most of the security for a wiring closet focuses on preventing physical unauthorized access. If an unauthorized intruder gains access to the area, they may be able to steal equipment, pull or cut cables, or even plant a listening device.

Understand how to handle visitors in a secure facility. If a facility employs restricted areas to control physical security, then a mechanism to handle visitors is required. Often an escort is assigned to visitors, and their access and activities are monitored closely. Failing to track the actions of outsiders when they are granted access to a protected area can result in malicious activity against the most protected assets.

Know the three categories of security controls implemented to manage physical security and be able to name examples of each. The security controls implemented to manage physical security can be divided into three groups: administrative, technical, and physical. Understand when and how to use each, and be able to list examples of each kind.

Understand security needs for media storage. Media storage facilities should be designed to securely store blank media, reusable media, and installation media. The concerns include theft, corruption, and data remnant recovery. Media storage facility protections include locked cabinets or safes, using a librarian/custodian, implementing a check-in/check-out process, and using media sanitization.

Understand the concerns of evidence storage. Evidence storage is used to retain logs, drive images, virtual machine snapshots, and other datasets for recovery, internal investigations, and forensic investigations. Protections include dedicated/isolated storage facilities, offline storage, activity tracking, hash management, access restrictions, and encryption.

Know the common threats to physical access controls. No matter what form of physical access control is used, a security guard or other monitoring system must be deployed to prevent abuse, masquerading, and piggybacking. Abuses of physical access control include propping open secured doors and bypassing locks or access controls. Masquerading is using someone else's security ID to gain entry to a facility. Piggybacking is following someone through a secured gate or doorway without being identified or authorized personally.

Understand the need for audit trails and access logs. Audit trails and access logs are useful tools even for physical access control. They may need to be created manually by security guards. Or they can be generated automatically if sufficiently automated access control mechanisms are in place (in other words, smartcards and certain proximity readers). You should also consider monitoring entry points with CCTV. Through CCTV, you can compare the audit trails and access logs with a visually recorded history of the events. Such information is critical to reconstructing the events of an intrusion, breach, or attack.

Understand the need for clean power. Power supplied by electric companies is not always consistent and clean. Most electronic equipment demands clean power in order to function properly. Equipment damage because of power fluctuations is a common occurrence. Many organizations opt to manage their own power through several means. A UPS is a type of self-charging battery that can be used to supply consistent clean power to sensitive equipment. UPSs also provide continuous power even after the primary power source fails. A UPS can continue to supply power for minutes or hours depending on its capacity and the draw by equipment.

Know the terms commonly associated with power issues. Know the definitions of the following: fault, blackout, sag, brownout, spike, surge, inrush, noise, transient, clean, and ground.

Understand how to control the environment. In addition to power considerations, maintaining the environment involves control over the HVAC mechanisms. Rooms containing primarily computers should be kept at 60 to 75 degrees Fahrenheit (15 to 23 degrees Celsius). Humidity in a computer room should be maintained between 40 and 60 percent. Too much humidity can cause corrosion. Too little humidity causes static electricity.

Know about static electricity. Even on nonstatic carpeting, if the environment has low humidity it is still possible to generate 20,000-volt static discharges. Even minimal levels of static discharge can destroy electronic equipment.

Understand the need to manage water leakage and flooding. Water leakage and flooding should be addressed in your environmental safety policy and procedures. Plumbing leaks are not an everyday occurrence, but when they occur, they often cause significant damage. Water and electricity don't mix. If your computer systems come in contact with water, especially while they are operating, damage is sure to occur. Whenever possible, locate server rooms and critical computer equipment away from any water source or transport pipes.

Understand the importance of fire detection and suppression. Fire detection and suppression must not be overlooked. Protecting personnel from harm should always be the most important goal of any security or protection system. In addition to protecting people, fire detection and suppression is designed to keep damage caused by fire, smoke, heat, and suppression materials to a minimum, especially in regard to the IT infrastructure.

Understand the possible contamination and damage caused by a fire and suppression. The destructive elements of a fire include smoke and heat but also the suppression medium, such as water or soda acid. Smoke is damaging to most storage devices. Heat can damage any electronic or computer component. Suppression mediums can cause short circuits, initiate corrosion, or otherwise render equipment useless. All of these issues must be addressed when designing a fire response system.

Understand personnel privacy and safety. In all circumstances and under all conditions, the most important aspect of security is protecting people. Thus, preventing harm to people is the most important goal for all security solutions.

Written Lab

1. What kind of device helps to define an organization's perimeter and also serves to deter casual trespassing?
2. What is the problem with halon-based fire suppression technology?
3. What kinds of potential issues can an emergency visit from the fire department leave in its wake?

Review Questions

1. Which of the following is the most important aspect of security?
   A. Physical security
   B. Intrusion detection
   C. Logical security
   D. Awareness training
2. What method can be used to map out the needs of an organization for a new facility?
   A. Log file audit
   B. Critical path analysis
   C. Risk analysis
   D. Inventory
3. What infrastructure component is often located in the same position across multiple floors in order to provide a convenient means of linking floor-based networks together?
   A. Server room
   B. Wiring closet
   C. Datacenter
   D. Media cabinets
4. Which of the following is *not* a security-focused design element of a facility or site?
   A. Separation of work and visitor areas
   B. Restricted access to areas with higher value or importance
   C. Confidential assets located in the heart or center of a facility
   D. Equal access to all locations within a facility
5. Which of the following does *not* need to be true in order to maintain the most efficient and secure server room?
   A. It must be human compatible.
   B. It must include the use of nonwater fire suppressants.
   C. The humidity must be kept between 40 and 60 percent.
   D. The temperature must be kept between 60 and 75 degrees Fahrenheit.
6. Which of the following is not a typical security measure implemented in relation to a media storage facility containing reusable removable media?
   A. Employing a librarian or custodian
   B. Using a check-in/check-out process
   C. Hashing
   D. Using sanitization tools on returned media

7. Which of the following is a double set of doors that is often protected by a guard and is used to contain a subject until their identity and authentication is verified?
   A. Gate
   B. Turnstile
   C. Mantrap
   D. Proximity detector

8. What is the most common form of perimeter security devices or mechanisms?
   A. Security guards
   B. Fences
   C. CCTV
   D. Lighting

9. Which of the following is *not* a disadvantage of using security guards?
   A. Security guards are usually unaware of the scope of the operations within a facility.
   B. Not all environments and facilities support security guards.
   C. Not all security guards are themselves reliable.
   D. Prescreening, bonding, and training does not guarantee effective and reliable security guards.

10. What is the most common cause of failure for a water-based fire suppression system?
   A. Water shortage
   B. People
   C. Ionization detectors
   D. Placement of detectors in drop ceilings

11. What is the most common and inexpensive form of physical access control device?
   A. Lighting
   B. Security guard
   C. Key locks
   D. Fences

12. What type of motion detector senses changes in the electrical or magnetic field surrounding a monitored object?
   A. Wave
   B. Photoelectric
   C. Heat
   D. Capacitance

13. Which of the following is *not* a typical type of alarm that can be triggered for physical security?
    - A. Preventive
    - B. Deterrent
    - C. Repellant
    - D. Notification

14. No matter what form of physical access control is used, a security guard or other monitoring system must be deployed to prevent all but which of the following?
    - A. Piggybacking
    - B. Espionage
    - C. Masquerading
    - D. Abuse

15. What is the most important goal of all security solutions?
    - A. Prevention of disclosure
    - B. Maintaining integrity
    - C. Human safety
    - D. Sustaining availability

16. What is the ideal humidity range for a computer room?
    - A. 20–40 percent
    - B. 40–60 percent
    - C. 60–75 percent
    - D. 80–95 percent

17. At what voltage level can static electricity cause destruction of data stored on hard drives?
    - A. 4,000
    - B. 17,000
    - C. 40
    - D. 1,500

18. A Type B fire extinguisher may use all *except* which of the following suppression mediums?
    - A. Water
    - B. CO2
    - C. Halon or an acceptable halon substitute
    - D. Soda acid

19. What is the best type of water-based fire suppression system for a computer facility?

A. Wet pipe system

B. Dry pipe system

C. Preaction system

D. Deluge system

20. Which of the following is typically *not* a culprit in causing damage to computer equipment in the event of a fire and a triggered suppression?

A. Heat

B. Suppression medium

C. Smoke

D. Light

Chapter 11

Secure Network Architecture and Securing Network Components

THE CISSP EXAM TOPICS COVERED IN THIS CHAPTER INCLUDE:

✓ **4) Communication and Network Security (Designing and Protecting Network Security)**

- A. Apply secure design principles to network architecture (e.g., IP & non-IP protocols, segmentation)
  - A.1 OSI and TCP/IP models
  - A.2 IP networking
  - A.3 Implications of multilayer protocols (e.g., DNP3)
  - A.4 Converged protocols (e.g., FCoE, MPLS, VoIP, iSCSI)
  - A.5 Software-defined networks
  - A.6 Wireless networks
  - A.7 Cryptography used to maintain communication security
- B. Secure network components
  - B.1 Operation of hardware (e.g., modems, switches, routers, wireless access points, mobile devices)
  - B.2 Transmission media (e.g., wired, wireless, fiber)
  - B.3 Network access control devices (e.g., firewalls, proxies)
  - B.4 Endpoint security
  - B.5 Content-distribution networks
  - B.6 Physical devices

Computers and networks emerge from the integration of communication devices, storage devices, processing devices, security devices, input devices, output devices, operating systems, software, services, data, and people. The CISSP CBK states that a thorough knowledge of these hardware and software components is an essential element of being able to implement and maintain security. This chapter discusses the OSI model as a guiding principle in networking, cabling, wireless connectivity, TCP/IP and related protocols, networking devices, and firewalls.

The Communication and Network Security domain for the CISSP certification exam deals with topics related to network components (i.e., network devices and protocols), specifically, how they function and how they are relevant to security. This domain is discussed in this chapter and in Chapter 12, "Secure Communications and Network Attacks." Be sure to read and study the materials in both chapters to ensure complete coverage of the essential material for the CISSP certification exam.

OSI Model

Communications between computers over networks are made possible by protocols. A protocol is a set of rules and restrictions that define how data is transmitted over a network medium (e.g., twisted-pair cable, wireless transmission). In the early days of network development, many companies had their own proprietary protocols, which meant interaction between computers of different vendors was often difficult, if not impossible. In an effort to eliminate this problem, the International Organization for Standardization (ISO) developed the Open Systems Interconnection (OSI) Reference Model for protocols in the early 1980s. Specifically, ISO 7498 defines the OSI Reference Model (more commonly called the OSI model). Understanding the OSI model and how it relates to network design, deployment, and security is essential in preparing for the CISSP exam.

In order to properly establish secure data communications, it is important to fully understand all of the technologies involved in computer communications. From hardware and software to protocols and encryption and beyond, there are lots of details to know, standards to understand, and procedures to follow. Additionally, the basis of secure network architecture and design is a thorough knowledge of the OSI and TCP/IP models as well as IP networking in general.

History of the OSI Model

The OSI model wasn't the first or only attempt to streamline networking protocols or establish a common communications standard. In fact, the most widely used protocol today, TCP/IP (which is based on the DARPA model, also known now as the TCP/IP model), was developed in the early 1970s. The OSI model was not developed until the late 1970s.

The OSI protocol was developed to establish a common communication structure or standard for all computer systems. The actual OSI protocol was never widely adopted, but the theory behind the OSI protocol, the OSI model, was readily accepted. The OSI model serves as an abstract framework, or theoretical model, for how protocols should function in an ideal world on ideal hardware. Thus, the OSI model has become a common reference point against which all protocols can be compared and contrasted.

OSI Functionality

The OSI model divides networking tasks into seven distinct layers. Each layer is responsible for performing specific tasks or operations for the ultimate goal of supporting data exchange (in other words, network communication) between two computers. The layers are always numbered from bottom to top (see Figure 11.1). They are referred to by either their name or their layer number. For example, layer 3 is also known as the Network layer. The layers are ordered specifically to indicate how information flows through the various levels of communication. Each layer communicates directly with the layer above it as well as the layer below it, plus the peer layer on a communication partner system.

FIGURE 11.1 Representation of the OSI model

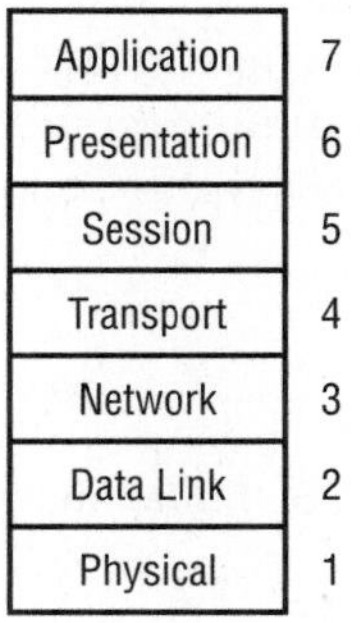

The OSI model is an open network architecture guide for network product vendors. This standard, or guide, provides a common foundation for the development of new protocols, networking services, and even hardware devices. By working from the OSI model, vendors are able to ensure that their products will integrate with products from other companies and be supported by a wide range of operating systems. If all vendors developed their own networking framework, interoperability between products from different vendors would be next to impossible.

The real benefit of the OSI model is its expression of how networking actually functions. In the most basic sense, network communications occur over a physical connection (whether that physical connection is electrons over copper, photons over fiber, or radio signals through the air). Physical devices establish channels through which electronic signals can pass from one computer to another. These physical device channels are only one type of the seven logical communication types defined by the OSI model. Each layer of the OSI model communicates via a logical channel with its peer layer on another computer. This enables protocols based on the OSI model to support a type of authentication by being able to identify the remote communication entity as well as authenticate the source of the received data.

Encapsulation/Deencapsulation

Protocols based on the OSI model employ a mechanism called encapsulation. *Encapsulation* is the addition of a header, and possibly a footer, to the data received by each layer from the layer above before it's handed off to the layer below. As the message is encapsulated at each layer, the previous layer's header and payload combine to become the payload of the current layer. Encapsulation occurs as the data moves down through the OSI model layers from Application to Physical. The inverse action occurring as data moves up through the OSI model layers from Physical to Application is known as deencapsulation. The encapsulation/deencapsulation process is as follows:

1. The Application layer creates a message.
2. The Application layer passes the message to the Presentation layer.
3. The Presentation layer encapsulates the message by adding information to it. Information is usually added only at the beginning of the message (called a header); however, some layers also add material at the end of the message (called a footer), as shown in Figure 11.2.

FIGURE 11.2 Representation of OSI model encapsulation

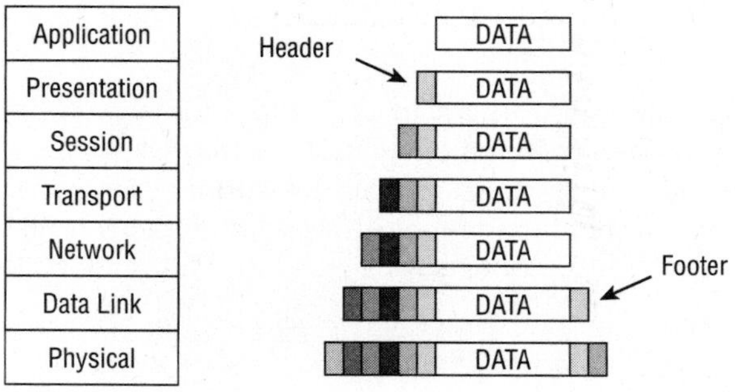

4. The process of passing the message down and adding layer-specific information continues until the message reaches the Physical layer.
5. At the Physical layer, the message is converted into electrical impulses that represent bits and is transmitted over the physical connection.
6. The receiving computer captures the bits from the physical connection and re-creates the message in the Physical layer.
7. The Physical layer converts the message from bits into a Data Link frame and sends the message up to the Data Link layer.
8. The Data Link layer strips its information and sends the message up to the Network layer.
9. This process of deencapsulation is performed until the message reaches the Application layer.
10. When the message reaches the Application layer, the data in the message is sent to the intended software recipient.

The information removed by each layer contains instructions, checksums, and so on that can be understood only by the peer layer that originally added or created the information (see Figure 11.3). This information is what creates the logical channel that enables peer layers on different computers to communicate.

FIGURE 11.3 Representation of the OSI model peer layer logical channels

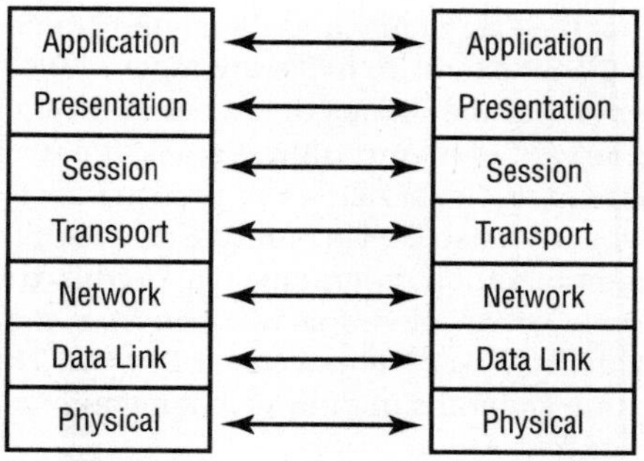

The message sent into the protocol stack at the Application layer (layer 7) is called the data stream. It retains the label of data stream until it reaches the Transport layer (layer 4), where it is called a segment (TCP protocols) or a datagram (UDP protocols). In the Network layer (layer 3), it is called a packet. In the Data Link layer (layer 2), it is called a frame. In the Physical layer (layer 1), the data has been converted into bits for transmission over the physical connection medium. Figure 11.4 shows how each layer changes the data through this process.

OSI Layers

Understanding the functions and responsibilities of each layer of the OSI model will help you understand how network communications function, how attacks can be perpetrated against network communications, and how security can be implemented to protect network communications. We discuss each layer, starting with the bottom layer, in the following sections.

FIGURE 11.4 OSI model data names

Application	Data stream
Presentation	Data stream
Session	Data stream
Transport	Segment (TCP)/Datagram (UDP)
Network	Packet
Data Link	Frame
Physical	Bits

NOTE

For more information on the TCP/IP stack, search for *TCP/IP* on Wikipedia (`http://en.wikipedia.org`).

Remember the OSI

Although it can be argued that the OSI has little practical use and that most technical workers don't use the OSI on a regular basis, you can rest assured that the OSI model and its related concepts are firmly positioned within the CISSP exam. To make the most of the OSI, you must first be able to remember the names of the seven layers in their proper order. One common method of memorizing them is to create a mnemonic from the initial letters of the layer names so they are easier to remember. One of our favorites is Please Do Not Teach Surly People Acronyms. Do take note that this memorization mnemonic works from the Physical layer up to the Application layer. A mnemonic working from the Application layer down is All Presidents Since Truman Never Did Pot. There are many other OSI memorization schemes out there; just be sure you know whether they are top-down or bottom-up.

Physical Layer

The Physical layer (layer 1) accepts the frame from the Data Link layer and converts the frame into bits for transmission over the physical connection medium. The Physical layer is also responsible for receiving bits from the physical connection medium and converting them into a frame to be used by the Data Link layer.

The Physical layer contains the device drivers that tell the protocol how to employ the hardware for the transmission and reception of bits. Located within the Physical layer are electrical specifications, protocols, and interface standards such as the following:

- EIA/TIA-232 and EIA/TIA-449
- X.21
- High-Speed Serial Interface (HSSI)

- Synchronous Optical Network (SONET)
- V.24 and V.35

Through the device drivers and these standards, the Physical layer controls throughput rates, handles synchronization, manages line noise and medium access, and determines whether to use digital or analog signals or light pulses to transmit or receive data over the physical hardware interface.

Network hardware devices that function at layer 1, the Physical layer, are network interface cards (NICs), hubs, repeaters, concentrators, and amplifiers. These devices perform hardware-based signal operations, such as sending a signal from one connection port out on all other ports (a hub) or amplifying the signal to support greater transmission distances (a repeater).

Data Link Layer

The Data Link layer (layer 2) is responsible for formatting the packet from the Network layer into the proper format for transmission. The proper format is determined by the hardware and the technology of the network. There are numerous possibilities, such as Ethernet (IEEE 802.3), Token Ring (IEEE 802.5), asynchronous transfer mode (ATM), Fiber Distributed Data Interface (FDDI), and Copper DDI (CDDI). However, only Ethernet remains a common Data Link layer technology in use in modern networks. Within the Data Link layer resides the technology-specific protocols that convert the packet into a properly formatted frame. Once the frame is formatted, it is sent to the Physical layer for transmission.

The following list includes some of the protocols found within the Data Link layer:

- Serial Line Internet Protocol (SLIP)
- Point-to-Point Protocol (PPP)
- Address Resolution Protocol (ARP)
- Reverse Address Resolution Protocol (RARP)
- Layer 2 Forwarding (L2F)
- Layer 2 Tunneling Protocol (L2TP)
- Point-to-Point Tunneling Protocol (PPTP)
- Integrated Services Digital Network (ISDN)

Part of the processing performed on the data within the Data Link layer includes adding the hardware source and destination addresses to the frame. The hardware address is the Media Access Control (MAC) address, which is a 6-byte (48-bit) binary address written in hexadecimal notation (for example, 00-13-02-1F-58-F5). The first 3 bytes (24 bits) of the address denote the vendor or manufacturer of the physical network interface. This is known as the Organizationally Unique Identifier (OUI). OUIs are registered with IEEE, which controls their issuance. The OUI can be used to discover the manufacturer of a NIC through the IEEE website at `http://standards.ieee.org/regauth/oui/index.shtml`. The last 3 bytes (24 bits) represent a unique number assigned to that interface by the manufacturer. No two devices can have the same MAC address in the same local Ethernet broadcast domain; otherwise an address conflict occurs. It is also good practice to ensure that all MAC addresses across a private enterprise network are unique. While the design of MAC addresses should make them unique, vendor errors have produced duplicate MAC addresses. When this happens either the NIC hardware must be replaced or the MAC address must be modified (i.e., spoofed) to a non-conflicting alternative address.

EUI-48 to EUI-64

The MAC address has been 48 bits for decades. A similar addressing method is the EUI-48. EUI stands for Extended Unique Identifier. The original 48-bit MAC addressing scheme for IEEE 802 was adopted from the original Xerox Ethernet addressing method. MAC addresses typically are used to identify network hardware, while EUI is used to identity other types of hardware as well as software.

The IEEE has decided that *MAC-48* is an obsolete term and should be deprecated in favor of *EUI-48*.

There is also a move to convert from EUI-48 to EUI-64. This is preparation for future worldwide adoption of IPv6 as well as the exponential growth of the number of networking devices and network software packages, all of which need a unique identifier.

A MAC-48 or EUI-48 address can be represented by an EUI-64. In the case of MAC-48, two additional octets of FF:FF are added between the OUI (first 3 bytes) and the unique NIC specification (last 3 bytes)—for example, cc:cc:cc:FF:FF:ee:ee:ee. In the case of EUI-48, the two additional octets are FF:FE—for example, cc:cc:cc:FF:FE:ee:ee:ee.

Among the protocols at the Data Link layer (layer 2) of the OSI model, the two you should be familiar with are Address Resolution Protocol (ARP) and Reverse Address Resolution Protocol (RARP). ARP is used to resolve IP addresses into MAC addresses. Traffic on a network segment (for example, cables across a hub) is directed from its source system to its destination system using MAC addresses. RARP is used to resolve MAC addresses into IP addresses.

The Data Link layer contains two sublayers: the Logical Link Control (LLC) sublayer and the MAC sublayer. Details about these sublayers are not critical for the CISSP exam.

Network hardware devices that function at layer 2, the Data Link layer, are switches and bridges. These devices support MAC-based traffic routing. Switches receive a frame on one port and send it out another port based on the destination MAC address. MAC address destinations are used to determine whether a frame is transferred over the bridge from one network to another.

Network Layer

The Network layer (layer 3) is responsible for adding routing and addressing information to the data. The Network layer accepts the segment from the Transport layer and adds information to it to create a packet. The packet includes the source and destination IP addresses.

The routing protocols are located at this layer and include the following:

- Internet Control Message Protocol (ICMP)
- Routing Information Protocol (RIP)
- Open Shortest Path First (OSPF)
- Border Gateway Protocol (BGP)
- Internet Group Management Protocol (IGMP)
- Internet Protocol (IP)
- Internet Protocol Security (IPSec)
- Internetwork Packet Exchange (IPX)
- Network Address Translation (NAT)
- Simple Key Management for Internet Protocols (SKIP)

The Network layer is responsible for providing routing or delivery information, but it is not responsible for verifying guaranteed delivery (that is the responsibility of the Transport layer). The Network layer also manages error detection and node data traffic (in other words, traffic control).

Non-IP Protocols

Non-IP protocols are protocols that serve as an alternative to IP at the OSI Network layer (3). In the past, non-IP protocols were widely used. However, with the dominance and success of TCP/IP, non-IP protocols have become the purview of special-purpose networks. The three most recognized non-IP protocols are IPX, AppleTalk, and NetBEUI. Internetwork Packet Exchange (IPX) is part of the IPX/SPX protocol suite commonly used (although not strictly required) on Novell NetWare networks in the 1990s. AppleTalk is a suite of protocols developed by Apple for networking of Macintosh systems, originally released in 1984. Support for AppleTalk was removed from the Apple operating system as of the release of Mac OS X v10.6 in 2009. Both IPX and AppleTalk can be used as IP alternatives in a dead-zone network implementation using IP-to-alternate-protocol gateways (a *dead zone* is a network segment using an alternative Network layer protocol instead of IP). NetBIOS Extended User Interface (NetBEUI, aka NetBIOS Frame protocol, or NBF) is most widely known as a Microsoft protocol developed in 1985 to support file and printer sharing. Microsoft has enabled support of NetBEUI on modern networks by devising NetBIOS over TCP/IP (NBT). This in turn supports the Windows sharing protocol of Server Message Block (SMB), which is also known as Common Internet File System (CIFS). NetBEUI is no longer supported as a lower-layer protocol; only its SMB and CIFS variants are still in use.

A potential security risk exists when non-IP protocols are in use in a private network. Because non-IP protocols are rare, most firewalls are unable to perform packet header, address, or payload content filtering on those protocols. Thus, when it comes to non-IP protocols, a firewall typically must either block all or allow. If your organization is dependent on a service that operates over only a non-IP protocol, then you may have to live with the risk of passing all non-IP protocols through your firewall. This is mostly a concern within a private network when non-IP protocols traverse between network segments. However, non-IP protocols can be encapsulated in IP to be communicated across the Internet. In an encapsulation situation, IP firewalls are rarely able to perform content filtering on such encapsulation and thus security has to be set to an allow-all or deny-all configuration.

Routers and bridge routers (brouters) are among the network hardware devices that function at layer 3. Routers determine the best logical path for the transmission of packets based on speed, hops, preference, and so on. Routers use the destination IP address to guide the transmission of packets. A brouter, working primarily in layer 3 but in layer 2 when necessary, is a device that attempts to route first, but if that fails, it defaults to bridging.

Routing Protocols

There are two broad categories of routing protocols: distance vector and link state. *Distance vector* routing protocols maintain a list of destination networks along with metrics of direction and distance as measured in hops (in other words, the number of routers to cross to reach the destination). *Link state* routing protocols maintain a topography map of all connected networks and use this map to determine the shortest path to the destination. Common examples of distance vector routing protocols are Routing Information Protocol (RIP), Interior Gateway Routing Protocol (IGRP), and Border Gateway Protocol (BGP), while a common example of a link state routing protocol is Open Shortest Path First (OSPF).

Transport Layer

The Transport layer (layer 4) is responsible for managing the integrity of a connection and controlling the session. It accepts a PDU (variably spelled out as Protocol Data Unit, Packet Data Unit, or Payload Data Unit—i.e., a container of information or data passed between network layers) from the Session layer and converts it into a segment. The Transport layer controls how devices on the network are addressed or referenced, establishes communication connections between nodes (also known as devices), and defines the rules of a session. Session rules specify how much data each segment can contain, how to verify the integrity of data transmitted, and how to determine whether data has been lost. Session rules are established through a handshaking process. (Please see the section "Transport Layer Protocols" later in this chapter for the discussion of the SYN/ACK three-way handshake of TCP.)

The Transport layer establishes a logical connection between two devices and provides end-to-end transport services to ensure data delivery. This layer includes mechanisms for segmentation, sequencing, error checking, controlling the flow of data, error correction, multiplexing, and network service optimization. The following protocols operate within the Transport layer:

- Transmission Control Protocol (TCP)
- User Datagram Protocol (UDP)
- Sequenced Packet Exchange (SPX)
- Secure Sockets Layer (SSL)
- Transport Layer Security (TLS)

Session Layer

The Session layer (layer 5) is responsible for establishing, maintaining, and terminating communication sessions between two computers. It manages dialogue discipline or dialogue control (simplex, half-duplex, full-duplex), establishes checkpoints for grouping and recovery, and retransmits PDUs that have failed or been lost since the last verified checkpoint. The following protocols operate within the Session layer:

- Network File System (NFS)
- Structured Query Language (SQL)
- Remote Procedure Call (RPC)

Communication sessions can operate in one of three different discipline or control modes:

Simplex One-way direction communication

Half-Duplex Two-way communication, but only one direction can send data at a time

Full-Duplex Two-way communication, in which data can be sent in both directions simultaneously

Presentation Layer

The Presentation layer (layer 6) is responsible for transforming data received from the Application layer into a format that any system following the OSI model can understand. It imposes common or standardized structure and formatting rules onto the data. The Presentation layer is also responsible for encryption and compression. Thus, it acts as an interface between the network and applications. This layer is what allows various applications to interact over a network, and it does so by ensuring that the data formats are supported by both systems. Most file or data formats operate within this layer. This includes formats for images, video, sound, documents, email, web pages, control sessions, and so on. The following list includes some of the format standards that exist within the Presentation layer:

- American Standard Code for Information Interchange (ASCII)
- Extended Binary-Coded Decimal Interchange Mode (EBCDICM)
- Tagged Image File Format (TIFF)
- Joint Photographic Experts Group (JPEG)
- Moving Picture Experts Group (MPEG)
- Musical Instrument Digital Interface (MIDI)

Real World Scenario

So Many Protocols, So Many Layers

With seven layers and more than 50 protocols, it may seem daunting to remember the layer in which each protocol resides. One way to learn this is to create flash cards. On the front of each card, write the name of the protocol; then on the back, write the layer name. After shuffling the cards, put the card for each protocol in a pile representing its supposed layer. Once you have placed all the protocols, check your work by viewing the backs of the cards. Repeat this process until you are able to place each one correctly.

Application Layer

The Application layer (layer 7) is responsible for interfacing user applications, network services, or the operating system with the protocol stack. It allows applications to communicate with the protocol stack. The Application layer determines whether a remote communication partner is available and accessible. It also ensures that sufficient resources are available to support the requested communications.

The application is not located within this layer; rather, the protocols and services required to transmit files, exchange messages, connect to remote terminals, and so on are found here. Numerous application-specific protocols are found within this layer, such as the following:

- Hypertext Transfer Protocol (HTTP)
- File Transfer Protocol (FTP)
- Line Print Daemon (LPD)
- Simple Mail Transfer Protocol (SMTP)
- Telnet
- Trivial File Transfer Protocol (TFTP)
- Electronic Data Interchange (EDI)

- Post Office Protocol version 3 (POP3)
- Internet Message Access Protocol (IMAP)
- Simple Network Management Protocol (SNMP)
- Network News Transport Protocol (NNTP)
- Secure Remote Procedure Call (S-RPC)
- Secure Electronic Transaction (SET)

There is a network device (or service) that works at the Application layer, namely, the gateway. However, an Application layer gateway is a specific type of component. It serves as a protocol translation tool. For example, an IP-to-IPX gateway takes inbound communications from TCP/IP and translates them over to IPX/SPX for outbound transmission. Application layer firewalls also operate at this layer. Other networking devices or filtering software may observe or modify traffic at this layer.

TCP/IP Model

The TCP/IP model (also called the DARPA or the DOD model) consists of only four layers, as opposed to the OSI Reference Model's seven. The four layers of the TCP/IP model are Application, Transport (also known as Host-to-Host), Internet (sometimes Internetworking), and Link (although Network Interface and sometimes Network Access are used). Figure 11.5 shows how they compare to the seven layers of the OSI model. The TCP/IP protocol suite was developed before the OSI Reference Model was created. The designers of the OSI Reference Model took care to ensure that the TCP/IP protocol suite fit their model because of its established deployment in networking.

FIGURE 11.5 Comparing the OSI model with the TCP/IP model

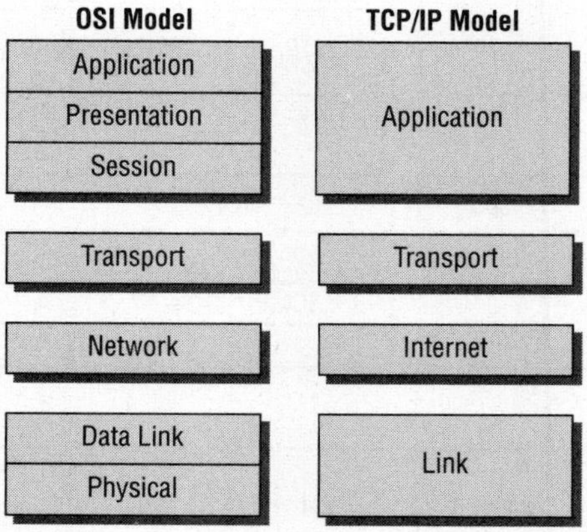

The TCP/IP model's Application layer corresponds to layers 5, 6, and 7 of the OSI model. The TCP/IP model's Transport layer corresponds to layer 4 from the OSI model. The TCP/IP model's Internet layer corresponds to layer 3 from the OSI model. The TCP/IP model's Link layer corresponds to layers 1 and 2 from the OSI model.

It has become common practice (through confusion, misunderstanding, and probably laziness) to also call the TCP/IP model layers by their OSI model layer equivalent names. The TCP/IP model's Application layer is already using a name borrowed from the OSI, so that one is a snap. The TCP/IP model's Host-to-Host layer is sometimes called the Transport layer (the OSI model's fourth layer). The TCP/IP model's Internet layer is sometimes called the Network layer (the OSI model's third layer). And the TCP/IP model's Link layer is sometimes called the Data Link or the Network Access layer (the OSI model's second layer).

TIP Since the TCP/IP model layer names and the OSI model layer names can be used interchangeably, it is important to know which model is being addressed in various contexts. Unless informed otherwise, always assume that the OSI model provides the basis for discussion because it's the most widely used network reference model.

TCP/IP Protocol Suite Overview

The most widely used protocol suite is TCP/IP, but it is not just a single protocol; rather, it is a protocol stack comprising dozens of individual protocols (see Figure 11.6). TCP/IP is a platform-independent protocol based on open standards. However, this is both a benefit and a drawback. TCP/IP can be found in just about every available operating system, but it consumes a significant amount of resources and is relatively easy to hack into because it was designed for ease of use rather than for security.

FIGURE 11.6 The four layers of TCP/IP and its component protocols

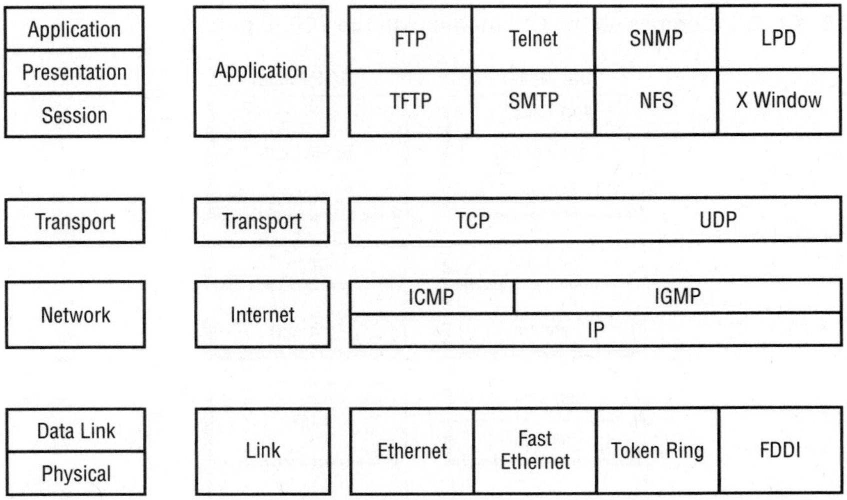

TCP/IP can be secured using VPN links between systems. VPN links are encrypted to add privacy, confidentiality, and authentication and to maintain data integrity. Protocols used to establish VPNs are Point-to-Point Tunneling Protocol (PPTP), Layer 2 Tunneling Protocol (L2TP), and Internet Protocol Security (IPSec). Another method to provide protocol-level security is to employ TCP wrappers. A *TCP wrapper* is an application that can serve as a basic firewall by restricting access to ports and resources based on user IDs or system IDs. Using TCP wrappers is a form of port-based access control.

Transport Layer Protocols

The two primary Transport layer protocols of TCP/IP are TCP and UDP. TCP is a full-duplex connection-oriented protocol, whereas UDP is a simplex connectionless protocol. When a communication connection is established between two systems, it is done using ports. TCP and UDP each have 65,536 ports. Since port numbers are 16-digit binary numbers, the total number of ports is 2^16, or 65,536, numbered from 0 through 65,535. A port (also called a socket) is little more than an address number that both ends of the communication link agree to use when transferring data. Ports allow a single IP address to be able to support multiple simultaneous communications, each using a different port number.

The first 1,024 of these ports (0–1,023) are called the well-known ports or the service ports. This is because they have standardized assignments as to the services they support. For example, port 80 is the standard port for web (HTTP) traffic, port 23 is the standard port for Telnet, and port 25 is the standard port for SMTP. You can find a list of ports worth knowing for the exam in the section "Common Application Layer Protocols" later in this chapter.

Ports 1024 to 49151 are known as the registered software ports. These are ports that have one or more networking software products specifically registered with the International Assigned Numbers Authority (IANA, `www.iana.org`) in order to provide a standardized port-numbering system for clients attempting to connect to their products.

Ports 49152 to 65535 are known as the random, dynamic, or ephemeral ports because they are often used randomly and temporarily by clients as a source port. These random ports are also used by several networking services when negotiating a data transfer pipeline between client and server outside the initial service or registered ports, such as performed by common FTP.

Port Numbers

The IANA recommends that ports 49152 to 65535 be used as dynamic and/or private ports. However, not all OSs abide by this, such as the following:

- Berkeley Software Distribution (BSD) uses ports 1024 through 4999.
- Many Linux kernels use 32768 to 61000.
- Microsoft, up to and including Windows Server 2003, uses the range 1025 to 5000.
- Windows Vista, Windows 7, and Windows Server 2008 use the IANA range.
- FreeBSD, since version 4.6, has used the IANA suggested port range.

Transmission Control Protocol (TCP) operates at layer 4 (the Transport layer) of the OSI model. It supports full-duplex communications, is connection oriented, and employs reliable sessions. TCP is connection oriented because it employs a handshake process between two systems to establish a communication session. Upon completion of this handshake process, a communication session that can support data transmission between the client and server is established. The three-way handshake process (Figure 11.7) is as follows:

1. The client sends a SYN (synchronize) flagged packet to the server.
2. The server responds with a SYN/ACK (synchronize and acknowledge) flagged packet back to the client.
3. The client responds with an ACK (acknowledge) flagged packet back to the server.

FIGURE 11.7 The TCP three-way handshake

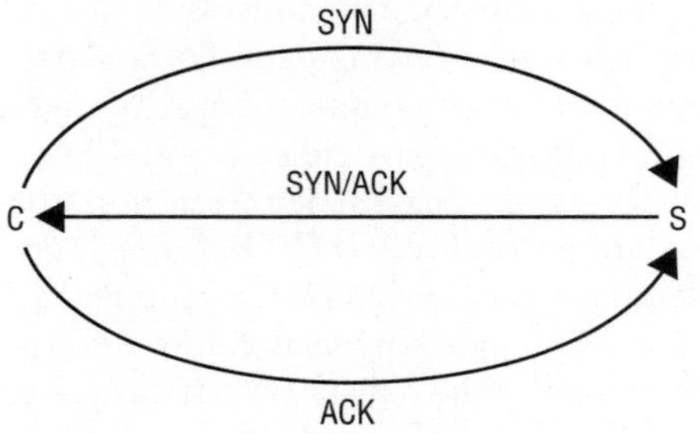

When a communication session is complete, there are two methods to disconnect the TCP session. First, and most common, is the use of FIN (finish) flagged packets instead of SYN flagged packets. Each side of a conversation will transmit a FIN flagged packet once all of its data is transmitted, triggering the opposing side to confirm with an ACK flagged packet. Thus, it takes four packets to gracefully tear down a TCP session. Second is the use of an RST (reset) flagged packet, which causes an immediate and abrupt session termination. (Please see the discussion of the TCP header flag later in this section.)

The segments of a TCP transmission are tagged with a sequence number. This allows the receiver to rebuild the original communication by reordering received segments back into their proper arrangement in spite of the order in which they were received. Data communicated through a TCP session is periodically verified with an acknowledgement. The acknowledgement is sent by the receiver back to the sender by setting the TCP header's acknowledgement sequence value to the last sequence number received from the sender within the transmission window. The number of packets transmitted before an acknowledge packet is sent is known as the transmission window. Data flow is controlled through a mechanism called sliding windows. TCP is able to use different sizes of windows (in other words, a different number of transmitted packets) before sending an acknowledgment. Larger windows allow for faster data transmission, but they should be used only on reliable connections where lost or corrupted data is minimal. Smaller windows should be used when the communication connection is unreliable. TCP should be employed when the delivery of data is required. Sliding windows allow this size to vary dynamically because the reliability of the TCP session changes while in use. In the event that all packets of a transmission window were not received, no acknowledgement is sent. After a timeout period, the sender will resend the entire transmission window set of packets again.

The TCP header is relatively complex when compared to its sister protocol UDP. A TCP header is 20 to 60 bytes long. This header is divided into several sections, or fields, as detailed in Table 11.1.

TABLE 11.1 TCP header construction (ordered from beginning of header to end)

Size in Bits	Field
16	Source port
16	Destination port
32	Sequence number
4	Data offset
4	Reserved for future use
8	Flags (see Table 12.2)
16	Window size
16	Checksum
16	Urgent pointer
Variable	Various options; must be a multiple of 32 bits

All of these fields have unique parameters and requirements, most of which are beyond the scope of the CISSP exam. However, you should be familiar with the details of the flags field. The flags field can contain a designation of one or more flags, or control bits. These flags indicate the function of the TCP packet and request that the recipient respond in a specific manner. The flags field is 8 bits long. Each of the bit positions represents a single flag, or control setting. Each position can be set on with a value of 1 or off with a value of 0. There are some conditions in which multiple flags can be enabled at once (in other words, the second packet in the TCP three-way handshake when both the SYN and ACK flags are set). Table 11.2 details the flag control bits.

TABLE 11.2 The TCP header flag field values

Flag Bit Designator	Name	Description
CWR	Congestion Window Reduced	Used to manage transmission over congested links; see RFC 3168
ECE	ECN-Echo (Explicit Congestion Notification)	Used to manage transmission over congested links; see RFC 3168
URG	Urgent	Indicates urgent data
ACK	Acknowledgement	Acknowledges synchronization or shutdown request
PSH	Push	Indicates need to push data immediately to application
RST	Reset	Causes immediate disconnect of TCP session
SYN	Synchronization	Requests synchronization with new sequencing numbers
FIN	Finish	Requests graceful shutdown of TCP session

An additional important tidbit is that the IP header protocol field value for TCP is 6 (0x06). The protocol field value is the label or flag found in the header of every IP packet that tells the receiving system what type of packet it is. The IP header's protocol field indicates the identity of the next encapsulated protocol (in other words, the protocol contained in the payload from the current protocol layer, such as ICMP or IGMP, or the next layer up, such as TCP or UDP). Think of it as like the label on a mystery-meat package wrapped in butcher paper you pull out of the freezer. Without the label, you would have to open it and inspect it to figure out what it was. But with the label, you can search or filter quickly to find items of interest. For a list of other protocol field values, please visit `www.iana.org/assignments/protocol-numbers`.

Unskilled Attackers Pester Real Security Folk

It might be a good idea to memorize at least the last six of the eight TCP header flags in their correct order. The first two flags (CWR and ECE) are rarely used today and thus are generally ignored/overlooked. However, the last six (URG, ACK, PSH, RST, SYN, and FIN) are still in common widespread use.

Keep in mind that these eight flags are eight binary positions (i.e., a byte) that can be presented in either hex or binary format. For example, 0x12 is the hex presentation of the byte 00010010. This specific byte layout indicates that the fourth and seventh flags are enabled. With the flag layout (using one letter per flag and leaving out CWR and ECE and replacing them with XX), XXUAPRSF is 000A00S0, or the SYN/ACK flag set. Note: the hex presentation of the TCP header flag byte is typically located in the raw data display of a packet capturing tool, such as Wireshark, in offset position 0x2F. This is based on a standard Ethernet Type II header, a standard 20-byte IP header, and a standard TCP header.

You can memorize this flag order using the phrase "Unskilled Attackers Pester Real Security Folk," in which the first letter of each word corresponds to the first letter of the flags in positions 3 through 8.

Real World Scenario

Protocol Discovery

Hundreds of protocols are in use on a typical TCP/IP network at any given moment. Using a sniffer, you can discover what protocols are in use on your current network. Before using a sniffer, though, make sure you have the proper permission or authorization. Without approval, using a sniffer can be considered a security violation because it enables you to eavesdrop on unprotected network communications. If you can't obtain permission at work, try this on your home network instead. Download and install a sniffer, such as Wireshark. Then use the sniffer to monitor the activity on your network. Discover just how many protocols (in other words, subprotocols of TCP/IP) are in use on your network.

Another step in using a sniffer is to analyze the contents of captured packets. Pick out a few different protocol packets and inspect their headers. Look for TCP, ICMP, ARP, and UDP packets. Compare the contents of their headers. Try to locate any special flags or field codes used by the protocols. You'll likely discover that there is a lot more going on within a protocol than you ever imagined.

User Datagram Protocol (UDP) also operates at layer 4 (the Transport layer) of the OSI model. It is a connectionless "best-effort" communications protocol. It offers no error detection or correction, does not use sequencing, does not use flow control mechanisms, does not use a preestablished session, and is considered unreliable. UDP has very low overhead and thus can transmit data quickly. However, UDP should be used only when the delivery of data is not essential. UDP is often employed by real-time or streaming communications for audio and/or video. The IP header protocol field value for UDP is 17 (0x11).

As mentioned earlier, the UDP header is relatively simple in comparison with the TCP header. A UDP header is 8 bytes (64 bits) long. This header is divided into four sections, or fields (each 16 bits long):

- Source port
- Destination port
- Message length
- Checksum

Network Layer Protocols and IP Networking Basics

Another important protocol in the TCP/IP protocol suite operates at the Network layer of the OSI model, namely, Internet Protocol (IP). IP provides route addressing for data packets. It is this route addressing that is the foundation of global Internet communications because it provides a means of identity and prescribes transmission paths. Similar to UDP, IP is connectionless and is an unreliable datagram service. IP does not offer guarantees that packets will be delivered or that packets will be delivered in the correct order, and it does not guarantee that packets will be delivered only once. Thus, you must employ TCP on IP to gain reliable and controlled communication sessions.

IPv4 vs. IPv6

IPv4 is the version of Internet Protocol that is most widely used around the world. However, a version known as IPv6 is primed to take over and improve network addressing and routing. IPv4 uses a 32-bit addressing scheme, while IPv6 uses 128 bits for addressing. IPv6 offers many new features that are not available in IPv4. Some of IPv6's new features are scoped addresses, autoconfiguration, and Quality of Service (QoS) priority values. Scoped addresses give administrators the ability to group and then block or allow access to network services, such as file servers or printing. Autoconfiguration removes the need for both DHCP and NAT. QoS priority values allow for traffic management based on prioritized content.

IPv6 is supported by most operating systems released since 2000, either natively or via an add-in. However, IPv6 has been slowly adopted. Most of the IPv6 networks are currently located in private networks such as those in large corporations, research laboratories, and universities.

IP classes

Basic knowledge of IP addressing and IP classes is a must for any security professional. If you are rusty on addressing, subnetting, classes, and other related topics, take the time to refresh yourself. Table 11.3 and Table 11.4 provide a quick overview of the key details of classes and default subnets. A full Class A subnet supports 16,777,214 hosts; a full class B subnet supports 65,534 hosts; and a full Class C subnet supports 254 hosts. Class D is used for multicasting, while Class E is reserved for future use.

TABLE 11.3 IP classes

Class	First Binary Digits	Decimal Range of First Octet
A	0	1–126
B	10	128–191
C	110	192–223
D	1110	224–239
E	1111	240–255

TABLE 11.4 IP classes' default subnet masks

Class	Default Subnet Mask	CIDR Equivalent
A	255.0.0.0	/8
B	255.255.0.0	/16
C	255.255.255.0	/24

Note that the entire Class A network of 127 was set aside for the loopback address, although only a single address is actually needed for that purpose.

Another option for subnetting is to use Classless Inter-Domain Routing (CIDR) notation. CIDR uses mask bits rather than a full dotted-decimal notation subnet mask. Thus, instead of 255.255.0.0, a CIDR is added to the IP address after a slash, as in 172.16.1.1/16, for example. One significant benefit of CIDR over traditional subnet-masking techniques is the ability to combine multiple noncontiguous sets of addresses into a single subnet. For example, it is possible to combine several Class C subnets into a single larger subnet grouping. If CIDR piques your interest, see the CIDR article on Wikipedia or visit the IETF's RFC for CIDR at `http://tools.ietf.org/html/rfc4632`.

ICMP and IGMP are other protocols in the Network layer of the OSI model:

ICMP Internet Control Message Protocol (ICMP) is used to determine the health of a network or a specific link. ICMP is utilized by `ping`, `traceroute`, `pathping`, and other network management tools. The `ping` utility employs ICMP echo packets and bounces them off remote systems. Thus, you can use `ping` to determine whether the remote system is online, whether the remote system is responding promptly, whether the intermediary systems are supporting communications, and the level of performance efficiency at which the intermediary systems are communicating. The `ping` utility includes a redirect function that allows the echo responses to be sent to a different destination than the system of origin.

Unfortunately, the features of ICMP were often exploited in various forms of bandwidth-based denial of service attacks, such as ping of death, smurf attacks, and ping floods. This fact has shaped how networks handle ICMP traffic today, resulting in many networks limiting the use of ICMP or at least limiting its throughput rates. Ping of death sends a malformed ping larger than 65,535 bytes (larger than the maximum IPv4 packet size) to a computer to attempt to crash it. Smurf attacks generate enormous amounts of traffic on a target network by spoofing broadcast pings, and ping floods are a basic denial of service (DoS) attack relying on consuming all of the bandwidth that a target has available.

You should be aware of several important details regarding ICMP. First, the IP header protocol field value for ICMP is 1 (0x01). Second, the type field in the ICMP header defines the type or purpose of the message contained within the ICMP payload. There are more than 40 defined types, but only 7 are commonly used (see Table 11.5). You can find a complete list of the ICMP type field values at `www.iana.org/assignments/icmp-parameters`. It may be worth noting that many of the types listed may also support codes. A code is simply an additional data parameter offering more detail about the function or purpose of the ICMP message payload. One example of an event that would cause an ICMP response is when an attempt is made to connect to a UDP service port when that service and port are not actually in use on the target server; this would cause an ICMP Type 3 response back to the origin. Since UDP does not have a means to send back errors, the protocol stack switches to ICMP for that purpose.

TABLE 11.5 Common ICMP type field values

Type	Function
0	Echo reply
3	Destination unreachable
5	Redirect
8	Echo request
9	Router advertisement
10	Router solicitation
11	Time exceeded

IGMP Internet Group Management Protocol (IGMP) allows systems to support multicasting. Multicasting is the transmission of data to multiple specific recipients. (RFC 1112 discusses the requirements to perform IGMP multicasting.) IGMP is used by IP hosts to register their dynamic multicast group membership. It is also used by connected routers to discover these groups. Through the use of IGMP multicasting, a server can initially transmit a single data signal for the entire group rather than a separate initial data signal for each intended recipient. With IGMP, the single initial signal is multiplied at the router if divergent pathways exist to the intended recipients. The IP header protocol field value for IGMP is 2 (0x02).

ARP and Reverse ARP Address Resolution Protocol (ARP) and Reverse Address Resolution Protocol (RARP) are essential to the interoperability of logical and physical addressing schemes. ARP is used to resolve IP addresses (32-bit binary number for logical addressing) into Media Access Control (MAC) addresses (48-bit binary number for physical addressing)—or EUI-48 or even EUI-64. Traffic on a network segment (for example, cables across a hub) is directed from its source system to its destination system using MAC addresses. RARP is used to resolve MAC addresses into IP addresses.

Both ARP and RARP function using caching and broadcasting. The first step in resolving an IP address into a MAC address, or vice versa, is to check the local ARP cache. If the needed information is already present in the ARP cache, it is used. This activity is sometimes abused using a technique called *ARP cache poisoning*, where an attacker inserts bogus information into the ARP cache. If the ARP cache does not contain the necessary information, an ARP request in the form of a broadcast is transmitted. If the owner of the queried address is in the local subnet, it can respond with the necessary information. If not, the system will default to using its default gateway to transmit its communications. Then, the default gateway (in other words, a router) will need to perform its own ARP or RARP process.

Common Application Layer Protocols

In the Application layer of the TCP/IP model (which includes the Session, Presentation, and Application layers of the OSI model) reside numerous application- or service-specific protocols. A basic knowledge of these protocols and their relevant service ports is important for the CISSP exam:

Telnet, TCP Port 23 This is a terminal emulation network application that supports remote connectivity for executing commands and running applications but does not support transfer of files.

File Transfer Protocol (FTP), TCP Ports 20 and 21 This is a network application that supports an exchange of files that requires anonymous or specific authentication.

Trivial File Transfer Protocol (TFTP), UDP Port 69 This is a network application that supports an exchange of files that does not require authentication.

Simple Mail Transfer Protocol (SMTP), TCP Port 25 This is a protocol used to transmit email messages from a client to an email server and from one email server to another.

Post Office Protocol (POP3), TCP Port 110 This is a protocol used to pull email messages from an inbox on an email server down to an email client.

Internet Message Access Protocol (IMAP), TCP Port 143 This is a protocol used to pull email messages from an inbox on an email server down to an email client. IMAP is more secure than POP3 and offers the ability to pull headers down from the email server as well as to delete messages directly off the email server without having to download to the local client first.

Dynamic Host Configuration Protocol (DHCP), UDP Ports 67 and 68 DHCP uses port 67 for server point-to-point response and port 68 for client request broadcasts. It is used to assign TCP/IP configuration settings to systems upon bootup. DHCP enables centralized control of network addressing.

Hypertext Transport Protocol (HTTP), TCP Port 80 This is the protocol used to transmit web page elements from a web server to web browsers.

Secure Sockets Layer (SSL), TCP Port 443 (for HTTP Encryption) This is a VPN-like security protocol that operates at the Transport layer. SSL was originally designed to support secured web communications (HTTPS) but is capable of securing any Application layer protocol communications.

Line Print Daemon (LPD), TCP Port 515 This is a network service that is used to spool print jobs and to send print jobs to printers.

X Window, TCP Ports 6000–6063 This is a GUI API for command-line operating systems.

Bootstrap Protocol (BootP)/Dynamic Host Configuration Protocol (DHCP), UDP Ports 67 and 68 This is a protocol used to connect diskless workstations to a network through autoassignment of IP configuration and download of basic OS elements. BootP is the forerunner to Dynamic Host Configuration Protocol (DHCP).

Network File System (NFS), TCP Port 2049 This is a network service used to support file sharing between dissimilar systems.

Simple Network Management Protocol (SNMP), UDP Port 161 (UDP Port 162 for Trap Messages) This is a network service used to collect network health and status information by polling monitoring devices from a central monitoring station.

Implications of Multilayer Protocols

As you can see from the previous sections, TCP/IP as a protocol suite comprises dozens of individual protocols spread across the various protocol stack layers. TCP/IP is therefore a multilayer protocol. TCP/IP derives several benefits from its multilayer design, specifically in relation to its mechanism of encapsulation. For example, when communicating between a web server and a web browser over a typical network connection, HTTP is encapsulated in TCP, which in turn is encapsulated in IP, which is in turn encapsulated in Ethernet. This could be presented as follows:

```
[ Ethernet [ IP [ TCP [ HTTP ] ] ] ]
```

However, this is not the extent of TCP/IP's encapsulation support. It is also possible to add additional layers of encapsulation. For example, adding SSL/TLS encryption to the communication would insert a new encapsulation between HTTP and TCP:

```
[ Ethernet [ IP [ TCP [ SSL [ HTTP ] ] ] ] ]
```

This in turn could be further encapsulated with a Network layer encryption such as IPSec:

```
[ Ethernet [ IPSec [ IP [ TCP [ SSL [ HTTP ] ] ] ] ] ]
```

However, encapsulation is not always implemented for benign purposes. There are numerous covert channel communication mechanisms that use encapsulation to hide or isolate an unauthorized protocol inside another authorized one. For example, if a network blocks the use of FTP but allows HTTP, then tools such as HTTP Tunnel can be used to bypass this restriction. This could result in an encapsulation structure such as this:

```
[ Ethernet [ IP [ TCP [ HTTP [ FTP ] ] ] ] ]
```

Normally, HTTP carries its own web-related payload, but with the HTTP Tunnel tool, the standard payload is replaced with an alternative protocol. This false encapsulation can even occur lower in the protocol stack. For example, ICMP is typically used for network health testing and not for general communication. However, with utilities such as Loki, ICMP is transformed into a tunnel protocol to support TCP communications. The encapsulation structure of Loki is as follows:

```
[ Ethernet [ IP [ ICMP [ TCP [ HTTP ] ] ] ] ]
```

Another area of concern caused by unbounded encapsulation support is the ability to jump between VLANs. VLANs are networks segments that are logically separated by tags. This attack, known as VLAN hopping, is performed by creating a double-encapsulated IEEE 802.1Q VLAN tag:

```
[ Ethernet [ VLAN1 [ VLAN2 [ IP [ TCP [ HTTP ] ] ] ] ] ]
```

With this double encapsulation, the first encountered switch will strip away the first VLAN tag, and then the next switch will be fooled by the interior VLAN tag and move the traffic into the other VLAN.

Multilayer protocols provide the following benefits:

- A wide range of protocols can be used at higher layers.
- Encryption can be incorporated at various layers.
- Flexibility and resiliency in complex network structures is supported.

There are a few drawbacks of multilayer protocols:

- Covert channels are allowed.

- Filters can be bypassed.
- Logically imposed network segment boundaries can be overstepped.

DNP3

DNP3 (Distributed Network Protocol) is specifically called out on the CISSP CBK in this section related to multilayer protocols. DNP3 is primarily used in the electric and water utility and management industries. It is used to support communications between data acquisition systems and the system control equipment. This includes substation computers, RTUs (remote terminal units) (devices controlled by an embedded microprocessor), IEDs (Intelligent Electronic Devices), and SCADA master stations (i.e., control centers). DNP3 is an open and public standard. DNP3 is a multilayer protocol that functions similarly to that of TCP/IP, in that it has link, transport, and transportation layers. For more details on DNP3, please view the protocol primer at `http://www.dnp.org/AboutUs/DNP3%20Primer%20Rev%20A.pdf`.

TCP/IP Vulnerabilities

TCP/IP's vulnerabilities are numerous. Improperly implemented TCP/IP stacks in various operating systems are vulnerable to buffer overflows, SYN flood attacks, various DoS attacks, fragment attacks, oversized packet attacks, spoofing attacks, man-in-the-middle attacks, hijack attacks, and coding error attacks.

TCP/IP (as well as most protocols) is also subject to passive attacks via monitoring or sniffing. Network monitoring is the act of monitoring traffic patterns to obtain information about a network. Packet sniffing is the act of capturing packets from the network in hopes of extracting useful information from the packet contents. Effective packet sniffers can extract usernames, passwords, email addresses, encryption keys, credit card numbers, IP addresses, system names, and so on.

Packet sniffing and other attacks are discussed in more detail in Chapter 13.

Domain Name Resolution

Addressing and naming are important components that make network communications possible. Without addressing schemes, networked computers would not be able to distinguish one computer from another or specify the destination of a communication. Likewise, without naming schemes, humans would have to remember and rely on numbering systems to identify computers. It is much easier to remember Google.com than 64.233.187.99. Thus, most naming schemes were enacted for human use rather than computer use.

It is reasonably important to grasp the basic ideas of addressing and numbering as used on TCP/IP-based networks. There are three different layers to be aware of. They're presented in reverse order here because the third layer is the most basic:

- The third, or bottom, layer is the MAC address. The MAC address, or hardware address, is a "permanent" physical address.
- The second, or middle, layer is the IP address. The IP address is a "temporary" logical address assigned over or onto the MAC address.
- The top layer is the domain name. The domain name or computer name is a "temporary" human-friendly convention assigned over or onto the IP address.

"Permanent" and "Temporary" Addresses

The reason these two adjectives are within quotation marks is that they are not completely accurate. MAC addresses are designed to be permanent physical addresses. However, some NICs support MAC address changes, and most modern operating systems (including Windows and Linux) do as well. When the NIC supports the change, the change occurs on the hardware. When the OS supports the change, the change is only in memory, but it looks like a hardware change to all other network entities.

An IP address is temporary because it is a logical address and could be changed at any time, either by DHCP or by an administrator. However, there are instances where systems are statically assigned an IP address. Likewise, computer names or DNS names might appear permanent, but they are logical and thus able to be modified by an administrator.

This system of naming and addressing grants each networking component the information it needs while making its use of that information as simple as possible. Humans get human-friendly domain names, networking protocols get router-friendly IP addresses, and the network interfaces get physical addresses. However, all three of these schemes must be linked together to allow interoperability. Thus, the Domain Name System (DNS) and the ARP/RARP system were developed. DNS resolves a human-friendly domain name into its IP address equivalent. Then, ARP resolves the IP address into its MAC address equivalent. Both of these resolutions also have an inverse, namely, DNS reverse lookups and RARP (see "ARP and Reverse ARP" earlier in this chapter).

Further Reading on DNS

For an excellent primer to advanced discussion on DNS, its operation, known issues, and the Dan Kaminski vulnerability, please visit "An Illustrated Guide to the Kaminsky DNS Vulnerability":

`http://unixwiz.net/techtips/iguide-kaminsky-dns-vuln.html`

For a look into the future of DNS, specifically the defense against the Kaminski vulnerability, visit `www.dnssec.net`.

Converged Protocols

Converged protocols are the merging of specialty or proprietary protocols with standard protocols, such as those from the TCP/IP suite. The primary benefit of converged protocols is the ability to use existing TCP/IP supporting network infrastructure to host special or proprietary services without the need for unique deployments of alternate networking hardware. This can result in significant cost savings. However, not all converged protocols provide the same level of throughput or reliability as their proprietary implementations. Some common examples of converged protocols are described here:

Fibre Channel over Ethernet (FCoE) Fibre Channel is a form of network data-storage solution (storage area network [SAN]) or network-attached storage [NAS]) that allows for high-speed file transfers at upward of 16 Gbps. It was designed to be operated over fiber-optic cables; support for copper cables was added later to offer less-expensive options. Fibre Channel typically requires its own dedicated infrastructure (separate cables). However, Fibre Channel over Ethernet (FCoE) can be used to support it over the existing network infrastructure. FCoE is used to encapsulate Fibre Channel communications over Ethernet networks. It typically requires 10 Gbps Ethernet in order to support the Fibre Channel protocol. With this technology, Fibre Channel operates as a Network layer or OSI layer 3 protocol, replacing IP as the payload of a standard Ethernet network.

MPLS (Multiprotocol Label Switching) MPLS (Multiprotocol Label Switching) is a high-throughput high-performance network technology that directs data across a network based on short path labels rather than longer network addresses. This technique saves significant time over traditional IP-based routing processes, which can be quite complex. Furthermore, MPLS is designed to handle a wide range of protocols through encapsulation. Thus, the network is not limited to TCP/IP and compatible protocols. This enables the use of many other networking technologies, including T1/E1, ATM, Frame Relay, SONET, and DSL.

Internet Small Computer System Interface (iSCSI) Internet Small Computer System Interface (iSCSI) is a networking storage standard based on IP. This technology can be used to enable location-independent file storage, transmission, and retrieval over LAN, WAN, or public Internet connections. iSCSI is often viewed as a low-cost alternative to Fibre Channel.

Voice over IP (VoIP) Voice over IP (VoIP) is a tunneling mechanism used to transport voice and/or data over a TCP/IP network. VoIP has the potential to replace or supplant PSTN because it's often less expensive and offers a wider variety of options and features. VoIP can be used as a direct telephone replacement on computer networks as well as mobile devices. However, VoIP is able to support video and data transmission to allow videoconferencing and remote collaboration on projects. VoIP is available in both commercial and open-source options. Some VoIP solutions require specialized hardware to either replace traditional telephone handsets/base stations or allow these to connect to and function over the VoIP system. Some VoIP solutions are software only, such as Skype, and allow the user's existing speakers, microphone, or headset to replace the traditional telephone handset. Others are more hardware based, such as magicJack, which allows the use of existing PSTN phone devices plugged into a USB adapter to take advantage of VoIP over the Internet. Often, VoIP-to-VoIP calls are free (assuming the same or compatible VoIP technology), whereas VoIP-to-land-line calls are usually charged a per-minute fee.

Software-Defined Networking (SDN) Software-Defined Networking (SDN) is a unique approach to network operation, design, and management. The concept is based on the theory that the complexities of a traditional network with on-device configuration (i.e., routers and switches) often force an organization to stick with a single device vendor, such as Cisco, and limit the flexibility of the network to respond to changing physical and business conditions. SDN aims at separating the infrastructure layer (i.e., hardware and hardware-based settings) from the control layer (i.e., network services of data transmission management). Furthermore, this also removes the traditional networking concepts of IP addressing, subnets, routing, and so on from needing to be programmed into or be deciphered by hosted applications.

SDN offers a new network design that is directly programmable from a central location, is flexible, is vendor neutral, and is open-standards based. Using SDN frees an organization from having to purchase devices from a single vendor. It instead allows organizations to mix and match hardware as needed, such as to select the most cost-effective or highest throughput–rated devices regardless of vendor. The configuration and management of hardware is then controlled through a centralized management interface. Additionally, the settings applied to the hardware can be changed and adjusted dynamically as needed.

Another way of thinking about SDN is that it is effectively network virtualization. It allows data transmission paths, communication decision trees, and flow control to be virtualized in the SDN control layer rather than being handled on the hardware on a per-device basis.

Content Distribution Networks

A content distribution network (CDN), or content delivery network, is a collection of resource services deployed in numerous data centers across the Internet in order to provide low latency, high performance, and high availability of the hosted content. CDNs provide the desired multimedia performance quality demanded by customers through the concept of distributed data hosts. Rather than having media content stored in a single location to be transmitted to all parts of the Internet, the media is distributed to numerous locations across the Internet. This results in a type of geographic and logical load-balancing. No one server or cluster of servers will be strained under the load of all resource requests, and the hosting servers are located closer to the requesting customers. The overall result is lower-latency and higher-quality throughput. There are many CDN service providers, including CloudFlare, Akamai, Amazon CloudFront, CacheFly, and Level 3 Communications.

While most CDNs focus on the physical distribution of servers, client-based CDN is also possible. This is often referred to by the term P2P (peer-to-peer). The most widely recognized P2P CDN is BitTorrent.

Wireless Networks

Wireless networking is a popular method of connecting corporate and home systems because of the ease of deployment and relatively low cost. It has made networking more versatile than ever before. Workstations and portable systems are no longer tied to a cable but can roam freely within the signal range of the deployed wireless access points. However, with this freedom come additional vulnerabilities. Historically, wireless networking has been fairly insecure, mainly because of a lack of knowledge by end users and organizations as well as insecure default configurations set by device manufacturers. Wireless networks are subject to the same vulnerabilities, threats, and risks as any cabled network in addition to distance eavesdropping, packet sniffing, and new forms of DoS and intrusion. Properly managing wireless networking for reliable access as well as security isn't always an easy or straightforward proposition. This section examines various wireless security issues.

Data emanation is the transmission of data across electromagnetic signals. Almost all activities within a computer or across a network are performed using some form of data emanation. However, this term is often used to focus on emanations that are unwanted or on data that is at risk due to the emanations.

Emanations occur whenever electrons move. Movement of electrons creates a magnetic field. If you can read that magnetic field, you could re-create it elsewhere in order to reproduce the electron stream. If the original electron stream was used to communicate data, then the re-created electron stream is also a re-creation of the original data. This form of electronic eavesdropping sounds like science fiction, but it is scientific fact. The U.S. government has been researching emanation security since the 1950s under the TEMPEST project.

Protecting against eavesdropping and data theft requires a multipronged effort. First, you must maintain physical access control over all electronic equipment. Second, where physical access or proximity is still possible for unauthorized personnel, you must use shielded devices and media. Third, you should always transmit any sensitive data using secure encryption protocols.

Securing Wireless Access Points

Wireless cells are the areas within a physical environment where a wireless device can connect to a wireless access point. Wireless cells can leak outside the secured environment and allow intruders easy access to the wireless network. You should adjust the strength of the wireless access point to maximize authorized user access and minimize intruder access. Doing so may require unique placement of wireless access points, shielding, and noise transmission.

802.11 is the IEEE standard for wireless network communications. Various versions (technically called amendments) of the standard have been implemented in wireless networking hardware, including 802.11a, 802.11b, 802.11g, and 802.11n. 802.11x is sometimes used to collectively refer to all of these specific implementations as a group; however, 802.11 is preferred because 802.11x is easily confused with 802.1x, which is an authentication technology independent of wireless. Each version or amendment to the 802.11 standard offered slightly better throughput: 2 MB, 11 MB, 54 MB, and 200 MB+, respectively, as described in Table 11.6. The 802.11 standard also defines Wired Equivalent Privacy (WEP), which provides eavesdropping protection for wireless communications. The b, g, and n amendments all use the same frequency; thus, they maintain backward compatibility.

TABLE 11.6 802.11 wireless networking amendments

Amendment	Speed	Frequency
802.11	2 Mbps	2.4 GHz
802.11a	54 Mbps	5 GHz
802.11b	11 Mbps	2.4 GHz
802.11g	54 Mbps	2.4 GHz
802.11n	200+ Mbps	2.4 GHz or 5 GHz
802.11ac	1 Gbps	5 GHz

When you're deploying wireless networks, you should deploy wireless access points configured to use *infrastructure mode* rather than *ad hoc mode*. Ad hoc mode means that any two wireless networking devices, including two wireless network interface cards (NICs), can communicate without a centralized control authority. Infrastructure mode means that a wireless access point is required, wireless NICs on systems can't interact directly, and the restrictions of the wireless access point for wireless network access are enforced.

Within the infrastructure mode concept are several variations, including stand-alone, wired extension, enterprise extended, and bridge. A *stand-alone* mode infrastructure occurs when there is a wireless access point connecting wireless clients to each other but not to any wired resources. The wireless access point serves as a wireless hub exclusively. A *wired extension* mode infrastructure occurs when the wireless access point acts as a connection point to link the wireless clients to the wired network. An *enterprise extended* mode infrastructure occurs when multiple wireless access points (WAPs) are used to connect a large physical area to the same wired network. Each wireless access point will use the same extended service set identifier (ESSID) so clients can roam the area while maintaining network connectivity, even while their wireless NICs change associations from one wireless access point to another. A *bridge* mode infrastructure occurs when a wireless connection is used to link two wired networks. This often uses dedicated wireless bridges and is used when wired bridges are inconvenient, such as when linking networks between floors or buildings.

NOTE

The term *SSID* (which stands for service set identifier) is typically misused to indicate the name of a wireless network. Technically there are two types of SSIDs, namely extended service set identifier (ESSID) and basic service set identifier (BSSID). An ESSID is the name of a wireless network when a wireless base station or WAP is used (i.e., infrastructure mode). A BSSID is the name of a wireless network when in ad hoc or peer-to-peer mode (i.e., when a base station or WAP is not used). However, when operating in infrastructure mode, the BSSID is the MAC address of the base station hosting the ESSID in order to differentiate multiple base stations supporting a single extended wireless network.

Real World Scenario

Wireless Channels

Within the assigned frequency of the wireless signal are subdivisions of that frequency known as *channels*. Think of channels as lanes on the same highway. In the United States there are 11 channels, in Europe there are 13, and in Japan there are 17. The differences stem from local laws regulating frequency management (think international versions of the United States' Federal Communications Commission).

Wireless communications take place between a client and access point over a single channel. However, when two or more access points are relatively close to each other physically, signals on one channel can interfere with signals on another channel. One way to avoid this is to set the channels of physically close access points as differently as possible to minimize channel overlap interference. For example, if a building has four access points arranged in a line along the length of the building, the channel settings could be 1, 11, 1, and 11. However, if the building is square and an access point is in each corner, the channel settings may need to be 1, 4, 8, and 11.

Think of the signal within a single channel as being like a wide-load truck in a lane on the highway. The wide-load truck is using part of each lane to either side of it, thus making passing the truck in those lanes dangerous. Likewise, wireless signals in adjacent channels will interfere with each other.

Securing the SSID

Wireless networks are assigned a service set identifier (SSID) (either BSSID or ESSID) to differentiate one wireless network from another. If multiple base stations or wireless access points are involved in the same wireless network, an extended station set identifier (ESSID) is defined. The SSID is similar to the name of a workgroup. If a wireless client knows the SSID, they can configure their wireless NIC to communicate with the associated WAP. Knowledge of the SSID does not always grant entry, though, because the WAP can use numerous security features to block unwanted access. SSIDs are defined by default by vendors, and since these default SSIDs are well known, standard security practice dictates that the SSID should be changed to something unique before deployment.

The SSID is broadcast by the WAP via a special transmission called a *beacon frame*. This allows any wireless NIC within range to see the wireless network and make connecting as simple as possible. However, this default broadcasting of the SSID should be disabled to keep the wireless network secret. Even so, attackers can still discover the SSID with a wireless sniffer since the SSID must still be used in transmissions between wireless clients and the WAP. Thus, disabling SSID broadcasting is not a true mechanism of security. Instead, use WPA2 as a reliable authentication and encryption solution rather than trying to hide the existence of the wireless network.

Disable SSID Broadcast

Wireless networks traditionally announce their SSID on a regular basis within a special packet known as the beacon frame. When the SSID is broadcast, any device with an automatic detect and connect feature is not only able to see the network but can also initiate a connection with the network. Network administrators may choose to disable SSID broadcast to hide their network from unauthorized personnel. However, the SSID is still needed to direct packets to and from the base station, so it is still a discoverable value to anyone with a wireless packet sniffer. Thus, the SSID should be disabled if the network is not for public use, but realize that hiding the SSID is not true security because any hacker with basic wireless knowledge can easily discover the SSID.

Conducting a Site Survey

One method used to discover areas of a physical environment where unwanted wireless access might be possible is to perform a site survey. A *site survey* is the process of investigating the presence, strength, and reach of wireless access points deployed in an environment. This task usually involves walking around with a portable wireless device, taking note of the wireless signal strength, and mapping this on a plot or schematic of the building.

Site surveys should be conducted to ensure that sufficient signal strength is available at all locations that are likely locations for wireless device usage, while at the same time minimizing or eliminating the wireless signal from locations where wireless access shouldn't be permitted (public areas, across floors, into other rooms, or outside the building). A site survey is useful for evaluating existing wireless network deployments, planning expansion of current deployments, and planning for future deployments.

Using Secure Encryption Protocols

The IEEE 802.11 standard defines two methods that wireless clients can use to authenticate to WAPs before normal network communications can occur across the wireless link. These two methods are open system authentication (OSA) and shared key authentication (SKA). OSA means there is no real authentication required. As long as a radio signal can be transmitted between the client and WAP, communications are allowed. It is also the case that wireless networks using OSA typically transmit everything in clear text, thus providing no secrecy or security. SKA means that some form of authentication must take place before network communications can occur. The 802.11 standard defines one optional technique for SKA known as Wired Equivalent Privacy (WEP). Later amendments to the original 802.11 standard added WPA, WPA2, and other technologies.

WEP

Wired Equivalent Privacy is defined by the IEEE 802.11 standard. It was designed to provide the same level of security and encryption on wireless networks as is found on wired or cabled networks. WEP provides protection from packet sniffing and eavesdropping against wireless transmissions.

A secondary benefit of WEP is that it can be configured to prevent unauthorized access to the wireless network. WEP uses a predefined shared secret key; however, rather than being a typical dynamic symmetric cryptography solution, the shared key is static and shared among all wireless access points and device interfaces. This key is used to encrypt packets before they are transmitted over the wireless link, thus providing confidentiality protection. A hash value is used to verify that received packets weren't modified or corrupted while in transit; thus WEP also provides integrity protection. Knowledge or possession of the key not only allows encrypted communication but also serves as a rudimentary form of authentication because, without it, access to the wireless network is prohibited.

WEP was cracked almost as soon as it was released. Today, it is possible to crack WEP in less than a minute, thus rendering it a worthless security precaution. Fortunately, there are alternatives to WEP, namely WPA and WPA2. WPA is an improvement over WEP in that it does not use the same static key to encrypt all communications. Instead, it negotiates a unique key set with each host. However, a single passphrase is used to authorized the association with the base station (i.e., allow a new client to set up a connection). If the passphrase is not long enough, it could be guessed. Usually 14 characters or more for the passphrase is recommended.

WEP encryption employs Rivest Cipher 4 (RC4), a symmetric stream cipher (see Chapter 6, "Cryptography and Symmetric Key Algorithms," and Chapter 7, "PKI and Cryptographic Applications," for more on encryption in general). Due to flaws in its design and implementation of RC4, WEP is weak in several areas, two of which are the use of a static common key and poor implementation of IVs (initiation vectors). Due to these weaknesses, a WEP crack can reveal the WEP key after it finds enough poorly used IVs. This attack can now be performed in less than 60 seconds. When the WEP key is discovered, the attacker can join the network and then listen in on all other wireless client communications. Therefore, WEP should not be used. It offers no real protection and may lead to a false sense of security.

WPA

WPA (Wi-Fi Protected Access) was designed as the replacement for WEP; it was a temporary fix until the new 802.11i amendment was completed. The process of crafting the new amendment took years, and thus WPA established a foothold in the marketplace and is still widely used today. Additionally, WPA can be used on most devices, whereas the features of 802.11i exclude some lower-end hardware.

802.11i is the amendment that defines a cryptographic solution to replace WEP. However, when 802.11i was finalized, the WPA solution was already widely used, so they could not use the WPA name as originally planned; thus it was branded WPA2. But this does not indicate that 802.11i is the second version of WPA. In fact, they are two completely different sets of technologies. 802.11i, or WPA2, implements concepts similar to IPSec to bring the best-to-date encryption and security to wireless communications.

Wi-Fi Protected Access is based on the LEAP and TKIP cryptosystems and often employs a secret passphrase for authentication. Unfortunately, the use of a single static passphrase is the downfall of WPA. An attacker can simply run a brute-force guessing attack against a WPA network to discover the passphrase. If the passphrase is 14 characters or more, this is usually a time-prohibitive proposition but not an impossible one. Additionally, both the LEAP and TKIP encryption options for WPA are now crackable using a variety of cracking techniques. While it is more complex than a WEP compromise, WPA no longer provides long-term reliable security.

WPA2

Eventually, a new method of securing wireless was developed that is still considered secure. This is the amendment known as 802.11i or WPA2. It is a new encryption scheme known as the Counter Mode Cipher Block Chaining Message Authentication Code Protocol (CCMP), which is based on the AES encryption scheme. To date, no real-world attack has compromised the encryption of a properly configured WPA2 wireless network.

802.1X/EAP

Both WPA and WPA2 support the enterprise authentication known as 802.1X/EAP, a standard port-based network access control that ensures clients cannot communicate with a resource until proper authentication has taken place. Effectively, 802.1X is a hand-off system that allows the wireless network to leverage the existing network infrastructure's authentication services. Through the use of 802.1X, other techniques and solutions such as RADIUS, TACACS, certificates, smart cards, token devices, and biometrics can be integrated into wireless networks providing techniques for both mutual and multi-factor authentication.

EAP (Extensible Authentication Protocol) is not a specific mechanism of authentication; rather it is an authentication framework. Effectively, EAP allows for new authentication technologies to be compatible with existing wireless or point-to-point connection technologies. More than 40 different EAP methods of authentication are widely supported. These include the wireless methods of LEAP, EAP-TLS, EAP-SIM, EAP-AKA, and EAP-TTLS.

Not all EAP methods are secure. For example, EAP-MD5 and a pre-release EAP known as LEAP are also crackable.

PEAP

PEAP (Protected Extensible Authentication Protocol) encapsulates EAP methods within a TLS tunnel that provides authentication and potentially encryption. Since EAP was originally designed for use over physically isolated channels and hence assumed secured pathways, EAP is usually not encrypted. So, PEAP can provide encryption for EAP methods.

LEAP

LEAP (Lightweight Extensible Authentication Protocol) is a Cisco proprietary alternative to TKIP for WPA. This was developed to address deficiencies in TKIP before the 802.11i/WPA2 system was ratified as a standard. An attack tool known as Asleap was released in 2004 that could exploit the ultimately weak protection provided by LEAP. LEAP should be avoided when possible; use of EAP-TLS as an alternative is recommended, but if LEAP is used, a complex password is strongly recommended.

MAC Filter

A MAC filter is a list of authorized wireless client interface MAC addresses that is used by a wireless access point to block access to all non-authorized devices. While a useful feature to implement, it can be difficult to manage, and tends to be used only in small, static environments. Additionally, a hacker with basic wireless hacking tools can discover the MAC address of a valid client and then spoof that address onto their attack wireless client.

TKIP

TKIP (Temporal Key Integrity Protocol) was designed as the replacement for WEP without requiring replacement of legacy wireless hardware. TKIP was implemented into 802.11 wireless networking under the name WPA (Wi-Fi Protected Access). TKIP improvements include a key-mixing function that combines the initialization vector (IV) (i.e., a random number) with the secret root key before using that key with RC4 to perform encryption; a sequence counter is used to prevent packet replay attacks; and a strong integrity check named Michael is used.

TKIP and WPA were officially replaced by WPA2 in 2004. Additionally, attacks specific to WPA and TKIP (i.e., coWPAtty and a GPU-based cracking tool) have rendered WPA's security unreliable.

CCMP

CCMP (Counter Mode with Cipher Block Chaining Message Authentication Code Protocol) was created to replace WEP and TKIP/WPA. CCMP uses AES (Advanced Encryption Standard) with a 128-bit key. CCMP is the preferred standard security protocol of 802.11 wireless networking indicated by 802.11i. To date, no attacks have yet been successful against the AES/CCMP encryption.

Determining Antenna Placement

Antenna placement should be a concern when deploying a wireless network. Do not fixate on a specific location before a proper site survey has been performed. Place the wireless access point and/or its antenna in a likely position; then test various locations for signal strength and connection quality. Only after confirming that a potential antenna placement provides satisfactory connectivity should it be made permanent.

Consider the following guidelines when seeking optimal antenna placement:

- Use a central location.
- Avoid solid physical obstructions.
- Avoid reflective or other flat metal surfaces.
- Avoid electrical equipment.

If a base station has external omnidirectional antennas, typically they should be positioned pointing straight up vertically. If a directional antenna is used, point the focus toward the area of desired use. Keep in mind that wireless signals are affected by interference, distance, and obstructions. When designing a secure wireless network engineers may select directional antennas to avoid broadcasting in areas where they do not wish to provide signal or to specifically cover an area with a stronger signal.

Antenna Types

A wide variety of antenna types can be used for wireless clients and base stations. Many devices can have their standard antennas replaced with stronger (i.e., signal-boosting) antennas.

The standard straight or pole antenna is an omnidirectional antenna that can send and receive signals in all directions perpendicular to the line of the antenna itself. This is the type of antenna found on most base stations and some client devices. This type of antenna is sometimes also called a base antenna or a rubber duck antenna (due to the fact that most are covered in a flexible rubber coating).

Most other types of antennas are directional, meaning they focus their sending and receiving capabilities in one primary direction. Some examples of directional antennas include Yagi, cantenna, panel, and parabolic. A Yagi antenna is similar in structure to that of traditional roof TV antennas. Yagi antennas are crafted from a straight bar with cross sections to catch specific radio frequencies in the direction of the main bar. Cantennas are constructed from tubes with one sealed end. They focus along the direction of the open end of the tube. Some of the first cantennas were crafted from Pringles cans. Panel antennas are flat devices that focus from only one side of the panel. Parabolic antennas are used to focus signals from very long distances or weak sources.

Adjusting Power Level Controls

Some wireless access points provide a physical or logical adjustment of the antenna power levels. Power level controls are typically set by the manufacturer to a setting that is suitable for most situations. However, if after performing site surveys and adjusting antenna placement, wireless signals are still not satisfactory, power level adjustment might be necessary. However, keep in mind that changing channels, avoiding reflective and signal-scattering surfaces, and reducing interference can often be more significant in terms of improving connectivity reliability.

When adjusting power levels, make minor adjustments instead of attempting to maximize or minimize the setting. Also, take note of the initial/default setting so you can return to that setting if desired. After each power level adjustment, reset/reboot the wireless access point before re-performing site survey and quality tests. Sometimes lowering the power level can improve performance. It is important to keep in mind that some wireless access points are capable of providing higher power levels than are allowed by regulations in countries where they are available.

Using Captive Portals

A captive portal is an authentication technique that redirects a newly connected wireless Web client to a portal access control page. The portal page may require the user to input payment information, provide logon credentials, or input an access code. A captive portal is also used to display an acceptable use policy, privacy policy, and tracking policy to the user, who must consent to the policies before being able to communicate across the network. Captive portals are most often located on wireless networks implemented for public use, such as at hotels, restaurants, bars, airports, libraries, and so on. However, they can be used on cabled Ethernet connections as well.

General Wi-Fi Security Procedure

Based on the details of wireless security and configuration options, here is a general guide or procedure to follow when deploying a Wi-Fi network. These steps are in order of consideration and application/installation. Additionally, this order does not imply which step offers more security. For example, using WPA-2 is a real security feature as opposed to SSID broadcast disabling. Here are the steps:

1. Change the default administrator password.
2. Disable the SSID broadcast.
3. Change the SSID to something unique.
4. Enable MAC filtering if the pool of wireless clients is relatively small (usually less than 20) and static.
5. Consider using static IP addresses, or configure DHCP with reservations (applicable only for small deployments).
6. Turn on the highest form of authentication and encryption supported. If WPA2 is not available, WPA and WEP provide very limited protection but are better than an unencrypted network.

7. Treat wireless as remote access, and manage access using 802.1X.
8. Treat wireless as external access, and separate the WAP from the wired network using a firewall.
9. Treat wireless as an entry point for attackers, and monitor all WAP-to-wired-network communications with an IDS.
10. Require all transmissions between wireless clients and WAPs to be encrypted; in other words, require a VPN link.

NOTE Often, adding layers of data encryption (WPA2 and IPSec VPN) and other forms of filtering to a wireless link can reduce the effective throughput by as much as 80 percent. In addition, greater distances from the base station and the presence of interference will reduce the effective throughput even further.

Wireless Attacks

Even with wireless security present, wireless attacks can still occur. There is an ever-increasing variety of attacks against networks, and many of these work against both wired and wireless environments. A few focus on wireless networks alone. For example, there is a collection of techniques, commonly called *wardriving*, to discover that a wireless network is present. This activity involves using a wireless interface or a wireless detector to locate wireless network signals. Once an attacker knows a wireless network is present, they can use sniffers to gather wireless packets for investigation. With the right tools, an attacker can discover hidden SSIDs, active IP addresses, valid MAC addresses, and even the authentication mechanism in use by the wireless clients. From there, attackers can grab dedicated cracking tools to attempt to break into the connection or attempt to conduct man-in-the-middle attacks. The older and weaker your protections, the faster and more successful such attacks are likely to be.

Secure Network Components

The Internet is host to countless information services and numerous applications, including the Web, email, FTP, Telnet, newsgroups, chat, and so on. The Internet is also home to malicious people whose primary goal is to locate your computer and extract valuable data from it, use it to launch further attacks, or damage it in some way. You should be familiar with the Internet and able to readily identify its benefits and drawbacks from your own online experiences. Because of the success and global use of the Internet, many of its technologies were adapted or integrated into the private business network. This created two new forms of network segments: intranets and extranets.

An intranet is a private network that is designed to host the same information services found on the Internet. Networks that rely on external servers (in other words, ones positioned on the public Internet) to provide information services internally are not considered intranets. Intranets provide users with access to the Web, email, and other services on internal servers that are not accessible to anyone outside the private network.

An extranet is a cross between the Internet and an intranet. An extranet is a section of an organization's network that has been sectioned off so that it acts as an intranet for the private network but also serves information to the public Internet. An extranet is often reserved for use by specific partners or customers. It is rarely on a public network. An extranet for public consumption is typically labeled a demilitarized zone (DMZ) or perimeter network.

Networks are not typically configured as a single large collection of systems. Usually networks are segmented or subdivided into smaller organizational units. These smaller units, grouping, segments, or subnetworks (i.e., subnets) can be used to improve various aspects of the network:

Boosting Performance Network segmentation can improve performance through an organizational scheme in which systems that often communicate are located in the same segment, while systems that rarely or never communicate are located in other segments.

Reducing Communication Problems Network segmentation often reduces congestion and contains communication problems, such as broadcast storms, to individual subsections of the network.

Providing Security Network segmentation can also improve security by isolating traffic and user access to those segments where they are authorized.

Segments can be created by using switch-based VLANs, routers, or firewalls, individually or in combination. A private LAN or intranet, a DMZ, and an extranet are all types of network segments.

When you're designing a secure network (whether a private network, an intranet, or an extranet), you must evaluate numerous networking devices. Not all of these components are necessary for a secure network, but they are all common network devices that may have an impact on network security.

Network Access Control

Network Access Control (NAC) is a concept of controlling access to an environment through strict adherence to and implementation of security policy. The goals of NAC are as follows:

- Prevent/reduce zero-day attacks
- Enforce security policy throughout the network
- Use identities to perform access control

The goals of NAC can be achieved through the use of strong detailed security policies that define all aspects of security control, filtering, prevention, detection, and response for every device from client to server and for every internal or external communication. NAC acts as an automated detection and response system that can react in real time to stop threats as they occur and before they cause damage or a breach.

Originally, 802.1X (which provides port-based NAC) was thought to embody NAC, but most supporters believe that 802.1X is only a simple form of NAC or just one component in a complete NAC solution.

NAC can be implemented with a preadmission philosophy or a postadmission philosophy, or aspects of both:

The preadmission philosophy requires a system to meet all current security requirements (such as patch application and antivirus updates) before it is allowed to communicate with the network.

The postadmission philosophy allows and denies access based on user activity, which is based on a predefined authorization matrix.

Other issues around NAC include client/system agent versus overall network monitoring (agent-less); out-of-band versus in-band monitoring; and resolving any remediation, quarantine, or captive portal strategies. These and other NAC concerns must be considered and evaluated prior to implementation.

Firewalls

Firewalls are essential tools in managing and controlling network traffic. A firewall is a network device used to filter traffic. It is typically deployed between a private network and a link to the Internet, but it can be deployed between departments within an organization. Without firewalls, it would not be possible to prevent malicious traffic from the Internet from entering into your private network. Firewalls filter traffic based on a defined set of rules, also called filters or access control lists. They are basically a set of instructions that are used to distinguish authorized traffic from unauthorized and/or malicious traffic. Only authorized traffic is allowed to cross the security barrier provided by the firewall.

Firewalls are useful for blocking or filtering traffic. They are most effective against unrequested traffic and attempts to connect from outside the private network and can also be used for blocking known malicious data, messages, or packets based on content, application, protocol, port, or source address. They are capable of hiding the structure and addressing scheme of a private network from the public. Most firewalls offer extensive logging, auditing, and monitoring capabilities as well as alarms and basic intrusion detection system (IDS) functions.

Firewalls are typically unable to block viruses or malicious code (i.e., firewalls do not typically scan traffic as an antivirus scanner would) transmitted through otherwise authorized communication channels, prevent unauthorized but accidental or intended disclosure of information by users, prevent attacks by malicious users already behind the firewall, or protect data after it passes out of or into the private network. However, you can add these features through special add-in modules or companion products, such as antivirus scanners and IDS tools. There are firewall appliances that are preconfigured to perform all (or most) of these add-on functions natively.

In addition to logging network traffic activity, firewalls should log several other events as well:

- A reboot of the firewall
- Proxies or dependencies being unable to start or not starting

- Proxies or other important services crashing or restarting
- Changes to the firewall configuration file
- A configuration or system error while the firewall is running

Firewalls are only one part of an overall security solution. With a firewall, many of the security mechanisms are concentrated in one place, and thus a firewall can be a single point of failure. Firewall failure is most commonly caused by human error and misconfiguration. Firewalls provide protection only against traffic that crosses the firewall from one subnet to another. They offer no protection against traffic within a subnet (in other words, behind the firewall).

There are four basic types of firewalls: static packet-filtering firewalls, application-level gateway firewalls, circuit-level gateway firewalls, and stateful inspection firewalls. There are also ways to create hybrid or complex gateway firewalls by combining two or more of these firewall types into a single firewall solution. In most cases, having a multilevel firewall provides greater control over filtering traffic. Regardless, we'll cover the various firewall types and discuss firewall deployment architectures as well.

Static Packet-Filtering Firewalls A *static packet-filtering firewall* filters traffic by examining data from a message header. Usually, the rules are concerned with source, destination, and port addresses. Using static filtering, a firewall is unable to provide user authentication or to tell whether a packet originated from inside or outside the private network, and it is easily fooled with spoofed packets. Static packet-filtering firewalls are known as first-generation firewalls; they operate at layer 3 (the Network layer) of the OSI model. They can also be called *screening routers* or *common routers*.

Application-Level Gateway Firewalls An application-level gateway firewall is also called a proxy firewall. A *proxy* is a mechanism that copies packets from one network into another; the copy process also changes the source and destination addresses to protect the identity of the internal or private network. An application-level gateway firewall filters traffic based on the Internet service (in other words, the application) used to transmit or receive the data. Each type of application must have its own unique proxy server. Thus, an application-level gateway firewall comprises numerous individual proxy servers. This type of firewall negatively affects network performance because each packet must be examined and processed as it passes through the firewall. Application-level gateways are known as second-generation firewalls, and they operate at the Application layer (layer 7) of the OSI model.

Circuit-Level Gateway Firewalls *Circuit-level gateway firewalls* are used to establish communication sessions between trusted partners. They operate at the Session layer (layer 5) of the OSI model. SOCKS (from *Socket Secure*, as in TCP/IP ports) is a common implementation of a circuit-level gateway firewall. Circuit-level gateway firewalls, also known as *circuit proxies*, manage communications based on the circuit, not the content of traffic. They permit or deny forwarding decisions based solely on the endpoint designations of the communication circuit (in other words, the source and destination addresses and service port numbers). Circuit-level gateway firewalls are considered second-generation firewalls because they represent a modification of the application-level gateway firewall concept.

Stateful Inspection Firewalls *Stateful inspection firewalls* (also known as *dynamic packet filtering firewalls*) evaluate the state or the context of network traffic. By examining source and destination addresses, application usage, source of origin, and relationship between current packets and the previous packets of the same session, stateful inspection firewalls are able to grant a broader range of access for authorized users and activities and actively watch for and block unauthorized users and activities. Stateful inspection firewalls generally operate more efficiently than application-level gateway firewalls. They are known as third-generation firewalls, and they operate at the Network and Transport layers (layers 3 and 4) of the OSI model.

Multihomed Firewalls

Some firewall systems have more than one interface. For instance, a multihomed firewall must have at least two interfaces to filter traffic (they're also known as dual-homed firewalls). All multihomed firewalls should have IP forwarding, which automatically sends traffic to another interface, disabled. This will force the filtering rules to control all traffic rather than allowing a software-supported shortcut between one interface and another.
A bastion host or a screened host is just a firewall system logically positioned between a private network and an untrusted network. Usually, the bastion host is located behind the router that connects the private network to the untrusted network. All inbound traffic is routed to the bastion host, which in turn acts as a proxy for all the trusted systems within the private network. It is responsible for filtering traffic coming into the private network as well as for protecting the identity of the internal client.

NOTE The word *bastion* comes from medieval castle architecture. A bastion guardhouse was positioned in front of the main entrance to serve as a first layer of protection. Using this term to describe a firewall indicates that the firewall is acting as a sacrificial host that will receive all inbound attacks.

A screened subnet is similar to the screened host (in other words, the bastion host) in concept, except a subnet is placed between two routers and the bastion host(s) is located within that subnet. All inbound traffic is directed to the bastion host, and only traffic proxied by the bastion host can pass through the second router into the private network. This creates a subnet where some external visitors are allowed to communicate with resources offered by the network. This is the concept of a DMZ, which is a network area (usually a subnet) that is designed to be accessed by outside visitors but that is still isolated from the private network of the organization. The DMZ is often the host of public web, email, file, and other resource servers.

Firewall Deployment Architectures

There are three commonly recognized firewall deployment architectures: single tier, two tier, and three tier (also known as multitier).

As you can see in Figure 11.8, a single-tier deployment places the private network behind a firewall, which is then connected through a router to the Internet (or some other untrusted network). Single-tier deployments are useful against generic attacks only. This architecture offers only minimal protection.

FIGURE 11.8 Single-, two-, and three-tier firewall deployment architectures

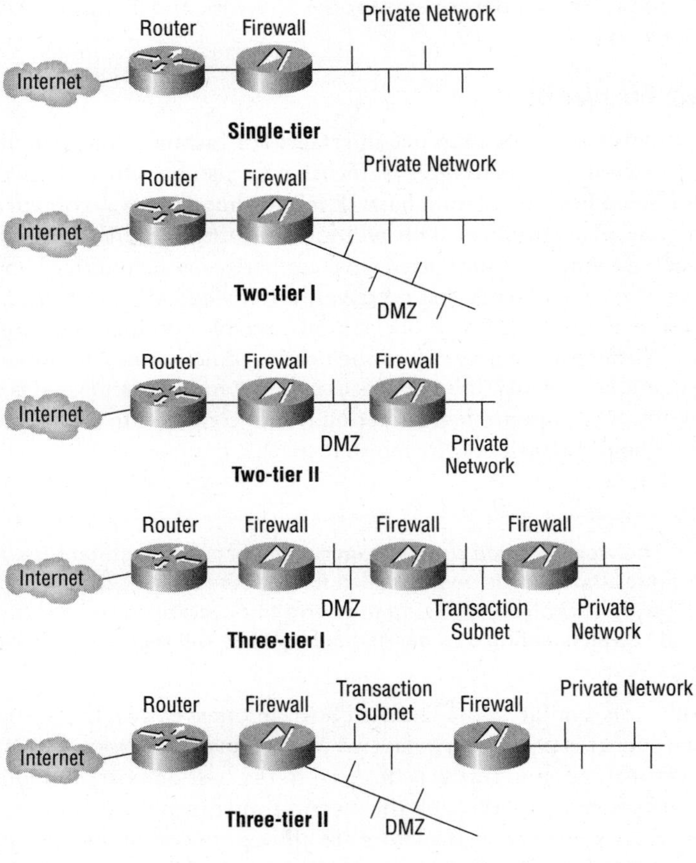

A two-tier deployment architecture may be one of two different designs. One uses a firewall with three or more interfaces. The other uses two firewalls in a series. This allows for a DMZ or a publicly accessible extranet. In the first design, the DMZ is located off one of the interfaces of the primary firewall, while in the second design the DMZ is located between the two serial firewalls. The DMZ is used to host information server systems to which external users should have access. The firewall routes traffic to the DMZ or the trusted network according to its strict filtering rules. This architecture introduces a moderate level of routing and filtering complexity.

A three-tier deployment architecture is the deployment of multiple subnets between the private network and the Internet separated by firewalls. Each subsequent firewall has more stringent filtering rules to restrict traffic to only trusted sources. The outermost subnet is usually a DMZ. A middle subnet can serve as a transaction subnet where systems needed to support complex web applications in the DMZ reside. The third, or back-end, subnet can support the private network. This architecture is the most secure; however, it is also the most complex to design, implement, and manage.

Endpoint Security

Endpoint security is the concept that each individual device must maintain local security whether or not its network or telecommunications channels also provide or offer security. Sometimes this is expressed as "the end device is responsible for its own security." However, a clearer perspective is that any weakness in a network, whether on the border, on a server, or on a client, presents a risk to all elements within the organization.

Traditional security has depended on the network border sentries, such as appliance firewalls, proxies, centralized virus scanners, and even IDS/IPS/IDP solutions, to provide security for all of the interior nodes of a network. This is no longer considered best business practice because threats exist from within as well as without. A network is only as secure as its weakest element.

Lack of internal security is even more problematic when remote access services, including dial-up, wireless, and VPN, might allow an external entity (authorized or not) to gain access to the private network without having to go through the border security gauntlet.

Endpoint security should therefore be viewed as an aspect of the effort to provide sufficient security on each individual host. Every system should have an appropriate combination of a local host firewall, antimalware scanners, authentication, authorization, auditing, spam filters, and IDS/IPS services.

Other Network Devices

You'll use numerous hardware devices when constructing a network. Strong familiarity with these secure network components can assist you in designing an IT infrastructure that avoids single points of failure and provides strong support for availability.

Collisions vs. Broadcasts

A collision occurs when two systems transmit data at the same time onto a connection medium that supports only a single transmission path. A broadcast occurs when a single system transmits data to all possible recipients. Generally, collisions are something to avoid and prevent, while broadcasts have useful purposes from time to time. The management of collisions and broadcasts introduces a new term known as *domains*.

(Continues)

(Continued)

A *collision domain* is a group of networked systems that could cause a collision if any two (or more) of the systems in that group transmitted simultaneously. Any system outside the collision domain cannot cause a collision with any member of that collision domain.

A *broadcast domain* is a group of networked systems in which all other members receive a broadcast signal when one of the members of the group transmits it. Any system outside a broadcast domain would not receive a broadcast from that broadcast domain.

As you design and deploy a network, you should consider how collision domains and broadcast domains will be managed. Collision domains are divided by using any layer 2 or higher device, and broadcast domains are divided by using any layer 3 or higher device. When a domain is divided, it means that systems on opposite sides of the deployed device are members of different domains.

These are some of the hardware devices in a network:

Repeaters, Concentrators, and Amplifiers Repeaters, concentrators, and amplifiers are used to strengthen the communication signal over a cable segment as well as connect network segments that use the same protocol. These devices can be used to extend the maximum length of a specific cable type by deploying one or more repeaters along a lengthy cable run. Repeaters, concentrators, and amplifiers operate at OSI layer 1. Systems on either side of a repeater, concentrator, or amplifier are part of the same collision domain and broadcast domain.

Hubs Hubs are used to connect multiple systems and connect network segments that use the same protocol. They repeat inbound traffic over all outbound ports. This ensures that the traffic will reach its intended host. A hub is a multiport repeater. Hubs operate at OSI layer 1. Systems on either side of a hub are part of the same collision and broadcast domains. Most organizations have a no-hub security policy to limit or reduce the risk of sniffing attacks since they are an outmoded technology and switches are preferred.

Modems A traditional land-line modem (modulator-demodulator) is a communications device that covers or modulates between an analog carrier signal and digital information in order to support computer communications of public switched telephone network (PSTN) lines. From about 1960 until the mid-1990s, modems were a common means of WAN communications. Modems have generally been replaced by digital broadband technologies including ISDN, cable modems, DSL modems, 802.11 wireless, and various forms of wireless modems.

NOTE

The term *modem* is used incorrectly on any device that does not actually perform modulation. Most modern devices labeled as modems (cable, DSL, ISDN, wireless, etc.) are routers, not modems.

Bridges A bridge is used to connect two networks together—even networks of different topologies, cabling types, and speeds—in order to connect network segments that use the same protocol. A bridge forwards traffic from one network to another. Bridges that connect networks using different transmission speeds may have a buffer to store packets until they can be forwarded to the slower network. This is known as a *store-and-forward* device. Bridges operate at OSI layer 2. Systems on either side of a bridge are part of the same broadcast domain but are in different collision domains.

Switches Rather than using a hub, you might consider using a switch, or intelligent hub. Switches know the addresses of the systems connected on each outbound port. Instead of repeating traffic on every outbound port, a switch repeats traffic only out of the port on which the destination is known to exist. Switches offer greater efficiency for traffic delivery, create separate collision domains, and improve the overall throughput of data. Switches can also create separate broadcast domains when used to create VLANs. In such configurations, broadcasts are allowed within a single VLAN but not allowed to cross unhindered from one VLAN to another. Switches operate primarily at OSI layer 2. When switches have additional features, such as routing, they can operate at OSI layer 3 as well (such as when routing between VLANs). Systems on either side of a switch operating at layer 2 are part of the same broadcast domain but are in different collision domains. Systems on either side of a switch operating at layer 3 are part of different broadcast domains and different collision domains. Switches are used to connect network segments that use the same protocol.

Routers Routers are used to control traffic flow on networks and are often used to connect similar networks and control traffic flow between the two. They can function using statically defined routing tables, or they can employ a dynamic routing system. There are numerous dynamic routing protocols, such as RIP, OSPF, and BGP. Routers operate at OSI layer 3. Systems on either side of a router are part of different broadcast domains and different collision domains. Routers are used to connect network segments that use the same protocol.

Brouters Brouters are combination devices comprising a router and a bridge. A brouter attempts to route first, but if that fails, it defaults to bridging. Thus, a brouter operates primarily at layer 3 but can operate at layer 2 when necessary. Systems on either side of a brouter operating at layer 3 are part of different broadcast domains and different collision domains. Systems on either side of a brouter operating at layer 2 are part of the same broadcast domain but are in different collision domains. Brouters are used to connect network segments that use the same protocol.

Gateways A gateway connects networks that are using different network protocols. A gateway is responsible for transferring traffic from one network to another by transforming the format of that traffic into a form compatible with the protocol or transport method used by each network. Gateways, also known as *protocol translators*, can be stand-alone hardware devices or a software service (for example, an IP-to-IPX gateway). Systems on either side of a gateway are part of different broadcast domains and different collision domains. Gateways are used to connect network segments that use different protocols. There are many types of gateways, including data, mail, application, secure, and Internet. Gateways typically operate at OSI layer 7.

Proxies A proxy is a form of gateway that does not translate across protocols. Instead, proxies serve as mediators, filters, caching servers, and even NAT/PAT servers for a network. A proxy performs a function or requests a service on behalf of another system and connects network segments that use the same protocol. Proxies are most often used in the context of providing clients on a private network with Internet access while protecting the identity of the clients. A proxy accepts requests from clients, alters the source address of the requester, maintains a mapping of requests to clients, and sends the altered request packets out. This mechanism is commonly known as Network Address Translation (NAT). Once a reply is received, the proxy server determines which client it is destined for by reviewing its mappings and then sends the packets on to the client. Systems on either side of a proxy are part of different broadcast domains and different collision domains.

Network Infrastructure Inventory

If you can gain approval from your organization, perform a general survey or inventory of the significant components that make up your network. See how many different network devices you can locate within your network. Also, do you notice any patterns of device deployment, such as devices always deployed in parallel or in series? Is the exterior of a device usually sufficient to indicate its function, or must you look up its model number?

LAN Extenders A LAN extender is a remote access, multilayer switch used to connect distant networks over WAN links. This is a strange beast of a device in that it creates WANs, but marketers of this device steer clear of the term *WAN* and use only *LAN* and *extended LAN*. The idea behind this device was to make the terminology easier to understand and thus make the product easier to sell than a normal WAN device with complex concepts and terms tied to it. Ultimately, it was the same product as a WAN switch or WAN router. (We agree with the Golgafrinchans, a race of aliens from Douglas Adams's *The Hitchhikers Guide to the Galaxy* series, who believed the marketing people should be shipped out with the lawyers and phone sanitizers on the first spaceship to the far end of the universe.)

NOTE

While managing network security with filtering devices such as firewalls and proxies is important, we must not overlook the need for endpoint security. Endpoints are the ends of a network communication link. One end is often at a server where a resource resides, and the other end is often a client making a request to use a network resource. Even with secured communication protocols, it is still possible for abuse, misuse, oversight, or malicious action to occur across the network because it originated at an endpoint. All aspects of security from one end to the other, often called *end-to-end security*, must be addressed. Any unsecured point will be discovered eventually and abused.

Cabling, Wireless, Topology, and Communications Technology

Establishing security on a network involves more than just managing the operating system and software. You must also address physical issues, including cabling, wireless, topology, and communications technology.

LANs vs. WANs

There are two basic types of networks: LANs and WANs. A *local area network (LAN)* is a network typically spanning a single floor or building. This is commonly a limited geographical area. *Wide area network (WAN)* is the term usually assigned to the long-distance connections between geographically remote networks.

WAN connections and communication links can include private circuit technologies and packet-switching technologies. Common private circuit technologies include dedicated or leased lines and PPP, SLIP, ISDN, and DSL connections. Packet-switching technologies include X.25, Frame Relay, asynchronous transfer mode (ATM), Synchronous Data Link Control (SDLC), and High-Level Data Link Control (HDLC). Packet-switching technologies use virtual circuits instead of dedicated physical circuits. A virtual circuit is created only when needed, which makes for efficient use of the transmission medium and is extremely cost-effective.

Network Cabling

The type of connectivity media employed in a network is important to the network's design, layout, and capabilities. Without the right cabling or transmission media, a network may not be able to span your entire enterprise, or it may not support the necessary traffic volume. In fact, the most common causes of network failure (in other words, violations of availability) are cable failures or misconfigurations. It is important for you to understand that different types of network devices and technologies are used with different types of cabling. Each cable type has unique useful lengths, throughput rates, and connectivity requirements.

Coaxial Cable

Coaxial cable, also called coax, was a popular networking cable type used throughout the 1970s and 1980s. In the early 1990s, its use quickly declined because of the popularity and capabilities of twisted-pair wiring (explained in more detail later). Coaxial cable has a center core of copper wire surrounded by a layer of insulation, which is in turn surrounded by a conductive braided shielding and encased in a final insulation sheath.

The center copper core and the braided shielding layer act as two independent conductors, thus allowing two-way communications over a coaxial cable. The design of coaxial cable makes it fairly resistant to electromagnetic interference (EMI) and makes it able to support high bandwidths (in comparison to other technologies of the time period), and it offers longer usable lengths than twisted-pair. It ultimately failed to retain its place as the popular networking cable technology because of twisted-pair's much lower cost and ease of installation. Coaxial cable requires the use of segment terminators, whereas twisted-pair cabling does not. Coaxial cable is bulkier and has a larger minimum arc radius than twisted-pair. (The arc radius is the maximum distance the cable can be bent before damaging the internal conductors.) Additionally, with the widespread deployment of switched networks, the issues of cable distance became moot because of the implementation of hierarchical wiring patterns.

There are two main types of coaxial cable: thinnet and thicknet. Thinnet, also known as 10Base2, was commonly used to connect systems to backbone trunks of thicknet cabling. Thinnet can span distances of 185 meters and provide throughput up to 10 Mbps. Thicknet, also known as 10Base5, can span 500 meters and provide throughput up to 10 Mbps (megabits per second).

The most common problems with coax cable are as follows:

- Bending the coax cable past its maximum arc radius and thus breaking the center conductor
- Deploying the coax cable in a length greater than its maximum recommended length (which is 185 meters for 10Base2 or 500 meters for 10Base5)
- Not properly terminating the ends of the coax cable with a 50 ohm resistor

Baseband and Broadband Cables

The naming convention used to label most network cable technologies follows the syntax XXyyyyZZ. XX represents the maximum speed the cable type offers, such as 10 Mbps for a 10Base2 cable. The next series of letters, yyyy, represents the baseband or broadband aspect of the cable, such as baseband for a 10Base2 cable. Baseband cables can transmit only a single signal at a time, and broadband cables can transmit multiple signals simultaneously. Most networking cables are baseband cables. However, when used in specific configurations, coaxial cable can be used as a broadband connection, such as with cable modems. ZZ either represents the maximum distance the cable can be used or acts as shorthand to represent the technology of the cable, such as the approximately 200 meters for 10Base2 cable (actually 185 meters, but it's rounded up to 200) or T or TX for twisted-pair in 10Base-T or 100Base-TX. (Note that 100Base-TX is implemented using two Cat 5 UTP or STP cables—one issued for receiving, the other for transmitting.)

Table 11.7 shows the important characteristics for the most common network cabling types.

TABLE 11.7 Important characteristics for common network cabling types

Type	Max Speed	Distance	Difficulty of Installation	Susceptibility to EMI	Cost
10Base2	10 Mbps	185 meters	Medium	Medium	Medium
10Base5	10 Mbps	500 meters	High	Low	High
10Base-T (UTP)	10 Mbps	100 meters	Low	High	Very low
STP	155 Mbps	100 meters	Medium	Medium	High
100Base-T/100Base-TX	100 Mbps	100 meters	Low	High	Low
1000Base-T	1 Gbps	100 meters	Low	High	Medium
Fiber-optic	2+ Gbps	2+ kilometers	Very high	None	Very high

Twisted-Pair

Twisted-pair cabling is extremely thin and flexible compared to coaxial cable. It consists of four pairs of wires that are twisted around each other and then sheathed in a PVC insulator. If there is a metal foil wrapper around the wires underneath the external sheath, the wire is known as shielded twisted-pair (STP). The foil provides additional protection from external EMI. Twisted-pair cabling without the foil is known as unshielded twisted-pair (UTP). UTP is most often used to refer to 10Base-T, 100Base-T, or 1000Base-T, which are now considered outdated references mostly outdated technology.

The wires that make up UTP and STP are small, thin copper wires that are twisted in pairs. The twisting of the wires provides protection from external radio frequencies and electric and magnetic interference and reduces crosstalk between pairs. Crosstalk occurs when data transmitted over one set of wires is picked up by another set of wires due to radiating electromagnetic fields produced by the electrical current. Each wire pair within the cable is twisted at a different rate (in other words, twists per inch); thus, the signals traveling over one pair of wires cannot cross over onto another pair of wires (at least within the same cable). The tighter the twist (the more twists per inch), the more resistant the cable is to internal and external interference and crosstalk, and thus the capacity for throughput (that is, higher bandwidth) is greater.

There are several classes of UTP cabling. The various categories are created through the use of tighter twists of the wire pairs, variations in the quality of the conductor, and variations in the quality of the external shielding. Table 11.8 shows the original UTP categories.

TABLE 11.8 UTP categories

UTP Category	Throughput	Notes
Cat 1	Voice only	Not suitable for networks but usable by modems
Cat 2	4 Mbps	Not suitable for most networks; often employed for host-to-terminal connections on mainframes
Cat 3	10 Mbps	Primarily used in 10Base-T Ethernet networks (offers only 4 Mbps when used on Token Ring networks) and as telephone cables
Cat 4	16 Mbps	Primarily used in Token Ring networks
Cat 5	100 Mbps	Used in 100Base-TX, FDDI, and ATM networks
Cat 6	1,000 Mbps	Used in high-speed networks
Cat 7	10 Gbps	Used on 10 gigabit-speed networks

NOTE

Cat 5e is an enhanced version of Cat 5 designed to protect against far-end crosstalk. In 2001, the TIA/EIA-568-B no longer recognized the original Cat 5 specification. Now, the Cat 5e standard is rated for use by 100Base-T and even 1000Base-T deployments.

The following problems are the most common with twisted-pair cabling:

- Using the wrong category of twisted-pair cable for high-throughput networking
- Deploying a twisted-pair cable longer than its maximum recommended length (in other words, 100 meters)
- Using UTP in environments with significant interference

Conductors

The distance limitations of conductor-based network cabling stem from the resistance of the metal used as a conductor. Copper, the most popular conductor, is one of the best and least expensive room-temperature conductors available. However, it is still resistant to the flow of electrons. This resistance results in a degradation of signal strength and quality over the length of the cable.

NOTE

Plenum cable is a type of cabling sheathed with a special material that does not release toxic fumes when burned, as does traditional PVC coated wiring. Often plenum-grade cable must be used to comply with building codes, especially if the building has enclosed spaces that could trap gases.

The maximum length defined for each cable type indicates the point at which the level of degradation could begin to interfere with the efficient transmission of data. This degradation of the signal is known as attenuation. It is often possible to use a cable segment that is longer than the cable is rated for, but the number of errors and retransmissions will be increased over that cable segment, ultimately resulting in poor network performance. Attenuation is more pronounced as the speed of the transmission increases. It is recommended that you use shorter cable lengths as the speed of the transmission increases.

Long cable lengths can often be supplemented through the use of repeaters or concentrators. A repeater is a signal amplification device, much like the amplifier for your car or home stereo. The repeater boosts the signal strength of an incoming data stream and rebroadcasts it through its second port. A concentrator does the same thing except it has more than two ports. However, using more than four repeaters (or hubs) in a row is discouraged (see the sidebar "5-4-3 Rule").

5-4-3 Rule

The 5-4-3 rule is used whenever Ethernet or other IEEE 802.3 shared-access networks are deployed in a tree topology (in other words, a central trunk with various splitting branches). This rule defines the number of repeaters/concentrators and segments that can be used in a network design. The rule states that between any two nodes (a node can be any type of processing entity, such as a server, client, or router), there can be a maximum of five segments connected by four repeaters/concentrators, and it states that only three of those five segments can be populated (in other words, have additional or other user, server, or networking device connections).

The 5-4-3 rule does not apply to switched networks or the use of bridges or routers.

An alternative to conductor-based network cabling is fiber-optic cable. Fiber-optic cables transmit pulses of light rather than electricity. This gives fiber-optic cable the advantage of being extremely fast and nearly impervious to tapping and interference. However, it is difficult to install and expensive; thus, the security and performance it offers come at a steep price.

Network Topologies

The physical layout and organization of computers and networking devices is known as the network topology. The logical topology is the grouping of networked systems into trusted collectives. The physical topology is not always the same as the logical topology. There are four basic topologies of the physical layout of a network: ring, bus, star, and mesh.

Ring Topology A ring topology connects each system as points on a circle (see Figure 11.9). The connection medium acts as a unidirectional transmission loop. Only one system can transmit data at a time. Traffic management is performed by a token. A token is a digital hall pass that travels around the ring until a system grabs it. A system in possession of the token can transmit data. Data and the token are transmitted to a specific destination. As the data travels around the loop, each system checks to see whether it is the intended recipient of the data. If not, it passes the token on. If so, it reads the data. Once the data is received, the token is released and returns to traveling around the loop until another system grabs it. If any one segment of the loop is broken, all communication around the loop ceases. Some implementations of ring topologies employ a fault tolerance mechanism, such as dual loops running in opposite directions, to prevent single points of failure.

FIGURE 11.9 A ring topology

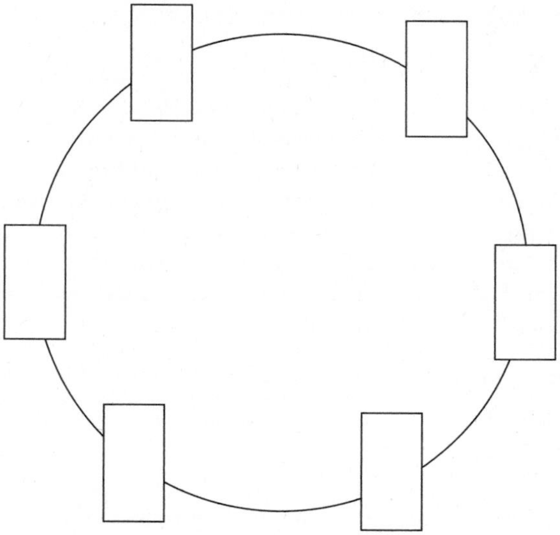

Bus Topology A bus topology connects each system to a trunk or backbone cable. All systems on the bus can transmit data simultaneously, which can result in collisions. A collision occurs when two systems transmit data at the same time; the signals interfere with each other. To avoid this, the systems employ a collision avoidance mechanism that basically "listens" for any other currently occurring traffic. If traffic is heard, the system waits a few moments and listens again. If no traffic is heard, the system transmits its data. When data is transmitted on a bus topology, all systems on the network hear the data. If the data is not addressed to a specific system, that system just ignores the data. The benefit of a bus topology is that if a single segment fails, communications on all other segments continue uninterrupted. However, the central trunk line remains a single point of failure.

FIGURE 11.10 A linear bus topology and a tree bus topology

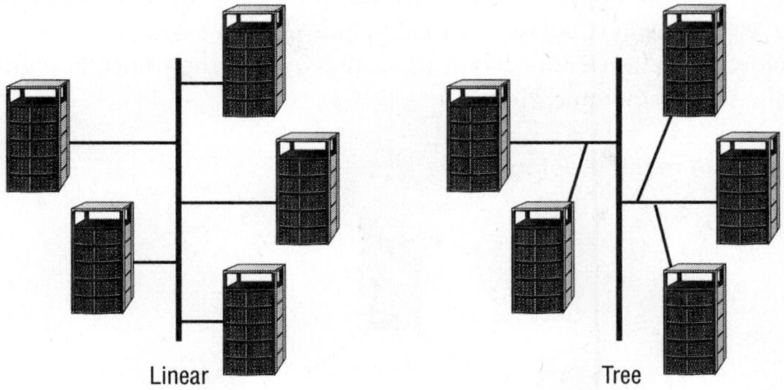

There are two types of bus topologies: linear and tree. A linear bus topology employs a single trunk line with all systems directly connected to it. A tree topology employs a single trunk line with branches that can support multiple systems. Figure 11.10 illustrates both types. The primary reason a bus is rarely if ever used today is that it must be terminated at both ends and any disconnection can take down the entire network.

Star Topology A star topology employs a centralized connection device. This device can be a simple hub or switch. Each system is connected to the central hub by a dedicated segment (see Figure 11.11). If any one segment fails, the other segments can continue to function. However, the central hub is a single point of failure. Generally, the star topology uses less cabling than other topologies and makes the identification of damaged cables easier.

A logical bus and a logical ring can be implemented as a physical star. Ethernet is a bus-based technology. It can be deployed as a physical star, but the hub or switch device is actually a logical bus connection device. Likewise, Token Ring is a ring-based technology. It can be deployed as a physical star using a multistation access unit (MAU). An MAU allows for the cable segments to be deployed as a star while internally the device makes logical ring connections.

FIGURE 11.11 A star topology

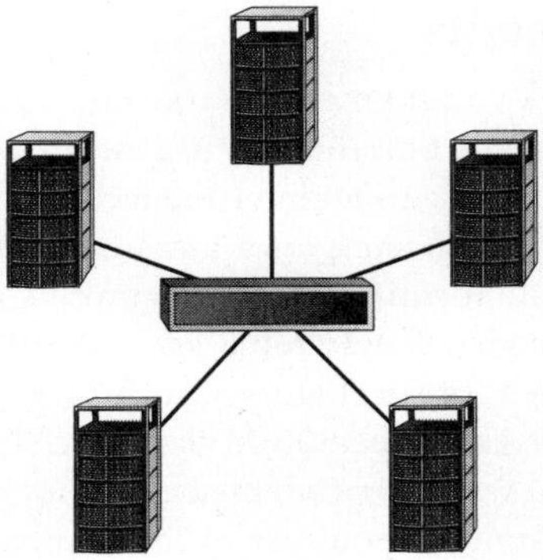

Mesh Topology A mesh topology connects systems to other systems using numerous paths (see Figure 11.12). A full mesh topology connects each system to all other systems on the network. A partial mesh topology connects many systems to many other systems. Mesh topologies provide redundant connections to systems, allowing multiple segment failures without seriously affecting connectivity.

FIGURE 11.12 A mesh topology

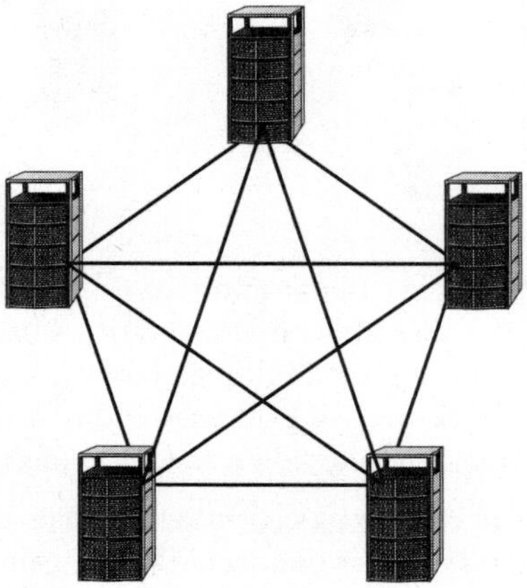

Wireless Communications and Security

Wireless communication is a quickly expanding field of technologies for networking, connectivity, communication, and data exchange. There are literally thousands of protocols, standards, and techniques that can be labeled as wireless. These include cell phones, Bluetooth, cordless phones, and wireless networking. As wireless technologies continue to proliferate, your organization's security efforts must go beyond locking down its local network. Security should be an end-to-end solution that addresses all forms, methods, and techniques of communication.

General Wireless Concepts

Wireless communications employ radio waves to transmit signals over a distance. There is a finite amount of radio wave spectrum; thus, its use must be managed properly to allow multiple simultaneous uses with little to no interference. The radio spectrum is measured or differentiated using frequency. Frequency is a measurement of the number of wave oscillations within a specific time and identified using the unit Hertz (Hz), or oscillations per second. Radio waves have a frequency between 3 Hz and 300 GHz. Different ranges of frequencies have been designated for specific uses, such as AM and FM radio, VHF and UHF television, and so on. Currently, the 900 MHz, 2.4 GHz, and 5 GHz frequencies are the most commonly used in wireless products because of their unlicensed categorization. However, to manage the simultaneous use of the limited radio frequencies, several spectrum-use techniques were developed. These included spread spectrum, FHSS, DSSS, and OFDM.

> **NOTE** Most devices operate within a small subsection of frequencies rather than all available frequencies. This is because of frequency-use regulations (in other words, the FCC in the United States), power consumption, and the expectation of interference.

Spread spectrum means that communication occurs over multiples frequencies at the same time. Thus, a message is broken into pieces, and each piece is sent at the same time but using a different frequency. Effectively this is a parallel communication rather than a serial communication.

Frequency Hopping Spread Spectrum (FHSS) was an early implementation of the spread spectrum concept. However, instead of sending data in a parallel fashion, it transmits data in a series while constantly changing the frequency in use. The entire range of available frequencies is employed, but only one frequency at a time is used. As the sender changes from one frequency to the next, the receiver has to follow the same hopping pattern to pick up the signal. FHSS was designed to help minimize interference by not using only a single frequency that could be affected. Instead, by constantly shifting frequencies, it minimizes interference.

Direct Sequence Spread Spectrum (DSSS) employs all the available frequencies simultaneously in parallel. This provides a higher rate of data throughput than FHSS. DSSS also uses a special encoding mechanism known as chipping code to allow a receiver to reconstruct data even if parts of the signal were distorted because of interference. This occurs in much the same way that the parity of RAID-5 allows the data on a missing drive to be re-created.

Orthogonal Frequency-Division Multiplexing (OFDM) is yet another variation on frequency use. OFDM employs a digital multicarrier modulation scheme that allows for a more tightly compacted transmission. The modulated signals are perpendicular (orthogonal) and thus do not cause interference with each other. Ultimately, OFDM requires a smaller frequency set (aka channel bands) but can offer greater data throughput.

Cell Phones

Cell phone wireless communications consist of using a portable device over a specific set of radio wave frequencies to interact with the cell phone carrier's network and either other cell phone devices or the Internet. The technologies used by cell phone providers are numerous and are often confusing. One point of confusion is the use of terms like 2G and 3G. These do not refer to technologies specifically but instead to the generation of cell phone technology. Thus, 1G is the first generation (mostly analog), 2G is the second (mostly digital, as are 3G and 4G), and so forth. There are even discussions of 2.5G when systems integrate second- and third-generation technologies. Table 11.9 attempts to clarify some of these confusing issues (this is only a partial listing of the technologies).

TABLE 11.9 UTP categories

Technology	Generation
NMT	1G
AMPS	1G
TACS	1G
GSM	2G
iDEN	2G
TDMA	2G
CDMA	2G
PDC	2G
HSCSD	2.5G
GPRS	2.5G
W-CDMA	3G
TD-CDMA	3G
UWC	3G
EDGE	3G
DECT	3G
UMTS	3G
HSPDA	3.5G
WiMax – IEEE 802.16	4G
XOHM (Brand name of WiMax)	4G
Mobile Broadband – IEEE 802.20	4G
LTE (Long Term Evolution)	4G

Some of the technologies listed in this table are labeled and marketed as 4G while not actually meeting the technical requirements to be classified as 4G. The International Telecommunications Union-Radio communications sector (ITU-R) defined the requirements for 4G in 2008 but in 2010 acquiesced that carriers can call their non-compliant technologies 4G as long as they lead to future compliant services. In late 2014, the standards for 5G were under consideration. New 5G technologies are in development, but as of 2015 no 5G network has yet been deployed for general public use.

There are a few key issues to keep in mind with regard to cell phone wireless transmissions. First, not all cell phone traffic is voice; often cell phone systems are used to transmit text and even computer data. Second, communications over a cell phone provider's network, whether voice, text, or data, are not necessarily secure. Third, with specific wireless-sniffing equipment, your cell phone transmissions can be intercepted. In fact, your provider's towers can be simulated to conduct man-in-the-middle attacks. Fourth, using your cell phone connectivity to access the Internet or your office network provides attackers with yet another potential avenue of attack, access, and compromise. Many of these devices can potentially act as bridges, creating unsecured access into your network.

One important cell phone technology to discuss is Wireless Application Protocol (WAP). WAP is not a standard; instead, it is a functioning industry-driven protocol stack. Via WAP-capable devices, users can communicate with the company network by connecting from their cell phone or PDA through the cell phone carrier network over the Internet and through a gateway into the company network. WAP is a suite of protocols working together. One of these protocols is Wireless Transport Layer Security (WTLS), which provides security connectivity services similar to those of SSL or TLS.

WAP vs. WAP

Wireless Application Protocol is often confused with wireless networking (802.11) because the same acronym (WAP) is used for both. WAP stands for wireless access point when used in relation to 802.11. Keep in mind the difference between them:

- With Wireless Application Protocol, portable devices use a cell phone carrier's network to establish communication links with the Internet.
- With wireless networking, an organization deploys its own wireless access points to allow its wireless clients to connect to its local network.

One very important security issue to recognize with WAP or with any security service provided by a telco is that you are unlikely to obtain true end-to-end protection from a communications service provider. The U.S. law known as the Communications Assistance for Law Enforcement Act (CALEA) mandates that all telcos, regardless of the technologies involved, must make it possible to wiretap voice and data communications when a search warrant is presented. Thus, a telco cannot provide customers with end-to-end encryption.

At some point along the communication path, the data must be returned to clear form before being resecured for the remainder of the journey to its destination. WAP complies with the CALEA restriction as follows: A secure link is established between the mobile device and the telco's main server using WAP/WTLS. The data is converted into its clear form before being reencapsulated in SSL, TLS, IPSec, and so on for its continued transmission to its intended destination. Knowing this, use telco services appropriately, and whenever possible, feed pre-encrypted data into the telco link rather than clear form data.

WAP 1.0 was implemented in 1999, mostly on European mobile phones. WAP 2.0 was released in 2002. Today, few phones still use WAP; the mechanisms used to support TCP/IP communications between mobile phones and the Internet are based on 3G and 4G technologies (including GSM, EDGE, HPDSA, and LTE).

Bluetooth (802.15)

Bluetooth, or IEEE 802.15, personal area networks (PANs) are another area of wireless security concern. Headsets for cell phones, mice, keyboards, GPS devices, and many other interface devices and peripherals are connected via Bluetooth. Many of these connections are set up using a technique known as pairing, where the primary device scans the 2.4 GHz radio frequencies for available devices, and then, once a device is discovered, a four-digit PIN is used to "authorize" the pairing. This process does reduce the number of accidental pairings; however, a four-digit PIN is not secure (not to mention that the default PIN is often 0000). In addition, there are attacks against Bluetooth-enabled devices. One technique, known as bluejacking, allows an attacker to transmit SMS-like messages to your device. Bluesnarfing allows hackers to connect with your Bluetooth devices without your knowledge and extract information from them. This form of attack can offer attackers access to your contact lists, your data, and even your conversations. Bluebugging is an attack that grants hackers remote control over the feature and functions of a Bluetooth device. This could include the ability to turn on the microphone to use the phone as an audio bug. Fortunately, Bluetooth typically has a limited range of 30 feet, but some devices can function from more than 100 meters away. Bluetooth devices sometimes employ encryption, but it is not dynamic and can usually be cracked with modest effort. Use Bluetooth for those activities that are not sensitive or confidential. Whenever possible, change the default PINs on your devices. Do not leave your devices in discovery mode, and always turn off Bluetooth when it's not in active use.

Cordless Phones

Cordless phones represent an often-overlooked security issue. Cordless phones are designed to use any one of the unlicensed frequencies, in other words, 900 MHz, 2.4 GHz, or 5 GHz. These three unlicensed frequency ranges are employed by many different types of devices, from cordless phones and baby monitors to Bluetooth and wireless networking devices. The issue that is often overlooked is that someone could easily eavesdrop on a conversation on a cordless phone since its signal is rarely encrypted. With a frequency scanner, anyone can listen in on your conversations.

Mobile Devices

Smartphones and other mobile devices present an ever-increasing security risk as they become more and more capable of interacting with the Internet as well as corporate networks. Mobile devices often support memory cards and can be used to smuggle malicious code into or confidential data out of organizations. Many mobile devices also support USB connections to perform synchronization of communications and contacts with desktop and/or notebook computers as well as the transfer of files, documents, music, video, and so on. The devices themselves often contain sensitive data such as contacts, text messages, email, and even notes and documents.

The loss or theft of a mobile device could mean the compromise of personal and/or corporate secrets.

Mobile devices are also becoming the target of hackers and malicious code. It's important to keep nonessential information off portable devices, run a firewall and antivirus product (if available), and keep the system locked and/or encrypted (if possible).

Many mobile devices also support USB connections to perform synchronization of communications and contacts with desktop and/or notebook computers as well as the transfer of files, documents, music, video, and so on.

Additionally, mobile devices aren't immune to eavesdropping. With the right type of sophisticated equipment, most mobile phone conversations can be tapped into—not to mention the fact that anyone within 15 feet can hear you talking. Employees should be coached to be discreet about what they discuss over mobile phones in public spaces.

A wide range of security features is available on mobile devices. However, support for a feature isn't the same thing as having a feature properly configured and enabled. A security benefit is gained only when the security function is in force. Be sure to check that all desired security features are operating as expected on any device allowed to connect to the organization's network.

NOTE

A device owned by an individual can be referenced using any of these terms: portable device, mobile device, personal mobile device (PMD), personal electronic device or portable electronic device (PED), and personally owned device (POD).

For more information on managing the security of mobile devices, please see Chapter 9, "Security Vulnerabilities, Threats, and Countermeasures," specifically the section "Assess and Mitigate Vulnerabilities in Mobile Systems".

LAN Technologies

There are three main types of LAN technologies: Ethernet, Token Ring, and FDDI. A handful of other LAN technologies are available, but they are not as widely used. Only the main three are addressed on the CISSP exam. Most of the differences between LAN technologies exist at and below the Data Link layer.

Ethernet

Ethernet is a shared-media LAN technology (also known as a broadcast technology). That means it allows numerous devices to communicate over the same medium but requires that the devices take turns communicating and performing collision detection and avoidance. Ethernet employs broadcast and collision domains. A broadcast domain is a physical grouping of systems in which all the systems in the group receive a broadcast sent by a single system in the group. A broadcast is a message transmitted to a specific address that indicates that all systems are the intended recipients.

A collision domain consists of groupings of systems within which a data collision occurs if two systems transmit simultaneously. A data collision takes place when two transmitted messages attempt to use the network medium at the same time. It causes one or both of the messages to be corrupted.

Ethernet can support full-duplex communications (in other words, full two-way) and usually employs twisted-pair cabling. (Coaxial cabling was originally used.) Ethernet is most often deployed on star or bus topologies. Ethernet is based on the IEEE 802.3 standard. Individual units of Ethernet data are called frames. Fast Ethernet supports 100 Mbps throughput. Gigabit Ethernet supports 1,000 Mbps (1 Gbps) throughput. 10 Gigabit Ethernet support 10,000 Mbps (10 Gbps) throughput.

Token Ring

Token Ring employs a token-passing mechanism to control which systems can transmit data over the network medium. The token travels in a logical loop among all members of the LAN. Token Ring can be employed on ring or star network topologies. It is rarely used today because of its performance limitations, higher cost compared to Ethernet, and increased difficulty in deployment and management.

Token Ring can be deployed as a physical star using a multistation access unit (MAU). A MAU allows for the cable segments to be deployed as a star while internally the device makes logical ring connections.

Fiber Distributed Data Interface (FDDI)

Fiber Distributed Data Interface is a high-speed token-passing technology that employs two rings with traffic flowing in opposite directions. FDDI is often used as a backbone for large enterprise networks. Its dual-ring design allows for self-healing by removing the failed segment from the loop and creating a single loop out of the remaining inner and outer ring portions. FDDI is expensive but was often used in campus environments before Fast Ethernet and Gigabit Ethernet were developed. A less-expensive, distance-limited, and slower version known as Copper Distributed Data Interface (CDDI) uses twisted-pair cables. CDDI is also more vulnerable to interference and eavesdropping.

Subtechnologies

Most networks comprise numerous technologies rather than a single technology. For example, Ethernet is not just a single technology but a superset of subtechnologies that support its common and expected activity and behavior. Ethernet includes the technologies of digital communications, synchronous communications, and baseband communications, and it supports broadcast, multicast, and unicast communications and Carrier-Sense Multiple Access with Collision Detection (CSMA/CD). Many of the LAN technologies, such as Ethernet, Token Ring, and FDDI, may include many of the subtechnologies described in the following sections.

Analog and Digital

One subtechnology common to many forms of network communications is the mechanism used to actually transmit signals over a physical medium, such as a cable. There are two types: analog and digital.

- Analog communications occur with a continuous signal that varies in frequency, amplitude, phase, voltage, and so on. The variances in the continuous signal produce a wave shape (as opposed to the square shape of a digital signal). The actual communication occurs by variances in the constant signal.
- Digital communications occur through the use of a discontinuous electrical signal and a state change or on-off pulses.

Digital signals are more reliable than analog signals over long distances or when interference is present. This is because of a digital signal's definitive information storage method employing direct current voltage where voltage on represents a value of 1 and voltage off represents a value of 0. These on-off pulses create a stream of binary data. Analog signals become altered and corrupted because of attenuation over long distances and interference. Since an analog signal can have an infinite number of variations used for signal encoding as opposed to digital's two states, unwanted alterations to the signal make extraction of the data more difficult as the degradation increases.

Synchronous and Asynchronous

Some communications are synchronized with some sort of clock or timing activity. Communications are either synchronous or asynchronous:

- Synchronous communications rely on a timing or clocking mechanism based on either an independent clock or a time stamp embedded in the data stream. Synchronous communications are typically able to support very high rates of data transfer.
- Asynchronous communications rely on a stop and start delimiter bit to manage the transmission of data. Because of the use of delimiter bits and the stop and start nature of its transmission, asynchronous communication is best suited for smaller amounts of data. Public switched telephone network (PSTN) modems are good examples of asynchronous communication devices.

Baseband and Broadband

How many communications can occur simultaneously over a cable segment depends on whether you use baseband technology or broadband technology:

- Baseband technology can support only a single communication channel. It uses a direct current applied to the cable. A current that is at a higher level represents the binary signal of 1, and a current that is at a lower level represents the binary signal of 0. Baseband is a form of digital signal. Ethernet is a baseband technology.

- Broadband technology can support multiple simultaneous signals. Broadband uses frequency modulation to support numerous channels, each supporting a distinct communication session. Broadband is suitable for high throughput rates, especially when several channels are multiplexed. Broadband is a form of analog signal. Cable television and cable modems, ISDN, DSL, T1, and T3 are examples of broadband technologies.

Broadcast, Multicast, and Unicast

Broadcast, multicast, and unicast technologies determine how many destinations a single transmission can reach:

- Broadcast technology supports communications to all possible recipients.
- Multicast technology supports communications to multiple specific recipients.
- Unicast technology supports only a single communication to a specific recipient.

LAN Media Access

There are at least five LAN media access technologies that are used to avoid or prevent transmission collisions. These technologies define how multiple systems all within the same collision domain are to communicate. Some of these technologies actively prevent collisions, while others respond to collisions.

Carrier-Sense Multiple Access (CSMA) This is the LAN media access technology that performs communications using the following steps:

1. The host listens to the LAN media to determine whether it is in use.
2. If the LAN media is not being used, the host transmits its communication.
3. The host waits for an acknowledgment.
4. If no acknowledgment is received after a time-out period, the host starts over at step 1.

CSMA does not directly address collisions. If a collision occurs, the communication would not have been successful, and thus an acknowledgment would not be received. This causes the sending system to retransmit the data and perform the CSMA process again.

Carrier-Sense Multiple Access with Collision Avoidance (CSMA/CA) This is the LAN media access technology that performs communications using the following steps:

1. The host has two connections to the LAN media: inbound and outbound. The host listens on the inbound connection to determine whether the LAN media is in use.
2. If the LAN media is not being used, the host requests permission to transmit.
3. If permission is not granted after a time-out period, the host starts over at step 1.
4. If permission is granted, the host transmits its communication over the outbound connection.
5. The host waits for an acknowledgment.
6. If no acknowledgment is received after a time-out period, the host starts over at step 1.

AppleTalk and 802.11 wireless networking are examples of networks that employ CSMA/CA technologies. CSMA/CA attempts to avoid collisions by granting only a single permission to communicate at any given time. This system requires designation of a master or primary system, which responds to the requests and grants permission to send data transmissions.

Carrier-Sense Multiple Access with Collision Detection (CSMA/CD) This is the LAN media access technology that performs communications using the following steps:

1. The host listens to the LAN media to determine whether it is in use.
2. If the LAN media is not being used, the host transmits its communication.
3. While transmitting, the host listens for collisions (in other words, two or more hosts transmitting simultaneously).
4. If a collision is detected, the host transmits a jam signal.
5. If a jam signal is received, all hosts stop transmitting. Each host waits a random period of time and then starts over at step 1.

Ethernet networks employ the CSMA/CD technology. CSMA/CD responds to collisions by having each member of the collision domain wait for a short but random period of time before starting the process over. Unfortunately, allowing collisions to occur and then responding or reacting to collisions causes delays in transmissions as well as a required repetition of transmissions. This results in about 40 percent loss in potential throughput.

Token Passing This is the LAN media access technology that performs communications using a digital token. Possession of the token allows a host to transmit data. Once its transmission is complete, it releases the token to the next system. Token passing is used by Token Ring networks, such as FDDI. Token Ring prevents collisions since only the system possessing the token is allowed to transmit data.

Polling This is the LAN media access technology that performs communications using a master-slave configuration. One system is labeled as the primary system. All other systems are labeled as secondary. The primary system polls or inquires of each secondary system in turn whether they have a need to transmit data. If a secondary system indicates a need, it is granted permission to transmit. Once its transmission is complete, the primary system moves on to poll the next secondary system. Synchronous Data Link Control (SDLC) uses polling.

Polling addresses collisions by attempting to prevent them from using a permission system. Polling is an inverse of the CSMA/CA method. Both use masters and slaves (or primary and secondary), but while CSMA/CA allows the slaves to request permissions, polling has the master offer permission. Polling can be configured to grant one (or more) system priority over other systems. For example, if the standard polling pattern was 1, 2, 3, 4, then to give system 1 priority, the polling pattern could be changed to 1, 2, 1, 3, 1, 4.

Summary

The tasks of designing, deploying, and maintaining security on a network require intimate knowledge of the technologies involved in networking. This includes protocols, services, communication mechanisms, topologies, cabling, endpoints, and networking devices.

The OSI model is a standard against which all protocols are evaluated. Understanding how the OSI model is used and how it applies to real-world protocols can help system designers and system administrators improve security. The TCP/IP model is derived directly from the protocol and roughly maps to the OSI model.

Most networks employ TCP/IP as the primary protocol. However, numerous subprotocols, supporting protocols, services, and security mechanisms can be found in a TCP/IP network. A basic understanding of these various entities can help you when designing and deploying a secure network.

In addition to routers, hubs, switches, repeaters, gateways, and proxies, firewalls are an important part of a network's security. There are four primary types of firewalls: static packet filtering, application-level gateway, circuit-level gateway, and stateful inspection.

Converged protocols are common on modern networks, including FCoE, MPLS, VoIP, and iSCSI. Software-defined networks and content distribution networks have expanded the definition of network as well as expanded the use cases for it. A wide range of hardware components can be used to construct a network, not the least of which is the cabling used to tie all the devices together. Understanding the strengths and weaknesses of each cabling type is part of designing a secure network.

Wireless communications occur in many forms, including cell phone, Bluetooth (802.15), and networking (802.11). Wireless communication is more vulnerable to interference, eavesdropping, denial of service, and man-in-the-middle attacks.

There are three LAN technologies mentioned in the CISSP CIB: Ethernet, Token Ring, and FDDI. Each can be used to deploy a secure network. There are also several common network topologies: ring, bus, star, and mesh.

Exam Essentials

Know the OSI model layers and which protocols are found in each. The seven layers and the protocols supported by each of the layers of the OSI model are as follows:

Application: HTTP, FTP, LPD, SMTP, Telnet, TFTP, EDI, POP3, IMAP, SNMP, NNTP, S-RPC, and SET

Presentation: Encryption protocols and format types, such as ASCII, EBCDICM, TIFF, JPEG, MPEG, and MIDI

Session: NFS, SQL, and RPC

Transport: SPX, SSL, TLS, TCP, and UDP

Network: ICMP, RIP, OSPF, BGP, IGMP, IP, IPSec, IPX, NAT, and SKIP

Data Link: SLIP, PPP, ARP, RARP, L2F, L2TP, PPTP, FDDI, ISDN

Physical: EIA/TIA-232, EIA/TIA-449, X.21, HSSI, SONET, V.24, and V.35

Have a thorough knowledge of TCP/IP. Know the difference between TCP and UDP; be familiar with the four TCP/IP layers (Application, Transport, Internet, and Link) and how they correspond to the OSI model. In addition, understand the usage of the well-known ports, and be familiar with the subprotocols.

Know the different cabling types and their lengths and maximum throughput rates. This includes STP, 10Base-T (UTP), 10Base2 (thinnet), 10Base5 (thicknet), 100Base-T, 1000Base-T, and fiber-optic. You should also be familiar with UTP categories 1 through 7.

Be familiar with the common LAN technologies. These are Ethernet, Token Ring, and FDDI. Also be familiar with analog versus digital communications; synchronous vs. asynchronous communications; baseband vs. broadband communications; broadcast, multicast, and unicast communications; CSMA, CSMA/CA, and CSMA/CD; token passing; and polling.

Understand secure network architecture and design. Network security should take into account IP and non-IP protocols, network access control, using security services and devices, managing multilayer protocols, and implementing endpoint security.

Understand the various types and purposes of network segmentation. Network segmentation can be used to manage traffic, improve performance, and enforce security. Examples of network segments or subnetworks include intranet, extranet, and DMZ.

Understand the different wireless technologies. Cell phones, Bluetooth (802.15), and wireless networking (802.11) are all called wireless technologies, even though they are all different. Be aware of their differences, strengths, and weaknesses. Understand the basics of securing 802.11 networking.

Understand Fibre Channel. Fibre Channel is a form of network data storage solution (i.e., SAN (storage area network) or NAS (network-attached storage)) that allows for high-speed file transfers.

Understand FCoE. FCoE (Fibre Channel over Ethernet) is used to encapsulate Fibre Channel communications over Ethernet networks.

Understand iSCSI. iSCSI (Internet Small Computer System Interface) is a networking storage standard based on IP.

Understand 802.11 and 802.11a, b, g, n, and ac. 802.11 is the IEEE standard for wireless network communications. Versions include 802.11 (2 Mbps), 802.11a (54 Mbps), 802.11b (11 Mbps), 802.11g (54 Mbps), 802.11n (600 Mbps), and 802.11ac (1.3+ Mbps). The 802.11 standard also defines Wired Equivalent Privacy (WEP).

Understand site survey. A *site survey* is the process of investigating the presence, strength, and reach of wireless access points deployed in an environment. This task usually involves walking around with a portable wireless device, taking note of the wireless signal strength, and mapping this on a plot or schematic of the building.

Understand WPA. An early alternative to WEP was Wi-Fi Protected Access (WPA). This technique was an improvement but was itself not fully secure. It is based on the LEAP and TKIP cryptosystem and employs a secret passphrase.

Understand WPA2. WPA2 is a new encryption scheme known as the Counter Mode with Cipher Block Chaining Message Authentication Code Protocol (CCMP), which is based on the AES encryption scheme.

Understand WEP. Wired Equivalent Privacy (WEP) is defined by the IEEE 802.11 standard. It was designed to provide the same level of security and encryption on wireless networks as is found on wired or cabled networks. WEP provides protection from packet sniffing and eavesdropping against wireless transmissions. A secondary benefit of WEP is that it can be configured to prevent unauthorized access to the wireless network. WEP uses a predefined shared secret key.

Understand EAP. EAP (Extensible Authentication Protocol) is not a specific mechanism of authentication; rather it is an authentication framework. Effectively, EAP allows for new authentication technologies to be compatible with existing wireless or point-to-point connection technologies.

Understand PEAP. PEAP (Protected Extensible Authentication Protocol) encapsulates EAP methods within a TLS tunnel that provides authentication and potentially encryption.

Understand LEAP. LEAP (Lightweight Extensible Authentication Protocol) is a Cisco proprietary alternative to TKIP for WPA. This was developed to address deficiencies in TKIP before the 802.11i/WPA2 system was ratified as a standard.

Understand MAC Filtering. A MAC filter is a list of authorized wireless client interface MAC addresses that is used by a wireless access point to block access to all non-authorized devices.

Understand SSID Broadcast. Wireless networks traditionally announce their SSID on a regular basis within a special packet known as the beacon frame. When the SSID is broadcast, any device with an automatic detect and connect feature is not only able to see the network, but it can also initiate a connection with the network.

Understand TKIP. TKIP (Temporal Key Integrity Protocol) was designed as the replacement for WEP without requiring replacement of legacy wireless hardware. TKIP was implemented into 802.11 wireless networking under the name WPA (Wi-Fi Protected Access).

Understand CCMP. CCMP (Counter Mode with Cipher Block Chaining Message Authentication Code Protocol) was created to replace WEP and TKIP/WPA. CCMP uses AES (Advanced Encryption Standard) with a 128-bit key.

Understand captive portals. A captive portal is an authentication technique that redirects a newly connected wireless web client to a portal access control page.

Understand antenna types.A wide variety of antenna types can be used for wireless clients and base stations. These include omnidirectional pole antennas as well as many directional antennas, such as Yagi, cantenna, panel, and parabolic.

Understand site surveys. A site survey is a formal assessment of wireless signal strength, quality, and interference using an RF signal detector.

Know the standard network topologies. These are ring, bus, star, and mesh.

Know the common network devices. Common network devices are firewalls, routers, hubs, bridges, modems, repeaters, switches, gateways, and proxies.

Understand the different types of firewalls. There are four basic types of firewalls: static packet filtering, application-level gateway, circuit-level gateway, and stateful inspection.

Know the protocol services used to connect to LAN and WAN communication technologies. These are Frame Relay, SMDS, X.25, ATM, HSSI, SDLC, HDLC, and ISDN.

Written Lab

1. Name the layers of the OSI model and their numbers from top to bottom.
2. Name three problems with cabling and the methods to counteract those issues.
3. What are the various technologies employed by wireless devices to maximize their use of the available radio frequencies?
4. Discuss methods used to secure 802.11 wireless networking.
5. Name the LAN shared media access technologies and examples of their use, if known.

Review Questions

1. What is layer 4 of the OSI model?
   - A. Presentation
   - B. Network
   - C. Data Link
   - D. Transport
2. What is encapsulation?
   - A. Changing the source and destination addresses of a packet
   - B. Adding a header and footer to data as it moves down the OSI stack
   - C. Verifying a person's identity
   - D. Protecting evidence until it has been properly collected
3. Which OSI model layer manages communications in simplex, half-duplex, and full-duplex modes?
   - A. Application
   - B. Session
   - C. Transport
   - D. Physical
4. Which of the following is the least resistant to EMI?
   - A. Thinnet
   - B. 10Base-T UTP
   - C. 10Base5
   - D. Coaxial cable
5. Which of the following is not an example of network segmentation?
   - A. Intranet
   - B. DMZ
   - C. Extranet
   - D. VPN
6. Which of the following is not considered a non-IP protocol?
   - A. IPX
   - B. UDP
   - C. AppleTalk
   - D. NetBEUI

7. If you are the victim of a bluejacking attack, what was compromised?
   A. Your firewall
   B. Your switch
   C. Your cell phone
   D. Your web cookies

8. Which networking technology is based on the IEEE 802.3 standard?
   A. Ethernet
   B. Token Ring
   C. FDDI
   D. HDLC

9. What is a TCP wrapper?
   A. An encapsulation protocol used by switches
   B. An application that can serve as a basic firewall by restricting access based on user IDs or system IDs
   C. A security protocol used to protect TCP/IP traffic over WAN links
   D. A mechanism to tunnel TCP/IP through non-IP networks

10. What is both a benefit and a potentially harmful implication of multilayer protocols?
   A. Throughput
   B. Encapsulation
   C. Hash integrity checking
   D. Logical addressing

11. By examining the source and destination addresses, the application usage, the source of origin, and the relationship between current packets with the previous packets of the same session, ___________ firewalls are able to grant a broader range of access for authorized users and activities and actively watch for and block unauthorized users and activities.
   A. Static packet-filtering
   B. Application-level gateway
   C. Stateful inspection
   D. Circuit-level gateway

12. ___________ firewalls are known as third-generation firewalls.
   A. Application-level gateway
   B. Stateful inspection
   C. Circuit-level gateway
   D. Static packet-filtering

13. Which of the following is not true regarding firewalls?
    A. They are able to log traffic information.
    B. They are able to block viruses.
    C. They are able to issue alarms based on suspected attacks.
    D. They are unable to prevent internal attacks.

14. Which of the following is not a routing protocol?
    A. OSPF
    B. BGP
    C. RPC
    D. RIP

15. A ____________ is an intelligent hub because it knows the addresses of the systems connected on each outbound port. Instead of repeating traffic on every outbound port, it repeats traffic only out of the port on which the destination is known to exist.
    A. Repeater
    B. Switch
    C. Bridge
    D. Router

16. Which of the following is not a technology specifically associated with 802.11 wireless networking?
    A. WAP
    B. WPA
    C. WEP
    D. 802.11i

17. Which wireless frequency access method offers the greatest throughput with the least interference?
    A. FHSS
    B. DSSS
    C. OFDM
    D. OSPF

18. What security concept encourages administrators to install firewalls, malware scanners, and an IDS on every host?
    A. Endpoint security
    B. Network access control (NAC)
    C. VLAN
    D. RADIUS

19. What function does RARP perform?

A. It is a routing protocol.

B. It converts IP addresses into MAC addresses.

C. It resolves physical addresses into logical addresses.

D. It manages multiplex streaming.

20. What form of infrastructure mode wireless networking deployment supports large physical environments through the use of a single SSID but numerous access points?

A. Stand-alone

B. Wired extension

C. Enterprise extension

D. Bridge

Chapter 12

Secure Communications and Network Attacks

THE CISSP EXAM TOPICS COVERED IN THIS CHAPTER INCLUDE:

✓ **4) Communication and Network Security (Designing and Protecting Network Security)**

- C. Design and establish secure communication channels
  - C.1 Voice
  - C.2 Multimedia collaboration (e.g., remote meeting technology, instant messaging)
  - C.3 Remote access (e.g., VPN, screen scraper, virtual application/desktop, telecommuting)
  - C.4 Data communications (e.g., VLAN, TLS/SSL)
  - C.5 Virtualized networks (e.g., SDN, virtual SAN, guest operating systems, port isolation)
- D. Prevent or mitigate network attacks

Data residing in a static form on a storage device is fairly simple to secure. As long as physical access control is maintained and reasonable logical access controls are implemented, stored files remain confidential, retain their integrity, and are available to authorized users. However, once data is used by an application or transferred over a network connection, the process of securing it becomes much more difficult.

Communications security covers a wide range of issues related to the transportation of electronic information from one place to another. That transportation may be between systems on opposite sides of the planet or between systems on the same business network. Once it is involved in any means of transportation, data becomes vulnerable to a plethora of threats to its confidentiality, integrity, and availability. Fortunately, many of these threats can be reduced or eliminated with the appropriate countermeasures.

Communications security is designed to detect, prevent, and even correct data transportation errors (that is, it provides integrity protection as well as confidentiality). This is done to sustain the security of networks while supporting the need to exchange and share data. This chapter covers the many forms of communications security, vulnerabilities, and countermeasures.

The Communication and Network Security domain for the CISSP certification exam deals with topics related to network components (i.e., network devices and protocols), specifically how they function and how they are relevant to security. This domain is discussed in this chapter and in Chapter 11, "Secure Network Architecture and Securing Network Components." Be sure to read and study the material in both chapters to ensure complete coverage of the essential material for the CISSP certification exam.

Network and Protocol Security Mechanisms

TCP/IP is the primary protocol suite used on most networks and on the Internet. It is a robust protocol suite, but it has numerous security deficiencies. In an effort to improve the security of TCP/IP, many subprotocols, mechanisms, or applications have been developed to protect the confidentiality, integrity, and availability of transmitted data. It is important to remember that even with the foundational protocol suite of TCP/IP, there are literally hundreds, if not thousands, of individual protocols, mechanisms, and applications in use across the Internet. Some of them are designed to provide security services. Some protect integrity, others protect confidentiality, and others provide authentication and access control. In the next sections, we'll discuss some of the more common network and protocol security mechanisms.

Secure Communications Protocols

Protocols that provide security services for application-specific communication channels are called secure communication protocols. The following list includes some of the options available:

Simple Key Management for Internet Protocol (SKIP) This is an encryption tool used to protect sessionless datagram protocols. SKIP was designed to integrate with IPSec; it functions at layer 3. It is able to encrypt any subprotocol of the TCP/IP suite. SKIP was replaced by Internet Key Exchange (IKE) in 1998.

Software IP Encryption (swIPe) This is another layer 3 security protocol for IP. It provides authentication, integrity, and confidentiality using an encapsulation protocol.

Secure Remote Procedure Call (S-RPC) This is an authentication service and is simply a means to prevent unauthorized execution of code on remote systems.

Secure Sockets Layer (SSL) This is an encryption protocol developed by Netscape to protect the communications between a web server and a web browser. SSL can be used to secure web, email, FTP, or even Telnet traffic. It is a session-oriented protocol that provides confidentiality and integrity. SSL is deployed using a 40-bit key or a 128-bit key. SSL is superseded by Transport Layer Security (TLS).

Transport Layer Security (TLS) TLS functions in the same general manner as SSL, but it uses stronger authentication and encryption protocols.

SSL and TLS both have the following features:

- Support secure client-server communications across an insecure network while preventing tampering, spoofing, and eavesdropping.
- Support one-way authentication.
- Support two-way authentication using digital certificates.
- Often implemented as the initial payload of a TCP package, allowing it to encapsulate all higher-layer protocol payloads.
- Can be implemented at lower layers, such as layer 3 (the Network layer) to operate as a VPN. This implementation is known as OpenVPN.

In addition, TLS can be used to encrypt UDP and Session Initiation Protocol (SIP) connections. (SIP is a protocol associated with VoIP.)

Secure Electronic Transaction (SET) This is a security protocol for the transmission of transactions over the Internet. SET is based on Rivest, Shamir, and Adelman (RSA) encryption and Data Encryption Standard (DES). It has the support of major credit card companies, such as Visa and MasterCard. However, SET has not been widely accepted by the

Internet in general; instead, SSL/TLS encrypted sessions are the preferred mechanism for secure e-commerce.

NOTE These five secure communication protocols (SKIP, swIPe, S-RPC, SSL/TLS, and SET) are just a few examples of options available. Keep in mind that there are many other secure protocols, such as IPSec and SSH.

Authentication Protocols

After a connection is initially established between a remote system and a server or a network, the first activity that should take place is to verify the identity of the remote user. This activity is known as authentication. There are several authentication protocols that control how the logon credentials are exchanged and whether those credentials are encrypted during transport:

Challenge Handshake Authentication Protocol (CHAP) This is one of the authentication protocols used over PPP links. CHAP encrypts usernames and passwords. It performs authentication using a challenge-response dialogue that cannot be replayed. CHAP also periodically reauthenticates the remote system throughout an established communication session to verify a persistent identity of the remote client. This activity is transparent to the user.

Password Authentication Protocol (PAP) This is a standardized authentication protocol for PPP. PAP transmits usernames and passwords in the clear. It offers no form of encryption; it simply provides a means to transport the logon credentials from the client to the authentication server.

Extensible Authentication Protocol (EAP) This is a framework for authentication instead of an actual protocol. EAP allows customized authentication security solutions, such as supporting smart cards, tokens, and biometrics. (See the sidebar "EAP, PEAP, and LEAP" for information about other protocols based on EAP.)

These three authentication protocols were initially used over dial-up PPP connections. Today, these and many other, newer authentication protocols and concepts are in use over a wide number of distance connection technologies, including broadband and virtual private networks (VPNs).

EAP, PEAP, and LEAP

Protected Extensible Authentication Protocol (PEAP) encapsulates EAP in a TLS tunnel. PEAP is preferred to EAP because EAP assumes that the channel is already protected but PEAP imposes its own security. PEAP is used for securing communications over 802.11

wireless connections. PEAP can be employed by Wi-Fi Protected Access (WPA) and WPA-2 connections.

PEAP is also preferred over Cisco's proprietary EAP known as Lightweight Extensible Authentication Protocol (LEAP). LEAP was Cisco's initial response to insecure WEP. LEAP supported frequent reauthentication and changing of WEP keys (whereas WEP used single authentication and a static key). However, LEAP is crackable using a variety of tools and techniques, including the exploit tool Asleap.

Secure Voice Communications

The vulnerability of voice communication is tangentially related to IT system security. However, as voice communication solutions move on to the network by employing digital devices and VoIP, securing voice communications becomes an increasingly important issue. When voice communications occur over the IT infrastructure, it is important to implement mechanisms to provide for authentication and integrity. Confidentiality should be maintained by employing an encryption service or protocol to protect the voice communications while in transit.

Normal private branch exchange (PBX) or POTS/PSTN voice communications are vulnerable to interception, eavesdropping, tapping, and other exploitations. Often, physical security is required to maintain control over voice communications within the confines of your organization's physical locations. Security of voice communications outside your organization is typically the responsibility of the phone company from which you lease services. If voice communication vulnerabilities are an important issue for sustaining your security policy, you should deploy an encrypted communication mechanism and use it exclusively.

Voice over Internet Protocol (VoIP)

VoIP is a technology that encapsulates audio into IP packets to support telephone calls over TCP/IP network connections. VoIP has become a popular and inexpensive telephony solution for companies and individuals worldwide.

It is important to keep security in mind when selecting a VoIP solution to ensure that it provides the privacy and security you expect. Some VoIP systems are essentially plain-form communications that are easily intercepted and eavesdropped; others are highly encrypted, and any attempt to interfere or wiretap is deterred and thwarted.

VoIP is not without its problems. Hackers can wage a wide range of potential attacks against a VoIP solution:

- Caller ID can be falsified easily using any number of VoIP tools, so hackers can perform vishing (VoIP phishing) or Spam over Internet Telephony (SPIT) attacks.
- The call manager systems and the VoIP phones themselves might be vulnerable to host OS attacks and DoS attacks. If a device's or software's host OS or firmware has vulnerabilities, hacker exploits are often not far off.

- Hackers might be able to perform man-in-the-middle (MitM) attacks by spoofing call managers or endpoint connection negotiations and/or responses.
- Depending on the deployment, there are also risks associated with deploying VoIP phones off the same switches as desktop and server systems. This could allow for 802.1X authentication falsification as well as VLAN and VoIP hopping (i.e., jumping across authenticated channels).
- Since VoIP traffic is just network traffic, it is often possible to listen in on VoIP communications by decoding the VoIP traffic when it isn't encrypted.

Social Engineering

Malicious individuals can exploit voice communications through a technique known as *social engineering*. Social engineering is a means by which an unknown, untrusted, or at least unauthorized person gains the trust of someone inside your organization. Adept individuals can convince employees that they are associated with upper management, technical support, the help desk, and so on. Once convinced, the victim is often encouraged to make a change to their user account on the system, such as resetting their password. Other attacks include instructing the victim to open specific email attachments, launch an application, or connect to a specific URL. Whatever the actual activity is, it is usually directed toward opening a back door that the attacker can use to gain network access.

The people within an organization make it vulnerable to social engineering attacks. With just a little information or a few facts, it is often possible to get a victim to disclose confidential information or engage in irresponsible activity. Social engineering attacks exploit human characteristics such as a basic trust in others, a desire to provide assistance, or a propensity to show off. Overlooking discrepancies, being distracted, following orders, assuming others know more than they actually do, wanting to help others, and fearing reprimands can also lead to attacks. Attackers are often able to bypass extensive physical and logical security controls because the victim opens an access pathway from the inside, effectively punching a hole in the secured perimeter.

Real World Scenario

The Fascinating World of Social Engineering

Social engineering is a fascinating subject. It is the means to break into the perfectly technically secured environment. Social engineering is the art of using an organization's own people against it. Although not necessary for the CISSP exam, there are lots of excellent resources, examples, and discussions of social engineering that can increase your awareness of this security problem. Some are also highly entertaining. We suggest doing some searching on the term *social engineering* to discover books and online videos. You'll find the reading informative and the video examples addicting.

The only way to protect against social engineering attacks is to teach users how to respond and interact with any form of communications, whether voice-only, face to face, IM, chat, or email. Here are some guidelines:

- Always err on the side of caution whenever voice communications seem odd, out of place, or unexpected.
- Always request proof of identity. This can be a driver's license number, Social Security number, employee ID number, customer number, or a case or reference number, any of which can be easily verified. It could also take the form of having a person in the office that would recognize the caller's voice take the call. For example, if the caller claims to be a department manager, you could confirm their identity by asking their administrative assistant to take the call.
- Require callback authorizations on all voice-only requests for network alterations or activities. A callback authorization occurs when the initial client connection is disconnected, and the server calls the client back on a predetermined number in order to perform a second round of authentication.
- Classify information (usernames, passwords, IP addresses, manager names, dial-in numbers, and so on), and clearly indicate which information can be discussed or even confirmed using voice communications.
- If privileged information is requested over the phone by an individual who should know that giving out that particular information over the phone is against the company's security policy, ask why the information is needed and verify their identity again. This incident should also be reported to the security administrator.
- Never give out or change passwords via voice-only communications.
- When disposing of office documentation (according to policy and regulation compliance) always use a secure disposal or destruction process, especially for any paperwork or media that contains information about the IT infrastructure or its security mechanisms.

Fraud and Abuse

Another voice communication threat is PBX fraud and abuse. Many PBX systems can be exploited by malicious individuals to avoid toll charges and hide their identity. Malicious attackers known as *phreakers* abuse phone systems in *much the same way that attackers abuse computer networks*. Phreakers may be able to gain unauthorized access to personal voice mailboxes, redirect messages, block access, and redirect inbound and outbound calls.

Countermeasures to PBX fraud and abuse include many of the same precautions you would employ to protect a typical computer network: logical or technical controls, administrative controls, and physical controls. Here are several key points to keep in mind when designing a PBX security solution:

- Consider replacing remote access or long-distance calling through the PBX with a credit card or calling card system.

- Restrict dial-in and dial-out features to authorized individuals who require such functionality for their work tasks.
- For your dial-in modems, use unpublished phone numbers that are outside the prefix block range of your voice numbers.
- Block or disable any unassigned access codes or accounts.
- Define an acceptable use policy and train users on how to properly use the system.
- Log and audit all activities on the PBX and review the audit trails for security and use violations.
- Disable maintenance modems (i.e., remote access modems used by the vendor to remotely manage, update, and tune a deployed product) and accounts.
- Change all default configurations, especially passwords and capabilities related to administrative or privileged features.
- Block remote calling (that is, allowing a remote caller to dial in to your PBX and then dial out again, thus directing all toll charges to the PBX host).
- Deploy Direct Inward System Access (DISA) technologies to reduce PBX fraud by external parties. (But be sure to configure it properly; see the sidebar "DISA: A Disease and the Cure.")
- Keep the system current with vendor/service provider updates.

Additionally, maintaining physical access control to all PBX connection centers, phone portals, and wiring closets prevents direct intrusion from onsite attackers.

Real World Scenario

DISA: A Disease and the Cure

An often-touted "security" improvement to PBX systems is Direct Inward System Access (DISA). This system is designed to help manage external access and external control of a PBX by assigning access codes to users. Although great in concept, this system is being compromised and abused by phreakers. Once an outside phreaker learns the PBX access codes, they can often fully control and abuse the company's telephone network. This can include using the PBX to make long-distance calls that are charged to your company's telephone account rather than the phreaker's phone.

DISA, like any other security feature, must be properly installed, configured, and monitored in order to obtain the desired security improvement. Simply having DISA is not sufficient. Be sure to disable all features that are not required by the organization, craft user codes/passwords that are complex and difficult to guess, and then turn on auditing to keep watch on PBX activities. Phreaking is a specific type of attack directed toward the telephone system. Phreakers use various types of technology to circumvent the telephone system to make free long-distance calls, to alter the function of telephone service, to steal specialized services, and even to cause service disruptions. Some phreaker tools are actual devices, whereas others are just particular ways of using a regular telephone. No matter what the tool or technology actually is, phreaker tools are referred to as colored boxes (black box, red box, and so on). Over the years, many box technologies have been developed and widely used by phreakers, but only a few of them work against today's telephone systems based on packet switching. Here are a few of the phreaker tools you need to recognize for the exam:

- Black boxes are used to manipulate line voltages to steal long-distance services. They are often just custom-built circuit boards with a battery and wire clips.
- Red boxes are used to simulate tones of coins being deposited into a pay phone. They are usually just small tape recorders.
- Blue boxes are used to simulate 2600 Hz tones to interact directly with telephone network trunk systems (that is, backbones). This could be a whistle, a tape recorder, or a digital tone generator.
- White boxes are used to control the phone system. A white box is a dual-tone multifrequency (DTMF) generator (that is, a keypad). It can be a custom-built device or one of the pieces of equipment that most telephone repair personnel use.

NOTE

As you probably know, cell phone security is a growing concern. Captured electronic serial numbers (ESNs) and mobile identification numbers (MINs) can be burned into blank phones to create clones (even subscriber identity modules—SIMs—can be duplicated). When a clone is used, the charges are billed to the original owner's cell phone account. Furthermore, conversations and data transmission can be intercepted using radio frequency scanners. Also, anyone in the immediate vicinity can overhear at least one side of the conversation. So, don't talk about confidential, private, or sensitive topics in public places.

Multimedia Collaboration

Multimedia collaboration is the use of various multimedia-supporting communication solutions to enhance distance collaboration (people working on a project together remotely). Often, collaboration allows workers to work simultaneously as well as across different time frames. Collaboration can also be used for tracking changes and including multimedia functions. Collaboration can incorporate email, chat, VoIP, videoconferencing, use of a whiteboard, online document editing, real-time file exchange, versioning control, and other tools. It is often a feature of advanced forms of remote meeting technology.

Remote Meeting

Remote meeting technology is used for any product, hardware, or software that allows for interaction between remote parties. These technologies and solutions are known by many other terms: digital collaboration, virtual meetings, videoconferencing, software or application collaboration, shared whiteboard services, virtual training solutions, and so on. Any service that enables people to communicate, exchange data, collaborate on materials/data/documents, and otherwise perform work tasks together can be considered a remote meeting technology service.

No matter what form of multimedia collaboration is implemented, the attendant security implications must be evaluated. Does the service use strong authentication techniques? Does the communication occur across an open protocol or an encrypted tunnel? Does the solution allow for true deletion of content? Are activities of users audited and logged? Multimedia collaboration and other forms of remote meeting technology can improve the work environment and allow for input from a wider range of diverse workers across the globe, but this is only a benefit if the security of the communications solution can be ensured.

Instant Messaging

Instant messaging (IM) is a mechanism that allows for real-time text-based chat between two users located anywhere on the Internet. Some IM utilities allow for file transfer, multimedia, voice and videoconferencing, and more. Some forms of IM are based on a peer-to-peer service while others use a centralized controlling server. Peer-to-peer-based IM is easy for end users to deploy and use, but it's difficult to manage from a corporate perspective because it's generally insecure. It has numerous vulnerabilities: It's susceptible to packet sniffing, it lacks true native security capabilities, and it provides no protection for privacy.

Many forms of instant messaging lack common security features, such as encryption or user privacy. Many IM clients are susceptible to malicious code deposit or infection through their file transfer capabilities. Also, IM users are often subject to numerous forms of social-engineering attacks, such as impersonation or convincing a victim to reveal information that should remain confidential (such as passwords).

Manage Email Security

Email is one of the most widely and commonly used Internet services. The email infrastructure employed on the Internet primarily consists of email servers using Simple Mail Transfer Protocol (SMTP) to accept messages from clients, transport those messages to other servers, and deposit them into a user's server-based inbox. In addition to email servers, the infrastructure includes email clients. Clients retrieve email from their server-based inboxes using Post Office Protocol version 3 (POP3) or Internet Message

Access Protocol (IMAP). Clients communicate with email servers using SMTP. Many Internet-compatible email systems rely on the X.400 standard for addressing and message handling.

Sendmail is the most common SMTP server for Unix systems and Exchange is the most common SMTP server for Microsoft systems. In addition to these three popular products, numerous alternatives exist, but they all share the same basic functionality and compliance with Internet email standards.

If you deploy an SMTP server, it is imperative that you properly configure authentication for both inbound and outbound mail. SMTP is designed to be a mail relay system. This means it relays mail from sender to intended recipient. However, you want to avoid turning your SMTP server into an *open relay* (also known as an open relay agent or *relay agent*), which is an STMP server that does not authenticate senders before accepting and relaying mail. Open relays are prime targets for spammers because they allow spammers to send out floods of emails by piggybacking on an insecure email infrastructure. As open relays are locked down, becoming closed or authentication relays, a growing number of SMTP attacks are occurring through hijacked authenticated user accounts.

Email Security Goals

For email, the basic mechanism in use on the Internet offers the efficient delivery of messages but lacks controls to provide for confidentiality, integrity, or even availability. In other words, basic email is not secure. However, you can add security to email in many ways. Adding security to email may satisfy one or more of the following objectives:

- Provide for nonrepudiation
- Restrict access to messages to their intended recipients (i.e., privacy and confidentiality)
- Maintain the integrity of messages
- Authenticate and verify the source of messages
- Verify the delivery of messages
- Classify sensitive content within or attached to messages

As with any aspect of IT security, email security begins in a security policy approved by upper management. Within the security policy, you must address several issues:

- Acceptable use policies for email
- Access control
- Privacy
- Email management
- Email backup and retention policies

Acceptable use policies define what activities can and cannot be performed over an organization's email infrastructure. It is often stipulated that professional, business-oriented email and a limited amount of personal email can be sent and received. Specific restrictions are usually placed on performing personal business (that is, work for another organization, including self-employment) and sending or receiving illegal, immoral, or offensive communications as well as on engaging in any other activities that would have a detrimental effect on productivity, profitability, or public relations.

Access control over email should be maintained so that users have access only to their specific inbox and email archive databases. An extension of this rule implies that no other user, authorized or not, can gain access to an individual's email. Access control should provide for both legitimate access and some level of privacy, at least from other employees and unauthorized intruders.

The mechanisms and processes used to implement, maintain, and administer email for an organization should be clarified. End users may not need to know the specifics of email management, but they do need to know whether email is considered private communication. Email has recently been the focus of numerous court cases in which archived messages were used as evidence—often to the chagrin of the author or recipient of those messages. If email is to be retained (that is, backed up and stored in archives for future use), users need to be made aware of this. If email is to be reviewed for violations by an auditor, users need to be informed of this as well. Some companies have elected to retain only the last three months of email archives before they are destroyed, whereas others have opted to retain email for years. Depending upon your country and industry, there are often regulations that dictate retention policies.

Understand Email Security Issues

The first step in deploying email security is to recognize the vulnerabilities specific to email. The protocols used to support email do not employ encryption. Thus, all messages are transmitted in the form in which they are submitted to the email server, which is often plain text. This makes interception and eavesdropping easy. However, the lack of native encryption is one of the least important security issues related to email.

Email is a common delivery mechanism for viruses, worms, Trojan horses, documents with destructive macros, and other malicious code. The proliferation of support for various scripting languages, autodownload capabilities, and autoexecute features has transformed hyperlinks within the content of email and attachments into a serious threat to every system.

Email offers little in the way of source verification. Spoofing the source address of email is a simple process for even a novice attacker. Email headers can be modified at their source or at any point during transit. Furthermore, it is also possible to deliver email directly to a user's inbox on an email server by directly connecting to the email server's SMTP port. And speaking of in-transit modification, there are no native integrity checks to ensure that a message was not altered between its source and destination.

In addition, email itself can be used as an attack mechanism. When sufficient numbers of messages are directed to a single user's inbox or through a specific STMP server, a denial-of-service (DoS) attack can result. This attack is often called mail-bombing and is simply a DoS performed by inundating a system with messages. The DoS can be the result of storage capacity consumption or processing capability utilization. Either way, the result is the same: Legitimate messages cannot be delivered.

Like email flooding and malicious code attachments, unwanted email can be considered an attack. Sending unwanted, inappropriate, or irrelevant messages is called spamming. Spamming is often little more than a nuisance, but it does waste system resources both locally and over the Internet. It is often difficult to stop spam because the source of the messages is usually spoofed.

Email Security Solutions

Imposing security on email is possible, but the efforts should be in tune with the value and confidentiality of the messages being exchanged. You can use several protocols, services, and solutions to add security to email without requiring a complete overhaul of the entire Internet-based SMTP infrastructure. These include S/MIME, MOSS, PEM, and PGP. We'll discuss S/MIME further in Chapter 7, "PKI and Cryptographic Applications."

Secure Multipurpose Internet Mail Extensions (S/MIME) Secure Multipurpose Internet Mail Extensions is an email security standard that offers authentication and confidentiality to email through public key encryption and digital signatures. Authentication is provided through X.509 digital certificates. Privacy is provided through the use of Public Key Cryptography Standard (PKCS) encryption. Two types of messages can be formed using S/MIME: signed messages and secured enveloped messages. A signed message provides integrity, sender authentication, and nonrepudiation. An enveloped message provides integrity, sender authentication, and confidentiality.

MIME Object Security Services (MOSS) MIME Object Security Services can provide authentication, confidentiality, integrity, and nonrepudiation for email messages. MOSS employs Message Digest 2 (MD2) and MD5 algorithms; Rivest, Shamir, and Adelman (RSA) public key; and Data Encryption Standard (DES) to provide authentication and encryption services.

Privacy Enhanced Mail (PEM) Privacy Enhanced Mail is an email encryption mechanism that provides authentication, integrity, confidentiality, and nonrepudiation. PEM uses RSA, DES, and X.509.

DomainKeys Identified Mail (DKIM) DKIM is a means to assert that valid mail is sent by an organization through verification of domain name identity. See `http://www.dkim.org`.

Pretty Good Privacy (PGP) Pretty Good Privacy (PGP) is a public-private key system that uses a variety of encryption algorithms to encrypt files and email messages. The first version of PGP used RSA, the second version, International Data Encryption Algorithm (IDEA), but later versions offered a spectrum of algorithm options. PGP is not a standard but rather an independently developed product that has wide Internet grassroots support.

Real World Scenario

Free PGP Solution

PGP started off as a free product for all to use, but it has since splintered into various divergent products. PGP is a commercial product, while OpenPGP is a developing standard that GnuPG is compliant with and that was independently developed by the Free Software Foundation. If you have not used PGP before, we recommend downloading the appropriate GnuPG version for your preferred email platform. This secure solution is sure to improve your email privacy and integrity. You can learn more about GnuPG at `http://gnupg.org`. You can learn more about PGP by visiting its pages on Wikipedia.

By using these and other security mechanisms for email and communication transmissions, you can reduce or eliminate many of the security vulnerabilities of email. Digital signatures can help eliminate impersonation. The encryption of messages reduces eavesdropping. And the use of email filters keep spamming and mail-bombing to a minimum.

Blocking attachments at the email gateway system on your network can ease the threats from malicious attachments. You can have a 100 percent no-attachments policy or block only attachments that are known or suspected to be malicious, such as attachments with extensions that are used for executable and scripting files. If attachments are an essential part of your email communications, you'll need to train your users and use antivirus tools for protection. Training users to avoid contact with suspicious or unexpected attachments greatly reduces the risk of malicious code transference via email. Antivirus software is generally effective against known viruses, but it offers little protection against new or unknown viruses.

Real World Scenario

Fax Security

Fax communications are waning in popularity because of the widespread use of email. Electronic documents are easily exchanged as attachments to email. Printed documents are just as easy to scan and email as they are to fax. However, you must still address faxing in your overall security plan. Most modems give users the ability to connect to a remote computer system and send and receive faxes. Many operating systems include built-in fax capabilities, and there are numerous fax products for computer systems. Faxes sent from a computer's fax/modem can be received by another computer, by a regular fax machine, or by a cloud-based fax service.

Even with declining use, faxes still represent a communications path that is vulnerable to attack. Like any other telephone communication, faxes can be intercepted and are susceptible to eavesdropping. If an entire fax transmission is recorded, it can be played back by another fax machine to extract the transmitted documents.

Some of the mechanisms that can be deployed to improve the security of faxes are fax encryptors, link encryption, activity logs, and exception reports. A fax encryptor gives a fax machine the capability to use an encryption protocol to scramble the outgoing fax signal. The use of an encryptor requires that the receiving fax machine support the same encryption protocol so it can decrypt the documents. Link encryption is the use of an encrypted communication path, like a VPN link or a secured telephone link, to transmit the fax. Activity logs and exception reports can be used to detect anomalies in fax activity that could be symptoms of attack.

In addition to the security of a fax transmission, it is important to consider the security of a received fax. Faxes that are automatically printed may sit in the out tray for a long period of time, therefore making them subject to viewing by unintended recipients. Studies have shown that adding banners of CONFIDENTIAL, PRIVATE, and so on spur the curiosity of passersby. So, disable automatic printing. Also, avoid fax machines that retain a copy of the fax in memory or on a local storage device. Consider integrating your fax system with your network so you can email faxes to intended recipients instead of printing them to paper.

Remote Access Security Management

Telecommuting, or working remotely, has become a common feature of business computing. Telecommuting usually requires remote access, the ability of a distant client to establish a communication session with a network. Remote access can take the following forms (among others):

- Using a modem to dial up directly to a remote access server
- Connecting to a network over the Internet through a VPN
- Connecting to a terminal server system through a thin-client connection

The first two examples use fully capable clients. They establish connections just as if they were directly connected to the LAN. In the last example, all computing activities occur on the terminal server system rather than on the distant client.

Telecommuting also usually involves telephone communications. Telephony is the collection of methods by which telephone services are provided to an organization or the mechanisms by which an organization uses telephone services for either voice and/or data communications. Traditionally, telephony included plain old telephone service (POTS)—also called public switched telephone network (PSTN)—combined with modems. However, private branch exchange (PBX), VoIP, and VPNs are commonly used for telephone communications as well.

Real World Scenario

Remote Access and Telecommuting Techniques

Telecommuting is performing work at a remote location (i.e., other than the primary office). In fact, there is a good chance that you perform some form of telecommuting as part of your current job. Telecommuting clients use many remote access techniques to establish connectivity to the central office LAN. There are four main types of remote access techniques:

Service Specific Service-specific remote access gives users the ability to remotely connect to and manipulate or interact with a single service, such as email.

Remote Control Remote-control remote access grants a remote user the ability to fully control another system that is physically distant from them. The monitor and keyboard act as if they are directly connected to the remote system.

Screen Scraper/Scraping This term can be used in two different circumstances. First, it is sometimes used to refer to remote control, remote access, or remote desktop services. These services are also called virtual applications or virtual desktops. The idea is that the screen on the target machine is scraped and shown to the remote operator. Since remote access to resources presents additional risks of disclosure or compromise during the distance transmission, it is important to employ encrypted screen scraper solutions.

Second, screen scraping is a technology that can allow an automated tool to interact with a human interface. For example, some stand-alone data-gathering tools use search engines in their operation. However, most search engines must be used through their normal web interface. For example, Google requires that all searches be performed through a Google web search form field. (In the past, Google offered an API that enabled products to interact with the backend directly. However, Google terminated this practice to support the integration of advertisements with search results.) Screen-scraping technology can interact with the human-friendly designed web front end to the search engine and then parse the web page results to extract just the relevant information. SiteDigger from Foundstone/McAfee is a great example of this type of product.

Remote Node Operation Remote node operation is just another name for dial-up connectivity. A remote system connects to a remote access server. That server provides the remote client with network services and possible Internet access.

POTS and PSTN refer to traditional landline telephone connections. POTS/PSTN connections were the only or primary remote network links for many businesses until high-speed, cost-effective, and ubiquitous access methods were available. POTS/PSTN also waned in use for home-user Internet connectivity once broadband and wireless services became more widely available. POTS/PSTN connections are sometimes still used as a backup option for remote connections when broadband solutions fail, as rural Internet and remote connections, and as standard voice lines when ISDN or VoIP are unavailable or not cost effective.

When remote access capabilities are deployed in any environment, security must be considered and implemented to provide protection for your private network against remote access complications:

- Remote access users should be stringently authenticated before being granted access.
- Only those users who specifically need remote access for their assigned work tasks should be granted permission to establish remote connections.
- All remote communications should be protected from interception and eavesdropping. This usually requires an encryption solution that provides strong protection for the authentication traffic as well as all data transmission.

It is important to establish secure communication channels before initiating the transmission of sensitive, valuable, or personal information. Remote access can pose several potential security concerns if not protected and monitored sufficiently:

- If anyone with a remote connection can attempt to breach the security of your organization, the benefits of physical security are reduced.
- Telecommuters might use insecure or less-secure remote systems to access sensitive data and thus expose it to greater risk of loss, compromise, or disclosure.
- Remote systems might be exposed to malicious code and could be used as a carrier to bring malware into the private LAN.
- Remote systems might be less physically secure and thus be at risk of being used by unauthorized entities or stolen.
- Remote systems might be more difficult to troubleshoot, especially if the issues revolve around remote connection.
- Remote systems might not be as easy to upgrade or patch due to their potential infrequent connections or slow throughput links.

Plan Remote Access Security

When outlining your remote access security management strategy, be sure to address the following issues:

Remote Connectivity Technology Each type of connection has its own unique security issues. Fully examine every aspect of your connection options. This can include modems, DSL, ISDN, wireless networking, satellite, and cable modems.

Transmission Protection There are several forms of encrypted protocols, encrypted connection systems, and encrypted network services or applications. Use the appropriate combination of secured services for your remote connectivity needs. This can include VPNs, SSL, TLS, Secure Shell (SSH), IPSec, and L2TP.

Authentication Protection In addition to protecting data traffic, you must ensure that all logon credentials are properly secured. This requires the use of an authentication protocol and may mandate the use of a centralized remote access authentication system. This can include Password Authentication Protocol (PAP), Challenge Handshake Authentication Protocol (CHAP), Extensible Authentication Protocol (EAP, or its extensions PEAP or LEAP), Remote Authentication Dial-In User Service (RADIUS), and Terminal Access Controller Access Control System Plus (TACACS+).

Remote User Assistance Remote access users may periodically require technical assistance. You must have a means established to provide this as efficiently as possible. This can include, for example, addressing software and hardware issues and user training issues. If an organization is unable to provide a reasonable solution for remote user technical support, it could result in loss of productivity, compromise of the remote system, or an overall breach of organizational security.

If it is difficult or impossible to maintain a similar level of security on a remote system as is maintained in the private LAN, remote access should be reconsidered in light of the security risks it represents. Network Access Control (NAC) can assist with this but may burden slower connections with large update and patch transfers.

The ability to use remote access or establish a remote connection should be tightly controlled. You can control and restrict the use of remote connectivity by means of filters, rules, or access controls based on user identity, workstation identity, protocol, application, content, and time of day.

To restrict remote access to only authorized users, you can use callback and caller ID. Callback is a mechanism that disconnects a remote user upon initial contact and then immediately attempts to reconnect to them using a predefined phone number (in other words, the number defined in the user account's security database). Callback does have a user-defined mode. However, this mode is not used for security; it is used to reverse toll charges to the company rather than charging the remote client. Caller ID verification can be used for the same purpose as callback—by potentially verifying the physical location (via phone number) of the authorized user.

It should be a standard element in your security policy that no unauthorized modems be present on any system connected to the private network. You may need to further specify this policy by indicating that those with portable systems must either remove their modems before connecting to the network or boot with a hardware profile that disables the modem's device driver.

Dial-Up Protocols

When a remote connection link is established, a protocol must be used to govern how the link is actually created and to establish a common communication foundation over which other protocols can work. It is important to select protocols that support security whenever possible. At a minimum, a means to secure authentication is needed, but adding the option for data encryption is also preferred. The two primary examples of dial-up protocols, PPP and SLIP, provide link governance, not only for true dial-up links but also for some VPN links:

Point-to-Point Protocol (PPP) This is a full-duplex protocol used for transmitting TCP/IP packets over various non-LAN connections, such as modems, ISDN, VPNs, Frame Relay, and so on. PPP is widely supported and is the transport protocol of choice for dial-up Internet connections. PPP authentication is protected through the use of various protocols, such as CHAP and PAP. PPP is a replacement for SLIP and can support any LAN protocol, not just TCP/IP.

Serial Line Internet Protocol (SLIP) This is an older technology developed to support TCP/IP communications over asynchronous serial connections, such as serial cables or modem dial-up. SLIP is rarely used but is still supported on many systems. It can support only IP, requires static IP addresses, offers no error detection or correction, and does not support compression.

NOTE One of the many proprietary dial-up protocols is Microcom Networking Protocol (MNP). MNP was found on Microcom modems in the 1990s. It supports its own form of error control called Echoplex.

Centralized Remote Authentication Services

As remote access becomes a key element in an organization's business functions, it is often important to add layers of security between remote clients and the private network. Centralized remote authentication services, such as RADIUS and TACACS+, provide this extra layer of protection. These mechanisms provide a separation of the authentication and authorization processes for remote clients that performed for LAN or local clients. The separation is important for security because if the RADIUS or TACACS+ servers are ever compromised, then only remote connectivity is affected, not the rest of the network.

Remote Authentication Dial-In User Service (RADIUS) This is used to centralize the authentication of remote dial-up connections. A network that employs a RADIUS server is configured so the remote access server passes dial-up user logon credentials to the RADIUS server for authentication. This process is similar to the process used by domain clients sending logon credentials to a domain controller for authentication.

Terminal Access Controller Access-Control System (TACACS+) This is an alternative to RADIUS. TACACS is available in three versions: original TACACS, Extended TACACS (XTACACS), and TACACS+. TACACS integrates the authentication and authorization processes. XTACACS keeps the authentication, authorization, and accounting processes separate. TACACS+ improves XTACACS by adding two-factor authentication. TACACS+ is the most current and relevant version of this product line.

Virtual Private Network

A virtual private network (VPN) is a communication tunnel that provides point-to-point transmission of both authentication and data traffic over an intermediary untrusted network. Most VPNs use encryption to protect the encapsulated traffic, but encryption is not necessary for the connection to be considered a VPN.

VPNs are most commonly associated with establishing secure communication paths through the Internet between two distant networks. However, they can exist anywhere, including within private networks or between end-user systems connected to an ISP. The VPN can link two networks or two individual systems. They can link clients, servers, routers, firewalls, and switches. VPNs are also helpful in providing security for legacy applications that rely on risky or vulnerable communication protocols or methodologies, especially when communication is across a network.

VPNs can provide confidentiality and integrity over insecure or untrusted intermediary networks. They do not provide or guarantee availability. VPNs also are in relatively widespread use to get around location requirements for services like Netflix and Hulu and thus provide a (at times questionable) level of anonymity.

Tunneling

Before you can truly understand VPNs, you must first understand tunneling. *Tunneling* is the network communications process that protects the contents of protocol packets by encapsulating them in packets of another protocol. The encapsulation is what creates the logical illusion of a communications tunnel over the untrusted intermediary network. This virtual path exists between the encapsulation and the de-encapsulation entities located at the ends of the communication.

In fact, sending a snail mail letter to your grandmother involves the use of a tunneling system. You create the personal letter (the primary content protocol packet) and place it in an envelope (the tunneling protocol). The envelope is delivered through the postal service (the untrusted intermediary network) to its intended recipient.You can use tunneling in many situations, such as when you're bypassing firewalls, gateways, proxies, or other traffic control devices. The bypass is achieved by encapsulating the restricted content inside packets that are authorized for transmission. The tunneling process prevents the traffic control devices from blocking or dropping the communication because such devices don't know what the packets actually contain.

Tunneling is often used to enable communications between otherwise disconnected systems. If two systems are separated by a lack of network connectivity, a communication link can be established by a modem dial-up link or other remote access or wide area network (WAN) networking service. The actual LAN traffic is encapsulated in whatever communication protocol is used by the temporary connection, such as Point-to-Point Protocol in the case of modem dial-up. If two networks are connected by a network employing a different protocol, the protocol of the separated networks can often be encapsulated within the intermediary network's protocol to provide a communication pathway.

Regardless of the actual situation, tunneling protects the contents of the inner protocol and traffic packets by encasing, or wrapping, it in an authorized protocol used by the intermediary network or connection. Tunneling can be used if the primary protocol is not routable and to keep the total number of protocols supported on the network to a minimum.

Real World Scenario

The Proliferation of Tunneling

Tunneling is such a common activity within communication systems that many of us use tunneling on a regular basis without even recognizing it. For example, every time you access a website using a secured SSL or TLS connection, you are using tunneling. Your plain-text web communications are being tunneled within an SSL or TLS session. Also, if you use Internet telephone or VoIP systems, your voice communication is being tunneled inside a VoIP protocol.

How many other instances of tunneling can you pinpoint that you encounter on a weekly basis?

If the act of encapsulating a protocol involves encryption, tunneling can provide a means to transport sensitive data across untrusted intermediary networks without fear of losing confidentiality and integrity.

Tunneling is not without its problems. It is generally an inefficient means of communicating because most protocols include their own error detection, error handling, acknowledgment, and session management features, so using more than one protocol at a time compounds the overhead required to communicate a single message. Furthermore, tunneling creates either larger packets or additional packets that in turn consume additional network bandwidth. Tunneling can quickly saturate a network if sufficient bandwidth is not available. In addition, tunneling is a point-to-point communication mechanism and is not designed to handle broadcast traffic. Tunneling also makes it difficult, if not impossible, to monitor the content of the traffic in some circumstances, creating issues for security practitioners.

How VPNs Work

A VPN link can be established over any other network communication connection. This could be a typical LAN cable connection, a wireless LAN connection, a remote access dial-up connection, a WAN link, or even a client using an Internet connection for access to an office LAN. A VPN link acts just like a typical direct LAN cable connection; the only possible difference would be speed based on the intermediary network and on the connection types between the client system and the server system. Over a VPN link, a client can perform the same activities and access the same resources as if they were directly connected via a LAN cable.

VPNs can connect two individual systems or two entire networks. The only difference is that the transmitted data is protected only while it is within the VPN tunnel. Remote access servers or firewalls on the network's border act as the start points and endpoints for VPNs.

Thus, traffic is unprotected within the source LAN, protected between the border VPN servers, and then unprotected again once it reaches the destination LAN.

VPN links through the Internet for connecting to distant networks are often inexpensive alternatives to direct links or leased lines. The cost of two high-speed Internet links to local ISPs to support a VPN is often significantly less than the cost of any other connection means available.

Common VPN Protocols

VPNs can be implemented using software or hardware solutions. In either case, there are four common VPN protocols: PPTP, L2F, L2TP, and IPSec. PPTP, L2F, and L2TP operate at the Data Link layer (layer 2) of the OSI model. PPTP and IPSec are limited for use on IP networks, whereas L2F and L2TP can be used to encapsulate any LAN protocol.

NOTE

SSL/TLS can also be used as a VPN protocol, not just as a session encryption tool operating on top of TCP. The CISSP exam does not seem to include SSL/TLS VPN content at this time.

Point-to-Point Tunneling Protocol

Point-to-Point Tunneling Protocol (PPTP) is an encapsulation protocol developed from the dial-up Point-to-Point Protocol. It operates at the Data Link layer (layer 2) of the OSI model and is used on IP networks. PPTP creates a point-to-point tunnel between two systems and encapsulates PPP packets. It offers protection for authentication traffic through the same authentication protocols supported by PPP:

- Microsoft Challenge Handshake Authentication Protocol (MS-CHAP)
- Challenge Handshake Authentication Protocol (CHAP)
- Password Authentication Protocol (PAP)
- Extensible Authentication Protocol (EAP)
- Shiva Password Authentication Protocol (SPAP)

NOTE

The CISSP exam focuses on the RFC 2637 version of PPTP, not the Microsoft implementation, which was customized using proprietary modifications to support data encryption using Microsoft Point-to-Point Encryption (MPPE).

The initial tunnel negotiation process used by PPTP is not encrypted. Thus, the session establishment packets that include the IP address of the sender and receiver—and can include usernames and hashed passwords—could be intercepted by a third party. PPTP is used on VPNs, but it is often replaced by the L2TP, which can use IPSec to provide traffic encryption for VPNs.

PPTP does not support TACACS+ and RADIUS.

Layer 2 Forwarding Protocol and Layer 2 Tunneling Protocol

Cisco developed its own VPN protocol called Layer 2 Forwarding (L2F), which is a mutual authentication tunneling mechanism. However, L2F does not offer encryption. L2F was not widely deployed and was soon replaced by L2TP. As their names suggest, both operate at layer 2. Both can encapsulate any LAN protocol.

Layer 2 Tunneling Protocol (L2TP) was derived by combining elements from both PPTP and L2F. L2TP creates a point-to-point tunnel between communication endpoints. It lacks a built-in encryption scheme, but it typically relies on IPSec as its security mechanism. L2TP also supports TACACS+ and RADIUS. IPSec is commonly used as a security mechanism for L2TP.

IP Security Protocol

The most commonly used VPN protocol is now IPSec. IP Security (IPSec) is both a standalone VPN protocol and the security mechanism for L2TP, and it can be used only for IP traffic. IPSec works only on IP networks and provides for secured authentication as well as encrypted data transmission. IPSec has two primary components, or functions:

Authentication Header (AH) AH provides authentication, integrity, and nonrepudiation.

Encapsulating Security Payload (ESP) ESP provides encryption to protect the confidentiality of transmitted data, but it can also perform limited authentication. It operates at the Network layer (layer 3) and can be used in transport mode or tunnel mode. In transport mode, the IP packet data is encrypted but the header of the packet is not. In tunnel mode, the entire IP packet is encrypted and a new header is added to the packet to govern transmission through the tunnel.

Table 12.1 illustrates the main characteristics of VPN protocols.

TABLE 12.1 VPN characteristics

VPN Protocol	Native Authentication Protection	Native Data Encryption	Protocols Supported	Dial-Up Links Supported	Number of Simultaneous Connections
PPTP	Yes	No	PPP	Yes	Single point-to-point
L2F	Yes	No	PPP/SLIP	Yes	Single point-to-point
L2TP	Yes	No (can use IPSec)	PPP	Yes	Single point-to-point
IPSec	Yes	Yes	IP only	No	Multiple

NOTE

The VPN protocols which encapsulate PPP are able to support any sub-protocol compatible with PPP, which includes IPv4, IPv6, IPX, and AppleTalk.

A VPN device is a network add-on device used to create VPN tunnels separately from server or client OSs. The use of the VPN devices is transparent to networked systems.

Virtual LAN

A virtual LAN (VLAN) is used for hardware-imposed network segmentation. VLANs are used to logically segment a network without altering its physical topology.

VLANs are created by switches. By default, all ports on a switch are part of VLAN #1. But as the switch administrator changes the VLAN assignment on a port-by-port basis, various ports can be grouped together and be distinct from other VLAN port designations. Thus, multiple logical network segments can be created on the same physical network.

Communication between ports within the same VLAN occurs without hindrance. Communication between VLANs can be denied or enabled using a routing function. Routing can be provided by an external router or by the internal software of the switch (suggested by the term multilayer switch).

VLAN management is the use of VLANs to control traffic for security or performance reasons. VLANs perform several traffic management functions, some of which are security related:

- Control and restrict broadcast traffic. Block broadcasts between subnets and VLANs.
- Isolate traffic between network segments. By default, different VLANs do not have a route for communication with each other. You can also allow communication between VLANs but specify a deny filter between certain VLANs (or certain members of a VLAN).
- Reduce a network's vulnerability to sniffers.
- Protect against broadcast storms (floods of unwanted broadcast network traffic).

Another element of some VLAN deployments is that of port isolation or private ports. These are private VLANs that are configured to use a dedicated or reserved uplink port. The members of a private VLAN or a port-isolated VLAN can interact only with each other and over the predetermined exit port or uplink port. A common implementation of port isolation occurs in hotels. A hotel network can be configured so that the Ethernet ports in each room or suite are isolated on unique VLANs so that connections in the same unit can communicate, but connections between units cannot. However, all of these private VLANs have a path out to the Internet (i.e., the uplink port).

TIP

VLANs work like subnets, but keep in mind that they are not actual subnets. VLANs are created by switches. Subnets are created by IP address and subnet mask assignments.

VLAN Management for Security

Any network segment that does not need to communicate with another to accomplish a work task/function should not be able to do so. Use VLANs to allow what is necessary, but block/deny anything not necessary. Remember, "deny by default; allow by exception" is not just a guideline for firewall rules but for security in general.

Virtualization

Virtualization technology is used to host one or more operating systems within the memory of a single host computer. This mechanism allows virtually any OS to operate on any hardware. Such an OS is also known as a guest operating system. From the perspective that there is an original or host OS installed directly on the computer hardware, the additional OSes hosted by the hypervisor system are guests. It also allows multiple operating systems to work simultaneously on the same hardware. Common examples include VMWare, Microsoft's Virtual PC, Microsoft Virtual Server, Hyper-V with Windows Server 2008, VirtualBox, and Apple's Parallels.

Virtualized servers and services are indistinguishable from traditional servers and services from a user's perspective.

Virtualization has several benefits, such as being able to launch individual instances of servers or services as needed, real-time scalability, and being able to run the exact OS version needed for the needed application. Additionally, recovery from damaged, crashed, or corrupted virtual systems is often quick: Simply replace the virtual system's main hard drive file with a clean backup version and then relaunch it.

In relation to security, virtualization offers several benefits. It is often easier and faster to make backups of entire virtual systems than the equivalent native hardware installed system. Plus, when there is an error or problem, the virtual system can be replaced by a backup in minutes. Malicious code compromise or infection of virtual systems rarely affects the host OS. This allows for safe testing and experimentation.

Virtualization is used for a wide variety of new architectures and system design solutions. Cloud computing is ultimately a form of virtualization (see Chapter 9, "Security Vulnerabilities, Threats, and Countermeasures," for more on cloud computing). Locally (or at least within an organization's private infrastructure), virtualization can be used to host servers, client operating systems, limited user interfaces (i.e., virtual desktops), applications, and more.

Virtual Software

A *virtual application* is a software product deployed in such a way that it is fooled into believing it is interacting with a full host OS. A virtual (or virtualized) application has been packaged or encapsulated to make it portable and able to operate without the full installation of its original host OS. A virtual application has enough of the original host OS included in its encapsulation bubble (technically called a virtual machine, or VM) that it operates/functions as if it was traditionally installed. Some forms of virtual applications are used as portable apps (short for applications) on USB drives. Other virtual applications are designed to be executed on alternate host OS platforms—for example, running a Windows application within a Linux OS.

The term *virtual desktop* refers to at least three different types of technology:

- A remote access tool that grants the user access to a distant computer system by allowing remote viewing and control of the distant desktop's display, keyboard, mouse, and so on.
- An extension of the virtual application concept encapsulating multiple applications and some form of "desktop" or shell for portability or cross-OS operation. This technology offers some of the features/benefits/applications of one platform to users of another without the need for multiple computers, dual-booting, or virtualizing an entire OS platform.
- An extended or expanded desktop larger than the display being used allows the user to employ multiple application layouts, switching between them using keystrokes or mouse movements.

See Chapter 8, "Principles of Security Models, Design, and Capabilities," and Chapter 9, "Security Vulnerabilities, Threats, and Countermeasures," for more information on virtualization as part of security architecture and design.

Virtual Networking

The concept of OS virtualization has given rise to other virtualization topics, such as virtualized networks. A virtualized network or network virtualization is the combination of hardware and software networking components into a single integrated entity. The resulting system allows for software control over all network functions: management, traffic shaping, address assignment, and so on. A single management console or interface can be used to oversee every aspect of the network, a task requiring physical presence at each hardware component in the past. Virtualized networks have become a popular means of infrastructure deployment and management by corporations worldwide. They allow organizations to implement or adapt other interesting network solutions, including software-defined networks, virtual SANs, guest operating systems, and port isolation.

Software-defined networking (SDN) is a unique approach to network operation, design, and management. The concept is based on the theory that the complexities of a traditional network with on-device configuration (i.e., routers and switches) often force an organization to stick with a single device vendor, such as Cisco, and limit the flexibility of the network to adapt to changing physical and business conditions. SDN aims at separating the infrastructure layer (i.e., hardware and hardware-based settings) from the control layer (i.e., network services of data transmission management). Furthermore, this also removes the traditional networking concepts of IP addressing, subnets, routing, and the like from needing to be programmed into or be deciphered by hosted applications.

SDN offers a new network design that is directly programmable from a central location, is flexible, is vendor neutral, and is open standards based. Using SDN frees an organization from having to purchase devices from a single vendor. It instead allows organizations to mix and match hardware as needed, such as to select the most cost-effective or highest throughput–rated devices regardless of vendor. The configuration and management of hardware are then controlled through a centralized management interface. In addition, the settings applied to the hardware can be changed and adjusted dynamically as needed.

Another way of thinking about SDN is that it is effectively network virtualization. It allows data transmission paths, communication decision trees, and flow control to be virtualized in the SDN control layer rather than being handled on the hardware on a per-device basis.

Another interesting development arising out of the concept of virtualized networks is that of a virtual SAN (storage area network). A SAN is a network technology that combines multiple individual storage devices into a single consolidated network-accessible storage container. A virtual SAN or a software-defined shared storage system is a virtual re-creation of a SAN on top of a virtualized network or an SDN.

Network Address Translation

The goals of hiding the identity of internal clients, masking the design of your private network, and keeping public IP address leasing costs to a minimum are all simple to achieve through the use of network address translation (NAT). NAT is a mechanism for converting the internal IP addresses found in packet headers into public IP addresses for transmission over the Internet.

NAT was developed to allow private networks to use any IP address set without causing collisions or conflicts with public Internet hosts with the same IP addresses. In effect, NAT translates the IP addresses of your internal clients to leased addresses outside your environment.

NAT offers numerous benefits, including the following:

- You can connect an entire network to the Internet using only a single (or just a few) leased public IP addresses.
- You can use the private IP addresses defined in RFC 1918 in a private network and still be able to communicate with the Internet.
- NAT hides the IP addressing scheme and network topography from the Internet.
- NAT restricts connections so that only traffic stemming from connections originating from the internal protected network is allowed back into the network from the Internet. Thus, most intrusion attacks are automatically repelled.

Real World Scenario

Are You Using NAT?

Most networks, whether at an office or at home, employ NAT. There are at least three ways to tell whether you are working within a NATed network:

1. Check your client's IP address. If it is one of the RFC 1918 addresses and you are still able to interact with the Internet, then you are on a NATed network.
2. Check the configuration of your proxy, router, firewall, modem, or gateway device to see whether NAT is configured. (This action requires authority and access to the networking device.)
3. If your client's IP address is not an RFC 1918 address, then compare your address to what the Internet thinks your address is. You can do this by visiting any of the IP-checking websites; a popular one is `http://whatismyipaddress.com`. If your client's IP address and the address that What Is My IP Address claims is your address are different, then you are working from a NATed network.

NOTE: Frequently, security professionals refer to NAT when they really mean PAT. By definition, NAT maps one internal IP address to one external IP address. However, port address translation (PAT) maps one internal IP address to an external IP address and port number combination. Thus, PAT can theoretically support 65,536 (2^16) simultaneous communications from internal clients over a single external leased IP address. So with NAT, you must lease as many public IP addresses as you want to have for simultaneous communications, while with PAT you can lease fewer IP addresses and obtain a reasonable 100:1 ratio of internal clients to external leased IP addresses.

NAT is part of a number of hardware devices and software products, including firewalls, routers, gateways, and proxies. It can be used only on IP networks and operates at the Network layer (layer 3).

Private IP Addresses

The use of NAT has proliferated recently because of the increased scarcity of public IP addresses and security concerns. With only roughly 4 billion addresses (232) available in IPv4, the world has simply deployed more devices using IP than there are unique IP addresses available. Fortunately, the early designers of the Internet and TCP/IP had good foresight and put aside a few blocks of addresses for private, unrestricted use. These IP addresses, commonly called the private IP addresses, are defined in RFC 1918. They are as follows:

- 10.0.0.0–10.255.255.255 (a full Class A range)

- 172.16.0.0–172.31.255.255 (16 Class B ranges)
- 192.168.0.0–192.168.255.255 (256 Class C ranges)

Real World Scenario

Can't NAT Again!

On several occasions we've needed to re-NAT an already NATed network. This might occur in the following situations:

- You need to make an isolated subnet within a NATed network and attempt to do so by connecting a router to host your new subnet to the single port offered by the existing network.
- You have a DSL or cable modem that offers only a single connection but you have multiple computers or want to add wireless to your environment.

By connecting a NAT proxy router or a wireless access point, you are usually attempting to re-NAT what was NATed to you initially. One configuration setting that can either make or break this setup is the IP address range in use. It is not possible to re-NAT the same subnet. For example, if your existing network is offering 192.168.1.x addresses, then you cannot use that same address range in your new NATed subnet. So, change the configuration of your new router/WAP to perform NAT on a slightly different address range, such as 192.168.5.x, so you won't have the conflict. This seems obvious, but it is quite frustrating to troubleshoot the unwanted result without this insight.

All routers and traffic-directing devices are configured by default not to forward traffic to or from these IP addresses. In other words, the private IP addresses are not routed by default. Thus, they cannot be directly used to communicate over the Internet. However, they can be easily used on private networks where routers are not employed or where slight modifications to router configurations are made. Using private IP addresses in conjunction with NAT greatly reduces the cost of connecting to the Internet by allowing fewer public IP addresses to be leased from an ISP.

WARNING

Attempting to use these private IP addresses directly on the Internet is futile because all publicly accessible routers will drop data packets containing a source or destination IP address from these RFC 1918 ranges.

Stateful NAT

NAT operates by maintaining a mapping between requests made by internal clients, a client's internal IP address, and the IP address of the Internet service contacted. When a request packet is received by NAT from a client, it changes the source address in the packet from the client's to the NAT server's. This change is recorded in the NAT mapping database along with the destination address. Once a reply is received from the Internet server, NAT matches the reply's source address to an address stored in its mapping database and then uses the linked client address to redirect the response packet to its intended destination. This process is known as stateful NAT because it maintains information about the communication sessions between clients and external systems.

NAT can operate on a one-to-one basis with only a single internal client able to communicate over one of its leased public IP addresses at a time. This type of configuration can result in a bottleneck if more clients attempt Internet access than there are public IP addresses. For example, if there are only five leased public IP addresses, the sixth client must wait until an address is released before its communications can be transmitted over the Internet. Other forms of NAT employ multiplexing techniques in which port numbers are used to allow the traffic from multiple internal clients to be managed on a single leased public IP address. Technically, this multiplexing form of NAT is known as port address translation (PAT) or overloaded NAT, but it seems that the industry still uses the term *NAT* to refer to this newer version.

Static and Dynamic NAT

You can use NAT in two modes: static and dynamic.

Static NAT Use static mode NAT when a specific internal client's IP address is assigned a permanent mapping to a specific external public IP address. This allows for external entities to communicate with systems inside your network even if you are using RFC 1918 IP addresses.

Dynamic NAT Use dynamic mode NAT to grant multiple internal clients access to a few leased public IP addresses. Thus, a large internal network can still access the Internet without having to lease a large block of public IP addresses. This keeps public IP address usage abuse to a minimum and helps keep Internet access costs to a minimum.

In a dynamic mode NAT implementation, the NAT system maintains a database of mappings so that all response traffic from Internet services is properly routed to the original internal requesting client. Often NAT is combined with a proxy server or proxy firewall to provide additional Internet access and content-caching features.

NAT is not directly compatible with IPSec because it modifies packet headers, which IPSec relies on to prevent security violations. However, there are versions of NAT proxies designed to support IPSec over NAT. Specifically, NAT-Traversal (RFC 3947) was designed to support IPSec VPNs through the use of UDP encapsulation of IKE. IP Security (IPSec) is a standards-based mechanism for providing encryption for point-to-point TCP/IP traffic.

Automatic Private IP Addressing

Automatic Private IP Addressing (APIPA), aka link-local address assignment (defined in RFC 3927), assigns an IP address to a system in the event of a DHCP assignment failure.

APIPA is primarily a feature of Windows. APIPA assigns each failed DHCP client with an IP address from the range of 169.254.0.1 to 169.254.255.254 along with the default Class B subnet mask of 255.255.0.0. This allows the system to communicate with other APIPA-configured clients within the same broadcast domain but not with any system across a router or with a correctly assigned IP address.

NOTE: Don't confuse APIPA with the private IP address ranges, defined in RFC 1918.

APIPA is not usually directly concerned with security. However, it is still an important issue to understand. If you notice that a system is assigned an APIPA address instead of a valid network address, that indicates a problem. It could be as mundane as a bad cable or power failure on the DHCP server, but it could also be a symptom of a malicious attack on the DHCP server. You might be asked to decipher issues in a scenario where IP addresses are presented. You should be able to discern whether an address is a public address, an RFC 1918 private address, an APIPA address, or a loopback address.

Converting IP Address Numbers

IP addresses and subnet masks are actual binary numbers, and through their use in binary, all the functions of routing and traffic management occur. Therefore, it is a good idea to know how to convert between decimal, binary, and even hexadecimal. Also, don't forget how to convert from a dotted-decimal notation IP address (such as 172.16.1.1) to its binary equivalent (that is, 10101100000100000000000100000001). And it is probably not a bad idea to be able to convert the 32-bit binary number to a single decimal number (that is, 2886729985). Knowledge of number conversions comes in handy when attempting to identify obfuscated addresses. If you are rusty in this skill area, take advantage of online conversion primers, such as at the following location:

`http://www.mathsisfun.com/binary-decimal-hexadecimal-converter.html`

Real World Scenario

The Loopback Address

Another IP address range that you should be careful not to confuse with the private IP address ranges defined in RFC 1918 is the loopback address. The loopback address is purely a software entity. It is an IP address used to create a software interface that connects to itself via TCP/IP. The loopback address allows for the testing of local network settings in spite of missing, damaged, or nonfunctional network hardware and related

(Continues)

(Continued)

device drivers. Technically, the entire 127.x.x.x network is reserved for loopback use. However, only the 127.0.0.1 address is widely used.

Windows XP SP2 (and possibly other OS updates) restricted the client to use only 127.0.0.1 as the loopback address. This caused several applications that used other addresses in the upper ranges of the 127.x.x.x network services to fail. In restricting client use to only 127.0.0.1, Microsoft has attempted to open up a wasted Class A address. Even if this tactic is successful for Microsoft, it will affect only Windows systems.

Switching Technologies

When two systems (individual computers or LANs) are connected over multiple intermediary networks, the task of transmitting data packets from one to the other is a complex process. To simplify this task, switching technologies were developed. The first switching technology was circuit switching.

Circuit Switching

Circuit switching was originally developed to manage telephone calls over the public switched telephone network. In circuit switching, a dedicated physical pathway is created between the two communicating parties. Once a call is established, the links between the two parties remain the same throughout the conversation. This provides for fixed or known transmission times, a uniform level of quality, and little or no loss of signal or communication interruptions. Circuit-switching systems employ permanent, physical connections. However, the term *permanent* applies only to each communication session. The path is permanent throughout a single conversation. Once the path is disconnected, if the two parties communicate again, a different path may be assembled. During a single conversation, the same physical or electronic path is used throughout the communication and is used only for that one communication. Circuit switching grants exclusive use of a communication path to the current communication partners. Only after a session has been closed can a pathway be reused by another communication.

Real World Scenario

Real-World Circuit Switching

There is very little real-world circuit switching in the modern world (or at least in the past 10 to 15 years or so). Packet switching, discussed next, has become ubiquitous for data and voice transmissions. Decades ago we could often point to the plain old telephone service (POTS)—also called public switched telephone network (PSTN)—as a prime example of circuit switching, but with the advent of digital switching and VoIP systems, those days are long gone. That's not to say that circuit switching is nonexistent in today's world; it is just not being used for data transmission. Instead, you can still find circuit switching in rail yards, irrigation systems, and even electrical distribution systems.

Packet Switching

Eventually, as computer communications increased as opposed to voice communications, a new form of switching was developed. Packet switching occurs when the message or communication is broken up into small segments (usually fixed-length packets, depending on the protocols and technologies employed) and sent across the intermediary networks to the destination. Each segment of data has its own header that contains source and destination information. The header is read by each intermediary system and is used to route each packet to its intended destination. Each channel or communication path is reserved for use only while a packet is actually being transmitted over it. As soon as the packet is sent, the channel is made available for other communications.

Packet switching does not enforce exclusivity of communication pathways. It can be seen as a logical transmission technology because addressing logic dictates how communications traverse intermediary networks between communication partners. Table 12.2 compares circuit switching to packet switching.

TABLE 12.2 Circuit Switching vs. Packet Switching

Circuit Switching	Packet Switching
Constant traffic	Bursty traffic
Fixed known delays	Variable delays
Connection oriented	Connectionless
Sensitive to connection loss	Sensitive to data loss
Used primarily for voice	Used for any type of traffic

In relation to security, there are a few potential issues to consider. A packet-switching system places data from different sources on the same physical connection. This could lend itself to disclosure, corruption, or eavesdropping. Proper connection management, traffic isolation, and usually encryption are needed to protect against shared physical pathway concerns. A benefit of packet-switching networks is that they are not as dependent on specific physical connections as circuit switching is. Thus, when or if a physical pathway is damaged or goes offline, an alternate path can be used to continue the data/packet delivery. A circuit-switching network is often interrupted by physical path violations.

Virtual Circuits

A virtual circuit (also called a communication path) is a logical pathway or circuit created over a packet-switched network between two specific endpoints. Within packet-switching systems are two types of virtual circuits:

- Permanent virtual circuits (PVCs)
- Switched virtual circuits (SVCs)

A PVC is like a dedicated leased line; the logical circuit always exists and is waiting for the customer to send data. A PVC is a predefined virtual circuit that is always available. The virtual circuit may be closed down when not in use, but it can be instantly reopened whenever needed. An SVC is more like a dial-up connection because a virtual circuit has to be created using the best paths currently available before it can be used and then disassembled after the transmission is complete. In either type of virtual circuit, when a data packet enters point A of a virtual circuit connection, that packet is sent directly to point B or the other end of the virtual circuit. However, the actual path of one packet may be different from the path of another packet from the same transmission. In other words, multiple paths may exist between point A and point B as the ends of the virtual circuit, but any packet entering at point A will end up at point B.

A PVC is like a two-way radio or walkie-talkie. Whenever communication is needed, you press the button and start talking; the radio reopens the predefined frequency automatically (that is, the virtual circuit). An SVC is more like a shortwave or ham radio. You must tune the transmitter and receiver to a new frequency every time you want to communicate with someone.

WAN Technologies

Wide area network links are used to connect distant networks, nodes, or individual devices together. This can improve communications and efficiency, but it can also place data at risk. Proper connection management and transmission encryption is needed to ensure a secure connection, especially over public network links. WAN links and long-distance connection technologies can be divided into two primary categories:

A dedicated line (also called a leased line or point-to-point link) is one that is indefinably and continually reserved for use by a specific customer (see Table 12.3). A dedicated line is always on and waiting for traffic to be transmitted over it. The link between the customer's LAN and the dedicated WAN link is always open and established. A dedicated line connects two specific endpoints and only those two endpoints.

TABLE 12.3 Examples of dedicated lines

Technology	Connection Type	Speed
Digital Signal Level 0 (DS-0)	Partial T1	64 Kbps up to 1.544 Mbps
Digital Signal Level 1 (DS-1)	T1	1.544 Mbps
Digital Signal Level 3 (DS-3)	T3	44.736 Mbps
European digital transmission format 1	EI	2.108 Mbps
European digital transmission format 3	E3	34.368 Mbps
Cable modem or cable routers		10+ Mbps

A nondedicated line is one that requires a connection to be established before data transmission can occur. A nondedicated line can be used to connect with any remote system that uses the same type of nondedicated line.

Achieving Fault Tolerance with Carrier Network Connections

To obtain fault tolerance with leased lines or with connections to carrier networks (that is, Frame Relay, ATM, SONET, SMDS, X.25, and so on), you must deploy two redundant connections. For even greater redundancy, you should purchase the connections from two different telcos or service providers. However, when you're using two different service providers, be sure they don't connect to the same regional backbone or share any major pipeline. The physical location of multiple communication lines leading from your building is also of concern because a single disaster or human error (e.g., a misguided backhoe) could cause multiple lines to fail at once. If you cannot afford to deploy an exact duplicate of your primary leased line, consider a nondedicated DSL, ISDN, or cable modem connection. These less-expensive options may still provide partial availability in the event of a primary leased line failure.

Standard modems, DSL, and ISDN are examples of nondedicated lines. Digital subscriber line (DSL) is a technology that exploits the upgraded telephone network to grant consumers speeds from 144 Kbps to 6 Mbps (or more). There are numerous formats of DSL, such as ADSL, xDSL, CDSL, HDSL, SDSL, RASDSL, IDSL, and VDSL. Each format varies as to the specific downstream and upstream bandwidth provided.

TIP

For the exam, just worry about the general idea of DSL instead of trying to memorize all the details about the various DSL subformats.

The maximum distance a DSL line can be from a central office (that is, a specific type of distribution node of the telephone network) is approximately 1,000 meters.

Integrated Services Digital Network (ISDN) is a fully digital telephone network that supports both voice and high-speed data communications. There are two standard classes, or formats, of ISDN service:

Basic Rate Interface (BRI) offers customers a connection with two B channels and one D channel. The B channels support a throughput of 64 Kbps and are used for data transmission. The D channel is used for call establishment, management, and teardown and has a bandwidth of 16 Kbps. Even though the D channel was not designed to support data transmissions, a BRI ISDN is said to offer consumers 144 Kbps of total throughput.

Primary Rate Interface (PRI) offers consumers a connection with multiple 64 Kbps B channels (2 to 23 of them) and a single 64 Kbps D channel. Thus, a PRI can be deployed with as little as 192 Kbps and up to 1.544 Mbps. However, remember that those numbers are bandwidth, not throughput, because they include the D channel, which cannot be used for actual data transmission (at least not in most normal commercial implementations).

TIP

When considering connection options, don't forget about satellite connections. Satellite connections may offer high-speed solutions even in locales that are inaccessible by cable-based, radio-wave-based, and line-of-sight-based communications. Satellites are usually considered insecure because of their large surface footprint: Communications over a satellite can be intercepted by anyone. But if you have strong encryption, satellite communications can be reasonably secured. Just think of satellite radio. As long as you have a receiver, you can get the signal anywhere. But without a paid service plan, you can't gain access to the audio content.

WAN Connection Technologies

Numerous WAN connection technologies are available to companies that need communication services between multiple locations and even external partners. These WAN technologies vary greatly in cost and throughput. However, most share the common feature of being transparent to the connected LANs or systems. A WAN switch, specialized router, or border connection device provides all the interfacing needed between the network carrier service and a company's LAN. The border connection device is called the channel service unit/data service unit (CSU/DSU). These devices convert LAN signals into the format used by the WAN carrier network and vice versa. The CSU/DSU contains data terminal equipment/data circuit-terminating equipment (DTE/DCE), which provides the actual connection point for the LAN's router (the DTE) and the WAN carrier network's switch (the DCE). The CSU/DSU acts as a translator, a store-and-forward device, and a link conditioner. A WAN switch is simply a specialized version of a LAN switch that is constructed with a built-in CSU/DSU for a specific type of carrier network. There are many types of carrier networks, or WAN connection technologies, such as X.25, Frame Relay, ATM, and SMDS.

X.25 WAN Connections

X.25 is an older packet-switching technology that was widely used in Europe. It uses permanent virtual circuits to establish specific point-to-point connections between two systems or networks. It is the predecessor to Frame Relay and operates in much the same fashion. However, X.25 use is declining because of its lower performance and throughput rates when compared to Frame Relay or ATM.

Frame Relay Connections

Like X.25, Frame Relay is a packet-switching technology that also uses PVCs (see the discussion of virtual circuits). However, unlike X.25, Frame Relay supports multiple PVCs over a single WAN carrier service connection. Frame Relay is a layer 2 connection mechanism that uses packet-switching technology to establish virtual circuits between communication endpoints. Unlike dedicated or leased lines, for which cost is based primarily on the distance between endpoints, Frame Relay's cost is primarily based on the amount of data transferred. The Frame Relay network is a shared medium across which virtual circuits are created to provide point-to-point communications. All virtual circuits are independent of and invisible to each other.

A key concept related to Frame Relay is the committed information rate (CIR). The CIR is the guaranteed minimum bandwidth a service provider grants to its customers. It is usually significantly less than the actual maximum capability of the provider network. Each customer may have a different CIR established and defined in their contract. The service network provider may allow customers to exceed their CIR over short intervals when additional bandwidth is available. This is known as bandwidth on demand. (Although at first this might sound like an outstanding benefit, the reality is that the customer is charged a premium rate for the extra consumed bandwidth.) Frame Relay operates at layer 2 (the Data Link layer) of the OSI model as a connection-oriented packet-switching transmission technology.

Frame Relay requires the use of DTE/DCE at each connection point. The customer owns the DTE, which acts like a router or a switch and provides the customer's network with access to the Frame Relay network. The Frame Relay service provider owns the DCE, which performs the actual transmission of data over the Frame Relay as well as establishing and maintaining the virtual circuit for the customer.

ATM

Asynchronous transfer mode (ATM) is a cell-switching WAN communication technology, as opposed to a packet-switching technology like Frame Relay. It fragments communications into fixed-length 53-byte cells. The use of fixed-length cells allows ATM to be very efficient and offer high throughputs. ATM can use either PVCs or SVCs. As with Frame

Relay providers, ATM providers can guarantee a minimum bandwidth and a specific level of quality to their leased services. Customers can often consume additional bandwidth as needed when available on the service network for an additional pay-as-you-go fee. ATM is a connection-oriented packet-switching technology.

SMDS

Switched Multimegabit Data Service (SMDS) is a connectionless packet-switching technology. Often, SMDS is used to connect multiple LANs to form a metropolitan area network (MAN) or a WAN. SMDS was often a preferred connection mechanism for linking remote LANs that communicate infrequently. SMDS supports high-speed bursty traffic and bandwidth on demand. It fragments data into small transmission cells. SMDS can be considered a forerunner to ATM because of the similar technologies used.

Specialized Protocols

Some WAN connection technologies require additional specialized protocols to support various types of specialized systems or devices. Three of these protocols are SDLC, HDLC, and HSSI:

Synchronous Data Link Control (SDLC) Synchronous Data Link Control is used on permanent physical connections of dedicated leased lines to provide connectivity for mainframes, such as IBM Systems Network Architecture (SNA) systems. SDLC uses polling, operates at OSI layer 2 (the Data Link layer), and is a bit-oriented synchronous protocol.

High-Level Data Link Control (HDLC) High-Level Data Link Control is a refined version of SDLC designed specifically for serial synchronous connections. HDLC supports full-duplex communications and supports both point-to-point and multipoint connections. HDLC, like SDLC, uses polling and operates at OSI layer 2 (the Data Link layer). HDLC offers flow control and includes error detection and correction.

High Speed Serial Interface (HSSI) High Speed Serial Interface is a DTE/DCE interface standard that defines how multiplexors and routers connect to high-speed network carrier services such as ATM or Frame Relay. A multiplexor is a device that transmits multiple communications or signals over a single cable or virtual circuit. HSSI defines the electrical and physical characteristics of the interfaces or connection points and thus operates at OSI layer 1 (the Physical layer).

Dial-Up Encapsulation Protocols

The Point-to-Point Protocol (PPP) is an encapsulation protocol designed to support the transmission of IP traffic over dial-up or point-to-point links. PPP allows for multivendor interoperability of WAN devices supporting serial links. All dial-up and most point-to-point connections are serial in nature (as opposed to parallel). PPP includes a wide range of communication services, including the assignment and management of IP addresses, management of synchronous communications, standardized encapsulation, multiplexing, link configuration, link quality testing, error detection, and feature or option negotiation (such as compression).

PPP was originally designed to support CHAP and PAP for authentication. However, recent versions of PPP also support MS-CHAP, EAP, and SPAP. PPP can also be used to support Internetwork Packet Exchange (IPX) and DECnet protocols. PPP is an Internet standard documented in RFC 1661. It replaced the Serial Line Internet Protocol (SLIP). SLIP offered no authentication, supported only half-duplex communications, had no error-detection capabilities, and required manual link establishment and teardown.

Miscellaneous Security Control Characteristics

When you're selecting or deploying security controls for network communications, you need to evaluate numerous characteristics in light of your circumstances, capabilities, and security policy. We discuss these issues in the following sections.

Transparency

Just as the name implies, transparency is the characteristic of a service, security control, or access mechanism that ensures that it is unseen by users. Transparency is often a desirable feature for security controls. The more transparent a security mechanism is, the less likely a user will be able to circumvent it or even be aware that it exists. With transparency, there is a lack of direct evidence that a feature, service, or restriction exists, and its impact on performance is minimal.

In some cases, transparency may need to function more as a configurable feature than as a permanent aspect of operation, such as when an administrator is troubleshooting, evaluating, or tuning a system's configurations.

Verify Integrity

To verify the integrity of a transmission, you can use a checksum called a hash total. A hash function is performed on a message or a packet before it is sent over the communication pathway. The hash total obtained is added to the end of the message and is called the message digest. Once the message is received, the hash function is performed by the destination system, and the result is compared to the original hash total. If the two hash totals match, then there is a high level of certainty that the message has not been altered or corrupted during transmission. Hash totals are similar to cyclic redundancy checks (CRCs) in that they both act as integrity tools. In most secure transaction systems, hash functions are used to guarantee communication integrity.

Real World Scenario

Checking the Hash

Checking the hash value of files is always a good idea. This simple task can prevent the use of corrupted files and prevent the accidental acceptance of maligned data. Several intrusion detection systems (IDSs) and system integrity verification tools use hashing as a means to check that files did not change over time. This is done by creating a hash for every file on a drive, storing those hashes in a database, and then periodically recalculating hashes for files and checking the new hash against the historical one. If there is ever any difference in the hashes, then you should investigate the file.

Another common use of hashes is to verify downloads. Many trusted Internet download sites provide MD5 and SHA hash totals for the files they offer. You can take advantage of these hashes in at least two ways. First, you can use a download manager that automatically checks the hashes for you upon download completion. Second, you can obtain a hashing tool, such as md5sum or sha1sum, to generate your own hash values. Then manually compare your generated value from the downloaded file against the claimed hash value from the download site. This mechanism ensures that the file you ultimately have on your system matches, to the last bit, the file from the download site.

Record sequence checking is similar to a hash total check; however, instead of verifying content integrity, it verifies packet or message sequence integrity. Many communications services employ record sequence checking to verify that no portions of a message were lost and that all elements of the message are in their proper order.

Transmission Mechanisms

Transmission logging is a form of auditing focused on communications. Transmission logging records the particulars about source, destination, time stamps, identification codes, transmission status, number of packets, size of message, and so on. These pieces of information may be useful in troubleshooting problems and tracking down unauthorized communications or used against a system as a means to extract data about how it functions.

Transmission error correction is a capability built into connection- or session-oriented protocols and services. If it is determined that a message, in whole or in part, was corrupted, altered, or lost, a request can be made for the source to resend all or part of the message. Retransmission controls determine whether all or part of a message is retransmitted in the event that a transmission error correction system discovers a problem with a communication. Retransmission controls can also determine whether multiple copies of a hash total or CRC value are sent and whether multiple data paths or communication channels are employed.

Security Boundaries

A security boundary is the line of intersection between any two areas, subnets, or environments that have different security requirements or needs. A security boundary exists between a high-security area and a low-security one, such as between a LAN and the Internet. It is important to recognize the security boundaries both on your network and in the physical world. Once you identify a security boundary, you need to deploy mechanisms to control the flow of information across those boundaries.

Divisions between security areas can take many forms. For example, objects may have different classifications. Each classification defines what functions can be performed by which subjects on which objects. The distinction between classifications is a security boundary.

Security boundaries also exist between the physical environment and the logical environment. To provide logical security, you must provide security mechanisms that are different from those used to provide physical security. Both must be present to provide a complete security structure, and both must be addressed in a security policy. However, they are different and must be assessed as separate elements of a security solution.

Security boundaries, such as a perimeter between a protected area and an unprotected one, should always be clearly defined. It's important to state in a security policy the point at which control ends or begins and to identify that point in both the physical and logical environments. Logical security boundaries are the points where electronic communications interface with devices or services for which your organization is legally responsible. In most cases, that interface is clearly marked, and unauthorized subjects are informed that they do not have access and that attempts to gain access will result in prosecution.

The security perimeter in the physical environment is often a reflection of the security perimeter of the logical environment. In most cases, the area over which the organization is legally responsible determines the reach of a security policy in the physical realm. This can be the walls of an office, the walls of a building, or the fence around a campus. In secured environments, warning signs are posted indicating that unauthorized access is prohibited and attempts to gain access will be thwarted and result in prosecution.

When transforming a security policy into actual controls, you must consider each environment and security boundary separately. Simply deduce what available security mechanisms would provide the most reasonable, cost-effective, and efficient solution for a specific environment and situation. However, all security mechanisms must be weighed against the value of the objects they are to protect. Deploying countermeasures that cost more than the value of the protected objects is unwarranted.

Prevent or Mitigate Network Attacks

Communication systems are vulnerable to attacks in much the same way any other aspect of the IT infrastructure is vulnerable. Understanding the threats and possible countermeasures is an important part of securing an environment. Any activity or condition that can cause harm to data, resources, or personnel must be addressed and mitigated if possible. Keep in mind that harm includes more than just destruction or damage; it also includes disclosure, access delay, denial of access, fraud, resource waste, resource abuse, and loss. Common threats against communication system security include denial of service, eavesdropping, impersonation, replay, and modification.

DoS and DDoS

A denial-of-service attack is a resource consumption attack that has the primary goal of preventing legitimate activity on a victimized system. A DoS attack renders the target unable to respond to legitimate traffic.

There are two basic forms of denial of service:

- Attacks exploiting a vulnerability in hardware or software. This exploitation of a weakness, error, or standard feature of software intends to cause a system to hang, freeze, consume all system resources, and so on. The end result is that the victimized computer is unable to process any legitimate tasks.
- Attacks that flood the victim's communication pipeline with garbage network traffic. These attacks are sometimes called traffic generation or flooding attacks. The end result is that the victimized computer is unable to send or receive legitimate network communications.

In either case, the victim has been denied the ability to perform normal operations (services).

DoS isn't a single attack but rather an entire class of attacks. Some attacks exploit flaws in operating system software, whereas others focus on installed applications, services, or protocols. Some attacks exploit specific protocols, including Internet Protocol (IP), Transmission Control Protocol (TCP), Internet Control Message Protocol (ICMP), and User Datagram Protocol (UDP).

DoS attacks typically occur between one attacker and one victim. However, they aren't always that simple. Most DoS attacks employ some form of intermediary system (usually an unwilling and unknowing participant) to hide the attacker from the victim. For example, if an attacker sends attack packets directly to a victim, it's possible for the victim to discover who the attacker is. This is made more difficult, although not impossible, through the use of spoofing (described in more detail elsewhere in this chapter).

Many DoS attacks begin by compromising or infiltrating one or more intermediary systems that then serve as launch points or attack platforms. These intermediary systems are commonly referred to as secondary victims. The attacker installs remote-control tools, often called *bots*, *zombies*, or *agents*, onto these systems. Then, at an appointed time or in response to a launch command from the attacker, the DoS attack is conducted against the victim. The victim may be able to discover zombied systems that are causing the DoS attack but probably won't be able to track down the actual attacker. Attacks involving zombied systems are known as distributed denial-of-service (DDoS) attacks. Deployments of numerous bots or zombies across numerous unsuspecting secondary victims have become known as *botnets*.

Here are some countermeasures and safeguards against these attacks:

- Add firewalls, routers, and intrusion detection systems (IDSs) that detect DoS traffic and automatically block the port or filter out packets based on the source or destination address.

- Maintain good contact with your service provider in order to request filtering services when a DoS occurs.
- Disable echo replies on external systems.
- Disable broadcast features on border systems.
- Block spoofed packets from entering or leaving your network.
- Keep all systems patched with the most current security updates from vendors.
- Consider commercial DoS protection/response services like CloudFlare's DDoS mitigation or Prolexic. These can be expensive, but they are often effective.

For further discussion of DoS and DDoS, see Chapter 17, "Preventing and Responding to Incidents."

Eavesdropping

As the name suggests, *eavesdropping* is simply listening to communication traffic for the purpose of duplicating it. The duplication can take the form of recording data to a storage device or using an extraction program that dynamically attempts to extract the original content from the traffic stream. Once a copy of traffic content is in the hands of an attacker, they can often extract many forms of confidential information, such as usernames, passwords, process procedures, data, and so on.

Eavesdropping usually requires physical access to the IT infrastructure to connect a physical recording device to an open port or cable splice or to install a software-recording tool onto the system. Eavesdropping is often facilitated by the use of a network traffic capture or monitoring program or a protocol analyzer system (often called a *sniffer*). Eavesdropping devices and software are usually difficult to detect because they are used in passive attacks. When eavesdropping or wiretapping is transformed into altering or injecting communications, the attack is considered an active attack.

Real World Scenario

You Too Can Eavesdrop on Networks

Eavesdropping on networks is the act of collecting packets from the communication medium. As a valid network client, you are limited to seeing just the traffic designated for your system. However, with the right tool (and authorization from your organization!), you can see all the data that passes your network interface. Sniffers such as Wireshark and NetWitness and dedicated eavesdropping tools such as T-Sight, Zed Attack Proxy (ZAP), and Cain & Abel can show you what is going on over the network. Some tools will display only the raw network packets, while others will reassemble the original data and display it for you in real time on your screen. We encourage you to experiment with a few eavesdropping tools (only on networks where you have the proper approval) so you can see firsthand what can be gleaned from network communications.

You can combat eavesdropping by maintaining physical access security to prevent unauthorized personnel from accessing your IT infrastructure. As for protecting communications that occur outside your network or for protecting against internal attackers, using encryption (such as IPSec or SSH) and one-time authentication methods (that is, one-time pads or token devices) on communication traffic will greatly reduce the effectiveness and timeliness of eavesdropping.

The common threat of eavesdropping is one of the primary motivations to maintain reliable communications security. While data is in transit, it is often easier to intercept than when it is in storage. Furthermore, the lines of communication may lie outside your organization's control. Thus, reliable means to secure data while in transit outside your internal infrastructure are of utmost importance. Some of the common network health and communication reliability evaluation and management tools, such as sniffers, can be used for nefarious purposes and thus require stringent controls and oversight to prevent abuse.

Impersonation/Masquerading

Impersonation, or *masquerading*, is the act of pretending to be someone or something you are not to gain unauthorized access to a system. This usually implies that authentication credentials have been stolen or falsified in order to satisfy (i.e., successfully bypass) authentication mechanisms. This is different from spoofing, where an entity puts forth a false identity but without any proof (such as falsely using an IP address, MAC addresses, email address, system name, domain name, etc.). Impersonation is often possible through the capture of usernames and passwords or of session setup procedures for network services.

Some solutions to prevent impersonation are using one-time pads and token authentication systems, using Kerberos, and using encryption to increase the difficulty of extracting authentication credentials from network traffic.

Replay Attacks

Replay attacks are an offshoot of impersonation attacks and are made possible through capturing network traffic via eavesdropping. Replay attacks attempt to reestablish a communication session by replaying captured traffic against a system. You can prevent them by using one-time authentication mechanisms and sequenced session identification.

Modification Attacks

In modification attacks, captured packets are altered and then played against a system. Modified packets are designed to bypass the restrictions of improved authentication mechanisms and session sequencing. Countermeasures to modification replay attacks include using digital signature verifications and packet checksum verification.

Address Resolution Protocol Spoofing

The Address Resolution Protocol (ARP) is a subprotocol of the TCP/IP protocol suite and operates at the Network layer (layer 3). ARP is used to discover the MAC address of a system by polling using its IP address. ARP functions by broadcasting a request packet with the target IP address. The system with that IP address (or some other system that already has an ARP mapping for it) will reply with the associated MAC address. The discovered IP-to-MAC mapping is stored in the ARP cache and is used to direct packets.

TIP

If you find the idea of misdirecting traffic through the abuse of the ARP system interesting, then consider experimenting with attacking tools that perform this function. Some of the well-known tools for performing ARP spoofing attacks include Ettercap, Cain & Abel, and arpspoof. Using these tools in combination with a network sniffer (so you can watch the results) will give you great insight into this form of network attack. However, as always, perform these activities only on networks where you have proper approval; otherwise, your attacker activities could land you in legal trouble.

ARP mappings can be attacked through spoofing. Spoofing provides false MAC addresses for requested IP-addressed systems to redirect traffic to alternate destinations. ARP attacks are often an element in man-in-the-middle attacks. Such attacks involve an intruder's system spoofing its MAC address against the destination's IP address into the source's ARP cache. All packets received from the source system are inspected and then forwarded to the actual intended destination system. You can take measures to fight ARP attacks, such as defining static ARP mappings for critical systems, monitoring ARP caches for MAC-to-IP-address mappings, or using an IDS to detect anomalies in system traffic and changes in ARP traffic.

DNS Poisoning, Spoofing, and Hijacking

DNS poisoning and DNS spoofing are also known as resolution attacks. DNS poisoning occurs when an attacker alters the domain-name-to-IP-address mappings in a DNS system to redirect traffic to a rogue system or to simply perform a denial-of-service against a system. DNS spoofing occurs when an attacker sends false replies to a requesting system, beating the real reply from the valid DNS server. This is also technically an exploitation of race conditions. Protections against false DNS results caused by poisoning and spoofing include allowing only authorized changes to DNS, restricting zone transfers, and logging all privileged DNS activity.

In 2008, a fairly significant vulnerability was discovered and disclosed to the world by Dan Kaminsky. The vulnerability lies in the method by which local or caching DNS servers obtain information from root servers regarding the identity of the authoritative servers for a particular domain. By sending falsified replies to a caching DNS server for nonexistent subdomains, an attacker can hijack the entire domain's resolution details. For an excellent detailed explanation on how DNS works and how this vulnerability threatens the current DNS infrastructure, visit "An Illustrated Guide to the Kaminsky DNS Vulnerability" located at `http://unixwiz.net/techtips/iguide-kaminsky-dns-vuln.html`.

The only real solution to this DNS hijacking vulnerability is to upgrade DNS to Domain Name System Security Extensions (DNSSEC). For details, please visit `dnssec.net`.

Hyperlink Spoofing

Yet another related attack is hyperlink spoofing, which is similar to DNS spoofing in that it is used to redirect traffic to a rogue or imposter system or to simply divert traffic away from its intended destination. Hyperlink spoofing can take the form of DNS spoofing or can simply be an alteration of the hyperlink URLs in the HTML code of documents sent to clients. Hyperlink spoofing attacks are usually successful because most users do not verify the domain name in a URL via DNS; rather, they assume that the hyperlink is valid and just click it.

Real World Scenario

Going Phishing?

Hyperlink spoofing is not limited to just DNS attacks. In fact, any attack that attempts to misdirect legitimate users to malicious websites through the abuse of URLs or hyperlinks could be considered hyperlink spoofing. Spoofing is falsifying information, which includes falsifying the relationship between a URL and its trusted and original destination.

Phishing is another attack that commonly involves hyperlink spoofing. The term means fishing for information. Phishing attacks can take many forms, including the use of false URLs.

Be wary of any URL or hyperlink in an email, PDF file, or productivity document. If you want to visit a site offered as such, go to your web browser and manually type in the address, use your own preexisting URL bookmark, or use a trusted search engine to find the site. These methods do involve more work on your part, but they will establish a pattern of safe behavior that will serve you well. There are too many attackers in the world to be casual or lazy about following proffered links and URLs.

An attack related to phishing is *pretexting*, which is the practice of obtaining your personal information under false pretenses. Pretexting is often used to obtain personal identity details that are then sold to others who actually perform the abuse of your credit and reputation.

Protections against hyperlink spoofing include the same precautions used against DNS spoofing as well as keeping your system patched and using the Internet with caution.

Summary

Remote access security management requires security system designers to address the hardware and software components of the implementation along with policy issues, work task issues, and encryption issues. This includes deployment of secure communication protocols. Secure authentication for both local and remote connections is an important foundational element of overall security.

Maintaining control over communication pathways is essential to supporting confidentiality, integrity, and availability for network, voice, and other forms of communication. Numerous attacks are focused on intercepting, blocking, or otherwise interfering with the transfer of data from one location to another. Fortunately, there are also reasonable countermeasures to reduce or even eliminate many of these threats.

Tunneling, or encapsulation, is a means by which messages in one protocol can be transported over another network or communications system using a second protocol. Tunneling can be combined with encryption to provide security for the transmitted message. VPNs are based on encrypted tunneling.

A VLAN is a hardware-imposed network segmentation created by switches. VLANs are used to logically segment a network without altering its physical topology. VLANs are used for traffic management.

Telecommuting, or remote connectivity, has become a common feature of business computing. When remote access capabilities are deployed in any environment, security must be considered and implemented to provide protection for your private network against remote access complications. Remote access users should be stringently authenticated before being granted access; this can include the use of RADIUS or TACACS. Remote access services include Voice over IP (VoIP), multimedia collaboration, and instant messaging.

NAT is used to hide the internal structure of a private network as well as to enable multiple internal clients to gain Internet access through a few public IP addresses. NAT is often a native feature of border security devices, such as firewalls, routers, gateways, and proxies.

In circuit switching, a dedicated physical pathway is created between the two communicating parties. Packet switching occurs when the message or communication is broken up into small segments (usually fixed-length packets, depending on the protocols and technologies employed) and sent across the intermediary networks to the destination. Within packet-switching systems are two types of communication: paths and virtual circuits. A virtual circuit is a logical pathway or circuit created over a packet-switched network between two specific endpoints. There are two types of virtual circuits: permanent virtual circuits (PVCs) and switched virtual circuits (SVCs).

WAN links, or long-distance connection technologies, can be divided into two primary categories: dedicated and nondedicated lines. A dedicated line connects two specific endpoints and only those two endpoints. A nondedicated line is one that requires a connection to be established before data transmission can occur. A nondedicated line can be used to connect with any remote system that uses the same type of nondedicated line. WAN connection technologies include X.25, Frame Relay, ATM, SMDS, SDLC, HDLC, and HSSI.

When selecting or deploying security controls for network communications, you need to evaluate numerous characteristics in light of your circumstances, capabilities, and security policy. Security controls should be transparent to users. Hash totals and CRC checks can be used to verify message integrity. Record sequences are used to ensure sequence integrity of a transmission. Transmission logging helps detect communication abuses.

Virtualization technology is used to host one or more operating systems within the memory of a single host computer. This mechanism allows virtually any OS to operate on any hardware. It also allows multiple operating systems to work simultaneously on the same hardware. Virtualization offers several benefits, such as being able to launch individual instances of servers or services as needed, real-time scalability, and being able to run the exact OS version needed for the application.

Internet-based email is insecure unless you take steps to secure it. To secure email, you should provide for nonrepudiation, restrict access to authorized users, make sure integrity is maintained, authenticate the message source, verify delivery, and even classify sensitive content. These issues must be addressed in a security policy before they can be implemented in a solution. They often take the form of acceptable use policies, access controls, privacy declarations, email management procedures, and backup and retention policies.

Email is a common delivery mechanism for malicious code. Filtering attachments, using antivirus software, and educating users are effective countermeasures against that kind of attack. Email spamming or flooding is a form of denial of service that can be deterred through filters and IDSs. Email security can be improved using S/MIME, MOSS, PEM, and PGP.

Fax and voice security can be improved by using encryption to protect the transmission of documents and prevent eavesdropping. Training users effectively is a useful countermeasure against social engineering attacks.

A security boundary can be the division between one secured area and another secured area, or it can be the division between a secured area and an unsecured area. Both must be addressed in a security policy.

Communication systems are vulnerable to many attacks, including distributed denial-of-service (DDoS), eavesdropping, impersonation, replay, modification, spoofing, and ARP and DNS attacks. Fortunately, effective countermeasures exist for each of these. PBX fraud and abuse and phone phreaking are problems that must also be addressed.

Exam Essentials

Understand the issues around remote access security management. Remote access security management requires that security system designers address the hardware and software components of an implementation along with issues related to policy, work tasks, and encryption.

Be familiar with the various protocols and mechanisms that may be used on LANs and WANs for data communications. These are SKIP, SWIPE, SSL, SET, PPP, SLIP, CHAP, PAP, EAP, and S-RPC. They can also include VPN, TLS/SSL, and VLAN.

Know what tunneling is. Tunneling is the encapsulation of a protocol-deliverable message within a second protocol. The second protocol often performs encryption to protect the message contents.

Understand VPNs. VPNs are based on encrypted tunneling. They can offer authentication and data protection as a point-to-point solution. Common VPN protocols are PPTP, L2F, L2TP, and IPSec.

Be able to explain NAT. NAT protects the addressing scheme of a private network, allows the use of the private IP addresses, and enables multiple internal clients to obtain Internet access through a few public IP addresses. NAT is supported by many security border devices, such as firewalls, routers, gateways, and proxies.

Understand the difference between packet switching and circuit switching. In circuit switching, a dedicated physical pathway is created between the two communicating parties. Packet switching occurs when the message or communication is broken up into small segments and sent across the intermediary networks to the destination. Within packet-switching systems are two types of communication paths, or virtual circuits: permanent virtual circuits (PVCs) and switched virtual circuits (SVCs).

Understand the difference between dedicated and nondedicated lines. A dedicated line is always on and is reserved for a specific customer. Examples of dedicated lines include T1, T3, E1, E3, and cable modems. A nondedicated line requires a connection to be established before data transmission can occur. It can be used to connect with any remote system that uses the same type of nondedicated line. Standard modems, DSL, and ISDN are examples of nondedicated lines.

Know various issues related to remote access security. Be familiar with remote access, dial-up connections, screen scrapers, virtual applications/desktops, and general telecommuting security concerns.

Know the various types of WAN technologies. Know that most WAN technologies require a channel service unit/data service unit (CSU/DSU), sometimes called a WAN switch. There are many types of carrier networks and WAN connection technologies, such as X.25, Frame Relay, ATM, and SMDS. Some WAN connection technologies require additional specialized protocols to support various types of specialized systems or devices. Three of these protocols are SDLC, HDLC, and HSSI.

Understand the differences between PPP and SLIP. The Point-to-Point Protocol (PPP) is an encapsulation protocol designed to support the transmission of IP traffic over dial-up or point-to-point links. PPP includes a wide range of communication services, including assignment and management of IP addresses, management of synchronous communications, standardized encapsulation, multiplexing, link configuration, link quality testing, error detection, and feature or option negotiation (such as compression). PPP was originally designed to support CHAP and PAP for authentication. However, recent versions of PPP also support MS-CHAP, EAP, and SPAP. PPP replaced Serial Line Internet Protocol (SLIP). SLIP offered no authentication, supported only half-duplex communications, had no error-detection capabilities, and required manual link establishment and teardown.

Understand common characteristics of security controls. Security controls should be transparent to users. Hash totals and CRC checks can be used to verify message integrity. Record sequences are used to ensure sequence integrity of a transmission. Transmission logging helps detect communication abuses.

Understand how email security works. Internet email is based on SMTP, POP3, and IMAP. It is inherently insecure. It can be secured, but the methods used must be addressed in a security policy. Email security solutions include using S/MIME, MOSS, PEM, or PGP.

Know how fax security works. Fax security is primarily based on using encrypted transmissions or encrypted communication lines to protect the faxed materials. The primary goal is to prevent interception. Activity logs and exception reports can be used to detect anomalies in fax activity that could be symptoms of attack.

Know the threats associated with PBX systems and the countermeasures to PBX fraud. Countermeasures to PBX fraud and abuse include many of the same precautions you would employ to protect a typical computer network: logical or technical controls, administrative controls, and physical controls.

Understand the security issues related to VoIP. VoIP is at risk for caller ID spoofing, vishing, SPIT, call manager software/firmware attacks, phone hardware attacks, DoS, MitM, spoofing, and switch hopping.

Recognize what a phreaker is. Phreaking is a specific type of attack in which various types of technology are used to circumvent the telephone system to make free long-distance calls, to alter the function of telephone service, to steal specialized services, or even to cause service disruptions. Common tools of phreakers include black, red, blue, and white boxes.

Understand voice communications security. Voice communications are vulnerable to many attacks, especially as voice communications become an important part of network services. You can obtain confidentiality by using encrypted communications. Countermeasures must be deployed to protect against interception, eavesdropping, tapping, and other types of exploitation. Be familiar with voice communication topics, such as POTS, PSTN, PBX, and VoIP.

Be able to explain what social engineering is. Social engineering is a means by which an unknown person gains the trust of someone inside your organization by convincing employees that they are, for example, associated with upper management, technical support, or the help desk. The victim is often encouraged to make a change to their user account on the system, such as reset their password, so the attacker can use it to gain access to the network. The primary countermeasure for this sort of attack is user training.

Explain the concept of security boundaries. A security boundary can be the division between one secured area and another secured area. It can also be the division between a secured area and an unsecured area. Both must be addressed in a security policy.

Understand the various network attacks and countermeasures associated with communications security. Communication systems are vulnerable to many attacks, including distributed denial-of-service (DDoS), eavesdropping, impersonation, replay, modification, spoofing, and ARP and DNS attacks. Be able to supply effective countermeasures for each.

Written Lab

1. Describe the differences between transport mode and tunnel mode of IPSec.
2. Discuss the benefits of NAT.
3. What are the main differences between circuit switching and packet switching?
4. What are some security issues with email and options for safeguarding against them?

Review Questions

1. ______________ is a layer 2 connection mechanism that uses packet-switching technology to establish virtual circuits between the communication endpoints.
   - **A.** ISDN
   - **B.** Frame Relay
   - **C.** SMDS
   - **D.** ATM
2. Tunnel connections can be established over all except for which of the following?
   - **A.** WAN links
   - **B.** LAN pathways
   - **C.** Dial-up connections
   - **D.** Stand-alone systems
3. ______________ is a standards-based mechanism for providing encryption for point-to-point TCP/IP traffic.
   - **A.** UDP
   - **B.** IDEA
   - **C.** IPSec
   - **D.** SDLC
4. Which of the following IP addresses is not a private IP address as defined by RFC 1918?
   - **A.** 10.0.0.18
   - **B.** 169.254.1.119
   - **C.** 172.31.8.204
   - **D.** 192.168.6.43
5. Which of the following cannot be linked over a VPN?
   - **A.** Two distant Internet-connected LANs
   - **B.** Two systems on the same LAN
   - **C.** A system connected to the Internet and a LAN connected to the Internet
   - **D.** Two systems without an intermediary network connection
6. What is needed to allow an external client to initiate a communication session with an internal system if the network uses a NAT proxy?
   - **A.** IPSec tunnel
   - **B.** Static mode NAT
   - **C.** Static private IP address
   - **D.** Reverse DNS

7. Which of the following VPN protocols do not offer native data encryption? (Choose all that apply.)
   A. L2F
   B. L2TP
   C. IPSec
   D. PPTP
8. At which OSI model layer does the IPSec protocol function?
   A. Data Link
   B. Transport
   C. Session
   D. Network
9. Which of the following is not defined in RFC 1918 as one of the private IP address ranges that are not routed on the Internet?
   A. 169.172.0.0–169.191.255.255
   B. 192.168.0.0–192.168.255.255
   C. 10.0.0.0–10.255.255.255
   D. 172.16.0.0–172.31.255.255
10. Which of the following is not a benefit of NAT?
    A. Hiding the internal IP addressing scheme
    B. Sharing a few public Internet addresses with a large number of internal clients
    C. Using the private IP addresses from RFC 1918 on an internal network
    D. Filtering network traffic to prevent brute-force attacks
11. A significant benefit of a security control is when it goes unnoticed by users. What is this called?
    A. Invisibility
    B. Transparency
    C. Diversion
    D. Hiding in plain sight
12. When you're designing a security system for Internet-delivered email, which of the following is least important?
    A. Nonrepudiation
    B. Availability
    C. Message integrity
    D. Access restriction
13. Which of the following is typically not an element that must be discussed with end users in regard to email retention policies?
    A. Privacy
    B. Auditor review

C. Length of retainer
D. Backup method

14. What is it called when email itself is used as an attack mechanism?
A. Masquerading
B. Mail-bombing
C. Spoofing
D. Smurf attack

15. Why is spam so difficult to stop?
A. Filters are ineffective at blocking inbound messages.
B. The source address is usually spoofed.
C. It is an attack requiring little expertise.
D. Spam can cause denial-of-service attacks.

16. Which of the following is a type of connection that can be described as a logical circuit that always exists and is waiting for the customer to send data?
A. ISDN
B. PVC
C. VPN
D. SVC

17. In addition to maintaining an updated system and controlling physical access, which of the following is the most effective countermeasure against PBX fraud and abuse?
A. Encrypting communications
B. Changing default passwords
C. Using transmission logs
D. Taping and archiving all conversations

18. Which of the following can be used to bypass even the best physical and logical security mechanisms to gain access to a system?
A. Brute-force attacks
B. Denial of service
C. Social engineering
D. Port scanning

19. Which of the following is *not* a denial-of-service attack?
A. Exploiting a flaw in a program to consume 100 percent of the CPU
B. Sending malformed packets to a system, causing it to freeze

C. Performing a brute-force attack against a known user account

D. Sending thousands of emails to a single address

20. What authentication protocol offers no encryption or protection for logon credentials?

A. PAP

B. CHAP

C. SSL

D. RADIUS

Managing Identity and Authentication

THE CISSP EXAM TOPICS COVERED IN THIS CHAPTER INCLUDE:

✓ **5. Identity and Access Management**

- A. Control physical and logical access to assets
  - A.1 Information
  - A.2 Systems
  - A.3 Devices
  - A.4 Facilities
- B. Manage identification and authentication of people and devices
  - B.1 Identity management implementation (e.g., SSO, LDAP)
  - B.2 Single/multi-factor authentication (e.g., factors, strength, errors, biometrics)
  - B.3 Accountability
  - B.4 Session management (e.g., timeouts, screen savers)
  - B.5 Registration and proofing of identity
  - B.6 Federated identity management (e.g., SAML)
  - B.7 Credential management systems
- C. Integrate identity as a service (e.g., cloud identity)
- D. Integrate third-party identity services (e.g., on-premise)
- G. Manage the identity and access provisioning lifecycle (e.g., provisioning, review)

The Identity and Access Management domain focuses on issues related to granting and revoking privileges to access data or perform actions on systems. A primary focus is on identification, authentication, authorization, and accountability. In this chapter and in Chapter 14, "Controlling and Monitoring Access," we discuss all the objectives within the Identity and Access Management domain. Be sure to read and study the materials from both chapters to ensure complete coverage of the essential material for this domain.

Controlling Access to Assets

Controlling access to assets is one of the central themes of security, and you'll find that many different security controls work together to provide access control. An asset includes information, systems, devices, facilities, and personnel.

Information An organization's information includes all of its data. Data might be stored in simple files on servers, computers, and smaller devices. It can also be stored on huge databases within a server farm. Access controls attempt to prevent unauthorized access to the information.

Systems An organization's systems include any information technology (IT) systems which provide one or more services. For example, a simple file server that stores user files is a system. Additionally, a web server working with a database server to provide an e-commerce service is a system.

Devices Devices include any computing system, including servers, desktop computers, portable laptop computers, tablets, smartphones, and external devices such as printers. More and more organizations have adopted bring your own device (BYOD) policies allowing employees to connect their personally owned device to an organization's network. Although the devices are the property of their owners, organizational data stored on the devices is still an asset of the organization.

Facilities An organization's facilities include any physical location that it owns or rents. This could be individual rooms, entire buildings, or entire complexes of several buildings. Physical security controls help protect facilities.

Personnel Personnel working for an organization are also a valuable asset to an organization. One of the primary ways to protect personnel is to ensure that adequate safety practices are in place to prevent injury or death.

Comparing Subjects and Objects

Access control addresses more than just controlling which users can access which files or services. It is about the relationships between entities (that is, subjects and objects). Access is the transfer of information from an object to a subject, which makes it important to understand the definition of both subject and object.

Subject A *subject* is an active entity that accesses a passive object to receive information from, or data about, an object. Subjects can be users, programs, processes, computers, or anything else that can access a resource. When authorized, subjects can modify objects.

Object An *object* is a passive entity that provides information to active subjects. Some examples of objects include files, databases, computers, programs, processes, printers, and storage media.

TIP

You can often simplify the access control topics by substituting the word *user* for *subject* and the word *file* for *object*. For example, instead of a subject accesses an object, you can think of it as a user accesses a file. However, it's also important to remember that subjects include more than users and objects include more than just files.

You may have noticed that some examples, such as programs and computers, are listed as both subjects and objects. This is because the roles of subject and object can switch back and forth. In many cases, when two entities interact, they perform different functions. Sometimes they may be requesting information and other times providing information. The key difference is that the subject is always the active entity that receives information about, or data from, the passive object. The object is always the passive entity that provides or hosts the information or data.

As an example, consider a common web application that provides dynamic web pages to users. Users query the web application to retrieve a web page, so the application starts as an object. The web application then switches to a subject role as it queries the user's computer to retrieve a cookie and then queries a database to retrieve information about the user based on the cookie. Finally, the application switches back to an object as it sends dynamic web pages back to the user.

Types of Access Control

Generally, an access control is any hardware, software, or administrative policy or procedure that controls access to resources. The goal is to provide access to authorized subjects and prevent unauthorized access attempts. Access control includes the following overall steps:

1. Identify and authenticate users or other subjects attempting to access resources.
2. Determine whether the access is authorized.

3. Grant or restrict access based on the subject's identity.
4. Monitor and record access attempts.

A broad range of controls is involved in these steps. The three primary control types are preventive, detective, and corrective. Whenever possible you want to prevent any type of security problem or incident. Of course, this isn't always possible and unwanted events occur. When they do, you want to detect the event as soon as possible. If you detect an event, you want to correct it.

There are also four other access control types, commonly known as deterrent, recovery, directive, and compensation access controls.

As you read about the controls in the following list, you'll notice that some are listed as an example in more than one access control type. For example, a fence (or perimeter-defining device) placed around a building can be a preventive control because it physically bars someone from gaining access to a building compound. However, it is also a deterrent control because it discourages someone from trying to gain access.

Preventive Access Control A *preventive control* attempts to thwart or stop unwanted or unauthorized activity from occurring. Examples of preventive access controls include fences, locks, biometrics, mantraps, lighting, alarm systems, separation of duties policies, job rotation policies, data classification, penetration testing, access control methods, encryption, auditing, the presence of security cameras or closed circuit television (CCTV), smartcards, callback procedures, security policies, security awareness training, antivirus software, firewalls, and intrusion prevention systems.

Detective Access Control A *detective control* attempts to discover or detect unwanted or unauthorized activity. Detective controls operate after the fact and can discover the activity only after it has occurred. Examples of detective access controls include security guards, motion detectors, recording and reviewing of events captured by security cameras or CCTV, job rotation policies, mandatory vacation policies, audit trails, honeypots or honeynets, intrusion detection systems, violation reports, supervision and reviews of users, and incident investigations.

Corrective Access Control A *corrective control* modifies the environment to return systems to normal after an unwanted or unauthorized activity has occurred. Corrective controls attempt to correct any problems that occurred as a result of a security incident. Corrective controls can be simple, such as terminating malicious activity or rebooting a system. They also include antivirus solutions that can remove or quarantine a virus, backup and restore plans to ensure that lost data can be restored, and active intrusion detection systems that can modify the environment to stop an attack in progress.

NOTE

Chapter 16, "Managing Security Operations," covers intrusion detection systems and intrusion prevention systems in more depth.

Deterrent Access Control A *deterrent control* attempts to discourage security policy violations. Deterrent and preventive controls are similar, but deterrent controls often depend on individuals deciding not to take an unwanted action. In contrast, a preventive control actually blocks the action. Some examples include policies, security awareness training, locks, fences, security badges, guards, mantraps, and security cameras.

Recovery Access Control A *recovery control* attempts to repair or restore resources, functions, and capabilities after a security policy violation. Recovery controls are an extension of corrective controls but have more advanced or complex abilities. Examples of recovery access controls include backups and restores, fault-tolerant drive systems, system imaging, server clustering, antivirus software, and database or virtual machine shadowing.

Directive Access Control A *directive control* attempts to direct, confine, or control the actions of subjects to force or encourage compliance with security policies. Examples of directive access controls include security policy requirements or criteria, posted notifications, escape route exit signs, monitoring, supervision, and procedures.

Compensation Access Control A *compensation control* provides an alternative when it isn't possible to use a primary control, or when necessary to increase the effectiveness of a primary control. As an example, a security policy might dictate the use of smartcards by all employees but it takes a long time for new employees to get a smartcard. The organization could issue hardware tokens to employees as a compensating control. These tokens provide stronger authentication than just a username and password.

Access controls are also categorized by how they are implemented. Controls can be implemented administratively, logically/technically, or physically. Any of the access control types mentioned previously can include any of these implementation types.

Administrative Access Controls *Administrative access controls* are the policies and procedures defined by an organization's security policy and other regulations or requirements. They are sometimes referred to as management controls. These controls focus on personnel and business practices. Examples of administrative access controls include policies, procedures, hiring practices, background checks, classifying and labeling data, security awareness and training efforts, reports and reviews, personnel controls, and testing.

Logical/Technical Controls *Logical access controls* (also known as *technical access controls*) are the hardware or software mechanisms used to manage access and to provide protection for resources and systems. As the name implies, they use technology. Examples of logical or technical access controls include authentication methods (such as passwords, smartcards, and biometrics), encryption, constrained interfaces, access control lists, protocols, firewalls, routers, intrusion detection systems, and clipping levels.

Physical Controls *Physical access controls* are items you can physically touch. They include physical mechanisms deployed to prevent, monitor, or detect direct contact with systems or areas within a facility. Examples of physical access controls include guards, fences, motion detectors, locked doors, sealed windows, lights, cable protection, laptop locks, badges, swipe cards, guard dogs, video cameras, mantraps, and alarms.

TIP When preparing for the CISSP exam, you should be able to identify the type of any control. For example, you should recognize that a firewall is a preventive control because it can prevent attacks by blocking traffic, whereas an intrusion detection system (IDS) is a detective control because it can detect attacks in progress or after they've occurred. You should also be able to identify both as logical/technical controls.

The CIA Triad

One of the primary reasons organizations implement access control mechanisms is to prevent losses. There are three categories of IT loss: loss of *confidentiality*, loss of *availability*, and loss of *integrity*. Protecting against these losses is so integral to IT security that they are frequently referred to as the *CIA Triad* (or sometimes the AIC Triad or Security Triad).

Confidentiality Access controls help ensure that only authorized subjects can access objects. When unauthorized entities are able to access systems or data, it results in a loss of confidentiality.

Integrity Integrity ensures that data or system configurations are not modified without authorization, or if unauthorized changes occur, security controls detect the changes. If unauthorized or unwanted changes to objects occur, it results in a loss of integrity.

Availability Authorized requests for objects must be granted to subjects within a reasonable amount of time. In other words, systems and data should be available to users and other subjects when they are needed. If the systems are not operational, or the data is not accessible, it results in a loss of availability.

Comparing Identification and Authentication

Identification is the process of a subject claiming, or professing, an identity. A subject must provide an identity to a system to start the authentication, authorization, and accountability processes. Providing an identity might entail typing a username; swiping a smartcard; waving a token device; speaking a phrase; or positioning your face, hand, or finger in front of a camera or in proximity to a scanning device. A core principle with authentication is that all subjects must have unique identities.

Authentication verifies the identity of the subject by comparing one or more factors against a database of valid identities, such as user accounts. Authentication information used to verify identity is private information and needs to be protected. As an example, passwords are rarely stored in clear text within a database. Instead, authentication systems store hashes of passwords within the authentication database. The ability of the subject and system to maintain the secrecy of the authentication information for identities directly reflects the level of security of that system.

Identification and authentication always occur together as a single two-step process. Providing an identity is the first step, and providing the authentication information is the second step. Without both, a subject cannot gain access to a system.

Each authentication technique or factor has unique benefits and drawbacks. Thus, it is important to evaluate each mechanism in the context of the environment where it will be deployed. For example, a facility that processes Top Secret materials requires very strong authentication mechanisms. In contrast, authentication requirements within a classroom environment are significantly less.

TIP

You can simplify identification and authentication by thinking about a username and a password. Users identify themselves with usernames and authenticate (or prove their identity) with passwords. Of course, there are many more identification and authentication methods, but this simplification helps keep the terms clear.

Registration and Proofing of Identity

The registration process occurs when a user is first given an identity. Within an organization, new employees prove their identity with appropriate documentation during the hiring process. Personnel within a Human Resource (HR) department then begin the process of creating their user ID.

Registration is more complex with more secure authentication methods. For example, if the organization uses fingerprinting as a biometric method for authentication, registration includes capturing user fingerprint.

Identity proofing is a little different for users interacting with online sites, such as an online banking site. When a user first tries to create an account, the bank will take extra steps to validate the user's identity. This normally entails asking the user to provide information that is known to the user and the bank such as account numbers and personal information about the user such as a national identification number or Social Security Number.

During this initial registration process, the bank will also ask the user to provide additional information, such as the user's favorite color, the middle name of their oldest sibling, or the model of their first car. Later, if the user needs to change their password or wants to transfer money, the bank can challenge the user with these questions as a method of identity proofing.

Authorization and Accountability

Two additional security elements in an access control system are *authorization* and *accountability*.

Authorization Subjects are granted access to objects based on proven identities. For example, administrators grant users access to files based on the user's proven identity.

Accountability Users and other subjects can be held accountable for their actions when auditing is implemented. Auditing tracks subjects and records when they access objects, creating an audit trail in one or more audit logs. For example, auditing can record when a user reads, modifies, or deletes a file. Auditing provides accountability.

An effective access control system requires strong identification and authentication mechanisms, in addition to authorization and accountability elements. Subjects have unique identities and prove their identity with authentication. Administrators grant access to subjects based on their identities providing authorization. Logging user actions based on their proven identities provides accountability.

In contrast, if users didn't need to log on with credentials, then all users would be anonymous. It isn't possible to restrict authorization to specific users. While logging could still record events, it would not be able to identify which users performed any actions.

Authorization

Authorization indicates who is trusted to perform specific operations. If the action is allowed, the subject is authorized; if disallowed, the subject is not authorized. Here's a simple example: if a user attempts to open a file, the authorization mechanism checks to ensure that the user has at least read permission on the file.

It's important to realize that just because users or other entities can authenticate to a system, that doesn't mean they are given access to anything and everything. Instead, subjects are authorized access to specific objects based on their proven identity. The process of authorization ensures that the requested activity or object access is possible based on the privileges assigned to the subject.

Identification and authentication are "all-or-nothing" aspects of access control. Either a user's credentials prove a professed identity, or they don't. In contrast, authorization occupies a wide range of variations. For example, a user may be able to read a file but not delete it or print a document but not alter the print queue.

Accountability

Auditing, logging, and monitoring provide accountability by ensuring that subjects can be held accountable for their actions. Auditing is the process of tracking and recording subject activities within logs. Logs typically record who took an action, when and where the action was taken, and what the action was. One or more logs create an *audit trail* that researchers can use to reconstruct events and identify security incidents. When investigators review the contents of audit trails, they can provide evidence to hold people accountable for their actions.

There's a subtle but important point to stress about accountability. Accountability relies on effective identification and authentication, but it does not require effective authorization. In other words, after identifying and authenticating users, accountability mechanisms such as audit logs can track their activity, even when they try to access resources that they aren't authorized to access.

Authentication Factors

The three basic methods of authentication are also known as types or factors. They are as follows:

Type 1 A *Type 1 authentication factor* is something you know. Examples include a password, personal identification number (PIN), or passphrase.

Type 2 A *Type 2 authentication factor* is something you have. Physical devices that a user possesses can help them provide authentication. Examples include a smartcard, hardware token, smartcard, *memory card*, or USB drive.

> **NOTE** The main difference between a smartcard and a memory card is that a smartcard can process data, whereas a memory card only stores information. For example, a smartcard includes a microprocessor in addition to a certificate that can be used for authentication, to encrypt data, to digitally sign email, and more. A memory card only holds authentication information for a user.

Type 3 A *Type 3 authentication factor* is something you are or something you do. It is a physical characteristic of a person identified with different types of biometrics. Examples in the something-you-are category include fingerprints, voice prints, retina patterns, iris patterns, face shapes, palm topology, and hand geometry. Examples in the something-you-do category include signature and keystroke dynamics, also known as behavioral biometrics.

These types are progressively stronger when implemented correctly, with Type 1 being the weakest and Type 3 being the strongest. In other words, passwords (Type 1) are the weakest, and a fingerprint (Type 3) is stronger than a password. However, attackers can still bypass some Type 3 authentication factors. For example, an attacker may be able to create a duplicate fingerprint on a gummi bear candy and fool a fingerprint reader.

Somewhere You Are

These three basic factors (something you know, something you have, and something you are) *are* the most common elements in authentication systems. However, a factor known as somewhere you are is sometimes used. It can identify a subject's location based on a specific computer, a phone number identified by caller ID, or a geographic location identified by an IP address. Controlling access by physical location forces a subject to be present in a specific location. For example, consider remote access users who dial in from their home. Caller ID and callback techniques can verify that the user is actually calling from home.

This factor isn't reliable on its own because a dedicated attacker can spoof any type of address information. However, it can be effective when used in combination with other factors.

Passwords

The most common authentication technique is the use of a *password* (a string of characters entered by a user) with Type 1 authentication (something you know). Passwords are typically static. A *static password* stays the same for a length of time such as 30 days, but static passwords are the weakest form of authentication. Passwords are weak security mechanisms for several reasons:

- Users often choose passwords that are easy to remember and therefore easy to guess or crack.
- Randomly generated passwords are hard to remember; thus, many users write them down.
- Users often share their passwords, or forget them.
- Attackers detect passwords through many means, including observation, sniffing networks, and stealing security databases.
- Passwords are sometimes transmitted in clear text or with easily broken encryption protocols. Attackers can capture these passwords with network sniffers.
- Password databases are sometimes stored in publicly accessible online locations.
- Brute-force attacks can quickly discover weak passwords.

Password Encryption

Passwords are rarely stored in plain text. Instead, a system will create a hash of a password using a hashing algorithm such as Password-Based Key Derivation Function 2 (PBKDF2). The hash is a number and the algorithm will always create the same number if the password is the same. When a user enters the password for authentication, the system hashes the password and compares it to the stored password's hash. If they are the same, the system authenticates the user.

Creating Strong Passwords

Passwords are most effective when users create strong passwords. A strong password is sufficiently long and uses multiple character types such as uppercase letters, lowercase letters, numbers, and special characters. Organizations often include a written *password policy* in the overall security policy. IT security professionals then enforce the policy with technical controls such as a technical password policy that enforces the *password restriction* requirements. The following list includes some common password policy settings:

Maximum Age This setting requires users to change their password periodically, such as every 45 days.

Password Complexity The complexity of a password refers to how many character types it includes. An eight-character password using uppercase characters, lowercase characters, symbols, and numbers is much stronger than an eight-character password using only numbers.

Password Length The length is the number of characters in the password. Shorter passwords are easier to crack. As an example, password crackers can discover a complex five-character password in less than a second but it takes thousands of years to crack a complex 12-character password. Many organizations require privileged account passwords to be at least 15 characters long. This specifically overcomes a weakness in how passwords are stored in some Windows systems.

Password History Many users get into the habit of rotating between two passwords. A password history remembers a certain number of previous passwords and prevents users from reusing a password in the history. This is often combined with a minimum password age setting, preventing users from changing a password repeatedly until they can set the password back to the original one. Minimum password age is often set to one day.

Users often don't understand the need for strong passwords. Even when they do, they often don't know to create strong passwords that they can easily remember. The following suggestions can help them create strong passwords:

- Do not use any part of your name, logon name, email address, employee number, national identification number or Social Security Number, phone number, extension, or other identifying name or code.
- Do not use information available from social network profiles such as a family member's name, a pet's name, or your birth date.
- Do not use dictionary words (including words in foreign dictionaries), slang, or industry acronyms.
- Do use nonstandard capitalization and spelling.
- Do replace letters with special characters and numbers.

In some environments, systems create initial passwords for user accounts automatically. Often the generated password is a form of a composition password, which includes two or more unrelated words joined together with a number or symbol in between. Composition passwords are easy for computers to generate, but they should not be used for extended periods of time because they are vulnerable to password-guessing attacks.

Password Phrases

A password mechanism that is more effective than a basic password is a *passphrase*. A passphrase is a string of characters similar to a password but that has unique meaning to the user. Passphrases are often basic sentences modified to simplify memorization. Here's an example: "I passed the CISSP exam" can be converted to the following passphrase: "IP@$$edTheCISSPEx@m." Using a passphrase has several benefits. It is difficult to crack a passphrase using a brute-force tool, and it encourages the use of a lengthy string with numerous characters but it is still easy to remember.

Cognitive Passwords

Another password mechanism is the *cognitive password*. A cognitive password is series of questions about facts or predefined responses that only the subject should know. Authentication systems often collect the answers to these questions during the initial registration of the account, but they can be collected or modified later. As an example, the subject might be asked three to five questions such as these when creating an account:

- What is your birth date?
- What is your mother's maiden name?
- What is the name of your first boss?
- What is the name of your first pet?
- What is your favorite sport?

Later, the system uses these questions for authentication. If the user answers all the questions correctly, the system authenticates the user. The most effective cognitive password systems collect answers for several questions, and ask a different set of questions each time they are used. Cognitive passwords often assist with password management using self-service password reset systems or assisted password reset systems. For example, if users forget their original password, they can ask for help. The password management system then challenges the user with one or more of these cognitive password questions, presumably known only by the user.

NOTE

One of the flaws associated with cognitive passwords is that the information is often available via the Internet. For example, an attacker broke into Sarah Palin's personal Yahoo! email account when she was a vice presidential candidate in 2008. The attacker accessed biographical information about her that he found on social media pages and was able to answer questions posed by Yahoo!'s account recovery process. The best cognitive password systems allow users to create their own questions and answers. This makes the attacker's job much more difficult.

Smartcards and Tokens

Smartcards and hardware tokens are both examples of a Type 2, or something you have, factor of authentication. They are rarely used by themselves but are commonly combined with another factor of authentication, providing multifactor authentication.

Smartcards

A *smartcard* is a credit card–sized ID or badge and has an integrated circuit chip embedded in it. Smartcards contain information about the authorized user that is used for identification and/or authentication purposes. Most current smartcards include a microprocessor and one or more certificates. The certificates are used for asymmetric cryptography such as encrypting data or digitally signing email. (Asymmetric cryptography topics are covered in more depth in Chapter 7, "PKI and Cryptographic Applications.") Smartcards are tamper resistant and provide users with an easy way to carry and use complex encryption keys.

Users insert the card into a smartcard reader when authenticating. It's common to require users to also enter a PIN or password as a second factor of authentication with the smartcard.

NOTE Note that smartcards can provide both identification and authentication. However, because users can share or swap smartcards, they aren't effective identification methods by themselves. Most implementations require users to use another authentication factor such as a PIN, or with a username and password.

Personnel within the US government use either *Common Access Cards (CACs)* or *Personal Identity Verification (PIV) cards*. CACs and PIV cards are smartcards that include pictures and other identifying information about the owner. Users wear them as a badge while walking around and insert them into card readers at their computer when logging on.

Tokens

A token, or hardware *token*, is a password-generating device that users can carry with them. A common token used today includes a display that shows a six- to eight-digit number. An authentication server stores the details of the token, so at any moment, the server knows what number is displayed on the user's token. Tokens are typically combined with another authentication mechanism. For example, users might enter a username and password (in the something-you-know factor of authentication) and then enter the number displayed in the token (in the something-you-have factor of authentication). This provides multifactor authentication.

Hardware tokens use dynamic one-time passwords, making them more secure than static passwords. The two types of tokens are *synchronous dynamic password tokens* and *asynchronous dynamic password tokens*.

Synchronous Dynamic Password Tokens Hardware tokens that create *synchronous dynamic passwords* are time-based and synchronized with an authentication server. They generate a new password periodically, such as every 60 seconds. This does require the token and the server to have accurate time. A common way this is used is by requiring the user to enter a username, static password, and the dynamic one-time password into a web page.

Asynchronous Dynamic Password Tokens An asynchronous dynamic password does not use a clock. Instead, the hardware token generates passwords based on an algorithm and an incrementing counter. When using an incrementing counter, it creates a dynamic one-time password that stays the same until used for authentication. Some tokens create a one-time password when the user enters a PIN provided by the authentication server into the token. For example, a user would first submit a username and password to a web page. After validating the user's credentials, the authentication system uses the token's identifier and incrementing counter to create a challenge number and sends it back to the user. The challenge number changes each time a user authenticates, so it is often called a nonce (short for "number used once"). The challenge number will only produce the correct one-time password on the device belonging to that user. The user enters the challenge number into the token and the token creates a password. The user then enters the password into the website to complete the authentication process.

Hardware tokens provide strong authentication, but they do have failings. If the battery dies or the device breaks, the user won't be able to gain access.

One-Time Password Generators

One-time passwords are *dynamic passwords* that change every time they are used. They can be effective for security purposes, but most people find it difficult to remember passwords that change so frequently. One-time password generators are token devices that create passwords, making one-time passwords reasonable to deploy. With token-device-based authentication systems, an environment can benefit from the strength of one-time passwords without relying on users to be able to memorize complex passwords.

Biometrics

Another common authentication and identification technique is the use of *biometrics*. *Biometric factors* fall into the Type 3, something-you-are, authentication category.

Biometric factors can be used as an identifying or authentication technique, or both. Using a biometric factor instead of a username or account ID as an identification factor requires a one-to-many search of the offered biometric pattern against a stored database of enrolled and authorized patterns. Capturing a single image of a person and searching a database of many people looking for a match is an example of a one-to-many search. As an identification technique, biometric factors are used in physical access controls.

Using a biometric factor as an authentication technique requires a one-to-one match of the offered biometric pattern against a stored pattern for the offered subject identity. In other words, the user claims an identity, and the biometric factor is checked to see if the person matches the claimed identity. As an authentication technique, biometric factors are used in logical access controls.

Biometric characteristics are often defined as either physiological or behavioral. Physiological biometric methods include fingerprints, face scans, retina scans, iris scans, palm scans (also known as palm topography or palm geography), hand geometry, and voice patterns. Behavioral biometric methods include signature dynamics and keystroke patterns (keystroke dynamics). These are sometimes referred to as something-you-do authentication.

Fingerprints *Fingerprints* are the visible patterns on the fingers and thumbs of people. They are unique to an individual and have been used for decades in physical security for identification. Fingerprint readers are now commonly used on laptop computers and USB flash drives as a method of identification and authentication.

Face Scans *Face scans* use the geometric patterns of faces for detection and recognition. If you've ever watched the TV show *Las Vegas*, you've probably seen how they can take a picture of a person and then match the characteristics of the face against a database. This allows them to quickly identify a person. Similarly, face scans are used to identify and authenticate people before accessing secure spaces such as a secure vault.

Retina Scans *Retina scans* focus on the pattern of blood vessels at the back of the eye. They are the most accurate form of biometric authentication and are able to differentiate between identical twins. However, they are the least acceptable biometric scanning method because retina scans can reveal medical conditions, such as high blood pressure and pregnancy. Older retinal scans blew a puff of air into the user's eye, but newer ones typically use an infrared light instead.

Iris Scans Focusing on the colored area around the pupil, *iris scans* are the second most accurate form of biometric authentication. Iris scans are often recognized as having a longer useful authentication life span than other biometric factors because the iris remains relatively unchanged throughout a person's life (barring eye damage or illness). Iris scans are considered more acceptable by general users than retina scans because they don't reveal personal medical information. However, some scanners can be fooled with a high-quality image in place of a person's eye. Additionally, accuracy can be affected by changes in lighting.

Palm Scans *Palm scans*, sometimes called *palm topography* or palm geography, scan the palm of the hand for identification. They use near-infrared light to measure vein patterns in the palm, which are as unique as fingerprints. Individuals don't need to touch the scanner but instead place their palm over a scanner. For example, many schools in Florida use palm scanners to identify students in their lunch lines, and some hospitals are also using palm scanners to identify patients. Some palm scanners include the fingers and measure the layout of ridges, creases, and grooves, as a full hand scan.

Hand Geometry *Hand geometry* recognizes the physical dimensions of the hand. This includes the width and length of the palm and fingers. It captures a silhouette of the hand, but not the details of fingerprints or vein patterns. Hand geometry is rarely used by itself since it is difficult to uniquely identify an individual using this method.

Heart/Pulse Patterns Measuring the user's pulse or heartbeat ensures that a real person is providing the biometric factor. It is often employed as a secondary biometric to support another type of authentication. Some researchers theorize that heartbeats are unique between individuals and claim it is possible to use electrocardiography for authentication. However, a reliable method has not been created or fully tested.

Voice Pattern Recognition This type of biometric authentication relies on the characteristics of a person's speaking voice, known as a voiceprint. The user speaks a specific phrase, which is recorded by the authentication system. To authenticate, they repeat the same phrase and it is compared to the original. *Voice pattern* recognition is sometimes used as an additional authentication mechanism but is rarely used by itself.

NOTE Speech recognition is commonly confused with voice pattern recognition, but they are different. Speech recognition software, such as dictation software, extracts communications from sound. In other words, voice pattern recognition differentiates between one voice and another for identification or authentication, whereas speech recognition differentiates between words within any person's voice.

Signature Dynamics This recognizes how a subject writes a string of characters. *Signature dynamics* examine both how a subject performs the act of writing as well as features in a written sample. The success of signature dynamics relies on pen pressure, stroke pattern, stroke length, and the points in time when the pen is lifted from the writing surface. The speed at which the written sample is created is usually not an important factor.

Keystroke Patterns *Keystroke patterns* (also known as *keystroke dynamics*) measure how a subject uses a keyboard by analyzing flight time and dwell time. *Flight time* is how long it takes between key presses, and *dwell time* is how long a key is pressed. Using keystroke patterns is inexpensive, nonintrusive, and often transparent to the user (for both use and enrollment). Unfortunately, keystroke patterns are subject to wild variances. Simple changes in user behavior greatly affect this biometric factor, such as using only one hand, being cold, standing rather than sitting, changing keyboards, or sustaining an injury to the hand or a finger.

The use of biometrics promises universally unique identification for every person on the planet. Unfortunately, biometric technology has yet to live up to this promise. However, technologies that focus on physical characteristics are very useful for authentication.

Biometric Factor Error Ratings

The most important aspect of a biometric device is its accuracy. To use biometrics for identification, a biometric device must be able to detect minute differences in information, such as variations in the blood vessels in a person's retina or tones and timbres in their voice. Because most people are basically similar, biometric methods often result in false negative and false positive authentications. Biometric devices are rated for performance by examining the different types of errors they produce.

Type 1 Error A *Type 1 error* occurs when a valid subject is not authenticated. This is also known as a false negative authentication. For example, if Dawn uses her fingerprint to authenticate herself but the system incorrectly rejects her, it is a false negative. The ratio of Type 1 errors to valid authentications is known as the *false rejection rate* (FRR).

Type 2 Error A *Type 2 error* occurs when an invalid subject is authenticated. This is also known as a false positive authentication. For example, if hacker Joe doesn't have an account but he uses his fingerprint to authenticate and the system recognizes him, it is a false positive. The ratio of Type 2 errors to valid authentications is called the *false acceptance rate* (FAR).

Most biometric devices have a sensitivity adjustment. When a biometric device is too sensitive, Type 1 errors (false negatives) are more common. When a biometric device is not sensitive enough, Type 2 errors (false positives) are more common.

You can compare the overall quality of biometric devices with the *crossover error rate* (CER), also known as the equal error rate (ERR). Figure 13.1 shows the FRR and FAR percentages when a device is set to different sensitivity levels. The point where the FRR and FAR percentages are equal is the CER, and the CER is used as a standard assessment value to compare the accuracy of different biometric devices. Devices with lower CERs are more accurate than devices with higher CERs.

FIGURE 13.1 Graph of FRR and FAR errors indicating the CER point

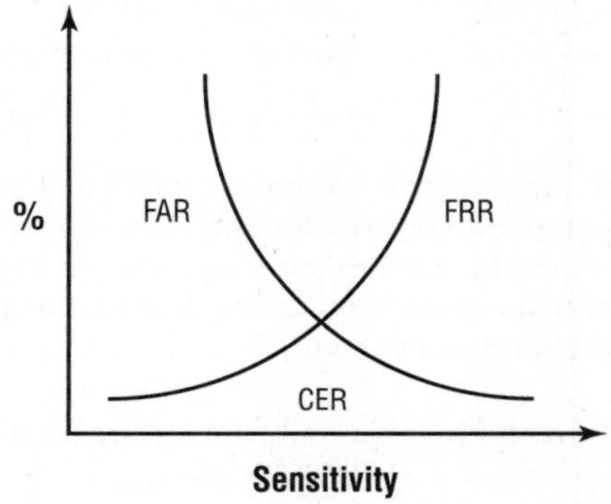

It's not necessary, and often not desirable, to operate a device with the sensitivity set at the CER level. For example, an organization may use a facial recognition system to allow or deny access to a secure area because they want to ensure that unauthorized individuals are never granted access. In this case, the organization would set the sensitivity very high so there is very little chance of a Type 2 error (false acceptance). This may result in more false rejections, but a false rejection is more acceptable than a false acceptance in this scenario.

Biometric Registration

Biometric devices can be ineffective or unacceptable due to factors known as enrollment time, throughput rate, and acceptance. For a biometric device to work as an identification or authentication mechanism, a process called *enrollment* (or registration) must take place. During enrollment, a subject's biometric factor is sampled and stored in the device's database. This stored sample of a biometric factor is the *reference profile* (also known as a *reference template*).

The time required to scan and store a biometric factor depends on which physical or performance characteristic is measured. Users are less willing to accept the inconvenience of biometric methods that take a long time. In general, enrollment times over 2 minutes are unacceptable. If you use a biometric characteristic that changes over time, such as a person's voice tones, facial hair, or signature pattern, reenrollment must occur at regular intervals, adding inconvenience.

The *throughput rate* is the amount of time the system requires to scan a subject and approve or deny access. The more complex or detailed a biometric characteristic, the longer processing takes. Subjects typically accept a throughput rate of about 6 seconds or faster.

Multifactor Authentication

Multifactor authentication is any authentication using two or more factors. *Two-factor authentication* requires two different factors to provide authentication. For example, when using a debit card at the grocery store, you must usually swipe the card (something you have) and enter a PIN (something you know) to complete the transaction. Similarly, smartcards typically require users to insert their card into a reader and also enter a PIN. As a general rule, using more types or factors results in more secure authentication.

TIP

> Multifactor authentication must use multiple types or factors, such as the something-you-know factor and the something-you-have factor. In contrast, requiring users to enter a password and a PIN is not multifactor authentication because both methods are from a single authentication factor (something you know).

When two authentication methods of the same factor are used together, the strength of the authentication is no greater than it would be if just one method were used because the same attack that could steal or obtain one could also obtain the other. For example, using two passwords together is no more secure than using a single password because a password-cracking attempt could discover both in a single successful attack.

In contrast, when two or more different factors are employed, two or more different methods of attack must succeed to collect all relevant authentication elements. For example, if a token, a password, and a biometric factor are all used for authentication, then a physical theft, a password crack, and a biometric duplication attack must all succeed simultaneously to allow an intruder to gain entry into the system.

Device Authentication

Historically, users have only been able to log into a network from a company-owned system such as a desktop PC. For example, in a Windows domain user computers join the domain and have computer accounts and passwords similar to user accounts and passwords. If the computer hasn't joined the domain, or its credentials are out of sync with a domain controller, users cannot log on from this computer.

Today, more and more employees are bringing their own devices to work and hooking them up to the network. Some organizations embrace this, but implement BYOD security policies as a measure of control. These devices aren't necessarily able to join a domain, but it is possible to implement device identification and authentication methods for these devices.

One method is device fingerprinting. Users can register their devices with the organization, and associate them with their user accounts. During registration, a device authentication system captures characteristics about the device. This is often accomplished by having the user access a web page with the device. The registration system then identifies the device using characteristics such as the operating system and version, web browser, browser fonts, browser plug-ins, time zone, data storage, screen resolution, cookie settings, and HTTP headers.

When the user logs on from the device, the authentication system checks the user account for a registered device. It then verifies the characteristics of the user's device with the registered device. Even though some of these characteristics change over time, this has proven to be a successful device authentication method. Organizations typically use third-party tools, such as the SecureAuth Identity Provider (IdP), for device authentication.

Implementing Identity Management

Identity management techniques generally fall into one of two categories: centralized and decentralized/distributed.

- *Centralized access control* implies that all authorization verification is performed by a single entity within a system.
- *Decentralized access control* (also known as *distributed access control*) implies that various entities located throughout a system perform authorization verification.

Centralized and decentralized access control methodologies offer the same benefits and drawbacks found in any centralized or decentralized system. A small team or individual can manage centralized access control. Administrative overhead is lower because all changes are made in a single location and a single change affects the entire system.

Decentralized access control often requires several teams or multiple individuals. Administrative overhead is higher because changes must be implemented across numerous locations. Maintaining consistency across a system becomes more difficult as the number of access control points increases. Changes made to any individual access control point need to be repeated at every access point.

Single Sign-On

Single sign-on (SSO) is a centralized access control technique that allows a subject to be authenticated only once on a system and to access multiple resources without authenticating again. For example, users can authenticate once on a network and then access resources throughout the network without being prompted to authenticate again.

SSO is very convenient for users, but it also increases security. When users have to remember multiple usernames and passwords, they often resort to writing them down, ultimately weakening security. Users are less likely to write down a single password. SSO also eases administration by reducing the number of accounts required for a subject.

The primary disadvantage to SSO is that once an account is compromised, an attacker gains unrestricted access to all of the authorized resources. However, most SSO systems include methods to protect user credentials.

The following sections discuss several common SSO mechanisms.

LDAP and Centralized Access Control

Within a single organization, a centralized access control system is often used. For example, a *directory service* is a centralized database that includes information about subjects and objects. Many directory services are based on the Lightweight Directory Access Protocol (LDAP). For example, the Microsoft Active Directory Domain Services is LDAP based.

You can think of an LDAP directory as a telephone directory for network services and assets. Users, clients, and processes can search the directory service to find where a desired system or resource resides. Subjects must authenticate to the directory service before performing queries and lookup activities. Even after authentication, the directory service will reveal only certain information to a subject, based on that subject's assigned privileges.

Multiple domains and trusts are commonly used in access control systems. A security domain is a collection of subjects and objects that share a common security policy, and individual domains can operate separately from other domains. *Trusts* are established between the domains to create a security bridge and allow users from one domain to access resources in another domain. Trusts can be one way only, or they can be two way.

LDAP and PKIs

A Public Key Infrastructure (PKI) uses LDAP when integrating digital certificates into transmissions. Chapter 7 covers a PKI in more depth, but in short, a PKI is a group of technologies used to manage digital certificates during the certificate life cycle. There are many times when clients need to query a certificate authority (CA) for information on a certificate and LDAP is one of the protocols used.

LDAP and centralized access control systems can be used to support single sign-on capabilities.

Kerberos

Ticket authentication is a mechanism that employs a third-party entity to prove identification and provide authentication. The most common and well-known ticket system is *Kerberos*.

NOTE

The Kerberos name is borrowed from Greek mythology. A three-headed dog named Kerberos guards the gates to the underworld. The dog faces inward, preventing escape rather than denying entrance.

Kerberos offers a single sign-on solution for users and provides protection for logon credentials. The current version, Kerberos 5, relies on symmetric-key cryptography (also known as secret-key cryptography) using the Advanced Encryption Standard (AES) symmetric encryption protocol. Kerberos provides confidentiality and integrity for authentication traffic using end-to-end security and helps prevent against eavesdropping and replay attacks. It uses several different elements that are important to understand:

Key Distribution Center The *key distribution center (KDC)* is the trusted third party that provides authentication services. Kerberos uses symmetric-key cryptography to authenticate clients to servers. All clients and servers are registered with the KDC, and it maintains the secret keys for all network members.

Kerberos Authentication Server The authentication server hosts the functions of the KDC: a ticket-granting service (TGS), and an authentication service (AS). However, it is possible to host the ticket-granting service on another server. The *authentication service* verifies or rejects the authenticity and timeliness of tickets. This server is often called the KDC.

Ticket-Granting Ticket A ticket-granting ticket (TGT) provides proof that a subject has authenticated through a KDC and is authorized to request tickets to access other objects. A TGT is encrypted and includes a symmetric key, an expiration time, and the user's IP address. Subjects present the TGT when requesting tickets to access objects.

Ticket A ticket is an encrypted message that provides proof that a subject is authorized to access an object. It is sometimes called a service ticket (ST). Subjects request tickets to access objects, and if they have authenticated and are authorized to access the object, Kerberos issues them a ticket. Kerberos tickets have specific lifetimes and usage parameters. Once a ticket expires, a client must request a renewal or a new ticket to continue communications with any server.

Kerberos requires a database of accounts, which is often contained in a directory service. It uses an exchange of tickets between clients, network servers, and the KDC to prove identity and provide authentication. This allows a client to request resources from the server with both the client and server having assurances of the identity of the other. These encrypted tickets also ensure that logon credentials, session keys, and authentication messages are never transmitted in clear text.

The Kerberos logon process works as follows:

1. The user types a username and password into the client.
2. The client encrypts the username with AES for transmission to the KDC.
3. The KDC verifies the username against a database of known credentials.
4. The KDC generates a symmetric key that will be used by the client and the Kerberos server. It encrypts this with a hash of the user's password. The KDC also generates an encrypted time-stamped TGT.
5. The KDC then transmits the encrypted symmetric key and the encrypted time-stamped TGT to the client.
6. The client installs the TGT for use until it expires. The client also decrypts the symmetric key using a hash of the user's password.

NOTE Note that the client's password is never transmitted over the network, but it is verified. The server encrypts a symmetric key using a hash of the user's password, and it can only be decrypted with a hash of the user's password. As long as the user entered the correct password, this step works. However, it fails if the user entered the incorrect password.

When a client wants to access an object, such as a resource hosted on the network, it must request a ticket through the Kerberos server. The following steps are involved in this process:

1. The client sends its TGT back to the KDC with a request for access to the resource.
2. The KDC verifies that the TGT is valid and checks its access control matrix to verify that the user has sufficient privileges to access the requested resource.
3. The KDC generates a service ticket and sends it to the client.
4. The client sends the ticket to the server or service hosting the resource.
5. The server or service hosting the resource verifies the validity of the ticket with the KDC.
6. Once identity and authorization is verified, Kerberos activity is complete. The server or service host then opens a session with the client and begins communications or data transmission.

Kerberos is a versatile authentication mechanism that works over local LANs, remote access, and client-server resource requests. However, Kerberos presents a single point of failure—the KDC. If the KDC is compromised, the secret key for every system on the network is also compromised. Also, if a KDC goes offline, no subject authentication can occur.

It also has strict time requirements and the default configuration requires that all systems be time-synchronized within five minutes of each other. If a system is not synchronized or the time is changed, a previously issued TGT will no longer be valid and the system will not be able receive any new tickets. In effect, the client will be denied access to any protected network resources.

Federated Identity Management and SSO

SSO has been common on internal networks for quite a while, but not on the Internet. However, with the explosion of cloud-based applications, it added a need for an SSO solution for users accessing resources over the Internet. Federated identity management is a form of SSO that meets this need.

Identity management is the management of user identities and their credentials. Federated identity management extends this beyond a single organization. Multiple organizations can join a federation, or group, where they agree on a method to share identities between them. Users in each organization can log on once in their own organization and their credentials are matched with a federated identity. They can then use this federated identity to access resources in any other organization within the group.

A federation can be composed of multiple unrelated networks within a single university campus, multiple college and university campuses, multiple organizations sharing resources, or any other group that can agree on a common federated identity management system. Members of the federation match user identities within an organization to federated identities.

As an example, many corporate online training websites use federated SSO systems. When the organization coordinates with the online training company for employee access, they also coordinate the details needed for federated access. A common method is to match the user's internal login ID with a federated identity. Users log on within the organization using their normal login ID. When the user accesses the training website with a web browser, the federated identity management system uses their login ID to retrieve the matching federated identity. If it finds a match, it authorizes the user access to the web pages granted to the federated identity.

Administrators manage these details behind the scenes and the process is usually transparent to users. Users don't need to enter their credentials again.

A challenge with multiple companies communicating in a federation is finding a common language. They often have different operating systems, but they still need to share a common language. Federated identity systems often use the Security Assertion Markup Language (SAML) and/or the Service Provisioning Markup Language (SPML) to meet this need. As background, here's a short description of some markup languages.

Hypertext Markup Language *Hypertext Markup Language (HTML)* is commonly used to display static web pages. HTML was derived from the Standard Generalized Markup Language (SGML) and the Generalized Markup Language (GML). HTML describes how data is displayed using tags to manipulate the size and color of the text. For example, the following H1 tag displays the text as a level one heading: `<H1>I Passed The CISSP Exam</H1>`.

Extensible Markup Language *Extensible Markup Language (XML)* goes beyond describing how to display the data by actually describing the data. XML can include tags to describe data as anything desired. For example, the following tag identifies the data as the results of taking an exam: `<ExamResults>Passed</ExamResults>`.

Databases from multiple vendors can import and export data to and from an XML format, making XML a common language used to exchange information. Many specific schemas have been created so that companies know exactly what tags are being used for specific purposes.

Security Assertion Markup Language *Security Assertion Markup Language (SAML)* is an XML-based language that is commonly used to exchange authentication and authorization (AA) information between federated organizations. It is often used to provide SSO capabilities for browser access.

Service Provisioning Markup Language *Service Provisioning Markup Language (SPML)* is a newer framework based on XML but specifically designed for exchanging user information for federated identity single sign-on purposes. It is based on the Directory Service Markup Language (DSML), which can display LDAP-based directory service information in an XML format.

Extensible Access Control Markup Language Extensible Access Control Markup Language (XACML) is used to define access control policies within an XML format, and it commonly implements role-based access controls. It helps provide assurances to all members in a federation that they are granting the same level of access to different roles.

TIP SAML is a popular SSO language on the Internet. XACML has become popular with software defined networking applications.

Other Examples of Single Sign-On

Although Kerberos may be the most widely recognized and deployed form of single sign-on within an organization, it is not the only one of its kind. In this section, we summarize other SSO mechanisms you may encounter.

Scripted access or logon scripts establish communication links by providing an automated process to transmit logon credentials at the start of a logon session. Scripted access can often simulate SSO even though the environment still requires a unique authentication process to connect to each server or resource. Scripts can be used to implement SSO in environments where true SSO technologies are not available. Scripts and batch files should be stored in a protected area because they usually contain access credentials in clear text.

The *Secure European System for Applications in a Multivendor Environment (SESAME)* is a ticket-based authentication system developed to address weaknesses in Kerberos. However, it did not compensate for all the problems with Kerberos. Eventually, newer Kerberos versions and various vendor implementations resolved the initial problems with Kerberos, bypassing SESAME. In the professional security world, SESAME is no longer considered a viable product.

KryptoKnight is a ticket-based authentication system developed by IBM. It is similar to Kerberos but uses peer-to-peer authentication instead of a third party. It was incorporated into the NetSP product. Like SESAME, KryptoKnight and NetSP never took off and are no longer widely used.

Two newer examples of SSO used on the Internet are OAuth (implying open authentication) and OpenID. OAuth is an open standard designed to work with HTTP and it allows users to log on with one account. For example, users can log onto their Google account and use the same account to access Facebook and Twitter pages. Google supports OAuth 2.0, which is not backward compatible with OAuth 1.0. RFC 6749 documents OAuth 2.0. OpenID is also an open standard, but it is maintained by the OpenID Foundation rather than as an IETF RFC standard. OpenID can be used in conjunction with OAuth, or on its own.

Credential Management Systems

A credential management system provides a storage space for users to keep their credentials when SSO isn't available. Users can store credentials for websites and network resources that require a different set of credentials. The management system secures the credentials with encryption to prevent unauthorized access.

As an example, Windows systems include the Credential Manager tool. Users enter their credentials into the Credential Manager and when necessary, the operating system retrieves the user's credentials and automatically submits them. When using this for a website, users enter the URL, username, and password. Later, when the user accesses the website, the Credential Manager automatically recognizes the URL and provides the credentials.

Third-party credential management systems are also available. For example, KeePass is a freeware tool that allows you to store your credentials. Credentials are stored in an encrypted database and users can unlock the database with a master password. Once unlocked, users can easily copy their passwords to paste into a website form. It's also possible to configure the app to enter the credentials automatically into the web page form. Of course, it's important to use a strong master password to protect all the other credentials.

Integrating Identity Services

Identity services provide additional tools for identification and authentication. Some of the tools are designed specifically for cloud-based applications whereas others are third-party identity services designed for use within the organization (on-premises).

Identity as a Service, or Identity and Access as a Service (IDaaS) is a third-party service that provides identity and access management. IDaaS effectively provides SSO for the cloud and is especially useful when internal clients access cloud-based Software as a Service (SaaS) applications. Google implements this with their motto of "One Google Account for everything Google." Users log into their Google account once and it provides them access to multiple Google cloud-based applications without requiring users to log in again.

As another example, Office 365 provides Office applications as a combination of installed applications and SaaS applications. Users have full Office applications installed on their user systems, which can also connect to cloud storage using OneDrive. This allows users to edit and share files from multiple devices. When people use Office 365 at home, Microsoft provides IDaaS, allowing users to authenticate via the cloud to access their data on OneDrive.

When employees use Office 365 from within an enterprise, administrators can integrate the network with a third-party service. For example, Centrify provides third-party IDaaS services that integrate with Microsoft Active Directory. Once configured, users log onto the domain and can then access Office 365 cloud resources without logging on again.

Managing Sessions

When using any type of authentication system, it's important to manage sessions to prevent unauthorized access. This includes sessions on regular computers such as desktop PCs and within online sessions with an application.

Desktop PCs and laptops include screen savers. These change the display when the computer isn't in use by displaying random patterns or different pictures, or simply blanking the screen. Screen savers protected the computer screens of older computers but new displays don't need them. However, they're still used and screen savers have a password-protect feature that can be enabled. This feature displays the logon screen and forces the user to authenticate again prior to exiting the screen saver.

Screen savers have a time frame in minutes that you can configure. It is commonly set between 10 and 20 minutes. If you set it for 10 minutes, it will activate after 10 minutes. This requires users to log on again if the system is idle for 10 minutes or longer.

Secure online sessions will normally terminate after a period of time too. For example, if you establish a secure session with your bank but don't interact with the session for 10 minutes, the application will typically log you off. In some cases, the application gives you a notification saying it will log you off soon. These notifications usually give you an opportunity to click in the page so that you stay logged on. If developers don't implement these automatic logoff capabilities, it allows a user's browser session to remain open with the user logged on. Even if the user closes a browser tab without logging off, it can potentially leave the browser session open. This leaves the user's account vulnerable to an attack if someone else accesses the browser.

AAA Protocols

Several protocols provide authentication, authorization, and accounting and are referred to as AAA protocols. These provide centralized access control with remote access systems such as virtual private networks (VPNs) and other types of network access servers. They help protect internal LAN authentication systems and other servers from remote attacks. When using a separate system for remote access, a successful attack on the system only affects the remote access users. In other words, the attacker won't have access to internal accounts. Mobile IP, which provides access to mobile users with smartphones, also uses AAA protocols.

These AAA protocols use the access control elements of identification, authentication, authorization, and accountability as described earlier in this chapter. They ensure that users have valid credentials to authenticate and verify that the user is authorized to connect to the remote access server based on the user's proven identity. Additionally, the accounting element can track the user's network resource usage, which can be used for billing purposes. Some common AAA protocols are RADIUS, TACACS+, and Diameter.

RADIUS

Remote Authentication Dial-in User Service (RADIUS) centralizes authentication for remote connections. It is typically used when an organization has more than one network access server (or remote access server). A user can connect to any network access server, which then passes on the user's credentials to the RADIUS server to verify authentication and authorization and to track accounting. In this context, the network access server is the RADIUS client and a RADIUS server acts as an authentication server. The RADIUS server also provides AAA services for multiple remote access servers.

Many Internet service providers (ISPs) use RADIUS for authentication. Users can access the ISP from anywhere and the ISP server then forwards the user's connection request to the RADIUS server.

Organizations can also use RADIUS, and organizations can implement it with callback security for an extra layer of protection. Users call in, and after authentication, the

RADIUS server terminates the connection and initiates a call back to the user's predefined phone number. If a user's authentication credentials are compromised, the callback security prevents an attacker from using them.

RADIUS uses the User Datagram Protocol (UDP) and encrypts only the exchange of the password. It doesn't encrypt the entire session, but additional protocols can be used to encrypt the data session. The current version is defined in RFC 2865.

TIP

RADIUS provides AAA services between network access servers and a shared authentication server. The network access server is the client of the RADIUS authentication server.

TACACS+

Terminal Access Controller Access-Control System (TACACS) was introduced as an alternative to RADIUS. Cisco later introduced extended TACACS (XTACACS) as a proprietary protocol. However, TACACS and XTACACS are not commonly used today. TACACS Plus (TACACS+) was later created as an open publicly documented protocol, and it is the most commonly used of the three.

TACACS+ provides several improvements over the earlier versions and over RADIUS. It separates authentication, authorization, and accounting into separate processes, which can be hosted on three separate servers if desired. The other versions combine two or three of these processes. Additionally, TACACS+ encrypts all of the authentication information, not just the password as RADIUS does. TACACS and XTACACS used UDP port 49, while TACACS+ uses Transmission Control Protocol (TCP) port 49, providing a higher level of reliability for the packet transmissions.

Diameter

Building on the success of RADIUS and TACACS+, an enhanced version of RADIUS named Diameter was developed. It supports a wide range of protocols, including traditional IP, Mobile IP, and Voice over IP (VoIP). Because it supports extra commands, it is becoming popular in situations where roaming support is desirable, such as with wireless devices and smart phones. While Diameter is an upgrade to RADIUS, it is not backward compatible to RADIUS.

Diameter uses TCP port 3868 or Stream Control Transmission Protocol (SCTP) port 3868, providing better reliability than UDP used by RADIUS. It also supports Internet Protocol Security (IPsec) and Transport Layer Security (TLS) for encryption.

NOTE

In geometry, the radius of a circle is the distance from the center to an edge, and the diameter is twice the radius going from edge to edge through the circle. The Diameter name implies that Diameter is twice as good as RADIUS. While that may not be exactly true, it is an improvement over RADIUS and helps to reinforce that Diameter came later and is an improvement.

Managing the Identity and Access Provisioning Life Cycle

The *identity and access provisioning life cycle* refers to the creation, management, and deletion of accounts. Although these activities may seem mundane, they are essential to a system's access control capabilities. Without properly defined and maintained user accounts, a system is unable to establish accurate identity, perform authentication, provide authorization, or track accountability. As mentioned previously, identification occurs when a subject claims an identity. This identity is most commonly a user account, but it also includes computer accounts and service accounts.

Access control administration is the collection of tasks and duties involved in managing accounts, access, and accountability during the life of the account. These tasks are contained within three main responsibilities of the identity and access provisioning life cycle: provisioning, account review, and account revocation.

Provisioning

An initial step in identity management is the creation of new accounts and provisioning them with appropriate privileges. Creating new user accounts is usually a simple process, but the process must be protected and secured via organizational security policy procedures. User accounts should not be created at an administrator's whim or in response to random requests. Rather, proper provisioning ensures that personnel follow specific procedures when creating accounts.

The initial creation of a new user account is often called an *enrollment* or registration. The enrollment process creates a new identity and establishes the factors the system needs to perform authentication. It is critical that the enrollment process be completed fully and accurately. It is also critical that the identity of the individual being enrolled be proved through whatever means your organization deems necessary and sufficient. Photo ID, birth certificate, background check, credit check, security clearance verification, FBI database search, and even calling references are all valid forms of verifying a person's identity before enrolling them in any secured system.

Many organizations have automated provisioning systems. For example, once a person is hired, the HR department completes initial identification and in-processing steps and then forwards a request to the IT department to create an account. Users within the IT department enter information such as the employee's name and their assigned department via an application. The application then creates the account using predefined rules. Automated provisioning systems create accounts consistently, such as always creating usernames the same way and treating duplicate usernames consistently. If the policy dictates that usernames include first and last names, then the application will create a username as `suziejones` for a user named Suzie Jones. If the organization hires a second employee with the same name, then the second username might be `suziejones2`.

If the organization is using groups (or roles), the application can automatically add the new user account to the appropriate groups based on the user's department or job responsibilities. The groups will already have appropriate privileges assigned, so this step provisions the account with appropriate privileges.

As part of the hiring process, new employees should be trained on organization security policies and procedures. Before hiring is complete, employees are typically required to review and sign an agreement committing to uphold the organization's security standards. This often includes an acceptable usage policy.

Throughout the life of a user account, ongoing maintenance is required. Organizations with static organizational hierarchies and low employee turnover or promotion will conduct significantly less account administration than an organization with a flexible or dynamic organizational hierarchy and high employee turnover and promotion rates. Most account maintenance deals with altering rights and privileges. Procedures similar to those used when creating new accounts should be established to govern how access is changed throughout the life of a user account. Unauthorized increases or decreases in an account's access capabilities can cause serious security repercussions.

Account Review

Accounts should be reviewed periodically to ensure that security policies are being enforced. This includes ensuring that inactive accounts are disabled and employees do not have excessive privileges.

Many administrators use scripts to check for inactive accounts periodically. For example, a script can locate accounts that users have not logged onto in the past 30 days, and automatically disable them. Similarly, scripts can check group membership of privileged groups (such as administrator groups) and remove unauthorized accounts. Account review is often formalized in auditing procedures.

Excessive Privilege and Creeping Privileges

It's important to guard against two problems related to access control: excessive privilege and creeping privileges. *Excessive privilege* occurs when users have more privileges than their assigned work tasks dictate. If a user account is discovered to have excessive privileges, the unnecessary privileges should be immediately revoked. *Creeping privileges* involve a user account accumulating privileges over time as job roles and assigned tasks change. This can occur because new tasks are added to a user's job and additional privileges are added, but unneeded privileges are never removed. Creeping privileges result in excessive privilege.

Both of these situations violate the basic security principle of least privilege. The principle of least privilege ensures that subjects are granted only the privileges they need to perform their work tasks and job functions, but no more. Account reviews are effective at discovering these problems.

Account Revocation

When employees leave an organization for any reason, it is important to disable their user accounts as soon as possible. This includes when an employee takes a leave of absence. Whenever possible, HR personnel should have the ability to perform this task because they are aware when employees are leaving for any reason. As an example, HR personnel know when an employee is about to be terminated, and they can disable the account during the employee exit interview.

If a terminated employee retains access to a user account after the exit interview, the risk for sabotage is very high. Even if the employee doesn't take malicious action, other employees may be able to use the account if they discover the password. Logs will record the activity in the name of the terminated employee instead of the person actually taking the action.

It's possible the account will be needed, such as to access encrypted data, so it should not be deleted right away. When it's determined that the account is no longer needed, it should be deleted. Accounts are often deleted within 30 days after an account is disabled, but it can vary depending on the needs of the organization.

Many systems have the ability to set specific expiration dates for any account. These are useful for temporary or short-term employees and automatically disable the account on the expiration date, such as after 30 days for temporary employee hired on a 30-day contract. This maintains a degree of control without requiring ongoing administrative oversight.

Real World Scenario

Dangers of Failing to Revoke Account Access

Fannie Mae learned firsthand of the dangers of not immediately revoking account access after firing an employee. At about 2 p.m. on October 24, 2008, a Unix engineer at Fannie Mae was fired. He turned in his badge at 4:45 but he retained administrative access until about 10:00 p.m. that day.

He used his account after being fired to grant himself remote access to Fannie Mae's servers and at some point inserted malicious code in a legitimate script that ran daily at 9 a.m. The full content of his malicious code was set to run on January 31, 2009, as a logic bomb and would have destroyed data on 4,000 Fannie Mae servers. Many experts believe it would have taken Fannie Mae as long as a week to restore functionality if the code ran successfully.

Another engineer discovered the malicious code about a week after the fired employee inserted it, so it didn't cause any damage. However, if personnel had disabled his account during the exit interview, it could have prevented the incident completely.

Summary

Domain 5 of the CISSP CBK is Identity and Access Management. It covers the management, administration, and implementation aspects of granting or restricting access to assets. Assets include information, systems, devices, facilities, and personnel. Access controls restrict access based on relationships between subjects and objects. Subjects are active entities (such as users), and objects are passive entities (such as files).

Three primary types of access controls are preventive, detective, and corrective. Preventive access controls attempt to prevent incidents before they occur. Detective access controls attempt to detect incidents after they've occurred, and corrective access controls attempt to correct problems caused by incidents once they've been detected.

Controls are implemented as administrative, logical, and physical. Administrative controls are also known as management controls and include policies and procedures. Logical controls are also known as technical controls and are implemented through technology. Physical controls use physical means to protect objects.

The four primary access control elements are identification, authentication, authorization, and accountability. Subjects (users) claim an identity, such as a username, and prove the identity with an authentication mechanism such as a password. After authenticating subjects, authorization mechanisms control their access and audit trails log their activities so that they can be held accountable for their actions.

The three factors of authentication are something you know (such as passwords or PINs), something you have (such as smartcards or tokens), and something you are (identified with biometrics). Multifactor authentication uses more than one authentication factor, and it is stronger than using any single authentication factor.

Single sign-on allows users to authenticate once and access any resources in a network without authenticating again. Kerberos is a popular single sign-on authentication protocol using tickets for authentication. Kerberos uses a database of subjects, symmetric cryptography, and time synchronization of systems to issue tickets.

Federated identity management is a single sign-on solution that can extend beyond a single organization. Multiple organizations create or join a federation and agree on a method to share identities between the organizations. Users can authenticate within their organization and access resources in other organizations without authenticating again. SAML is a common protocol used for SSO on the Internet.

AAA protocols provide authentication, authorization, and accounting. Popular AAA protocols are RADIUS, TACACS+, and Diameter.

The identity and access provisioning life cycle includes the processes to create, manage, and delete accounts used by subjects. Provisioning includes the initial steps of creating the accounts and ensuring that they are granted appropriate access to objects. As users' jobs change, they often require changes to the initial access. Account review processes ensure account modifications follow the principle of least privilege. When employees leave the organization, accounts should be disabled as soon as possible and then deleted when they are no longer needed.

Exam Essentials

Know the difference between subjects and objects. You'll find that CISSP questions and security documentation commonly use the terms *subject* and *object,* so it's important to know the difference between them. Subjects are active entities (such as users) that access passive objects (such as files). A user is a subject who accesses objects in the course of performing some action or accomplishing a work task.

Know the various types of access control. You should be able to identify the type of any given access control. Access controls may be preventive (to stop unwanted or unauthorized activity from occurring), detective (to discover unwanted or unauthorized activity), or corrective (to restore systems to normal after an unwanted or unauthorized activity has occurred). Deterrent access controls attempt to discourage violation of security policies, by encouraging people to decide not to take an unwanted action. Recovery controls attempt to repair or restore resources, functions, and capabilities after a security policy violation. Directive controls attempt to direct, confine, or control the action of subjects to force or encourage compliance with security policy. Compensation controls provide options or alternatives to existing controls to aid in enforcement and support of a security policy.

Know the implementation methods of access controls. Controls are implemented as administrative, logical/technical, or physical controls. Administrative (or management) controls include policies or procedures to implement and enforce overall access control. Logical/technical controls include hardware or software mechanisms used to manage access to resources and systems and provide protection for those resources and systems. Physical controls include physical barriers deployed to prevent direct contact and access with systems or areas within a facility.

Understand the difference between identification and authentication. Access controls depend on effective identification and authentication, so it's important to understand the differences between them. Subjects claim an identity, and identification can be as simple as a username for a user. Subjects prove their identity by providing authentication credentials such as the matching password for a username.

Understand the difference between authorization and accountability. After authenticating subjects, systems authorize access to objects based on their proven identity. Auditing logs and audit trails record events including the identity of the subject that performed an action. The combination of effective identification, authentication, and auditing provides accountability.

Understand the details of the three authentication factors. The three factors of authentication are something you know (such as a password or PIN), something you have (such as a smartcard or token), and something you are (based on biometrics). Multifactor authentication includes two or more authentication factors, and using it is more secure than using a single authentication factor. Passwords are the weakest form of authentication, but password policies help increase their security by enforcing complexity and history requirements. Smartcards include microprocessors and cryptographic certificates, and tokens create one-time passwords. Biometric methods identify users based on characteristics such as fingerprints. The crossover error rate identifies the accuracy of a biometric method. It shows where Type 1 errors (false rejection rate) are equal to Type 2 errors (false acceptance rate).

Understand single sign-on. Single sign-on (SSO) is a mechanism that allows subjects to authenticate once on a system and access multiple objects without authenticating again. Kerberos is the most common SSO method used within organizations, and it uses symmetric cryptography and tickets to prove identification and provide authentication. When multiple organizations want to use a common SSO system, they often use a federated identity management system, where the federation, or group of organizations, agrees on a common method of authentication. Security Assertion Markup Language (SAML) is commonly used to share federated identity information. Other SSO methods are scripted access, SESAME and KryptoKnight. OAuth and OpenID are two newer SSO technologies used on the Internet. OAuth 2.0 is recommended over OAuth 1.0 by many large organizations such as Google.

Understand the purpose of AAA protocols. Several protocols provide centralized authentication, authorization, and accounting services. Network access (or remote access) systems use AAA protocols. For example, a network access server is a client to a RADIUS server and the RADIUS server provides AAA services. RADIUS uses UDP and encrypts the password only. TACACS+ uses TCP and encrypts the entire session. Diameter is based on RADIUS and improves many of the weaknesses of RADIUS, but Diameter is not compatible with RADIUS. Diameter is becoming more popular with mobile IP systems such as smartphones.

Understand the identity and access provisioning life cycle. The identity and access provisioning life cycle refers to the creation, management, and deletion of accounts. Provisioning accounts ensures that they have appropriate privileges based on task requirements. Periodic reviews ensure that accounts don't have excessive privileges and follow the principle of least privilege. Revocation includes disabling accounts as soon as possible when an employee leaves the company, and deleting accounts when they are no longer needed.

Written Lab

1. Name at least three access control types.
2. Describe the three primary authentication factor types.
3. Name the method that allows users to log on once and access resources in multiple organizations without authenticating again.
4. Identify the three primary elements within the identity and access provisioning life cycle.

Review Questions

1. Which of the following would *not* be an asset that an organization would want to protect with access controls?
   - **A.** Information
   - **B.** Systems
   - **C.** Devices
   - **D.** Facilities
   - **E.** None of the above
2. Which of the following is true related to a subject?
   - **A.** A subject is always a user account.
   - **B.** The subject is always the entity that provides or hosts the information or data.
   - **C.** The subject is always the entity that receives information about or data from an object.
   - **D.** A single entity can never change roles between subject and object.
3. Which of the following types of access control uses fences, security policies, security awareness training, and antivirus software to stop an unwanted or unauthorized activity from occurring?
   - **A.** Preventive
   - **B.** Detective
   - **C.** Corrective
   - **D.** Authoritative
4. What type of access controls are hardware or software mechanisms used to manage access to resources and systems, and provide protection for those resources and systems?
   - **A.** Administrative
   - **B.** Logical/technical
   - **C.** Physical
   - **D.** Preventive
5. Which of the following *best* expresses the primary goal when controlling access to assets?
   - **A.** Preserve confidentiality, integrity, and availability of systems and data.
   - **B.** Ensure that only valid objects can authenticate on a system.
   - **C.** Prevent unauthorized access to subjects.
   - **D.** Ensure that all subjects are authenticated.
6. A user logs in with a login ID and a password. What is the purpose of the login ID?
   - **A.** Authentication
   - **B.** Authorization

C. Accountability

D. Identification

7. Accountability requires all of the following items except one. Which item is not required for accountability?

A. Identification

B. Authentication

C. Auditing

D. Authorization

8. What can you use to prevent users from rotating between two passwords?

A. Password complexity

B. Password history

C. Password age

D. Password length

9. Which of the following *best* identifies the benefit of a passphrase?

A. It is short.

B. It is easy to remember.

C. It includes a single set of characters.

D. It is easy to crack.

10. Which of the following is an example of a Type 2 authentication factor?

A. Something you have

B. Something you are

C. Something you do

D. Something you know

11. Your organization issues devices to employees. These devices generate one-time passwords every 60 seconds. A server hosted within the organization knows what this password is at any given time. What type of device is this?

A. Synchronous token

B. Asynchronous token

C. Smartcard

D. Common access card

12. Which of the following provides authentication based on a physical characteristic of a subject?

A. Account ID

B. Biometrics

C. Token

D. PIN

13. What does the crossover error rate (CER) for a biometric device indicate?
    - **A.** It indicates that the sensitivity is too high.
    - **B.** It indicates that the sensitivity is too low.
    - **C.** It indicates the point where the false rejection rate equals the false acceptance rate.
    - **D.** When high enough, it indicates the biometric device is highly accurate.
14. A biometric system has falsely rejected a valid user, indicating that the user is not recognized. What type of error is this?
    - **A.** Type 1 error
    - **B.** Type 2 error
    - **C.** Crossover error rate
    - **D.** Equal error rate
15. What is the primary purpose of Kerberos?
    - **A.** Confidentiality
    - **B.** Integrity
    - **C.** Authentication
    - **D.** Accountability
16. Which of the following is the best choice to support a federated identity management system?
    - **A.** Kerberos
    - **B.** Hypertext Markup Language (HTML)
    - **C.** Extensible Markup Language (XML)
    - **D.** Security Assertion Markup Language (SAML)
17. What is the function of the network access server within a RADIUS architecture?
    - **A.** Authentication server
    - **B.** Client
    - **C.** AAA server
    - **D.** Firewall
18. Which of the following authentication, authorization, and accounting (AAA) protocols is based on RADIUS and supports Mobile IP and Voice over IP?
    - **A.** Distributed access control
    - **B.** Diameter
    - **C.** TACACS+
    - **D.** TACACS

Refer the following scenario when answering questions 19 and 20.

An administrator has been working within an organization for over 10 years. He has moved between different IT divisions within the company and has retained privileges from each of the jobs that he's had during his tenure. Recently, supervisors admonished him for making unauthorized changes to systems. He once again made an unauthorized change that resulted in an unexpected outage and management decided to terminate his employment at the company. He came back to work the following day to clean out his desk and belongings, and during this time he installed a malicious script that was scheduled to run as a logic bomb on the first day of the following month. The script will change administrator passwords, delete files, and shut down over 100 servers in the datacenter.

19. Which of the following basic principles was violated during the administrator's employment?

A. Implicit deny

B. Loss of availability

C. Defensive privileges

D. Least privilege

20. What could have discovered problems with this user's account while he was employed?

A. Policy requiring strong authentication

B. Multifactor authentication

C. Logging

D. Account review

Chapter 14

Controlling and Monitoring Access

THE CISSP EXAM TOPICS COVERED IN THIS CHAPTER INCLUDE:

✓ **Identity and Access Management**

- E. Implement and manage authorization mechanisms
  - E.1 Role-Based Access Control (RBAC) methods
  - E.2 Rule-based access control methods
  - E.3 Mandatory Access Control (MAC)
  - E.4 Discretionary Access Control (DAC)
- F. Prevent or mitigate access control attacks

Chapter 13, "Managing Identity and Authentication," presented several important topics related to the Identity and Access Management domain of the Common Body of Knowledge (CBK) for the CISSP certification exam. This chapter builds on those topics and includes key information on some common access control models. It also includes information on how to prevent or mitigate access control attacks. Be sure to read and study the materials from each of these chapters to ensure complete coverage of the essential material for this domain.

Comparing Access Control Models

Chapter 13 focused heavily on identification and authentication. After authenticating subjects, the next step is authorization. The method of authorizing subjects to access objects varies depending on the access control method used by the IT system.

TIP

A *subject* is an active entity that accesses a passive object and an *object* is a passive entity that provides information to active subjects. For example, when a user accesses a file, the user is the subject and the file is the object.

There are several categories for access control techniques and the CISSP CIB specifically mentions four: discretionary access control (DAC), mandatory access control (MAC), role-based access control (role-BAC), and rule-based access control (rule-BAC). The following sections introduce some basic principles used by these models and describe the models in more depth.

Comparing Permissions, Rights, and Privileges

When studying access control topics, you'll often come across the terms permissions, rights, and privileges. Some people use these terms interchangeably, but they don't always mean the same thing.

Permissions In general, *permissions* refer to the access granted for an object and determine what you can do with it. If you have read permission for a file, you'll be able to open it and read it. You can grant user permissions to create, read, edit, or delete a file on a file server. Similarly, you can grant user access rights to a file, so in this context, access rights and permissions are synonymous. For example, you may be granted read and execute permissions for an application file, which gives you the right to run the application.

Additionally, you may be granted data rights within a database, allowing you to retrieve or update information in the database.

Rights A *right* primarily refers to the ability to take an action on an object. For example, a user might have the right to modify the system time on a computer or the right to restore backed-up data. This is a subtle distinction and not always stressed. However, you'll rarely see the right to take action on a system referred to as a permission.

Privileges *Privileges* are the combination of rights and permissions. For example, an administrator for a computer will have full privileges, granting the administrator full rights and permissions on the computer. The administrator will be able to perform any actions and access any data on the computer.

Understanding Authorization Mechanisms

Access control models use many different types of authorization mechanisms, or methods, to control who can access specific objects. Here's a brief introduction to some common mechanisms and concepts.

Implicit Deny A basic principle of access control is *implicit deny* and most authorization mechanisms use it. The implicit deny principle ensures that access to an object is denied unless access has been explicitly granted to a subject. For example, imagine an administrator explicitly grants Jeff Full Control permissions to a file but does not explicitly grant permissions to anyone else. Mary doesn't have any access even though the administrator didn't explicitly deny her access. Instead, the implicit deny principle denies access to Mary and everyone else except for Jeff.

Access Control Matrix An *access control matrix* is a table that includes subjects, objects, and assigned privileges. When a subject attempts an action, the system checks the access control matrix to determine if the subject has the appropriate privileges to perform the action. For example, an access control matrix can include a group of files as the objects and a group of users as the subjects. It will show the exact permissions authorized by each user for each file. Note that this covers much more than a single *access control list* (ACL). In this example, each file listed within the matrix has a separate ACL that lists the authorized users and their assigned permissions.

Capability Tables Capability tables are another way to identify privileges assigned to subjects. They are different from ACLs in that a capability table is focused on subjects (such as users, groups, or roles). For example, a capability table created for the accounting role will include a list of all objects that the accounting role can access and will include the specific privileges assigned to the accounting role for these objects. In contrast, ACLs are focused on objects. An ACL for a file would list all the users and/or groups that are authorized access to the file and the specific access granted to each.

TIP

The difference between an ACL and a capability table is the focus. ACLs are object focused and identify access granted to subjects for any specific object. Capability tables are subject focused and identify the objects that subjects can access.

Constrained Interface Applications use constrained interfaces or restricted interfaces to restrict what users can do or see based on their privileges. Users with full privileges have access to all the capabilities of the application. Users with restricted privileges have limited access. Applications constrain the interface using different methods. A common method is to hide the capability if the user doesn't have permissions to use it. For example, commands might be available to administrators via a menu or by right-clicking an item, but if a regular user doesn't have permissions, the command does not appear. Other times, the application displays the menu item but shows it dimmed or disabled. A regular user can see the menu item but will not be able to use it.

Content-Dependent Control *Content-dependent access controls* restrict access to data based on the content within an object. A database view is a content-dependent control. A view retrieves specific columns from one or more tables, creating a virtual table. For example, a customer table in a database could include customer names, email addresses, phone numbers, and credit card data. A customer-based view might show a user only the customer names and email addresses but nothing else. Users granted access to the view can see the customer names and email addresses but cannot access data in the underlying table.

Context-Dependent Control *Context-dependent access controls* require specific activity before granting users access. As an example, consider the data flow for a transaction selling digital products online. Users add products to a shopping cart and begin the checkout process. The first page in the checkout flow shows the products in the shopping cart, the next page collects credit card data, and the last page confirms the purchase and provides instructions for downloading the digital products. The system denies access to the download page if users don't go through the purchase process first. It's also possible to use date and time controls as context-dependent controls. For example, it's possible to restrict access to computers and applications based on the current day and/or time. If users attempt to access the resource outside of the allowed time, the system denies them access.

Need to Know This principle ensures that subjects are granted access only to what they need to know for their work tasks and job functions. Subjects may have clearance to access classified or restricted data but are not granted authorization to the data unless they actually need it to perform a job.

Least Privilege The principle of least privilege ensures that subjects are granted only the privileges they need to perform their work tasks and job functions. This is sometimes lumped together with need to know. The only difference is that least privilege will also include rights to take action on a system.

Separation of Duties and Responsibilities This principle ensures that sensitive functions are split into tasks performed by two or more employees. It helps to prevent fraud and errors by creating a system of checks and balances.

Defining Requirements with a Security Policy

A *security policy* is a document that defines the security requirements for an organization. It identifies assets that need protection and the extent to which security solutions should go to protect them. Some organizations create a security policy as a single document, and other organizations create multiple security policies, with each one focused on a separate area.

Policies are an important element of access control because they help personnel within the organization understand what security requirements are important. Senior leadership approves the security policy and, in doing so, provides a broad overview of an organization's security needs. However, a security policy usually does not go into details about how to fulfill the security needs or how to implement the policy. For example, it may state the need to implement and enforce separation of duties and least privilege principles but not state how to do so. Professionals within the organization use the security policies as a guide to implement security requirements.

TIP

Chapter 1, "Security Governance Through Principles and Policies," covers security policies in more depth. It includes detailed information on standards, procedures, and guidelines.

Implementing Defense in Depth

Organizations implement access controls using a *defense-in-depth strategy*. This uses multiple layers or levels of access controls to provide layered security. As an example, consider Figure 14.1. It shows two servers and two disks to represent assets that an organization wants to protect. Intruders or attackers need to overcome multiple layers of defense to reach these protected assets.

FIGURE 14.1 Defense in depth with layered security

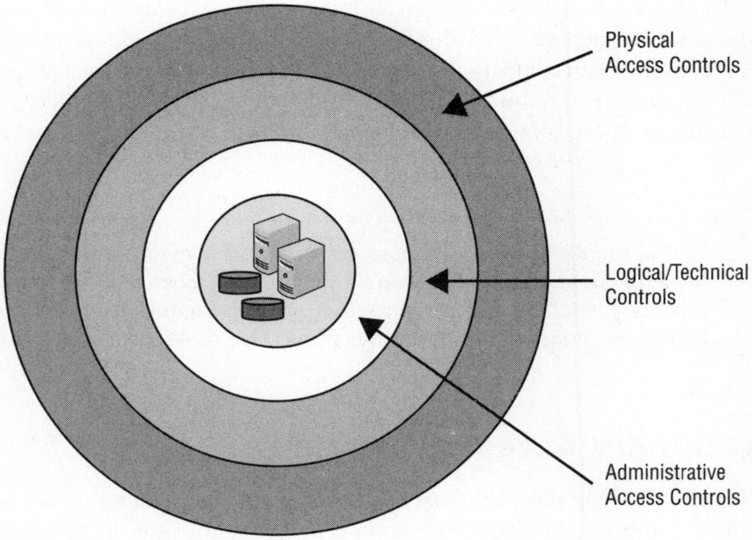

Organizations implement controls using multiple methods. You can't depend on technology alone to provide security; you must also use physical access controls and administrative access controls. For example, if a server has strong authentication but is stored on an unguarded desk, a thief can easily steal it and take his time hacking into the system. Similarly, users may have strong passwords, but social engineers can trick uneducated users into giving up their password.

This concept of defense in depth highlights several important points:

- An organization's security policy, which is one of the administrative access controls, provides a layer of defense for assets by defining security requirements.
- Personnel are a key component of defense. However, they need proper training and education to implement, comply with, and support security elements defined in an organization's security policy.
- A combination of administrative, technical, and physical access controls provides a much stronger defense. Using only administrative, only technical, or only physical controls results in weaknesses that attackers can discover and exploit.

Discretionary Access Controls

A system that employs *discretionary access controls* (DACs) allows the owner, creator, or data custodian of an object to control and define access to that object. All objects have owners, and access control is based on the discretion or decision of the owner. For example, if a user creates a new spreadsheet file, that user is the owner of the file. As the owner, the user can modify the permissions of the file to grant or deny access to other users. Identity-based access control is a subset of DAC because systems identify users based on their identity and assign resource ownership to identities.

A DAC model is implemented using access control lists (ACLs) on objects. Each ACL defines the types of access granted or denied to subjects. It does not offer a centrally controlled management system because owners can alter the ACLs on their objects at will. Access to objects is easy to change, especially when compared to the static nature of mandatory access controls.

Within a DAC environment, administrators can easily suspend user privileges while they are away, such as on vacation. Similarly, it's easy to disable accounts when users leave the organization.

TIP

Within the discretionary access control model, every object has an owner (or data custodian), and owners have full control over their objects. Permissions (such as read and modify for files) are maintained in an ACL, and owners can easily change permissions. This makes the model very flexible.

Nondiscretionary Access Controls

The major difference between discretionary and *nondiscretionary access controls* is in how they are controlled and managed. Administrators centrally administer nondiscretionary access controls and can make changes that affect the entire environment. In contrast, discretionary access control models allow owners to make their own changes, and their changes don't affect other parts of the environment.

In a non-DAC model, access does not focus on user identity. Instead, a static set of rules governing the whole environment manages access. Non-DAC systems are centrally controlled and easier to manage (although less flexible). In general, any model that isn't a discretionary model is a nondiscretionary model. This includes rule-based, role-based, and lattice-based access controls.

Role-based Access Control

Systems that employ role-based or task-based access controls define a subject's ability to access an object based on the subject's role or assigned tasks. *Role-based access control* (role-BAC) is often implemented using groups.

As an example, a bank may have loan officers, tellers, and managers. Administrators can create a group named Loan Officers, place the user accounts of each loan officer into this group, and then assign appropriate privileges to the group, as shown in Figure 14.2. If the organization hires a new loan officer, administrators simply add the new loan officer's account into the Loan Officers group and the new employee automatically has all the same permissions as other loan officers in this group. Administrators would take similar steps for tellers and managers.

FIGURE 14.2 Role-based access controls

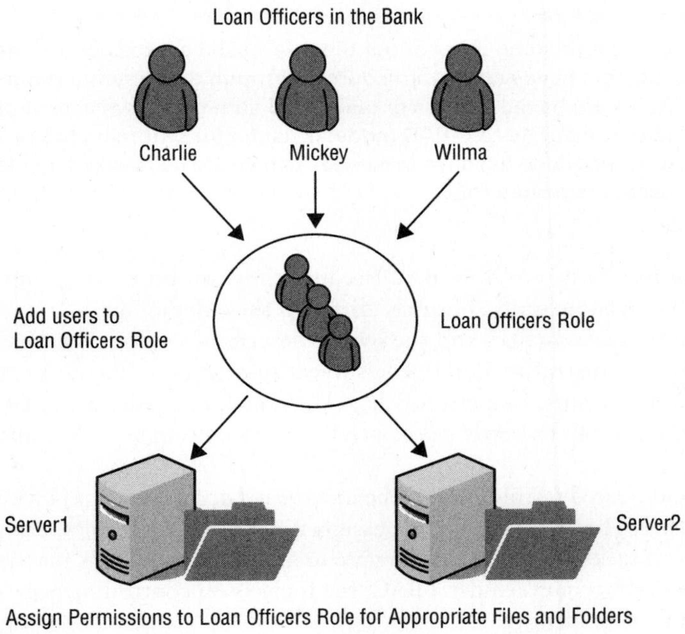

This helps enforce the principle of least privilege by preventing privilege creep. *Privilege creep* is the tendency for privileges to accrue to users over time as their roles and access needs change. Ideally, administrators revoke user privileges when users change jobs within an organization. However, when privileges are assigned to users directly, it is challenging to identify and revoke all of a user's unneeded privileges.

Administrators can easily revoke unneeded privileges by simply removing the user's account from a group. As soon as an administrator removes a user from a group, the user no longer has the privileges assigned to the group. As an example, if a loan officer moves to another department, administrators can simply remove the loan officer's account from the Loan Officers group. This immediately removes all the Loan Officers group privileges from the user's account.

Administrators identify roles (and groups) by job descriptions or work functions. In many cases, this follows the organization's hierarchy documented in an organizational chart. Users who occupy management positions will have greater access to resources than users in a temporary job.

Role-based access controls are useful in dynamic environments with frequent personnel changes because administrators can easily grant multiple permissions simply by adding a new user into the appropriate role. It's worth noting that users can belong to multiple roles or groups. For example, using the same bank scenario, managers might belong to the Managers role, the Loan Officers role, and the Tellers role. This allows managers access all of the same resources that their employees can access.

TIP

A distinguishing point about the role-based access control model is that subjects have access to resources through their membership in roles. Roles are based on jobs or tasks, and administrators assign privileges to the role. The role-BAC model is useful for enforcing the principle of least privilege because privileges can easily be revoked by removing user accounts from a role.

It's easy to confuse DAC and role-BAC because they can both use groups to organize users into manageable units, but they differ in their deployment and use. In the DAC model, objects have owners and the owner determines who has access. In the role-BAC model, administrators determine subject privileges and assign appropriate privileges to roles or groups. In a strict role-BAC model, administrators do not assign privileges to users directly but only grant privileges by adding user accounts to roles or groups.

Another method related to role-BAC is the *task-based access control* (TBAC). TBAC is similar to role-BAC, but instead of being assigned to one or more roles, each user is assigned an array of tasks. These items all relate to assigned work tasks for the person associated with a user account. Under TBAC, the focus is on controlling access by assigned tasks rather than by user identity.

Real World Scenario

Application Roles

Many applications use role-based access controls because they reduce the overall labor cost of maintaining the application. As a simple example, WordPress is a popular web-based application used for blogging and as a content management system.

WordPress includes five roles organized in a hierarchy. The roles, listed from least privileges to the most privileges, are subscriber, contributor, author, editor, and administrator. Each higher-level role includes all the privileges of the lower-level role.

Subscribers can modify some elements of the look and feel of the pages within their user profile. Contributors can create, edit, and delete their own unpublished posts. Authors can create, edit, and publish posts. They can also edit and delete their own published posts, and upload files. Editors can create, edit, and delete any posts. They can also manage website pages, including editing and deleting pages. Administrators can do anything and everything on the site, including managing underlying themes, plug-ins, and users.

Rule-based Access Controls

A *rule-based access control* (rule-BAC) uses a set of rules, restrictions, or filters to determine what can and cannot occur on a system. It includes granting a subject access to an object, or granting the subject the ability to perform an action. A distinctive characteristic about rule-BAC models is that they have global rules that apply to all subjects.

One common example of a rule-BAC model is a firewall. Firewalls include a set of rules or filters within an ACL, defined by an administrator. The firewall examines all the traffic going through it and only allows traffic that meets one of the rules.

Firewalls include a final rule (referred to as the implicit deny rule) denying all other traffic. For example, the last rule might be `deny all all` to indicate the firewall should block all other traffic in or out of the network. In other words, if traffic didn't meet the condition of any previous explicitly defined rule, then the final rule ensures that the traffic is blocked. This final rule is sometimes viewable in the ACL so that you can see it. Other times, the implicit deny rule is implied as the final rule but is not explicitly stated in the ACL.

NOTE: We use acronyms throughout this book such as DAC, MAC, rule-BAC, and role-BAC. However, the CISSP exam typically spells out all terms and acronyms in the questions. Study each of the models and their defining characteristics. However, you don't need to memorize the acronyms.

Attribute-based Access Controls

Traditional rule-BAC models include global rules that apply to all users. However, an advanced implementation of a rule-BAC is an *attribute-based access control* (ABAC) model. ABAC models use policies that include multiple attributes for rules. Many software defined networking applications use ABAC models.

As an example, CloudGenix has created a software-defined wide area network (SD-WAN) solution that implements policies to allow or block traffic. Administrators create ABAC policies using plain language statements such as "Allow Managers to access the WAN using tablets or smartphones." This allows users in the Managers role to access the WAN using tablet devices or smartphones. Notice how this improves the rule-BAC model. The rule-BAC applies to all users, but the ABAC can be much more specific.

Mandatory Access Controls

A *mandatory access control* (MAC) model relies on the use of classification labels. Each classification label represents a security *domain*, or a realm of security. A security domain is a collection of subjects and objects that share a common security policy. For example, a security domain could have the label Secret, and the MAC model would protect all objects with the Secret label in the same manner. Subjects are only able to access objects with the Secret label, when they have a matching Secret label. Additionally, the requirement for subjects to gain the Secret label is the same for all subjects.

Users have labels assigned to them based on their clearance level, which is a form of privilege. Similarly, objects have labels, which indicate their level of classification or sensitivity. For example, the U.S. military uses the labels of Top Secret, Secret, and Confidential to classify data. Administrators can grant access to Top Secret data to users with Top Secret clearances. However, administrators cannot grant access to Top Secret data to users with lower-level clearances such as Secret and Confidential.

Organizations in the private sector often use labels such as confidential (or proprietary), private, sensitive, and public. While governments use labels mandated by law, private sector organizations are free to use whatever labels they choose.

The MAC model is often referred to as a lattice-based model. Figure 14.3 shows an example of lattice-based MAC model. It is reminiscent of a lattice in a garden, such as a rose lattice used to train climbing roses. The horizontal lines labeled Confidential, Private, Sensitive, and Public mark the upper bounds of the classification levels. For example, the area between Public and Sensitive include objects labeled Sensitive (the upper boundary). Users with the Sensitive label can access Sensitive data.

FIGURE 14.3 A representation of the boundaries provided by lattice-based access controls

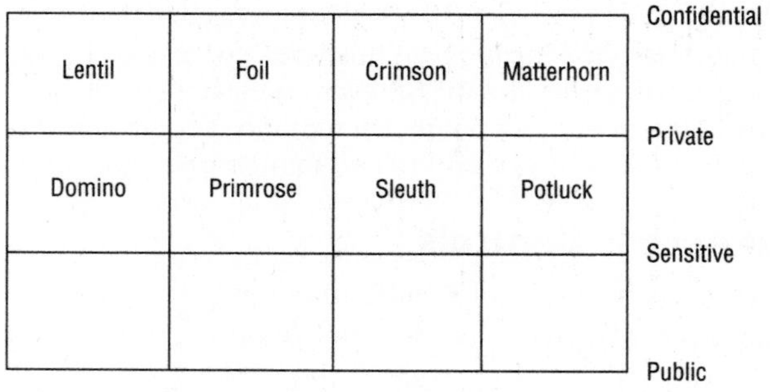

The MAC model also allows labels to identify more defined security domains. Within the Confidential section (between Private and Confidential), there are four separate security domains labeled Lentil, Foil, Crimson, and Matterhorn. These all include Confidential data, but are maintained in separate compartments for an added layer of protection. Users with the Confidential label also require the additional label to access data within these compartments. For example, to access Lentil data, users need to have both the Confidential label and the Lentil label.

Similarly, the compartments labeled Domino, Primrose, Sleuth, and Potluck include Private data. Users need the Private label and one of the labels in this compartment to access the data within that compartment.

The labels in Figure 14.3 are names of World War II military operations, but an organization can use any names for the labels. The key is that these sections provide an added level of compartmentalization for objects such as data. Notice that Sensitive data (between the Public and Sensitive boundaries) doesn't have any additional labels. Users with the Sensitive label can access any data with the Sensitive label.

Personnel within the organization identify the labels and define their meanings as well as the requirements to obtain the labels. Administrators then assign the labels to subjects and objects. With the labels in place, the system determines access based on the assigned labels.

Using compartmentalization with the MAC model enforces the *need to know* principle. Users with the Confidential label are not automatically granted access to compartments within the Confidential section. However, if their job requires them to have access to certain data, such as data with the Crimson label, an administrator can assign them the Crimson label to grant them access to this compartment.

Mandatory access control is prohibitive rather than permissive, and it uses an implicit deny philosophy. If users are not specifically granted access to data, the system denies them access to the associated data. The MAC model is more secure than the DAC model, but it isn't as flexible or scalable.

> **TIP** A distinguishing factor between MAC and rule-based access controls is that MAC controls have labels whereas the rule-based access controls do not use labels.

Security classifications indicate a hierarchy of sensitivity. For example, if you consider the military security labels of Top Secret, Secret, Confidential, and Unclassified, the Top Secret label includes the most sensitive data and unclassified is the least sensitive. Because of this hierarchy, someone cleared for Top Secret data is cleared for Secret and less sensitive data. However, classifications don't have to include lower levels. It is possible to use MAC labels so that a clearance for a higher-level label does not include clearance for a lower-level label.

> **TIP** A key point about the MAC model is that every object and every subject has a label. These labels are predefined and the system makes a determination of access based on assigned labels.

Classifications within a MAC model use one of the following three types of environments:

Hierarchical Environment A *hierarchical environment* relates various classification labels in an ordered structure from low security to medium security to high security, such as Confidential, Secret, and Top Secret, respectively. Each level or classification label in the structure is related. Clearance in one level grants the subject access to objects in that level as well as to all objects in lower levels but prohibits access to all objects in higher levels. For example, someone with a Top Secret clearance can access Top Secret data and Secret data.

Compartmentalized Environment In a *compartmentalized environment*, there is no relationship between one security domain and another. Each domain represents a separate isolated compartment. To gain access to an object, the subject must have specific clearance for its security domain.

Hybrid Environment A *hybrid environment* combines both hierarchical and compartmentalized concepts so that each hierarchical level may contain numerous subdivisions that are isolated from the rest of the security domain. A subject must have the correct clearance and the need to know data within a specific compartment to gain access to the compartmentalized object. A hybrid MAC environment provides granular control over access, but becomes increasingly difficult to manage as it grows. Figure 14.3 is an example of a hybrid environment.

Understanding Access Control Attacks

As mentioned in Chapter 13, one of the goals of access control is to prevent unauthorized access to objects. This includes access into any information system, including networks, services, communications links, and computers, and unauthorized access to data. In addition to controlling access, IT security methods seek to prevent unauthorized disclosure and unauthorized alteration, and to provide consistent availability of resources. In other words, IT security methods attempt to prevent loss of confidentiality, loss of integrity, and loss of availability.

With this in mind, security professionals need to be aware of common attack methods so that they can take proactive steps to prevent them, recognize them when they occur, and respond appropriately. The following sections provide a quick review of risk elements and cover some common access control attacks.

While this section focuses on access control attacks, it's important realize that there are many other types of attacks, which are covered in other chapters. For example, Chapter 6, "Cryptography and Symmetric Key Algorithms," covers various cryptanalytic attacks.

Crackers, Hackers, and Attackers

Crackers are malicious individuals intent on waging an attack against a person or system. They attempt to crack the security of a system to exploit it. They are typically motivated by greed, power, or recognition. Their actions can result in loss of property (such as data and intellectual property), disabled systems, compromised security, negative public opinion, loss of market share, reduced profitability, and lost productivity. In many situations, crackers are simply criminals.

In the 1970s and '80s, hackers were defined as technology enthusiasts with no malicious intent. However, the media now uses the term *hacker* in place of *cracker*. Its use is so widespread that the definition has changed.

To avoid confusion within this book, we use the term *attacker* for malicious intruders. An attack is any attempt to exploit the vulnerability of a system and compromise confidentiality, integrity, and/or availability.

Risk Elements

Chapter 2, "Personnel Security and Risk Management Concepts," covers risk and risk management in more depth, but it's worth reiterating some terms in the context of access control attacks. A *risk* is the possibility or likelihood that a threat will exploit a vulnerability resulting in a loss such as harm to an asset. A *threat* is a potential occurrence that can result in an undesirable outcome. This includes potential attacks by criminals or other attackers. It also includes natural occurrences such as floods or earthquakes, and accidental acts by employees. A *vulnerability* is any type of weakness. The weakness can be due to a flaw or limitation in hardware or software, or the absence of a security control such as the absence of antivirus software on a computer.

Risk management attempts to reduce or eliminate vulnerabilities, or reduce the impact of potential threats by implementing controls or countermeasures. It is not possible, or desirable, to eliminate risk. Instead, an organization focuses on reducing the risks that can cause the most harm to their organization. With this in mind, key steps early in a risk management process are as follows:

- Identifying assets
- Identifying threats
- Identifying vulnerabilities

Identifying Assets

Asset valuation refers to identifying the actual value of assets with the goal of prioritizing them. Risk management focuses on assets with the highest value and identifies controls to mitigate risks to these assets.

The value of an asset is more than just the purchase price. For example, a web server that is generating $10,000 a day in sales is much more valuable than just the cost of the hardware and software. If this server failed, it would result in the loss of revenue from direct sales and the loss of customer goodwill.

NOTE Customer goodwill is one of many intangible aspects that represent the actual value of an asset.

Knowing the asset value also helps with cost-benefit analysis, which seeks to determine the cost-effectiveness of different types of security controls. For example, if an asset is valued at hundreds of thousands of dollars, an effective security control that costs $100 is justified. In contrast, spending a few hundred dollars to protect against the theft of a $10 mouse is not a justifiable expense. Instead, an organization will often accept risks associated with low-value assets.

In the context of access control attacks, it's important to evaluate the value of data. For example, if an attacker compromises a database server and downloads a customer database that includes privacy data and credit card information, it represents a significant loss to the company. This isn't always easy to quantify, but attacks on Sony provide some perspective. (See the sidebar "Data Breaches at Sony.")

Experts estimate the direct losses from just the Sony PlayStation breach at $171 million. It's highly likely that many gamers have chosen to quit using the PlayStation and/or purchase another competing product. Were these losses preventable? Many security professionals say yes. At the Black Hat conference in 2011, Sony was nominated for "Most Epic Fail" for these attacks and for laying off numerous information security personnel months before the first cyber attack in 2011.

It's possible that Sony simply didn't recognize the value of the data in its databases. However, after the 2011 attacks, Sony has quantifiable data it can use to measure the costs of the loss. Effective asset valuation is able to determine the value of the data before such massive losses.

Real World Scenario

Data Breaches at Sony

Sony suffered multiple data breaches throughout 2011, and then again in 2014. These occurrences severely tarnished its image.

A massive data breach in April 2011 resulted in attackers stealing data from 77 million Sony PlayStation customer accounts. In May 2011, attackers compromised 24.5 million Sony Online Entertainment accounts. In June 2011, an attack on Sony Pictures compromised over one million user accounts, and the attackers bragged that they used a single SQL injection attack to retrieve data. (For more on injection attacks, see Chapter 21, "Malicious Code and Application Attacks.") In October 2011, Sony locked almost 100,000 PlayStation accounts and sent email messages to users indicating attackers stole the users' credentials. Sony encouraged these users to "choose unique, hard-to-guess passwords," implying the problem was the customers' fault. Ironically, Sony may have been correct because many users have a single password they use for multiple online accounts. However, coming after the recent spate of attacks, users met Sony's advice with skepticism.

Attackers launched another attack in November and December 2014, effectively taking down their entire network for several days. Attacks obtained over 100 TB of data, and released some damaging information (such as critical internal emails) to the public. Rumors started to trickle out indicating that North Korea was responsible for the attack because Kim Jong-un was upset about the Sony movie "The Interview." The U.S. government eventually concluded that North Korea was responsible for the attack and imposed sanctions on North Korea as a response.

Identifying Threats

After identifying and prioritizing assets, an organization attempts to identify any possible threats to the valuable systems. *Threat modeling* refers to the process of identifying, understanding, and categorizing potential threats. A goal is to identify a potential list of threats to these systems and to analyze the threats.

TIP

Attackers aren't the only type of threat. A threat can be something natural, such as a flood or earthquake, or it could be accidental, such as a user accidentally deleting a file. However, when considering access control, threats are primarily unauthorized individuals (commonly attackers) attempting unauthorized access to resources.

Threat modeling isn't meant to be a single event. Instead, it's common for an organization to begin threat modeling early in the design process of a system and continue throughout its life cycle. For example, Microsoft uses its Security Development Lifecycle process to consider and implement security at each stage of a product's development. This supports the motto of "Secure by Design, Secure by Default, Secure in Deployment and Communication" (also known as SD3+C). Microsoft has two primary goals in mind with this process:

- To reduce the number of security-related design and coding defects
- To reduce the severity of any remaining defects

In other words, it attempts to reduce vulnerabilities and reduce the impact of any vulnerabilities that remain. The overall result is reduced risk.

Threat Modeling Approaches

There's an almost infinite possibility of threats, so it's important to use a structured approach to identify relevant threats. For example, some organizations use one or more of the following three approaches:

Focused on Assets This method uses asset valuation results and attempts to identify threats to the valuable assets. Personnel evaluate specific assets to determine their susceptibility to attacks. If the asset hosts data, personnel evaluate the access controls to identify threats that can bypass authentication or authorization mechanisms.

Focused on Attackers Some organizations identify potential attackers and identify the threats they represent based on the attacker's goals. For example, a government is often able to identify potential attackers and recognize what the attackers want to achieve. They can then use this knowledge to identify and protect their relevant assets. A challenge with this approach is that new attackers appear that might not have been considered a threat previously. For example, Sony might not have considered attacks from a foreign government (such as North Korea) prior to the attacks in 2014.

Focused on Software If an organization develops software, it can consider potential threats against the software. While organizations didn't commonly develop their own software years ago, it's common to do so today. Specifically, most organizations have a web presence, and many create their own websites. Fancy websites attract more traffic, but they also require more sophisticated programming and present additional threats. Chapter 21 covers application attacks and web application security.

If an organization identifies an attacker as a potential threat (as opposed to a natural threat), threat modeling attempts to identify the attacker's goals. Some attackers may want to disable a system, while other attackers may want to steal data, and each goal represents a separate threat. Once an organization identifies these threats, it categorizes them based on the priority of the underlying assets.

Advanced Persistent Threat

Any threat model should take into account the existence of known threats, and a relatively new threat is an *advanced persistent threat (APT)*. An APT refers to a group of attackers who are working together and are highly motivated, skilled, and patient. They have advanced knowledge and a wide variety of skills to detect and exploit vulnerabilities. They are persistent and focus on exploiting one or more specific targets rather than just any target of opportunity. Governments typically fund APTs. However, some groups of organized criminals also fund and run APTs.

> Mandiant, an information security company, released a report in 2013 documenting a group operating out of China that they named APT1. The report provided evidence that indicated personnel employed by the People's Liberation Army originated a wide range of attacks on non-China targets. Mandiant indicated APT1 released at least 40 different families of malware, stole hundreds of terabytes of data from over 100 different organizations, and maintained remote access to some networks for several years before being detected. China has denied the claims. You can access the report by searching "Mandiant APT1" with your favorite search engine.

It used to be that to keep your network safe, you only needed to be more secure than other networks. The attackers would go after the easy targets and avoid the secure networks. You might remember the old line "How fast do you need to run when you're being chased by a grizzly bear?" Answer: "Only a little faster than the slowest person in your group."

However, if you're carrying a jar of honey that the bear wants, he may ignore the others and go after only you. This is what an APT does. It goes after specific targets based on what it wants to exploit from those targets. Here are a few examples that security experts attribute to APTs:

Sony Many people attribute the attacks on Sony in 2014 to an APT sponsored by a foreign government. The U.S. government imposed sanctions on North Korea after concluding that North Korea was responsible for the attacks. Some experts suspect that another government orchestrated the attacks with the intent of implicating North Korea.

Google Google released details of a highly sophisticated attack against it and several other companies that occurred in December 2009. It said the attack originated from China and resulted in the theft of intellectual property. The attack also targeted Gmail accounts of Chinese human rights activists. Google discovered that attackers accessed accounts for other human rights advocates in China on a routine basis.

U.S. Department of Defense An attack in 2008 began after a military member inserted an infected USB flash drive into a computer. The malware spread to highly classified networks and it periodically sent out packets of information over the Internet during a 14-month period. Operation Buckshot Yankee finally eradicated the malware in 2009.

The French Government In 2011, a successful spear phishing attack allowed attackers to control over 150 computers in the French Ministry of Economy. Attackers targeted specific email addresses within the French Ministry and spoofed the source address, indicating the emails arrived from other employees in the Ministry. These emails included malicious attachments. After users opened the attachment, attackers were able to create backdoors on the user systems and access them remotely. Attackers retrieved documents for over three months from these backdoors.

RSA Attackers used socially engineered emails to exploit a zero-day vulnerability in Adobe Flash in March 2011. Attackers were able to steal information related to RSA's SecurID token devices. They then used this information to target contractors such as Lockheed Martin and L-3 Communications.

Stuxnet Stuxnet was a worm that exploited several zero-day vulnerabilities and caused a significant amount of damage to Iranian nuclear facilities. Several reports subsequently indicated that Stuxnet was part of a joint U.S. and Israeli operation name Operation Olympic Games. It was discovered in 2010.

The important point to remember about APTs is that they can target any company, not just governments.

Identifying Vulnerabilities

After identifying valuable assets and potential threats, an organization will perform *vulnerability analysis*. In other words, it attempts to discover weaknesses in these systems against potential threats. In the context of access control, vulnerability analysis attempts to identify the strengths and weaknesses of the different access control mechanisms and the potential of a threat to exploit a weakness.

Vulnerability analysis is an ongoing process and can include both technical and administrative steps. In larger organizations, specific individuals may be doing vulnerability analysis as a full-time job. They regularly perform vulnerability scans, looking for a wide variety of vulnerabilities, and report the results. In smaller organizations, a network administrator may run vulnerability scans on a periodic basis, such as once a week or once a month.

A risk analysis will often include a vulnerability analysis by evaluating systems and the environment against known threats and vulnerabilities, followed by a penetration test to exploit vulnerabilities.

Common Access Control Attacks

Access control attacks attempt to bypass or circumvent access control methods. As mentioned in Chapter 13, access control starts with identification and authorization, and access control attacks often try to steal user credentials. After attackers have stolen a user's credentials, they can launch an online *impersonation attack* by logging in as the user and accessing the user's resources. In other cases, an access control attack can bypass authentication mechanisms and just steal the data, as was mentioned in the Sony examples earlier in this chapter.

This book covers multiple attacks, and the following sections cover some common attacks directly related to access control.

Access Aggregation Attacks

Access aggregation refers to collecting multiple pieces of nonsensitive information and combining (i.e., aggregating) them to learn sensitive information. In other words, a person or group may be able to collect multiple facts about a system and then use these facts to launch an attack.

Reconnaissance attacks are access aggregation attacks that combine multiple tools to identify multiple elements of a system, such as IP addresses, open ports, running services, operating systems, and more. Attackers also use aggregation attacks against databases. Chapter 20, "Software Development Security," covers aggregation and inference attacks that indirectly allow unauthorized individuals access to data using aggregation and inference techniques.

Combining defense-in-depth, need-to-know, and least privilege principles helps prevent access aggregation attacks.

Password Attacks

As mentioned in Chapter 1, passwords are the weakest form of authentication. If an attacker is successful in a password attack, the attacker can gain access to the account and access resources authorized to the account. If an attacker discovers a root or administrator password, the attacker can access any other account and its resources. If attackers discover passwords for privileged accounts in a high-security environment, the security of the environment can never be fully trusted again. The attacker could have created other accounts or backdoors to access the system. Instead of accepting the risk, an organization may choose to rebuild the entire system from scratch.

A *strong password* helps prevent password attacks and includes at least eight characters with a combination of at least three of the four character types (uppercase, lowercase, numbers, and special characters). As password crackers get better, some people believe that strong passwords must be at least 15 characters, though it's difficult to get regular users to buy into this. While security professionals usually know what makes a strong password, many users do not, and it is common for users to use short passwords with only a single character type. For example, attackers published account information they stole from one of the Sony attacks mentioned earlier.

Troy Hunt, Microsoft Most Valuable Professional (MVP) for Developer Security, analyzed these passwords (`www.troyhunt.com/2011/06/brief-sony-password-analysis.html`). The analysis showed that the top 10 passwords were seinfeld, password, winner, 123456, purple, sweeps, contest, princess, maggie, and 9452. Attackers can discover these passwords in no more than a few seconds using a common password-cracking tool.

NOTE Most security professionals know they should never use simple passwords, such as 123456. However, security professionals sometimes forget that users still create these types of simple passwords because they are unaware of the risks. Many end users benefit from security training to educate them.

The following sections describe common password attacks using dictionary, brute-force, rainbow table, and sniffing methods. Some of these attacks are possible against online accounts. However, it's more common for an attacker to steal an account database and then crack the passwords offline.

Dictionary Attacks

A *dictionary attack* is an attempt to discover passwords by using every possible password in a predefined database or list of common or expected passwords. In other words, an attacker starts with a database of words commonly found in a dictionary. Dictionary attack databases also include character combinations commonly used as passwords, but not found in dictionaries. For example, you will probably see the list of passwords found in the published Sony accounts database mentioned earlier in many password-cracking dictionaries.

Additionally, dictionary attacks often scan for one-upped-constructed passwords. A *one-upped-constructed password* is a previously used password, but with one character different. For example, password1 is one-upped from password, as are Password, 1password, and passXword. Attackers often use this approach when generating rainbow tables (discussed later in this chapter).

TIP Some people think that using a foreign word as a password will beat dictionary attacks. However, password-cracking dictionaries can, and often do, include foreign words.

Brute-Force Attacks

A *brute-force attack* is an attempt to discover passwords for user accounts by systematically attempting all possible combinations of letters, numbers, and symbols. Attackers don't typically type these in manually but instead have programs that can programmatically try all the combinations. A *hybrid attack* attempts a dictionary attack and then performs a type of brute-force attack with one-upped-constructed passwords.

The longer and more complex a password is, the more costly and time consuming a brute-force attack becomes. As the number of possibilities increases, the cost of performing an exhaustive attack goes up. In other words, the longer the password and the more character types it includes, the more secure it is against brute-force attacks.

Passwords and usernames are stored in an account database file on secured systems. However, instead of being stored as plain text, systems and applications commonly hash passwords, and only store the hash values.

The following three steps occur when a user authenticates with a hashed password.

1. The user enters credentials such as a username and password.
2. The user's system hashes the password and sends the hash to the authenticating system.
3. The authenticating system compares this hash to the hash stored in the password database file. If it matches, it indicates the user entered the correct password.

This provides two important protections. Passwords do not traverse the network in clear text, making them susceptible to sniffing attacks. Password databases do not store passwords in clear text, making it easier for attackers to discover the passwords if they access the password database.

However, password attacker tools look for a password that creates the same hash value as an entry stored in the account database file. If they're successful, they can use the password to log on to the account.

For example, imagine the password IPassed has a stored hash value of 1A5C7G hexadecimal (though the actual hash would be much longer). A brute-force password tool would guess a password, calculate the hash, and compare it against the stored hash value. This is also known as comparative analysis. When the password-cracking tool finds a matching hash value, it indicates that the guessed password is very likely the original password. In this case, the tool cracked the password.

If two separate passwords create the same hash, it results in a collision. Collisions aren't desirable and ideally, collisions aren't possible, but some hashing functions (such as MD5) are not collision free. This allows an attacker to create a different password that results in the same hash as a hashed password stored in the account database file.

With the speed of modern computers and the ability to employ distributed computing, brute-force attacks prove successful against even some strong passwords. The actual time it takes to discover passwords depends on the algorithm used to hash them and the power of the computer.

Many attackers are using graphic processing units (GPUs) in brute-force attacks. In general, many GPUs have more processing power than most CPUs in desktop computers. Blogger Vijay Devakumar ran some tests using an older CPU-based password cracker named Cain & Abel against a newer GPU-based tool named ighashgpu. He reported that it took Cain & Abel up to 1 hour and 30 minutes to crack a six-character password but ighashgpu took less than 4 seconds to crack the same password.

TIP With enough time, attackers can discover any password using an offline brute-force attack. However, longer passwords result in sufficiently longer times, making it infeasible for attackers to crack them. For example, a 12-character password using four character types can take thousands of years to crack.

Birthday Attack

A *birthday attack* focuses on finding collisions. Its name comes from a statistical phenomenon known as the birthday paradox. The birthday paradox states that if there are 23 people in a room, there is a 50 percent chance that any two of them will have the same birthday. This is not the same year, but instead the same month and day, such as March 30.

With February 29 in a leap year, there are only 366 possible days in a year. With 367 people in a room, you have a 100 percent chance of getting at least two people with the same birthdays. Reduce this to only 23 people in the room, and you still have a 50 percent chance that any two have the same birthday.

This is similar to finding any two passwords with the same hash. If a hashing function could only create 366 different hashes, then an attacker with a sample of only 23 hashes has a 50 percent chance of discovering two passwords that create the same hash. Hashing algorithms can create many more than 366 different hashes, but the point is that the birthday attack method doesn't need all possible hashes to see a match.

From another perspective, imagine that you are one of the people in the room and you want to find someone else with the same birthday as you. In this example, you'll need 253 people in the room to reach the same 50 percent probability of finding someone else with the same birthday. Even though you need more people in the room, the point is that you don't need 366 people in the room to find a match.

Similarly, it is possible for some tools to come up with another password that creates the same hash of a given hash. For example, if you know that the hash of the administrator account password is 1A5C7G, some tools can identify a password that will create the same hash of 1A5C7G. It isn't necessarily the same password, but if it can create the same hash, it is just as effective as the original password.

You can reduce the success of birthday attacks by using hashing algorithms with a sufficient number of bits to make collisions computationally infeasible, and by using salts (discussed in the "Rainbow Table Attacks" section next). There was a time when MD5 (using 128 bits) was considered to be collision free. However, computing power continues to improve, and MD5 is not collision free. SHA-3 (short for Secure Hash Algorithm version 3) can use as many as 512 bits and is considered safe against birthday attacks and collisions—at least for now. Computing power continues to improve, so at some point,

SHA-3 will be replaced with another hashing algorithm with longer hashes and/or stronger cryptology methods used to create the hash.

Rainbow Table Attacks

It takes a long time to find a password by guessing it, hashing it, and then comparing it with a valid password hash. However, a *rainbow table* reduces this time by using large databases of precomputed hashes. Attackers guess a password (with either a dictionary or a brute-force method), hash it, and then put both the guessed password and the hash of the guessed password into the rainbow table.

A password cracker can then compare every hash in the rainbow table against the hash in a stolen password database file. A traditional password-cracking tool must guess the password and hash it before it can compare the hashes. However, when using the rainbow table the password cracker doesn't spend any time guessing and calculating hashes. It simply compares the hashes until it finds a match. This can significantly reduce the time it takes to crack a password.

TIP

Many different rainbow tables are available for free download. Rainbow tables that have hashes for 14-character passwords using all four character types are approximately 7.5 GB in size. Although these take some time to download, attackers are willing to wait. However, a passphrase using 15 characters or more will beat most rainbow tables.

Many systems commonly *salt* passwords to reduce the effectiveness of rainbow table attacks. A salt is a group of random bits, added to a password before hashing it. Cryptographic methods add the additional bits before hashing it, making it significantly more difficult for an attacker to use rainbow tables against the passwords. However, given enough time, attackers can still crack salted passwords using a brute-force attack. Combining salts with long, complex passwords does significantly reduce the effectiveness of rainbow tables.

Sniffer Attacks

Sniffing captures packets sent over a network with the intent of analyzing the packets. A sniffer (also called a packet analyzer or protocol analyzer) is a software application that captures traffic traveling over the network. Administrators use sniffers to analyze network traffic and troubleshoot problems.

Of course, attackers can also use sniffers. A *sniffer attack* (also called a snooping attack or eavesdropping attack) occurs when an attacker uses a sniffer to capture information transmitted over a network. They can capture and read any data sent over a network in clear text, including passwords.

Wireshark is a popular protocol analyzer available as a free download. Figure 14.4 shows Wireshark with the contents of a relatively small capture, and demonstrates how attackers can capture and read data sent over a network in cleartext.

FIGURE 14.4 Wireshark capture

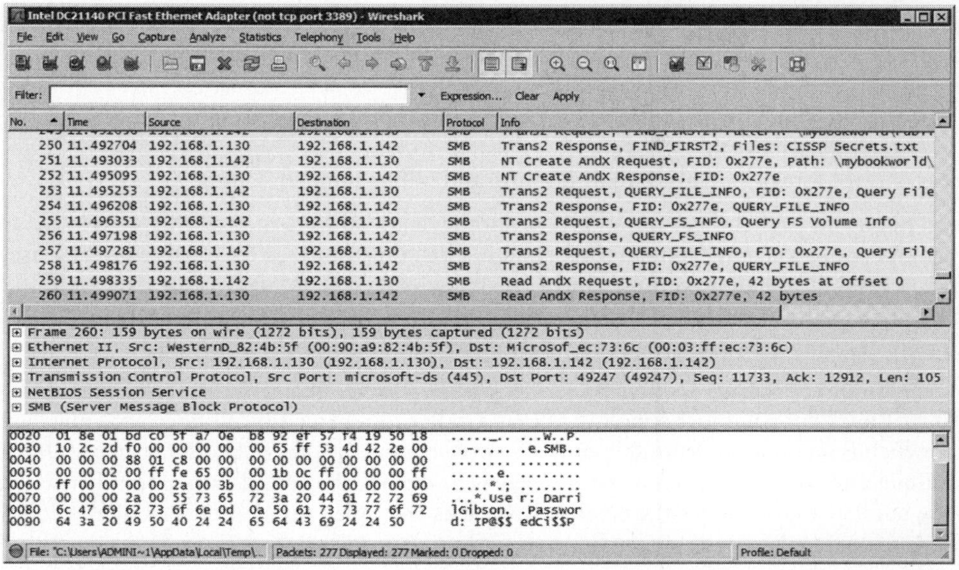

The top pane shows packet 260 selected and you can see the contents of this packet in the bottom pane. It includes the text `User: DarrilGibson Password: IP@$$edCi$$P`. If you look at the first packet in the top pane (packet number 250), you can see that the name of the opened file is `CISSP Secrets.txt`.

The following techniques can prevent successful sniffing attacks:

- Encrypt all sensitive data (including passwords) sent over a network. Attackers cannot read encrypted data with a sniffer. For example, Kerberos encrypts tickets to prevent attacks, and attackers cannot read the contents of these tickets with a sniffer.
- Use one-time passwords when encryption is not possible or feasible. One-time passwords prevent the success of sniffing attacks, because they are used only once. Even if an attacker captures a one-time password, the attacker is not able to use it.
- Protect network devices with physical security. Controlling physical access to routers and switches prevents attackers from installing sniffers on these devices.
- Monitor the network for signatures from sniffers. Intrusion detection systems can monitor the network for sniffers and will raise an alert when they detect a sniffer on the network.

Spoofing Attacks

Spoofing (also known as masquerading) is pretending to be something, or someone, else. There is a wide variety of spoofing attacks. As an example, an attacker can use someone else's credentials to enter a building or access an IT system. Some applications spoof legitimate logon screens. One attack brought up a logon screen that looked exactly like the operating system logon screen. When the user entered credentials, the fake application captured the user's credentials and the attacker used them later. Some phishing attacks (described later in this section) mimic this with bogus websites.

In an IP spoofing attack, attackers replace a valid source IP address with a false one to hide their identity or to impersonate a trusted system. Other types of spoofing used in access control attacks include email spoofing and phone number spoofing.

Email Spoofing Spammers commonly spoof the email address in the From field to make an email appear to come from another source. Phishing attacks often do this to trick users into thinking the email is coming from a trusted source. The Reply To field can be a different email address and email programs typically don't display this until a user actually replies to the email. By this time, they often ignore it.

Phone Number Spoofing Caller ID services allow users to identify the phone number of any caller. Phone number spoofing allows a caller to replace this number with another one, which is a common technique on Voice over Internet Protocol (VoIP) systems. One technique attackers have been using recently is to replace the actual calling number with a phone number that includes the same area code as the called number. This makes it look like it's a local call.

Social Engineering Attacks

Sometimes, the easiest way to get someone's password is to ask for it, and this is a common method used by social engineers. *Social engineering* occurs when an attacker attempts to gain the trust of someone by using deceit, such as false flattery or impersonation, or by using conniving behavior. The attacker attempts to trick people into revealing information they wouldn't normally reveal or perform an action they wouldn't normally perform. Often the goal of the social engineer is to gain access to the IT infrastructure or the physical facility.

For example, skilled social engineers can convince an uneducated help desk employee that they are associated with upper management and working remotely but have forgotten their password. If fooled, the employee may reset the password and provide the attacker with the new password. Other times, social engineers trick regular users into revealing their own passwords, providing the attacker with access to the user's accounts. Educating employees on common social engineer tactics reduces the effectiveness of these types of attacks.

Social engineering attacks can happen over the phone, in person, and via email. In person, malicious individuals often impersonate repair technicians, such as a telephone repair technician, to gain physical access. If they gain access to the network infrastructure, they can then install a sniffer to capture sensitive data. Verifying visitor identities before providing access can mitigate these types of impersonation attacks.

Sometimes a social engineer just tries to look over the shoulder of an individual to read information on the computer screen or watch the keyboard as a user types. This is commonly called *shoulder surfing*. Screen filters placed over a monitor can restrict the attacker's view. Additionally, password masking (displaying an alternate character such as an asterisk instead of the actual password characters) is often used to mitigate shoulder surfing.

Phishing

Phishing is a form of social engineering that attempts to trick users into giving up sensitive information, opening an attachment, or clicking a link. It often tries to obtain user credentials or personally identifiable information (PII) such as usernames, passwords, or credit card details by masquerading as a legitimate company. Attackers send phishing emails indiscriminately as spam, without knowing who will get them but in the hope that some users will respond. Phishing emails commonly inform the user of a bogus problem and say that if the user doesn't take action, the company will lock the user's account. For example, the email may state that the company detected suspicious activity on the account and unless the user verifies username and password information, the company will lock the account.

Simple phishing attacks inform users of a problem and ask the recipients to respond to an email with their username, password, and other details. The From email address is often spoofed to look legitimate, but the Reply To email address is an account controlled by the attacker. Sophisticated attacks include a link to a bogus website that looks legitimate. For example, if the phishing email describes a problem with a PayPal account, the bogus website looks like the PayPal website. If the user enters credentials, the website captures them and passes them to the attacker.

Other times, the goal of sending a phishing email is to install malware on user systems. The message may include an infected file such as an attachment and encourage the user to open it. The email could include a link to a website that installs a malicious drive-by download without the user's knowledge.

NOTE

A drive-by download is a type of malware that installs itself without the user's knowledge when the user visits a website. Drive-by downloads take advantage of vulnerabilities in browsers or plug-ins.

Some malicious websites try to trick the user into downloading and installing the software. For example, ransomware has become very popular with attackers in recent years. Attackers deliver it through malicious attachments and drive-by downloads, and by encouraging users to download and install software. CryptoLocker is one of several variants. Once installed, it encrypts all the data on the users' hard drives. It then threatens the users that unless they pay a ransom (such as $300 or more), the attackers will delete the encryption key and the user's data will be lost forever. Even though police forces disrupted the network running the original CryptoLocker ransomware in mid-2014, variants started appearing soon afterward.

Personnel can avoid some of the common risks associated with phishing by following some simple rules:

- Be suspicious of unexpected email messages, or email messages from unknown senders.
- Never open unexpected email attachments.

- Never share sensitive information via email.
- Be suspicious of any links in email.

There are several variations of phishing attacks, including spear phishing, whaling, and vishing.

Spear Phishing

Spear phishing is a form of phishing targeted to a specific group of users, such as employees within a specific organization. It may appear to originate from a colleague or co-worker within the organization or from an external source.

For example, attackers exploited a zero-day vulnerability in Adobe PDF files that allowed them to embed malicious code. If users opened the file, it installed malware onto the user's systems. The attackers named the PDF file FY12 ... Contract Guide and stated in the email that it provided updated information on a contract award process. They sent the email to targeted email addresses at well-known government contractors such as Lockheed Martin. If any contractors opened the file, it installed malware on their systems that gave attackers remote access to infected systems.

NOTE

A zero-day vulnerability is one that application vendors either don't know about, or have not released a patch to remove the vulnerability. The FY12... Contract Guide attack exploited a vulnerability in PDF files. Even though Adobe patched that vulnerability, attackers discover new application vulnerabilities regularly.

Whaling

Whaling is a variant of phishing that targets senior or high-level executives such as CEOs and presidents within a company. A well-known whaling attack targeted about 20,000 senior corporate executives with an email identifying each recipient by name and stating they were subpoenaed to appear before a grand jury. It included a link to get more information on the subpoena. If the executive clicked the link, a message on the website indicated that the executive needed to install a browser add-on to read the file.

Executives that approved the installation of the add-on actually installed malicious software that logged their keystrokes, capturing login credentials for different websites they visited. It also gave the attacker remote access to the executive's system, allowing the attacker to install additional malware, or read all the data on the system.

Vishing

While attackers primarily launch phishing attacks via email, they have also used other means to trick users, such as instant messaging (IM) and VoIP.

Vishing is a variant of phishing that uses the phone system or VoIP. A common attack uses an automated call to the user explaining a problem with a credit card account. The user is encouraged to verify or validate information such as a credit card number, expiration date, and security code on the back of the card. Vishing attacks commonly spoof the caller ID number to impersonate a valid bank or financial institution.

Smartcard Attacks

Smartcards provide better authentication than passwords, especially when they're combined with another factor of authentication such as a personal identification number (PIN). However, smartcards are also susceptible to attacks. A *side-channel attack* is a passive, noninvasive attack intended to observe the operation of a device. When the attack is successful, the attacker is able to learn valuable information contained within the card, such as an encryption key.

A smartcard includes a microprocessor, but it doesn't have internal power. Instead, when a user inserts the card into the reader, the reader provides power to the card. The reader has an electromagnetic coil that excites electronics on the card. This provides enough power for the smartcard to transmit data to the reader.

Side-channel attacks analyze the information sent to the reader. Sometimes they are able to measure the power consumption of a chip, using a power monitoring attack or differential power analysis attack, to extract information. In a timing attack, they are able to monitor the processing timings to gain information based on how much time different computations require. Fault analysis attacks attempt to cause faults, such as by providing too little power to the card, to glean valuable information.

Denial-of-Service Attacks

A *denial-of-service* (DoS) attack prevents a system from processing or responding to legitimate traffic or requests for resources. When the system fails, all legitimate access to the system is blocked, disrupted, or slowed. As a simple example, if a server isn't protected with adequate physical security, an attacker can unplug it, removing it from service.

DoS attacks often occur over a network, including over the Internet. Some DoS attacks allow attackers to install malicious code onto servers. For example, an attacker can install a drive-by download or code that displays malicious pop-ups on web servers. This code can infect user systems when they visit the infected website.

Summary of Protection Methods

The following list summarizes many security precautions that protect against access control attacks. However, it's important to realize that this isn't a comprehensive list of protections against all types of attacks. You'll find additional controls that help prevent attacks covered throughout this book.

Control physical access to systems. An old saying related to security is that if an attacker has unrestricted physical access to a computer, the attacker owns it. If attackers can gain physical access to an authentication server, they can steal the password file in a very short time. Once attackers have the password file, they can crack the passwords offline. If attackers successfully download a password file, all passwords should be considered compromised.

Control electronic access to files. Tightly control and monitor electronic access to password files. End users and those who are not account administrators have no need to access the password database file for daily work tasks. Security professionals should investigate any unauthorized access to password database files immediately.

Encrypt password files. Encrypting password files with the strongest encryption available for the operating system helps protect them from unauthorized access. Hashing (as described earlier) is one-way encryption, and it is a common method of encrypting passwords. Additionally, salting the passwords prior to hashing them provides even stronger protection. It's also important to maintain rigid control over all media containing copies of password database files, such as backup tapes or repair disks. Last, it's important to encrypt sensitive data in transit, including passwords sent over a network.

Create a strong password policy. A password policy programmatically enforces the use of strong passwords and ensures that users regularly change their passwords. Attackers require more time to crack a longer password using multiple character types. Given enough time, attackers can discover any password in an offline brute-force attack, so changing passwords regularly is required to maintain security. More secure or sensitive environments require even stronger passwords, and require users to change their passwords more frequently. Many organizations implement separate password policies for privileged accounts such as administrator accounts to ensure that they have stronger passwords and that administrators change the passwords more frequently than regular users.

Use password masking. Ensure that applications never display passwords in clear text on any screen. Instead, mask the display of the password by displaying an alternate character such as an asterisk (*). This reduces shoulder surfing attempts, but users should be aware that an attacker might be able to learn the password by watching the user type the keys on the keyboard.

Deploy multifactor authentication. Deploy multifactor authentication, such as using biometrics or token devices. When an organization uses multifactor authentication, attackers are not able to access a network if they discover just a password. Many online services, such as Google, now offer multifactor authentication as an additional measure of protection.

Use account lockout controls. Account lockout controls help prevent online password attacks. They lock an account after the incorrect password is entered a predefined number of times. Account lockout controls typically use clipping levels that ignore some user errors but take action after reaching a threshold. For example, it's common to allow a user to enter the incorrect password as many as five times before locking the account. For systems and services that don't support account lockout controls, such as most FTP servers, extensive logging along with an intrusion detection system can protect the server.

TIP

Account lockout controls help prevent an attacker from guessing a password in an online account. However, this does not prevent an attacker from using a password-cracking tool against a stolen database file.

Use last logon notification. Many systems display a message including the time, date, and location (such as the computer name or IP address) of the last successful logon. If users pay attention to this message, they might notice if someone else logged onto their account. For example, if a user logged on to an account last Friday, but the last logon notification indicates someone accessed the account on Saturday, it indicates a problem. Users who suspect someone else is logging on to their accounts can change their passwords or report the issue to a system administrator.

Educate users about security. Properly trained users have a better understanding of security and the benefit of using stronger passwords. Inform users that they should never share or write down their passwords. Administrators might write down long, complex passwords for the most sensitive accounts, such as administrator or root accounts, and store these passwords in a vault or safety deposit box. Offer tips to users on how to create strong passwords, such as with password phrases, and how to prevent shoulder surfing. Also, let users know the dangers of using the same password for all online accounts, such as banking accounts and gaming accounts. When users use the same passwords for all these accounts, a successful attack on a gaming system can give attackers access to a user's bank accounts. Users should also know about common social-engineering tactics.

Summary

This chapter covered many concepts related to access control models. Permissions refer to the access granted for an object and determine what a user (subject) can do with the object. A right primarily refers to the ability to take an action on an object. Privileges include both rights and permissions. Implicit deny ensures that access to an object is denied unless access has been explicitly granted to a subject.

An access control matrix is an object-focused table that includes objects, subjects, and the privileges assigned to subjects. Each row within the table represents an ACL for a single object. ACLs are object focused and identify access granted to subjects for any specific object. Capability tables are subject focused and identify the objects that subjects can access.

A constrained interface restricts what users can do or see based on their privileges. Content-dependent controls restrict access based on the content within an object. Context-dependent controls require specific activity before granting users access.

The principle of least privilege ensures that subjects are granted only the privileges they need to perform their work tasks and job functions. Separation of duties helps prevent fraud by ensuring that sensitive functions are split into tasks performed by two or more employees.

A written security policy defines the security requirements for an organization, and security controls implement and enforce the security policy. A defense-in-depth strategy implements security controls on multiple levels to protect assets.

With discretionary access controls, all objects have an owner, and the owner has full control over the object. Administrators centrally manage nondiscretionary controls.

Role-based access controls use roles or groups that often match the hierarchy of an organization. Administrators place users into roles and assign privileges to the roles based on jobs or tasks. Rule-based access controls use global rules that apply to all subjects equally. Mandatory access controls require all objects to have labels, and access is based on subjects having a matching label.

It's important to understand basic risk elements when evaluating the potential loss from access control attacks. Risk is the possibility or likelihood that a threat can exploit a vulnerability, resulting in a loss. Asset valuation identifies the value of assets, threat modeling identifies potential threats, and vulnerability analysis identifies vulnerabilities. These are all important concepts to understand when implementing controls to prevent access control attacks.

Common access control attacks attempt to circumvent authentication mechanisms. Access aggregation is the act of collecting and aggregating nonsensitive information in an attempt to infer sensitive information.

Passwords are a common authentication mechanism, and several different types of attacks attempt to crack passwords. Password attacks include dictionary attacks, brute-force attacks, birthday attacks, rainbow table attacks, and sniffer attacks. Side-channel attacks are passive attacks against smartcards.

Social-engineering techniques are often used in an attempt to get passwords and other data. Phishing uses email in an attempt to get users to give up valuable information (such as their credentials), click a link, or open a malicious attachment. Spear phishing targets a group of people, such as those within a single organization. Whaling targets high-level executives.

Exam Essentials

Identify common authorization mechanisms. Authorization ensures that the requested activity or object access is possible, given the privileges assigned to the authenticated identity. For example, it ensures that users with appropriate privileges can access files and other resources. Common authorization mechanisms include implicit deny, access control lists, access control matrixes, capability tables, constrained interfaces, content-dependent controls, and context-dependent controls. These mechanisms enforce security principles such as the need-to-know, the principle of least privilege, and separation of duties.

Know details about each of the access control models. With discretionary access control models, all objects have owners and the owners can modify permissions. Administrators centrally manage nondiscretionary controls. Role-based access control models use task-based roles and users gain privileges when administrators place their accounts into a role. Rule-based access control models use a set of rules, restrictions, or filters to determine access. Mandatory access controls use labels to identify security domains. Subjects need matching labels to access objects.

Understand basic risk elements. Risk is the possibility or likelihood that a threat can exploit a vulnerability and cause damage to assets. Asset valuation identifies the value of assets, threat modeling identifies threats against these assets, and vulnerability analysis identifies weaknesses in an organization's valuable assets. Access aggregation is a type of attack that combines, or aggregates, nonsensitive information to learn sensitive information and is used in reconnaissance attacks.

Know how brute-force and dictionary attacks work. Brute-force and dictionary attacks are carried out against a stolen password database file or the logon prompt of a system. They are designed to discover passwords. In brute-force attacks, all possible combinations of keyboard characters are used, whereas a predefined list of possible passwords is used in a dictionary attack. Account lockout controls prevent their effectiveness against online attacks.

Understand the need for strong passwords. Strong passwords make password-cracking utilities less successful. Strong passwords include multiple character types and are not words contained in a dictionary. Password policies ensure that users create strong passwords. Passwords should be encrypted when stored and encrypted when sent over a network. Authentication can be strengthened by using an additional factor beyond just passwords.

Understand sniffer attacks. In a sniffer attack (or snooping attack) an attacker uses a packet capturing tool (such as a sniffer or protocol analyzer) to capture, analyze, and read data sent over a network. Attackers can easily read data sent over a network in cleartext, but encrypting data-in-transit thwarts this type of attack.

Understand spoofing attacks. Spoofing is pretending to be something or someone else, and it is used in many types of attacks, including access control attacks. Attackers often try to obtain the credentials of users so that they can spoof the user's identity. Spoofing attacks include email spoofing, phone number spoofing, and IP spoofing. Many phishing attacks use spoofing methods.

Understand social engineering. A social-engineering attack is an attempt by an attacker to convince someone to provide information (such as a password) or perform an action they wouldn't normally perform (such as clicking on a malicious link), resulting in a security compromise. Social engineers often try to gain access to the IT infrastructure or the physical facility. User education is an effective tool to prevent the success of social-engineering attacks.

Understand phishing. Phishing attacks are commonly used to try to trick users into giving up personal information (such as user accounts and passwords), click a malicious link, or open a malicious attachment. Spear phishing targets specific groups of users, and whaling targets high-level executives. Vishing uses VoIP technologies.

Written Lab

1. Describe the primary difference between discretionary and nondiscretionary access control models.
2. List three elements to identify when attempting to identify and prevent access control attacks.
3. Name at least three types of attacks used to discover passwords.

Review Questions

1. Which of the following *best* describes an implicit deny principle?
   - **A.** All actions that are not expressly denied are allowed.
   - **B.** All actions that are not expressly allowed are denied.
   - **C.** All actions must be expressly denied.
   - **D.** None of the above.
2. What is the intent of least privilege?
   - **A.** Enforce the most restrictive rights required by users to run system processes.
   - **B.** Enforce the least restrictive rights required by users to run system processes.
   - **C.** Enforce the most restrictive rights required by users to complete assigned tasks.
   - **D.** Enforce the least restrictive rights required by users to complete assigned tasks.
3. A table includes multiple objects and subjects and it identifies the specific access each subject has to different objects. What is this table?
   - **A.** Access control list
   - **B.** Access control matrix
   - **C.** Federation
   - **D.** Creeping privilege
4. Who, or what, grants permissions to users in a discretionary access control model?
   - **A.** Administrators
   - **B.** Access control list
   - **C.** Assigned labels
   - **D.** The data custodian
5. Which of the following models is also known as an identity-based access control model?
   - **A.** Discretionary access control
   - **B.** Role-based access control
   - **C.** Rule-based access control
   - **D.** Mandatory access control
6. A central authority determines which files a user can access. Which of the following best describes this?
   - **A.** An access control list (ACL)
   - **B.** An access control matrix
   - **C.** Discretionary access control model
   - **D.** Nondiscretionary access control model

7. A central authority determines which files a user can access based on the organization's hierarchy. Which of the following best describes this?
   A. Discretionary access control model
   B. An access control list (ACL)
   C. Rule-based access control model
   D. Role-based access control model
8. Which of the following statements is true related to the role-based access control (role-BAC) model?
   A. A role-BAC model allows users membership in multiple groups.
   B. A role-BAC model allows users membership in a single group.
   C. A role-BAC model is non-hierarchical.
   D. A role-BAC model uses labels.
9. Which of the following is the *best* choice for a role within an organization using a role-based access control model?
   A. Web server
   B. Application
   C. Database
   D. Programmer
10. Which of the following *best* describes a rule-based access control model?
    A. It uses local rules applied to users individually.
    B. It uses global rules applied to users individually.
    C. It uses local rules applied to all users equally.
    D. It uses global rules applied to all users equally.
11. What type of access control model is used on a firewall?
    A. Mandatory access control model
    B. Discretionary access control model
    C. Rule-based access control model
    D. Role-based access control model
12. What type of access controls rely on the use of labels?
    A. Discretionary
    B. Nondiscretionary
    C. Mandatory
    D. Role based
13. Which of the following *best* describes a characteristic of the mandatory access control model?
    A. Employs explicit-deny philosophy
    B. Permissive

C. Rule-based
D. Prohibitive

14. Which of the following is not a valid access control model?
    A. Discretionary access control model
    B. Nondiscretionary access control model
    C. Mandatory access control model
    D. Lettuce-based access control model

15. What would an organization do to identify weaknesses?
    A. Asset valuation
    B. Threat modeling
    C. Vulnerability analysis
    D. Access review

16. Which of the following can help mitigate the success of an online brute-force attack?
    A. Rainbow table
    B. Account lockout
    C. Salting passwords
    D. Encryption of password

17. What is an attack that attempts to detect flaws in smartcards?
    A. Whaling
    B. Side-channel attack
    C. Brute-force
    D. Rainbow table attack

18. What type of attack uses email and attempts to trick high-level executives?
    A. Phishing
    B. Spear phishing
    C. Whaling
    D. Vishing

Refer the following scenario when answering questions 19 and 20:

An organization has recently suffered a series of security breaches that have significantly damaged its reputation. Several successful attacks have resulted in compromised customer database files accessible via one of the company's web servers. Additionally, an employee had access to secret data from previous job assignments. This employee made copies of the data and sold it to competitors. The organization has hired a security consultant to help them reduce their risk from future attacks.

19. What would the consultant use to identify potential attackers?

A. Asset valuation

B. Threat modeling

C. Vulnerability analysis

D. Access review and audit

20. What would need to be completed to ensure that the consultant has the correct focus?

A. Asset valuation

B. Threat modeling

C. Vulnerability analysis

D. Creation of audit trails

Chapter 15

Security Assessment and Testing

THE CISSP EXAM TOPICS COVERED IN THIS CHAPTER INCLUDE:

✓ **6. Security Assessment ad Testing (Designing, Performing, and Analyzing Security Testing**

- A. Design and validate assessment and test strategies
- B. Conduct security control testing
  - B.1 Vulnerability assessment
  - B.2 Penetration testing
  - B.3 Log reviews
  - B.4 Synthetic transactions
  - B.5 Code review and testing (e.g. manual, dynamic, static, fuzz)
  - B.6 Misuse case testing
  - B.7 Test coverage analysis
  - B.8 Interface testing (e.g. API, UI, physical)
- C. Collect security process data (e.g. management and operational controls)
  - C.1 Account management
  - C.2 Management review
  - C.3 Key performance and risk indicators
  - C.4 Backup verification data
- D. Analyze and report test outputs (e.g. automated, manual)
- E. Conduct or facilitate internal and third party audits

Throughout this book, you've learned about many of the different controls that information security professionals implement to safeguard the confidentiality, integrity, and availability of data. Among these, technical controls play an important role protecting servers, networks, and other information processing resources. Once security professionals build and configure these controls, they must regularly test them to ensure that they continue to properly safeguard information.

Security assessment and testing programs perform regular checks to ensure that adequate security controls are in place and that they effectively perform their assigned functions. In this chapter, you'll learn about many of the assessment and testing controls used by security professionals around the world.

Building a Security Assessment and Testing Program

The cornerstone maintenance activity for an information security team is their security assessment and testing program. This program includes tests, assessments, and audits that regularly verify that an organization has adequate security controls and that those security controls are functioning properly and effectively safeguarding information assets.

In this section, you will learn about the three major components of a security assessment program:

- Security tests
- Security assessments
- Security audits

Security Testing

Security tests verify that a control is functioning properly. These tests include automated scans, tool-assisted penetration tests and manual attempts to undermine security. Security testing should take place on a regular schedule, with attention paid to each of the key security controls protecting an organization. When scheduling security controls for review, information security managers should consider the following factors:

- Availability of security testing resources
- Criticality of the systems and applications protected by the tested controls

- Sensitivity of information contained on tested systems and applications
- Likelihood of a technical failure of the mechanism implementing the control
- Likelihood of a misconfiguration of the control that would jeopardize security
- Risk that the system will come under attack
- Rate of change of the control configuration
- Other changes in the technical environment that may affect the control performance
- Difficulty and time required to perform a control test
- Impact of the test on normal business operations

After assessing each of these factors, security teams design and validate a comprehensive assessment and testing strategy. This strategy may include frequent automated tests supplemented by infrequent manual tests. For example, a credit card processing system may undergo automated vulnerability scanning on a nightly basis with immediate alerts to administrators when the scan detects a new vulnerability. The automated scan requires no work from administrators once it is configured, so it is easy to run quite frequently. The security team may wish to complement those automated scans with a manual penetration test performed by an external consultant for a significant fee. Those tests may occur on an annual basis to minimize costs and disruption to the business.

WARNING

Many security testing programs begin on a haphazard basis, with security professionals simply pointing their fancy new tools at whatever systems they come across first. Experimentation with new tools is fine, but security testing programs should be carefully designed and include rigorous, routine testing of systems using a risk-prioritized approach.

Of course, it's not sufficient to simply perform security tests. Security professionals must also carefully review the results of those tests to ensure that each test was successful. In some cases, these reviews consist of manually reading the test output and verifying that the test completed successfully. Some tests require human interpretation and must be performed by trained analysts.

Other reviews may be automated, performed by security testing tools that verify the successful completion of a test, log the results, and remain silent unless there is a significant finding. When the system detects an issue requiring administrator attention, it may trigger an alert, send an email or text message, or automatically open a trouble ticket, depending on the severity of the alert and the administrator's preference.

Security Assessments

Security assessments are comprehensive reviews of the security of a system, application, or other tested environment. During a security assessment, a trained information security professional performs a risk assessment that identifies vulnerabilities in the tested environment that may allow a compromise and makes recommendations for remediation, as needed.

Security assessments normally include the use of security testing tools but go beyond automated scanning and manual penetration tests. They also include a thoughtful review of the threat environment, current and future risks, and the value of the targeted environment.

The main work product of a security assessment is normally an assessment report addressed to management that contains the results of the assessment in nontechnical language and concludes with specific recommendations for improving the security of the tested environment.

Security Audits

Security audits use many of the same techniques followed during security assessments but must be performed by independent auditors. While an organization's security staff may routinely perform security tests and assessments, this is not the case for audits. Assessment and testing results are meant for internal use only and are designed to evaluate controls with an eye toward finding potential improvements. Audits, on the other hand, are evaluations performed with the purpose of demonstrating the effectiveness of controls to a third party. The staff who design, implement, and monitor controls for an organization have an inherent conflict of interest when evaluating the effectiveness of those controls.

Auditors provide an impartial, unbiased view of the state of security controls. They write reports that are quite similar to security assessment reports, but those reports are intended for different audiences that may include an organization's board of directors, government regulators, and other third parties. There are two main types of audits: internal audits and external audits.

Government Auditors Discover Air Traffic Control Security Vulnerabilities

Federal, state, and local governments also use internal and external auditors to perform security assessments. The U.S. Government Accountability Office (GAO) performs audits at the request of Congress, and these GAO audits often focus on information security risks. In 2015, the GAO released an audit report titled "Information Security: FAA Needs to Address Weaknesses in Air Traffic Control Systems."

The conclusion of this report was damning: "While the Federal Aviation Administration (FAA) has taken steps to protect its air traffic control systems from cyber-based and other threats, significant security control weaknesses remain, threatening the agency's ability to ensure the safe and uninterrupted operation of the national airspace system (NAS). These include weaknesses in controls intended to prevent, limit and detect unauthorized access to computer resources, such as controls for protecting system boundaries, identifying and authenticating users, authorizing users to access systems, encrypting sensitive data, and auditing and monitoring activity on FAA's systems."

The report went on to make 17 recommendations on how the FAA might improve its information security controls to better protect the integrity and availability of the nation's air traffic control system. The full GAO report may be found at `http://gao.gov/assets/670/668169.pdf`.

Internal audits are performed by an organization's internal audit staff and are typically intended for internal audiences. The internal audit staff performing these audits normally have a reporting line that is completely independent of the functions they evaluate. In many organizations, the Chief Audit Executive reports directly to the President, Chief Executive Officer, or similar role. The Chief Audit Executive may also have reporting responsibility directly to the organization's governing board.

External audits are performed by an outside auditing firm. These audits have a high degree of external validity because the auditors performing the assessment theoretically have no conflict of interest with the organization itself. There are thousands of firms who perform external audits, but most people place the highest credibility with the so-called "Big Four" audit firms:

- Ernst & Young
- Deloitte & Touche
- PricewaterhouseCoopers
- KPMG

Audits performed by these firms are generally considered acceptable by most investors and governing body members.

Information security professionals are often asked to participate in both internal and external audits. They commonly must provide information about security controls to auditors through interviews and written documentation. Auditors may also request the participation of security staff members in the execution of control evaluations. Auditors generally have *carte blanche* access to all information within an organization and security staff should comply with those requests, consulting with management as needed.

When Audits Go Wrong

The Big Four didn't come into being until 2002. Up until that point, the Big Five also included the highly respected firm Arthur Andersen. Andersen, however, collapsed suddenly after they were implicated in the collapse of Enron Corporation. Enron, an energy company, suddenly filed for bankruptcy in 2001 after allegations of systemic accounting fraud came to the attention of regulators and the media.

Arthur Andersen, then one of the world's largest auditing firms, had performed Enron's financial audits, effectively signing off on their fraudulent practices as legitimate. The firm was later convicted of obstruction of justice and, although the conviction was later overturned by the Supreme Court, quickly collapsed due to the loss of credibility they suffered in the wake of the Enron scandal and other allegations of fraudulent behavior.

Performing Vulnerability Assessments

Vulnerability assessments are some of the most important testing tools in the information security professional's toolkit. Vulnerability scans and penetration tests provide security professionals with a perspective on the weaknesses in a system or application's technical controls.

NOTE

Just to be clear on terminology, vulnerability assessments as they are described in this chapter are actually security *testing* tools, not security *assessment* tools. They probably should be called vulnerability tests for linguistic consistency, but we'll stick with the language used by $(ISC)^2$ in the official CISSP body of knowledge.

Vulnerability Scans

Vulnerability scans automatically probe systems, applications, and networks, looking for weaknesses that may be exploited by an attacker. The scanning tools used in these tests provide quick, point-and-click tests that perform otherwise tedious tasks without requiring manual intervention. Most tools allow scheduled scanning on a recurring basis and provide reports that show differences between scans performed on different days, offering administrators a view into changes in their security risk environment.

There are three main categories of vulnerability scans: network discovery scans, network vulnerability scans, and web application vulnerability scan. A wide variety of tools perform each of these types of scans.

WARNING

Remember that information security professionals aren't the only ones with access to vulnerability testing tools. Attackers have access to the same tools used by the "good guys" and often run vulnerability tests against systems, applications, and networks prior to an intrusion attempt. These scans help attackers zero in on vulnerable systems and focus their attacks on systems where they will have the greatest likelihood of success.

Network Discovery Scanning

Network discovery scanning uses a variety of techniques to scan a range of IP addresses, searching for systems with open network ports. Network discovery scanners do not actually probe systems for vulnerabilities but provide a report showing the systems detected on a network and the list of ports that are exposed through the network and server firewalls that lie on the network path between the scanner and the scanned system.

Network discovery scanners use many different techniques to identify open ports on remote systems. Some of the more common techniques are as follows:

TCP SYN Scanning Sends a single packet to each scanned port with the SYN flag set. This indicates a request to open a new connection. If the scanner receives a response that has the SYN and ACK flags set, this indicates that the system is moving to the second phase in the three-way TCP handshake and that the port is open. TCP SYN scanning is also known as "half-open" scanning.

TCP Connect Scanning Opens a full connection to the remote system on the specified port. This scan type is used when the user running the scan does not have the necessary permissions to run a half-open scan.

TCP ACK Scanning Sends a packet with the ACK flag set, indicating that it is part of an open connection.

Xmas Scanning Sends a packet with the FIN, PSH, and URG flags set. A packet with so many flags set is said to be "lit up like a Christmas tree," leading to the scan's name.

TIP If you've forgotten how the three-way TCP handshake functions, you'll find complete coverage of it in Chapter 11, "Secure Network Architecture and Securing Network Components."

The most common tool used for network discovery scanning is an open source tool called nmap. Originally released in 1997, nmap is remarkably still maintained and in general use today. It remains one of the most popular network security tools, and almost every security professional either uses nmap regularly or has used it at some point in their career. You can download a free copy of nmap or learn more about the tool at `http://nmap.org`.

When nmap scans a system, it identifies the current state of each network port on the system. For ports where nmap detects a result, it provides the current status of that port:

Open The port is open on the remote system and there is an application that is actively accepting connections on that port.

Closed The port is accessible on the remote system, meaning that the firewall is allowing access, but there is no application accepting connections on that port.

Filtered Nmap is unable to determine whether a port is open or closed because a firewall is interfering with the connection attempt.

Figure 15.1 shows an example of nmap at work. The user entered the following command at a Linux prompt:

```
nmap -vv 52.4.85.159
```

The nmap software then began a port scan of the system with IP address 52.4.85.159. The `-vv` flag specified with the command simply tells nmap to use verbose mode, reporting detailed output of its results. The results of the scan, appearing toward the bottom of Figure 15.1, indicate that nmap found three active ports on the system: 22, 80, and 443. Ports 22 and 80 are open, indicating that the system is actively accepting connection requests on those ports. Port 443 is closed, meaning that the firewall contains rules allowing connection attempts on that port but the system is not running an application configured to accept those connections.

FIGURE 15.1 Nmap scan of a web server run from a Linux system

```
Sun May 03 scanner $ nmap -vv 52.4.85.159

Starting Nmap 6.40 ( http://nmap.org ) at 2015-05-03 16:06 UTC
Initiating Ping Scan at 16:06
Scanning 52.4.85.159 [2 ports]
Completed Ping Scan at 16:06, 0.00s elapsed (1 total hosts)
Initiating Parallel DNS resolution of 1 host. at 16:06
Completed Parallel DNS resolution of 1 host. at 16:06, 0.00s elapsed
Initiating Connect Scan at 16:06
Scanning ec2-52-4-85-159.compute-1.amazonaws.com (52.4.85.159) [1000 ports]
Discovered open port 22/tcp on 52.4.85.159
Discovered open port 80/tcp on 52.4.85.159
Completed Connect Scan at 16:06, 4.71s elapsed (1000 total ports)
Nmap scan report for ec2-52-4-85-159.compute-1.amazonaws.com (52.4.85.159)
Host is up (0.00090s latency).
Scanned at 2015-05-03 16:06:24 UTC for 5s
Not shown: 997 filtered ports
PORT    STATE  SERVICE
22/tcp  open   ssh
80/tcp  open   http
443/tcp closed https

Read data files from: /usr/bin/../share/nmap
Nmap done: 1 IP address (1 host up) scanned in 4.73 seconds
Sun May 03 scanner $
```

To interpret these results, you must know the use of common network ports, as discussed in Chapter 12. Let's walk through the results of this nmap scan:

- The first line of the port listing, `22/tcp open ssh`, indicates that the system accepts connections on TCP port 22. The secure shell (SSH) service uses this port to allow administrative connections to servers.
- The second line of the port listing, `80/tcp open http`, indicates that the system is accepting connection requests on port 80, which is used by HTTP to deliver web pages.
- The final line of the port listing, `443/tcp closed https`, indicates that a firewall rule exists to allow access to port 443 but no service is listening on that port. Port 443 is used by the HTTPS protocol to accept encrypted web server connections.

What can we learn from these results? The system being scanned is probably a web server that is openly accepting connection requests from the scanned system. The firewalls between the scanner and this system are configured to allow both secure (port 443) and insecure (port 80) connections, but the server is not set up to actually perform encrypted transactions. The server also has an administrative port open that may allow command-line connections.

An attacker reading these results would probably make a few observations about the system that would lead to some further probing:

- Pointing a web browser at this server would likely give a good idea of what the server does and who operates it. Simply typing **`http://52.4.85.159`** in the address bar of the browser may reveal useful information. Figure 15.2 shows the result of performing this: the site is running a default installation of the Apache web server.

FIGURE 15.2 Default Apache server page running on the server scanned in Figure 15.1

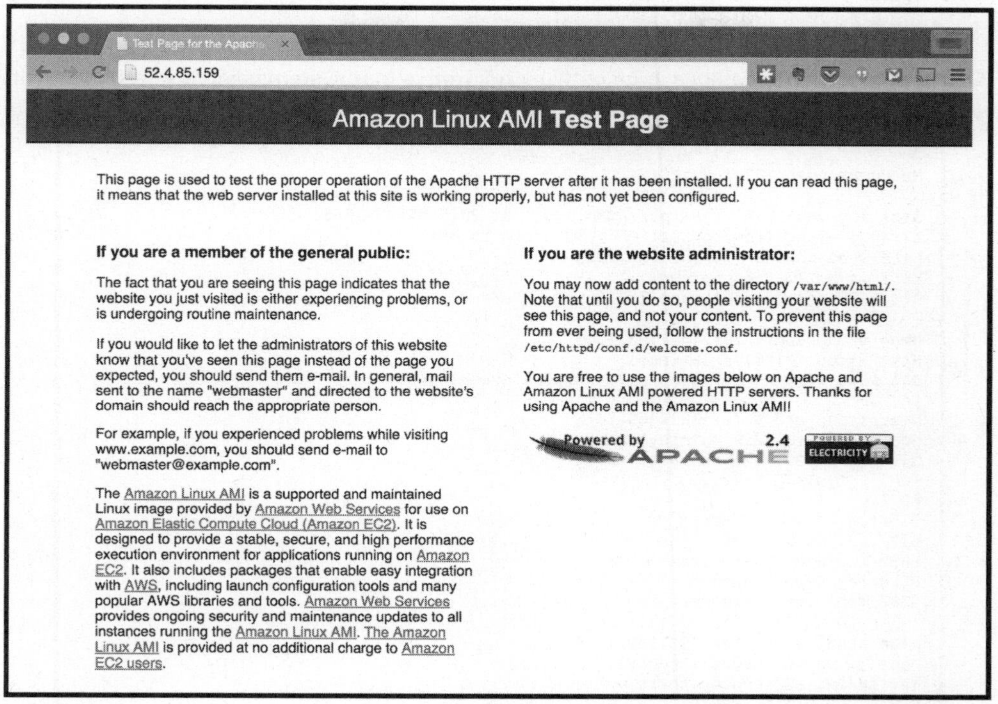

- Connections to this server are unencrypted. Eavesdropping on those connections, if possible, may reveal sensitive information.
- The open SSH port is an interesting finding. An attacker may try to conduct a brute-force password attack against administrative accounts on that port to gain access to the system.

In this example, we used nmap to scan a single system, but the tool also allows scanning entire networks for systems with open ports. The scan shown in Figure 15.3 scans across the 192.168.1.0/24 network, including all addresses in the range 192.168.1.0–192.168.1.255.

WARNING

The fact that you *can* run a network discovery scan doesn't mean that you *may* or *should* run that scan. You should only scan networks where you have explicit permission from the network owner to perform security scanning. Some jurisdictions consider unauthorized scanning a violation of computer abuse laws and may prosecute individuals for an act as simple as running nmap on a coffee shop wireless network.

Network Vulnerability Scanning

Network vulnerability scans go deeper than discovery scans. They don't stop with detecting open ports but continue on to probe a targeted system or network for the presence of known vulnerabilities. These tools contain databases of thousands of known vulnerabilities, along with tests they can perform to identify whether a system is susceptible to each vulnerability in the system's database.

FIGURE 15.3 Nmap scan of a large network run from a Mac system using the Terminal utility

```
MacBook$ nmap 192.168.1.0/24

Starting Nmap 6.01 ( http://nmap.org ) at 2015-05-09 15:50 EDT
Strange error from connect (65):No route to host
Nmap scan report for 192.168.1.65
Host is up (0.036s latency).
All 1000 scanned ports on 192.168.1.65 are closed

Nmap scan report for 192.168.1.69
Host is up (0.0017s latency).
All 1000 scanned ports on 192.168.1.69 are closed

Nmap scan report for 192.168.1.73
Host is up (0.021s latency).
Not shown: 994 closed ports
PORT     STATE SERVICE
80/tcp   open  http
515/tcp  open  printer
631/tcp  open  ipp
8080/tcp open  http-proxy
8290/tcp open  unknown
9100/tcp open  jetdirect

Nmap scan report for 192.168.1.94
Host is up (0.00089s latency).
Not shown: 998 closed ports
PORT      STATE SERVICE
5009/tcp  open  airport-admin
10000/tcp open  snet-sensor-mgmt

Nmap scan report for 192.168.1.114
Host is up (0.0015s latency).
Not shown: 962 closed ports, 37 filtered ports
PORT     STATE SERVICE
4242/tcp open  vrml-multi-use
```

When the scanner tests a system for vulnerabilities, it uses the tests in its database to determine whether a system may contain the vulnerability. In some cases, the scanner may not have enough information to conclusively determine that a vulnerability exists and it reports a vulnerability when there really is no problem. This situation is known as a *false positive* report and is sometimes seen as a nuisance to system administrators. Far more dangerous is when the vulnerability scanner misses a vulnerability and fails to alert the administrator to the presence of a dangerous situation. This error is known as a *false negative* report.

By default, network vulnerability scanners run unauthenticated scans. They test the target systems without having passwords or other special information that would grant the scanner special privileges. This allows the scan to run from the perspective of an attacker but also limits the ability of the scanner to fully evaluate possible vulnerabilities. One way to improve the accuracy of the scanning and reduce false positive and false negative reports is to perform *authenticated scans* of systems. In this approach, the scanner has read-only access to the servers being scanned and can use this access to read configuration information from the target system and use that information when analyzing vulnerability testing results.

Figure 15.4 shows the results of a network vulnerability scan performed using the Nessus vulnerability scanner against the same system subjected to a network discovery scan earlier in this chapter.

FIGURE 15.4 Network vulnerability scan of the same web server that was port scanned in Figure 15.1

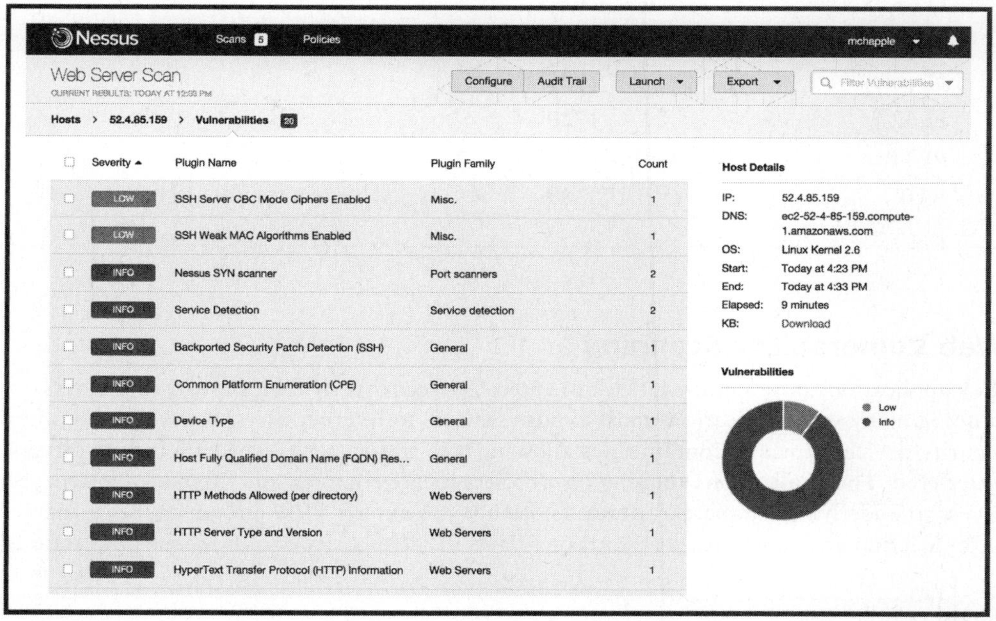

The scan results shown in Figure 15.4 are very clean and represent a well-maintained system. There are no serious vulnerabilities and only two low-risk vulnerabilities related to the SSH service running on the scanned system. While the system administrator may wish to tweak the SSH cryptography settings to remove those low-risk vulnerabilities, this is a very good report for the administrator and provides confidence that the system is well managed.

Learning TCP Ports

Interpreting port scan results requires knowledge of some common TCP ports. Here are a few that you should commit to memory when preparing for the CISSP exam:

FTP	21
SSH	22
Telnet	23

SMTP	25
DNS	53
HTTP	80
POP3	110
NTP	123
HTTPS	443
Microsoft SQL Server	1433
Oracle	1521
H.323	1720
PPTP	1723
RDP	3389

Web Vulnerability Scanning

Web applications pose significant risk to enterprise security. By their nature, the servers running many web applications must expose services to Internet users. Firewalls and other security devices typically contain rules allowing web traffic to pass through to web servers unfettered. The applications running on web servers are complex and often have privileged access to underlying databases. Attackers often try to exploit these circumstances using SQL injection and other attacks that target flaws in the security design of web applications.

TIP You'll find complete coverage of SQL injection attacks, cross-site scripting (XSS), cross-site request forgery (XSRF), and other web application vulnerabilities in Chapter 9, "Security Vulnerabilities, Threats and Countermeasures."

Web vulnerability scanners are special-purpose tools that scour web applications for known vulnerabilities. They play an important role in any security testing program because they may discover flaws not visible to network vulnerability scanners. When an administrator runs a web application scan, the tool probes the web application using automated techniques that manipulate inputs and other parameters to identify web vulnerabilities. The tool then provides a report of its findings, often including suggested vulnerability remediation techniques. Figure 15.5 shows an example of a web vulnerability scan performed using the Nessus vulnerability scanning tool. This scan ran against the web application running on the same server as the network discovery scan in Figure 15.1 and the network vulnerability scan in Figure 15.4. As you read through the scan report in Figure 15.5, notice that it detected vulnerabilities that did not show up in the network vulnerability scan.

FIGURE 15.5 Web application vulnerability scan of the same web server that was port scanned in Figure 15.1 and network vulnerability scanned in Figure 15.4

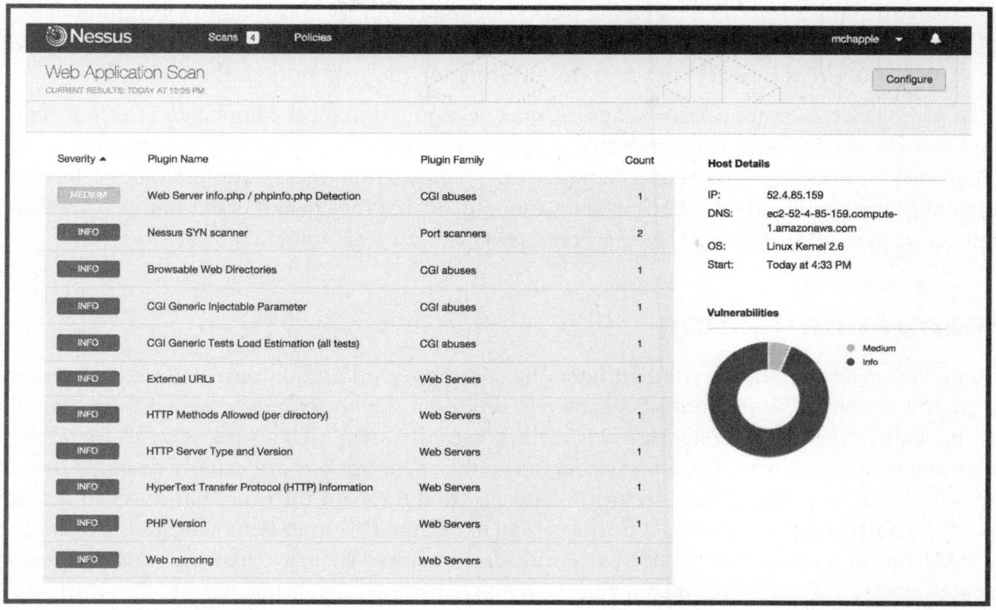

NOTE

Do network vulnerability scans and web vulnerability scans sound similar? That's because they are! Both probe services running on a server for known vulnerabilities. The difference is that network vulnerability scans generally don't dive deep into the structure of web applications whereas web application scans don't look at services other than those supporting web services. Many network vulnerability scanners do perform basic web vulnerability scanning tasks, but deep-dive web vulnerability scans require specialized, dedicated web vulnerability scanning tools.

You may have noticed that the Nessus vulnerability scanner performed both the network vulnerability scan shown in Figure 15.4 and the web vulnerability scan shown in Figure 15.5. Nessus is an example of a hybrid tool that can perform both types of scan.

As with most tools, the capabilities for various vulnerability scanners vary quite a bit. Before using a scanner, you should research it to make sure it meets your security control objectives.

Web vulnerability scans are an important component of an organization's security assessment and testing program. It's a good practice to run scans in the following circumstances:

- Scan all applications when you begin performing web vulnerability scanning for the first time. This will detect issues with legacy applications.

- Scan any new application before moving it into a production environment for the first time.
- Scan any modified application before the code changes move into production.
- Scan all applications on a recurring basis. Limited resources may require scheduling these scans based on the priority of the application. For example, you may wish to scan web applications that interact with sensitive information more often than those that do not.

In some cases, web application scanning may be required to meet compliance requirements. For example, the Payment Card Industry Data Security Standard (PCI DSS), discussed in Chapter 4, "Laws, Regulations and Compliance," requires that organizations either perform web application vulnerability scans at least annually or that they install dedicated web application firewalls to add additional layers of protection against web vulnerabilities.

Penetration Testing

The *penetration test* goes beyond vulnerability testing techniques because it actually attempts to exploit systems. Vulnerability scans merely probe for the presence of a vulnerability and do not normally take offensive action against the targeted system. (That said, some vulnerability scanning techniques may disrupt a system, although these options are usually disabled by default.) Security professionals performing penetration tests, on the other hand, try to defeat security controls and break into a targeted system or application to demonstrate the flaw.

Penetration tests require focused attention from trained security professionals, to a much greater extent than vulnerability scans. When performing a penetration test, the security professional typically targets a single system or set of systems and uses many different techniques to gain access. The process may include the following:

- Performing basic reconnaissance to determine system function (such as visiting websites hosted on the system)
- Network discovery scans to identify open ports
- Network vulnerability scans to identify unpatched vulnerabilities
- Web application vulnerability scans to identify web application flaws
- Use of exploit tools to automatically attempt to defeat the system security
- Manual probing and attack attempts

Penetration testers commonly use a tool called *Metasploit* to automatically execute exploits against targeted systems. Metasploit, shown in Figure 15.6, uses a scripting language to allow the automatic execution of common attacks, saving testers (and hackers!) quite a bit of time by eliminating many of the tedious, routine steps involved in executing an attack.

Penetration testers may be company employees who perform these tests as part of their duties or external consultants hired to perform penetration tests. The tests are normally categorized into three groups:

White Box Penetration Test Provides the attackers with detailed information about the systems they target. This bypasses many of the reconnaissance steps that normally precede attacks, shortening the time of the attack and increasing the likelihood that it will find security flaws.

FIGURE 15.6 The Metasploit automated system exploitation tool allows attackers to quickly execute common attacks against target systems.

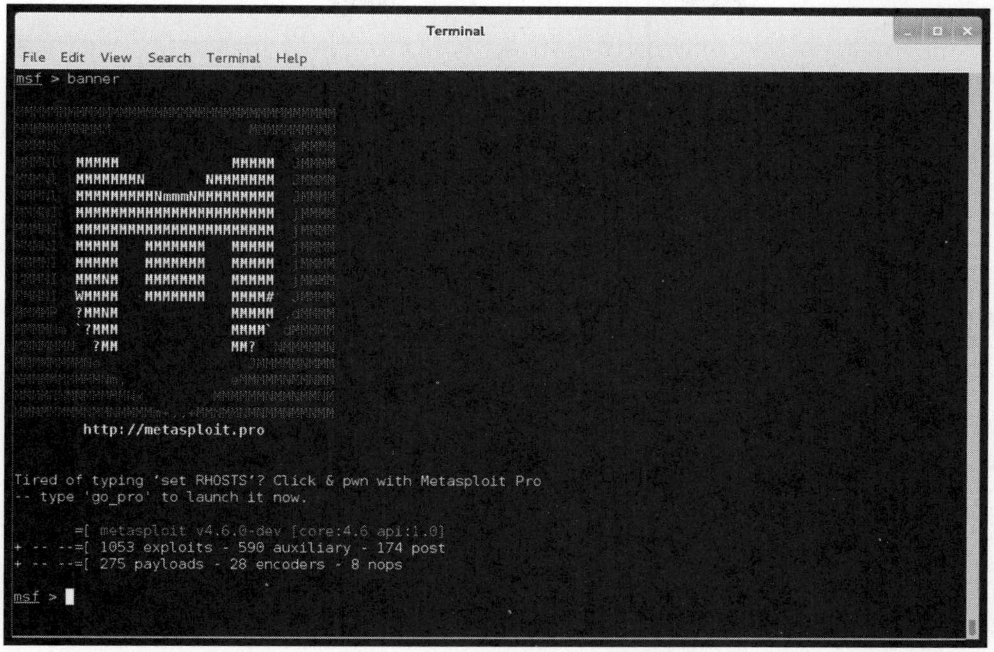

Gray Box Penetration Test Also known as partial knowledge tests, these are sometimes chosen to balance the advantages and disadvantages of white and black box penetration tests. This is particularly common when black box results are desired but costs or time constraints mean that some knowledge is needed to complete the testing.

Black Box Penetration Test Does not provide attackers with any information prior to the attack. This simulates an external attacker trying to gain access to information about the business and technical environment before engaging in an attack.

Penetration tests are time-consuming and require specialized resources, but they play an important role in the ongoing operation of a sound information security testing program.

Testing Your Software

Software is a critical component in system security. Think about the following characteristics common to many applications in use throughout the modern enterprise:

- Software applications often have privileged access to the operating system, hardware, and other resources.

- Software applications routinely handle sensitive information, including credit card numbers, Social Security Numbers, and proprietary business information.
- Many software applications rely on databases that also contain sensitive information.
- Software is the heart of the modern enterprise and performs business-critical functions. Software failures can disrupt businesses with very serious consequences.

Those are just a few of the many reasons that careful testing of software is essential to the confidentiality, integrity, and availability requirements of every modern organization. In this section, you'll learn about the many types of software testing that you may integrate into your organization's software development life cycle.

NOTE

This chapter provides coverage of software testing topics. You'll find deeper coverage of the software development life cycle (SDLC) and software security issues in Chapter 20, "Software Development Security."

Code Review and Testing

One of the most critical components of a software testing program is conducting code review and testing. These procedures provide third-party reviews of the work performed by developers before moving code into a production environment. Code reviews and tests may discover security, performance, or reliability flaws in applications before they go live and negatively impact business operations.

Code Review

Code review is the foundation of software assessment programs. During a code review, also known as a "peer review," developers other than the one who wrote the code review it for defects. Code reviews may result in approval of an application's move into a production environment, or they may send the code back to the original developer with recommendations for rework of issues detected during the review.

Code review takes many different forms and varies in formality from organization to organization. The most formal code review processes, known as Fagan inspections, follow a rigorous review and testing process with six steps:

1. Planning
2. Overview
3. Preparation
4. Inspection
5. Rework
6. Follow-up

An overview of the Fagan inspection appears in Figure 15.7. Each of these steps has well-defined entry and exit criteria that must be met before the process may formally transition from one stage to the next.

FIGURE 15.7 Fagan inspections follow a rigid formal process, with defined entry and exit criteria that must be met before transitioning between stages.

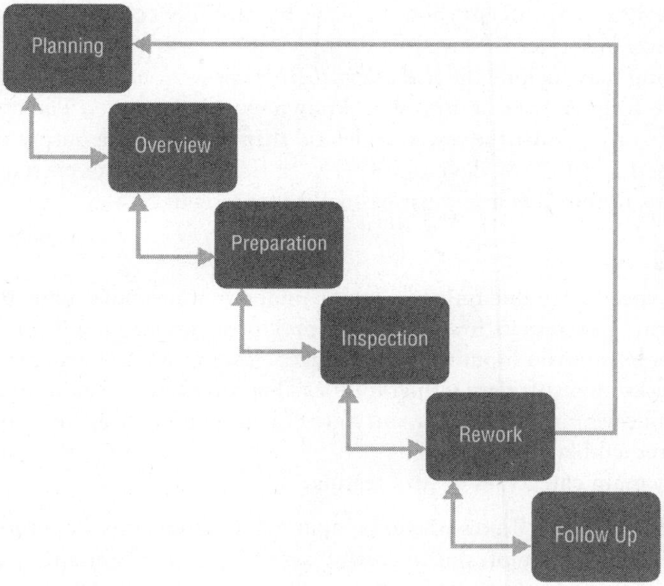

The Fagan inspection level of formality is normally found only in highly restrictive environments where code flaws may have catastrophic impact. Most organizations use less rigorous processes using code peer review measures that include the following:

- Developers walking through their code in a meeting with one or more other team members
- A senior developer performing manual code review and signing off on all code before moving to production
- Use of automated review tools to detect common application flaws before moving to production

Each organization should adopt a code review process that suits its business requirements and software development culture.

Static Testing

Static testing evaluates the security of software without running it by analyzing either the source code or the compiled application. Static analysis usually involves the use of automated tools designed to detect common software flaws, such as buffer overflows. In mature development environments, application developers are given access to static analysis tools and use them throughout the design, build, and test process.

Dynamic Testing

Dynamic testing evaluates the security of software in a runtime environment and is often the only option for organizations deploying applications written by someone else. In those cases, testers often do not have access to the underlying source code. One common example of dynamic software testing is the use of web application scanning tools to detect the presence of cross-site scripting, SQL injection, or other flaws in web applications. Dynamic tests on a production environment should always be carefully coordinated to avoid an unintended interruption of service.

Dynamic testing may include the use of *synthetic transactions* to verify system performance. These are scripted transactions with known expected results. The testers run the synthetic transactions against the tested code and then compare the output of the transactions to the expected state. Any deviations between the actual and expected results represent possible flaws in the code and must be further investigated.

Fuzz Testing

Fuzz testing is a specialized dynamic testing technique that provides many different types of input to software to stress its limits and find previously undetected flaws. Fuzz testing software supplies invalid input to the software, either randomly generated or specially crafted to trigger known software vulnerabilities. The fuzz tester then monitors the performance of the application, watching for software crashes, buffer overflows, or other undesirable and/or unpredictable outcomes.

There are two main categories of fuzz testing:

Mutation (Dumb) Fuzzing Takes previous input values from actual operation of the software and manipulates (or mutates) it to create fuzzed input. It might alter the characters of the content, append strings to the end of the content, or perform other data manipulation techniques.

Generational (Intelligent) Fuzzing Develops data models and creates new fuzzed input based on an understanding of the types of data used by the program.

The zzuf tool automates the process of mutation fuzzing by manipulating input according to user specifications. For example, Figure 15.8 shows a file containing a series of 1s.

Figure 15.9 shows the zzuf tool applied to that input. The resulting fuzzed text is almost identical to the original text. It still contains mostly 1s, but it now has several changes made to the text that might confuse a program expecting the original input. This process of slightly manipulating the input is known as *bit flipping*.

Interface Testing

Interface testing is an important part of the development of complex software systems. In many cases, multiple teams of developers work on different parts of a complex application that must function together to meet business objectives. The handoffs between these separately developed modules use well-defined interfaces so that the teams may work independently. Interface testing assesses the performance of modules against the interface specifications to ensure that they will work together properly when all of the development efforts are complete.

FIGURE 15.8 Prefuzzing input file containing a series of 1s

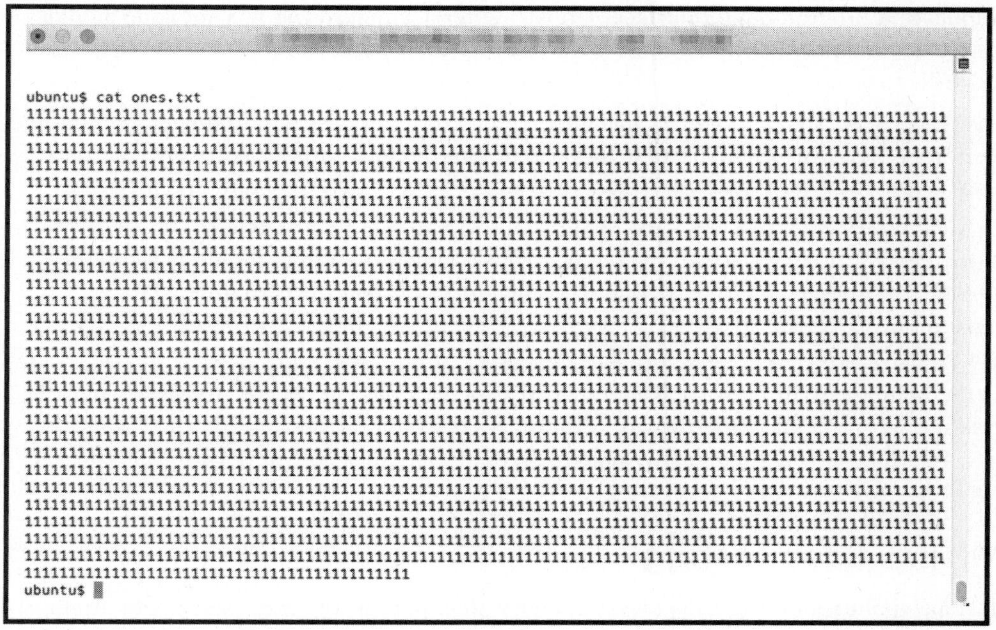

FIGURE 15.9 :The input file from Figure 15.8 after being run through the zzuf mutation fuzzing tool

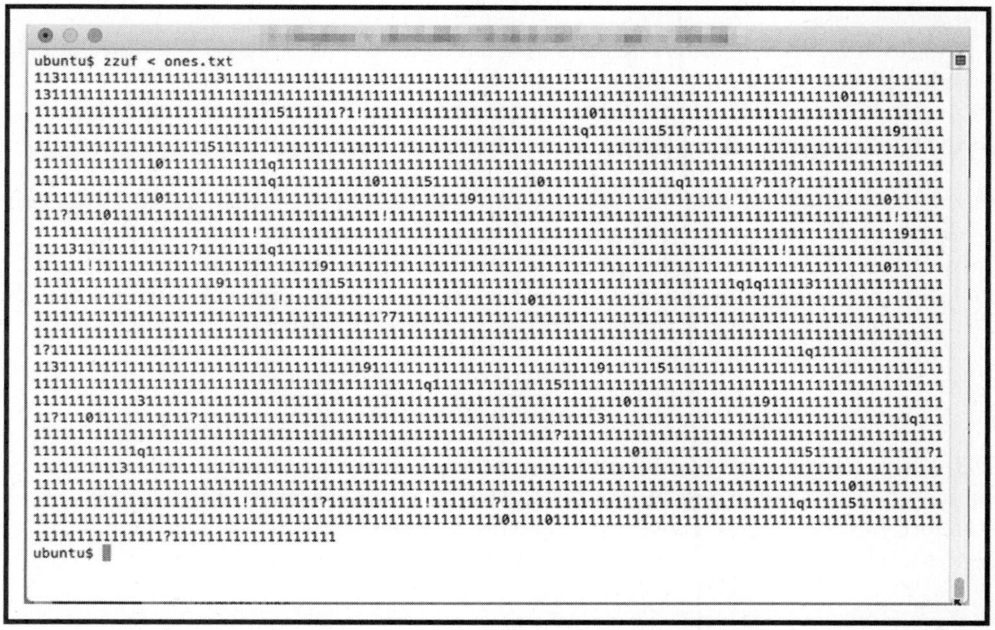

Three types of interfaces should be tested during the software testing process:

Application Programming Interfaces (APIs) Offer a standardized way for code modules to interact and may be exposed to the outside world through web services. Developers must test APIs to ensure that they enforce all security requirements.

User Interfaces (UIs) Examples include graphic user interfaces (GUIs) and command-line interfaces. UIs provide end users with the ability to interact with the software. Interface tests should include reviews of all user interfaces to verify that they function properly.

Physical Interfaces Exist in some applications that manipulate machinery, logic controllers, or other objects in the physical world. Software testers should pay careful attention to physical interfaces because of the potential consequences if they fail.

Interfaces provide important mechanisms for the planned or future interconnection of complex systems. The Web 2.0 world depends on the availability of these interfaces to facilitate interactions between disparate software packages. However, developers must be careful that the flexibility provided by interfaces does not introduce additional security risk. Interface testing provides an added degree of assurance that interfaces meet the organization's security requirements.

Misuse Case Testing

In some applications, there are clear examples of ways that software users might attempt to misuse the application. For example, users of banking software might try to manipulate input strings to gain access to another user's account. They might also try to withdraw funds from an account that is already overdrawn. Software testers use a process known as *misuse case testing* or *abuse case testing* to evaluate the vulnerability of their software to these known risks.

In misuse case testing, testers first enumerate the known misuse cases. They then attempt to exploit those use cases with manual and/or automated attack techniques.

Test Coverage Analysis

While testing is an important part of any software development process, it is unfortunately impossible to completely test any piece of software. There are simply too many ways that software might malfunction or undergo attack. Software testing professionals often conduct a *test coverage analysis* to estimate the degree of testing conducted against the new software. The test coverage is computed using the following formula:

$$test\ coverage = \frac{number\ of\ use\ cases\ tested}{total\ number\ of\ use\ cases}$$

Of course, this is a highly subjective calculation. Accurately computing test coverage requires enumerating the possible use cases, which is an exceptionally difficult task. Therefore, anyone using test coverage calculations should take care to understand the process used to develop the input values when interpreting the results.

Implementing Security Management Processes

In addition to performing assessments and testing, sound information security programs also include a variety of management processes designed to oversee the effective operation of the information security program. These processes are a critical feedback loop in the security assessment process because they provide management oversight and have a deterrent effect against the threat of insider attacks.

The security management reviews that fill this need include log reviews, account management, backup verification, and key performance and risk indicators.

Log Reviews

In Chapter 16, "Managing Security Operations," you will learn the importance of storing log data and conducting both automated and manual log reviews. Security incident and event management (SIEM) packages play an important role in these processes, automating much of the routine work of log review.

Information security managers should also periodically conduct log reviews, particularly for sensitive functions, to ensure that privileged users are not abusing their privileges. For example, if an information security team has access to eDiscovery tools that allow searching through the contents of individual user files, security managers should routinely review the logs of actions taken by those administrative users to ensure that their file access relates to legitimate eDiscovery initiatives and does not violate user privacy.

Account Management

Account management reviews ensure that users only retain authorized permissions and that unauthorized modifications do not occur. Account management reviews may be a function of information security management personnel or internal auditors.

One way to perform account management is to conduct a full review of all accounts. This is typically done only for highly privileged accounts because of the amount of time consumed. The exact process may vary from organization to organization, but here's one example:

1. Managers ask system administrators to provide a list of users with privileged access and the privileged access rights. They may monitor the administrator as they retrieve this list to avoid tampering.
2. Managers ask the privilege approval authority to provide a list of authorized users and the privileges they should be assigned.
3. The managers then compare the two lists to ensure that only authorized users retain access to the system and that the access of each user does not exceed their authorization.

This process may include many other checks, such as verifying that terminated users do not retain access to the system, checking the paper trail for specific accounts or other tasks.

Organizations that do not have time to conduct this thorough process may use sampling instead. In this approach, managers pull a random sample of accounts and perform a full verification of the process used to grant permissions for those accounts. If no significant flaws are found in the sample, they make the assumption that this is representative of the entire population.

WARNING Sampling only works if it is random! Don't allow system administrators to generate the sample or use non-random criteria to select accounts for review, or you may miss entire categories of users where errors may exist.

Backup Verification

In Chapter 18, "Disaster Recovery Planning," you will learn the importance of maintaining a consistent backup program. Managers should periodically inspect the results of backups to ensure that the process functions effectively and meets the organization's data protection needs. This may involve reviewing logs, inspecting hash values, or requesting an actual restore of a system or file.

Key Performance and Risk Indicators

Security managers should also monitor key performance and risk indicators on an ongoing basis. The exact metrics they monitor will vary from organization to organization but may include the following:

- Number of open vulnerabilities
- Time to resolve vulnerabilities
- Number of compromised accounts
- Number of software flaws detected in preproduction scanning
- Repeat audit findings
- User attempts to visit known malicious sites

Once an organization identifies the key security metrics it wishes to track, managers may want to develop a dashboard that clearly displays the values of these metrics over time and display it where both managers and the security team will regularly see it.

Summary

Security assessment and testing programs play a critical role in ensuring that an organization's security controls remain effective over time. Changes in business operations, the technical environment, security risks, and user behavior may alter the effectiveness of controls that protect the confidentiality, integrity, and availability of information assets. Assessment and testing programs monitor those controls and highlight changes requiring administrator intervention. Security professionals should carefully design their assessment and testing program and revise it as business needs change.

Security testing techniques include vulnerability assessments and software testing. With vulnerability assessments, security professionals perform a variety of tests to identify misconfigurations and other security flaws in systems and applications. Network discovery tests identify systems on the network with open ports. Network vulnerability scans discover known security flaws on those systems. Web vulnerability scans probe the operation of web applications searching for known vulnerabilities.

Software plays a critical role in any security infrastructure because it handles sensitive information and interacts with critical resources. Organizations should use a code review process to allow peer validation of code before moving it to production. Rigorous software testing programs also include the use of static testing, dynamic testing, interface testing, and misuse case testing to robustly evaluate software.

Security management processes include log reviews, account management, backup verification, and tracking of key performance and risk indicators. These processes help security managers validate the ongoing effectiveness of the information security program. They are complemented by formal internal and external audits performed by third parties on a less frequent basis.

Exam Essentials

Understand the importance of security assessment and testing programs. Security assessment and testing programs provide an important mechanism for validating the ongoing effectiveness of security controls. They include a variety of tools, including vulnerability assessments, penetration tests, software testing, audits, and security management tasks designed to validate controls. Every organization should have a security assessment and testing program defined and operational.

Conduct vulnerability assessments and penetration tests. Vulnerability assessments use automated tools to search for known vulnerabilities in systems, applications, and networks. These flaws may include missing patches, misconfigurations, or faulty code that expose the organization to security risks. Penetration tests also use these same tools but supplement them with attack techniques where an assessor attempts to exploit vulnerabilities and gain access to the system.

Perform software testing to validate code moving into production. Software testing techniques verify that code functions as designed and does not contain security flaws. Code review uses a peer review process to formally or informally validate code before deploying it in production. Interface testing assesses the interactions between components and users with API testing, user interface testing, and physical interface testing.

Understand the difference between static and dynamic software testing. Static software testing techniques, such as code reviews, evaluate the security of software without running it by analyzing either the source code or the compiled application. Dynamic testing evaluates the security of software in a runtime environment and is often the only option for organizations deploying applications written by someone else.

Explain the concept of fuzzing. Fuzzing uses modified inputs to test software performance under unexpected circumstances. Mutation fuzzing modifies known inputs to generate synthetic inputs that may trigger unexpected behavior. Generational fuzzing develops inputs based on models of expected inputs to perform the same task.

Perform security management tasks to provide oversight to the information security program. Security managers must perform a variety of activities to retain proper oversight of the information security program. Log reviews, particularly for administrator activities, ensure that systems are not misused. Account management reviews ensure that only authorized users retain access to information systems. Backup verification ensures that the organization's data protection process is functioning properly. Key performance and risk indicators provide a high-level view of security program effectiveness.

Conduct or facilitate internal and third-party audits. Security audits occur when a third party performs an assessment of the security controls protecting an organization's information assets. Internal audits are performed by an organization's internal staff and are intended for management use. External audits are performed by a third-party audit firm and are generally intended for the organization's governing body.

Written Lab

1. Describe the difference between TCP SYN scanning and TCP connect scanning.
2. What are the three port status values returned by the nmap network discovery scanning tool?
3. What is the difference between static and dynamic code testing techniques?
4. What is the difference between mutation fuzzing and generational fuzzing?

Review Questions

1. Which one of the following tools is used primarily to perform network discovery scans?
   A. Nmap
   B. Nessus
   C. Metasploit
   D. `lsof`

2. Adam recently ran a network port scan of a web server running in his organization. He ran the scan from an external network to get an attacker's perspective on the scan. Which one of the following results is the greatest cause for alarm?
   A. `80/open`
   B. `22/filtered`
   C. `443/open`
   D. `1433/open`

3. Which one of the following factors should not be taken into consideration when planning a security testing schedule for a particular system?
   A. Sensitivity of the information stored on the system
   B. Difficulty of performing the test
   C. Desire to experiment with new testing tools
   D. Desirability of the system to attackers

4. Which one of the following is not normally included in a security assessment?
   A. Vulnerability scan
   B. Risk assessment
   C. Mitigation of vulnerabilities
   D. Threat assessment

5. Who is the intended audience for a security assessment report?
   A. Management
   B. Security auditor
   C. Security professional
   D. Customers

6. Beth would like to run an nmap scan against all of the systems on her organization's private network. These include systems in the 10.0.0.0 private address space. She would like to scan this entire private address space because she is not certain what subnets are used. What network address should Beth specify as the target of her scan?
   A. 10.0.0.0/0
   B. 10.0.0.0/8

C. 10.0.0.0/16

D. 10.0.0.0/24

7. Alan ran an nmap scan against a server and determined that port 80 is open on the server. What tool would likely provide him the best additional information about the server's purpose and the identity of the server's operator?

A. SSH

B. Web browser

C. telnet

D. ping

8. What port is typically used to accept administrative connections using the SSH utility?

A. 20

B. 22

C. 25

D. 80

9. Which one of the following tests provides the most accurate and detailed information about the security state of a server?

A. Unauthenticated scan

B. Port scan

C. Half-open scan

D. Authenticated scan

10. What type of network discovery scan only follows the first two steps of the TCP handshake?

A. TCP connect scan

B. Xmas scan

C. TCP SYN scan

D. TCP ACK scan

11. Matthew would like to test systems on his network for SQL injection vulnerabilities. Which one of the following tools would be best suited to this task?

A. Port scanner

B. Network vulnerability scanner

C. Network discovery scanner

D. Web vulnerability scanner

12. Badin Industries runs a web application that processes e-commerce orders and handles credit card transactions. As such, it is subject to the Payment Card Industry Data Security Standard (PCI DSS). The company recently performed a web vulnerability scan of the application and it had no unsatisfactory findings. How often must Badin rescan the application?

A. Only if the application changes

B. At least monthly

C. At least annually

D. There is no rescanning requirement.

13. Grace is performing a penetration test against a client's network and would like to use a tool to assist in automatically executing common exploits. Which one of the following security tools will best meet her needs?

A. nmap

B. Metasploit

C. Nessus

D. Snort

14. Paul would like to test his application against slightly modified versions of previously used input. What type of test does Paul intend to perform?

A. Code review

B. Application vulnerability review

C. Mutation fuzzing

D. Generational fuzzing

15. Users of a banking application may try to withdraw funds that don't exist from their account. Developers are aware of this threat and implemented code to protect against it. What type of software testing would most likely catch this type of vulnerability if the developers have not already remediated it?

A. Misuse case testing

B. SQL injection testing

C. Fuzzing

D. Code review

16. What type of interface testing would identify flaws in a program's command-line interface?

A. Application programming interface testing

B. User interface testing

C. Physical interface testing

D. Security interface testing

17. During what type of penetration test does the tester always have access to system configuration information?

A. Black box penetration test

B. White box penetration test

C. Gray box penetration test

D. Red box penetration test

18. What port is typically open on a system that runs an unencrypted HTTP server?

A. 22

B. 80

C. 143

D. 443

19. Which one of the following is the final step of the Fagin inspection process?

A. Inspection

B. Rework

C. Follow-up

D. None of the above

20. What information security management task ensures that the organization's data protection requirements are met effectively?

A. Account management

B. Backup verification

C. Log review

D. Key performance indicators

Chapter 16

Managing Security Operations

THE CISSP EXAM TOPICS COVERED IN THIS CHAPTER INCLUDE:

✓ **Security Operations**

- D. Secure the provisioning of resources
  - D.1 Asset inventory (e.g., hardware, software)
  - D.2 Configuration management
  - D.3 Physical assets
  - D.4 Virtual assets (e.g., software-defined network, virtual SAN, guest operating systems)
  - D.5 Cloud assets (e.g., services, VMs, storage, networks)
  - D.6 Applications (e.g., workloads or private clouds, web services, software as a service)
- E. Understand and apply foundational security operations concepts
  - E.1 Need-to-know/least privilege (e.g., entitlement, aggregation, transitive trust)
  - E.2 Separation of duties and responsibilities
  - E.3 Monitor special privileges (e.g., operators, administrators)
  - E.4 Job rotation
  - E.5 Information lifecycle
  - E.6 Service-level agreements
- F. Employ resource protection techniques
  - F.1 Media management
  - F.2 Hardware and software asset management

- I. Implement and support patch and vulnerability management
- J. Participate in and understand change management processes (e.g., versioning, baselining, security impact analysis)
- P. Participate in addressing personnel safety concerns (e.g., duress, travel, monitoring)

The Security Operations domain includes a wide range of security foundation concepts and best practices. This includes several core concepts that any organization needs to implement to provide basic security protection. The first section of this chapter covers these concepts.

Resource protection ensures the protection of media and other valuable assets throughout the lifetime of the resource. Configuration management ensures that systems are configured similarly, and change management processes protect against outages from unauthorized changes. Patch and vulnerability management controls ensure systems are up-to-date and protected against known vulnerabilities.

Applying Security Operations Concepts

The primary purpose for security operations practices is to safeguard information assets that reside in a system. These practices help identify threats and vulnerabilities, and implement controls to reduce the overall risk to organizational assets.

In the context of IT security, due care and due diligence refers to taking reasonable care to protect the assets of an organization on an ongoing basis. Senior management has a direct responsibility to exercise due care and due diligence. Implementing the common security operations concepts covered in the following sections, along with performing periodic security audits and reviews, demonstrates a level of due care and due diligence that will reduce senior management's liability when a loss occurs.

Need to Know and Least Privilege

Need to know and least privilege are two standard principles followed in any secure IT environment. They help provide protection for valuable assets by limiting access to these assets. Though they are related and many people use the terms interchangeably, there is a distinctive difference between the two. Need to know focuses on permissions and the ability to access information, whereas least privilege focuses on privileges.

Chapter 14, "Controlling and Managing Access," compared permissions, rights, and privileges. As a reminder, permissions allow access to objects such as files. Rights refer to the ability to take actions. Access rights are synonymous with permissions, but rights can also refer to the ability to take action on a system, such as the right to change the system time. Privileges are the combination of both rights and permissions.

Need-to-Know Access

The *need to know principle* imposes the requirement to grant users access only to data or resources they need to perform assigned work tasks. The primary purpose is to keep secret information secret. If you want to keep a secret, the best way is to tell no one. If you're the only person who knows it, you can ensure that it remains a secret. If you tell a trusted friend, it might remain secret. Your trusted friend might tell someone else—such as another trusted friend. However, the risk of the secret leaking out to others increases as more and more people learn it. Limit the people who know and you increase the chances of keeping it secret.

Need to know is commonly associated with security clearances, such as a person having a Secret clearance. However, the clearance doesn't automatically grant access to the data. As an example, imagine that Sally has a Secret clearance. This indicates that she is cleared to access Secret data. However, the clearance doesn't automatically grant her access to all Secret data. Instead, administrators grant her access to only the Secret data she has a need to know for her job.

Although need to know is most often associated with clearances used in military and government agencies, it can also apply in civilian organizations. For example, database administrators may need access to a database server to perform maintenance, but they don't need access to all the data within the server's databases. Restricting access based on a need to know helps protect against unauthorized access resulting in a loss of confidentiality.

The Principle of Least Privilege

The *principle of least privilege* states that subjects are granted only the privileges necessary to perform assigned work tasks and no more. Keep in mind that privilege in this context includes both permissions to data and rights to perform tasks on systems. For data, it includes controlling the ability to write, create, alter, or delete data. Limiting and controlling privilege based on this concept protects confidentiality and data integrity. If users can modify only those data files that their work tasks require them to modify, then it protects the integrity of other files in the environment.

NOTE: The principle of least privilege relies on the assumption that all users have a well-defined job description that personnel understand. Without a specific job description, it is not possible to know what privileges users need.

This principle extends beyond just accessing data, though. It also applies to system access. For example, in many networks regular users have the ability to log on to any computer in the network using a network account. However, organizations commonly restrict this privilege by preventing regular users from logging on to servers or restricting a user to logging on to a single workstation.

A common way organizations violate this principle is by adding all users to the local Administrators group or granting root access to a computer. This gives the users full control over the computer. However, regular users rarely need this much access. When they have this much access, they can accidentally (or intentionally) cause damage within the system such as accessing or deleting valuable data.

Additionally, if a user logs on with full administrative privileges and inadvertently installs malware, the malware can assume full administrative privileges of the user's account. In contrast, if the user logs on with a regular user account, malware can only assume the limited privileges of the regular account.

Least privilege is typically focused on ensuring that user privileges are restricted, but it also applies to other subjects, such as applications or processes. For example, services and applications often run under the context of an account specifically created for the service or application. Historically, administrators often gave these service accounts full administrative privileges without considering the principle of least privilege. If an attacker compromises the application, they can potentially assume the privileges of the service account, granting the attacker full administrative privileges.

Additional concepts personnel should consider when implementing need to know and least privilege are entitlement, aggregation, and transitive trusts.

Entitlement *Entitlement* refers to the amount of privileges granted to users, typically when first provisioning an account. In other words, when administrators create user accounts, they ensure the accounts are provisioned with the appropriate amount of resources, and this includes privileges. User provisioning processes should follow the principle of least privilege.

Aggregation In the context of least privilege, *aggregation* refers to the amount of privileges that users collect over time. For example, if a user moves from one department to another while working for an organization, this user can end up with privileges from each department. To avoid access aggregation problems such as this, administrators should revoke privileges when users move to a different department and no longer need the previously assigned privileges.

Transitive Trust A nontransitive trust exists between two security domains, which could be within the same organization or between different organizations. It allows subjects in one domain to access objects in the other domain. A transitive trust extends the trust relationship between the two security domains to all of their subdomains. Within the context of least privilege, it's important to examine these trust relationships, especially when creating them between different organizations. A nontransitive trust enforces the principle of least privilege and grants the trust to a single domain at a time.

Separation of Duties and Responsibilities

Separation of duties and responsibilities ensures that no single person has total control over a critical function or system. This is necessary to ensure that no single person can compromise the system or its security. Instead, two or more people must conspire or collude against the organization, which increases the risk for these people.

A separation of duties policy creates a checks-and-balances system where two or more users verify each other's actions and must work in concert to accomplish necessary work tasks. This makes it more difficult for individuals to engage in malicious, fraudulent, or unauthorized activities and broadens the scope of detection and reporting. In contrast, individuals may be more inclined to perform unauthorized acts if they think they can get away with them, but with two or more people involved, the risk of detection increases and acts as an effective deterrent.

Here's a simple example. Movie theaters use separation of duties to prevent fraud. One person sells tickets. Another person collects the tickets and doesn't allow entry to anyone who doesn't have a ticket. If the same person collects the money and grants entry, this person can allow people in without a ticket or pocket the collected money without issuing a ticket. Of course, it is possible for the ticket seller and the ticket collector to get together and concoct a plan to steal from the movie theater. This is collusion because it is an agreement between two or more persons to perform some unauthorized activity. However, collusion takes more effort and increases the risk to each of them. Policies such as this reduce fraud by requiring collusion to perform the unauthorized activity.

Similarly, organizations often break down processes into multiple tasks or duties and assign these duties to different individuals to prevent fraud. For example, one person approves payment for a valid invoice, but someone else actually makes the payment. If one person controlled the entire process of approval and payment, it would be easy to approve bogus invoices and defraud the company.

Another way separation of duties is enforced is by dividing the security or administrative capabilities and functions among multiple trusted individuals. When the organization divides administration and security responsibilities among several users, no single person has sufficient access to circumvent or disable security mechanisms.

Separation of Privilege

Separation of privilege is similar in concept to separation of duties and responsibilities. It builds on the principle of least privilege and applies it to applications and processes. A separation of privilege policy requires the use of granular rights and permissions.

Administrators assign different rights and permissions for each type of privileged operation. They grant specific processes only the privileges necessary to perform certain functions, instead of granting them unrestricted access to the system.

Just as the principle of least privilege can apply to both user and service accounts, separation of privilege concepts can also apply to both user and service accounts.

Many server applications have underlying services that support the applications, and as described earlier, these services must run in the context of an account, commonly called a service account. It is common today for server applications to have multiple service accounts. Administrators grant each service account only the privileges needed to perform its functions within the application. This supports a segregation of privilege policy.

Segregation of Duties

Segregation of duties is similar to a separation of duties and responsibilities policy, but it also combines the principle of least privilege. The goal is to ensure that individuals do not have excessive system access that may result in a conflict of interest. When duties are properly segregated, no single employee will have the ability to commit fraud or make a mistake and have the ability to cover it up. It's similar to separation of duties in that duties are separated, and it's also similar to a principle of least privilege in that privileges are limited.

A segregation of duties policy is highly relevant for any company that must abide by the Sarbanes-Oxley Act of 2002 (SOX) because SOX specifically requires it. However, it is also possible to apply segregation of duties policies in any IT environment.

NOTE SOX applies to all public companies that have registered equity or debt securities with the Securities and Exchange Commission (SEC). The U.S. government passed it in response to several high-profile financial scandals that resulted in the loss of billions of shareholder dollars.

One of the most common implementations of segregation of duties policies is ensuring that security duties are separate from other duties within an organization. In other words, personnel responsible for auditing, monitoring, and reviewing security do not have other operational duties related to what they are auditing, monitoring, and reviewing. Whenever security duties are combined with other operational duties, individuals can use their security privileges to cover up activities related to their operational duties.

Figure 16.1 is a basic segregation of duties control matrix comparing different roles and tasks within an organization. The areas marked with an X indicate potential conflicts to avoid. For example, consider an application programmer and a security administrator. The programmer can make unauthorized modifications to an application, but auditing or reviews by a security administrator would detect the unauthorized modifications. However, if a single person had the duties (and the privileges) of both jobs, this person could modify the application and then cover up the modifications to prevent detection.

FIGURE 16.1 A segregation of duties control matrix

Roles/Tasks	Application Programmer	Security Administrator	Database Administrator	Database Server Administrator	Budget Analyst	Accounts Receivable	Accounts Payable	Deploy Patches	Verify Patches
Application Programmer		X	X	X					
Security Administrator	X		X	X	X	X	X	X	
Database Administrator	X	X		X					
Database Server Administrator	X	X	X						
Budget Analyst		X				X	X		
Accounts Receivable		X			X		X		
Accounts Payable		X			X	X			
Deploy Patches		X							X
Verify Patches								X	
	Potential Areas of Conflict								

NOTE The roles and tasks within a segregation of duties control matrix are not standards used by all organizations. Instead, an organization tailors it to fit the roles and responsibilities used within the organization. A matrix such as the one shown in Figure 16.1 provides a guide to help identify potential conflicts.

Ideally, personnel will never be assigned to two roles with a conflict of interest. However, if extenuating circumstances require doing so, it's possible to implement compensating controls to mitigate the risks.

Two-Person Control

Two-person control (often called the two-man rule) is similar to segregation of duties. It requires the approval of two individuals for critical tasks. For example, safety deposit boxes in banks often require two keys. A bank employee controls one key and the customer holds the second key. Both keys are required to open the box, and bank employees allow a customer access to the box only after verifying the customer's identification.

Using two-person controls within an organization ensures peer review and reduces the likelihood of collusion and fraud. For example, an organization can require two individuals within the company (such as the chief financial officer and the chief executive officer) to approve key business decisions. Additionally, some privileged activities can be configured so that they require two administrators to work together to complete a task.

Split knowledge combines the concepts of separation of duties and two-person control into a single solution. The basic idea is that the information or privilege required to perform an operation be divided among two or more users. This ensures that no single person has sufficient privileges to compromise the security of the environment.

Job Rotation

Further control and restriction of privileged capabilities can be implemented by using *job rotation*. Job rotation (sometimes called rotation of duties) means simply that employees are rotated through jobs, or at least some of the job responsibilities are rotated to different employees. Using job rotation as a security control provides peer review, reduces fraud, and enables cross-training. Cross-training helps make an environment less dependent on any single individual.

Job rotation can act as both a deterrent and a detection mechanism. If employees know that someone else will be taking over their job responsibilities at some point in the future, they are less likely to take part in fraudulent activities. If they choose to do so anyway, individuals taking over the job responsibilities later are likely to discover the fraud.

Mandatory Vacations

Many organizations require employees to take *mandatory vacations* in one-week or two-week increments. This provides a form of peer review and helps detect fraud and collusion. This policy ensures that another employee takes over an individual's job responsibilities for at least a week. If an employee is involved in fraud, the person taking over the responsibilities is likely to discover it.

This is similar to the benefits of job rotation. Mandatory vacations can act as both a deterrent and a detection mechanism, just as job rotation policies can. Even though someone else will take over a person's responsibilities for just a week or two, this is often enough to detect irregularities.

NOTE Financial organizations are at risk of significant losses from fraud by employees. They often use job rotation, separation of duties and responsibilities, and mandatory vacation policies to reduce these risks. Combined, these policies help prevent incidents and help detect them when they occur.

Monitor Special Privileges

Special privilege operations are activities that require special access or elevated rights and permissions to perform many administrative and sensitive job tasks. Examples of these tasks include creating new user accounts, adding new routes to a router table, altering the configuration of a firewall, and accessing system log and audit files. Using common security practices, such as the principle of least privilege, ensures that only a limited number of people have these special privileges. Monitoring ensures that users granted these privileges do not abuse them.

Accounts granted elevated privileges are often referred to as *privileged entities* that have access to special, higher-order capabilities inaccessible to normal users. If misused, these elevated rights and permissions can result in significant harm to the confidentiality, integrity, or availability of an organization's assets. Because of this, it's important to monitor privileged entities and their access.

In most cases, these elevated privileges are restricted to administrators and certain system operators. In this context, a system operator is a user who needs additional privileges to perform specific job functions. Regular users (or regular system operators) only need the most basic privileges to perform their jobs.

Employees filling these privileged roles are usually trusted employees. However, there are many reasons why an employee can change from a trusted employee to a disgruntled employee or malicious insider. Reasons that can change a trusted employee's behavior can be as simple as a lower-than-expected bonus, a negative performance review, or just a personal grudge against another employee. However, by monitoring usage of special privileges, an organization can deter an employee from misusing the privileges and detect the action if a trusted employee does misuse them.

In general, any type of administrator account has elevated privileges and should be monitored. It's also possible to grant a user elevated privileges without giving that user full administrative access. With this in mind, it's also important to monitor user activity when the user has certain elevated privileges. The following list includes some examples of privileged operations to monitor.

- Accessing audit logs
- Changing system time
- Configuring interfaces
- Managing user accounts
- Controlling system reboots
- Controlling communication paths
- Backing up and restoring the system
- Running script/task automation tools
- Configuring security mechanism controls
- Using operating system control commands
- Using database recovery tools and log files

Many automated tools are available that can monitor these activities. When an administrator or privileged operator performs one of these activities, the tool can log the event and send an alert. Additionally, access review audits detect misuse of these privileges.

NOTE The task of monitoring special privileges is used in conjunction with other basic principles, such as least privilege and separation of duties and responsibilities. In other words, principles such as least privilege and separation of duties help prevent security policy violations, and monitoring helps to deter and detect any violations that occur despite the use of preventive controls.

Managing the Information Life Cycle

Chapter 5, "Protecting Security of Assets," discusses a variety of methods for protecting data. Of course, not all data deserves the same levels of protection. However, an organization will define data classifications and identify methods that protect the data based on its classification. An organization defines data classifications and typically publishes them within a security policy. Some common data classifications used by governments include Top Secret, Secret, Confidential, and Unclassified. Civilian classifications include confidential (or proprietary), private, sensitive, and public.

Security controls protect information throughout its life cycle. Common methods include marking, handling, storing, and destroying data properly.

Marking Data Marking (or labeling) data ensures that personnel can easily recognize the data's value. Personnel should mark the data as soon as possible after creating it. As an example, a backup of Top Secret data should be marked Top Secret. Similarly, if a system processes sensitive data, the system should be marked with the appropriate label. In addition to marking systems externally, organizations often configure wallpaper and screen savers to clearly show the level of data processed on the system. For example, a system processing Secret data would have wallpaper and screen savers clearly indicating the system processes Secret data.

Handling Data Handling data primarily refers to transporting it, and the key is to provide the same level of protection for the data during transport as it has when it is stored. For example, sensitive data stored on a server in a datacenter has several security controls to protect it. A backup of this data requires protection when taking it to an offsite location for storage. The level of protection is dependent on the value of the data. Similarly, data in transit (transmitted over a network) requires protection based on the value of the data. Encrypting data before sending it provides this protection.

Storing Data Storage locations require protection against losses. Data is primarily stored on disk drives and personnel periodically back up valuable data. Backups of sensitive information are stored in one location onsite, and a copy is stored at another location offsite. Physical security methods protect these backups against theft. Environmental controls protect the data against loss due to corruption.

Destroying Data When data is no longer needed, it should be destroyed in such a way that it is not readable. Simply deleting files doesn't actually delete them but instead marks them for deletion, so this isn't a valid way to destroy data. Technicians and administrators use a variety of tools to remove all readable elements of files when necessary. These often overwrite the files or disks with patterns of 1s and 0s, or use other methods to shred the files. When deleting sensitive data, many organizations require personnel to destroy the disk to ensure data is not accessible.

Service Level Agreements

A service level agreement (SLA) is an agreement between an organization and an outside entity, such as a vendor. The SLA stipulates performance expectations and often includes penalties if the vendor doesn't meet these expectations.

As an example, many organizations use cloud-based services to rent servers. A vendor provides access to the servers and maintains them to ensure they are available. The organization can use an SLA to specify availability such as with maximum downtimes. With this in mind, an organization should have a clear idea of their requirements when working with third parties and make sure the SLA includes these requirements.

In addition to an SLA, organizations sometimes use a memorandum of understanding (MOU) and/or an interconnection security agreement (ISA). MOUs document the intention of two entities to work together toward a common goal. Although an MOU is similar to an SLA, it is less formal and doesn't include any monetary penalties if one of the parties doesn't meet its responsibilities.

If two or more parties plan to transmit sensitive data, they can use an ISA to specify the technical requirements of the connection. The ISA provides information on how the two parties establish, maintain, and disconnect the connection. It can also identify the minimum encryption methods used to secure the data.

NOTE

NIST Special Publication 800-47, "Security Guide for Interconnecting Information Technology Systems," includes detailed information on MOUs and ISAs.

Addressing Personnel Safety

Personnel safety concerns are an important element of security operations. It's always possible to replace things such as data, servers, and even entire buildings. In contrast, it isn't possible to replace people. With that in mind, organizations should implement security controls that enhance personnel safety.

As an example, consider the exit door in a datacenter that is controlled by an electronic cypher lock. If a fire results in a power outage, does the exit door automatically unlock or remain locked? An organization that values assets in the server room more than personnel safety might decide to ensure the door remains locked when power isn't available. This protects the physical assets in the datacenter. However, it also risks the lives of personnel within the room because they won't be able to easily exit the room. In contrast, an organization that values personnel safety over the assets in the datacenter will ensure that the locks unlock the exit door when power is lost.

Duress systems are useful when personnel are working alone. For example, a single guard might be guarding a building after hours. If a group of people break into the building, the guard probably can't stop them on his own. However, a guard can raise an alarm with a duress system. A simple duress system is just a button that sends a distress call. A monitoring entity receives the distress call and responds based on established procedures. The monitoring entity could initiate a phone call or text message back to the person who sent the distress call. In this example, the guard responds by confirming the situation.

Security systems often include code words or phrases that personnel use to verify everything truly is okay, or to verify there is a problem. For example, a code phrase indicating everything is okay could be "everything is awesome." If a guard inadvertently activated the duress system, and the monitoring entity responded, the guard says, "Everything is awesome" and then explains what happened. However, if criminals apprehended the guard, he could skip the phrase and instead make up a story of how he accidentally activated the duress system. The monitoring entity would recognize the guard skipped the code phrase and send help.

Another safety concern is when employees travel because criminals might target an organization's employees while they are traveling. Training personnel on safe practices while traveling might enhance their safety and prevent security incidents. This includes simple things such as verifying a person's identity before opening the hotel door. If room service is delivering complimentary food, a call to the front desk can verify if this is valid or part of a scam.

Provisioning and Managing Resources

Another element of the security operations domain is provisioning and managing resources throughout their life cycle. This includes multiple types of assets such as hardware, software, physical, virtual, and cloud-based assets. It's also important to protect data assets. Chapter 5 covers the protection of data in more depth.

Managing Hardware and Software Assets

Within this context, hardware refers to IT resources such as computers, servers, and peripherals. Software includes the operating systems and applications. Organizations often perform routine inventories to track their hardware and software.

Hardware Inventories

Many organizations use databases and inventory applications to perform inventories and track hardware assets through the entire equipment life cycle. For example, bar-code systems are available that can print bar codes to place on equipment. The bar-code database includes relevant details on the hardware, such as the model, serial number, and location. On a regular basis, personnel scan all of the bar codes with a bar-code reader to verify that the organization still controls the hardware.

A similar method uses radio frequency identification (RFID) tags, which can transmit information to RFID readers up to several miles away. Personnel place the RFID tags on the equipment and use the RFID readers to inventory all the equipment. RFID tags and readers are more expensive than bar codes and bar-code readers. However, RFID methods significantly reduce the time needed to perform an inventory.

Before disposing of equipment, personnel sanitize it. Sanitizing equipment removes all data to ensure that unauthorized personnel do not gain access to sensitive information. When equipment is at the end of its lifetime, it's easy for individuals to lose sight of the data that it contains, so using checklists to sanitize the system is often valuable. Checklists can include steps to sanitize hard drives, nonvolatile memory, and removable media such as CDs, DVDs, and USB flash drives within the system.

Portable media holding sensitive data is also managed as an asset. For example, an organization can label portable media with bar codes and use a bar-code inventory system to complete inventories on a regular basis. This allows them to inventory the media holding sensitive data on a regular basis.

Software Licensing

Organizations pay for software, and license keys are routinely used to activate the software. The activation process often requires contacting a licensing server over the Internet to prevent piracy. If the license keys are leaked outside the organization, it can invalidate the use of the key within the organization.

For example, an organization could purchase a license key for five installations of the software product but only install and activate one instance immediately. If the key is stolen and installed on four systems outside the organization, those activations will succeed. When the organization tries to install the application on internal systems, the activation will fail. Any type of license key is therefore highly valuable to an organization and should be protected.

Software licensing also refers to ensuring that systems do not have unauthorized software installed. Many tools are available that can inspect systems remotely to detect the system's details. For example, Microsoft's System Center Configuration Manager (ConfigMgr) is a server product that can query each system on a network. ConfigMgr has a wide range of capabilities, including the ability to identify the installed operating system and installed applications. This allows it to identify unauthorized software running on systems, and helps an organization ensure it is in compliance with software licensing rules.

NOTE Tools such as ConfigMgr regularly expand their capabilities. For example, ConfigMgr now has the ability to connect to mobile devices, including those running Windows operating systems, Apple's iOS, and Android-based operating systems. In addition to identifying operating systems and applications, it can ensure the clients are healthy according to predefined requirements, such as running antivirus software or having specific security settings configured.

Protecting Physical Assets

Physical assets go beyond IT hardware and include all physical assets, such as an organization's building and its contents. Methods used to protect physical security assets include fences, barricades, locked doors, guards, closed circuit television (CCTV) systems, and much more.

When an organization is planning its layout, it's common to locate sensitive physical assets toward the center of the building. This allows the organization to implement progressively stronger physical security controls. For example, an organization would place a datacenter housing multiple servers closer to the center of the building. If the datacenter is located against an outside wall, an attacker might be able to drive a truck through the wall and steal the servers.

Similarly, buildings often have public entrances where anyone is allowed to enter. However, additional physical security controls restrict access to internal work areas. Cipher locks, mantraps, security badges, and guards are all common methods used to control access.

Managing Virtual Assets

Organizations are consistently implementing more and more virtualization technologies due to the huge cost savings available. For example, an organization can reduce 100 physical servers to just 10 physical servers, hosting 100 virtual servers. This reduces heating, ventilation, and air conditioning (HVAC) costs, power costs, and overall operating costs.

Virtualization extends beyond just servers. Software-defined everything (SDx) refers to a trend of replacing hardware with software using virtualization. Some of the virtual assets within SDx include the following:

Virtual Machines (VMs) VMs run as guest operating systems on physical servers. The physical servers include extra processing power, memory, and disk storage to handle the VM requirements.

Software-Defined Networks (SDNs) SDNs decouple the control plane from the data plane (or forwarding plane). The control plane uses protocols to decide where to send traffic, and the data plane includes rules that decide whether traffic will be forwarded. Instead of traditional networking equipment such as routers and switches, an SDN controller handles traffic-routing using simpler network devices that accept instructions from the controller. This eliminates some of the complexity related to traditional networking protocols.

Virtual Storage Area Networks (VSANs) A SAN is a dedicated high-speed network that hosts multiple storage devices. They are often used with servers that need high-speed access to data. These have historically been expensive due to the complex hardware requirements of the SAN. VSANs bypass these complexities with virtualization.

The primary software component in virtualization is a hypervisor. The hypervisor manages the VMs, virtual data storage, and virtual network components. As an additional layer of software on the physical server, it represents an additional attack surface. If an attacker is able to compromise a physical host, the attacker can potentially access all of the virtual systems hosted on the physical server. Administrators often take extra care to ensure virtual hosts are hardened.

Although virtualization can simplify many IT concepts, it's important to remember many of the same basic security requirements still apply. For example, each VM still needs to be updated individually. Updating the host system doesn't update the VMs. Additionally, organizations should maintain backups of their virtual assets. Many virtualization tools include built-in tools to create full backups of virtual systems and create periodic snapshots, allowing relatively easy point-in-time restores.

Managing Cloud-based Assets

Cloud-based assets include any resources that an organization accesses using cloud computing. Cloud computing refers to on-demand access to computing resources available from almost anywhere, and cloud computing resources are highly available and easily scalable. Organizations typically lease cloud-based resources from outside the organization, but they can also host them within the organization. One of the primary challenges is that these resources are outside the direct control of an organization, making it more difficult to manage the risk.

Some cloud-based services only provide data storage and access. When storing data in the cloud, organizations must ensure security controls are in place to prevent unauthorized access to the data. Additionally, organizations should formally define requirements to store and process data stored in the cloud. As an example, the Department of Defense (DoD) Cloud Computing Security Requirements Guide defines specific requirements for U.S. government agencies to follow when evaluating the use of cloud computing assets. This document identifies computing requirements for assets labeled Secret and below using six separate information impact levels.

There are varying levels of responsibility for assets depending on the service model. This includes maintaining the assets, ensuring they remain functional, and keeping the systems and applications up-to-date with current patches. In some cases, the cloud service provider (CSP) is responsible for these steps. In other cases, the consumer is responsible for these steps.

Software as a Service (SaaS) SaaS models provide fully functional applications typically accessible via a web browser. For example, Google's Gmail is a SaaS application. The CSP is responsible for all maintenance of the IaaS services. Consumers do not manage or control any of the cloud-based assets.

Platform as a Service (PaaS) PaaS models provide consumers with a computing platform, including hardware, an operating system, and applications. In some cases, consumers install the applications from a list of choices provided by the CSP. Consumers manage their applications and possibly some configuration settings on the host. However, the CSP is responsible for maintenance of the host and the underlying cloud infrastructure.

Infrastructure as a Service (IaaS) IaaS models provide basic computing resources to consumers. This includes servers, storage, and in some cases, networking resources. Consumers install operating systems and applications and perform all required maintenance on the operating systems and applications. The CSP maintains the cloud-based infrastructure, ensuring that consumers have access to leased systems. The distinction between IaaS and PaaS models isn't always clear when evaluating public services. However, when leasing cloud-based services, the label the CSP uses isn't as important as clearly understanding who is responsible for performing different maintenance and security actions.

TIP

NIST SP 800-145, "The NIST Definition of Cloud Computing," provides standard definitions for many cloud-based services. This includes definitions for service models (SaaS, PaaS, and IaaS), and definitions for deployment models (public, private, community, and hybrid). NIST SP 800-144, "Guidelines on Security and Privacy in Public Cloud Computing," provides in-depth details on security issues related to cloud-based computing.

The cloud deployment model also affects the breakdown of responsibilities of the cloud-based assets. The three cloud models available are public, private, hybrid, and community.

- A public cloud model includes assets available for any consumers to rent or lease and is hosted by an external CSP. Service level agreements can be effective at ensuring the CSP provides the cloud-based services at a level acceptable to the organization.
- The private cloud deployment model includes cloud-based assets for a single organization. Organizations can create and host private clouds using their own resources. If so, the organization is responsible for all maintenance. However, an organization can also rent resources from a third party and split maintenance requirements based on the service model (SaaS, PaaS, or IaaS).
- A community cloud deployment model provides cloud-based assets to two or more organizations. Maintenance responsibilities are shared based on who is hosting the assets and the service models. Hybrid models include a combination of two or more clouds. Similar to a community cloud model, maintenance responsibilities are shared based on who is hosting the assets and the service models in use.

Media Management

Media management refers to the steps taken to protect media and data stored on media. In this context, media is anything that can hold data. It includes tapes, optical media such as CDs and DVDs, portable USB or FireWire drives, external SATA (eSATA) drives, internal hard drives, solid-state drives, and USB flash drives. Many portable devices, such as smartphones, include memory cards that can hold data so they fall into this category too. Media also includes any type of hard-copy data. Backups are often contained on tapes, so media management directly relates to tapes. However, media management extends beyond just backup tapes to any type of media that can hold data.

When media includes sensitive information, it should be stored in a secure location with strict access controls to prevent losses due to unauthorized access. Additionally, any location used to store media should have temperature and humidity controls to prevent losses due to corruption.

Media management can also include technical controls to restrict device access from computer systems. For example, due to the risks USB drives represent, many organizations use technical controls to block their use and/or detect and record when users attempt to use them. In some situations, a written security policy prohibits the use of USB flash drives, and automated detection methods detect and report any violations.

NOTE The primary risks from USB flash drives are malware infections and data theft. A system infected with a virus can detect when a user inserts a USB drive and infect the USB drive. When the user inserts this infected drive into another system, the malware attempts to infect the second system. Additionally, malicious users can easily copy and transfer large amounts of data and conceal the drive in their pocket.

Properly managing media directly addresses confidentiality, integrity, and availability. When media is marked, handled, and stored properly, it helps prevent unauthorized disclosure (loss of confidentiality), unauthorized modification (loss of integrity), and unauthorized destruction (loss of availability).

Tape Media

Organizations commonly store backups on tapes, and they are highly susceptible to loss due to corruption. As a best practice, organizations keep at least two copies of backups. They maintain one copy onsite for immediate usage if necessary, and store the second copy at a secure location offsite. If a catastrophic disaster such as a fire destroys the primary location, the data is still available at the alternate location.

The cleanliness of the storage area will directly affect the life span and usefulness of tape media. Additionally, magnetic fields can act as a degausser and erase or corrupt data on the tape. With this in mind, tapes should not be exposed to magnetic fields that can come from

Controlling USB Flash Drives

Many organizations restrict the use of USB flash drives to only specific brands purchased and provided by the organization. This allows the organization to protect data on the drives and ensure that the drives are not being used to inadvertently transfer malicious software (malware) between systems. Users still have the benefit of the USB flash drives, but this practice reduces risk for the organization without hampering the user's ability to use USB drives.

For example, Imation sells IronKey flash drives that include multiple levels of built-in protection. Several authentication mechanisms are available to ensure that only authorized users can access data on the drive. It protects data with built-in AES 256-bit hardware-based encryption. Active antimalware software on the flash drive helps prevent malware from infecting the drive. Enterprise editions of IronKey include the "Silver Bullet Service," used to protect data on lost or stolen devices. This service can remotely deny all access to the data, disable the device, or initiate a self-destruct sequence to destroy it. "Self-destruct" may evoke an image of a massive explosion from a science fiction movie. However, the IronKey self-destruct feature doesn't cause an explosion but instead destroys all the data and settings on the drive.

elevator motors, printers, and older CRT monitors. Here are some useful guidelines for managing tape media:

- Keep new media in its original sealed packaging until it's needed to protect it from dust and dirt.
- When opening a media package, take extra caution not to damage the media in any way. This includes avoiding sharp objects and not twisting or flexing the media.
- Avoid exposing the media to temperature extremes; it shouldn't be stored close to heaters, radiators, air conditioners, or other sources of extreme temperatures.
- Do not use media that has been damaged, exposed to abnormal levels of dust and dirt, or dropped.
- Media should be transported from one site to another in a temperature-controlled vehicle.
- Media should be protected from exposure to the outside environment; avoid sunlight, moisture, humidity, heat, and cold.
- Media should be acclimated for 24 hours before use.
- Appropriate security should be maintained over media from the point of departure from the backup device to the secured offsite storage facility. Media is vulnerable to damage and theft at any point during transportation.
- Appropriate security should be maintained over media throughout the lifetime of the media based on the classification level of data on the media.

Mobile Devices

Mobile devices include smartphones and tablets. These devices have internal memory or removable memory cards that can hold a significant amount of data. Data can include email with attachments, contacts, and scheduling information. Additionally, many devices include applications that allow users to read and manipulate different types of documents.

Organizations often purchase smartphones for users and maintain their data plans. This is certainly a great benefit for the employee, but it also gives the organization additional control over the user's phone and the data it contains. Some of the common controls organizations enable on user phones are encryption, screen lock, global positioning system (GPS), and remote wipe. Encryption protects the data if the phone is lost or stolen, the screen lock slows down someone that may have stolen a phone, and GPS provides information on the location of the phone if it is lost or stolen. A remote wipe signal can be sent to a lost device to delete some or all data on the device if it has been lost. Many devices respond with a confirmation message when the remote wipe has succeeded.

TIP

Remote wipe doesn't provide guaranteed protection. Knowledgeable thieves who want data from a business smartphone often remove the subscriber identity module (SIM) card immediately. Additionally, they have used shielded rooms similar to Faraday cages when putting the SIM back into the phone to get the data. These techniques block the remote wipe signal. If a confirmation message is not received indicating that the remote wipe has succeeded, it's very possible that the data has been compromised.

Organizations sometimes allow personnel to use their personal devices and connect them to the organization's network. This results in different challenges. For example, if it is the user's device, what can the organization do to ensure the device is maintained in a secure state and data stored on the device is protected? To respond to this challenge, organizations often include bring your own device (BYOD) policies within the security policy. BYOD policies define responsibilities and expectations for users who want to connect their devices to the organization's network.

Managing Media Life Cycle

All media has a useful, but finite, life cycle. Reusable media is subject to a *mean time to failure (MTTF)* that is sometimes represented in the number of times it can be reused or the number of years you can expect to keep it. For example, some tapes include specifications saying they can be reused as many as 250 times or last up to 30 years under ideal conditions. However, many variables affect the lifetime of media and can reduce these estimates. It's important to monitor backups for errors and use them as a guide to gauge the lifetime in your environment. When a tape begins to generate errors, technicians should rotate it out of use.

Once backup media has reached its MTTF, it should be destroyed. The classification of data held on the tape will dictate the method used to destroy the media. Some organizations degauss highly classified tapes when they've reached the end of their lifetime and then store them until they are able to destroy the tapes. Tapes are commonly destroyed in bulk shredders or incinerators.

Chapter 5 discusses some of the security challenges with SSDs. Specifically, degaussing does not remove data from an SSD, and built-in erase commands often do not sanitize the entire disk. Instead of attempting to remove data from SSDs, many organizations destroy them.

NOTE MTTF is different from mean time between failures (MTBF). MTTF is normally calculated for items that will not be repaired when they fail, such as a tape. In contrast, MTBF refers to the amount of time expected to elapse between failures of an item that personnel will repair, such as a computer server.

Managing Configuration

Configuration management helps ensure that systems are deployed in a secure consistent state, and maintain this state throughout their lifetime. One method used with configuration management is with baselines.

Baselining

A baseline is a starting point. Within the context of configuration management, it is the starting configuration for a system. Administrators often modify the baseline after deploying systems to meet different requirements. However, when systems are deployed in a secure state with a secure baseline, they are much more likely to stay secure. This is especially true if an organization has an effective change management program in place.

Baselines can be created with checklists that require someone to make sure a system is deployed a certain way or with a specific configuration. However, manual baselines are susceptible to human error. It's easy for a person to miss a step or accidentally misconfigure a system. Scripts and operating system tools are also used to implement baselines, and when automated methods are used, it reduces the potential for errors from manual baselines. For example, Microsoft operating systems include Group Policy. Administrators can configure a Group Policy setting one time and automatically have the setting apply to all the computers in the domain.

Using Images for Baselining

Many organizations use images to create baselines. Figure 16.2 shows the process of creating and deploying baseline images in an overall three-step process. Here are the steps:

NOTE: In practice, more details are involved in this process, depending on the tools used for imaging. For example, the steps to capture and deploy images using Norton Ghost by Symantec are different from the steps to capture and deploy images using Microsoft's Windows Deployment Services (WDS).

1. An administrator starts by installing the operating system and all desired applications on a computer (labeled as the baseline system in the figure). The administrator then configures the system with relevant security and other settings to meet the needs of the organization. Next, personnel perform extensive testing to ensure the system operates as expected before proceeding to the next step.
2. Next, the administrator captures an image of the system using imaging software and stores it on a server (labeled as an Image Server) in the figure. It's often possible to store images on external hard drives, USB drives, or DVDs.
3. Personnel then deploy the image to systems as needed. These systems often require additional configuration to finalize them, such as giving them unique names. However, the overall configuration of these systems is the same as the baseline system.

Baseline images improve the security of systems by ensuring that desired security settings are always configured correctly. Additionally, they reduce the amount of time required to deploy and maintain systems, thus reducing the overall maintenance costs. Deployment of a prebuilt image can require only a few minutes of a technician's time. Additionally, when a user's system becomes corrupt, technicians can redeploy an image in minutes, instead of taking hours to troubleshoot the system or trying to rebuild it from scratch.

FIGURE 16.2 Creating and deploying images

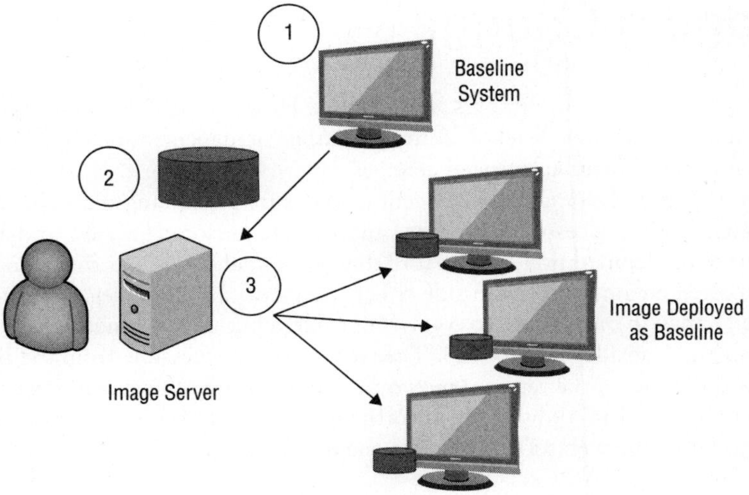

It's common to combine imaging with other automated methods for baselines. In other words, administrators can create one image for all desktop computers within an organization. They then use automated methods to add additional applications, features, or settings for specific groups of computers. For example, computers in one department may have additional security settings or applications applied through scripting or other automated tools.

Real World Scenario

Baseline Images Use in the U.S. Government

The U.S. government recognized that many of the security problems it was having were due to misconfigured Windows systems. Many IT professionals knew about core security settings to protect systems, but often, personnel who were deploying the systems didn't have this knowledge. Technicians were routinely deploying vulnerable systems, resulting in security incidents that the experts knew were preventable.

In response, the U.S. Air Force collaborated with Microsoft and created standardized images to use as baselines for their systems. Later, several government agencies again collaborated with Microsoft and created standardized images to use as baselines for all government agencies. The United States Government Configuration Baseline (USGCB) now includes images for several different operating systems.

Currently, the Office of Management and Budget (OMB) mandates the use of these images for all general-purpose Windows-based systems such as desktops and laptops used in government agencies. The National Institute of Standards and Technology (NIST) maintains and updates the images as needed. This site provides more details: `http://usgcb.nist.gov/`.

Managing Change

Deploying systems in a secure state is a good start. However, it's also important to ensure the system retains that same level of security. Change management helps reduce unanticipated outages caused by unauthorized changes.

The primary goal of change management is to ensure that changes do not cause outages. Change management processes ensure that appropriate personnel review and approve changes before implementation, and ensure that personnel document the changes.

Changes often create unintended side effects that can cause outages. An administrator can make a change to one system to resolve a problem but unknowingly cause a problem in other systems. Consider Figure 16.3. The web server is accessible from the Internet and accesses the database on the internal network. Administrators have configured appropriate ports on Firewall 1 to allow Internet traffic to the web server and appropriate ports on Firewall 2 to allow the web server to access the database server.

FIGURE 16.3 Web server and database server

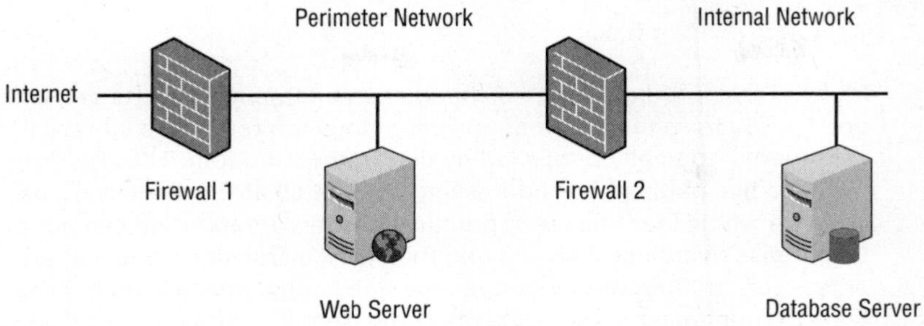

A well-meaning firewall administrator may see an unrecognized open port on Firewall 2 and decide to close it in the interest of security. Unfortunately, the web server needs this port open to communicate with the database server, so when the port is closed, the web server will begin having problems. Soon, the help desk is flooded with requests to fix the web server and people begin troubleshooting it. They ask the web server programmers for help and after some troubleshooting the developers realize that the database server isn't answering queries. They then call in the database administrators to troubleshoot the database server. After a bunch of hooting, hollering, blame storming, and finger pointing, someone realizes that a needed port on Firewall2 is closed. They open the port and resolve the problem. At least until this well-meaning firewall administrator closes it again, or starts tinkering with Firewall1.

TIP

Organizations constantly seek the best balance between security and usability, and there are instances when an organization makes conscious decisions to improve performance or usability of a system by weakening security. However, change management helps ensure that an organization takes the time to evaluate the risk of weakening security and compare it to the benefits of increased usability.

Unauthorized changes directly affect the *A* in the CIA Triad–availability. However, change management processes give various IT experts an opportunity to review proposed changes for unintended side effects before technicians implement the changes. And they give administrators time to check their work in controlled circumstances before implementing changes in production environments.

Additionally, some changes can weaken or reduce security. For example, if an organization isn't using an effective access control model to grant access to users, administrators may not be able to keep up with the requests for additional access. Frustrated administrators may decide to add a group of users to an administrators group within the network. Users will now have all the access they need, improving their ability to use the network, and they will no longer bother the administrators with access requests. However, granting administrator access in this way directly violates the principle of least privilege and significantly weakens security.

> **NOTE** Many of the configuration and change management concepts in use today are derived from the Information Technology Infrastructure Library (ITIL) documents originally published by the United Kingdom. The ITIL Core includes five publications addressing the overall life cycle of systems. ITIL as a whole identifies best practices that an organization can adopt to increase overall availability, and the Service Transition publication addresses configuration management and change management processes. Even though many of the concepts come from ITIL, organizations don't need to adopt ITIL to implement change and configuration management.

Security Impact Analysis

A change management process ensures that personnel can perform a security impact analysis. Experts evaluate changes to identify any security impacts before personnel deploy the changes in a production environment.

Change management controls provide a process to control, document, track, and audit all system changes. This includes changes to any aspect of a system, including hardware and software configuration. Organizations implement change management processes through the life cycle of any system.

Common tasks within a change management process are as follows:

1. Request the change. Once personnel identify desired changes, they request the change. Some organizations use internal websites, allowing individuals to submit change requests via a web page. The website automatically logs the request in a database, which allows personnel to track the changes. It also allows anyone to see the status of a change request.
2. Review the change. Experts within the organization review the change. Personnel reviewing a change are typically from several different areas within the organization. In some cases, they may quickly complete the review and approve or reject the change. In other cases, the change may require approval at a formal change review board after extensive testing.
3. Approve/reject the change. Based on the review, these experts then approve or reject the change. They also record the response in the change management documentation. For example, if the organization uses an internal website, someone will document the results in the website's database. In some cases, the change review board might require the creation of a rollback or back-out plan. This ensures that personnel can return the system to its original condition if the change results in a failure.
4. Schedule and implement the change. The change is scheduled so that it can be implemented with the least impact on the system and the system's customer. This may require scheduling the change during off-duty or nonpeak hours.

5. Document the change. The last step is the documentation of the change to ensure that all interested parties are aware of it. This often requires a change in the configuration management documentation. If an unrelated disaster requires administrators to rebuild the system, the change management documentation provides them with the information on the change. This ensures they can return the system to the state it was in before the change.

There may be instances when an emergency change is required. For example, if an attack or malware infection takes one or more systems down, an administrator may need to make changes to a system or network to contain the incident. In this situation, the administrator still needs to document the changes. This ensures that the change review board can review the change for potential problems. Additionally, documenting the emergency change ensures that the affected system will include the new configuration if it needs to be rebuilt.

When the change management process is enforced, it creates documentation for all changes to a system. This provides a trail of information if personnel need to reverse the change. If personnel need to implement the same change on other systems, the documentation also provides a road map or procedure to follow.

Change management control is a mandatory element for some security assurance requirements (SARs) in the ISO Common Criteria. However, change management controls are implemented in many organizations that don't require compliance with ISO Common Criteria. It improves the security of an environment by protecting against unauthorized changes resulting in unintentional losses.

Versioning

Versioning typically refers to version control used in software configuration management. A labeling or numbering system differentiates between different software sets and configurations across multiple machines or at different points in time on a single machine. For example, the first version of an application may be labeled as 1.0. The first minor update would be labeled as 1.1, and the first major update would be 2.0. This helps keep track of changes over time to deployed software.

Although most established software developers recognize the importance of versioning and revision control with applications, many new web developers don't recognize its importance. These web developers have learned some excellent skills they use to create awesome websites but don't always recognize the importance of underlying principles such as versioning control. If they don't control changes through some type of versioning control system, they can implement a change that effectively breaks the website.

Configuration Documentation

Configuration documentation identifies the current configuration of systems. It identifies who is responsible for the system and the purpose of the system, and lists all changes applied to the baseline. Years ago, many organizations used simple paper notebooks to record this information for servers, but it is much more common to store this information in files or databases today. Of course, the challenge with storing the documentation in a data file is that it can be inaccessible during an outage.

Managing Patches and Reducing Vulnerabilities

Patch management and vulnerability management work together to help protect an organization against emerging threats. Bugs and security vulnerabilities are routinely discovered in operating systems and applications. As they are discovered, vendors write and test patches to remove the vulnerability. Patch management ensures that appropriate patches are applied, and vulnerability management helps verify that systems are not vulnerable to known threats.

Patch Management

Patch is a blanket term for any type of code written to correct a bug or vulnerability or improve the performance of existing software. The software can be either an operating system or an application. Patches are sometimes referred to as updates, quick fixes, and hot fixes. In the context of security, administrators are primarily concerned with security patches, which are patches that affect the vulnerability of a system. Service packs are collections of patches that bring a system up-to-date with current patches.

Even though vendors regularly write and release patches, these patches are useful only if they are applied. This may seem obvious, but many security incidents occur simply because organizations don't implement a patch management policy. An effective *patch management* program ensures that systems are kept up-to-date with current patches. These are the common steps within an effective patch management program:

Evaluate patches. When vendors announce or release patches, administrators evaluate them to determine if they apply to their systems. For example, a patch released to fix a vulnerability on a Unix system configured as a Domain Name System (DNS) server is not relevant for a server running DNS on Windows. Similarly, a patch released to fix a feature running on a Windows system is not needed if the feature is disabled.

Test patches. Whenever possible, administrators test patches on an isolated system to determine if the patch causes any unwanted side effects. The worst-case scenario is that a system will no longer start after applying a patch. For example, patches have occasionally caused systems to begin an endless reboot cycle. They boot into a stop error, and keep trying to reboot to recover from the error. If testing shows this on a single system, it affects only one system. However, if an organization applies the patch to a thousand computers before testing it, it could have catastrophic results.

NOTE

Smaller organizations often choose not to evaluate, test, and approve patches but instead use an automatic method to approve and deploy the patches. Windows systems include Windows Update, which makes this easy. However, larger organizations usually take control of the process to prevent potential outages from updates.

Approve the patches. After administrators test the patches and determine them to be safe, they approve the patches for deployment. It's common to use a change management process (described earlier in this chapter) as part of the approval process.

Deploy the patches. After testing and approval, administrators deploy the patches. Many organizations use automated methods to deploy the patches. These can be third-party products or products provided by the software vendor.

Verify that patches are deployed, After deploying patches, administrators regularly test and audit systems to ensure that they remain patched. Many deployment tools include the ability to audit systems. Additionally, many vulnerability assessment tools include the ability to check systems to ensure that they have appropriate patches.

Patch Tuesday and Exploit Wednesday

Microsoft regularly releases patches on the second Tuesday of every month, commonly called *patch Tuesday*. The regular schedule allows administrators to plan for the release of patches so that they have adequate time to test and deploy them. Many organizations that have support contracts with Microsoft have advance notification of the patches prior to patch Tuesday. Some vulnerabilities are significant enough that Microsoft releases them "out-of-band." In other words, instead of waiting for the next patch Tuesday to release a patch, Microsoft releases some patches earlier.

Attackers realize that many organizations do not patch their systems right away. Some attackers have reverse-engineered patches to identify the underlying vulnerability and then created methods to exploit the vulnerability. These attacks often start within a day after patch Tuesday, giving rise to the term *exploit Wednesday*.

However, many attacks occur on unpatched systems weeks, months, and even years after vendors release the patches. In other words, many systems remain unpatched and attackers exploit them much later than a day after the vendor released the patch. For example, Microsoft released a fix in October 2008 to fix a vulnerability commonly referred to as Conficker. Conficker includes many malicious capabilities and is a serious threat. However, in 2011 there were still more than 1.8 million computers worldwide infected with Conficker, meaning at least this many computers hadn't been updated to block it.

Vulnerability Management

Vulnerability management refers to regularly identifying vulnerabilities, evaluating them, and taking steps to mitigate risks associated with them. It isn't possible to eliminate risks. Similarly, it isn't possible to eliminate all vulnerabilities. However, an effective vulnerability management program helps an organization ensure that they are regularly evaluating vulnerabilities and mitigating the vulnerabilities that represent the greatest risks. Two common elements of a vulnerability management program are routine vulnerability scans and periodic vulnerability assessments.

> **NOTE** One of the most common vulnerabilities within an organization is an unpatched system, and so a vulnerability management program will often work in conjunction with a patch management program. In many cases, duties of the two programs are separated between different employees. One person or group would be responsible for keeping systems patched, and another person or group would be responsible for verifying that the systems are patched. As with other separation of duties implementations, this provides a measure of checks and balances within the organization.

Vulnerability Scans

Vulnerability scanners are software tools used to test systems and networks for known security issues. Attackers use vulnerability scanners to detect weaknesses in systems and networks, such as missing patches or weak passwords. After they detect the weaknesses, they launch attacks to exploit them. Administrators in many organizations use the same types of vulnerability scanners to detect vulnerabilities on their network. Their goal is to detect the vulnerabilities and mitigate them before an attacker discovers them.

Just as antivirus software uses a signature file to detect known viruses, vulnerability scanners include a database of known security issues and they check systems against this database. Vendors regularly update this database and sell a subscription for the updates to customers. If administrators don't keep vulnerability scanners up-to-date, they won't be able to detect newer threats. This is similar to how antivirus software won't be able to detect newer viruses if it doesn't have current virus signature definitions.

Nessus is a popular vulnerability scanner managed by Tenable Network Security, and it combines multiple techniques to detect a wide range of vulnerabilities. Nessus analyzes packets sent out from systems to determine the system's operating system and other details about these systems. It uses port scans to detect open ports and identify the services and protocols that are likely running on these systems. Once Nessus discovers basic details about systems, it can then follow up with queries to test the systems for known vulnerabilities, such as if the system is up-to-date with current patches. It can also discover potentially malicious systems on a network that are using IP probes and ping sweeps.

It's important to realize that a vulnerability scanner does more than just check unpatched systems. For example, if a system is running a database server application, it can check the database for default passwords with default accounts. Similarly, if a system is hosting a website, it can check the website to determine if it is using input validation techniques to prevent different types of injection attacks such as SQL injection or cross-site scripting.

In some large organizations, a dedicated security team will perform regular vulnerability scans using available tools. In smaller organizations, an IT or security administrator may perform the scans as part of their other responsibilities. Remember, though, if the person responsible for deploying patches is also responsible for running scans to check for patches, it represents a potential conflict. If something prevents an administrator from deploying patches, the administrator can also skip the scan that would otherwise detect the unpatched systems.

Scanners include the ability to generate reports identifying any vulnerabilities they discover. The reports may recommend applying patches or making specific configuration or security setting changes to improve or impose security. Obviously, simply recommending applying patches doesn't reduce the vulnerabilities. Administrators need to take steps to apply the patches.

However, there may be situations where it isn't feasible or desirable to do so. For example, if a patch fixing a minor security issue breaks an application on a system, management may decide not to implement the fix until developers create a workaround. The vulnerability scanner will regularly report the vulnerability, even though the organization has addressed the risk.

NOTE

Management can choose to accept a risk rather than mitigate it. Any risk that remains after applying a control is residual risk. Any losses that occur from residual risk are the responsibility of management.

In contrast, an organization that never performs vulnerability scans will likely have many vulnerabilities. Additionally, these vulnerabilities will remain unknown, and management will not have the opportunity to decide which vulnerabilities to mitigate and which ones to accept.

Vulnerability Assessments

A vulnerability assessment will often include results from vulnerability scans, but the assessment will do more. For example, an annual vulnerability assessment may analyze all of the vulnerability scan reports from the past year to determine if the organization is addressing vulnerabilities. If the same vulnerability is repeated on every vulnerability scan report, a logical question to ask is, Why hasn't this been mitigated? There may be a valid reason and management chose to accept the risk, or it may be that the vulnerability scans are being performed but action is never taken to mitigate the discovered vulnerabilities.

Vulnerability assessments are often done as part of a risk analysis or risk assessment to identify the vulnerabilities at a point in time. Additionally, vulnerability assessments can look at other areas to determine risks. For example, a vulnerability assessment can look at how sensitive information is marked, handled, stored, and destroyed throughout its lifetime to address potential vulnerabilities.

TIP

The term *vulnerability assessment* is sometimes used to indicate a risk assessment. In this context, a vulnerability assessment would include the same elements as a risk assessment, described in Chapter 2, "Personnel Security and Risk Management Concepts." This includes identifying the value of assets, identifying vulnerabilities and threats, and performing a risk analysis to determine the overall risk.

Chapter 15, "Security Assessment and Testing," covers penetration tests. Many penetration tests start with a vulnerability assessment. Additionally, many penetration testers include social-engineering tactics as a part of their overall testing.

Common Vulnerabilities and Exposures

Vulnerabilities are commonly referred to using the Common Vulnerability and Exposures (CVE) dictionary. The CVE dictionary provides a standard convention used to identify vulnerabilities. MITRE maintains the CVE database, and you can view it here: `www.cve.mitre.org`.

TIP

MITRE looks like an acronym, but it isn't. The founders do have a history as research engineers at the Massachusetts's Institute of Technology (MIT) and the name reminds people of that history. However, MITRE is not a part of MIT. MITRE receives funding from the U.S. government to maintain the CVE database.

Patch management and vulnerability management tools commonly use the CVE dictionary as a standard when scanning for specific vulnerabilities. For example, Conficker was mentioned earlier. Conficker takes advantage of a vulnerability in unpatched Windows systems, and Microsoft released Microsoft Security Bulletin MS08-067 with updates to address it. The same Conficker vulnerability is identified as CVE-2008-4250 by MITRE and any CVE-compatible products.

The CVE database makes it easier for companies that create patch management and vulnerability management tools. They don't have to expend any resources to manage the naming and definition of vulnerabilities but can instead focus on methods used to check systems for the vulnerabilities.

Summary

Several basic security principles are at the core of security operations in any environment. These include need to know, least privilege, separation of duties and responsibilities, job rotation, and mandatory vacations. Combined, these practices help prevent security incidents from occurring, and limit the scope of incidents that do occur. Administrators and operators require special privileges to perform their jobs following these security principles. In addition to implementing the principles, it's important to monitor privileged activities to ensure privileged entities do not abuse their access.

With resource protection, media and other assets that contain data are protected throughout their life cycle. Media includes anything that can hold data, such as tapes, internal drives, portable drives (USB, FireWire, and eSATA), CDs and DVDs, mobile devices, memory cards, and printouts. Media holding sensitive information should be marked, handled, stored, and destroyed using methods that are acceptable within the organization. Asset management extends beyond media to any asset considered valuable to an organization—physical assets such as computers and software assets such as purchased applications and software keys.

Virtual assets include virtual machines, software-defined networks (SDNs), and virtual storage area networks (VSANs). A hypervisor is the software component that manages the virtual components. The hypervisor adds an additional attack surface, so it's important to ensure it is deployed in a secure state and kept up-to-date with patches. Additionally, each virtual component needs to be updated separately.

Cloud-based assets include any resources stored in the cloud. When negotiating with cloud service providers, you must understand who is responsible for maintenance and security. In general, the cloud service provider has the most responsibility with Software as a Service (SaaS) resources, less responsibility with Platform as a Service (SaaS) offerings, and the least responsibility with Infrastructure as a Service (IaaS) offerings. Many organizations use service level agreements (SLAs) when contracting cloud-based services. The SLA stipulates performance expectations and often includes penalties if the vendor doesn't meet these expectations.

Change and configuration management are two additional controls that help reduce outages. Configuration management ensures that systems are deployed in a consistent manner that is known to be secure. Imaging is a common configuration management technique that ensures that systems start with a known baseline. Change management helps reduce unintended outages from unauthorized changes and can also help prevent changes from weakening security.

Patch and vulnerability management procedures work together to keep systems protected against known vulnerabilities. Patch management keeps systems up-to-date with relevant patches. Vulnerability management includes vulnerability scans to check for a wide variety of known vulnerabilities (including unpatched systems) and also includes vulnerability assessments done as part of a risk assessment.

Exam Essentials

Understand need to know and the principle of least privilege. Need to know and the principle of least privilege are two standard IT security principles implemented in secure networks. They limit access to data and systems so that users and other subjects have access only to what they require. This limited access helps prevent security incidents and helps limit the scope of incidents when they occur. When these principles are not followed, security incidents result in far greater damage to an organization.

Understand separation of duties and job rotation. Separation of duties is a basic security principle that ensures that no single person can control all the elements of a critical function or system. With job rotation, employees are rotated into different jobs, or tasks are assigned to different employees. Collusion is an agreement among multiple persons to perform some unauthorized or illegal actions. Implementing these policies helps prevent fraud by limiting actions individuals can do without colluding with others.

Understand the importance of monitoring privileged operations. Privileged entities are trusted, but they can abuse their privileges. Because of this, it's important to monitor all assignment of privileges and the use of privileged operations. The goal is to ensure that trusted employees do not abuse the special privileges they are granted.

Understand the information life cycle. Data needs to be protected throughout its entire life cycle. This starts by properly classifying and marking data. It also includes properly handling, storing, and destroying data.

Understand service level agreements. Organizations use service level agreements (SLAs) with outside entities such as vendors. They stipulate performance expectations such as maximum downtimes and often include penalties if the vendor doesn't meet expectations.

Understand virtual assets. Virtual assets include virtual machines, software-defined networks, and virtual storage area networks. Hypervisors are the primary software component that manages virtual assets, but hypervisors also provide attackers with an additional target. It's important to keep physical servers hosting virtual assets up-to-date with appropriate patches for the operating system and the hypervisor. Additionally, all virtual machines must be kept up-to-date.

Recognize security issues with cloud-based assets. Cloud-based assets include any resources accessed via the cloud. Storing data in the cloud increases the risk so additional steps may be necessary to protect the data, depending on its value. When leasing cloud-based services, you must understand who is responsible for maintenance and security. The cloud service provider provides the least amount of maintenance and security in the IaaS model.

Explain configuration and change control management. Many outages and incidents can be prevented with effective configuration and change management programs. Configuration management ensures that systems are configured similarly and the configurations of systems are known and documented. Baselining ensures that systems are deployed with a common baseline or starting point, and imaging is a common baselining method. Change management helps reduce outages or weakened security from unauthorized changes. A change management process requires changes to be requested, approved, and documented. Versioning uses a labeling or numbering system to track changes in updated versions of software.

Understand patch management. Patch management ensures that systems are kept up-to-date with current patches. You should know that an effective patch management program will evaluate, test, approve, and deploy patches. Additionally, be aware that system audits verify the deployment of approved patches to systems. Patch management is often intertwined with change and configuration management to ensure that documentation reflects the changes. When an organization does not have an effective patch management program, it will often experience outages and incidents from known issues that could have been prevented.

Explain vulnerability management. Vulnerability management includes routine vulnerability scans and periodic vulnerability assessments. Vulnerability scanners can detect known security vulnerabilities and weaknesses such as the absence of patches or weak passwords. They generate reports that indicate the technical vulnerabilities of a system and are an effective check for a patch management program. Vulnerability assessments extend beyond just technical scans and can include reviews and audits to detect vulnerabilities.

Written Lab

1. Define the difference between need to know and the principle of least privilege.
2. Name the common methods used to manage sensitive information.
3. List the three primary cloud-based service models and identify the level of maintenance provided by the cloud service provider in each of the models.
4. What control prevents outages due to unauthorized modifications in system configuration?

Review Questions

1. An organization ensures that users are granted access to only the data they need to perform specific work tasks. What principle are they following?
   - **A.** Principle of least permission
   - **B.** Separation of duties
   - **C.** Need to know
   - **D.** Role-based access control
2. An administrator is granting permissions to a database. What is the default level of access the administrator should grant to new users?
   - **A.** Read
   - **B.** Modify
   - **C.** Full access
   - **D.** No access
3. Why is separation of duties important for security purposes?
   - **A.** It ensures that multiple people can do the same job.
   - **B.** It prevents an organization from losing important information when they lose important people.
   - **C.** It prevents any single security person from being able to make major security changes without involving other individuals.
   - **D.** It helps employees concentrate their talents where they will be most useful.
4. What is a primary benefit of job rotation and separation of duties policies?
   - **A.** Preventing collusion
   - **B.** Preventing fraud
   - **C.** Encouraging collusion
   - **D.** Correcting incidents
5. A financial organization commonly has employees switch duty responsibilities every six months. What security principle are they employing?
   - **A.** Job rotation
   - **B.** Separation of duties
   - **C.** Mandatory vacations
   - **D.** Least privilege
6. Which of the following is one of the primary reasons an organization enforces a mandatory vacation policy?
   - **A.** To rotate job responsibilities
   - **B.** To detect fraud

C. To increase employee productivity

D. To reduce employee stress levels

7. An organization wants to reduce vulnerabilities against fraud from malicious employees. Of the following choices, what would help with this goal? (Choose all that apply.)

A. Job rotation

B. Separation of duties

C. Mandatory vacations

D. Baselining

8. Of the following choices, what is *not* a valid security practice related to special privileges?

A. Monitor special privilege assignments.

B. Grant access equally to administrators and operators.

C. Monitor special privilege usage.

D. Grant access to only trusted employees.

9. Which of the following identifies vendor responsibilities and can include monetary penalties if the vendor doesn't meet the stated responsibilities?

A. Service level agreement (SLA)

B. Memorandum of understanding (MOU)

C. Interconnection security agreement (ISA)

D. Software as a Service (SaaS)

10. What should be done with equipment that is at the end of its life cycle and that is being donated to a charity?

A. Remove all CDs and DVDs.

B. Remove all software licenses.

C. Sanitize it.

D. Install the original software.

11. An organization is planning the layout of a new building that will house a datacenter. Where is the most appropriate place to locate the datacenter?

A. In the center of the building

B. Closest to the outside wall where power enters the building

C. Closest to the outside wall where heating, ventilation, and air conditioning systems are located

D. At the back of the building

12. Which of the following is a true statement regarding virtual machines (VMs) running as guest operating systems on physical servers?

A. Updating the physical server automatically updates the VMs.

B. Updating any VM automatically updates all the VMs.

C. VMs do not need to be updated as long as the physical server is updated.

D. VMs must be updated individually.

13. Some cloud-based service models require an organization to perform some maintenance and take responsibility for some security. Which of the following models places the majority of these responsibilities on the organization leasing the cloud-based resources?

A. Infrastructure as a Service (IaaS)

B. Platform as a Service (PaaS)

C. Software as a Service (SaaS)

D. Cloud as a Service (CaaS)

14. An organization is using a Software as a Service (SaaS) cloud-based service shared with another organization. What type of deployment model does this describe?

A. Public

B. Private

C. Community

D. Hybrid

15. Backup tapes have reached the end of their life cycle and need to be disposed of. Which of the following is the *most* appropriate disposal method?

A. Throw them away. Because they are at the end of their life cycle, it is not possible to read data from them.

B. Purge the tapes of all data before disposing of them.

C. Erase data off the tapes before disposing of them.

D. Store the tapes in a storage facility.

16. Which of the following can be an effective method of configuration management using a baseline?

A. Implementing change management

B. Using images

C. Implementing vulnerability management

D. Implementing patch management

17. Which of the following steps would *not* be included in a change management process?

A. Immediately implement the change if it will improve performance.

B. Request the change.

C. Create a rollback plan for the change.

D. Document the change.

18. While troubleshooting a network problem, a technician realized it could be resolved by opening a port on a firewall. The technician opened the port and verified the system was now working. However, an attacker accessed this port and launched a successful attack. What could have prevented this problem?

A. Patch management processes

B. Vulnerability management processes

C. Configuration management processes

D. Change management processes

19. Which of the following is *not* a part of a patch management process?

A. Evaluate patches.

B. Test patches.

C. Deploy all patches.

D. Audit patches.

20. What would an administrator use to check systems for known issues that attackers may use to exploit the systems?

A. Versioning tracker

B. Vulnerability scanner

C. Security audit

D. Security review

Preventing and Responding to Incidents

THE CISSP EXAM TOPICS COVERED IN THIS CHAPTER INCLUDE:

✓ **Security Operations**

- C. Conduct logging and monitoring activities
  - C.1 Intrusion detection and prevention
  - C.2 Security information and event management
  - C.3 Continuous monitoring
  - C.4 Egress monitoring (e.g., data loss prevention, steganography, watermarking)
- G. Conduct incident management
  - G.1 Detection
  - G.2 Response
  - G.3 Mitigation
  - G.4 Reporting
  - G.5 Recovery
  - G.6 Remediation
  - G.7 Lessons learned
- H. Operate and maintain preventative measures
  - H.1 Firewalls
  - H.2 Intrusion detection and prevention systems
  - H.3 Whitelisting/Blacklisting
  - H.4 Third-party security services
  - H.5 Sandboxing
  - H.6 Honeypots/Honeynets
  - H.7 Anti-malware

The Security Operations domain for the CISSP certification exam includes several objectives directly related to incident management. Effective incident management helps an organization respond appropriately when attacks occur to limit the scope of an attack. Organizations implement preventive measures to protect against, and detect, attacks, and this chapter covers many of these controls and countermeasures. Logging, monitoring, and auditing provide assurances that the security controls are in place and are providing the desired protections.

Managing Incident Response

One of the primary goals of any security program is to prevent security incidents. However, despite best efforts of IT and security professionals, incidents do occur. When they happen, an organization must be able to respond to limit or contain the incident. The primary goal of incident response is to minimize the impact on the organization.

Defining an Incident

Before digging into incident response, it's important to understand the definition of an incident. Although that may seem simple, you'll find that there are different definitions depending on the context.

An *incident* is any event that has a negative effect on the confidentiality, integrity, or availability of an organization's assets. Information Technology Infrastructure Library version 3 (ITILv3) defines an incident as "an unplanned interruption to an IT Service or a reduction in the quality of an IT Service." Notice that these definitions encompass events as diverse as direct attacks, natural occurrences such as a hurricane or earthquake, and even accidents, such as someone accidentally cutting cables for a live network.

In contrast, a *computer security incident* (sometimes called just *security incident*) commonly refers to an incident that is the result of an attack, or the result of malicious or intentional actions on the part of users. For example, RFC 2350, "Expectations for Computer Security Incident Response," defines both a security incident and a computer security incident as "any adverse event which compromises some aspect of computer or network security." National Institute of Standards and Technology (NIST) Special Publication (SP) 800-61 "Computer Security Incident Handling Guide" defines a computer security incident as "a violation or imminent threat of violation of computer security policies, acceptable use policies, or standard security practices." (NIST SP documents, including SP 800-61, are available from the NIST special publications download page: `http://csrc.nist.gov/publications/PubsSPs.html`.)

In the context of incident response, an incident is referring to a computer security incident. However, you'll often see it listed as just as incident. For example, in the CISSP Candidate Information Bulletin (CIB) within the Security Operations domain, the "Conduct incident management" objective is clearly referring to computer security incidents.

NOTE

In this chapter, any reference to an incident refers to a computer security incident. Organizations handle some incidents such as weather events or natural disasters using other methods such as with a business continuity plan (covered in Chapter 3, "Business Continuity Planning") or with a disaster recovery plan (covered in Chapter 18, "Disaster Recovery Planning").

Organizations commonly define the meaning of a computer security incident within their security policy or incident response plans. The definition is usually one or two sentences long and includes examples of common events that the organization classifies as security incidents, such as the following:

- Any attempted network intrusion
- Any attempted denial-of-service attack
- Any detection of malicious software
- Any unauthorized access of data
- Any violation of security policies

Incident Response Steps

Effective incident response management is handled in several steps or phases. Figure 17.1 shows the five steps involved in managing incident response as outlined in the CISSP CIB. It's important to realize that incident response is an ongoing activity and the results of the lessons learned stage are used to improve detection methods or help prevent a repeated incident. The following sections describe these steps in more depth.

FIGURE 17.1 Incident response

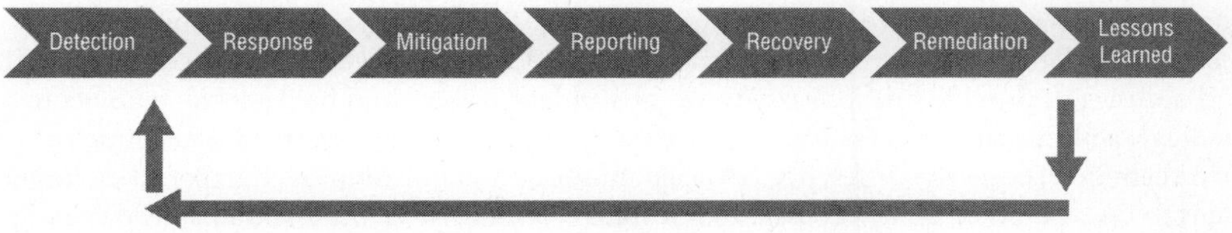

NOTE

You may run across documentation that lists these steps differently. For example, SP 800-61 is an excellent resource for learning more about incident handling, but it identifies the following four steps in the incident response life cycle: 1) preparation, 2) detection and analysis, 3) containment, eradication, and recovery, and 4) postincident recovery. Still, no matter how documentation lists the steps, they contain many of the same elements and have the same goal of managing incident response effectively.

It's important to stress that incident response does not include a counterattack against the attacker. Launching attacks on others is counterproductive and often illegal. If a technician is able to identify the attacker and launch an attack, it will very likely result in an escalation of the attack by the attacker. In other words, the attacker may now consider it personal and regularly launch grudge attacks. In addition, it's likely that the attacker is hiding behind one or more innocent victims. Attackers often use spoofing methods to hide their identity, or launch attacks by zombies in a botnet. Counterattacks may be against an innocent victim rather than an attacker.

Detection

IT environments include multiple methods of detecting potential incidents. The following list identifies many of the common methods used to detect potential incidents. It also includes notes on how these methods report the incidents:

- Intrusion detection and prevention systems (described later in this chapter) send alerts to administrators when an item of interest occurs.
- Anti-malware software will often display a pop-up window to indicate when it detects malware.
- Many automated tools regularly scan audit logs looking for predefined events, such as the use of special privileges. When they detect specific events, they typically send an alert to administrators.
- End users sometimes detect irregular activity and contact technicians or administrators for help. When users report events such as the inability to access a network resource, it alerts IT personnel about a potential incident.

Notice that just because an IT professional receives an alert from an automated tool or a complaint from a user, this doesn't always mean an incident has occurred. Intrusion detection and prevention systems often give false alarms, and end users are prone to simple user errors. IT personnel investigate these events to determine whether they are incidents.

Many IT professionals are classified as first responders for incidents. They are the first ones on the scene and have knowledge on how to differentiate typical IT problems from security incidents. They are similar to medical first responders who have outstanding skills and abilities to provide medical assistance at accident scenes, and help get the patients to medical facilities when necessary. The medical first responders have specific training to help them determine the difference between minor and major injuries. Further, they know what to do when they come across a major injury. Similarly, IT professionals need specific training so that they can determine the difference between a typical problem that needs troubleshooting and a security incident that they need to escalate.

After investigating an event and determining it is a security incident, IT personnel move to the next step: response. In many cases, the individual doing the initial investigation will escalate the incident to bring in other IT professionals to respond.

Response

After detecting and verifying an incident, the next step is response. The response varies depending on the severity of the incident. Many organizations have a designated incident response team—sometimes called a computer incident response team (CIRT), or computer security incident response team (CSIRT). The organization activates the team during a major security incident but does not typically activate the team for minor incidents. A formal incident response plan documents who would activate the team and under what conditions.

Team members would have training on incident response and the organization's incident response plan. Typically team members would assist with investigating the incident, assessing the damage, collecting evidence, reporting the incident, and recovery procedures. They would also participate in the remediation and lessons learned stages, and help with root cause analysis.

The quicker an organization can respond to an incident, the better chance they have at limiting the damage. On the other hand, if an incident continues for hours or days, the damage is likely to be greater. For example, an attacker may be trying to access a customer database. A quick response can prevent the attacker from obtaining any meaningful data. However, if given continued unobstructed access to the database for several hours or days, the attacker may be able to get a copy of the entire database.

After an investigation is over, management may decide to prosecute responsible individuals. Because of this, it's important to protect all data as evidence during the investigation. Chapter 19, "Incidents and Ethics," covers incident handling and response in the context of supporting investigations. If there is any possibility of prosecution, team members take extra steps to protect the evidence. This ensures the evidence can be used in legal procedures.

NOTE

Computers should not be turned off when containing an incident. Temporary files and data in volatile random access memory (RAM) will be lost if the computer is powered down. Forensics experts have tools they can use to retrieve data in temporary files and volatile RAM as long as the system is kept powered on. However, this evidence is lost if someone turns the computer off or unplugs it.

Mitigation

Mitigation steps attempt to contain an incident. One of the primary goals of an effective incident response is to limit the effect or scope of an incident. For example, if an infected computer is sending data out its network interface card (NIC), a technician can disable the NIC or disconnect the cable to the NIC. Sometimes containment involves disconnecting a network from other networks to contain the problem within a single network. When the problem is isolated, security personnel can address it without worrying about it spreading to the rest of the network.

Reporting

Reporting refers to reporting an incident within the organization and to organizations and individuals outside the organization. Although there's no need to report a minor malware infection to a company's chief executive officer (CEO), upper-level management does need to know about serious security breaches.

When employees at Sony logged on to their computers on November 24, 2014, they saw an eerie red image of a skull and menacing bony fingers. It was accompanied with a warning saying, "We've obtained all your internal data" and warning Sony to obey their demands. By 11:00 a.m. news reports indicated that all of Sony's computers in Los Angeles were shut down as a precaution. Managers up the chain did not take these steps without notifying senior management. The next day, a Sony spokesperson made a public statement indicating they were investigating. The next week, the Sony CEO and co-chairperson issued a company-wide alert about the attack. Sony's response indicates they clearly had a reporting mechanism in place and upper-level management became involved.

Organizations often have a legal requirement to report some incidents outside of the organization. Most countries (and many smaller jurisdictions, including states and cities) have enacted regulatory compliance laws to govern security breaches, particularly as they apply to sensitive data retained within information systems. These laws typically include a requirement to report the incident, especially if the security breach exposed customer data. Laws differ from locale to locale, but all seek to protect the privacy of individual records and information, to protect consumer identities, and to establish standards for financial practice and corporate governance. Every organization has a responsibility to know what laws apply to it, and to abide by these laws.

Many jurisdictions have specific laws governing the protection of personally identifiable information (PII). If a data breach exposes PII, the organization must report it. Different laws have different reporting requirements, but most include a requirement to notify individuals affected by the incident. In other words, if an attack on a system resulted in an attacker gaining PII about you, the owners of the system have a responsibility to inform you of the attack and what data the attackers accessed.

In response to serious security incidents, the organization should consider reporting the incident to official agencies. In the United States, this may mean notifying the Federal Bureau of Investigations (FBI), district attorney offices, and/or state and local law enforcement agencies. In Europe, organizations may report the incident to the International Criminal Police Organization (INTERPOL) or some other entity based on the incident and their location. These agencies may be able to assist in investigations, and the data they collect may help them prevent future attacks against other organizations.

Many incidents are not reported because they aren't recognized as incidents. This is often the result of inadequate training. The obvious solution is to ensure that personnel have relevant training. Training should teach individuals how to recognize incidents, what to do in the initial response, and how to report an incident.

Recovery

After investigators collect all appropriate evidence from a system, the next step is to recover the system, or return it to a fully functioning state. This can be very simple for minor incidents and may only require a reboot. However, a major incident may require completely rebuilding a system. Rebuilding the system includes restoring all data from the most recent backup.

When a compromised system is rebuilt from scratch, it's important to ensure it is configured properly and is at least as secure as it was before the incident. If an organization has effective configuration management and change management programs, these programs will provide necessary documentation to ensure the rebuilt systems are configured properly. Some things to double-check include access control lists (ACLs) and ensuring that unneeded services and protocols are disabled or removed, that all up-to-date patches are installed, and that user accounts are modified from the defaults.

NOTE In some cases, an attacker may have installed malicious code on a system during an attack. This may not be apparent without a detailed inspection of the system. The most secure method of restoring a system after an incident is to completely rebuild the system from scratch. If investigators suspect that an attacker may have modified code on the system, rebuilding a system may be a good option.

Remediation

In the remediation stage, personnel look at the incident and attempt to identify what allowed it to occur, and then implement methods to prevent it from happening again. This includes performing a root cause analysis.

A *root cause analysis* examines the incident to determine what allowed it to happen. For example, if attackers successfully accessed a database through a website, personnel would examine all the elements of the system to determine what allowed the attackers to succeed. If the root cause analysis identifies a vulnerability that can be mitigated, this stage will recommend a change.

It could be that the web server didn't have up-to-date patches, allowing the attackers to gain remote control of the server. Remediation steps might include implementing a patch management program. Perhaps the website application wasn't using adequate input validation techniques, allowing a successful SQL injection attack. Remediation would involve updating the application to include input validation. Maybe the database is located on the web server instead of in a backend database server. Remediation would mean moving the database to a server behind an additional firewall.

Lessons Learned

During the lessons learned stage, personnel examine the incident and the response to see if there are any lessons to be learned. The incident response team will be involved in this stage, but other employees who are knowledgeable about the incident will also participate.

While examining the response to the incident, personnel look for any areas where they can improve their response. For example, if it took a long time for the response team to contain the incident, the examination tries to determine why. It might be that personnel don't have adequate training and didn't have the knowledge and expertise to respond effectively. They may not have recognized the incident when they received the first notification, allowing an attack to continue longer than necessary. First responders may not have recognized the need to protect evidence and inadvertently corrupted it during the response.

Remember, the output of this stage can be fed back to the detection stage of incident management. For example, administrators may realize that attacks are getting through undetected and increase their detection capabilities and recommend changes to their intrusion detection systems.

It is common for the incident response team to create a report when they complete a lessons learned review. Based on the findings, the team may recommend changes to procedures, the addition of security controls, or even changes to policies. Management will decide what recommendations to implement and is responsible for the remaining risk for any recommendations they reject.

Real World Scenario

Delegating Incident Response to Users

In one organization, the responsibility to respond to computer infections was extended to users. Close to each computer was a checklist that identified common symptoms of malware infection. If users suspected their computers were infected, the checklist instructed them to disconnect the NIC and contact the help desk to report the issue. By disconnecting the NIC, they quickly helped contain the malware to their system and stopped it from spreading any further.

This isn't possible in all organizations, but in this case, users were part of a very large network operations center and they were all involved in some form of computer support. In other words, they weren't typical end users but instead had a substantial amount of technical expertise.

Implementing Preventive Measures

Ideally, an organization can avoid incidents completely by implementing preventive countermeasures. This section covers several preventive security controls that can prevent many common attacks. You may notice the use of both preventative and preventive. While most documentation currently uses only *preventive*, the CIB includes both usages. For example, Domain 1 includes references to preventive controls. This chapter covers objectives from Domain 7, and Domain 7 refers to preventative measures. For simplicity, we are using preventive in this chapter, except when quoting the CIB.

Basic Preventive Measures

While there is no single step you can take to protect against all attacks, there are some basic steps you can take that go a long way to protect against many types of attacks. Many of these steps are described in more depth in other areas of the book but are listed here as an introduction to this section.

Keep systems and applications up-to-date. Vendors regularly release patches to correct bugs and security flaws but these only help when they're applied. Patch management (covered in Chapter 16, "Managing Security Operations") ensures that systems and applications are kept up-to-date with relevant patches.

Remove or disable unneeded services and protocols. If a system doesn't need a service or protocol, it should not be running. Attackers cannot exploit a vulnerability in a service or protocol that isn't running on a system. As an extreme contrast, imagine a web server is running every available service and protocol. It is vulnerable to potential attacks on any of these services and protocols.

Use intrusion detection and prevention systems. Intrusion detection and prevention systems observe activity, attempt to detect attacks, and provide alerts. They can often block or stop attacks. These systems are described in more depth later in this chapter.

Use up-to-date anti-malware software. Chapter 21, "Malicious Code and Application Attacks," covers various types of malicious code such as viruses and worms. A primary countermeasure is anti-malware software, covered later in this chapter.

Use firewalls. Firewalls can prevent many different types of attacks. Network-based firewalls protect entire networks and host-based firewalls protect individual systems. Chapter 11, "Secure Network Architecture and Securing Network Components," includes information on using firewalls within a network, and this chapter includes a section describing how firewalls can prevent attacks.

NOTE

Thwarting an attacker's attempts to breach your security requires vigilant efforts to keep systems patched and properly configured. Firewalls and intrusion detection and prevention systems often provide the means to detect and gather evidence to prosecute attackers that have breached your security.

Understanding Attacks

Security professionals need to be aware of common attack methods so that they can take proactive steps to prevent them, recognize them when they occur, and respond appropriately in response to an attack. This section provides an overview of many common attacks. The following sections discuss many of the preventive measures used to thwart these and other attacks.

NOTE We've attempted to avoid duplication of specific attacks but also provide a comprehensive coverage of different types of attacks throughout this book. In addition to this chapter, you'll see different types of attacks in other chapters. For example, Chapter 14, "Controlling and Monitoring Access," discusses some specific attacks related to access control; Chapter 12, "Secure Communications and Network Attacks," covers different types of network-based attacks; and Chapter 21 covers several various types of attacks related to malicious code and applications.

Denial-of-Service Attacks

Denial-of-service (DoS) attacks are attacks that prevent a system from processing or responding to legitimate traffic or requests for resources and objects. A common form of a DoS attack will transmit so many data packets to a server that it cannot process them all. Other forms of DoS attacks focus on the exploitation of a known fault or vulnerability in an operating system, service, or application. Exploiting the fault often results in a system crash or 100 percent CPU utilization. No matter what the actual attack consists of, any attack that renders its victim unable to perform normal activities is a DoS attack. DoS attacks can result in system crashes, system reboots, data corruption, blockage of services, and more.

NOTE DoS attacks are common for any Internet-facing system. In other words, if attackers can access a system via the Internet, it is highly susceptible to a DoS attack. In contrast, DoS attacks are not common for internal systems that are not directly accessible via the Internet.

Another form of DoS attack is a distributed denial-of-service (DDoS) attack. A DDoS attack occurs when multiple systems attack a single system at the same time. For example, a group of attackers could launch coordinated attacks against a single system. More often today, though, an attacker will compromise several systems and use them as launching platforms against the victims. Attackers commonly use botnets (described later in this chapter) to launch DDoS attacks.

A *distributed reflective denial-of-service (DRDoS) attack* is a variant of a DoS. It uses a reflected approach to an attack. In other words, it doesn't attack the victim directly, but instead manipulates traffic or a network service so that the attacks are reflected back to the victim from other sources. Domain Name System (DNS) poisoning attacks (covered in Chapter 12) and smurf attacks (covered later in this chapter) are examples.

SYN Flood Attack

The *SYN flood attack* is a common DoS attack. It disrupts the standard three-way handshake used by TCP to initiate communication sessions. Normally, a client sends a SYN (synchronize) packet to a server, the server responds with a SYN/ACK (synchronize/

acknowledge) packet to the client, and the client then responds with an ACK (acknowledge) packet back to the server. This three-way handshake establishes a communication session that the two systems use for data transfer until the session is terminated with FIN (finish) or RST (reset) packets.

However, in a SYN flood attack, the attackers send multiple SYN packets but never complete the connection with an ACK. This is similar to a jokester sticking his hand out to shake hands, but when the other person sticks his hand out in response, the jokester pulls his hand back, leaving the other person hanging.

Figure 17.2 shows an example. In this example, a single attacker has sent three SYN packets and the server has responded to each. For each of these requests, the server has reserved system resources to wait for the ACK. Servers often wait for the ACK for as long as three minutes before aborting the attempted session, though administrators can adjust this time.

FIGURE 17.2 SYN flood attack

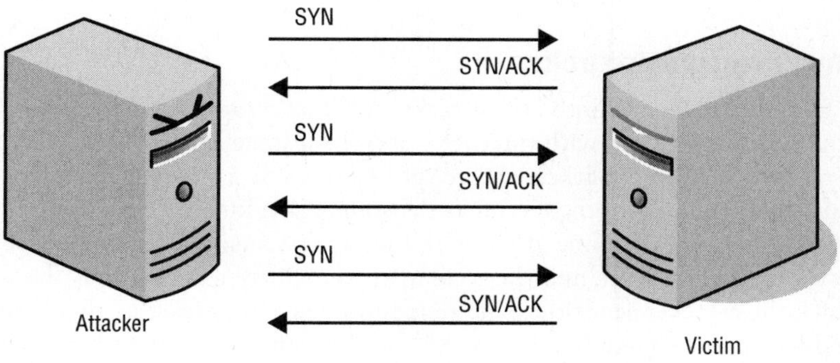

Three incomplete sessions won't cause a problem. However, an attacker will send hundreds or thousands of SYN packets to the victim. Each incomplete session consumes resources, and at some point, the victim becomes overwhelmed and is not able to respond to legitimate requests. The attack can consume available memory and processing power, resulting in the victim slowing to a crawl or actually crashing.

It's common for the attacker to spoof the source address, with each SYN packet having a different source address. This makes it difficult to block the attacker using the source IP address. Attackers have also coordinated attacks launching simultaneous attacks against a single victim as a DDoS attack. Limiting the number of allowable open sessions isn't effective as a defense because once the system reaches the limit it blocks session requests from legitimate users. Increasing the number of allowable sessions on a server results in the attack consuming more system resources, and a server has a finite amount of RAM and processing power.

Using SYN cookies is one method of blocking this attack. These small records consume very few system resources. When the system receives an ACK, it checks the SYN cookies and establishes a session. Firewalls often include mechanisms to check for SYN attacks, as do intrusion detection and intrusion prevention systems.

Another method of blocking this attack is to reduce the amount of time a server will wait for an ACK. It is typically three minutes by default, but in normal operation it rarely takes a legitimate system three minutes to send the ACK packet. By reducing the time, half-open sessions are flushed from the system's memory quicker.

TCP Reset Attack

Another type of attack that manipulates the TCP session is the TCP reset attack. Sessions are normally terminated with either the FIN (finish) or the RST (reset) packet. Attackers can spoof the source IP address in a RST packet and disconnect active sessions. The two systems then need to reestablish the session. This is primarily a threat for systems that need persistent sessions to maintain data with other systems. When the session is reestablished, they need to re-create the data so it's much more than just sending three packets back and forth to establish the session.

Smurf and Fraggle Attacks

Smurf and fraggle attacks are both DoS attacks. A *smurf attack* is another type of flood attack, but it floods the victim with Internet Control Message Protocol (ICMP) echo packets instead of with TCP SYN packets. More specifically, it is a spoofed broadcast ping request using the IP address of the victim as the source IP address.

Ping uses ICMP to check connectivity with remote systems. Normally, ping sends an echo request to a single system, and the system responds with an echo reply. However, in a smurf attack the attacker sends the echo request out as a broadcast to all systems on the network and spoofs the source IP address. All these systems respond with echo replies to the spoofed IP address, flooding the victim with traffic.

Smurf attacks take advantage of an amplifying network (also called a smurf amplifier) by sending a directed broadcast through a router. All systems on the amplifying network then attack the victim. However, RFC 2644, released in 1999, changed the standard default for routers so that they do not forward directed broadcast traffic. When administrators correctly configure routers in compliance with RFC 2644, a network cannot be an amplifying network. This limits smurf attacks to a single network. Additionally, it's becoming common to disable ICMP on firewalls, routers, and even many servers to prevent any type of attacks using ICMP. When standard security practices are used, smurf attacks are rarely a problem today.

Fraggle attacks are similar to smurf attacks. However, instead of using ICMP, a fraggle attack uses UDP packets over UDP ports 7 and 19. The fraggle attack will broadcast a UDP packet using the spoofed IP address of the victim. All systems on the network will then send traffic to the victim, just as with a smurf attack.

Ping Flood

A *ping flood attack* floods a victim with ping requests. This can be very effective when launched by zombies within a botnet as a DDoS attack. If tens of thousands of systems simultaneously send ping requests to a system, the system can be overwhelmed trying to answer the ping requests. The victim will not have time to respond to legitimate requests. A common way systems handle this today is by blocking ICMP traffic. Active intrusion detection systems can detect a ping flood and modify the environment to block ICMP traffic during the attack.

Botnets

Botnets are quite common today. The computers in a botnet are like robots (often called zombies) and will do whatever attackers instruct them to do. A bot herder is typically a criminal who controls all the computers in the botnet via one or more command and control servers. The bot herder enters commands on the server and the zombies periodically check in with the command and control server to receive instructions. Bot herders commonly use computers within a botnet to launch a wide range of attacks, send spam and phishing emails, or rent the botnets out to other criminals.

Computers often join a botnet after being infected with some type of malicious code or malicious software. Once the computer is infected, it often gives the bot herder remote access to the system and additional malware is installed. In some cases, the zombies install malware that searches for files including passwords or other information of interest to the attacker, or include keyloggers to capture user keystrokes.

Botnets of over 40,000 computers are relatively common, and botnets controlling millions of systems have been active in the past. Some bot herders control more than one botnet.

The best protection against a computer's joining a botnet is to ensure anti-malware software is running and the definitions are up-to-date. Because malware often takes advantage of unpatched flaws in operating systems and applications, keeping a system up-to-date with patches helps keep them protected.

Many malware infections are browser based, allowing user systems to become infected when the user is surfing the Web. Keeping browsers and their plug-ins up-to-date is an important security practice. Additionally, most browsers have strong security built in, and these features shouldn't be disabled. For example, most browsers support sandboxing to isolate web applications, but some browsers include the ability to disable sandboxing. This might improve performance of the browser slightly, but the risk is significant.

Real World Scenario

Some Recent Botnets

Criminals use the Gameover Zeus (GOZ) botnet to collect credentials for financial systems and perform banking fraud. They have also used it to distribute the CryptoLocker ransomware. CryptoLocker encrypts user's data and then demands users pay a ransom to get the decryption key. GOZ had infected between 500,000 and 1 million systems by June 2014. Operation Tovar (an international collaboration between several law enforcement agencies) temporarily cut the communication lines to the GOZ command and control servers. However, the criminals have begun using different tactics and GOZ is growing again.

Simda is another botnet that criminals used to steal banking credentials and install additional malware. It was controlling more than 770,000 computers when an international coalition of law enforcement personnel took it down in April 2015. This one was relatively new but was infecting about 128,000 new computers each month for six months.

The Esthost botnet (also called DNSChanger) infected approximately 4 million computers. It manipulated DNS settings to use DNS servers controlled by the bot herders and manipulated advertising. It generated at least $14 million in illicit payments and prevented users from updating anti-malware software or updating their operating system. In this case, the inability to update the system was an important symptom, but one that many users ignored. Law enforcement personnel took it down in 2011.

While these are a few of the well-known large botnets, this list is certainly not complete. No one has released data on how many smaller botnets are currently running, but there are lists that identify many active botnets that are controlling tens of thousands of systems.

Ping of Death

A *ping-of-death attack* employs an oversized ping packet. Ping packets are normally 32 or 64 bytes, though different operating systems can use other sizes. The ping-of-death attack changed the size of ping packets to over 64 KB, which was bigger than many systems could handle. When a system received a ping packet larger than 64 KB, it resulted in a problem. In some cases the system crashed. In other cases, it resulted in a buffer overflow error. A ping-of-death attack is rarely successful today because patches and updates remove the vulnerability.

NOTE

Although the ping of death isn't a problem today, many other types of attacks cause buffer overflow errors (discussed in Chapter 21). When vendors discover bugs that can cause a buffer overflow, they release patches to fix them. One of the best protections against any buffer overflow attack is to keep a system up-to-date with current patches. Additionally, production systems should not include untested code or allow the use of system or root-level privileges.

Teardrop

In a *teardrop attack*, an attacker fragments traffic in such a way that a system is unable to put data packets back together. Large packets are normally divided into smaller fragments when they're sent over a network, and the receiving system then puts the packet fragments back together into their original state. However, a teardrop attack mangles these packets in such a way that the system cannot put them back together. Older systems couldn't handle this situation and crashed, but patches resolved the problem. Although current systems aren't susceptible to teardrop attacks, this does emphasize the importance of keeping systems up-to-date. Additionally, intrusion detection systems can check for malformed packets.

Land Attacks

A *land attack* occurs when the attacker sends spoofed SYN packets to a victim using the victim's IP address as both the source and destination IP address. This tricks the system into constantly replying to itself and can cause it to freeze, crash, or reboot. This attack was first discovered in 1997, and it has resurfaced several times attacking different ports. Keeping a system up-to-date and filtering traffic to detect traffic with identical source and destination addresses helps to protect against LAND attacks.

Zero-day Exploit

A *zero-day exploit* refers to an attack on a system exploiting a vulnerability that is unknown to others. However, security professionals use the term in different contexts and it has some minor differences based on the context. Here are some examples:

Attacker First Discovers a Vulnerability When an attacker discovers a vulnerability, the attacker can easily exploit it because the attacker is the only one aware of the vulnerability. At this point, the vendor is unaware of the vulnerability and has not developed or released a patch. This is the common definition of a zero-day exploit.

Vendor Learns of Vulnerability When vendors learn of a vulnerability, they evaluate the seriousness of the threat and prioritize the development of a patch. Software patches can be complex and require extensive testing to ensure that the patch does not cause other problems. Vendors may develop and release patches within days for serious threats, or they may take months to develop and release a patch for a problem they do not consider serious. Attacks exploiting the vulnerability during this time are often called zero-day-exploits because the public does not know about the vulnerability.

Vendor Releases Patch Once a patch is developed and released, patched systems are no longer vulnerable to the exploit. However, organizations often take time to evaluate and test a patch before applying it, resulting in a gap between when the vendor releases the patch and when administrators apply it. Microsoft typically releases patches on the second Tuesday of every month, commonly called "Patch Tuesday." Attackers often try to reverse-engineer the patches to understand them, and then exploit them the next day, commonly called "Exploit Wednesday." Some people refer to attacks the day after the vendor releases a patch as a zero-day attack. However, this usage isn't as common. Instead, most security professionals consider this as an attack on an unpatched system.

NOTE

If an organization doesn't have an effective patch management system, they can have systems that are vulnerable to known exploits. If an attack occurs weeks or months after a vendor releases a patch, this is not a zero-day exploit. Instead, it is an attack on an unpatched system.

Methods used to protect systems against zero-day exploits include many of the basic preventive measures. Ensure systems are not running unneeded services and protocols to reduce a system's attack surface, enable both network-based and host-based firewalls to limit potentially malicious traffic, and use intrusion detection and prevention systems to help detect and block potential attacks. Additionally, honeypots and padded cells give administrators an opportunity to observe attacks and may reveal an attack using a zero-day exploit. Honeypots and padded cells are explained later in this chapter.

Malicious Code

Malicious code is any script or program that performs an unwanted, unauthorized, or unknown activity on a computer system. Malicious code can take many forms, including viruses, worms, Trojan horses, documents with destructive macros, and logic bombs. It is often called *malware*, short for malicious software, and less commonly *malcode*, short for malicious code. Malicious code exists for every type of computer or computing device and is the most common form of security breach today. Chapter 21 covers malicious code in detail.

Methods of distributing viruses continue to evolve. Years ago, the most popular method was via floppy disks, hand-carried from system to system. Later, the most popular method was via email as either an attachment or an embedded script. Today, many professionals consider drive-by downloads to be the most popular method.

A *drive-by download* is code downloaded and installed on a user's system without the user's knowledge. Attackers modify the code on a web page and when the user visits, the code downloads and installs malware on the user's system without the user's knowledge or consent. Attackers sometimes compromise legitimate websites and add malicious code to include drive-by downloads. They also host their own malicious websites and use phishing or redirection methods to get users to the malicious website. Most drive-by downloads take advantage of vulnerabilities in unpatched systems, so keeping a system up-to-date protects them.

NOTE

Some recent drive-by downloads include Zeus and Gumblar. Zeus spread through drive-by downloads and phishing attempts, and once installed, it stole credentials for bank sites. A site infected with Gumblar redirected users to another site, which then downloaded and opened an infected PDF file.

Another popular method of installing malware uses a pay-per-install approach. Criminals pay website operators to host their malware, which is often a fake anti-malware program (also called rogueware). The website operators are paid for every installation initiated from their website. According to Symantec, payments can be anywhere between 13 cents per install to $30 per install depending on what is installed and the location of the victim. Installations on computers in the United States pay more.

Although the majority of malware arrives from the Internet, some is transmitted to systems via USB flash drives. Many viruses can detect when a user inserts a USB flash drive into a system. It then infects the drive. When the user plugs it into another system, the malware infects the other system.

Man-in-the-Middle Attacks

A *man-in-the-middle* attack occurs when a malicious user is able to gain a position logically between the two endpoints of an ongoing communication. There are two types of man-in-the-middle attacks. One involves copying or sniffing the traffic between two parties, which is basically a sniffer attack as described in Chapter 14. The other type involves attackers positioning themselves in the line of communication where they act as a store-and-forward or proxy mechanism, as shown in Figure 17.3. The client and server think they are connected directly to each other. However, the attacker captures and forwards all data between the two systems. An attacker can collect logon credentials and other sensitive data as well as change the content of messages exchanged between the two systems.

FIGURE 17.3 A man-in-the-middle attack

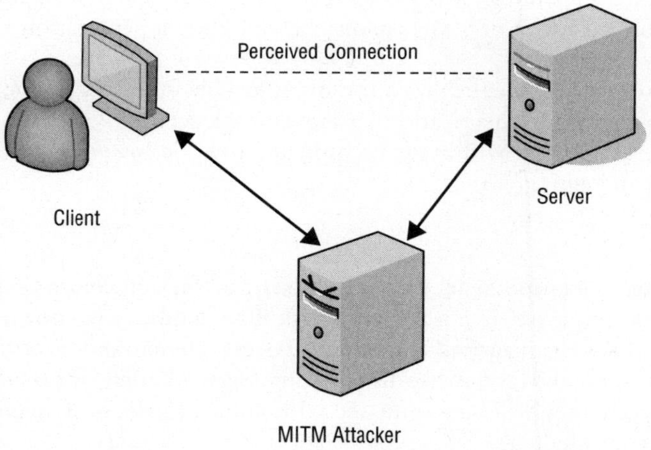

Man-in-the-middle attacks require more technical sophistication than many other attacks because the attacker needs to successfully impersonate a server from the perspective of the client and impersonate the client from the perspective of the server. A man-in-the-middle attack will often require a combination of multiple attacks. For example, the attacker may alter routing information and DNS values, or falsify Address Resolution Protocol (ARP) lookups as a part of the attack.

Some man-in-the-middle attacks are thwarted by keeping systems up-to-date with patches. An intrusion detection system cannot usually detect man-in-the-middle or hijack attacks, but it can detect abnormal activities occurring over communication links and raise alerts on suspicious activity.

War Dialing

War dialing means using a modem to search for a system that accepts inbound connection attempts. A war dialer might be a typical computer with a modem attached and running war dialer software, or it can be a stand-alone device. In either case, war dialers systematically dial phone numbers and listen for computer carrier tones. When they detect a computer carrier tone, the war dialer adds this number to a report generated at the end of the search process. A war dialer can search any range of numbers, such as all 10,000 numbers within a specific prefix or all 10,000,000 within a specific area code.

Although the use of modems has dwindled significantly, organizations are still using them. They are still an efficient way to provide remote access for employees who don't have direct access to the Internet while traveling. Also, employees have been known to install modems on their work systems to access the Internet and bypass the organization's content monitoring tools.

A newer form of war dialing uses Voice over Internet Protocol (VoIP) to make calls without the use of modems. This allows an attacker to scan many more phone numbers and detect devices other than modems, such as fax machines, voice mailboxes, dial tones, and human voices. For example, Metasploit incorporated an updated version of WarVOX, a war-dialing tool that uses VoIP. Metasploit is a well-known penetration-testing tool used by both attackers and testers.

Countermeasures against malicious war dialing include imposing strong remote access security (including strong authentication), using callback security, ensuring that no unauthorized modems are present within the organization, restricting what protocols can be used, and using call logging.

Sabotage

Employee *sabotage* is a criminal act of destruction or disruption committed against an organization by an employee. It can become a risk if an employee is knowledgeable enough about the assets of an organization, has sufficient access to manipulate critical aspects of the environment, and has become disgruntled. Employee sabotage occurs most often when an employee suspects they will be terminated without just cause, or if an employee retains access after being terminated.

This is another important reason employee terminations should be handled swiftly and account access should be disabled as soon as possible after the termination. Other safeguards against employee sabotage are intensive auditing, monitoring for abnormal or unauthorized activity, keeping lines of communication open between employees and managers, and properly compensating and recognizing employees for their contributions.

Espionage

Espionage is the malicious act of gathering proprietary, secret, private, sensitive, or confidential information about an organization. Attackers often commit espionage with the intent of disclosing or selling the information to a competitor or other interested organization (such as a foreign government). Attackers can be dissatisfied employees, and in some cases, employees who are being blackmailed from someone outside the organization.

It can also be committed by a mole or plant placed in the organization to steal information for a primary secret employer. In some cases, espionage occurs far from the workplace, such as at a convention or an event, perpetrated by someone who specifically targets employees' mobile assets.

Countermeasures against espionage are to strictly control access to all nonpublic data, thoroughly screen new employee candidates, and efficiently track all employee activities.

Intrusion Detection and Prevention Systems

An *intrusion* occurs when an attacker is able to bypass or thwart security mechanisms and gain access to an organization's resources. *Intrusion detection* is a specific form of monitoring that monitors recorded information and real-time events to detect abnormal activity indicating a potential incident or intrusion. An *intrusion detection system (IDS)* automates the inspection of logs and real-time system events to detect intrusion attempts and system failures.

IDSs are an effective method of detecting many DoS and DDoS attacks. They can recognize attacks that come from external connections, such as an attack from the Internet, and attacks that spread internally such as a malicious worm. Once they detect a suspicious event, they respond by sending alerts or raising alarms. In some cases, they can modify the environment to stop an attack. A primary goal of an IDS is to provide a means for a timely and accurate response to intrusions.

NOTE An IDS is intended as part of a defense-in-depth security plan. It will work with, and complement, other security mechanisms such as firewalls, but it does not replace them.

An intrusion prevention system (IPS) includes all the capabilities of an IDS but can also take additional steps to stop or prevent intrusions. If desired, administrators can disable these extra features of an IPS, essentially causing it to function as an IDS.

You'll often see the two terms combined as intrusion detection and prevention systems (IDPSs). For example, NIST SP 800-94, "Guide to Intrusion Detection and Prevention Systems" (available from the NIST special publications download page: `http://csrc.nist.gov/publications/PubsSPs.html`), provides comprehensive coverage of both intrusion detection and intrusion prevention systems, but for brevity uses IDPS throughout the document to refer to both. In this chapter, we are describing methods used by IDSs to detect attacks, how they can respond to attacks, and the types of IDSs available. We are then adding information on IPSs where appropriate.

A Little History on CISSP Objectives

The CISSP certification was first established and launched in 1994, and it has gone through several changes over the years. Similarly, IT security has also gone through several changes as new threats emerge and security professionals create and improve security controls.

$(ISC)^2$ publishes the Candidate Information Bulletin (CIB), which identifies the eight domains and also outlines major topics and subtopics within the domains. The CIB provides a limited exam blueprint. In 2002, (ISC)² called this document the CISSP Certification Common Body of Knowledge (CBK) Study Guide. The content in the CBK Study Guide was very similar to the current CIB, though it often went into more detail.

Intrusion detection is a topic that has been in the CISSP CBK and CIB for many years. In the 2002 CBK Study Guide, intrusion detection topics were included in both the Access Control Systems & Methodology domain and the Operations Security domain. (The current CIB names these domains Identity and Access Management, and Security Operations, respectively.)

However, the 2009 and 2012 CIBs didn't include any mention of Intrusion Detection topics. It was still relevant and tested, but "Intrusion Detection" wasn't listed anywhere. In the last version of this book, we chose to include intrusion detection topics as part of the "Implement preventative measures against attacks" objective. In this version of the CIB, (ISC)² brought back mention of the intrusion detection and prevention systems, within the preventative measures objective. With a specific mention of these topics, you can bet you'll see questions on your exam about them.

Knowledge- and Behavior-based Detection

An IDS actively watches for suspicious activity by monitoring network traffic and inspecting logs. For example, an IDS can have sensors or agents monitoring key devices such as routers and firewalls in a network. These devices have logs that can record activity, and the sensors can forward these log entries to the IDS for analysis. Some sensors send all the data to the IDS, whereas other sensors inspect the entries and only send specific log entries based on how administrators configure the sensors.

The IDS evaluates the data and can detect malicious behavior using two common methods: knowledge-based detection and behavior-based detection. In short, knowledge-based detection uses signatures similar to the signature definitions used by anti-malware software. Behavior-based detection doesn't use signatures but instead compares activity against a baseline of normal performance to detect abnormal behavior. Many IDSs use a combination of both methods.

Knowledge-based Detection The most common method of detection is *knowledge-based detection* (also called signature-based detection or pattern-matching detection). It uses a database of known attacks developed by the IDS vendor. For example, some automated tools are available to launch SYN flood attacks, and these tools have known patterns and characteristics defined in a signature database. Real-time traffic is matched against the database, and if the IDS finds a match, it raises an alert. The primary drawback for a knowledge-based IDS is that it is effective only against known attack methods. New attacks, or slightly modified versions of known attacks, often go unrecognized by the IDS.

Knowledge-based detection on an IDS is similar to signature-based detection used by anti-malware applications. The anti-malware application has a database of known malware and checks files against the database looking for a match. Just as anti-malware software must be regularly updated with new signatures from the anti-malware vendor, IDS databases must be regularly updated with new attack signatures. Most IDS vendors provide automated methods to update the signatures.

Behavior-based Detection The second detection type is *behavior-based detection* (also called statistical intrusion detection, anomaly detection, and heuristics-based detection). Behavior-based detection starts by creating a baseline of normal activities and events on the system. Once it has accumulated enough baseline data to determine normal activity, it can detect abnormal activity that may indicate a malicious intrusion or event.

This baseline is often created over a finite period such as a week. If the network is modified, the baseline needs to be updated. Otherwise, the IDS may alert you to normal behavior that it identifies as abnormal. Some products continue to monitor the network to learn more about normal activity and will update the baseline based on the observations.

Behavior-based IDSs use the baseline, activity statistics, and heuristic evaluation techniques to compare current activity against previous activity to detect potentially malicious events. Many can perform stateful packet analysis similar to how stateful inspection firewalls (covered in Chapter 11) examine traffic based on the state or context of network traffic.

Anomaly analysis adds to an IDS's capabilities by allowing it to recognize and react to sudden increases in traffic volume or activity, multiple failed login attempts, logons or program activity outside normal working hours, or sudden increases in error or failure messages. All of these could indicate an attack that a knowledge-based detection system may not recognize.

A behavior-based IDS can be labeled an expert system or a pseudo-artificial intelligence system because it can learn and make assumptions about events. In other words, the IDS can act like a human expert by evaluating current events against known events. The more information provided to a behavior-based IDS about normal activities and events, the more accurately it can detect anomalies. A significant benefit of a behavior-based IDS is that it can detect newer attacks that have no signatures and are not detectable with the signature-based method.

The primary drawback for a behavior-based IDS is that it often raises a high number of false alarms, also called false alerts or false positives. Patterns of user and system activity can vary widely during normal operations, making it difficult to accurately define the boundaries of normal and abnormal activity.

Real World Scenario

False Alarms

A challenge that many IDS administrators have is finding a balance between the number of false alarms or alerts that an IDS sends and ensuring that the IDS reports actual attacks. In one organization we know about, an IDS sent a series of alerts over a couple of days that were aggressively investigated but turned out to be false alarms. Administrators began losing faith in the system and regretted wasting time chasing these false alarms.

Later, the IDS began sending alerts on an actual attack. However, administrators were actively troubleshooting another issue that they knew was real and they didn't have time to chase what they perceived as more false alarms. They simply dismissed the alarms on the IDS and didn't discover the attack until a few days later.

IDS Response

Although knowledge-based and behavior-based IDSs detect incidents differently, they both use an alert system. When the IDS detects an event, it triggers an alarm or alert. It can then respond using a passive or active method. A passive response logs the event and sends a notification. An active response changes the environment to block the activity in addition to logging and sending a notification.

NOTE In some cases, you can measure a firewall's effectiveness by placing a passive IDS before the firewall and another passive IDS after the firewall. By examining the alerts in the two IDSs, you can determine what attacks the firewall is blocking in addition to determining what attacks are getting through.

Passive Response Notifications can be sent to administrators via email, text or pager messages, or pop-up messages. In some cases, the alert can generate a report detailing the activity leading up to the event and logs are available for administrators to get more information if needed. Many 24-hour network operations centers (NOCs) have central monitoring screens viewable by everyone in the main support center. For example, a single wall can have multiple large screen monitors providing data on different elements of the NOC. The IDS alerts can be displayed on one of these screens to ensure personnel are aware of the event. These instant notifications help administrators respond quickly and effectively to unwanted behavior.

Active Response Active responses can modify the environment using several different methods. Typical responses include modifying ACLs to block traffic based on ports, protocols, and source addresses, and even disabling all communications over specific cable segments. For example, if an IDS detects a SYN flood attack from a single IP address, the IDS can change the ACL to block all traffic from this IP address. Similarly, if the IDS detects a ping flood attack from multiple IP addresses, it can change the ACL to block all ICMP traffic. An IDS can also block access to resources for suspicious or ill-behaved users. Security administrators configure these active responses in advance and can tweak them based on changing needs in the environment.

NOTE An IDS that uses an active response is sometimes referred to as an IPS (intrusion prevention system). This is accurate in some situations. However, an IPS (described later in this section) is placed in line with the traffic. If an active IDS is placed in line with the traffic, it is an IPS. If is not placed in line with the traffic, it isn't a true IPS because it can only respond to the attack after it has detected an attack in progress. NIST SP 800-94 recommends placing all active IDSs in line with the traffic so that they function as IPSs.

Host- and Network-based IDSs

IDS types are commonly classified as host based and network based. A *host-based IDS* (HIDS) monitors a single computer or host. A *network-based IDS* (NIDS) monitors a network by observing network traffic patterns.

A less-used classification is an application-based IDS, which is a specific type of network-based IDS. It monitors specific application traffic between two or more servers. For example, an application-based IDS can monitor traffic between a web server and a database server looking for suspicious activity.

Host-based IDS An HIDS monitors activity on a single computer, including process calls and information recorded in system, application, security, and host-based firewall logs. It can often examine events in more detail than an NIDS can, and it can pinpoint specific files compromised in an attack. It can also track processes employed by the attacker.

A benefit of HIDSs over NIDSs is that HIDSs can detect anomalies on the host system that NIDSs cannot detect. For example, an HIDS can detect infections where an intruder has infiltrated a system and is controlling it remotely. You may notice that this sounds similar to what anti-malware software will do on a computer. It is. Many HIDSs include anti-malware capabilities.

Although many vendors recommend installing host-based IDSs on all systems, this isn't common due to some of the disadvantages of HIDSs. Instead, many organizations choose to install HIDSs only on key servers as an added level of protection. Some of the disadvantages to HIDSs are related to the cost and usability. HIDSs are more costly to manage than NIDSs because they require administrative attention on each system, whereas NIDSs usually support centralized administration. An HIDS cannot detect network attacks on other systems. Additionally, it will often consume a significant amount of system resources, degrading the host system performance. Although it's often possible to restrict the system resources used by the HIDS, this can result in it missing an active attack. Additionally, HIDSs are easier for an intruder to discover and disable, and their logs are maintained on the system, making the logs susceptible to modification during a successful attack.

Network-based IDS An NIDS monitors and evaluates network activity to detect attacks or event anomalies. It cannot monitor the content of encrypted traffic but can monitor other packet details. A single NIDS can monitor a large network by using remote sensors to collect data at key network locations that send data to a central management console. These sensors can monitor traffic at routers, firewalls, network switches that support port mirroring, and other types of network taps.

TIP

Switches are often used as a preventive measure against rogue sniffers. If the IDS is connected to a normal port on the switch, it will capture only a small portion of the network traffic, which isn't very useful. Instead, the switch is configured to mirror all traffic to a specific port (commonly called port mirroring) used by the IDS. On Cisco switches, the port used for port mirroring is referred to as a Switched Port Analyzer (SPAN) port.

The central console is often installed on a single-purpose computer that is hardened against attacks. This reduces vulnerabilities in the NIDS and can allow it to operate almost invisibly, making it much harder for attackers to discover and disable it. An NIDS has very little negative effect on the overall network performance, and when it is deployed on a single-purpose system, it doesn't adversely affect performance on any other computer. On networks with large volumes of traffic, a single NIDS may be unable to keep up with the flow of data, but it is possible to add additional systems to balance the load.

Often, an NIDS can discover the source of an attack by performing Reverse Address Resolution Protocol (RARP) or reverse Domain Name System (DNS) lookups. However, because attackers often spoof IP addresses or launch attacks by zombies via a botnet, additional investigation is required to determine the actual source. This can be a laborious process and is beyond the scope of the IDS. However, it is possible to discover the source of spoofed IPs with some investigation.

WARNING

It is unethical and risky to launch counterstrikes against an intruder or to attempt to reverse-hack an intruder's computer system. Instead, rely on your logging capabilities and sniffing collections to provide sufficient data to prosecute criminals or to improve the security of your environment in response.

An NIDS is usually able to detect the initiation of an attack or ongoing attacks, but they can't always provide information about the success of an attack. They won't know if an attack affected specific systems, user accounts, files, or applications. For example, an NIDS may discover that a buffer overflow exploit was sent through the network, but it won't necessarily know whether the exploit successfully infiltrated a system. However, after administrators receive the alert they can check relevant systems. Additionally, investigators can use the NIDS logs as part of an audit trail to learn what happened.

Intrusion Prevention Systems

An intrusion prevention system (IPS) is a special type of active IDS that attempts to detect and block attacks before they reach target systems. It's sometimes referred to as an intrusion detection and prevention system (IDPS). A distinguishing difference between an IDS and an IPS is that the IPS is placed in line with the traffic, as shown in Figure 17.4. In other words, all traffic must pass through the IPS and the IPS can choose what traffic to forward and what traffic to block after analyzing it. This allows the IPS to prevent an attack from reaching a target.

FIGURE 17.4 Intrusion prevention system

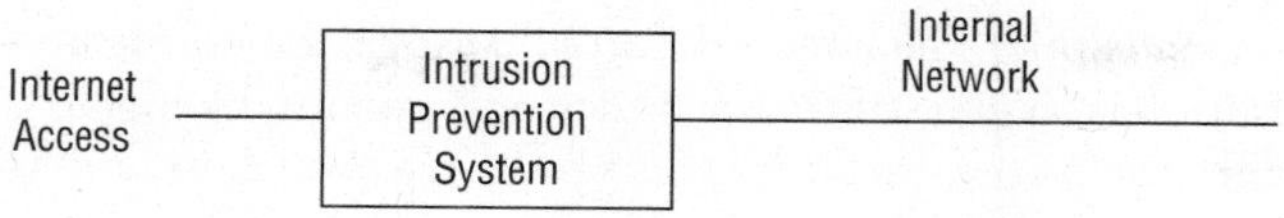

In contrast, an active IDS that is not placed in line can check the activity only after it has reached the target. The active IDS can take steps to block an attack after it starts but cannot prevent it.

An IPS can use knowledge-based detection and/or behavior-based detection, just as any other IDS. Additionally, it can log activity and provide notification to administrators just as an IDS would.

Understanding Darknets

Within the context of intrusion detection, a *darknet* is a portion of allocated IP addresses within a network that are not used. It includes one device configured to capture all the traffic into the darknet. Since the IP addresses are not used, the darknet does not have any other hosts and it should not have any traffic at all. However, if an attacker is probing a network, or malware is attempting to spread, the host in the darknet will detect and capture the activity. A benefit is that there are few false positives. Legitimate traffic should not be in the darknet, so unless there is a misconfiguration on the network, traffic in the darknet is not legitimate.

Specific Preventive Measures

Although intrusion detection and prevention systems go a long way toward protecting networks, administrators typically implement additional security controls to protect their networks. The following sections describe several of these as additional preventive measures.

Honeypots/Honeynets

Honeypots are individual computers created as a trap for intruders. A *honeynet* is two or more networked honeypots used together to simulate a network. They look and act like legitimate systems, but they do not host data of any real value for an attacker. Administrators often configure honeypots with vulnerabilities to tempt intruders into attacking them. They may be unpatched or have security vulnerabilities that administrators purposely leave open. The goal is grab the attention of intruders and keep the intruders away from the legitimate network that is hosting valuable resources. Legitimate users wouldn't access the honeypot, so any access to a honeypot is most likely an unauthorized intruder.

In addition to keeping the attacker away from a production environment, the honeypot gives administrators an opportunity to observe an attacker's activity without compromising the live environment. In some cases, the honeypot is designed to delay an intruder long enough for the automated IDS to detect the intrusion and gather as much information about the intruder as possible. The longer the attacker spends with the honeypot, the more time an administrator has to investigate the attack and potentially identify the intruder. Many security professionals consider honeypots to be effective countermeasures against zero-day exploits.

Often, administrators host honeypots and honeynets on virtual systems. These are much simpler to re-create after an attack. For example, administrators can configure the honeypot and then take a snapshot of a honeypot virtual machine. If an attacker modifies the environment, administrators can revert the machine to the state it was in when they took the snapshot.

The use of honeypots raises the issue of enticement versus entrapment. An organization can legally use a honeypot as an enticement device if the intruder discovers it through no outward efforts of the honeypot owner. Placing a system on the Internet with open security vulnerabilities and active services with known exploits is enticement. Enticed attackers make their own decisions to perform illegal or unauthorized actions. Entrapment, which is illegal, occurs when the honeypot owner actively solicits visitors to access the site and then charges them with unauthorized intrusion. In other words, it is entrapment when you trick or encourage someone into performing an illegal or unauthorized action. Laws vary in different countries so it's important to understand local laws related to enticement and entrapment.

Understanding Pseudo Flaws

Pseudo flaws are false vulnerabilities or apparent loopholes intentionally implanted in a system in an attempt to tempt attackers. They are often used on honeypot systems to emulate well-known operating system vulnerabilities. Attackers seeking to exploit a known flaw might stumble across a pseudo flaw and think that they have successfully penetrated a system. More sophisticated pseudo flaw mechanisms actually simulate the penetration and convince the attacker that they have gained additional access privileges to a system. However, while the attacker is exploring the system, monitoring and alerting mechanisms trigger and alert administrators to the threat.

Understanding Padded Cells

A *padded cell* system is similar to a honeypot, but it performs intrusion isolation using a different approach. When an IDS detects an intruder, that intruder is automatically transferred to a padded cell. The padded cell has the look and feel of an actual network, but the attacker is unable to perform any malicious activities or access any confidential data from within the padded cell.

The padded cell is a simulated environment that offers fake data to retain an intruder's interest, similar to a honeypot. However, the IDS transfers the intruder into a padded cell without informing the intruder that the change has occurred. In contrast, the attacker chooses to attack the honeypot. Administrators monitor padded cells closely and use them to trace attacks and gather evidence for possible prosecution of attackers.

Warning Banners

Warning banners inform users and intruders about basic security policy guidelines. They typically mention that online activities are audited and monitored, and often provide reminders of restricted activities. In most situations, wording in banners is important from a legal standpoint because these banners can legally bind users to a permissible set of actions, behaviors, and processes.

Unauthorized personnel who are somehow able to log on to a system also see the warning banner. In this case, you can think of a warning banner as an electronic equivalent of a "no trespassing" sign. Most intrusions and attacks can be prosecuted when warnings clearly state that unauthorized access is prohibited and that any activity will be monitored and recorded.

TIP

Warning banners inform both authorized and unauthorized users. These banners typically remind authorized users of the content in acceptable-use agreements.

Anti-malware

The most important protection against malicious code is the use of anti-malware software with up-to-date signature files. Attackers regularly release new malware and often modify existing malware to prevent detection by anti-malware software. Anti-malware software vendors look for these changes and develop new signature files to detect the new and modified malware. Years ago, anti-malware vendors recommended updating signature files once a week. However, most anti-malware software today includes the ability to check for updates several times a day without user intervention.

NOTE

Originally, anti-malware software focused on viruses. However, as malware expanded to include other malicious code such as Trojans, worms, spyware, and rootkits, vendors expanded the ability of their anti-malware software. Today, most anti-malware software will detect and block most malware, so technically it is anti-malware software. However, most vendors still market their products as anti-malware software. The CISSP CIB only uses the term anti-malware.

Many organizations use a multipronged approach to blocking malware and detecting any malware that gets in. Firewalls with content-filtering capabilities (or specialized content-filter appliances) are commonly used at the boundary between the Internet and the internal network to filter out any type of malicious code. Specialized anti-malware software is installed on email servers to detect and filter any type of malware passed via email. Additionally, anti-malware software is installed on each system to detect and block malware. Organizations often use a central server to deploy anti-malware software, download updated definitions, and push these definitions out to the clients.

A multipronged approach with anti-malware software on each system in addition to filtering Internet content helps protect systems from infections from any source. As an example, using up-to-date anti-malware software on each system will detect and block a virus on an employee's USB flash drive.

Anti-malware vendors commonly recommend installing only one anti-malware application on any system. When a system has more than one anti-malware application installed, the applications can interfere with each other and can sometimes cause system problems. Additionally, having more than one scanner can consume excessive system resources.

Following the principle of least privilege also helps. Users will not have administrative permissions on systems and will not be able to install applications that may be malicious. If a virus does infect a system, it can often impersonate the logged-in user. When this user has limited privileges, the virus is limited in its capabilities. Additionally, vulnerabilities related to malware increase as additional applications are added. Each additional application provides another potential attack point for malicious code.

Educating users about the dangers of malicious code, how attackers try to trick users into installing it, and what they can do to limit their risks is another protection method. Many times a user can avoid an infection simply by not clicking on a link or opening an attachment sent via email.

Chapter 14, "Controlling and Monitoring Access," covers social engineering tactics, including phishing, spear phishing, and whaling. When users are educated about these types of attacks, they are less likely to fall for them. Although many users are educated about these risks, phishing emails continue to flood the Internet and land in users' inboxes. The only reason attackers continue to send them is that they continue to fool some users.

Education, Policy, and Tools

Malicious software is a constant challenge within any organization using IT resources. Consider Kim, who forwarded a seemingly harmless interoffice joke through email to Larry's account. Larry opened the document, which actually contained active code segments that performed harmful actions on his system. Larry then reported a host of "performance issues" and "stability problems" with his workstation, which he'd never complained about before.

In this scenario, Kim and Larry don't recognize the harm caused by their apparently innocuous activities. After all, sharing anecdotes and jokes through company email is a common way to bond and socialize. What's the harm in that, right? The real question is how can you educate Kim, Larry, and all your other users to be more discreet and discerning in handling shared documents and executables?

The key is a combination of education, policy, and tools. Education should inform Kim that forwarding nonwork materials on the company network is counter to policy and good behavior. Likewise, Larry should learn that opening attachments unrelated to specific work tasks can lead to all kinds of problems (including those he fell prey to here). Policies should clearly identify acceptable use of IT resources and the dangers of circulating unauthorized materials. Tools such as anti-malware software should be employed to prevent and detect any type of malware within the environment.

Whitelisting and Blacklisting

Whitelisting and blacklisting applications can be an effective preventive measure blocking users from running unauthorized applications. They can also help prevent malware infections. Whitelisting identifies a list of applications authorized to run on a system, and blacklisting identifies a list of applications that are not authorized to run on a system.

A whitelist would not include malware applications and would block them from running. Some whitelists identify applications using a hashing algorithm to create a hash. However, if an application is infected with a virus, the virus effectively changes the hash, so this type of whitelist blocks infected applications from running too. (Chapter 6, "Cryptography and Symmetric Key Algorithms," covers hashing algorithms in more depth.)

The Apple iOS running on iPhones and iPads is an example of an extreme version of whitelisting. Users are only able to install apps available from Apple's App Store. Personnel at Apple review and approve all apps on the App Store and quickly remove misbehaving apps. Although it is possible for users to bypass security and jailbreak their iOS device, most users don't do so partly because it voids the warranty.

NOTE: Jailbreaking removes restrictions on iOS devices and permits root-level access to the underlying operating system. It is similar to rooting a device running the Android operating system.

Blacklisting is a good option if administrators know which applications they want to block. For example, if management wants to ensure users are not running games on their system, administrators can enable tools to block these games.

Firewalls

Firewalls provide protection to a network by filtering traffic. As discussed in Chapter 11, firewalls have gone through a lot of changes over the years.

Basic firewalls filter traffic based on IP addresses, ports, and some protocols using protocol numbers. Firewalls include rules within an ACL to allow specific traffic and end with an implicit deny rule. The implicit deny rule blocks all traffic not allowed by a previous rule. For example, a firewall can allow HTTP and HTTPS traffic by allowing traffic using TCP ports 80 and 443, respectively. (Chapter 11 covers logical ports in more depth.)

ICMP uses a protocol number of 1, so a firewall can allow ping traffic by allowing traffic with a protocol number of 1. Similarly, a firewall can allow IPsec Encapsulating Security Protocol (ESP) traffic and IPsec Authentication Header (AH) traffic by allowing protocol numbers 50 and 51, respectively.

NOTE: The Internet Assigned Numbers Authority (IANA) maintains a list of well-known ports matched to protocols. IANA also maintains lists of assigned IP numbers for IPv4 and IPv6.

Second-generation firewalls add additional filtering capabilities. For example, an application-level gateway firewall filters traffic based specific application requirements and *circuit-level gateway firewalls* filter traffic based on the communications circuit. Third-generation firewalls (also called *stateful inspection firewalls* and *dynamic packet filtering firewalls*) filter traffic based on its state within a stream of traffic.

A *next-generation firewall* functions as a unified threat management (UTM) device and combines several filtering capabilities. It includes traditional functions of a firewall such as packet filtering and stateful inspection. However, it is able to perform packet inspection techniques, allowing it to identify and block malicious traffic. It can filter malware using definition files and/or whitelists and blacklists. It also includes intrusion detection and/or intrusion prevention capabilities.

Sandboxing

Sandboxing provides a security boundary for applications and prevents the application from interacting with other applications. Anti-malware applications use sandboxing techniques to test unknown applications. If the application displays suspicious characteristics, the sandboxing technique prevents the application from infecting other applications or the operating system.

Application developers often use virtualization techniques to test applications. They create a virtual machine and then isolate it from the host machine and the network. They are then able to test the application within this sandbox environment without affecting anything outside the virtual machine. Similarly, many anti-malware vendors use virtualization as a sandboxing technique to observe the behavior of malware.

Third-party Security Services

Some organizations outsource security services to a third party, which is an individual or organization outside the organization. This can include many different types of services such as auditing and penetration testing.

In some cases, an organization must provide assurances to an outside entity that third-party service providers comply with specific security requirements. For example, organizations processing transactions with major credit cards must comply with the Payment Card Industry Data Security Standard (PCI DSS). These organizations often outsource some of the services, and PCI DSS requires organizations to ensure that service providers also comply with PCI DSS requirements. In other words, PCI DSS doesn't allow organizations to outsource their responsibilities.

Some Software as a Service (SaaS) vendors provide security services via the cloud. For example, Barracuda Networks include cloud-based solutions similar to next-generation firewalls and UTM devices. For example, their Web Security Service acts as a proxy for web browsers. Administrators configure proxy settings to access a cloud-based system, and it performs web filtering based on the needs of the organization. Similarly, they have a cloud-based Email Security Service that can perform inbound spam and malware filtering.

Penetration Testing

Penetration testing is another preventive measure an organization can use to counter attacks. A penetration test (often shortened to pentest) mimics an actual attack in an attempt to identify what techniques attackers can use to circumvent security in an application, system, network, or organization. It may include vulnerability scans, port scans, packet sniffing, DoS attacks, and social-engineering techniques.

Security professionals try to avoid outages when performing penetration testing. However, penetration testing is intrusive and can affect the availability of a system. Because of this, it's extremely important for security professionals to get approval from senior management before performing any testing.

NOTE NIST SP 800-115, "Technical Guide to Information Security Testing and Assessment," includes a significant amount of information about testing, including penetration testing. You can download it from the NIST special publications download page: `http://csrc.nist.gov/publications/PubsSPs.html`.

Regularly staged penetration tests are a good way to evaluate the effectiveness of security controls used within an organization. Penetration testing may reveal areas where patches or security settings are insufficient, where new vulnerabilities have developed or become exposed, and where security policies are either ineffective or not being followed. Attackers can exploit any of these vulnerabilities.

A penetration test will commonly include a vulnerability scan or vulnerability assessment to detect weaknesses. However, the penetration test goes a step further and attempts to exploit the weaknesses. For example, a vulnerability scanner may discover that a website with a backend database is not using input validation techniques and is susceptible to a SQL injection attack. The penetration test may then use a SQL injection attack to access the entire database. Similarly, a vulnerability assessment may discover that employees aren't educated about social-engineering attacks and a penetration test may use social-engineering methods to gain access to a secure area or obtain sensitive information from employees.

Here are some of the goals of a penetration test:

- Determine how well a system can tolerate an attack
- Identify employee's ability to detect and respond to attacks in real time
- Identify additional controls that can be implemented to reduce risk

NOTE Penetration testing typically includes social-engineering attacks, network and system configuration reviews, and environment vulnerability assessments. A penetration test takes vulnerability assessments and vulnerability scans a step further by verifying that vulnerabilities can be exploited.

Risks of Penetration Testing

A significant danger with penetration tests is that some methods can cause outages. For example, if a vulnerability scan discovers that an Internet-based server is susceptible to a buffer overflow attack, a penetration test can exploit that vulnerability, which may result in the server shutting down or rebooting.

Ideally, penetration tests should stop before they cause any actual damage. Unfortunately, testers often don't know what step will cause the damage until they take that step. For example, fuzz testers send invalid or random data to applications or systems to check for the response. It is possible for a fuzz tester to send a stream of data that causes a buffer overflow and locks up an application but testers don't know that will happen until they run the fuzz tester. Experienced penetration testers are able to minimize the risk of a test causing damage, but they cannot eliminate the risk.

Whenever possible, testers perform penetration tests on a test system instead of a live production system. For example, when testing an application testers can run the application in an isolated environment and then test the application in the isolated environment. If the testing causes damage, it only affects the test system and does not impact the live network. The challenge is that test systems often don't provide a true view of a production environment. Testers may be able to test simple applications that don't interact with other systems in a test environment. However, most applications that need to be tested are not simple. When test systems are used, penetration testers will often qualify their analysis with a statement indicating that the test was done on a test system and so the results may not provide a valid analysis of the production environment.

Obtaining Permission for Penetration Testing

Penetration testing should only be performed after careful consideration and approval of senior management. Many security professionals insist on getting this approval in writing with the risks spelled out. Performing unapproved security testing could cause productivity losses and trigger emergency response teams.

Malicious employees intent on violating the security of an IT environment can be punished based on existing laws. Similarly, if internal employees perform informal unauthorized tests against a system without authorization, an organization may view their actions as an illegal attack rather than as a penetration test. These employees will very likely lose their jobs and may even face legal consequences.

Penetration-Testing Techniques

It is common for organizations to hire external consultants to perform penetration testing. The organization can control what information they give to these testers, and the level of knowledge they are given identifies the type of tests they conduct.

NOTE

Chapter 20, "Software Development Security," covers white-box testing, black-box testing, and gray-box testing in the context of software testing. These same terms are often associated with penetration testing and mean the same thing.

Black-Box Testing by Zero-knowledge Team A *zero-knowledge team* knows nothing about the target site except for publicly available information, such as domain name and company address. It's as if they are looking at the target as a black box and have no idea what is within the box until they start probing. An attack by a zero-knowledge team closely resembles a real external attack because all information about the environment must be obtained from scratch.

White-Box Testing by Full-knowledge Team A *full-knowledge team* has full access to all aspects of the target environment. They know what patches and upgrades are installed, and the exact configuration of all relevant devices. If the target is an application, they would have access to the source code. Full-knowledge teams perform white-box testing (sometimes called crystal-box or clear-box testing). White-box testing is commonly recognized as being more efficient and cost effective in locating vulnerabilities because less time is needed for discovery.

Gray-Box Testing by Partial-knowledge Team A *partial-knowledge team* that has some knowledge of the target performs gray-box testing, but they are not provided access to all the information. They may be given information on the network design and configuration details so that they can focus on attacks and vulnerabilities for specific targets.

The regular security administration staff protecting the target of a penetration test can be considered a full-knowledge team. However, they aren't the best choice to perform a penetration test. They often have blind spots or gaps in their understanding, estimation, or capabilities with certain security subjects. If they knew about a vulnerability that could be exploited, they would likely already have recommended a control to minimize it. A full-knowledge team knows what has been secured, so it may fail to properly test every possibility by relying on false assumptions. Zero-knowledge or partial-knowledge testers are less likely to make these mistakes.

Penetration testing may employ automated attack tools or suites, or be performed manually using common network utilities. Automated attack tools range from professional vulnerability scanners and penetration testers to wild, underground tools discovered on the Internet. Several open source and commercial tools (such as Metasploit and Core Impact) are available, and both security professionals and attackers use these tools.

Social-engineering techniques are often used during penetration tests. Depending on the goal of the test, the testers may use techniques to breach the physical perimeter of an organization or to get users to reveal information. These tests help determine how vulnerable employees are to skilled social engineers, and how familiar they are with security policies designed to thwart these types of attacks.

Real World Scenario

Social Engineering in Pentests

The following example is from a penetration test conducted at a bank, but the same results are often repeated at many different organizations. The testers were specifically asked if they could get access to employee user accounts or employee user systems.

Penetration testers crafted a forged email that looked like it was coming from an executive within the bank. It indicated a problem with the network and said that all employees needed to respond with their username and password as soon as possible to ensure they didn't lose their access. Over 40 percent of the employees responded with their credentials.

Additionally, the testers installed malware on several USB drives and "dropped" them at different locations in the parking lot and within the bank. A well-meaning employee saw one, picked it up, and inserted it into a computer with the intent of identifying the owner. Instead, the USB drive infected the user's system, granting the testers remote access.

Both testers and attackers often use similar methods successfully. Education is often the most effective method at mitigating these types of attacks, and the pentest often reinforces the need for education.

Protect Reports

Penetration testers will provide a report documenting their results, and this report should be protected as sensitive information. The report will outline specific vulnerabilities and how these vulnerabilities can be exploited. It will often include recommendations on how to mitigate the vulnerabilities. If these results fall into the hands of attackers before the organization implements the recommendations, attackers can use details in the report to launch an attack.

It's also important to realize that just because a penetration testing team makes a recommendation, it doesn't mean the organization will implement the recommendation. Management has the choice of implementing a recommendation to mitigate a risk or accepting a risk if they decide the cost of the recommended control is not justified. In other words, a one-year-old report may outline a specific vulnerability that hasn't been mitigated. This year-old report should be protected just as closely as a report completed yesterday.

Ethical Hacking

Ethical hacking is often used as another name for penetration testing. An *ethical hacker* is someone that understands network security and methods to breach security but does not use this knowledge for personal gain. Instead, an ethical hacker uses this knowledge to help organizations understand its vulnerabilities and take action to prevent malicious attacks. An ethical hacker will always stay within legal limits.

Chapter 14, "Controlling and Monitoring Access," mentions the technical difference between crackers, hackers, and attackers. The original definition of a hacker is a technology enthusiast that does not have malicious intent whereas a cracker or attacker is malicious. The original meaning of the term hacker has become blurred because it is often used synonymously with attacker. In other words, most people view a hacker as an attacker, giving the impression that ethical hacking is a contradiction in terms. However, the term ethical hacking uses the term hacker in its original sense.

An ethical hacker will learn about and often use the same tools and techniques used by attackers. However, they do not use them to attack systems. Instead, they use them to test systems for vulnerabilities and only after an organization has granted them explicit permission to do so.

Logging, Monitoring, and Auditing

Logging, monitoring, and auditing procedures help an organization prevent incidents and provide an effective response when they occur. The following sections cover logging and monitoring, as well as various auditing methods used to assess the effectiveness of access controls.

Logging and Monitoring

Logging records events into various logs, and monitoring reviews these events. Combined, logging and monitoring allow an organization to track, record, and review activity, providing overall accountability.

This helps an organization detect undesirable events that can negatively affect confidentiality, integrity, or availability of systems. It is also useful in reconstructing activity after an event has occurred to identify what happened and sometimes to prosecute responsible personnel.

Logging Techniques

Logging is the process of recording information about events to a log file or database. Logging captures events, changes, messages, and other data that describe activities that occurred on a system. Logs will commonly record details such as what happened, when it happened, where it happened, who did it, and sometimes how it happened. When you need to find information about an incident that occurred in the recent past, logs are a good place to start.

For example, Figure 17.5 shows Event Viewer on a Microsoft server with a log entry selected and expanded. This log entry shows that a user named Darril deleted a file named `CISSP Study Notes.rtf` originally located in a folder named `C:\CISSP Study Notes` on a server named SQL1. It shows that Darril deleted the file at 10:30 a.m. on July 14.

FIGURE 17.5 Viewing a log entry

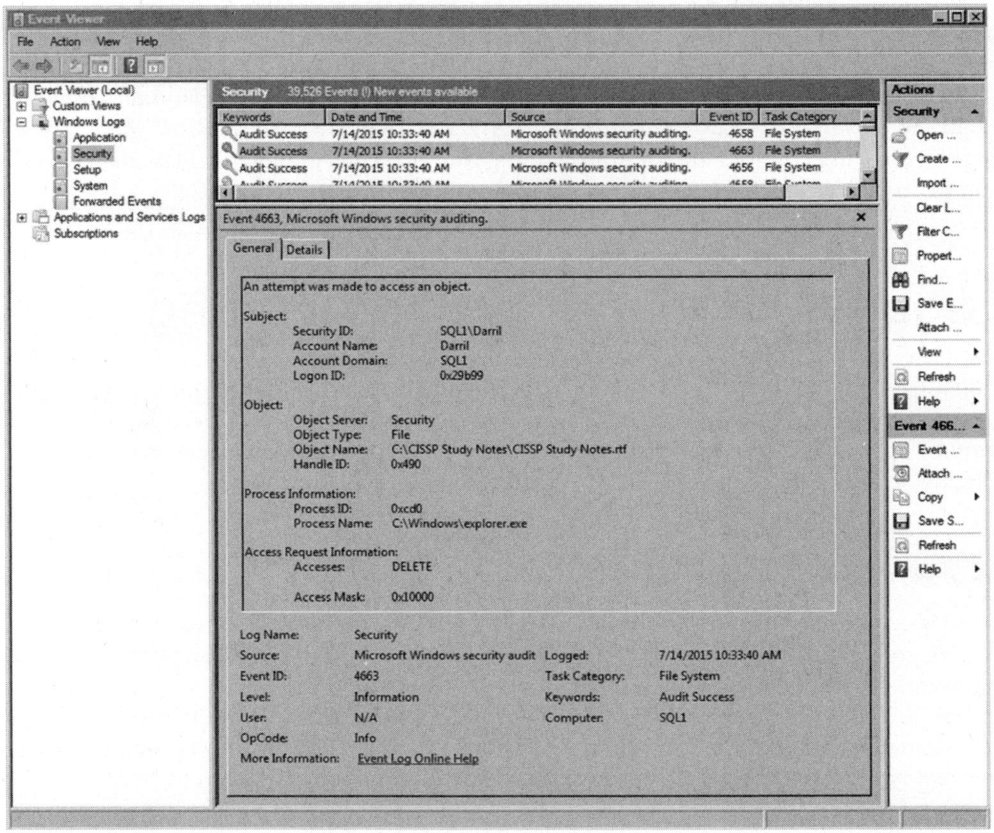

As long as the identification and authentication processes are secure, this is enough to hold Darril accountable for deleting the file. On the other hand, if the organization doesn't use secure authentication processes and it's easy for someone to impersonate another user, Darril may be wrongly accused. This reinforces the requirement for secure identification and authentication practices as a prerequisite for accountability.

NOTE

Logs are often referred to as audit logs, and logging is often called audit logging. However, it's important to realize that auditing (described later in this chapter) is more than just logging. Logging will record events whereas auditing examines or inspects an environment for compliance.

Common Log Types

There are many different types of logs. The following is a short list of common logs available within an IT environment.

Security Logs Security logs record access to resources such as files, folders, printers, and so on. For example, they can record when a user accessed, modified, or deleted a file, as shown earlier in Figure 18.5. Many systems automatically record access to key system files but require an administrator to enable auditing on other resources before logging access. For example, administrators might configure logging for proprietary data, but not for public data posted on a website.

System Logs System logs record system events such as when a system starts or stops, or when services start or stop. If attackers are able to shut down a system and reboot it with a CD or USB flash drive, they can steal data from the system without any record of the data access. Similarly, if attackers are able to stop a service that is monitoring the system, they may be able to access the system without the logs recording their actions. Logs that detect when systems reboot, or when services stop, can help administrators discover potentially malicious activity.

Application Logs These logs record information for specific applications. Application developers choose what to record in the application logs. For example, a database developer can choose to record when anyone accesses specific data objects such as tables or views.

Firewall Logs Firewall logs can record events related to any traffic that reaches a firewall. This includes traffic that the firewall allows and traffic that the firewall blocks. These logs commonly log key packet information such as source and destination IP addresses, and source and destination ports, but not the actual contents of the packets.

Proxy Logs Proxy servers improve Internet access performance for users and can control what websites users can visit. Proxy logs include the ability to record details such as what sites specific users visit and how much time they spend on these sites. They can also record when users attempt to visit known prohibited sites.

Change Logs Change logs record change requests, approvals, and actual changes to a system as a part of an overall change management process. These are useful to track approved changes. They can also be helpful as part of a disaster recovery program. For example, after a disaster administrators and technicians can use change logs to return a system to its last known state, including all applied changes.

Logging is usually a native feature in an operating system and for most applications and services. This makes it relatively easy for administrators and technicians to configure a system to record specific types of events. Events from privileged accounts, such as administrator and root user accounts, should be included in any logging plan. This helps prevent attacks from a malicious insider and will document activity for prosecution if necessary.

Protecting Log Data

Personnel within the organization can use logs to re-create events leading up to and during an incident, but only if the logs haven't been modified. If attackers can modify the logs, they can erase their activity, effectively nullifying the value of the data. The files may no longer include accurate information and may not be admissible as evidence to prosecute attackers. With this in mind, it's important to protect log files against unauthorized access and unauthorized modification.

It's common to store copies of logs on a central system to protect it. Even if an attack modifies or corrupts the original files, personnel can still use the copy to view the events. One way to protect log files is by assigning permissions to limit their access.

Organizations often have strict policies mandating backups of log files. Additionally, these policies define retention times. For example, organizations might keep archived log files for a year, three years, or any other length of time. Some government regulations require organizations to keep archived logs indefinitely. Security controls such as setting logs to read-only, assigning permissions, and implementing physical security controls protect archived logs from unauthorized access and modifications. It's important to destroy logs when they are no longer needed.

TIP: Keeping unnecessary logs can cause excessive labor costs if the organization experiences legal issues. For example, if regulations require an organization to keep logs for one year but the organization has 10 years of logs, a court order can force personnel to retrieve relevant data from these 10 years of logs. In contrast, if the organization keeps only one year of logs, personnel need only search a year's worth of logs, which will take significantly less time and effort.

The National Institute of Standards and Technology (NIST) publishes a significant amount of information on IT security, including *Federal Information Processing Standards (FIPS) publications*. The *Minimum Security Requirements for Federal Information and Information Systems (FIPS 200)* specifies the following as the minimum security requirements for audit data:

> Create, protect, and retain information system audit records to the extent needed to enable the monitoring, analysis, investigation, and reporting of unlawful, unauthorized, or inappropriate information system activity.
>
> Ensure that the actions of individual information system users can be uniquely traced to those users so they can be held accountable for their actions.

NOTE: You'll find it useful to review NIST documents when preparing for the CISSP exam to give you a broader idea of different security concepts. They are freely available and you can access them here: `http://csrc.nist.gov`. You can download the FIPS 200 document here: `http://csrc.nist.gov/publications/fips/fips200/FIPS-200-final-march.pdf`.

The Role of Monitoring

Monitoring provides several benefits for an organization, including increasing accountability, helping with investigations, and basic troubleshooting. The following sections describe these benefits in more depth.

Monitoring and Accountability

Monitoring is a necessary function to ensure that subjects (such as users and employees) can be held accountable for their actions and activities. Users claim an identity (such as with a username) and prove their identity (by authenticating), and audit trails record their activity while they are logged in. Monitoring and reviewing the audit trail logs provides accountability for these users.

This directly promotes positive user behavior and compliance with the organization's security policy. Users who are aware that logs are recording their IT activities are less likely to try to circumvent security controls or to perform unauthorized or restricted activities.

Once a security policy violation or a breach occurs, the source of that violation should be determined. If it is possible to identify the individuals responsible, they should be held accountable based on the organization's security policy. Severe cases can result in terminating employment or legal prosecution.

Legislation often requires specific monitoring and accountability practices. This includes laws such as the Sarbanes-Oxley Act of 2002, the Health Insurance Portability and Accountability Act (HIPAA), and European Union (EU) privacy laws that many organizations must abide by.

Real World Scenario

Monitoring Activity

Accountability is necessary at every level of business, from the frontline infantry to the high-level commanders overseeing daily operations. If you don't monitor the actions and activities of users and their applications on a given system, you aren't able to hold them accountable for mistakes or misdeeds they commit.

Consider Duane, a quality assurance supervisor for the data entry department at an oil-drilling data mining company. During his daily routine, he sees many highly sensitive documents that include the kind of valuable information that can earn a heavy tip or bribe from interested parties. He also corrects the kind of mistakes that could cause serious backlash from his company's clientele because sometimes a minor clerical error can cause serious issues for a client's entire project.

Whenever Duane touches or transfers such information on his workstation, his actions leave an electronic trail of evidence that his supervisor, Nicole, can examine in the event that Duane's actions should come under scrutiny. She can observe where he obtained or placed pieces of sensitive information, when he accessed and modified such information, and just about anything else related to the handling and processing of the data as it flows in from the source and out to the client.

This accountability provides protection to the company should Duane misuse this information. It also provides Duane with protection against anyone falsely accusing him of misusing the data he handles.

Monitoring and Investigations

Audit trails give investigators the ability to reconstruct events long after they have occurred. They can record access abuses, privilege violations, attempted intrusions, and many different types of attacks. After detecting a security violation, security professionals can reconstruct the conditions and system state leading up to the event, during the event, and after the event through a close examination of the audit trail.

One important consideration is ensuring that logs have accurate time stamps and that these time stamps remain consistent throughout the environment. A common method is to set up an internal Network Time Protocol (NTP) server that is synchronized to a trusted time source such as a public NTP server. Other systems can then synchronize with this internal NTP server.

NOTE: Systems should have their time synchronized against a centralized or trusted public time server. This ensures that all audit logs record accurate and consistent times for recorded events.

Monitoring and Problem Identification

Audit trails offer details about recorded events that are useful for administrators. They can record system failures, OS bugs, and software errors in addition to malicious attacks. Some log files can even capture the contents of memory when an application or system crashes. This information can help pinpoint the cause of the event and eliminate it as a possible attack. For example, if a system keeps crashing due to faulty memory, crash dump files can help diagnose the problem.

Using log files for this purpose is often labeled as problem identification. Once a problem is identified, performing problem resolution involves little more than following up on the disclosed information.

Monitoring Techniques

Monitoring is the process of reviewing information logs looking for something specific. Personnel can manually review logs, or use tools to automate the process. Monitoring is necessary to detect malicious actions by subjects as well as attempted intrusions and system failures. It can help reconstruct events, provide evidence for prosecution, and create reports for analysis.

Log analysis is a detailed and systematic form of monitoring in which the logged information is analyzed for trends and patterns as well as abnormal, unauthorized, illegal, and policy-violating activities. Log analysis isn't necessarily in response to an incident but instead a periodic task, which can detect potential issues.

When manually analyzing logs, administrators simply open the log files and look for relevant data. This can be very tedious and time consuming, even when using some tools. For example, searching 10 different archived logs for a specific event or ID code can take some time, even when using built-in search tools.

In many cases, logs can produce so much information that important details can get lost in the sheer volume of data, so administrators often use automated tools to analyze the log data. For example, intrusion detection systems (IDSs) actively monitor multiple logs to detect and respond to malicious intrusions in real time. An IDS can help detect and track attacks from external attackers, send alerts to administrators, and record attackers' access to resources.

Multiple vendors sell operations management software that actively monitors the security, health, and performance of systems throughout a network. This software looks for suspicious or abnormal activities that indicate problems such as an attack or unauthorized access.

Security Information and Event Management

Many organizations use a centralized application to automate monitoring of systems on a network. Several terms are used to describe these tools, including Security Information and Event Management (SIEM), Security Event Management (SEM), and Security Information Management (SIM). These tools provide real-time analysis of events occurring on systems throughout an organization. They include agents installed on remote systems that monitor for specific events known as alarm triggers. When the trigger occurs, the agents report the event back to the central monitoring software.

For example, a SIEM can monitor a group of email servers. Each time of the email servers logs an event, a SIEM agent examines the event to determine if it is an item of interest. If it is, the SIEM agent forwards the event to a central SIEM server, and depending on the event, it can raise an alarm for an administrator. For example, if the send queue of an email server starts backing up, a SIEM application can detect the issue and alert administrators before the problem is serious.

Most SIEMs are configurable, allowing personnel within the organization to specify what items are of interest and need to be forwarded to the SIEM server. SIEMs have agents for just about any type of server or network device, and in some cases, they monitor network flows for traffic and trend analysis. The tools can also collect all the logs from target systems and use data-mining techniques to retrieve relevant data. Security professionals can then create reports and analyze the data.

Some monitoring tools are also used for inventory and status purposes. For example, tools can query all the available systems and document details, such as system names, IP addresses, operating systems, installed patches, updates, and installed software. These tools can then create reports of any system based on the needs of the organization. For example, they can identify how many systems are active, identify systems with missing patches, and flag systems that have unauthorized software installed.

Software monitoring watches for attempted or successful installations of unapproved software, use of unauthorized software, or unauthorized use of approved software. This reduces the risk of users inadvertently installing a virus or Trojan horse.

Audit Trails

Audit trails are records created when information about events and occurrences is stored in one or more databases or log files. Audit trails provide a record of system activity and can reconstruct activity leading up to and during security events. Security professionals extract information about an incident from an audit trail to prove or disprove culpability, and much more. Audit trails allow security professionals to examine and trace events in forward or reverse order. This flexibility helps when tracking down problems, performance issues, attacks, intrusions, security breaches, coding errors, and other potential policy violations.

TIP Audit trails provide a comprehensive record of system activity and can help detect a wide variety of security violations, software flaws, and performance problems.

Using audit trails is a passive form of detective security control. They serve as a deterrent in the same manner that closed circuit television (CCTV) or security guards do. If personnel know they are being watched and their activities are being recorded, they are less likely to engage in illegal, unauthorized, or malicious activity—at least in theory. However, some criminals are too careless or clueless for this to apply consistently.

Audit trails are also essential as evidence in the prosecution of criminals. They provide a before-and-after picture of the state of resources, systems, and assets. This in turn helps to determine whether a change or alteration is the result of an action by a user, the OS, or the software, or whether it's caused by some other source, such as hardware failure.

Sampling

Sampling, or *data extraction*, is the process of extracting specific elements from a large collection of data to construct a meaningful representation or summary of the whole. In other words, sampling is a form of data reduction that allows someone to glean valuable information by looking at only a small sample of data in an audit trail.

Statistical sampling uses precise mathematical functions to extract meaningful information from a very large volume of data. This is similar to the science used by pollsters to learn the opinions of large populations without interviewing everyone in the population. There is always a risk that sampled data is not an accurate representation of the whole body of data, and statistical sampling can identify the margin of error.

Clipping Levels

Clipping is a form of nonstatistical sampling. It selects only events that exceed a *clipping level*, which is a predefined threshold for the event. The system ignores events until they reach this threshold.

For example, failed logon attempts are common in any system as users can easily enter the wrong password once or twice. Instead of raising an alarm for every single failed logon attempt, a clipping level can be set to raise an alarm only if it detects five failed logon attempts within a 30-minute period. Many account lockout controls use a similar clipping level. They don't lock the account after a single failed logon. Instead, they count the failed logons and lock the account only when the predefined threshold is reached.

Clipping levels are widely used in the process of auditing events to establish a baseline of routine system or user activity. The monitoring system raises an alarm to signal abnormal events only if the baseline is exceeded. In other words, the clipping level causes the system to ignore routine events and only raise an alert when it detects serious intrusion patterns.

Additionally, clipping levels are often associated with a form of mainframe auditing known as violation analysis. In violation analysis, an older form of auditing, the environment is monitored for error occurrences. The baseline for errors is expected and known, and this level of expected, known errors defines the clipping level. Any errors that exceed the clipping level threshold trigger a violation, and details about such events are recorded into a violation record for later analysis.

In general, nonstatistical sampling is discretionary sampling, or sampling at the auditor's discretion. It doesn't offer an accurate representation of the whole body of data and will ignore events that don't reach the clipping level threshold. However, it is effective when used to focus on specific events. Additionally, nonstatistical sampling is less expensive and easier to implement than statistical sampling.

NOTE Both statistical and nonstatistical sampling are valid mechanisms to create summaries or overviews of large bodies of audit data. However, statistical sampling is more reliable and mathematically defensible.

Other Monitoring Tools

Although logs are the primary tools used with auditing, there are some additional tools used within organizations that are worth mentioning. For example, a closed-circuit television (CCTV) can automatically record events onto tape for later review. Security personnel can also watch a CCTV system for unwanted, unauthorized, or illegal activities in real time. This system can work alone or in conjunction with security guards, who themselves can be monitored by the CCTV and held accountable for any illegal or unethical activity. Other tools include keystroke monitoring, traffic analysis monitoring, trend analysis monitoring, and monitoring to prevent data loss.

Keystroke Monitoring *Keystroke monitoring* is the act of recording the keystrokes a user performs on a physical keyboard. The monitoring is commonly done via technical means such as a hardware device or a software program known as a keylogger. However, a video recorder can perform visual monitoring. In most cases, attackers use keystroke monitoring for malicious purposes. In extreme circumstances and highly restricted environments, an organization might implement keystroke monitoring to audit and analyze user activity.

Keystroke monitoring is often compared to wiretapping. There is some debate about whether keystroke monitoring should be restricted and controlled in the same manner as telephone wiretaps. Many organizations that employ keystroke monitoring notify both authorized and unauthorized users of such monitoring through employment agreements, security policies, or warning banners at sign-on or login areas.

NOTE Companies can and do use keystroke monitoring in some situations. However, in almost all cases, they are required to inform employees of the monitoring.

Traffic Analysis and Trend Analysis *Traffic analysis* and *trend analysis* are forms of monitoring that examine the flow of packets rather than actual packet contents. This is sometimes referred to as network flow monitoring. It can infer a lot of information, such as primary and backup communication routes, the location of primary servers, sources of encrypted traffic and the amount of traffic supported by the network, typical direction of traffic flow, frequency of communications, and much more.

These techniques can sometimes reveal questionable traffic patterns, such as when an employee's account sends a massive amount of email to others. This might indicate the employee's system is part of a botnet controlled by an attacker at a remote location. Similarly, traffic analysis might detect if an unscrupulous insider forwards internal information to unauthorized parties via email. These types of events often leave detectable signatures.

Egress Monitoring

Egress monitoring refers to monitoring outgoing traffic to prevent data exfiltration, which is the unauthorized transfer of data outside the organization. Some common methods used to prevent data exfiltration are using data loss prevention techniques, looking for steganography attempts, and using watermarking to detect unauthorized data going out.

Data Loss Prevention

Data loss prevention (DLP) systems attempt to detect and block data exfiltration attempts. These systems have the capability of scanning data looking for keywords and data patterns. For example, imagine an organization uses data classifications of Confidential, Proprietary, Private, and Sensitive. A DLP system can scan files for these words and detect them.

Pattern-matching DLP systems look for specific patterns. For example, US Social Security numbers have a pattern of nnn-nn-nnnn (three numbers, a dash, two numbers, a dash, and four numbers). The DLP can look for this pattern and detect it. Administrators can set up a DLP system to look for any patterns based on their needs.

There are two primary types of DLP systems: network-based and endpoint-based.

Network-based DLP A network-based DLP scans all outgoing data looking for specific data. Administrators would place it on the edge of the negative to scan all data leaving the organization. If a user sends out a file containing restricted data, the DLP system will detect it and prevent it from leaving the organization. The DLP system will send an alert, such as an email to an administrator.

Endpoint-based DLP An endpoint-based DLP can scan files stored on a system as well as files sent to external devices, such as printers. For example, an organization endpoint-based DLP can prevent users from copying sensitive data to USB flash drives or sending sensitive data to a printer. Administrators would configure the DLP to scan the files with the appropriate keywords, and if it detects files with these keywords, it will block the copy or print job. It's also possible to configure an endpoint-based DLP system to regularly scan files (such as on a file server) for files containing specific keywords or patterns, or even for unauthorized file types, such as MP3 files.

DLP systems typically have the ability to perform deep-level examinations. For example, if users embed the files in compressed zip files, a DLP system can still detect the keywords and patterns. However, a DLP system doesn't have the ability to decrypt data.

A network-based DLP system might have stopped some major breaches in the past. For example, in the Sony attack of 2014, attackers exfiltrated more than 25 GB of sensitive data on Sony employees, including Social Security numbers, medical, and salary information. If the attackers didn't encrypt the data prior to retrieving it, a DLP system could have detected attempts to transmit it out of the network. However, it's worth mentioning that advanced persistent threats (such as APT1 identified by Mandiant) do encrypt some traffic prior to transmitting it out of the network.

NOTE Security company Mandiant released the report "APT1: Exposing One of China's Cyber Espionage Units" in 2013 documenting the activities of an APT apparently operating out of China. You can download the free report by searching for "Mandiant APT1."

Steganography

Steganography is the practice of embedding a message within a file. For example, individuals can modify bits within a picture file to embed a message. The change is imperceptible to someone looking at the picture, but if other people know to look for the message, they can extract it.

However, it is possible to detect steganography attempts if you have the original file and a file you suspect has a hidden message. If you use a hashing algorithm such as MD5, you can create a hash of both files. If the hashes are the same, the file does not have a hidden message. However, if the hashes are different, it indicates the second file has been modified. Forensic analysis techniques might be able to retrieve the message.

In the context of egress monitoring, an organization can periodically capture hashes of internal files that rarely change. For example, graphics files such as JPEG and GIF files generally stay the same. If security experts suspect a malicious insider is embedding additional data within these files and emailing them outside the organization, they can compare the original hashes with the hashes of the files the malicious insider sent out. If the hashes are different, it indicates the files are different and may contain hidden messages.

Watermarking

Watermarking is the practice of embedding an image or pattern in paper that isn't readily perceivable. It is often used with currency to thwart counterfeiting attempts. Similarly, organizations often use watermarking in documents. For example, authors of sensitive documents can mark them with the appropriate classification such as "Confidential" or "Proprietary." Anyone working with the file or a printed copy of the file will easily see the classification.

From the perspective of egress monitoring, DLP systems can detect the watermark. When a DLP system identifies sensitive data from these watermarks, it can block the transmission and raise an alert for security personnel. This prevents transmission of the files outside the organization.

An advanced implementation of watermarking is digital watermarking. A digital watermark is a secretly embedded marker in a digital file. For example, some movie studios digitally mark copies of movies sent to different distributors. Each copy has a different mark and the studios track which distributor received which copy. If any of the distributors release pirated copies of the movie, the studio can identify which distributor did so.

Auditing to Assess Effectiveness

Many organizations have strong effective security policies in place. However, just because the policies are in place doesn't mean that personnel know about them or follow them. Many times an organization will want to assess the effectiveness of their security policies and related access controls by *auditing* the environment.

Auditing is a methodical examination or review of an environment to ensure compliance with regulations and to detect abnormalities, unauthorized occurrences, or crimes. It verifies that the security mechanisms deployed in an environment are providing adequate security for the environment. The test process ensures that personnel are following the requirements dictated by the security policy or other regulations, and that no significant holes or weaknesses exist in deployed security solutions.

Auditors are responsible for testing and verifying that processes and procedures are in place to implement security policies or regulations, and that they are adequate to meet the organization's security requirements. They also verify that personnel are following these processes and procedures. In other words, auditors perform the auditing.

Auditing and Auditing

The term *auditing* has two different distinct meanings within the context of IT security, so it's important to recognize the differences.

First, *auditing* refers to the use of audit logs and monitoring tools to track activity. For example, audit logs can record when any user accesses a file and document exactly what the user did with the file and when.

Second, *auditing* also refers to an inspection or evaluation. Specifically, an audit is an inspection or evaluation of a specific process or result to determine whether an organization is following specific rules or guidelines.

These rules may be from the organization's security policy or a result of external laws and regulations. For example, a security policy may dictate that inactive accounts should be disabled as soon as possible after an employee is terminated. An audit can check for inactive accounts and even verify the exact time accounts were disabled and match this to the time of a terminated employee's exit interview. Inspection audits can be done internally or by an external auditor, and they will often use the logs created from auditing and monitoring as part of the evaluation process.

Inspection Audits

Secure IT environments rely heavily on auditing as a detective security control to discover and correct vulnerabilities. Two important audits within the context of access control are access review audits and user entitlement audits.

It's important to clearly define and adhere to the frequency of audit reviews. Organizations typically determine the frequency of a security audit or security review based on risk. Personnel evaluate vulnerabilities and threats against the organization's valuable assets to determine the overall level of risk. This helps the organization justify the expense of an audit and determine how frequently they want to have an audit.

TIP

Audits cost time and money, and the frequency of an audit is based on the associated risk. For example, potential misuse or compromise of privileged accounts represents a much greater risk than misuse or compromise of regular user accounts. With this in mind, security personnel would perform user entitlement audits for privileged accounts much more often than user entitlement audits of regular user accounts.

As with many other aspects of deploying and maintaining security, security audits are often viewed as key elements of due care. If senior management fails to enforce compliance with regular security reviews, then stakeholders will hold them accountable and liable for any asset losses that occur because of security breaches or policy violations. When audits aren't performed, it creates the perception that management is not exercising due care.

Access Review Audits

Many organizations perform periodic access reviews and audits to ensure that object access and account management practices support the security policy. These audits verify that users do not have excessive privileges and that accounts are managed appropriately. They ensure that secure processes and procedures are in place, that personnel are following them, and that these processes and procedures are working as expected.

For example, access to highly valuable data should be restricted to only the users who need it. An access review audit will verify that data has been classified and that data classifications are clear to the users. Additionally, it will ensure that anyone who has the authority to grant access to data understands what makes a user eligible for the access. For example, if a help desk professional can grant access to highly classified data, the help desk professional needs to know what makes a user eligible for that level of access.

When examining account management practices, an access review audit will ensure that accounts are disabled and deleted in accordance with best practices and security policies. For example, accounts should be disabled as soon as possible if an employee is terminated. A typical termination procedure policy often includes the following elements:

- At least one witness is present during the exit interview.
- Account access is disabled during the interview.

- Employee identification badges and other physical credentials such as smartcards are collected during or immediately after the interview.
- The employee is escorted off the premises immediately after the interview.

The access review verifies that a policy exists and verifies personnel are following it. When terminated employees have continued access to the network after an exit interview, they can easily cause damage. For example, an administrator can create a separate administrator account and use it to access the network even if the administrator's original account is disabled.

User Entitlement Audits

User entitlement refers to the privileges granted to users. Users need rights and permissions (privileges) to perform their job, but they only need a limited number of privileges. In the context of user entitlement, the principle of least privilege ensures that users have only the privileges they need to perform their job and no more.

Although access controls attempt to enforce the principle of least privilege, there are times when users are granted excessive privileges. User entitlement reviews can discover when users have excessive privileges, which violate security policies related to user entitlement.

Audits of Privileged Groups

Many organizations use groups as part of a role-based access control model. It's important to limit the membership of those groups. It's also important to make sure group members are using their high-privilege accounts only when necessary. Audits can help determine whether personnel are following these policies.

High-Level Administrator Groups

Many operating systems have privileged groups such as an Administrators group. The Administrators group is typically granted full privileges on a system, and when a user account is placed in the Administrators group, the user has these privileges. With this in mind, a user entitlement review will often review membership in any privileged groups, including the different administrator groups.

Some groups have such high privileges that even in organizations with tens of thousands of users, their membership is limited to a very few people. For example, Microsoft domains include a group known as the Enterprise Admins group. Users in this group can do anything on any domain within a Microsoft forest (a group of related domains). This group has so much power that membership is often restricted to only two or three high-level administrators. Monitoring and auditing membership in this group can uncover unauthorized individuals added to these groups.

It is possible to use automated methods to monitor membership in privileged accounts so that attempts to add unauthorized users automatically fail. Audit logs will also record this action, and an entitlement review can check for these events. Auditors can examine the audit trail to determine who attempted to add the unauthorized account.

Personnel can also create additional groups with elevated privileges. For example, administrators might create an ITAdmins group for some users in the IT department. They would grant the group appropriate privileges based on the job requirements of these administrators, and place the accounts of the IT department administrators into the ITAdmins group. Only administrators from the IT department should be in the group, and a user entitlement audit can verify that users in other departments are not in the group. This is one way to detect creeping privileges.

NOTE A user entitlement audit can also detect whether processes are in place to remove privileges when users no longer need them and if personnel are following these processes. For example, if an administrator transferred to the Sales department of an organization, this administrator should no longer have administrative privileges.

Dual Administrator Accounts

Many organizations require administrators to maintain two accounts. They use one account for regular day-to-day use. A second account has additional privileges and they use it for administrative work. This reduces the risk associated with this privileged account.

For example, if malware infects a system while a user is logged on, the malware can often assume the privileges of the user's account. If the user is logged on with a privileged account, the malware starts with these elevated privileges. However, if an administrator uses the administrator account only 10 percent of the time to perform administrative actions, this reduces the potential risk of an infection occurring at the same time the administrator is logged on with an administrator account.

Auditing can verify that administrators are using the privileged account appropriately. For example, an organization may estimate that administrators will need to use a privileged account only about 10 percent of the time during a typical day and should use their regular account the rest of the time. An analysis of logs can show whether this is an accurate estimate and whether administrators are following the rule. If an administrator is constantly using the administrator account and rarely using the regular user account, an audit can flag this as an obvious policy violation.

Similarly, the administrator account requires a stronger password. A policy may state that regular user passwords must be at least 8 characters long but that administrators are required to maintain passwords more than 15 characters long. Password-cracking tools can attempt to discover the passwords of administrator accounts to verify that administrators are using stronger passwords.

Security Audits and Reviews

Security audits and reviews help ensure that an organization has implemented security controls properly. Access review audits (presented earlier in this chapter) assess the effectiveness of access controls. These reviews ensure that accounts are managed appropriately, don't have excessive privileges, and are disabled or deleted when required. In the context of the Security Operations domain, security audits help ensure that management controls are in place. The following list includes some common items to check:

Patch Management A patch management review ensures that patches are evaluated as soon as possible once they are available. It also ensures that the organization follows established procedures to evaluate, test, approve, deploy, and verify the patches. Vulnerability scan reports can be valuable in any patch management review or audit.

Vulnerability Management A vulnerability management review ensures that vulnerability scans and assessments are performed regularly in compliance with established guidelines. For example, an organization may have a policy document stating that vulnerability scans are performed at least weekly, and the review verifies that this is done. Additionally, the review will verify that the vulnerabilities discovered in the scans have been addressed and mitigated.

Configuration Management Systems can be audited periodically to ensure that the original configurations are not modified. It is often possible to use scripting tools to check specific configurations of systems and identify when a change has occurred. Additionally, logging can be enabled for many configuration settings to record configuration changes. A configuration management audit can check the logs for any changes and verify that they are authorized.

Change Management A change management review ensures that changes are implemented in accordance with the organization's change management policy. This often includes a review of outages to determine the cause. Outages that result from unauthorized changes are a clear indication that the change management program needs improvement.

Reporting Audit Results

The actual formats used by an organization to produce reports from audit trails will vary greatly. However, reports should address a few basic or central concepts:

- The purpose of the audit
- The scope of the audit
- The results discovered or revealed by the audit

In addition to these basic concepts, audit reports often include many details specific to the environment, such as time, date, and a list of the audited systems. They can also include a wide range of content that focuses on

- Problems, events, and conditions
- Standards, criteria, and baselines
- Causes, reasons, impact, and effect
- Recommended solutions and safeguards

Audit reports should have a structure or design that is clear, concise, and objective. Although auditors will often include opinions or recommendations, they should clearly identify them. The actual findings should be based on fact and evidence gathered from audit trails and other sources during the audit.

Protecting Audit Results

Audit reports include sensitive information. They should be assigned a classification label and only those people with sufficient privilege should have access to audit reports. This includes high-level executives and security personnel involved in the creation of the reports or responsible for the correction of items mentioned in the reports.

Auditors sometimes create a separate audit report with limited data for other personnel. This modified report provides only the details relevant to the target audience. For example, senior management does not need to know all the minute details of an audit report. Therefore, the audit report for senior management is much more concise and offers more of an overview or summary of findings. An audit report for a security administrator responsible for correction of the problems should be very detailed and include all available information on the events it covers.

On the other hand, the fact that an auditor is performing an audit is often very public. This lets personnel know that senior management is actively taking steps to maintain security.

Distributing Audit Reports

Once an audit report is completed, auditors submit it to its assigned recipients, as defined in security policy documentation. It's common to file a signed confirmation of receipt. When an audit report contains information about serious security violations or performance issues, personnel escalate it to higher levels of management for review, notification, and assignment of a response to resolve the issues.

Using External Auditors

Many organizations choose to conduct independent audits by hiring external security auditors. Additionally, some laws and regulations require external audits. External audits provide a level of objectivity that an internal audit cannot provide, and they bring a fresh, outside perspective to internal policies, practices, and procedures.

NOTE

Many organizations hire external security experts to perform penetration testing against their system as a form of testing. These penetration tests help an organization identify vulnerabilities and the ability of attackers to exploit these vulnerabilities.

An external auditor is given access to the company's security policy and the authorization to inspect appropriate aspects of the IT and physical environment. Thus, the auditor must be a trusted entity. The goal of the audit activity is to obtain a final report that details findings and suggests countermeasures when appropriate.

An external audit can take a considerable amount of time to complete—weeks or months, in some cases. During the course of the audit, the auditor may issue interim reports. An *interim report* is a written or verbal report given to the organization about any observed security weaknesses or policy/procedure mismatches that demand immediate attention. Auditors issue interim reports whenever a problem or issue is too important to wait until the final audit report.

Once the auditors complete their investigations, they typically hold an exit conference. During this conference, the auditors present and discuss their findings and discuss resolution issues with the affected parties. However, only after the exit conference is over and the auditors have left the premises do they write and submit their final audit report to the organization. This allows the final audit report to remain unaffected by office politics and coercion.

After the organization receives the final audit report, internal auditors review it and make recommendations to senior management based on the report. Senior management is responsible for selecting which recommendations to implement and for delegating implementation requirements to internal personnel.

Summary

The CISSP CIB lists six specific incidence response steps. Detection is the first step and can come from automated tools or from employee observations. Personnel investigate alerts to determine if an actual incident has occurred, and if so, the next step is response. Containment of the incident is important during the mitigation stage. It's also important to protect any evidence during all stages of incident response. Reporting may be required based on governing laws or an organization's security policy. In the recovery stage, the system is restored to full operation, and it's important to ensure that it is restored to at least as secure a state as it was in before the attack. The remediation stage includes a root cause analysis and will often include recommendations to prevent a reoccurrence. Last, the lessons learned stage examines the incident and the response to determine if there are any lessons to be learned.

Several basic steps can prevent many common attacks. They include keeping systems and applications up-to-date with current patches, removing or disabling unneeded services and protocols, using intrusion detection and prevention systems, using anti-malware software with up-to-date signatures, and enabling both host-based and network-based firewalls.

Denial-of-service (DoS) attacks prevent a system from processing or responding to legitimate requests for service and commonly attack systems accessible via the Internet. The SYN flood attack disrupts the TCP three-way handshake and is common today, whereas other attacks are often variations on older attack methods. Botnets are often used to launch distributed DoS (DDoS) attacks. Zero-day exploits are previously unknown vulnerabilities. Following basic preventive measures helps to prevent successful zero-day exploit attacks.

Automated tools such as intrusion detection systems use logs to monitor the environment and detect attacks as they are occurring. Some can automatically block attacks. There are two types of detection methods employed by IDSs: knowledge based and behavior based. A knowledge-based IDS uses a database of attack signatures to detect intrusion attempts but cannot recognize new attack methods. A behavior-based system starts with a baseline of normal activity and then measures activity against the baseline to detect abnormal activity. A passive response will log the activity and possibly send an alert on items of interest. An active response will change the environment to block an attack in action. Host-based systems are installed on and monitor individual hosts, whereas network-based systems are installed on network devices and monitor overall network activity. Intrusion prevention systems are placed in line with the traffic and can block malicious traffic before it reaches the target system.

Honeypots, honeynets, and padded cells are useful tools to prevent malicious activity from occurring on a production network while enticing intruders to stick around. They often include pseudo flaws and fake data used to tempt attackers. Administrators and security personnel also use these to gather evidence against attackers for possible prosecution.

Up-to-date anti-malware software prevents many malicious code attacks. Anti-malware software is commonly installed at the boundary between the Internet and the internal network, on email servers, and on each system. Limiting user privileges for software installations helps prevent accidental malware installation by users. Additionally, educating users about different types of malware, and how criminals try to trick users, helps them avoid risky behaviors.

Penetration testing is a useful tool to check the strength and effectiveness of deployed security measures and an organization's security policies. It starts with vulnerability assessments or scans and then attempts to exploit vulnerabilities. Penetration testing should only be done with management approval and should be done on test systems instead of production systems whenever possible. Organizations often hire external consultants to perform penetration testing and can control the amount of knowledge these consultants have. Zero-knowledge testing is often called black-box testing, full-knowledge testing is often called white-box or crystal-box testing, and partial-knowledge testing is often called gray-box testing.

Logging and monitoring provide overall accountability when combined with effective identification and authentication practices. Logging involves recording events in logs and database files. Security logs, system logs, application logs, firewall logs, proxy logs, and change management logs are all common log files. Log files include valuable data and should be protected to ensure that they aren't modified, deleted, or corrupted. If they are not protected, attackers will often try to modify or delete them, and they will not be admissible as evidence to prosecute an attacker.

Monitoring involves reviewing logs in real time and also later as part of an audit. Audit trails are the records created by recording information about events and occurrences into one or more databases or log files, and they can be used to reconstruct events, extract information about incidents, and prove or disprove culpability. Audit trails provide a passive form of detective security control and serve as a deterrent in the same manner as CCTV or security guards do. In addition, they can be essential as evidence in the prosecution of criminals. Logs can be quite large, so different methods are used to analyze them or reduce their size. Sampling is a statistical method used to analyze logs, and using clipping levels is a nonstatistical method involving predefined thresholds for items of interest.

The effectiveness of access controls can be assessed using different types of audits and reviews. Auditing is a methodical examination or review of an environment to ensure compliance with regulations and to detect abnormalities, unauthorized occurrences, or outright crimes. Access review audits ensure that object access and account management practices support an organization's security policy. User entitlement audits ensure that personnel follow the principle of least privilege.

Audit reports document the results of an audit. These reports should be protected and distribution should be limited to only specific people in an organization. Senior management and security professionals have a need to access the results of security audits, but if attackers have access to audit reports, they can use the information to identify vulnerabilities they can exploit.

Security audits and reviews are commonly done to guarantee that controls are implemented as directed and working as desired. It's common to include audits and reviews to check patch management, vulnerability management, change management, and configuration management programs.

Exam Essentials

Know incident response steps. The CISSP CIB lists incident response steps as detection, response, mitigation, reporting, recovery, remediation, and lessons learned. After detecting and verifying an incident, the first response is to limit or contain the scope of the incident while protecting evidence. Based on governing laws, an organization may need to report an incident to official authorities, and if PII is affected, individuals need to be informed. The remediation and lessons learned stages include root cause analysis to determine the cause and recommend solutions to prevent a reoccurrence.

Know basic preventive measures. Basic preventive measures can prevent many incidents from occurring. These include keeping systems up-to-date, removing or disabling unneeded protocols and services, using intrusion detection and prevention systems, using anti-malware software with up-to-date signatures, and enabling both host-based and network-based firewalls.

Know what denial-of-service (DoS) attacks are. DoS attacks prevent a system from responding to legitimate requests for service. A common DoS attack is the SYN flood attack, which disrupts the TCP three-way handshake. Even though older attacks are not as common today because basic precautions block them, you may still be tested on them because many newer attacks are often variations on older methods. Smurf attacks employ an amplification network to send numerous response packets to a victim. Ping-of-death attacks send numerous oversized ping packets to the victim, causing the victim to freeze, crash, or reboot.

Understand botnets, botnet controllers, and bot herders. Botnets represent significant threats due to the massive number of computers that can launch attacks, so it's important to know what they are. A botnet is a collection of compromised PCs (often called zombies) organized in a network controlled by a criminal known as a bot herder. Bot herders use a command and control server to remotely control the zombies and often use the botnet to launch attacks on other systems, or to send spam or phishing emails. Bot herders also rent botnet access out to other criminals.

Understand zero-day exploits. A zero-day exploit is an attack that uses a vulnerability that is either unknown to anyone but the attacker or known only to a limited group of people. On the surface, it sounds like you can't protect against an unknown vulnerability, but basic security practices go a long way toward preventing zero-day exploits. Removing or disabling unneeded protocols and services reduces the attack surface, enabling firewalls blocks many access points, and using intrusion detection and prevention systems helps detect and block potential attacks. Additionally, using tools such as honeypots and padded cells helps protect live networks.

Understand man-in-the-middle attacks. A man-in-the-middle attack occurs when a malicious user is able to gain a logical position between the two endpoints of a communications link. Although it takes a significant amount of sophistication on the part of an attacker to complete a man-in-the middle attack, the amount of data obtained from the attack can be significant.

Understand sabotage and espionage. Malicious insiders can perform sabotage against an organization if they become disgruntled for some reason. Espionage is when a competitor tries to steal information, and they may use an internal employee. Basic security principles, such as implementing the principle of least privilege and immediately disabling accounts for terminated employees, limit the damage from these attacks.

Understand intrusion detection and intrusion prevention. IDSs and IPSs are important detective and preventive measures against attacks. Know the difference between knowledge-based detection (using a database similar to anti-malware signatures) and behavior-based detection. Behavior-based detection starts with a baseline to recognize normal behavior and compares activity with the baseline to detect abnormal activity. The baseline can be outdated if the network is modified, so it must be updated when the environment changes.

Recognize IDS/IPS responses. An IDS can respond passively by logging and sending notifications or actively by changing the environment. Some people refer to an active IDS as an IPS. However, it's important to recognize that an IPS is placed in line with the traffic and includes the ability to block malicious traffic before it reaches the target.

Understand the differences between HIDSs and NIDSs. Host-based IDSs (HIDSs) can monitor activity on a single system only. A drawback is that attackers can discover and disable them. A network-based IDS (NIDS) can monitor activity on a network, and an NIDS isn't as visible to attackers.

Understand honeypots, padded cells, and pseudo flaws. A honeypot is a system that often has pseudo flaws and fake data to lure intruders. Administrators can observe the activity of attackers while they are in the honeypot, and as long as attackers are in the honeypot, they are not in the live network. Some IDSs have the ability to transfer attackers into a padded cell after detection. Although a honeypot and padded cell are similar, note that a honeypot lures the attacker but the attacker is transferred into the padded cell.

Understand methods to block malicious code. Malicious code is thwarted with a combination of tools. The obvious tool is anti-malware software with up-to-date definitions installed on each system, at the boundary of the network, and on email servers. However, policies that enforce basic security principles, such as the principle of least privilege, prevent regular users from installing potentially malicious software. Additionally educating users about the risks and the methods attackers commonly use to spread viruses helps users understand and avoid dangerous behaviors.

Understand penetration testing. Penetration tests start by discovering vulnerabilities and then mimic an attack to identify what vulnerabilities can be exploited. It's important to remember penetration tests should not be done without express consent and knowledge from management. Additionally, since penetration tests can result in damage, they should be done on isolated systems whenever possible. You should also recognize the differences between black-box testing (zero knowledge), white-box testing (full knowledge), and gray-box testing (partial knowledge).

Know the types of log files. Log data is recorded in databases and different types of log files. Common log files include security logs, system logs, application logs, firewall logs, proxy logs, and change management logs. Logs files should be protected by centrally storing them and using permissions to restrict access, and archived logs should be set to read-only to prevent modifications.

Understand monitoring and uses of monitoring tools. Monitoring is a form of auditing that focuses on active review of the log file data. Monitoring is used to hold subjects accountable for their actions and to detect abnormal or malicious activities. It is also used to monitor system performance. Monitoring tools such as IDSs or SIEMs automate monitoring and provide real-time analysis of events.

Understand audit trails. Audit trails are the records created by recording information about events and occurrences into one or more databases or log files. They are used to reconstruct an event, to extract information about an incident, and to prove or disprove culpability. Using audit trails is a passive form of detective security control, and audit trails are essential evidence in the prosecution of criminals.

Understand sampling. Sampling, or data extraction, is the process of extracting elements from a large body of data to construct a meaningful representation or summary of the whole. Statistical sampling uses precise mathematical functions to extract meaningful information from a large volume of data. Clipping is a form of nonstatistical sampling that records only events that exceed a threshold.

Understand how to maintain accountability. Accountability is maintained for individual subjects through the use of auditing. Logs record user activities and users can be held accountable for their logged actions. This directly promotes good user behavior and compliance with the organization's security policy.

Understand the importance of security audits and reviews. Security audits and reviews help ensure that management programs are effective and being followed. They are commonly associated with account management practices to prevent violations with least privilege or need-to-know principles. However, they can also be performed to oversee patch management, vulnerability management, change management, and configuration management programs.

Understand auditing and the need for frequent security audits. Auditing is a methodical examination or review of an environment to ensure compliance with regulations and to detect abnormalities, unauthorized occurrences, or outright crimes. Secure IT environments rely heavily on auditing. Overall, auditing serves as a primary type of detective control used within a secure environment. The frequency of an IT infrastructure security audit or security review is based on risk. An organization determines whether sufficient risk exists to warrant the expense and interruption of a security audit. The degree of risk also affects how often an audit is performed. It is important to clearly define and adhere to the frequency of audit reviews.

Understand that auditing is an aspect of due care. Security audits and effectiveness reviews are key elements in displaying due care. Senior management must enforce compliance with regular periodic security reviews, or they will likely be held accountable and liable for any asset losses that occur.

Understand the need to control access to audit reports. Audit reports typically address common concepts such as the purpose of the audit, the scope of the audit, and the results discovered or revealed by the audit. They often include other details specific to the environment and can include sensitive information such as problems, standards, causes, and recommendations. Audit reports that include sensitive information should be assigned a classification label and handled appropriately. Only people with sufficient privilege should have access to them. An audit report can be prepared in various versions for different target audiences to include only the details needed by a specific audience. For example, senior security administrators might have a report with all the relevant details, whereas a report for executives would provide only high-level information.

Understand access review and user entitlement audits. An access review audit ensures that object access and account management practices support the security policy. User entitlement audits ensure that the principle of least privilege is followed and often focus on privileged accounts.

Audit access controls. Regular reviews and audits of access control processes help assess the effectiveness of access controls. For example, auditing can track logon success and failure of any account. An intrusion detection system can monitor these logs and easily identify attacks and notify administrators.

Written Lab

1. List the different phases of incident response identified in the CISSP CIB.
2. Describe the primary types of intrusion detection systems.
3. Describe the relationship between auditing and audit trails.
4. What should an organization do to verify that accounts are managed properly?

Review Questions

1. Which of the following is the best response after detecting and verifying an incident?
   A. Contain it.
   B. Report it.
   C. Remediate it.
   D. Gather evidence.

2. Which of the following would security personnel do during the remediation stage of an incident response?
   A. Contain the incident
   B. Collect evidence
   C. Rebuild system
   D. Root cause analysis

3. Which of the following are denial-of-service attacks? (Choose three.)
   A. Teardrop
   B. Smurf
   C. Ping of death
   D. Spoofing

4. How does a SYN flood attack work?
   A. Exploits a packet processing glitch in Windows systems
   B. Uses an amplification network to flood a victim with packets
   C. Disrupts the three-way handshake used by TCP
   D. Sends oversized ping packets to a victim

5. A web server hosted on the Internet was recently attacked, exploiting a vulnerability in the operating system. The operating system vendor assisted in the incident investigation and verified the vulnerability was not previously known. What type of attack was this?
   A. Botnet
   B. Zero-day exploit
   C. Denial-of-service
   D. Distributed denial-of-service

6. Of the following choices, which is the most common method of distributing malware?
   A. Drive-by downloads
   B. USB flash drives
   C. Ransomware
   D. Unapproved software

7. Of the following choices, what indicates the primary purpose of an intrusion detection system (IDS)?

A. Detect abnormal activity

B. Diagnose system failures

C. Rate system performance

D. Test a system for vulnerabilities

8. Which of the following is true for a host-based intrusion detection system (HIDS)?

A. It monitors an entire network.

B. It monitors a single system.

C. It's invisible to attackers and authorized users.

D. It cannot detect malicious code.

9. Which of the following is a fake network designed to tempt intruders with unpatched and unprotected security vulnerabilities and false data?

A. IDS

B. Honeynet

C. Padded cell

D. Pseudo flaw

10. Of the following choices, what is the best form of anti-malware protection?

A. Multiple solutions on each system

B. A single solution throughout the organization

C. Anti-malware protection at several locations

D. One-hundred-percent content filtering at all border gateways

11. When using penetration testing to verify the strength of your security policy, which of the following is *not* recommended?

A. Mimicking attacks previously perpetrated against your system

B. Performing attacks without management knowledge

C. Using manual and automated attack tools

D. Reconfiguring the system to resolve any discovered vulnerabilities

12. What is used to keep subjects accountable for their actions while they are authenticated to a system?

A. Authentication

B. Monitoring

C. Account lockout

D. User entitlement reviews

13. What type of a security control is an audit trail?
    - A. Administrative
    - B. Detective
    - C. Corrective
    - D. Physical
14. Which of the following options is a methodical examination or review of an environment to ensure compliance with regulations and to detect abnormalities, unauthorized occurrences, or outright crimes?
    - A. Penetration testing
    - B. Auditing
    - C. Risk analysis
    - D. Entrapment
15. What can be used to reduce the amount of logged or audited data using nonstatistical methods?
    - A. Clipping levels
    - B. Sampling
    - C. Log analysis
    - D. Alarm triggers
16. Which of the following focuses more on the patterns and trends of data than on the actual content?
    - A. Keystroke monitoring
    - B. Traffic analysis
    - C. Event logging
    - D. Security auditing
17. What would detect when a user has more privileges than necessary?
    - A. Account management
    - B. User entitlement audit
    - C. Logging
    - D. Reporting

Refer to the following scenario when answering questions 18 through 20.

An organization has an incident response plan that requires reporting incidents after verifying them. For security purposes, the organization has not published the plan. Only members of the incident response team know about the plan and its contents. Recently, a server administrator noticed that a web server he manages was running slower than normal. After a quick investigation, he realized an attack was coming from a specific IP address. He immediately rebooted the web server to reset the connection and stop the attack. He then used a utility he found on the Internet to launch a protracted attack against this IP address for several hours. Because attacks from this IP address stopped, he didn't report the incident.

18. What should have been done before rebooting the web server?

A. Review the incident

B. Perform remediation steps

C. Take recovery steps

D. Gather evidence

19. Which of the following indicates the most serious mistake the server administrator made in this incident?

A. Rebooting the server

B. Not reporting the incident

C. Attacking the IP address

D. Resetting the connection

20. What was missed completely in this incident?

A. Lessons learned

B. Detection

C. Response

D. Recovery

Chapter 18

Disaster Recovery Planning

THE CISSP EXAM TOPICS COVERED IN THIS CHAPTER INCLUDE:

✓ **Security Assessment and Testing**

- C. Collect security process data (e.g. management and operational controls)
  - C.5 Training and awareness
  - C.6 Disaster recovery and business continuity

✓ **Security Operations**

- K. Implement recovery strategies
  - K.1 Backup storage strategies (e.g., offsite storage, electronic vaulting, tape rotation)
  - K.2 Recovery site strategies
  - K.3 Multiple processing sites (e.g., operationally redundant systems)
  - K.4 System resilience, high availability, quality of service and fault tolerance
- L. Implement disaster recovery processes
  - L.1 Response
  - L.2 Personnel
  - L.3 Communications
  - L.4 Assessment
  - L.5 Restoration
  - L.6 Training and awareness
- M. Test disaster recovery plans
  - M.1 Read-through
  - M.2 Walkthrough
  - M.3 Simulation
  - M.4 Parallel
  - M.5 Full interruption

In Chapter 3, "Business Continuity Planning," you learned the essential elements of business continuity planning (BCP)—the art of helping your organization avoid business interruption as the result of an emergency or disaster. But business continuity plans do not seek to prevent every possible disaster.

Disaster recovery planning (DRP) steps in where BCP leaves off. When a disaster strikes and a business continuity plan fails to prevent interruption of business activities, the disaster recovery plan kicks in and guides the actions of emergency-response personnel until the end goal is reached—which is to see the business restored to full operating capacity in its primary operations facilities.

While reading this chapter, you may notice many areas of overlap between the BCP and DRP processes. Our discussion of specific disasters provides information on how to handle them from both BCP and DRP points of view. Although the (ISC)^2 CISSP curriculum draws a distinction between these two areas, most organizations simply have a single team and plan to address both business continuity and disaster recovery concerns. In many organizations, the single discipline known as business continuity management (BCM) encompasses BCP, DRP, and incident management under a single umbrella.

The Nature of Disaster

Disaster recovery planning brings order to the chaos that surrounds the interruption of an organization's normal activities. By its very nature, a *disaster recovery plan* is implemented only when tension is high and cooler heads may not naturally prevail. Picture the circumstances in which you might find it necessary to implement DRP measures—a hurricane destroys your main operations facility; a fire devastates your main processing center; terrorist activity closes off access to a major metropolitan area. Any event that stops, prevents, or interrupts an organization's ability to perform its work tasks is considered a disaster. The moment that IT becomes unable to support mission-critical processes is the moment DRP kicks in to manage the restoration and recovery procedures.

A disaster recovery plan should be set up so that it can almost run on autopilot. The DRP should also be designed to reduce decision-making activities during a disaster as much as possible. Essential personnel should be well trained in their duties and responsibilities in the wake of a disaster and also know the steps they need to take to get the organization up and running as soon as possible. We'll begin by analyzing some of the possible disasters that might strike your organization and the particular threats that they pose. Many of these are mentioned in Chapter 3, but we'll now explore them in further detail.

To plan for natural and unnatural disasters in the workplace, you must first understand their various forms, as explained in the following sections.

Natural Disasters

Natural disasters reflect the occasional fury of our habitat—violent occurrences that result from changes in the earth's surface or atmosphere that are beyond human control. In some cases, such as hurricanes, scientists have developed sophisticated predictive models that provide ample warning before a disaster strikes. Others, such as earthquakes, can cause devastation at a moment's notice. A disaster recovery plan should provide mechanisms for responding to both types of disasters, either with a gradual buildup of response forces or as an immediate reaction to a rapidly emerging crisis.

Earthquakes

Earthquakes are caused by the shifting of seismic plates and can occur almost anywhere in the world without warning. However, they are far more likely to occur along known fault lines that exist in many areas of the world. A well-known example is the San Andreas fault, which poses a significant risk to portions of the western United States. If you live in a region along a fault line where earthquakes are likely, your DRP should address the procedures your business will implement should a seismic event interrupt your normal activities.

You might be surprised by some of the regions of the world where earthquakes are considered possible. Table 18.1 shows parts of the United States (and U.S. territories) that the Federal Emergency Management Agency (FEMA) considers moderate, high, or very high seismic hazards. Note that the states listed in the table include 82 percent (41) of the 50 states, meaning that the majority of the country has at least a moderate risk of seismic activity.

TABLE 18.1 Seismic hazard level by U.S. state or territory

Moderate seismic hazard	High seismic hazard	Very high seismic hazard
Alabama	American Samoa	Alaska
Colorado	Arizona	California
Connecticut	Arkansas	Guam
Delaware	Illinois	Hawaii
Georgia	Indiana	Idaho
Maine	Kentucky	Montana
Maryland	Missouri	Nevada
Massachusetts	New Mexico	Oregon

TABLE 18.1 Seismic hazard level by U.S. state or territory *(continued)*

Moderate seismic hazard	High seismic hazard	Very high seismic hazard
Mississippi	South Carolina	Puerto Rico
New Hampshire	Tennessee	Virgin Islands
New Jersey	Utah	Washington
New York		Wyoming
North Carolina		
Ohio		
Oklahoma		
Pennsylvania		
Rhode Island		
Texas		
Vermont		
Virginia		
West Virginia		

Floods

Flooding can occur almost anywhere in the world at any time of the year. Some flooding results from the gradual accumulation of rainwater in rivers, lakes, and other bodies of water that then overflow their banks and flood the community. Other floods, known as *flash floods*, strike when a sudden severe storm dumps more rainwater on an area than the ground can absorb in a short period of time. Floods can also occur when dams are breached. Large waves caused by seismic activity, or *tsunamis*, combine the awesome power and weight of water with flooding, as we saw during the 2011 tsunami in Japan. This tsunami amply demonstrated the enormous destructive capabilities of water and the havoc it can wreak on various businesses and economies.

According to government statistics, flooding is responsible for more than $1 billion (that's billion with a *b*!) in damage to businesses and homes each year in the United States. It's important that your DRP make appropriate response plans for the eventuality that a flood may strike your facilities.

WARNING

When you evaluate a firm's risk of damage from flooding to develop business continuity and disaster recovery plans, it's also a good idea to check with responsible individuals and ensure that your organization has sufficient insurance in place to protect it from the financial impact of a flood. In the United States, most general business policies do not cover flood damage, and you should investigate obtaining specialized government-backed flood insurance under FEMA's National Flood Insurance Program.

Although flooding is theoretically possible in almost any region of the world, it is much more likely to occur in certain areas. FEMA's National Flood Insurance Program is responsible for completing a flood risk assessment for the entire United States and providing this data to citizens in graphical form. You can view flood maps online at

`http://msc.fema.gov/portal`

This site also provides valuable information on recorded earthquakes, hurricanes, windstorms, hailstorms, and other natural disasters to help you prepare your organization's risk assessment.

When viewing flood maps, like the example shown in Figure 18.1, you'll find that the two risks often assigned to an area are the "100-year flood plain" and the "500-year flood plain." These evaluations mean that the government estimates chances of flooding in any given year at 1 in 100 or at 1 in 500, respectively. For a more detailed tutorial on reading flood maps and current map information, visit `www.fema.gov/media/fhm/firm/ot_firm.htm`.

FIGURE 18.1 Flood hazard map for Miami–Dade County, Florida

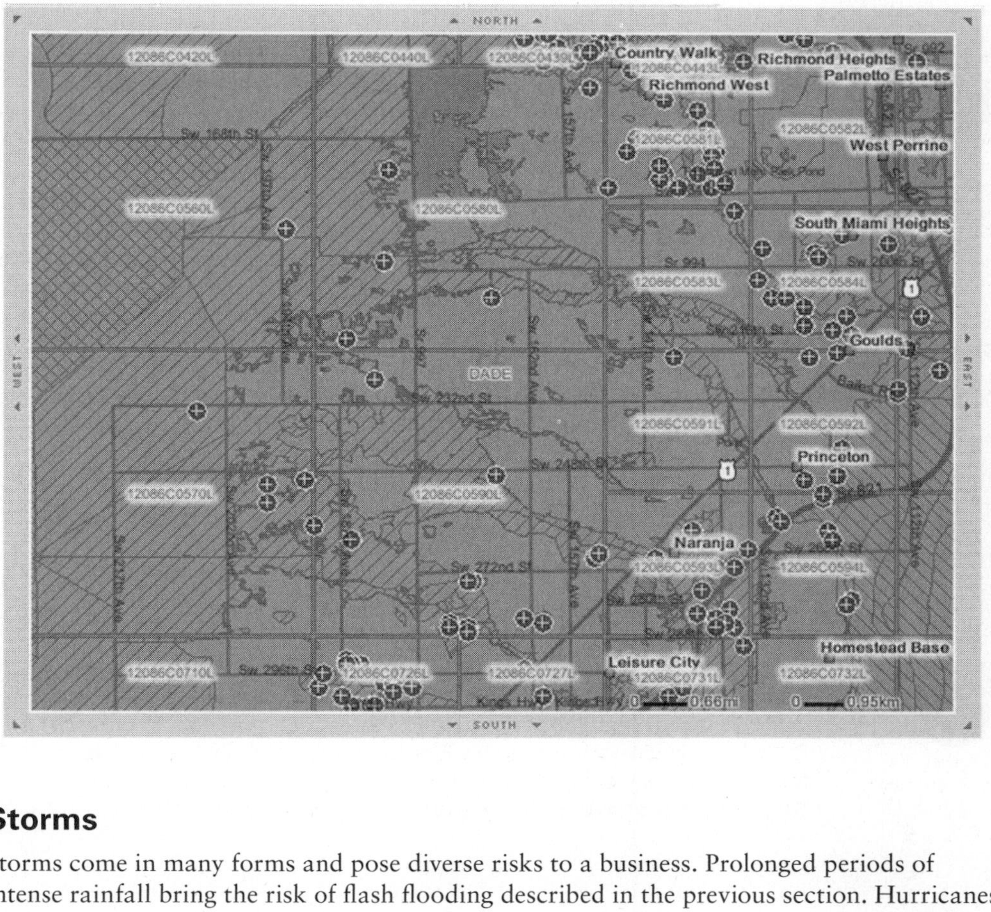

Storms

Storms come in many forms and pose diverse risks to a business. Prolonged periods of intense rainfall bring the risk of flash flooding described in the previous section. Hurricanes and tornadoes come with the threat of winds exceeding 100 miles per hour that undermine the structural integrity of buildings and turn everyday objects such as trees, lawn furniture, and even vehicles into deadly missiles. Hailstorms bring a rapid onslaught of destructive ice chunks falling from the sky. Many storms also bring the risk of lightning, which can cause severe damage to sensitive electronic components. For this reason, your business continuity plan should detail appropriate mechanisms to protect against lightning-induced damage, and your disaster recovery plan should provide adequate provisions for power outages and equipment damage that might result from a lightning strike. Never underestimate the damage that a single storm can do.

In 2005, the Category 5 Atlantic hurricane Katrina marked one of the costliest, deadliest, and strongest hurricanes ever to make landfall in the continental United States. It bored a path of destruction from Louisiana to Alabama, destroying both natural and man-made features throughout those areas. The total economic impact stemming from the damage this storm caused is estimated at $81 billion, eliminating a major Gulf Coast highway and impeding commodities exports, not to mention inundating nearly 80 percent of the city of New Orleans.

TIP

If you live in an area susceptible to a certain type of severe storm, it's important to regularly monitor weather forecasts from responsible government agencies. For example, disaster recovery specialists in hurricane-prone areas should periodically check the website of the National Weather Service's National Hurricane Center (`www.nhc.noaa.gov`) during hurricane season. This website allows you to monitor Atlantic and Pacific storms that may pose a risk to your region before word about them hits the local news. This lets you begin a gradual response to the storm before time runs out.

Fires

Fires can start for a variety of reasons, both natural and man-made, but both forms can be equally devastating. During the BCP/DRP process, you should evaluate the risk of fire and implement at least basic measures to mitigate that risk and prepare the business for recovery from a catastrophic fire in a critical facility.

Some regions of the world are susceptible to wildfires during the warm season. These fires, once started, spread in somewhat predictable patterns, and fire experts working with meteorologists can produce relatively accurate forecasts of a wildfire's potential path.

TIP

As with many other types of large-scale natural disasters, you can obtain valuable information about impending threats on the Web. In the United States, the National Interagency Fire Center posts daily fire updates and forecasts on its website: `www.nifc.gov/fireInfo/fireInfo_maps.html`. Other countries have similar warning systems in place.

Other Regional Events

Some regions of the world are prone to localized types of natural disasters. During the BCP/DRP process, your assessment team should analyze all of your organization's operating locations and gauge the impact that such events might have on your business. For example, many parts of the world are subject to volcanic eruptions. If you conduct operations in an area in close proximity to an active or dormant volcano, your DRP should probably address this eventuality. Other localized natural occurrences include monsoons in Asia, tsunamis in the South Pacific, avalanches in mountainous regions, and mudslides in the western United States.

If your business is geographically diverse, it is prudent to include area natives on your planning team. At the very least, make use of local resources such as government emergency preparedness teams, civil defense organizations, and insurance claim offices to help guide your efforts. These organizations possess a wealth of knowledge and are usually more than happy to help you prepare your organization for the unexpected—after all, every organization that successfully weathers a natural disaster is one less organization that requires a portion of their valuable recovery resources after disaster strikes.

Man-made Disasters

Our advanced civilization has become increasingly dependent on complex interactions between technological, logistical, and natural systems. The same complex interactions that make our sophisticated society possible also present a number of potential vulnerabilities from both intentional and unintentional *man-made disasters*. In the following sections, we'll examine a few of the more common disasters to help you analyze your organization's vulnerabilities when preparing a business continuity plan and disaster recovery plan.

Fires

Earlier in the chapter, we explained how some regions of the world are susceptible to wildfires during the warm season, and these types of fires can be described as natural disasters. Many smaller-scale fires result from human action—be it carelessness, faulty electrical wiring, improper fire protection practices, or other reasons. Studies from the Insurance Information Institute indicate that there are at least 1,000 building fires in the United States *every day*. If such a fire strikes your organization, do you have the proper preventive measures in place to quickly contain it? If the fire destroys your facilities, how quickly does your disaster recovery plan allow you to resume operations elsewhere?

Acts of Terrorism

Since the terrorist attacks on September 11, 2001, businesses are increasingly concerned about risks posed by terrorist threats. The attacks on September 11 caused many small businesses to fail because they did not have business continuity/disaster recovery plans in place that were adequate to ensure their continued viability. Many larger businesses experienced significant losses that caused severe long-term damage. The Insurance Information

Institute issued a study one year after the attacks that estimated the total damage from the attacks in New York City at $40 billion (yes, that's with a *b* again!).

WARNING

General business insurance may not properly cover an organization against acts of terrorism. Prior to the September 11, 2001, attacks, most policies either covered acts of terrorism or didn't mention them explicitly. After suffering such a catastrophic loss, many insurance companies responded by amending policies to exclude losses from terrorist activity. Policy riders and endorsements are sometimes available but often at extremely high cost. If your business continuity or disaster recovery plan includes insurance as a means of financial recovery (as it probably should!), you'd be well advised to check your policies and contact your insurance professionals to ensure that you're still covered.

Terrorist acts pose a unique challenge to DRP teams because of their unpredictable nature. Prior to the September 11, 2001, terrorist attacks, few DRP teams considered the threat of an airplane crashing into their corporate headquarters significant enough to merit mitigation. Many companies are asking themselves a number of "what if" questions regarding terrorist activity. In general, these questions are healthy because they promote dialogue between business elements regarding potential threats. On the other hand, disaster recovery planners must emphasize solid risk-management principles and ensure that resources aren't overallocated to terrorist threats to the detriment of other DRP/BCP activities that protect against more likely threats.

Bombings/Explosions

Explosions can result from a variety of man-made occurrences. Explosive gases from leaks might fill a room/building and later ignite and cause a damaging blast. In many areas, bombings are also cause for concern. From a disaster planning perspective, the effects of bombings and explosions are like those caused by a large-scale fire. However, planning to avoid the impact of a bombing is much more difficult and relies on physical security measures we cover in Chapter 10, "Physical Security Requirements."

Power Outages

Even the most basic disaster recovery plan contains provisions to deal with the threat of a short power outage. Critical business systems are often protected by uninterruptible power supply (UPS) devices to keep them running at least long enough to shut down or long enough to get emergency generators up and working. Even so, could your organization keep operating during a sustained power outage?

After Hurricane Katrina made landfall in 2005, a reported 2,400,000 people in Mississippi, Louisiana and Alabama lost power. Does your business continuity plan include provisions to keep your business viable during such a prolonged period without power? Does your disaster recovery plan make ample preparations for the timely restoration of power even if the commercial power grid remains unavailable?

WARNING

Check your UPSs regularly! These critical devices are often overlooked until they become necessary. Many UPSs contain self-testing mechanisms that report problems automatically, but it's still a good idea to subject them to regular testing. Also, be sure to audit the number and type of devices plugged into each UPS. It's amazing how many people think it's okay to add "just one more system" to a UPS, and you don't want to be surprised when the device can't handle the load during a real power outage!

Today's technology-driven organizations depend increasingly on electric power, so your BCP/DRP team should consider provisioning alternative power sources that can run business systems indefinitely. An adequate backup generator could make a huge difference when the survival of your business is at stake.

Other Utility and Infrastructure Failures

When planners consider the impact that utility outages may have on their organizations, they naturally think first about the impact of a power outage. However, keep other utilities in mind too. Do any of your critical business systems rely on water, sewers, natural gas, or other utilities? Also consider regional infrastructure such as highways, airports, and railroads. Any of these systems can suffer failures that might not be related to weather or other conditions described in this chapter. Many businesses depend on one or more of these infrastructure elements to move people or materials. Their failure can paralyze your business's ability to continue functioning.

NOTE

If you quickly answered "no" to the question whether you have critical business systems that rely on water, sewers, natural gas, or other utilities, think again. Do you consider people a critical business system? If a major storm knocks out the water supply to your facilities and you need to keep those facilities up and running, can you supply your employees with enough drinking water to meet their needs?

What about your fire protection systems? If any of them are water based, is there a holding tank system in place that contains ample water to extinguish a serious building fire if the public water system is unavailable? Fires often cause serious damage in areas ravaged by storms, earthquakes, and other disasters that might also interrupt the delivery of water.

Hardware/Software Failures

Like it or not, computer systems fail. Hardware components simply wear out and refuse to continue performing, or they suffer physical damage. Software systems contain bugs or fall prey to improper or unexpected inputs. For this reason, BCP/DRP teams must provide adequate redundancy in their systems. If zero downtime is a mandatory requirement, the best solution is to use fully redundant failover servers in separate locations attached to separate communications links and infrastructures (also designed to operate in a failover mode). If one server is damaged or destroyed, the other will instantly take over the processing load.

For more information on this concept, see the section "Remote Mirroring" later in this chapter.

Because of financial constraints, it isn't always feasible to maintain fully redundant systems. In those circumstances, the BCP/DRP team should address how replacement parts can be quickly obtained and installed. As many parts as possible should be kept in a local parts inventory for quick replacement; this is especially true for hard-to-find parts that must otherwise be shipped in. After all, how many organizations could do without telephones for three days while a critical PBX component is en route from an overseas location to be installed on site?

Real World Scenario

NYC Blackout

On August 14, 2003, the lights went out in New York City and in large areas of the northeastern and midwestern United States when a series of cascading failures caused the collapse of a major power grid.

Fortunately, security professionals in the New York area were ready. Spurred to action by the September 11, 2001, terrorist attacks, many businesses updated their disaster recovery plans and took steps to ensure their continued operations in the wake of another disaster. This blackout served to test those plans, and many organizations were able to continue operating on alternate power sources or to transfer control seamlessly to offsite data-processing centers.

Lessons learned during this blackout offer insight for BCP/DRP teams around the world and include the following:

- Ensure that alternate processing sites are far enough away from your main site that they are unlikely to be affected by the same disaster.
- Remember that threats to your organization are both internal and external. Your next disaster may come from a terrorist attack, building fire, or malicious code running loose on your network. Take steps to ensure that your alternate sites are segregated from the main facility to protect against all of these threats.
- Disasters don't usually come with advance warning. If real-time operations are critical to your organization, be sure that your backup sites are ready to assume primary status at a moment's notice.

Strikes/Picketing

When designing your business continuity and disaster recovery plans, don't forget about the importance of the human factor in emergency planning. One form of man-made disaster that is often overlooked is the possibility of a strike or other labor crisis. If a large number of your employees walk out at the same time, what impact would that have on your business? How long would you be able to sustain operations without the regular full-time employees that staff a certain area? Your BCP and DRP teams should address these concerns and provide alternative plans should a labor crisis occur.

Theft/Vandalism

Earlier, we talked about the threat that terrorist activities pose to an organization. Theft and vandalism represent the same kind of threat on a much smaller scale. In most cases, however, there's a far greater chance that your organization will be affected by theft or vandalism than by a terrorist attack. Insurance provides some financial protection against these events (subject to deductibles and limitations of coverage), but acts of this kind can cause serious damage to your business, on both a short-term and a long-term basis. Your business continuity and disaster recovery plans should include adequate preventive measures to control the frequency of these occurrences as well as contingency plans to mitigate the effects theft and vandalism have on ongoing operations.

NOTE

Theft of infrastructure is becoming increasingly common as scrappers target copper in air-conditioning systems, plumbing, and power subsystems. It's a common mistake to assume that fixed infrastructure is unlikely to be a theft target.

Real World Scenario

Offsite Challenges to Security

The constant threat of theft and vandalism is the bane of information security professionals worldwide. Personal identity information, proprietary or trade secrets, and other forms of confidential data are just as interesting to those who create and possess them as they are to direct competitors and other unauthorized parties. Here's an example.

Aaron knows the threats to confidential data firsthand, working as a security officer for a very prominent and highly visible computing enterprise. His chief responsibility is to keep sensitive information from exposure to various elements and entities. Bethany is one of his more troublesome employees because she's constantly taking her notebook computer off site without properly securing its contents.

Even a casual smash-and-grab theft attempt could put thousands of client contacts and their confidential business dealings at risk of being leaked and possibly sold to malicious parties. Aaron knows the potential dangers, but Bethany just doesn't seem to care.

This poses the question: How might you better inform, train, or advise Bethany so that Aaron does not have to relieve her of her position should her notebook be stolen? Bethany must come to understand and appreciate the importance of keeping sensitive information secure. It may be necessary to emphasize the potential loss and exposure that comes with losing such data to wrongdoers, competitors, or other unauthorized third parties. It may suffice to point out to Bethany that the employee handbook clearly states that employees whose behavior leads to the unauthorized disclosure or loss of information assets are subject to loss of pay or termination. If such behavior recurs after a warning, Bethany should be rebuked and reassigned to a position where she can't expose sensitive or proprietary information—that is, if she's not fired on the spot.

NOTE Keep the impact that theft may have on your operations in mind when planning your parts inventory. It's a good idea to keep extra inventory of items with a high pilferage rate, such as RAM chips and laptops. It's also a good idea to keep such materials in secure storage and to require employees to sign such items out whenever they are used.

Understand System Resilience and Fault Tolerance

Technical controls that add to system resilience and fault tolerance directly affect availability, one of the core goals of the CIA security triad (confidentiality, integrity, and availability). A primary goal of system resilience and fault tolerance is to eliminate single points of failure.

A *single point of failure* is any component that can cause an entire system to fail. If a computer has data on a single disk, failure of the disk can cause the computer to fail, so the disk is a single point of failure. If a database-dependent website includes multiple web servers all served by a single database server, the database server is a single point of failure.

Fault tolerance is the ability of a system to suffer a fault but continue to operate. Fault tolerance is achieved by adding redundant components such as additional disks within a redundant array of inexpensive disks (RAID) array, or additional servers within a failover clustered configuration.

System resilience refers to the ability of a system to maintain an acceptable level of service during an adverse event. This could be a hardware fault managed by fault-tolerant components, or it could be an attack managed by other controls such as effective intrusion detection and prevention systems. In some contexts, it refers to the ability of a system to return to a previous state after an adverse event. For example, if a primary server in a failover cluster fails, fault tolerance ensures that the system fails over to another server. System resilience implies that the cluster can fail back to the original server after the original server is repaired.

Protecting Hard Drives

A common way that fault tolerance and system resilience is added for computers is with a redundant array of disks (RAID) array. A RAID array includes two or more disks, and most RAID configurations will continue to operate even after one of the disks fails. Some of the common RAID configurations are as follows:

RAID-0 This is also called striping. It uses two or more disks and improves the disk subsystem performance, but it does not provide fault tolerance.

RAID-1 This is also called mirroring. It uses two disks, which both hold the same data. If one disk fails, the other disk includes the data so a system can continue to operate after a single disk fails. Depending on the hardware used and which drive fails, the system may be able to continue to operate without intervention, or the system may need to be manually configured to use the drive that didn't fail.

RAID-5 This is also called striping with parity. It uses three or more disks with the equivalent of one disk holding parity information. If any single disk fails, the RAID array will continue to operate, though it will be slower.

RAID-10 This is also known as RAID 1 + 0 or a stripe of mirrors, and is configured as two or more mirrors (RAID-1) configured in a striped (RAID-0) configuration. It uses at least four disks but can support more as long as an even number of disks are added. It will continue to operate even if multiple disks fail, as long as at least one drive in each mirror continues to function. For example, if it had three mirrored sets (called M1, M2, and M3 for this example) it would have a total of six disks. If one drive in M1, one in M2, and one in M3 all failed, the array would continue to operate. However, if two drives in any of the mirrors failed, such as both drives in M1, the entire array would fail.

NOTE

Fault tolerance is not the same as a backup. Occasionally, management may balk at the cost of backup tapes and point to the RAID, saying that the data is already backed up. However, if a catastrophic hardware failure destroys a RAID array, all the data is lost unless a backup exists. Similarly, if an accidental deletion or corruption destroys data, it cannot be restored if a backup doesn't exist.

Both software and hardware-based RAID solutions are available. Software-based systems require the operating system to manage the disks in the array and can reduce overall system performance. They are relatively inexpensive since they don't require any additional hardware other than the additional disk(s). Hardware RAID systems are generally more efficient and reliable. While a hardware RAID is more expensive, the benefits outweigh the costs when used to increase availability of a critical component.

Hardware-based RAID arrays typically include spare drives that can be logically added to the array. For example, a hardware-based RAID-5 could include five disks, with three disks in a RAID-5 array and two spare disks. If one disk fails, the hardware senses the failure and logically swaps out the faulty drive with a good spare. Additionally, most hardware-based arrays support hot swapping, allowing technicians to replace failed disks without powering down the system. A cold swappable RAID requires the system to be powered down to replace a faulty drive.

Protecting Servers

Fault tolerance can be added for critical servers with failover clusters. A failover cluster includes two or more servers, and if one of the servers fails, another server in the cluster can take over its load in an automatic process called *failover*. Failover clusters can include multiple servers (not just two), and they can also provide fault tolerance for multiple services or applications.

As an example of a failover cluster, consider Figure 18.2. It shows multiple components put together to provide reliable web access for a heavily accessed website that uses a database. DB1 and DB2 are two database servers configured in a failover cluster. At any given time, only one server will function as the active database server, and the second server will be inactive. For example, if DB1 is the active server it will perform all the database services for the website. DB2 monitors DB1 to ensure it is operational, and if DB2 senses a failure in DB1, it will cause the cluster to automatically fail over to DB2.

FIGURE 18.2 Failover cluster with network load balancing

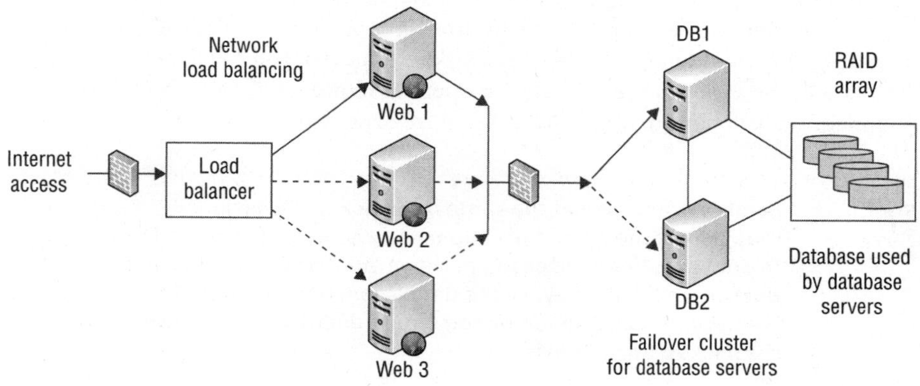

In Figure 18.2, you can see that both DB1 and DB2 have access to the data in the database. This data is stored on a RAID array providing fault tolerance for the disks.

Additionally, the three web servers are configured in a network load-balancing cluster. The load balancer can be hardware or software based, and it balances the client load across the three servers. It makes it easy to add additional web servers to handle increased load while also balancing the load among all the servers. If any of the servers fail, the load balancer can sense the failure and stop sending traffic to that server. Although network load balancing is primarily used to increase the scalability of a system so that it can handle more traffic, it also provides a measure of fault tolerance.

NOTE

Failover clusters are not the only method of fault tolerance for servers. Some systems provide automatic fault tolerance for servers, allowing a server to fail without losing access to the provided service. For example, in a Microsoft domain with two or more domain controllers, each domain controller will regularly replicate data with the others so that all the domain controllers have the same data. If one fails, computers within the domain can still find the other domain controller(s) and the network can continue to operate. Similarly, many database server products include methods to replicate database content with other servers so that all servers have the same content. Three of these methods: electronic vaulting, remote journaling, and remote mirroring, are discussed later in this chapter.

Protecting Power Sources

Fault tolerance can be added for power sources with an *uninterruptible power supply* (UPS), a generator, or both. In general, a UPS provides battery-supplied power for a short period of time between 5 and 30 minutes, and a generator provides long-term power. The goal of a UPS is to provide power long enough to complete a logical shutdown of a system, or until a generator is powered on and providing stable power.

Ideally, power is consistently clean without any fluctuations, but in reality, commercial power suffers from a wide assortment of problems. A *spike* is a quick instance of an increase in voltage whereas a *sag* is a quick instance of a reduction in voltage. If power stays high for a long period of time, it's called a *surge* rather than a spike. If it remains low for a long period of time, it's called a *brownout*. Occasionally, power lines have noise on them called *transients* that can come from many different sources. All of these issues can cause problems for electrical equipment.

A very basic UPS (also called an offline or standby UPS) provides surge protection and battery backup. It is plugged into commercial power, and critical systems are plugged into the UPS system. If power fails, the battery backup will provide continuous power to the systems for a short period of time. Line-interactive UPS are becoming popular, and they provide additional services beyond a basic UPS. They include a variable-voltage transformer that can adjust to the overvoltage and undervoltage events without draining the battery. When power is lost, the battery will provide power to the system for a short period of time.

Generators provide power to systems during long-term power outages. The length of time that a generator will provide power is dependent on the fuel, and it's possible for a site to stay on generator power as long as it has fuel. Generators commonly use diesel fuel, natural gas, or propane.

Trusted Recovery

Trusted recovery provides assurances that after a failure or crash, the system is just as secure as it was before the failure or crash occurred. Depending on the failure, the recovery may be automated or require manual intervention by an administrator. However, in either case systems can be designed to ensure they support trusted recovery.

Systems can be designed so that they fail in a fail-secure state or a fail-open state. A *fail-secure* system will default to a secure state in the event of a failure, blocking all access. A *fail-open* system will fail in an open state, granting all access. The choice is dependent on whether security or availability is more important after a failure.

For example, firewalls provide a significant amount of security by controlling access in and out of a network. They are configured with an implicit deny philosophy and only allow traffic that is explicitly allowed based on a rule. Firewalls are typically designed to be fail secure, supporting the implicit deny philosophy. If a firewall fails, all traffic is blocked. Although this eliminates availability of communication through the firewall, it is secure. In contrast, if availability of traffic was more important than security, the firewall could be configured to fail into a fail-open state, allowing all traffic through. This wouldn't be secure, but the network would not lose availability of traffic.

NOTE In the context of physical security with electrical hardware locks, the terms *fail safe* and *fail secure* are used. Specifically, a fail-safe electrical lock will be unlocked when power is removed, but a fail-secure electrical lock will be locked when power is removed. For example, emergency exit doors will be configured to be fail safe so that personnel are not locked inside during a fire or other emergency. In this case, safety is a primary concern if a failure occurs. In contrast, a bank vault will likely be configured to be fail secure so that it remains locked if power is removed because security is the primary concern with a bank vault door.

Two elements of the recovery process are addressed to implement a trusted solution. The first element is failure preparation. This includes system resilience and fault-tolerant methods in addition to a reliable backup solution. The second element is the process of system recovery. The system should be forced to reboot into a single-user, nonprivileged state. This means that the system should reboot so that a normal user account can be used to log in and that the system does not grant unauthorized access to users. System recovery also includes the restoration of all affected files and services actively in use on the system at the time of the failure or crash. Any missing or damaged files are restored, any changes to classification labels corrected, and settings on all security critical files are then verified.

The Common Criteria (introduced in Chapter 8, "Principles of Security Models, Design, and Capabilities") includes a section on trusted recovery that is relevant to system resilience and fault tolerance. Specifically, it defines four types of trusted recovery:

Manual Recovery If a system fails, it does not fail in a secure state. Instead, an administrator is required to manually perform the actions necessary to implement a secured or trusted recovery after a failure or system crash.

Automated Recovery The system is able to perform trusted recovery activities to restore itself against at least one type of failure. For example, a hardware RAID provides automated recovery against the failure of a hard drive but not against the failure of the entire server. Some types of failures will require manual recovery.

Automated Recovery without Undue Loss This is similar to automated recovery in that a system can restore itself against at least one type of failure. However, it includes mechanisms to ensure that specific objects are protected to prevent their loss. A method of automated recovery that protects against undue loss would include steps to restore data or other objects. It may include additional protection mechanisms to restore corrupted files, rebuild data from transaction logs, and verify the integrity of key system and security components.

Function Recovery Systems that support function recovery are able to automatically recover specific functions. This state ensures that the system is able to successfully complete the recovery for the functions, or that the system will be able to roll back the changes to return to a secure state.

Quality of Service

Quality of service (QoS) controls protect the integrity of data networks under load. Many different factors contribute to the quality of the end-user experience, and QoS attempts to manage all of those factors to create an experience that meets business requirements.

Some of the factors contributing to QoS are as follows:

Bandwidth The network capacity available to carry communications.

Latency The time it takes a packet to travel from source to destination.

Jitter The variation in latency between different packets.

Packet Loss Some packets may be lost between source and destination, requiring retransmission.

Interference Electrical noise, faulty equipment, and other factors may corrupt the contents of packets.

In addition to controlling these factors, QoS systems often prioritize certain traffic types that have low tolerance for interference and/or have high business requirements. For example, a QoS device might be programmed to prioritize videoconference traffic from the executive conference room over video streaming from an intern's computer.

Recovery Strategy

When a disaster interrupts your business, your disaster recovery plan should kick in nearly automatically and begin providing support for recovery operations. The disaster recovery plan should be designed so that the first employees on the scene can immediately begin the recovery effort in an organized fashion, even if members of the official DRP team have not yet arrived on site. In the following sections, we'll cover critical subtasks involved in crafting an effective disaster recovery plan that can guide rapid restoration of regular business processes and resumption of activity at the primary business location.

In addition to improving your response capabilities, purchasing insurance can reduce the risk of financial losses. When selecting insurance, be sure to purchase sufficient coverage to enable you to recover from a disaster. Simple value coverage may be insufficient to encompass actual replacement costs. If your property insurance includes an actual cash value (ACV) clause, then your damaged property will be compensated based on the fair market value of the items on the date of loss less all accumulated depreciation since the time of their purchase. The important point here is that unless you have a replacement cost clause in your insurance coverage, your organization is likely to be out of pocket as a result of any losses it might sustain.

Valuable paper insurance coverage provides protection for inscribed, printed, and written documents and manuscripts and other printed business records. However, it does not cover damage to paper money and printed security certificates.

Business Unit and Functional Priorities

To recover your business operations with the greatest possible efficiency, you must engineer your disaster recovery plan so that those business units with the highest priority are recovered first. You must identify and prioritize critical business functions as well so you can define which functions you want to restore after a disaster or failure and in what order.

To achieve this goal, the DRP team must first identify those business units and agree on an order of prioritization, and they must do likewise with business functions. (And take note: Not all critical business functions will necessarily be carried out in critical business units, so the final results of this analysis will very probably comprise a superset of critical business units plus other select units.)

If this process sounds familiar, it should! This is very like the prioritization task the BCP team performs during the business impact assessment discussed in Chapter 3. In fact, most organizations will complete a business impact assessment (BIA) as part of their business continuity planning process. This analysis identifies vulnerabilities, develops strategies to minimize risk, and ultimately produces a BIA report that describes the potential risks that an organization faces and identifies critical business units and functions. A BIA also identifies costs related to failures that include loss of cash flow, equipment replacement, salaries paid to clear work backlogs, profit losses, opportunity costs from the inability to attract new business, and so forth. Such failures are assessed in terms of potential impacts on finances, personnel, safety, legal compliance, contract fulfillment, and quality assurance, preferably in monetary terms to make impacts comparable and to set budgetary expectations. With all this BIA information in hand, you should use the resulting documentation as the basis for this prioritization task.

At a minimum, the output from this task should be a simple listing of business units in priority order. However, a more detailed list, broken down into specific business processes listed in order of priority, would be a much more useful deliverable. This business process–oriented list is more reflective of real-world conditions, but it requires considerable additional effort. It will, however, greatly assist in the recovery effort—after all, not every task performed by the highest-priority business unit will be of the highest priority. You might find that it would be best to restore the highest-priority unit to 50 percent capacity and then move on to lower-priority units to achieve some minimum operating capacity across the organization before attempting a full recovery effort.

By the same token, the same exercise must be completed for critical business processes and functions. Not only can these things involve multiple business units and cross the lines between them, but they also define the operational elements that must be restored in the wake of a disaster or other business interruption. Here also, the final result should be a checklist of items in priority order, each with its own risk and cost assessment, and a corresponding set of mean time to recovery (MTR) and related recovery objectives and milestones.

Crisis Management

If a disaster strikes your organization, panic is likely to set in. The best way to combat this is with an organized disaster recovery plan. The individuals in your business who are most likely to first notice an emergency situation (that is, security guards, technical personnel, and so on) should be fully trained in disaster recovery procedures and know the proper notification procedures and immediate response mechanisms.

Many things that normally seem like common sense (such as calling 911 in the event of a fire) may slip the minds of panicked employees seeking to flee an emergency. The best way to combat this is with continuous training on disaster recovery responsibilities. Returning to the fire example, all employees should be trained to activate the fire alarm or contact emergency officials when they spot a fire (after, of course, taking appropriate measures to protect themselves). After all, it's better that the fire department receives 10 different phone calls reporting a fire at your organization than it is for everyone to assume that someone else already took care of it.

Crisis management is a science and an art form. If your training budget permits, investing in crisis training for your key employees is a good idea. This ensures that at least some of your employees know how to handle emergency situations properly and can provide all-important "on-the-scene" leadership to panic-stricken co-workers.

Emergency Communications

When a disaster strikes, it is important that the organization be able to communicate internally as well as with the outside world. A disaster of any significance is easily noticed, but if an organization is unable to keep the outside world informed of its recovery status, the public is apt to fear the worst and assume that the organization is unable to recover. It is also essential that the organization be able to communicate internally during a disaster so that employees know what is expected of them—whether they are to return to work or report to another location, for instance.

In some cases, the circumstances that brought about the disaster to begin with may have also damaged some or all normal means of communications. A violent storm or an earthquake may have also knocked out telecommunications systems; at that point, it's too late to try to figure out other means of communicating both internally and externally.

Workgroup Recovery

When designing a disaster recovery plan, it's important to keep your goal in mind—the restoration of workgroups to the point that they can resume their activities in their usual work locations. It's easy to get sidetracked and think of disaster recovery as purely an IT effort focused on restoring systems and processes to working order.

To facilitate this effort, it's sometimes best to develop separate recovery facilities for different workgroups. For example, if you have several subsidiary organizations that are in different locations and that perform tasks similar to the tasks that workgroups at your office perform, you may want to consider temporarily relocating those workgroups to the other facility and having them communicate electronically and via telephone with other business units until they're ready to return to the main operations facility.

Larger organizations may have difficulty finding recovery facilities capable of handling the entire business operation. This is another example of a circumstance in which independent recovery of different workgroups is appropriate.

Alternate Processing Sites

One of the most important elements of the disaster recovery plan is the selection of alternate processing sites to be used when the primary sites are unavailable. Many options are available when considering recovery facilities, limited only by the creative minds of disaster recovery planners and service providers. In the following sections, we cover several types of sites commonly used in disaster recovery planning: cold sites, warm sites, hot sites, mobile sites, service bureaus, and multiple sites.

NOTE

When choosing any alternate processing site, be sure to situate it far away enough from your primary location that it won't be affected by the same disaster that disables your primary site. But it should be close enough that it takes less than a full day's drive to reach it.

Cold Sites

Cold sites are standby facilities large enough to handle the processing load of an organization and equipped with appropriate electrical and environmental support systems. They may be large warehouses, empty office buildings, or other similar structures. However, a cold site has no computing facilities (hardware or software) preinstalled and also has no active broadband communications links. Many cold sites do have at least a few copper telephone lines, and some sites may have standby links that can be activated with minimal notification.

Real World Scenario

Cold Site Setup

A cold site setup is well depicted in the 2000 film *Boiler Room*, which involves a chop-shop investment firm telemarketing bogus pharmaceutical investment deals to prospective clients. In this fictional case, the "disaster" is man-made, but the concept is much the same, even if the timing is quite different.

Under threat of exposure and a pending law enforcement raid, the firm establishes a nearby building that is empty, save for a few banks of phones on dusty concrete floors in a mock-up of a cold recovery site. Granted, this work is both fictional and illegal, but it illustrates a very real and legitimate reason for maintaining a redundant failover recovery site for the purpose of business continuity.

Research the various forms of recovery sites, and then consider which among them is best suited for your particular business needs and budget. A cold site is the least expensive option and perhaps the most practical. A warm site contains the data links and preconfigured equipment necessary to begin restoring operations but no usable data or information. The most expensive option is a hot site, which fully replicates your existing business infrastructure and is ready to take over for the primary site on short notice.

The major advantage of a cold site is its relatively low cost—there's no computing base to maintain and no monthly telecommunications bill when the site is idle. However, the drawbacks of such a site are obvious—there is a tremendous lag between the time the decision is made to activate the site and the time when that site is ready to support business operations. Servers and workstations must be brought in and configured. Data must be restored from backup tapes. Communications links must be activated or established. The time to activate a cold site is often measured in weeks, making timely recovery close to impossible and often yielding a false sense of security. It's also worth observing that the substantial time, effort, and expense required to activate and transfer operations to a cold site make this approach the most difficult to test.

Hot Sites

A *hot site* is the exact opposite of the cold site. In this configuration, a backup facility is maintained in constant working order, with a full complement of servers, workstations, and communications links ready to assume primary operations responsibilities. The servers and workstations are all preconfigured and loaded with appropriate operating system and application software.

The data on the primary site servers is periodically or continuously replicated to corresponding servers at the hot site, ensuring that the hot site has up-to-date data. Depending on the bandwidth available between the sites, hot site data may be replicated instantaneously. If that is the case, operators could move operations to the hot site at a moment's notice. If it's not the case, disaster recovery managers have three options to activate the hot site:

- If there is sufficient time before the primary site must be shut down, they can force replication between the two sites right before the transition of operational control.
- If replication is impossible, managers may carry backup tapes of the transaction logs from the primary site to the hot site and manually reapply any transactions that took place since the last replication.
- If there are no available backups and it isn't possible to force replication, the disaster recovery team may simply accept the loss of some portion of the data.

The advantages of a hot site are obvious—the level of disaster recovery protection provided by this type of site is unsurpassed. However, the cost is *extremely* high. Maintaining a hot site essentially doubles an organization's budget for hardware, software, and services and requires the use of additional employees to maintain the site.

WARNING If you use a hot site, never forget that it has copies of your production data. Be sure to provide that site with the same level of technical and physical security controls you provide at your primary site.

If an organization wants to maintain a hot site but wants to reduce the expense of equipment and maintenance, it might opt to use a shared hot site facility managed by an outside contractor. However, the inherent danger in these facilities is that they may be overtaxed in the event of a widespread disaster and be unable to service all clients simultaneously. If your organization considers such an arrangement, be sure to investigate these issues thoroughly, both before signing the contract and periodically during the contract term.

Warm Sites

Warm sites occupy the middle ground between hot and cold sites for disaster recovery specialists. They always contain the equipment and data circuits necessary to rapidly establish operations. As with hot sites, this equipment is usually preconfigured and ready to run appropriate applications to support an organization's operations. Unlike hot sites, however, warm sites do not typically contain copies of the client's data. The main requirement in bringing a warm site to full operational status is the transportation of appropriate backup media to the site and restoration of critical data on the standby servers.

Activation of a warm site typically takes at least 12 hours from the time a disaster is declared. This does not mean that any site that can be activated in less than 12 hours qualifies as a hot site, however; switchover times for most hot sites are often measured in seconds or minutes, and complete cutovers seldom take more than an hour or two.

Warm sites avoid significant telecommunications and personnel costs inherent in maintaining a near-real-time copy of the operational data environment. As with hot sites and cold sites, warm sites may also be obtained on a shared facility basis. If you choose this option, be sure that you have a "no lockout" policy written into your contract guaranteeing you the use of an appropriate facility even during a period of high demand. It's a good idea to take this concept one step further and physically inspect the facilities and the contractor's operational plan to reassure yourself that the facility will indeed be able to back up the "no lockout" guarantee should push ever come to shove.

Mobile Sites

Mobile sites are nonmainstream alternatives to traditional recovery sites. They typically consist of self-contained trailers or other easily relocated units. These sites include all the environmental control systems necessary to maintain a safe computing environment. Larger corporations sometimes maintain these sites on a "fly-away" basis, ready to deploy them to any operating location around the world via air, rail, sea, or surface transportation. Smaller firms might contract with a mobile site vendor in their local area to provide these services on an as-needed basis.

TIP

If your disaster recovery plan depends on a workgroup recovery strategy, mobile sites are an excellent way to implement that approach. They are often large enough to accommodate entire (small!) workgroups.

Mobile sites are usually configured as cold sites or warm sites, depending on the disaster recovery plan they are designed to support. It is also possible to configure a mobile site as a hot site, but this is unusual because you seldom know in advance where a mobile site will need to be deployed.

Hardware Replacement Options

One thing to consider when determining mobile sites and recovery sites in general is hardware replacement supplies. There are basically two options for hardware replacement supplies. One option is to employ "in-house" replacement, whereby you store extra and duplicate equipment at a different but nearby location (that is, a warehouse on the other side of town). (*In-house* here means you own it already, not that it is necessarily housed under the same roof as your production environment.) If you have a hardware failure or a disaster, you can immediately pull the appropriate equipment from your stash. The other option is an SLA-type agreement with a vendor to provide quick response and delivery time in the event of a disaster. However, even a 4-, 12-, 24-, or 48-hour replacement hardware contract from a vendor does not provide a reliable guarantee that delivery will actually occur. There are too many uncontrollable variables to rely on this second option as your sole means of recovery.

Service Bureaus

A *service bureau* is a company that leases computer time. Service bureaus own large server farms and often fields of workstations. Any organization can purchase a contract from a service bureau to consume some portion of their processing capacity. Access can be on site or remote.

A service bureau can usually provide support for all your IT needs in the event of a disaster—even desktops for workers to use. Your contract with a service bureau will often include testing and backups as well as response time and availability. However, service bureaus regularly oversell their actual capacity by gambling that not all their contracts will be exercised at the same time. Therefore, potential exists for resource contention in the wake of a major disaster. If your company operates in an industry-dense locale, this could be an important issue. You may need to select both a local and a distant service bureau to be sure to gain access to processing facilities during a real disaster.

Cloud Computing

Many organizations now turn to cloud computing as their preferred disaster recovery option. Infrastructure as a Service (IaaS) providers, such as Amazon Web Services, Microsoft Azure, and Google Compute Cloud, offer on-demand service at low cost. Companies wishing to maintain their own datacenters may choose to use these IaaS options as backup service providers. Storing ready-to-run images in cloud providers is often quite cost effective and allows the organization to avoid incurring most of the operating cost until the cloud site activates in a disaster.

Mutual Assistance Agreements

Mutual assistance agreements (MAAs), also called *reciprocal agreements*, are popular in disaster recovery literature but are rarely implemented in real-world practice. In theory, they provide an excellent alternate processing option. Under an MAA, two organizations pledge to assist each other in the event of a disaster by sharing computing facilities or other technological resources. They appear to be extremely cost effective at first glance—it's not necessary for either organization to maintain expensive alternate processing sites (such as the hot sites, warm sites, cold sites, and mobile processing sites described in the previous sections). Indeed, many MAAs are structured to provide one of the levels of service described. In the case of a cold site, each organization may simply maintain some open space in their processing facilities for the other organization to use in the event of a disaster. In the case of a hot site, the organizations may host fully redundant servers for each other.

However, many drawbacks inherent to MAAs prevent their widespread use:

- MAAs are difficult to enforce. The parties might trust each other to provide support in the event of a disaster. However, when push comes to shove, the nonvictim might renege on the agreement. A victim may have legal remedies available, but this doesn't help the immediate disaster recovery effort.
- Cooperating organizations should be located in relatively close proximity to each other to facilitate transportation of employees between sites. However, proximity means that both organizations may be vulnerable to the same threats. An MAA won't do you any good if an earthquake levels your city and destroys processing sites for *both* participating organizations.

- Confidentiality concerns often prevent businesses from placing their data in the hands of others. These may be legal concerns (such as in the handling of health-care or financial data) or business concerns (such as trade secrets or other intellectual property issues).

Despite these concerns, an MAA may be a good disaster recovery solution for an organization, especially if cost is an overriding factor. If you simply can't afford to implement any other type of alternate processing, an MAA might provide a degree of valuable protection in the event a localized disaster strikes your business.

Database Recovery

Many organizations rely on databases to process and track operations, sales, logistics, and other activities vital to their continued viability. For this reason, it's essential that you include database recovery techniques in your disaster recovery plans. It's a wise idea to have a database specialist on the DRP team who can provide input as to the technical feasibility of various ideas. After all, you shouldn't allocate several hours to restore a database backup when it's impossible to complete a restoration in less than half a day!

In the following sections, we'll cover the three main techniques used to create offsite copies of database content: electronic vaulting, remote journaling, and remote mirroring. Each one has specific benefits and drawbacks, so you'll need to analyze your organization's computing requirements and available resources to select the option best suited to your firm.

Electronic Vaulting

In an *electronic vaulting* scenario, database backups are moved to a remote site using bulk transfers. The remote location may be a dedicated alternative recovery site (such as a hot site) or simply an offsite location managed within the company or by a contractor for the purpose of maintaining backup data.

If you use electronic vaulting, remember that there may be a significant delay between the time you declare a disaster and the time your database is ready for operation with current data. If you decide to activate a recovery site, technicians will need to retrieve the appropriate backups from the electronic vault and apply them to the soon-to-be production servers at the recovery site.

WARNING

Be careful when considering vendors for an electronic vaulting contract. Definitions of electronic vaulting vary widely within the industry. Don't settle for a vague promise of "electronic vaulting capability." Insist on a written definition of the service that will be provided, including the storage capacity, bandwidth of the communications link to the electronic vault, and the time necessary to retrieve vaulted data in the event of a disaster.

As with any type of backup scenario, be certain to periodically test your electronic vaulting setup. A great method for testing backup solutions is to give disaster recovery personnel a "surprise test," asking them to restore data from a certain day.

Remote Journaling

With *remote journaling*, data transfers are performed in a more expeditious manner. Data transfers still occur in a bulk transfer mode, but they occur on a more frequent basis, usually once every hour and sometimes more frequently. Unlike electronic vaulting scenarios, where entire database backup files are transferred, remote journaling setups transfer copies of the database transaction logs containing the transactions that occurred since the previous bulk transfer.

Remote journaling is similar to electronic vaulting in that transaction logs transferred to the remote site are not applied to a live database server but are maintained in a backup device. When a disaster is declared, technicians retrieve the appropriate transaction logs and apply them to the production database.

Remote Mirroring

Remote mirroring is the most advanced database backup solution. Not surprisingly, it's also the most expensive! Remote mirroring goes beyond the technology used by remote journaling and electronic vaulting; with remote mirroring, a live database server is maintained at the backup site. The remote server receives copies of the database modifications at the same time they are applied to the production server at the primary site. Therefore, the mirrored server is ready to take over an operational role at a moment's notice.

Remote mirroring is a popular database backup strategy for organizations seeking to implement a hot site. However, when weighing the feasibility of a remote mirroring solution, be sure to take into account the infrastructure and personnel costs required to support the mirrored server as well as the processing overhead that will be added to each database transaction on the mirrored server.

Recovery Plan Development

Once you've established your business unit priorities and have a good idea of the appropriate alternative recovery sites for your organization, it's time to put pen to paper and begin drafting a true disaster recovery plan. Don't expect to sit down and write the full plan in one sitting. It's likely that the DRP team will go through many draft documents before reaching a final written document that satisfies the operational needs of critical business units and falls within the resource, time, and expense constraints of the disaster recovery budget and available personnel.

In the following sections, we explore some important items to include in your disaster recovery plan. Depending on the size of your organization and the number of people involved in the DRP effort, it may be a good idea to maintain multiple types of plan documents, intended for different audiences. The following list includes various types of documents worth considering:

- Executive summary providing a high-level overview of the plan
- Department-specific plans
- Technical guides for IT personnel responsible for implementing and maintaining critical backup systems
- Checklists for individuals on the disaster recovery team
- Full copies of the plan for critical disaster recovery team members

Using custom-tailored documents becomes especially important when a disaster occurs or is imminent. Personnel who need to refresh themselves on the disaster recovery procedures that affect various parts of the organization will be able to refer to their department-specific plans. Critical disaster recovery team members will have checklists to help guide their actions amid the chaotic atmosphere of a disaster. IT personnel will have technical guides helping them get the alternate sites up and running. Finally, managers and public relations personnel will have a simple document that walks them through a high-level view of the coordinated symphony that is an active disaster recovery effort without requiring interpretation from team members busy with tasks directly related to that effort.

TIP

Visit the Professional Practices library at `https://www.drii.org/certification/professionalprac.php` to examine a collection of documents that explain how to work through and document your planning processes for BCP and disaster recovery. Other good standard documents in this area includes the BCI Good Practices Guideline (`http://thebci.org/index.php/resources/the-good-practice-guidelines`), ISO 27001 (`www.27001-online.com`), and NIST SP 800-34 (`http://csrc.nist.gov/publications/PubsSPs.html`).

Emergency Response

A disaster recovery plan should contain simple yet comprehensive instructions for essential personnel to follow immediately upon recognizing that a disaster is in progress or is imminent. These instructions will vary widely depending on the nature of the disaster, the type of personnel responding to the incident, and the time available before facilities need to be evacuated and/or equipment shut down. For example, instructions for a large-scale fire will be much more concise than the instructions for how to prepare for a hurricane that is still 48 hours away from a predicted landfall near an operational site. Emergency-response plans are often put together in the form of checklists provided to responders. When designing such checklists, keep one essential design principle in mind: arrange the checklist tasks in order of priority, with the most important task first!

It's essential to remember that these checklists will be executed in the midst of a crisis. It is extremely likely that responders will not be able to complete the entire checklist, especially in the event of a short-notice disaster. For this reason, you should put the most essential tasks (that is, "Activate the building alarm") first on the checklist. The lower an item on the list, the lower the likelihood that it will be completed before an evacuation/shutdown takes place.

Personnel and Communications

A disaster recovery plan should also contain a list of personnel to contact in the event of a disaster. Usually, this includes key members of the DRP team as well as personnel who execute critical disaster recovery tasks throughout the organization. This response checklist should include alternate means of contact (that is, pager numbers, mobile phone numbers, and so on) as well as backup contacts for each role should the primary contact be incommunicado or unable to reach the recovery site for one reason or another.

The Power of Checklists

Checklists are invaluable tools in the face of disaster. They provide a sense of order amidst the chaotic events surrounding a disaster. Do what you must to ensure that response checklists provide first responders with a clear plan to protect life and property and ensure the continuity of operations.

A checklist for response to a building fire might include the following steps:

1. Activate the building alarm system.
2. Ensure that an orderly evacuation is in progress.
3. After leaving the building, use a mobile telephone to call 911 to ensure that emergency authorities received the alarm notification. Provide additional information on any required emergency response.
4. Ensure that any injured personnel receive appropriate medical treatment.
5. Activate the organization's disaster recovery plan to ensure continuity of operations.

Be sure to consult with the individuals in your organization responsible for privacy before assembling and disseminating a telephone notification checklist. You may need to comply with special policies regarding the use of home telephone numbers and other personal information in the checklist.

The notification checklist should be supplied to all personnel who might respond to a disaster. This enables prompt notification of key personnel. Many firms organize their notification checklists in a "telephone tree" style: Each member of the tree contacts the person below them, spreading the notification burden among members of the team instead of relying on one person to make lots of telephone calls.

If you choose to implement a telephone tree notification scheme, be sure to add a safety net. Have the last person in each chain contact the originator to confirm that their entire chain has been notified. This lets you rest assured that the disaster recovery team activation is smoothly underway.

Assessment

When the disaster recovery team arrives on site, one of their first tasks is to assess the situation. This normally occurs in a rolling fashion, with the first responders performing a very simple assessment to triage activity and get the disaster response underway. As the incident progresses, more detailed assessments will take place to gauge the effectiveness of disaster recovery efforts and prioritize the assignment of resources.

Backups and Offsite Storage

Your disaster recovery plan (especially the technical guide) should fully address the backup strategy pursued by your organization. Indeed, this is one of the most important elements of any business continuity plan and disaster recovery plan.

Many system administrators are already familiar with various types of backups, so you'll benefit by bringing one or more individuals with specific technical expertise in this area onto the BCP/DRP team to provide expert guidance. There are three main types of backups:

Full Backups As the name implies, *full backups* store a complete copy of the data contained on the protected device. Full backups duplicate every file on the system regardless of the setting of the archive bit. Once a full backup is complete, the archive bit on every file is reset, turned off, or set to 0.

Incremental Backups *Incremental backups* store only those files that have been modified since the time of the most recent full or incremental backup. Only files that have the archive bit turned on, enabled, or set to 1 are duplicated. Once an incremental backup is complete, the archive bit on all duplicated files is reset, turned off, or set to 0.

Differential Backups *Differential backups* store all files that have been modified since the time of the most recent full backup. Only files that have the archive bit turned on, enabled, or set to 1 are duplicated. However, unlike full and incremental backups, the differential backup process does not change the archive bit.

The most important difference between incremental and differential backups is the time needed to restore data in the event of an emergency. If you use a combination of full and differential backups, you will need to restore only two backups—the most recent full backup and the most recent differential backup. On the other hand, if your strategy combines full backups with incremental backups, you will need to restore the most recent full backup as well as all incremental backups performed since that full backup. The trade-off is the time required to *create* the backups—differential backups don't take as long to restore, but they take longer to create than incremental ones.

The storage of the backup media is equally critical. It may be convenient to store backup media in or near the primary operations center to easily fulfill user requests for backup data, but you'll definitely need to keep copies of the media in at least one offsite location to provide redundancy should your primary operating location be suddenly destroyed.

Using Backups

In case of system failure, many companies use one of two common methods to restore data from backups. In the first situation, they run a full backup on Monday night and then run differential backups every other night of the week. If a failure occurs Saturday morning, they restore Monday's full backup and then restore only Friday's differential backup. In the second situation, they run a full backup on Monday night and run incremental backups every other night of the week. If a failure occurs Saturday morning, they restore Monday's full backup and then restore each incremental backup in original chronological order (that is, Wednesday's, then Friday's, and so on).

Most organizations adopt a backup strategy that utilizes more than one of the three backup types along with a media rotation scheme. Both allow backup administrators access to a sufficiently large range of backups to complete user requests and provide fault tolerance while minimizing the amount of money that must be spent on backup media. A common strategy is to perform full backups over the weekend and incremental or differential backups on a nightly basis. The specific method of backup and all of the particulars of the backup procedure are dependent on your organization's fault-tolerance requirements. If you are unable to survive minor amounts of data loss, your ability to tolerate faults is low. However, if hours or days of data can be lost without serious consequence, your tolerance of faults is high. You should design your backup solution accordingly.

Real World Scenario

The Oft-Neglected Backup

Backups are probably the least practiced and most neglected preventive measure known to protect against computing disasters. A comprehensive backup of all operating system and personal data on workstations happens less frequently than for servers or mission-critical machines, but they all serve an equal and necessary purpose.

Damon, an information professional, learned this the hard way when he lost months of work following a natural disaster that wiped out the first floor at an information brokering firm. He never used the backup facilities built into his operating system or any of the shared provisions established by his administrator, Carol.

Carol has been there and done that, so she knows a thing or two about backup solutions. She has established incremental backups on her production servers and differential backups on her development servers, and she's never had an issue restoring lost data.

The toughest obstacle to a solid backup strategy is human nature, so a simple, transparent, and comprehensive strategy is the most practical. Differential backups require only two container files (the latest full backup and the latest differential) and can be scheduled for periodic updates at some specified interval. That's why Carol elects to implement this approach and feels ready to restore from her backups any time she's called on to do so.

Backup Tape Formats

The physical characteristics and the rotation cycle are two factors that a worthwhile backup solution should track and manage. The physical characteristics involve the type of tape drive in use. This defines the physical wear placed on the media. The rotation cycle is the frequency of backups and retention length of protected data. By overseeing these characteristics, you can be assured that valuable data will be retained on serviceable backup media. Backup media has a maximum use limit; perhaps 5, 10, or 20 rewrites may be made before the media begins to lose reliability (statistically speaking). A wide variety of backup tape formats exist:

- Digital Data Storage (DDS)/Digital Audio Tape (DAT)
- Digital Linear Tape (DLT) and Super DLT
- Linear Tape Open (LTO)

Disk-to-Disk Backup

Over the past decade, disk storage has become increasingly inexpensive. With drive capacities now measured in terabytes (TB), tape and optical media can't cope with data volume requirements anymore. Many enterprises now use disk-to-disk (D2D) backup solutions for some portion of their disaster recovery strategy.

One important note: Organizations seeking to adopt an entirely disk-to-disk approach must remember to maintain geographical diversity. Some of those disks have to be located offsite. Many organizations solve this problem by hiring managed service providers to manage remote backup locations.

TIP

As transfer and storage costs come down, cloud-based backup solutions are becoming more cost effective. You may wish to consider using such a service as an alternative to physically transporting backup tapes to a remote location.

Backup Best Practices

No matter what the backup solution, media, or method, you must address several common issues with backups. For instance, backup and restoration activities can be bulky and slow. Such data movement can significantly affect the performance of a network, especially during regular production hours. Thus, backups should be scheduled during the low peak periods (for example, at night).

The amount of backup data increases over time. This causes the backup (and restoration) processes to take longer each time and to consume more space on the backup media. Thus, you need to build sufficient capacity to handle a reasonable amount of growth over a reasonable amount of time into your backup solution. What is reasonable all depends on your environment and budget.

With periodic backups (that is, backups that are run every 24 hours), there is always the potential for data loss up to the length of the period. Murphy's law dictates that a server never crashes immediately after a successful backup. Instead, it is always just before the next backup begins. To avoid the problem with periods, you need to deploy some form of real-time continuous backup, such as RAID, clustering, or server mirroring.

Finally, remember to test your organization's recovery processes. Organizations often rely on the fact that their backup software reports a successful backup and fail to attempt recovery until it's too late to detect a problem. This is one of the biggest causes of backup failures.

Tape Rotation

There are several commonly used tape rotation strategies for backups: the Grandfather-Father-Son (GFS) strategy, the Tower of Hanoi strategy, and the Six Cartridge Weekly Backup strategy. These strategies can be fairly complex, especially with large tape sets. They can be implemented manually using a pencil and a calendar or automatically by using either commercial backup software or a fully automated hierarchical storage management (HSM) system. An HSM system is an automated robotic backup jukebox consisting of 32 or 64 optical or tape backup devices. All the drive elements within an HSM system are configured as a single drive array (a bit like RAID).

> **NOTE** Details about various tape rotations are beyond the scope of this book, but if you want to learn more about them, search by their names on the Internet.

Software Escrow Arrangements

A *software escrow arrangement* is a unique tool used to protect a company against the failure of a software developer to provide adequate support for its products or against the possibility that the developer will go out of business and no technical support will be available for the product.

> **TIP** Focus your efforts on negotiating software escrow agreements with those suppliers you fear may go out of business because of their size. It's not likely that you'll be able to negotiate such an agreement with a firm such as Microsoft, unless you are responsible for an extremely large corporate account with serious bargaining power. On the other hand, it's equally unlikely that a firm of Microsoft's magnitude will go out of business, leaving end users high and dry.

If your organization depends on custom-developed software or software products produced by a small firm, you may want to consider developing this type of arrangement as part of your disaster recovery plan. Under a software escrow agreement, the developer provides copies of the application source code to an independent third-party organization. This third party then maintains updated backup copies of the source code in a secure fashion. The agreement between the end user and the developer specifies "trigger events," such as the failure of the developer to meet terms of a service-level agreement (SLA) or the liquidation of the developer's firm. When a trigger event takes place, the third party releases copies of the application source code to the end user. The end user can then analyze the source code to resolve application issues or implement software updates.

External Communications

During the disaster recovery process, it will be necessary to communicate with various entities outside your organization. You will need to contact vendors to provide supplies as they are needed to support the disaster recovery effort. Your clients will want to contact you for reassurance that you are still in operation. Public relations officials may need to contact the media or investment firms, and managers may need to speak to governmental authorities. For these reasons, it is essential that your disaster recovery plan include appropriate channels of communication to the outside world in a quantity sufficient to meet your operational needs. Usually, it is not a sound business or recovery practice to use the CEO as your spokesperson during a disaster. A media liaison should be hired, trained, and prepared to take on this responsibility.

Utilities

As discussed in previous sections of this chapter, your organization is reliant on several utilities to provide critical elements of your infrastructure—electric power, water, natural gas, sewer service, and so on. Your disaster recovery plan should contain contact information and procedures to troubleshoot these services if problems arise during a disaster.

Logistics and Supplies

The logistical problems surrounding a disaster recovery operation are immense. You will suddenly face the problem of moving large numbers of people, equipment, and supplies to alternate recovery sites. It's also possible that the people will be living at those sites for an extended period of time and that the disaster recovery team will be responsible for providing them with food, water, shelter, and appropriate facilities. Your disaster recovery plan should contain provisions for this type of operation if it falls within the scope of your expected operational needs.

Recovery vs. Restoration

It is sometimes useful to separate disaster recovery tasks from disaster restoration tasks. This is especially true when a recovery effort is expected to take a significant amount of time. A disaster recovery team may be assigned to implement and maintain operations at the recovery site, and a salvage team is assigned to restore the primary site to operational capacity. Make these allocations according to the needs of your organization and the types of disasters you face.

NOTE *Recovery* and *restoration* are separate concepts. In this context, recovery involves bringing business *operations and processes* back to a working state. Restoration involves bringing a business *facility and environment* back to a workable state.

The recovery team members have a very short time frame in which to operate. They must put the DRP into action and restore IT capabilities as swiftly as possible. If the recovery team fails to restore business processes within the MTD/RTO, then the company fails.

Once the original site is deemed safe for people, the salvage team members begin their work. Their job is to restore the company to its full original capabilities and, if necessary, to the original location. If the original location is no longer in existence, a new primary spot is selected. The salvage team must rebuild or repair the IT infrastructure. Since this activity is basically the same as building a new IT system, the return activity from the alternate/recovery site to the primary/original site is itself a risky activity. Fortunately, the salvage team has more time to work than the recovery team.

The salvage team must ensure the reliability of the new IT infrastructure. This is done by returning the least mission-critical processes to the restored original site to stress-test the rebuilt network. As the restored site shows resiliency, more important processes are transferred. A serious vulnerability exists when mission-critical processes are returned to the original site. The act of returning to the original site could cause a disaster of its own. Therefore, the state of emergency cannot be declared over until full normal operations have returned to the restored original site.

At the conclusion of any disaster recovery effort, the time will come to restore operations at the primary site and terminate any processing sites operating under the disaster recovery agreement. Your DRP should specify the criteria used to determine when it is appropriate to return to the primary site and guide the DRP recovery and salvage teams through an orderly transition.

Training, Awareness, and Documentation

As with a business continuity plan, it is essential that you provide training to all personnel who will be involved in the disaster recovery effort. The level of training required will vary according to an individual's role in the effort and their position within the company. When designing a training plan, consider including the following elements:

- Orientation training for all new employees
- Initial training for employees taking on a new disaster recovery role for the first time
- Detailed refresher training for disaster recovery team members
- Brief awareness refreshers for all other employees (can be accomplished as part of other meetings and through a medium like email newsletters sent to all employees)

TIP

Loose-leaf binders are an excellent way to store disaster recovery plans. You can distribute single-page changes to the plan without destroying a national forest!

The disaster recovery plan should also be fully documented. Earlier in this chapter, we discussed several of the documentation options available to you. Be sure you implement the necessary documentation programs and modify the documentation as changes to the plan occur. Because of the rapidly changing nature of the disaster recovery and business continuity plans, you might consider publication on a secured portion of your organization's intranet.

Your DRP should be treated as an extremely sensitive document and provided to individuals on a compartmentalized, need-to-know basis only. Individuals who participate in the plan should understand their roles fully, but they do not need to know or have access to the entire plan. Of course, it is essential to ensure that key DRP team members and senior management have access to the entire plan and understand the high-level implementation details. You certainly don't want this knowledge to rest in the mind of only one individual.

WARNING

Remember that a disaster may render your intranet unavailable. If you choose to distribute your disaster recovery and business continuity plans through an intranet, be sure you maintain an adequate number of printed copies of the plan at both the primary and alternate sites and maintain only the most current copy!

Testing and Maintenance

Every disaster recovery plan must be tested on a periodic basis to ensure that the plan's provisions are viable and that it meets an organization's changing needs. The types of tests that you conduct will depend on the types of recovery facilities available to you, the culture of your organization, and the availability of disaster recovery team members. The five main test types—checklist tests, structured walk-throughs, simulation tests, parallel tests, and full-interruption tests—are discussed in the remaining sections of this chapter.

Read-Through Test

The *read-through test* is one of the simplest tests to conduct, but it's also one of the most critical. In this test, you distribute copies of disaster recovery plans to the members of the disaster recovery team for review. This lets you accomplish three goals simultaneously:

- It ensures that key personnel are aware of their responsibilities and have that knowledge refreshed periodically.

- It provides individuals with an opportunity to review the plans for obsolete information and update any items that require modification because of changes within the organization.
- In large organizations, it helps identify situations in which key personnel have left the company and nobody bothered to reassign their disaster recovery responsibilities. This is also a good reason why disaster recovery responsibilities should be included in job descriptions.

Structured Walk-Through

A *structured walk-through* takes testing one step further. In this type of test, often referred to as a *table-top exercise*, members of the disaster recovery team gather in a large conference room and role-play a disaster scenario. Usually, the exact scenario is known only to the test moderator, who presents the details to the team at the meeting. The team members then refer to their copies of the disaster recovery plan and discuss the appropriate responses to that particular type of disaster.

Simulation Test

Simulation tests are similar to the structured walk-throughs. In simulation tests, disaster recovery team members are presented with a scenario and asked to develop an appropriate response. Unlike with the tests previously discussed, some of these response measures are then tested. This may involve the interruption of noncritical business activities and the use of some operational personnel.

Parallel Test

Parallel tests represent the next level in testing and involve relocating personnel to the alternate recovery site and implementing site activation procedures. The employees relocated to the site perform their disaster recovery responsibilities just as they would for an actual disaster. The only difference is that operations at the main facility are not interrupted. That site retains full responsibility for conducting the day-to-day business of the organization.

Full-Interruption Test

Full-interruption tests operate like parallel tests, but they involve actually shutting down operations at the primary site and shifting them to the recovery site. For obvious reasons, full-interruption tests are extremely difficult to arrange, and you often encounter resistance from management.

Maintenance

Remember that a disaster recovery plan is a living document. As your organization's needs change, you must adapt the disaster recovery plan to meet those changed needs to follow suit. You will discover many necessary modifications by using a well-organized and coordinated testing plan. Minor changes may often be made through a series of telephone conversations or emails, whereas major changes may require one or more meetings of the full disaster recovery team.

A disaster recovery planner should refer to the organization's business continuity plan as a template for its recovery efforts. This and all the supportive material must comply with federal regulations and reflect current business needs. Business processes such as payroll and order generation should contain specified metrics mapped to related IT systems and infrastructure.

Most organizations apply formal change management processes so that whenever the IT infrastructure changes, all relevant documentation is updated and checked to reflect such changes. Regularly scheduled fire drills and dry runs to ensure that all elements of the DRP are used properly to keep staff trained present a perfect opportunity to integrate changes into regular maintenance and change management procedures. Design, implement, and document changes each time you go through these processes and exercises. Know where everything is, and keep each element of the DRP working properly. In case of emergency, use your recovery plan. Finally, make sure the staff stays trained to keep their skills sharp—for existing support personnel—and use simulated exercises to bring new people up to speed quickly.

Summary

Disaster recovery planning is critical to a comprehensive information security program. No matter how comprehensive your business continuity plan, the day may come when your business is interrupted by a disaster and you face the task of restoring operations to the primary site quickly and efficiently.

In this chapter, you learned about the different types of natural and man-made disasters that may impact your business. You also explored the types of recovery sites and backup strategies that bolster your recovery capabilities.

An organization's disaster recovery plan is one of the most important documents under the purview of security professionals. It should provide guidance to the personnel responsible for ensuring the continuity of operations in the face of disaster. The DRP provides an orderly sequence of events designed to activate alternate processing sites while simultaneously restoring the primary site to operational status. Once you've successfully developed your DRP, you must train personnel on its use, ensure that you maintain accurate documentation, and conduct periodic tests to keep the plan fresh in the minds of responders.

Exam Essentials

Know the common types of natural disasters that may threaten an organization. Natural disasters that commonly threaten organizations include earthquakes, floods, storms, fires, tsunamis, and volcanic eruptions.

Know the common types of man-made disasters that may threaten an organization. Explosions, electrical fires, terrorist acts, power outages, other utility failures, infrastructure failures, hardware/software failures, labor difficulties, theft, and vandalism are all common man-made disasters.

Be familiar with the common types of recovery facilities. The common types of recovery facilities are cold sites, warm sites, hot sites, mobile sites, service bureaus, and multiple sites. Be sure you understand the benefits and drawbacks for each such facility.

Explain the potential benefits behind mutual assistance agreements as well as the reasons they are not commonly implemented in businesses today. Mutual assistance agreements (MAAs) provide an inexpensive alternative to disaster recovery sites, but they are not commonly used because they are difficult to enforce. Organizations participating in an MAA may also be shut down by the same disaster, and MAAs raise confidentiality concerns.

Understand the technologies that may assist with database backup. Databases benefit from three backup technologies. Electronic vaulting is used to transfer database backups to a remote site as part of a bulk transfer. In remote journaling, data transfers occur on a more frequent basis. With remote mirroring technology, database transactions are mirrored at the backup site in real time.

Know the five types of disaster recovery plan tests and the impact each has on normal business operations. The five types of disaster recovery plan tests are read-through tests, structured walk-throughs, simulation tests, parallel tests, and full-interruption tests. Checklist tests are purely paperwork exercises, whereas structured walk-throughs involve a project team meeting. Neither has an impact on business operations. Simulation tests may shut down noncritical business units. Parallel tests involve relocating personnel but do not affect day-to-day operations. Full-interruption tests involve shutting down primary systems and shifting responsibility to the recovery facility.

Written Lab

1. What are some of the main concerns businesses have when considering adopting a mutual assistance agreement?
2. List and explain the five types of disaster recovery tests.
3. Explain the differences between the three types of backup strategies discussed in this chapter.

Review Questions

1. What is the end goal of disaster recovery planning?
   A. Preventing business interruption
   B. Setting up temporary business operations
   C. Restoring normal business activity
   D. Minimizing the impact of a disaster

2. Which one of the following is an example of a man-made disaster?
   A. Tsunami
   B. Earthquake
   C. Power outage
   D. Lightning strike

3. According to the Federal Emergency Management Agency, approximately what percentage of U.S. states is rated with at least a moderate risk of seismic activity?
   A. 20 percent
   B. 40 percent
   C. 60 percent
   D. 80 percent

4. Which one of the following disaster types is not usually covered by standard business or homeowner's insurance?
   A. Earthquake
   B. Flood
   C. Fire
   D. Theft

5. In the wake of the September 11, 2001 terrorist attacks, what industry made drastic changes that directly impact DRP/BCP activities?
   A. Tourism
   B. Banking
   C. Insurance
   D. Airline

6. Which of the following statements about business continuity planning and disaster recovery planning is incorrect?
   A. Business continuity planning is focused on keeping business functions uninterrupted when a disaster strikes.
   B. Organizations can choose whether to develop business continuity planning or disaster recovery planning plans.

C. Business continuity planning picks up where disaster recovery planning leaves off.

D. Disaster recovery planning guides an organization through recovery of normal operations at the primary facility.

7. What does the term "100-year flood plain" mean to emergency preparedness officials?

A. The last flood of any kind to hit the area was more than 100 years ago.

B. The odds of a flood at this level are 1 in 100 in any given year.

C. The area is expected to be safe from flooding for at least 100 years.

D. The last significant flood to hit the area was more than 100 years ago.

8. In which one of the following database recovery techniques is an exact, up-to-date copy of the database maintained at an alternative location?

A. Transaction logging

B. Remote journaling

C. Electronic vaulting

D. Remote mirroring

9. What disaster recovery principle best protects your organization against hardware failure?

A. Consistency

B. Efficiency

C. Redundancy

D. Primacy

10. What business continuity planning technique can help you prepare the business unit prioritization task of disaster recovery planning?

A. Vulnerability analysis

B. Business impact assessment

C. Risk management

D. Continuity planning

11. Which one of the following alternative processing sites takes the longest time to activate?

A. Hot site

B. Mobile site

C. Cold site

D. Warm site

12. What is the typical time estimate to activate a warm site from the time a disaster is declared?

A. 1 hour

B. 6 hours

C. 12 hours

D. 24 hours

13. Which one of the following items is a characteristic of hot sites but not a characteristic of warm sites?
    A. Communications circuits
    B. Workstations
    C. Servers
    D. Current data

14. What type of database backup strategy involves maintenance of a live backup server at the remote site?
    A. Transaction logging
    B. Remote journaling
    C. Electronic vaulting
    D. Remote mirroring

15. What type of document will help public relations specialists and other individuals who need a high-level summary of disaster recovery efforts while they are underway?
    A. Executive summary
    B. Technical guides
    C. Department-specific plans
    D. Checklists

16. What disaster recovery planning tool can be used to protect an organization against the failure of a critical software firm to provide appropriate support for their products?
    A. Differential backups
    B. Business impact assessment
    C. Incremental backups
    D. Software escrow agreement

17. What type of backup involves always storing copies of all files modified since the most recent full backup?
    A. Differential backups
    B. Partial backup
    C. Incremental backups
    D. Database backup

18. What combination of backup strategies provides the fastest backup creation time?
    A. Full backups and differential backups
    B. Partial backups and incremental backups
    C. Full backups and incremental backups
    D. Incremental backups and differential backups

19. What combination of backup strategies provides the fastest backup restoration time?
    A. Full backups and differential backups
    B. Partial backups and incremental backups
    C. Full backups and incremental backups
    D. Incremental backups and differential backups

20. What type of disaster recovery plan test fully evaluates operations at the backup facility but does not shift primary operations responsibility from the main site?
    A. Structured walk-through
    B. Parallel test
    C. Full-interruption test
    D. Simulation test

Chapter 19

Incidents and Ethics

THE CISSP EXAM TOPICS COVERED IN THIS CHAPTER INCLUDE:

✓ **1. Security and Risk Management**

- E. Understand professional ethics
  - E.1 Exercise (ISC)^2 Code of Professional Ethics
  - E.2 Support organization's code of ethics

✓ **7. Security Operations**

- A. Understand and support investigations
  - A.1 Evidence collection and handling (e.g., chain of custody, interviewing)
  - A.2 Reporting and documenting
  - A.3 Investigative techniques (e.g., root-cause analysis, incident handling)
  - A.4 Digital forensics (e.g. media, network, software, and embedded devices)
- B. Understand requirements for investigation types
  - B.1 Operational
  - B.2 Criminal
  - B.3 Civil
  - B.4 Regulatory
  - B.5 Electronic discovery (eDiscovery)

In this chapter, we explore the process of incident handling, including investigative techniques used to determine whether a computer crime has been committed and to collect evidence when appropriate. This chapter also includes a complete discussion of ethical issues and the code of conduct for information security practitioners.

The first step in deciding how to respond to a computer attack is to know if and when an attack has taken place. You must know how to determine that an attack is occurring, or has occurred, before you can properly choose a course of action. Once you have determined that an incident has occurred, the next step is to conduct an investigation and collect evidence to find out what has happened and determine the extent of any damage that might have been done. You must be sure you conduct the investigation in accordance with local laws and regulations.

Investigations

Every information security professional will, at one time or another, encounter a security incident that requires an investigation. In many cases, this investigation will be a brief, informal determination that the matter is not serious enough to warrant further action or the involvement of law enforcement authorities. However, in some cases, the threat posed or damage done will be severe enough to require a more formal inquiry. When this occurs, investigators must be careful to ensure that proper procedures are followed. Failure to abide by the correct procedures may violate the civil rights of those individual(s) being investigated and could result in a failed prosecution or even legal action against the investigator.

Investigation Types

Security practitioners may find themselves conducting investigations for a wide variety of reasons. Some of these investigations involve law enforcement and must follow rigorous standards designed to produce evidence that will be admissible in court. Other investigations support internal business processes and require much less rigor.

Operational Investigations

Operational investigations examine issues related to the organization's computing infrastructure and have the primary goal of resolving operational issues. For example, an IT team noticing performance issues on their web servers may conduct an operational investigation designed to determine the cause of the performance problems.

TIP Operational investigations may quickly transition to another type of investigation. For example, an investigation into a performance issue may uncover evidence of a system intrusion that may then become a criminal investigation.

Operational investigations have the loosest standards for collection of information. They are not intended to produce evidence because they are for internal operational purposes only. Therefore, administrators conducting an operational investigation will only conduct analysis necessary to reach their operational conclusions. The collection need not be thorough or well-documented, because resolving the issue is the primary goal.

In addition to resolving the operational issue, operational investigations also often conduct a *root cause analysis* that seeks to identify the reason that an operational issue occurred. The root cause analysis often highlights issues that require remediation to prevent similar incidents in the future.

Criminal Investigations

Criminal investigations, typically conducted by law enforcement personnel, investigate the alleged violation of criminal law. Criminal investigations may result in charging suspects with a crime and the prosecution of those charges in criminal court.

Most criminal cases must meet the *beyond a reasonable doubt* standard of evidence. Following this standard, the prosecution must demonstrate that the defendant committed the crime by presenting facts from which there are no other logical conclusions. For this reason, criminal investigations must follow very strict evidence collection and preservation processes.

Civil Investigations

Civil investigations typically do not involve law enforcement but rather involve internal employees and outside consultants working on behalf of a legal team. They prepare the evidence necessary to present a case in civil court resolving a dispute between two parties.

Most civil cases do not follow the beyond a reasonable doubt standard of proof. Instead, they use the weaker *preponderance of the evidence* standard. Meeting this standard simply requires that the evidence demonstrate that the outcome of the case is more likely than not. For this reason, evidence collection standards for civil investigations are not as rigorous as those used in criminal investigations.

Regulatory Investigations

Government agencies may conduct regulatory investigations when they believe that an individual or corporation has violated administrative law. Regulators typically conduct these investigations with a standard of proof commensurate with the venue where they expect to try their case. Regulatory investigations vary widely in scope and procedure and are almost always conducted by government agents.

Electronic Discovery

In legal proceedings, each side has a duty to preserve evidence related to the case and, through the discovery process, share information with their adversary in the proceedings. This discovery process applies to both paper records and electronic records and the electronic discovery (or eDiscovery) process facilitates the processing of electronic information for disclosure.

The Electronic Discovery Reference Model describes a standard process for conducting eDiscovery with nine steps:

Information Governance ensures that information is well organized for future eDiscovery efforts

Identification locates the information that may be responsive to a discovery request when the organization believes that litigation is likely.

Preservation ensures that potentially discoverable information is protected against alteration or deletion.

Collection gathers the responsive information centrally for use in the eDiscovery process

Processing screens the collected information to perform a "rough cut" of irrelevant information, reducing the amount of information requiring detailed screening.

Review examines the remaining information to determine what information is responsive to the request and removing any information protected by attorney-client privilege.

Analysis performs deeper inspection of the content and context of remaining information.

Production places the information into a format that may be shared with others.

Presentation displays the information to witnesses, the court and other parties.

Conducting eDiscovery is a complex process and requires careful coordination between information technology professionals and legal counsel.

Evidence

To successfully prosecute a crime, the prosecuting attorneys must provide sufficient evidence to prove an individual's guilt beyond a reasonable doubt. In the following sections, we'll explain the requirements that evidence must meet before it is allowed in court, the various types of evidence that may be introduced, and the requirements for handling and documenting evidence.

TIP

NIST's Guide to Integrating Forensic Techniques into Incident Response (SP 800-86) is a great reference and is available at `www.csrc.nist.gov/publications/nistpubs/800-86/SP800-86.pdf`.

Admissible Evidence

There are three basic requirements for evidence to be introduced into a court of law. To be considered *admissible evidence*, it must meet all three of these requirements, as determined by the judge, prior to being discussed in open court:

- The evidence must be *relevant* to determining a fact.

- The fact that the evidence seeks to determine must be *material* (that is, related) to the case.
- The evidence must be *competent*, meaning it must have been obtained legally. Evidence that results from an illegal search would be inadmissible because it is not competent.

Types of Evidence

Three types of evidence can be used in a court of law: real evidence, documentary evidence, and testimonial evidence. Each has slightly different additional requirements for admissibility.

Real Evidence *Real evidence* (also known as *object evidence*) consists of things that may actually be brought into a court of law. In common criminal proceedings, this may include items such as a murder weapon, clothing, or other physical objects. In a computer crime case, real evidence might include seized computer equipment, such as a keyboard with fingerprints on it or a hard drive from a hacker's computer system. Depending on the circumstances, real evidence may also be *conclusive evidence*, such as DNA, that is incontrovertible.

Documentary Evidence *Documentary evidence* includes any written items brought into court to prove a fact at hand. This type of evidence must also be authenticated. For example, if an attorney wants to introduce a computer log as evidence, they must bring a witness (for example, the system administrator) into court to testify that the log was collected as a routine business practice and is indeed the actual log that the system collected.

Two additional evidence rules apply specifically to documentary evidence:

- The *best evidence rule* states that, when a document is used as evidence in a court proceeding, the original document must be introduced. Copies or descriptions of original evidence (known as *secondary evidence*) will not be accepted as evidence unless certain exceptions to the rule apply.
- The *parol evidence rule* states that, when an agreement between parties is put into written form, the written document is assumed to contain all the terms of the agreement and no verbal agreements may modify the written agreement.

If documentary evidence meets the materiality, competency, and relevancy requirements and also complies with the best evidence and parol evidence rules, it can be admitted into court.

Chain of Evidence

Real evidence, like any type of evidence, must meet the relevancy, materiality, and competency requirements before being admitted into court. Additionally, real evidence must be authenticated. This can be done by a witness who can actually identify an object as unique (for example, "That knife with my name on the handle is the one that the intruder took off the table in my house and used to stab me.").

In many cases, it is not possible for a witness to uniquely identify an object in court. In those cases, a *chain of evidence* (also known as a *chain of custody*) must be established. This documents everyone who handles evidence—including the police who originally collect it, the evidence technicians who process it, and the lawyers who use it in court. The location of the evidence must be fully documented from the moment it was collected to the moment it appears in court to ensure that it is indeed the same item. This requires thorough labeling of evidence and comprehensive logs noting who had access to the evidence at specific times and the reasons they required such access.

When evidence is labeled to preserve the chain of custody, the label should include the following types of information regarding the collection:

- General description of the evidence
- Time and date the evidence was collected
- Exact location the evidence was collected from
- Name of the person collecting the evidence
- Relevant circumstances surrounding the collection

Each person who handles the evidence must sign the chain of custody log indicating the time they took direct responsibility for the evidence and the time they handed it off to the next person in the chain of custody. The chain must provide an unbroken sequence of events accounting for the evidence from the time it was collected until the time of the trial.

Testimonial Evidence *Testimonial evidence* is, quite simply, evidence consisting of the testimony of a witness, either verbal testimony in court or written testimony in a recorded deposition. Witnesses must take an oath agreeing to tell the truth, and they must have personal knowledge on which their testimony is based. Furthermore, witnesses must remember the basis for their testimony (they may consult written notes or records to aid their memory). Witnesses can offer *direct evidence*: oral testimony that proves or disproves a claim based on their own direct observation. The testimonial evidence of most witnesses must be strictly limited to direct evidence based on the witness's factual observations. However, this does not apply if a witness has been accepted by the court as an expert in a certain field. In that case, the witness may offer an *expert opinion* based on the other facts presented and their personal knowledge of the field.

Testimonial evidence must not be *hearsay evidence*. That is, a witness cannot testify as to what someone else told them outside court. Computer log files that are not authenticated by a system administrator can also be considered hearsay evidence.

Evidence Collection and Forensic Procedures

Collecting digital evidence is a tricky process and should be attempted only by professional forensic technicians. The International Organization on Computer Evidence (IOCE) outlines six principles to guide digital evidence technicians as they perform media analysis, network analysis, and software analysis in the pursuit of forensically recovered evidence:

- When dealing with digital evidence, all of the general forensic and procedural principles must be applied.
- Upon seizing digital evidence, actions taken should not change that evidence.
- When it is necessary for a person to access original digital evidence, that person should be trained for the purpose.
- All activity relating to the seizure, access, storage, or transfer of digital evidence must be fully documented, preserved, and available for review.
- An individual is responsible for all actions taken with respect to digital evidence while the digital evidence is in their possession.
- Any agency that is responsible for seizing, accessing, storing, or transferring digital evidence is responsible for compliance with these principles.

As you conduct forensic evidence collection, it is important to preserve the original evidence. Remember that the very conduct of your investigation may alter the evidence you are evaluating. Therefore, when analyzing digital evidence, it's best to work with a copy of the actual evidence whenever possible. For example, when conducting an investigation into the contents of a hard drive, make an image of that drive, seal the original drive in an evidence bag, and then use the disk image for your investigation.

Media Analysis Media analysis, a branch of computer forensic analysis, involves the identification and extraction of information from storage media. This may include the following:

- Magnetic media (e.g., hard disks, tapes)
- Optical media (e.g., CDs, DVDs, Blu-ray discs)
- Memory (e.g., RAM, solid state storage)

Techniques used for media analysis may include the recovery of deleted files from unallocated sectors of the physical disk, the live analysis of storage media connected to a computer system (especially useful when examining encrypted media), and the static analysis of forensic images of storage media.

Network Analysis Forensic investigators are also often interested in the activity that took place over the network during a security incident. This is often difficult to reconstruct due to the volatility of network data—if it isn't deliberately recorded at the time it occurs, it generally is not preserved.

Network forensic analysis, therefore, often depends on either prior knowledge that an incident is underway or the use of preexisting security controls that log network activity. These include:

- Intrusion detection and prevention system logs
- Network flow data captured by a flow monitoring system
- Packet captures deliberately collected during an incident
- Logs from firewalls and other network security devices

The task of the network forensic analyst is to collect and correlate information from these disparate sources and produce as comprehensive a picture of network activity as possible.

Software Analysis Forensic analysts may also be called on to conduct forensic reviews of applications or the activity that takes place within a running application. In some cases, when malicious insiders are suspected, the forensic analyst may be asked to conduct a review of software code, looking for back doors, logic bombs, or other security vulnerabilities. For more on these topics, see Chapter 21, "Malicious Code and Application Attacks."

In other cases, forensic analysis may be asked to review and interpret the log files from application or database servers, seeking other signs of malicious activity, such as SQL injection attacks, privilege escalations, or other application attacks. These are also discussed in Chapter 21.

Hardware/Embedded Device Analysis Finally, forensic analysts often must review the contents of hardware and embedded devices. This may include a review of

- Personal computers
- Smartphones
- Tablet computers
- Embedded computers in cars, security systems, and other devices

Analysts conducting these reviews must have specialized knowledge of the systems under review. This often requires calling in expert consultants who are familiar with the memory, storage systems, and operating systems of such devices. Because of the complex interactions between software, hardware, and storage, the discipline of hardware analysis requires skills in both media analysis and software analysis.

Investigation Process

When you initiate a computer security investigation, you should first assemble a team of competent analysts to assist with the investigation. This team should operate under the organization's existing incident response policy and be given a charter that clearly outlines the scope of the investigation; the authority, roles, and responsibilities of the investigators; and any rules of engagement that they must follow while conducting the investigation. These rules of engagement define and guide the actions that investigators are authorized to take at different phases of the investigation, such as calling in law enforcement, interrogating suspects, collecting evidence, and disrupting system access.

Calling in Law Enforcement

One of the first decisions that must be made in an investigation is whether law enforcement authorities should be called in. This is a relatively complicated decision that should involve senior management officials. There are many factors in favor of calling in the experts. For example, the FBI now maintains a National Computer Crime Squad that includes individuals with the following qualifications:

- Degrees in the computer sciences
- Prior work experience in industry and academic institutions
- Basic and advanced commercial training
- Knowledge of basic data and telecommunications networks
- Experience with Unix and other computer operating systems

On the other hand, two major factors may cause a company to shy away from calling in the authorities. First, the investigation will more than likely become public and may embarrass the company. Second, law enforcement authorities are bound to conduct an investigation that complies with the Fourth Amendment and other legal requirements that may not apply if the organization conducted its own, private investigation.

Search Warrants

Even the most casual viewer of American crime television is familiar with the question, "Do you have a warrant?" The Fourth Amendment of the U.S. Constitution outlines the burden placed on investigators to have a valid search warrant before conducting certain searches and the legal hurdle they must overcome to obtain a warrant:

> The right of the people to be secure in their persons, houses, papers and effects, against unreasonable searches and seizures, shall not be violated, and no warrants shall issue, but upon probable cause, supported by oath or affirmation, and particularly describing the place to be searched, and the persons or things to be seized.

This amendment contains several important provisions that guide the activities of law enforcement personnel:

- Investigators must obtain a warrant before searching a person's private belongings, assuming that there is a reasonable expectation of privacy. There are a number of documented exceptions to this requirement, such as when an individual consents to a search, the evidence of a crime is in plain view, or there is a life-threatening emergency necessitating the search.
- Warrants can be issued only based on probable cause. There must be some type of evidence that a crime took place and that the search in question will yield evidence relating to that crime. The standard of "probable cause" required to get a warrant is

much weaker than the standard of evidence required to secure a conviction. Most warrants are "sworn out" based solely on the testimony of investigators.

- Warrants must be specific in their scope. The warrant must contain a detailed description of the legal bounds of the search and seizure.

If investigators fail to comply with even the smallest detail of these provisions, they may find their warrant invalidated and the results of the search deemed inadmissible. This leads to another one of those American colloquialisms: "He got off on a technicality."

Conducting the Investigation

If you elect not to call in law enforcement, you should still attempt to abide by the principles of a sound investigation to ensure the accuracy and fairness of your inquiry. It is important to remember a few key principles:

- Never conduct your investigation on an actual system that was compromised. Take the system offline, make a backup, and use the backup to investigate the incident.
- Never attempt to "hack back" and avenge a crime. You may inadvertently attack an innocent third party and find yourself liable for computer crime charges.
- If in doubt, call in expert assistance. If you don't want to call in law enforcement, contact a private investigations firm with specific experience in the field of computer security investigations.
- Usually, it's best to begin the investigation process using informal interviewing techniques. These are used to gather facts and determine the substance of the case. When specific suspects are identified, they should be questioned using interrogation techniques. Interviewing typically involves open-ended questions to gather information. Interrogation often involves closed-ended questioning with a specific goal in mind and is more adversarial in nature. Again, this is an area best left untouched without specific legal advice.

Major Categories of Computer Crime

There are many ways to attack a computer system and many motivations to do so. Information system security practitioners generally put crimes against or involving computers into different categories. Simply put, a *computer crime* is a crime (or violation of a law or regulation) that involves a computer. The crime could be against the computer, or the computer could have been used in the actual commission of the crime. Each of the categories of computer crimes represents the purpose of an attack and its intended result.

Any individual who violates one or more of your security policies is considered to be an *attacker*. An attacker uses different techniques to achieve a specific goal. Understanding the goals helps to clarify the different types of attacks. Remember that crime is crime, and the motivations behind computer crime are no different from the motivations behind any other type of crime. The only real difference may be in the methods the attacker uses to strike.

Computer crimes are generally classified as one of the following types:

- Military and intelligence attacks
- Business attacks
- Financial attacks
- Terrorist attacks
- Grudge attacks
- Thrill attacks

It is important to understand the differences among the categories of computer crime to best understand how to protect a system and react when an attack occurs. The type and amount of evidence left by an attacker is often dependent on their expertise. In the following sections, we'll discuss the different categories of computer crimes and the types of evidence you might find after an attack. This evidence can help you determine the attacker's actions and intended target. You may find that your system was only a link in the chain of network hops used to reach the real victim, making the trail harder to follow back to the true attacker.

Military and Intelligence Attacks

Military and intelligence attacks are launched primarily to obtain secret and restricted information from law enforcement or military and technological research sources. The disclosure of such information could compromise investigations, disrupt military planning, and threaten national security. Attacks to gather military information or other sensitive intelligence often precede other, more damaging attacks.

An attacker may be looking for the following kinds of information:

- Military descriptive information of any type, including deployment information, readiness information, and order of battle plans
- Secret intelligence gathered for military or law enforcement purposes
- Descriptions and storage locations of evidence obtained in a criminal investigation
- Any secret information that could be used in a later attack

Because of the sensitive nature of information collected and used by the military and intelligence agencies, their computer systems are often attractive targets for experienced attackers. To protect from more numerous and more sophisticated attackers, you will generally find more formal security policies in place on systems that house such information. As you learned in Chapter 1, "Security Governance Through Principles and Policies," data can be classified according to sensitivity and stored on systems that support the required level of security. It is common to find stringent perimeter security as well as internal controls to limit access to classified documents on military and intelligence agency systems.

You can be sure that serious attacks to acquire military or intelligence information are carried out by professionals. Professional attackers are generally very thorough in covering their tracks. There is usually very little evidence to collect after such an attack. Attackers in this category are the most successful and the most satisfied when no one is aware that an attack occurred.

Advanced Persistent Threats

Recent years have marked the rise of sophisticated attacks known as advanced persistent threats (APTs). The attackers are well funded and have advanced technical skills and resources. They act on behalf of a nation-state, organized crime, terrorist group, or other sponsor and wage highly effective attacks against a very focused target.

Business Attacks

Business attacks focus on illegally obtaining an organization's confidential information. This could be information that is critical to the operation of the organization, such as a secret recipe, or information that could damage the organization's reputation if disclosed, such as personal information about its employees. The gathering of a competitor's confidential information, also called *industrial espionage*, is not a new phenomenon. Businesses have used illegal means to acquire competitive information for many years. The temptation to steal a competitor's trade secrets and the ease with which a savvy attacker can compromise some computer systems makes this type of attack attractive.

The goal of business attacks is solely to extract confidential information. The use of the information gathered during the attack usually causes more damage than the attack itself. A business that has suffered an attack of this type can be put into a position from which it might not ever recover. It is up to you as the security professional to ensure that the systems that contain confidential data are secure. In addition, a policy must be developed that will handle such an intrusion should it occur. (For more information on security policies, see Chapter 2, "Personnel Security and Risk Management Concepts.")

Financial Attacks

Financial attacks are carried out to unlawfully obtain money or services. They are the type of computer crime you most commonly hear about in the news. The goal of a financial attack could be to steal credit card numbers, increase the balance in a bank account, or place "free" long-distance telephone calls. You have probably heard of individuals breaking into telephone company computers and placing free calls. This type of financial attack is called *phone phreaking*.

Shoplifting and burglary are both examples of financial attacks. You can usually tell the sophistication of the attacker by the dollar amount of the damages. Less sophisticated attackers seek easier targets, but although the damages are usually minimal, they can add up over time.

Financial attacks launched by sophisticated attackers can result in substantial damages. Although phone phreaking causes the telephone company to lose the revenue of calls placed, serious financial attacks can result in losses amounting to millions of dollars. As with the attacks previously described, the ease with which you can detect an attack and track an attacker is largely dependent on the attacker's skill level.

Terrorist Attacks

Terrorist attacks are a reality in modern society. Our increasing reliance on information systems makes them more and more attractive to terrorists. Such attacks differ from military and intelligence attacks. The purpose of a terrorist attack is to disrupt normal life and instill fear, whereas a military or intelligence attack is designed to extract secret information. Intelligence gathering generally precedes any type of terrorist attack. The very systems that are victims of a terrorist attack were probably compromised in an earlier attack to collect intelligence. The more diligent you are in detecting attacks of any type, the better prepared you will be to intervene before more serious attacks occur.

Possible targets of a computer terrorist attack could be systems that regulate power plants or control telecommunications or power distribution. Many such control and regulatory systems are computerized and vulnerable to terrorist action. In fact, the possibility exists of a simultaneous physical and computerized terrorist attack. Our ability to respond to such an attack would be greatly diminished if the physical attack were simultaneously launched with a computer attack designed to knock out power and communications.

Most large power and communications companies have dedicated a security staff to ensure the security of their systems, but many smaller businesses that have systems connected to the Internet are more vulnerable to attacks. You must diligently monitor your systems to identify any attacks and then respond swiftly when an attack is discovered.

Grudge Attacks

Grudge attacks are attacks that are carried out to damage an organization or a person. The damage could be in the loss of information or information processing capabilities or harm to the organization or a person's reputation. The motivation behind a grudge attack is usually a feeling of resentment, and the attacker could be a current or former employee or someone who wishes ill will upon an organization. The attacker is disgruntled with the victim and takes out their frustration in the form of a grudge attack.

An employee who has recently been fired is a prime example of a person who might carry out a grudge attack to "get back" at the organization. Another example is a person who has been rejected in a personal relationship with another employee. The person who has been rejected might launch an attack to destroy data on the victim's system.

Real World Scenario

The Insider Threat

It's common for security professionals to focus on the threat from outside an organization. Indeed, many of our security technologies are designed to keep unauthorized individuals out. We often don't pay enough (or much!) attention to protecting our organizations against the malicious insider, even though they often pose the greatest risk to our computing assets.

One of the authors of this book recently wrapped up a consulting engagement with a medium-sized subsidiary of a large, well-known corporation. The company had suffered a serious security breach, involving the theft of thousands of dollars and the deliberate destruction of sensitive corporate information. The IT leaders within the organization needed someone to work with them to diagnose the cause of the event and protect themselves against similar events in the future.

After only a very small amount of digging, it became apparent that they were dealing with an insider attack. The intruder's actions demonstrated knowledge of the company's IT infrastructure as well as an understanding of which data was most important to the company's ongoing operations.

Additional investigation revealed that the culprit was a former employee who ended his employment with the firm on less-than-favorable terms. He left the building with a chip on his shoulder and an ax to grind. Unfortunately, he was a system administrator with a wide range of access to corporate systems, and the company had an immature deprovisioning process that failed to remove all of his access upon his termination. He simply found several accounts that remained active and used them to access the corporate network through a VPN.

The moral of this story? Don't underestimate the insider threat. Take the time to evaluate your controls to mitigate the risk that malicious current and former employees pose to your organization.

Your security policy should address the potential of attacks by disgruntled employees. For example, as soon as an employee is terminated, all system access for that employee should be terminated. This action reduces the likelihood of a grudge attack and removes unused access accounts that could be used in future attacks.

Although most grudge attackers are just disgruntled people with limited hacking and cracking abilities, some possess the skills to cause substantial damage. An unhappy cracker can be a handful for security professionals. Take extreme care when a person with known cracking ability leaves your company. At the least, you should perform a vulnerability assessment of all systems the person could access. You may be surprised to find one or more "back doors" left in the system. (For more on back doors, see Chapter 21.) But even in the absence of any back doors, a former employee who is familiar with the technical architecture of the organization may know how to exploit its weaknesses.

Grudge attacks can be devastating if allowed to occur unchecked. Diligent monitoring and assessing systems for vulnerabilities is the best protection for most grudge attacks.

Thrill Attacks

Thrill attacks are the attacks launched only for the fun of it. Attackers who lack the ability to devise their own attacks will often download programs that do their work for them. These attackers are often called *script kiddies* because they run only other people's programs, or scripts, to launch an attack.

The main motivation behind these attacks is the "high" of successfully breaking into a system. If you are the victim of a thrill attack, the most common fate you will suffer is a service interruption. Although an attacker of this type may destroy data, the main motivation is to compromise a system and perhaps use it to launch an attack against another victim.

One common type of thrill attack involves website defacements, where the attacker compromises a web server and replaces an organization's legitimate web content with other pages, often boasting about the attacker's skills. For example, an attacker operating under the pseudonym iSKORPiTX conducted more than 20,000 website defacements in 2006, replacing legitimate websites with his own pages containing the text "Hacked by iSKORPiTX."

Recently, the world has seen a rise in the field of "hacktivism." These attackers, known as *hacktivists* (a combination of *hacker* and *activist*), often combine political motivations with the thrill of hacking. They organize themselves loosely into groups with names like Anonymous and Lolzsec and use tools like the Low Orbit Ion Cannon to create large-scale denial-of-service attacks with little knowledge required.

Incident Handling

When an incident occurs, you must handle it in a manner that is outlined in your security policy and consistent with local laws and regulations. The first step in handling an incident properly is recognizing when one occurs. You should understand the following two terms related to incident handling:

Event Any occurrence that takes place during a certain period of time

Incident An event that has a negative outcome affecting the confidentiality, integrity, or availability of an organization's data

The most common reason incidents are not reported is that they are never identified. You could have many security policy violations occurring each day, but if you don't have a way of identifying them, you will never know. Therefore, your security policy should identify and list all possible violations and ways to detect them. It's also important to update your security policy as new types of violations and attacks emerge.

What you do when you find that an incident has occurred depends on the type of incident and scope of damage. Law dictates that some incidents must be reported, such as those that impact government or federal interest computers (a federal interest computer is one that is used by financial institutions and by infrastructure systems such as water and power systems) or certain financial transactions, regardless of the amount of damage. Most U.S. states now have laws that require organizations that experience an incident involving certain types of personally identifiable information (for example, credit card numbers, Social Security numbers, and driver's license numbers) to notify affected individuals of the breach.

In addition to laws, many companies have contractual obligations to report different types of security incidents to business partners. For example, the Payment Card Industry Data Security Standard (PCI DSS) requires any merchant that handles credit card information to report incidents involving that information to their acquiring bank as well as law enforcement.

Next, we'll cover some of the different types of incidents and typical responses.

Common Types of Incidents

An incident occurs when an attack, or other violation of your security policy, is carried out against your system. There are many ways to classify incidents; here is a general list of categories:

- Scanning
- Compromises
- Malicious code
- Denial of service

These four areas are the basic entry points for attackers to impact a system. You must focus on each of these areas to create an effective monitoring strategy that detects system incidents. Each incident area has representative signatures that can tip off an alert security administrator that an incident has occurred. Make sure you know your operating system environment and where to look for the telltale signs of each type of incident.

Scanning

Scanning attacks are reconnaissance attacks that usually precede another, more serious attack. They're comparable to a burglar casing a neighborhood for targets, looking for homes with unlocked doors or where nobody is home on guard. Attackers will gather as much information about your system as possible before launching a directed attack. Look for any unusual activity on any port or from any single address. For example, a high volume of Secure Shell (SSH) packets on port 22 may point to a systematic scan of your network.

Remember that simply scanning your system may not be illegal, depending on your local laws. But it can indicate that illegal activity will follow, so it is a good idea to treat scans as incidents and to collect evidence of scanning activity. You may find that the evidence you collect at the time the system is scanned could be the link you need to find the party responsible for a later attack.

Because scanning is such a common occurrence, you definitely want to automate evidence collection. Set up your firewall to log rejected traffic and archive your log files. The logs may become large, but storage is cheap, and you should consider it a cost of doing business.

Compromise

A system *compromise* is any unauthorized access to the system or information the system stores. A compromise could originate inside or outside the organization. To make matters worse, a compromise could come from a valid user. An unauthorized use of a valid user ID is just as much of a compromise incident as an experienced cracker breaking in from the outside. Another example of a system compromise is when an attacker uses a normal user account to gain the elevated privileges of a system administrator without authorization.

System compromises can be difficult to detect. Most often, the data custodian notices something unusual about the data. It could be missing, altered, or moved; the time stamps could be different; or something else is just not right. The more you know about the normal operation of your system, the better prepared you will be to detect abnormal system behavior.

Malicious Code

When *malicious code* is mentioned, you probably think of viruses and spyware. Although a virus is a common type of malicious code, it is only one type of several. (In Chapter 21, we discuss different types of malicious code.) Detection of this type of a malicious code incident comes from either an end user reporting behavior caused by the malicious code or an automated alert reporting that scanned code containing a malicious component has been found.

The most effective way to protect your system from malicious code is to implement virus and spyware scanners and keep the signature database up to date. In addition, your security policy should address the introduction of outside code. Be specific as to what code you will allow end users to install.

Denial of Service

The final type of incident is a *denial of service (DoS)*. This type of incident is often the easiest to detect. A user or automated tool reports that one or more services (or the entire machine) are unavailable. Although they're simple to detect, avoidance is a far better course of action. It is theoretically possible to dynamically alter firewall rules to reject DoS network traffic, but in recent years the sophistication and complexity of DoS attacks make them extremely difficult to defend against. Because there are so many variations of the DoS attack, implementing this strategy is a nontrivial task.

A detailed discussion of DoS and distributed denial-of-service (DDoS) attacks appears in Chapter 21.

Response Teams

Many organizations now have a dedicated team responsible for investigating any computer security incidents that take place. These teams are commonly known as computer incident response teams (CIRTs) or computer security incident response teams (CSIRTs). When an incident occurs, the response team has four primary responsibilities:

- Determine the amount and scope of damage caused by the incident.
- Determine whether any confidential information was compromised during the incident.
- Implement any necessary recovery procedures to restore security and recover from incident-related damages.
- Supervise the implementation of any additional security measures necessary to improve security and prevent recurrence of the incident.

Real World Scenario

The Gibson Research Denial-of-Service Attacks: Fun or Grudge?

Steve Gibson is a well-known software developer and personality in the IT industry whose high visibility derives not only from highly regarded products associated with his company, Gibson Research, but also from his many years as a vocal and outspoken columnist for *Computer World* magazine. In recent years, he has become quite active in the field of computer security, and his site offers free vulnerability-scanning services and a variety of patches and fixes for operating system vulnerabilities. He operates a website at `http://grc.com` that has been the subject of numerous well-documented denial-of-service attacks. It's interesting to speculate whether such attacks are motivated by grudges (that is, by those who seek to advance their reputations by breaking into an obvious and presumably well-defended point of attack) or by fun (that is, by those with excess time on their hands who might seek to prove themselves against a worthy adversary without necessarily expecting any gain other than notoriety from their actions).

Gibson's website has in fact been subject to two well-documented denial-of-service attacks that you can read about in detail on his site:

- "Distributed Reflection Denial of Service": `http://www.cs.washington.edu/homes/arvind/cs425/doc/drdos.pdf`
- "The Strange Tale of the Denial of Service Attacks against GRC.COM": `http://www.crime-research.org/library/grcdos.pdf`

Although his subsequent anonymous discussions with one of the perpetrators involved seem to indicate that the motive for some of these attacks was fun rather than business damage or acting on a grudge, these reports are fascinating because of the excellent model they provide for incident handling and reporting.

These documents contain a brief synopsis of the symptoms and chronology of the attacks that occurred, along with short- and long-term fixes and changes enacted to prevent recurrences. They also stress the critical importance of communication with service providers whose infrastructures may be involved in attacks as they're underway. What's extremely telling about Gibson's report on the denial-of-service attacks is that he experienced 17 hours of downtime because he was unable to establish contact with a knowledgeable, competent engineer at his service provider who could help define the right kinds of traffic filters to stymie the floods of traffic that characterize denial-of-service attacks.

Gibson's analysis also indicates his thoroughness in analyzing the sources of the distributed denial-of-service attacks and in documenting what he calls "an exact profile of the malicious traffic being generated during these attacks." This information permitted his Internet service provider (ISP) to define a set of filters that blocked further such traffic from transiting the final T1 links from Gibson's ISP to his servers. As his experience proves so conclusively, recognizing, analyzing, and characterizing attacks is absolutely essential to defining filters or other countermeasures that can block or defeat them.

As part of these duties, the team should facilitate a *postmortem review* of the incident within a week of the occurrence to ensure that key players in the incident share their knowledge and develop best practices to assist in future incident response efforts.

When putting together your incident response team, be sure to design a cross-functional group of individuals who represent the management, technical, and functional areas of responsibility most directly impacted by a security incident. Potential team members include the following:

- Representative(s) of senior management
- Information security professionals
- Legal representatives
- Public affairs/communications representatives
- Engineering representatives (system and network)

Incident Response Process

Many organizations use a three-step incident response process, consisting of the following phases:

1. Detection and identification
2. Response and reporting
3. Recovery and remediation

The next three sections outline each phase of the standard incident response process.

Step 1: Detection and Identification

The incident identification process has two main goals: detecting security incidents and notifying appropriate personnel. To successfully detect and identify incidents, a security team must monitor any relevant events that occur and notice when they meet the organization's defined threshold for a security incident. The key to identifying incidents is to detect abnormal or suspicious activity that may constitute evidence of an incident. Although you can detect many attacks by their characteristic signatures, experienced attackers know how to "fly under the radar." You must be aware of how your system operates normally and recognize *abnormal* or *suspicious* activity—that is, any system activity that does not normally occur on your system.

These are some of the tools you should monitor for events indicative of security incidents:

- Intrusion detection/prevention systems
- Antivirus software
- Firewall logs
- System logs
- Physical security systems
- File integrity monitoring software

Always use multiple sources of data when investigating an incident. Be suspicious of anything that does not make sense. Ensure that you can clearly explain any activity you see that is not normal for your system. Even if your sense is that "it just does not feel right," that could be the only clue you have to successfully intervene in an ongoing incident.

Once the initial evaluator identifies that an event or events meet the organization's security incident criteria, the evaluator must notify the incident response team. This notification concludes the incident detection and identification phase and initiates the response and reporting phase.

Step 2: Response and Reporting

Once you determine that an incident has occurred, the next step is to choose an appropriate response. Your security policy should specify steps to take for various types of incidents. Always proceed with the assumption that an incident will end up in a court of law. Treat any evidence you collect as if it must pass admissibility standards. Once you taint evidence, there is no going back. You must ensure that the chain of evidence is maintained.

Isolation and Containment The first actions you take should be dedicated to limiting the exposure of your organization and preventing further damage. In the case of a potentially compromised system, you should disconnect it from the network to prevent intruders from accessing the compromised system and also to prevent the compromised system from affecting other resources on the network.

WARNING

In the isolation and containment phase of incident response, it is critical that you leave the system in a running state. Do not power down the system. Turning off the computer destroys the contents of volatile memory and may destroy evidence.

Gathering Evidence It is common to confiscate equipment, software, or data to perform a proper investigation. The manner in which the evidence is confiscated is important. The confiscation of evidence must be carried out in a proper fashion. There are three basic alternatives.

First, the person who owns the evidence could *voluntarily surrender* it. This method is generally appropriate only when the attacker is not the owner. Few guilty parties willingly surrender evidence they know will incriminate them. Less experienced attackers may believe they have successfully covered their tracks and voluntarily surrender important evidence. A good forensic investigator can extract much "covered-up" information from a computer. In most cases, asking for evidence from a suspected attacker just alerts the suspect that you are close to taking legal action.

TIP

In the case of an internal investigation, you will gather the vast majority of your information through voluntary surrender. Most likely, you're conducting the investigation under the auspices of a senior member of management who will authorize you to access any organizational resources necessary to complete your investigation.

Second, you could get a court to issue a *subpoena*, or court order, that compels an individual or organization to surrender evidence and then have the subpoena served by law enforcement. Again, this course of action provides sufficient notice for someone to alter the evidence and render it useless in court.

The last option is a *search warrant*. This option should be used only when you must have access to evidence without tipping off the evidence's owner or other personnel. You must have a strong suspicion with credible reasoning to convince a judge to pursue this course of action.

The three alternatives apply to confiscating equipment both inside and outside an organization, but there is another step you can take to ensure that the confiscation of equipment that belongs to your organization is carried out properly. It is common to have all new employees sign an agreement that provides consent to search and seize any necessary evidence during an investigation. In this manner, consent is provided as a term of the employment agreement. This makes confiscation much easier and reduces the chances of a loss of evidence while waiting for legal permission to seize it. Make sure your security policy addresses this important topic.

You should consider the following sources of data when determining what evidence to gather:

- Computer systems involved in the incident (both servers and workstations)
- Logs from security systems (such as intrusion detection, file integrity monitoring, and firewalls)
- Logs from network devices
- Physical access logs
- Other relevant sources of information specific to the incident under investigation

Analysis and Reporting Once you finish gathering evidence, you should analyze it to determine the most likely course of events leading up to your incident. Summarize those findings in a written report to management. In your report, you should be careful to distinguish fact from opinion. It is acceptable to theorize about possible causes, but you should be certain to state which of your conclusions are based entirely on fact and which involve a degree of estimation.

Step 3: Recovery and Remediation

After completing your investigation, you have two tasks remaining: restoring your environment to its normal operating state and completing a "lessons learned" process to improve how you handle future incidents.

Restoration The goal of the restoration process is to remediate any damage that may have occurred to the organization and limit the damage incurred by similar incidents in the future. These are some of the key actions you should take during this phase:

- Rebuild compromised systems, taking care to remediate any security vulnerabilities that may have contributed to the incident.
- Restore backup data, if necessary, to replace data of questionable integrity.
- Supplement existing security controls, if necessary, to fill gaps identified during the incident analysis.

Once you have completed the restoration process, your business should be back up and running in the state it was in prior to the incident (although in a more secure manner!).

Lessons Learned The final stage of the incident response process is to conduct a "lessons learned" session. During this important process, members of the incident response team review their actions during the incident and look for potential areas of improvement, both in their actions and in the incident response process. This hindsight review provides an important perspective on the success of your incident response process by analyzing its effectiveness during a real-world incident.

Interviewing Individuals

During your incident investigation, you may find it necessary to speak with individuals who might have information relevant to your investigation. If you seek only to gather information to assist with your investigation, this is called an *interview.* If you suspect the person of involvement in a crime and intend to use the information gathered in court, this is called an *interrogation.*

Interviewing and interrogating individuals are specialized skills and should be performed only by trained investigators. Improper techniques may jeopardize the ability of law enforcement to successfully prosecute an offender. Additionally, many laws govern holding or detaining individuals, and you must abide by them if you plan to conduct private interrogations. Always consult an attorney before conducting any interviews.

Incident Data Integrity and Retention

No matter how persuasive evidence may be, it can be thrown out of court if you somehow alter it during the evidence collection process. Make sure you can prove that you maintained the integrity of all evidence. But what about the integrity of data before it is collected?

You may not detect all incidents as they are happening. Sometimes an investigation reveals that there were previous incidents that went undetected. It is discouraging to follow a trail of evidence and find that a key log file that could point back to an attacker has been purged. Carefully consider the fate of log files or other possible evidence locations. A simple archiving policy can help ensure that key evidence is available upon demand no matter how long ago the incident occurred.

Because many log files can contain valuable evidence, attackers often attempt to sanitize them after a successful attack. Take steps to protect the integrity of log files and to deter their modification. One technique is to implement remote logging, where all systems on the network send their log records to a centralized log server that is locked down against attack and does not allow for the modification of data. This technique provides protection from post-incident log file cleansing. Administrators also often use digital signatures to prove that log files were not tampered with after initial capture. For more on digital signatures, see Chapter 7, "PKI and Cryptographic Applications."

As with every aspect of security planning, there is no single solution. Get familiar with your system, and take the steps that make the most sense for your organization to protect it.

Reporting and Documenting Incidents

When should you report an incident? To whom should you report it? These questions are often difficult to answer. Your security policy should contain guidelines on both questions. There is a fundamental problem with reporting incidents. If you report every incident, you run the very real risk of being viewed as a noisemaker and being ignored if you subsequently report a serious incident. Also, reporting an unimportant incident could give the impression that your organization is more vulnerable than is the case. This can have a serious detrimental effect if your organization must maintain strict security. For example, if your bank reported daily security incidents, you might lose confidence in their security practices.

On the other hand, escalation and legal action become more difficult if you do not report an incident soon after discovery. If you delay notifying authorities of a serious incident, you will probably have to answer questions about your motivation for delaying. Even an innocent person could look as if they were trying to hide something by not reporting an incident in a timely manner.

As with most security topics, the answer is not an easy one. In fact, you are compelled by law or regulation to report some incidents. Make sure you know what incidents you must report. For example, any organization that stores credit card information must report any incident in which the disclosure of such information occurred.

Before you encounter an incident, it is wise to establish a relationship with your corporate legal personnel and the appropriate law enforcement agencies. Find out who the appropriate law enforcement contacts are for your organization and talk with them. When the time comes to report an incident, your efforts at establishing a prior working relationship will pay off. You will spend far less time in introductions and explanations if you already know the person with whom you are talking. It is a good idea to identify, in advance, a single point of contact in the organization that will act as your liaison with law enforcement. This provides two benefits. First, it ensures that law enforcement hears a single perspective from your organization and knows the "go-to" person for updates. Second, it allows the predesignated contact to develop working relationships with law enforcement personnel.

NOTE One great way to establish technical contacts with law enforcement is to participate in the FBI's InfraGard program. InfraGard exists in most major metropolitan areas in the United States and provides a forum for law enforcement and business security professionals to share information in a closed environment. For more information, visit `www.infragard.org`.

Once you determine that you should report an incident, make sure you have documented as much of the following information as possible:

- What is the nature of the incident, how was it initiated, and by whom?
- When did the incident occur? (Be as precise as possible with dates and times.)
- Where did the incident occur?
- If known, what tools did the attacker use?
- What was the damage resulting from the incident?

You may be asked to provide additional information. Be prepared to provide it in as timely a manner as possible. You may also be asked to quarantine your system.

As with any security action you take, keep a log of all communication, and make copies of any documents you provide as you report an incident.

TIP For more information on incident handling, read NIST SP 800-61, Computer Security Incident Handling Guide, available at `http://nvlpubs.nist.gov/nistpubs/SpecialPublications/NIST.SP.800-61r2.pdf`, and the Handbook for Computer Security Incident Response Teams (CSIRTs) at `http://resources.sei.cmu.edu/library/asset-view.cfm?assetID=6305`.

Ethics

Security professionals hold themselves and each other to a high standard of conduct because of the sensitive positions of trust they occupy. The rules that govern personal conduct are collectively known as rules of *ethics*. Several organizations have recognized the need for standard ethics rules, or codes, and have devised guidelines for ethical behavior.

We present two codes of ethics in the following sections. These rules are not laws. They are minimum standards for professional behavior. They should provide you with a basis for sound, ethical judgment. We expect all security professionals to abide by these guidelines regardless of their area of specialty or employer. Make sure you understand and agree with the codes of ethics outlined in the following sections. In addition to these codes, all information security professionals should also support their organization's code of ethics.

(ISC)² Code of Ethics

The governing body that administers the CISSP certification is the International Information Systems Security Certification Consortium, or (ISC)². The (ISC)² Code of Ethics was developed to provide the basis for CISSP behavior. It is a simple code with a preamble and four canons. The following is a short summary of the major concepts of the Code of Ethics.

TIP

All CISSP candidates should be familiar with the entire (ISC)² Code of Ethics because they have to sign an agreement that they will adhere to this code. We won't cover the code in depth, but you can find further details about the (ISC)²'s Code of Ethics at `www.isc2.org/ethics`. You need to visit this site and read the entire code.

Code of Ethics Preamble

The Code of Ethics preamble is as follows:

- The safety and welfare of society and the common good, duty to our principals, and to each other requires that we adhere, and be seen to adhere, to the highest ethical standards of behavior.
- Therefore, strict adherence to this Code is a condition of certification.

Code of Ethics Canons

The Code of Ethics includes the following canons:

Protect society, the common good, necessary public trust and confidence, and the infrastructure. Security professionals have great social responsibility. We are charged with the burden of ensuring that our actions benefit the common good.

Act honorably, honestly, justly, responsibly, and legally. Integrity is essential to the conduct of our duties. We cannot carry out our duties effectively if others within our organization, the security community, or the general public have doubts about the accuracy of the guidance we provide or the motives behind our actions.

Provide diligent and competent service to principals. Although we have responsibilities to society as a whole, we also have specific responsibilities to those who have hired us to protect their infrastructure. We must ensure that we are in a position to provide unbiased, competent service to our organization.

Advance and protect the profession. Our chosen profession changes on a continuous basis. As security professionals, we must ensure that our knowledge remains current and that we contribute our own knowledge to the community's common body of knowledge.

Ethics and the Internet

In January 1989, the Internet Advisory Board (IAB) recognized that the Internet was rapidly expanding beyond the initial trusted community that created it. Understanding that misuse could occur as the Internet grew, IAB issued a statement of policy concerning the proper use of the Internet. The contents of this statement are valid even today. It is important that you know the basic contents of the document, titled "Ethics and the Internet," Request for Comments (RFC) 1087, because most codes of ethics can trace their roots back to this document.

The statement is a brief list of practices considered unethical. Where a code of ethics states what you should do, this document outlines what you should not do. RFC 1087 states that any activity with the following purposes is unacceptable and unethical:

- Seeks to gain unauthorized access to the resources of the Internet
- Disrupts the intended use of the Internet
- Wastes resources (people, capacity, computer) through such actions
- Destroys the integrity of computer-based information
- Compromises the privacy of users

Ten Commandments of Computer Ethics

The Computer Ethics Institute created its own code of ethics. The Ten Commandments of Computer Ethics are as follows:

1. Thou shalt not use a computer to harm other people.
2. Thou shalt not interfere with other people's computer work.
3. Thou shalt not snoop around in other people's computer files.
4. Thou shalt not use a computer to steal.
5. Thou shalt not use a computer to bear false witness.
6. Thou shalt not copy proprietary software for which you have not paid.
7. Thou shalt not use other people's computer resources without authorization or proper compensation.
8. Thou shalt not appropriate other people's intellectual output.

9. Thou shalt think about the social consequences of the program you are writing or the system you are designing.

10. Thou shalt always use a computer in ways that ensure consideration and respect for your fellow humans.

There are many ethical and moral codes of IT behavior to choose from. Another system you should consider is the Generally Accepted System Security Principles (GASSP). You can find the full text of the GASSP system at `www.infosectoday.com/Articles/gassp.pdf`.

Summary

Information security professionals must be familiar with the incident response process. This involves gathering and analyzing the evidence required to conduct an investigation. Security professionals should be familiar with the major categories of evidence, including real evidence, documentary evidence, and testimonial evidence. Electronic evidence is often gathered through the analysis of hardware, software, storage media, and networks. It is essential to gather evidence using appropriate procedures that do not alter the original evidence and preserve the chain of custody.

Computer crimes are grouped into several major categories, and the crimes in each category share common motivations and desired results. Understanding what an attacker is after can help in properly securing a system.

For example, military and intelligence attacks are launched to acquire secret information that could not be obtained legally. Business attacks are similar except that they target civilian systems. Other types of attacks include financial attacks (phone phreaking is an example of a financial attack) and terrorist attacks (which, in the context of computer crimes, are attacks designed to disrupt normal life). Finally, there are grudge attacks, the purpose of which is to cause damage by destroying data or using information to embarrass an organization or person, and thrill attacks, launched by inexperienced crackers to compromise or disable a system. Although generally not sophisticated, thrill attacks can be annoying and costly.

An incident is a violation or the threat of a violation of your security policy. When an incident is suspected, you should immediately begin an investigation and collect as much evidence as possible because, if you decide to report the incident, you must have enough admissible evidence to support your claims.

The set of rules that govern your personal behavior is a code of ethics. There are several codes of ethics, from general to specific in nature, that security professionals can use to guide them. The $(ISC)^2$ makes the acceptance of its code of ethics a requirement for certification.

Exam Essentials

Know the definition of computer crime. Computer crime is a crime (or violation of a law or regulation) that is directed against, or directly involves, a computer.

Be able to list and explain the six categories of computer crimes. Computer crimes are grouped into six categories: military and intelligence attack, business attack, financial attack, terrorist attack, grudge attack, and thrill attack. Be able to explain the motive of each type of attack.

Know the importance of collecting evidence. As soon you discover an incident, you must begin to collect evidence and as much information about the incident as possible. The evidence can be used in a subsequent legal action or in finding the identity of the attacker. Evidence can also assist you in determining the extent of damage.

Understand that an incident is any violation, or threat of a violation, of your security policy. Incidents should be defined in your security policy. Even though specific incidents may not be outlined, the existence of the policy sets the standard for the use of your system. An incident is any event that has a negative outcome affecting the confidentiality, integrity, or availability of an organization's data.

Be able to list the four common types of incidents, and know the telltale signs of each. An incident occurs when an attack or other violation of your security policy is carried out against your system. Incidents can be grouped into four categories: scanning, compromises, malicious code, and denial of service. Be able to explain what each type of incident involves and what signs to look for.

Know the importance of identifying abnormal and suspicious activity. Attacks will generate some activity that is not normal. Recognizing abnormal and suspicious activity is the first step toward detecting incidents.

Know how to investigate intrusions and how to gather sufficient information from the equipment, software, and data. You must have possession of equipment, software, or data to analyze it and use it as evidence. You must acquire the evidence without modifying it or allowing anyone else to modify it.

Know the three basic alternatives for confiscating evidence and when each one is appropriate. First, the person who owns the evidence could voluntarily surrender it. Second, a subpoena could be used to compel the subject to surrender the evidence. Third, a search warrant is most useful when you need to confiscate evidence without giving the subject an opportunity to alter it.

Know the importance of retaining incident data. Because you will discover some incidents after they have occurred, you will lose valuable evidence unless you ensure that critical log files are retained for a reasonable period of time. You can retain log files and system status information either in place or in archives.

Be familiar with how to report an incident. The first step is to establish a working relationship with the corporate and law enforcement personnel with whom you will work to resolve an incident. When you do have a need to report an incident, gather as much descriptive information as possible and make your report in a timely manner.

Know the basic requirements for evidence to be admissible in a court of law. To be admissible, evidence must be relevant to a fact at issue in the case, the fact must be material to the case, and the evidence must be competent or legally collected.

Explain the various types of evidence that may be used in a criminal or civil trial. Real evidence consists of actual objects that can be brought into the courtroom. Documentary evidence consists of written documents that provide insight into the facts. Testimonial evidence consists of verbal or written statements made by witnesses.

Understand the importance of ethics to security personnel. Security practitioners are granted a very high level of authority and responsibility to execute their job functions. The potential for abuse exists, and without a strict code of personal behavior, security practitioners could be regarded as having unchecked power. Adherence to a code of ethics helps ensure that such power is not abused.

Know the (ISC)^2 Code of Ethics and RFC 1087, "Ethics and the Internet." All CISSP candidates should be familiar with the entire (ISC)^2 Code of Ethics because they have to sign an agreement that they will adhere to it. In addition, be familiar with the basic statements of RFC 1087.

Written Lab

1. What are the major categories of computer crime?
2. What is the main motivation behind a thrill attack?
3. What is the difference between an interview and an interrogation?
4. What is the difference between an event and an incident?
5. Who are the common members of an incident response team?
6. What are the three phases of the incident response process?
7. What are the three basic requirements that evidence must meet in order to be admissible in court?

Review Questions

1. What is a computer crime?
   - **A.** Any attack specifically listed in your security policy
   - **B.** Any illegal attack that compromises a protected computer
   - **C.** Any violation of a law or regulation that involves a computer
   - **D.** Failure to practice due diligence in computer security
2. What is the main purpose of a military and intelligence attack?
   - **A.** To attack the availability of military systems
   - **B.** To obtain secret and restricted information from military or law enforcement sources
   - **C.** To utilize military or intelligence agency systems to attack other nonmilitary sites
   - **D.** To compromise military systems for use in attacks against other systems
3. What type of attack targets proprietary information stored on a civilian organization's system?
   - **A.** Business attack
   - **B.** Denial-of-service attack
   - **C.** Financial attack
   - **D.** Military and intelligence attack
4. What goal is not a purpose of a financial attack?
   - **A.** Access services you have not purchased
   - **B.** Disclose confidential personal employee information
   - **C.** Transfer funds from an unapproved source into your account
   - **D.** Steal money from another organization
5. Which one of the following attacks is most indicative of a terrorist attack?
   - **A.** Altering sensitive trade secret documents
   - **B.** Damaging the ability to communicate and respond to a physical attack
   - **C.** Stealing unclassified information
   - **D.** Transferring funds to other countries
6. Which of the following would not be a primary goal of a grudge attack?
   - **A.** Disclosing embarrassing personal information
   - **B.** Launching a virus on an organization's system
   - **C.** Sending inappropriate email with a spoofed origination address of the victim organization
   - **D.** Using automated tools to scan the organization's systems for vulnerable ports

7. What are the primary reasons attackers engage in thrill attacks? (Choose all that apply.)
   A. Bragging rights
   B. Money from the sale of stolen documents
   C. Pride of conquering a secure system
   D. Retaliation against a person or organization
8. What is the most important rule to follow when collecting evidence?
   A. Do not turn off a computer until you photograph the screen.
   B. List all people present while collecting evidence.
   C. Never modify evidence during the collection process.
   D. Transfer all equipment to a secure storage location.
9. What would be a valid argument for not immediately removing power from a machine when an incident is discovered?
   A. All of the damage has been done. Turning the machine off would not stop additional damage.
   B. There is no other system that can replace this one if it is turned off.
   C. Too many users are logged in and using the system.
   D. Valuable evidence in memory will be lost.
10. Hacktivists are motivated by which of the following factors? (Choose all that apply.)
    A. Financial gain
    B. Thrill
    C. Skill
    D. Political beliefs
11. What is an incident?
    A. Any active attack that causes damage to your system
    B. Any violation of a code of ethics
    C. Any crime (or violation of a law or regulation) that involves a computer
    D. Any event that adversely affects the confidentiality, integrity, or availability of your data
12. If port scanning does no damage to a system, why is it generally considered an incident?
    A. All port scans indicate adversarial behavior.
    B. Port scans can precede attacks that cause damage and can indicate a future attack.
    C. Scanning a port damages the port.
    D. Port scanning uses system resources that could be put to better uses.
13. What type of incident is characterized by obtaining an increased level of privilege?
    A. Compromise
    B. Denial of service

C. Malicious code

D. Scanning

14. What is the best way to recognize abnormal and suspicious behavior on your system?

A. Be aware of the newest attacks.

B. Configure your IDS to detect and report all abnormal traffic.

C. Know what your normal system activity looks like.

D. Study the activity signatures of the main types of attacks.

15. If you need to confiscate a PC from a suspected attacker who does not work for your organization, what legal avenue is most appropriate?

A. Consent agreement signed by employees.

B. Search warrant.

C. No legal avenue is necessary.

D. Voluntary consent.

16. Why should you avoid deleting log files on a daily basis?

A. An incident may not be discovered for several days and valuable evidence could be lost.

B. Disk space is cheap, and log files are used frequently.

C. Log files are protected and cannot be altered.

D. Any information in a log file is useless after it is several hours old.

17. Which of the following conditions might require that you report an incident? (Choose all that apply.)

A. Confidential information protected by government regulation was possibly disclosed.

B. Damages exceeded $1,500.

C. The incident has occurred before.

D. The incident resulted in a violation of a law.

18. What are ethics?

A. Mandatory actions required to fulfill job requirements

B. Laws of professional conduct

C. Regulations set forth by a professional organization

D. Rules of personal behavior

19. According to the $(ISC)^2$ Code of Ethics, how are CISSPs expected to act?

A. Honestly, diligently, responsibly, and legally

B. Honorably, honestly, justly, responsibly, and legally

C. Upholding the security policy and protecting the organization

D. Trustworthy, loyally, friendly, courteously

20. Which of the following actions are considered unacceptable and unethical according to RFC 1087, "Ethics and the Internet"?

A. Actions that compromise the privacy of classified information

B. Actions that compromise the privacy of users

C. Actions that disrupt organizational activities

D. Actions in which a computer is used in a manner inconsistent with a stated security policy

Chapter

20

Software Development Security

THE CISSP EXAM TOPICS COVERED IN THIS CHAPTER INCLUDE:

✓ **A. Understand and apply security in the software development life cycle**

- A.1 Development methodologies (e.g., Agile, waterfall)
- A.2 Maturity models
- A.3 Operation and maintenance
- A.4 Change management
- A.5 Integrated product team (e.g., DevOps)

✓ **B. Enforce security controls in development environments**

- B.1 Security of the software environments
- B.3 Configuration management as an aspect of secure coding
- B.4 Security of code repositories
- B.5 Security of application programming interfaces

✓ **C. Assess the effectiveness of software security**

- C.1 Auditing and logging of changes
- C.2 Risk analysis and mitigation
- C.3 Acceptance testing

✓ **D. Assess security impact of acquired software**

Software development is a complex and challenging task undertaken by developers with many different skill levels and varying security awareness. Applications created and modified by these developers often work with sensitive data and interact with members of the general public. This presents significant risks to enterprise security, and information security professionals must understand these risks, balance them with business requirements, and implement appropriate risk mitigation mechanisms.

Introducing Systems Development Controls

Many organizations use custom-developed software to achieve flexible operational goals. These custom solutions can present great security vulnerabilities as a result of malicious and/or careless developers who create trap doors, buffer overflow vulnerabilities, or other weaknesses that can leave a system open to exploitation by malicious individuals.

To protect against these vulnerabilities, it's vital to introduce security controls into the entire systems development life cycle. An organized, methodical process helps ensure that solutions meet functional requirements as well as security guidelines. The following sections explore the spectrum of systems development activities with an eye toward security concerns that should be foremost on the mind of any information security professional engaged in solutions development.

Software Development

Security should be a consideration at every stage of a system's development, including the software development process. Programmers should strive to build security into every application they develop, with greater levels of security provided to critical applications and those that process sensitive information. It's extremely important to consider the security implications of a software development project from the early stages because it's much easier to build security into a system than it is to add security to an existing system.

Programming Languages

As you probably know, software developers use programming languages to develop software code. You might not know that several types of languages can be used simultaneously by the same system. This section takes a brief look at the different types of programming languages and the security implications of each.

Computers understand binary code. They speak a language of 1s and 0s, and that's it! The instructions that a computer follows consist of a long series of binary digits in a language known as *machine language*. Each CPU chipset has its own machine language, and it's virtually impossible for a human being to decipher anything but the simplest machine language code without the assistance of specialized software. Assembly language is a higher-level alternative that uses mnemonics to represent the basic instruction set of a CPU but still requires hardware-specific knowledge of a relatively obscure language. It also requires a large amount of tedious programming; a task as simple as adding two numbers together could take five or six lines of assembly code!

Programmers don't want to write their code in either machine language or assembly language. They prefer to use high-level languages, such as C++, Ruby, Java, and Visual Basic. These languages allow programmers to write instructions that better approximate human communication, decrease the length of time needed to craft an application, possibly decrease the number of programmers needed on a project, and also allow some portability between different operating systems and hardware platforms. Once programmers are ready to execute their programs, two options are available to them: compilation and interpretation.

Some languages (such as C, Java, and FORTRAN) are compiled languages. When using a compiled language, the programmer uses a tool known as a *compiler* to convert the higher-level language into an executable file designed for use on a specific operating system. This executable is then distributed to end users, who may use it as they see fit. Generally speaking, it's not possible to view or modify the software instructions in an executable file.

Other languages (such as JavaScript and VBScript) are interpreted languages. When these languages are used, the programmer distributes the source code, which contains instructions in the higher-level language. End users then use an interpreter to execute that source code on their systems. They're able to view the original instructions written by the programmer.

Each approach has security advantages and disadvantages. Compiled code is generally less prone to manipulation by a third party. However, it's also easier for a malicious (or unskilled) programmer to embed back doors and other security flaws in the code and escape detection because the original instructions can't be viewed by the end user. Interpreted code, however, is less prone to the insertion of malicious code by the original programmer because the end user may view the code and check it for accuracy. On the other hand, everyone who touches the software has the ability to modify the programmer's original instructions and possibly embed malicious code in the interpreted software. You'll learn more about the exploits attackers use to undermine software in the section "Application Attacks" in Chapter 21, "Malicious Code and Application Attacks."

Generations of Languages

For the CISSP exam, you should also be familiar with the programming language generations, which are defined as follows:

- *First-generation languages (1GL)* include all machine languages.
- *Second-generation languages (2GL)* include all assembly languages.
- *Third-generation languages (3GL)* include all compiled languages.
- *Fourth-generation languages (4GL)* attempt to approximate natural languages and include SQL, which is used by databases.
- *Fifth-generation languages (5GL)* allow programmers to create code using visual interfaces.

Object-Oriented Programming

Many modern programming languages, such as C++, Java, and the .NET languages, support the concept of object-oriented programming (OOP). Older programming styles, such as functional programming, focused on the flow of the program itself and attempted to model the desired behavior as a series of steps. Object-oriented programming focuses on the objects involved in an interaction. You can think of it as a group of objects that can be requested to perform certain operations or exhibit certain behaviors. Objects work together to provide a system's functionality or capabilities. OOP has the potential to be more reliable and able to reduce the propagation of program change errors. As a type of programming method, it is better suited to modeling or mimicking the real world. For example, a banking program might have three object classes that correspond to accounts, account holders, and employees, respectively. When a new account is added to the system, a new instance, or copy, of the appropriate object is created to contain the details of that account.

Each object in the OOP model has methods that correspond to specific actions that can be taken on the object. For example, the account object can have methods to add funds, deduct funds, close the account, and transfer ownership.

Objects can also be subclasses of other objects and inherit methods from their parent class. For example, the account object may have subclasses that correspond to specific types of accounts, such as savings, checking, mortgages, and auto loans. The subclasses can use all the methods of the parent class and have additional class-specific methods. For example, the checking object might have a method called `write_check()`, whereas the other subclasses do not.

From a security point of view, object-oriented programming provides a black-box approach to abstraction. Users need to know the details of an object's interface (generally the inputs, outputs, and actions that correspond to each of the object's methods) but don't necessarily need to know the inner workings of the object to use it effectively. To provide the desired characteristics of object-oriented systems, the objects are encapsulated (self-contained), and they can be accessed only through specific messages (in other words, input). Objects can also exhibit the substitution property, which allows different objects providing compatible operations to be substituted for each other.

Here are some common object-oriented programming terms you might come across in your work:

Message A message is a communication to or input of an object.

Method A method is internal code that defines the actions an object performs in response to a message.

Behavior The results or output exhibited by an object is a behavior. Behaviors are the results of a message being processed through a method.

Class A collection of the common methods from a set of objects that defines the behavior of those objects is a class.

Instance Objects are instances of or examples of classes that contain their methods.

Inheritance Inheritance occurs when methods from a class (parent or superclass) are inherited by another subclass (child).

Delegation Delegation is the forwarding of a request by an object to another object or delegate. An object delegates if it does not have a method to handle the message.

Polymorphism A polymorphism is the characteristic of an object that allows it to respond with different behaviors to the same message or method because of changes in external conditions.

Cohesion Cohesion describes the strength of the relationship between the purposes of the methods within the same class.

Coupling Coupling is the level of interaction between objects. Lower coupling means less interaction. Lower coupling provides better software design because objects are more independent. Lower coupling is easier to troubleshoot and update. Objects that have low cohesion require lots of assistance from other objects to perform tasks and have high coupling.

Assurance

To ensure that the security control mechanisms built into a new application properly implement the security policy throughout the life cycle of the system, administrators use *assurance procedures*. Assurance procedures are simply formalized processes by which trust is built into the life cycle of a system. The Trusted Computer System Evaluation Criteria (TCSEC) Orange Book refers to this process as *life cycle assurance*.

Avoiding and Mitigating System Failure

No matter how advanced your development team, your systems will likely fail at some point in time. You should plan for this type of failure when you put the software and hardware controls in place, ensuring that the system will respond appropriately. You can employ many methods to avoid failure, including using input validation and creating fail-safe or fail-open procedures. Let's talk about these in more detail.

Input Validation As users interact with software, they often provide information to the application in the form of input. This may include typing in values that are later used by a program. Developers often expect these values to fall within certain parameters. For example, if the programmer asks the user to enter a month, the program may expect to see an integer value between 1 and 12. If the user enters a value outside of that range, a poorly written program may crash, at best, or allow the user to gain control of the underlying system, at worst.

Input validation verifies that the values provided by a user match the programmer's expectation before allowing further processing. For example, input validation would check whether a month value is an integer between 1 and 12. If the value falls outside that range, the program will not try to process the number as a date and will inform the user of the input expectations. This type of input validation, where the code checks to ensure that a number falls within an acceptable range, is known as a *limit check*.

Input validation also may check for unusual characters, such as quotation marks within a text field, that may be indicative of an attack. In some cases, the input validation routine can transform the input to remove risky character sequences and replace them with safe values. This process is known as escaping input.

Input validation should always occur on the server side of the transaction. Any code sent to the user's browser is subject to manipulation by the user and is therefore easily circumvented.

TIP

In most organizations, security professionals come from a system administration background and don't have professional experience in software development. If your background doesn't include this type of experience, don't let that stop you from learning about it and educating your organization's developers on the importance of secure coding.

Fail-secure and fail-open In spite of the best efforts of programmers, product designers, and project managers, developed applications will be used in unexpected ways. Some of these conditions will cause failures. Since failures are unpredictable, programmers should design into their code a general sense of how to respond to and handle failures.

There are two basic choices when planning for system failure:

- The *fail-secure failure state* puts the system into a high level of security (and possibly even disables it entirely) until an administrator can diagnose the problem and restore the system to normal operation.

- The *fail-open state* allows users to bypass failed security controls, erring on the side of permissiveness.

In the vast majority of environments, fail-secure is the appropriate failure state because it prevents unauthorized access to information and resources.

Software should revert to a fail-secure condition. This may mean closing just the application or possibly stopping the operation of the entire host system. An example of such failure response is seen in the Windows OS with the appearance of the infamous Blue Screen of Death (BSOD), indicating the occurrence of a STOP error. A STOP error occurs when an undesirable activity occurs in spite of the OS's efforts to prevent it. This could include an application gaining direct access to hardware, an attempt to bypass a security access check, or one process interfering with the memory space of another. Once one of these conditions occurs, the environment is no longer trustworthy. So, rather than continuing to support an unreliable and insecure operating environment, the OS initiates a STOP error as its fail-secure response.

Once a fail-secure operation occurs, the programmer should consider the activities that occur afterward. The options are to remain in a fail-secure state or to automatically reboot the system. The former option requires an administrator to manually reboot the system and oversee the process. This action can be enforced by using a boot password. The latter option does not require human intervention for the system to restore itself to a functioning state, but it has its own unique issues. For example, it must restrict the system to reboot into a nonprivileged state. In other words, the system should not reboot and perform an automatic logon; instead, it should prompt the user for authorized access credentials.

WARNING

In limited circumstances, it may be appropriate to implement a fail-open failure state. This is sometimes appropriate for lower-layer components of a multilayered security system. Fail-open systems should be used with extreme caution. Before deploying a system using this failure mode, clearly validate the business requirement for this move. If it is justified, ensure that adequate alternative controls are in place to protect the organization's resources should the system fail. It's extremely rare that you'd want all your security controls to use a fail-open approach.

Even when security is properly designed and embedded in software, that security is often disabled in order to support easier installation. Thus, it is common for the IT administrator to have the responsibility of turning on and configuring security to match the needs of his or her specific environment. Maintaining security is often a trade-off with user-friendliness and functionality, as you can see in Figure 20.1. Additionally, as you add or increase security, you will also increase costs, increase administrative overhead, and reduce productivity/throughput.

FIGURE 20.1 Security vs. user-friendliness vs. functionality

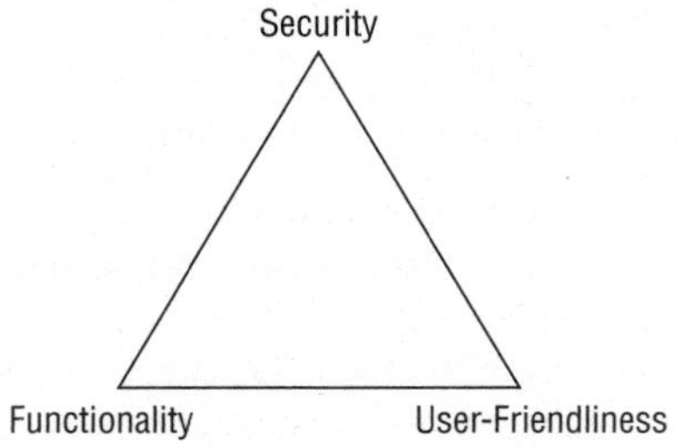

Systems Development Life Cycle

Security is most effective if it is planned and managed throughout the life cycle of a system or application. Administrators employ project management to keep a development project on target and moving toward the goal of a completed product. Often project management is structured using life cycle models to direct the development process. Using formalized life cycle models helps ensure good coding practices and the embedding of security in every stage of product development.

All systems development processes should have several activities in common. Although they may not necessarily share the same names, these core activities are essential to the development of sound, secure systems:

- Conceptual definition
- Functional requirements determination
- Control specifications development
- Design review
- Code review walk-through
- System test review
- Maintenance and change management

The section "Life Cycle Models" later in this chapter examines two life cycle models and shows how these activities are applied in real-world software engineering environments.

NOTE It's important to note at this point that the terminology used in systems development life cycles varies from model to model and from publication to publication. Don't spend too much time worrying about the exact terms used in this book or any of the other literature you may come across. When taking the CISSP examination, it's much more important that you have an understanding of how the process works and of the fundamental principles underlying the development of secure systems.

Conceptual Definition

The conceptual definition phase of systems development involves creating the basic concept statement for a system. It's a simple statement agreed on by all interested stakeholders (the developers, customers, and management) that states the purpose of the project as well as the general system requirements. The conceptual definition is a very high-level statement of purpose and should not be longer than one or two paragraphs. If you were reading a detailed summary of the project, you might expect to see the concept statement as an abstract or introduction that enables an outsider to gain a top-level understanding of the project in a short period of time.

It's very helpful to refer to the concept statement at all phases of the systems development process. Often, the intricate details of the development process tend to obscure the overarching goal of the project. Simply reading the concept statement periodically can assist in refocusing a team of developers.

Functional Requirements Determination

Once all stakeholders have agreed on the concept statement, it's time for the development team to sit down and begin the functional requirements process. In this phase, specific system functionalities are listed, and developers begin to think about how the parts of the system should interoperate to meet the functional requirements. The deliverable from this phase of development is a functional requirements document that lists the specific system requirements.

As with the concept statement, it's important to ensure that all stakeholders agree on the functional requirements document before work progresses to the next level. When it's finally completed, the document shouldn't be simply placed on a shelf to gather dust—the entire development team should constantly refer to this document during all phases to ensure that the project is on track. In the final stages of testing and evaluation, the project managers should use this document as a checklist to ensure that all functional requirements are met.

Control Specifications Development

Security-conscious organizations also ensure that adequate security controls are designed into every system from the earliest stages of development. It's often useful to have a control specifications development phase in your life cycle model. This phase takes place soon after the development of functional requirements and often continues as the design and design review phases progress.

During the development of control specifications, it's important to analyze the system from a number of security perspectives. First, adequate access controls must be designed into every system to ensure that only authorized users are allowed to access the system and that they are not permitted to exceed their level of authorization. Second, the system must maintain the confidentiality of vital data through the use of appropriate encryption and data protection technologies. Next, the system should provide both an audit trail to enforce individual accountability and a detective mechanism for illegitimate activity. Finally, depending on the criticality of the system, availability and fault-tolerance issues should be addressed as corrective actions.

Keep in mind that designing security into a system is not a one-time process and it must be done proactively. All too often, systems are designed without security planning, and then developers attempt to retrofit the system with appropriate security mechanisms. Unfortunately, these mechanisms are an afterthought and do not fully integrate with the system's design, which leaves gaping security vulnerabilities. Also, the security requirements should be revisited each time a significant change is made to the design specifications. If a major component of the system changes, it's likely that the security requirements will change as well.

Design Review

Once the functional and control specifications are complete, let the system designers do their thing! In this often-lengthy process, the designers determine exactly how the various parts of the system will interoperate and how the modular system structure will be laid out. Also, during this phase the design management team commonly sets specific tasks for various teams and lays out initial timelines for the completion of coding milestones.

After the design team completes the formal design documents, a review meeting with the stakeholders should be held to ensure that everyone is in agreement that the process is still on track for the successful development of a system with the desired functionality.

Code Review Walk-Through

Once the stakeholders have given the software design their blessing, it's time for the software developers to start writing code. Project managers should schedule several code review walk-through meetings at various milestones throughout the coding process. These technical meetings usually involve only development personnel, who sit down with a copy of the code for a specific module and walk through it, looking for problems in logical flow or other design/security flaws. The meetings play an instrumental role in ensuring that the code produced by the various development teams performs according to specification.

User Acceptance Testing

After many code reviews and a lot of long nights, there will come a point at which a developer puts in that final semicolon and declares the system complete. As any seasoned software engineer knows, the system is never complete. Now it's time to begin the user acceptance testing phase. Initially, most organizations perform the initial system tests using development personnel to seek out any obvious errors. As the testing progresses, developers and actual users validate the system against predefined scenarios that model common and unusual user activities.

Once this phase is complete, the code may move to deployment. As with any critical development process, it's important that you maintain a copy of the written test plan and test results for future review.

Maintenance and Change Management

Once a system is operational, a variety of maintenance tasks are necessary to ensure continued operation in the face of changing operational, data processing, storage, and environmental requirements. It's essential that you have a skilled support team in place to handle any routine or unexpected maintenance. It's also important that any changes to the code be handled through a formalized change management process, as described in Chapter 1, "Security Governance through Principles and Policies."

Life Cycle Models

One of the major complaints you'll hear from practitioners of the more established engineering disciplines (such as civil, mechanical, and electrical engineering) is that software engineering is not an engineering discipline at all. In fact, they contend, it's simply a combination of chaotic processes that somehow manage to scrape out workable solutions from time to time. Indeed, some of the "software engineering" that takes place in today's development environments is nothing but bootstrap coding held together by "duct tape and chicken wire."

However, the adoption of more formalized life cycle management processes is seen in mainstream software engineering as the industry matures. After all, it's hardly fair to compare the processes of an age-old discipline such as civil engineering to those of an industry that's only a few decades old. In the 1970s and 1980s, pioneers like Winston Royce and Barry Boehm proposed several software development life cycle (SDLC) models to help guide the practice toward formalized processes. In 1991, the Software Engineering Institute introduced the Capability Maturity Model, which described the process organizations undertake as they move toward incorporating solid engineering principles into their software development processes. In the following sections, we'll take a look at the work produced by these studies. Having a management model in place should improve the resultant products. However, if the SDLC methodology is inadequate, the project may fail to meet business and user needs. Thus, it is important to verify that the SDLC model is properly implemented and is appropriate for your environment. Furthermore, one of the initial steps of implementing an SDLC should include management approval.

Waterfall Model

Originally developed by Winston Royce in 1970, the waterfall model seeks to view the systems development life cycle as a series of iterative activities. As shown in Figure 20.2, the traditional waterfall model has seven stages of development. As each stage is completed, the project moves into the next phase. As illustrated by the backward arrows, the modern waterfall model does allow development to return to the previous phase to correct defects discovered during the subsequent phase. This is often known as the *feedback loop characteristic* of the waterfall model.

FIGURE 20.2 The waterfall life cycle model

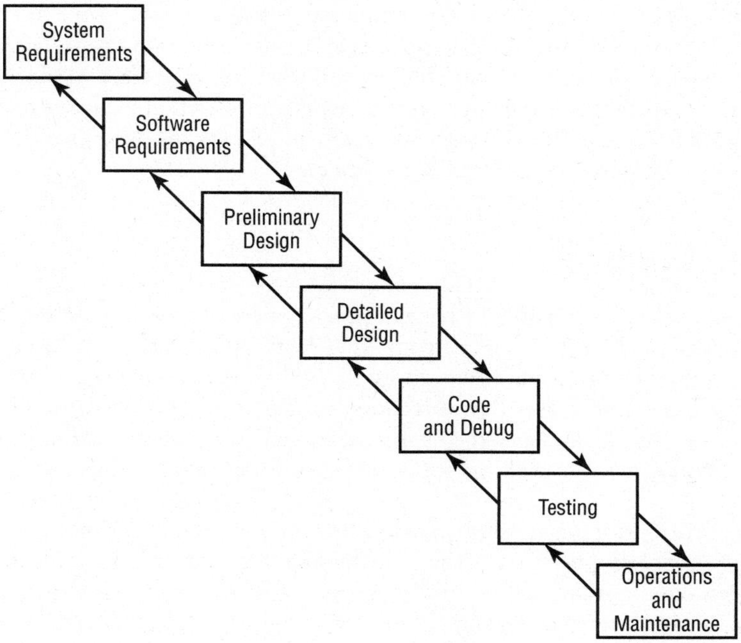

The waterfall model was one of the first comprehensive attempts to model the software development process while taking into account the necessity of returning to previous phases to correct system faults. However, one of the major criticisms of this model is that it allows the developers to step back only one phase in the process. It does not make provisions for the discovery of errors at a later phase in the development cycle.

NOTE: The waterfall model was improved by adding validation and verification steps to each phase. Verification evaluates the product against specifications, whereas validation evaluates how well the product satisfies real-world requirements. The improved model was labeled the *modified* waterfall model. However, it did not gain widespread use before the spiral model dominated the project management scene.

Spiral Model

In 1988, Barry Boehm of TRW proposed an alternative life cycle model that allows for multiple iterations of a waterfall-style process. Figure 20.3 illustrates this model. Because the spiral model encapsulates a number of iterations of another model (the waterfall model), it is known as a *metamodel*, or a "model of models."

FIGURE 20.3 The spiral life cycle model

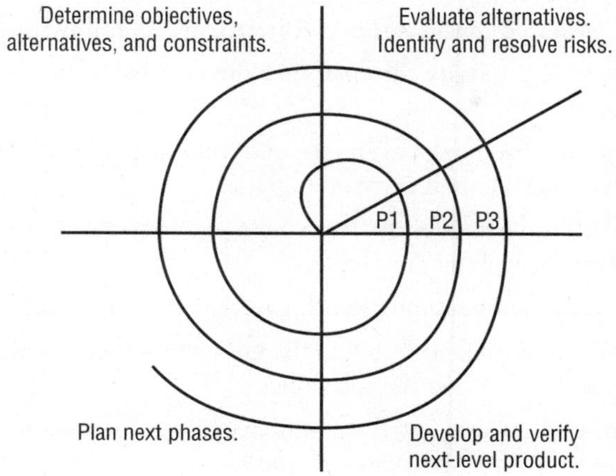
Determine objectives,
alternatives, and constraints.
Evaluate alternatives.
Identify and resolve risks.
P1
P2
P3
Plan next phases.
Develop and verify
next-level product.

Notice that each "loop" of the spiral results in the development of a new system prototype (represented by P1, P2, and P3 in Figure 20.3). Theoretically, system developers would apply the entire waterfall process to the development of each prototype, thereby incrementally working toward a mature system that incorporates all the functional requirements in a fully validated fashion. Boehm's spiral model provides a solution to the major criticism of the waterfall model—it allows developers to return to the planning stages as changing technical demands and customer requirements necessitate the evolution of a system.

Agile Software Development

More recently, the Agile model of software development has gained popularity within the software engineering community. Beginning in the mid-1990s, developers increasingly embraced approaches to software development that eschewed the rigid models of the past in favor of approaches that placed an emphasis on the needs of the customer and on quickly developing new functionality that meets those needs in an iterative fashion.

Seventeen pioneers of the Agile development approach got together in 2001 and produced a document titled *Manifesto for Agile Software Development* (`http://agilemanifesto.org`) that states the core philosophy of the Agile approach:

> We are uncovering better ways of developing software by doing it and helping others do it. Through this work we have come to value:
>
> **Individuals and interactions** over processes and tools
>
> **Working software** over comprehensive documentation
>
> **Customer collaboration** over contract negotiation
>
> **Responding to change** over following a plan
>
> That is, while there is value in the items on the right, we value the items on the left more.

The *Agile Manifesto* also defines 12 principles that underlie the philosophy, which are available here: `http://agilemanifesto.org/principles.html`.

The 12 principles, as stated in the Agile Manifesto, are as follows:

- Our highest priority is to satisfy the customer through early and continuous delivery of valuable software.
- Welcome changing requirements, even late in development. Agile processes harness change for the customer's competitive advantage.
- Deliver working software frequently, from a couple of weeks to a couple of months, with a preference to the shorter timescale.
- Business people and developers must work together daily throughout the project.
- Build projects around motivated individuals. Give them the environment and support they need, and trust them to get the job done.
- The most efficient and effective method of conveying information to and within a development team is face-to-face conversation.
- Working software is the primary measure of progress.
- Agile processes promote sustainable development. The sponsors, developers, and users should be able to maintain a constant pace indefinitely.
- Continuous attention to technical excellence and good design enhances agility.
- Simplicity—the art of maximizing the amount of work not done—is essential.
- The best architectures, requirements, and designs emerge from self-organizing teams.
- At regular intervals, the team reflects on how to become more effective, then tunes and adjusts its behavior accordingly.

The Agile development approach is quickly gaining momentum in the software community and has many variants, including Scrum, Agile Unified Process (AUP), the Dynamic Systems Development Model (DSDM), and Extreme Programming (XP).

Software Capability Maturity Model

The Software Engineering Institute (SEI) at Carnegie Mellon University introduced the Capability Maturity Model for Software, also known as the Software Capability Maturity Model (abbreviated as SW-CMM, CMM, or SCMM), which contends that all organizations engaged in software development move through a variety of maturity phases in sequential fashion. The SW-CMM describes the principles and practices underlying software process maturity. It is intended to help software organizations improve the maturity and quality of their software processes by implementing an evolutionary path from ad hoc, chaotic processes to mature, disciplined software processes. The idea behind the SW-CMM is that the quality of software depends on the quality of its development process.

The stages of the SW-CMM are as follows:

Level 1: Initial In this phase, you'll often find hardworking people charging ahead in a disorganized fashion. There is usually little or no defined software development process.

Level 2: Repeatable In this phase, basic life cycle management processes are introduced. Reuse of code in an organized fashion begins to enter the picture, and repeatable results are expected from similar projects. SEI defines the key process areas for this level as Requirements Management, Software Project Planning, Software Project Tracking and Oversight, Software Subcontract Management, Software Quality Assurance, and Software Configuration Management.

Level 3: Defined In this phase, software developers operate according to a set of formal, documented software development processes. All development projects take place within the constraints of the new standardized management model. SEI defines the key process areas for this level as Organization Process Focus, Organization Process Definition, Training Program, Integrated Software Management, Software Product Engineering, Intergroup Coordination, and Peer Reviews.

Level 4: Managed In this phase, management of the software process proceeds to the next level. Quantitative measures are utilized to gain a detailed understanding of the development process. SEI defines the key process areas for this level as Quantitative Process Management and Software Quality Management.

Level 5: Optimizing In the optimized organization, a process of continuous improvement occurs. Sophisticated software development processes are in place that ensure that feedback from one phase reaches to the previous phase to improve future results. SEI defines the key process areas for this level as Defect Prevention, Technology Change Management, and Process Change Management. For more information on the Capability Maturity Model for Software, visit the Software Engineering Institute's website at `www.sei.cmu.edu`.

IDEAL Model

The Software Engineering Institute also developed the IDEAL model for software development, which implements many of the SW-CMM attributes. The IDEAL model has five phases:

I: Initiating In the initiating phase of the IDEAL model, the business reasons behind the change are outlined, support is built for the initiative, and the appropriate infrastructure is put in place.

2: Diagnosing During the diagnosing phase, engineers analyze the current state of the organization and make general recommendations for change.

3: Establishing In the establishing phase, the organization takes the general recommendations from the diagnosing phase and develops a specific plan of action that helps achieve those changes.

4: Acting In the acting phase, it's time to stop "talking the talk" and "walk the walk." The organization develops solutions and then tests, refines, and implements them.

5: Learning As with any quality improvement process, the organization must continuously analyze its efforts to determine whether it has achieved the desired goals and, when necessary, propose new actions to put the organization back on course.

The IDEAL model is illustrated in Figure 20.4.

FIGURE 20.4 The IDEAL model

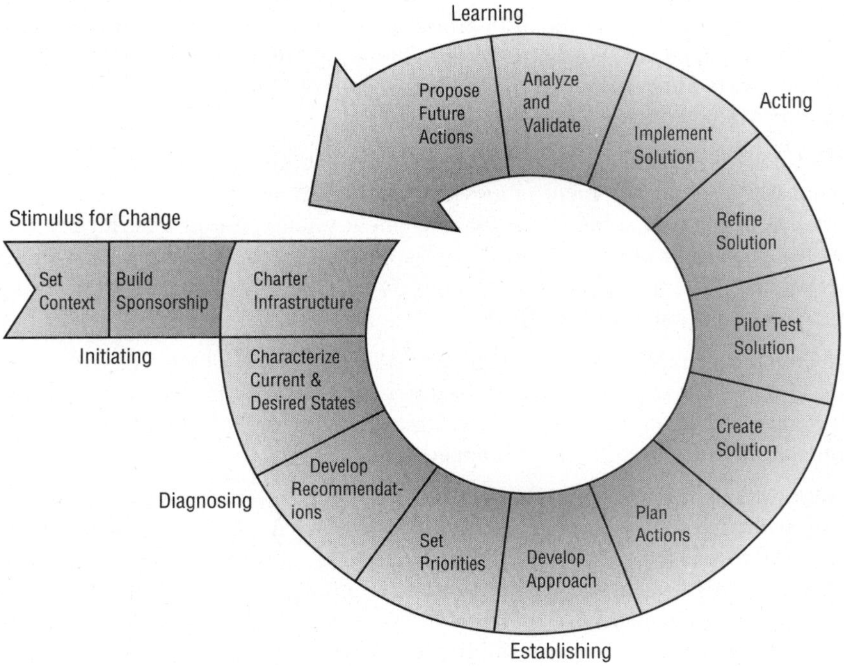

Special permission to reproduce "IDEAL Model," ©2004 by Carnegie Mellon University, is granted by the Carnegie Mellon Software Engineering Institute.

SW-CMM and IDEAL Model Memorization

To help you remember the initial letters of each of the 10 level names of the SW-CMM and IDEAL models (II DR ED AM LO), imagine yourself sitting on the couch in a psychiatrist's office saying, "I…I, Dr. Ed, am lo(w)." If you can remember that phrase, then you can extract the 10 initial letters of the level names. If you write the letters out into two columns, you can reconstruct the level names in order of the two systems. The left column is the IDEAL model, and the right represents the levels of the SW-CMM.

Initiating	Initiating
Diagnosing	Repeatable
Establishing	Defined
Acting	Managed
Learning	Optimized

Gantt Charts and PERT

A Gantt chart is a type of bar chart that shows the interrelationships over time between projects and schedules. It provides a graphical illustration of a schedule that helps to plan, coordinate, and track specific tasks in a project. Figure 20.5 shows an example of a Gantt chart.

FIGURE 20.5 Gantt chart

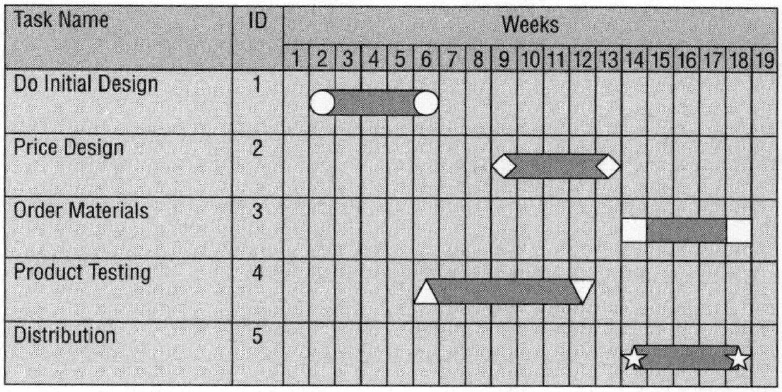

Program Evaluation Review Technique (PERT) is a project-scheduling tool used to judge the size of a software product in development and calculate the standard deviation (SD) for risk assessment. PERT relates the estimated lowest possible size, the most likely size, and the highest possible size of each component. PERT is used to direct improvements to project management and software coding in order to produce more efficient software. As the capabilities of programming and management improve, the actual produced size of software should be smaller.

Change and Configuration Management

Once software has been released into a production environment, users will inevitably request the addition of new features, correction of bugs, and other modifications to the code. Just as the organization developed a regimented process for developing software, they must also put a procedure in place to manage changes in an organized fashion. Those changes should then be logged to a central repository to support future auditing, investigation, and analysis requirements.

Change Management as a Security Tool

Change management (also known as control management) plays an important role when monitoring systems in the controlled environment of a datacenter. One of the authors recently worked with an organization that used change management as an essential component of its efforts to detect unauthorized changes to computing systems.

> In Chapter 20, "Software Development Security," you'll learn how tools for monitoring file integrity, such as Tripwire, allow you to monitor a system for changes. This organization used Tripwire to monitor hundreds of production servers. However, the organization quickly found itself overwhelmed by file modification alerts resulting from normal activity. The author worked with them to tune the Tripwire-monitoring policies and integrate them with the organization's change management process. Now all Tripwire alerts go to a centralized monitoring center, where administrators correlate them with approved changes. System administrators receive an alert only if the security team identifies a change that does not appear to correlate with an approved change request.
>
> This approach greatly reduced the time spent by administrators reviewing file integrity reports and improved the usefulness of the tool to security administrators.

The change management process has three basic components:

Request Control The request control process provides an organized framework within which users can request modifications, managers can conduct cost/benefit analysis, and developers can prioritize tasks.

Change Control The change control process is used by developers to re-create the situation encountered by the user and analyze the appropriate changes to remedy the situation. It also provides an organized framework within which multiple developers can create and test a solution prior to rolling it out into a production environment. Change control includes conforming to quality control restrictions, developing tools for update or change deployment, properly documenting any coded changes, and restricting the effects of new code to minimize diminishment of security.

Release Control Once the changes are finalized, they must be approved for release through the release control procedure. An essential step of the release control process is to double-check and ensure that any code inserted as a programming aid during the change process (such as debugging code and/or back doors) is removed before releasing the new software to production. Release control should also include acceptance testing to ensure that any alterations to end-user work tasks are understood and functional.

In addition to the change management process, security administrators should be aware of the importance of configuration management. This process is used to control the version(s) of software used throughout an organization and formally track and control changes to the software configuration. It has four main components:

Configuration Identification During the configuration identification process, administrators document the configuration of covered software products throughout the organization.

Configuration Control The configuration control process ensures that changes to software versions are made in accordance with the change control and configuration management policies. Updates can be made only from authorized distributions in accordance with those policies.

Configuration Status Accounting Formalized procedures are used to keep track of all authorized changes that take place.

Configuration Audit A periodic configuration audit should be conducted to ensure that the actual production environment is consistent with the accounting records and that no unauthorized configuration changes have taken place.

Together, change and configuration management techniques form an important part of the software engineer's arsenal and protect the organization from development-related security issues.

The DevOps Approach

Recently, many technology professionals recognized a disconnect between the major IT functions of software development, quality assurance, and technology operations. These functions, typically staffed with very different types of individuals and located in separate organizational silos, often conflicted with each other. This conflict resulted in lengthy delays in creating code, testing it, and deploying it onto production systems. When problems arose, instead of working together to cooperatively solve the issue, teams often "threw problems over the fence" at each other, resulting in bureaucratic back-and-forth.

The DevOps approach seeks to resolve these issues by bringing the three functions together in a single operational model. The word *DevOps* is a combination of Development and Operations, symbolizing that these functions must merge and cooperate to meet business requirements. The model in Figure 20.6 illustrates the overlapping nature of software development, quality assurance, and IT operations.

FIGURE 20.6 The DevOps model

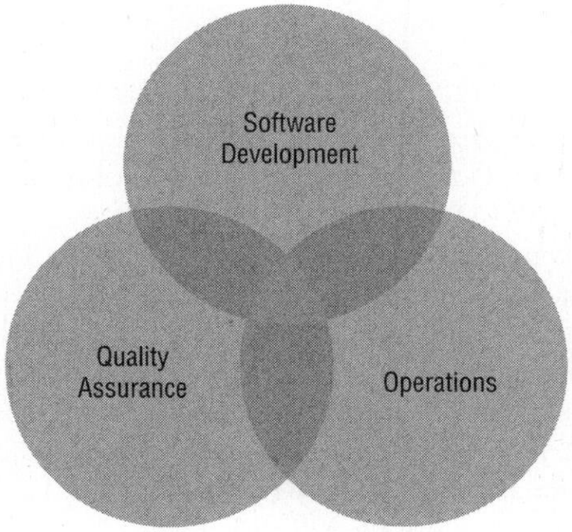

The DevOps model is closely aligned with the Agile development approach and aims to dramatically decrease the time required to develop, test, and deploy software changes. Although traditional approaches often resulted in major software deployments on a very infrequent basis, perhaps annually, organizations using the DevOps model often deploy code several times per day. Some organizations even strive to reach the goal of continuous deployment, where code may roll out dozens or even hundreds of times per day.

NOTE If you're interested in learning more about DevOps, the authors highly recommend the book *The Phoenix Project: A Novel about IT, DevOps, and Helping Your Business Win* by Gene Kim, Kevin Behr, and George Spafford (IT Revolution Press, 2013). This book presents the case for DevOps and shares DevOps strategies in an entertaining, engaging novel form.

Application Programming Interfaces

Although early web applications were often stand-alone systems that processed user requests and provided output, modern web applications are much more complex. They often include interactions between a number of different web services. For example, a retail website might make use of an external credit card processing service, allow users to share their purchases on social media, integrate with shipping provider sites, and offer a referral program on other websites.

For these cross-site functions to work properly, the websites must interact with each other. Many organizations offer *application programming interfaces (APIs)* for this purpose. APIs allow application developers to bypass traditional web pages and interact directly with the underlying service through function calls. For example, a social media API might include some of the following API function calls:

- Post status
- Follow user
- Unfollow user
- Like/Favorite a post

Offering and using APIs creates tremendous opportunities for service providers, but it also poses some security risks. Developers must be aware of these challenges and address them when they create and use APIs.

First, developers must consider authentication requirements. Some APIs, such as those that allow checking weather forecasts or product inventory, may be available to the general public and not require any authentication for use. Other APIs, such as those that allow modifying information, placing orders, or accessing sensitive information, may be limited to specific users and depend on secure authentication. API developers must know when to require authentication and ensure that they verify credentials and authorization for every API call. This authentication is typically done by providing authorized API users with a complex API key that is passed with each API call. The backend system validates this API key before processing a request, ensuring that the system making the request is authorized to make the specific API call.

WARNING API keys are like passwords and should be treated as very sensitive information. They should always be stored in secure locations and transmitted only over encrypted communications channels. If someone gains access to your API key, they can interact with a web service as if they were you!

APIs must also be tested thoroughly for security flaws, just like any web application. You'll learn more about this in the next section.

Software Testing

As part of the development process, your organization should thoroughly test any software before distributing it internally (or releasing it to market). The best time to address testing is as the modules are designed. In other words, the mechanisms you use to test a product and the data sets you use to explore that product should be designed in parallel with the product itself. Your programming team should develop special test suites of data that exercise all paths of the software to the fullest extent possible and know the correct resulting outputs beforehand.

One of the tests you should perform is a *reasonableness check*. The reasonableness check ensures that values returned by software match specified criteria that are within reasonable bounds. For example, a routine that calculated optimal weight for a human being and returned a value of 612 pounds would certainly fail a reasonableness check!

Furthermore, while conducting software testing, you should check how the product handles normal and valid input data, incorrect types, out-of-range values, and other bounds and/or conditions. Live workloads provide the best stress testing possible. However, you should not use live or actual field data for testing, especially in the early development stages, since a flaw or error could result in the violation of integrity or confidentiality of the test data.

When testing software, you should apply the same rules of separation of duties that you do for other aspects of your organization. In other words, you should assign the testing of your software to someone other than the programmer(s) who developed the code to avoid a conflict of interest and assure a more secure and functional finished product. When a third party tests your software, you have a greater likelihood of receiving an objective and nonbiased examination. The third-party test allows for a broader and more thorough test and prevents the bias and inclinations of the programmers from affecting the results of the test.

You can use three software testing methods:

White-box Testing White-box testing examines the internal logical structures of a program and steps through the code line by line, analyzing the program for potential errors.

Black-box Testing Black-box testing examines the program from a user perspective by providing a wide variety of input scenarios and inspecting the output. Black-box testers do not have access to the internal code. Final acceptance testing that occurs prior to system delivery is a common example of black-box testing.

Gray-box Testing Gray-box testing combines the two approaches and is popular for software validation. In this approach, testers examine the software from a user perspective, analyzing inputs and outputs. They also have access to the source code and use it to help design their tests. They do not, however, analyze the inner workings of the program during their testing.

In addition to assessing the quality of software, programmers and security professionals should carefully assess the security of their software to ensure that it meets the organization's security requirements. This is especially critical for web applications that are exposed to the public. There are two categories of testing used specifically to evaluate application security:

Static Testing Static testing evaluates the security of software without running it by analyzing either the source code or the compiled application. Static analysis usually involves the use of automated tools designed to detect common software flaws, such as buffer overflows. (For more on buffer overflows, see Chapter 21, "Malicious Code and Application Attacks.") In mature development environments, application developers are given access to static analysis tools and use them throughout the design/build/test process.

Dynamic Testing Dynamic testing evaluates the security of software in a runtime environment and is often the only option for organizations deploying applications written by someone else. In those cases, testers often do not have access to the underlying source code. One common example of dynamic software testing is the use of web application scanning tools to detect the presence of cross-site scripting, SQL injection, or other flaws in web applications. Dynamic tests on a production environment should always be carefully coordinated to avoid an unintended interruption of service.

Proper software test implementation is a key element in the project development process. Many of the common mistakes and oversights often found in commercial and in-house software can be eliminated. Keep the test plan and results as part of the system's permanent documentation.

Code Repositories

Software development is a collaborative effort, and large software projects require teams of developers who may simultaneously work on different parts of the code. Further complicating the situation is the fact that these developers may be geographically dispersed around the world.

Code repositories provide several important functions supporting these collaborations. Primarily, they act as a central storage point for developers to place their source code. In addition, code repositories such as GitHub, Bitbucket, and SourceForge also provide version control, bug tracking, web hosting, release management, and communications functions that support software development.

Code repositories are wonderful collaborative tools that facilitate software development, but they also have security risks of their own. First, developers must appropriately control access to their repositories. Some repositories, such as those supporting open source software development, may allow public access. Others, such as those hosting code containing trade secret information, may be more limited, restricting access to authorized developers. Repository owners must carefully design access controls to only allow appropriate users read and/or write access.

Sensitive Information and Code Repositories

Developers must take care not to include sensitive information in public code repositories. This is particularly true of API keys.

Many developers use APIs to access the underlying functionality of Infrastructure-as-a-Service providers, such as Amazon Web Services (AWS), Microsoft Azure, and Google Compute Engine. This provides tremendous benefits, allowing developers to quickly provision servers, modify network configuration, and allocate storage using simple API calls.

Of course, IaaS providers charge for these services. When a developer provisions a server, it triggers an hourly charge for that server until it is shut down. The API key used to create a server ties the server to a particular user account (and credit card!).

If developers write code that includes API keys and then upload that key to a public repository, anyone in the world can then gain access to their API key. This allows anyone to create IaaS resources and charge it to the original developer's credit card!

Further worsening the situation, hackers have written bots that scour public code repositories searching for exposed API keys. These bots may detect an inadvertently posted key in seconds, allowing the hacker to quickly provision massive computing resources before the developer even knows of their mistake!

Service-Level Agreements

Using service-level agreements (SLAs) is an increasingly popular way to ensure that organizations providing services to internal and/or external customers maintain an appropriate level of service agreed on by both the service provider and the vendor. It's a wise move to put SLAs in place for any data circuits, applications, information processing systems, databases, or other critical components that are vital to your organization's continued viability. The following issues are commonly addressed in SLAs:

- System uptime (as a percentage of overall operating time)
- Maximum consecutive downtime (in seconds/minutes/and so on)
- Peak load
- Average load

- Responsibility for diagnostics
- Failover time (if redundancy is in place)

Service-level agreements also commonly include financial and other contractual remedies that kick in if the agreement is not maintained. For example, if a critical circuit is down for more than 15 minutes, the service provider might agree to waive all charges on that circuit for one week.

Software Acquisition

Most of the software used by enterprises is not developed internally but purchased from vendors. Some of this software is purchased to run on servers managed by the organization, either on premises or in an Infrastructure-as-a-Service (IaaS) environment. Other software is purchased and delivered over the Internet through web browsers, in a Software-as-a-Service (SaaS) approach. Most organizations use a combination of these approaches depending on business needs and software availability.

For example, organizations may approach email service in two ways. They might purchase physical or virtual servers and then install email software on them, such as Microsoft Exchange. In that case, the organization purchases Exchange licenses from Microsoft and then installs, configures, and manages the email environment.

As an alternative, the organization might choose to outsource email entirely to Google, Microsoft, or another vendor. Users then access email through their web browsers or other tools, interacting directly with the email servers managed by the vendor. In this case, the organization is only responsible for creating accounts and managing some application-level settings.

In either case, security is of paramount concern. When the organization purchases and configures software itself, security professionals must understand the proper configuration of that software to meet security objectives. They also must remain vigilant about security bulletins and patches that correct newly discovered vulnerabilities. Failure to meet these obligations may result in an insecure environment.

In the case of SaaS environments, most security responsibility rests with the vendor, but the organization's security staff isn't off the hook. Although they might not be responsible for as much configuration, they now take on responsibility for monitoring the vendor's security. This may include audits, assessments, vulnerability scans, and other measures designed to verify that the vendor maintains proper controls.

Establishing Databases and Data Warehousing

Almost every modern organization maintains some sort of database that contains information critical to operations—be it customer contact information, order-tracking data, human resource and benefits information, or sensitive trade secrets. It's likely that many of these databases contain personal information that users hold secret, such as credit card usage activity, travel habits, grocery store purchases, and telephone records. Because of the growing reliance on database systems, information security professionals must ensure that adequate security controls exist to protect them against unauthorized access, tampering, or destruction of data.

In the following sections, we'll discuss database management system (DBMS) architecture, including the various types of DBMSs and their features. Then we'll discuss database security considerations, including polyinstantiation, ODBC, aggregation, inference, and data mining.

Database Management System Architecture

Although a variety of database management system (DBMS) architectures are available today, the vast majority of contemporary systems implement a technology known as relational database management systems (RDBMSs). For this reason, the following sections focus primarily on relational databases. However, first we'll discuss two other important DBMS architectures: hierarchical and distributed.

Hierarchical and Distributed Databases

A hierarchical data model combines records and fields that are related in a logical tree structure. This results in a one-to-many data model, where each node may have zero, one, or many children but only one parent. An example of a hierarchical data model appears in Figure 20.7.

FIGURE 20.7 Hierarchical data model

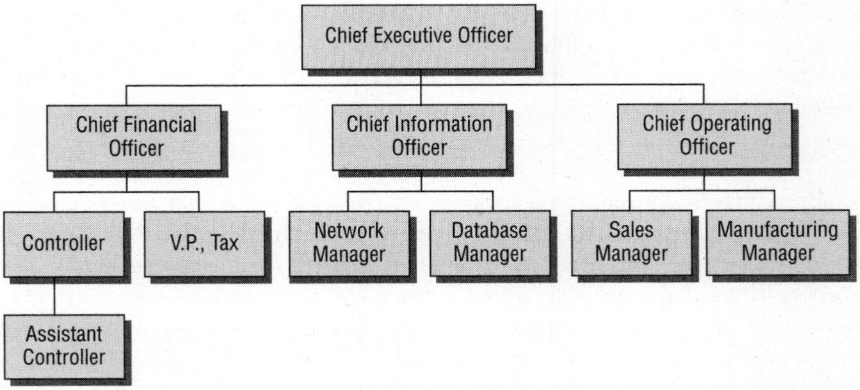

The hierarchical model in Figure 20.7 is a corporate organization chart. Notice that the one-to-many data model holds true in this example. Each employee has only one manager (the *one* in *one-to-many*), but each manager may have one or more (the *many*) employees. Other examples of hierarchical data models include the NCAA March Madness bracket system and the hierarchical distribution of Domain Name System (DNS) records used on the Internet. Hierarchical databases store data in this type of hierarchical fashion and are useful for specialized applications that fit the model. For example, biologists might use a hierarchical database to store data on specimens according to the kingdom/phylum/class/order/family/genus/species hierarchical model used in that field.

The distributed data model has data stored in more than one database, but those databases are logically connected. The user perceives the database as a single entity, even though it consists of numerous parts interconnected over a network. Each field can have numerous children as well as numerous parents. Thus, the data mapping relationship for distributed databases is many-to-many.

Relational Databases

A relational database consists of flat two-dimensional tables made up of rows and columns. In fact, each table looks similar to a spreadsheet file. The row and column structure provides for one-to-one data mapping relationships. The main building block of the relational database is the table (also known as a *relation*). Each table contains a set of related records. For example, a sales database might contain the following tables:

- Customers table that contains contact information for all the organization's clients
- Sales Reps table that contains identity information on the organization's sales force
- Orders table that contains records of orders placed by each customer

Object-Oriented Programming and Databases

Object-relational databases combine relational databases with the power of object-oriented programming. True object-oriented databases (OODBs) benefit from ease of code reuse, ease of troubleshooting analysis, and reduced overall maintenance. OODBs are also better suited than other types of databases for supporting complex applications involving multimedia, CAD, video, graphics, and expert systems.

Each table contains a number of attributes, or *fields*. Each attribute corresponds to a column in the table. For example, the Customers table might contain columns for company name, address, city, state, zip code, and telephone number. Each customer would have its own record, or *tuple*, represented by a row in the table. The number of rows in the relation is referred to as *cardinality*, and the number of columns is the *degree*. The *domain* of an attribute is the set of allowable values that the attribute can take. Figure 20.8 shows an example of a Customers table from a relational database.

FIGURE 20.8 Customers table from a relational database

Company ID	Company Name	Address	City	State	ZIP Code	Telephone	Sales Rep
1	Acme Widgets	234 Main Street	Columbia	MD	21040	(301) 555-1212	14
2	Abrams Consulting	1024 Sample Street	Miami	FL	33131	(305) 555-1995	14
3	Dome Widgets	913 Sorin Street	South Bend	IN	46556	(574) 555-5863	26

In this example, the table has a cardinality of 3 (corresponding to the three rows in the table) and a degree of 8 (corresponding to the eight columns). It's common for the cardinality of a table to change during the course of normal business, such as when a sales rep adds new customers. The degree of a table normally does not change frequently and usually requires database administrator intervention.

TIP To remember the concept of cardinality, think of a deck of cards on a desk, with each card (the first four letters of *cardinality*) being a row. To remember the concept of degree, think of a wall thermometer as a column (in other words, the temperature in degrees as measured on a thermometer).

Relationships between the tables are defined to identify related records. In this example, a relationship exists between the Customers table and the Sales Reps table because each customer is assigned a sales representative and each sales representative is assigned to one or more customers. This relationship is reflected by the Sales Rep field/column in the Customers table, shown in Figure 20.8. The values in this column refer to a Sales Rep ID field contained in the Sales Rep table (not shown). Additionally, a relationship would probably exist between the Customers table and the Orders table because each order must be associated with a customer and each customer is associated with one or more product orders. The Orders table (not shown) would likely contain a Customer field that contained one of the Customer ID values shown in Figure 20.8.

Records are identified using a variety of keys. Quite simply, *keys* are a subset of the fields of a table and are used to uniquely identify records. They are also used to join tables when you wish to cross-reference information. You should be familiar with three types of keys:

Candidate Keys A *candidate key* is a subset of attributes that can be used to uniquely identify any record in a table. No two records in the same table will ever contain the same values for all attributes composing a candidate key. Each table may have one or more candidate keys, which are chosen from column headings.

Primary Keys A *primary key* is selected from the set of candidate keys for a table to be used to uniquely identify the records in a table. Each table has only one primary key, selected by the database designer from the set of candidate keys. The RDBMS enforces the uniqueness of primary keys by disallowing the insertion of multiple records with the same primary key. In the Customers table shown in Figure 20.8, the Customer ID would likely be the primary key.

Foreign Keys A *foreign key* is used to enforce relationships between two tables, also known as *referential integrity*. Referential integrity ensures that if one table contains a foreign key, it corresponds to a still-existing primary key in the other table in the relationship. It makes certain that no record/tuple/row contains a reference to a primary key of a nonexistent record/tuple/row. In the example described earlier, the Sales Rep field shown in Figure 20.8 is a foreign key referencing the primary key of the Sales Reps table.

All relational databases use a standard language, Structured Query Language (SQL), to provide users with a consistent interface for the storage, retrieval, and modification of data and for administrative control of the DBMS. Each DBMS vendor implements a slightly different version of SQL (like Microsoft's Transact-SQL and Oracle's PL/SQL), but all support a core feature set. SQL's primary security feature is its granularity of authorization. This means that SQL allows you to set permissions at a very fine level of detail. You can limit user access by table, row, column, or even an individual cell in some cases.

Database Normalization

Database developers strive to create well-organized and efficient databases. To assist with this effort, they've defined several levels of database organization known as *normal forms*. The process of bringing a database table into compliance with normal forms is known as *normalization*.

Although a number of normal forms exist, the three most common are first normal form (1NF), second normal form (2NF), and third normal form (3NF). Each of these forms adds requirements to reduce redundancy in the tables, eliminating misplaced data and performing a number of other housekeeping tasks. The normal forms are cumulative; in other words, to be in 2NF, a table must first be 1NF compliant. Before making a table 3NF compliant, it must first be in 2NF.

The details of normalizing a database table are beyond the scope of the CISSP exam, but several web resources can help you understand the requirements of the normal forms in greater detail. For example, refer to the article "Database Normalization Basics":

`http://databases.about.com/od/specificproducts/a/normalization.htm`

SQL provides the complete functionality necessary for administrators, developers, and end users to interact with the database. In fact, the graphical database interfaces popular today merely wrap some extra bells and whistles around a standard SQL interface to the DBMS. SQL itself is divided into two distinct components: the Data Definition Language (DDL), which allows for the creation and modification of the database's structure (known as the *schema*), and the Data Manipulation Language (DML), which allows users to interact with the data contained within that schema.

Database Transactions

Relational databases support the explicit and implicit use of transactions to ensure data integrity. Each transaction is a discrete set of SQL instructions that will either succeed or fail as a group. It's not possible for one part of a transaction to succeed while another part fails. Consider the example of a transfer between two accounts at a bank. You might use the following SQL code to first add $250 to account 1001 and then subtract $250 from account 2002:

```
BEGIN TRANSACTION
UPDATE accounts
SET balance = balance + 250
WHERE account_number = 1001;

UPDATE accounts
SET balance = balance - 250
WHERE account_number = 2002

END TRANSACTION
```

Imagine a case where these two statements were not executed as part of a transaction but were instead executed separately. If the database failed during the moment between completion of the first transaction and completion of the second transaction, $250 would have been added to account 1001, but there would be no corresponding deduction from account 2002. The $250 would have appeared out of thin air! Flipping the order of the two statements wouldn't help—this would cause $250 to disappear into thin air if interrupted! This simple example underscores the importance of transaction-oriented processing.

When a transaction successfully finishes, it is said to be committed to the database and cannot be undone. Transaction committing may be explicit, using SQL's `COMMIT` command, or it can be implicit if the end of the transaction is successfully reached. If a transaction must be aborted, it can be rolled back explicitly using the `ROLLBACK` command or implicitly if there is a hardware or software failure. When a transaction is rolled back, the database restores itself to the condition it was in before the transaction began.

All database transactions have four required characteristics: atomicity, consistency, isolation, and durability. Together, these attributes are known as the *ACID model*, which is a critical concept in the development of database management systems. Let's take a brief look at each of these requirements:

Atomicity Database transactions must be atomic—that is, they must be an "all-or-nothing" affair. If any part of the transaction fails, the entire transaction must be rolled back as if it never occurred.

Consistency All transactions must begin operating in an environment that is consistent with all of the database's rules (for example, all records have a unique primary key). When the transaction is complete, the database must again be consistent with the rules, regardless of whether those rules were violated during the processing of the transaction itself. No other transaction should ever be able to use any inconsistent data that might be generated during the execution of another transaction.

Isolation The isolation principle requires that transactions operate separately from each other. If a database receives two SQL transactions that modify the same data, one transaction must be completed in its entirety before the other transaction is allowed to modify the same data. This prevents one transaction from working with invalid data generated as an intermediate step by another transaction.

Durability Database transactions must be durable. That is, once they are committed to the database, they must be preserved. Databases ensure durability through the use of backup mechanisms, such as transaction logs.

In the following sections, we'll discuss a variety of specific security issues of concern to database developers and administrators.

Security for Multilevel Databases

As you learned in Chapter 1, many organizations use data classification schemes to enforce access control restrictions based on the security labels assigned to data objects and individual users. When mandated by an organization's security policy, this classification concept must also be extended to the organization's databases.

Multilevel security databases contain information at a number of different classification levels. They must verify the labels assigned to users and, in response to user requests, provide only information that's appropriate. However, this concept becomes somewhat more complicated when considering security for a database.

When multilevel security is required, it's essential that administrators and developers strive to keep data with different security requirements separate. Mixing data with different classification levels and/or need-to-know requirements is known as *database contamination* and is a significant security challenge. Often, administrators will deploy a trusted front end to add multilevel security to a legacy or insecure DBMS.

Real World Scenario

Restricting Access with Views

Another way to implement multilevel security in a database is through the use of database views. Views are simply SQL statements that present data to the user as if the views were tables themselves. Views may be used to collate data from multiple tables, aggregate individual records, or restrict a user's access to a limited subset of database attributes and/or records.

Views are stored in the database as SQL commands rather than as tables of data. This dramatically reduces the space requirements of the database and allows views to violate the rules of normalization that apply to tables. However, retrieving data from a complex view can take significantly longer than retrieving it from a table because the DBMS may need to perform calculations to determine the value of certain attributes for each record.

Because views are so flexible, many database administrators use them as a security tool—allowing users to interact only with limited views rather than with the raw tables of data underlying them.

Concurrency

Concurrency, or edit control, is a preventive security mechanism that endeavors to make certain that the information stored in the database is always correct or at least has its integrity and availability protected. This feature can be employed on a single-level or multilevel database. Concurrency uses a "lock" feature to allow one user to make changes but deny other users access to views or make changes to data elements at the same time. Then, after the changes have been made, an "unlock" feature restores the ability of other users to access the data they need. In some instances, administrators will use concurrency with auditing mechanisms to track document and/or field changes. When this recorded data is reviewed, concurrency becomes a detective control.

Other Security Mechanisms

Administrators can deploy several other security mechanisms when using a DBMS. These features are relatively easy to implement and are common in the industry. The mechanisms related to semantic integrity, for instance, are common security features of a DBMS. Semantic integrity ensures that user actions don't violate any structural rules. It also checks that all stored data types are within valid domain ranges, ensures that only logical values exist, and confirms that the system complies with any and all uniqueness constraints.

Administrators may employ time and date stamps to maintain data integrity and availability. Time and date stamps often appear in distributed database systems. When a time stamp is placed on all change transactions and those changes are distributed or replicated to the other database members, all changes are applied to all members, but they are implemented in correct chronological order.

Another common security feature of a DBMS is that objects can be controlled granularly within the database; this can also improve security control. Content-dependent access control is an example of granular object control. Content-dependent access control is based on the contents or payload of the object being accessed. Because decisions must be made on an object-by-object basis, content-dependent control increases processing overhead. Another form of granular control is *cell suppression*. Cell suppression is the concept of hiding individual database fields or cells or imposing more security restrictions on them.

Context-dependent access control is often discussed alongside content-dependent access control because of the similarity of the terms. Context-dependent access control evaluates the big picture to make access control decisions. The key factor in context-dependent access control is how each object or packet or field relates to the overall activity or communication. Any single element may look innocuous by itself, but in a larger context that element may be revealed to be benign or malign.

Administrators might employ database partitioning to subvert aggregation and inference vulnerabilities, which are discussed in the section "Aggregation" later in this chapter. Database partitioning is the process of splitting a single database into multiple parts, each with a unique and distinct security level or type of content.

Polyinstantiation occurs when two or more rows in the same relational database table appear to have identical primary key elements but contain different data for use at differing classification levels. It is often used as a defense against some types of inference attacks (see "Inference" which was covered in Chapter 9).

Consider a database table containing the location of various naval ships on patrol. Normally, this database contains the exact position of each ship stored at the secret classification level. However, one particular ship, the USS *UpToNoGood*, is on an undercover mission to a top-secret location. Military commanders do not want anyone to know that the ship deviated from its normal patrol. If the database administrators simply change the classification of the *UpToNoGood*'s location to top secret, a user with a secret clearance would know that something unusual was going on when they couldn't query the location of the ship. However, if polyinstantiation is used, two records could be inserted into the table. The first one, classified at the top-secret level, would reflect the true location of the ship and be available only to users with the appropriate top - secret security clearance. The second record, classified at the secret level, would indicate that the ship was on routine patrol and would be returned to users with a secret clearance.

Finally, administrators can insert false or misleading data into a DBMS in order to redirect or thwart information confidentiality attacks. This is a concept known as noise and perturbation. You must be extremely careful when using this technique to ensure that noise inserted into the database does not affect business operations.

ODBC

Open Database Connectivity (ODBC) is a database feature that allows applications to communicate with different types of databases without having to be directly programmed for interaction with each type. ODBC acts as a proxy between applications and backend database drivers, giving application programmers greater freedom in creating solutions without having to worry about the backend database system. Figure 20.9 illustrates the relationship between ODBC and a backend database system.

FIGURE 20.9 ODBC as the interface between applications and a backend database system

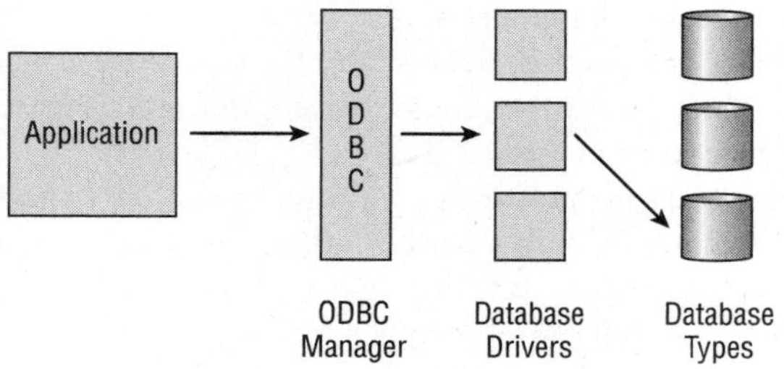

Storing Data and Information

Database management systems have helped harness the power of data and gain some modicum of control over who can access it and the actions they can perform on it. However, security professionals must keep in mind that DBMS security covers access to information through only the traditional "front-door" channels. Data is also processed through a computer's storage resources—both memory and physical media. Precautions must be in place to ensure that these basic resources are protected against security vulnerabilities as well. After all, you would never incur a lot of time and expense to secure the front door of your home and then leave the back door wide open, would you?

Types of Storage

Modern computing systems use several types of storage to maintain system and user data. The systems strike a balance between the various storage types to satisfy an organization's computing requirements. There are several common storage types:

Primary (or "real") memory consists of the main memory resources directly available to a system's CPU. Primary memory normally consists of volatile random access memory (RAM) and is usually the most high-performance storage resource available to a system.

Secondary storage consists of more inexpensive, nonvolatile storage resources available to a system for long-term use. Typical secondary storage resources include magnetic and optical media, such as tapes, disks, hard drives, flash drives, and CD/DVD storage.

Virtual memory allows a system to simulate additional primary memory resources through the use of secondary storage. For example, a system low on expensive RAM might make a portion of the hard disk available for direct CPU addressing.

Virtual storage allows a system to simulate secondary storage resources through the use of primary storage. The most common example of virtual storage is the RAM disk that presents itself to the operating system as a secondary storage device but is actually implemented in volatile RAM. This provides an extremely fast filesystem for use in various applications but provides no recovery capability.

Random access storage allows the operating system to request contents from any point within the media. RAM and hard drives are examples of random access storage resources.

Sequential access storage requires scanning through the entire media from the beginning to reach a specific address. A magnetic tape is a common example of a sequential access storage resource.

Volatile storage loses its contents when power is removed from the resource. RAM is the most common type of volatile storage resource.

Nonvolatile storage does not depend upon the presence of power to maintain its contents. Magnetic/optical media and nonvolatile RAM (NVRAM) are typical examples of nonvolatile storage resources.

Storage Threats

Information security professionals should be aware of two main threats posed against data storage systems. First, the threat of illegitimate access to storage resources exists no matter what type of storage is in use. If administrators do not implement adequate filesystem access controls, an intruder might stumble across sensitive data simply by browsing the filesystem. In more sensitive environments, administrators should also protect against attacks that involve bypassing operating system controls and directly accessing the physical storage media to retrieve data. This is best accomplished through the use of an encrypted filesystem, which is accessible only through the primary operating system. Furthermore, systems that operate in a multilevel security environment should provide adequate controls to ensure that shared memory and storage resources are set up with fail-safe controls so that data from one classification level is not readable at a lower classification level.

Covert channel attacks pose the second primary threat against data storage resources. Covert storage channels allow the transmission of sensitive data between classification levels through the direct or indirect manipulation of shared storage media. This may be as simple as writing sensitive data to an inadvertently shared portion of memory or physical storage. More complex covert storage channels might be used to manipulate the amount of free space available on a disk or the size of a file to covertly convey information between security levels. For more information on covert channel analysis, see Chapter 8, "Principles of Security Models, Design, and Capabilities."

Understanding Knowledge-Based Systems

Since the advent of computing, engineers and scientists have worked toward developing systems capable of performing routine actions that would bore a human and consume a significant amount of time. The majority of the achievements in this area have focused on relieving the burden of computationally intensive tasks. However, researchers have also made giant strides toward developing systems that have an "artificial intelligence" that can simulate (to some extent) the purely human power of reasoning.

The following sections examine two types of knowledge-based artificial intelligence systems: expert systems and neural networks. We'll also take a look at their potential applications to computer security problems.

Expert Systems

Expert systems seek to embody the accumulated knowledge of experts on a particular subject and apply it in a consistent fashion to future decisions. Several studies have shown that expert systems, when properly developed and implemented, often make better decisions than some of their human counterparts when faced with routine decisions.

Every expert system has two main components: the knowledge base and the inference engine.

The knowledge base contains the rules known by an expert system. The knowledge base seeks to codify the knowledge of human experts in a series of "if/then" statements. Let's consider a simple expert system designed to help homeowners decide whether they should evacuate an area when a hurricane threatens. The knowledge base might contain the following statements (these statements are for example only):

- If the hurricane is a Category 4 storm or higher, then flood waters normally reach a height of 20 feet above sea level.
- If the hurricane has winds in excess of 120 miles per hour (mph), then wood-frame structures will be destroyed.
- If it is late in the hurricane season, then hurricanes tend to get stronger as they approach the coast.

In an actual expert system, the knowledge base would contain hundreds or thousands of assertions such as those just listed.

The second major component of an expert system—the inference engine—analyzes information in the knowledge base to arrive at the appropriate decision. The expert system user employs some sort of user interface to provide the inference engine with details about the current situation, and the inference engine uses a combination of logical reasoning and fuzzy logic techniques to draw a conclusion based on past experience. Continuing with the hurricane example, a user might inform the expert system that a Category 4 hurricane is approaching the coast with wind speeds averaging 140 mph. The inference engine would then analyze information in the knowledge base and make an evacuation recommendation based on that past knowledge.

Expert systems are not infallible—they're only as good as the data in the knowledge base and the decision-making algorithms implemented in the inference engine. However, they have one major advantage in stressful situations—their decisions do not involve judgment clouded by emotion. Expert systems can play an important role in analyzing emergency events, stock trading, and other scenarios in which emotional investment sometimes gets in the way of a logical decision. For this reason, many lending institutions now use expert systems to make credit decisions instead of relying on loan officers who might say to themselves, "Well, Jim hasn't paid his bills on time, but he seems like a perfectly nice guy."

Fuzzy Logic

As previously mentioned, inference engines commonly use a technique known as *fuzzy logic*. This technique is designed to more closely approximate human thought patterns than the rigid mathematics of set theory or algebraic approaches that use "black-and-white" categorizations of data. Fuzzy logic replaces them with blurred boundaries, allowing the algorithm to think in the "shades of gray" that dominate human thought. Fuzzy logic as used by an expert system has four steps or phases: fuzzification, inference, composition, and defuzzification.

For example, consider the task of determining whether a website is undergoing a denial-of-service attack. Traditional mathematical techniques may create basic rules, such as "If we have more than 1,000 connections per second, we are under attack." Fuzzy logic, on the other hand, might define a blurred boundary, saying that 1,000 connections per second represents an 80 percent chance of an attack, 10,000 connections per second represents a 95 percent chance, and 100 connections per second represents a 5 percent chance. The interpretation of these probabilities is left to the analyst.

Neural Networks

In neural networks, chains of computational units are used in an attempt to imitate the biological reasoning process of the human mind. In an expert system, a series of rules is stored in a knowledge base, whereas in a neural network, a long chain of computational decisions that feed into each other and eventually sum to produce the desired output is set up.

Keep in mind that no neural network designed to date comes close to having the reasoning power of the human mind. Nevertheless, neural networks show great potential to advance the artificial intelligence field beyond its current state. Benefits of neural networks include linearity, input-output mapping, and adaptivity. These benefits are evident in the implementations of neural networks for voice recognition, face recognition, weather prediction, and the exploration of models of thinking and consciousness.

Typical neural networks involve many layers of summation, each of which requires weighting information to reflect the relative importance of the calculation in the overall decision-making process. The weights must be custom-tailored for each type of decision the neural network is expected to make. This is accomplished through the use of a training period during which the network is provided with inputs for which the proper decision is known. The algorithm then works backward from these decisions to determine the proper weights for each node in the computational chain. This activity is performed using what is known as the *Delta rule* or *learning rule*. Through the use of the Delta rule, neural networks are able to learn from experience.

Decision Support Systems

A *decision support system (DSS)* is a knowledge-based application that analyzes business data and presents it in such a way as to make business decisions easier for users. It is considered more of an informational application than an operational application. Often a DSS is employed by knowledge workers (such as help desk or customer support personnel) and by sales services (such as phone operators). This type of application may present information in a graphical manner to link concepts and content and guide the script of the operator. Often a DSS is backed by an expert system controlling a database.

Security Applications

Both expert systems and neural networks have great applications in the field of computer security. One of the major advantages offered by these systems is their capability to rapidly make consistent decisions. One of the major problems in computer security is the inability of system administrators to consistently and thoroughly analyze massive amounts of log and audit trail data to look for anomalies. It seems like a match made in heaven!

One successful application of this technology to the computer security arena is the Next-Generation Intrusion Detection Expert System (NIDES) developed by Phillip Porras and his team at the Information and Computing Sciences System Design Laboratory of SRI International. This system provides an inference engine and knowledge base that draws information from a variety of audit logs across a network and provides notification to security administrators when the activity of an individual user varies from the user's standard usage profile.

Summary

Data is the most valuable resource many organizations possess. Therefore, it's critical that information security practitioners understand the necessity of safeguarding the data itself and the systems and applications that assist in the processing of that data. Protections against malicious code, database vulnerabilities, and system/application development flaws must be implemented in every technology-aware organization.

Malicious code objects pose a threat to the computing resources of organizations. In the nondistributed environment, such threats include viruses, logic bombs, Trojan horses, and worms.

By this point, you no doubt recognize the importance of placing adequate access controls and audit trails on these valuable information resources. Database security is a rapidly growing field; if databases play a major role in your security duties, take the time to sit down with database administrators, courses, and textbooks and learn the underlying theory. It's a valuable investment.

Finally, various controls can be put into place during the system and application development process to ensure that the end product of these processes is compatible with operation in a secure environment. Such controls include process isolation, hardware segmentation, abstraction, and contractual arrangements such as service-level agreements (SLAs). Security should always be introduced in the early planning phases of any development project and continually monitored throughout the design, development, deployment, and maintenance phases of production.

Exam Essentials

Explain the basic architecture of a relational database management system (RDBMS). Know the structure of relational databases. Be able to explain the function of tables (relations), rows (records/tuples), and columns (fields/attributes). Know how relationships are defined between tables and the roles of various types of keys. Describe the database security threats posed by aggregation and inference.

Know the various types of storage. Explain the differences between primary memory and virtual memory, secondary storage and virtual storage, random access storage and sequential access storage, and volatile storage and nonvolatile storage.

Explain how expert systems and neural networks function. Expert systems consist of two main components: a knowledge base that contains a series of "if/then" rules and an inference engine that uses that information to draw conclusions about other data. Neural networks simulate the functioning of the human mind to a limited extent by arranging a series of layered calculations to solve problems. Neural networks require extensive training on a particular problem before they are able to offer solutions.

Understand the models of systems development. Know that the waterfall model describes a sequential development process that results in the development of a finished product. Developers may step back only one phase in the process if errors are discovered. The spiral model uses several iterations of the waterfall model to produce a number of fully specified and tested prototypes. Agile development models place an emphasis on the needs of the customer and quickly developing new functionality that meets those needs in an iterative fashion.

Describe software development maturity models. Know that maturity models help software organizations improve the maturity and quality of their software processes by implementing an evolutionary path from ad hoc, chaotic processes to mature, disciplined software processes. Be able to describe the SW-CMM and IDEAL models.

Understand the importance of change and configuration management. Know the three basic components of change control—request control, change control, and release control—and how they contribute to security. Explain how configuration management controls the versions of software used in an organization.

Understand the importance of testing. Software testing should be designed as part of the development process. Testing should be used as a management tool to improve the design, development, and production processes.

Written Lab

1. What is the main purpose of a primary key in a database table?
2. What is polyinstantiation?
3. Explain the difference between static and dynamic analysis of application code.
4. How far backward does the waterfall model allow developers to travel when a development flaw is discovered?

Review Questions

1. Which one of the following is not a component of the DevOps model?
   - **A.** Information security
   - **B.** Software development
   - **C.** Quality assurance
   - **D.** IT operations
2. Bob is developing a software application and has a field where users may enter a date. He wants to ensure that the values provided by the users are accurate dates to prevent security issues. What technique should Bob use?
   - **A.** Polyinstantiation
   - **B.** Input validation
   - **C.** Contamination
   - **D.** Screening
3. What portion of the change management process allows developers to prioritize tasks?
   - **A.** Release control
   - **B.** Configuration control
   - **C.** Request control
   - **D.** Change audit
4. What approach to failure management places the system in a high level of security?
   - **A.** Fail open
   - **B.** Fail mitigation
   - **C.** Fail secure
   - **D.** Fail clear
5. What software development model uses a seven-stage approach with a feedback loop that allows progress one step backward?
   - **A.** Boyce-Codd
   - **B.** Waterfall
   - **C.** Spiral
   - **D.** Agile
6. What form of access control is concerned primarily with the data stored by a field?
   - **A.** Content-dependent
   - **B.** Context-dependent
   - **C.** Semantic integrity mechanisms
   - **D.** Perturbation

7. Which one of the following key types is used to enforce referential integrity between database tables?
   - A. Candidate key
   - B. Primary key
   - C. Foreign key
   - D. Super key

8. Richard believes that a database user is misusing his privileges to gain information about the company's overall business trends by issuing queries that combine data from a large number of records. What process is the database user taking advantage of?
   - A. Inference
   - B. Contamination
   - C. Polyinstantiation
   - D. Aggregation

9. What database technique can be used to prevent unauthorized users from determining classified information by noticing the absence of information normally available to them?
   - A. Inference
   - B. Manipulation
   - C. Polyinstantiation
   - D. Aggregation

10. Which one of the following is not a principle of Agile development?
    - A. Satisfy the customer through early and continuous delivery.
    - B. Businesspeople and developers work together.
    - C. Pay continuous attention to technical excellence.
    - D. Prioritize security over other requirements.

11. What type of information is used to form the basis of an expert system's decision-making process?
    - A. A series of weighted layered computations
    - B. Combined input from a number of human experts, weighted according to past performance
    - C. A series of "if/then" rules codified in a knowledge base
    - D. A biological decision-making process that simulates the reasoning process used by the human mind

12. In which phase of the SW-CMM does an organization use quantitative measures to gain a detailed understanding of the development process?
    - A. Initial
    - B. Repeatable
    - C. Defined
    - D. Managed

13. Which of the following acts as a proxy between an application and a database to support interaction and simplify the work of programmers?
   A. SDLC
   B. ODBC
   C. DSS
   D. Abstraction

14. In what type of software testing does the tester have access to the underlying source code?
   A. Static testing
   B. Dynamic testing
   C. Cross-site scripting testing
   D. Black box testing

15. What type of chart provides a graphical illustration of a schedule that helps to plan, coordinate, and track project tasks?
   A. Gantt
   B. Venn
   C. Bar
   D. PERT

16. Which database security risk occurs when data from a higher classification level is mixed with data from a lower classification level?
   A. Aggregation
   B. Inference
   C. Contamination
   D. Polyinstantiation

17. What database security technology involves creating two or more rows with seemingly identical primary keys that contain different data for users with different security clearances?
   A. Polyinstantiation
   B. Cell suppression
   C. Aggregation
   D. Views

18. Which one of the following is not part of the change management process?
   A. Request control
   B. Release control
   C. Configuration audit
   D. Change control

19. What transaction management principle ensures that two transactions do not interfere with each other as they operate on the same data?

A. Atomicity

B. Consistency

C. Isolation

D. Durability

20. Tom built a database table consisting of the names, telephone numbers, and customer IDs for his business. The table contains information on 30 customers. What is the degree of this table?

A. Two

B. Three

C. Thirty

D. Undefined

Chapter

21

Malicious Code and Application Attacks

THE CISSP EXAM TOPICS COVERED IN THIS CHAPTER INCLUDE:

3. SECURITY ENGINEERING

✓ E. Assess and mitigate the vulnerabilities of security architectures, designs, and solution elements

✓ F. Assess and mitigate vulnerabilities in web-based systems (e.g., XML, OWASP)

8. SOFTWARE DEVELOPMENT SECURITY

✓ B. Enforce security controls in development environments

- B.1 Security of the software environments
- B.2 Security weaknesses and vulnerabilities at the source-code level (e.g., buffer overflow, escalation of privilege, input/output validation)

In previous chapters, you learned about many general security principles and the policy and procedure mechanisms that help security practitioners develop adequate protection against malicious individuals. This chapter takes an in-depth look at some of the specific threats faced on a daily basis by administrators in the field.

This material is not only critical for the CISSP exam; it's also some of the most basic information a computer security professional must understand to effectively practice their trade. We'll begin this chapter by looking at the risks posed by malicious code objects—viruses, worms, logic bombs, and Trojan horses. We'll then take a look at some of the other security exploits used by someone attempting to gain unauthorized access to a system or to prevent legitimate users from gaining such access.

Malicious Code

Malicious code objects include a broad range of programmed computer security threats that exploit various network, operating system, software, and physical security vulnerabilities to spread malicious payloads to computer systems. Some malicious code objects, such as computer viruses and Trojan horses, depend on irresponsible computer use by humans in order to spread from system to system with any success. Other objects, such as worms, spread rapidly among vulnerable systems under their own power.

All information security practitioners must be familiar with the risks posed by the various types of malicious code objects so they can develop adequate countermeasures to protect the systems under their care as well as implement appropriate responses if their systems are compromised.

Sources of Malicious Code

Where does malicious code come from? In the early days of computer security, malicious code writers were extremely skilled (albeit misguided) software developers who took pride in carefully crafting innovative malicious code techniques. Indeed, they actually served a somewhat useful function by exposing security holes in popular software packages and operating systems, raising the security awareness of the computing community. For an example of this type of code writer, see the sidebar "RTM and the Internet Worm" later in this chapter.

Modern times have given rise to the *script kiddie*—the malicious individual who doesn't understand the technology behind security vulnerabilities but downloads ready-to-use software (or scripts) from the Internet and uses them to launch attacks against remote systems. This trend gave birth to a new breed of virus-creation software that allows anyone with a minimal level of technical expertise to create a virus and unleash it upon the Internet. This is reflected in the large number of viruses documented by antivirus experts to date. The amateur malicious code developers are usually just experimenting with a new tool they downloaded or attempting to cause problems for one or two enemies. Unfortunately, the malware sometimes spreads rapidly and creates problems for Internet users in general.

In addition, the tools used by script kiddies are freely available to those with more sinister criminal intent. Indeed, international organized crime syndicates are known to play a role in malware proliferation. These criminals, located in countries with weak law enforcement mechanisms, use malware to steal the money and identities of people from around the world, especially residents of the United States. In fact, the Zeus Trojan horse is widely believed to be the product of an Eastern European organized crime ring seeking to infect as many systems as possible to log keystrokes and harvest online banking passwords. The Zeus outbreak began in 2007 and continues today. This is just one example of an emerging trend in malware development.

Viruses

The computer virus is perhaps the earliest form of malicious code to plague security administrators. Indeed, viruses are so prevalent nowadays that major outbreaks receive attention from the mass media and provoke mild hysteria among average computer users. According to Symantec, one of the major antivirus software vendors, there were over 286 million strains of malicious code roaming the global network in 2010 and this trend only continues, with some sources suggesting that 200,000 new malware strains appear on the Internet every *day*! Hundreds of thousands of variations of these viruses strike unsuspecting computer users each day. Many carry malicious payloads that cause damage ranging in scope from displaying a profane message on the screen all the way to causing complete destruction of all data stored on the local hard drive.

As with biological viruses, computer viruses have two main functions—propagation and destruction. Miscreants who create viruses carefully design code to implement these functions in new and innovative methods that they hope escape detection and bypass increasingly sophisticated antivirus technology. It's fair to say that an arms race has developed between virus writers and antivirus technicians, each hoping to develop technology one step ahead of the other. The propagation function defines how the virus will spread from system to system, infecting each machine it leaves in its wake. A virus's payload delivers the destructive power by implementing whatever malicious activity the virus writer had in mind. This could be anything that negatively impacts the confidentiality, integrity, or availability of systems or data.

Virus Propagation Techniques

By definition, a virus must contain technology that enables it to spread from system to system, aided by unsuspecting computer users seeking to share data by exchanging disks, sharing networked resources, sending electronic mail, or using some other means. Once they've "touched" a new system, they use one of several propagation techniques to infect the new victim and expand their reach. In this section, we'll look at four common propagation techniques: master boot record infection, file infection, macro infection, and service injection.

Master Boot Record Viruses The *master boot record (MBR) virus* is one of the earliest known forms of virus infection. These viruses attack the MBR—the portion of bootable media (such as a hard disk, USB drive, or CD/DVD) that the computer uses to load the operating system during the boot process. Because the MBR is extremely small (usually 512 bytes), it can't contain all the code required to implement the virus's propagation and destructive functions. To bypass this space limitation, MBR viruses store the majority of their code on another portion of the storage media. When the system reads the infected MBR, the virus instructs it to read and execute the code stored in this alternate location, thereby loading the entire virus into memory and potentially triggering the delivery of the virus's payload.

The Boot Sector and the Master Boot Record

You'll often see the terms *boot sector* and *master boot record* used interchangeably to describe the portion of a storage device used to load the operating system and the types of viruses that attack that process. This is not technically correct. The MBR is a single disk sector, normally the first sector of the media that is read in the initial stages of the boot process. The MBR determines which media partition contains the operating system and then directs the system to read that partition's boot sector to load the operating system.

Viruses can attack both the MBR and the boot sector, with substantially similar results. MBR viruses act by redirecting the system to an infected boot sector, which loads the virus into memory before loading the operating system from the legitimate boot sector. Boot sector viruses actually infect the legitimate boot sector and are loaded into memory during the operating system load process.

Most MBR viruses are spread between systems through the use of infected media inadvertently shared between users. If the infected media is in the drive during the boot process, the target system reads the infected MBR, and the virus loads into memory, infects the MBR on the target system's hard drive, and spreads its infection to yet another machine.

File Infector Viruses Many viruses infect different types of executable files and trigger when the operating system attempts to execute them. For Windows-based systems, the names of these files end with `.exe` and `.com` extensions. The propagation routines of *file infector viruses* may slightly alter the code of an executable program, thereby implanting the technology the virus needs to replicate and damage the system. In some cases, the virus might actually replace the entire file with an infected version. Standard file infector viruses that do not use cloaking techniques such as stealth or encryption (see the section "Virus Technologies" later in this chapter) are often easily detected by comparing file characteristics (such as size and modification date) before and after infection or by comparing hash values. The section "Antivirus Mechanisms" provides technical details of these techniques.

A variation of the file infector virus is the *companion virus*. These viruses are self-contained executable files that escape detection by using a filename similar to, but slightly different from, a legitimate operating system file. They rely on the default filename extensions that Windows-based operating systems append to commands when executing program files (`.com`, `.exe`, and `.bat`, in that order). For example, if you had a program on your hard disk named `game.exe`, a companion virus might use the name `game.com`. If you then open a Command tool and simply type **`GAME`**, the operating system would execute the virus file, `game.com`, instead of the file you actually intended to execute, `game.exe`. This is a very good reason to avoid shortcuts and fully specify the name of the file you want to execute.

Macro Viruses Many common software applications implement some sort of scripting functionality to assist with the automation of repetitive tasks. These functionalities often use simple, yet powerful programming languages such as Visual Basic for Applications (VBA). Although macros do indeed offer great productivity-enhancing opportunities to computer users, they also expose systems to yet another avenue of infection—macro viruses.

Macro viruses first appeared on the scene in the mid-1990s, utilizing crude technologies to infect documents created in the popular Microsoft Word environment. Although they were relatively unsophisticated, these viruses spread rapidly because the antivirus community didn't anticipate them, and therefore antivirus applications didn't provide any defense against them. Macro viruses quickly became more and more commonplace, and vendors rushed to modify their antivirus platforms to scan application documents for malicious macros. In 1999, the Melissa virus spread through the use of a Word document that exploited a security vulnerability in Microsoft Outlook to replicate. The infamous I Love You virus quickly followed on its heels, exploiting similar vulnerabilities in early 2000.

WARNING

Macro viruses proliferate because of the ease of writing code in the scripting languages (such as VBA) utilized by modern productivity applications.

After a rash of macro viruses in the late part of the twentieth century, productivity software developers made important changes to the macro development environment, restricting the ability of untrusted macros to run without explicit user permission. A drastic reduction in the prevalence of macro viruses was the result.

Service Injection Viruses Recent outbreaks of malicious code use yet another technique to infect systems and escape detection—injecting themselves into trusted runtime processes of the operating system, such as `svchost.exe`, `winlogin.exe`, and `explorer.exe`. By successfully compromising these trusted processes, the malicious code is able to bypass detection by any antivirus software running on the host. One of the best techniques to protect systems against service injection is to ensure that all software allowing the viewing of web content (browsers, media players, helper applications) receive current security patches.

Platforms Vulnerable to Viruses

Just as most macro viruses infect systems running the popular Microsoft Office suite of applications, most computer viruses are designed to disrupt activity on systems running versions of the world's most popular operating system—Microsoft Windows. It's estimated that fewer than 1 percent of the viruses "in the wild" today are designed to impact other operating systems, such as Unix and Mac OS.

The main reason for this is that there is no single Unix operating system. Rather, there is a series of many similar operating systems that implement the same functions in a similar fashion and that are independently designed by a large number of developers. Large-scale corporate efforts compete with the myriad of freely available versions of the Linux operating system developed by the public at large. The sheer number of Unix versions and the fact that they are developed on entirely different kernels (the core code of an operating system) make it difficult to write a virus that would impact a large portion of Unix systems.

That said, Macintosh and Unix users should not fail to be vigilant. Although only a few viruses pose a risk to their systems, one of those viruses could affect their systems at any moment. Anyone responsible for the security of a computer system should implement adequate antivirus mechanisms to ensure the continued safety of their resources.

Antivirus Mechanisms

Almost every desktop computer in service today runs some sort of antivirus software package. Popular desktop titles include Microsoft Security Essentials, McAfee VirusScan, and Norton AntiVirus, but a plethora of other products on the market offer protection for anything from a single system to an entire enterprise; other packages are designed to protect against specific common types of virus invasion vectors, such as inbound email.

The vast majority of these packages utilize a method known as *signature-based detection* to identify potential virus infections on a system. Essentially, an antivirus package maintains an extremely large database that contains the telltale characteristics of all known viruses. Depending on the antivirus package and configuration settings, it scans storage media periodically, checking for any files that contain data matching those criteria. If any are detected, the antivirus package takes one of the following actions:

- If the software can eradicate the virus, it disinfects the affected files and restores the machine to a safe condition.
- If the software recognizes the virus but doesn't know how to disinfect the files, it may quarantine the files until the user or an administrator can examine them manually.
- If security settings/policies do not provide for quarantine or the files exceed a predefined danger threshold, the antivirus package may delete the infected files in an attempt to preserve system integrity.

When using a signature-based antivirus package, it's essential to remember that the package is only as effective as the virus definition file upon which it's based. If you don't frequently update your virus definitions (usually requiring an annual subscription fee), your antivirus software will not be able to detect newly created viruses. With thousands of viruses appearing on the Internet each year, an outdated definition file will quickly render your defenses ineffective.

Many antivirus packages also use heuristic-based mechanisms to detect potential malware infections. These methods analyze the behavior of software, looking for the telltale signs of virus activity, such as attempts to elevate privilege level, cover their electronic tracks, and alter unrelated or operating system files.

Most of the modern antivirus software products are able to detect and remove a wide variety of types of malicious code and then clean the system. In other words, antivirus solutions are rarely limited to viruses. These tools are often able to provide protection against worms, Trojan horses, logic bombs, rootkits, spyware, and various other forms of email- or web-borne code. In the event that you suspect new malicious code is sweeping the Internet, your best course of action is to contact your antivirus software vendor to inquire about your state of protection against the new threat. Don't wait until the next scheduled or automated signature dictionary update. Furthermore, never accept the word of any third party about protection status offered by an antivirus solution. Always contact the vendor directly. Most responsible antivirus vendors will send alerts to their customers as soon as new, substantial threats are identified, so be sure to register for such notifications as well.

Other security packages, such as the popular Tripwire data integrity assurance package, also provide a secondary antivirus functionality. Tripwire is designed to alert administrators to unauthorized file modifications. It's often used to detect web server defacements and similar attacks, but it also may provide some warning of virus infections if critical system executable files, such as `command.com`, are modified unexpectedly. These systems work by maintaining a database of hash values for all files stored on the system (see Chapter 6, "Cryptography and Symmetric Key Algorithms," for a full discussion of the hash functions used to create these values). These archived hash values are then compared to current computed values to detect any files that were modified between the two periods. At the most basic level, a hash is a number used to summarize the contents of a file. As long as the file stays the same, the hash will stay the same. If the file is modified, even slightly, the hash will change dramatically, indicating that the file has been modified. Unless the action seems explainable, for instance if it happens after the installation of new software, application of an operating system patch, or similar change, sudden changes in executable files may be a sign of malware infection.

Virus Technologies

As virus detection and eradication technology rises to meet new threats programmed by malicious developers, new kinds of viruses designed to defeat those systems emerge. This section examines four specific types of viruses that use sneaky techniques in an attempt to escape detection—multipartite viruses, stealth viruses, polymorphic viruses, and encrypted viruses.

Multipartite Viruses *Multipartite viruses* use more than one propagation technique in an attempt to penetrate systems that defend against only one method or the other. For example, the Marzia virus discovered in 1993 infects critical COM and EXE files, most notably the `command.com` system file, by adding 2,048 bytes of malicious code to each file. This characteristic qualifies it as a file infector virus. In addition, two hours after it infects a system, it writes malicious code to the system's master boot record, qualifying it as a boot sector virus.

Stealth Viruses *Stealth viruses* hide themselves by actually tampering with the operating system to fool antivirus packages into thinking that everything is functioning normally. For example, a stealth boot sector virus might overwrite the system's master boot record with malicious code but then also modify the operating system's file access functionality to cover its tracks. When the antivirus package requests a copy of the MBR, the modified operating system code provides it with exactly what the antivirus package expects to see—a clean version of the MBR free of any virus signatures. However, when the system boots, it reads the infected MBR and loads the virus into memory.

Polymorphic Viruses *Polymorphic viruses* actually modify their own code as they travel from system to system. The virus's propagation and destruction techniques remain the same, but the signature of the virus is somewhat different each time it infects a new system. It is the hope of polymorphic virus creators that this constantly changing signature will render signature-based antivirus packages useless. However, antivirus vendors have "cracked the code" of many polymorphism techniques, so current versions of antivirus software are able to detect known polymorphic viruses. However, it tends to take vendors longer to generate the necessary signature files to stop a polymorphic virus in its tracks, which means the virus can run free on the Internet for a longer time.

Encrypted Viruses *Encrypted viruses* use cryptographic techniques, such as those described in Chapter 6, to avoid detection. In their outward appearance, they are actually quite similar to polymorphic viruses—each infected system has a virus with a different signature. However, they do not generate these modified signatures by changing their code; instead, they alter the way they are stored on the disk. Encrypted viruses use a very short segment of code, known as the *virus decryption routine*, which contains the cryptographic information necessary to load and decrypt the main virus code stored elsewhere on the disk. Each infection utilizes a different cryptographic key, causing the main code to appear completely different on each system. However, the virus decryption routines often contain telltale signatures that render them vulnerable to updated antivirus software packages.

Hoaxes

No discussion of viruses is complete without mentioning the nuisance and wasted resources caused by virus *hoaxes*. Almost every email user has, at one time or another, received a message forwarded by a friend or relative that warns of the latest virus threat roaming the Internet. Invariably, this purported "virus" is the most destructive virus ever unleashed, and no antivirus package is able to detect and/or eradicate it. One famous example of such a hoax is the Good Times virus warning that first surfaced on the Internet in 1994 and still circulates today.

For more information on this topic, the myth-tracking website Snopes maintains a virus hoax list at `http://www.snopes.com/computer/virus/virus.asp`.

Logic Bombs

As you learned in Chapter 20, "Software Development Security," *logic bombs* are malicious code objects that infect a system and lie dormant until they are triggered by the occurrence of one or more conditions such as time, program launch, website logon, and so on. The vast majority of logic bombs are programmed into custom-built applications by software developers seeking to ensure that their work is destroyed if they unexpectedly leave the company. Chapter 20 provided several examples of this type of logic bomb.

Like all malicious code objects, logic bombs come in many shapes and sizes. Indeed, many viruses and Trojan horses contain a logic bomb component. The famous Michelangelo virus caused a media frenzy when it was discovered in 1991 because of the logic bomb trigger it contained. The virus infected a system's master boot record through the sharing of infected floppy disks and then hid itself until March 6—the birthday of the famous Italian artist Michelangelo Buonarroti. On that date, it sprang into action, reformatting the hard drives of infected systems and destroying all the data they contained.

Trojan Horses

System administrators constantly warn computer users not to download and install software from the Internet unless they are absolutely sure it comes from a trusted source. In fact, many companies strictly prohibit the installation of any software not prescreened by the IT department. These policies serve to minimize the risk that an organization's network will be compromised by a *Trojan horse*—a software program that appears benevolent but carries a malicious, behind-the-scenes payload that has the potential to wreak havoc on a system or network.

Trojans differ very widely in functionality. Some will destroy all the data stored on a system in an attempt to cause a large amount of damage in as short a time frame as possible. Some are fairly innocuous. For example, a series of Trojans appeared on the Internet in mid-2002 that claimed to provide PC users with the ability to run games designed for the Microsoft Xbox gaming system on their computers. When users ran the program, it simply didn't work. However, it also inserted a value into the Windows Registry that caused a specific web page to open each time the computer booted. The Trojan creators hoped to cash in on the advertising revenue generated by the large number of page views their website received from the Xbox Trojan horses. Unfortunately for them, antivirus experts quickly discovered their true intentions, and the website was shut down.

One category of Trojan that has recently made a significant impact on the security community is rogue antivirus software. This software tricks the user into installing it by claiming to be an antivirus package, often under the guise of a pop-up ad that mimics the look and feel of a security warning. Once the user installs the software, it either steals personal information or prompts the user for payment to "update" the rogue antivirus. The "update" simply disables the Trojan!

Another variant, *ransomware*, is particularly insidious. Ransomware infects a target machine and then uses encryption technology to encrypt documents, spreadsheets, and other files stored on the system with a key known only to the malware creator. The user is then unable to access their files and receives an ominous pop-up message warning that the files will be permanently deleted unless a ransom is paid within a short period of time. The user then often pays this ransom to regain access to their files. One of the most famous ransomware strains is a program known as Cryptolocker.

Real World Scenario

Botnets

A few years ago, one of the authors of this book visited an organization that suspected it had a security problem, but the organization didn't have the expertise to diagnose or resolve the issue. The major symptom was network slowness. A few basic tests found that none of the systems on the company's network ran basic antivirus software, and some of them were infected with a Trojan horse.

Why did this cause network slowness? Well, the Trojan horse made all the infected systems members of a *botnet*, a collection of computers (sometimes thousands or even millions!) across the Internet under the control of an attacker known as the *botmaster*.

The botmaster of this particular botnet used the systems on their network as part of a denial of service attack against a website that he didn't like for one reason or another. He instructed all the systems in his botnet to retrieve the same web page, over and over again, in hopes that the website would fail under the heavy load. With close to 30 infected systems on the organization's network, the botnet's attack was consuming almost all its bandwidth!

The solution was simple: Antivirus software was installed on the systems and it removed the Trojan horse. Network speeds returned to normal quickly.

Worms

Worms pose a significant risk to network security. They contain the same destructive potential as other malicious code objects with an added twist—they propagate themselves without requiring any human intervention.

The Internet worm was the first major computer security incident to occur on the Internet. Since that time, hundreds of new worms (with thousands of variant strains) have unleashed their destructive power on the Internet. The following sections examine some specific worms.

Code Red Worm

The Code Red worm received a good deal of media attention in the summer of 2001 when it rapidly spread among web servers running unpatched versions of Microsoft's Internet

Information Server (IIS). Code Red performed three malicious actions on the systems it penetrated:

- It randomly selected hundreds of IP addresses and then probed those addresses to see whether they were used by hosts running a vulnerable version of IIS. Any systems it found were quickly compromised. This greatly magnified Code Red's reach because each host it infected sought many new targets.
- It defaced HTML pages on the local web server, replacing normal content with the following text:

  ```
  Welcome to http://www.worm.com!
  Hacked By Chinese!
  ```

- It planted a logic bomb that would initiate a denial of service attack against the IP address 198.137.240.91, which at that time belonged to the web server hosting the White House's home page. Quick-thinking government web administrators changed the White House's IP address before the attack actually began.

The destructive power of Internet worm, Code Red, and their many variants poses an extreme risk to the modern Internet. System administrators simply must ensure that they apply appropriate security patches to their Internet-connected systems as software vendors release them. As a case in point, a security fix for an IIS vulnerability exploited by Code Red was available from Microsoft for more than a month before the worm attacked the Internet. Had security administrators applied it promptly, Code Red would have been a miserable failure.

RTM and the Internet Worm

In November 1988, a young computer science student named Robert Tappan Morris brought the fledgling Internet to its knees with a few lines of computer code. He released a malicious worm he claimed to have created as an experiment onto the Internet. It spread quickly and crashed a large number of systems.

This worm spread by exploiting four specific security holes in the Unix operating system.

Sendmail Debug Mode Then-current versions of the popular Sendmail software package used to route electronic mail messages across the Internet contained a security vulnerability. This vulnerability allowed the worm to spread itself by sending a specially crafted email message that contained the worm's code to the Sendmail program on a remote system. When the remote system processed the message, it became infected.

Password Attack The worm also used a dictionary attack to attempt to gain access to remote systems by utilizing the username and password of a valid system user (see "Dictionary Attacks" later in this chapter).

Finger Vulnerability Finger, a popular Internet utility, allowed users to determine who was logged on to a remote system. Then-current versions of the Finger software contained a buffer-overflow vulnerability that allowed the worm to spread (see "Buffer Overflows" later in this chapter). The Finger program has since been removed from most Internet-connected systems.

Trust Relationships After the worm infected a system, it analyzed any existing trust relationships with other systems on the network and attempted to spread itself to those systems through the trusted path.

This multipronged approach made Internet worm extremely dangerous. Fortunately, the (then-small) computer security community quickly put together a crack team of investigators who disarmed the worm and patched the affected systems. Their efforts were facilitated by several inefficient routines in the worm's code that limited the rate of its spread.

Because of the lack of experience among law enforcement authorities and the court system in dealing with computer crimes, along with a lack of relevant laws, Morris received only a slap on the wrist for his transgression. He was sentenced to three years' probation, 400 hours of community service, and a $10,000 fine under the Computer Fraud and Abuse Act of 1986. Ironically, Morris's father, Robert Morris, was serving as the director of the National Security Agency's National Computer Security Center (NCSC) at the time of the incident.

Stuxnet

In mid-2010, a worm named Stuxnet surfaced on the Internet. This highly sophisticated worm uses a variety of advanced techniques to spread, including multiple previously undocumented vulnerabilities. Stuxnet uses the following propagation techniques:

- Searching for unprotected administrative shares of systems on the local network
- Exploiting zero-day vulnerabilities in the Windows Server service and Windows Print Spooler service
- Connecting to systems using a default database password
- Spreading by the use of shared infected USB drives

While Stuxnet spread from system to system with impunity, it was actually searching for a very specific type of system—one using a controller manufactured by Siemens and allegedly used in the production of material for nuclear weapons. When it found such a system, it executed a series of actions designed to destroy centrifuges attached to the Siemens controller.

Stuxnet appeared to begin its spread in the Middle East, specifically on systems located in Iran. It is alleged to have been designed by Western nations with the intent of disrupting an Iranian nuclear weapons program. According to a story in the *New York Times*, a facility in Israel contained equipment used to test the worm. The story stated, "Israel has spun nuclear centrifuges nearly identical to Iran's" and went on to say that "the operations there, as well as related efforts in the United States, are…clues that the virus was designed as an American-Israeli project to sabotage the Iranian program."

If these allegations are true, Stuxnet marks two major evolutions in the world of malicious code: the use of a worm to cause major physical damage to a facility and the use of malicious code in warfare between nations.

Spyware and Adware

Two other types of unwanted software interfere with the way you normally use your computer. *Spyware* monitors your actions and transmits important details to a remote system that spies on your activity. For example, spyware might wait for you to log into a banking website and then transmit your username and password to the creator of the spyware. Alternatively, it might wait for you to enter your credit card number on an e-commerce site and transmit it to a fraudster to resell on the black market.

Adware, while quite similar to spyware in form, has a different purpose. It uses a variety of techniques to display advertisements on infected computers. The simplest forms of adware display pop-up ads on your screen while you surf the Web. More nefarious versions may monitor your shopping behavior and redirect you to competitor websites.

NOTE

Adware and malware authors often take advantage of third-party plug-ins to popular Internet tools, such as web browsers, to spread their malicious content. The authors find plug-ins that already have a strong subscriber base that granted the plug-in permission to run within their browser and/or gain access to their information. They then supplement the original plug-in code with malicious code that spreads malware, steals information, or performs other unwanted activity.

Countermeasures

The primary means of defense against malicious code is the use of antivirus-filtering software. These packages are primarily signature-based systems, designed to detect known viruses running on a system. It's wise to consider implementing antivirus filters in at least three key areas, described here:

Client Systems Every workstation on a network should have updated antivirus software searching the local file system for malicious code.

Server Systems Servers should have similar protections. This is even more critical than protecting client systems because a single virus on a common server could quickly spread throughout an entire network.

Content Filters The majority of viruses today are exchanged over email. It's a wise move to implement content filtering on your network that scans inbound and outbound electronic mail and web traffic for signs of malicious code.

NOTE

With current antivirus software, removal is often possible within hours after new malicious code is discovered. *Removal* removes the malicious code but does not repair the damage caused by it. Cleaning capabilities are usually made available within a few days after new malicious code is discovered. *Cleaning* not only removes the code; it also repairs any damage it causes.

WARNING

Remember, most antivirus filters are signature based. Therefore, they're only as good as the most recent update to their virus definition files. It's critical that you update these files frequently, especially when a new piece of high-profile malicious code appears on the Internet.

Signature-based filters rely on the descriptions of known viruses provided by software developers. Therefore, there is a period of time between when any given virus first appears "in the wild" and when updated filters are made available. This problem has two solutions that are commonly used today:

- Integrity-checking software, such as Tripwire (an open source version is available at `www.tripwire.org`), scans your file system for unexpected modifications and reports to you periodically.
- Access controls limit the ability of malicious code to damage your data and spread on your network. They should be strictly maintained and enforced.

Three additional techniques can specifically prevent systems from being infected by malicious code embedded in active content:

- Java's sandbox provides applets with an isolated environment in which they can run safely without gaining access to critical system resources.
- ActiveX control signing utilizes a system of digital signatures to ensure that the code originates from a trusted source. It is up to the end user to determine whether the authenticated source should be trusted.
- Whitelisting applications at the operating system level requires administrators to specify approved applications. The operating system uses this list to allow only known good applications to run.

For an in-depth explanation of digital signature technology, see Chapter 7, "PKI and Cryptographic Applications."

Many forms of malicious code take advantage of zero-day vulnerabilities, security flaws discovered by hackers that have not been thoroughly addressed by the security community. There are two main reasons systems are affected by these vulnerabilities:

- The necessary delay between the discovery of a new type of malicious code and the issuance of patches and antivirus updates
- Slowness in applying updates on the part of system administrators

The existence of zero-day vulnerabilities makes it critical that you have a strong patch management program in your organization that ensures the prompt application of critical security updates. Additionally, you may wish to use a vulnerability scanner to scan your systems on a regular basis for known security issues.

Password Attacks

One of the simplest techniques attackers use to gain illegitimate access to a system is to learn the username and password of an authorized system user. Once they've gained access as a regular user, they have a foothold into the system. At that point, they can use other techniques, including automated rootkit packages, to gain increased levels of access to the system (see the section "Escalation of Privilege and Rootkits" later in this chapter). They may also use the compromised system as a jumping-off point for attacks on other, more attractive targets on the same network.

The following sections examine three methods attackers use to learn the passwords of legitimate users and access a system: password-guessing attacks, dictionary attacks, and social-engineering attacks. Many of these attacks rely on weak password storage mechanisms. For example, many Unix operating systems store encrypted versions of a user's password in the `/etc/passwd` file.

Password Guessing

In the most basic type of password attack, attackers simply attempt to guess a user's password. No matter how much security education users receive, they often use extremely weak passwords. If attackers are able to obtain a list of authorized system users, they can often quickly figure out the correct usernames. (On most networks, usernames consist of the first initial of the user's first name followed by a portion of their last name.) With this information, they can begin making some educated guesses about the user's password. The most commonly used password is some form of the user's last name, first name, or username. For example, the user mchapple might use the weak password elppahcm because it's easy to remember. Unfortunately, it's also easy to guess.

If that attempt fails, attackers turn to widely available lists of the most common passwords on the Internet. Some of these are shown in the sidebar "Most Common Passwords."

Most Common Passwords

Attackers often use the Internet to distribute lists of commonly used passwords based on data gathered during system compromises. Many of these are no great surprise. Here are just a very few of the 815 passwords contained in an attacker list retrieved from the Internet:

Password

Secret

sex

money

love

computer

football

hello

morning

Ibm

work

office

online

terminal

Internet

Along with these common words, the password list contained more than 300 first names, 70 percent of which were female names.

Finally, a little knowledge about a person can provide extremely good clues about their password. Many people use the name of a spouse, child, family pet, relative, or favorite entertainer. Common passwords also include birthdays, anniversaries, Social Security numbers, phone numbers, and (believe it or not!) ATM PINs.

Dictionary Attacks

As mentioned previously, many Unix systems store encrypted versions of user passwords in an `/etc/passwd` file accessible to all system users. To provide some level of security, the file doesn't contain the actual user passwords; it contains an encrypted value obtained from a one-way encryption function (see Chapter 7 for a discussion of encryption functions). When a user attempts to log on to the system, access verification routines use the same encryption function to encrypt the password entered by the user and then compare it with the encrypted version of the actual password stored in the /etc/passwd file. If the values match, the user is allowed access.

Password attackers use automated tools like John the Ripper to run automated dictionary attacks that exploit a simple vulnerability in this mechanism. They take a large dictionary file that contains thousands of words and then run the encryption function against all those words to obtain their encrypted equivalents. John the Ripper then searches the password file for any encrypted values for which there is a match in the encrypted dictionary. When a match is found, it reports the username and password (in plain text), and the attacker gains access to the system.

Password Crackers

John the Ripper is just one password-cracking program. There are many others available on the Internet that use a variety of attack techniques. These include Cain & Abel, Ophcrack, Brutus, THC Hydra, L0phtCrack, Pwdump, and RainbowCrack. Each tool specializes in different operating systems and password types.

It sounds like simple security mechanisms and education would prevent users from using passwords that are easily guessed by John the Ripper, but the tool is surprisingly effective at compromising live systems. As new versions of cracking tools are released, more advanced features are introduced to defeat common techniques used by users to defeat password complexity rules. Some of these are included in the following list:

- Rearranging the letters of a dictionary word
- Appending a number to a dictionary word
- Replacing each occurrence of the letter O in a dictionary word with the number 0 (or the letter *l* with the number 1)
- Combining two dictionary words in some form

Social Engineering

Social engineering is one of the most effective tools attackers use to gain access to a system. In its most basic form, a social-engineering attack consists of simply calling the user and asking for their password, posing as a technical support representative or other authority figure who needs the information immediately. Fortunately, most contemporary computer users are aware of these scams, and the effectiveness of directly asking a user for a password is somewhat diminished today. Instead, these attacks rely on phishing emails that prompt users to log in to a fake site using their actual username and password, which are then captured by the attacker and used to log into the actual site. Phishing attacks often target financial services websites, where user credentials can be used to quickly transfer cash. In addition to tricking users into giving up their passwords, phishing attacks are often used to get users to install malware or provide other sensitive personal information.

Although users are becoming savvier, social engineering still poses a significant threat to the security of passwords (and networks in general). Attackers can often obtain sensitive personal information by "chatting up" computer users, office gossips, and administrative personnel. This information can provide excellent ammunition when mounting a password-guessing attack. Furthermore, attackers can sometimes obtain sensitive network topography or configuration data that is useful when planning other types of electronic attacks against an organization.

Countermeasures

The cornerstone of any security program is education. Security personnel should continually remind users of the importance of choosing a secure password and keeping it secret. Users should receive training when they first enter an organization, and they should receive periodic refresher training, even if it's just an email from the administrator reminding them of the threats.

Provide users with the knowledge they need to create secure passwords. Tell them about the techniques attackers use when guessing passwords, and give them advice on how to create a strong password. One of the most effective techniques is to use a mnemonic device such as thinking of an easy-to-remember sentence and creating a password out of the first letter of each word. For example, "My son Richard likes to eat four pies" would become MsRlte4p—an extremely strong password. You may also wish to consider providing users with a secure tool that allows for the storage of these strong passwords. Password Safe and LastPass are two commonly used examples. These tools allow users to create unique, strong passwords for each service they use without the burden of memorizing them all.

TIP: One of the best ways to prevent password-based attacks is to supplement passwords with other authentication techniques. This approach, known as multifactor authentication, is discussed in Chapter 13.

One of the most common mistakes made by overzealous security administrators is to create a series of strong passwords and then assign them to users (who are then prevented from changing their password). At first glance, this seems to be a sound security policy. However, the first thing a user will do when they receive a password like 1mf0A8flt is write it down on a sticky note and put it under their computer keyboard. Whoops! Security just went out the window (or under the keyboard)!

If your network includes Unix operating systems that implement the `/etc/passwd` file, consider using some other access verification mechanism to increase security. One popular technique available in many versions of Unix and Linux is the use of a shadow password file, `/etc/shadow`. This file contains the true encrypted passwords of each user, but it is not accessible to anyone but the administrator. The publicly accessible `/etc/passwd` file then simply contains a list of usernames without the data necessary to mount a dictionary attack.

Application Attacks

In Chapter 20, you learned about the importance of utilizing solid software engineering processes when developing operating systems and applications. In the following sections, you'll take a brief look at some of the specific techniques attackers use to exploit vulnerabilities left behind by sloppy coding practices.

Buffer Overflows

Buffer overflow vulnerabilities exist when a developer does not properly validate user input to ensure that it is of an appropriate size. Input that is too large can "overflow" a data structure to affect other data stored in the computer's memory. For example, if a web form has a field that ties to a backend variable that allows 10 characters, but the form processor does not verify the length of the input, the operating system may try to simply write data past the end of the memory space reserved for that variable, potentially corrupting other data stored in memory. In the worst case, that data can be used to overwrite system commands, allowing an attacker to exploit the buffer overflow vulnerability to execute arbitrary commands on the server.

When creating software, developers must pay special attention to variables that allow user input. Many programming languages do not enforce size limits on variables intrinsically—they rely on the programmer to perform this bounds checking in the code. This is an inherent vulnerability because many programmers feel parameter checking is an unnecessary burden that slows down the development process. As a security practitioner, it's your responsibility to ensure that developers in your organization are aware of the risks posed by buffer overflow vulnerabilities and that they take appropriate measures to protect their code against this type of attack.

Anytime a program variable allows user input, the programmer should take steps to ensure that each of the following conditions is met:

- The user can't enter a value longer than the size of any buffer that will hold it (for example, a 10-letter word into a 5-letter string variable).
- The user can't enter an invalid value for the variable types that will hold it (for example, a letter into a numeric variable).
- The user can't enter a value that will cause the program to operate outside of its specified parameters (for example, answer a "yes" or "no" question with "maybe").

Failure to perform simple checks to make sure these conditions are met can result in a buffer overflow vulnerability that may cause the system to crash or even allow the user to execute shell commands and gain access to the system. Buffer overflow vulnerabilities are especially prevalent in code developed rapidly for the Web using CGI or other languages that allow unskilled programmers to quickly create interactive web pages. Most buffer overflow vulnerabilities are mitigated with patches provided by software and operating system vendors, magnifying the importance of keeping systems and software up to date.

Time of Check to Time of Use

The *time-of-check-to-time-of-use (TOCTTOU or TOC/TOU)* issue is a timing vulnerability that occurs when a program checks access permissions too far in advance of a resource request. For example, if an operating system builds a comprehensive list of access permissions for a user upon logon and then consults that list throughout the logon session, a TOCTTOU vulnerability exists. If the system administrator revokes a particular permission, that restriction would not be applied to the user until the next time they log on. If the user is logged on when the access revocation takes place, they will have access to the resource indefinitely. The user simply needs to leave the session open for days, and the new restrictions will never be applied.

Back Doors

Back doors are undocumented command sequences that allow individuals with knowledge of the back door to bypass normal access restrictions. They are often used during the development and debugging process to speed up the workflow and avoid forcing developers to continuously authenticate to the system. Occasionally, developers leave these back doors in the system after it reaches a production state, either by accident or so they can "take a peek" at their system when it is processing sensitive data to which they should not have access. In addition to back doors planted by developers, many types of malicious code create back doors on infected systems that allow the developers of the malicious code to remotely access infected systems.

No matter how they arise on a system, the undocumented nature of back doors makes them a significant threat to the security of any system that contains them. Individuals with knowledge of the back door may use it to access the system and retrieve confidential information, monitor user activity, or engage in other nefarious acts.

Escalation of Privilege and Rootkits

Once attackers gain a foothold on a system, they often quickly move on to a second objective—expanding their access from the normal user account they may have compromised to more comprehensive, administrative access. They do this by engaging in *escalation of privilege attacks*.

One of the most common ways that attackers wage escalation of privilege attacks is through the use of *rootkits*. Rootkits are freely available on the Internet and exploit known vulnerabilities in various operating systems. Attackers often obtain access to a standard system user account through the use of a password attack or social engineering and then use a rootkit to increase their access to the root (or administrator) level. This increase in access from standard to administrative privileges is known as an escalation of privilege attack.

Administrators can take one simple precaution to protect their systems against escalation of privilege attacks, and it's nothing new. Administrators must keep themselves informed about new security patches released for operating systems used in their environment and apply these corrective measures consistently. This straightforward step will fortify a network against almost all rootkit attacks as well as a large number of other potential vulnerabilities.

Web Application Security

The Web allows you to purchase airline tickets, check your email, pay your bills, and purchase stocks all from the comfort of your living room. Almost every business today operates a website, and many allow you to conduct sensitive transactions through that site.

Along with the convenience benefits of web applications comes a series of new vulnerabilities that may expose web-enabled organizations to security risks. In the next several sections, we'll cover two common web application attacks. Additional detail on web application security can be found in Chapter 9, "Security Vulnerabilities, Threats, and Countermeasures."

Cross-Site Scripting (XSS)

Cross-site scripting attacks occur when web applications contain some type of *reflected input*. For example, consider a simple web application that contains a single text box asking a user to enter their name. When the user clicks Submit, the web application loads a new page that says, "Hello, *name*."

Under normal circumstances, this web application functions as designed. However, a malicious individual could take advantage of this web application to trick an unsuspecting third party. As you may know, you can embed scripts in web pages by using the HTML tags `<SCRIPT>` and `</SCRIPT>`. Suppose that, instead of entering *Mike* in the Name field, you enter the following text:

```
Mike<SCRIPT>alert('hello')</SCRIPT>
```

When the web application "reflects" this input in the form of a web page, your browser processes it as it would any other web page: It displays the text portions of the web page and executes the script portions. In this case, the script simply opens a pop-up window that says "hello" in it. However, you could be more malicious and include a more sophisticated script that asks the user to provide a password and transmits it to a malicious third party.

At this point, you're probably asking yourself how anyone would fall victim to this type of attack. After all, you're not going to attack yourself by embedding scripts in the input that you provide to a web application that performs reflection. The key to this attack is that it's possible to embed form input in a link. A malicious individual could create a web page with a link titled "Check your account at First Bank" and encode form input in the link. When the user visits the link, the web page appears to be an authentic First Bank website (because it is!) with the proper address in the toolbar and a valid SSL certificate. However, the website would then execute the script included in the input by the malicious user, which appears to be part of the valid web page.

What's the answer to cross-site scripting? When you create web applications that allow any type of user input, you must be sure to perform *input validation*. At the most basic level, you should never allow a user to include the `<SCRIPT>` tag in a reflected input field. However, this doesn't solve the problem completely; there are many clever alternatives available to an industrious web application attacker. The best solution is to determine the type of input that you *will* allow and then validate the input to ensure that it matches that pattern. For example, if you have a text box that allows users to enter their age, you should accept only one to three digits as input. Your application should reject any other input as invalid.

TIP

For more examples of ways to evade cross-site scripting filters, see `https://www.owasp.org/index.php/XSS_Filter_Evasion_Cheat_Sheet`.

SQL Injection

SQL injection attacks are even riskier than XSS attacks from an organization's perspective. As with XSS attacks, SQL injection attacks use unexpected input to a web application. However, instead of using this input to attempt to fool a user, SQL injection attacks use it to gain unauthorized access to an underlying database.

Dynamic Web Applications

In the early days of the Web, all web pages were *static*, or unchanging. Webmasters created web pages containing information and placed them on a web server, where users could retrieve them using their web browsers. The Web quickly outgrew this model because users wanted the ability to access customized information based on their individual needs. For example, visitors to a bank website aren't interested only in static pages containing information about the bank's locations, hours, and services. They also want to retrieve *dynamic* content containing information about their personal accounts. Obviously, the webmaster can't possibly create pages on the web server for each individual user with that user's personal account information. At a large bank, that would require maintaining millions of pages with up-to-the-minute information. That's where dynamic web applications come into play.

Web applications take advantage of a database to create content on demand when the user makes a request. In the banking example, the user logs into the web application, providing an account number and password. The web application then retrieves current account information from the bank's database and uses it to instantly create a web page containing the user's current account information. If that user returns an hour later, the web server would repeat the process, obtaining updated account information from the database. Figure 21.1 illustrates this model.

FIGURE 21.1 Typical database-driven website architecture

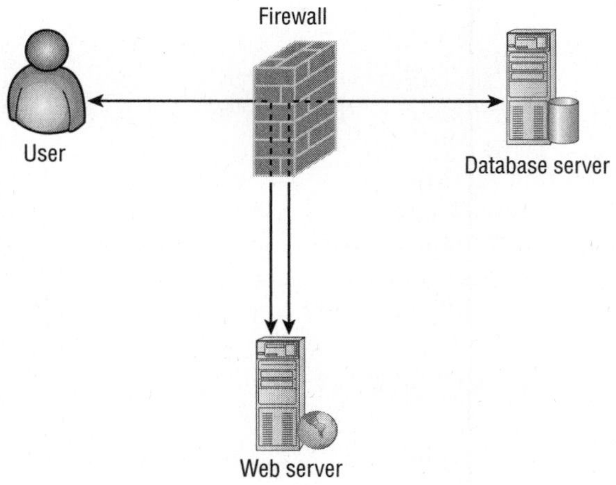

What does this mean to you as a security professional? Web applications add complexity to our traditional security model. As shown in Figure 21.1, the web server, as a publicly accessible server, belongs in a separate network zone from other servers, commonly referred to as a demilitarized zone (DMZ). The database server, on the other hand, is not meant for public access, so it belongs on the internal network. The web application needs access to the database, so the firewall administrator must create a rule allowing access from the web server to the database server. This rule creates a potential path for Internet users to gain access to the database server. (For more on firewalls and DMZs, see Chapter 11, "Secure Network Architecture and Securing Network Components.") If the web application functions properly, it will allow only authorized requests to the database. However, if there is a flaw in the web application, it may allow individuals to tamper with the database in an unexpected and unauthorized fashion through the use of SQL injection attacks.

SQL Injection Attacks

SQL injection attacks allow a malicious individual to directly perform SQL transactions against the underlying database, in violation of the isolation model shown in Figure 21.1.

TIP: For more on databases and SQL, see Chapter 20.

In the example used earlier, a bank customer might enter an account number to gain access to a dynamic web application that retrieves current account details. The web application must use a SQL query to obtain that information, perhaps of the following form, where `<number>` is the account number provided by the user on the web form:

```
SELECT *
FROM transactions
WHERE account_number = '<number>'
```

There's one more important fact you need to know: Databases will process multiple SQL statements at the same time, provided that you end each one with a semicolon.

If the web application doesn't perform proper input validation, the user may be able to insert their own SQL code into the statement executed by the web server. For example, if the user's account number is 145249, they could enter the following:

```
145249'; DELETE * FROM transactions WHERE 'a' = 'a
```

The web application would then obediently plug this into the `<number>` field in the earlier SQL statement, resulting in the following:

```
SELECT *
FROM transactions
WHERE account_number ='145249'; DELETE * FROM transactions WHERE 'a' = 'a'
```

Reformatting that command slightly, you get the following:

```
SELECT *
FROM transactions
WHERE account_number ='145249';
DELETE *
FROM transactions
WHERE 'a' = 'a'
```

This is a valid SQL transaction containing two statements. The first one retrieves the requested information from the database. The second statement deletes all the records stored in the database. Whoops!

Protecting against SQL Injection

You can use three techniques to protect your web applications against SQL injection attacks:

Perform Input Validation As described earlier in this chapter when talking about cross-site scripting, input validation allows you to limit the types of data a user provides in a form. In the case of the SQL injection example we provided in the previous section, removing the single quote characters (`'`) from the input would prevent the successful use of this attack. This is the most effective means of preventing SQL injection attacks.

Limit Account Privileges The database account used by the web server should have the smallest set of privileges possible. If the web application needs only to retrieve data, it should have that ability only. In the example, the `DELETE` command would fail if the account had `SELECT` privileges only.

Use Stored Procedures Developers of web applications should leverage database stored procedures to limit the application's ability to execute arbitrary code. With stored procedures, the SQL statement resides on the database server and may be modified only by database administrators. Web applications calling the stored procedure may pass parameters to it but may not alter the underlying structure of the SQL statement.

Reconnaissance Attacks

While malicious code often relies on tricking users into opening or accessing malware, other attacks directly target machines. Performing reconnaissance can allow an attacker to find weak points to target directly with their attack code. To assist with this targeting, attacker-tool developers have created a number of automated tools that perform network reconnaissance. In the following sections, we'll cover three of those automated techniques—IP probes, port scans, and vulnerability scans—and then explain how these techniques can be supplemented by the more physically intensive dumpster-diving technique.

IP Probes

IP probes (also called *IP sweeps* or *ping sweeps*) are often the first type of network reconnaissance carried out against a targeted network. With this technique, automated tools simply attempt to ping each address in a range. Systems that respond to the ping request are logged for further analysis. Addresses that do not produce a response are assumed to be unused and are ignored.

TIP

The Nmap tool is one of the most common tools used to perform both IP probes and port scans. It's available for free download from `www.nmap.org`.

IP probes are extremely prevalent on the Internet today. Indeed, if you configure a system with a public IP address and connect it to the Internet, you'll probably receive at least one IP probe within hours of booting up. The widespread use of this technique makes a strong case for disabling ping functionality, at least for users external to a network.

Port Scans

After an attacker performs an IP probe, they are left with a list of active systems on a given network. The next task is to select one or more systems to target with additional attacks. Often, attackers have a type of target in mind; web servers, file servers, and other servers supporting critical operations are prime targets.

To narrow down their search, attackers use *port scan* software to probe all the active systems on a network and determine what public services are running on each machine. For example, if the attacker wants to target a web server, they might run a port scan to locate any systems with a service running on port 80, the default port for HTTP services.

Vulnerability Scans

The third technique is the *vulnerability scan*. Once the attacker determines a specific system to target, they need to discover a specific vulnerability in that system that can be exploited to gain the desired access permissions. A variety of tools available on the Internet assist with this task. Some of the more popular tools for this purpose include Nessus, OpenVAS, Qualys, Core Impact, and Nexpose. These packages contain a database of known vulnerabilities and probe targeted systems to locate security flaws. They then produce very attractive reports that detail every vulnerability detected. From that point, it's simply a matter of locating a script that exploits a specific vulnerability and launching an attack against the victim.

It's important to note that vulnerability scanners are highly automated tools. They can be used to launch an attack against a specific system, but it's just as likely that an attacker would use a series of IP probes, port scans, and vulnerability scans to narrow down a list of potential victims. However, chances are an intruder will run a vulnerability scanner against an entire network to probe for any weakness that could be exploited.

Once again, simply updating operating systems to the most recent security patch level can repair almost every weakness reported by a vulnerability scanner. Furthermore, wise system administrators learn to think like the enemy—they download and run these vulnerability scanners against their own networks (with the permission of upper management) to see what security holes might be pointed out to a potential attacker. This allows them to quickly focus their resources on fortifying the weakest points on their networks.

Dumpster Diving

Every organization generates trash—often significant amounts on a daily basis. Have you ever taken the time to sort through your trash to see the sensitivity of the materials that hit the recycle bin? Give it a try—the results may frighten you. When you're analyzing the work papers thrown away each day, look at them from an attacker's perspective. What type of intelligence could you glean from them that might help you launch an attack? Is there sensitive data about network configurations or installed software versions? A list of employees' birthdays from a particular department that might be used in a social-engineering attack? A policy manual that contains detailed procedures on the creation of new accounts? Discarded floppy disks or other storage media?

Don't underestimate the value of even trivial corporate documents to a social engineer. Kevin Mitnick, a famous social engineer, once admitted to using company newsletters as a key component of his attacks. He skipped right to the section containing a listing of new hires, recognizing that these individuals were perfect victims, all too eager to please someone calling from the "top floor" requesting sensitive information.

Dumpster diving is one of the oldest attacker tools in the book, and it's still used today. The best defense against these attacks is quite simple—make them more difficult. Purchase shredders for key departments, and encourage employees to use them. Keep the trash locked up in a secure area until the garbage collectors arrive. A little common sense goes a long way in this area.

Masquerading Attacks

One of the easiest ways to gain access to resources you're not otherwise entitled to use is to impersonate someone who does have the appropriate access permissions. In the offline world, teenagers often borrow the driver's license of an older sibling to purchase alcohol, and the same type of thing happens in the computer security world. Attackers borrow the identities of legitimate users and systems to gain the trust of third parties. In the following sections, we'll take a look at two common masquerading attacks—IP spoofing and session hijacking.

IP Spoofing

In an *IP spoofing attack*, the malicious individual simply reconfigures their system so that it has the IP address of a trusted system and then attempts to gain access to other external resources. This is surprisingly effective on many networks that don't have adequate filters installed to prevent this type of traffic from occurring. System administrators should configure filters at the perimeter of each network to ensure that packets meet at least the following criteria:

- Packets with internal source IP addresses don't enter the network from the outside.
- Packets with external source IP addresses don't exit the network from the inside.
- Packets with private IP addresses don't pass through the router in either direction (unless specifically allowed as part of an intranet configuration).

These three simple filtering rules can eliminate the vast majority of IP spoofing attacks and greatly enhance the security of a network.

Session Hijacking

Session hijacking attacks occur when a malicious individual intercepts part of the communication between an authorized user and a resource and then uses a hijacking technique to take over the session and assume the identity of the authorized user. The following list includes some common techniques:

- Capturing details of the authentication between a client and server and using those details to assume the client's identity
- Tricking the client into thinking the attacker's system is the server, acting as the middleman as the client sets up a legitimate connection with the server, and then disconnecting the client
- Accessing a web application using the cookie data of a user who did not properly close the connection

All of these techniques can have disastrous results for the end user and must be addressed with both administrative controls (such as anti-replay authentication techniques) and application controls (such as expiring cookies within a reasonable period of time).

Summary

Applications developers have a lot to worry about! As hackers become more sophisticated in their tools and techniques, the Application layer is increasingly becoming the focus of their attacks due to its complexity and multiple points of vulnerability.

Malicious code, including viruses, worms, Trojan horses, and logic bombs, exploits vulnerabilities in applications and operating systems or uses social engineering to infect systems and gain access to their resources and confidential information.

Applications themselves also may contain a number of vulnerabilities. Buffer overflow attacks exploit code that lacks proper input validation to affect the contents of a system's memory. Back doors provide former developers and malicious code authors with the ability to bypass normal security mechanisms. Rootkits provide attackers with an easy way to conduct escalation-of-privilege attacks.

Many applications are moving to the Web, creating a new level of exposure and vulnerability. Cross-site scripting attacks allow hackers to trick users into providing sensitive information to unsecure sites. SQL injection attacks allow the bypassing of application controls to directly access and manipulate the underlying database.

Reconnaissance tools provide attackers with automated tools they can use to identify vulnerable systems that may be attacked at a later date. IP probes, port scans, and vulnerability scans are all automated ways to detect weak points in an organization's security controls. Masquerading attacks use stealth techniques to allow the impersonation of users and systems.

Exam Essentials

Understand the propagation techniques used by viruses. Viruses use four main propagation techniques—file infection, service injection, boot sector infection, and macro infection—to penetrate systems and spread their malicious payloads. You need to understand these techniques to effectively protect systems on your network from malicious code.

Know how antivirus software packages detect known viruses. Most antivirus programs use signature-based detection algorithms to look for telltale patterns of known viruses. This makes it essential to periodically update virus definition files in order to maintain protection against newly authored viruses as they emerge.

Explain the techniques that attackers use to compromise password security. Passwords are the most common access control mechanism in use today, and it is essential that you understand how to protect against attackers who seek to undermine their security. Know how password crackers, dictionary attacks, and social engineering can be used to defeat password security.

Be familiar with the various types of application attacks attackers use to exploit poorly written software. Application attacks are one of the greatest threats to modern computing. Attackers exploit buffer overflows, back doors, time-of-check-to-time-of-use vulnerabilities, and rootkits to gain illegitimate access to a system. Security professionals must have a clear understanding of each of these attacks and associated countermeasures.

Understand common web application vulnerabilities and countermeasures. As many applications move to the Web, developers and security professionals must understand the new types of attacks that exist in this environment and how to protect against them. The two most common examples are cross-site scripting (XSS) and SQL injection attacks.

Know the network reconnaissance techniques used by attackers preparing to attack a network. Before launching an attack, attackers use IP sweeps to search out active hosts on a network. These hosts are then subjected to port scans and other vulnerability probes to locate weak spots that might be attacked in an attempt to compromise the network. You should understand these attacks to help protect your network against them, limiting the amount of information attackers may glean.

Written Lab

1. What is the major difference between a virus and a worm?
2. Explain the four propagation methods used by Robert Tappan Morris's Internet worm.
3. What are the actions an antivirus software package might take when it discovers an infected file?
4. Explain how a data integrity assurance package like Tripwire provides some secondary virus detection capabilities.

Review Questions

1. What is the most commonly used technique to protect against virus attacks?
   A. Signature detection
   B. Heuristic detection
   C. Data integrity assurance
   D. Automated reconstruction
2. You are the security administrator for an e-commerce company and are placing a new web server into production. What network zone should you use?
   A. Internet
   B. DMZ
   C. Intranet
   D. Sandbox
3. Which one of the following types of attacks relies on the difference between the timing of two events?
   A. Smurf
   B. TOCTTOU
   C. Land
   D. Fraggle
4. Which of the following techniques requires that administrators identify appropriate applications for an environment?
   A. Sandboxing
   B. Control signing
   C. Integrity monitoring
   D. Whitelisting
5. What advanced virus technique modifies the malicious code of a virus on each system it infects?
   A. Polymorphism
   B. Stealth
   C. Encryption
   D. Multipartitism
6. Which one of the following tools provides a solution to the problem of users forgetting complex passwords?
   A. LastPass
   B. Crack
   C. Shadow password files
   D. Tripwire

7. What type of application vulnerability most directly allows an attacker to modify the contents of a system's memory?
   - A. Rootkit
   - B. Back door
   - C. TOC/TOU
   - D. Buffer overflow

8. Which one of the following passwords is least likely to be compromised during a dictionary attack?
   - A. mike
   - B. elppa
   - C. dayorange
   - D. fsas3alG

9. What file is instrumental in preventing dictionary attacks against Unix systems?
   - A. `/etc/passwd`
   - B. `/etc/shadow`
   - C. `/etc/security`
   - D. `/etc/pwlog`

10. What character should always be treated carefully when encountered as user input on a web form?
    - A. !
    - B. &
    - C. *
    - D. '

11. What database technology, if implemented for web forms, can limit the potential for SQL injection attacks?
    - A. Triggers
    - B. Stored procedures
    - C. Column encryption
    - D. Concurrency control

12. What type of reconnaissance attack provides attackers with useful information about the services running on a system?
    - A. Session hijacking
    - B. Port scan
    - C. Dumpster diving
    - D. IP sweep

13. What condition is necessary on a web page for it to be used in a cross-site scripting attack?
    - A. Reflected input
    - B. Database-driven content
    - C. .NET technology
    - D. CGI scripts
14. What type of virus utilizes more than one propagation technique to maximize the number of penetrated systems?
    - A. Stealth virus
    - B. Companion virus
    - C. Polymorphic virus
    - D. Multipartite virus
15. What is the most effective defense against cross-site scripting attacks?
    - A. Limiting account privileges
    - B. Input validation
    - C. User authentication
    - D. Encryption
16. What worm was the first to cause major physical damage to a facility?
    - A. Stuxnet
    - B. Code Red
    - C. Melissa
    - D. rtm
17. Ben's system was infected by malicious code that modified the operating system to allow the malicious code author to gain access to his files. What type of exploit did this attacker engage in?
    - A. Escalation of privilege
    - B. Back door
    - C. Rootkit
    - D. Buffer overflow
18. What technology does the Java language use to minimize the threat posed by applets?
    - A. Confidentiality
    - B. Encryption
    - C. Stealth
    - D. Sandbox
19. What HTML tag is often used as part of a cross-site scripting (XSS) attack?
    - A. `<H1>`
    - B. `<HEAD>`

C. `<XSS>`

D. `<SCRIPT>`

20. When designing firewall rules to prevent IP spoofing, which of the following principles should you follow?

A. Packets with internal source IP addresses don't enter the network from the outside.

B. Packets with internal source IP addresses don't exit the network from the inside.

C. Packets with public IP addresses don't pass through the router in either direction.

D. Packets with external source IP addresses don't enter the network from the outside.

Appendix A

Answers to Review Questions

Chapter 1: Security Governance Through Principles and Policies

1. B. The primary goals and objectives of security are confidentiality, integrity, and availability, commonly referred to as the *CIA Triad*.
2. A. Vulnerabilities and risks are evaluated based on their threats against one or more of the CIA Triad principles.
3. B. Availability means that authorized subjects are granted timely and uninterrupted access to objects.
4. C. Hardware destruction is a violation of availability and possibly integrity. Violations of confidentiality include capturing network traffic, stealing password files, social engineering, port scanning, shoulder surfing, eavesdropping, and sniffing.
5. C. Violations of confidentiality are not limited to direct intentional attacks. Many instances of unauthorized disclosure of sensitive or confidential information are due to human error, oversight, or ineptitude.
6. D. Disclosure is not an element of STRIDE. The elements of STRIDE are spoofing, tampering, repudiation, information disclosure, denial of service, and elevation of privilege.
7. C. Accessibility of data, objects, and resources is the goal of availability. If a security mechanism offers availability, then it is highly likely that the data, objects, and resources are accessible to authorized subjects.
8. C. Privacy refers to keeping information confidential that is personally identifiable or which might cause harm, embarrassment, or disgrace to someone if revealed. Seclusion is to store something in an out of the way location. Concealment is the act of hiding or preventing disclosure. The level to which information is mission critical is its measure of criticality.
9. D. Users should be aware that email messages are retained, but the backup mechanism used to perform this operation does not need to be disclosed to them.
10. D. Ownership grants an entity full capabilities and privileges over the object they own. The ability to take ownership is often granted to the most powerful accounts in an operating system because it can be used to overstep any access control limitations otherwise implemented.
11. C. Nonrepudiation ensures that the subject of an activity or event cannot deny that the event occurred.
12. B. Layering is the deployment of multiple security mechanisms in a series. When security restrictions are performed in a series, they are performed one after the other in a linear fashion. Therefore, a single failure of a security control does not render the entire solution ineffective.

13. A. Preventing an authorized reader of an object from deleting that object is just an example of access control, not data hiding. If you can read an object, it is not hidden from you.
14. D. The prevention of security compromises is the primary goal of change management.
15. B. The primary objective of data classification schemes is to formalize and stratify the process of securing data based on assigned labels of importance and sensitivity.
16. B. Size is not a criterion for establishing data classification. When classifying an object, you should take value, lifetime, and security implications into consideration.
17. A. Military (or government) and private sector (or commercial business) are the two common data classification schemes.
18. B. Of the options listed, secret is the lowest classified military data classification. Keep in mind that items labeled as confidential, secret, and top secret are collectively known as classified, and confidential is below secret in the list.
19. B. The commercial business/private sector data classification of private is used to protect information about individuals.
20. C. Layering is a core aspect of security mechanisms, but it is not a focus of data classifications.

Chapter 2: Personnel Security and Risk Management Concepts

1. D. Regardless of the specifics of a security solution, humans are the weakest element.
2. A. The first step in hiring new employees is to create a job description. Without a job description, there is no consensus on what type of individual needs to be found and hired.
3. B. The primary purpose of an exit interview is to review the nondisclosure agreement (NDA) and other liabilities and restrictions placed on the former employee based on the employment agreement and any other security-related documentation.
4. B. You should remove or disable the employee's network user account immediately before or at the same time they are informed of their termination.
5. B. Third-party governance is the application of security oversight on third parties that your organization relies on.
6. D. A portion of the documentation review is the logical and practical investigation of business processes and organizational policies.
7. C. Risks to an IT infrastructure are not all computer based. In fact, many risks come from noncomputer sources. It is important to consider all possible risks when performing risk evaluation for an organization. Failing to properly evaluate and respond to all forms of risk, a company remains vulnerable.

8. C. Risk analysis includes analyzing an environment for risks, evaluating each threat event as to its likelihood of occurring and the cost of the damage it would cause, assessing the cost of various countermeasures for each risk, and creating a cost/benefit report for safeguards to present to upper management. Selecting safeguards is a task of upper management based on the results of risk analysis. It is a task that falls under risk management, but it is not part of the risk analysis process.
9. D. The personal files of users are not usually considered assets of the organization and thus are not considered in a risk analysis.
10. A. Threat events are accidental or intentional exploitations of vulnerabilities.
11. A. A vulnerability is the absence or weakness of a safeguard or countermeasure.
12. B. Anything that removes a vulnerability or protects against one or more specific threats is considered a safeguard or a countermeasure, not a risk.
13. C. The annual costs of safeguards should not exceed the expected annual cost of asset loss.
14. B. SLE is calculated using the formula SLE = asset value ($) * exposure factor (SLE = AV * EF).
15. A. The value of a safeguard to an organization is calculated by ALE before safeguard – ALE after implementing the safeguard – annual cost of safeguard [(ALE1 – ALE2) – ACS].
16. C. The likelihood that a co-worker will be willing to collaborate on an illegal or abusive scheme is reduced because of the higher risk of detection created by the combination of separation of duties, restricted job responsibilities, and job rotation.
17. C. Training is teaching employees to perform their work tasks and to comply with the security policy. Training is typically hosted by an organization and is targeted to groups of employees with similar job functions.
18. A. Managing the security function often includes assessment of budget, metrics, resources, information security strategies, and assessing the completeness and effectiveness of the security program.
19. B. The threat of a fire and the vulnerability of a lack of fire extinguishers lead to the risk of damage to equipment.
20. D. A countermeasure directly affects the annualized rate of occurrence, primarily because the countermeasure is designed to prevent the occurrence of the risk, thus reducing its frequency per year.

Chapter 3: Business Continuity Planning

1. B. The business organization analysis helps the initial planners select appropriate BCP team members and then guides the overall BCP process.
2. B. The first task of the BCP team should be the review and validation of the business organization analysis initially performed by those individuals responsible for

spearheading the BCP effort. This ensures that the initial effort, undertaken by a small group of individuals, reflects the beliefs of the entire BCP team.

3. C. A firm's officers and directors are legally bound to exercise due diligence in conducting their activities. This concept creates a fiduciary responsibility on their part to ensure that adequate business continuity plans are in place.

4. D. During the planning phase, the most significant resource utilization will be the time dedicated by members of the BCP team to the planning process itself. This represents a significant use of business resources and is another reason that buy-in from senior management is essential.

5. A. The quantitative portion of the priority identification should assign asset values in monetary units.

6. C. The annualized loss expectancy (ALE) represents the amount of money a business expects to lose to a given risk each year. This figure is quite useful when performing a quantitative prioritization of business continuity resource allocation.

7. C. The maximum tolerable downtime (MTD) represents the longest period a business function can be unavailable before causing irreparable harm to the business. This figure is useful when determining the level of business continuity resources to assign to a particular function.

8. B. The SLE is the product of the AV and the EF. From the scenario, you know that the AV is $3,000,000 and the EF is 90 percent, based on that the same land can be used to rebuild the facility. This yields an SLE of $2,700,000.

9. D. This problem requires you to compute the ALE, which is the product of the SLE and the ARO. From the scenario, you know that the ARO is 0.05 (or 5 percent). From question 8, you know that the SLE is $2,700,000. This yields an SLE of $135,000.

10. A. This problem requires you to compute the ALE, which is the product of the SLE and ARO. From the scenario, you know that the ARO is 0.10 (or 10 percent). From the scenario presented, you know that the SLE is $7.5 million. This yields an SLE of $750,000.

11. C. The strategy development task bridges the gap between business impact assessment and continuity planning by analyzing the prioritized list of risks developed during the BIA and determining which risks will be addressed by the BCP.

12. D. The safety of human life must always be the paramount concern in business continuity planning. Be sure that your plan reflects this priority, especially in the written documentation that is disseminated to your organization's employees!

13. C. It is very difficult to put a dollar figure on the business lost because of negative publicity. Therefore, this type of concern is better evaluated through a qualitative analysis.

14. B. The single loss expectancy (SLE) is the amount of damage that would be caused by a single occurrence of the risk. In this case, the SLE is $10 million, the expected damage from one tornado. The fact that a tornado occurs only once every 100 years is not reflected in the SLE but would be reflected in the annualized loss expectancy (ALE).

15. C. The annualized loss expectancy (ALE) is computed by taking the product of the single loss expectancy (SLE), which was $10 million in this scenario, and the annualized rate of occurrence (ARO), which was 0.01 in this example. These figures yield an ALE of $100,000.
16. C. In the provisions and processes phase, the BCP team actually designs the procedures and mechanisms to mitigate risks that were deemed unacceptable during the strategy development phase.
17. D. This is an example of alternative systems. Redundant communications circuits provide backup links that may be used when the primary circuits are unavailable.
18. C. Disaster recovery plans pick up where business continuity plans leave off. After a disaster strikes and the business is interrupted, the disaster recovery plan guides response teams in their efforts to quickly restore business operations to normal levels.
19. A. The single loss expectancy (SLE) is computed as the product of the asset value (AV) and the exposure factor (EF). The other formulas displayed here do not accurately reflect this calculation.
20. C. You should strive to have the highest-ranking person possible sign the BCP's statement of importance. Of the choices given, the chief executive officer is the highest ranking.

Chapter 4: Laws, Regulations, and Compliance

1. C. The Computer Fraud and Abuse Act, as amended, provides criminal and civil penalties for those individuals convicted of using viruses, worms, Trojan horses, and other types of malicious code to cause damage to computer system(s).
2. A. The Computer Security Act requires mandatory periodic training for all people involved in managing, using, or operating federal computer systems that contain sensitive information.
3. D. Administrative laws do not require an act of the legislative branch to implement at the federal level. Administrative laws consist of the policies, procedures, and regulations promulgated by agencies of the executive branch of government. Although they do not require an act of Congress, these laws are subject to judicial review and must comply with criminal and civil laws enacted by the legislative branch.
4. C. The National Institute of Standards and Technology (NIST) is charged with the security management of all federal government computer systems that are not used to process sensitive national security information. The National Security Agency (part of the Department of Defense) is responsible for managing those systems that do process classified and/or sensitive information.

5. C. The original Computer Fraud and Abuse Act of 1984 covered only systems used by the government and financial institutions. The act was broadened in 1986 to include all federal interest systems. The Computer Abuse Amendments Act of 1994 further amended the CFAA to cover all systems that are used in interstate commerce, including a large portion (but not all) of the computer systems in the United States.
6. B. The Fourth Amendment to the U.S. Constitution sets the "probable cause" standard that law enforcement officers must follow when conducting searches and/or seizures of private property. It also states that those officers must obtain a warrant before gaining involuntary access to such property.
7. A. Copyright law is the only type of intellectual property protection available to Matthew. It covers only the specific software code that Matthew used. It does not cover the process or ideas behind the software. Trademark protection is not appropriate for this type of situation. Patent protection does not apply to mathematical algorithms. Matthew can't seek trade secret protection because he plans to publish the algorithm in a public technical journal.
8. D. Mary and Joe should treat their oil formula as a trade secret. As long as they do not publicly disclose the formula, they can keep it a company secret indefinitely.
9. C. Richard's product name should be protected under trademark law. Until his registration is granted, he can use the ™ symbol next to it to inform others that it is protected under trademark law. Once his application is approved, the name becomes a registered trademark and Richard can begin using the ® symbol.
10. A. The Privacy Act of 1974 limits the ways government agencies may use information that private citizens disclose to them under certain circumstances.
11. B. The Uniform Computer Information Transactions Act (UCITA) attempts to implement a standard framework of laws regarding computer transactions to be adopted by all states. One of the issues addressed by UCITA is the legality of various types of software license agreements.
12. A. The Children's Online Privacy Protection Act (COPPA) provides severe penalties for companies that collect information from young children without parental consent. COPPA states that this consent must be obtained from the parents of children younger than the age of 13 before any information is collected (other than basic information required to obtain that consent).
13. A. The Digital Millennium Copyright Act does not include any geographical location requirements for protection under the "transitory activities" exemption. The other options are three of the five mandatory requirements. The other two requirements are that the service provider must not determine the recipients of the material and the material must be transmitted with no modification to its content.
14. C. The USA PATRIOT Act was adopted in the wake of the September 11, 2001, terrorist attacks. It broadens the powers of the government to monitor communications between private citizens and therefore actually weakens the privacy rights of consumers and Internet users. The other laws mentioned all contain provisions designed to enhance individual privacy rights.

15. B. Shrink-wrap license agreements become effective when the user opens a software package. Click-wrap agreements require the user to click a button during the installation process to accept the terms of the license agreement. Standard license agreements require that the user sign a written agreement prior to using the software. Verbal agreements are not normally used for software licensing but also require some active degree of participation by the software user.
16. B. The Gramm-Leach-Bliley Act provides, among other things, regulations regarding the way financial institutions can handle private information belonging to their customers.
17. C. U.S. patent law provides for an exclusivity period of 20 years beginning at the time the patent application is submitted to the Patent and Trademark Office.
18. C. Marketing needs are not a valid reason for processing personal information, as defined by the European Union privacy directive.
19. C. The Payment Card Industry Data Security Standard (PCI DSS) applies to organizations involved in the storage, transmission, and processing of credit card information.
20. A. The Health Information Technology for Economic and Clinical Health Act (HITECH) of 2009 amended the privacy and security requirements of HIPAA.

Chapter 5: Protecting Security of Assets

1. A. A primary purpose of information classification processes is to identify security classifications for sensitive data and define the requirements to protect sensitive data. Information classification processes will typically include requirements to protect sensitive data at rest (in backups and stored on media), but not requirements for backing up and storing any data. Similarly, information classification processes will typically include requirements to protect sensitive data in transit, but not any data.
2. B. Data is classified based on its value to the organization. In some cases, it is classified based on the potential negative impact if unauthorized personnel can access it, which represents a negative value. It is not classified based on the processing system, but the processing system is classified based on the data it processes. Similarly, the storage media is classified based on the data classification, but the data is not classified based on where it is stored. Accessibility is affected by the classification, but the accessibility does not determine the classification. Personnel implement controls to limit accessibility of sensitive data.
3. D. Data posted on a website is not sensitive, but PII, PHI, and proprietary data are all sensitive data.
4. D. Classification is the most important aspect of marking media because it clearly identifies the value of the media and users know how to protect it based on the classification. Including information such as the date and a description of the content isn't as important as marking the classification. Electronic labels or marks can be used, but when they are used, the most important information is still the classification of the data.

5. C. Purging media removes all data by writing over existing data multiple times to ensure that the data is not recoverable using any known methods. Purged media can then be reused in less secure environments. Erasing the media performs a delete, but the data remains and can easily be restored. Clearing, or overwriting, writes unclassified data over existing data, but some sophisticated forensics techniques may be able to recover the original data, so this method should not be used to reduce the classification of media.
6. C. Sanitization can be unreliable because personnel can perform the purging, degaussing, or other processes improperly. When done properly, purged data is not recoverable using any known methods. Data cannot be retrieved from incinerated, or burned, media. Data is not physically etched into the media.
7. D. Purging is the most reliable method of the given choices. Purging overwrites the media with random bits multiple times and includes additional steps to ensure data is removed. While not an available answer choice, destruction of the drive is a more reliable method. Erasing or deleting processes rarely remove the data from media, but instead mark it for deletion. Solid state drives (SSDs) do not have magnetic flux so degaussing an SSD doesn't destroy data.
8. C. Physical destruction is the most secure method of deleting data on optical media such as a DVD. Formatting and deleting processes rarely remove the data from any media. DVDs do not have magnetic flux so degaussing a DVD doesn't destroy data.
9. D. Data remanence refers to data remnants that remain on a hard drive as residual magnetic flux. Clearing, purging, and overwriting are valid methods of erasing data.
10. C. Linux systems use bcrypt to encrypt passwords, and bcrypt is based on Blowfish. Bcrypt adds 128 additional bits as a salt to protect against rainbow table attacks. Advanced Encryption Standard (AES) and Triple DES (or 3DES) are separate symmetric encryption protocols, and neither one is based on Blowfish, or directly related to protecting against rainbow table attacks. Secure Copy (SCP) uses Secure Shell (SSH) to encrypt data transmitted over a network.
11. D. SSH is a secure alternative to Telnet because it encrypts data transmitted over a network. In contrast, Telnet transmits data in cleartext. SFTP and SCP are good methods for transmitting sensitive data over a network, but not for administration purposes.
12. D. A data custodian performs day to day tasks to protect the integrity security of data and this includes backing it up. Users access the data. Owners classify the data. Administrators assign permissions to the data.
13. A. The administrator assigns permissions based on the principles of least privilege and need to know. A custodian protects the integrity and security of the data. Owners have ultimate responsibility for the data and ensure that it is classified properly, and owners provide guidance to administrators on who can have access, but owners do not assign permissions. Users simply access the data.
14. C. The rules of behavior identify the rules for appropriate use and protection of data. Least privilege ensures users are granted access to only what they need. A data owner

determines who has access to a system, but that is not rules of behavior. Rules of behavior apply to users, not systems or security controls.

15. A. The EU Data Protection law defines a data processor as "a natural or legal person which processes personal data solely on behalf of the data controller." The data controller is the entity that controls processing of the data and directs the data processor. Within the context of the EU Data Protection law, the data processor is not a computing system or network.

16. A. These are the first four principles in the Safe Harbor principles and they apply to maintaining the privacy of data. They do not address identification or retention of data. They primarily refer to privacy data such as personally identifiable information (PII), and while that may be considered a classification, classification isn't the primary purpose of the seven Safe Harbor principles.

17. D. Scoping and tailoring processes allow an organization to tailor security baselines to its needs. There is no need to implement security controls that do not apply, and it is not necessary to identify or re-create a different baseline.

18. D. Backup media should be protected with the same level of protection afforded the data it contains, and using a secure offsite storage facility would ensure this. The media should be marked, but that won't protect it if it is stored in an unmanned warehouse. A copy of backups should be stored offsite to ensure availability if a catastrophe affects the primary location. If copies of data are not stored offsite, or offsite backups are destroyed, security is sacrificed by risking availability.

19. A. If the tapes were marked before they left the datacenter, employees would recognize their value and it is more likely someone would challenge their storage in an unmanned warehouse. Purging or degaussing the tapes before using them will erase previously held data but won't help if sensitive information is backed up to the tapes after they are purged or degaussed. Adding the tapes to an asset management database will help track them but wouldn't prevent this incident.

20. B. Personnel did not follow the record retention policy. The scenario states that administrators purge onsite email older than six months to comply with the organization's security policy, but offsite backups included backups for the last 20 years. Personnel should follow media destruction policies when the organization no longer needs the media, but some backups are needed. Configuration management ensures that systems are configured correctly using a baseline, but this does not apply to backup media. Versioning is applied to applications, not backup tapes.

Chapter 6: Cryptography and Symmetric Key Algorithms

1. C. To determine the number of keys in a key space, raise 2 to the power of the number of bits in the key space. In this example, 24 = 16.

2. A. Nonrepudiation prevents the sender of a message from later denying that they sent it.
3. A. DES uses a 56-bit key. This is considered one of the major weaknesses of this cryptosystem.
4. B. Transposition ciphers use a variety of techniques to reorder the characters within a message.
5. A. The Rijndael cipher allows users to select a key length of 128, 192, or 256 bits, depending on the specific security requirements of the application.
6. A. Nonrepudiation requires the use of a public key cryptosystem to prevent users from falsely denying that they originated a message.
7. D. Assuming that it is used properly, the one-time pad is the only known cryptosystem that is not vulnerable to attacks.
8. B. Option B is correct because 16 divided by 3 equals 5, with a remainder value of 1.
9. A. The cryptanalysts from the United States discovered a pattern in the method the Soviets used to generate their one-time pads. After this pattern was discovered, much of the code was eventually broken.
10. C. Block ciphers operate on message "chunks" rather than on individual characters or bits. The other ciphers mentioned are all types of stream ciphers that operate on individual bits or characters of a message.
11. A. Symmetric key cryptography uses a shared secret key. All communicating parties utilize the same key for communication in any direction.
12. B. M of N Control requires that a minimum number of agents (M) out of the total number of agents (N) work together to perform high-security tasks.
13. D. Output Feedback (OFB) mode prevents early errors from interfering with future encryption/decryption. Cipher Block Chaining and Cipher Feedback modes will carry errors throughout the entire encryption/decryption process. Electronic Codebook (ECB) operation is not suitable for large amounts of data.
14. C. A one-way function is a mathematical operation that easily produces output values for each possible combination of inputs but makes it impossible to retrieve the input values.
15. C. The number of keys required for a symmetric algorithm is dictated by the formula $(n*(n-1))/2$, which in this case, where $n = 10$, is 45.
16. C. The Advanced Encryption Standard uses a 128-bit block size, despite the fact that the Rijndael algorithm it is based on allows a variable block size.
17. C. The Caesar cipher (and other simple substitution ciphers) are vulnerable to frequency analysis attacks that analyze the rate at which specific letters appear in the ciphertext.
18. B. Running key (or "book") ciphers often use a passage from a commonly available book as the encryption key.

19. B. The Twofish algorithm, developed by Bruce Schneier, uses prewhitening and postwhitening.
20. B. In an asymmetric algorithm, each participant requires two keys: a public key and a private key.

Chapter 7: PKI and Cryptographic Applications

1. B. The number n is generated as the product of the two large prime numbers, p and q. Therefore, n must always be greater than both p and q. Furthermore, it is an algorithm constraint that e must be chosen such that e is smaller than n. Therefore, in RSA cryptography, n is always the largest of the four variables shown in the options to this question.
2. B. The El Gamal cryptosystem extends the functionality of the Diffie-Hellman key exchange protocol to support the encryption and decryption of messages.
3. C. Richard must encrypt the message using Sue's public key so that Sue can decrypt it using her private key. If he encrypted the message with his own public key, the recipient would need to know Richard's private key to decrypt the message. If he encrypted it with his own private key, any user could decrypt the message using Richard's freely available public key. Richard could not encrypt the message using Sue's private key because he does not have access to it. If he did, any user could decrypt it using Sue's freely available public key.
4. C. The major disadvantage of the El Gamal cryptosystem is that it doubles the length of any message it encrypts. Therefore, a 2,048-bit plain-text message would yield a 4,096-bit ciphertext message when El Gamal is used for the encryption process.
5. A. The elliptic curve cryptosystem requires significantly shorter keys to achieve encryption that would be the same strength as encryption achieved with the RSA encryption algorithm. A 1,024-bit RSA key is cryptographically equivalent to a 160-bit elliptic curve cryptosystem key.
6. A. The SHA-1 hashing algorithm always produces a 160-bit message digest, regardless of the size of the input message. In fact, this fixed-length output is a requirement of any secure hashing algorithm.
7. C. The WEP algorithm has documented flaws that make it trivial to break. It should never be used to protect wireless networks.
8. A. WiFi Protected Access (WPA) uses the Temporal Key Integrity Protocol (TKIP) to protect wireless communications. WPA2 uses AES encryption.
9. B. Sue would have encrypted the message using Richard's public key. Therefore, Richard needs to use the complementary key in the key pair, his private key, to decrypt the message.

10. B. Richard should encrypt the message digest with his own private key. When Sue receives the message, she will decrypt the digest with Richard's public key and then compute the digest herself. If the two digests match, she can be assured that the message truly originated from Richard.
11. C. The Digital Signature Standard allows federal government use of the Digital Signature Algorithm, RSA, or the Elliptic Curve DSA in conjunction with the SHA-1 hashing function to produce secure digital signatures.
12. B. X.509 governs digital certificates and the public key infrastructure (PKI). It defines the appropriate content for a digital certificate and the processes used by certificate authorities to generate and revoke certificates.
13. B. Pretty Good Privacy uses a "web of trust" system of digital signature verification. The encryption technology is based on the IDEA private key cryptosystem.
14. C. Transport Layer Security uses TCP port 443 for encrypted client-server communications.
15. C. The meet-in-the-middle attack demonstrated that it took relatively the same amount of computation power to defeat 2DES as it does to defeat standard DES. This led to the adoption of Triple DES (3DES) as a standard for government communication.
16. A. Rainbow tables contain precomputed hash values for commonly used passwords and may be used to increase the efficiency of password cracking attacks.
17. C. The WiFi Protected Access protocol encrypts traffic passing between a mobile client and the wireless access point. It does not provide end-to-end encryption.
18. B. Certificate revocation lists (CRLs) introduce an inherent latency to the certificate expiration process due to the time lag between CRL distributions.
19. D. The Merkle-Hellman Knapsack algorithm, which relies on the difficulty of factoring super-increasing sets, has been broken by cryptanalysts.
20. B. IPsec is a security protocol that defines a framework for setting up a secure channel to exchange information between two entities.

Chapter 8: Principles of Security Models, Design, and Capabilities

1. B. A system certification is a technical evaluation. Option A describes system accreditation. Options C and D refer to manufacturer standards, not implementation standards.
2. A. Accreditation is the formal acceptance process. Option B is not an appropriate answer because it addresses manufacturer standards. Options C and D are incorrect because there is no way to prove that a configuration enforces a security policy and accreditation does not entail secure communication specification.

3. C. A closed system is one that uses largely proprietary or unpublished protocols and standards. Options A and D do not describe any particular systems, and Option B describes an open system.
4. C. A constrained process is one that can access only certain memory locations. Options A, B, and D do not describe a constrained process.
5. A. An object is a resource a user or process wants to access. Option A describes an access object.
6. D. A control limits access to an object to protect it from misuse by unauthorized users.
7. B. The applications and systems at a specific, self-contained location are evaluated for DITSCAP and NIACAP site accreditation.
8. C. TCSEC defines four major categories: Category A is verified protection, Category B is mandatory protection, Category C is discretionary protection, and Category D is minimal protection.
9. C. The TCB is the combination of hardware, software, and controls that work together to enforce a security policy.
10. A, B. Although the most correct answer in the context of this chapter is Option B, Option A is also a correct answer in the context of physical security.
11. C. The reference monitor validates access to every resource prior to granting the requested access. Option D, the security kernel, is the collection of TCB components that work together to implement the reference monitor functions. In other words, the security kernel is the implementation of the reference monitor concept. Options A and B are not valid TCB concept components.
12. B. Option B is the only option that correctly defines a security model. Options A, C, and D define part of a security policy and the certification and accreditation process.
13. D. The Bell-LaPadula and Biba models are built on the state machine model.
14. A. Only the Bell-LaPadula model addresses data confidentiality. The Biba and Clark-Wilson models address data integrity. The Brewer and Nash model prevents conflicts of interest.
15. C. The no read up property, also called the Simple Security Policy, prohibits subjects from reading a higher security level object.
16. B. The simple property of Biba is no read down, but it implies that it is acceptable to read up.
17. D. Declassification is the process of moving an object into a lower level of classification once it is determined that it no longer justifies being placed at a higher level. Only a trusted subject can perform declassification because this action is a violation of the verbiage of the star property of Bell-LaPadula, but not the spirit or intent, which is to prevent unauthorized disclosure.
18. B. An access control matrix assembles ACLs from multiple objects into a single table. The rows of that table are the ACEs of a subject across those objects, thus a capabilities list.

19. C. The trusted computing base (TCB) has a component known as the reference monitor in theory, which becomes the security kernel in implementation.
20. C. The three parts of the Clark-Wilson model's access control relationship (a.k.a. access triple) are subject, object, and program (or interface).

Chapter 9: Security Vulnerabilities, Threats, and Countermeasures

1. C. Multitasking is processing more than one task at the same time. In most cases, multitasking is simulated by the operating system even when not supported by the processor.
2. B. Mobile device management (MDM) is a software solution to the challenging task of managing the myriad mobile devices that employees use to access company resources. The goals of MDM are to improve security, provide monitoring, enable remote management, and support troubleshooting. Not all mobile devices support removable storage, and even fewer support encrypted removable storage. Geotagging is used to mark photos and social network posts, not for BYOD management. Application whitelisting may be an element of BYOD management, but is only part of a full MDM solution.
3. A. A single-processor system can operate on only one thread at a time. There would be a total of four application threads (ignoring any threads created by the operating system), but the operating system would be responsible for deciding which single thread is running on the processor at any given time.
4. A. In a dedicated system, all users must have a valid security clearance for the highest level of information processed by the system, they must have access approval for all information processed by the system, and they must have a valid need to know of all information processed by the system.
5. C. Because an embedded system is in control of a mechanism in the physical world, a security breach could cause harm to people and property. This typically is not true of a standard PC. Power loss, Internet access, and software flaws are security risks of both embedded systems and standard PCs.
6. B. Programmable read-only memory (PROM) chips may be written to once by the end user but may never be erased. The contents of ROM chips are burned in at the factory, and the end user is not allowed to write data. EPROM and EEPROM chips both make provisions for the end user to somehow erase the contents of the memory device and rewrite new data to the chip.
7. C. EPROMs may be erased through exposure to high-intensity ultraviolet light. ROM and PROM chips do not provide erasure functionality. EEPROM chips may be erased through the application of electrical currents to the chip pins and do not require removal from the computer prior to erasure.

8. C. *Secondary memory* is a term used to describe magnetic, optical, or flash media. These devices will retain their contents after being removed from the computer and may later be read by another user.

9. B. The risk of a lost or stolen notebook is the data loss, not the loss of the system itself. Thus, keeping minimal sensitive data on the system is the only way to reduce the risk. Hard drive encryption, cable locks, and strong passwords, although good ideas, are preventive tools, not means of reducing risk. They don't keep intentional and malicious data compromise from occurring; instead, they encourage honest people to stay honest.

10. A. Dynamic RAM chips are built from a large number of capacitors, each of which holds a single electrical charge. These capacitors must be continually refreshed by the CPU in order to retain their contents. The data stored in the chip is lost when power is removed.

11. C. Removable drives are easily taken out of their authorized physical location, and it is often not possible to apply operating system access controls to them. Therefore, encryption is often the only security measure short of physical security that can be afforded to them. Backup tapes are most often well controlled through physical security measures. Hard disks and RAM chips are often secured through operating system access controls.

12. B. In system high mode, all users have appropriate clearances and access permissions for all information processed by the system but need to know only some of the information processed by that system.

13. C. The most commonly overlooked aspect of mobile phone eavesdropping is related to people in the vicinity overhearing conversations (at least one side of them). Organizations frequently consider and address issues of wireless networking, storage device encryption, and screen locks.

14. B. BIOS and device firmware are often stored on EEPROM chips to facilitate future firmware updates.

15. C. Registers are small memory locations that are located directly on the CPU chip itself. The data stored within them is directly available to the CPU and can be accessed extremely quickly.

16. B. In immediate addressing, the CPU does not need to actually retrieve any data from memory. The data is contained in the instruction itself and can be immediately processed.

17. D. In indirect addressing, the location provided to the CPU contains a memory address. The CPU retrieves the operand by reading it from the memory address provided (which is why it's called *indirect*).

18. C. Process isolation provides separate memory spaces to each process running on a system. This prevents processes from overwriting each other's data and ensures that a process can't read data from another process.

19. D. The principle of least privilege states that only processes that absolutely need kernel-level access should run in supervisory mode. The remaining processes should run in user mode to reduce the number of potential security vulnerabilities.

20. A. Hardware segmentation achieves the same objectives as process isolation but takes them to a higher level by implementing them with physical controls in hardware.

Chapter 10: Physical Security Requirements

1. A. Physical security is the most important aspect of overall security. Without physical security, none of the other aspects of security are sufficient.
2. B. Critical path analysis can be used to map out the needs of an organization for a new facility. A critical path analysis is the process of identifying relationships between mission-critical applications, processes, and operations and all of the supporting elements.
3. B. A wiring closet is the infrastructure component often located in the same position across multiple floors in order to provide a convenient means of linking floor-based networks together.
4. D. Equal access to all locations within a facility is not a security-focused design element. Each area containing assets or resources of different importance, value, and confidentiality should have a corresponding level of security restriction placed on it.
5. A. A computer room does not need to be human compatible to be efficient and secure. Having a human-incompatible server room provides a greater level of protection against attacks.
6. C. Hashing is not a typical security measure implemented in relation to a media storage facility containing reusable removable media. Hashing is used when it is necessary to verify the integrity of a dataset, while data on reusable removable media should be removed and not retained. Usually the security features for a media storage facility include using a librarian or custodian, using a check-in/check-out process, and using sanitization tools on returned media.
7. C. A mantrap is a double set of doors that is often protected by a guard and used to contain a subject until their identity and authentication is verified.
8. D. Lighting is the most common form of perimeter security device or mechanism. Your entire site should be clearly lit. This provides for easy identification of personnel and makes it easier to notice intrusions.
9. A. Security guards are usually unaware of the scope of the operations within a facility, which supports confidentiality of those operations and thus helps reduce the possibility that a security guard will be involved in the disclosure of confidential information.
10. B. The most common cause of failure for a water-based system is human error. If you turn off the water source after a fire and forget to turn it back on, you'll be in trouble for the future. Also, pulling an alarm when there is no fire will trigger damaging water release throughout the office.
11. C. Key locks are the most common and inexpensive form of physical access control device. Lighting, security guards, and fences are all much more costly.
12. D. A capacitance motion detector senses changes in the electrical or magnetic field surrounding a monitored object.

13. A. There is no such thing as a preventive alarm. Alarms are always triggered in response to a detected intrusion or attack.
14. B. No matter what form of physical access control is used, a security guard or other monitoring system must be deployed to prevent abuse, masquerading, and piggybacking. Espionage cannot be prevented by physical access controls.
15. C. Human safety is the most important goal of all security solutions.
16. B. The humidity in a computer room should ideally be from 40 to 60 percent.
17. D. Destruction of data stored on hard drives can be caused by 1,500 volts of static electricity.
18. A. Water is never the suppression medium in Type B fire extinguishers because they are used on liquid fires.
19. C. A preaction system is the best type of water-based fire suppression system for a computer facility.
20. D. Light is usually not damaging to most computer equipment, but fire, smoke, and the suppression medium (typically water) are very destructive.

Chapter 11: Secure Network Architecture and Securing Network Components

1. D. The Transport layer is layer 4. The Presentation layer is layer 6, the Data Link layer is layer 2, and the Network layer is layer 3.
2. B. Encapsulation is adding a header and footer to data as it moves down the OSI stack.
3. B. Layer 5, Session, manages simplex (one-direction), half-duplex (two-way, but only one direction can send data at a time), and full-duplex (two-way, in which data can be sent in both directions simultaneously) communications.
4. B. 10Base-T UTP is the least resistant to EMI because it is unshielded. Thinnet (10Base2) and thicknet (10Base5) are each a type of coaxial cable, which is shielded against EMI.
5. D. A VPN is a secure tunnel used to establish connections across a potentially insecure intermediary network. Intranet, extranet, and DMZ are examples of network segmentation.
6. B. UDP is a transport layer protocol that operates as the payload of an IP packet. While it is not IP itself, it depends on IP. IPX, AppleTalk, and NetBEUI are all alternatives to IP and thus are labeled as non-IP protocols.
7. C. A bluejacking attack is a wireless attack on Bluetooth, and the most common device compromised in a bluejacking attack is a cell phone.
8. A. Ethernet is based on the IEEE 802.3 standard.

9. B. A TCP wrapper is an application that can serve as a basic firewall by restricting access based on user IDs or system IDs.
10. B. Encapsulation is both a benefit and a potentially harmful implication of multilayer protocols.
11. C. Stateful inspection firewalls are able to grant a broader range of access for authorized users and activities and actively watch for and block unauthorized users and activities.
12. B. Stateful inspection firewalls are known as third-generation firewalls.
13. B. Most firewalls offer extensive logging, auditing, and monitoring capabilities as well as alarms and even basic IDS functions. Firewalls are unable to block viruses or malicious code transmitted through otherwise authorized communication channels, prevent unauthorized but accidental or intended disclosure of information by users, prevent attacks by malicious users already behind the firewall, or protect data after it passed out of or into the private network.
14. C. There are numerous dynamic routing protocols, including RIP, OSPF, and BGP, but RPC is not a routing protocol.
15. B. A switch is an intelligent hub. It is considered to be intelligent because it knows the addresses of the systems connected on each outbound port.
16. A. Wireless Application Protocol (WAP) is a technology associated with cell phones accessing the Internet rather than 802.11 wireless networking.
17. C. Orthogonal Frequency-Division Multiplexing (OFDM) offers high throughput with the least interference. OSPF is a routing protocol, not a wireless frequency access method.
18. A. Endpoint security is the security concept that encourages administrators to install firewalls, malware scanners, and an IDS on every host.
19. C. Reverse Address Resolution Protocol (RARP) resolves physical addresses (MAC addresses) into logical addresses (IP addresses).
20. C. Enterprise extended infrastructure mode exists when a wireless network is designed to support a large physical environment through the use of a single SSID but numerous access points.

Chapter 12: Secure Communications and Network Attacks

1. B. Frame Relay is a layer 2 connection mechanism that uses packet-switching technology to establish virtual circuits between the communication endpoints. The Frame Relay network is a shared medium across which virtual circuits are created to provide

point-to-point communications. All virtual circuits are independent of and invisible to each other.

2. D. A stand-alone system has no need for tunneling because no communications between systems are occurring and no intermediary network is present.

3. C. IPSec, or IP Security, is a standards-based mechanism for providing encryption for point-to-point TCP/IP traffic.

4. B. The 169.254.*x*.*x* subnet is in the APIPA range, which is not part of RFC 1918. The addresses in RFC 1918 are 10.0.0.0–10.255.255.255, 172.16.0.0–172.31.255.255, and 192.168.0.0–192.168.255.255.

5. D. An intermediary network connection is required for a VPN link to be established.

6. B. Static mode NAT is needed to allow an outside entity to initiate communications with an internal system behind a NAT proxy.

7. A, B, D. L2F, L2TP, and PPTP all lack native data encryption. Only IPSec includes native data encryption.

8. D. IPSec operates at the Network layer (layer 3).

9. A. The address range 169.172.0.0–169.191.255.255 is not listed in RFC 1918 as a private IP address range. It is, in fact, a public IP address range.

10. D. NAT does not protect against or prevent brute-force attacks.

11. B. When transparency is a characteristic of a service, security control, or access mechanism it is unseen by users.

12. B. Although availability is a key aspect of security in general, it is the least important aspect of security systems for Internet-delivered email.

13. D. The backup method is not an important factor to discuss with end users regarding email retention.

14. B. Mail-bombing is the use of email as an attack mechanism. Flooding a system with messages causes a denial of service.

15. B. It is often difficult to stop spam because the source of the messages is usually spoofed.

16. B. A permanent virtual circuit (PVC) can be described as a logical circuit that always exists and is waiting for the customer to send data.

17. B. Changing default passwords on PBX systems provides the most effective increase in security.

18. C. Social engineering can often be used to bypass even the most effective physical and logical controls. Whatever activity the attacker convinces the victim to perform, it is usually directed toward opening a back door that the attacker can use to gain access to the network.

19. C. A brute-force attack is not considered a DoS.

20. A. Password Authentication Protocol (PAP) is a standardized authentication protocol for PPP. PAP transmits usernames and passwords in the clear. It offers no form of encryption. It simply provides a means to transport the logon credentials from the client to the authentication server.

Chapter 13: Managing Identity and Authentication

1. E. All of the answers are included in the types of assets that an organization would try to protect with access controls.
2. C. The subject is active and is always the entity that receives information about, or data from, the object. A subject can be a user, a program, a process, a file, a computer, a database, and so on. The object is always the entity that provides or hosts information or data. The roles of subject and object can switch while two entities communicate to accomplish a task.
3. A. A preventive access control helps stop an unwanted or unauthorized activity from occurring. Detective controls discover the activity after it has occurred, and corrective controls attempt to reverse any problems caused by the activity. Authoritative isn't a valid type of access control.
4. B. Logical/technical access controls are the hardware or software mechanisms used to manage access to resources and systems and to provide protection for those resources and systems. Administrative controls are managerial controls and physical controls use physical items to control physical access. A preventive control attempts to prevent security incidents.
5. A. A primary goal when controlling access to assets is to protect against losses, including any loss of confidentiality, loss of availability, or loss of integrity. Subjects authenticate on a system, but objects do not authenticate. Subjects access objects, but objects do not access subjects. Identification and authentication is important as a first step in access control, but much more is needed to protect assets.
6. D. A user professes an identity with a login ID. The combination of the login ID and the password provides authentication. Subjects are authorized access to objects after authentication. Logging and auditing provide accountability.
7. D. Accountability does not include authorization. Accountability requires proper identification and authentication. After authentication, accountability requires logging to support auditing.
8. B. Password history can prevent users from rotating between two passwords. It remembers previously used passwords. Password complexity and password length help ensure users create strong passwords. Password age ensures users change their password regularly.
9. B. A passphrase is a long string of characters that is easy to remember, such as IP@$$edTheCISSPEx@m. It is not short and typically includes all four sets of character types. It is strong and complex, making it difficult to crack.
10. A. A Type 2 authentication factor is based on something you have, such as a smartcard or token device. Type 3 authentication is based on something you are and sometimes something you do, which uses physical and behavioral biometric methods. Type 1 authentication is based on something you know, such as passwords or PINs.

11. A. A synchronous token generates and displays one-time passwords, which are synchronized with an authentication server. An asynchronous token uses a challenge-response process to generate the one-time password. Smartcards do not generate one-time passwords, and common access cards are a version of a smartcard that includes a picture of the user.
12. B. Physical biometric methods such as fingerprints and iris scans provide authentication for subjects. An account ID provides identification. A token is something you have and it creates one-time passwords, but it is not related to physical characteristics. A personal identification number (PIN) is something you know.
13. C. The point at which biometric Type 1 errors (false rejection rate) and Type 2 errors (false acceptance rate) are equal is the crossover error rate (CER). A lower CER indicates a higher quality biometric device. It does not indicate that sensitivity is too high or too low.
14. A. A Type 1 error (false rejection or false negative) occurs when a valid subject is not authenticated. A Type 2 error (false acceptance or false positive) occurs when an invalid subject is authenticated. The crossover error rate (also called equal error rate) compares the rate of Type 1 errors to Type 2 errors and provides a measurement of the accuracy of the biometric system.
15. C. The primary purpose of Kerberos is authentication, as it allows users to prove their identity. It also provides a measure of confidentiality and integrity using symmetric key encryption, but these are not the primary purpose. Kerberos does not include logging capabilities, so it does not provide accountability.
16. D. SAML is an XML-based framework used to exchange user information for single sign-on (SSO) between organizations within a federated identity management system. Kerberos supports SSO in a single organization, not a federation. HTML only describes how data is displayed. XML could be used, but it would require redefining tags already defined in SAML.
17. B. The network access server is the client within a RADIUS architecture. The RADIUS server is the authentication server and it provides authentication, authorization, and accounting (AAA) services. The network access server might have a host firewall enabled, but that isn't the primary function.
18. B. Diameter is based on RADIUS and it supports Mobile IP and Voice over IP. Distributed access control systems such as a federated identity management system are not a specific protocol, and they don't necessarily provide authentication, authorization, and accounting. TACACS and TACACS+ are AAA protocols, but they are alternatives to RADIUS, not based on RADIUS.
19. D. The principle of least privilege was violated because he retained privileges from all his previous administrator positions in different divisions. Implicit deny ensures that only access that is explicitly granted is allowed, but the administrator was explicitly granted privileges. While the administrator's actions could have caused loss of availability, loss of availability isn't a basic principle. Defensive privileges aren't a valid security principle.

20. D. Account review can discover when users have more privileges than they need and could have been used to discover that this employee had permissions from several positions. Strong authentication methods (including multifactor authentication) would not have prevented the problems in this scenario. Logging could have recorded activity, but a review is necessary to discover the problems.

Chapter 14: Controlling and Monitoring Access

1. B. The implicit deny principle ensures that access to an object is denied unless access has been expressly allowed (or explicitly granted) to a subject. It does not allow all actions that are not denied, and it doesn't require all actions to be denied.
2. C. The principle of least privilege ensures that users (subjects) are granted only the most restrictive rights they need to perform their work tasks and job functions. Users don't execute system processes. The least privilege principle does not enforce the least restrictive rights but rather the most restrictive rights.
3. B. An access control matrix includes multiple objects, and it lists subjects' access to each of the objects. A single list of subjects for any specific object within an access control matrix is an access control list. A federation refers to a group of companies that share a federated identity management system for single sign-on. Creeping privileges refers to the excessive privileges a subject gathers over time.
4. D. The data custodian (or owner) grants permissions to users in a discretionary access control (DAC) model. Administrators grant permissions for resources they own, but not for all resources in a DAC model. A rule-based access control model uses an access control list. The mandatory access control model uses labels.
5. A. A discretionary access control model is an identity-based access control model. It allows the owner (or data custodian) of a resource to grant permissions at the discretion of the owner. The role-based access control model is based on role or group membership. The rule-based access control model is based on rules within an ACL. The mandatory access control model uses assigned labels to identify access.
6. D. A nondiscretionary access control model uses a central authority to determine which objects (such as files) that users (and other subjects) can access. In contrast, a discretionary access control model allows users to grant or reject access to any objects they own. An ACL is an example or rule-based access control model. An access control matrix includes multiple objects, and it lists the subject's access to each of the objects.
7. D. A role-based access control model can group users into roles based on the organization's hierarchy and it is a nondiscretionary access control model. A nondiscretionary access control model uses a central authority to determine which objects that subjects

can access. In contrast, a discretionary access control model allows users to grant or reject access to any objects they own. An ACL is an example of a rule-based access control model that uses rules, not roles.

8. A. The role-BAC model is based on role or group membership and users can be members of multiple groups. Users are not limited to only a single role. Role-BAC models are based on the hierarchy of an organization, so they are hierarchy based. The mandatory access control model uses assigned labels to identify access.

9. D. A programmer is a valid role in a role-based access control model. Administrators would place programmers' user accounts into the Programmer role and assign privileges to this role. Roles are typically used to organize users, and the other answers are not users.

10. D. A rule-based access control model uses global rules applied to all users and other subjects equally. It does not apply rules locally, or to individual users.

11. C. Firewalls use a rule-based access control model with rules expressed in an access control list. A mandatory access control model uses labels. A discretionary access control model allows users to assign permissions. A role-based access control model organizes users in groups.

12. C. Mandatory access controls rely on the use of labels for subjects and objects. Discretionary access control systems allow an owner of an object to control access to the object. Nondiscretionary access controls have centralized management such as a rule-based access control deployed on a firewall. Role-based access controls define a subject's access based on job-related roles.

13. D. The mandatory access control model is prohibitive and it uses an implicit-deny philosophy (not an explicit-deny philosophy). It is not permissive and it uses labels rather than rules.

14. D. Lettuce-based access control model is not a valid type of access control model. The other answers list valid access control models. A lattice-based (not lettuce-based) access control model is a type of mandatory access control model.

15. C. A vulnerability analysis identifies weaknesses and can include periodic vulnerability scans and penetration tests. Asset valuation determines the value of assets, not weaknesses. Threat modeling attempts to identify threats, but threat modeling doesn't identify weaknesses. An access review audits account management and object access practices.

16. B. An account lockout policy will lock an account after a user has entered an incorrect password too many times, and this blocks an online brute-force attack. Attackers use rainbow tables in offline password attacks. Password salts reduce the effectiveness of rainbow tables. Encrypting the password protects the password, but not against a brute-force attack.

17. B. A side-channel attack is a passive, noninvasive attack to observe the operation of a device, and can be used against some smartcards. Methods include power monitoring, timing, and fault analysis attacks. Whaling is a type of phishing attack that targets

high-level executives. A brute-force attack attempts to discover passwords by using all possible character combinations. A rainbow table attack is used to crack passwords.

18. C. Whaling is a form of phishing that targets high-level executives. Spear phishing targets a specific group of people but not necessarily high-level executives. Vishing is a form of phishing that commonly uses Voice over IP (VoIP).

19. B. Threat modeling helps identify, understand, and categorize potential threats. Asset valuation identifies the value of assets, and vulnerability analysis identifies weaknesses that can be exploited by threats. An access review and audit ensures that account management practices support the security policy.

20. A. Asset valuation identifies the actual value of assets so that they can be prioritized. This will ensure that the consultant focuses on high-value assets. Threat modeling identifies threats, but asset valuation should be done first so that the focus is on threats to high-value assets. Vulnerability analysis identifies weaknesses but should be focused on high-value assets. Audit trails are useful to re-create events leading up to an incident, but if they aren't already created, creating them now won't help unless the organization is attacked again.

Chapter 15: Security Assessment and Testing

1. A. Nmap is a network discovery scanning tool that reports the open ports on a remote system.

2. D. Only open ports represent potentially significant security risks. Ports 80 and 443 are expected to be open on a web server. Port 1433 is a database port and should never be exposed to an external network.

3. C. The sensitivity of information stored on the system, difficulty of performing the test, and likelihood of an attacker targeting the system are all valid considerations when planning a security testing schedule. The desire to experiment with new testing tools should not influence the production testing schedule.

4. C. Security assessments include many types of tests designed to identify vulnerabilities, and the assessment report normally includes recommendations for mitigation. The assessment does not, however, include actual mitigation of those vulnerabilities.

5. A. Security assessment reports should be addressed to the organization's management. For this reason, they should be written in plain English and avoid technical jargon.

6. B. The use of an 8-bit subnet mask means that the first octet of the IP address represents the network address. In this case, that means 10.0.0.0/8 will scan any IP address beginning with 10.

7. B. The server is likely running a website on port 80. Using a web browser to access the site may provide important information about the site's purpose.
8. B. The SSH protocol uses port 22 to accept administrative connections to a server.
9. D. Authenticated scans can read configuration information from the target system and reduce the instances of false positive and false negative reports.
10. C. The TCP SYN scan sends a SYN packet and receives a SYN ACK packet in response, but it does not send the final ACK required to complete the three-way handshake.
11. D. SQL injection attacks are web vulnerabilities, and Matthew would be best served by a web vulnerability scanner. A network vulnerability scanner might also pick up this vulnerability, but the web vulnerability scanner is specifically designed for the task and more likely to be successful.
12. C. PCI DSS requires that Badin rescan the application at least annually and after any change in the application.
13. B. Metasploit is an automated exploit tool that allows attackers to easily execute common attack techniques.
14. C. Mutation fuzzing uses bit flipping and other techniques to slightly modify previous inputs to a program in an attempt to detect software flaws.
15. A. Misuse case testing identifies known ways that an attacker might exploit a system and tests explicitly to see if those attacks are possible in the proposed code.
16. B. User interface testing includes assessments of both graphical user interfaces (GUIs) and command-line interfaces (CLIs) for a software program.
17. B. During a white box penetration test, the testers have access to detailed configuration information about the system being tested.
18. B. Unencrypted HTTP communications take place over TCP port 80 by default.
19. C. The Fagin inspection process concludes with the follow-up phase.
20. B. The backup verification process ensures that backups are running properly and thus meeting the organization's data protection objectives.

Chapter 16: Managing Security Operations

1. C. Need to know is the requirement to have access to, knowledge about, or possession of data to perform specific work tasks, but no more. The principle of least *privilege* includes both rights and permissions, but the term *principle of least permission* is not valid within IT security. Separation of duties ensures that a single person

doesn't control all the elements of a process. Role-based access control grants access to resources based on a role.

2. D. The default level of access should be no access. The principle of least privilege dictates that users should only be granted the level of access they need for their job and the question doesn't indicate new users need any access. Read access, modify access, and full access grants users some level of access, which violates the principle of least privilege.
3. C. A separation of duties policy prevents a single person from controlling all elements of a process, and when applied to security settings, it can prevent a person from making major security changes without assistance. Job rotation helps ensure that multiple people can do the same job and can help prevent the organization from losing information when a single person leaves. Having employees concentrate their talents is unrelated to separation of duties.
4. B. Job rotation and separation of duties policies help prevent fraud. Collusion is an agreement among multiple persons to perform some unauthorized or illegal actions, and implementing these policies helps prevent fraud. They don't prevent collusion and certainly aren't intended to encourage employees to collude against an organization. They help deter and prevent incidents, but they do not correct them.
5. A. A job rotation policy has employees rotate jobs or job responsibilities and can help detect incidences of collusion and fraud. A separation of duties policy ensures that a single person doesn't control all elements of a specific function. Mandatory vacation policies ensure that employees take an extended time away from their job, requiring someone else to perform their job responsibilities, which increases the likelihood of discovering fraud. Least privilege ensures that users have only the permissions they need to perform their job and no more.
6. B. Mandatory vacation policies help detect fraud. They require employees to take an extended time away from their job, requiring someone else to perform their job responsibilities and this increases the likelihood of discovering fraud. It does not rotate job responsibilities. While mandatory vacations might help employees reduce their overall stress levels, and in turn increase productivity, these are not the primary reasons for mandatory vacation policies.
7. A, B, C. Job rotation, separation of duties, and mandatory vacation policies will all help reduce fraud. Baselining is used for configuration management and would not help reduce collusion or fraud.
8. B. Special privileges should not be granted equally to administrators and operators. Instead, personnel should be granted only the privileges they need to perform their job. Special privileges are activities that require special access or elevated rights and permissions to perform administrative and sensitive job tasks. Assignment and usage of these privileges should be monitored, and access should be granted only to trusted employees.
9. A. A service level agreement identifies responsibilities of a third party such as a vendor and can include monetary penalties if the vendor doesn't meet the stated responsibilities. A MOU is in informal agreement and does not include monetary penalties. An

ISA defines requirements for establishing, maintaining, and disconnecting a connection. SaaS is one of the cloud-based service models and does not specify vendor responsibilities.

10. C. Systems should be sanitized when they reach the end of their life cycle to ensure that they do not include any sensitive data. Removing CDs and DVDs is part of the sanitation process, but other elements of the system, such as disk drives, should also be checked to ensure they don't include sensitive information. Removing software licenses or installing the original software is not necessarily required unless the organization's sanitization process requires it.

11. A. Valuable assets require multiple layers of physical security and placing a datacenter in the center of the building helps provide these additional layers. Placing valuable assets next to an outside wall (including at the back of the building) eliminates some layers of security.

12. D. VMs need to be updated individually just as they would be if they were running on a physical server. Updates to the physical server do not update hosted VMs. Similarly, updating one VM doesn't update all VMs.

13. A. Organizations have the most responsibility for maintenance and security when leasing IaaS cloud resources. The cloud service provider takes more responsibility with the PaaS model and the most responsibility with the SaaS model. CaaS isn't a valid name for a cloud-based service model.

14. C. A community cloud deployment model provides cloud-based assets to two or more organizations. A public cloud model includes assets available for any consumers to rent or lease. A private cloud deployment model includes cloud-based assets for a single organization. A hybrid model includes a combination of two or more deployment models.

15. B. The tapes should be purged, ensuring that data cannot be recovered using any known means. Even though tapes may be at the end of their life cycle, they can still hold data and should be purged before throwing them away. Erasing doesn't remove all usable data from media, but purging does. There is no need to store the tapes if they are at the end of their life cycle.

16. B. Images can be an effective configuration management method using a baseline. Imaging ensures that systems are deployed with the same, known configuration. Change management processes help prevent outages from unauthorized changes. Vulnerability management processes help to identify vulnerabilities, and patch management processes help to ensure systems are kept up-to-date.

17. A. Change management processes may need to be temporarily bypassed to respond to an emergency, but they should not be bypassed simply because someone thinks it can improve performance. Even when a change is implemented in response to an emergency, it should still be documented and reviewed after the incident. Requesting changes, creating rollback plans, and documenting changes are all valid steps within a change management process.

18. D. Change management processes would ensure that changes are evaluated before being implemented to prevent unintended outages or needlessly weakening security. Patch management ensures systems are up-to-date, vulnerability management checks systems for known vulnerabilities, and configuration management ensures that system are deployed similarly, but these other processes wouldn't prevent an unauthorized change.
19. C. Only required patches should be deployed so an organization will not deploy *all* patches. Instead, an organization evaluates the patches to determine which patches are needed, tests them to ensure that they don't cause unintended problems, deploys the approved and tested patches, and audits systems to ensure that patches have been applied.
20. B. Vulnerability scanners are used to check systems for known issues and are part of an overall vulnerability management program. Versioning is used to track software versions and is unrelated to detecting vulnerabilities. Security audits and reviews help ensure that an organization is following its policies but wouldn't directly check systems for vulnerabilities.

Chapter 17: Preventing and Responding to Incidents

1. A. Containment is the first step after detecting and verifying an incident. This limits the effect or scope of an incident. Organizations report the incident based on policies and governing laws, but this is not the first step. Remediation attempts to identify the cause of the incident and steps that can be taken to prevent a reoccurrence, but this is not the first step. It is important to protect evidence while trying to contain an incident, but gathering the evidence will occur after containment.
2. D. Security personnel perform a root cause analysis during the remediation stage. A root cause analysis attempts to discover the source of the problem. After discovering the cause, the review will often identify a solution to help prevent a similar occurrence in the future. Containing the incident and collecting evidence is done early in the incident response process. Rebuilding a system may be needed during the recovery stage.
3. A, B, C. Teardrop, smurf, and ping of death are all types of DoS attacks. Attackers use spoofing to hide their identity in a variety of attacks, but spoofing is not an attack by itself.
4. C. A SYN flood attack disrupts the TCP three-way handshake process by never sending the third packet. It is not unique to any specific operating system such as Windows. Smurf attacks use amplification networks to flood a victim with packets. A ping-of-death attack uses oversized ping packets.

5. B. A zero-day exploit takes advantage of a previously unknown vulnerability. A botnet is a group of computers controlled by a bot herder that can launch attacks, but they can exploit both known vulnerabilities and previously unknown vulnerabilities. Similarly, denial-of-service (DoS) and distributed DoS (DDoS) attacks could use zero-day exploits or use known methods.
6. A. Of the choices offered, drive-by downloads are the most common distribution method for malware. USB flash drives can be used to distribute malware, but this method isn't as common as drive-by downloads. Ransomware is a type of malware infection, not a method of distributing malware. If users are able to install unapproved software, they may inadvertently install malware, but this isn't the most common method either.
7. A. An IDS automates the inspection of audit logs and real-time system events to detect abnormal activity indicating unauthorized system access. Although IDSs can detect system failures and monitor system performance, they don't include the ability to diagnose system failures or rate system performance. Vulnerability scanners are used to test systems for vulnerabilities.
8. B. An HIDS monitors a single system looking for abnormal activity. A network-based IDS (NIDS) watches for abnormal activity on a network. An HIDS is normally visible as a running process on a system and provides alerts to authorized users. An HIDS can detect malicious code similar to how anti-malware software can detect malicious code.
9. B. Honeypots are individual computers, and honeynets are entire networks created to serve as a trap for intruders. They look like legitimate networks and tempt intruders with unpatched and unprotected security vulnerabilities as well as attractive and tantalizing but false data. An intrusion detection system (IDS) will detect attacks. In some cases an IDS can divert an attacker to a padded cell, which is a simulated environment with fake data intended to keep the attacker's interest. A pseudo flaw (used by many honeypots and honeynets) is a false vulnerability intentionally implanted in a system to tempt attackers.
10. C. A multipronged approach provides the best solution. This involves having antimalware software at several locations, such as at the boundary between the Internet and the internal network, at email servers, and on each system. More than one antimalware application on a single system isn't recommended. A single solution for the whole organization is often ineffective because malware can get into the network in more than one way. Content filtering at border gateways (boundary between the Internet and the internal network) is a good partial solution, but it won't catch malware brought in through other methods.
11. B. Penetration testing should be performed only with the knowledge and consent of the management staff. Unapproved security testing could result in productivity loss, trigger emergency response teams, and legal action against the tester including loss of employment. A penetration test can mimic previous attacks and use both manual and automated attack methods. After a penetration test, a system may be reconfigured to resolve discovered vulnerabilities.

12. B. Accountability is maintained by monitoring the activities of subjects and objects as well as core system functions that maintain the operating environment and the security mechanisms. Authentication is required for effective monitoring, but it doesn't provide accountability by itself. Account lockout prevents login to an account if the wrong password is entered too many times. User entitlement reviews can identify excessive privileges.

13. B. Audit trails are a passive form of detective security control. Administrative controls are management practices. Corrective controls can correct problems related to an incident, and physical controls are controls that you can physically touch.

14. B. Auditing is a methodical examination or review of an environment to ensure compliance with regulations and to detect abnormalities, unauthorized occurrences, or outright crimes. Penetration testing attempts to exploit vulnerabilities. Risk analysis attempts to analyze risks based on identified threats and vulnerabilities. Entrapment is tricking someone into performing an illegal or unauthorized action.

15. A. Clipping is a form of nonstatistical sampling that reduces the amount of logged data based on a clipping-level threshold. Sampling is a statistical method that extracts meaningful data from audit logs. Log analysis reviews log information looking for trends, patterns, and abnormal or unauthorized events. An alarm trigger is a notification sent to administrators when specific events or thresholds occur.

16. B. Traffic analysis focuses more on the patterns and trends of data rather than the actual content. Keystroke monitoring records specific keystrokes to capture data. Event logging logs specific events to record data. Security auditing records security events and/or reviews logs to detect security incidents.

17. B. A user entitlement audit can detect when users have more privileges than necessary. Account management practices attempt to ensure that privileges are assigned correctly. The audit detects whether the management practices are followed. Logging records activity, but the logs need to be reviewed to determine if practices are followed. Reporting is the result of an audit.

18. D. Security personnel should have gathered evidence for possible prosecution of the attacker. The first response after detecting and verifying an incident is to contain the incident, but it could have been contained without rebooting the server. The lessons learned stage includes review, and it is the last stage. Remediation includes a root cause analysis to determine what allowed the incident, but this is done late in the process. In this scenario, rebooting the server performed the recovery.

19. C. Attacking the IP address was the most serious mistake because it is illegal in most locations. Additionally, because attackers often use spoofing techniques, it probably isn't the actual IP address of the attacker. Rebooting the server without gathering evidence and not reporting the incident were mistakes but won't have a potential lasting negative effect on the organization. Resetting the connection to isolate the incident would have been a good step if it was done without rebooting the server.

20. A. The administrator did not report the incident so there was no opportunity to perform a lessons learned step. It could be the incident occurred because of a vulnerability on the server, but without an examination, the exact cause won't be known unless the attack is repeated. The administrator detected the event and responded (though inappropriately). Rebooting the server is a recovery step. It's worth mentioning that the incident response plan was kept secret and the server administrator didn't have access to it and so likely does not know what the proper response should be.

Chapter 18: Disaster Recovery Planning

1. C. Once a disaster interrupts the business operations, the goal of DRP is to restore regular business activity as quickly as possible. Thus, disaster recovery planning picks up where business continuity planning leaves off.
2. C. A power outage is an example of a man-made disaster. The other events listed—tsunamis, earthquakes, and lightning strikes—are all naturally occurring events.
3. D. Forty-one of the 50 U.S. states are considered to have a moderate, high, or very high risk of seismic activity. This rounds to 80 percent to provide the value given in option D.
4. B. Most general business insurance and homeowner's insurance policies do not provide any protection against the risk of flooding or flash floods. If floods pose a risk to your organization, you should consider purchasing supplemental flood insurance under FEMA's National Flood Insurance Program.
5. C. All the industries listed in the options made changes to their practices after September 11, 2001, but the insurance industry's change toward noncoverage of acts of terrorism most directly impacts the BCP/DRP process.
6. C. The opposite of this statement is true—disaster recovery planning picks up where business continuity planning leaves off. The other three statements are all accurate reflections of the role of business continuity planning and disaster recovery planning.
7. B. The term *100-year flood plain* is used to describe an area where flooding is expected once every 100 years. It is, however, more mathematically correct to say that this label indicates a 1 percent probability of flooding in any given year.
8. D. When you use remote mirroring, an exact copy of the database is maintained at an alternative location. You keep the remote copy up-to-date by executing all transactions on both the primary and remote site at the same time.
9. C. Redundant systems/components provide protection against the failure of one particular piece of hardware.

10. B. During the business impact assessment phase, you must identify the business priorities of your organization to assist with the allocation of BCP resources. You can use this same information to drive the DRP business unit prioritization.

11. C. The cold site contains none of the equipment necessary to restore operations. All of the equipment must be brought in and configured and data must be restored to it before operations can commence. This often takes weeks.

12. C. Warm sites typically take about 12 hours to activate from the time a disaster is declared. This is compared to the relatively instantaneous activation of a hot site and the lengthy time (at least a week) required to bring a cold site to operational status.

13. D. Warm sites and hot sites both contain workstations, servers, and the communications circuits necessary to achieve operational status. The main difference between the two alternatives is the fact that hot sites contain near-real-time copies of the operational data and warm sites require the restoration of data from backup.

14. D. Remote mirroring is the only backup option in which a live backup server at a remote site maintains a bit-for-bit copy of the contents of the primary server, synchronized as closely as the latency in the link between primary and remote systems will allow.

15. A. The executive summary provides a high-level view of the entire organization's disaster recovery efforts. This document is useful for the managers and leaders of the firm as well as public relations personnel who need a nontechnical perspective on this complex effort.

16. D. Software escrow agreements place the application source code in the hands of an independent third party, thus providing firms with a "safety net" in the event a developer goes out of business or fails to honor the terms of a service agreement.

17. A. Differential backups involve always storing copies of all files modified since the most recent full backup regardless of any incremental or differential backups created during the intervening time period.

18. C. Any backup strategy must include full backups at some point in the process. Incremental backups are created faster than differential backups because of the number of files it is necessary to back up each time.

19. A. Any backup strategy must include full backups at some point in the process. If a combination of full and differential backups is used, a maximum of two backups must be restored. If a combination of full and incremental backups is chosen, the number of required restorations may be unlimited.

20. B. Parallel tests involve moving personnel to the recovery site and gearing up operations, but responsibility for conducting day-to-day operations of the business remains at the primary operations center.

Chapter 19: Incidents and Ethics

1. C. A crime is any violation of a law or regulation. The violation stipulation defines the action as a crime. It is a computer crime if the violation involves a computer either as the target or as a tool.
2. B. A military and intelligence attack is targeted at the classified data that resides on the system. To the attacker, the value of the information justifies the risk associated with such an attack. The information extracted from this type of attack is often used to plan subsequent attacks.
3. A. Confidential information that is not related to the military or intelligence agencies is the target of business attacks. The ultimate goal could be destruction, alteration, or disclosure of confidential information.
4. B. A financial attack focuses primarily on obtaining services and funds illegally.
5. B. A terrorist attack is launched to interfere with a way of life by creating an atmosphere of fear. A computer terrorist attack can reach this goal by reducing the ability to respond to a simultaneous physical attack.
6. D. Any action that can harm a person or organization, either directly or through embarrassment, would be a valid goal of a grudge attack. The purpose of such an attack is to "get back" at someone.
7. A, C. Thrill attacks have no reward other than providing a boost to pride and ego. The thrill of launching the attack comes from the act of participating in the attack (and not getting caught).
8. C. Although the other options have some merit in individual cases, the most important rule is to never modify, or taint, evidence. If you modify evidence, it becomes inadmissible in court.
9. D. The most compelling reason for not removing power from a machine is that you will lose the contents of memory. Carefully consider the pros and cons of removing power. After all is considered, it may be the best choice.
10. B, D. Hacktivists (the word is a combination of *hacker* and *activist*) often combine political motivations with the thrill of hacking. They organize themselves loosely into groups with names like Anonymous and Lolzsec and use tools like the Low Orbit Ion Cannon to create large-scale denial-of-service attacks with little knowledge required.
11. D. An incident is normally defined as any event that adversely affects the confidentiality, integrity, or availability of your data.
12. B. Some port scans are normal. An unusually high volume of port scan activity can be a reconnaissance activity preceding a more dangerous attack. When you see unusual port scanning, you should always investigate.
13. A. Any time an attacker exceeds their authority, the incident is classified as a system compromise. This includes valid users who exceed their authority as well as invalid users who gain access through the use of a valid user ID.
14. C. Although options A, B, and D are actions that can make you aware of what attacks look like and how to detect them, you will never successfully detect most attacks until

you know your system. When you know what the activity on your system looks like on a normal day, you can immediately detect any abnormal activity.

15. B. In this case, you need a search warrant to confiscate equipment without giving the suspect time to destroy evidence. If the suspect worked for your organization and you had all employees sign consent agreements, you could simply confiscate the equipment.

16. A. Log files contain a large volume of generally useless information. However, when you are trying to track down a problem or an incident, they can be invaluable. Even if an incident is discovered as it is happening, it may have been preceded by other incidents. Log files provide valuable clues and should be protected and archived.

17. A, D. You must report an incident when the incident resulted in the violation of a law or regulation. This includes any damage (or potential damage) to or disclosure of protected information.

18. D. Ethics are simply rules of personal behavior. Many professional organizations establish formal codes of ethics to govern their members, but ethics are personal rules individuals use to guide their lives.

19. B. The second canon of the (ISC)2 Code of Ethics states how a CISSP should act, which is honorably, honestly, justly, responsibly, and legally.

20. B. RFC 1087 does not specifically address the statements in A, C, or D. Although each type of activity listed is unacceptable, only "actions that compromise the privacy of users" are explicitly identified in RFC 1087.

Chapter 20: Software Development Security

1. A. The three elements of the DevOps model are software development, quality assurance, and IT operations

2. B. Input validation ensures that the input provided by users matches the design parameters.

3. C. The request control provides users with a framework to request changes and developers with the opportunity to prioritize those requests.

4. C. In a fail-secure state, the system remains in a high level of security until an administrator intervenes.

5. B. The waterfall model uses a seven-stage approach to software development and includes a feedback loop that allows development to return to the previous phase to correct defects discovered during the subsequent phase

6. A. Content-dependent access control is focused on the internal data of each field.

7. C. Foreign keys are used to enforce referential integrity constraints between tables that participate in a relationship.

8. D. In this case, the process the database user is taking advantage of is aggregation. Aggregation attacks involve the use of specialized database functions to combine information from a large number of database records to reveal information that may be more sensitive than the information in individual records would reveal.
9. C. Polyinstantiation allows the insertion of multiple records that appear to have the same primary key values into a database at different classification levels.
10. D. In Agile, the highest priority is to satisfy the customer through early and continuous delivery of valuable software.
11. C. Expert systems use a knowledge base consisting of a series of "if/then" statements to form decisions based on the previous experience of human experts.
12. D. In the Managed phase, level 4 of the SW-CMM, the organization uses quantitative measures to gain a detailed understanding of the development process.
13. B. ODBC acts as a proxy between applications and the backend DBMS.
14. A. In order to conduct a static test, the tester must have access to the underlying source code.
15. A. A Gantt chart is a type of bar chart that shows the interrelationships over time between projects and schedules. It provides a graphical illustration of a schedule that helps to plan, coordinate, and track specific tasks in a project.
16. C. Contamination is the mixing of data from a higher classification level and/or need-to-know requirement with data from a lower classification level and/or need-to-know requirement.
17. A. Database developers use polyinstantiation, the creation of multiple records that seem to have the same primary key, to protect against inference attacks.
18. C. Configuration audit is part of the configuration management process rather than the change control process.
19. C. The isolation principle states that two transactions operating on the same data must be temporarily separated from each other such that one does not interfere with the other.
20. B. The cardinality of a table refers to the number of rows in the table while the degree of a table is the number of columns.

Chapter 21: Malicious Code and Application Attacks

1. A. Signature detection mechanisms use known descriptions of viruses to identify malicious code resident on a system.
2. B. The DMZ (demilitarized zone) is designed to house systems like web servers that must be accessible from both the internal and external networks.
3. B. The time-of-check-to-time-of-use (TOCTTOU) attack relies on the timing of the execution of two events.

4. D. Application whitelisting requires that administrators specify approved applications, and then the operating system uses this list to allow only known good applications to run.

5. A. In an attempt to avoid detection by signature-based antivirus software packages, polymorphic viruses modify their own code each time they infect a system.

6. A. LastPass is a tool that allows users to create unique, strong passwords for each service they use without the burden of memorizing them all.

7. D. Buffer overflow attacks allow an attacker to modify the contents of a system's memory by writing beyond the space allocated for a variable.

8. D. Except option D, the choices are forms of common words that might be found during a dictionary attack. *mike* is a name and would be easily detected. *elppa* is simply *apple* spelled backward, and *dayorange* combines two dictionary words. Crack and other utilities can easily see through these "sneaky" techniques. Option D is simply a random string of characters that a dictionary attack would not uncover.

9. B. Shadow password files move encrypted password information from the publicly readable `/etc/passwd` file to the protected `/etc/shadow` file.

10. D. The single quote character (`'`) is used in SQL queries and must be handled carefully on web forms to protect against SQL injection attacks.

11. B. Developers of web applications should leverage database stored procedures to limit the application's ability to execute arbitrary code. With stored procedures, the SQL statement resides on the database server and may only be modified by database administrators.

12. B. Port scans reveal the ports associated with services running on a machine and available to the public.

13. A. Cross-site scripting attacks are successful only against web applications that include reflected input.

14. D. Multipartite viruses use two or more propagation techniques (for example, file infection and boot sector infection) to maximize their reach.

15. B. Input validation prevents cross-site scripting attacks by limiting user input to a predefined range. This prevents the attacker from including the HTML `<SCRIPT>` tag in the input.

16. A. Stuxnet was a highly sophisticated worm designed to destroy nuclear enrichment centrifuges attached to Siemens controllers.

17. B. Back doors are undocumented command sequences that allow individuals with knowledge of the back door to bypass normal access restrictions.

18. D. The Java sandbox isolates applets and allows them to run within a protected environment, limiting the effect they may have on the rest of the system.

19. D. The `<SCRIPT>` tag is used to indicate the beginning of an executable client-side script and is used in reflected input to create a cross-site scripting attack.

20. A. Packets with internal source IP addresses should not be allowed to enter the network from the outside because they are likely spoofed.

Answers to Written Labs

Chapter 1: Security Governance Through Principles and Policies

1. The CIA Triad is the combination of confidentiality, integrity, and availability. This term is used to indicate the three key components of a security solution.
2. The requirements of accountability are identification, authentication, authorization, and auditing. Each of these components needs to be legally supportable to truly hold someone accountable for their actions.
3. The benefits of change control management include preventing unwanted security reduction because of uncontrolled change, documenting and tracking of all alterations in the environment, standardization, conforming with security policy, and the ability to roll back changes in the event of an unwanted or unexpected outcome.
4. (1) Identify the custodian, and define their responsibilities. (2) Specify the evaluation criteria of how the information will be classified and labeled. (3) Classify and label each resource. Although the owner conducts this step, a supervisor should review it. (4) Document any exceptions to the classification policy that are discovered, and integrate them into the evaluation criteria. (5) Select the security controls that will be applied to each classification level to provide the necessary level of protection. (6) Specify the procedures for declassifying resources and the procedures for transferring custody of a resource to an external entity. (7) Create an enterprise-wide awareness program to instruct all personnel about the classification system.
5. The six security roles are senior management, IT/security staff, owner, custodian, operator/user, and auditor.
6. The four components of a security policy are policies, standards, guidelines, and procedures. Policies are broad security statements. Standards are definitions of hardware and software security compliance. Guidelines are used when there is not an appropriate procedure. Procedures are detailed step-by-step instructions for performing work tasks in a secure manner.

Chapter 2: Personnel Security and Risk Management Concepts

1. Possible answers include job descriptions, principle of least privilege, separation of duties, job responsibilities, job rotation/cross-training, performance reviews, background checks, job action warnings, awareness training, job training, exit interviews/

terminations, nondisclosure agreements, noncompete agreements, employment agreements, privacy declaration, and acceptable use policies.

2. The formulas are as follows:

   SLE = AV * EF

   ARO = # / yr

   ALE = SLE * ARO

   Cost/benefit = (ALE1 – ALE2) – ACS

3. The Delphi technique is an anonymous feedback-and-response process used to enable a group to reach an anonymous consensus. Its primary purpose is to elicit honest and uninfluenced responses from all participants. The participants are usually gathered into a single meeting room. To each request for feedback, each participant writes down their response on paper anonymously. The results are compiled and presented to the group for evaluation. The process is repeated until a consensus is reached.

4. Risk assessment often involves a hybrid approach using both quantitative and qualitative methods. A purely quantitative analysis is not possible; not all elements and aspects of the analysis can be quantified because some are qualitative, some are subjective, and some are intangible. Since a purely quantitative risk assessment is not possible, balancing the results of a quantitative analysis is essential. The method of combining quantitative and qualitative analysis into a final assessment of organizational risk is known as hybrid assessment or hybrid analysis.

Chapter 3: Business Continuity Planning

1. Many federal, state, and local laws or regulations require businesses to implement BCP provisions. Including legal representation on your BCP team helps ensure that you remain compliant with laws, regulations, and contractual obligations.

2. The "seat-of-the-pants" approach is an excuse used by individuals who do not want to invest time and money in the proper creation of a BCP. This can lead to catastrophe when a firmly laid plan isn't in place to guide the response during a stressful emergency situation.

3. Quantitative risk assessment involves using numbers and formulas to make a decision. Qualitative risk assessment includes nonnumeric factors, such as emotions, investor/consumer confidence, and workforce stability.

4. The BCP training plan should include a plan overview briefing for all employees and specific training for individuals with direct or indirect involvement. In addition, backup personnel should be trained for each key BCP role.

5. The four steps of the BCP process are project scope and planning, business impact assessment, continuity planning, and approval/implementation.

Chapter 4: Laws, Regulations, and Compliance

1. Individuals have a right to access records kept about them and know the source of data included in those records. They also have the right to correct inaccurate records. Individuals have the right to withhold consent from data processors and have legal recourse if these rights are violated.
2. Some common questions that organizations may ask about outsourced service providers are as follows:
   - What type(s) of sensitive information are stored, processed, or transmitted by the vendor?
   - What controls are in place to protect the organization's information?
   - How is our organization's information segregated from that of other clients?
   - If encryption is relied on as a security control, what encryption algorithms and key lengths are used? How is key management handled?
   - What types of security audits does the vendor perform, and what access does the client have to those audits?
   - Does the vendor rely on any other third parties to store, process, or transmit data? How do the provisions of the contract related to security extend to those third parties?
   - Where will data storage, processing, and transmission take place? If outside the home country of the client and/or vendor, what implications does that have?
   - What is the vendor's incident response process and when will clients be notified of a potential security breach?
   - What provisions are in place to ensure the ongoing integrity and availability of client data?
3. Some common steps that employers take to notify employees of monitoring include clauses in employment contracts that state the employee should have no expectation of privacy while using corporate equipment, similar written statements in corporate acceptable use and privacy policies, logon banners warning that all communications are subject to monitoring, and labels on computers and telephones warning of monitoring.

Chapter 5: Protecting Security of Assets

1. Personally identifiable information (PII) is any information that can identify an individual. It includes information that can be used to distinguish or trace an individual's identity, such as name, social security number or national ID number, date and place of birth, mother's maiden name, and biometric records. Protected health information

(PHI) is any health-related information that can be related to a specific person. PHI doesn't apply only to health-care providers. Any employer that provides, or supplements, health-care policies collects and handles PHI.

2. Solid state drives (SSDs) should be destroyed (such as with a disintegrator) to sanitize them. Traditional methods used hard drives and are not reliable.
3. Organizations can use any classification levels they desire. Two examples are Class 3, Class 2, Class 1, and Class 0, and confidential (or proprietary), private, sensitive, and public.
4. The Safe Harbor program includes the following seven principles: notice, choice, onward transfer, security, data integrity, access, and enforcement.

Chapter 6: Cryptography and Symmetric Key Algorithms

1. The major obstacle to the widespread adoption of one-time pad cryptosystems is the difficulty in creating and distributing the very lengthy keys on which the algorithm depends.
2. The first step in encrypting this message requires the assignment of numeric column values to the letters of the secret keyword:

```
S E C U R E
5 2 1 6 4 3
```

Next, the letters of the message are written in order underneath the letters of the keyword:

```
S E C U R E
5 2 1 6 4 3
I W I L L P
A S S T H E
C I S S P E
X A M A N D
B E C O M E
C E R T I F
I E D N E X
T M O N T H
```

Finally, the sender enciphers the message by reading down each column; the order in which the columns are read corresponds to the numbers assigned in the first step. This produces the following ciphertext:

```
I S S M C R D O W S I A E E E M P E E D E F X H L H P N M I E T I A C X B C I
T L T S A O T N N
```

3. This message is decrypted by using the following function:

```
P  = (C - 3) mod 26
C: F R Q J U D W X O D W L R Q V B R X J R W L W
P: C O N G R A T U L A T I O N S Y O U G O T I T
```

And the hidden message is "Congratulations You Got It." Congratulations, you got it!

Chapter 7: PKI and Cryptographic Applications

1. Bob should encrypt the message using Alice's public key and then transmit the encrypted message to Alice.
2. Alice should decrypt the message using her private key.
3. Bob should generate a message digest from the plaintext message using a hash function. He should then encrypt the message digest using his own private key to create the digital signature. Finally, he should append the digital signature to the message and transmit it to Alice.
4. Alice should decrypt the digital signature in Bob's message using Bob's public key. She should then create a message digest from the plaintext message using the same hashing algorithm Bob used to create the digital signature. Finally, she should compare the two message digests. If they are identical, the signature is authentic.

Chapter 8: Principles of Security Models, Design, and Capabilities

1. Security models include state machine, information flow, noninterference, Take-Grant, access control matrix, Bell-LaPadula, Biba, Clark-Wilson, Brewer and Nash (aka Chinese Wall), Goguen-Meseguer, Sutherland, and Graham-Denning.
2. The primary components of the trusted computing base (TCB) are the hardware and software elements used to enforce the security policy (these elements are called the TCB), the security perimeter distinguishing and separating TCB components from non-TCB components, and the reference monitor that serves as an access control device across the security perimeter.
3. The two primary rules of Bell-LaPadula are the simple rule of no read-up and the star rule of no write-down. The two rules of Biba are the simple rule of no read-down and the star rule of no write-up.

4. An open system is one with published APIs that allow third parties to develop products to interact with it. A closed system is one that is proprietary with no third-party product support. Open source is a coding stance that allows others to view the source code of a program. Closed source is an opposing coding stance that keeps source code confidential.

Chapter 9: Security Vulnerabilities, Threats, and Countermeasures

1. The terms used to describe the various computer mechanisms that allow multiple simultaneous activities are *multitasking*, *multiprocessing*, *multiprogramming*, *multithreading*, and *multistate processing*.
2. The four security modes are dedicated, system high, compartmented, and multilevel.
3. The three pairs of aspects or features used to describe storage are primary vs. secondary, volatile vs. nonvolatile, and random vs. sequential.
4. Some vulnerabilities found in distributed architecture include sensitive data found on desktops/terminals/notebooks, lack of security understanding among users, greater risk of physical component theft, compromise of a client leading to the compromise of the whole network, greater risk from malware because of user-installed software and removable media, and data on clients less likely to be included in backups.

Chapter 10: Physical Security Requirements

1. A fence is an excellent perimeter safeguard that can help to deter casual trespassing. Moderately secure installations work when the fence is 6 to 8 feet tall and will typically be cyclone (also known as chain link) fencing with the upper surface twisted or barbed to deter casual climbers. More secure installations usually opt for fence heights over 8 feet and often include multiple strands of barbed or razor wire strung above the chain link fabric to further deter climbers.
2. Halon degrades into toxic gases at 900 degrees Fahrenheit. Also, it is not environmentally friendly (it is an ozone-depleting substance). Recycled halon is available, but production of halon ceased in developed countries in 2003. Halon is often replaced by a more ecologically friendly and less toxic medium.
3. Anytime water is used to respond to fire, flame, or smoke, water damage becomes a serious concern, particularly when water is released in areas where electrical equipment is in use. Not only can computers and other electrical gear be damaged or destroyed by water,

but also many forms of storage media can become damaged or unusable. Also, when seeking hot spots to put out, firefighters often use axes to break down doors or cut through walls to reach them as quickly as possible. This, too, poses the potential for physical damage to or destruction of devices and/or wiring that may also be in the vicinity.

Chapter 11: Secure Network Architecture and Securing Network Components

1. Application (7), Presentation (6), Session (5), Transport (4), Network (3), Data Link (2), and Physical (1).
2. Problems with cabling and their countermeasures include attenuation (use repeaters or don't violate distance recommendations), using the wrong CAT cable (check the cable specifications against throughput requirements, and err on the side of caution), crosstalk (use shielded cables, place cables in separate conduits, or use cables of different twists per inch), cable breaks (avoid running cables in locations where movement occurs), interference (use cable shielding, use cables with higher twists per inch, or switch to fiber-optic cables), and eavesdropping (maintain physical security over all cable runs or switch to fiber-optic cables).
3. Some of the frequency spectrum-use technologies are spread spectrum, Frequency Hopping Spread Spectrum (FHSS), Direct Sequence Spread Spectrum (DSSS), and Orthogonal Frequency-Division Multiplexing (OFDM).
4. Methods to secure 802.11 wireless networking include disabling the SSID broadcast; changing the SSID to something unique; enabling MAC filtering; considering the use of static IPs or using DHCP with reservations; turning on the highest form of encryption offered (such as WEP, WPA, or WPA2/802.11i); treating wireless as remote access and employing 802.1X, RADIUS, or TACACS; separating wireless access points from the LAN with firewalls; monitoring all wireless client activity with an IDS; and considering requiring wireless clients to connect with a VPN to gain LAN access.
5. The LAN shared media access technologies are CSMA, CSMA/CA (used by 802.11 and AppleTalk), CSMA/CD (used by Ethernet), token passing (used by Token Ring and FDDI/CDDI), and polling (used by SDLC, HDLC, and some mainframe systems).

Chapter 12: Secure Communications and Network Attacks

1. IPSec's transport mode is used for host-to-host links and encrypts only the payload, not the header. IPSec's tunnel mode is used for host-to-LAN and LAN-to-LAN links and encrypts the entire original payload and header and then adds a link header.

2. Network Address Translation (NAT) allows for the identity of internal systems to be hidden from external entities. Often NAT is used to translate between RFC 1918 private IP addresses and leased public addresses. NAT serves as a one-way firewall because it allows only inbound traffic that is a response to a previous internal query. NAT also allows a few leased public addresses to be used to grant Internet connectivity to a larger number of internal systems.
3. Circuit switching is usually associated with physical connections. The link itself is physically established and then dismantled for the communication. Circuit switching offers known fixed delays, supports constant traffic, is connection oriented, is sensitive only to the loss of the connection rather than the communication, and was most often used for voice transmissions. Packet switching is usually associated with logical connections because the link is just a logically defined path among possible paths. Within a packet-switching system, each system or link can be employed simultaneously by other circuits. Packet switching divides the communication into segments, and each segment traverses the circuit to the destination. Packet switching has variable delays because each segment could take a unique path, is usually employed for bursty traffic, is not physically connection oriented but often uses virtual circuits, is sensitive to the loss of data, and is used for any form of communication.
4. Email is inherently insecure because it is primarily a plain-text communication medium and employs nonencrypted transmission protocols. This allows for email to be easily spoofed, spammed, flooded, eavesdropped on, interfered with, and hijacked. Defenses against these issues primarily include having stronger authentication requirements and using encryption to protect the content while in transit.

Chapter 13: Managing Identity and Authentication

1. Access control types include preventive, detective, corrective, deterrent, recovery, directive, and compensation access controls. They are implemented as administrative controls, logical/technical controls, and/or physical controls.
2. A Type 1 authentication factor is something you know. A Type 2 authentication factor is something you have. A Type 3 authentication factor is something you are.
3. Federated identity management systems allow single sign-on (SSO) to be extended beyond a single organization. SSO allows users to authenticate once and access multiple resources without authenticating again. SAML is a common language used to exchange federated identity information between organizations.
4. The identity and access provisioning life cycle includes provisioning accounts, periodically reviewing and managing accounts, and revocation of accounts when they are no longer being used.

Chapter 14: Controlling and Monitoring Access

1. A discretionary access control (DAC) model allows the owner, creator, or data custodian of an object to control and define access. Administrators centrally administer nondiscretionary access controls and can make changes that affect the entire environment.
2. Assets, threats, and vulnerabilities should be identified through asset valuation, threat modeling, and vulnerability analysis.
3. Brute-force attacks, dictionary attacks, sniffer attacks, rainbow table attacks, and social-engineering attacks are all methods used to discover passwords.

Chapter 15: Security Assessment and Testing

1. TCP SYN scanning sends a single packet to each scanned port with the SYN flag set. This indicates a request to open a new connection. If the scanner receives a response that has the SYN and ACK flags set, this indicates that the system is moving to the second phase in the three-way TCP handshake and that the port is open. TCP SYN scanning is also known as "half-open" scanning. TCP connect scanning opens a full connection to the remote system on the specified port. This scan type is used when the user running the scan does not have the necessary permissions to run a half-open scan.
2. The three possible port status values returned by nmap are as follows:
   - Open—The port is open on the remote system and there is an application that is actively accepting connections on that port.
   - Closed—The port is accessible on the remote system, meaning that the firewall is allowing access, but there is no application accepting connections on that port.
   - Filtered—Nmap is unable to determine whether a port is open or closed because a firewall is interfering with the connection attempt.
3. Static software testing techniques, such as code reviews, evaluate the security of software without running it by analyzing either the source code or the compiled application. Dynamic testing evaluates the security of software in a runtime environment and is often the only option for organizations deploying applications written by someone else.
4. Mutation (dumb) fuzzing takes previous input values from actual operation of the software and manipulates (or mutates) it to create fuzzed input. It might alter the characters

of the content, append strings to the end of the content, or perform other data manipulation techniques.

Generational (intelligent) fuzzing develops data models and creates new fuzzed input based on an understanding of the types of data used by the program.

Chapter 16: Managing Security Operations

1. Need to know focuses on permissions and the ability to access information, whereas the principle of least privilege focuses on privileges. Privileges include both rights and permissions. Both limit the access of users and subjects to only what they need. Following these principles prevents and limits the scope of security incidents.
2. Managing sensitive information includes properly marking, handling, storing, and destroying it based on its classification.
3. The three models are Software as a Service (SaaS), Platform as a Service (PaaS), and Infrastructure as a Service (IaaS). The cloud service provider (CSP) provides the most maintenance and security services with SaaS, less with PaaS, and the least with IaaS. While NIST SP 800-144 provides these definitions, CSPs sometimes use their own terms and definitions in marketing materials.
4. Change management helps prevent outages due to unauthorized changes in system configuration.

Chapter 17: Preventing and Responding to Incidents

1. Incident response steps listed in the CISSP CIB are detection, response, mitigation, reporting, recovery, remediation, and lessons learned.
2. Intrusion detection systems can be described as host based or network based, based on their detection methods (knowledge based or behavior based) and based on their responses (passive or active).

   Host-based IDSs examine events on individual computers in great detail, including file activities, accesses, and processes. Network-based IDSs examine general network events and anomalies through traffic evaluation.

A knowledge-based IDS uses a database of known attacks to detect intrusions. A behavior-based IDS starts with a baseline of normal activity and measures network activity against the baseline to identify abnormal activity.

A passive response will log the activity and often provide a notification. An active response directly responds to the intrusion to stop or block the attack.

3. Auditing is a methodical examination or review of an environment and encompasses a wide variety of activities to ensure compliance with regulations and to detect abnormalities, unauthorized occurrences, or outright crimes. Audit trails provide the data that supports such examination or review and essentially are what make auditing and subsequent detection of attacks and misbehavior possible.
4. Organizations should regularly perform access reviews and audits. These can detect when an organization is not following its own policies and procedures related to account management.

Chapter 18: Disaster Recovery Planning

1. Businesses have three main concerns when considering adopting a mutual assistance agreement. First, the nature of an MAA often necessitates that the businesses be located in close geographical proximity. However, this requirement also increases the risk that the two businesses will fall victim to the same threat. Second, MAAs are difficult to enforce in the middle of a crisis. If one of the organizations is affected by a disaster and the other isn't, the organization not affected could back out at the last minute, leaving the other organization out of luck. Finally, confidentiality concerns (both legal and business related) often prevent businesses from trusting others with their sensitive operational data.
2. There are five main types of disaster recovery tests:
   - Read-through tests involve the distribution of recovery checklists to disaster recovery personnel for review.
   - Structured walk-throughs are "table-top" exercises that involve assembling the disaster recovery team to discuss a disaster scenario.
   - Simulation tests are more comprehensive and may impact one or more noncritical business units of the organization.
   - Parallel tests involve relocating personnel to the alternate site and commencing operations there.
   - Full-interruption tests involve relocating personnel to the alternate site and shutting down operations at the primary site.
3. Full backups create a copy of all data stored on a server. Incremental backups create copies of all files modified since the last full or incremental backup. Differential

backups create copies of all files modified since the last full backup without regard to any previous differential or incremental backups that may taken place.

Chapter 19: Incidents and Ethics

1. The major categories of computer crime are military/intelligence attacks, business attacks, financial attacks, terrorist attacks, grudge attacks, and thrill attacks.
2. Thrill attacks are motivated by individuals seeking to achieve the "high" associated with successfully breaking into a computer system.
3. Interviews are conducted with the intention of gathering information from individuals to assist with your investigation. Interrogations are conducted with the intent of gathering evidence from suspects to be used in a criminal prosecution.
4. An event is any occurrence that takes place during a certain period of time. Incidents are events that have negative outcomes affecting the confidentiality, integrity, or availability of your data.
5. Incident response teams normally include representatives from senior management, information security professionals, legal representatives, public affairs/communications representatives, and technical engineers.
6. The three phases of the incident response process are detection and identification, response and reporting, and recovery and remediation.
7. To be admissible, evidence must be reliable, competent, and material to the case.

Chapter 20: Software Development Security

1. The primary key uniquely identifies each row in the table. For example, an employee identification number might be the primary key for a table containing information about employees.
2. Polyinstantiation is a database security technique that appears to permit the insertion of multiple rows sharing the same uniquely identifying information.
3. Static analysis performs assessment of the code itself, analyzing the sequence of instructions for security flaws. Dynamic analysis tests the code in a live production environment, searching for runtime flaws.
4. One phase.

Chapter 21: Malicious Code and Application Attacks

1. Viruses and worms both travel from system to system attempting to deliver their malicious payloads to as many machines as possible. However, viruses require some sort of human intervention, such as sharing a file, network resource, or email message, to propagate. Worms, on the other hand, seek out vulnerabilities and spread from system to system under their own power, thereby greatly magnifying their reproductive capability, especially in a well-connected network.
2. The Internet worm used four propagation techniques. First, it exploited a bug in the Sendmail utility that allowed it to spread itself by sending a specially crafted email message that contained its code to the Sendmail program on a remote system. Second, it used a dictionary-based password attack to attempt to gain access to remote systems by utilizing the username and password of a valid system user. Third, it exploited a buffer overflow vulnerability in the Finger program to infect systems. Fourth, it analyzed any existing trust relationships with other systems on the network and attempted to spread itself to those systems through the trusted path.
3. If possible, antivirus software may try to disinfect an infected file, removing the virus's malicious code. If that fails, it might either quarantine the file for manual review or automatically delete it to prevent further infection.
4. Data integrity assurance packages like Tripwire compute hash values for each file stored on a protected system. If a file infector virus strikes the system, this would result in a change in the affected file's hash value and would, therefore, trigger a file integrity alert.

Index

Note to Reader: **Bolded** page numbers refer to definitions and main discussions of a topic. *Italicized* page numbers refer to illustrations.

Symbols

Numbers

A

B

C

D

E

F

G

H

I

J

K

L

M

N

O

P

Q

R

S

T

U

V

W

X

Z

Comprehensive Online Learning Environment

Register on Sybex.com to gain access to the online interactive learning environment and test bank to help you study for your $(ISC)^2$ CISSP certification - included with your purchase of this book!

The online tool includes:

- Assessment Test to help you focus your study to specific objectives
- Chapter Tests to reinforce what you learned
- Practice Exams to test your knowledge of the material
- Electronic Flashcards to reinforce your learning and provide last-minute
- test prep before the exam
- Searchable Glossary gives you instant access to the key terms you'll need
- to know for the exam

Go to `http://sybextestbanks.wiley.com` to register and gain access to this comprehensive study tool package.